GIBSONS & DISTRICT PUBLIC LIBRARY
604-886-2130

MAY 17 2018

All the books I could ever want!!!

...d me, "I will grant you anything in the world that you desire—just ask for it," I would answer without hesitation, "I want Japan's National Diet Library."

—*Hiromu Arakawa, 2008*

Born in Hokkaido (northern Japan), Hiromu Arakawa first attracted national attention in 1999 with her award-winning manga *Stray Dog*. Her series *Fullmetal Alchemist* debuted in 2001 in Square Enix's monthly manga anthology *Shonen Gangan*.

FULLMETAL ALCHEMIST
3-in-1 Edition

VIZ Media Omnibus Edition Volume 7
A compilation of the graphic novel volumes 19–21

Story and Art by Hiromu Arakawa

Translation/Akira Watanabe
English Adaptation/Jake Forbes
Touch-up Art & Lettering/Wayne Truman, Susan Daigle-Leach
Manga Design/Julie Behn
Omnibus Design/Yukiko Whitley
Manga Editors/Annette Roman, Alexis Kirsch
Omnibus Editor/Hope Donovan

FULLMETAL ALCHEMIST vol. 19–21
© 2007 Hiromu Arakawa/SQUARE ENIX.
First published in Japan in 2008 by SQUARE ENIX CO., LTD.
English translation rights arranged with SQUARE ENIX CO., LTD.
and VIZ Media, LLC.

The stories, characters and incidents mentioned in this publication
are entirely fictional.

No portion of this book may be reproduced or transmitted in any
form or by any means without written permission from the copyright
holders.

Printed in the U.S.A.

Published by VIZ Media, LLC
P.O. Box 77010
San Francisco, CA 94107

10 9 8 7 6 5 4 3
Omnibus edition first printing, March 2014
Third printing, December 2016

www.viz.com

PARENTAL ADVISORY
FULLMETAL ALCHEMIST is rated T for Teen and
is recommended for ages 13 and up. Contains mildly
strong language, tobacco/alcohol use and fantasy
violence.
ratings.viz.com

鋼の錬金術師

FULLMETAL ALCHEMIST

HIROMU ARAKAWA

荒川弘

19

■ アルフォンス・エルリック

Alphonse Elric

■ エドワード・エルリック

Edward Elric

■ アレックス・ルイ・アームストロング

Alex Louis Armstrong

■ ロイ・マスタング

Roy Mustang

OUTLINE
FULLMETAL ALCHEMIST

Using a forbidden alchemical ritual, the Elric brothers attempted to bring their dead mother back to life. But the ritual went wrong, consuming Edward Elric's leg and Alphonse Elric's entire body. At the cost of his arm, Edward was able to graft his brother's soul into a suit of armor. Equipped with mechanical "auto-mail" to replace his missing limbs, Edward becomes a state alchemist in hopes of finding a way to restore their bodies. Their search embroils them in a deadly conspiracy that threatens to take the innocence, if not the lives, of everyone involved.

Since their shocking discovery of the military's ties to the Homunculi, Ed and Al have been kept on a short leash, with Winry held hostage to buy their silence. In the snowbound Mountains of Briggs, the brothers, in a tenuous alliance with Scar, come up with a plan to get Winry out of the enemy's clutches by faking her death. But all their plotting could be for naught. Major General Armstrong, their ally at Fort Briggs, has been summoned to Central Command. Now, with the murderous alchemist Kimblee hot on their trail, Ed desperately plots their next move…

鋼の錬金術師
FULLMETAL ALCHEMIST

CHARACTERS
FULLMETAL ALCHEMIST

■ ウィンリィ・ロックベル

Winry Rockbell

■ スカー

Scar

■ オリヴィエ・ミラ・アームストロング

Olivier Mira Armstrong

■ キング・ブラッドレイ

King Bradley

■ ゾルフ・J・キンブリー

Solf J. Kimblee

■ メイ・チャン

May Chang

CONTENTS

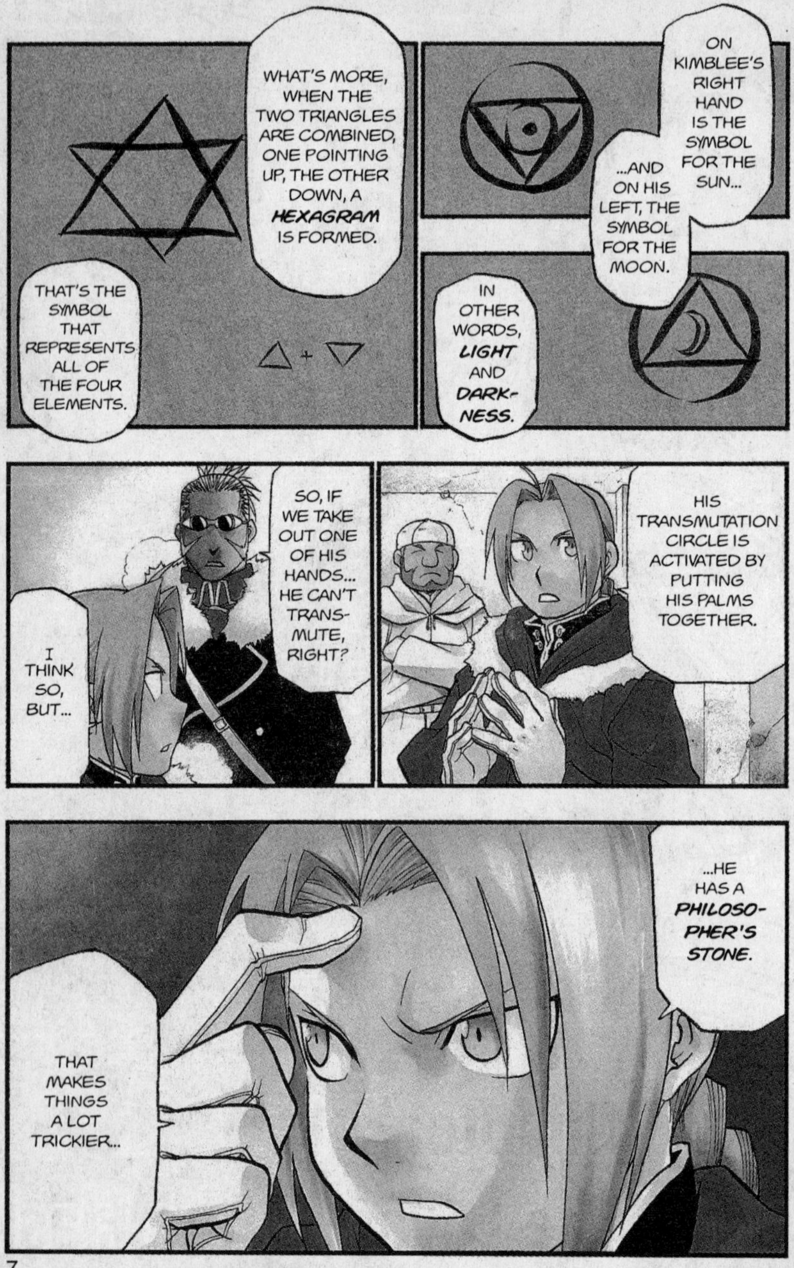
ON KIMBLEE'S RIGHT HAND IS THE SYMBOL FOR THE SUN...
...AND ON HIS LEFT, THE SYMBOL FOR THE MOON.
IN OTHER WORDS, LIGHT AND DARKNESS.
WHAT'S MORE, WHEN THE TWO TRIANGLES ARE COMBINED, ONE POINTING UP, THE OTHER DOWN, A HEXAGRAM IS FORMED.
THAT'S THE SYMBOL THAT REPRESENTS ALL OF THE FOUR ELEMENTS.
HIS TRANSMUTATION CIRCLE IS ACTIVATED BY PUTTING HIS PALMS TOGETHER.
SO, IF WE TAKE OUT ONE OF HIS HANDS... HE CAN'T TRANSMUTE, RIGHT?
I THINK SO, BUT...
...HE HAS A PHILOSOPHER'S STONE.
THAT MAKES THINGS A LOT TRICKIER...

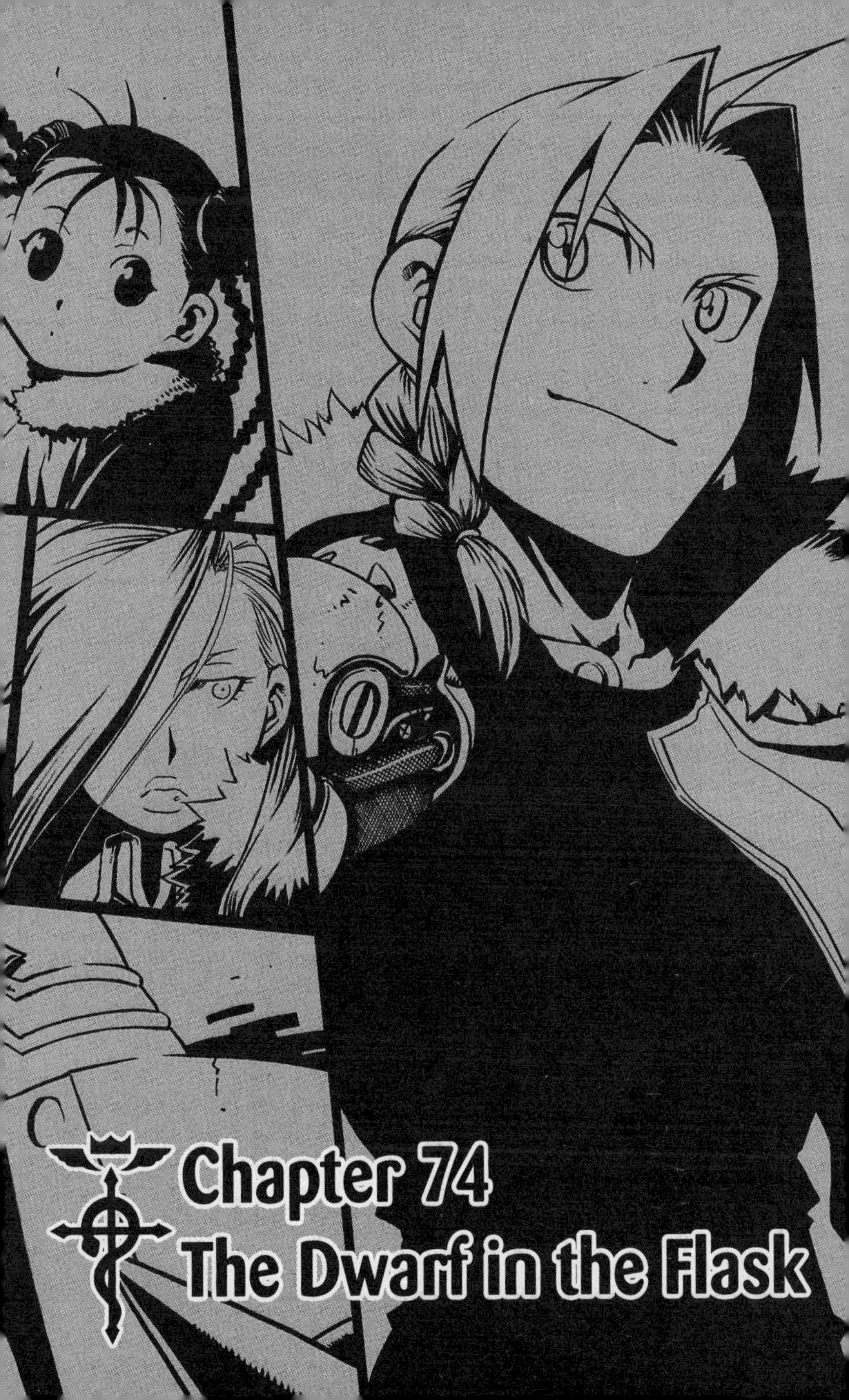
Chapter 74
The Dwarf in the Flask

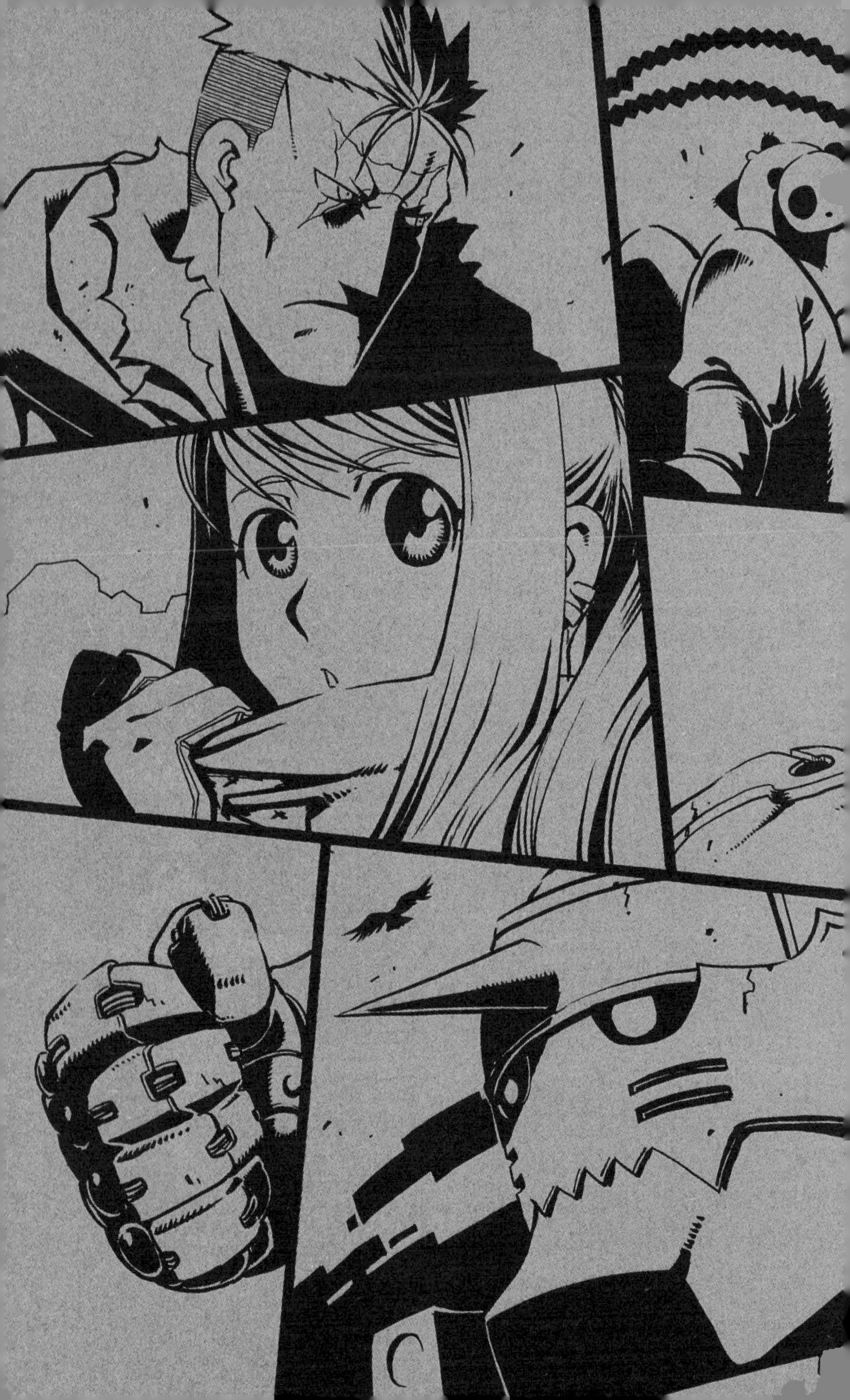

FULLMETAL
ALCHEMIST

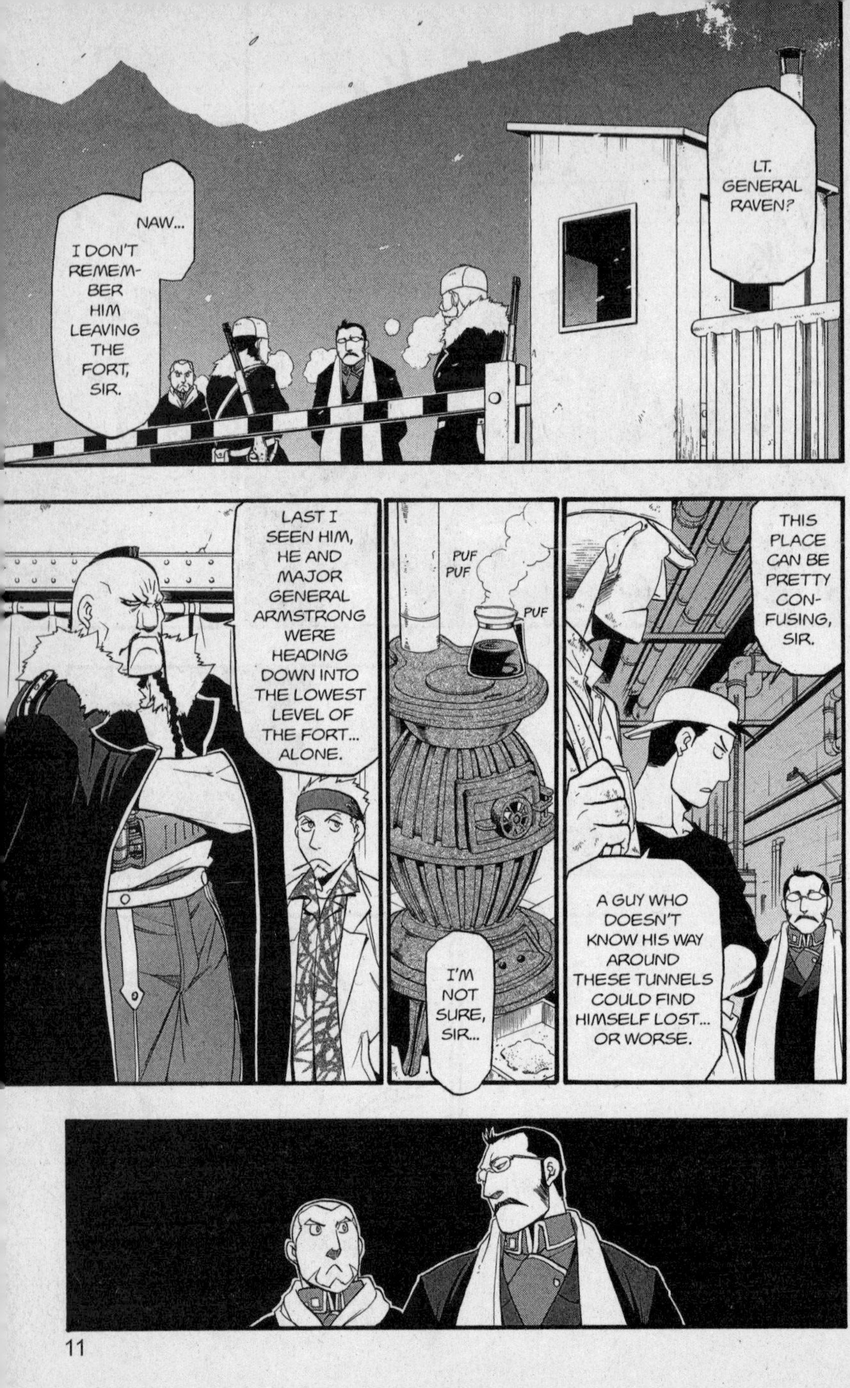
LT. GENERAL RAVEN?
NAW... I DON'T REMEM-BER HIM LEAVING THE FORT, SIR.
THIS PLACE CAN BE PRETTY CON-FUSING, SIR.
A GUY WHO DOESN'T KNOW HIS WAY AROUND THESE TUNNELS COULD FIND HIMSELF LOST... OR WORSE.
PUF PUF
PUF
I'M NOT SURE, SIR...
LAST I SEEN HIM, HE AND MAJOR GENERAL ARMSTRONG WERE HEADING DOWN INTO THE LOWEST LEVEL OF THE FORT... ALONE.

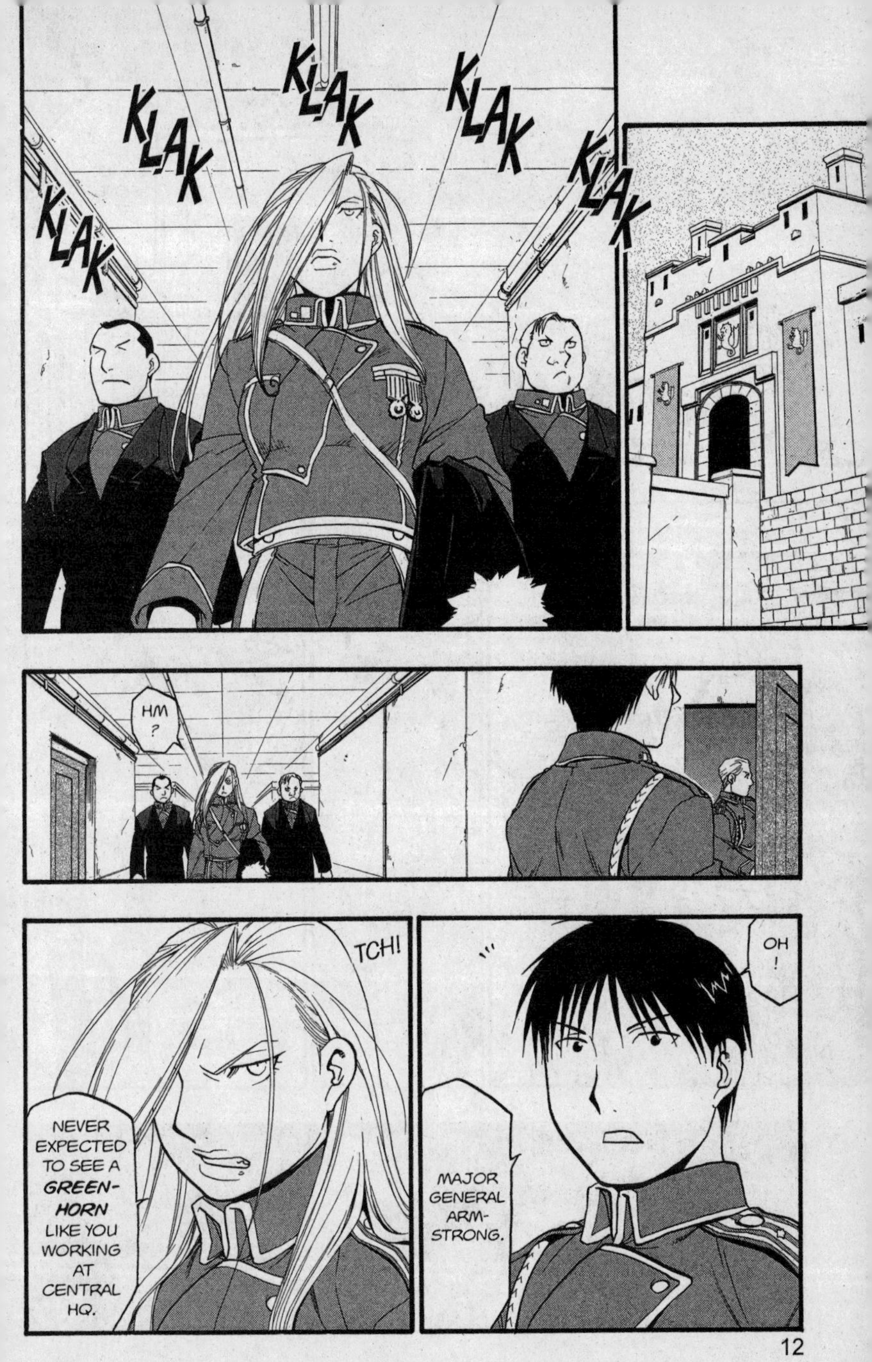
KLAK
KLAK
KLAK
KLAK
HM ?
OH !
MAJOR GENERAL ARM-STRONG.
TCH!
NEVER EXPECTED TO SEE A ***GREEN-HORN*** LIKE YOU WORKING AT CENTRAL HQ.

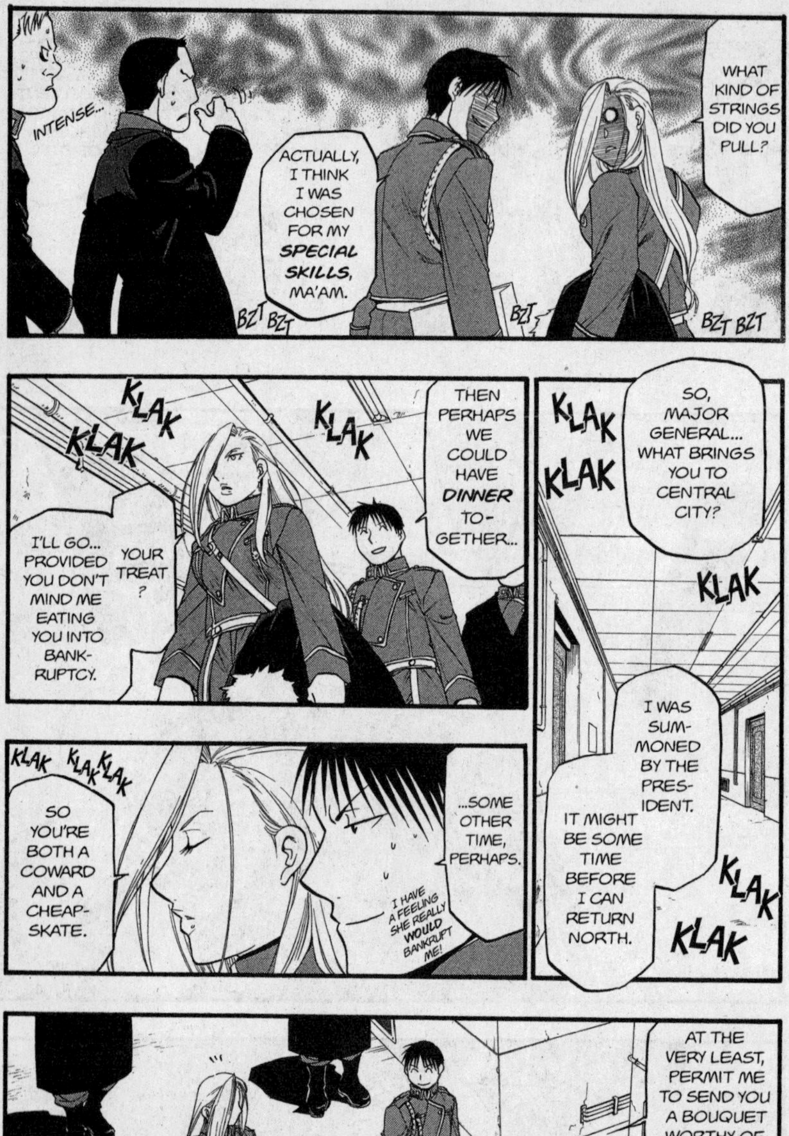
WHAT KIND OF STRINGS DID YOU PULL?
ACTUALLY, I THINK I WAS CHOSEN FOR MY **SPECIAL SKILLS**, MA'AM.
BZT BZT
BZT
BZT BZT
INTENSE...
KLAK KLAK
SO, MAJOR GENERAL... WHAT BRINGS YOU TO CENTRAL CITY?
KLAK
I WAS SUMMONED BY THE PRESIDENT.
IT MIGHT BE SOME TIME BEFORE I CAN RETURN NORTH.
KLAK KLAK
THEN PERHAPS WE COULD HAVE **DINNER** TOGETHER...
KLAK
KLAK KLAK
YOUR TREAT?
I'LL GO... PROVIDED YOU DON'T MIND ME EATING YOU INTO BANKRUPTCY.
...SOME OTHER TIME, PERHAPS.
I HAVE A FEELING SHE REALLY **WOULD** BANKRUPT ME!
KLAK KLAK
KLAK
SO YOU'RE BOTH A COWARD AND A CHEAPSKATE.
AT THE VERY LEAST, PERMIT ME TO SEND YOU A BOUQUET WORTHY OF YOUR BEAUTY, MAJOR GENERAL.

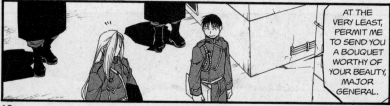

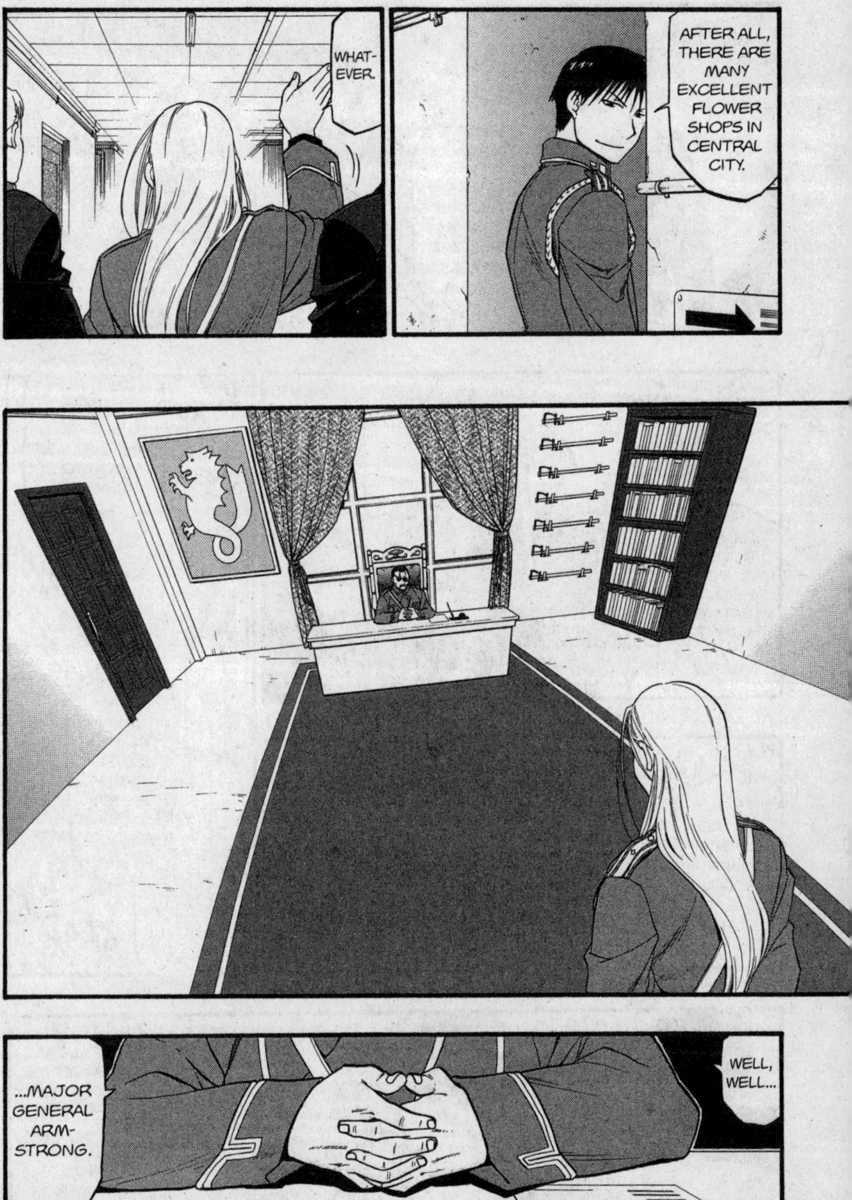
AFTER ALL, THERE ARE MANY EXCELLENT FLOWER SHOPS IN CENTRAL CITY.
WHAT-EVER.
WELL, WELL...
...MAJOR GENERAL ARM-STRONG.

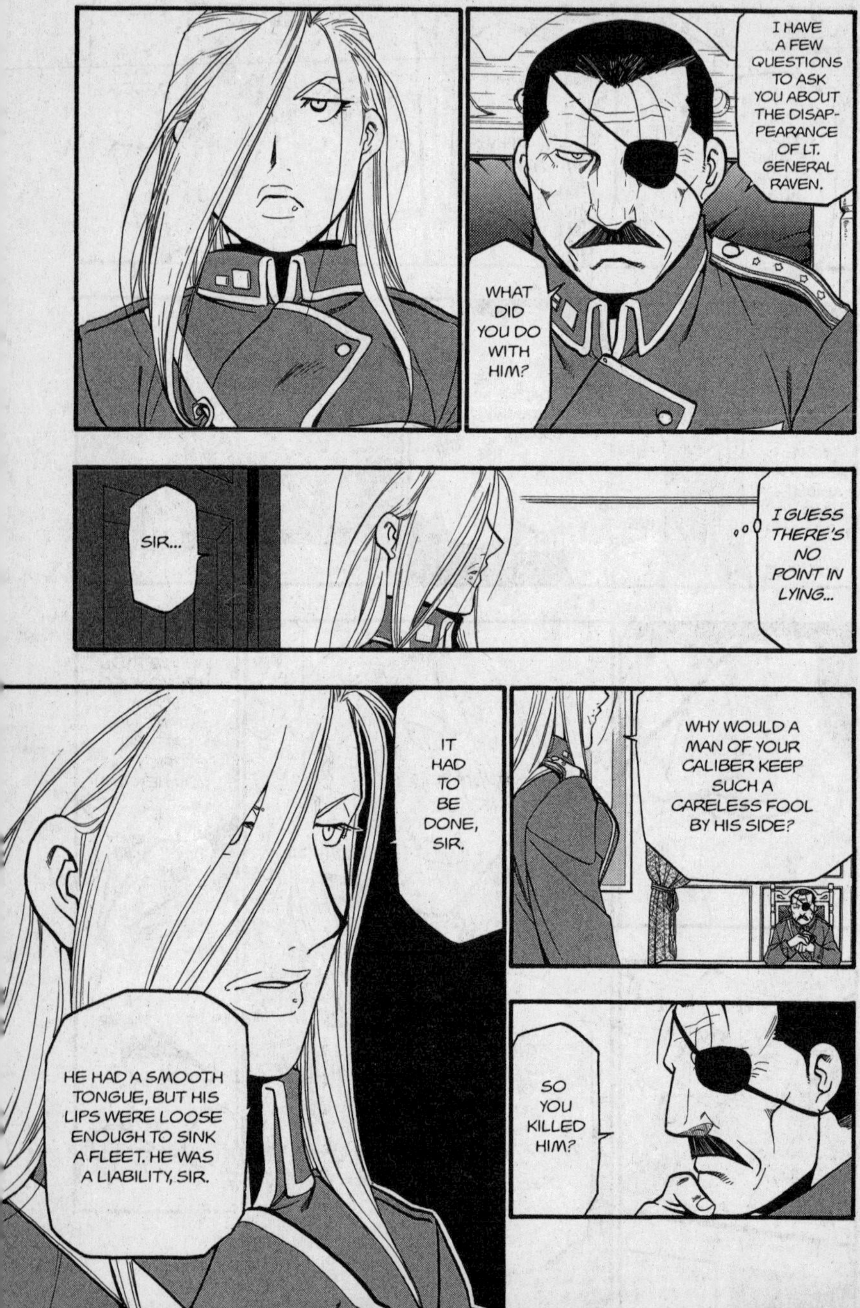
I HAVE A FEW QUESTIONS TO ASK YOU ABOUT THE DISAPPEARANCE OF LT. GENERAL RAVEN.
WHAT DID YOU DO WITH HIM?
I GUESS THERE'S NO POINT IN LYING...
SIR...
WHY WOULD A MAN OF YOUR CALIBER KEEP SUCH A CARELESS FOOL BY HIS SIDE?
SO YOU KILLED HIM?
IT HAD TO BE DONE, SIR.
HE HAD A SMOOTH TONGUE, BUT HIS LIPS WERE LOOSE ENOUGH TO SINK A FLEET. HE WAS A LIABILITY, SIR.

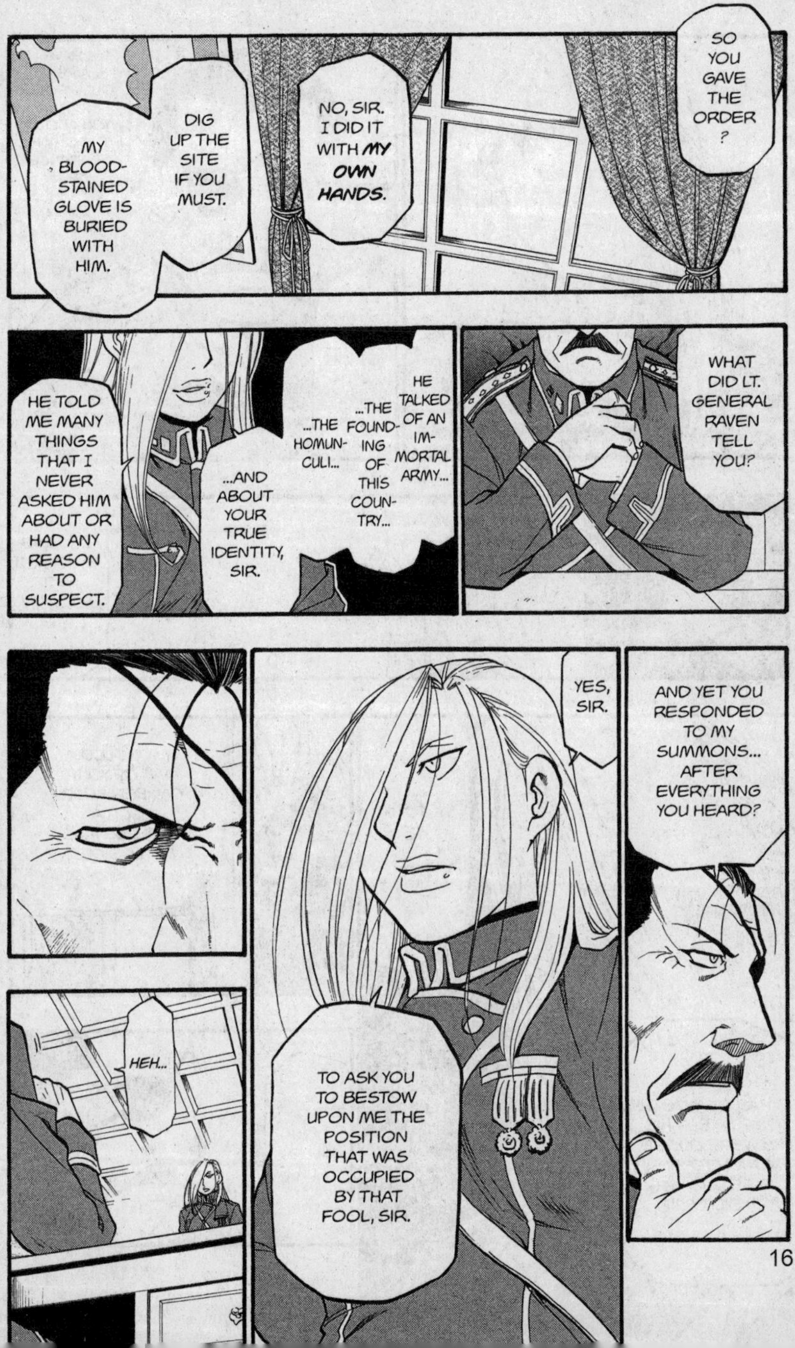
SO YOU GAVE THE ORDER?
NO, SIR. I DID IT WITH MY OWN HANDS.
DIG UP THE SITE IF YOU MUST.
MY BLOOD-STAINED GLOVE IS BURIED WITH HIM.
WHAT DID LT. GENERAL RAVEN TELL YOU?
HE TALKED OF AN IM-MORTAL ARMY...
...THE FOUND-ING OF THIS COUN-TRY...
...THE HOMUN-CULI...
...AND ABOUT YOUR TRUE IDENTITY, SIR.
HE TOLD ME MANY THINGS THAT I NEVER ASKED HIM ABOUT OR HAD ANY REASON TO SUSPECT.
AND YET YOU RESPONDED TO MY SUMMONS... AFTER EVERYTHING YOU HEARD?
YES, SIR.
TO ASK YOU TO BESTOW UPON ME THE POSITION THAT WAS OCCUPIED BY THAT FOOL, SIR.
HEH...

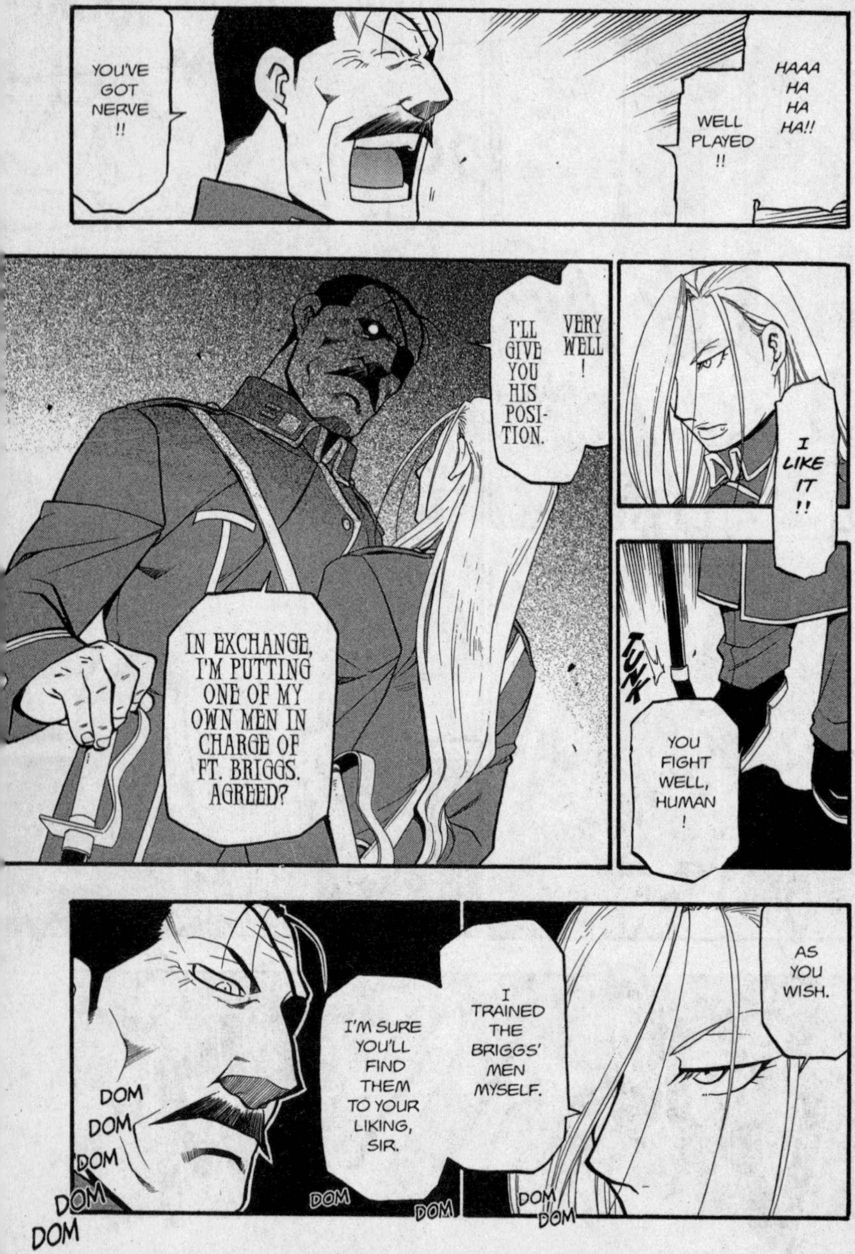
HAAA HA HA HA!!
WELL PLAYED !!
YOU'VE GOT NERVE !!
I LIKE IT !!
TUNK
YOU FIGHT WELL, HUMAN !
VERY WELL !
I'LL GIVE YOU HIS POSITION.
IN EXCHANGE, I'M PUTTING ONE OF MY OWN MEN IN CHARGE OF FT. BRIGGS. AGREED?
AS YOU WISH.
I TRAINED THE BRIGGS' MEN MYSELF.
I'M SURE YOU'LL FIND THEM TO YOUR LIKING, SIR.
DOM
DOM
DOM
DOM
DOM
DOM
DOM
DOM
DOM
DOM

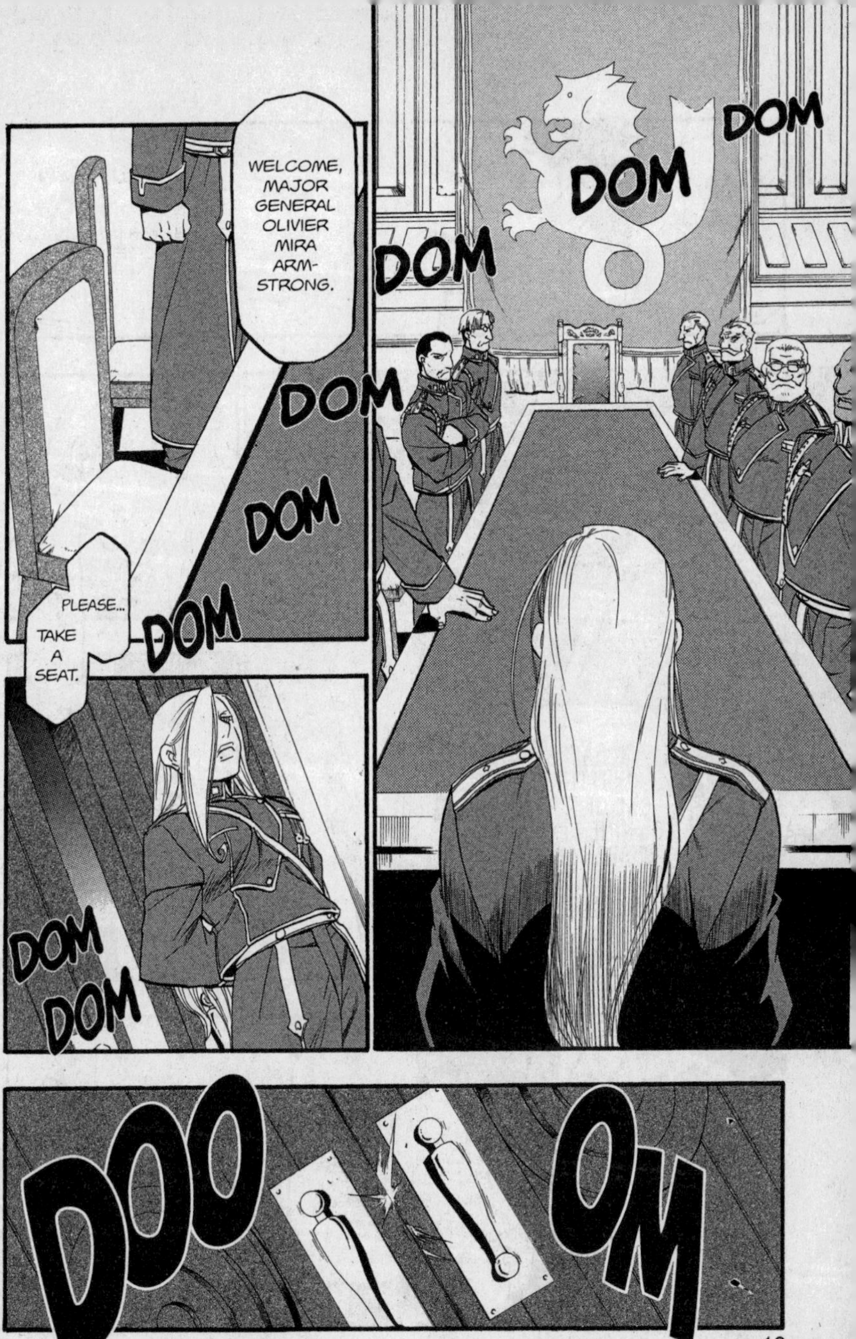
DOM
DOM
DOM
WELCOME, MAJOR GENERAL OLIVIER MIRA ARM-STRONG.
DOM
DOM
DOM
PLEASE... TAKE A SEAT.
DOM
DOM
DOOOM

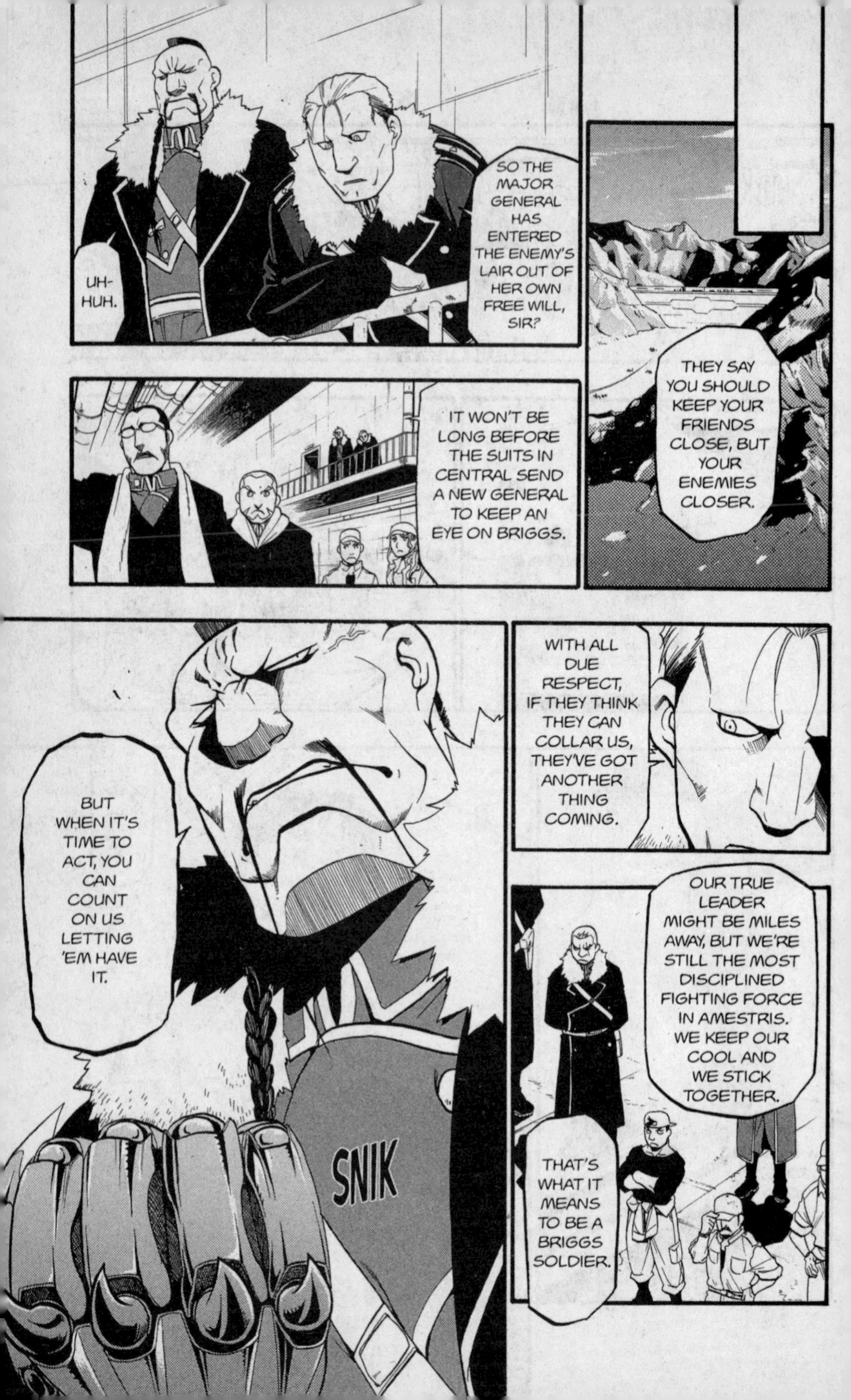
THEY SAY YOU SHOULD KEEP YOUR FRIENDS CLOSE, BUT YOUR ENEMIES CLOSER.
SO THE MAJOR GENERAL HAS ENTERED THE ENEMY'S LAIR OUT OF HER OWN FREE WILL, SIR?
UH-HUH.
IT WON'T BE LONG BEFORE THE SUITS IN CENTRAL SEND A NEW GENERAL TO KEEP AN EYE ON BRIGGS.
WITH ALL DUE RESPECT, IF THEY THINK THEY CAN COLLAR US, THEY'VE GOT ANOTHER THING COMING.
OUR TRUE LEADER MIGHT BE MILES AWAY, BUT WE'RE STILL THE MOST DISCIPLINED FIGHTING FORCE IN AMESTRIS. WE KEEP OUR COOL AND WE STICK TOGETHER.
THAT'S WHAT IT MEANS TO BE A BRIGGS SOLDIER.
BUT WHEN IT'S TIME TO ACT, YOU CAN COUNT ON US LETTING 'EM HAVE IT.
SNIK

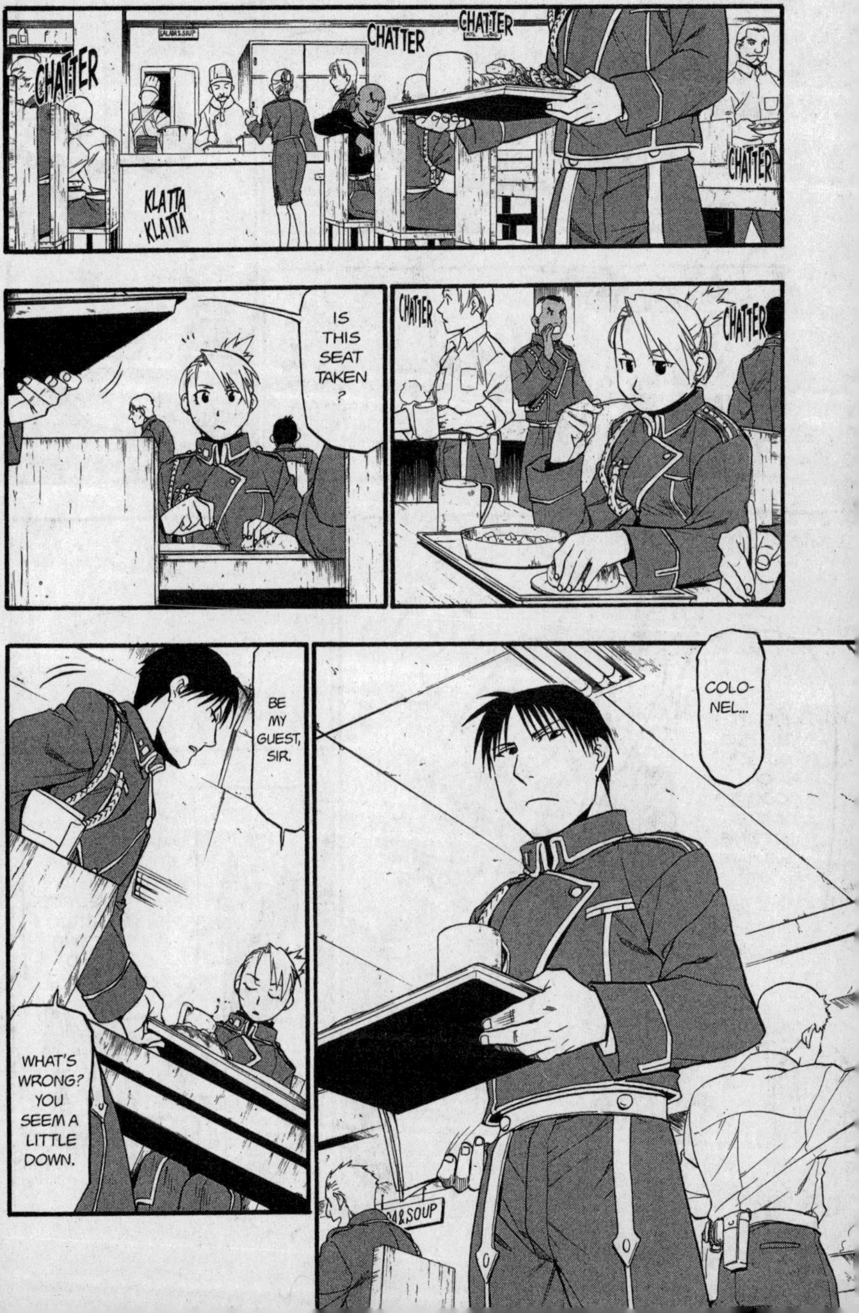
CHATTER
CHATTER
CHATTER
CHATTER
KLATTA KLATTA
CHATTER
CHATTER
IS THIS SEAT TAKEN?
COLO-NEL...
BE MY GUEST, SIR.
WHAT'S WRONG? YOU SEEM A LITTLE DOWN.

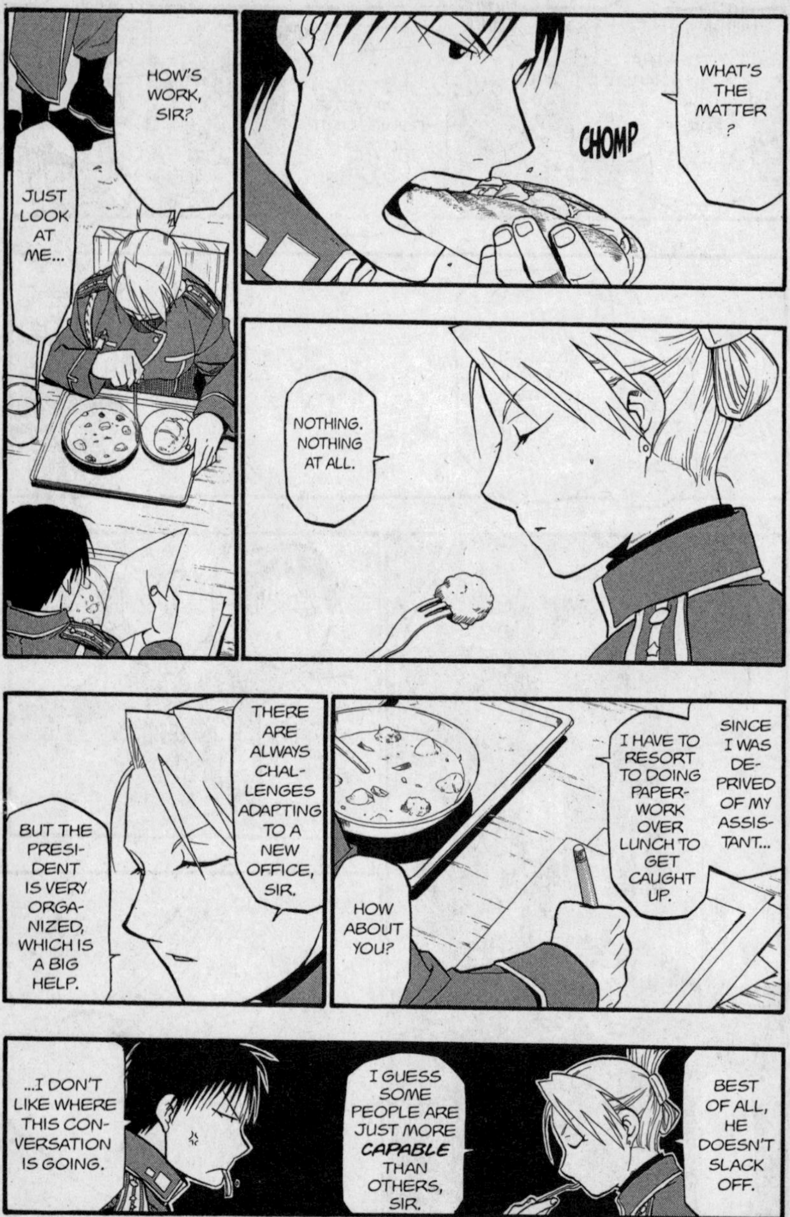
WHAT'S THE MATTER?
CHOMP
NOTHING. NOTHING AT ALL.
HOW'S WORK, SIR?
JUST LOOK AT ME...
SINCE I WAS DEPRIVED OF MY ASSISTANT...
I HAVE TO RESORT TO DOING PAPERWORK OVER LUNCH TO GET CAUGHT UP.
HOW ABOUT YOU?
THERE ARE ALWAYS CHALLENGES ADAPTING TO A NEW OFFICE, SIR.
BUT THE PRESIDENT IS VERY ORGANIZED, WHICH IS A BIG HELP.
BEST OF ALL, HE DOESN'T SLACK OFF.
I GUESS SOME PEOPLE ARE JUST MORE *CAPABLE* THAN OTHERS, SIR.
...I DON'T LIKE WHERE THIS CONVERSATION IS GOING.

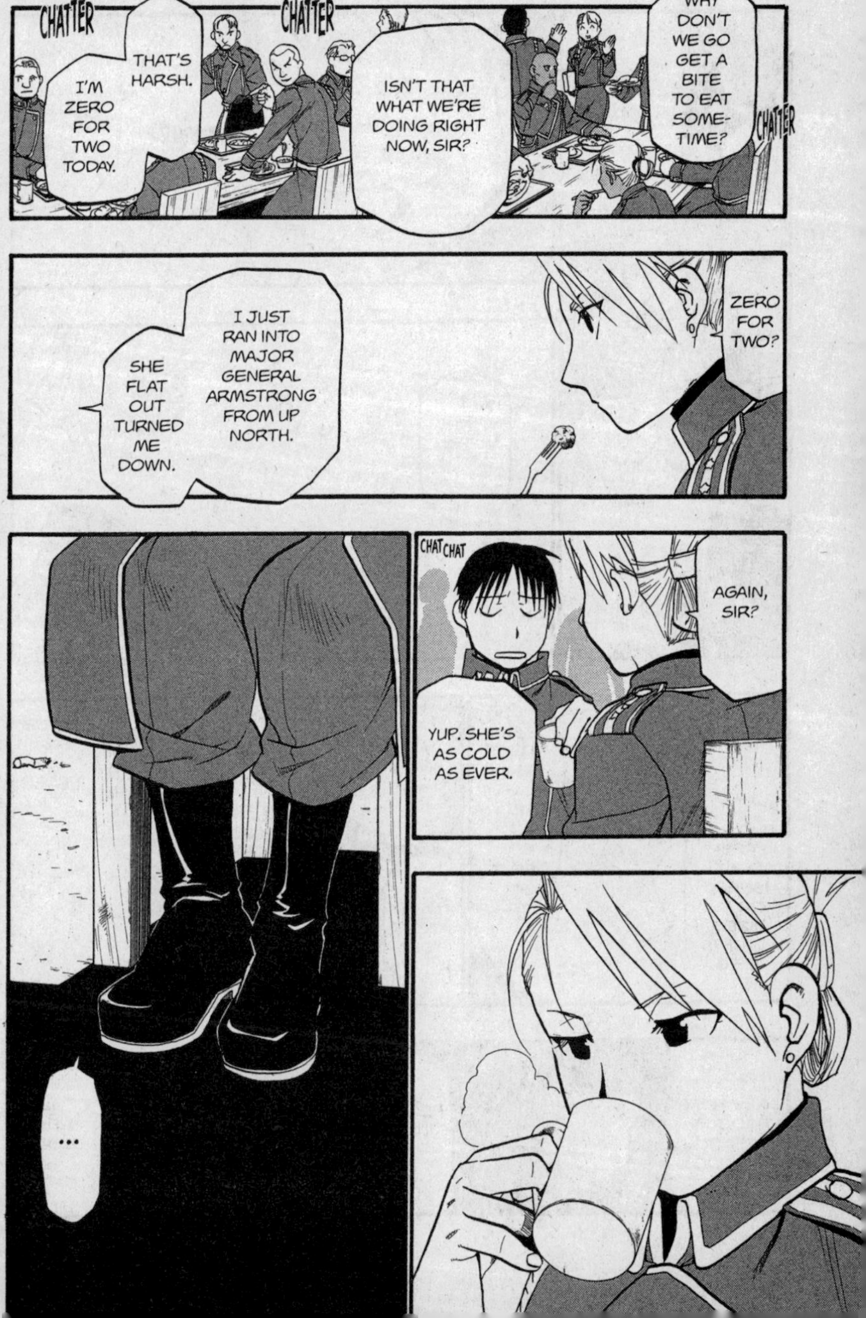
WHY DON'T WE GO GET A BITE TO EAT SOMETIME?
CHATTER
ISN'T THAT WHAT WE'RE DOING RIGHT NOW, SIR?
CHATTER
THAT'S HARSH.
I'M ZERO FOR TWO TODAY.
CHATTER
ZERO FOR TWO?
I JUST RAN INTO MAJOR GENERAL ARMSTRONG FROM UP NORTH.
SHE FLAT OUT TURNED ME DOWN.
CHAT CHAT
AGAIN, SIR?
YUP. SHE'S AS COLD AS EVER.
...

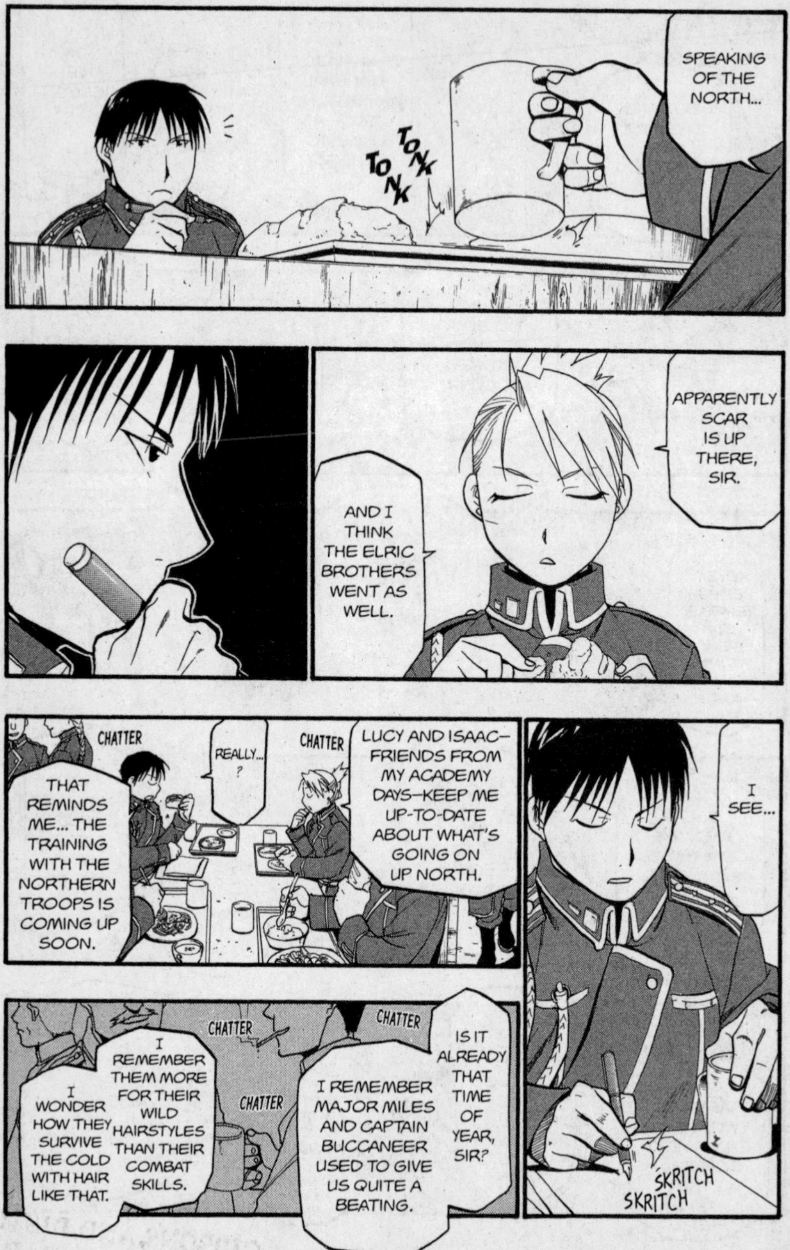
SPEAKING OF THE NORTH...
TONK TONK
APPARENTLY SCAR IS UP THERE, SIR.
AND I THINK THE ELRIC BROTHERS WENT AS WELL.
I SEE...
SKRITCH SKRITCH
LUCY AND ISAAC—FRIENDS FROM MY ACADEMY DAYS—KEEP ME UP-TO-DATE ABOUT WHAT'S GOING ON UP NORTH.
CHATTER
REALLY... ?
CHATTER
THAT REMINDS ME... THE TRAINING WITH THE NORTHERN TROOPS IS COMING UP SOON.
IS IT ALREADY THAT TIME OF YEAR, SIR?
CHATTER
I REMEMBER MAJOR MILES AND CAPTAIN BUCCANEER USED TO GIVE US QUITE A BEATING.
CHATTER
CHATTER
I REMEMBER THEM MORE FOR THEIR WILD HAIRSTYLES THAN THEIR COMBAT SKILLS.
I WONDER HOW THEY SURVIVE THE COLD WITH HAIR LIKE THAT.

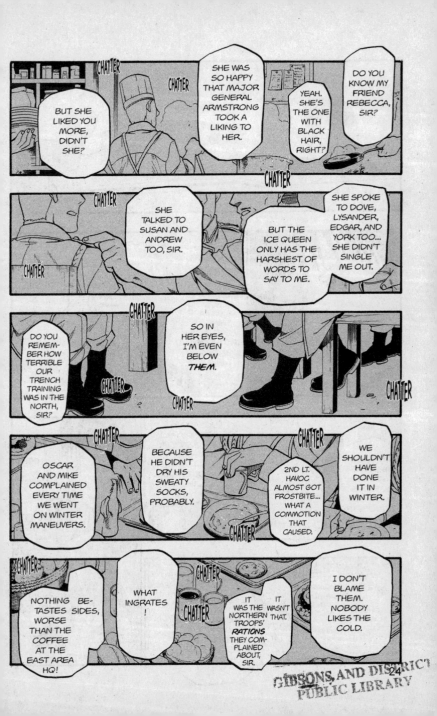

BUT SHE LIKED YOU MORE, DIDN'T SHE?

SHE WAS SO HAPPY THAT MAJOR GENERAL ARMSTRONG TOOK A LIKING TO HER.

YEAH. SHE'S THE ONE WITH BLACK HAIR, RIGHT?

DO YOU KNOW MY FRIEND REBECCA, SIR?

CHATTER

CHATTER

CHATTER

SHE TALKED TO SUSAN AND ANDREW TOO, SIR.

BUT THE ICE QUEEN ONLY HAS THE HARSHEST OF WORDS TO SAY TO ME.

SHE SPOKE TO DOVE, LYSANDER, EDGAR, AND YORK TOO... SHE DIDN'T SINGLE ME OUT.

CHATTER

CHATTER

DO YOU REMEMBER HOW TERRIBLE OUR TRENCH TRAINING WAS IN THE NORTH, SIR?

SO IN HER EYES, I'M EVEN BELOW *THEM*.

CHATTER

CHATTER

CHATTER

CHATTER

OSCAR AND MIKE COMPLAINED EVERY TIME WE WENT ON WINTER MANEUVERS.

BECAUSE HE DIDN'T DRY HIS SWEATY SOCKS, PROBABLY.

2ND LT. HAVOC ALMOST GOT FROSTBITE... WHAT A COMMOTION THAT CAUSED.

WE SHOULDN'T HAVE DONE IT IN WINTER.

CHATTER

CHATTER

CHATTER

NOTHING BE-TASTES SIDES, WORSE THAN THE COFFEE AT THE EAST AREA HQ!

WHAT INGRATES!

IT WAS THE NORTHERN TROOPS' *RATIONS* THEY COM-PLAINED ABOUT, SIR.

IT WASN'T THAT.

I DON'T BLAME THEM. NOBODY LIKES THE COLD.

CHATTER

CHATTER

GIBSONS AND DISTRICT PUBLIC LIBRARY

24

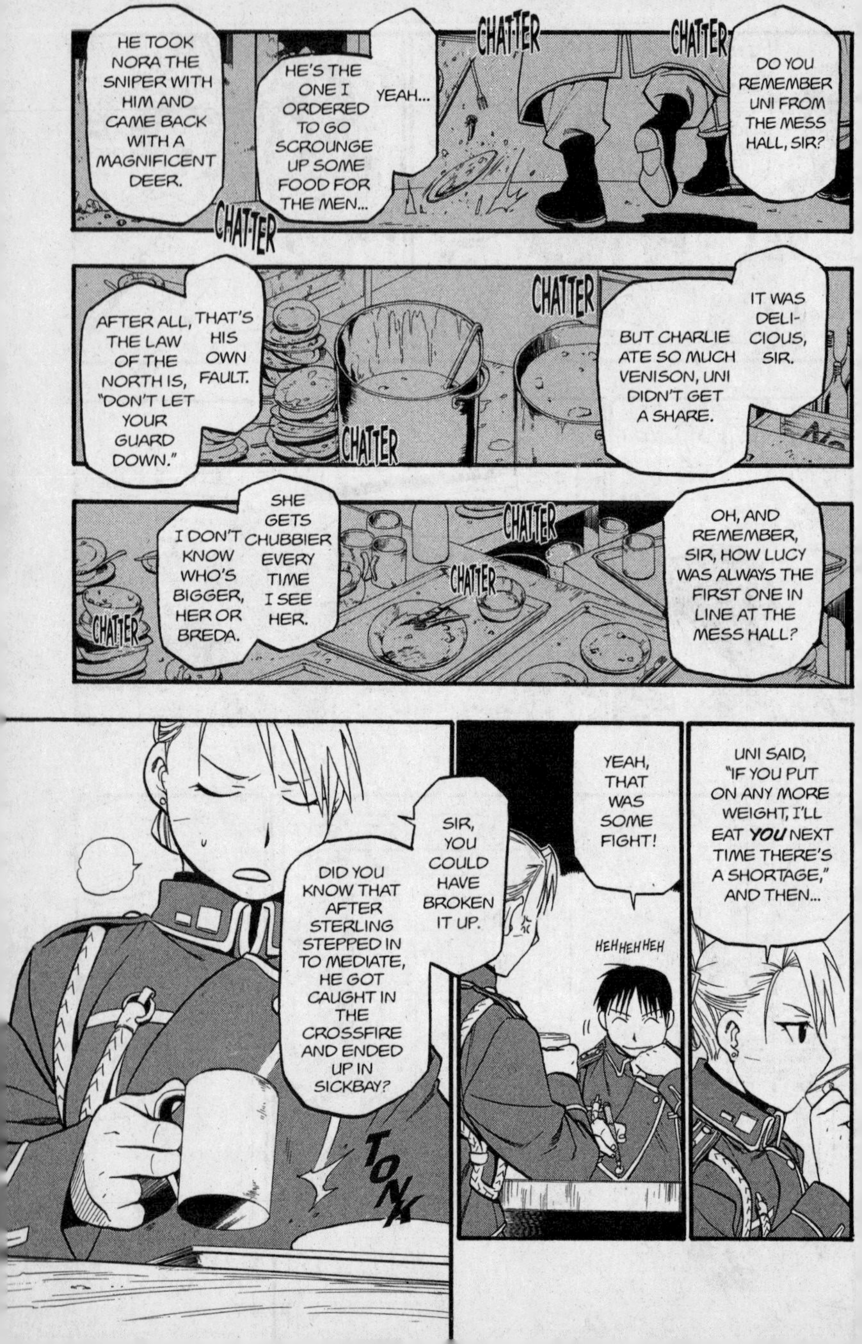
CHATTER
CHATTER
DO YOU REMEMBER UNI FROM THE MESS HALL, SIR?
YEAH...
HE'S THE ONE I ORDERED TO GO SCROUNGE UP SOME FOOD FOR THE MEN...
HE TOOK NORA THE SNIPER WITH HIM AND CAME BACK WITH A MAGNIFICENT DEER.
CHATTER
IT WAS DELICIOUS, SIR.
BUT CHARLIE ATE SO MUCH VENISON, UNI DIDN'T GET A SHARE.
CHATTER
CHATTER
THAT'S HIS OWN FAULT.
AFTER ALL, THE LAW OF THE NORTH IS, "DON'T LET YOUR GUARD DOWN."
OH, AND REMEMBER, SIR, HOW LUCY WAS ALWAYS THE FIRST ONE IN LINE AT THE MESS HALL?
CHATTER
CHATTER
SHE GETS CHUBBIER EVERY TIME I SEE HER.
I DON'T KNOW WHO'S BIGGER, HER OR BREDA.
CHATTER
UNI SAID, "IF YOU PUT ON ANY MORE WEIGHT, I'LL EAT **YOU** NEXT TIME THERE'S A SHORTAGE," AND THEN...
YEAH, THAT WAS SOME FIGHT!
HEH HEH HEH
SIR, YOU COULD HAVE BROKEN IT UP.
DID YOU KNOW THAT AFTER STERLING STEPPED IN TO MEDIATE, HE GOT CAUGHT IN THE CROSSFIRE AND ENDED UP IN SICKBAY?
TONK

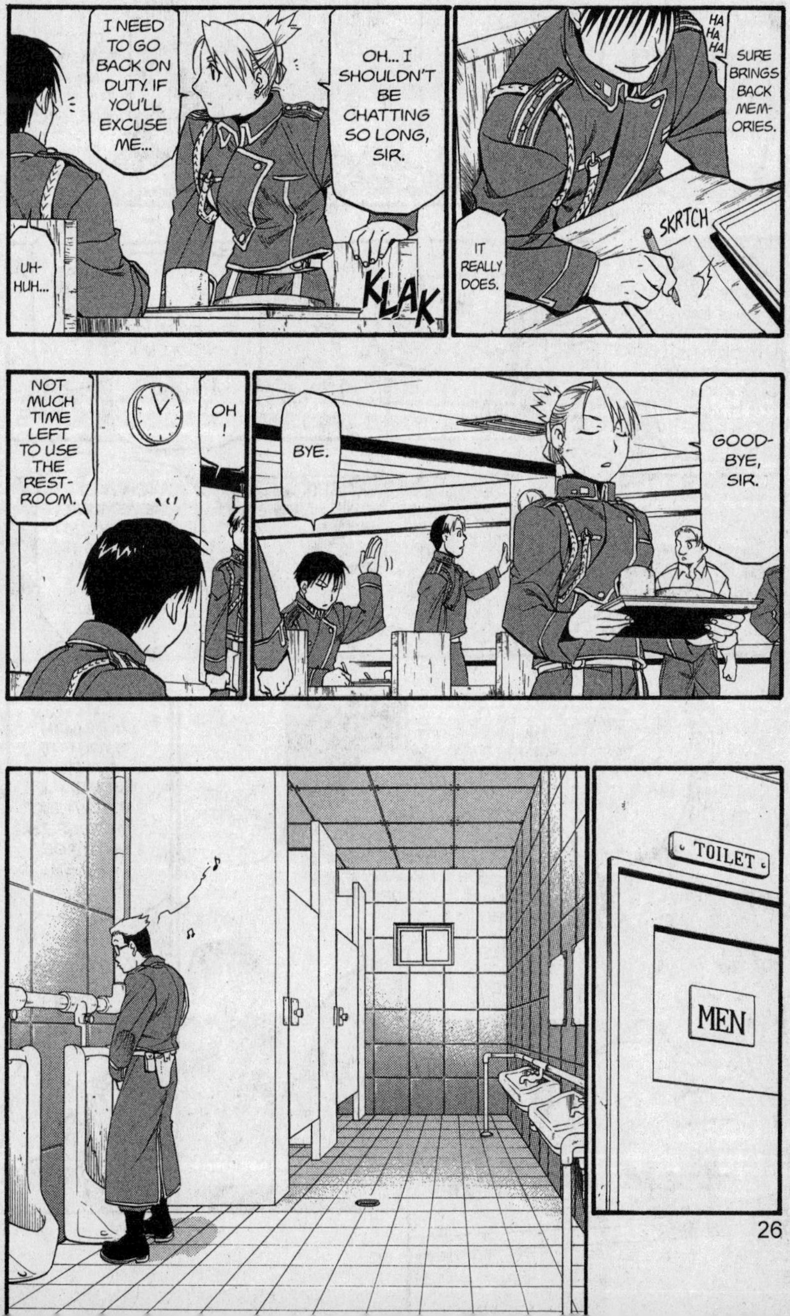
HA HA HA
SURE BRINGS BACK MEM-ORIES.
SKRTCH
IT REALLY DOES.
OH... I SHOULDN'T BE CHATTING SO LONG, SIR.
I NEED TO GO BACK ON DUTY. IF YOU'LL EXCUSE ME...
UH-HUH...
KLAK
GOOD-BYE, SIR.
BYE.
OH!
NOT MUCH TIME LEFT TO USE THE REST-ROOM.
TOILET
MEN

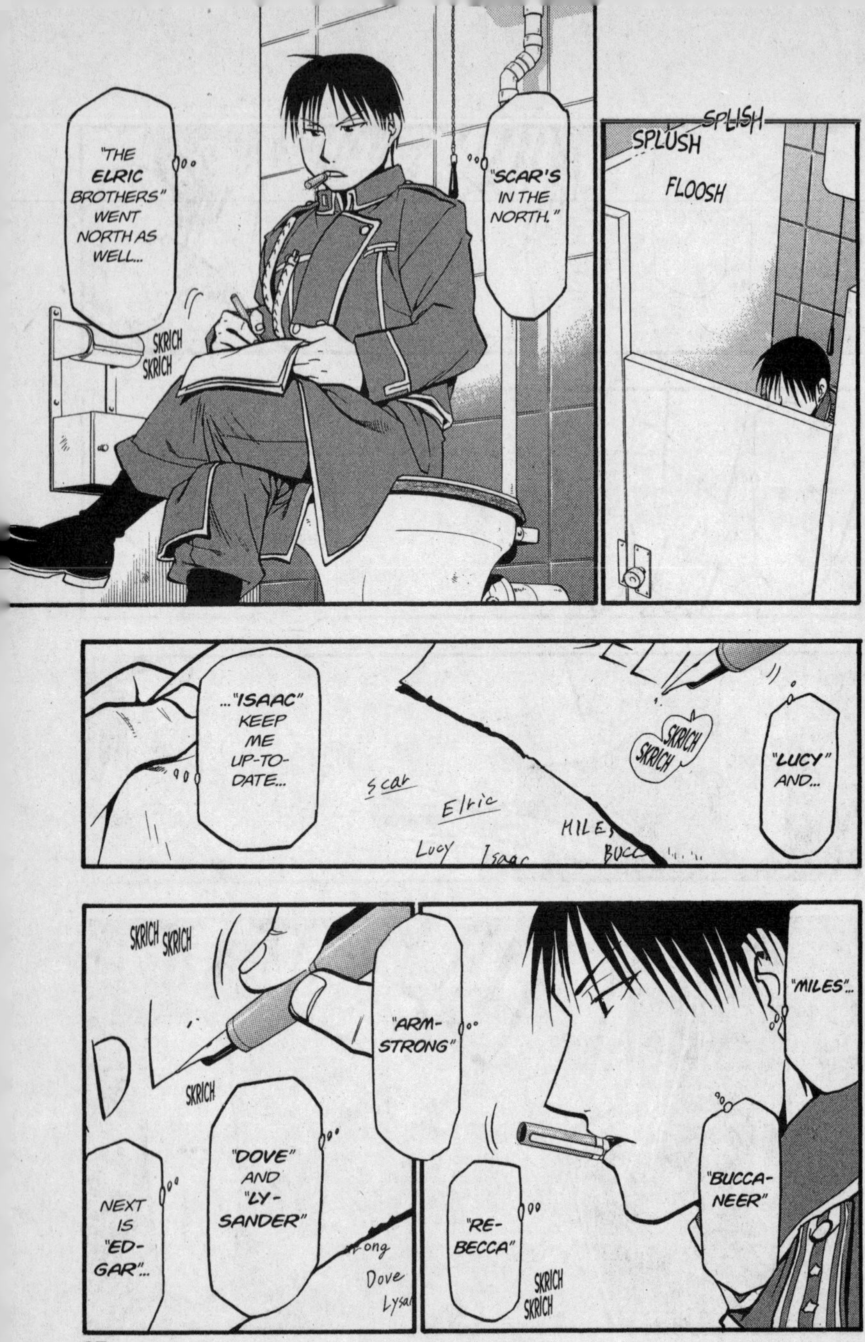
SPLISH
SPLUSH
FLOOSH
"SCAR'S IN THE NORTH."
"THE ELRIC BROTHERS" WENT NORTH AS WELL...
SKRICH SKRICH
"LUCY" AND...
SKRICH SKRICH
...."ISAAC" KEEP ME UP-TO-DATE...
Scar
Elric
Lucy
"MILES"...
"BUCCA-NEER"
"RE-BECCA"
SKRICH SKRICH
"ARM-STRONG"
SKRICH SKRICH
SKRICH
"DOVE" AND "LY-SANDER"
Dove
NEXT IS "ED-GAR"...

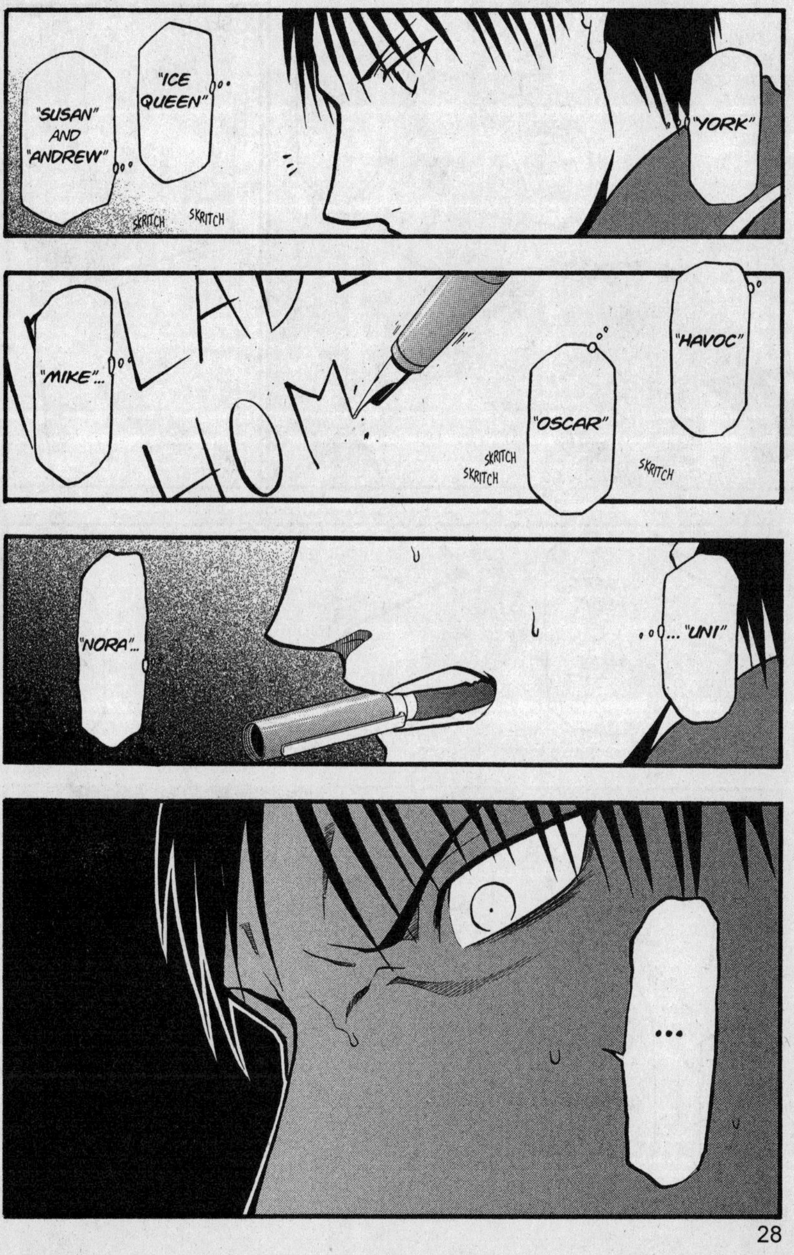
"YORK"
"ICE QUEEN"
"SUSAN" AND "ANDREW"
SKRITCH
SKRITCH
"HAVOC"
SKRITCH
"OSCAR"
SKRITCH
SKRITCH
"MIKE"...
..."UNI"
"NORA"...
...

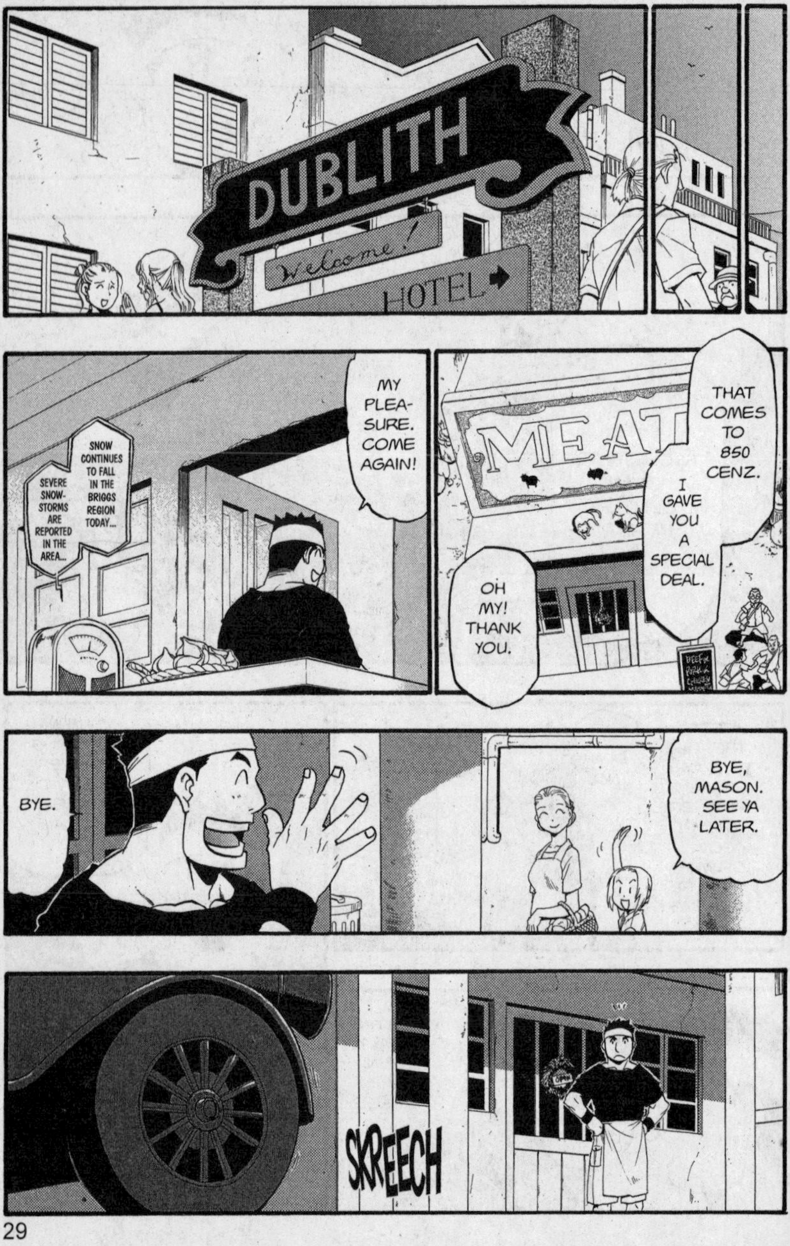
DUBLITH
Welcome!
HOTEL
THAT COMES TO 850 CENZ.
I GAVE YOU A SPECIAL DEAL.
OH MY! THANK YOU.
MY PLEASURE. COME AGAIN!
SNOW CONTINUES TO FALL IN THE BRIGGS REGION TODAY...
SEVERE SNOW-STORMS ARE REPORTED IN THE AREA...
MEAT
BYE, MASON. SEE YA LATER.
BYE.
SKREECH

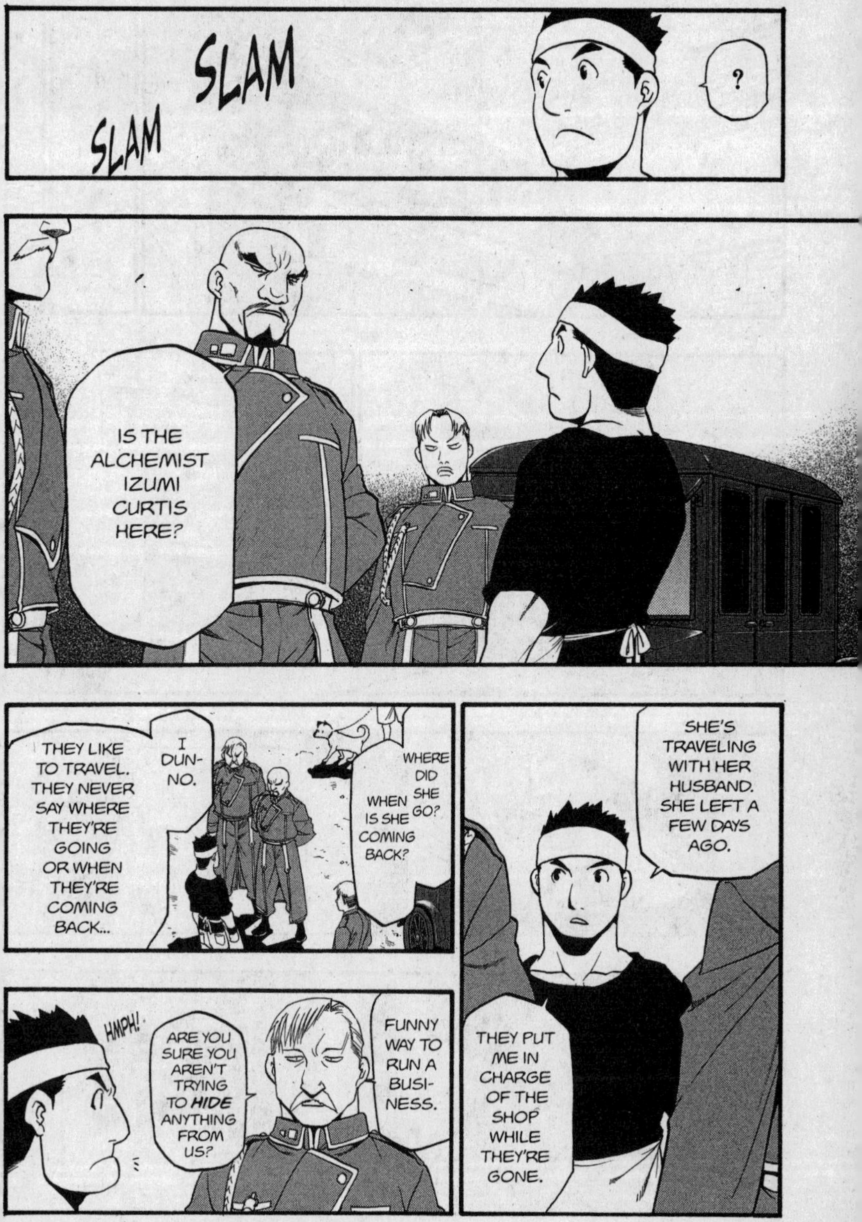
?
SLAM
SLAM
IS THE ALCHEMIST IZUMI CURTIS HERE?
SHE'S TRAVELING WITH HER HUSBAND. SHE LEFT A FEW DAYS AGO.
THEY PUT ME IN CHARGE OF THE SHOP WHILE THEY'RE GONE.
WHERE DID SHE GO?
WHEN IS SHE COMING BACK?
I DUN-NO.
THEY LIKE TO TRAVEL. THEY NEVER SAY WHERE THEY'RE GOING OR WHEN THEY'RE COMING BACK...
FUNNY WAY TO RUN A BUSI-NESS.
ARE YOU SURE YOU AREN'T TRYING TO *HIDE* ANYTHING FROM US?
HMPH!

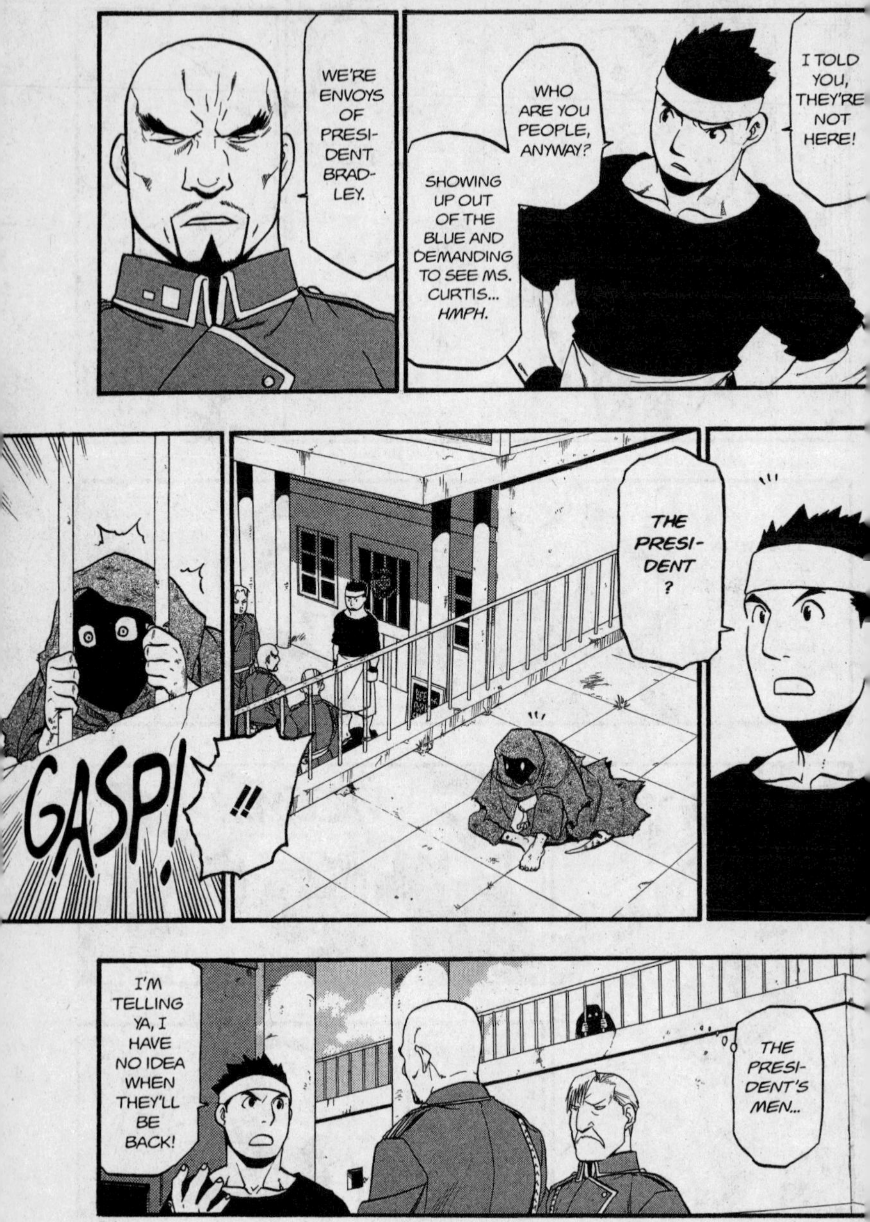
I TOLD YOU, THEY'RE NOT HERE!
WHO ARE YOU PEOPLE, ANYWAY?
SHOWING UP OUT OF THE BLUE AND DEMANDING TO SEE MS. CURTIS... HMPH.
WE'RE ENVOYS OF PRESIDENT BRADLEY.
THE PRESIDENT?
GASP!
!!
THE PRESIDENT'S MEN...
I'M TELLING YA, I HAVE NO IDEA WHEN THEY'LL BE BACK!

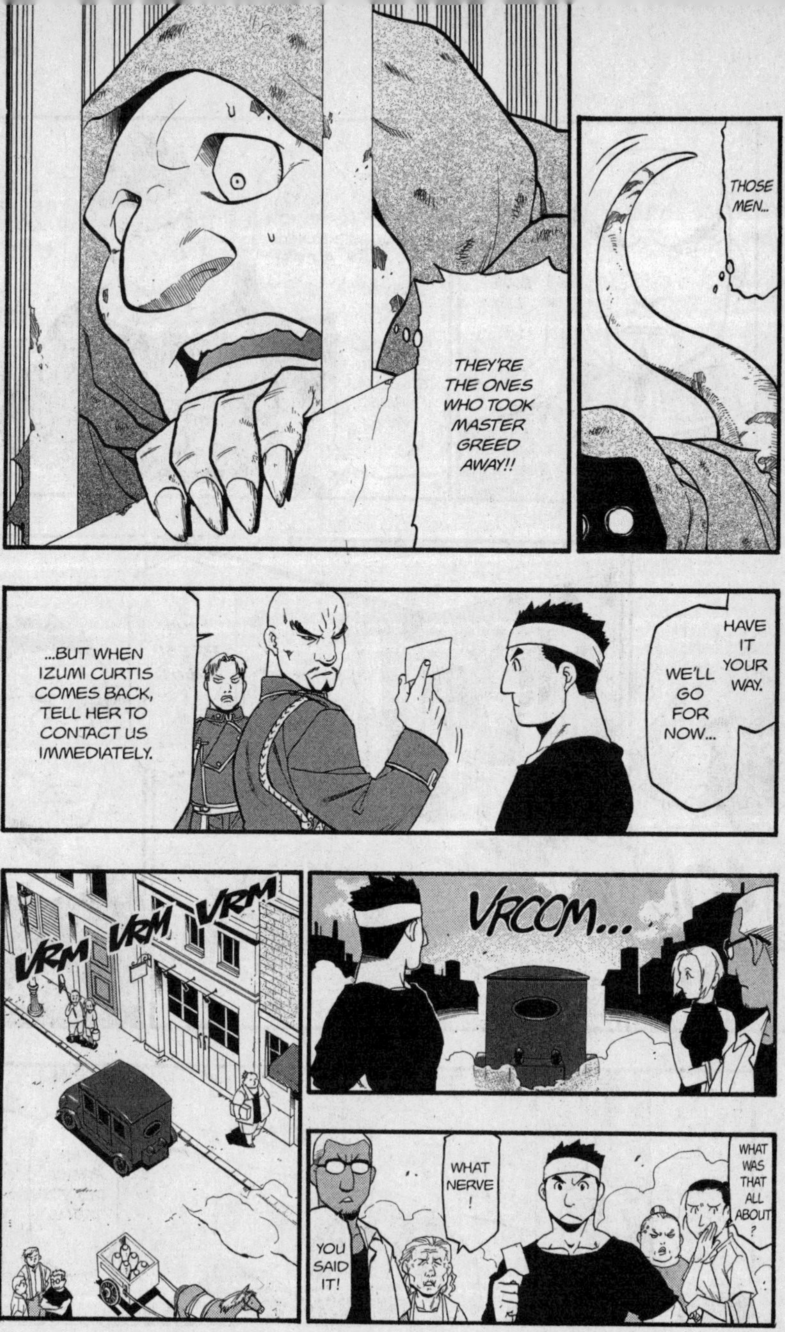
THOSE MEN...
THEY'RE THE ONES WHO TOOK MASTER GREED AWAY!!
HAVE IT YOUR WAY.
WE'LL GO FOR NOW...
...BUT WHEN IZUMI CURTIS COMES BACK, TELL HER TO CONTACT US IMMEDIATELY.
VRCOM...
WHAT WAS THAT ALL ABOUT?
WHAT NERVE!
YOU SAID IT!
VRM VRM VRM

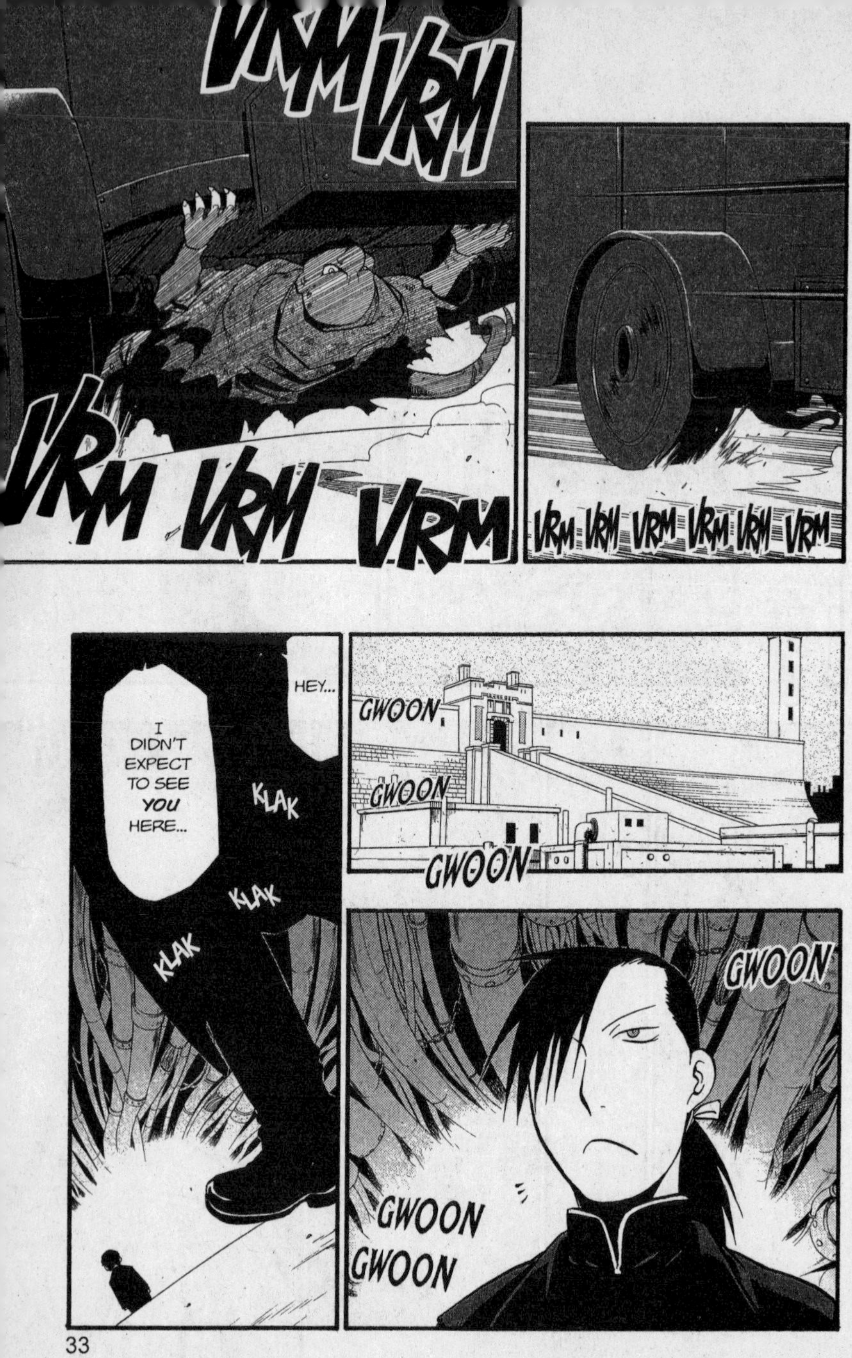
VRM VRM VRM VRM VRM VRM
VRM VRM
VRM VRM VRM
GWOON
GWOON
GWOON
GWOON
GWOON
GWOON
HEY...
I DIDN'T EXPECT TO SEE *YOU* HERE...
KLAK
KLAK
KLAK

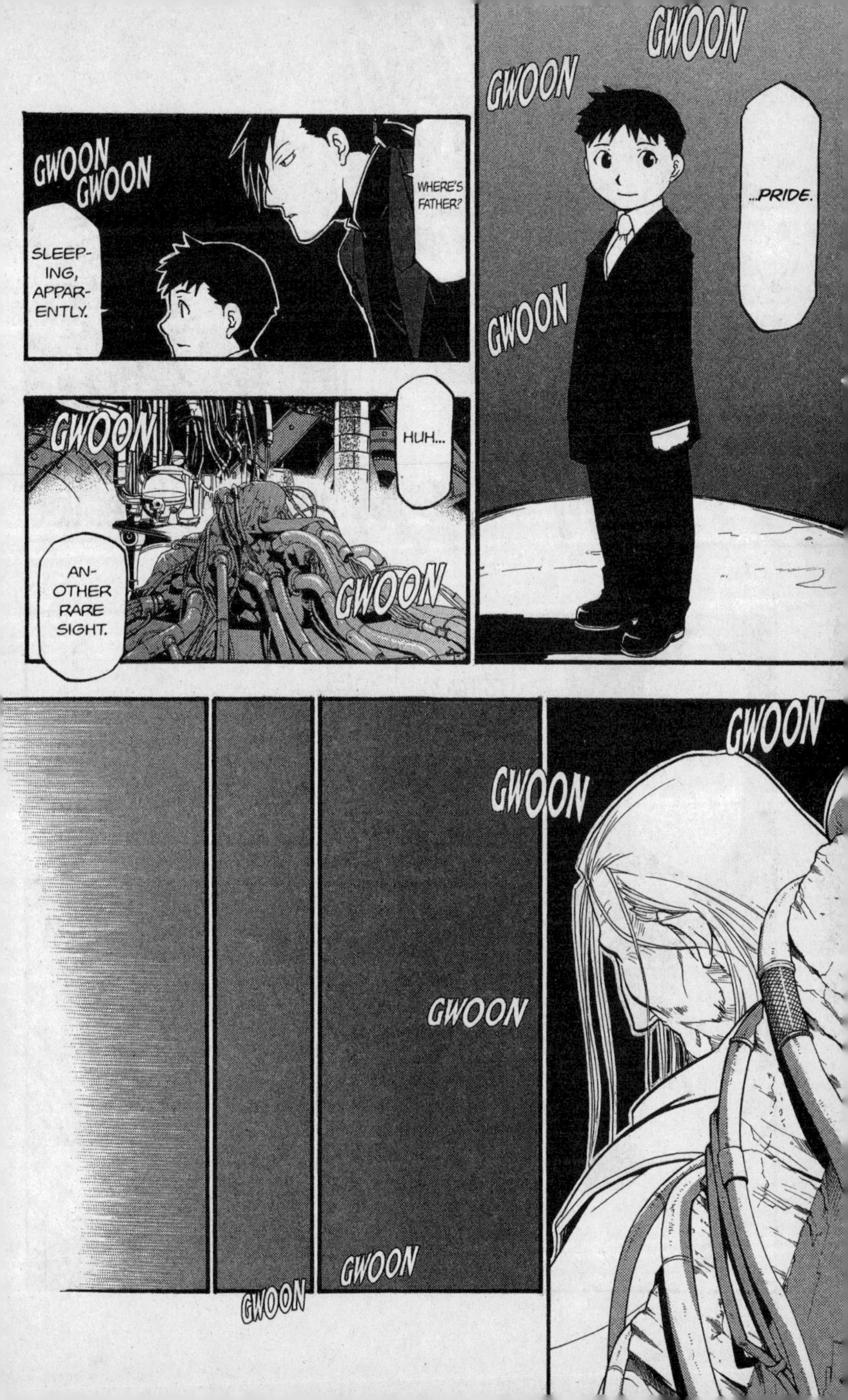
GWOON
GWOON
...PRIDE.
GWOON
GWOON
GWOON
WHERE'S FATHER?
SLEEP-ING, APPAR-ENTLY.
HUH...
GWOON
AN-OTHER RARE SIGHT.
GWOON
GWOON
GWOON
GWOON
GWOON
GWOON

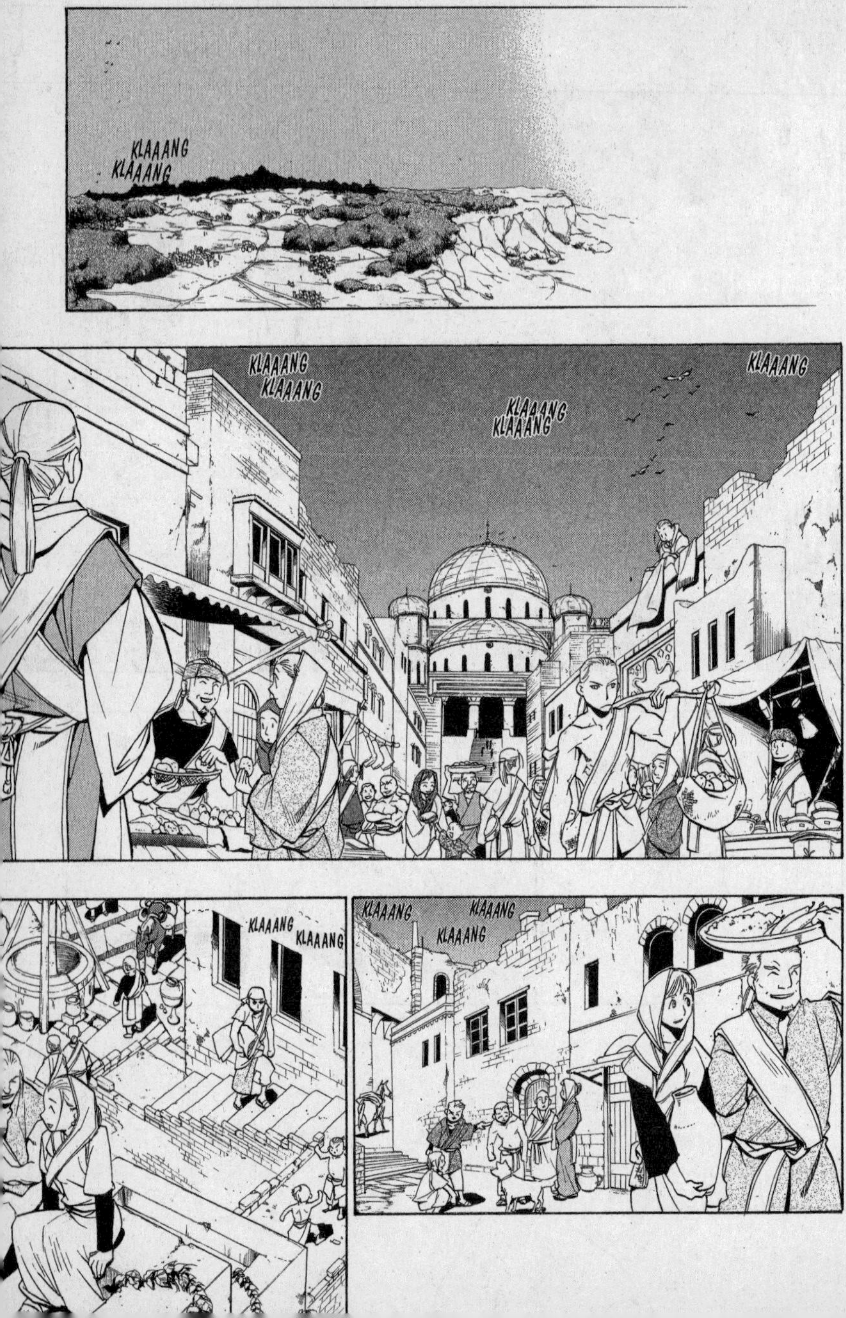
KLAAANG
KLAAANG
KLAAANG
KLAAANG
KLAAANG
KLAAANG
KLAAANG
KLAAANG
KLAAANG
KLAAANG
KLAAANG
KLAAANG
KLAAANG

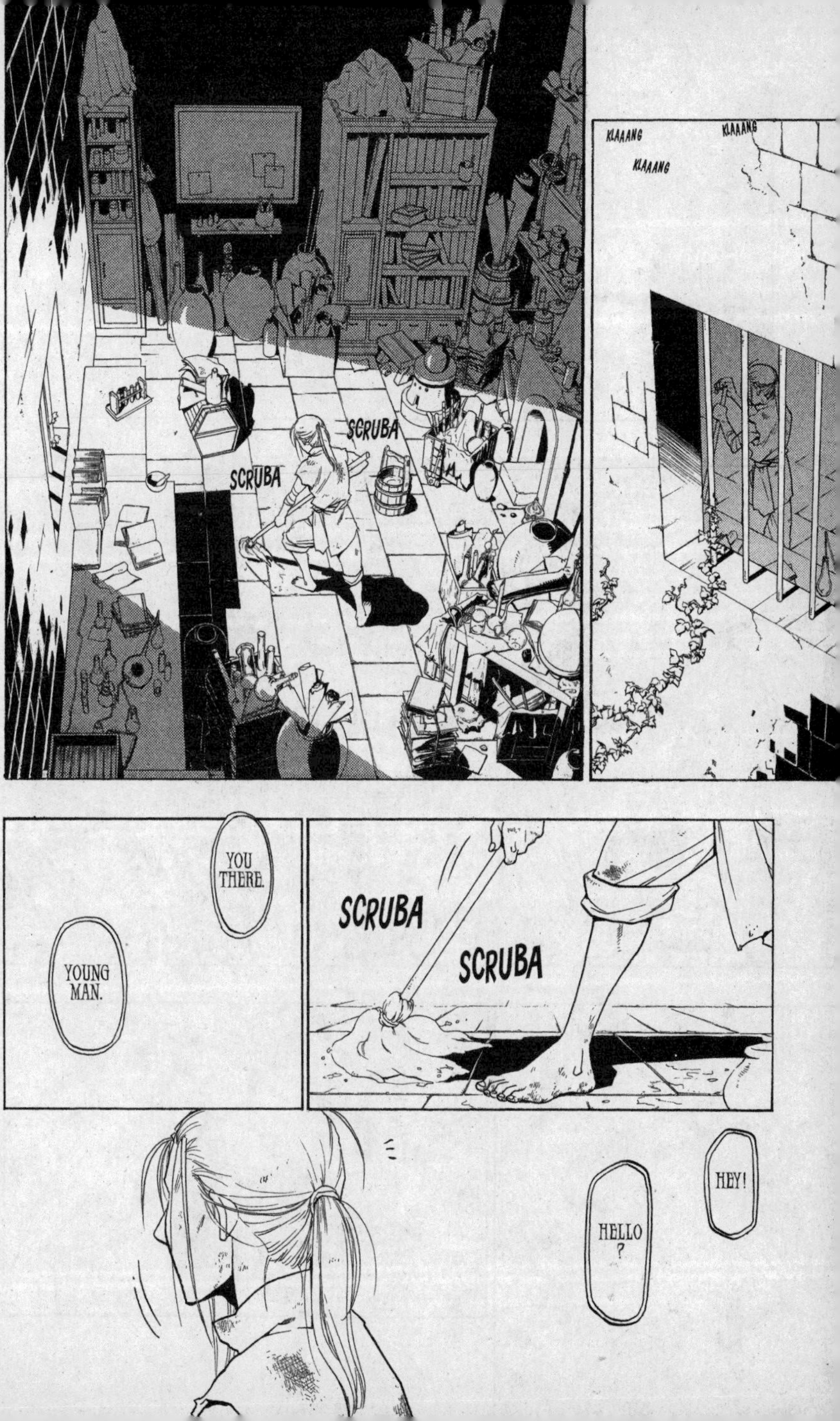
KLAAANG
KLAAANG
KLAAANG
SCRUBA
SCRUBA
SCRUBA
SCRUBA
YOU THERE.
YOUNG MAN.
HEY!
HELLO?

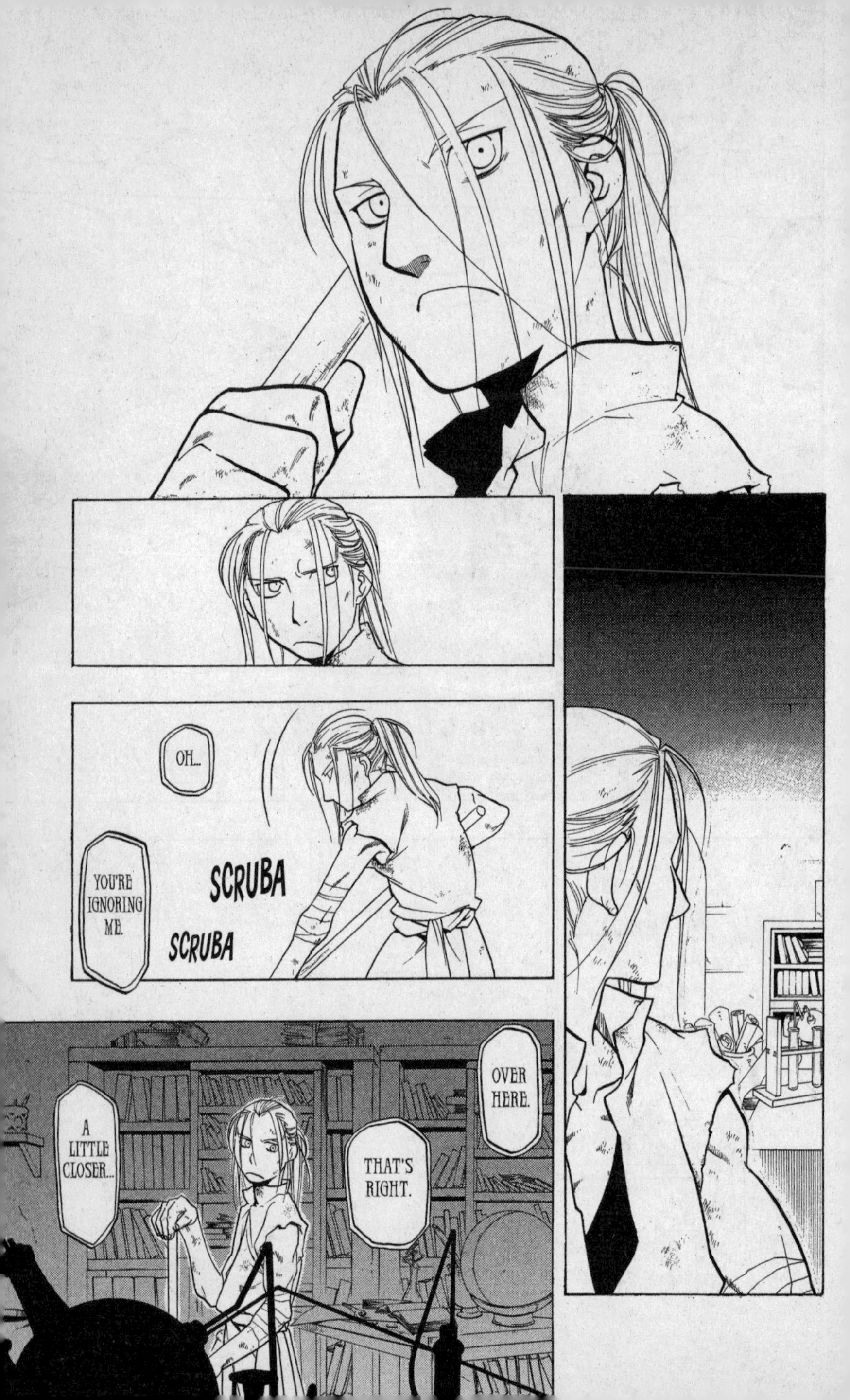
OH...
SCRUBA
YOU'RE IGNORING ME.
SCRUBA
OVER HERE.
THAT'S RIGHT.
A LITTLE CLOSER...

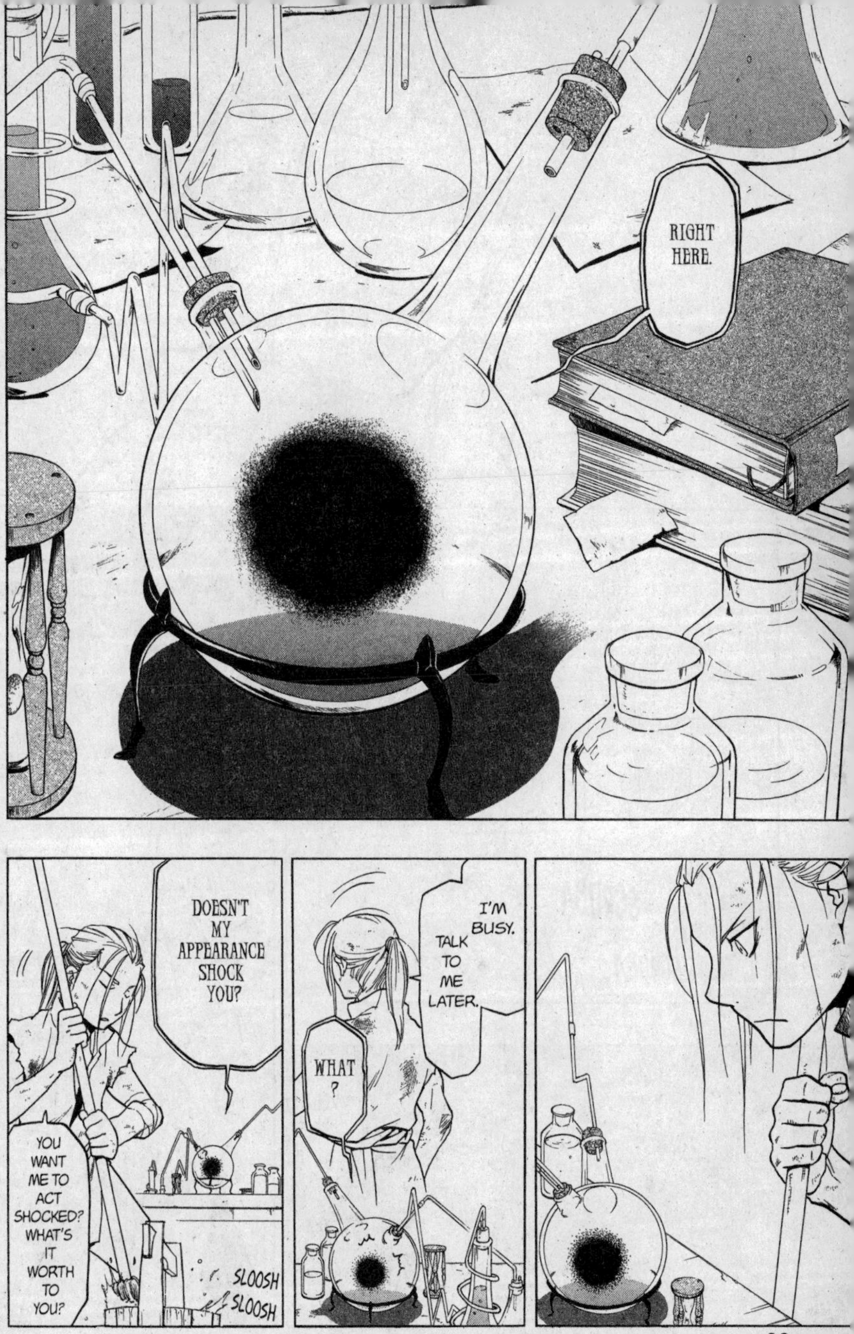
RIGHT HERE.
I'M BUSY. TALK TO ME LATER.
WHAT?
DOESN'T MY APPEARANCE SHOCK YOU?
YOU WANT ME TO ACT SHOCKED? WHAT'S IT WORTH TO YOU?
SLOSH SLOSH

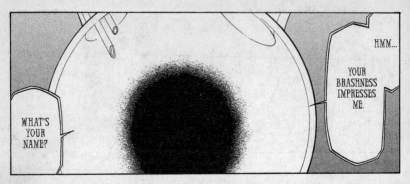

HMM...
YOUR BRASHNESS IMPRESSES ME.
WHAT'S YOUR NAME?
NUMBER TWENTY-THREE.
SCRUBA SCRUBA
MR. TWENTY-THREE?
DON'T TELL ME YOUR NUMBER, TELL ME YOUR NAME.
I DON'T HAVE ONE.
I'M A SLAVE.
A SLAVE...
YOU MEAN, "THOSE WHO HAVE BEEN DENIED THEIR FREEDOM AND RIGHTS, WHOSE OWNERSHIP IS TRANSFERRED AND SOLD TO OTHERS AS A COMMODITY"?
?
TRANS-FERRED?
"A CONVEYANCE, BY SALE, GIFT, OR OTHERWISE, OF REAL OR PERSONAL PROPERTY, TO ANOTHER."
HUH?
...
YOU'RE NOT VERY SMART, ARE YOU?
SHUT UP!!!

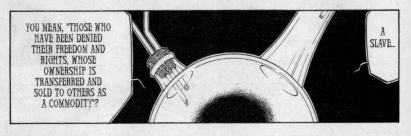

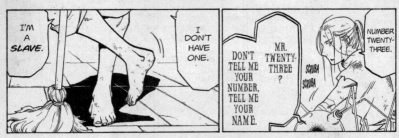

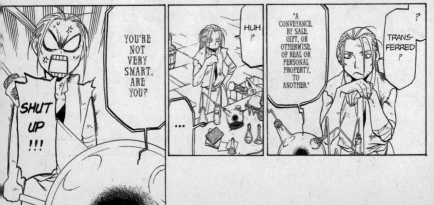

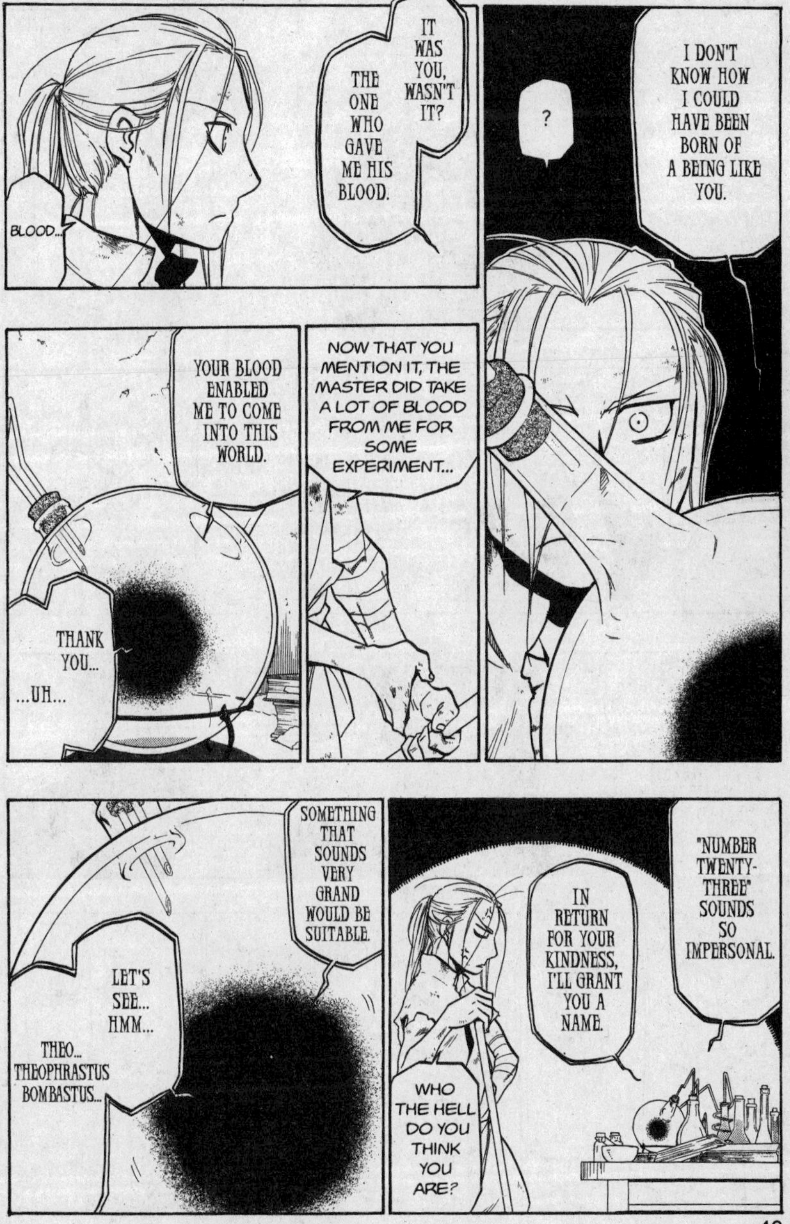
I DON'T KNOW HOW I COULD HAVE BEEN BORN OF A BEING LIKE YOU.
?
IT WAS YOU, WASN'T IT?
THE ONE WHO GAVE ME HIS BLOOD.
BLOOD...
NOW THAT YOU MENTION IT, THE MASTER DID TAKE A LOT OF BLOOD FROM ME FOR SOME EXPERIMENT...
YOUR BLOOD ENABLED ME TO COME INTO THIS WORLD.
THANK YOU...
...UH...
"NUMBER TWENTY-THREE" SOUNDS SO IMPERSONAL.
IN RETURN FOR YOUR KINDNESS, I'LL GRANT YOU A NAME.
WHO THE HELL DO YOU THINK YOU ARE?
SOMETHING THAT SOUNDS VERY GRAND WOULD BE SUITABLE.
LET'S SEE... HMM...
THEO... THEOPHRASTUS BOMBASTUS...

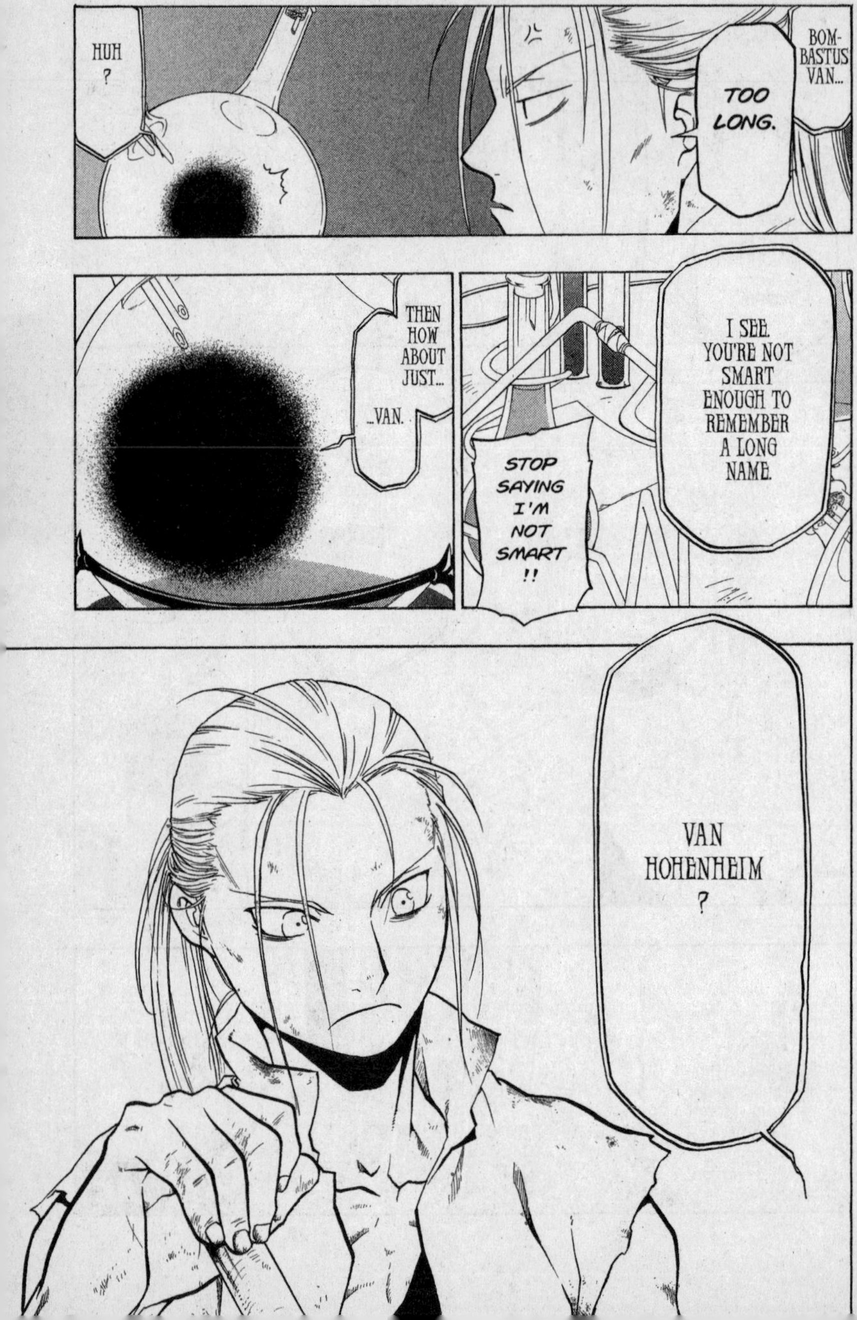
BOMBASTUS VAN...
TOO LONG.
HUH ?
I SEE. YOU'RE NOT SMART ENOUGH TO REMEMBER A LONG NAME.
STOP SAYING I'M NOT SMART !!
THEN HOW ABOUT JUST...
...VAN.
VAN HOHENHEIM ?

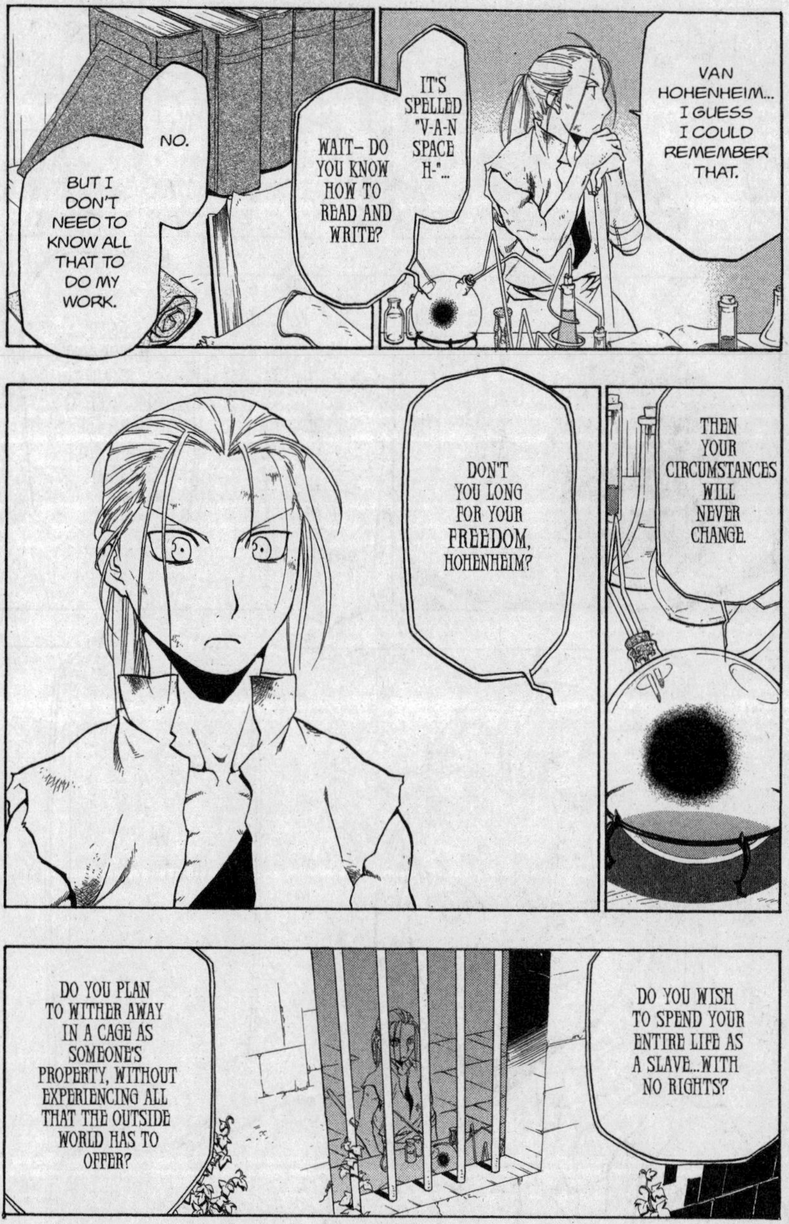
VAN HOHENHEIM... I GUESS I COULD REMEMBER THAT.
IT'S SPELLED "V-A-N SPACE H-"...
WAIT— DO YOU KNOW HOW TO READ AND WRITE?
NO.
BUT I DON'T NEED TO KNOW ALL THAT TO DO MY WORK.
THEN YOUR CIRCUMSTANCES WILL NEVER CHANGE.
DON'T YOU LONG FOR YOUR FREEDOM, HOHENHEIM?
DO YOU WISH TO SPEND YOUR ENTIRE LIFE AS A SLAVE...WITH NO RIGHTS?
DO YOU PLAN TO WITHER AWAY IN A CAGE AS SOMEONE'S PROPERTY, WITHOUT EXPERIENCING ALL THAT THE OUTSIDE WORLD HAS TO OFFER?

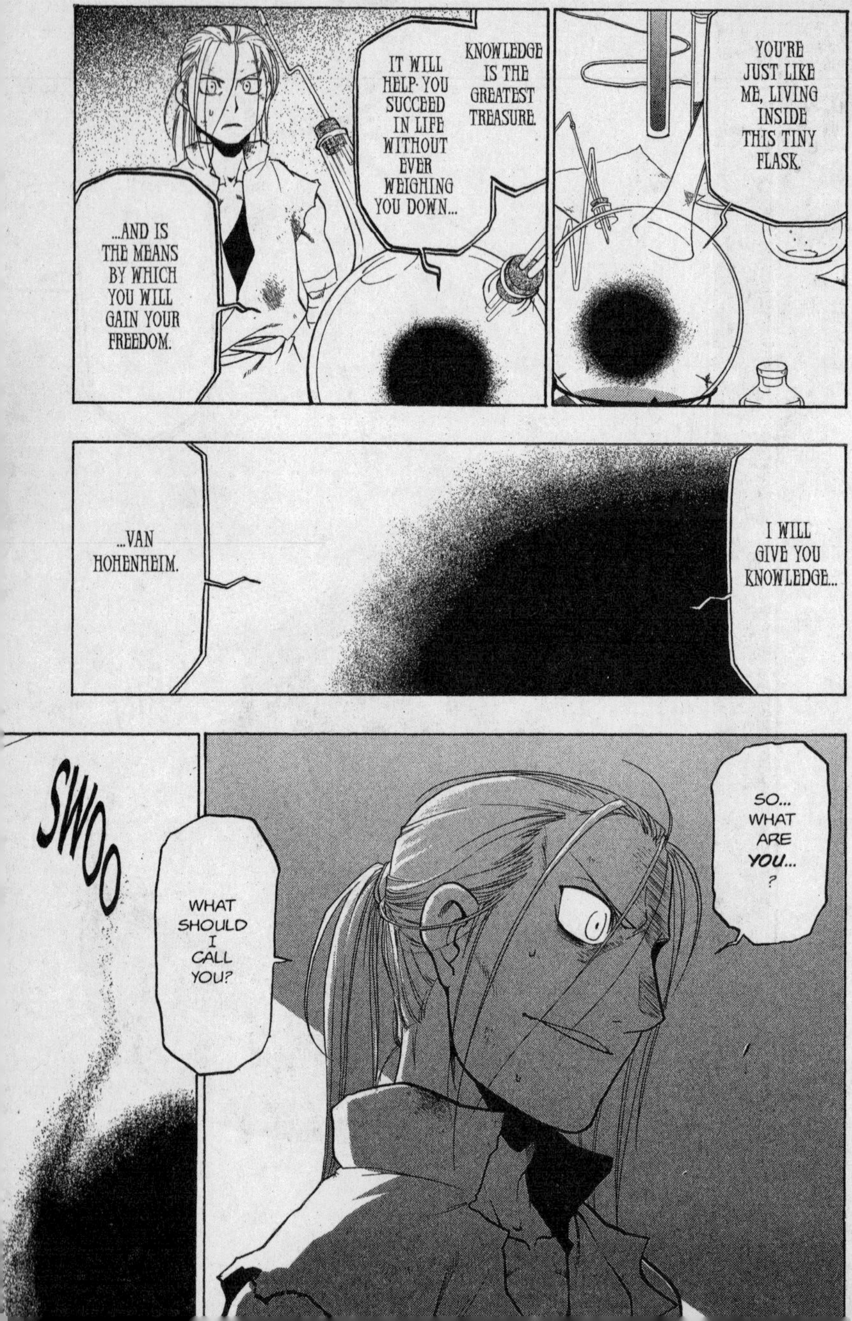
YOU'RE JUST LIKE ME, LIVING INSIDE THIS TINY FLASK.
KNOWLEDGE IS THE GREATEST TREASURE.
IT WILL HELP YOU SUCCEED IN LIFE WITHOUT EVER WEIGHING YOU DOWN...
...AND IS THE MEANS BY WHICH YOU WILL GAIN YOUR FREEDOM.
I WILL GIVE YOU KNOWLEDGE...
...VAN HOHENHEIM.
SO... WHAT ARE *YOU*...?
WHAT SHOULD I CALL YOU?
SWOO

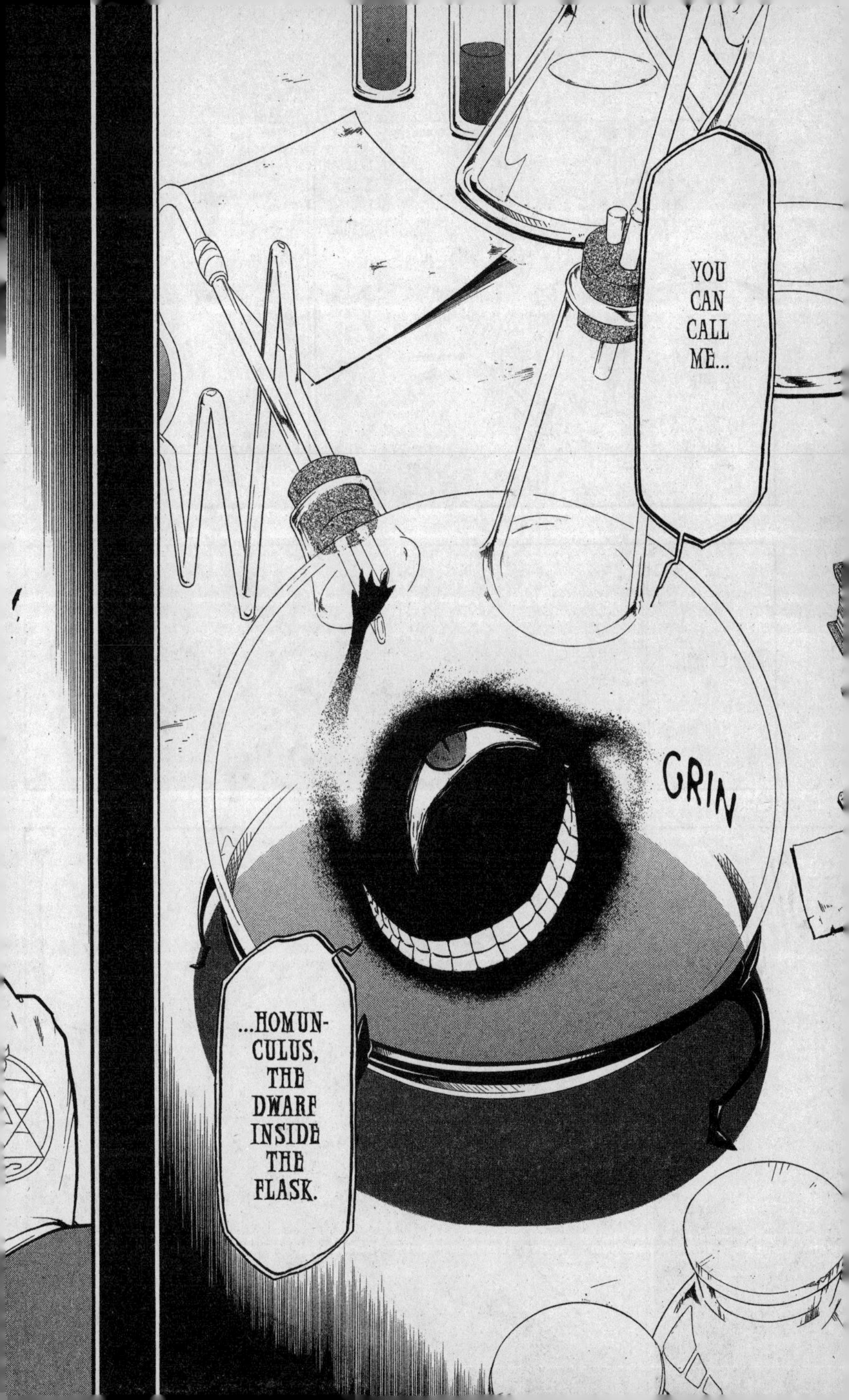
YOU CAN CALL ME...
GRIN
...HOMUNCULUS, THE DWARF INSIDE THE FLASK.

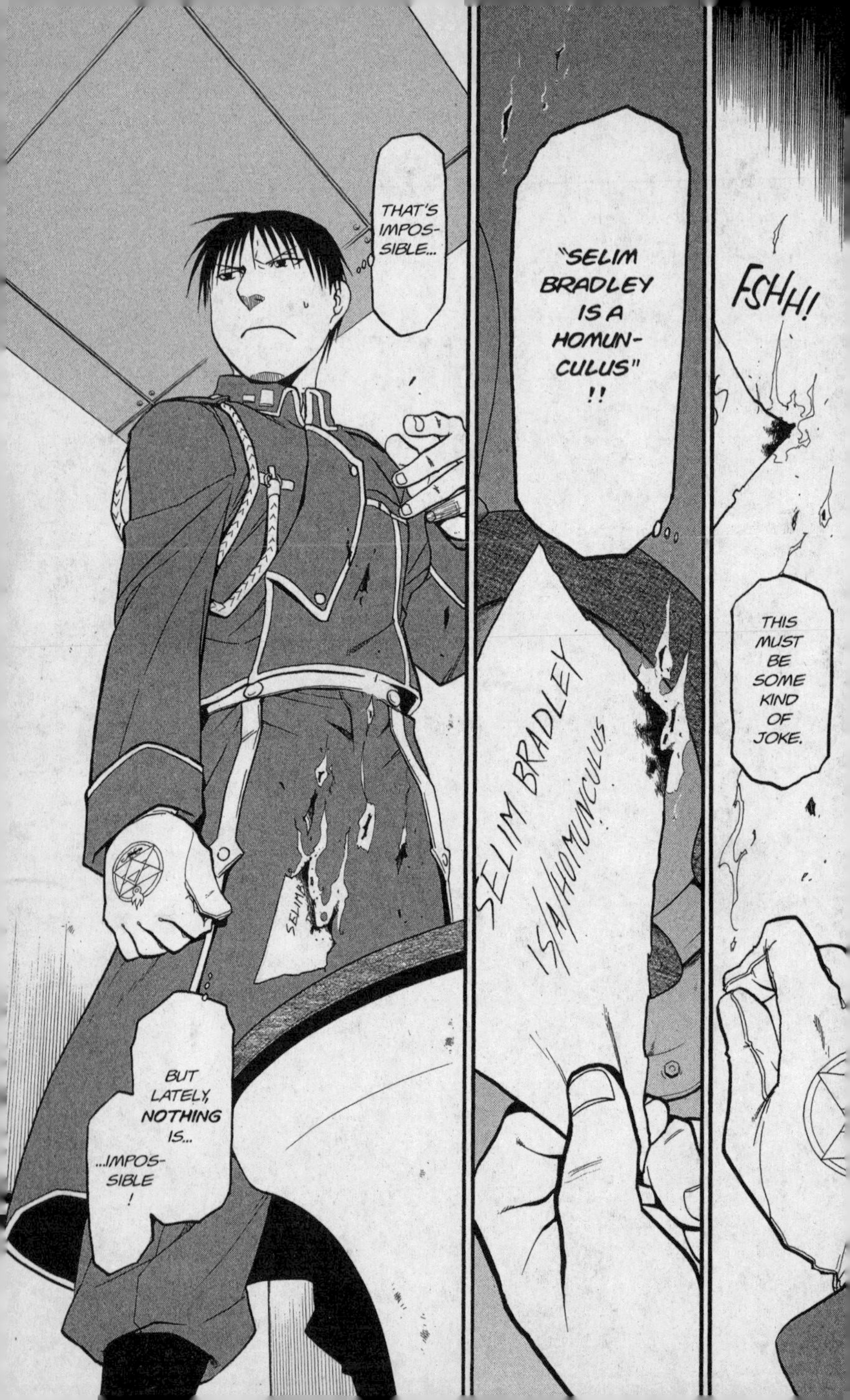
FSHH!
THIS MUST BE SOME KIND OF JOKE.
"SELIM BRADLEY IS A HOMUNCULUS" !!
SELIM BRADLEY IS/A/HOMUNCULUS
THAT'S IMPOSSIBLE...
SELIM
BUT LATELY, **NOTHING** IS...
...IMPOSSIBLE !

FULLMETAL
ALCHEMIST

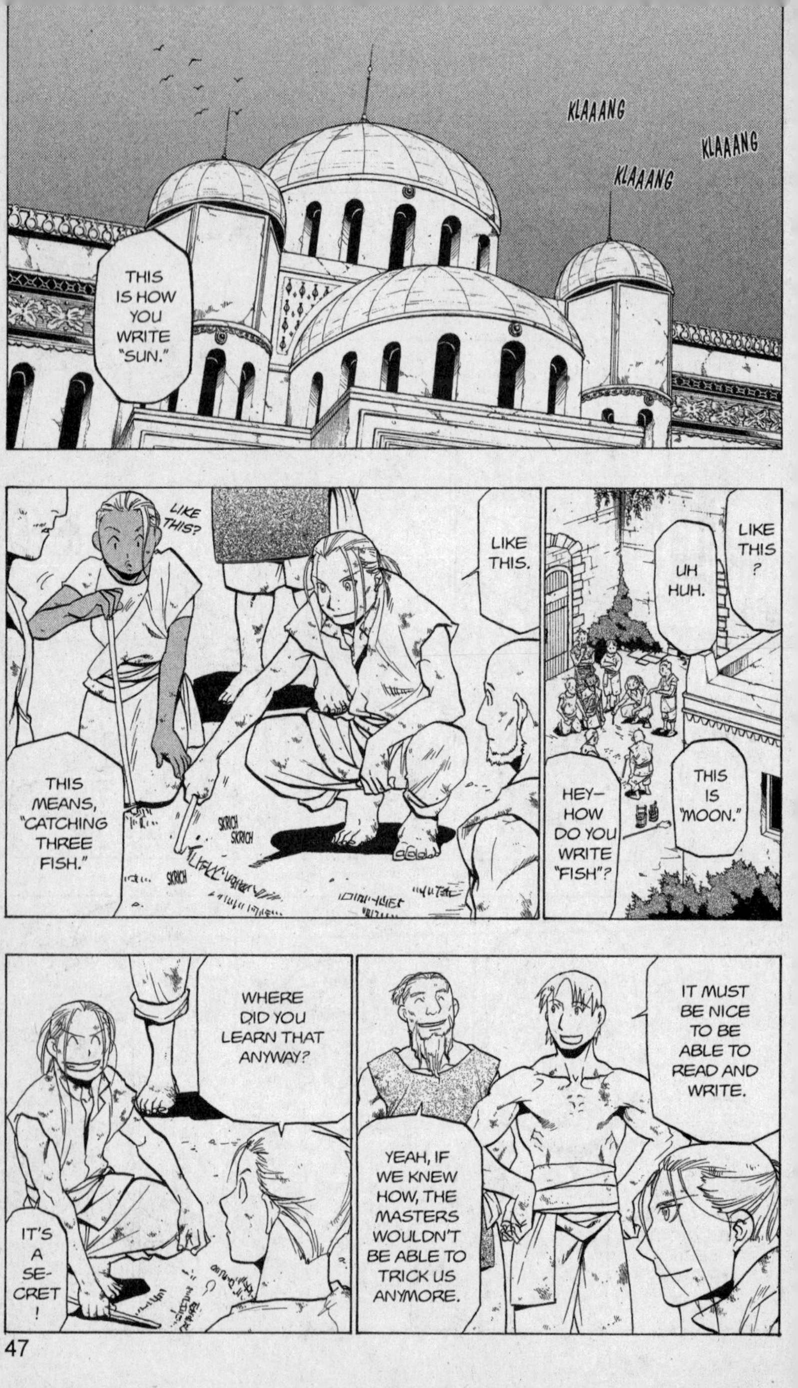
KLAAANG
KLAAANG
KLAAANG
THIS IS HOW YOU WRITE "SUN."
LIKE THIS?
UH HUH.
THIS IS "MOON."
HEY— HOW DO YOU WRITE "FISH"?
LIKE THIS.
LIKE THIS?
SKRICH SKRICH
THIS MEANS, "CATCHING THREE FISH."
SKRICH
IT MUST BE NICE TO BE ABLE TO READ AND WRITE.
YEAH, IF WE KNEW HOW, THE MASTERS WOULDN'T BE ABLE TO TRICK US ANYMORE.
WHERE DID YOU LEARN THAT ANYWAY?
IT'S A SE-CRET!

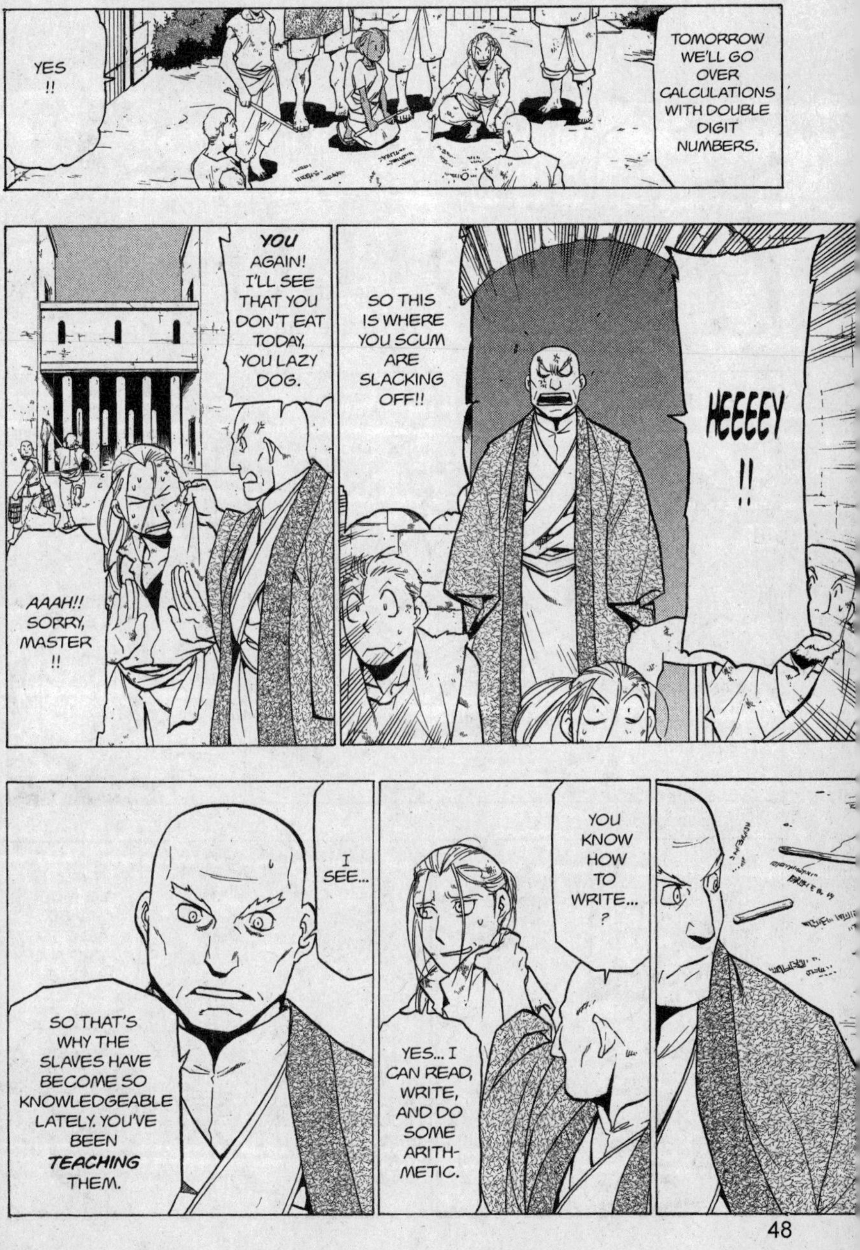
TOMORROW WE'LL GO OVER CALCULATIONS WITH DOUBLE DIGIT NUMBERS.
YES !!
HEEEEY !!
SO THIS IS WHERE YOU SCUM ARE SLACKING OFF!!
YOU AGAIN! I'LL SEE THAT YOU DON'T EAT TODAY, YOU LAZY DOG.
AAAH!! SORRY, MASTER !!
YOU KNOW HOW TO WRITE... ?
YES... I CAN READ, WRITE, AND DO SOME ARITHMETIC.
I SEE...
SO THAT'S WHY THE SLAVES HAVE BECOME SO KNOWLEDGEABLE LATELY. YOU'VE BEEN TEACHING THEM.

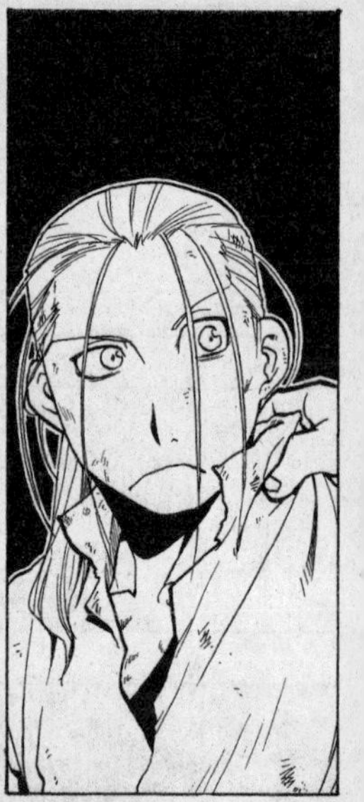
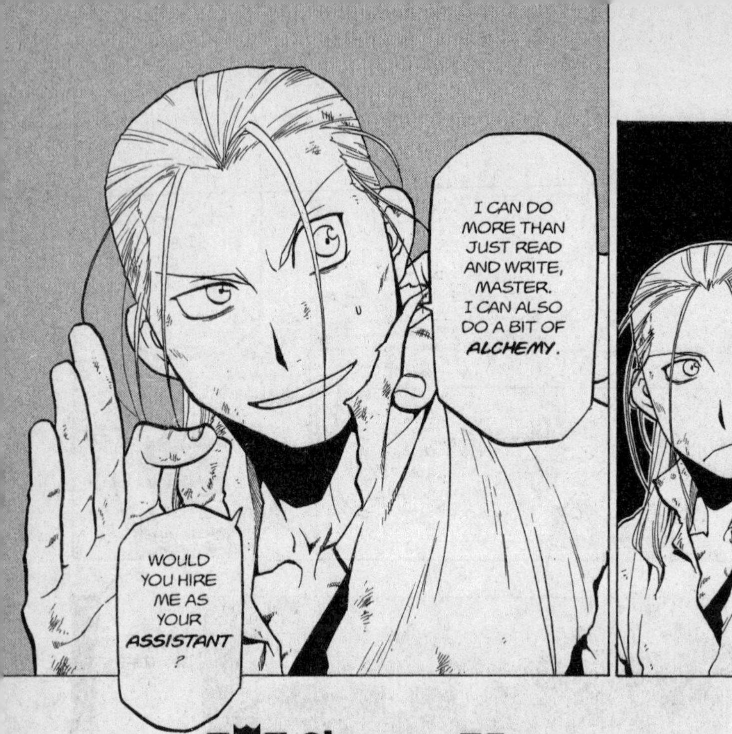
I CAN DO MORE THAN JUST READ AND WRITE, MASTER. I CAN ALSO DO A BIT OF ALCHEMY.
WOULD YOU HIRE ME AS YOUR ASSISTANT?

Chapter 75
The Last Days of Cselkcess

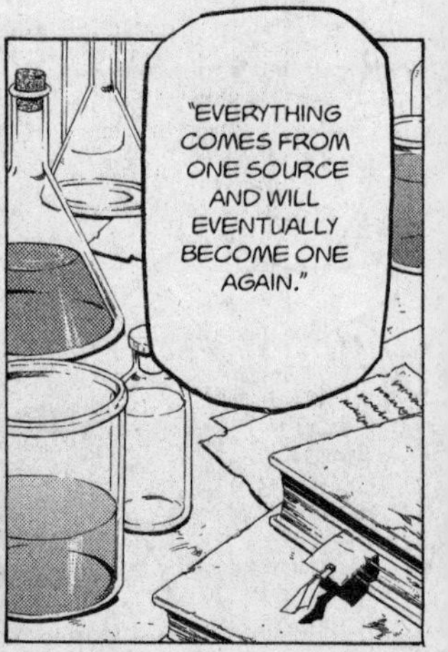
"EVERYTHING COMES FROM ONE SOURCE AND WILL EVENTUALLY BECOME ONE AGAIN."
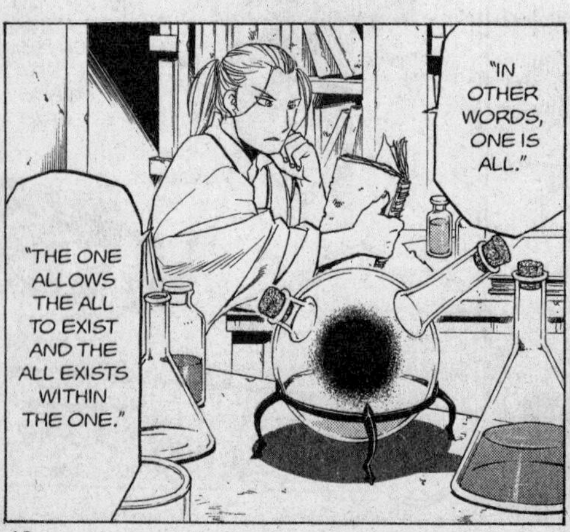
"IN OTHER WORDS, ONE IS ALL."
"THE ONE ALLOWS THE ALL TO EXIST AND THE ALL EXISTS WITHIN THE ONE."

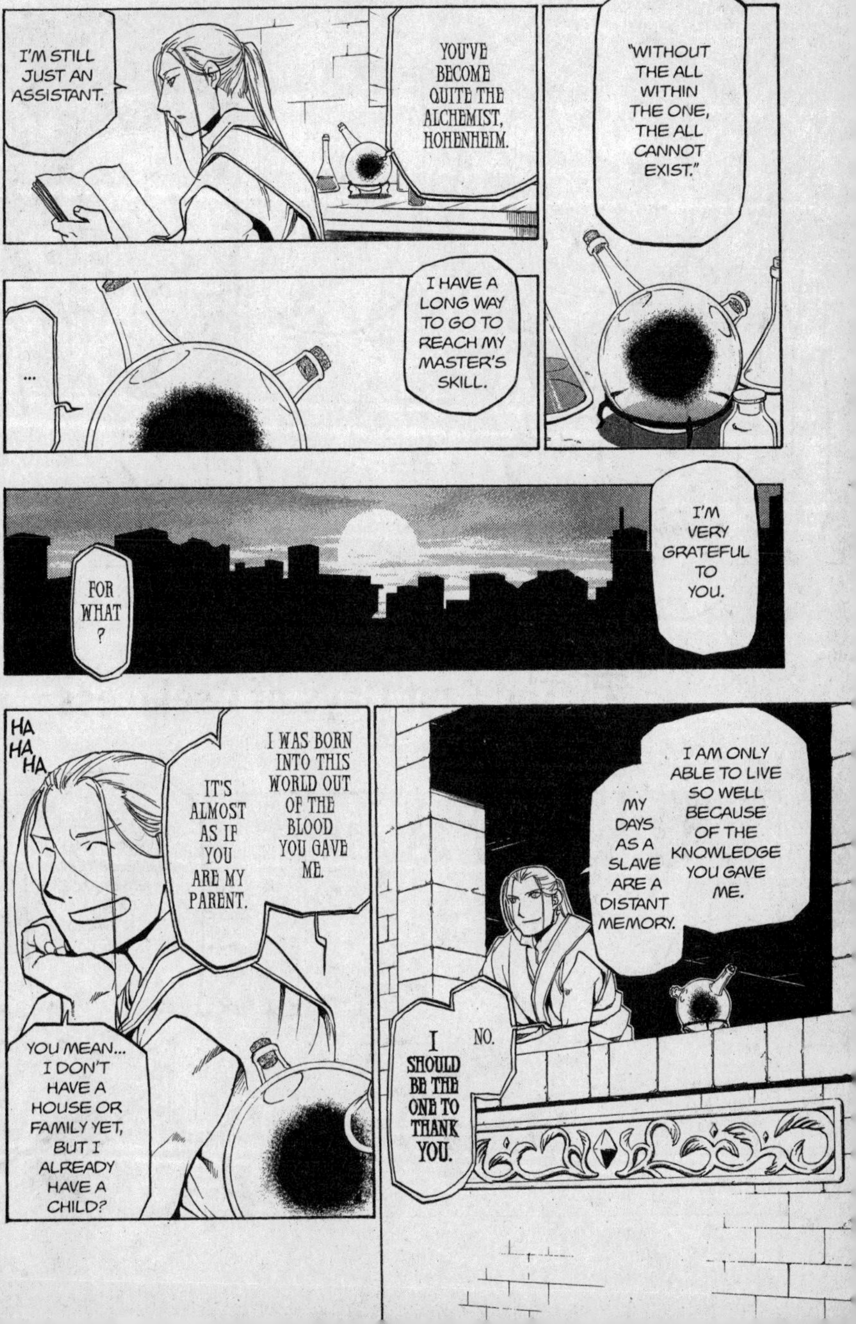
"WITHOUT THE ALL WITHIN THE ONE, THE ALL CANNOT EXIST."
YOU'VE BECOME QUITE THE ALCHEMIST, HOHENHEIM.
I'M STILL JUST AN ASSISTANT.
I HAVE A LONG WAY TO GO TO REACH MY MASTER'S SKILL.
...
I'M VERY GRATEFUL TO YOU.
FOR WHAT?
I AM ONLY ABLE TO LIVE SO WELL BECAUSE OF THE KNOWLEDGE YOU GAVE ME.
MY DAYS AS A SLAVE ARE A DISTANT MEMORY.
NO.
I SHOULD BE THE ONE TO THANK YOU.
I WAS BORN INTO THIS WORLD OUT OF THE BLOOD YOU GAVE ME.
IT'S ALMOST AS IF YOU ARE MY PARENT.
HA HA HA
YOU MEAN... I DON'T HAVE A HOUSE OR FAMILY YET, BUT I ALREADY HAVE A CHILD?

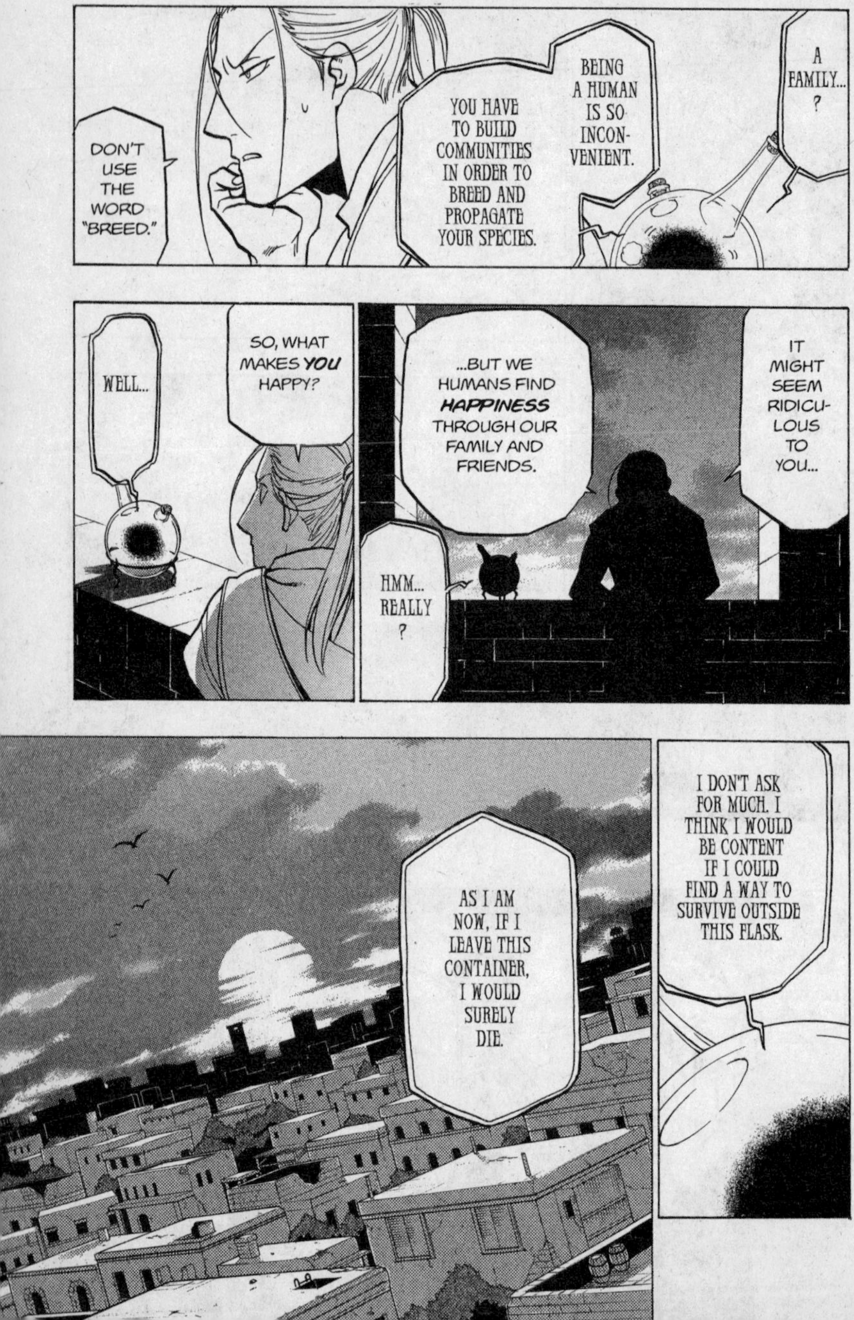
A FAMILY...?
BEING A HUMAN IS SO INCONVENIENT.
YOU HAVE TO BUILD COMMUNITIES IN ORDER TO BREED AND PROPAGATE YOUR SPECIES.
DON'T USE THE WORD "BREED."
IT MIGHT SEEM RIDICULOUS TO YOU...
...BUT WE HUMANS FIND HAPPINESS THROUGH OUR FAMILY AND FRIENDS.
HMM... REALLY?
SO, WHAT MAKES YOU HAPPY?
WELL...
I DON'T ASK FOR MUCH. I THINK I WOULD BE CONTENT IF I COULD FIND A WAY TO SURVIVE OUTSIDE THIS FLASK.
AS I AM NOW, IF I LEAVE THIS CONTAINER, I WOULD SURELY DIE.

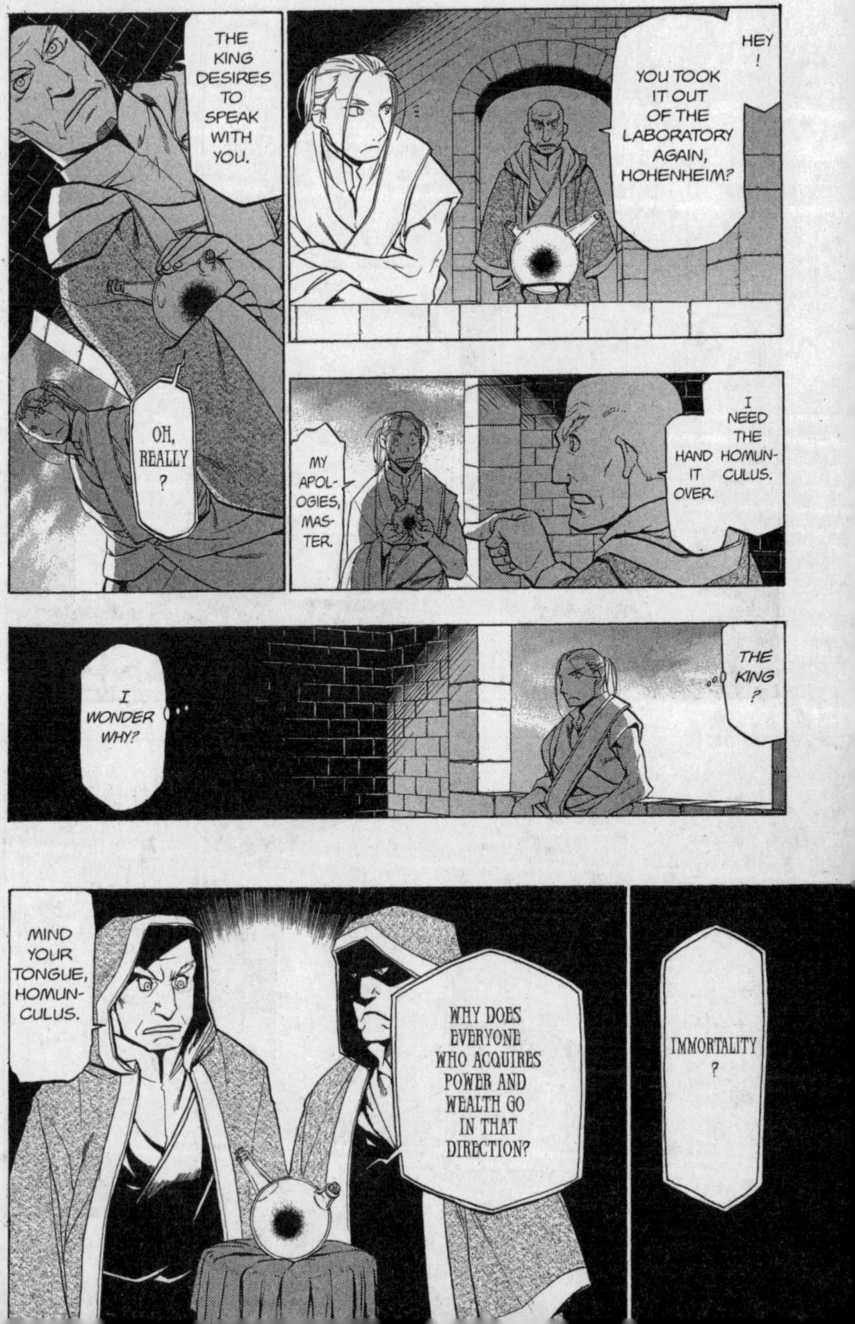
HEY!
YOU TOOK IT OUT OF THE LABORATORY AGAIN, HOHENHEIM?
I NEED THE HOMUNCULUS. HAND IT OVER.
MY APOLOGIES, MASTER.
THE KING DESIRES TO SPEAK WITH YOU.
OH, REALLY?
THE KING?
I WONDER WHY?
IMMORTALITY?
WHY DOES EVERYONE WHO ACQUIRES POWER AND WEALTH GO IN THAT DIRECTION?
MIND YOUR TONGUE, HOMUNCULUS.

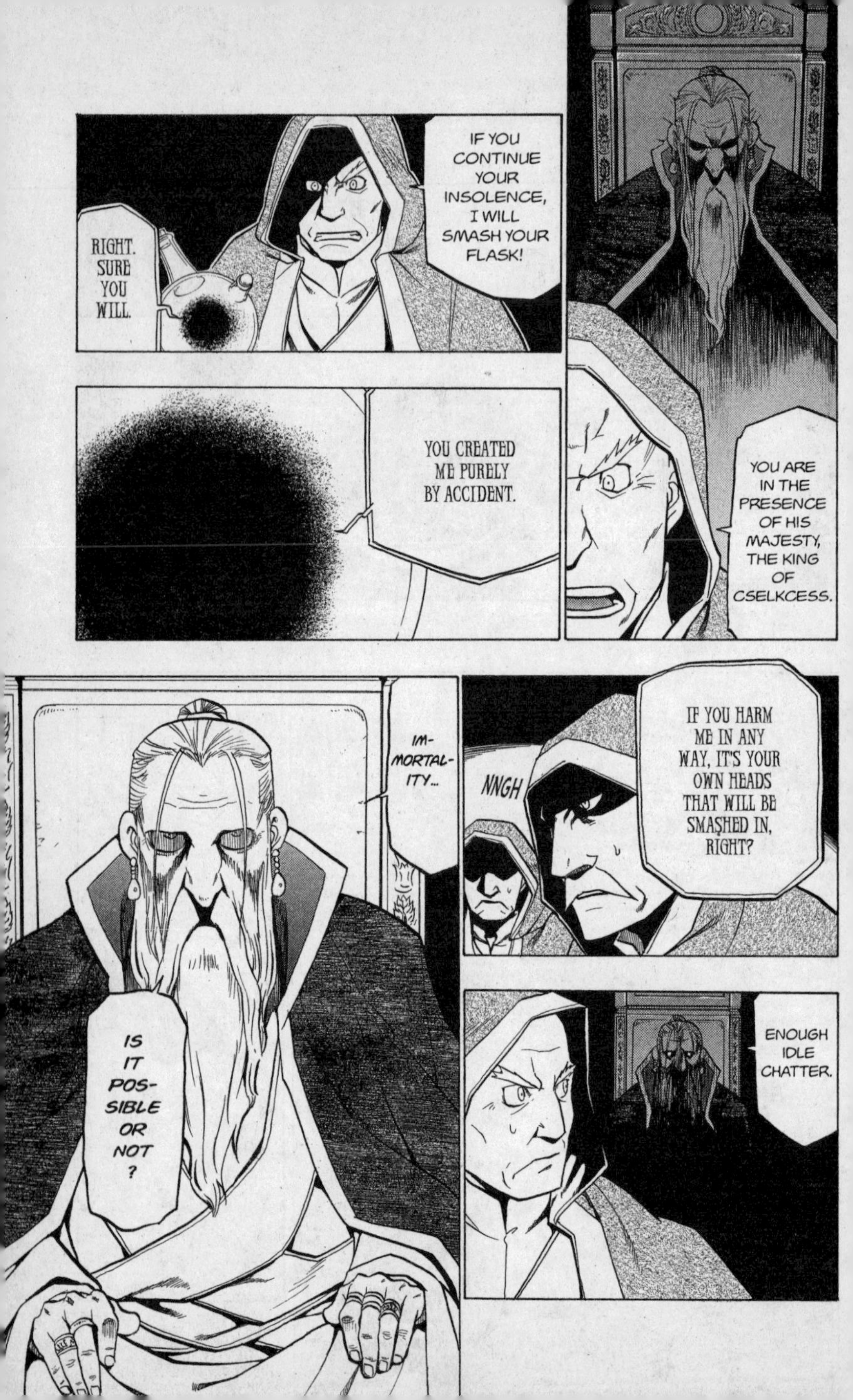
YOU ARE IN THE PRESENCE OF HIS MAJESTY, THE KING OF CSELKCESS.
IF YOU CONTINUE YOUR INSOLENCE, I WILL SMASH YOUR FLASK!
RIGHT. SURE YOU WILL.
YOU CREATED ME PURELY BY ACCIDENT.
IF YOU HARM ME IN ANY WAY, IT'S YOUR OWN HEADS THAT WILL BE SMASHED IN, RIGHT?
NNGH
ENOUGH IDLE CHATTER.
IM-MORTAL-ITY...
IS IT POS-SIBLE OR NOT?

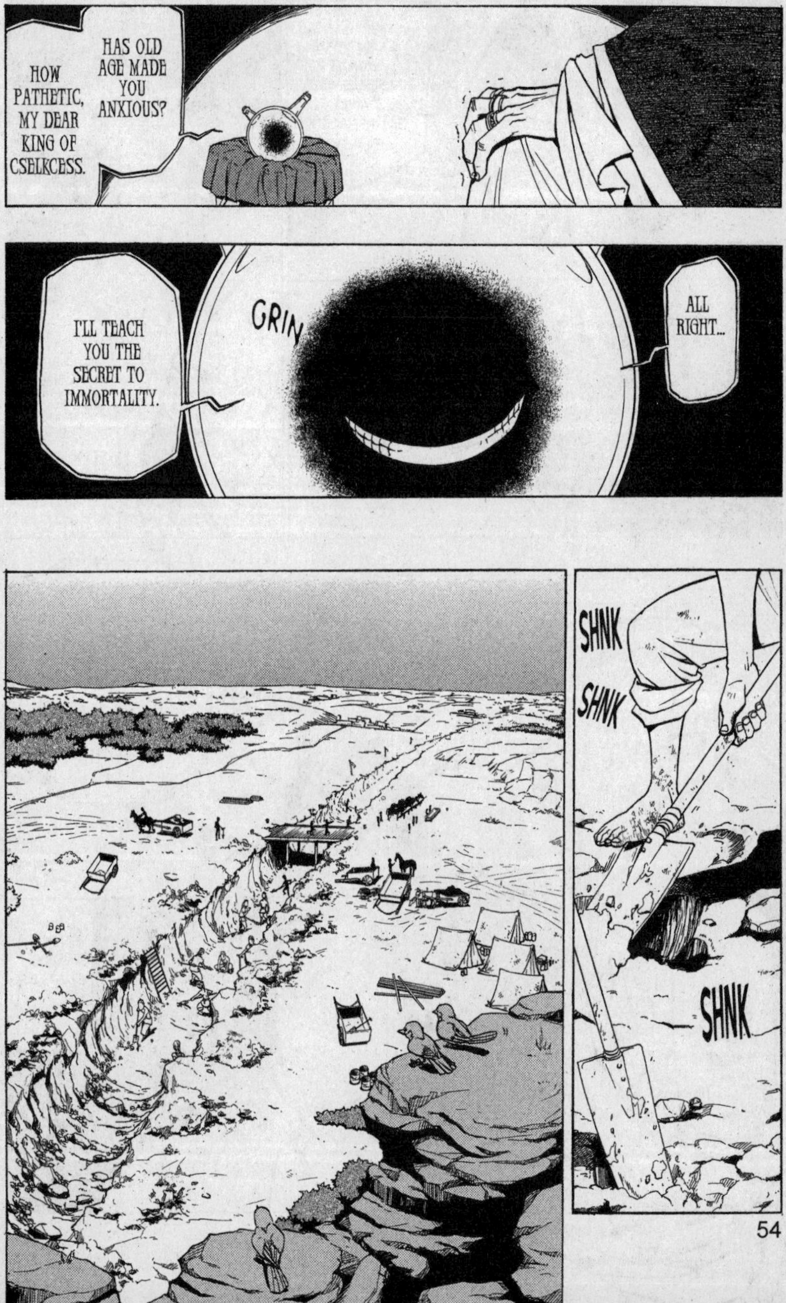

HAS OLD AGE MADE YOU ANXIOUS?
HOW PATHETIC, MY DEAR KING OF CSELKCESS.
ALL RIGHT...
GRIN
I'LL TEACH YOU THE SECRET TO IMMORTALITY.
SHNK
SHNK
SHNK

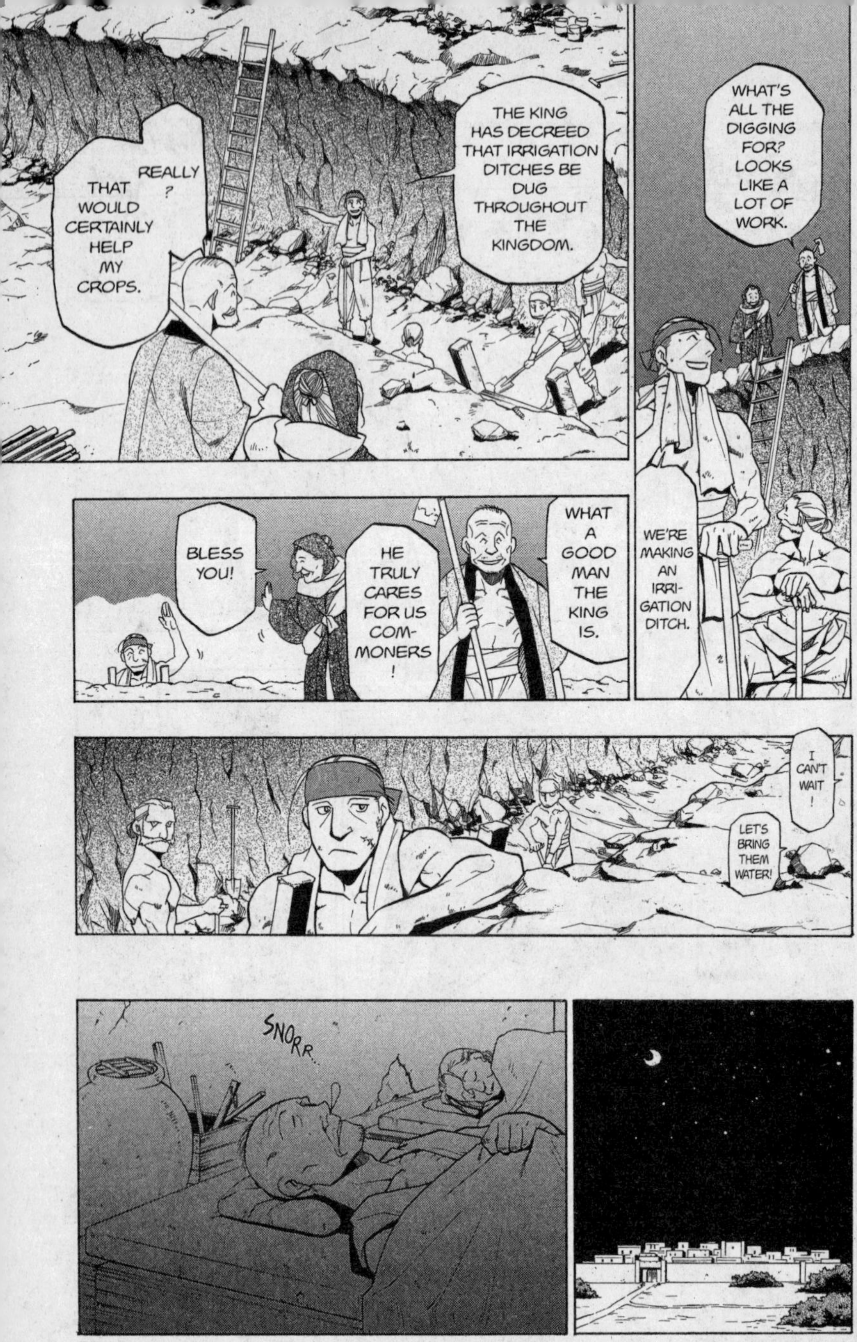
WHAT'S ALL THE DIGGING FOR? LOOKS LIKE A LOT OF WORK.
WE'RE MAKING AN IRRIGATION DITCH.
THE KING HAS DECREED THAT IRRIGATION DITCHES BE DUG THROUGHOUT THE KINGDOM.
REALLY? THAT WOULD CERTAINLY HELP MY CROPS.
WHAT A GOOD MAN THE KING IS.
HE TRULY CARES FOR US COMMONERS!
BLESS YOU!
I CAN'T WAIT!
LET'S BRING THEM WATER!
SNORR...

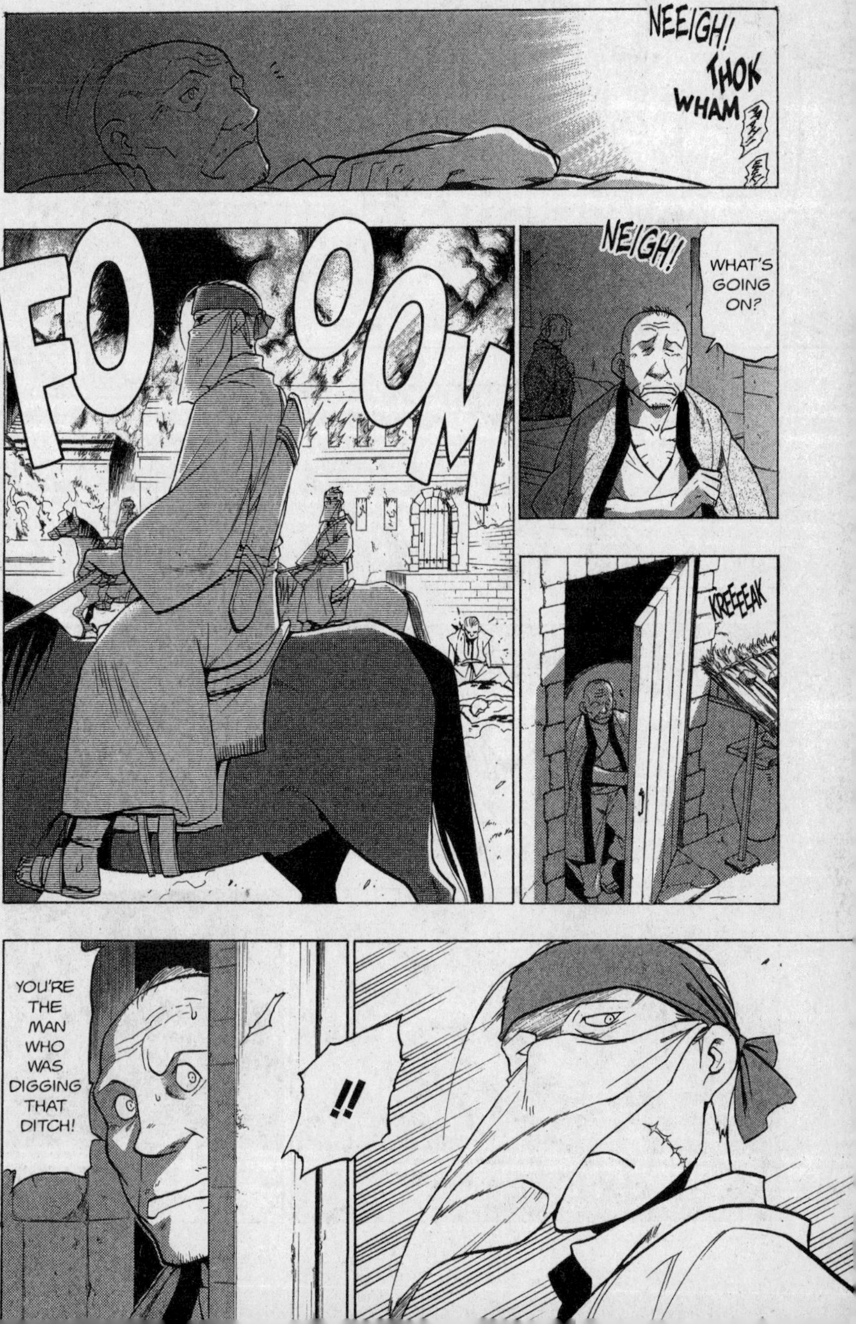
NEEIGH!
THOK
WHAM
NEIGH!
WHAT'S GOING ON?
FOOOM
KREEEEAK
!!
YOU'RE THE MAN WHO WAS DIGGING THAT DITCH!

AIEE!

WHAM

BOOM

AAA...

AAAAH...

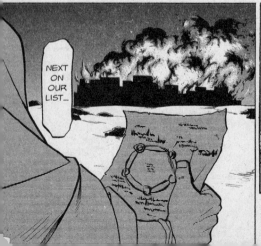

YES, SIR.

KILL THEM ALL.

NEXT ON OUR LIST...

GWOOOO

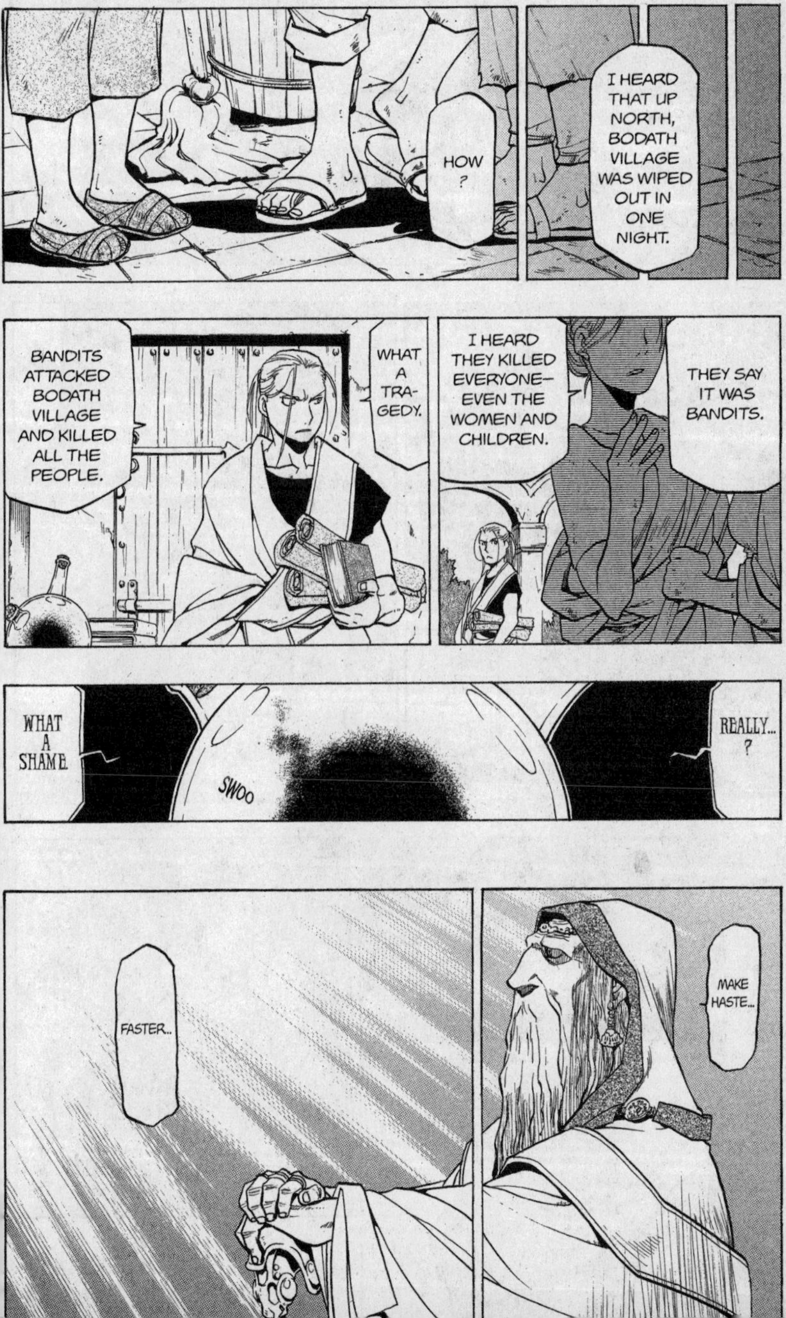
I HEARD THAT UP NORTH, BODATH VILLAGE WAS WIPED OUT IN ONE NIGHT.
HOW?
THEY SAY IT WAS BANDITS.
I HEARD THEY KILLED EVERYONE— EVEN THE WOMEN AND CHILDREN.
WHAT A TRA-GEDY.
BANDITS ATTACKED BODATH VILLAGE AND KILLED ALL THE PEOPLE.
REALLY...?
SWOO
WHAT A SHAME.
MAKE HASTE...
FASTER..

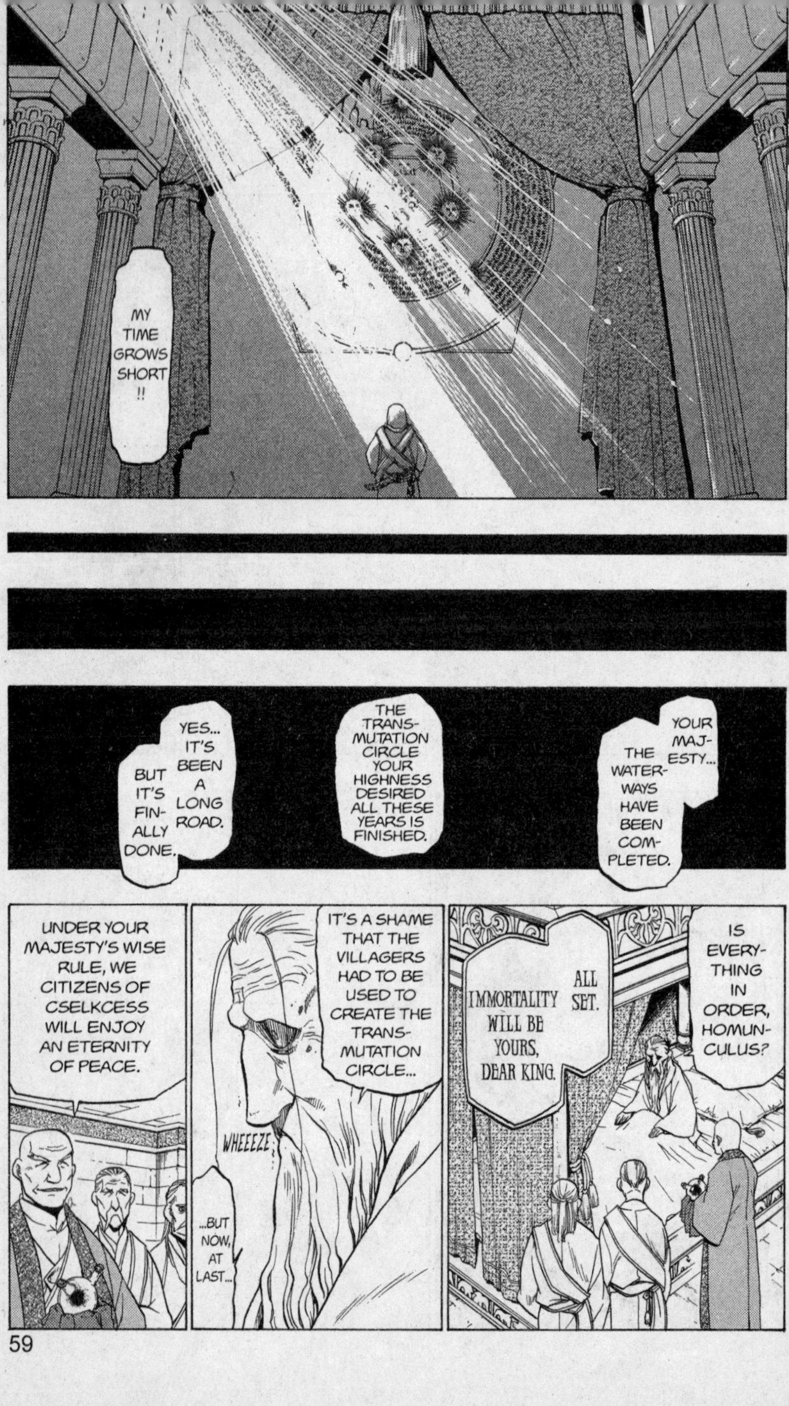
MY TIME GROWS SHORT!!
YOUR MAJESTY...
THE WATERWAYS HAVE BEEN COMPLETED.
THE TRANSMUTATION CIRCLE YOUR HIGHNESS DESIRED ALL THESE YEARS IS FINISHED.
YES... IT'S BEEN A LONG ROAD.
BUT IT'S FINALLY DONE.
IS EVERYTHING IN ORDER, HOMUNCULUS?
ALL SET.
IMMORTALITY WILL BE YOURS, DEAR KING.
IT'S A SHAME THAT THE VILLAGERS HAD TO BE USED TO CREATE THE TRANSMUTATION CIRCLE...
WHEEEZE
...BUT NOW, AT LAST...
UNDER YOUR MAJESTY'S WISE RULE, WE CITIZENS OF CSELKCESS WILL ENJOY AN ETERNITY OF PEACE.

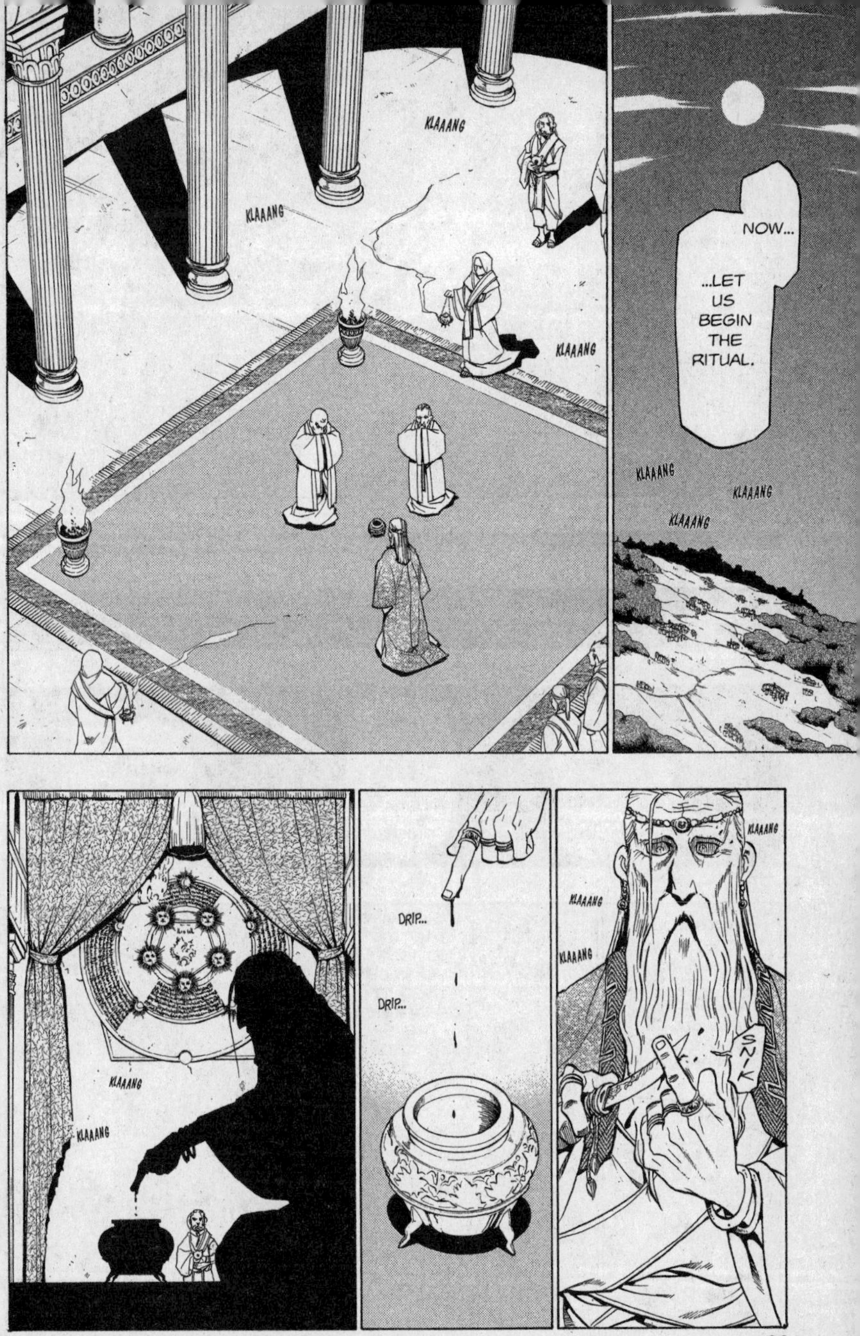
NOW...
...LET US BEGIN THE RITUAL.
KLAAANG
KLAAANG
KLAAANG
KLAAANG
KLAAANG
KLAAANG
KLAAANG
KLAAANG
KLAAANG
SNIK
DRIP...
DRIP...
KLAAANG
KLAAANG

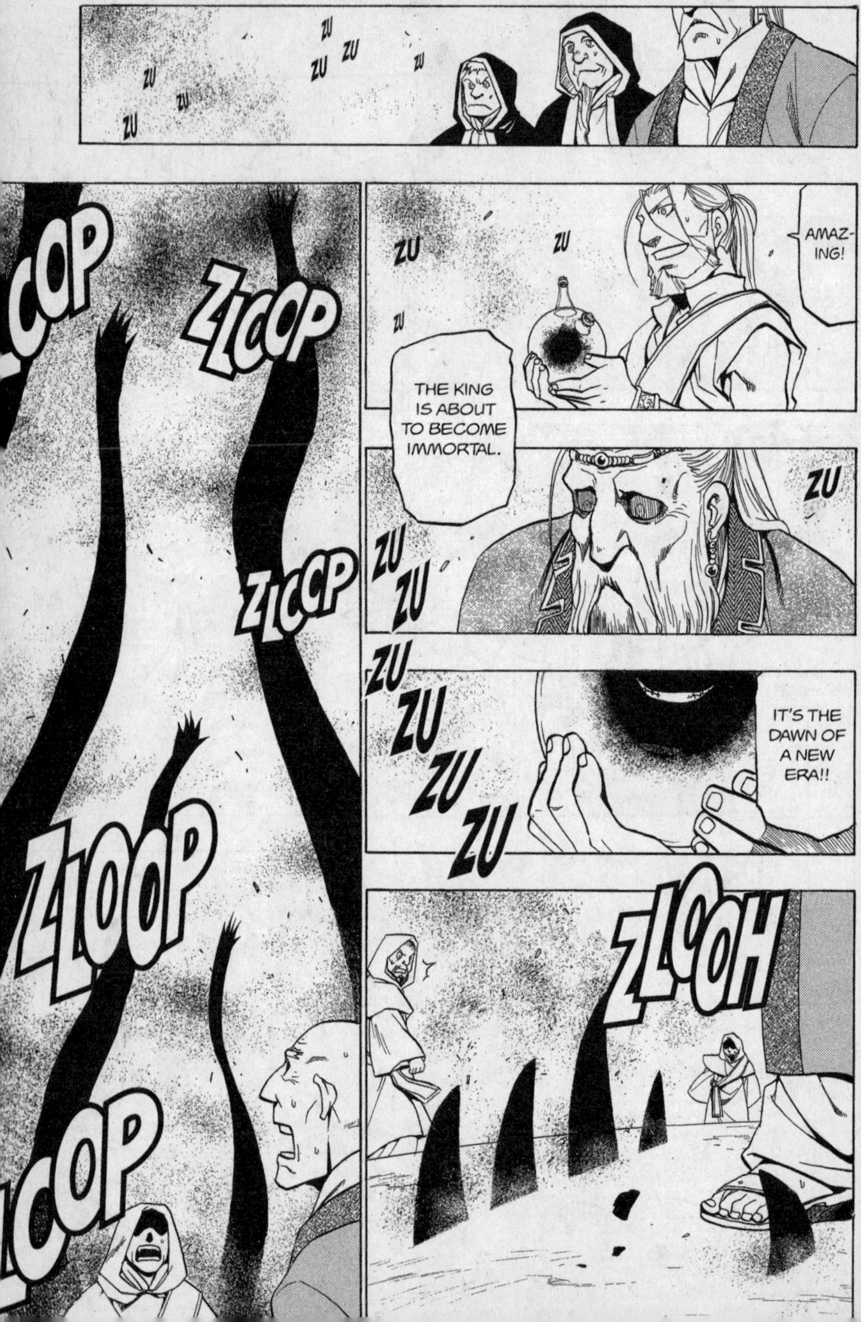
ZU
ZU
ZU
ZU
ZU
ZU
ZU
AMAZING!
ZU
ZU
ZU
THE KING IS ABOUT TO BECOME IMMORTAL.
ZU
ZU
ZU
IT'S THE DAWN OF A NEW ERA!!
ZU
ZU
ZU
ZU
ZU
ZLOOH
ZLOOP
ZLOOP
ZLOOP

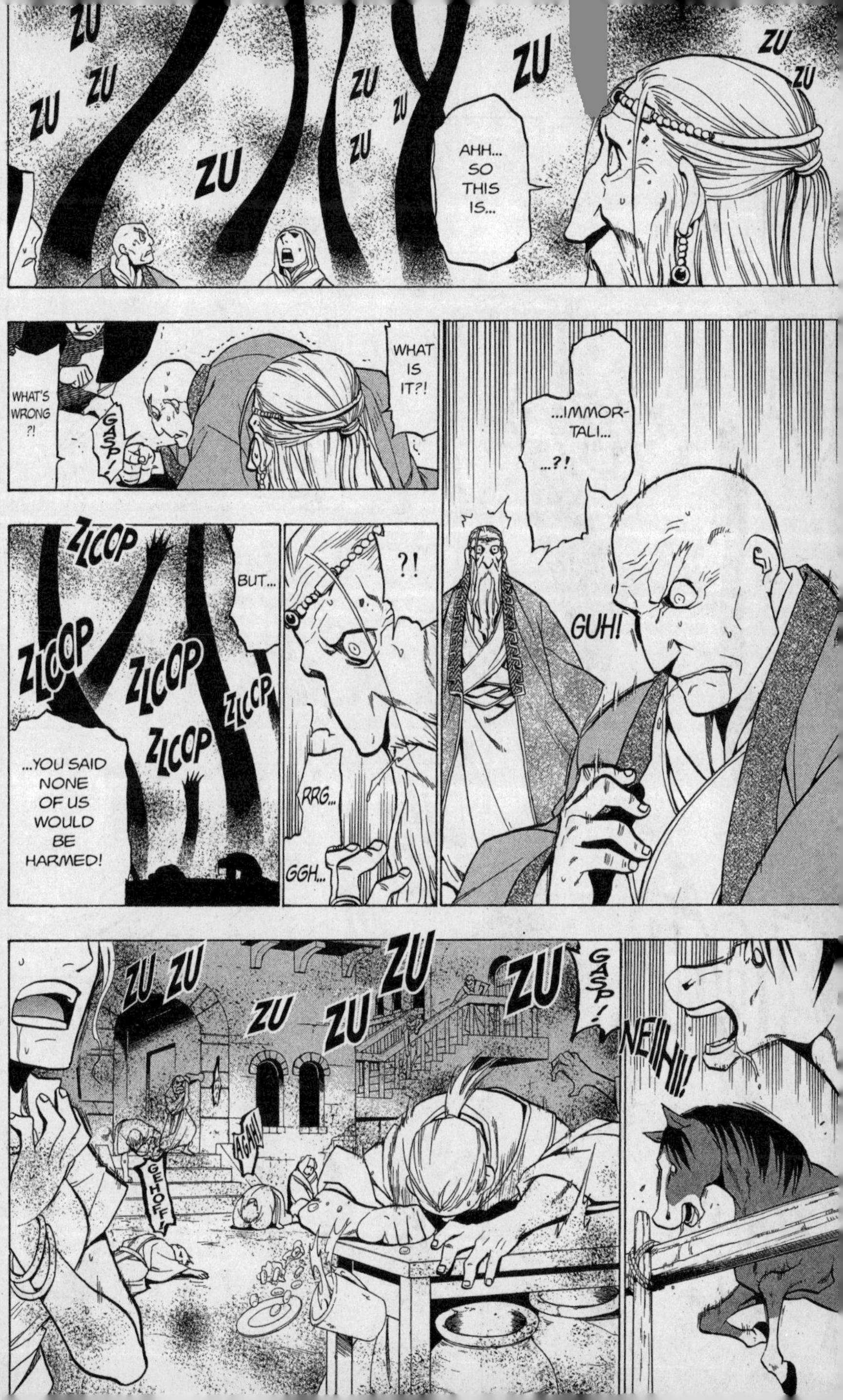
ZU ZU
ZU ZU ZU ZU ZU ZU ZU ZU
AHH... SO THIS IS...
...IMMORTALI...
...?!
GUH!
WHAT IS IT?!
GASP!
WHAT'S WRONG ?!
?!
RRG...
GGH...
BUT...
ZLCOP ZLCOP ZLCOP ZLCOP ZLCOP
...YOU SAID NONE OF US WOULD BE HARMED!
GASP!
NEIIHII!
ZU ZU ZU ZU ZU ZU
AGAH!
GEHOFF!

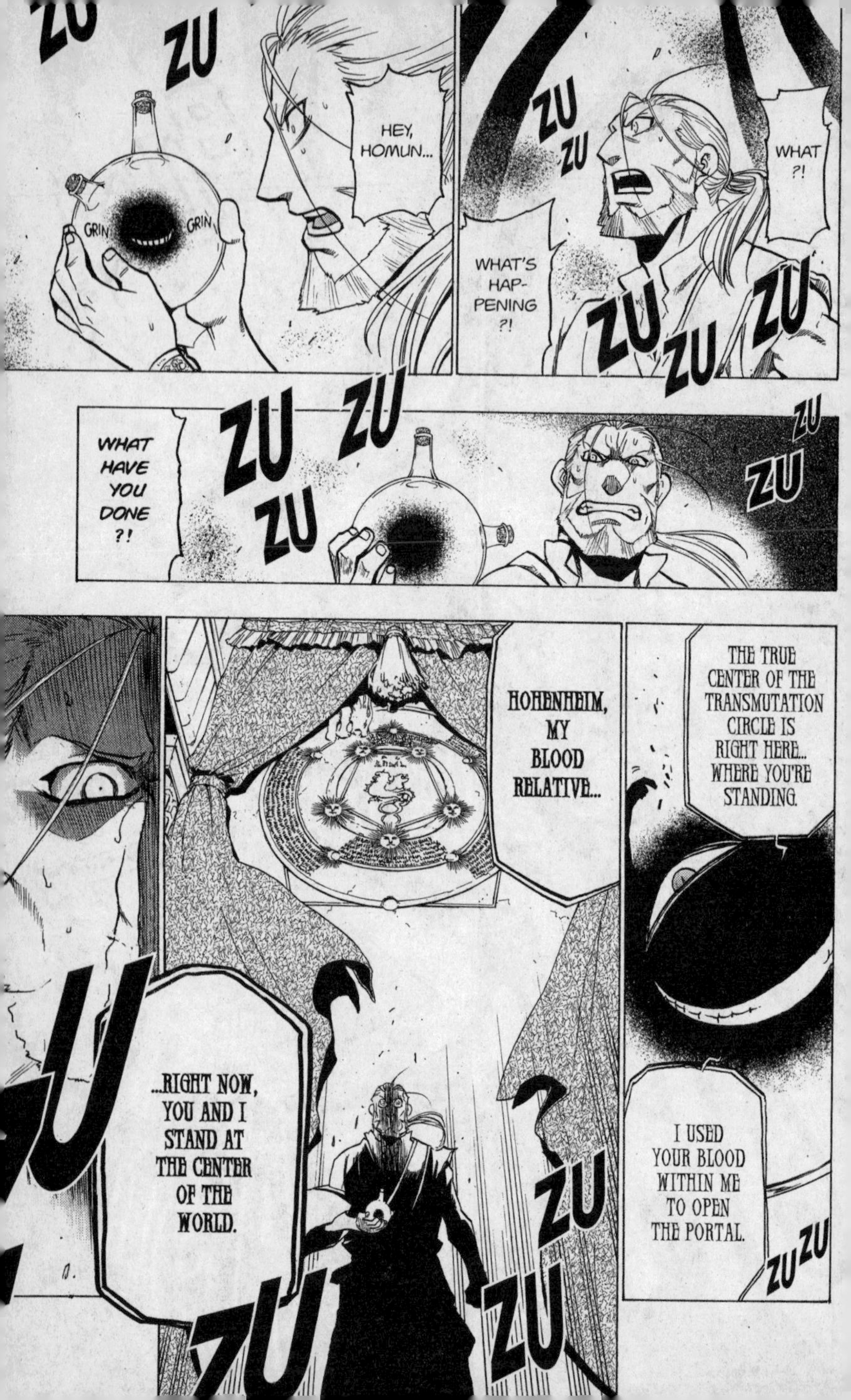
ZU
ZU
WHAT ?!
WHAT'S HAP-PENING ?!
ZU
ZU
ZU
ZU
HEY, HOMUN...
GRIN
GRIN
ZU
ZU
ZU
ZU
WHAT HAVE YOU DONE ?!
ZU
ZU
ZU
ZU
THE TRUE CENTER OF THE TRANSMUTATION CIRCLE IS RIGHT HERE... WHERE YOU'RE STANDING.
I USED YOUR BLOOD WITHIN ME TO OPEN THE PORTAL.
ZU ZU
HOHENHEIM, MY BLOOD RELATIVE...
...RIGHT NOW, YOU AND I STAND AT THE CENTER OF THE WORLD.
ZU
ZU
ZU
ZU

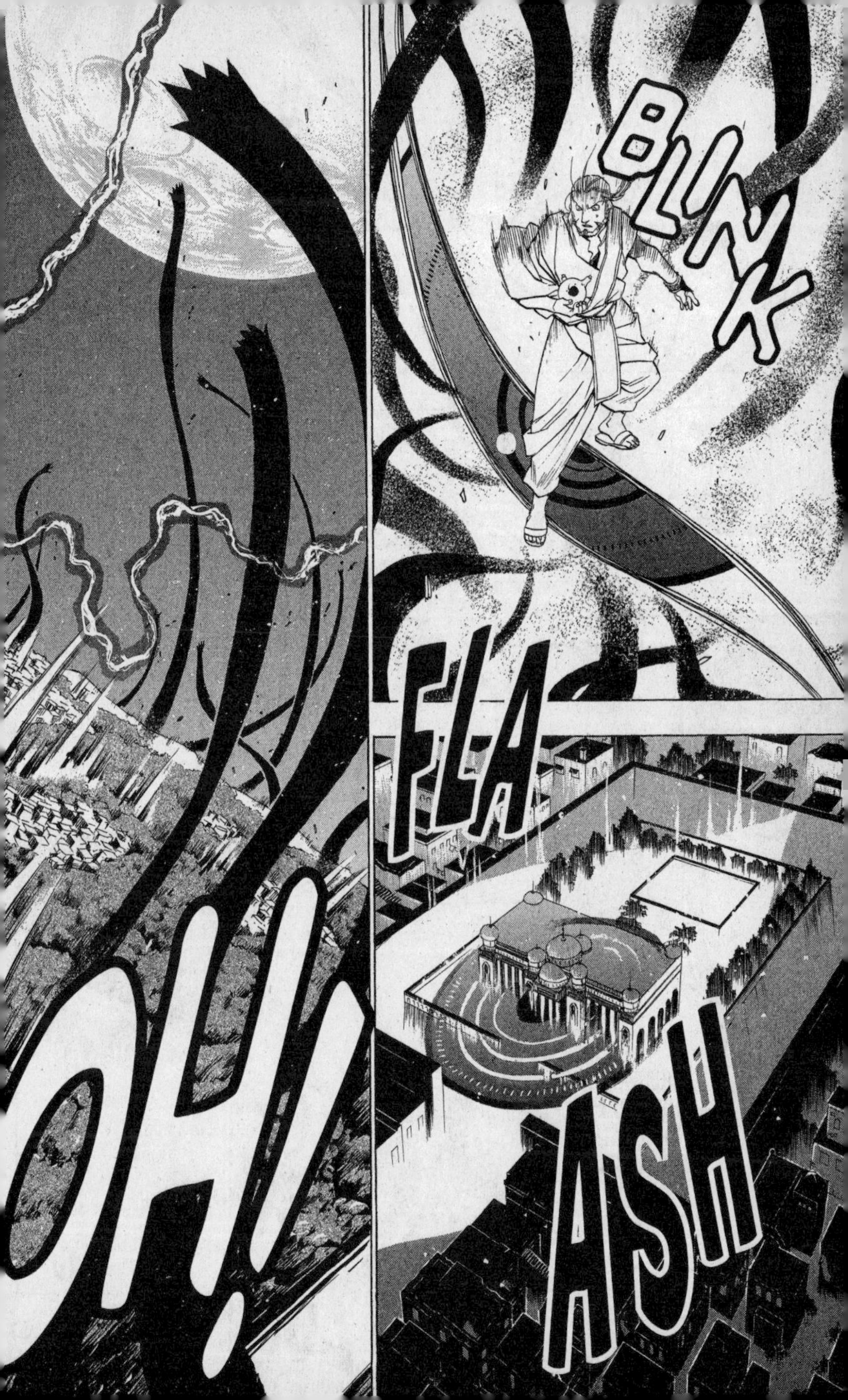
BLINK
FLA
ASH
OH!!

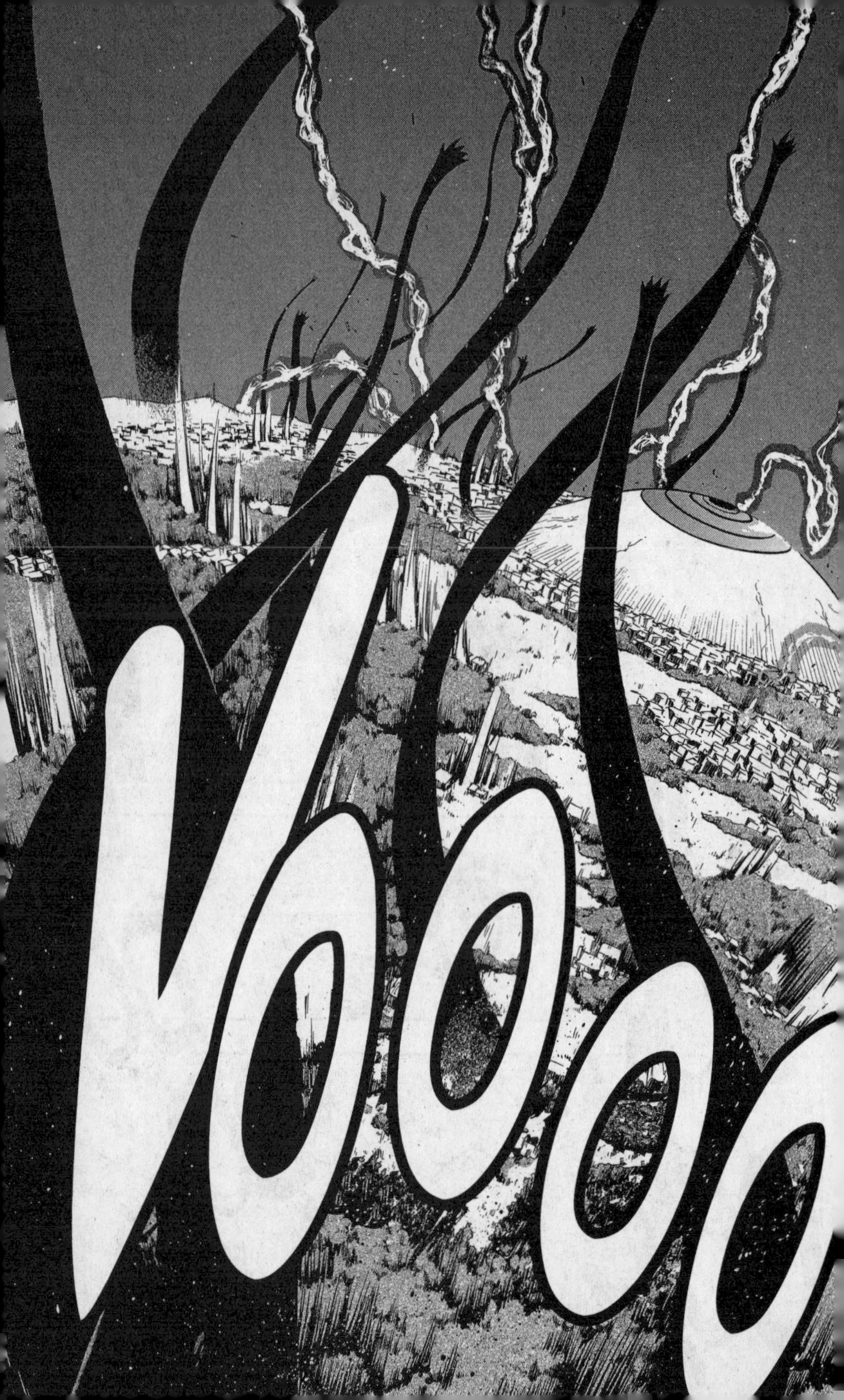

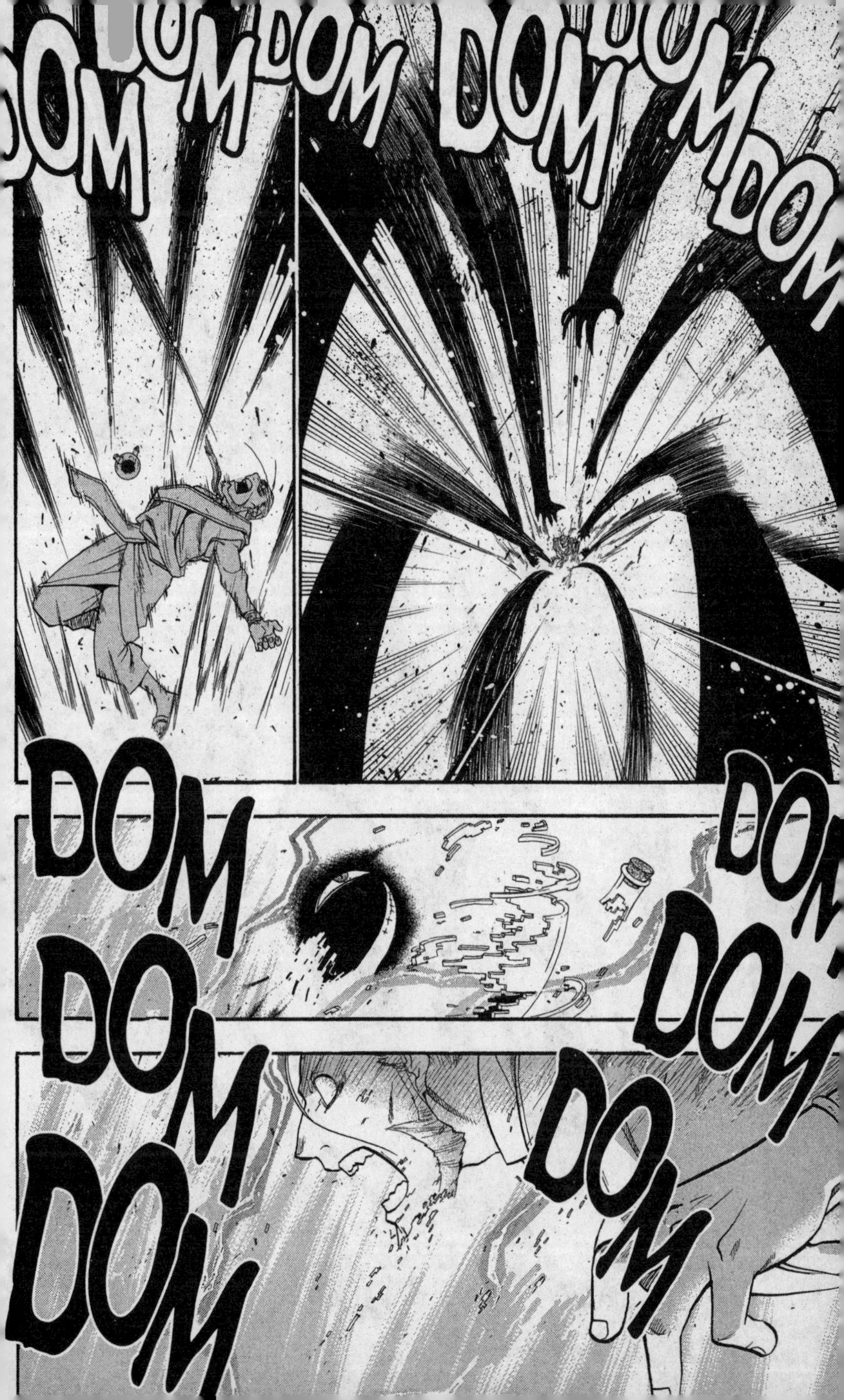
DOM DOM DOM DOM DOM DOM
DOM DOM DOM DOM
DOM DOM DOM DOM
DOM DOM DOM DOM

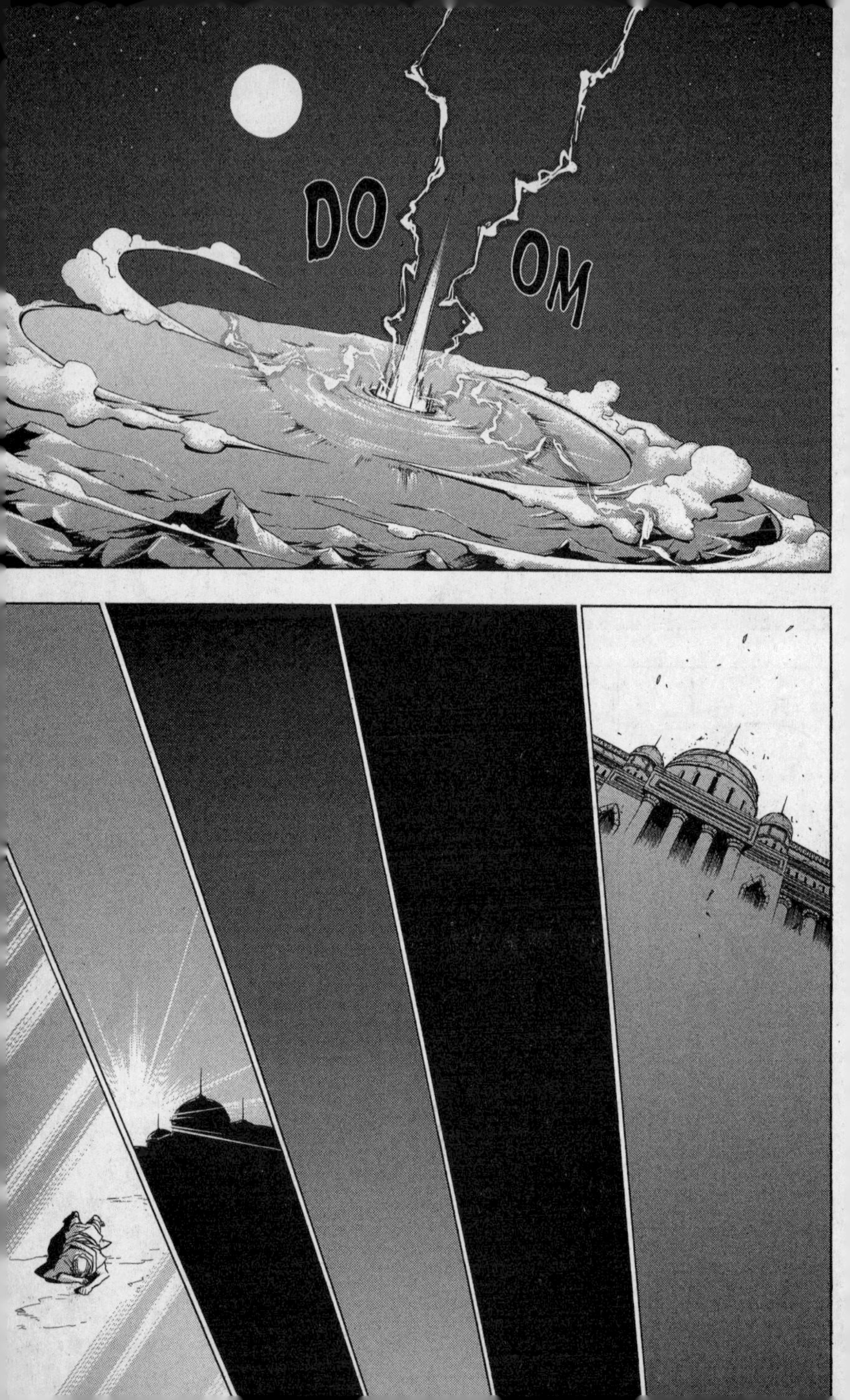
DO OM

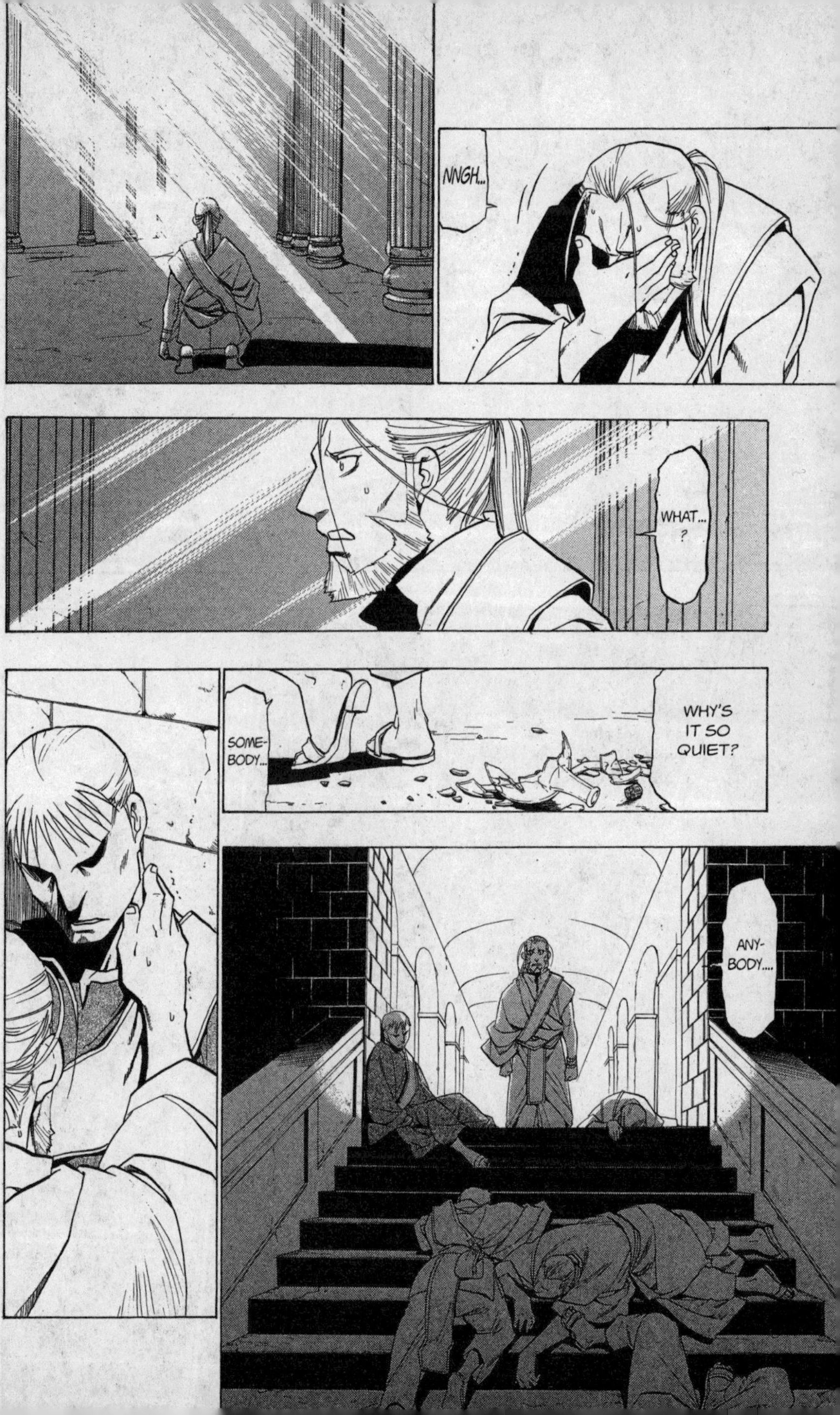
NNGH...
WHAT...?
WHY'S IT SO QUIET?
SOME-BODY...
ANY-BODY....

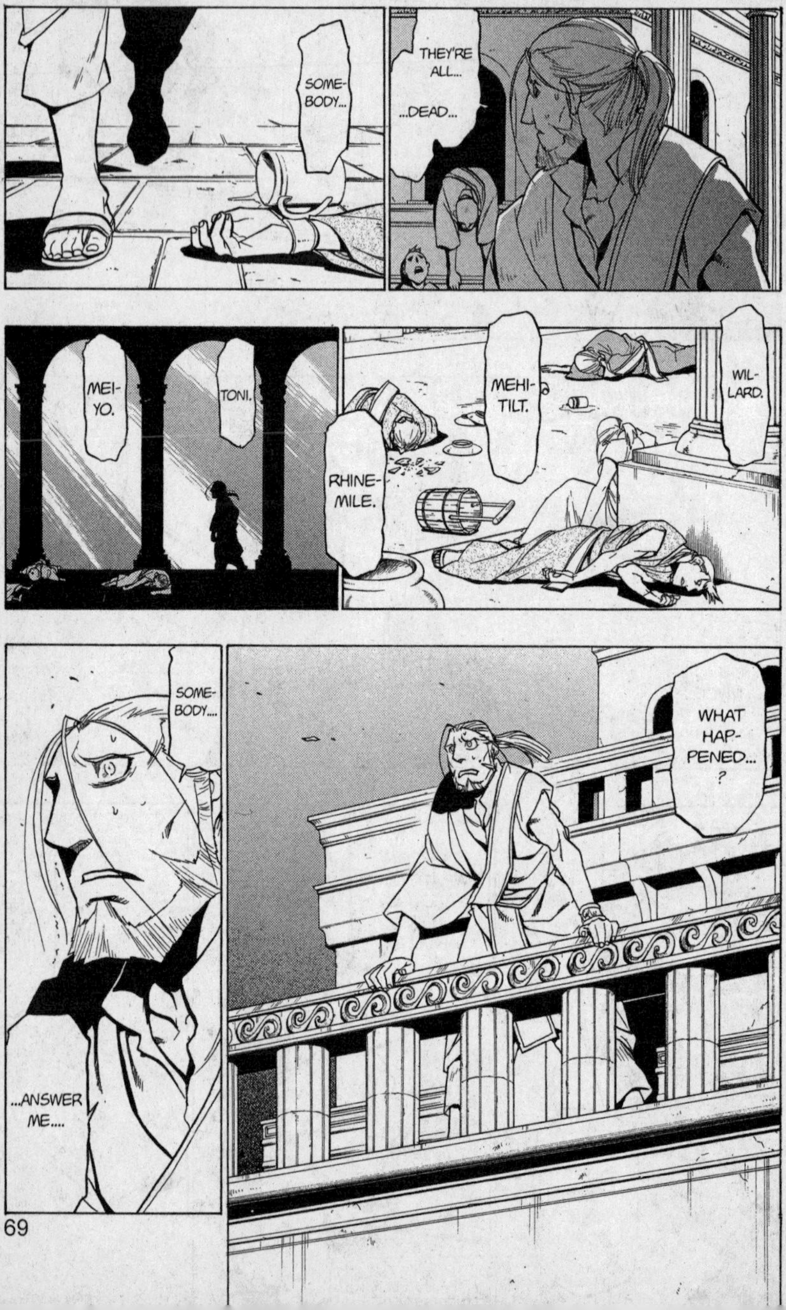
THEY'RE ALL...
...DEAD...
SOMEBODY...
WILLARD.
MEHITILT.
RHINEMILE.
TONI.
MEIYO.
WHAT HAPPENED...?
SOMEBODY....
...ANSWER ME....

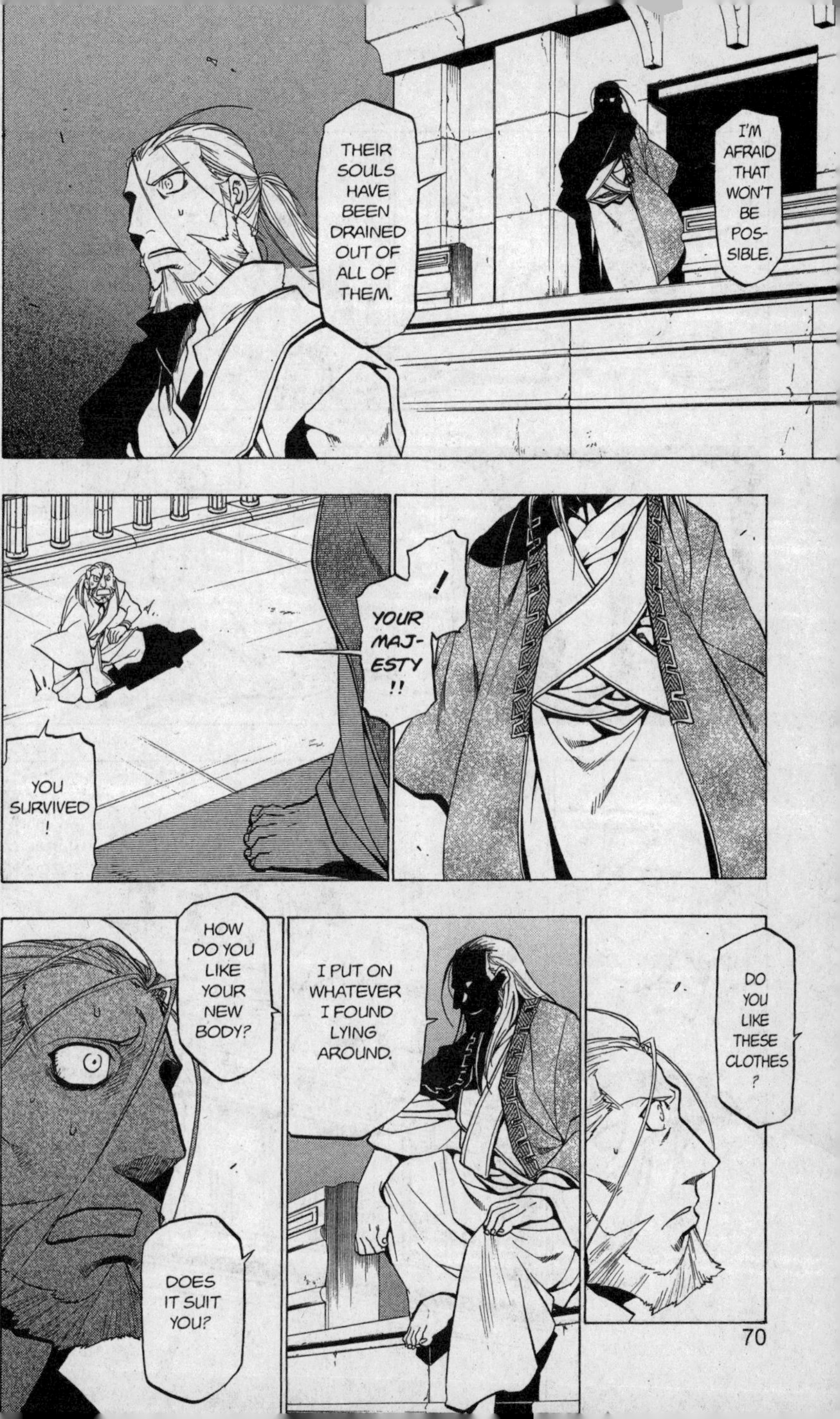
I'M AFRAID THAT WON'T BE POSSIBLE.
THEIR SOULS HAVE BEEN DRAINED OUT OF ALL OF THEM.
!
YOUR MAJESTY!!
YOU SURVIVED!
DO YOU LIKE THESE CLOTHES?
I PUT ON WHATEVER I FOUND LYING AROUND.
HOW DO YOU LIKE YOUR NEW BODY?
DOES IT SUIT YOU?

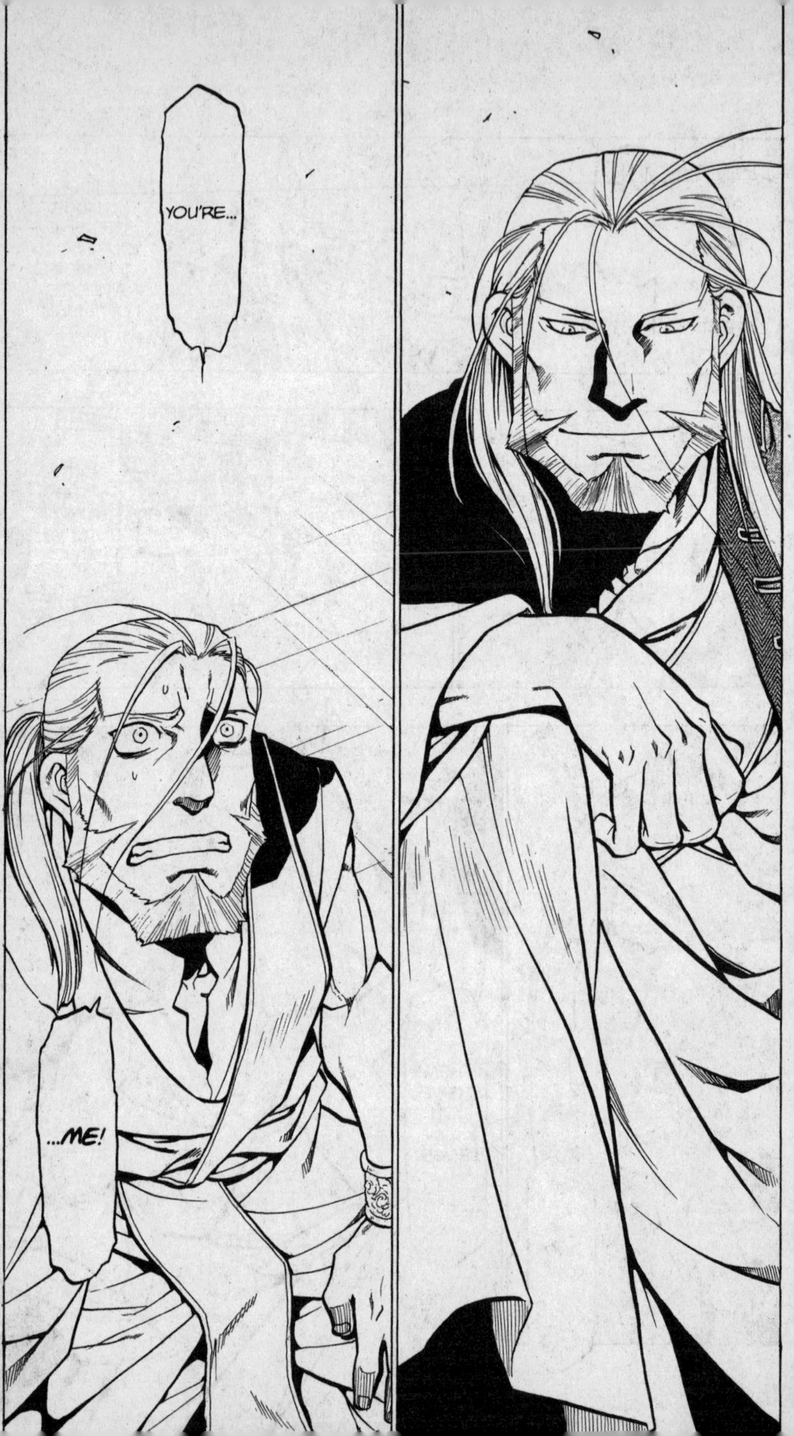
YOU'RE...
...ME!

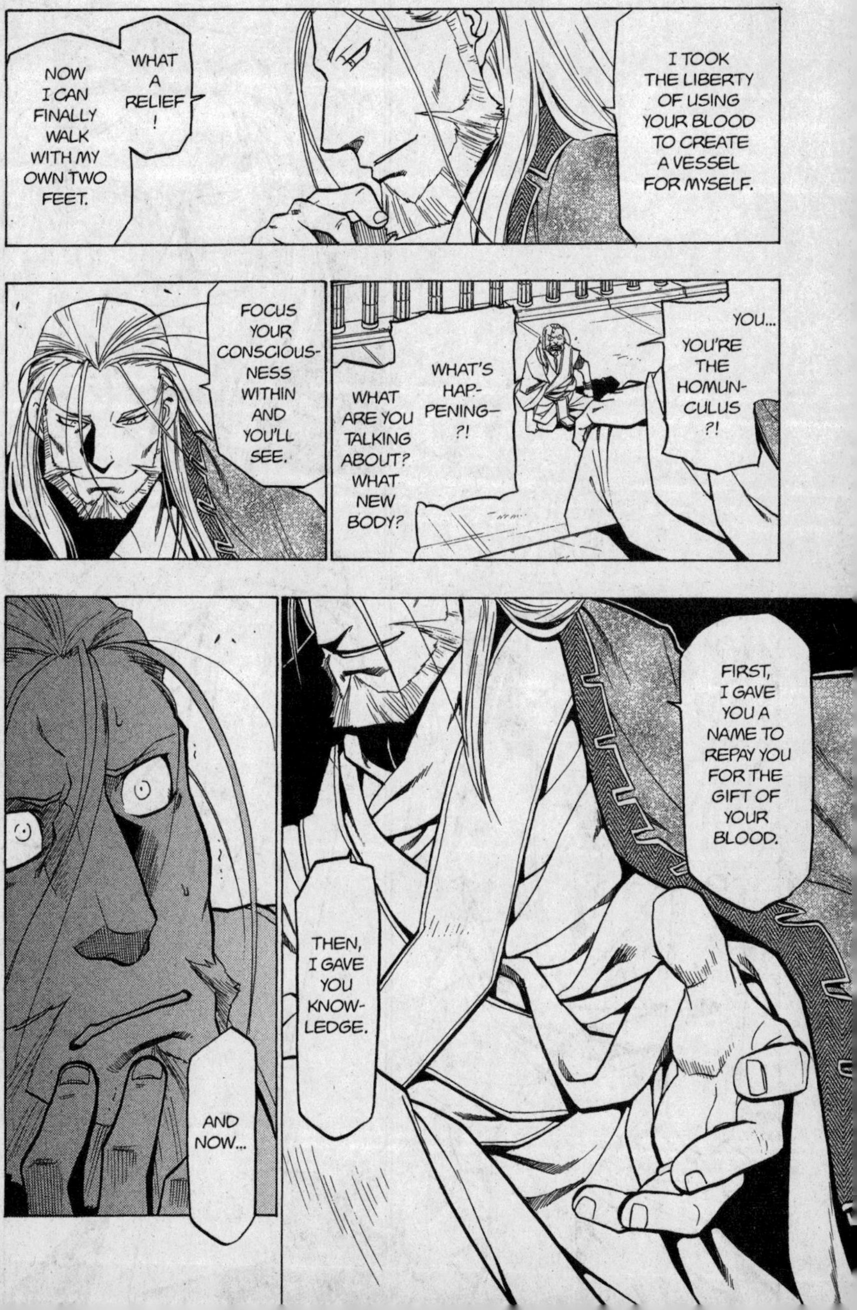
I TOOK THE LIBERTY OF USING YOUR BLOOD TO CREATE A VESSEL FOR MYSELF.
WHAT A RELIEF!
NOW I CAN FINALLY WALK WITH MY OWN TWO FEET.
YOU... YOU'RE THE HOMUNCULUS?!
WHAT'S HAPPENING—?!
WHAT ARE YOU TALKING ABOUT? WHAT NEW BODY?
FOCUS YOUR CONSCIOUSNESS WITHIN AND YOU'LL SEE.
FIRST, I GAVE YOU A NAME TO REPAY YOU FOR THE GIFT OF YOUR BLOOD.
THEN, I GAVE YOU KNOWLEDGE.
AND NOW...

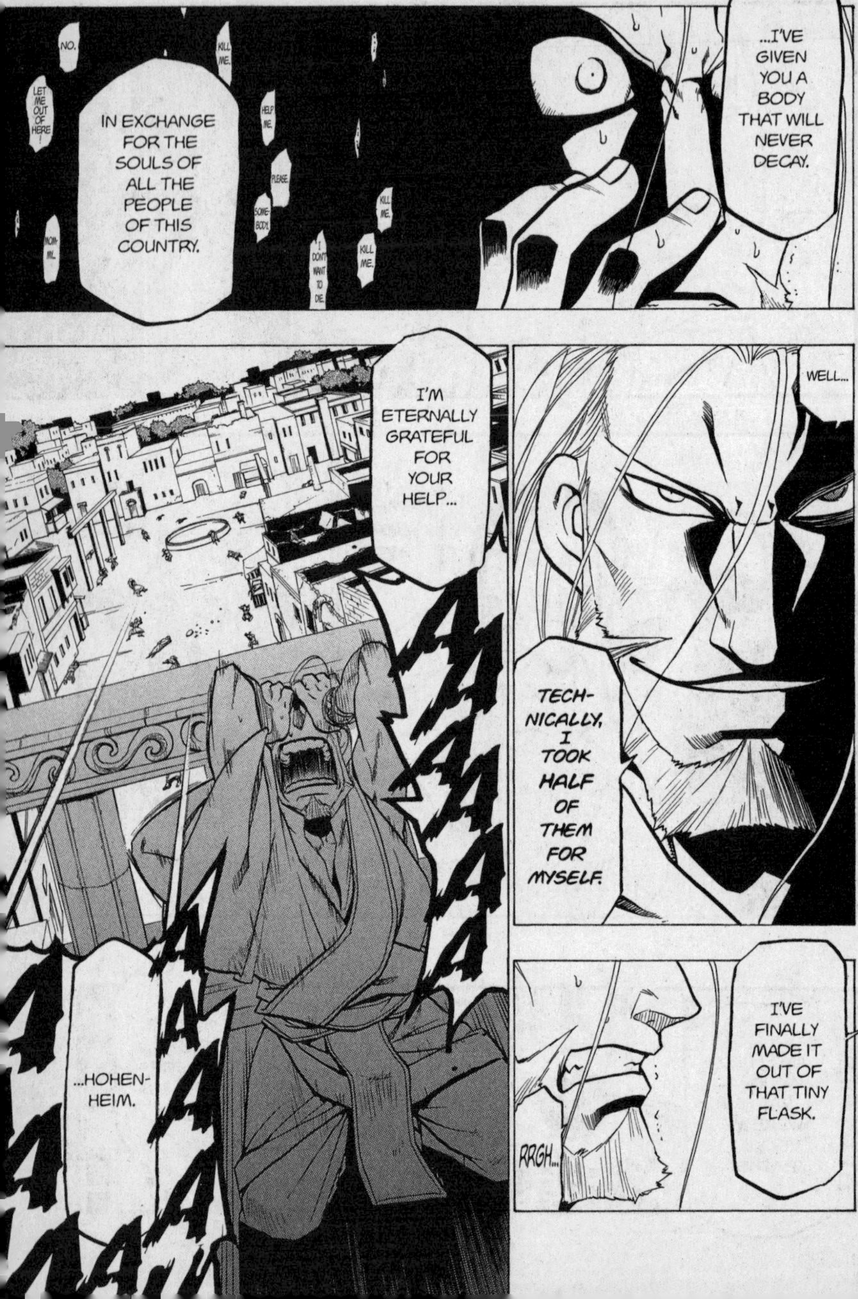
...I'VE GIVEN YOU A BODY THAT WILL NEVER DECAY.
KILL ME.
PLEASE.
HELP ME.
KILL ME.
NO.
IN EXCHANGE FOR THE SOULS OF ALL THE PEOPLE OF THIS COUNTRY.
LET ME OUT OF HERE!
KILL ME.
SOME-BODY.
I DON'T WANT TO DIE.
MOM-MY.
WELL...
TECH-NICALLY, I TOOK HALF OF THEM FOR MYSELF.
I'VE FINALLY MADE IT OUT OF THAT TINY FLASK.
RRGH...
I'M ETERNALLY GRATEFUL FOR YOUR HELP...
...HOHEN-HEIM.

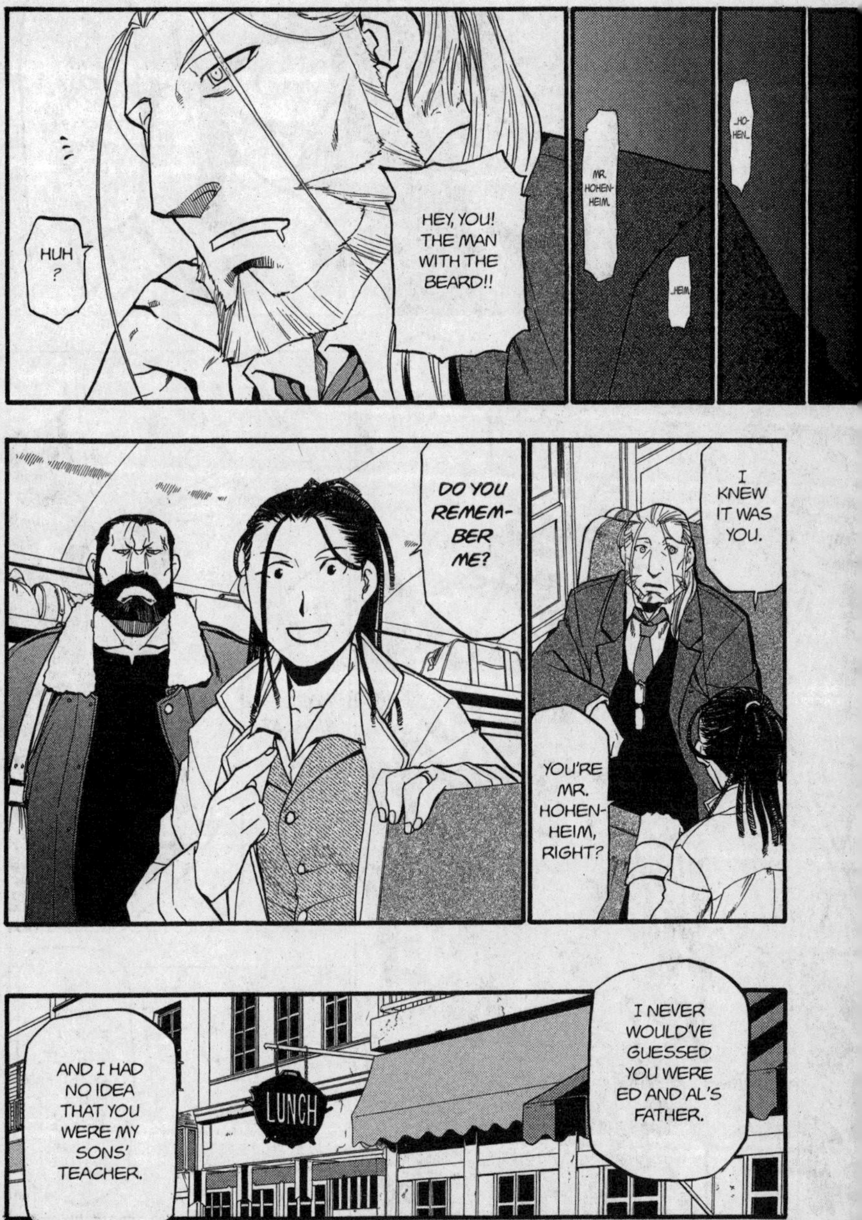
...HO-HEN...
MR. HOHEN-HEIM.
...HEIM
HEY, YOU! THE MAN WITH THE BEARD!!
HUH?
I KNEW IT WAS YOU.
YOU'RE MR. HOHEN-HEIM, RIGHT?
DO YOU REMEM-BER ME?
I NEVER WOULD'VE GUESSED YOU WERE ED AND AL'S FATHER.
LUNCH
AND I HAD NO IDEA THAT YOU WERE MY SONS' TEACHER.

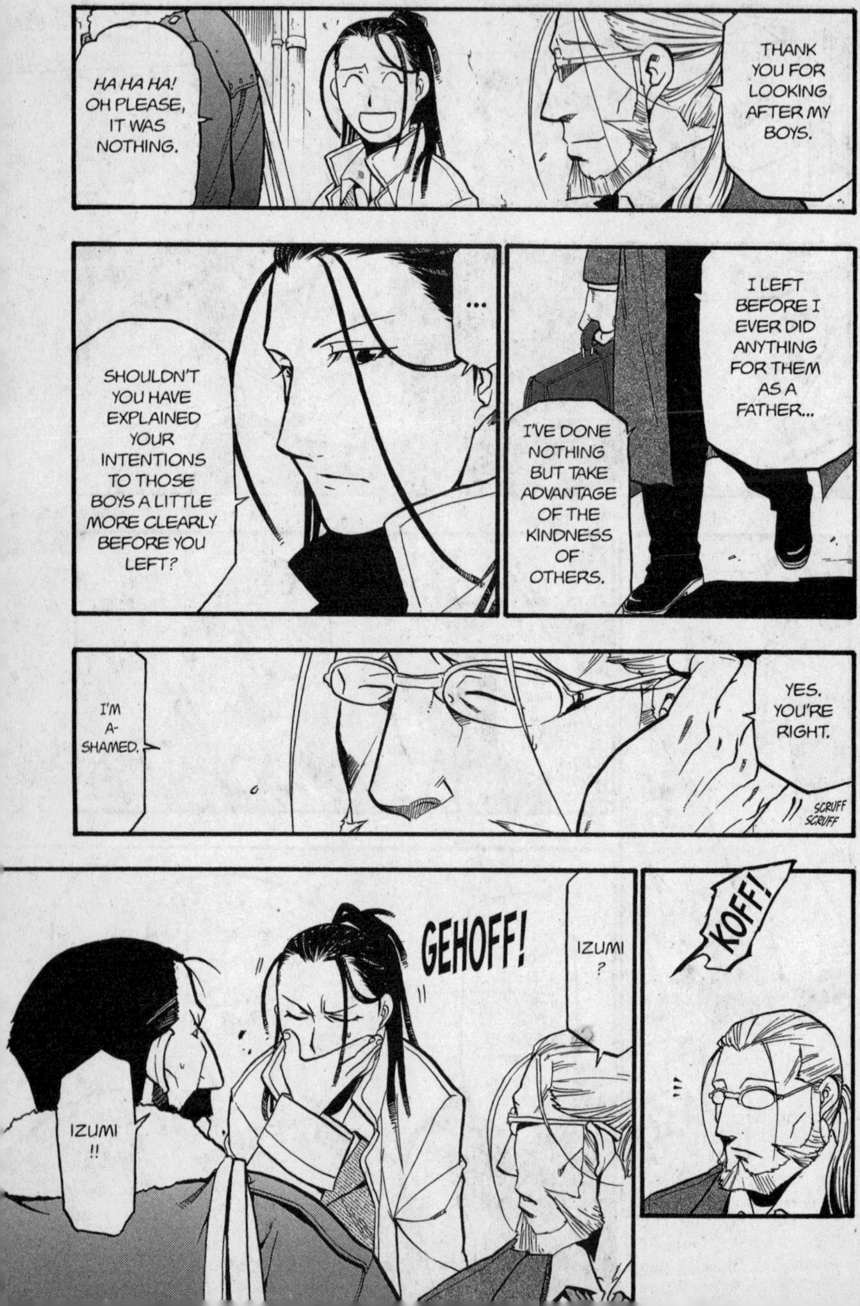
THANK YOU FOR LOOKING AFTER MY BOYS.
HA HA HA! OH PLEASE, IT WAS NOTHING.
I LEFT BEFORE I EVER DID ANYTHING FOR THEM AS A FATHER...
I'VE DONE NOTHING BUT TAKE ADVANTAGE OF THE KINDNESS OF OTHERS.
...
SHOULDN'T YOU HAVE EXPLAINED YOUR INTENTIONS TO THOSE BOYS A LITTLE MORE CLEARLY BEFORE YOU LEFT?
YES. YOU'RE RIGHT.
SCRUFF SCRUFF
I'M A-SHAMED.
KOFF!
IZUMI ?
GEHOFF!
IZUMI !!

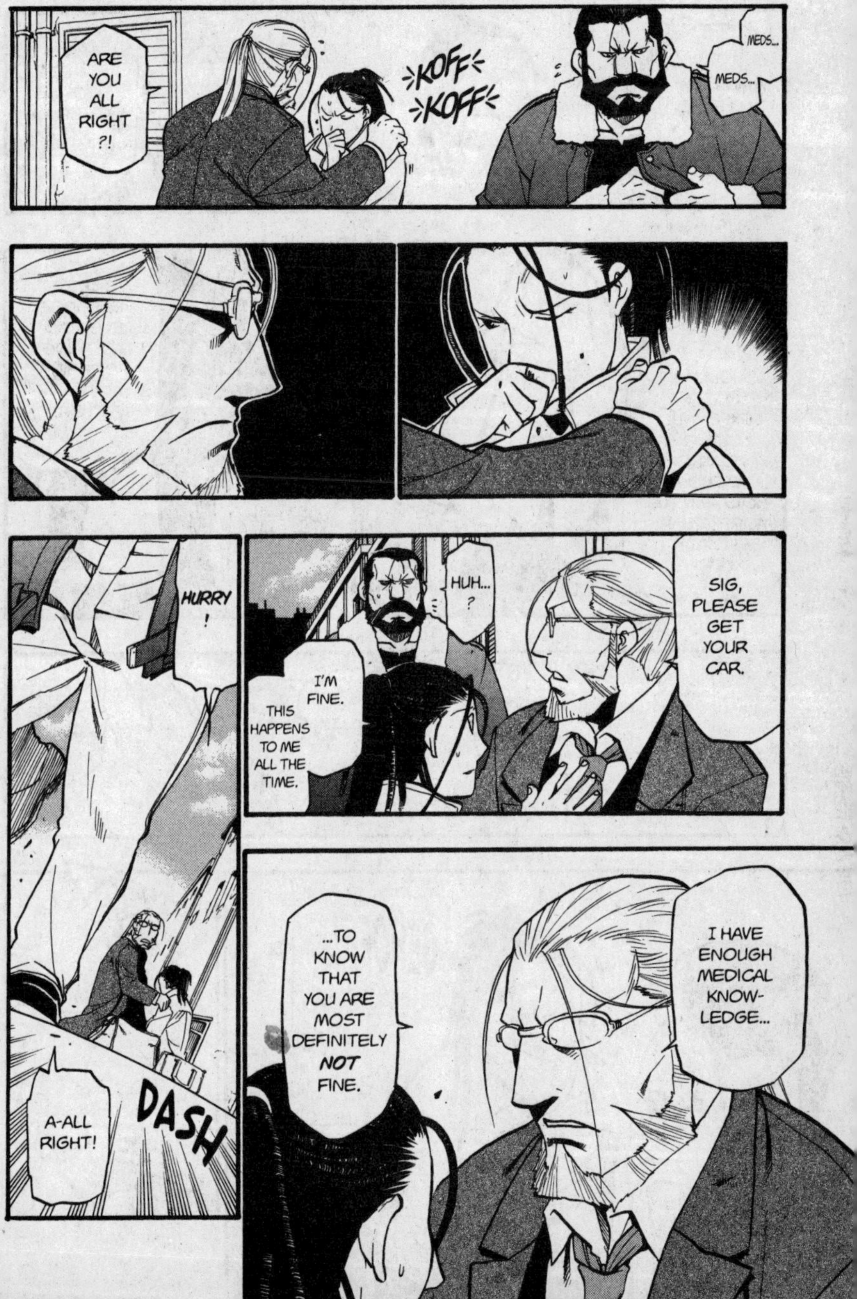
MEDS... MEDS...
KOFF KOFF
ARE YOU ALL RIGHT ?!
SIG, PLEASE GET YOUR CAR.
HUH... ?
I'M FINE. THIS HAPPENS TO ME ALL THE TIME.
I HAVE ENOUGH MEDICAL KNOW-LEDGE...
...TO KNOW THAT YOU ARE MOST DEFINITELY *NOT* FINE.
HURRY !
A-ALL RIGHT!
DASH

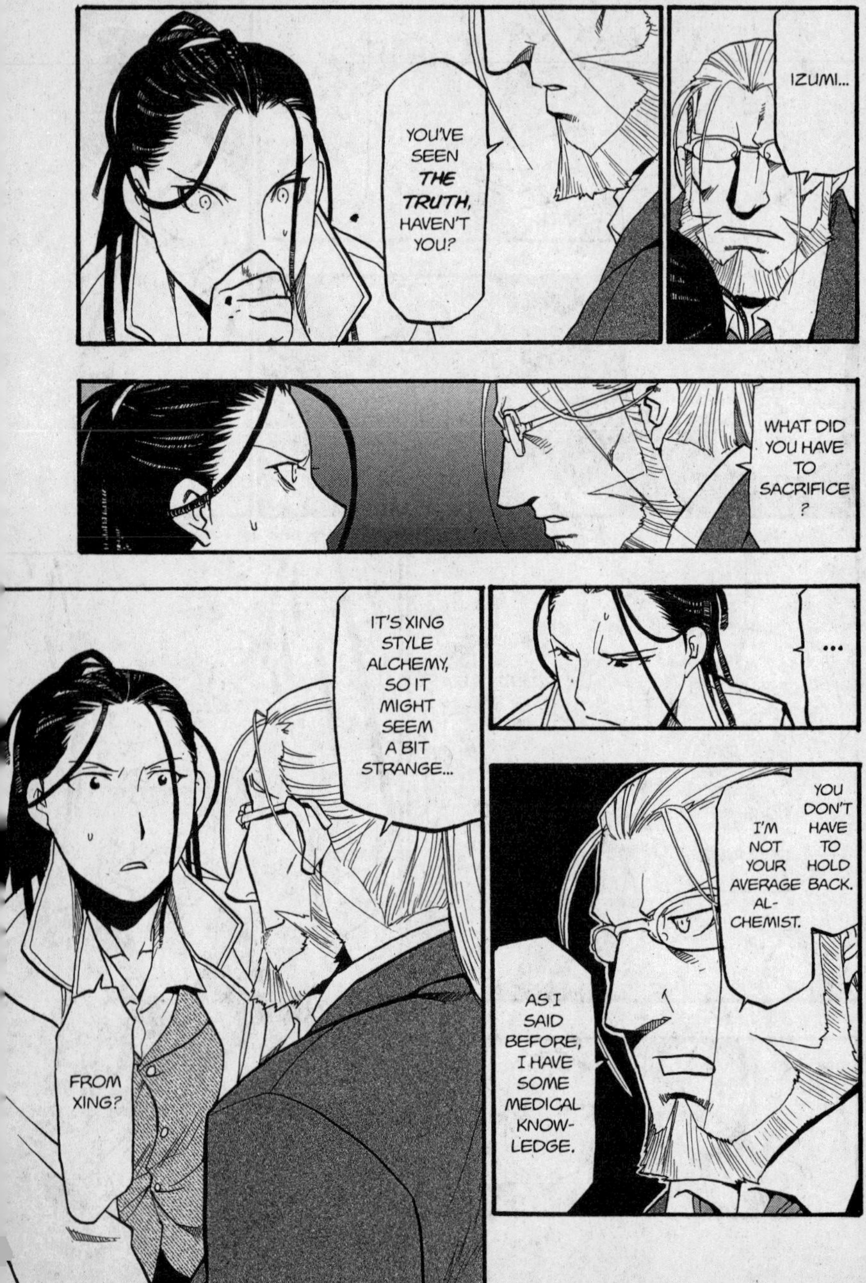
IZUMI...
YOU'VE SEEN THE TRUTH, HAVEN'T YOU?
WHAT DID YOU HAVE TO SACRIFICE?
...
YOU DON'T HAVE TO HOLD BACK.
I'M NOT YOUR AVERAGE AL-CHEMIST.
AS I SAID BEFORE, I HAVE SOME MEDICAL KNOW-LEDGE.
IT'S XING STYLE ALCHEMY, SO IT MIGHT SEEM A BIT STRANGE...
FROM XING?

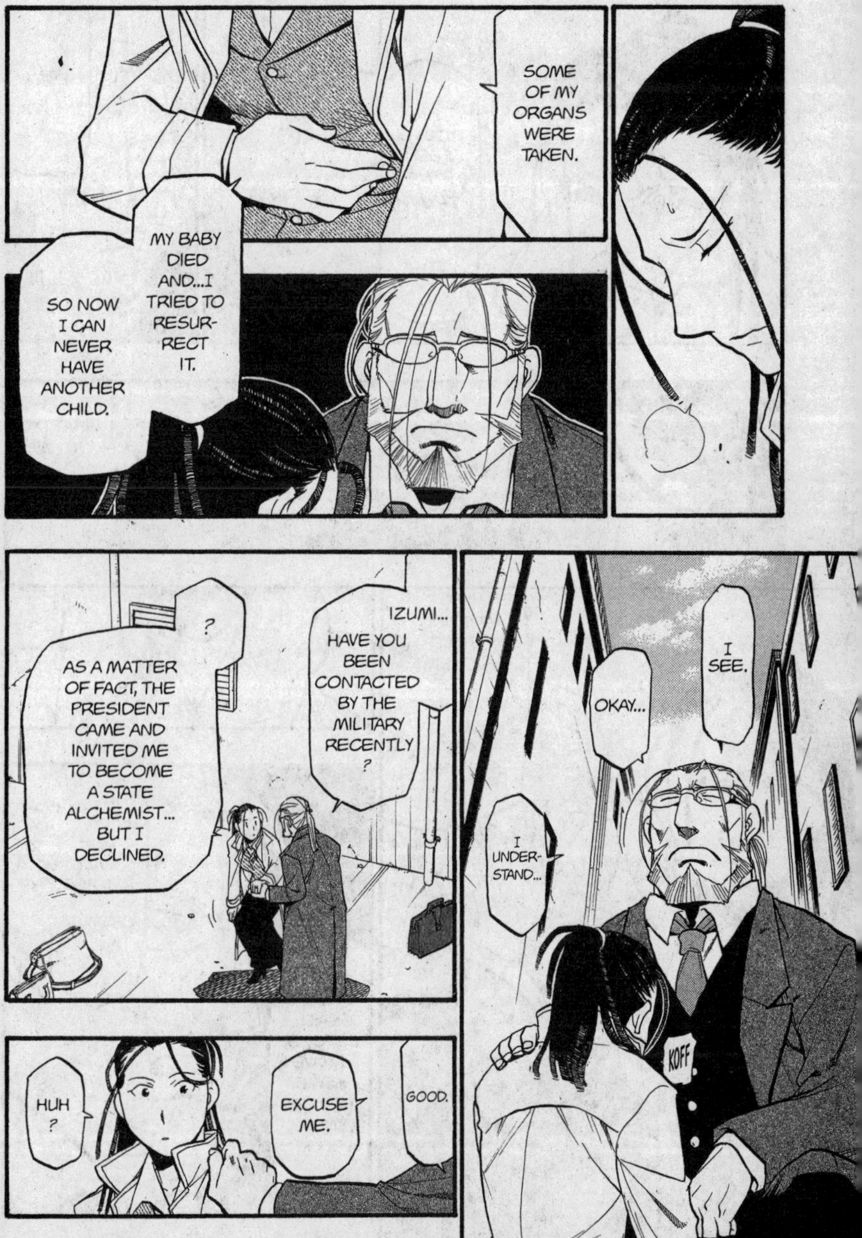
SOME OF MY ORGANS WERE TAKEN.
MY BABY DIED AND...I TRIED TO RESURRECT IT.
SO NOW I CAN NEVER HAVE ANOTHER CHILD.
I SEE.
OKAY...
I UNDERSTAND...
KOFF
IZUMI... HAVE YOU BEEN CONTACTED BY THE MILITARY RECENTLY?
?
AS A MATTER OF FACT, THE PRESIDENT CAME AND INVITED ME TO BECOME A STATE ALCHEMIST... BUT I DECLINED.
GOOD.
EXCUSE ME.
HUH?

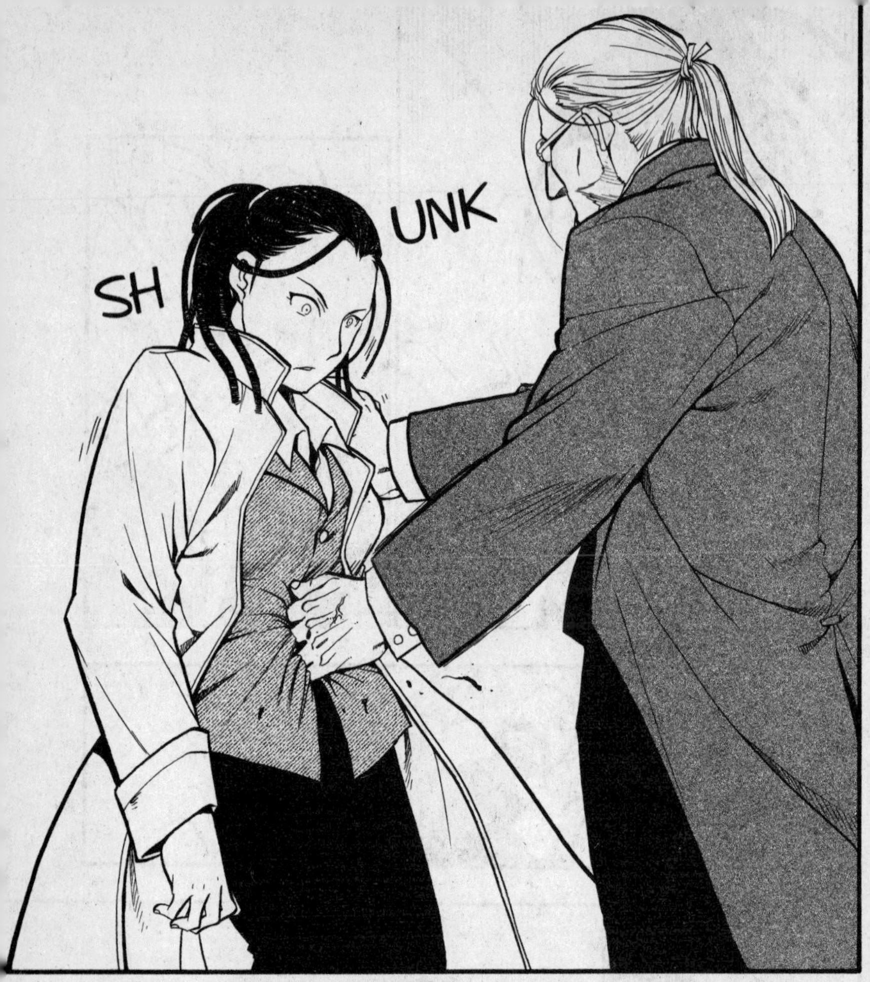
SH
UNK

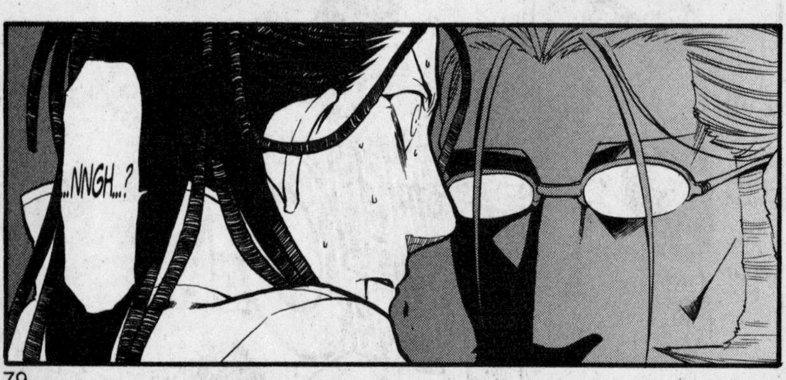
...NNGH...?

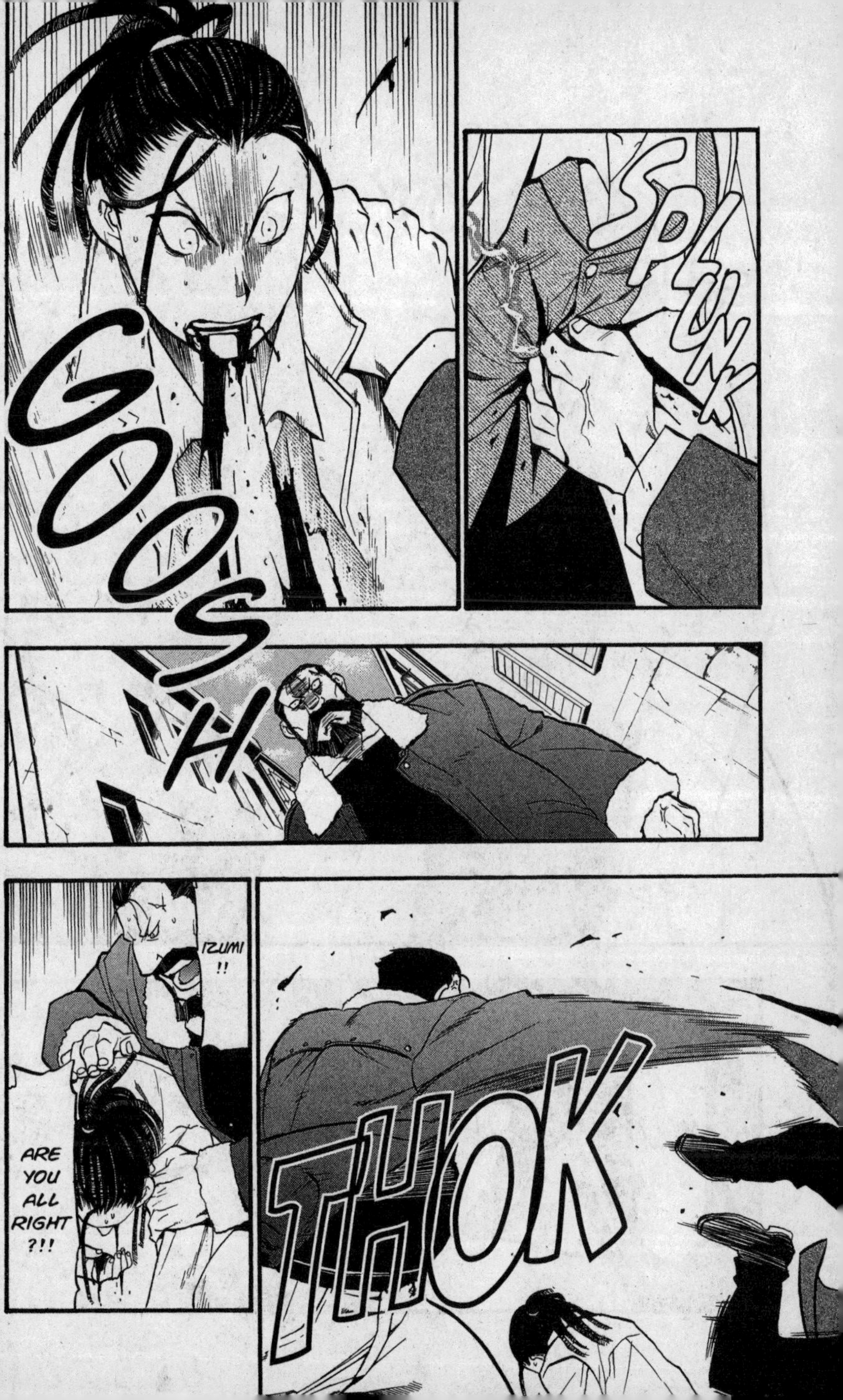
SPLUNK
GOOOSH
THOK
IZUMI!!
ARE YOU ALL RIGHT?!!

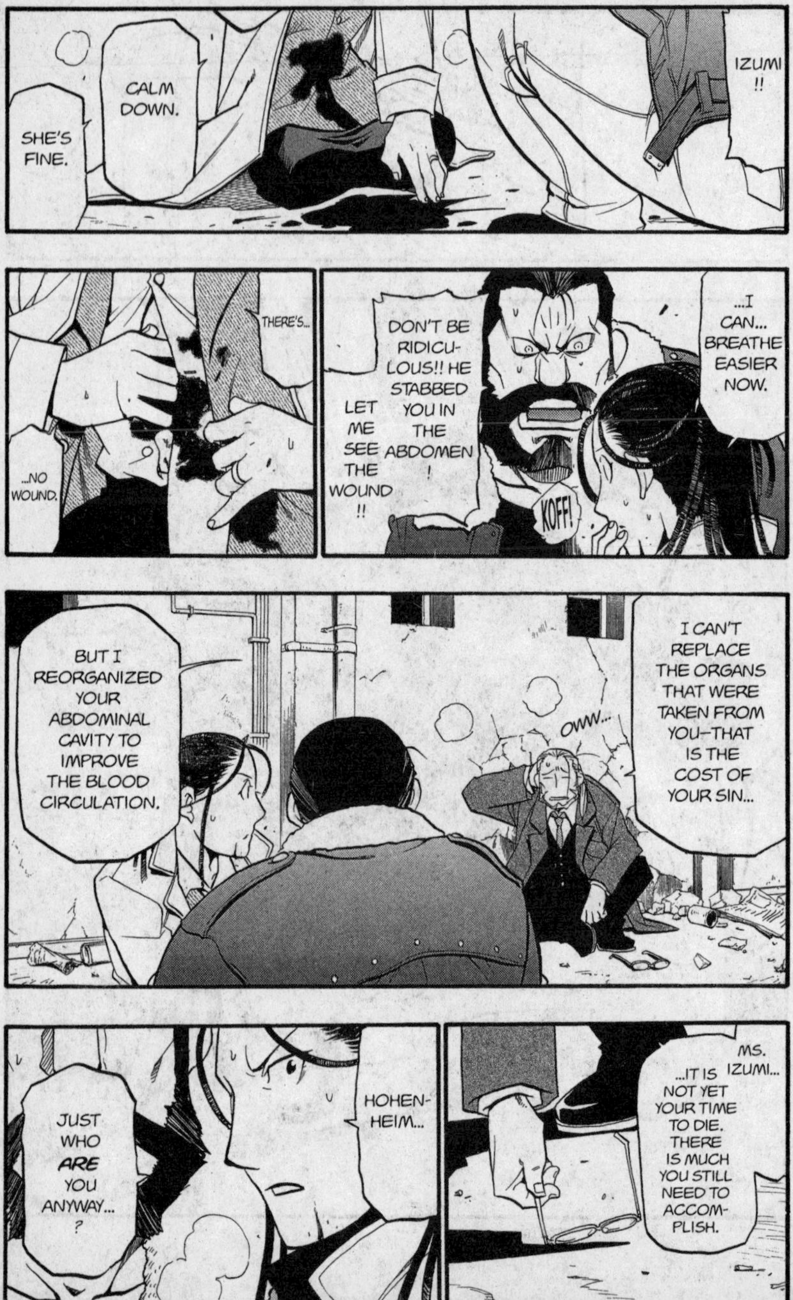
IZUMI!!
CALM DOWN.
SHE'S FINE.
...I CAN... BREATHE EASIER NOW.
DON'T BE RIDICULOUS!! HE STABBED YOU IN THE ABDOMEN!
LET ME SEE THE WOUND!!
KOFF!
THERE'S...
...NO WOUND.
I CAN'T REPLACE THE ORGANS THAT WERE TAKEN FROM YOU—THAT IS THE COST OF YOUR SIN...
OWW...
BUT I REORGANIZED YOUR ABDOMINAL CAVITY TO IMPROVE THE BLOOD CIRCULATION.
MS. IZUMI...
...IT IS NOT YET YOUR TIME TO DIE. THERE IS MUCH YOU STILL NEED TO ACCOMPLISH.
HOHENHEIM...
JUST WHO ARE YOU ANYWAY...?

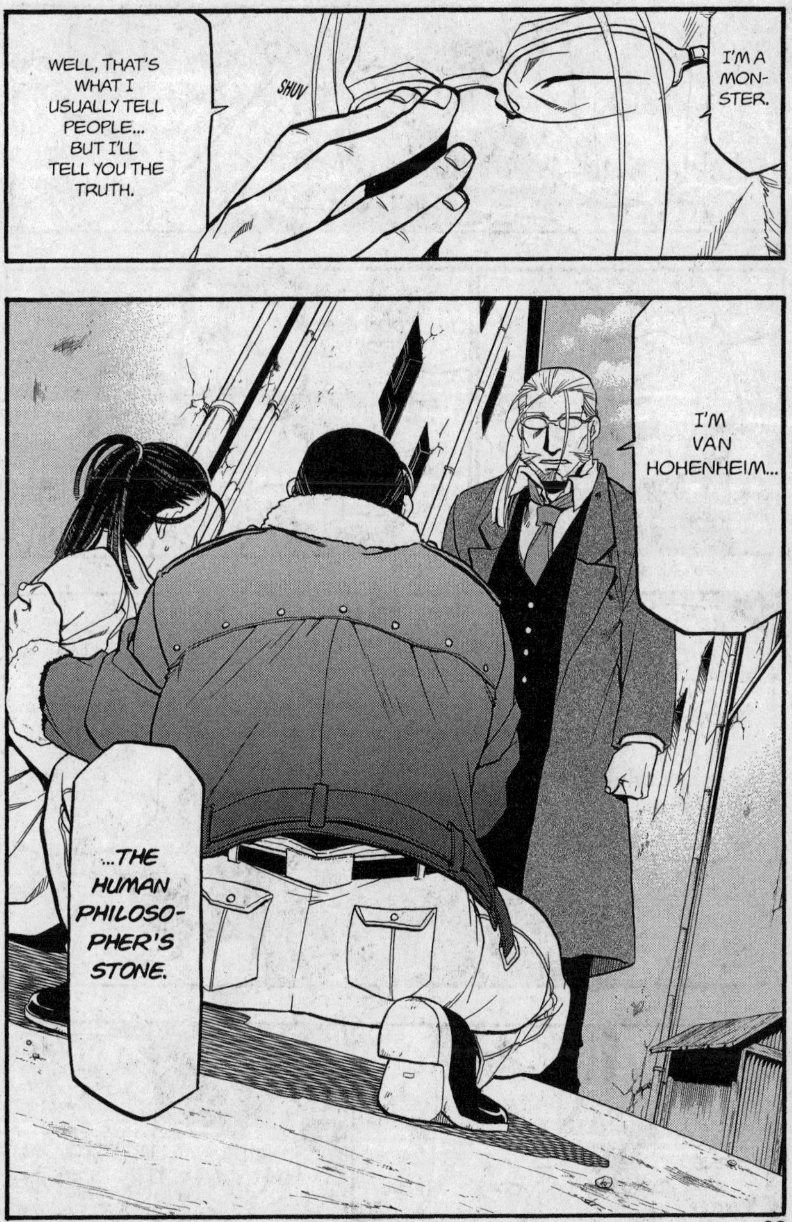
I'M A MONSTER.
SHUV
WELL, THAT'S WHAT I USUALLY TELL PEOPLE... BUT I'LL TELL YOU THE TRUTH.
I'M VAN HOHENHEIM...
...THE HUMAN PHILOSOPHER'S STONE.

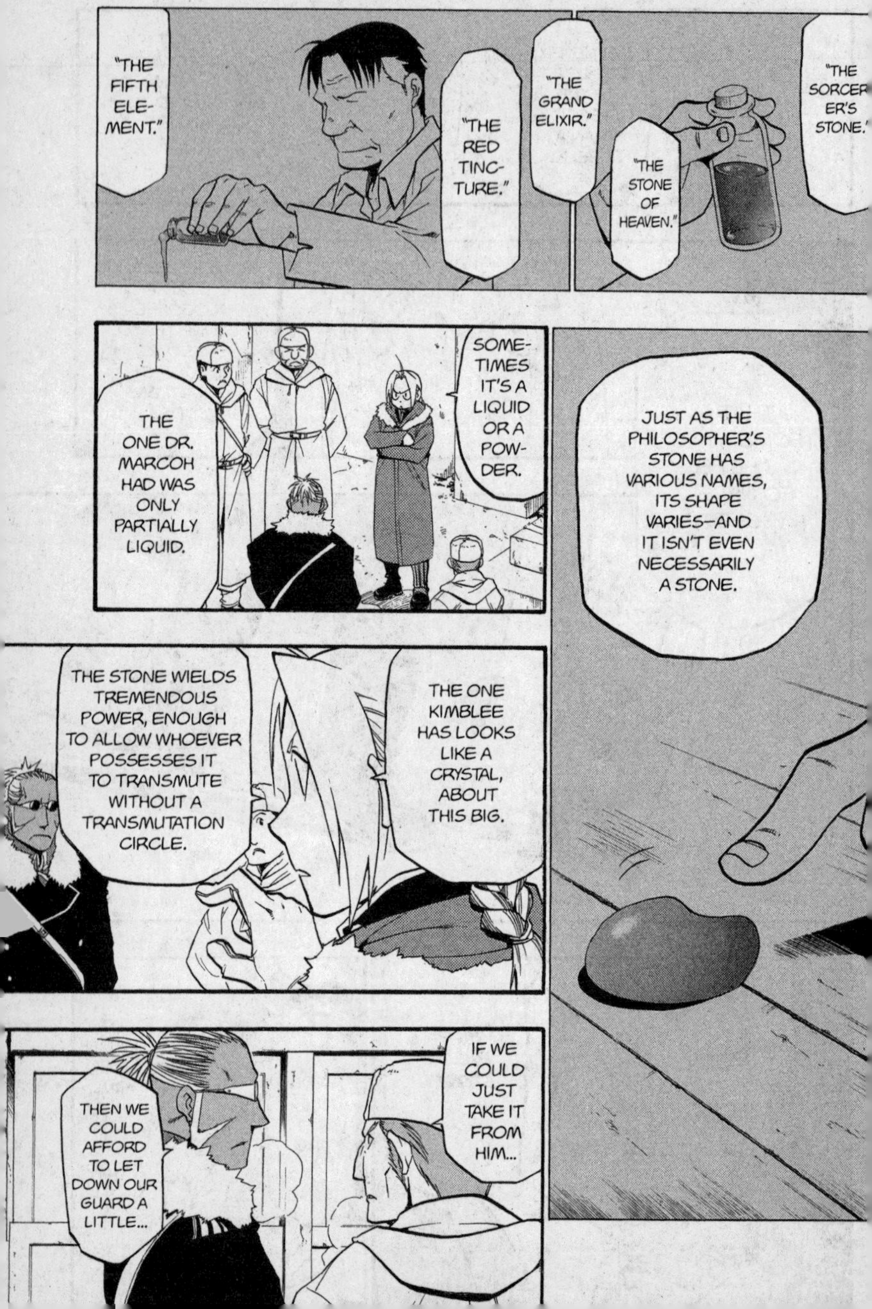
"THE SORCERER'S STONE."
"THE STONE OF HEAVEN."
"THE GRAND ELIXIR."
"THE RED TINCTURE."
"THE FIFTH ELEMENT."
JUST AS THE PHILOSOPHER'S STONE HAS VARIOUS NAMES, ITS SHAPE VARIES—AND IT ISN'T EVEN NECESSARILY A STONE.
SOMETIMES IT'S A LIQUID OR A POWDER.
THE ONE DR. MARCOH HAD WAS ONLY PARTIALLY LIQUID.
THE ONE KIMBLEE HAS LOOKS LIKE A CRYSTAL, ABOUT THIS BIG.
THE STONE WIELDS TREMENDOUS POWER, ENOUGH TO ALLOW WHOEVER POSSESSES IT TO TRANSMUTE WITHOUT A TRANSMUTATION CIRCLE.
IF WE COULD JUST TAKE IT FROM HIM...
THEN WE COULD AFFORD TO LET DOWN OUR GUARD A LITTLE...

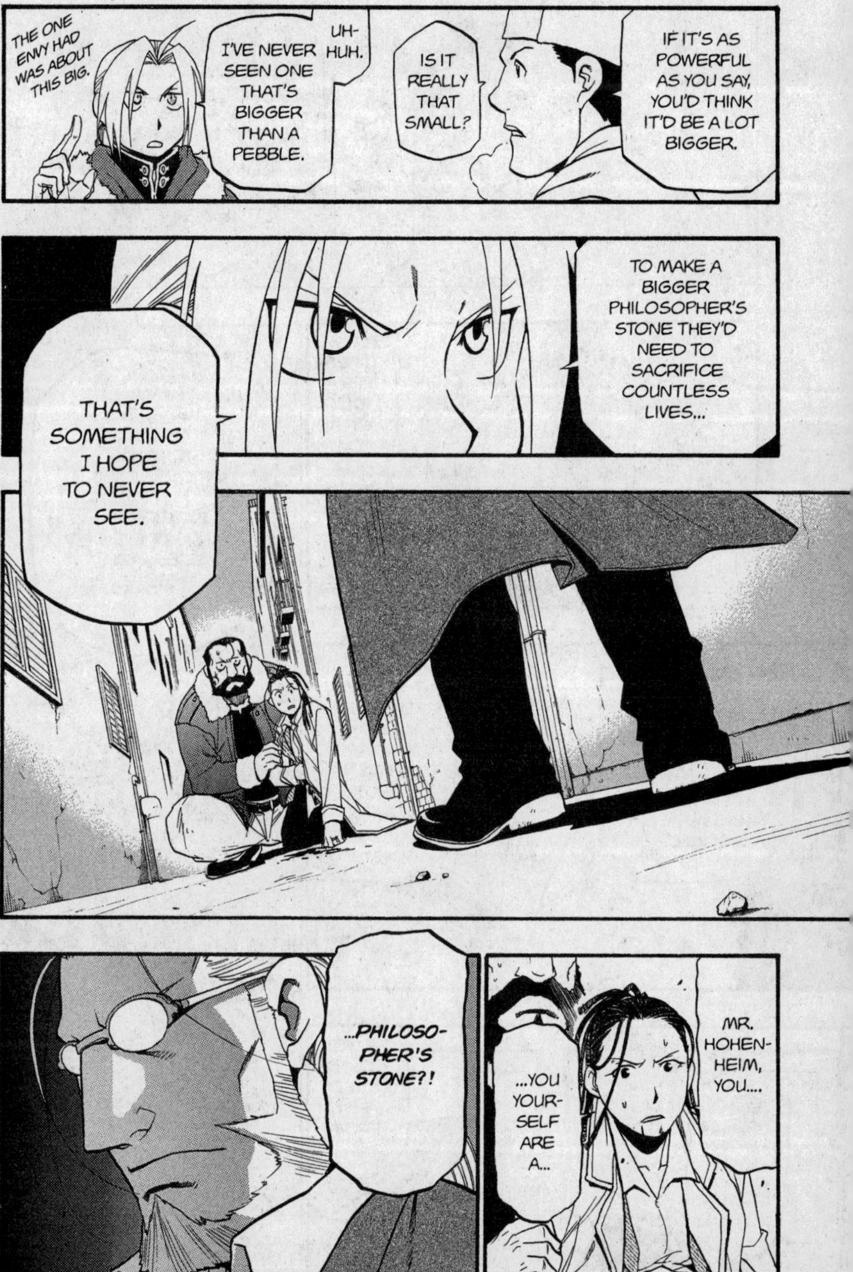
IF IT'S AS POWERFUL AS YOU SAY, YOU'D THINK IT'D BE A LOT BIGGER.
IS IT REALLY THAT SMALL?
UH-HUH.
I'VE NEVER SEEN ONE THAT'S BIGGER THAN A PEBBLE.
THE ONE ENVY HAD WAS ABOUT THIS BIG.
TO MAKE A BIGGER PHILOSOPHER'S STONE THEY'D NEED TO SACRIFICE COUNTLESS LIVES...
THAT'S SOMETHING I HOPE TO NEVER SEE.
MR. HOHENHEIM, YOU....
...YOU YOURSELF ARE A...
...PHILOSO-PHER'S STONE?!

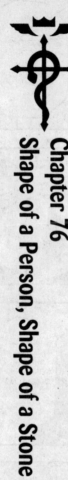

Chapter 76
Shape of a Person, Shape of a Stone

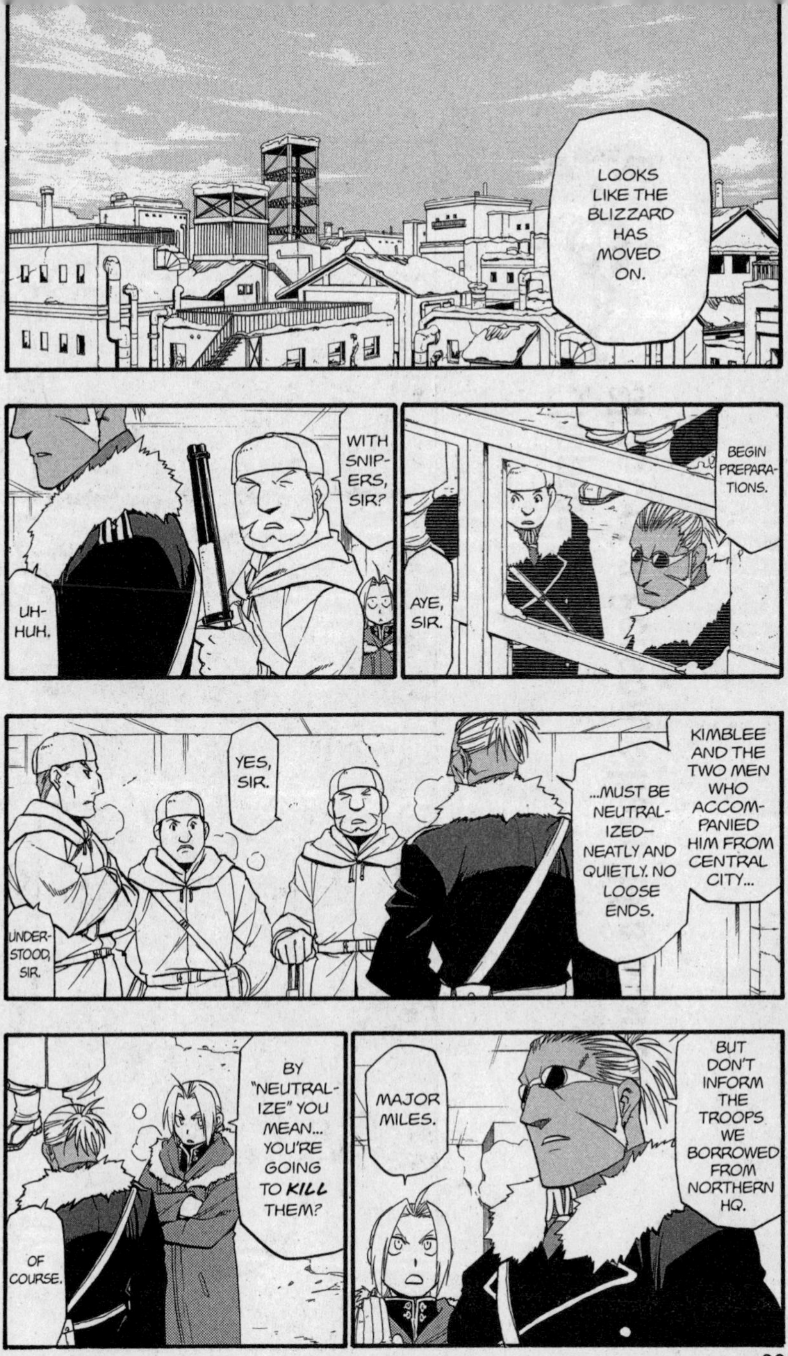
LOOKS LIKE THE BLIZZARD HAS MOVED ON.
BEGIN PREPARATIONS.
AYE, SIR.
WITH SNIPERS, SIR?
UH-HUH.
KIMBLEE AND THE TWO MEN WHO ACCOMPANIED HIM FROM CENTRAL CITY...
...MUST BE NEUTRALIZED—NEATLY AND QUIETLY. NO LOOSE ENDS.
YES, SIR.
UNDERSTOOD, SIR.
BUT DON'T INFORM THE TROOPS WE BORROWED FROM NORTHERN HQ.
MAJOR MILES.
BY "NEUTRALIZE" YOU MEAN... YOU'RE GOING TO **KILL** THEM?
OF COURSE.

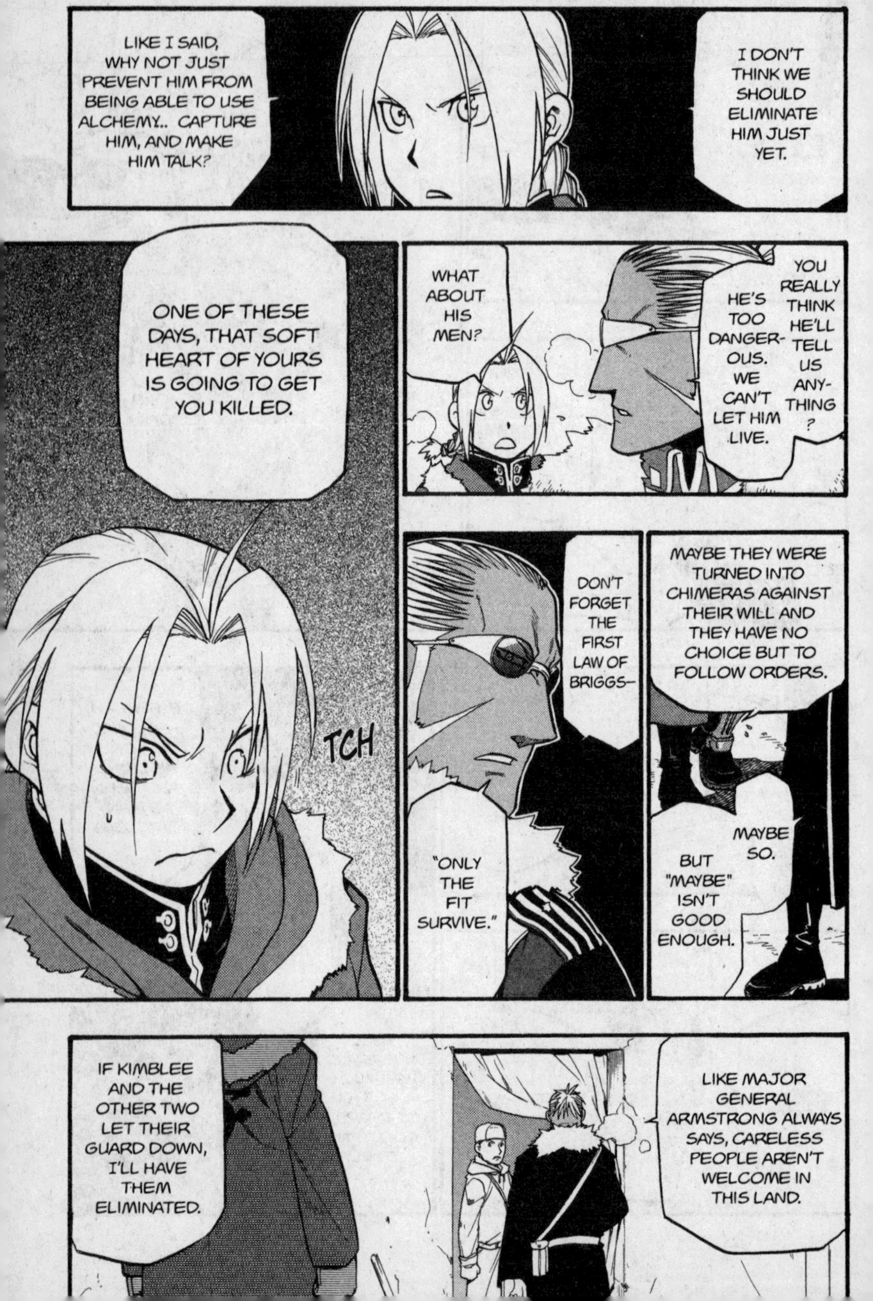

I DON'T THINK WE SHOULD ELIMINATE HIM JUST YET.
LIKE I SAID, WHY NOT JUST PREVENT HIM FROM BEING ABLE TO USE ALCHEMY.. CAPTURE HIM, AND MAKE HIM TALK?
YOU REALLY THINK HE'LL TELL US ANYTHING?
HE'S TOO DANGEROUS. WE CAN'T LET HIM LIVE.
WHAT ABOUT HIS MEN?
MAYBE THEY WERE TURNED INTO CHIMERAS AGAINST THEIR WILL AND THEY HAVE NO CHOICE BUT TO FOLLOW ORDERS.
MAYBE SO.
BUT "MAYBE" ISN'T GOOD ENOUGH.
DON'T FORGET THE FIRST LAW OF BRIGGS—
"ONLY THE FIT SURVIVE."
ONE OF THESE DAYS, THAT SOFT HEART OF YOURS IS GOING TO GET YOU KILLED.
TCH
LIKE MAJOR GENERAL ARMSTRONG ALWAYS SAYS, CARELESS PEOPLE AREN'T WELCOME IN THIS LAND.
IF KIMBLEE AND THE OTHER TWO LET THEIR GUARD DOWN, I'LL HAVE THEM ELIMINATED.

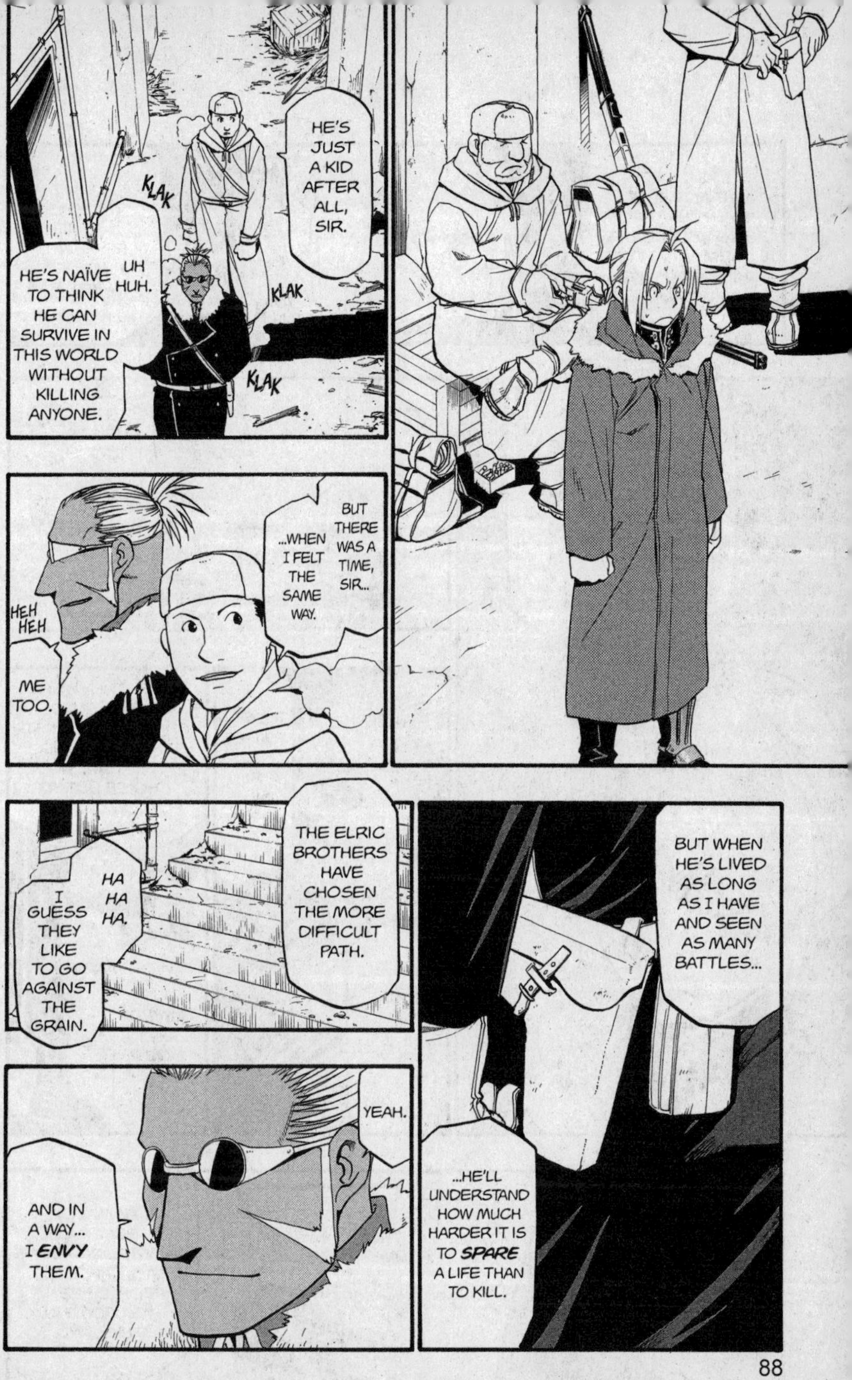
HE'S JUST A KID AFTER ALL, SIR.
KLAK
UH HUH.
KLAK
HE'S NAÏVE TO THINK HE CAN SURVIVE IN THIS WORLD WITHOUT KILLING ANYONE.
KLAK
BUT THERE WAS A TIME, SIR...
...WHEN I FELT THE SAME WAY.
HEH HEH
ME TOO.
BUT WHEN HE'S LIVED AS LONG AS I HAVE AND SEEN AS MANY BATTLES...
...HE'LL UNDERSTAND HOW MUCH HARDER IT IS TO **SPARE** A LIFE THAN TO KILL.
THE ELRIC BROTHERS HAVE CHOSEN THE MORE DIFFICULT PATH.
HA HA HA.
I GUESS THEY LIKE TO GO AGAINST THE GRAIN.
YEAH.
AND IN A WAY... I **ENVY** THEM.

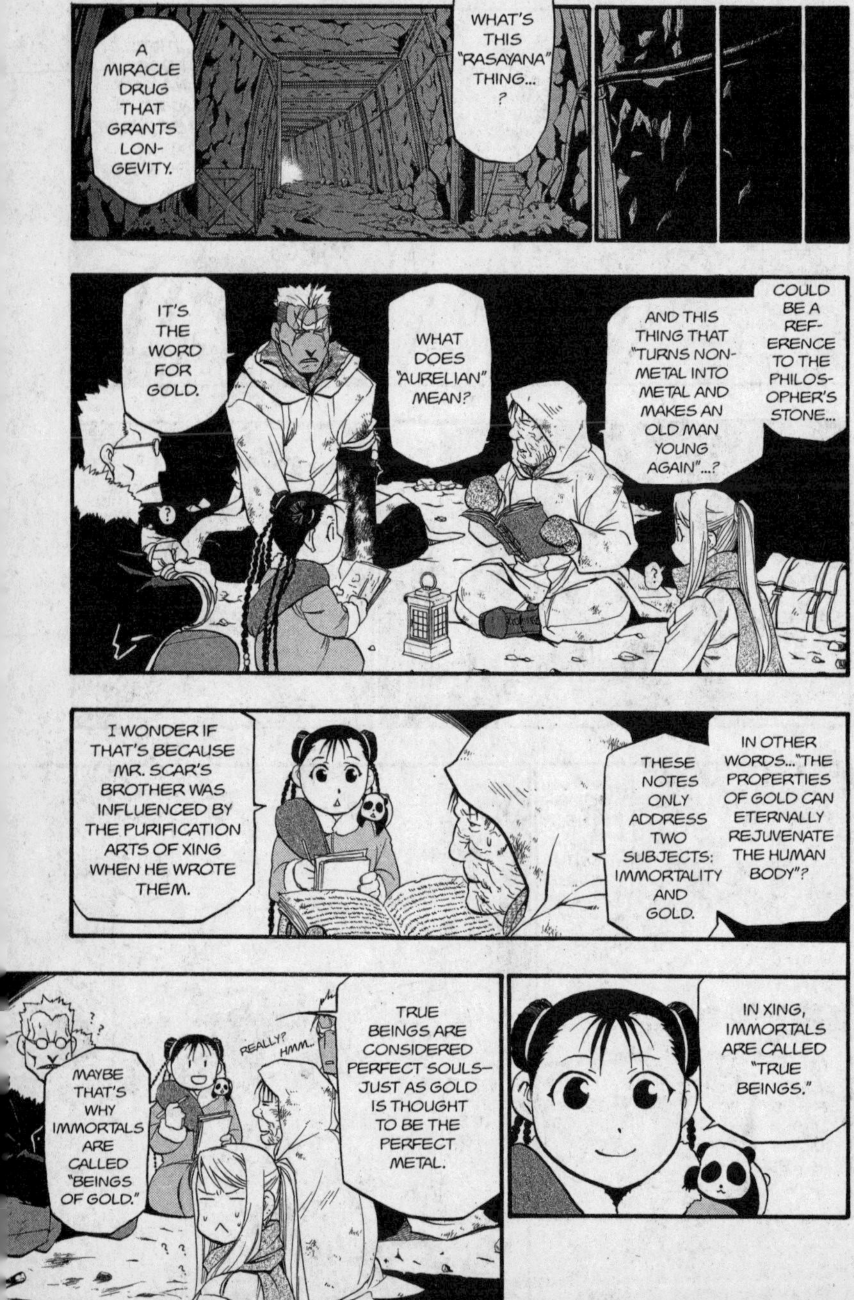
WHAT'S THIS "RASAYANA" THING...?
A MIRACLE DRUG THAT GRANTS LON-GEVITY.
AND THIS THING THAT "TURNS NON-METAL INTO METAL AND MAKES AN OLD MAN YOUNG AGAIN"...?
COULD BE A REF-ERENCE TO THE PHILOS-OPHER'S STONE...
WHAT DOES "AURELIAN" MEAN?
IT'S THE WORD FOR GOLD.
THESE NOTES ONLY ADDRESS TWO SUBJECTS: IMMORTALITY AND GOLD.
IN OTHER WORDS..."THE PROPERTIES OF GOLD CAN ETERNALLY REJUVENATE THE HUMAN BODY"?
I WONDER IF THAT'S BECAUSE MR. SCAR'S BROTHER WAS INFLUENCED BY THE PURIFICATION ARTS OF XING WHEN HE WROTE THEM.
IN XING, IMMORTALS ARE CALLED "TRUE BEINGS."
TRUE BEINGS ARE CONSIDERED PERFECT SOULS–JUST AS GOLD IS THOUGHT TO BE THE PERFECT METAL.
REALLY? HMM..
MAYBE THAT'S WHY IMMORTALS ARE CALLED "BEINGS OF GOLD."

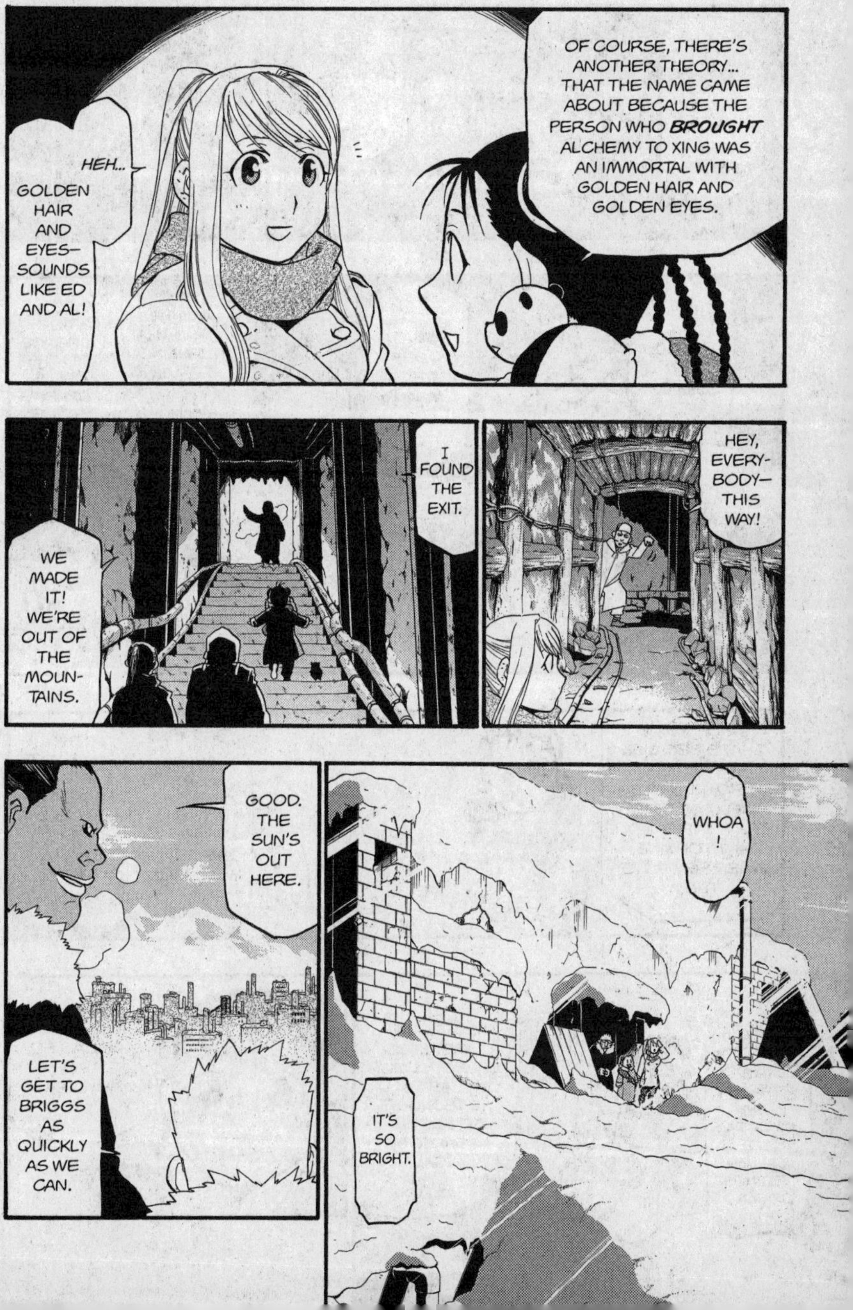
OF COURSE, THERE'S ANOTHER THEORY... THAT THE NAME CAME ABOUT BECAUSE THE PERSON WHO **BROUGHT** ALCHEMY TO XING WAS AN IMMORTAL WITH GOLDEN HAIR AND GOLDEN EYES.
HEH...
GOLDEN HAIR AND EYES—SOUNDS LIKE ED AND AL!
HEY, EVERYBODY—THIS WAY!
I FOUND THE EXIT.
WE MADE IT! WE'RE OUT OF THE MOUNTAINS.
WHOA!
IT'S SO BRIGHT.
GOOD. THE SUN'S OUT HERE.
LET'S GET TO BRIGGS AS QUICKLY AS WE CAN.

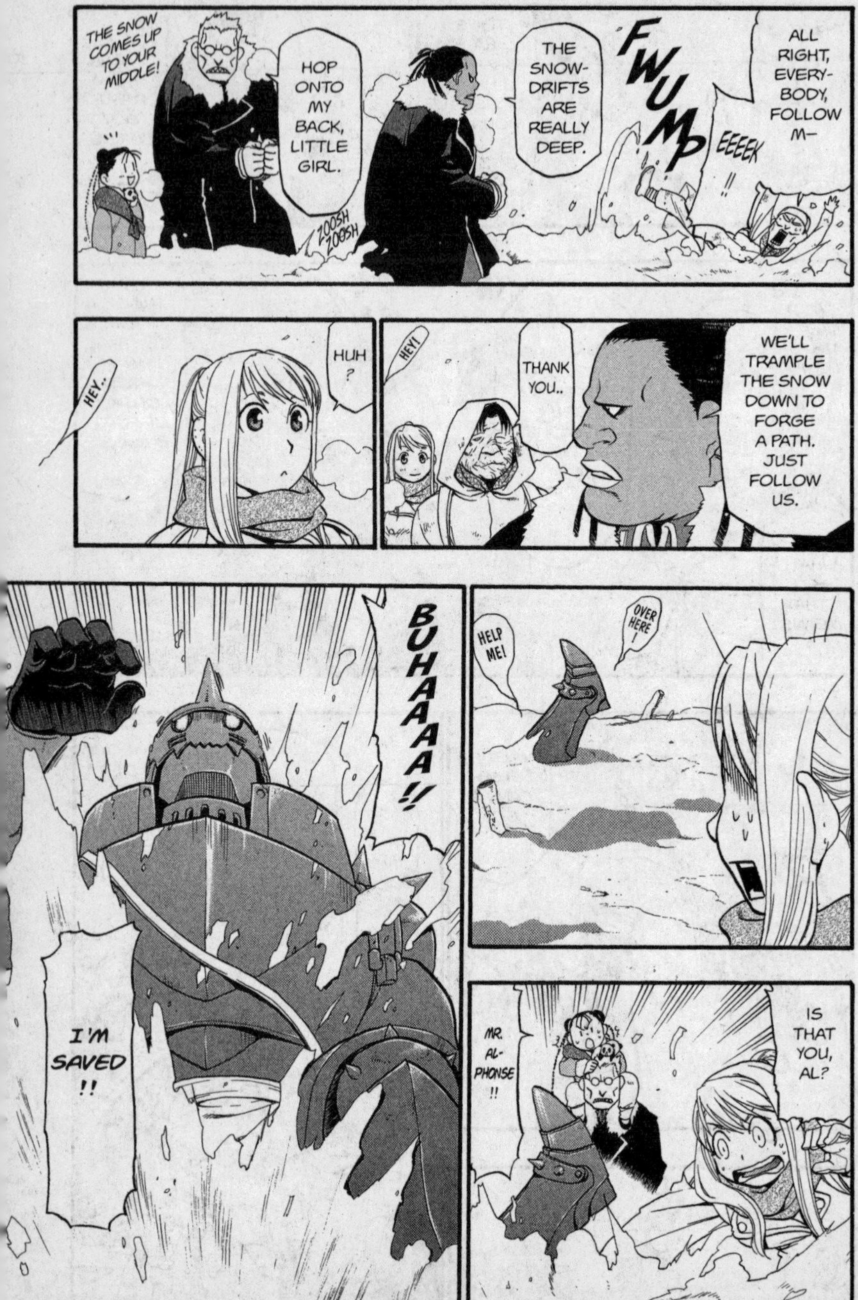
ALL RIGHT, EVERYBODY, FOLLOW M—
EEEEK !!
FWUMP
THE SNOW-DRIFTS ARE REALLY DEEP.
HOP ONTO MY BACK, LITTLE GIRL.
ZOOSH ZOOSH
THE SNOW COMES UP TO YOUR MIDDLE!
WE'LL TRAMPLE THE SNOW DOWN TO FORGE A PATH. JUST FOLLOW US.
THANK YOU..
HEY!
HUH ?
HEY..
OVER HERE !
HELP ME!
IS THAT YOU, AL?
MR. AL-PHONSE !!
BUHAAAAA!!
I'M SAVED !!

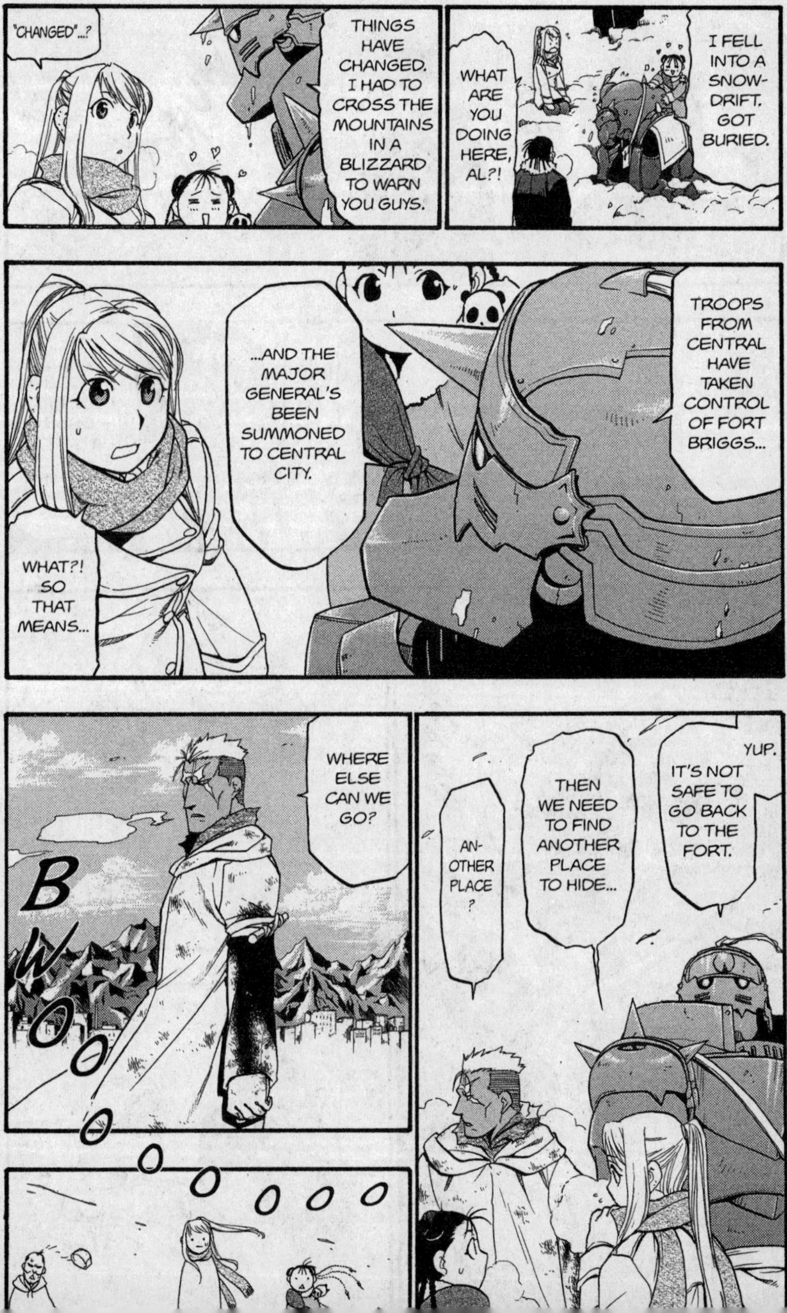
WHAT ARE YOU DOING HERE, AL?!
I FELL INTO A SNOW-DRIFT. GOT BURIED.
THINGS HAVE CHANGED. I HAD TO CROSS THE MOUNTAINS IN A BLIZZARD TO WARN YOU GUYS.
"CHANGED"...?
TROOPS FROM CENTRAL HAVE TAKEN CONTROL OF FORT BRIGGS...
...AND THE MAJOR GENERAL'S BEEN SUMMONED TO CENTRAL CITY.
WHAT?! SO THAT MEANS...
YUP. IT'S NOT SAFE TO GO BACK TO THE FORT.
THEN WE NEED TO FIND ANOTHER PLACE TO HIDE...
AN-OTHER PLACE?
WHERE ELSE CAN WE GO?
BWOOOOOOOOOO

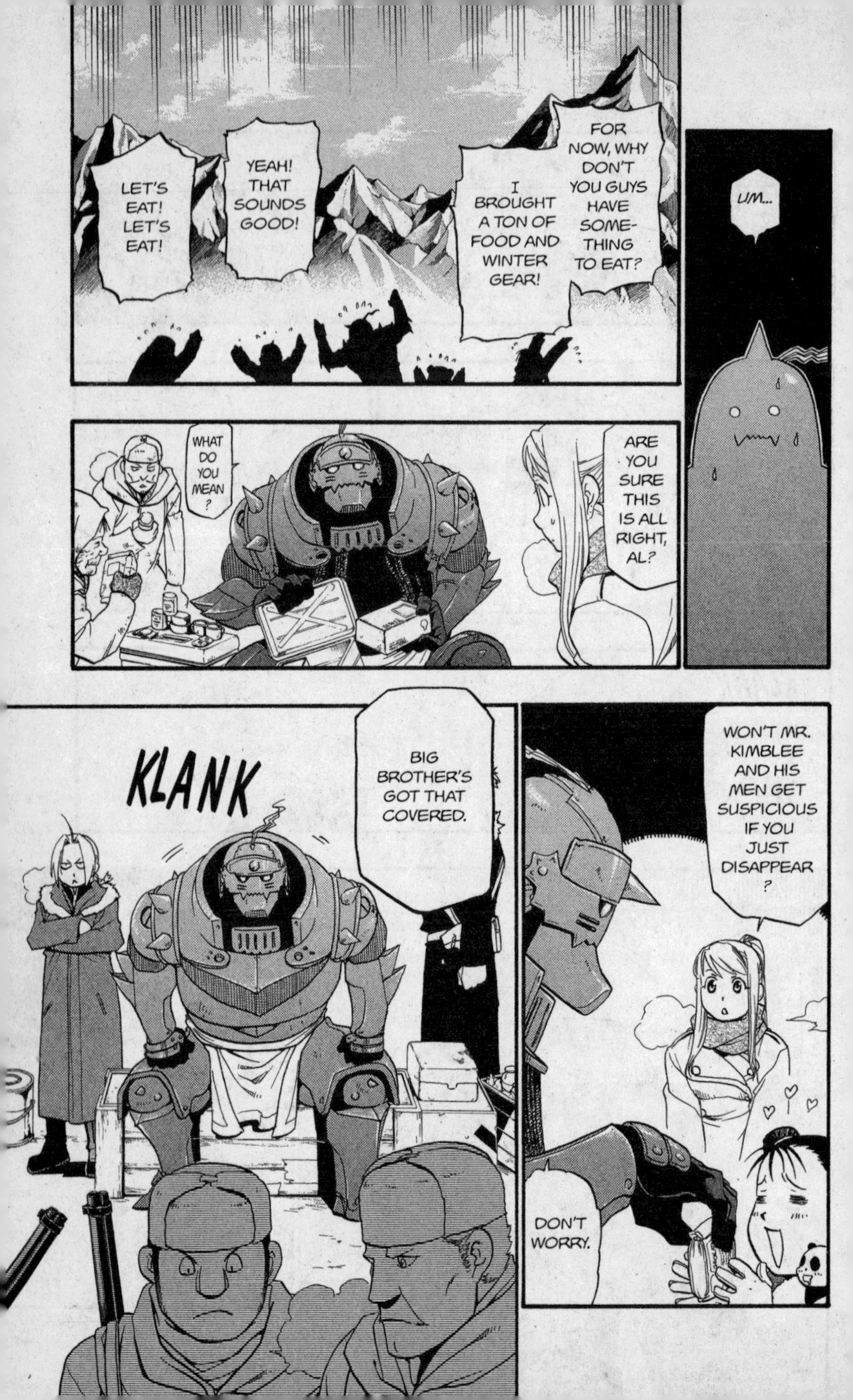

UM...
FOR NOW, WHY DON'T YOU GUYS HAVE SOME-THING TO EAT?
I BROUGHT A TON OF FOOD AND WINTER GEAR!
YEAH! THAT SOUNDS GOOD!
LET'S EAT! LET'S EAT!
ARE YOU SURE THIS IS ALL RIGHT, AL?
WHAT DO YOU MEAN?
WON'T MR. KIMBLEE AND HIS MEN GET SUSPICIOUS IF YOU JUST DISAPPEAR?
DON'T WORRY.
BIG BROTHER'S GOT THAT COVERED.
KLANK

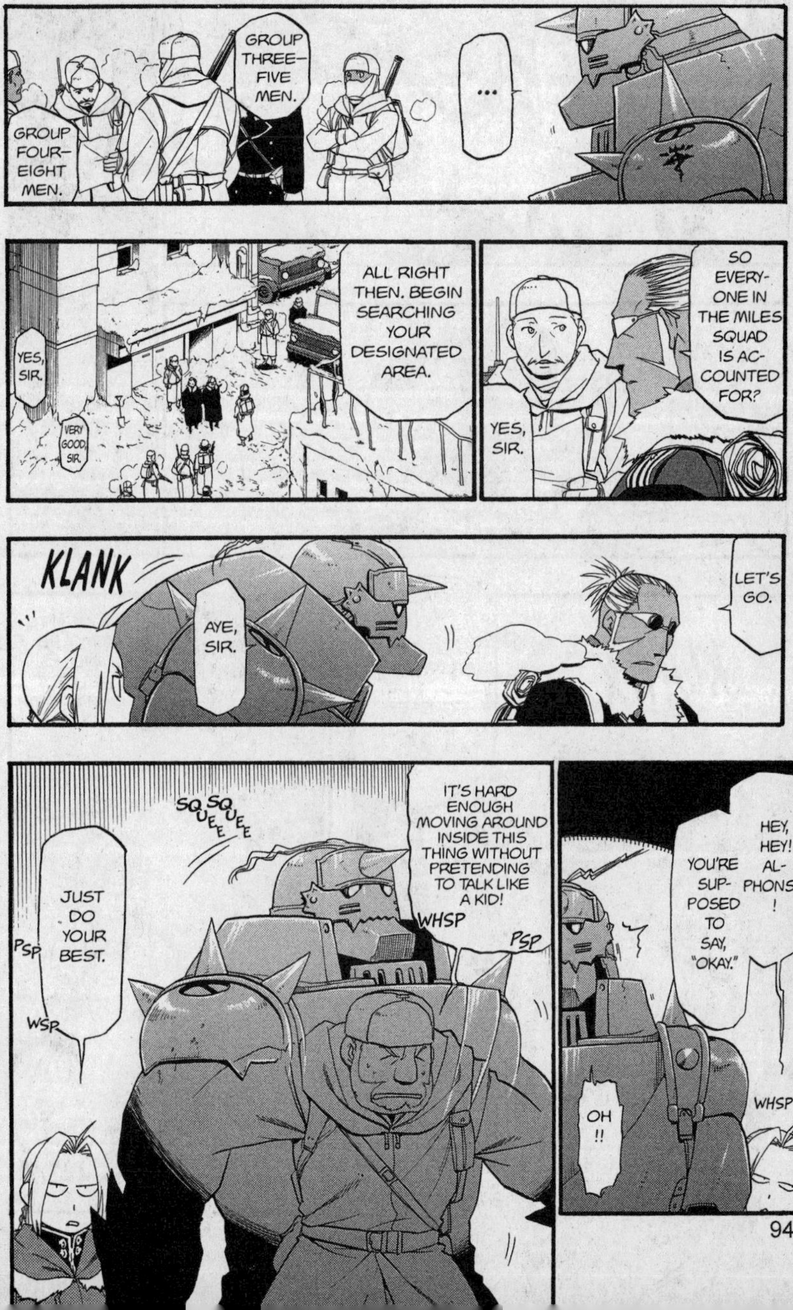
...
GROUP THREE—FIVE MEN.
GROUP FOUR—EIGHT MEN.
SO EVERYONE IN THE MILES SQUAD IS ACCOUNTED FOR?
YES, SIR.
ALL RIGHT THEN. BEGIN SEARCHING YOUR DESIGNATED AREA.
YES, SIR.
VERY GOOD, SIR.
LET'S GO.
AYE, SIR.
KLANK
HEY, HEY! ALPHONSE!
YOU'RE SUPPOSED TO SAY, "OKAY."
WHSP
OH!!
IT'S HARD ENOUGH MOVING AROUND INSIDE THIS THING WITHOUT PRETENDING TO TALK LIKE A KID!
WHSP
PSP
SQUEE SQUEE
JUST DO YOUR BEST.
PSP
WSP

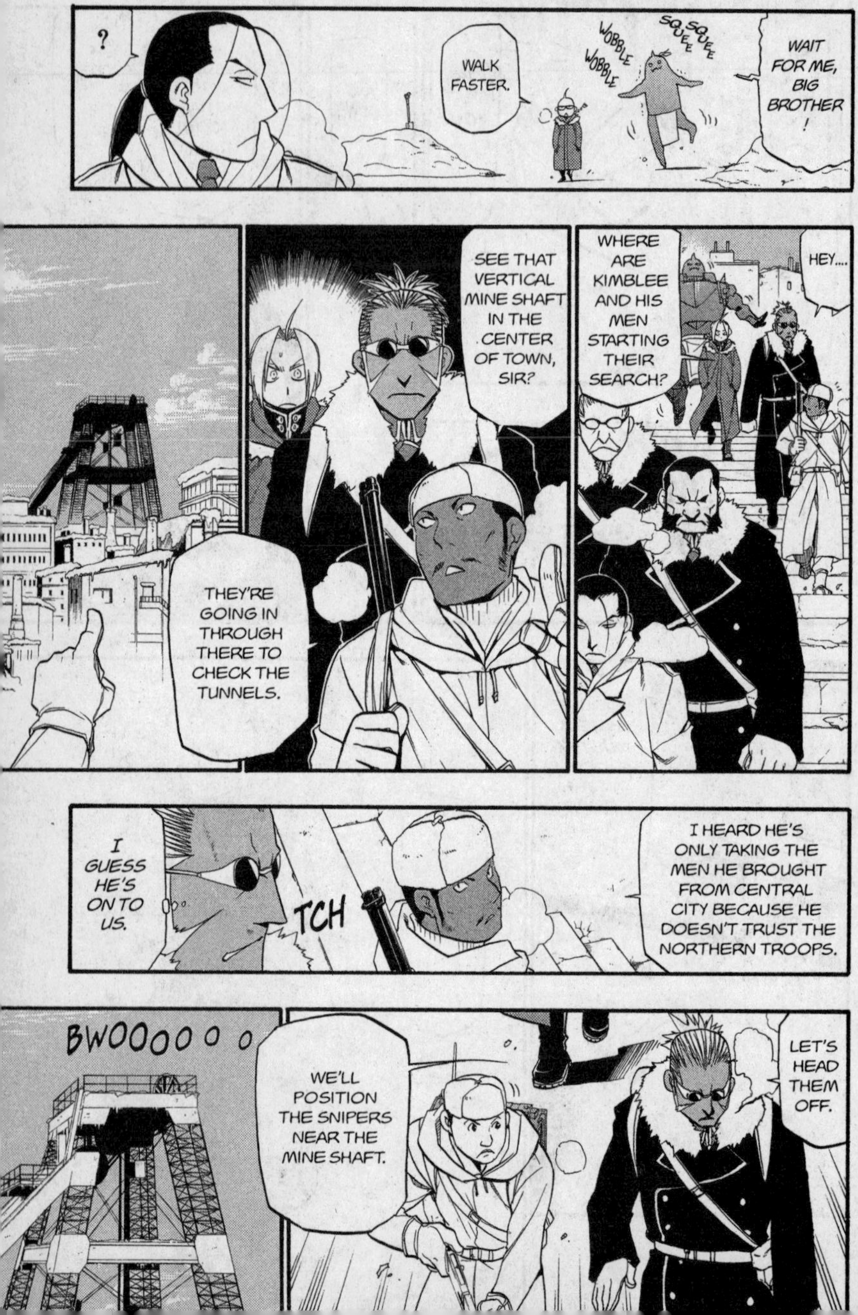
WAIT FOR ME, BIG BROTHER!
SQUEE SQUEE
WOBBLE WOBBLE
WALK FASTER.
?
HEY....
WHERE ARE KIMBLEE AND HIS MEN STARTING THEIR SEARCH?
SEE THAT VERTICAL MINE SHAFT IN THE CENTER OF TOWN, SIR?
THEY'RE GOING IN THROUGH THERE TO CHECK THE TUNNELS.
I HEARD HE'S ONLY TAKING THE MEN HE BROUGHT FROM CENTRAL CITY BECAUSE HE DOESN'T TRUST THE NORTHERN TROOPS.
TCH
I GUESS HE'S ON TO US.
LET'S HEAD THEM OFF.
WE'LL POSITION THE SNIPERS NEAR THE MINE SHAFT.
BWOOOOO O O

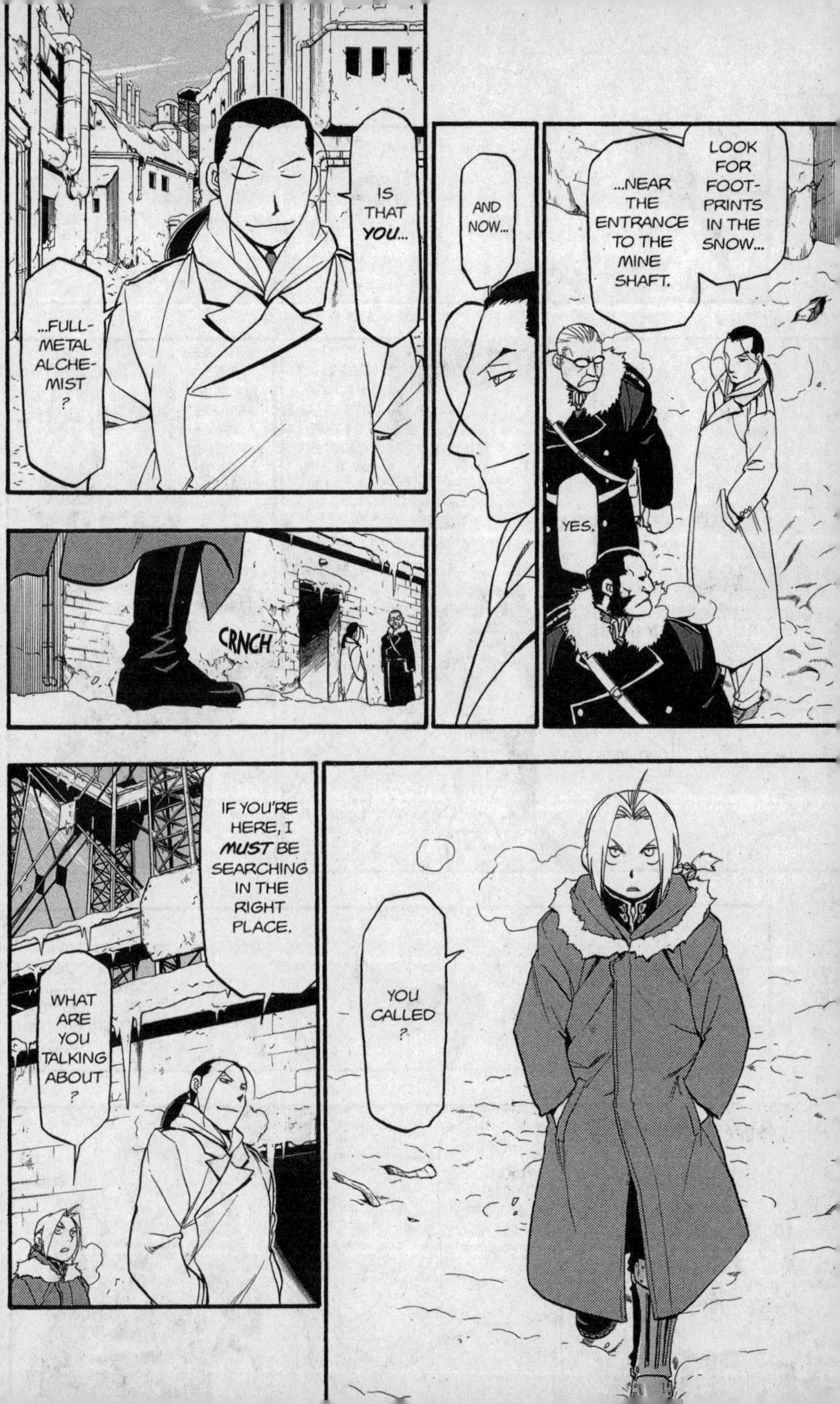
LOOK FOR FOOT-PRINTS IN THE SNOW...
...NEAR THE ENTRANCE TO THE MINE SHAFT.
YES.
AND NOW...
IS THAT *YOU*...
...FULL-METAL ALCHE-MIST?
CRNCH
YOU CALLED?
IF YOU'RE HERE, I *MUST* BE SEARCHING IN THE RIGHT PLACE.
WHAT ARE YOU TALKING ABOUT?

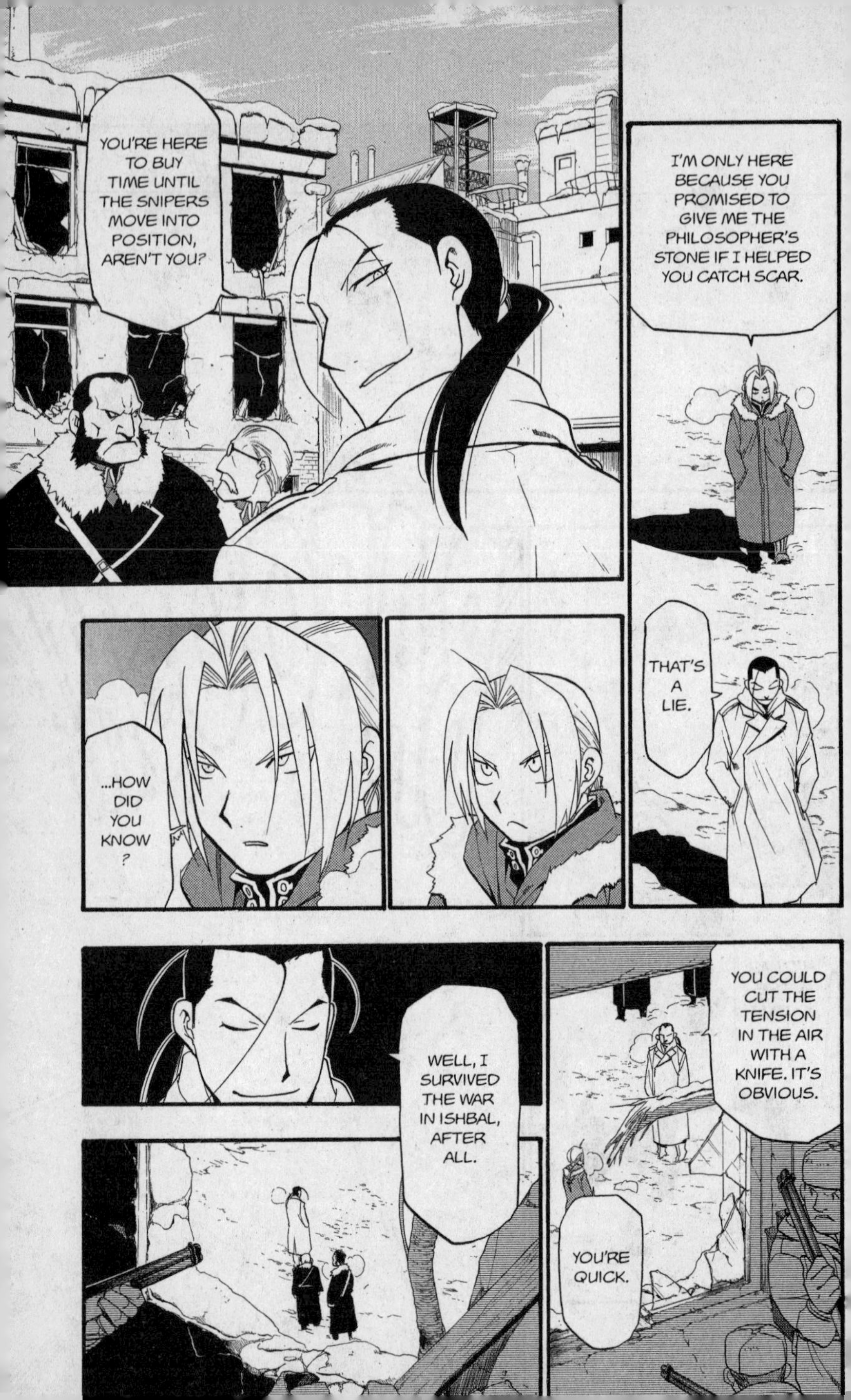
I'M ONLY HERE BECAUSE YOU PROMISED TO GIVE ME THE PHILOSOPHER'S STONE IF I HELPED YOU CATCH SCAR.
THAT'S A LIE.
YOU'RE HERE TO BUY TIME UNTIL THE SNIPERS MOVE INTO POSITION, AREN'T YOU?
...HOW DID YOU KNOW?
YOU COULD CUT THE TENSION IN THE AIR WITH A KNIFE. IT'S OBVIOUS.
YOU'RE QUICK.
WELL, I SURVIVED THE WAR IN ISHBAL, AFTER ALL.

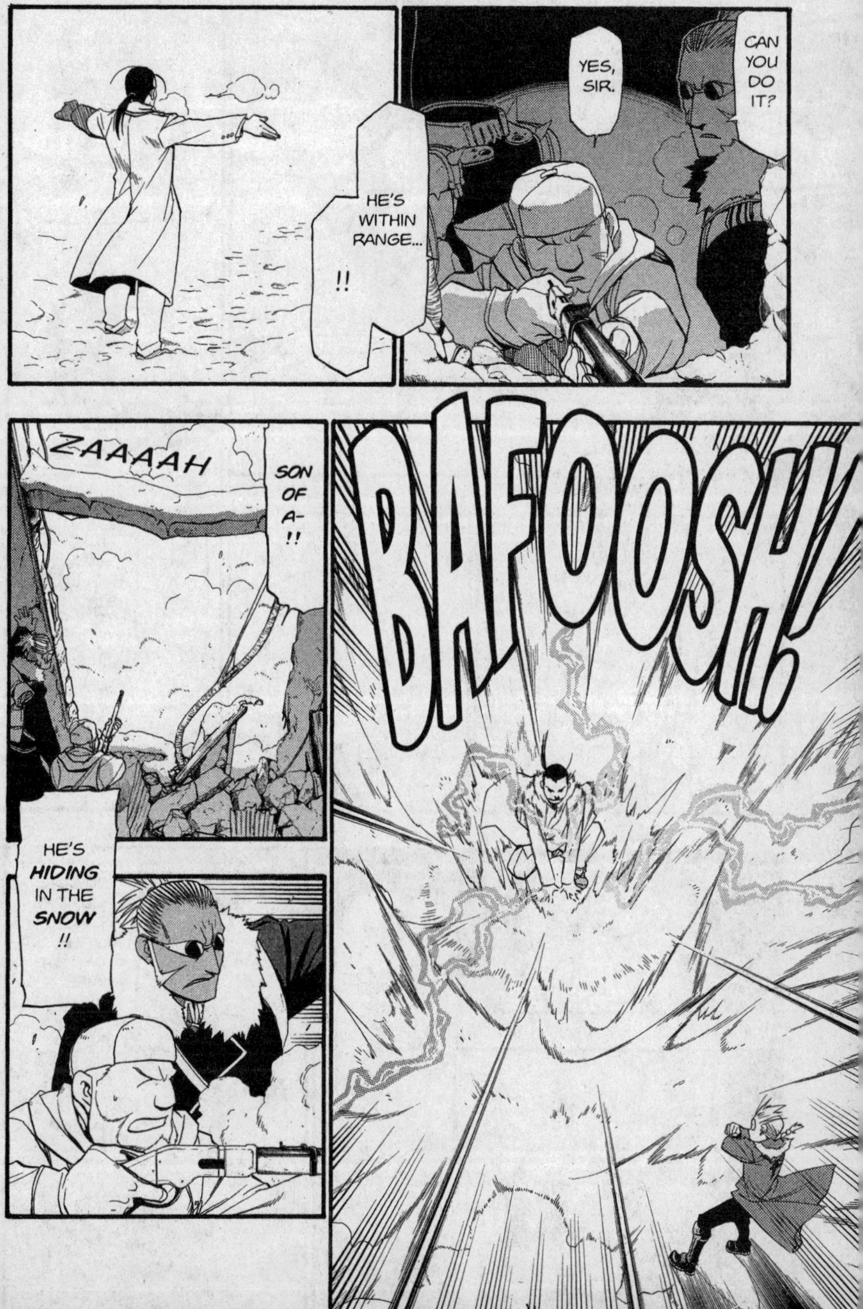
CAN YOU DO IT?
YES, SIR.
HE'S WITHIN RANGE...
!!
BAFOOSH!
ZAAAAH
SON OF A- !!
HE'S HIDING IN THE SNOW !!

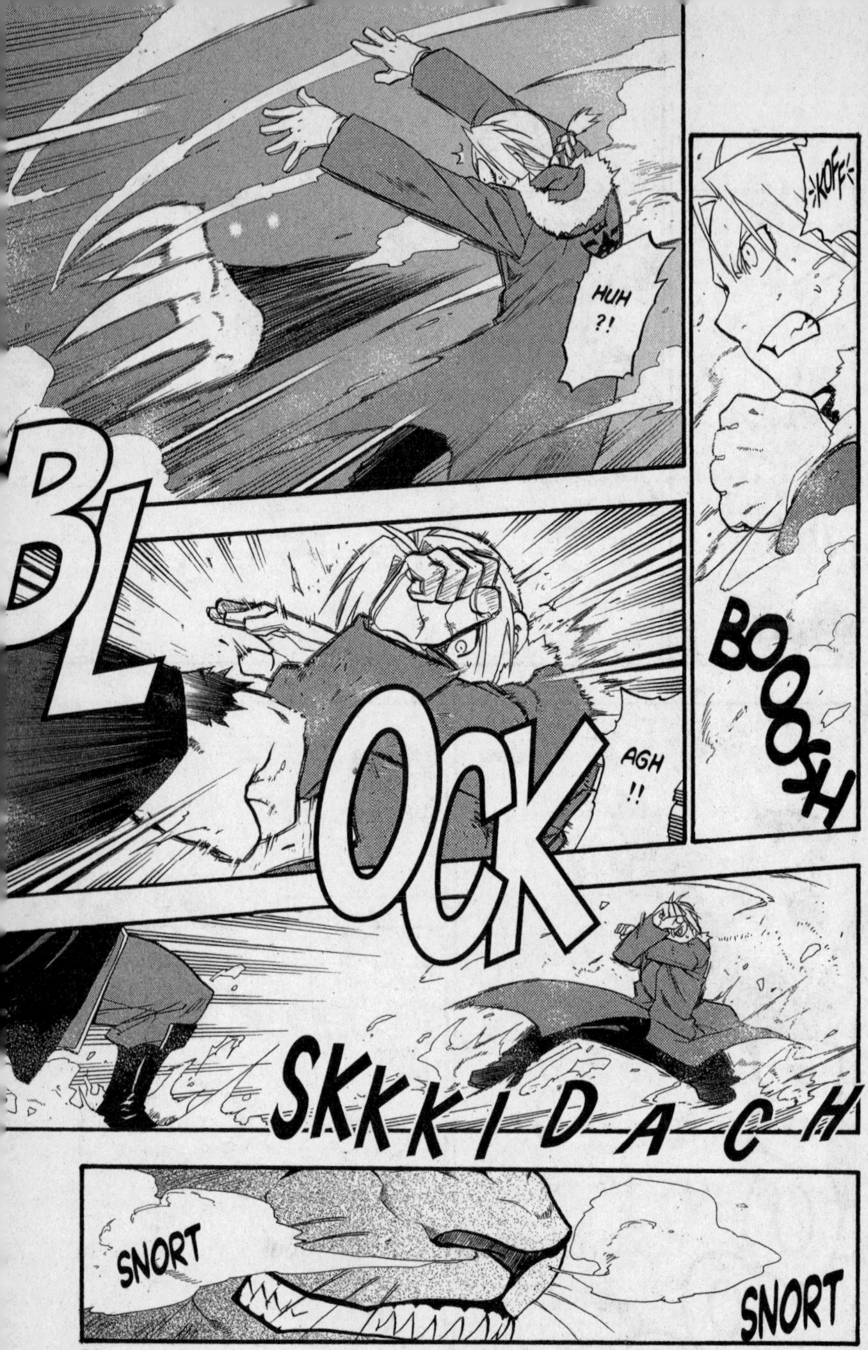
KOFF
BOOOOSH
HUH ?!
BLOCK
AGH !!
SKKIDACH
SNORT
SNORT

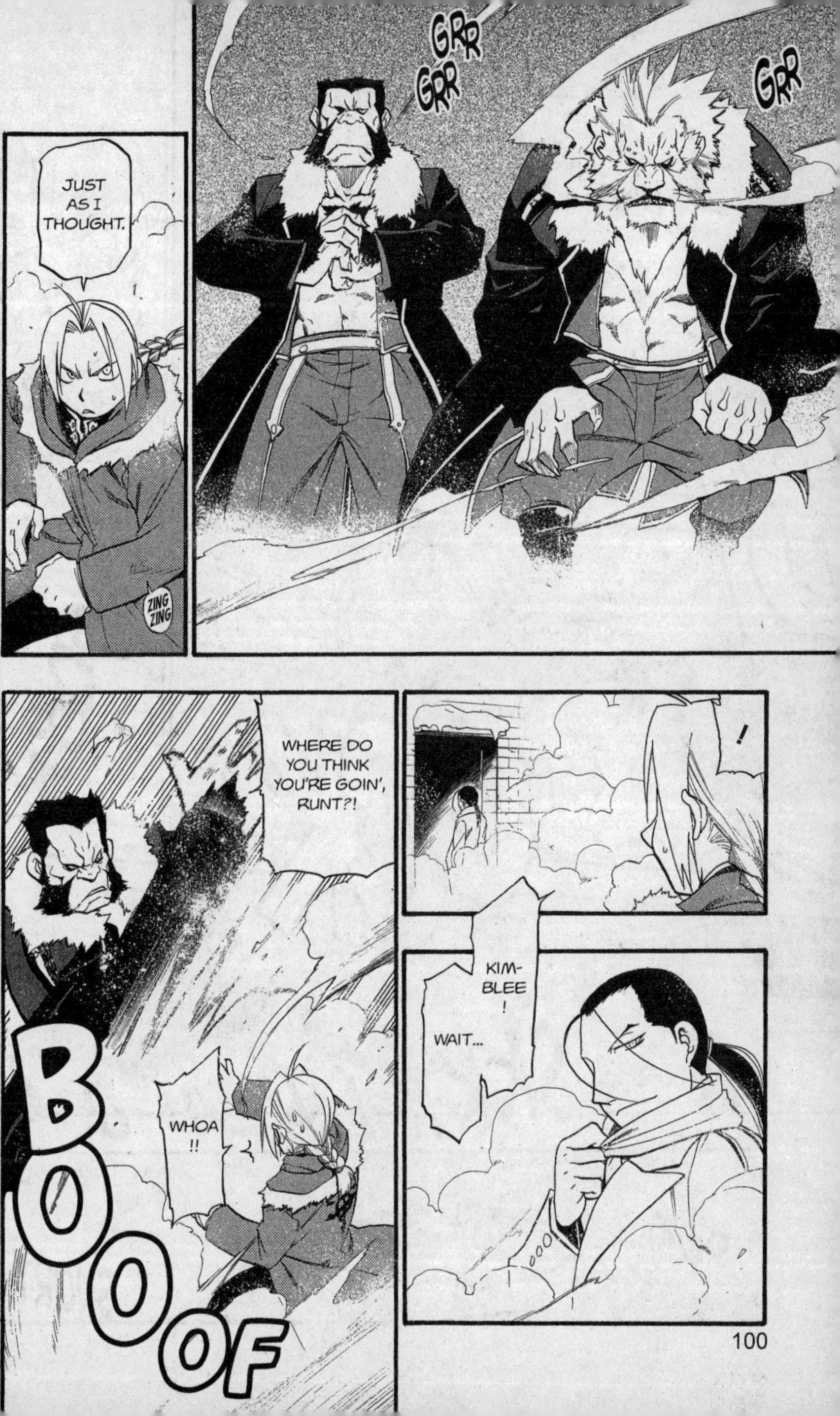
GRR GRR
GRR
JUST AS I THOUGHT.
ZING ZING
!
KIMBLEE!
WAIT...
WHERE DO YOU THINK YOU'RE GOIN', RUNT?!
WHOA!!
BOOOF

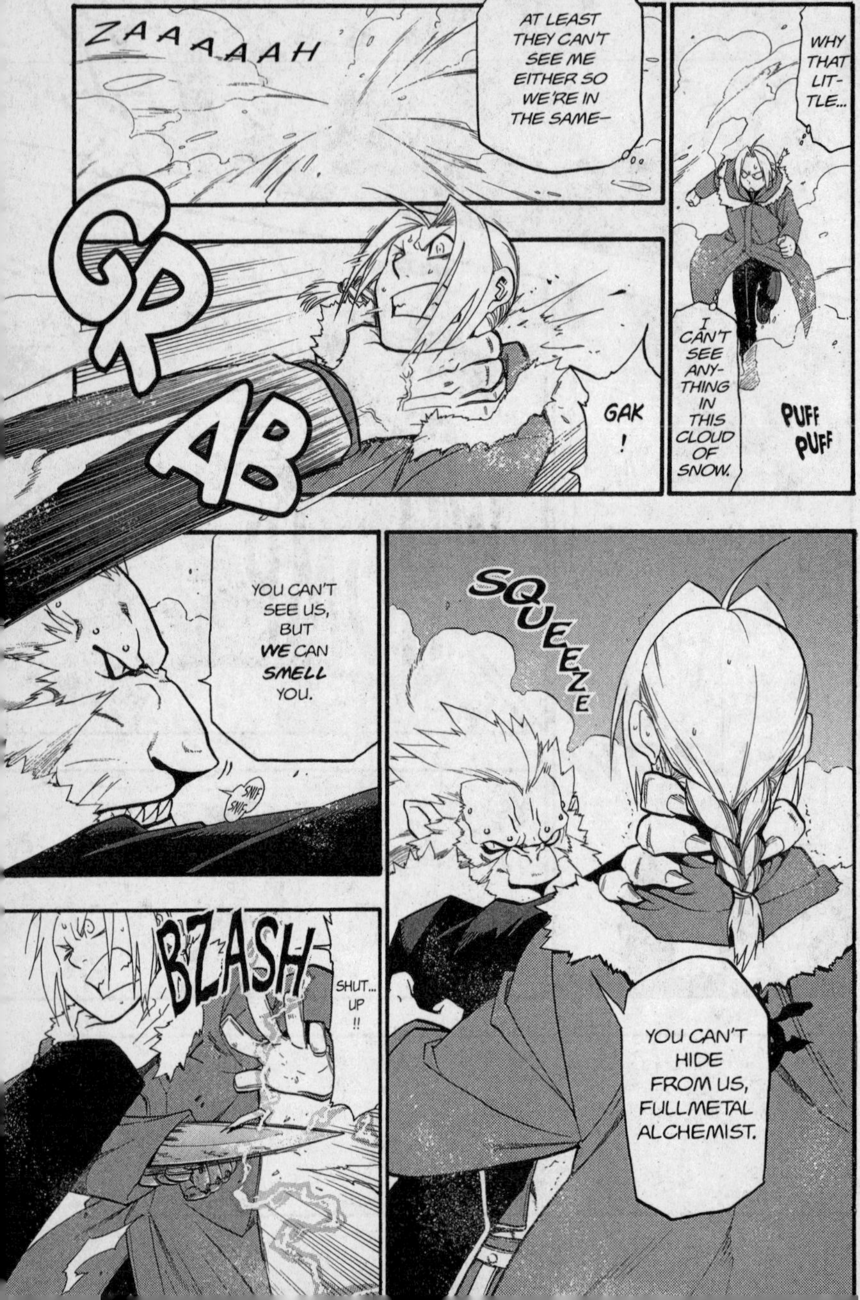
WHY THAT LIT-TLE...
I CAN'T SEE ANYTHING IN THIS CLOUD OF SNOW.
PUFF PUFF
ZAAAAAAH
AT LEAST THEY CAN'T SEE ME EITHER SO WE'RE IN THE SAME—
GRAB
GAK!
SQUEEZE
YOU CAN'T HIDE FROM US, FULLMETAL ALCHEMIST.
YOU CAN'T SEE US, BUT **WE** CAN **SMELL** YOU.
SNIF SNIF
BZASH
SHUT... UP!!

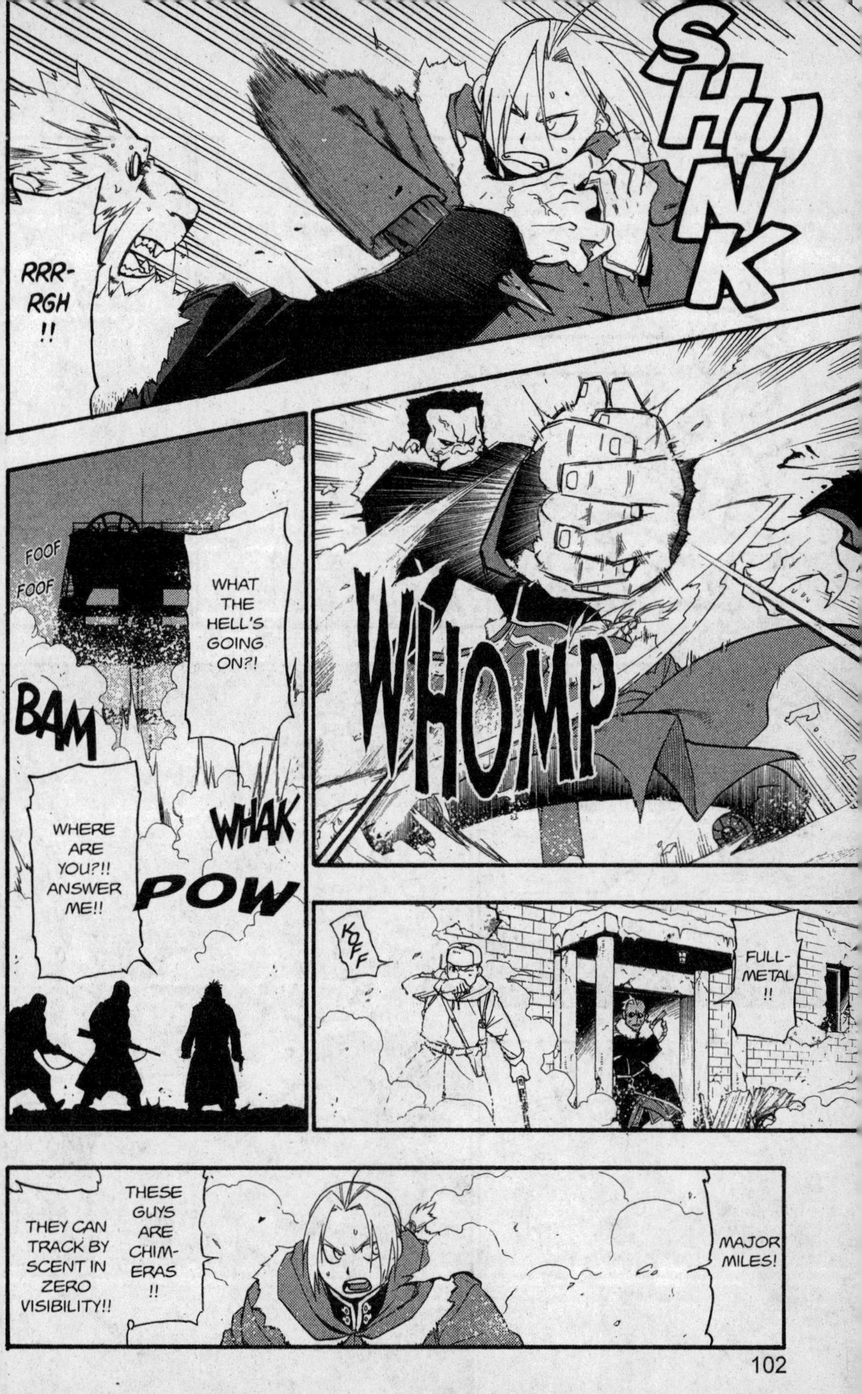
SHUNK
RRR-RGH!!
WHOMP
KOFF
FULL-METAL!!
FOOF FOOF
WHAT THE HELL'S GOING ON?!
BAM
WHAK
POW
WHERE ARE YOU?!! ANSWER ME!!
MAJOR MILES!
THESE GUYS ARE CHIM-ERAS!!
THEY CAN TRACK BY SCENT IN ZERO VISIBILITY!!

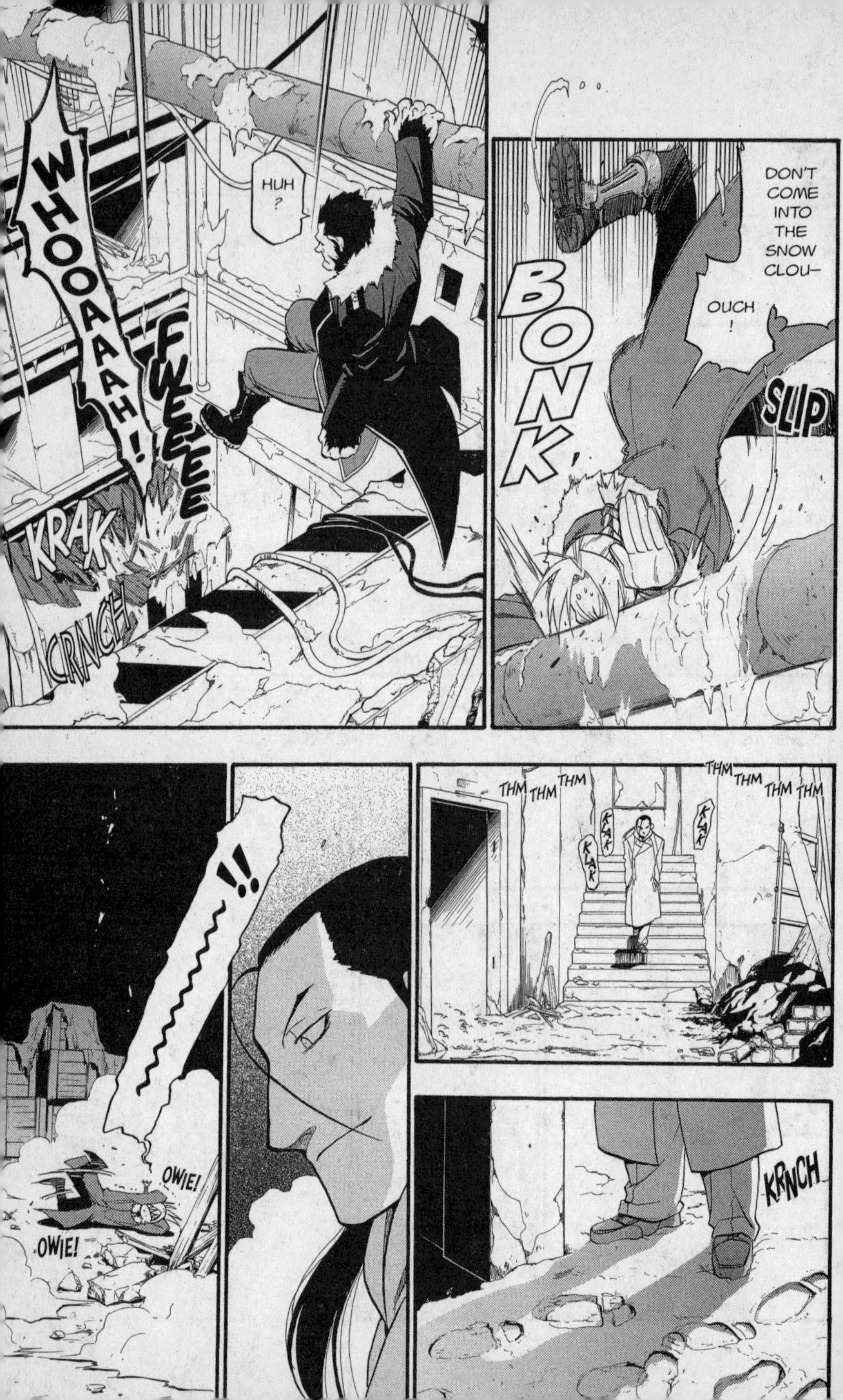
DON'T COME INTO THE SNOW CLOU—
OUCH!
BONK,
SLIP
HUH?
WHOOAAAAH!
FWEEEEE
KRAK
CRNCH
THM THM THM
THM THM THM THM
KLAK
KLAK
KLAK
KRNCH
~~~~!!
OWIE!
OWIE!
~~~~

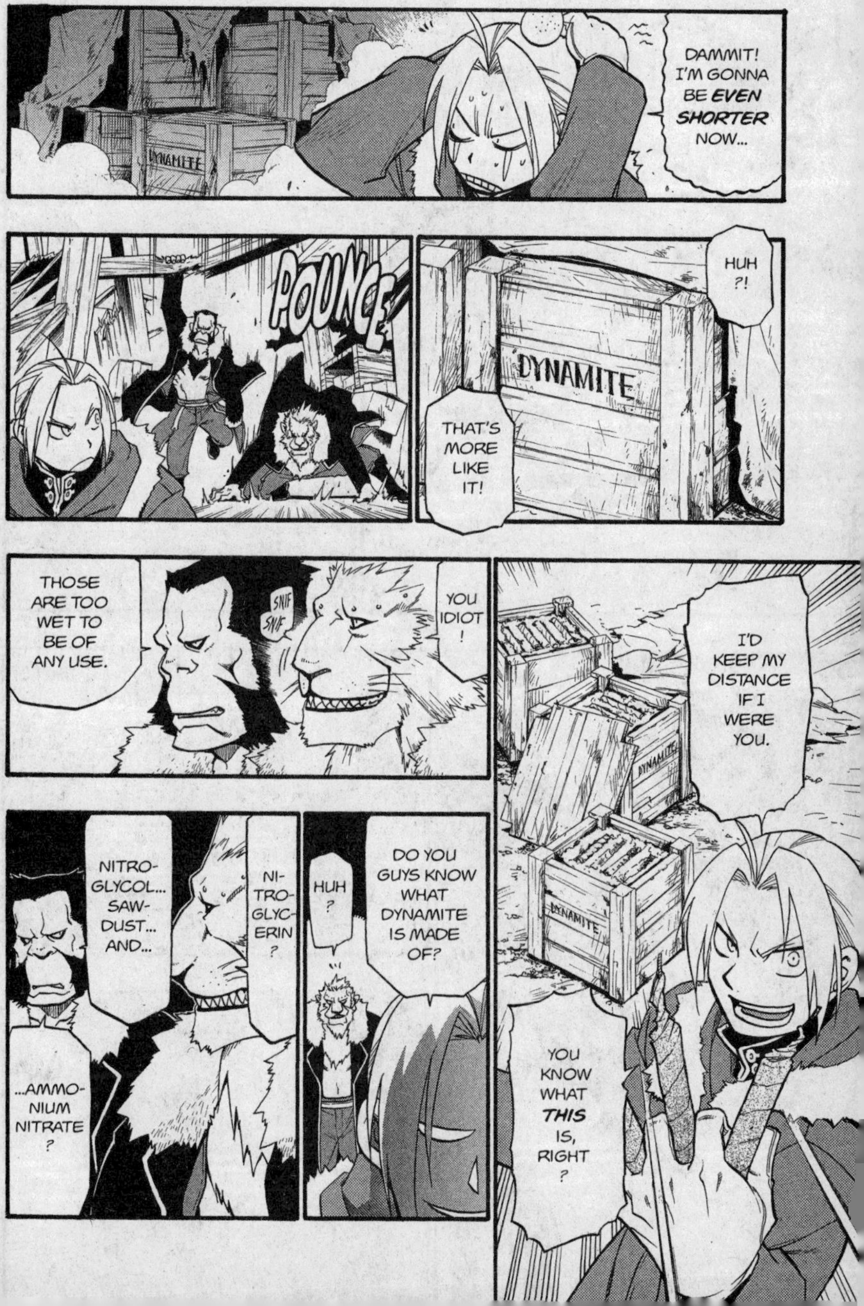
DAMMIT! I'M GONNA BE *EVEN SHORTER* NOW...
HUH ?!
THAT'S MORE LIKE IT!
POUNCE
I'D KEEP MY DISTANCE IF I WERE YOU.
YOU KNOW WHAT *THIS* IS, RIGHT ?
YOU IDIOT !
SNIF SNIF
THOSE ARE TOO WET TO BE OF ANY USE.
DO YOU GUYS KNOW WHAT DYNAMITE IS MADE OF?
HUH ?
NI-TRO-GLYC-ERIN ?
NITRO-GLYCOL... SAW-DUST... AND...
...AMMO-NIUM NITRATE ?

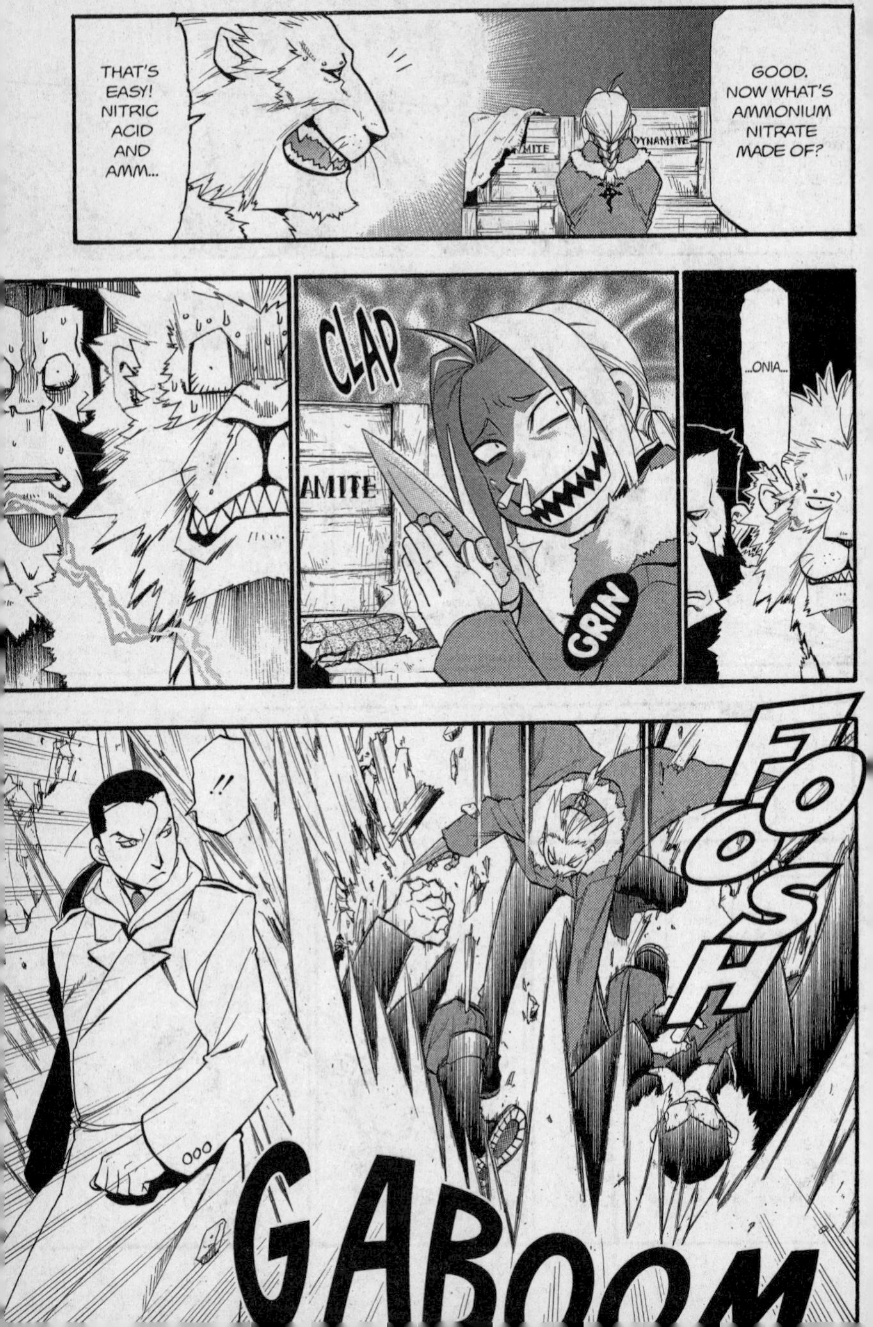
GOOD. NOW WHAT'S AMMONIUM NITRATE MADE OF?
DYNAMITE
THAT'S EASY! NITRIC ACID AND AMM...
...ONIA...
CLAP
AMITE
GRIN
FOOSH
!!
GABOOM

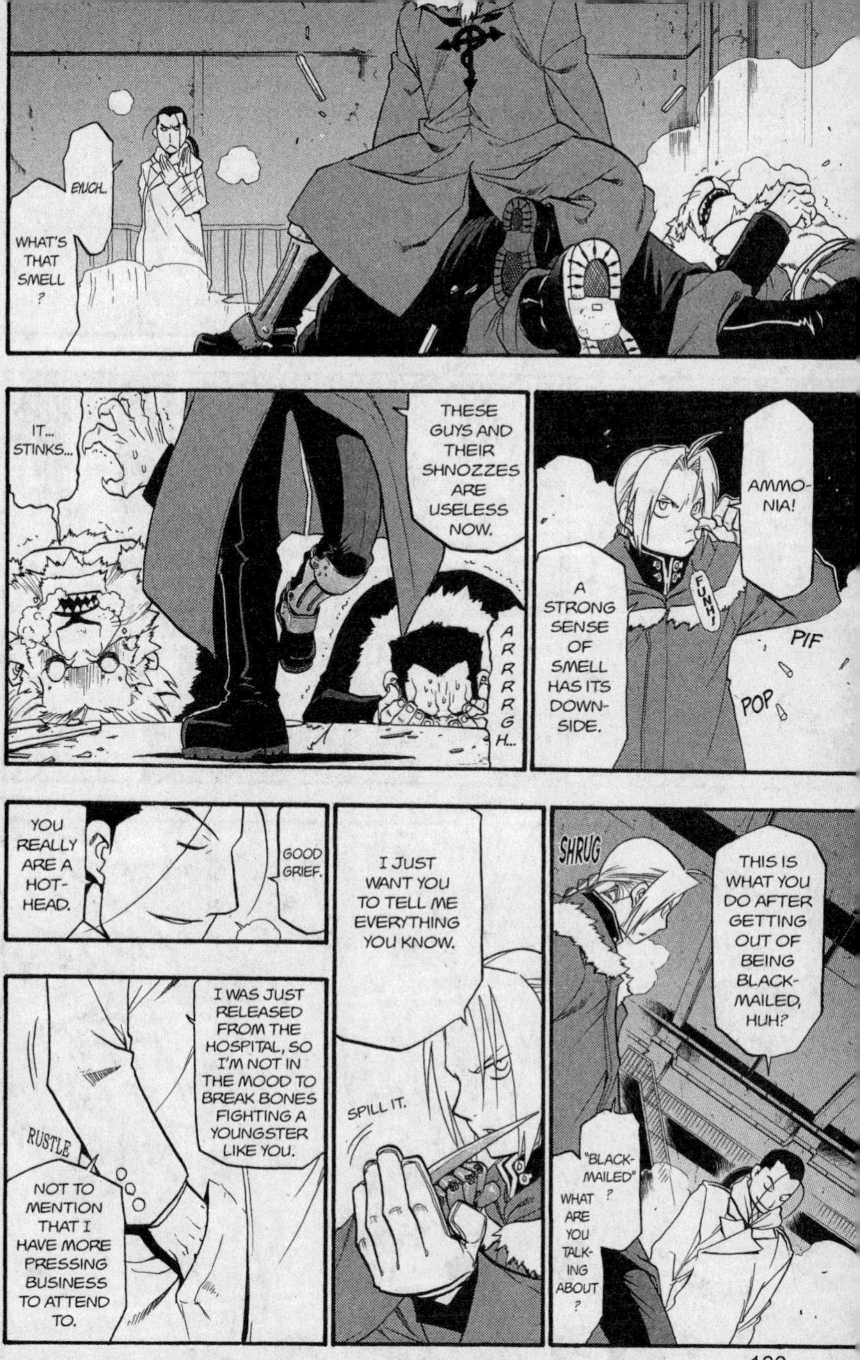
EYUCH...
WHAT'S THAT SMELL?
AMMONIA!
A STRONG SENSE OF SMELL HAS ITS DOWNSIDE.
FUNH!
PIF
POP
THESE GUYS AND THEIR SHNOZZES ARE USELESS NOW.
ARRRRGH...
IT... STINKS...
SHRUG
THIS IS WHAT YOU DO AFTER GETTING OUT OF BEING BLACKMAILED, HUH?
"BLACKMAILED"? WHAT ARE YOU TALKING ABOUT?
I JUST WANT YOU TO TELL ME EVERYTHING YOU KNOW.
SPILL IT.
GOOD GRIEF.
YOU REALLY ARE A HOT-HEAD.
I WAS JUST RELEASED FROM THE HOSPITAL, SO I'M NOT IN THE MOOD TO BREAK BONES FIGHTING A YOUNGSTER LIKE YOU.
RUSTLE
NOT TO MENTION THAT I HAVE MORE PRESSING BUSINESS TO ATTEND TO.

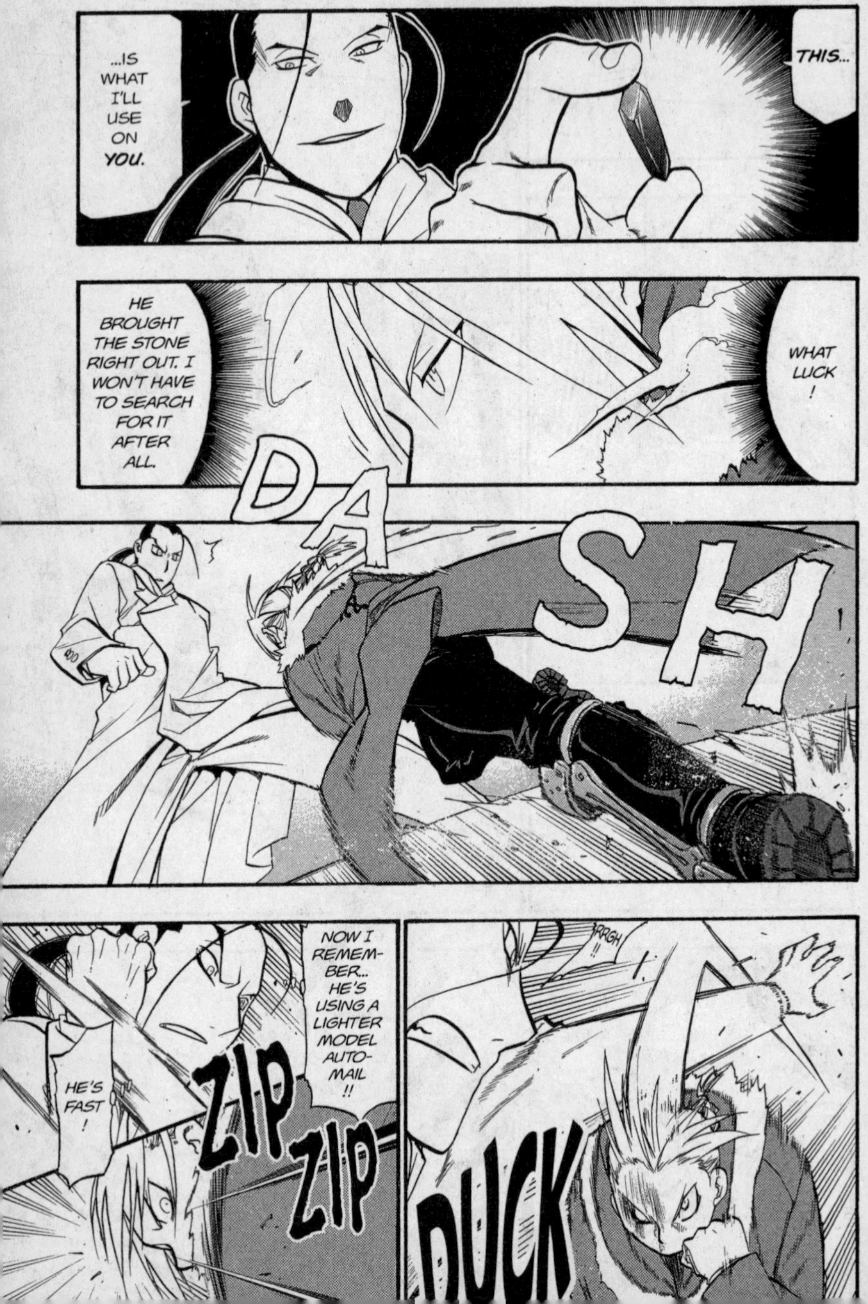
THIS...
...IS WHAT I'LL USE ON YOU.
WHAT LUCK!
HE BROUGHT THE STONE RIGHT OUT. I WON'T HAVE TO SEARCH FOR IT AFTER ALL.
DASH
RRGH!!
DUCK
NOW I REMEM-BER... HE'S USING A LIGHTER MODEL AUTO-MAIL!!
HE'S FAST!
ZIP
ZIP

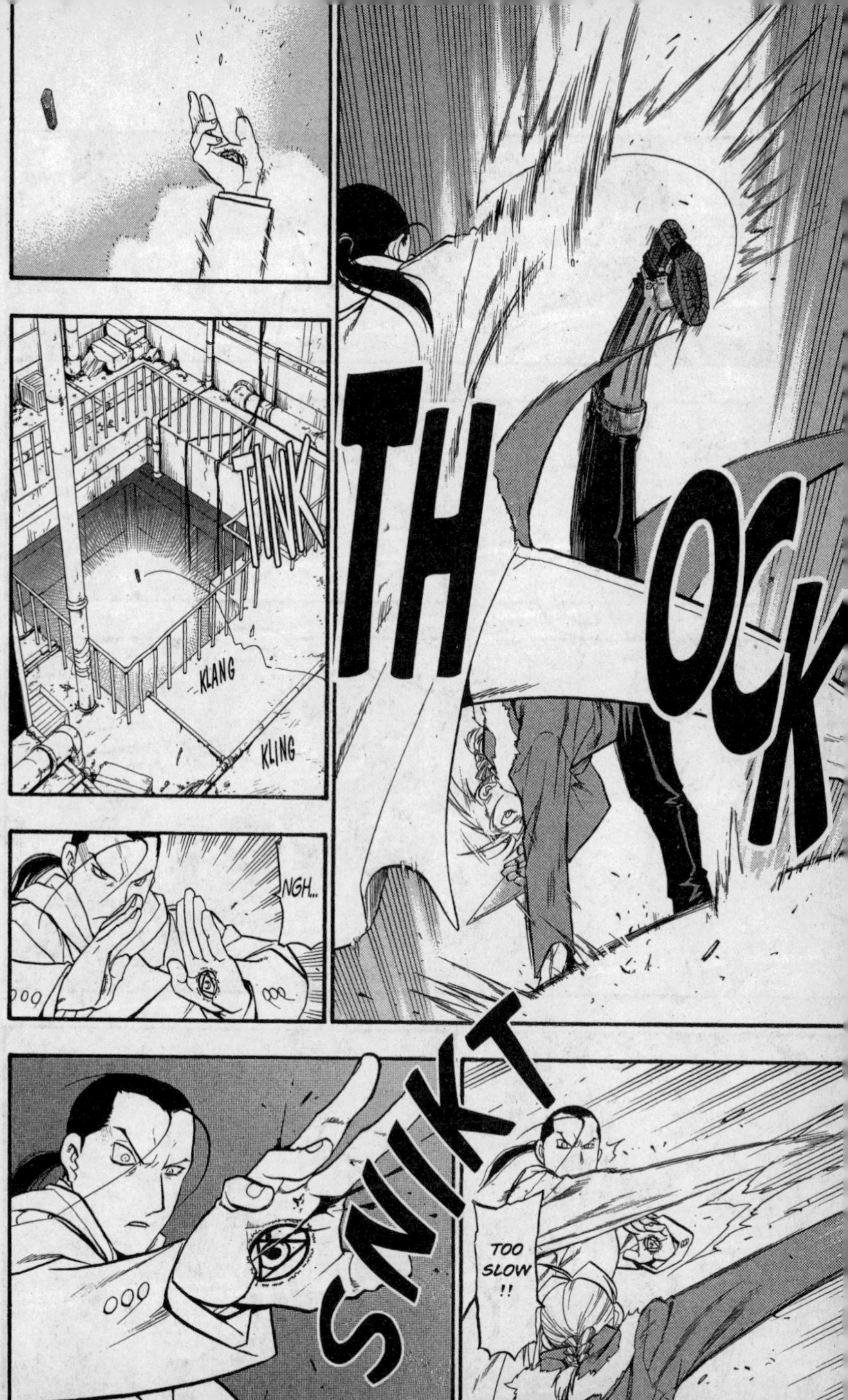
THOCK
TINK
KLANG
KLING
NGH...
SNIKT
TOO SLOW !!

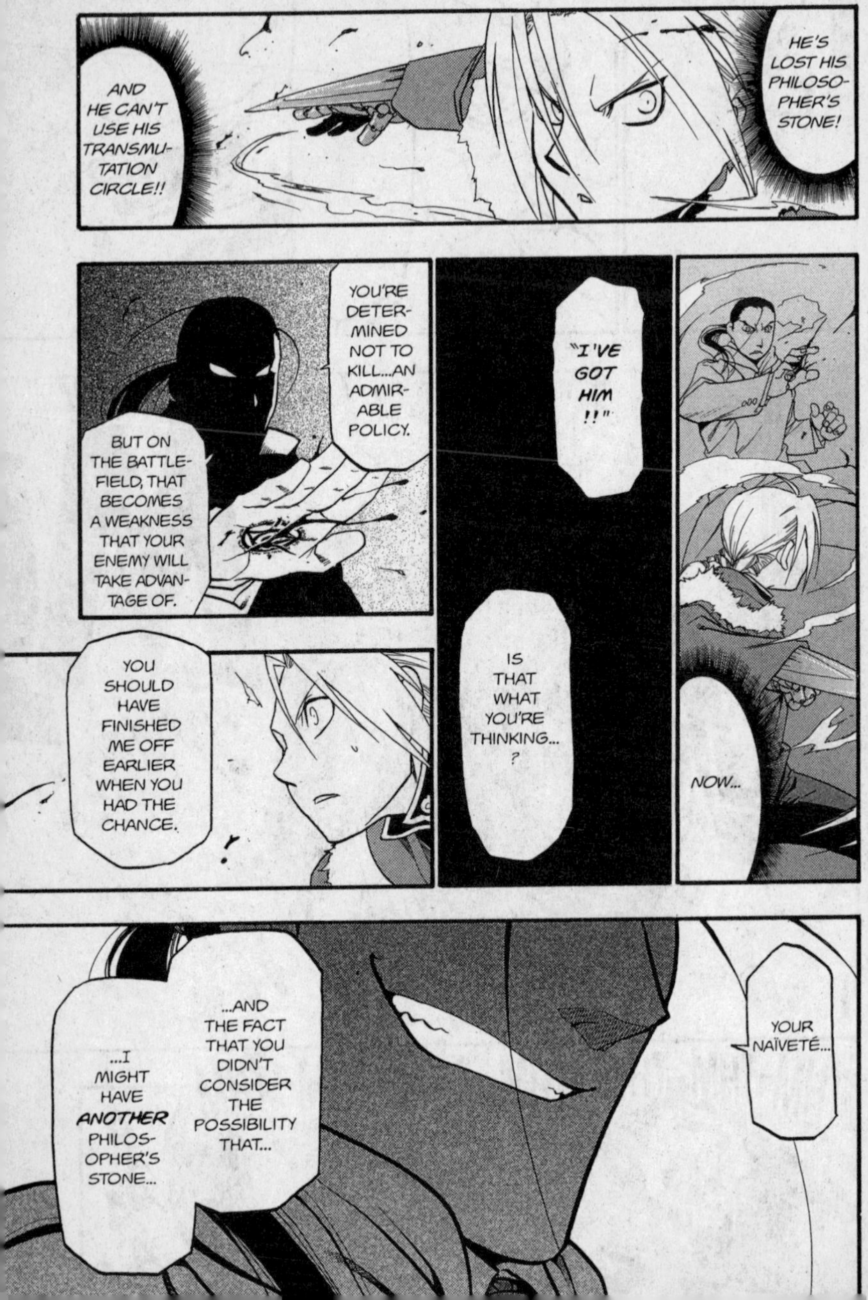
HE'S LOST HIS PHILOSOPHER'S STONE!
AND HE CAN'T USE HIS TRANSMUTATION CIRCLE!!
NOW...
"I'VE GOT HIM!!"
IS THAT WHAT YOU'RE THINKING...?
YOU'RE DETERMINED NOT TO KILL...AN ADMIRABLE POLICY.
BUT ON THE BATTLEFIELD, THAT BECOMES A WEAKNESS THAT YOUR ENEMY WILL TAKE ADVANTAGE OF.
YOU SHOULD HAVE FINISHED ME OFF EARLIER WHEN YOU HAD THE CHANCE.
YOUR NAÏVETÉ...
...AND THE FACT THAT YOU DIDN'T CONSIDER THE POSSIBILITY THAT...
...I MIGHT HAVE ANOTHER PHILOSOPHER'S STONE...

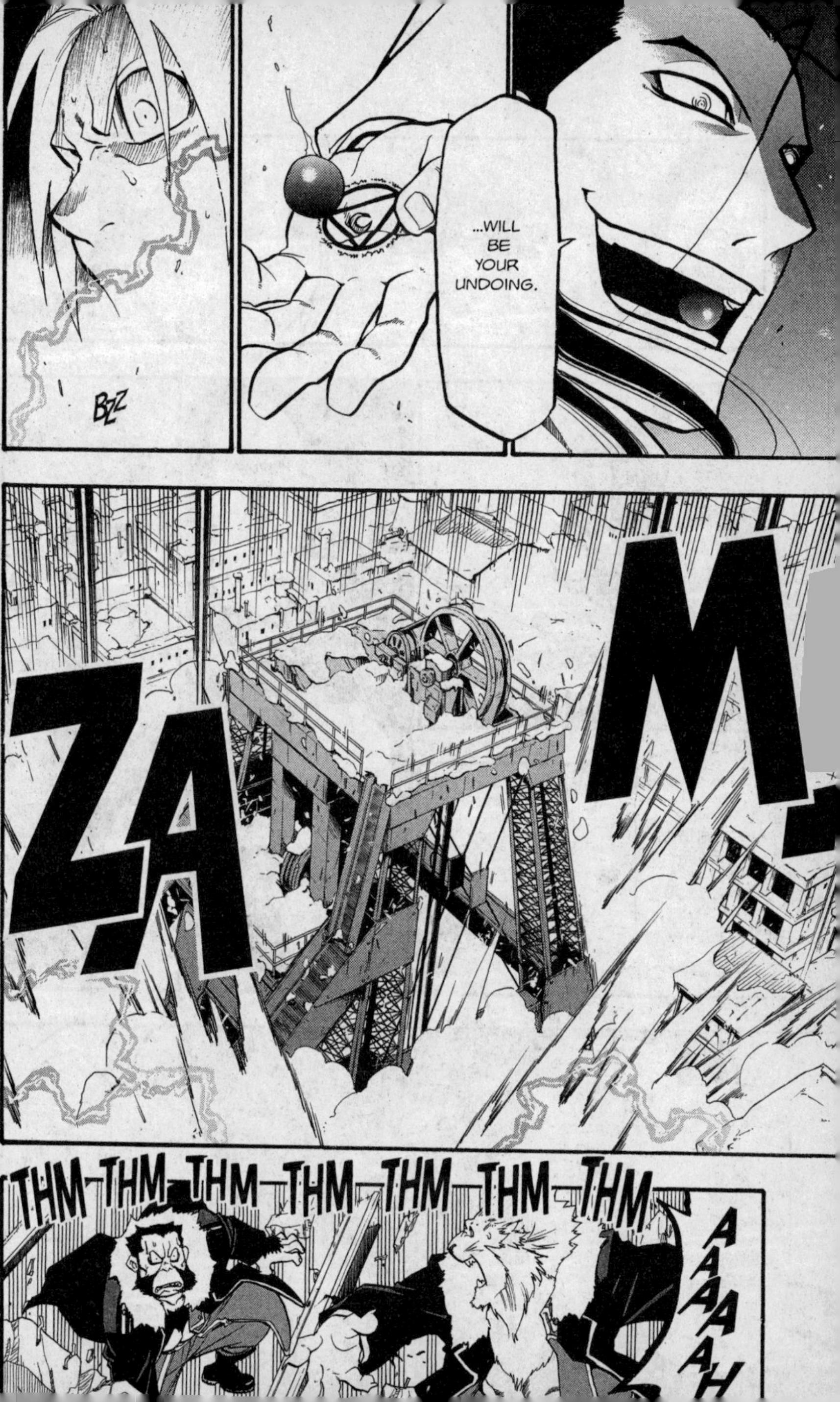
...WILL BE YOUR UNDOING.
BZZ
ZAM
THM THM THM THM THM THM THM
AAAAAH

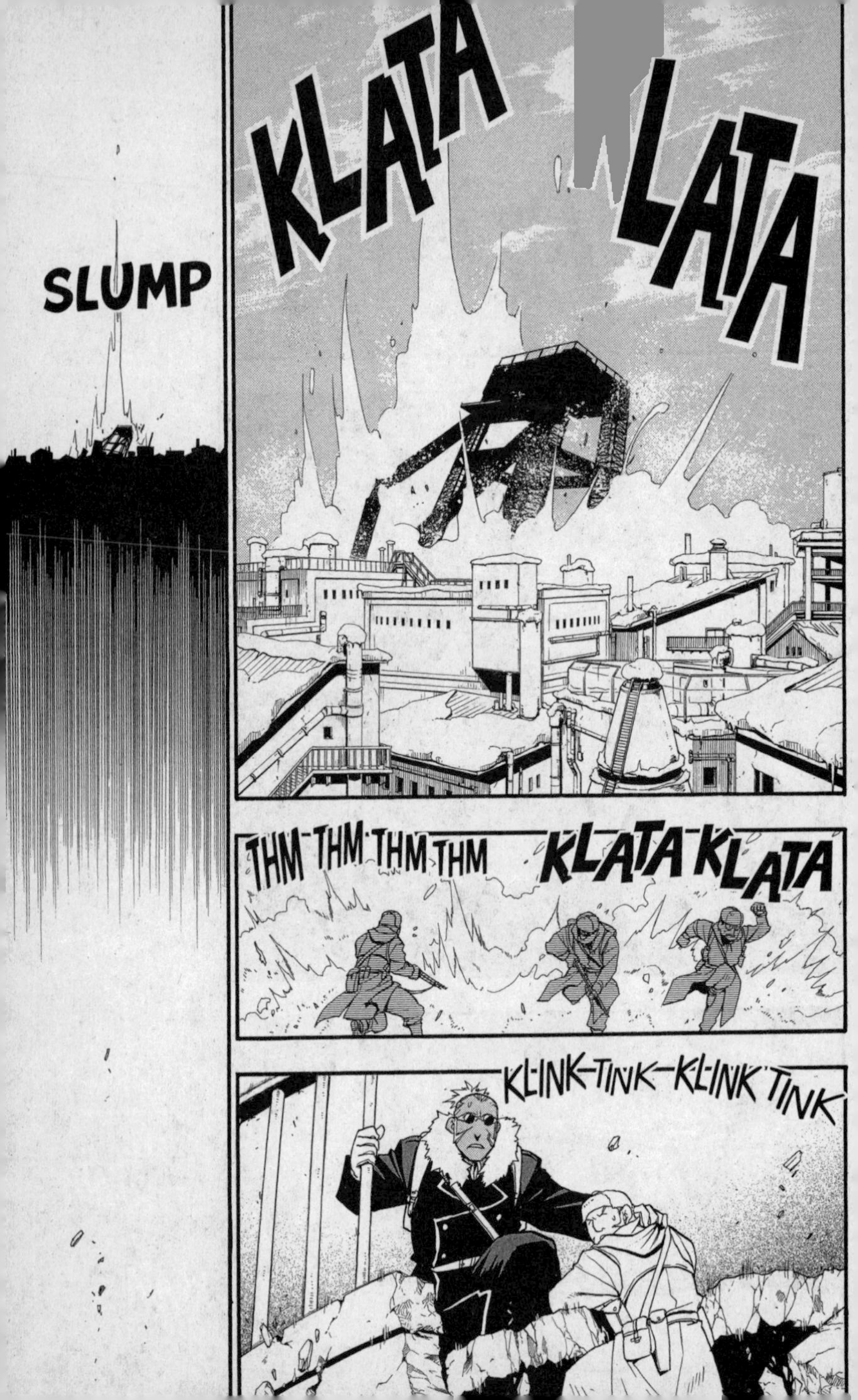
KLATA
LATA
KLATA KLATA
THM THM THM THM
KLINK-TINK-KLINK TINK
SLUMP

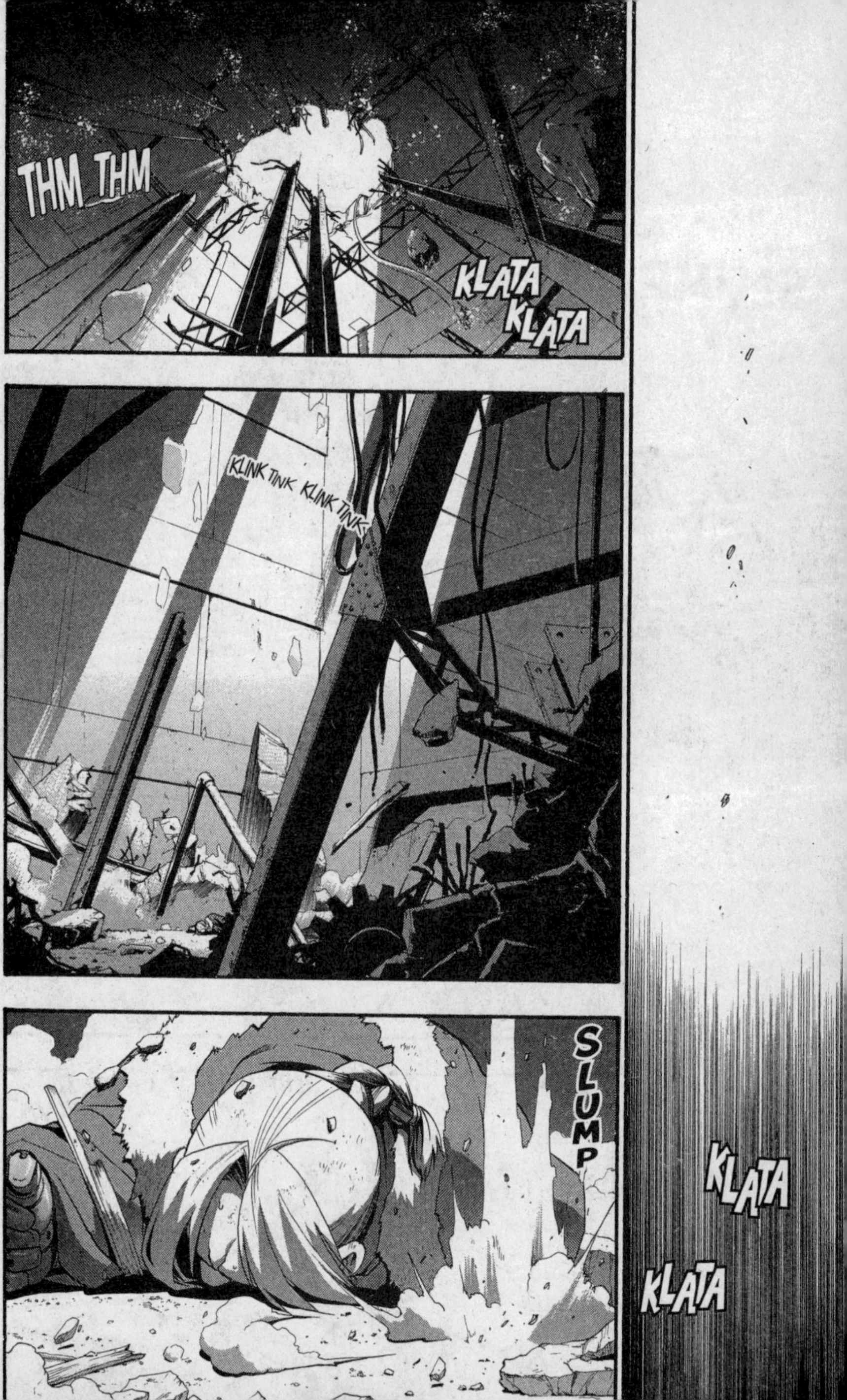
KLATA
KLATA
THM THM
KLATA KLATA
KLINK TINK KLINK TINK
SLUMP

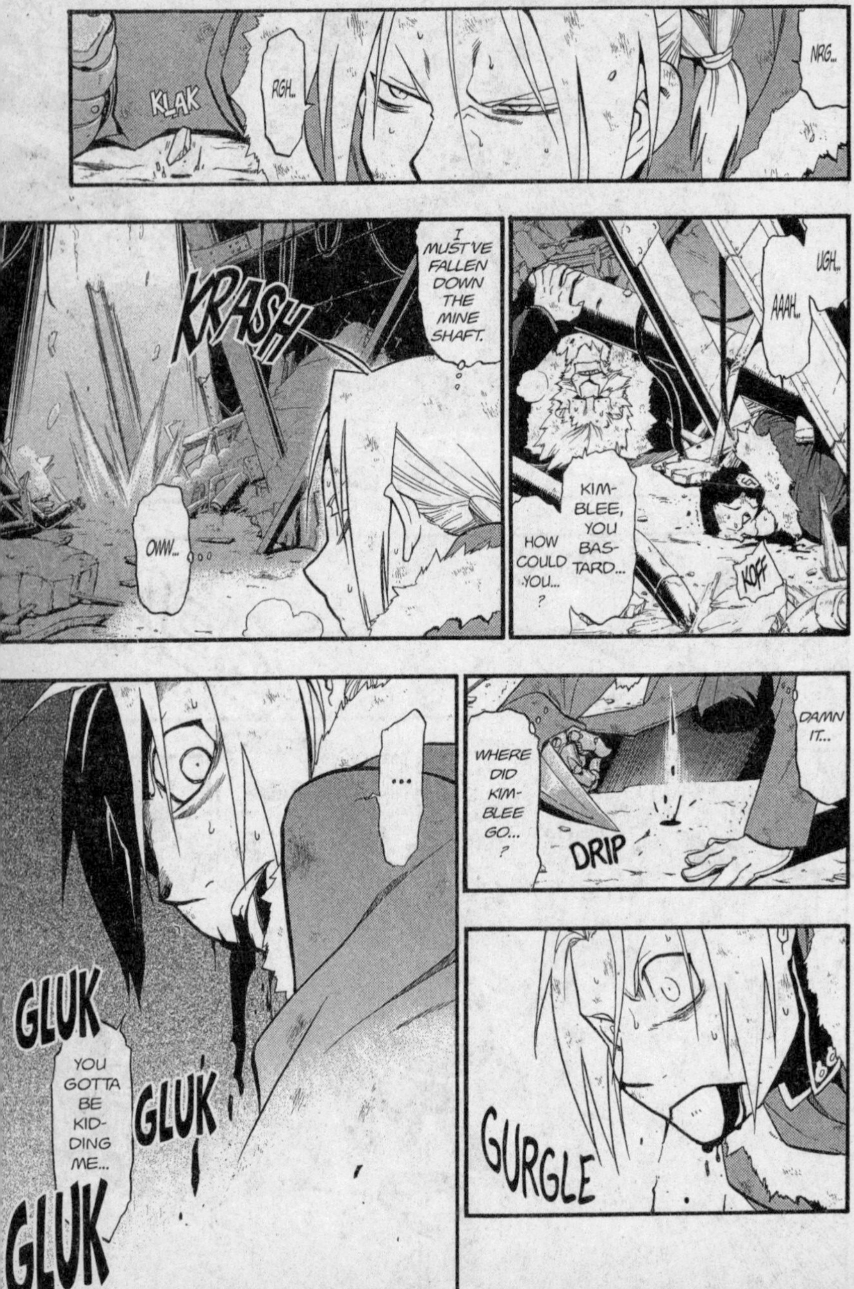
NRG...
RGH...
KLAK
UGH...
AAAH...
KIM-BLEE, YOU BAS-TARD...
HOW COULD YOU...?
KOFF
I MUST'VE FALLEN DOWN THE MINE SHAFT.
KRASH
OWW...
DAMN IT...
WHERE DID KIM-BLEE GO...?
DRIP
GURGLE
...
GLUK
YOU GOTTA BE KID-DING ME...
GLUK
GLUK

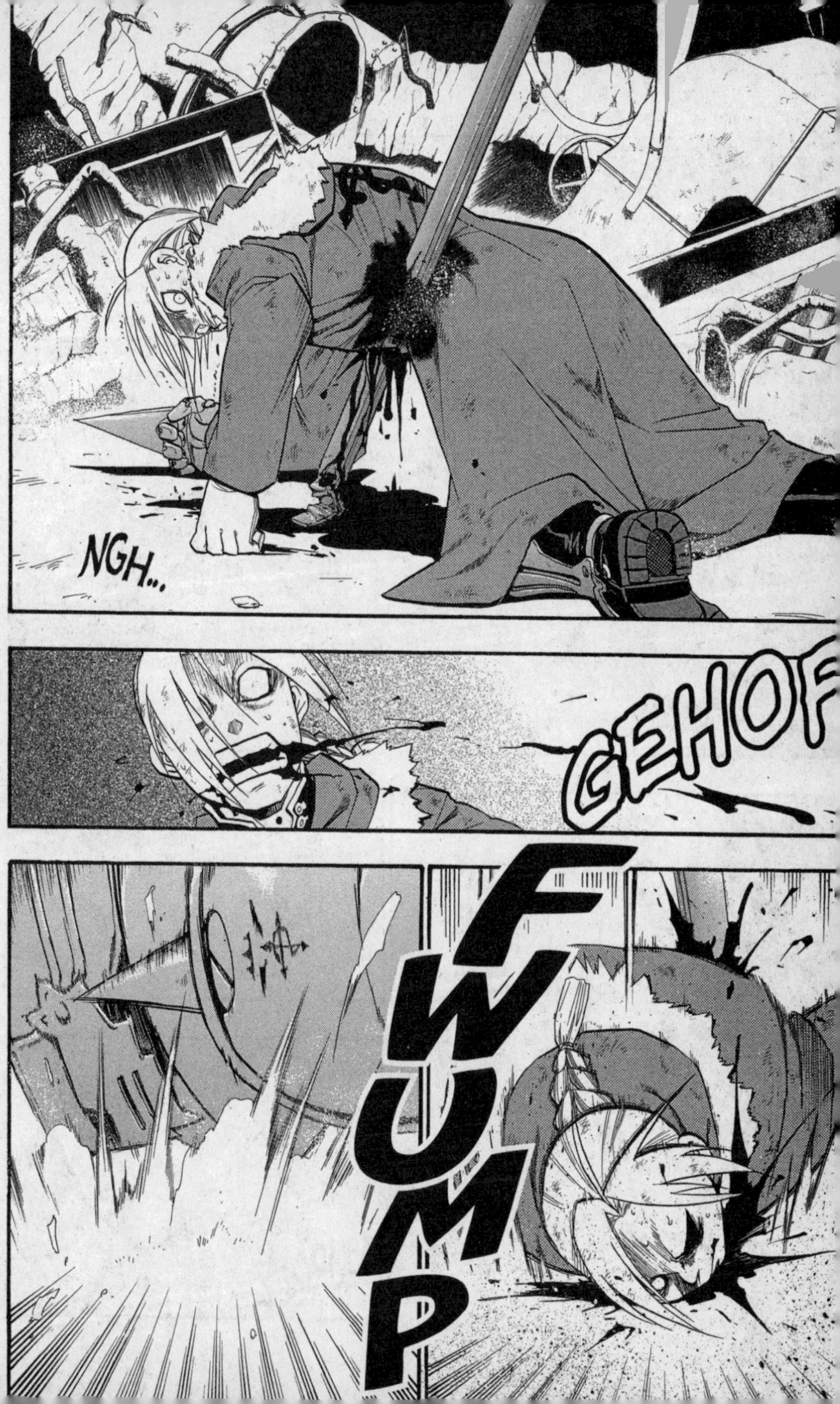
NGH...
GEHOF
FWUMP

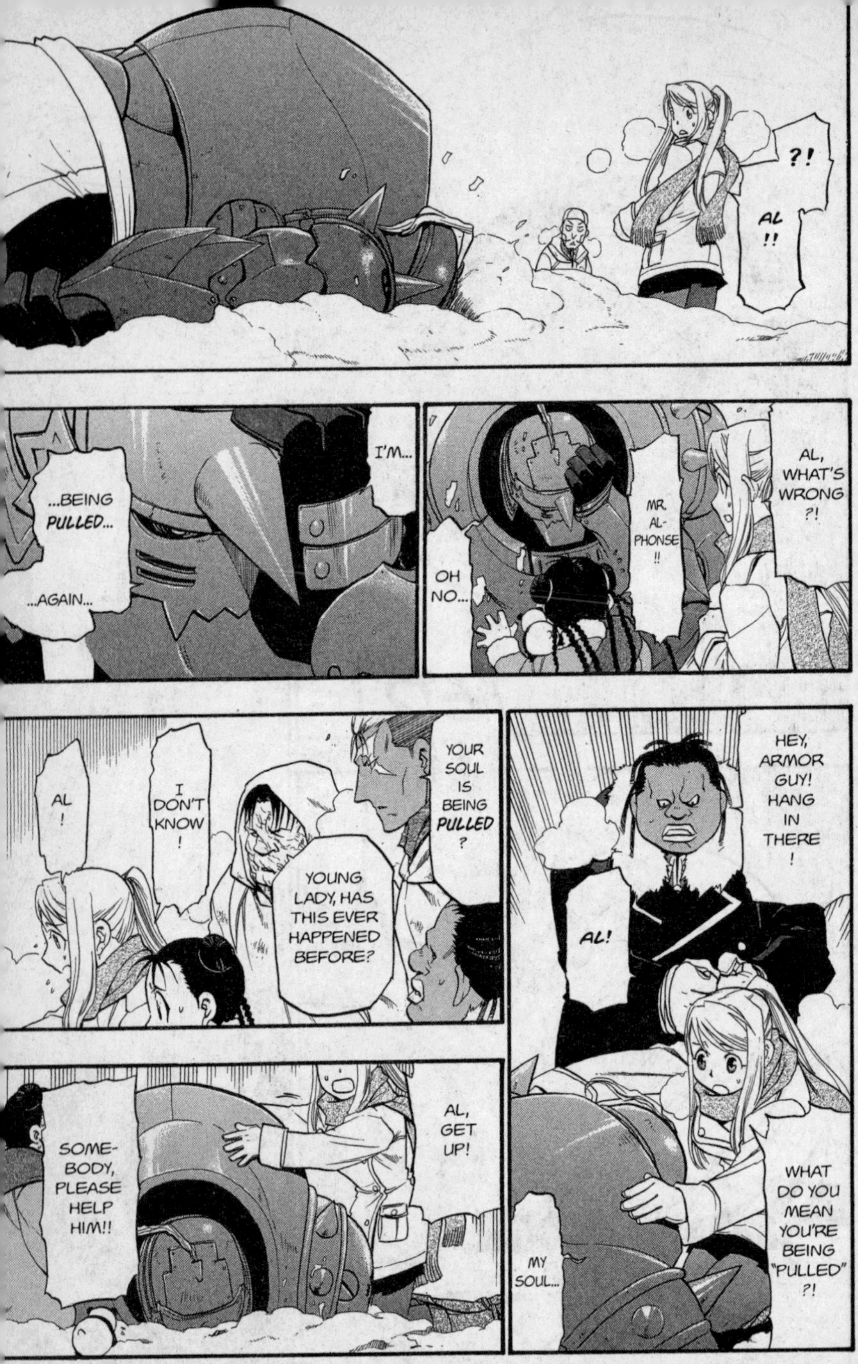
?!
AL !!
AL, WHAT'S WRONG ?!
MR. AL-PHONSE !!
OH NO...
I'M...
...BEING PULLED...
...AGAIN...
HEY, ARMOR GUY! HANG IN THERE!
AL!
WHAT DO YOU MEAN YOU'RE BEING "PULLED" ?!
MY SOUL...
YOUR SOUL IS BEING PULLED ?
YOUNG LADY, HAS THIS EVER HAPPENED BEFORE?
I DON'T KNOW !
AL !
AL, GET UP!
SOME-BODY, PLEASE HELP HIM!!

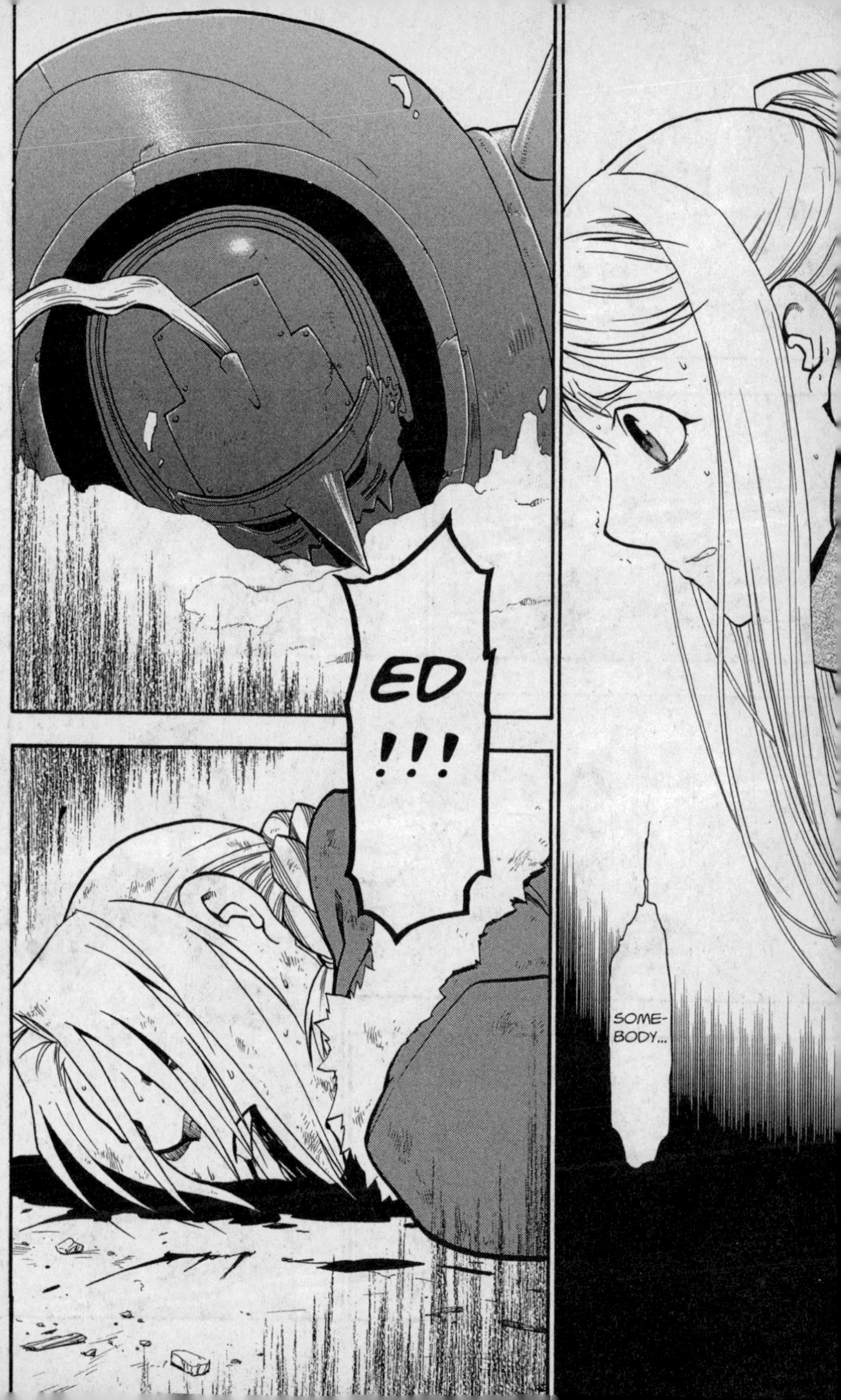
SOME-BODY...
ED!!!

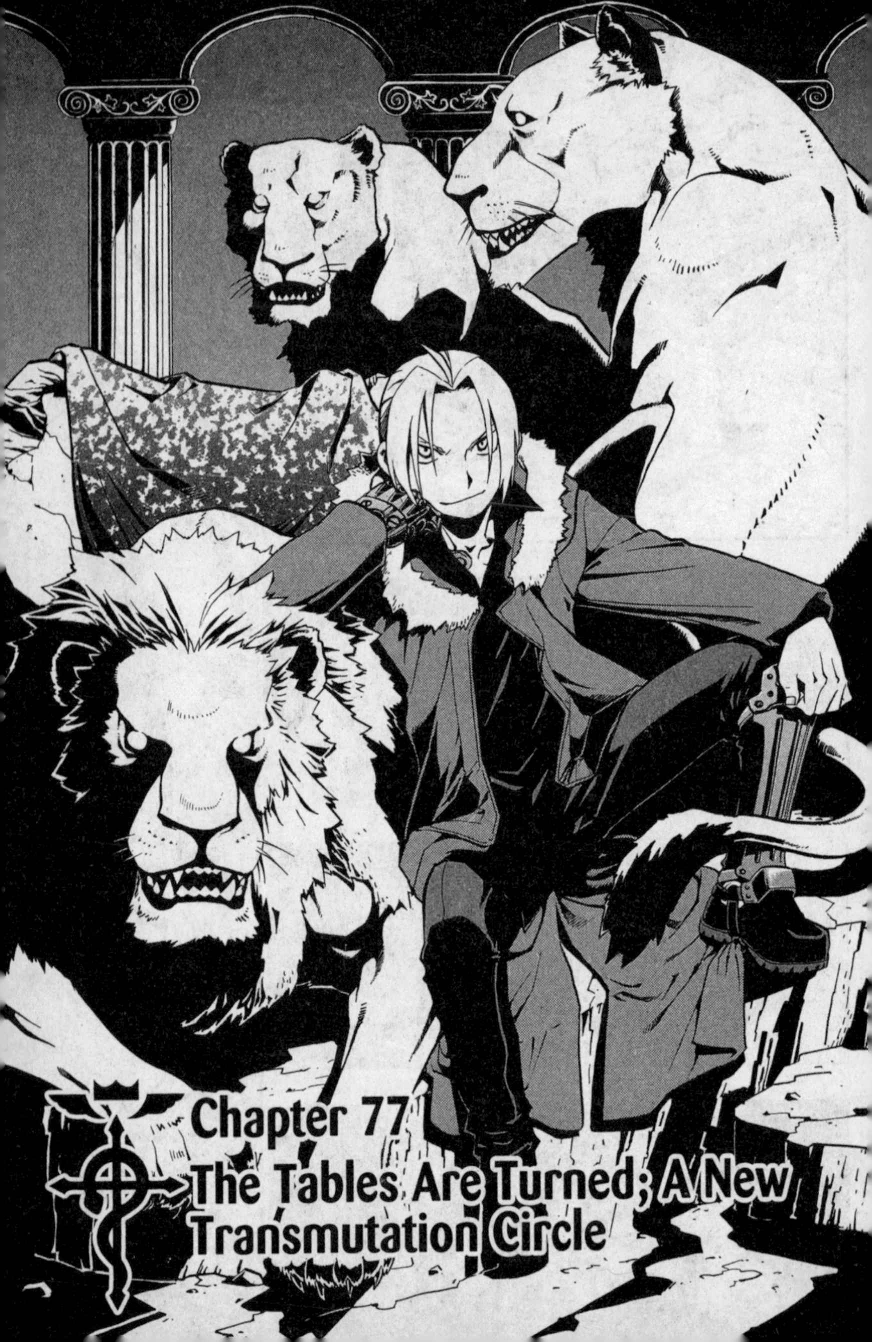
Chapter 77
The Tables Are Turned; A New Transmutation Circle

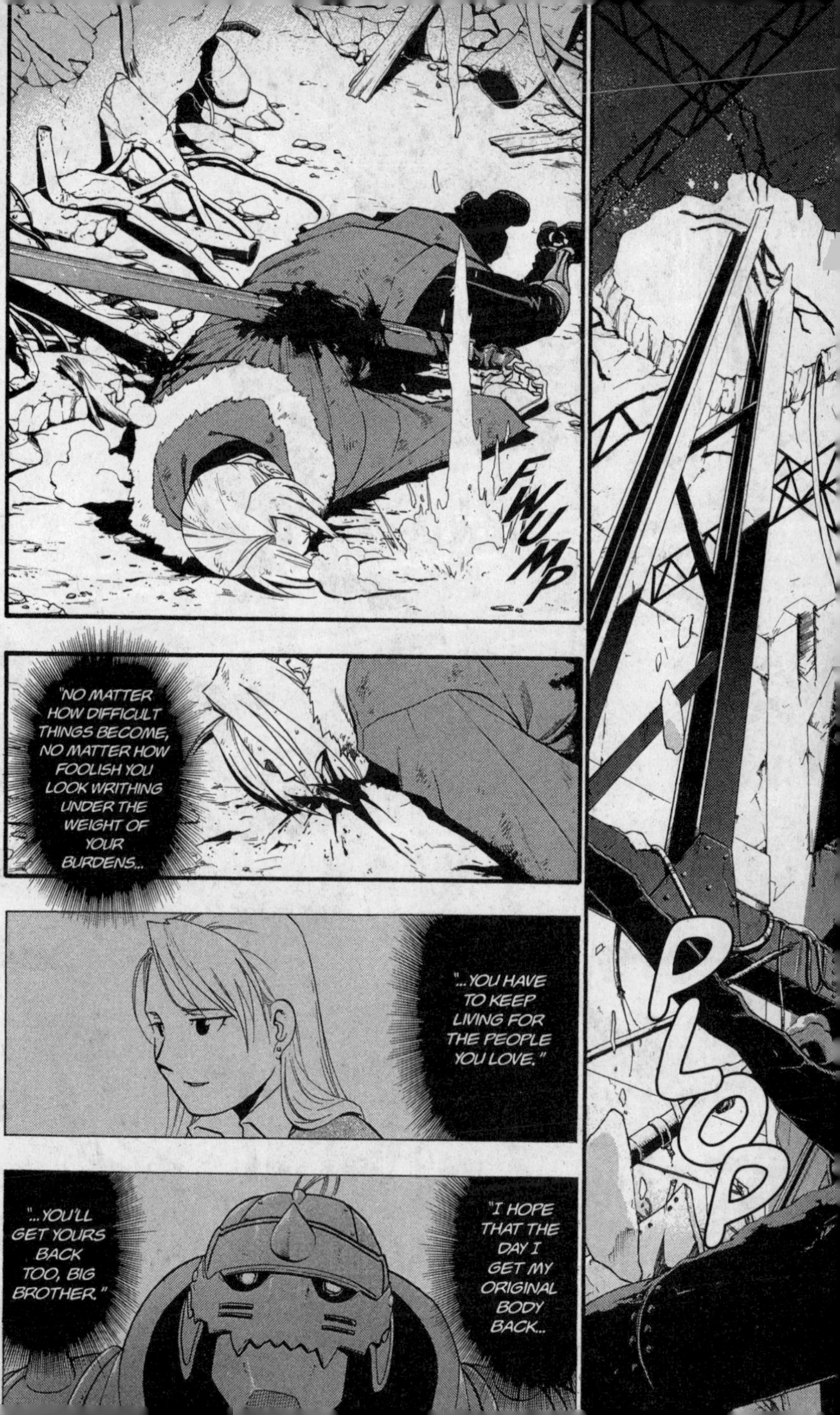
PLOP
FWUMP
"NO MATTER HOW DIFFICULT THINGS BECOME, NO MATTER HOW FOOLISH YOU LOOK WRITHING UNDER THE WEIGHT OF YOUR BURDENS...
"...YOU HAVE TO KEEP LIVING FOR THE PEOPLE YOU LOVE."
"I HOPE THAT THE DAY I GET MY ORIGINAL BODY BACK...
"...YOU'LL GET YOURS BACK TOO, BIG BROTHER."

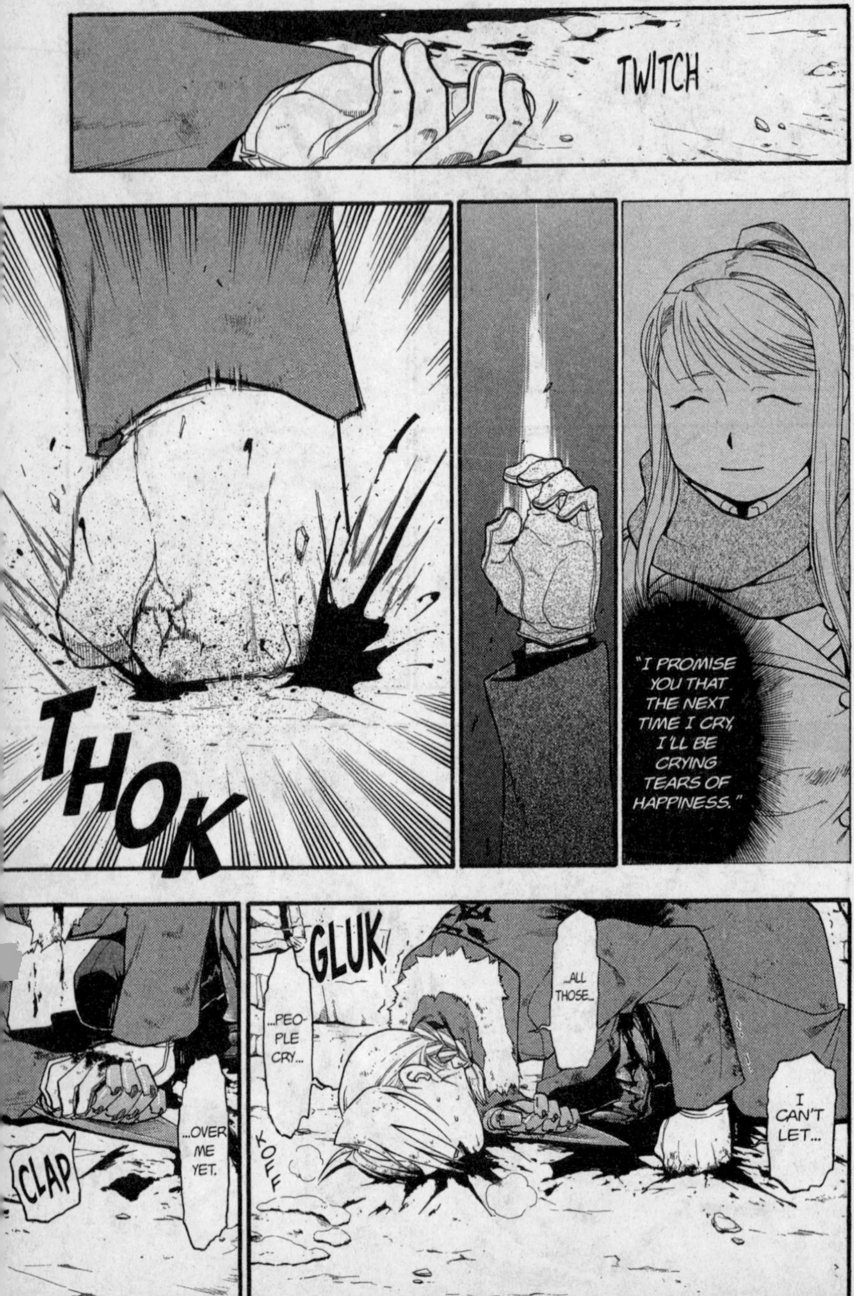
TWITCH
"I PROMISE YOU THAT THE NEXT TIME I CRY, I'LL BE CRYING TEARS OF HAPPINESS."
THOK
I CAN'T LET...
...ALL THOSE...
GLUK
...PEO-PLE CRY...
KOFF
...OVER ME YET.
CLAP

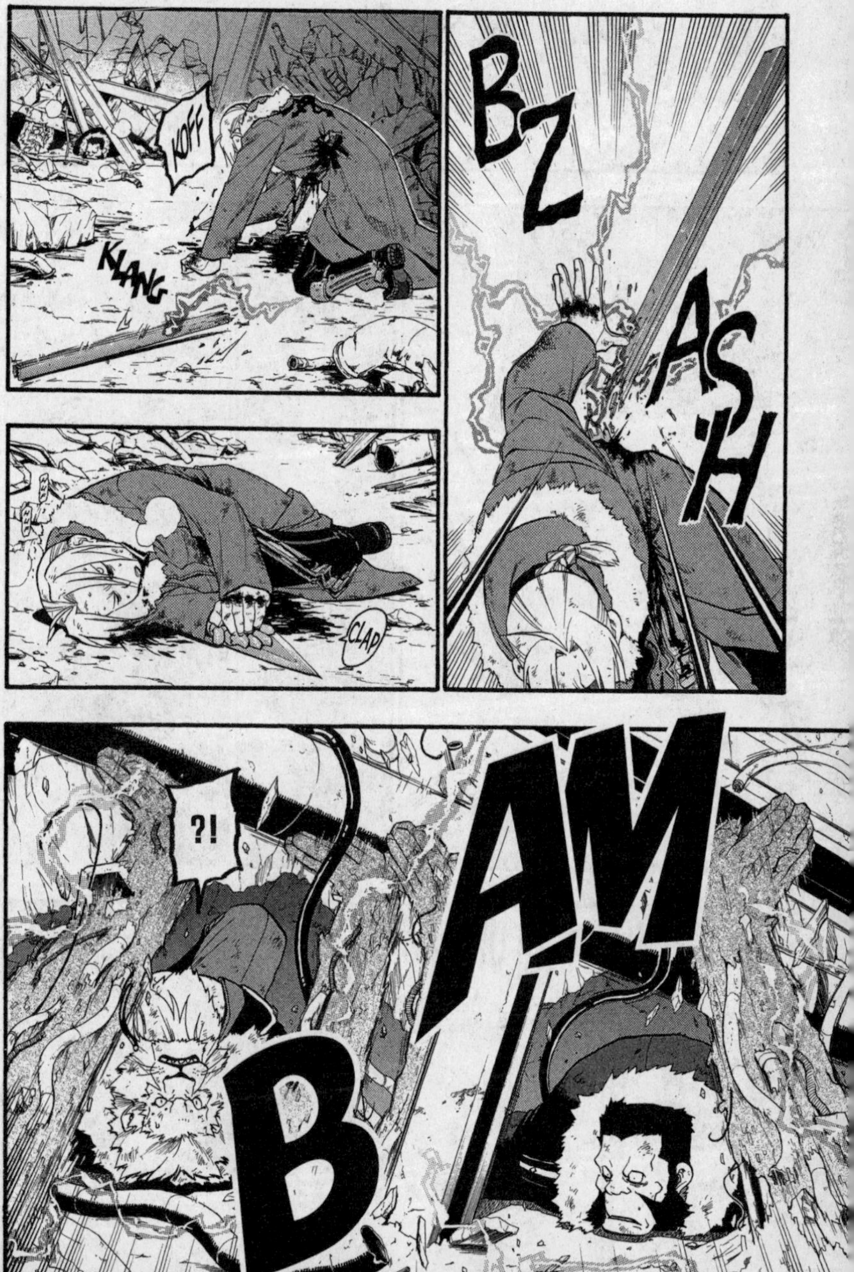
BZASH
KOFF
KLANG
CLAP
?!
BAM

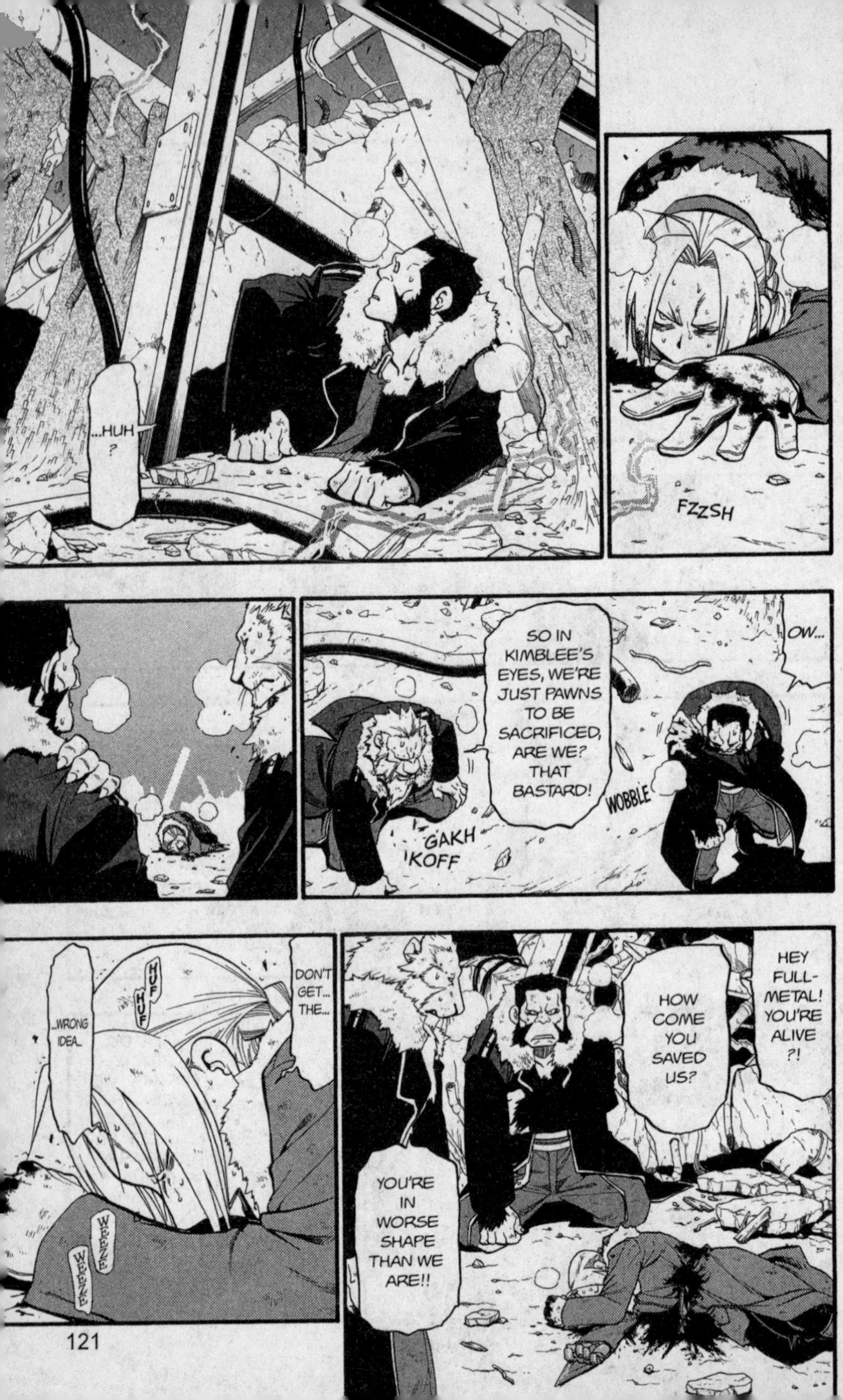
FZZSH
...HUH?
OW...
WOBBLE
SO IN KIMBLEE'S EYES, WE'RE JUST PAWNS TO BE SACRIFICED, ARE WE? THAT BASTARD!
GAKH KOFF
HEY FULL-METAL! YOU'RE ALIVE?!
HOW COME YOU SAVED US?
YOU'RE IN WORSE SHAPE THAN WE ARE!!
DON'T GET... THE...
HUF HUF
...WRONG IDEA.
WEEZE WEEZE

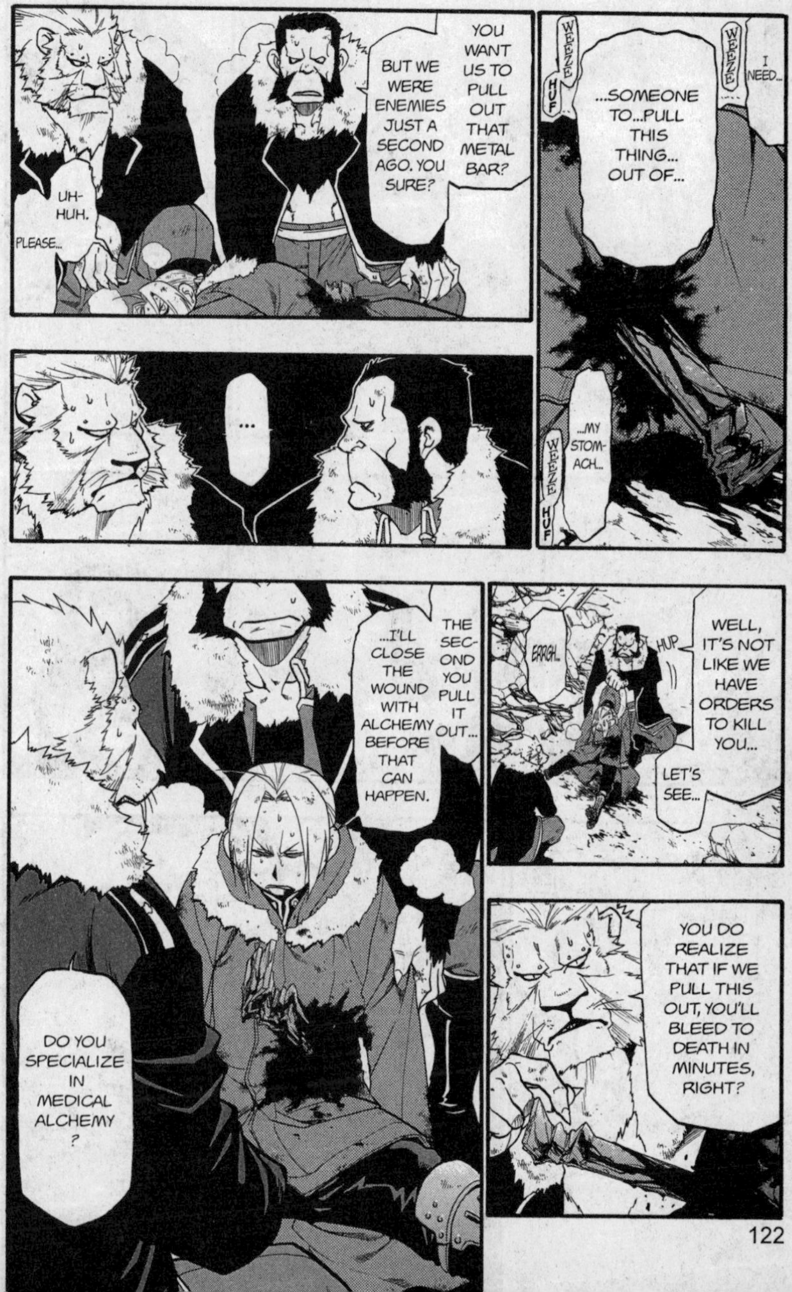
I NEED...
WEEZE
...SOMEONE TO...PULL THIS THING... OUT OF...
WEEZE
HUF
...MY STOMACH...
WEEZE
HUF
YOU WANT US TO PULL OUT THAT METAL BAR?
BUT WE WERE ENEMIES JUST A SECOND AGO. YOU SURE?
UH-HUH.
PLEASE...
...
WELL, IT'S NOT LIKE WE HAVE ORDERS TO KILL YOU...
LET'S SEE...
HUP
ERRGH.
YOU DO REALIZE THAT IF WE PULL THIS OUT, YOU'LL BLEED TO DEATH IN MINUTES, RIGHT?
THE SECOND YOU PULL IT OUT...
...I'LL CLOSE THE WOUND WITH ALCHEMY BEFORE THAT CAN HAPPEN.
DO YOU SPECIALIZE IN MEDICAL ALCHEMY?

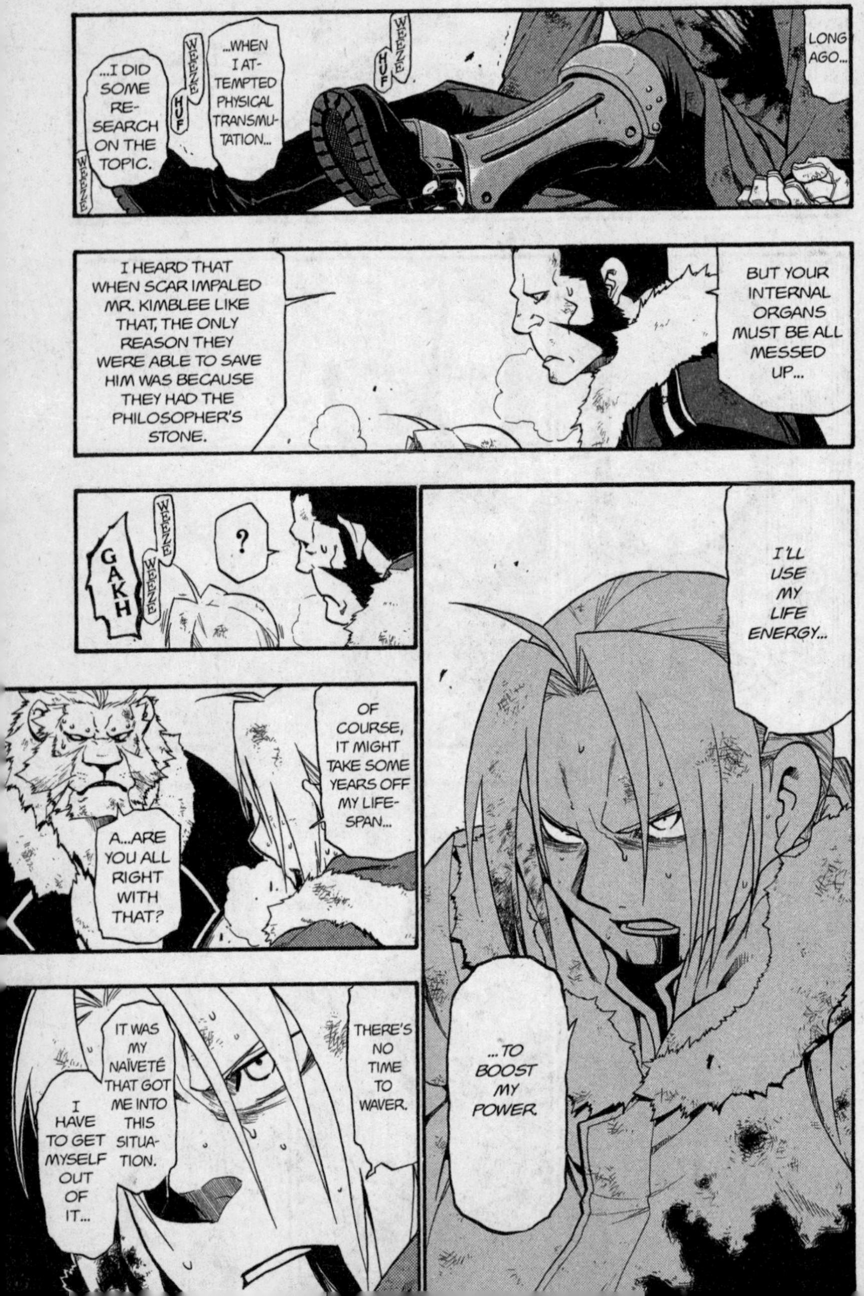
LONG AGO...
HUF
WEEZE
...WHEN I ATTEMPTED PHYSICAL TRANSMUTATION...
WEEZE
HUF
...I DID SOME RESEARCH ON THE TOPIC.
WEEZE
BUT YOUR INTERNAL ORGANS MUST BE ALL MESSED UP...
I HEARD THAT WHEN SCAR IMPALED MR. KIMBLEE LIKE THAT, THE ONLY REASON THEY WERE ABLE TO SAVE HIM WAS BECAUSE THEY HAD THE PHILOSOPHER'S STONE.
I'LL USE MY LIFE ENERGY...
...TO BOOST MY POWER.
?
WEEZE
WEEZE
GAKH
OF COURSE, IT MIGHT TAKE SOME YEARS OFF MY LIFESPAN...
A...ARE YOU ALL RIGHT WITH THAT?
THERE'S NO TIME TO WAVER.
IT WAS MY NAÏVETÉ THAT GOT ME INTO THIS SITUATION.
I HAVE TO GET MYSELF OUT OF IT...

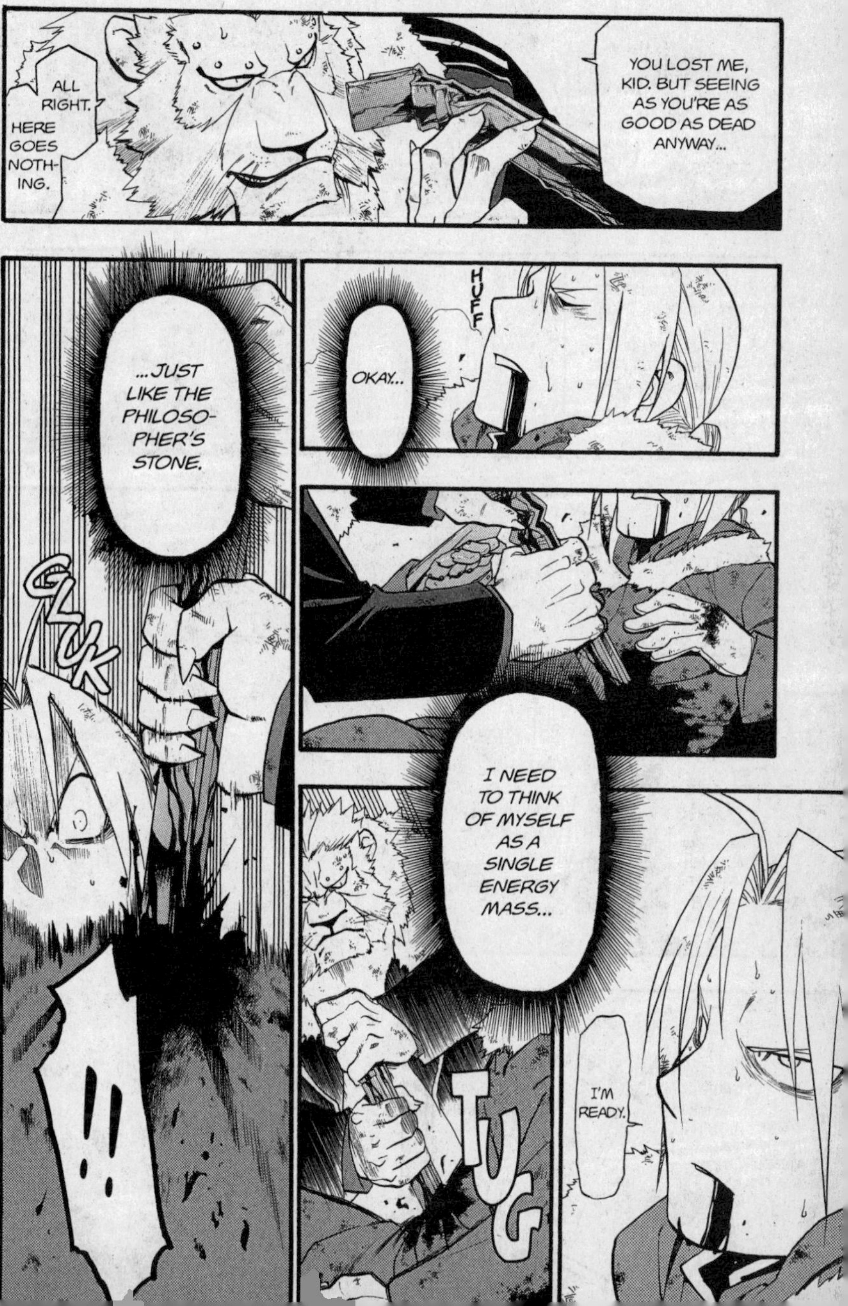
YOU LOST ME, KID. BUT SEEING AS YOU'RE AS GOOD AS DEAD ANYWAY...
ALL RIGHT. HERE GOES NOTH-ING.
HUFF
OKAY...
I NEED TO THINK OF MYSELF AS A SINGLE ENERGY MASS...
I'M READY.
TUG
...JUST LIKE THE PHILOSO-PHER'S STONE.
GLUK
!!

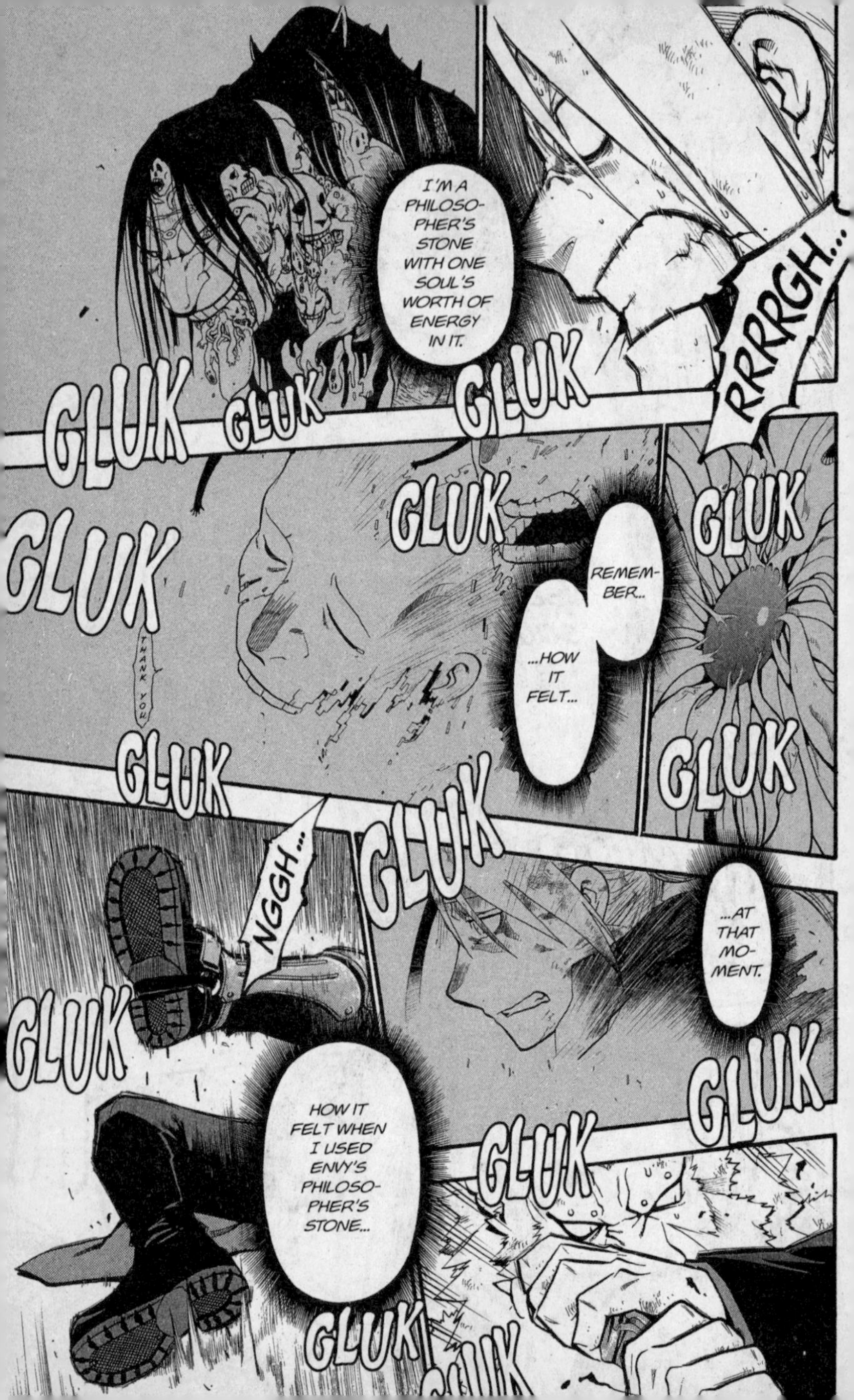
RRRRGH...
I'M A PHILOSOPHER'S STONE WITH ONE SOUL'S WORTH OF ENERGY IN IT.
GLUK
GLUK
GLUK
GLUK
GLUK
REMEMBER...
...HOW IT FELT...
GLUK
GLUK
THANK YOU
GLUK
...AT THAT MOMENT.
GLUK
GLUK
GLUK
NGGH...
GLUK
HOW IT FELT WHEN I USED ENVY'S PHILOSOPHER'S STONE...
GLUK

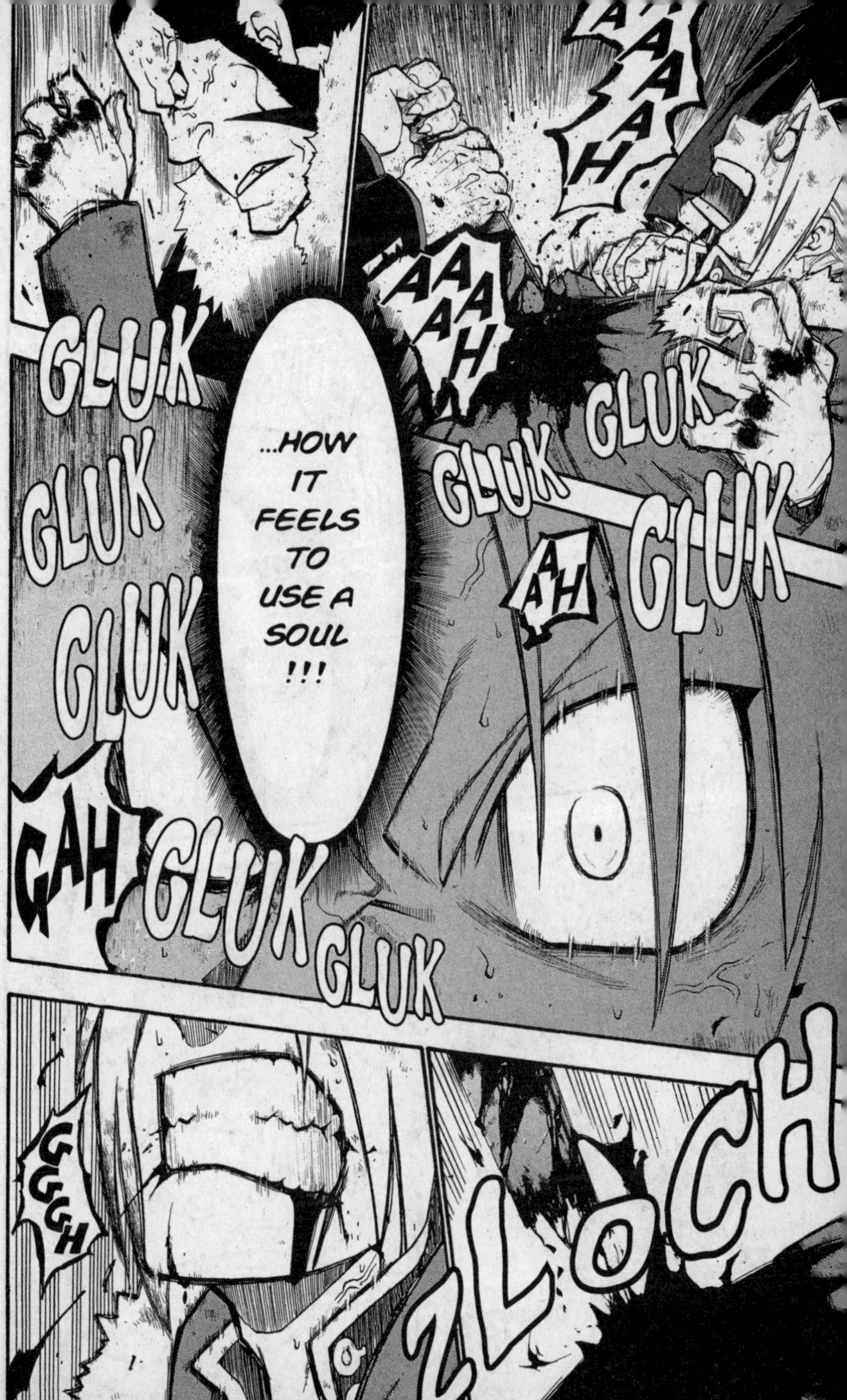
AAAAH
AAAAH
GLUK GLUK GLUK GLUK GLUK GLUK GLUK GLUK GLUK
AAH
...HOW IT FEELS TO USE A SOUL!!!
GAH
ZLOOCH
GGGH

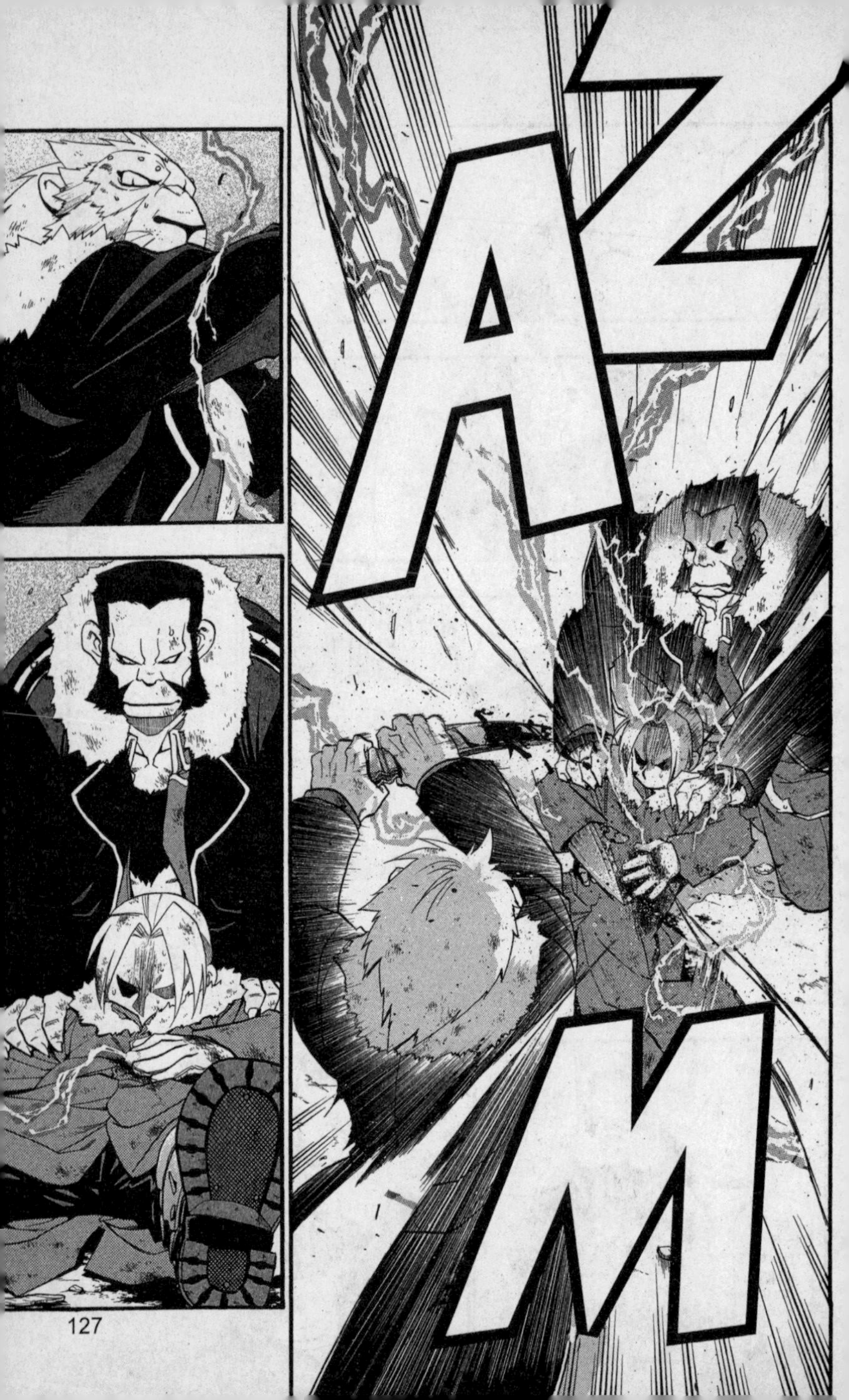
ZAM

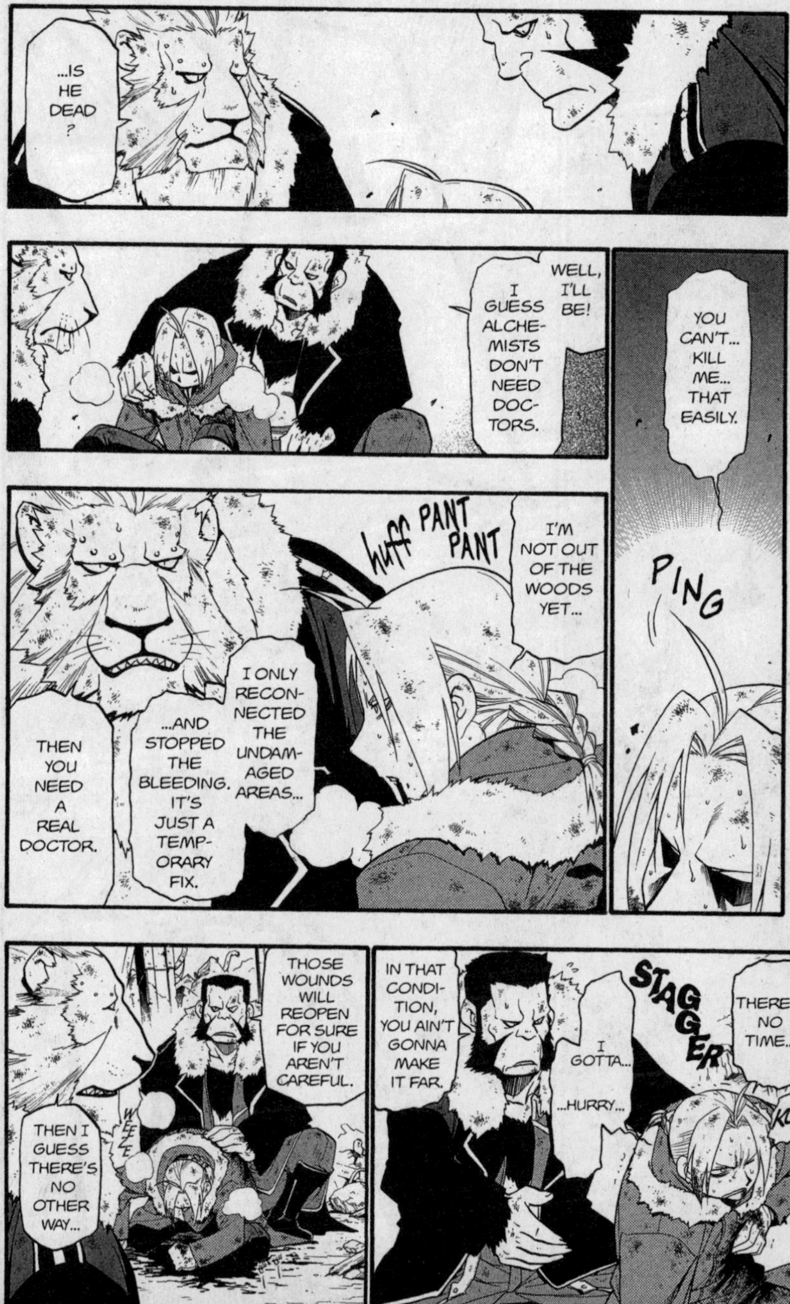
...IS HE DEAD ?
YOU CAN'T... KILL ME... THAT EASILY.
PING
WELL, I'LL BE!
I GUESS ALCHEMISTS DON'T NEED DOCTORS.
I'M NOT OUT OF THE WOODS YET...
huff PANT PANT
I ONLY RECONNECTED THE UNDAMAGED AREAS...
...AND STOPPED THE BLEEDING. IT'S JUST A TEMPORARY FIX.
THEN YOU NEED A REAL DOCTOR.
THERE'S NO TIME...
STAGGER
KOFF
I GOTTA...
...HURRY...
IN THAT CONDITION, YOU AIN'T GONNA MAKE IT FAR.
THOSE WOUNDS WILL REOPEN FOR SURE IF YOU AREN'T CAREFUL.
WEEZE
THEN I GUESS THERE'S NO OTHER WAY...

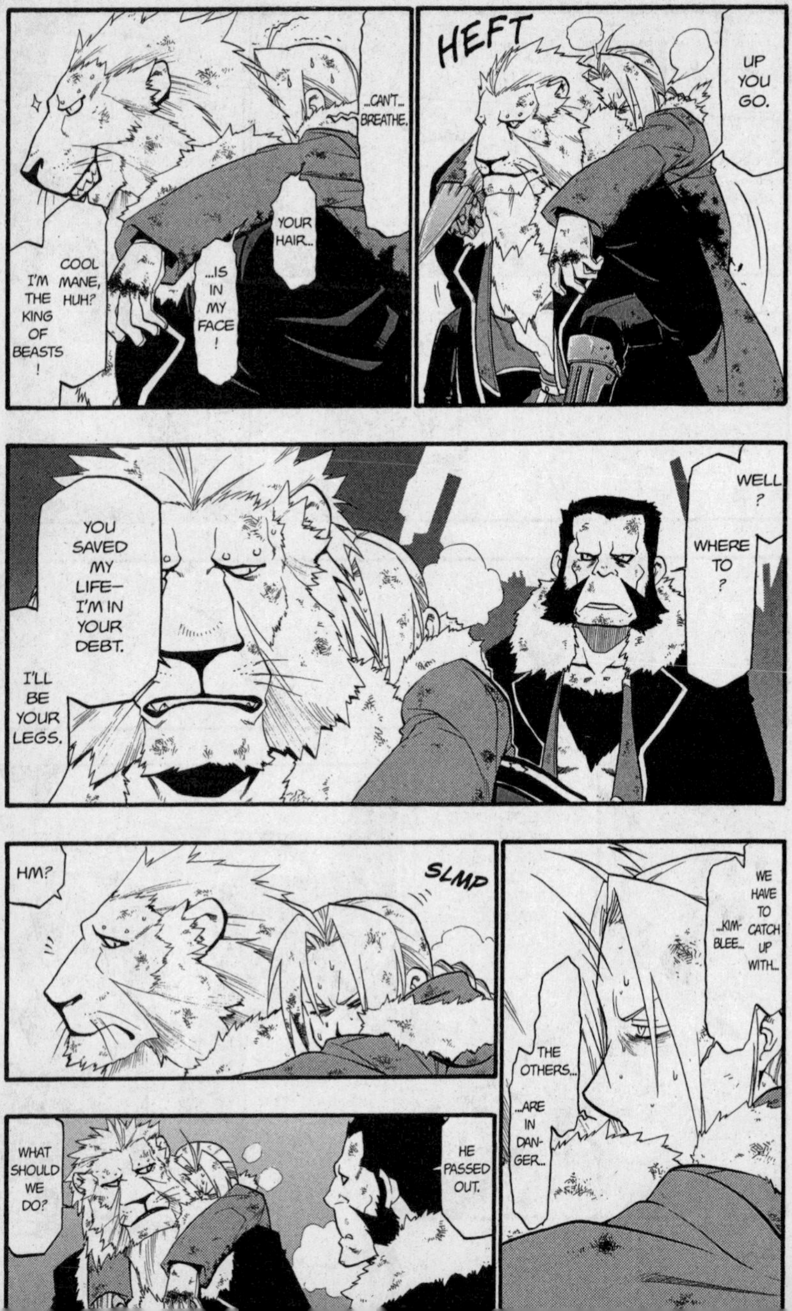
HEFT
UP YOU GO.
...CAN'T... BREATHE.
YOUR HAIR...
...IS IN MY FACE!
COOL MANE, HUH?
I'M THE KING OF BEASTS!
WELL? WHERE TO?
YOU SAVED MY LIFE—I'M IN YOUR DEBT.
I'LL BE YOUR LEGS.
WE HAVE TO CATCH UP WITH...
...KIM-BLEE...
THE OTHERS...
...ARE IN DAN-GER...
SLMP
HM?
HE PASSED OUT.
WHAT SHOULD WE DO?

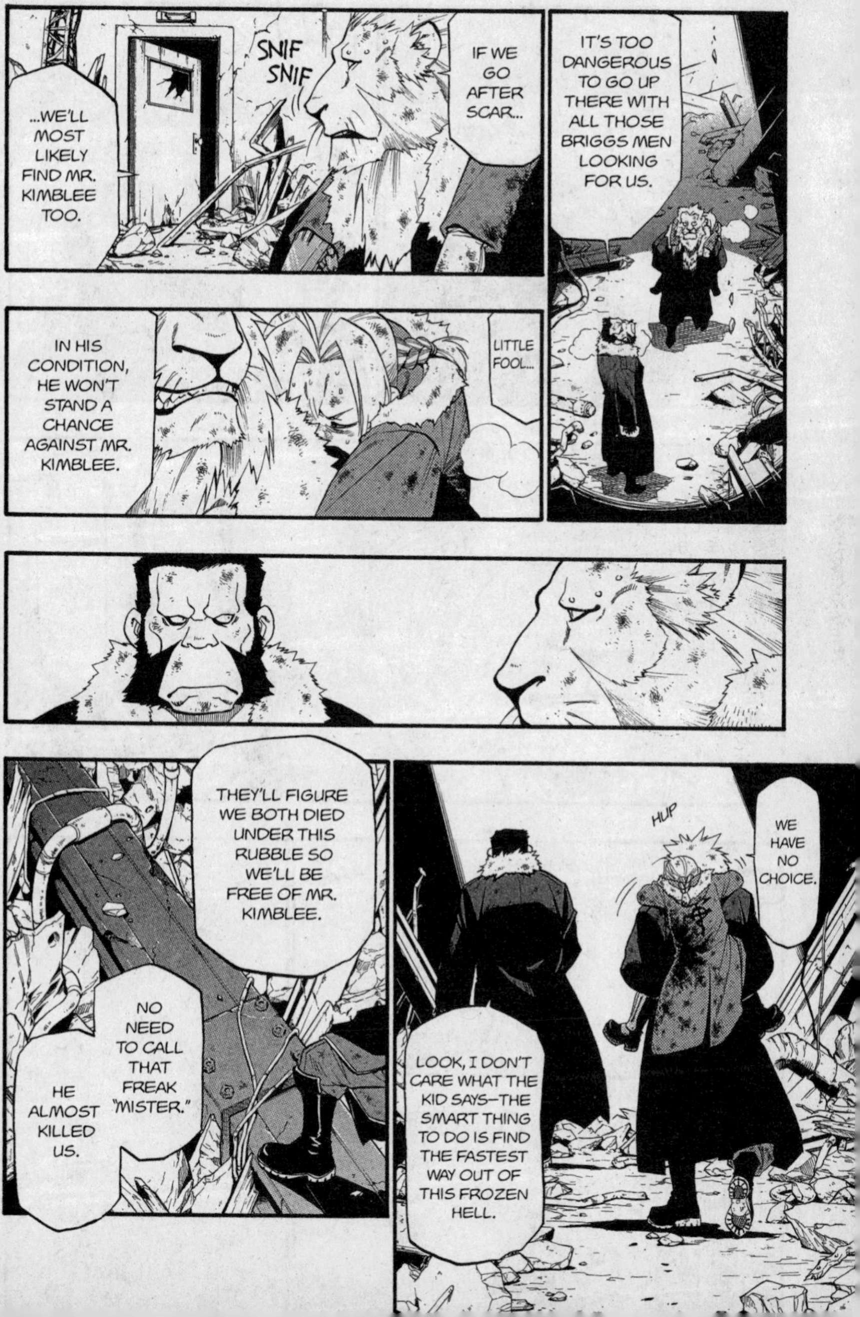
IT'S TOO DANGEROUS TO GO UP THERE WITH ALL THOSE BRIGGS MEN LOOKING FOR US.
IF WE GO AFTER SCAR...
SNIF SNIF
...WE'LL MOST LIKELY FIND MR. KIMBLEE TOO.
LITTLE FOOL...
IN HIS CONDITION, HE WON'T STAND A CHANCE AGAINST MR. KIMBLEE.
WE HAVE NO CHOICE.
HUP
LOOK, I DON'T CARE WHAT THE KID SAYS—THE SMART THING TO DO IS FIND THE FASTEST WAY OUT OF THIS FROZEN HELL.
THEY'LL FIGURE WE BOTH DIED UNDER THIS RUBBLE SO WE'LL BE FREE OF MR. KIMBLEE.
NO NEED TO CALL THAT FREAK "MISTER."
HE ALMOST KILLED US.

HM
?
WHAT IS IT?
THIS IS A...
CRNCH
CRNCH
CRNCH
CRNCH
CRNCH

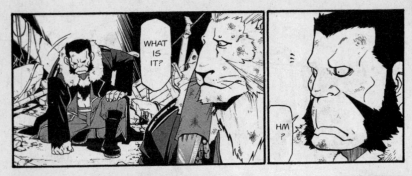

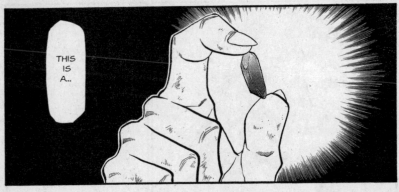

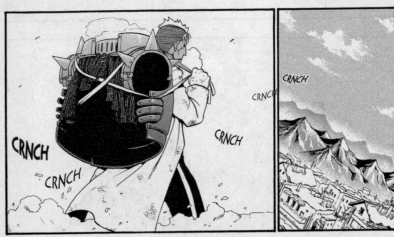

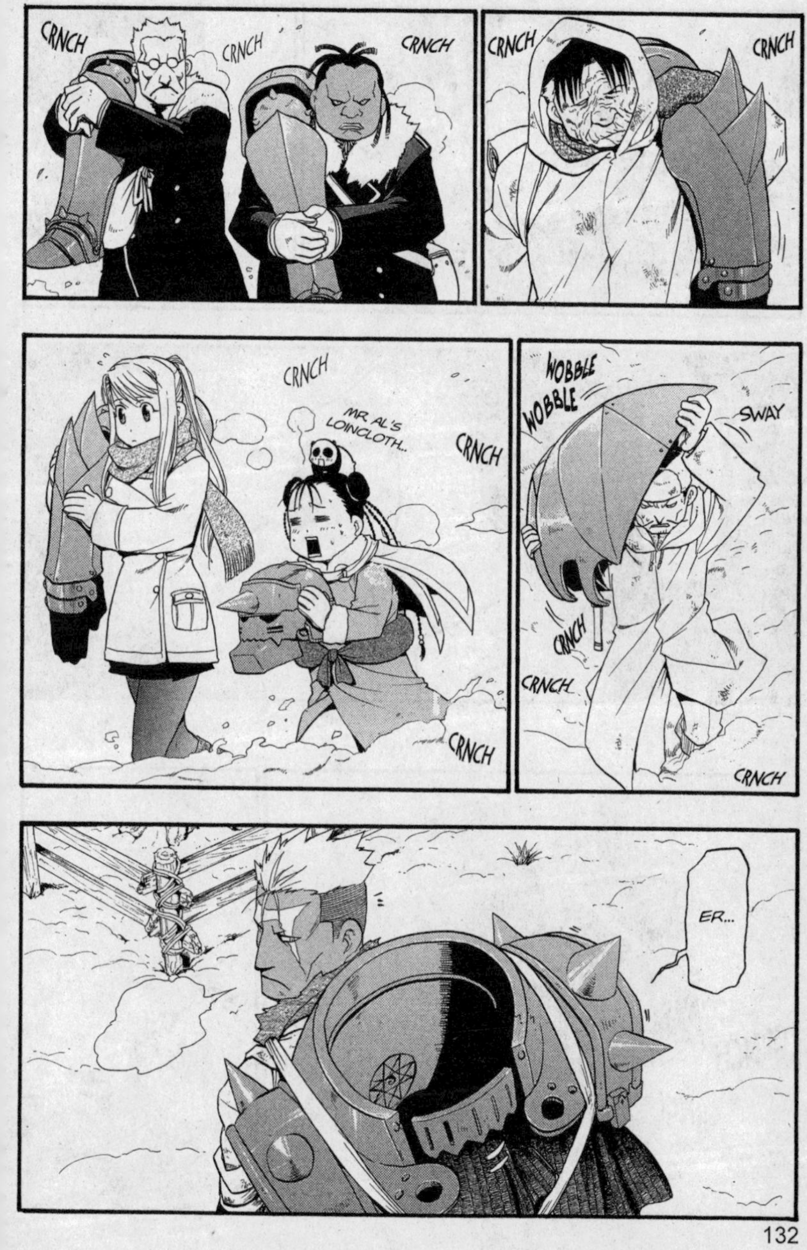
CRNCH
CRNCH
CRNCH
CRNCH
CRNCH
WOBBLE
WOBBLE
SWAY
CRNCH
CRNCH
CRNCH
CRNCH
MR. AL'S LOINCLOTH...
CRNCH
CRNCH
ER...

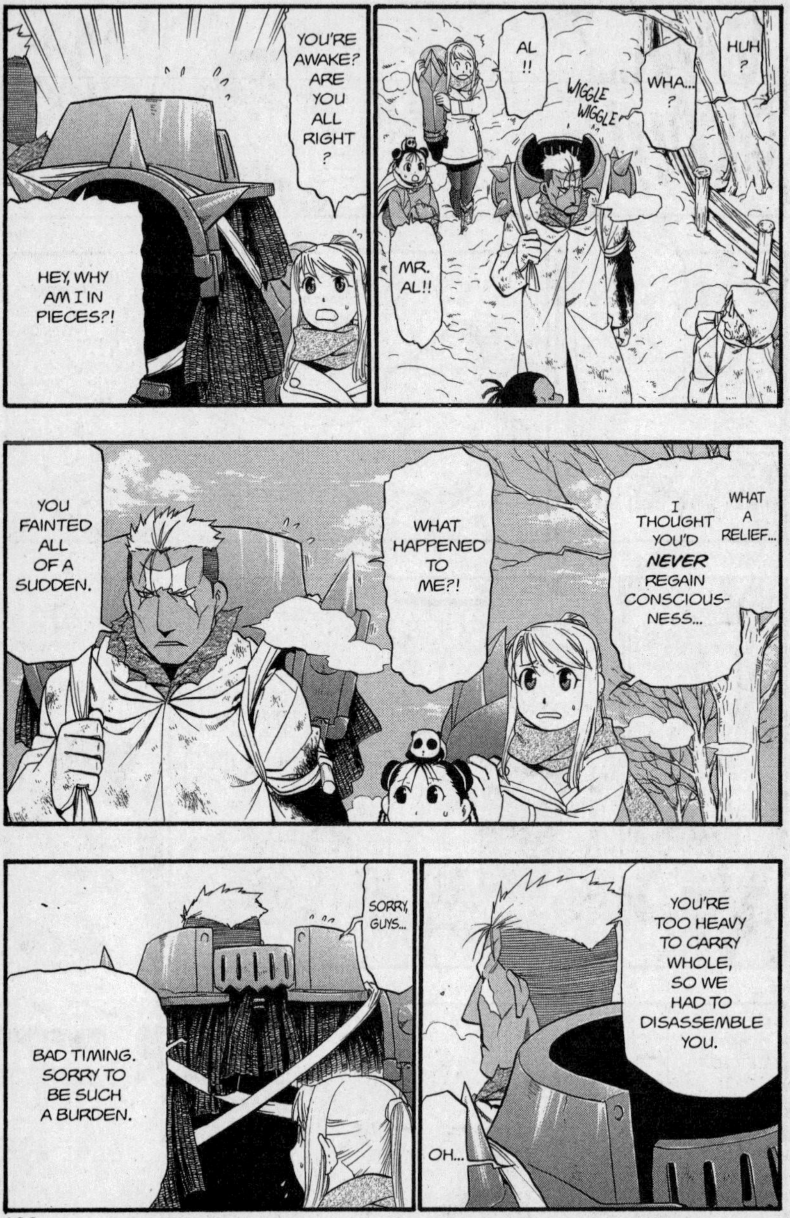
HUH ?
WHA... ?
AL !!
WIGGLE WIGGLE
MR. AL!!
YOU'RE AWAKE? ARE YOU ALL RIGHT ?
HEY, WHY AM I IN PIECES?!
WHAT A RELIEF...
I THOUGHT YOU'D NEVER REGAIN CONSCIOUSNESS...
WHAT HAPPENED TO ME?!
YOU FAINTED ALL OF A SUDDEN.
YOU'RE TOO HEAVY TO CARRY WHOLE, SO WE HAD TO DISASSEMBLE YOU.
OH...
SORRY, GUYS...
BAD TIMING. SORRY TO BE SUCH A BURDEN.

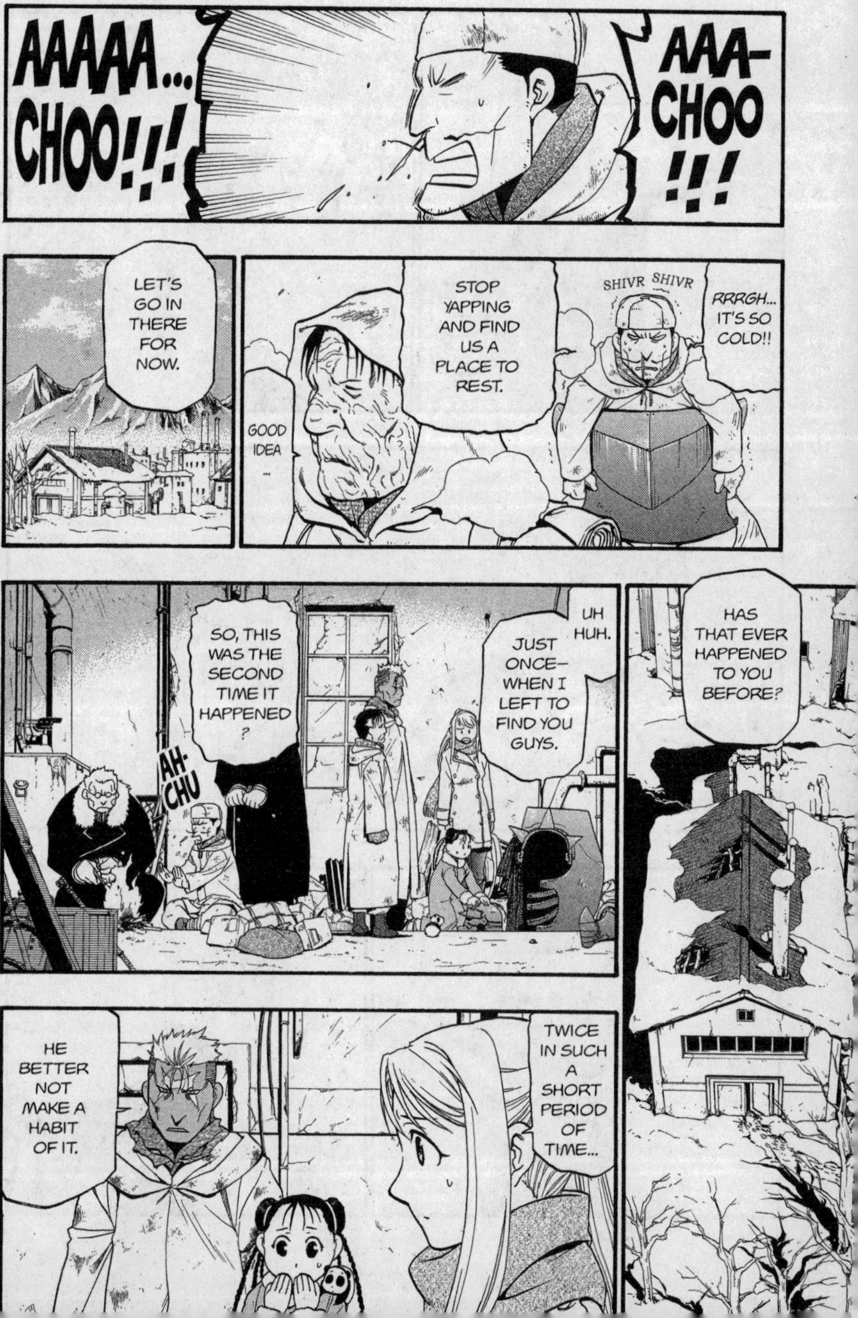
AAA-CHOO!!!
AAAAA... CHOO!!!
SHIVR SHIVR
RRRGH... IT'S SO COLD!!
STOP YAPPING AND FIND US A PLACE TO REST.
GOOD IDEA...
LET'S GO IN THERE FOR NOW.
HAS THAT EVER HAPPENED TO YOU BEFORE?
UH HUH.
JUST ONCE— WHEN I LEFT TO FIND YOU GUYS.
SO, THIS WAS THE SECOND TIME IT HAPPENED?
AH-CHU
TWICE IN SUCH A SHORT PERIOD OF TIME...
HE BETTER NOT MAKE A HABIT OF IT.

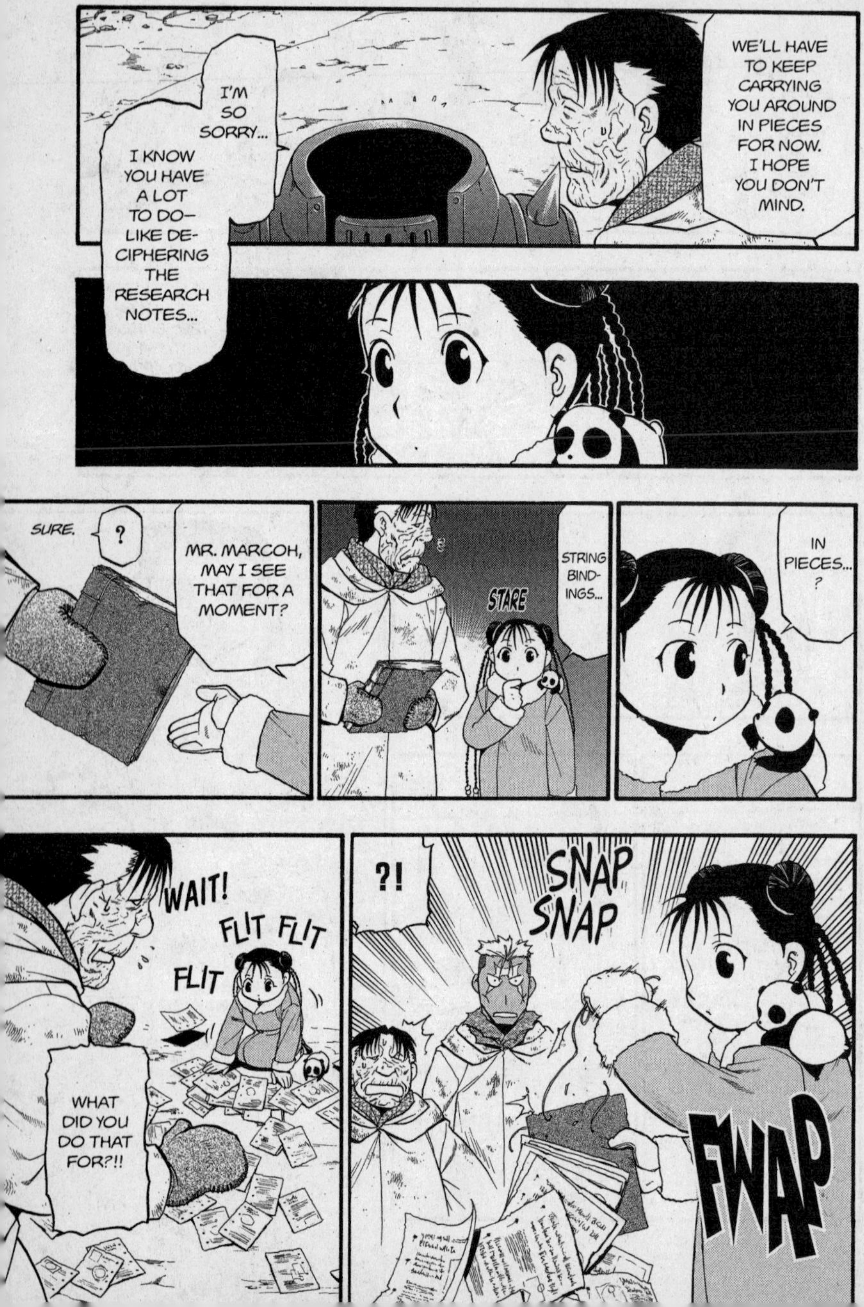
WE'LL HAVE TO KEEP CARRYING YOU AROUND IN PIECES FOR NOW. I HOPE YOU DON'T MIND.
I'M SO SORRY...
I KNOW YOU HAVE A LOT TO DO—LIKE DE-CIPHERING THE RESEARCH NOTES...
IN PIECES...?
STRING BIND-INGS...
STARE
MR. MARCOH, MAY I SEE THAT FOR A MOMENT?
?
SURE.
SNAP SNAP
?!
FWAP
WAIT!
FLIT FLIT
FLIT
WHAT DID YOU DO THAT FOR?!!

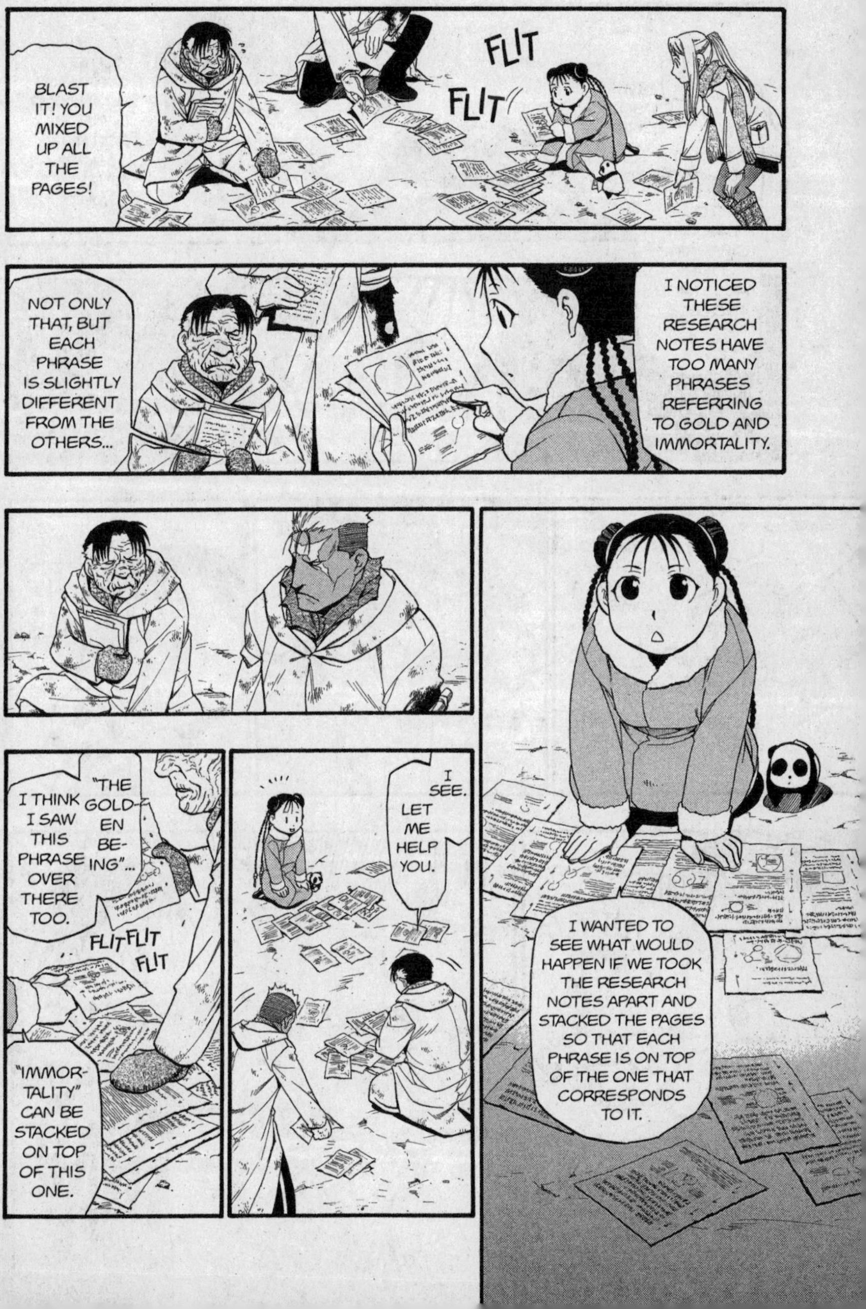
FLIT
FLIT
BLAST IT! YOU MIXED UP ALL THE PAGES!
I NOTICED THESE RESEARCH NOTES HAVE TOO MANY PHRASES REFERRING TO GOLD AND IMMORTALITY.
NOT ONLY THAT, BUT EACH PHRASE IS SLIGHTLY DIFFERENT FROM THE OTHERS...
I WANTED TO SEE WHAT WOULD HAPPEN IF WE TOOK THE RESEARCH NOTES APART AND STACKED THE PAGES SO THAT EACH PHRASE IS ON TOP OF THE ONE THAT CORRESPONDS TO IT.
I SEE. LET ME HELP YOU.
I THINK I SAW THIS PHRASE "THE GOLDEN BEING"... OVER THERE TOO.
FLIT FLIT FLIT
"IMMORTALITY" CAN BE STACKED ON TOP OF THIS ONE.

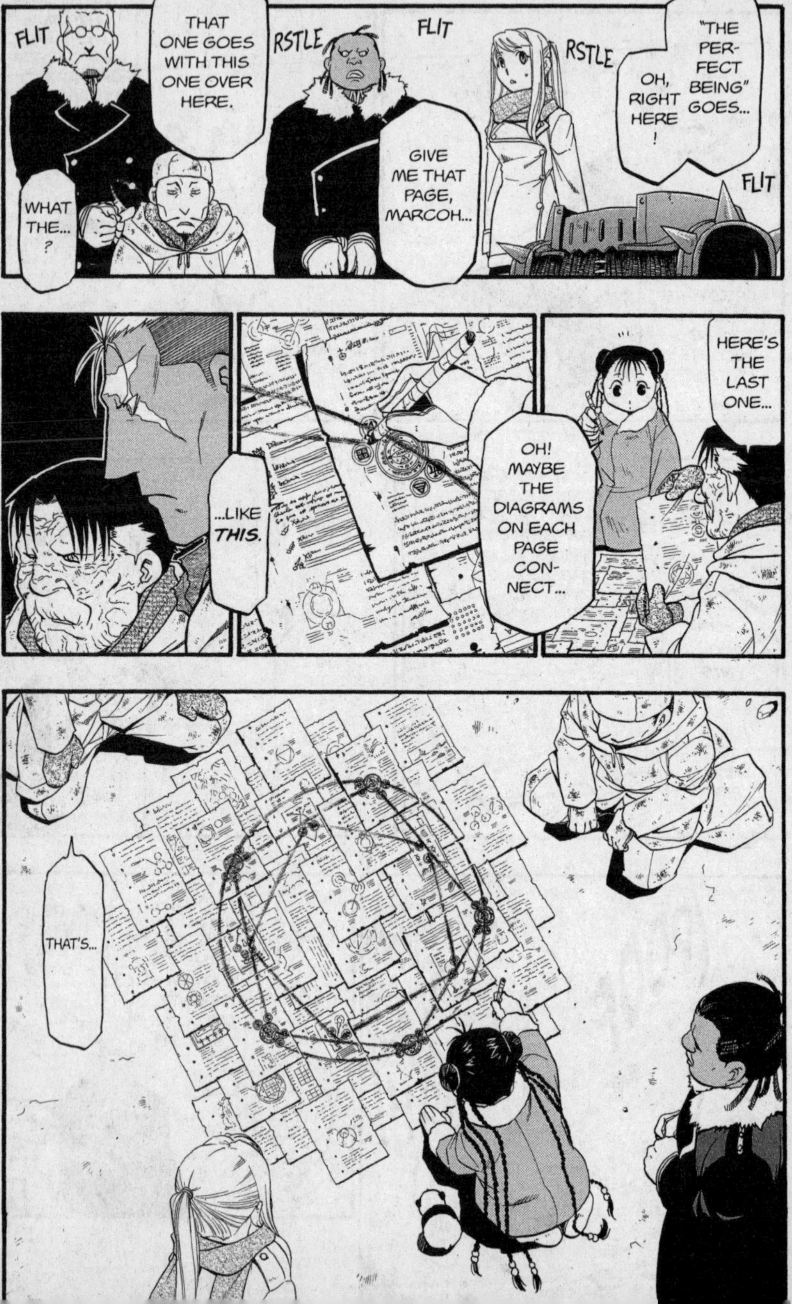
"THE PERFECT BEING" GOES...
OH, RIGHT HERE!
FLIT
RSTLE
FLIT
GIVE ME THAT PAGE, MARCOH...
RSTLE
THAT ONE GOES WITH THIS ONE OVER HERE.
FLIT
WHAT THE...?
HERE'S THE LAST ONE...
OH! MAYBE THE DIAGRAMS ON EACH PAGE CONNECT...
...LIKE *THIS.*
THAT'S...

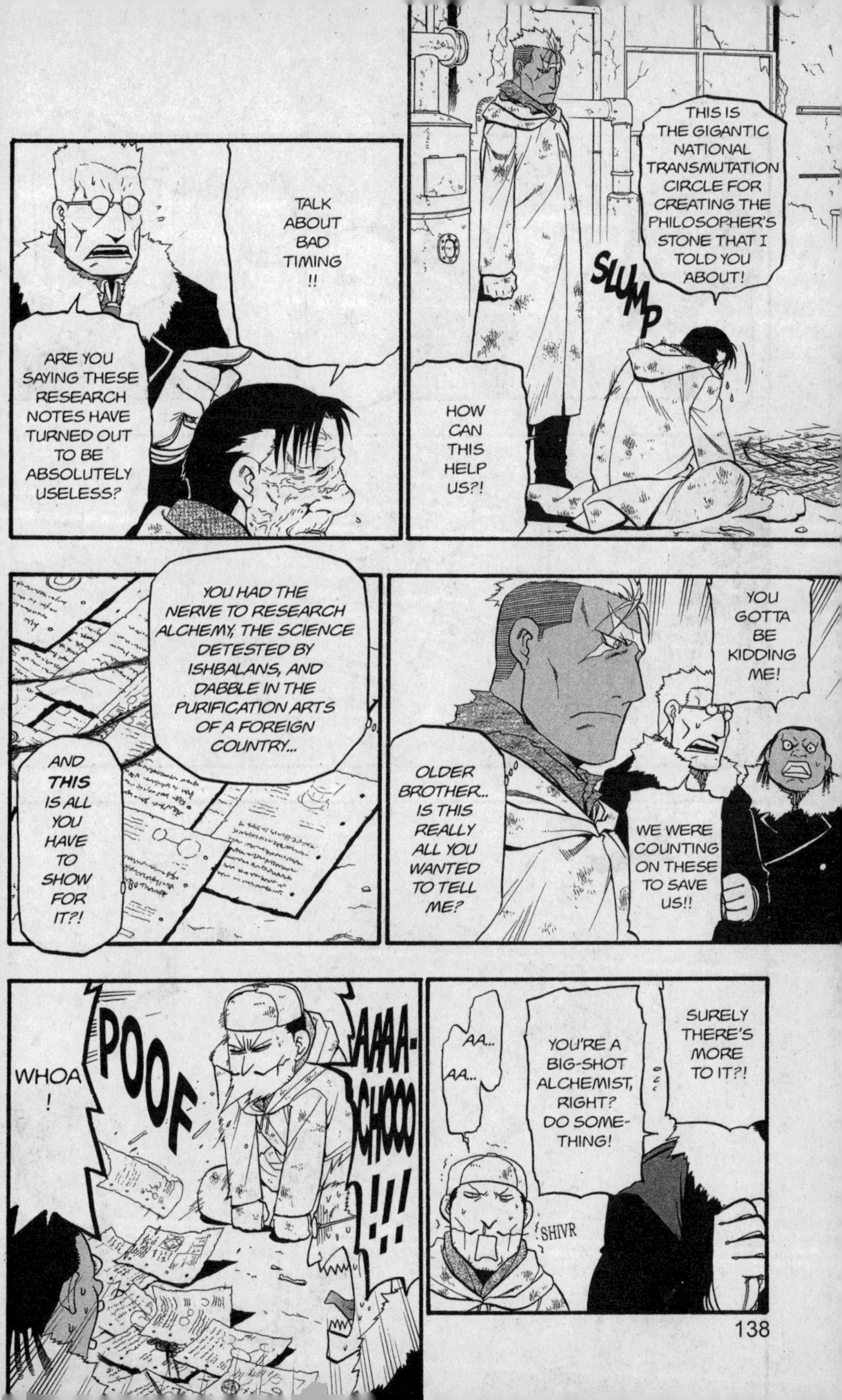
THIS IS THE GIGANTIC NATIONAL TRANSMUTATION CIRCLE FOR CREATING THE PHILOSOPHER'S STONE THAT I TOLD YOU ABOUT!
SLUMP
HOW CAN THIS HELP US?!
TALK ABOUT BAD TIMING!!
ARE YOU SAYING THESE RESEARCH NOTES HAVE TURNED OUT TO BE ABSOLUTELY USELESS?
YOU GOTTA BE KIDDING ME!
WE WERE COUNTING ON THESE TO SAVE US!!
OLDER BROTHER... IS THIS REALLY ALL YOU WANTED TO TELL ME?
YOU HAD THE NERVE TO RESEARCH ALCHEMY, THE SCIENCE DETESTED BY ISHBALANS, AND DABBLE IN THE PURIFICATION ARTS OF A FOREIGN COUNTRY...
AND THIS IS ALL YOU HAVE TO SHOW FOR IT?!
SURELY THERE'S MORE TO IT?!
YOU'RE A BIG-SHOT ALCHEMIST, RIGHT? DO SOME-THING!
AA... AA...
SHIVR
AAAA-CHOOO!!!
POOF
WHOA!

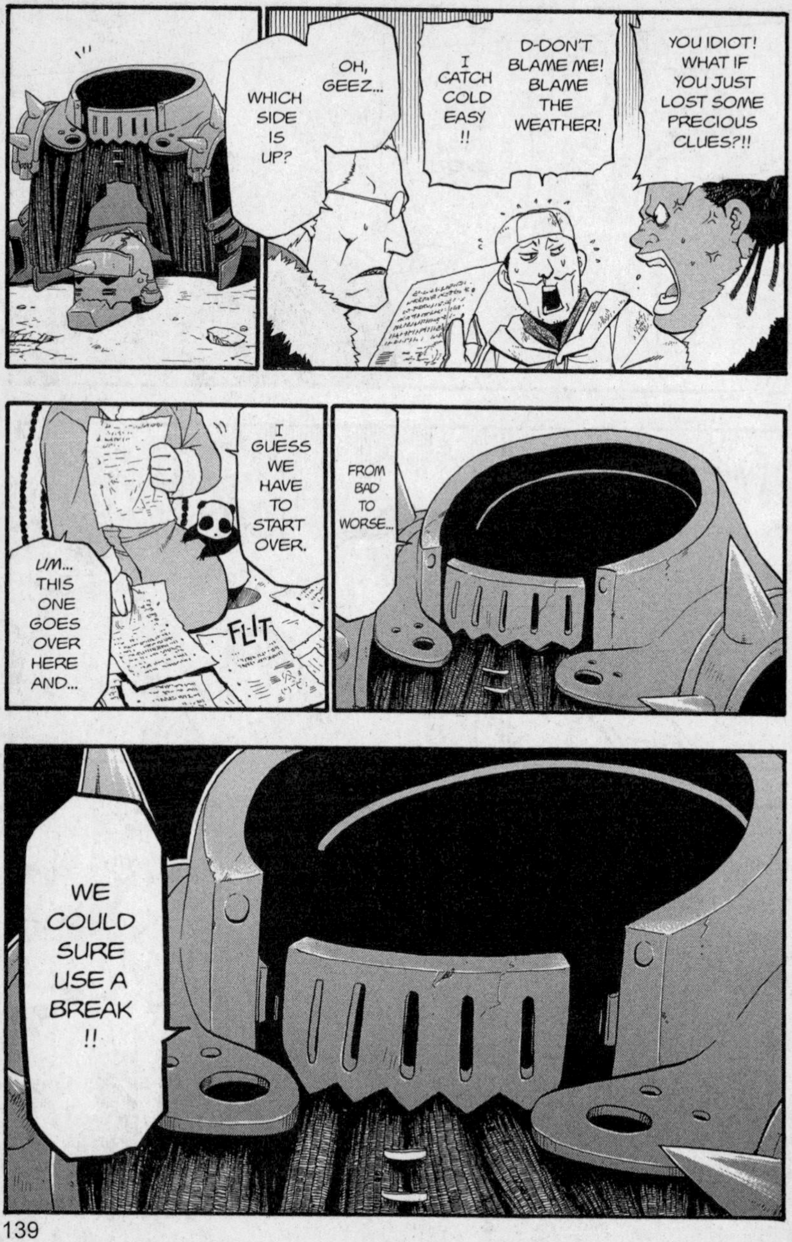
YOU IDIOT! WHAT IF YOU JUST LOST SOME PRECIOUS CLUES?!!
D-DON'T BLAME ME! BLAME THE WEATHER!
I CATCH COLD EASY !!
OH, GEEZ...
WHICH SIDE IS UP?
FROM BAD TO WORSE...
I GUESS WE HAVE TO START OVER.
FLIT
UM... THIS ONE GOES OVER HERE AND...
WE COULD SURE USE A BREAK !!

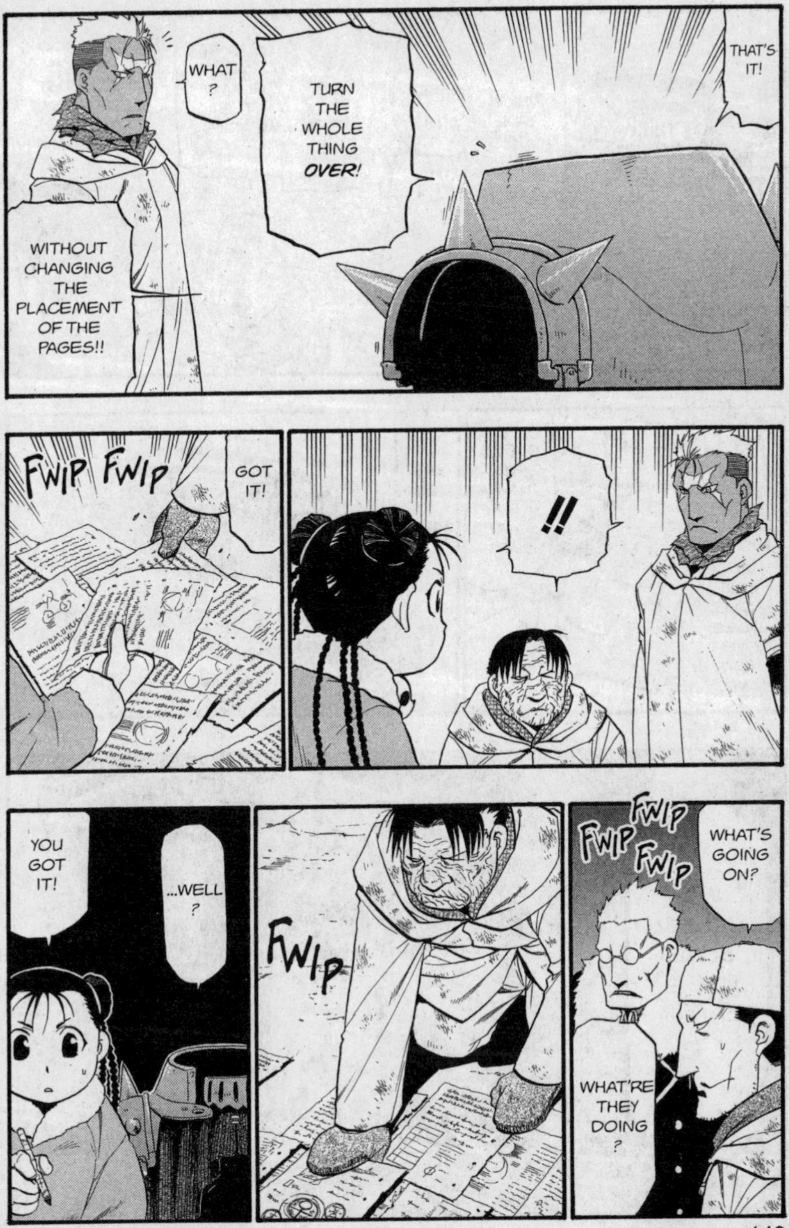
THAT'S IT!
TURN THE WHOLE THING OVER!
WHAT?
WITHOUT CHANGING THE PLACEMENT OF THE PAGES!!
!!
GOT IT!
FWIP FWIP
WHAT'S GOING ON?
FWIP FWIP FWIP
WHAT'RE THEY DOING?
FWIP
...WELL?
YOU GOT IT!

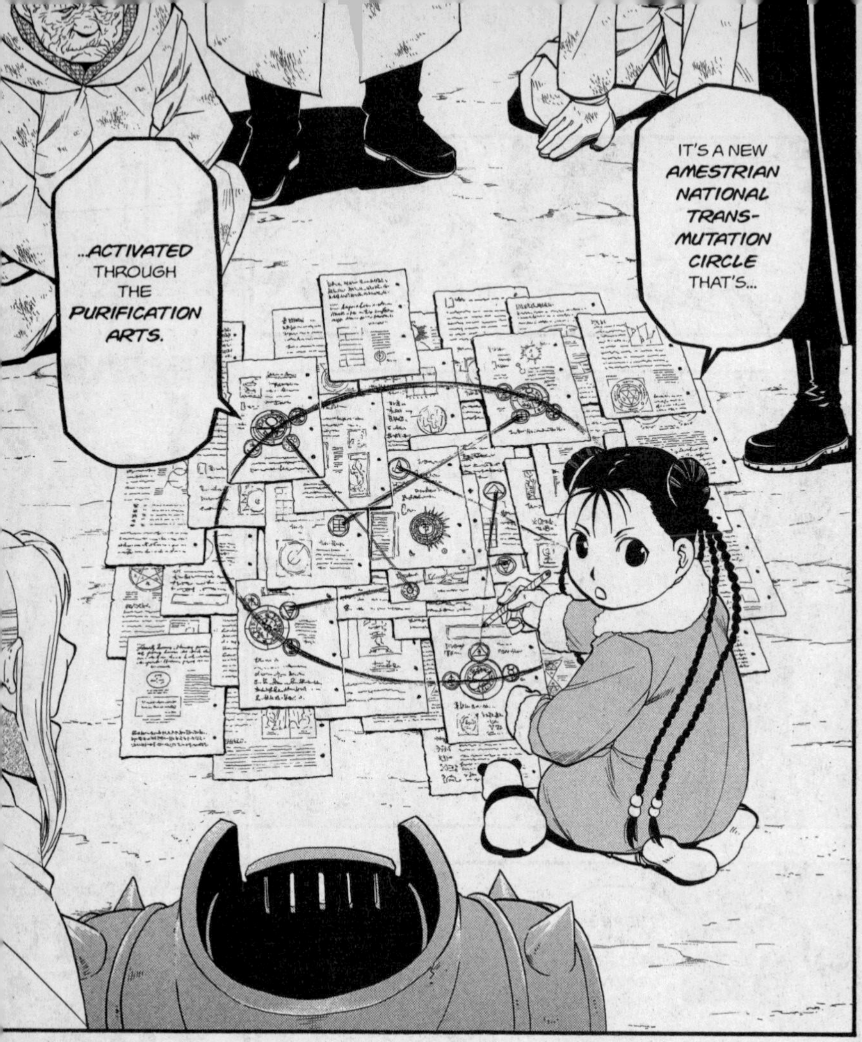
IT'S A NEW AMESTRIAN NATIONAL TRANS-MUTATION CIRCLE THAT'S...
...ACTIVATED THROUGH THE PURIFICATION ARTS.

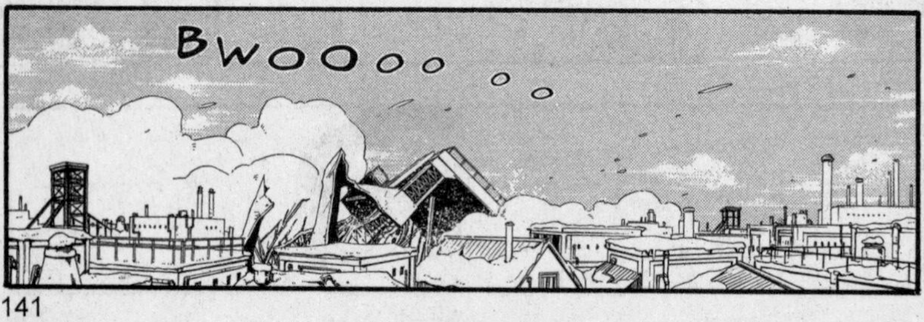
BWOOOOOOO

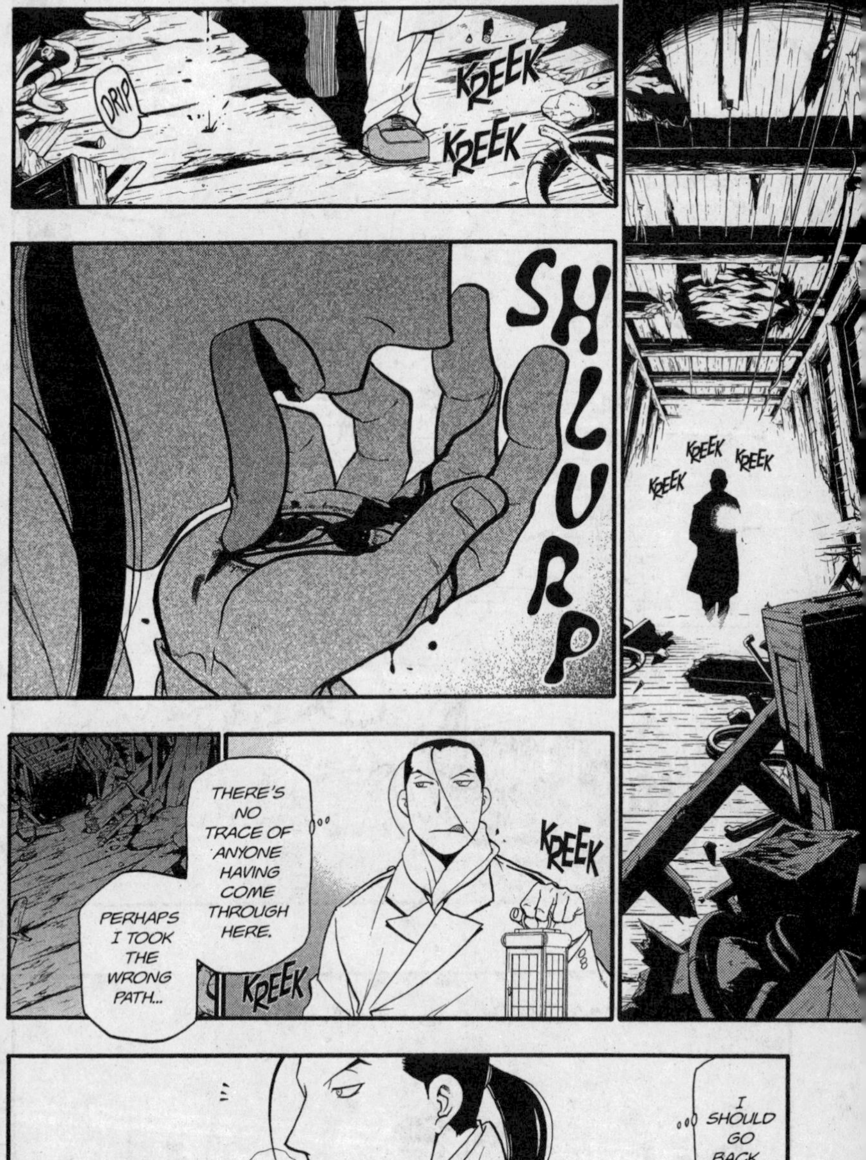
KREEK
KREEK
KREEK
KREEK
KREEK
DRIP
SHLURP
KREEK
THERE'S NO TRACE OF ANYONE HAVING COME THROUGH HERE.
PERHAPS I TOOK THE WRONG PATH...
KREEK
...I SHOULD GO BACK...

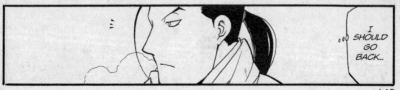

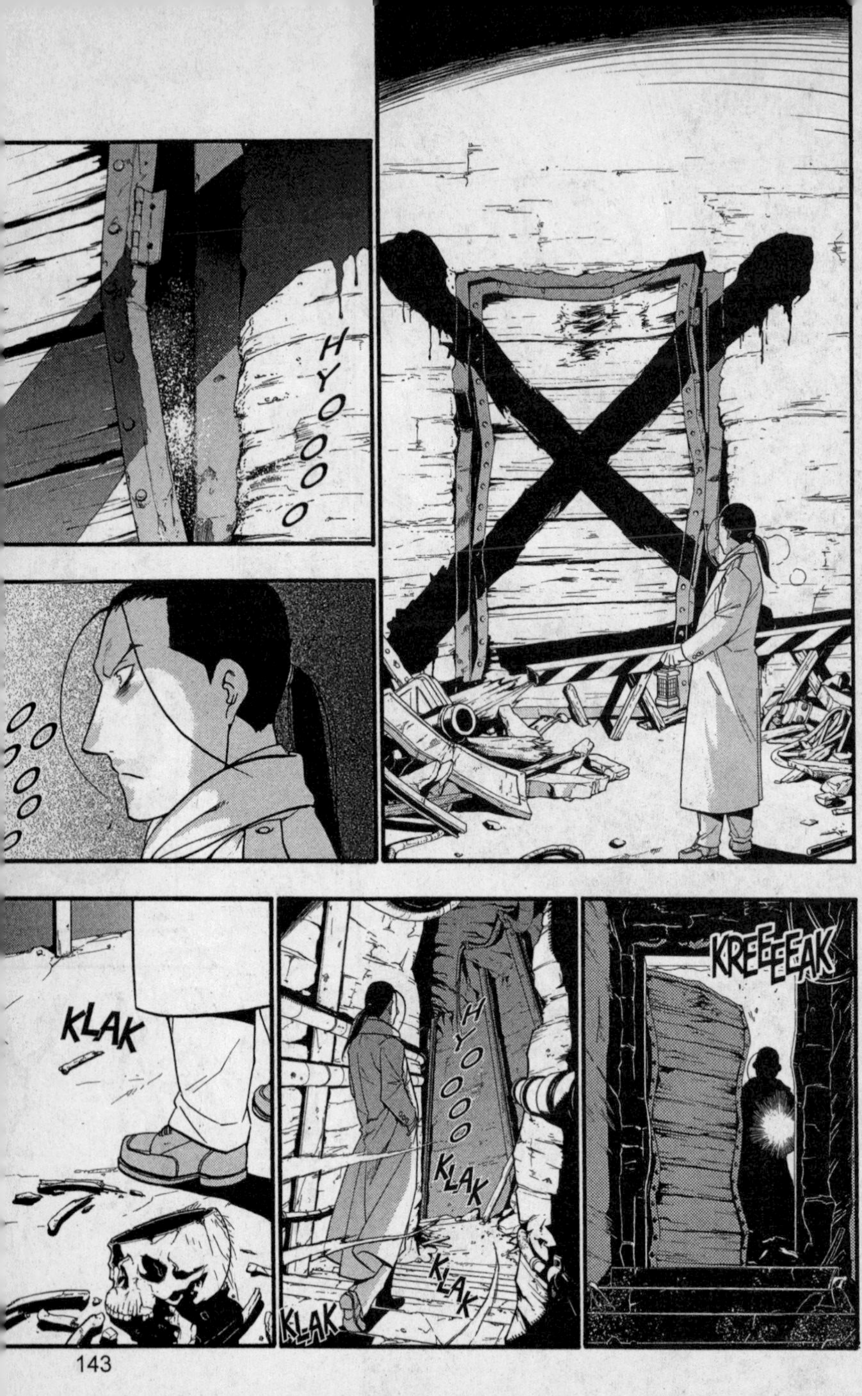
HYOOOOO
OOOOOO
KREEEEAK
HYOOOOO
KLAK
KLAK
KLAK
KLAK

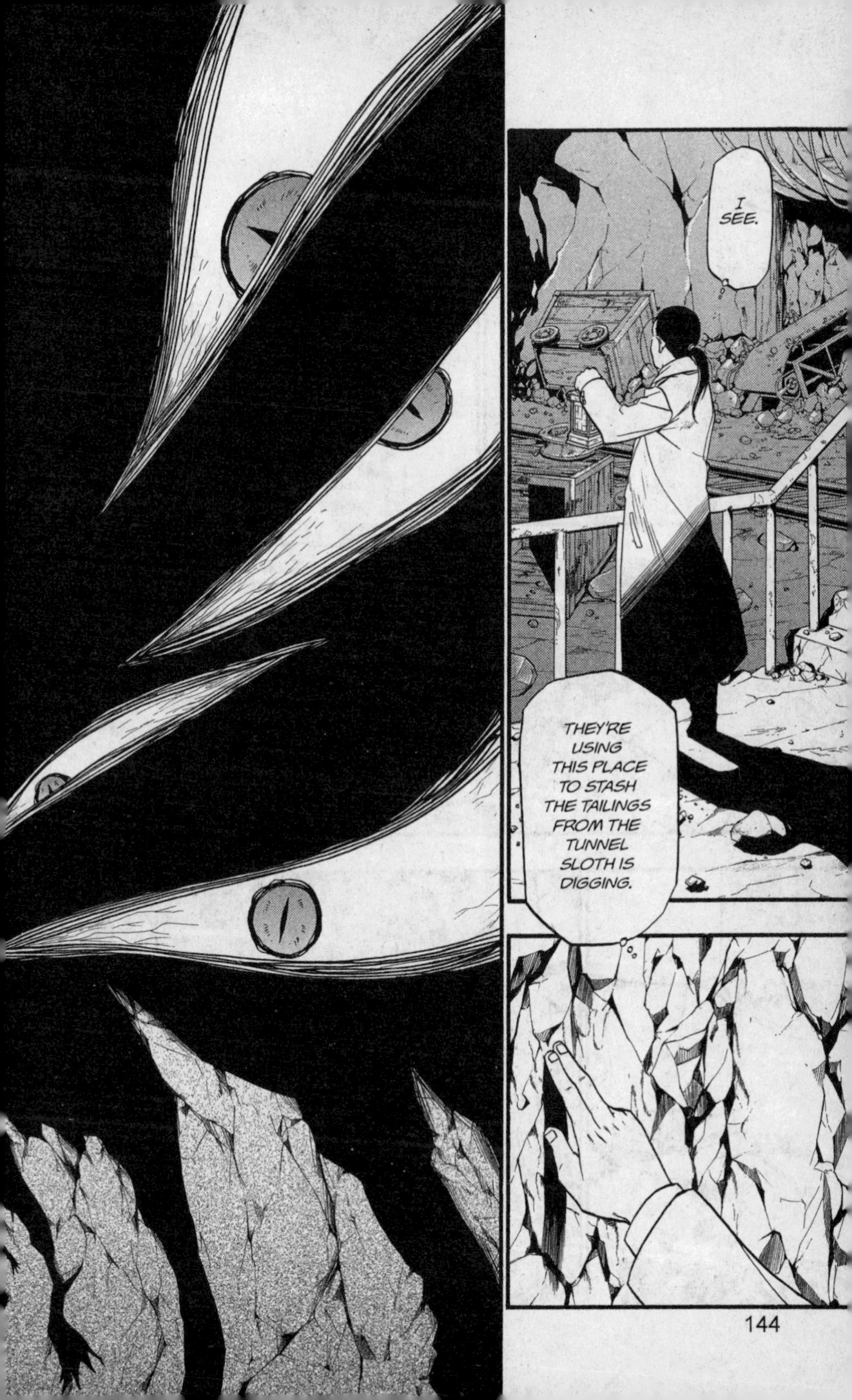
I SEE.
THEY'RE USING THIS PLACE TO STASH THE TAILINGS FROM THE TUNNEL SLOTH IS DIGGING.

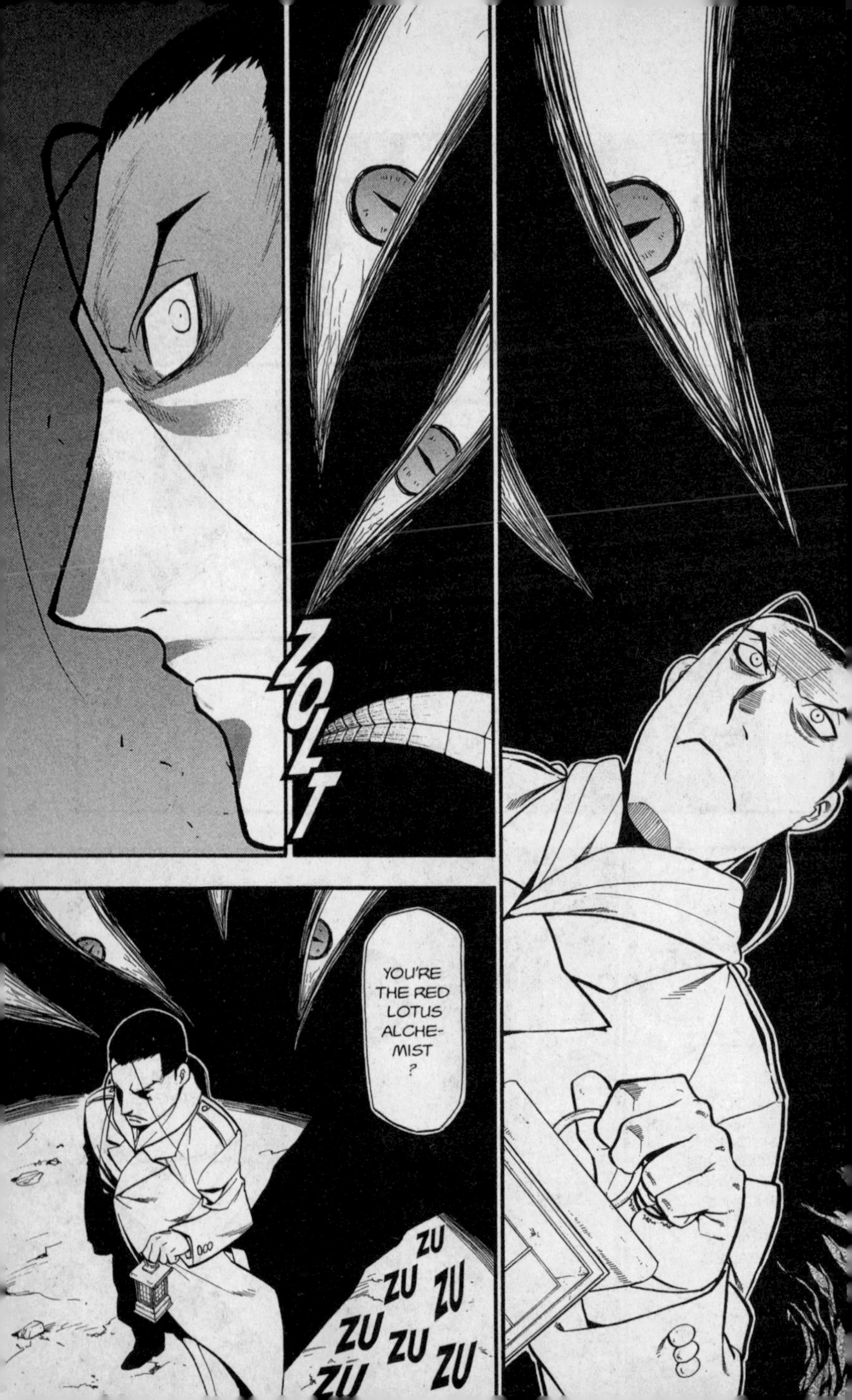
ZOLT
YOU'RE THE RED LOTUS ALCHE-MIST ?
ZU ZU ZU ZU ZU ZU ZU ZU ZU

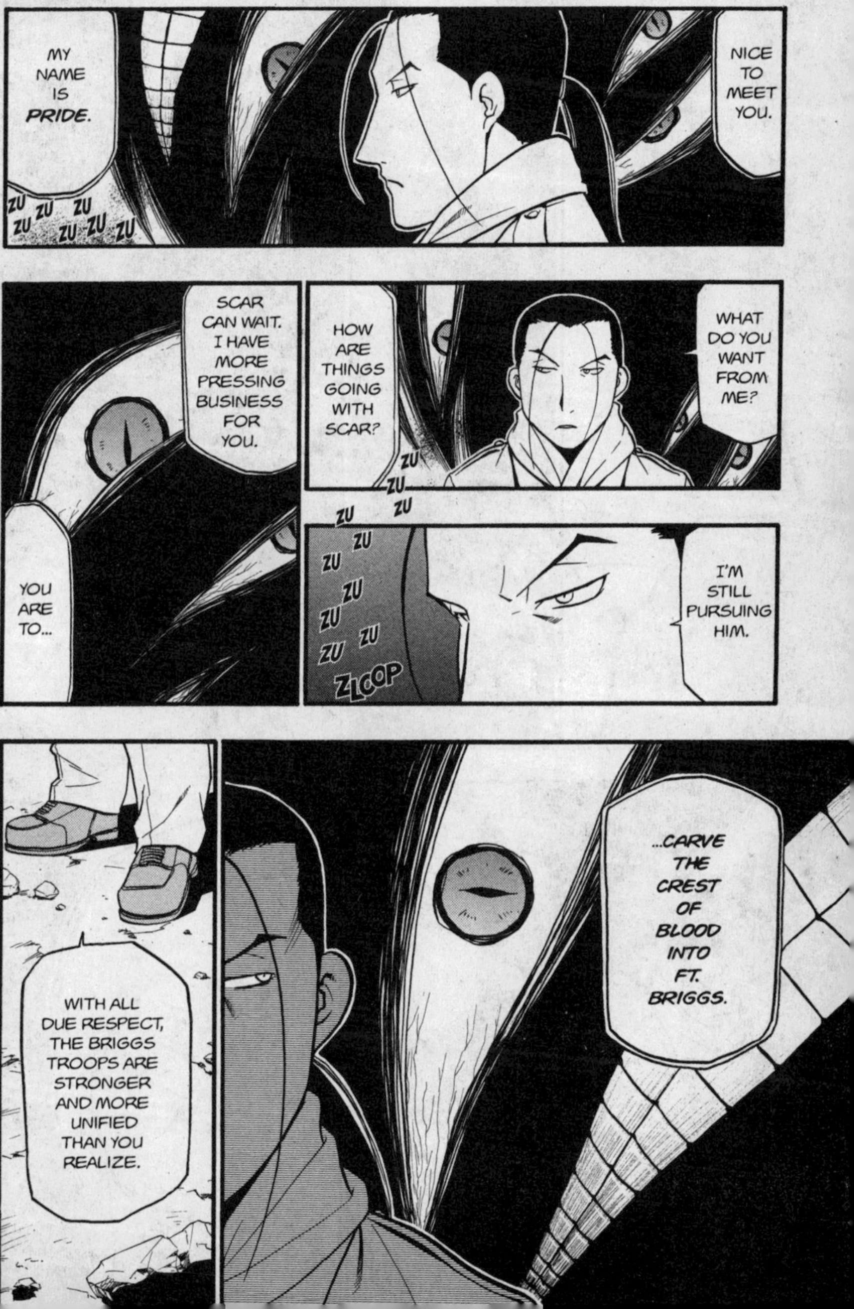
NICE TO MEET YOU.
MY NAME IS PRIDE.
ZU ZU ZU ZU ZU ZU ZU
WHAT DO YOU WANT FROM ME?
HOW ARE THINGS GOING WITH SCAR?
ZU ZU ZU
I'M STILL PURSUING HIM.
ZU ZU ZU ZU ZU ZU ZU ZU
ZLOOP
SCAR CAN WAIT. I HAVE MORE PRESSING BUSINESS FOR YOU.
YOU ARE TO...
...CARVE THE CREST OF BLOOD INTO FT. BRIGGS.
WITH ALL DUE RESPECT, THE BRIGGS TROOPS ARE STRONGER AND MORE UNIFIED THAN YOU REALIZE.

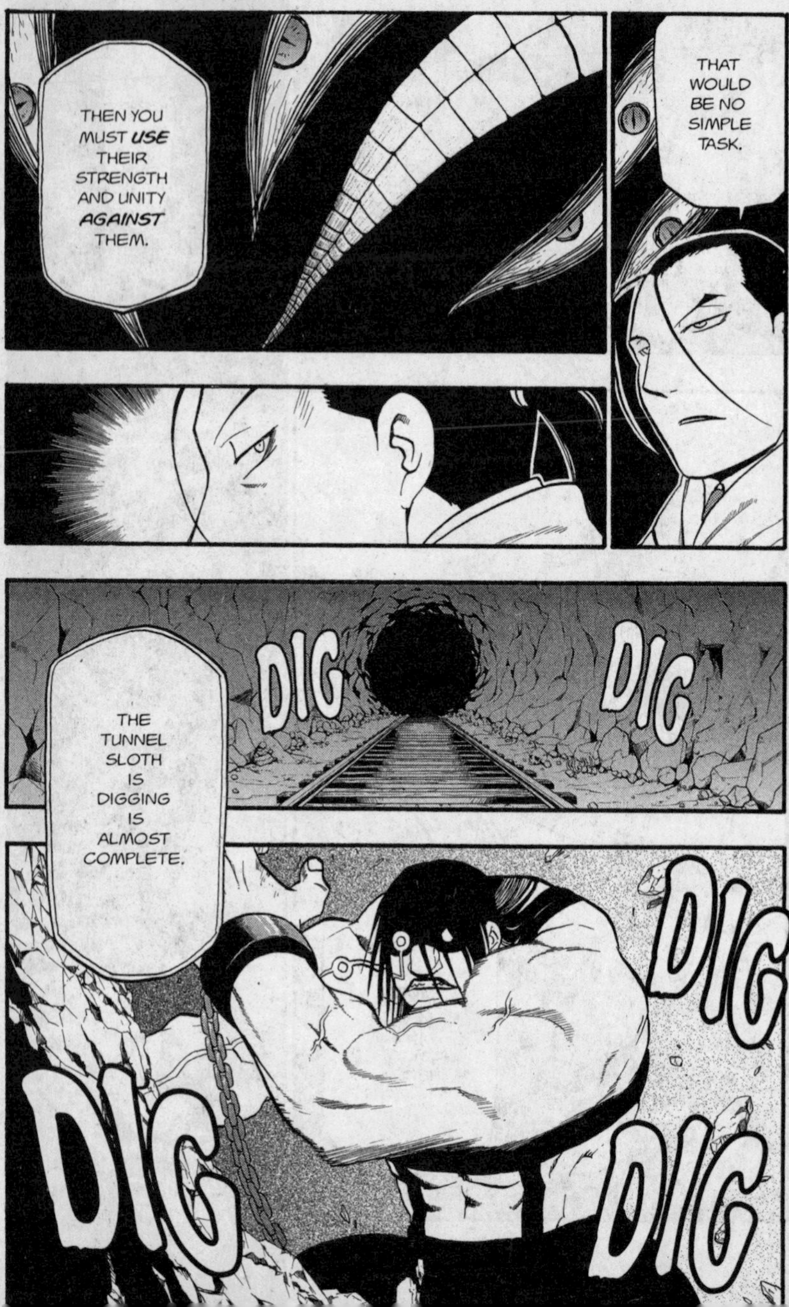
THAT WOULD BE NO SIMPLE TASK.
THEN YOU MUST *USE* THEIR STRENGTH AND UNITY *AGAINST* THEM.
DIG
DIG
THE TUNNEL SLOTH IS DIGGING IS ALMOST COMPLETE.
DIG
DIG
DIG
DIG

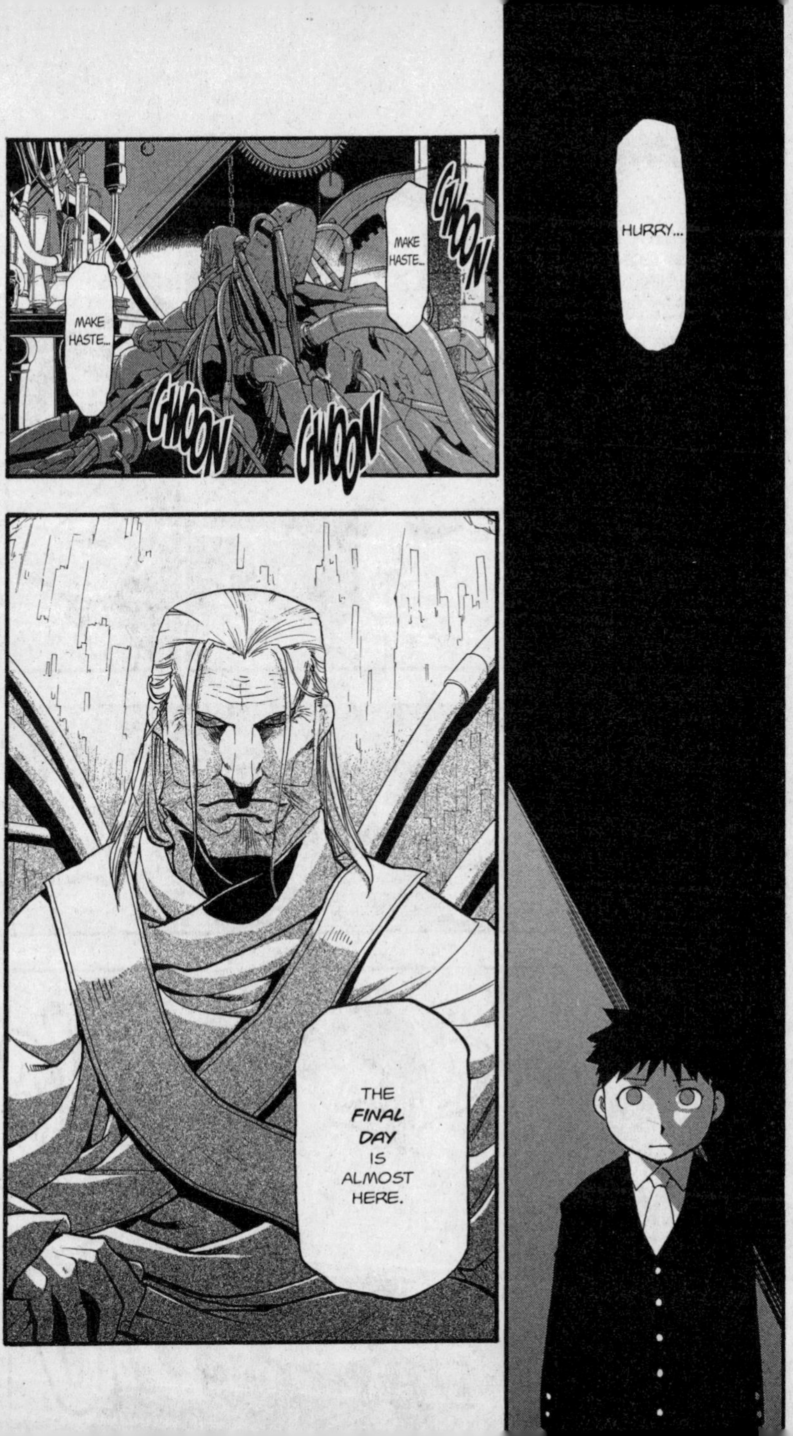
HURRY...
GWOON
MAKE HASTE...
MAKE HASTE...
GWOON
GWOON
THE FINAL DAY IS ALMOST HERE.

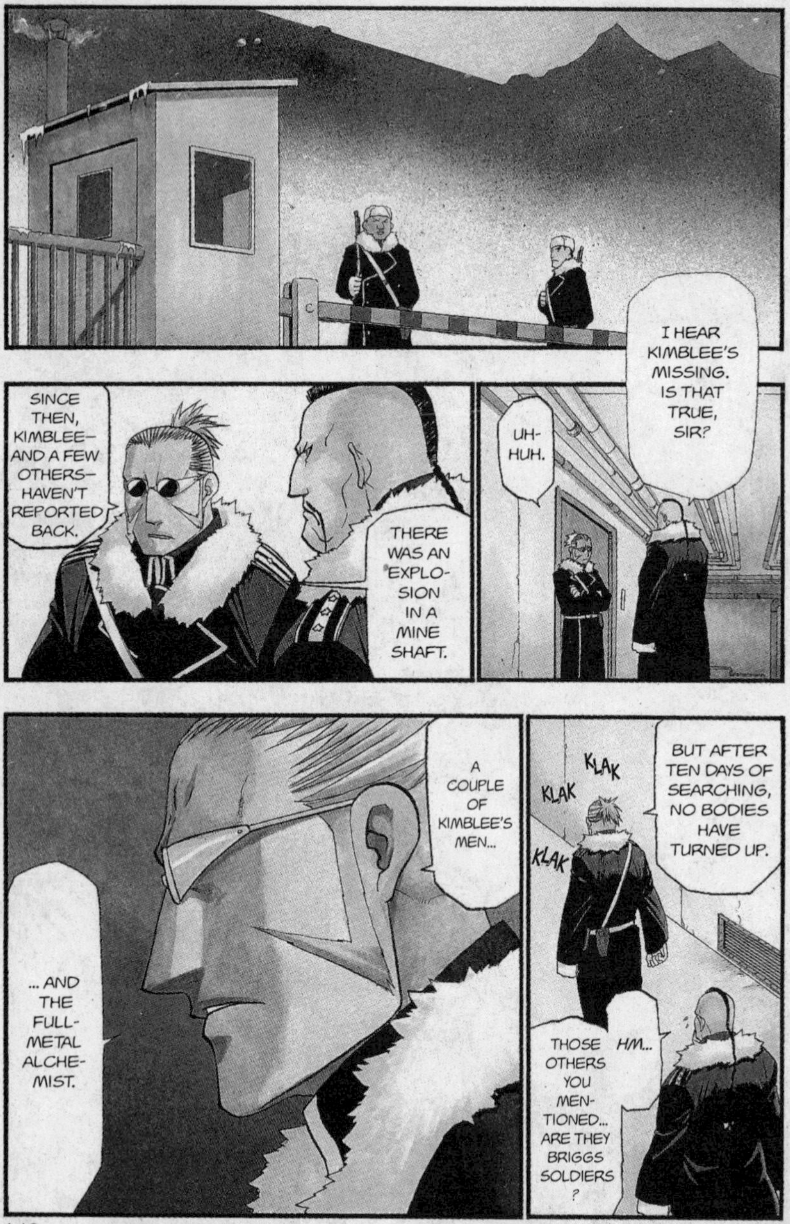
I HEAR KIMBLEE'S MISSING. IS THAT TRUE, SIR?
UH-HUH.
THERE WAS AN EXPLOSION IN A MINE SHAFT.
SINCE THEN, KIMBLEE— AND A FEW OTHERS— HAVEN'T REPORTED BACK.
BUT AFTER TEN DAYS OF SEARCHING, NO BODIES HAVE TURNED UP.
KLAK
KLAK
KLAK
HM...
THOSE OTHERS YOU MENTIONED... ARE THEY BRIGGS SOLDIERS?
A COUPLE OF KIMBLEE'S MEN...
... AND THE FULL-METAL ALCHE-MIST.

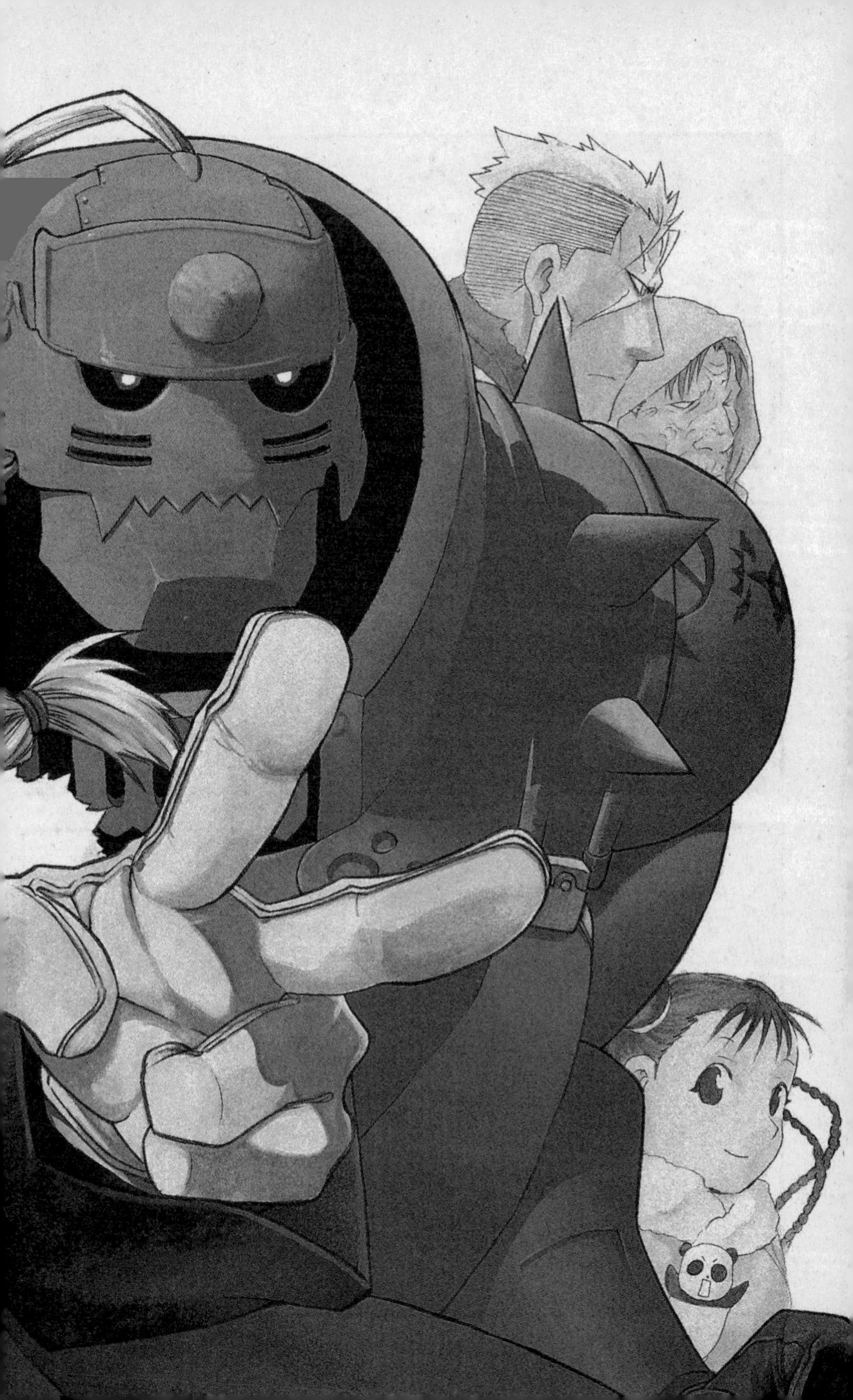

Chapter 78
The Seven Deadly Sins

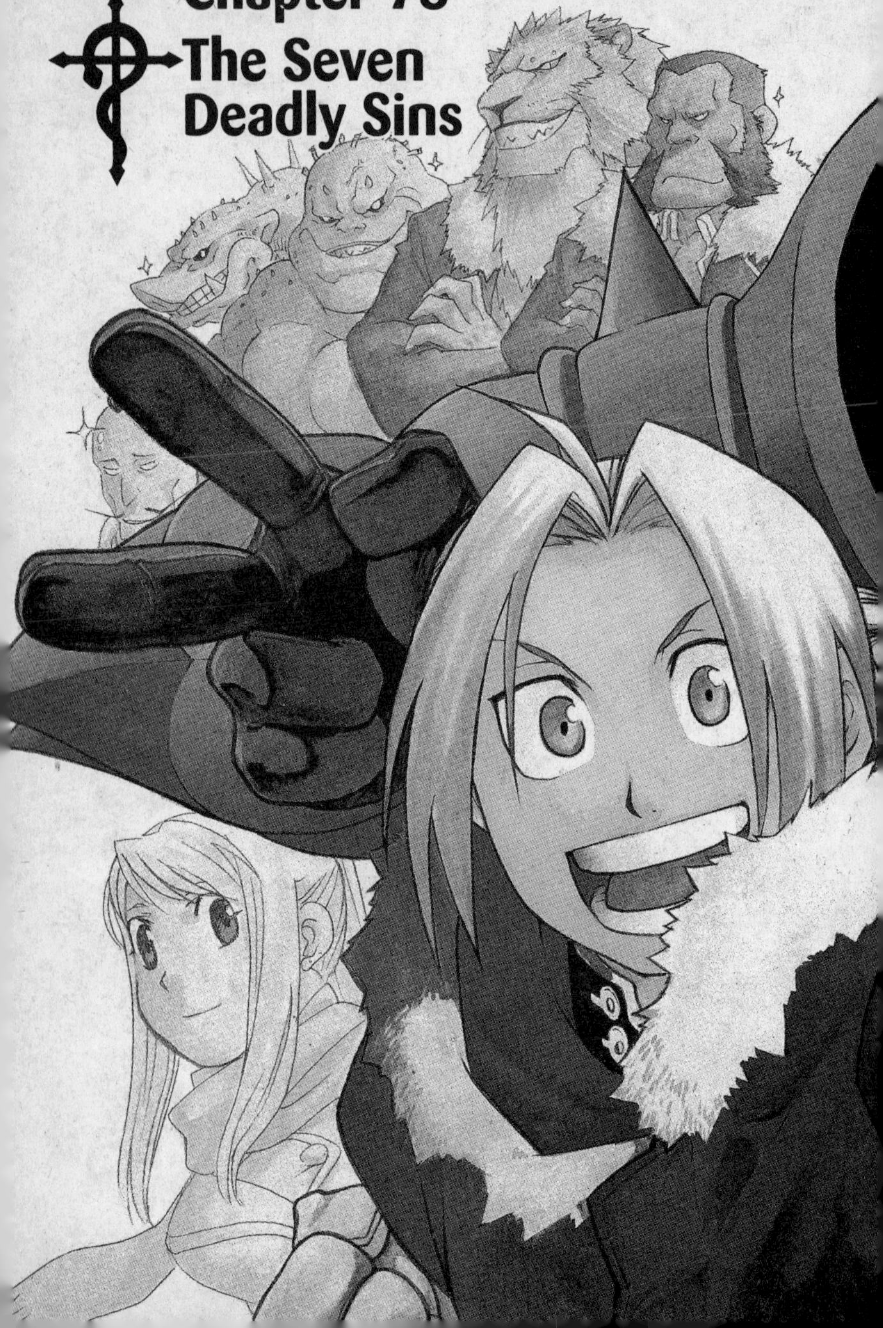

FULLMETAL
ALCHEMIST

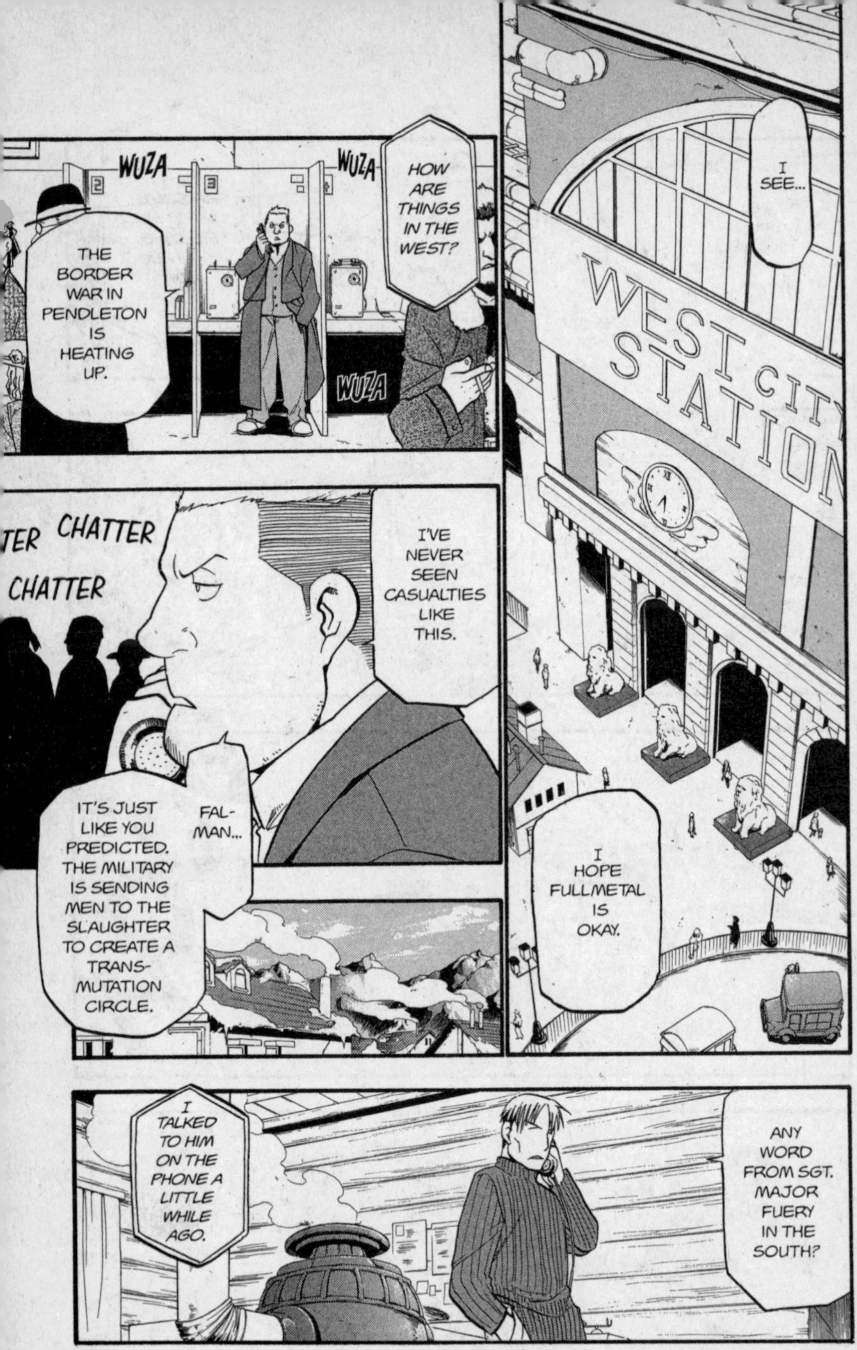
I SEE...
WEST CITY STATION
I HOPE FULLMETAL IS OKAY.
WUZA
WUZA
HOW ARE THINGS IN THE WEST?
THE BORDER WAR IN PENDLETON IS HEATING UP.
WUZA
I'VE NEVER SEEN CASUALTIES LIKE THIS.
CHATTER
CHATTER
FAL-MAN...
IT'S JUST LIKE YOU PREDICTED. THE MILITARY IS SENDING MEN TO THE SLAUGHTER TO CREATE A TRANS-MUTATION CIRCLE.
ANY WORD FROM SGT. MAJOR FUERY IN THE SOUTH?
I TALKED TO HIM ON THE PHONE A LITTLE WHILE AGO.

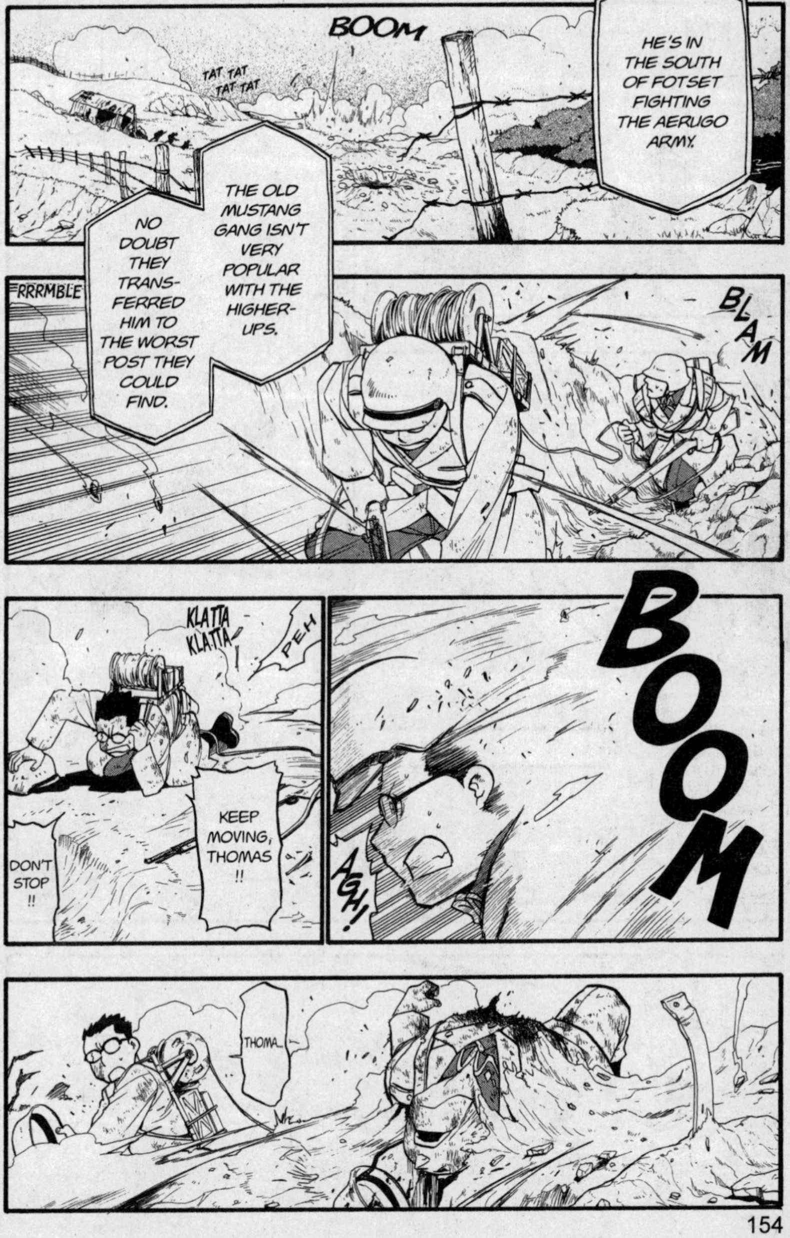
HE'S IN THE SOUTH OF FOTSET FIGHTING THE AERUGO ARMY.
BOOM
TAT TAT TAT TAT
THE OLD MUSTANG GANG ISN'T VERY POPULAR WITH THE HIGHER-UPS.
NO DOUBT THEY TRANS-FERRED HIM TO THE WORST POST THEY COULD FIND.
BLAM
RRRMBLE
BOOM
AGH!
KLATTA KLATTA
PEH
KEEP MOVING, THOMAS !!
DON'T STOP !!
THOMA...

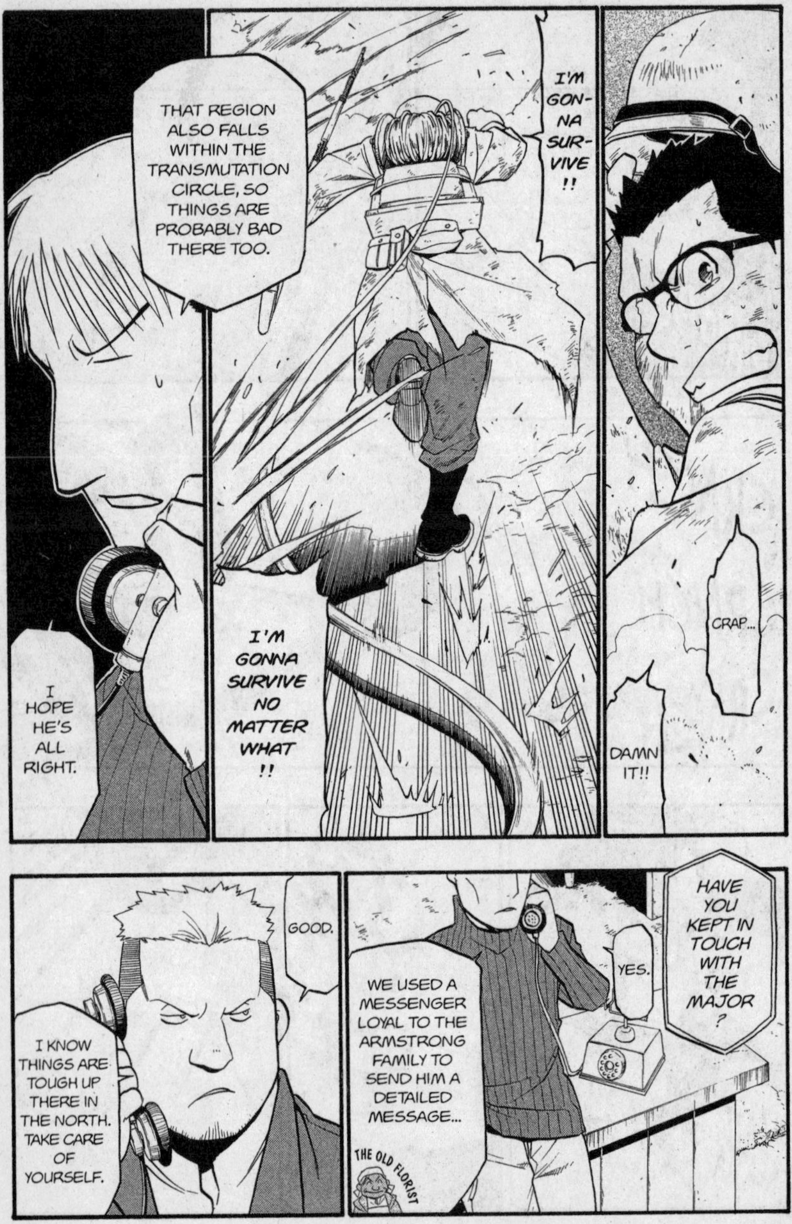
CRAP...
DAMN IT!!
I'M GONNA SURVIVE!!
I'M GONNA SURVIVE NO MATTER WHAT!!
THAT REGION ALSO FALLS WITHIN THE TRANSMUTATION CIRCLE, SO THINGS ARE PROBABLY BAD THERE TOO.
I HOPE HE'S ALL RIGHT.
HAVE YOU KEPT IN TOUCH WITH THE MAJOR?
YES.
WE USED A MESSENGER LOYAL TO THE ARMSTRONG FAMILY TO SEND HIM A DETAILED MESSAGE...
THE OLD FLORIST
GOOD.
I KNOW THINGS ARE TOUGH UP THERE IN THE NORTH. TAKE CARE OF YOURSELF.

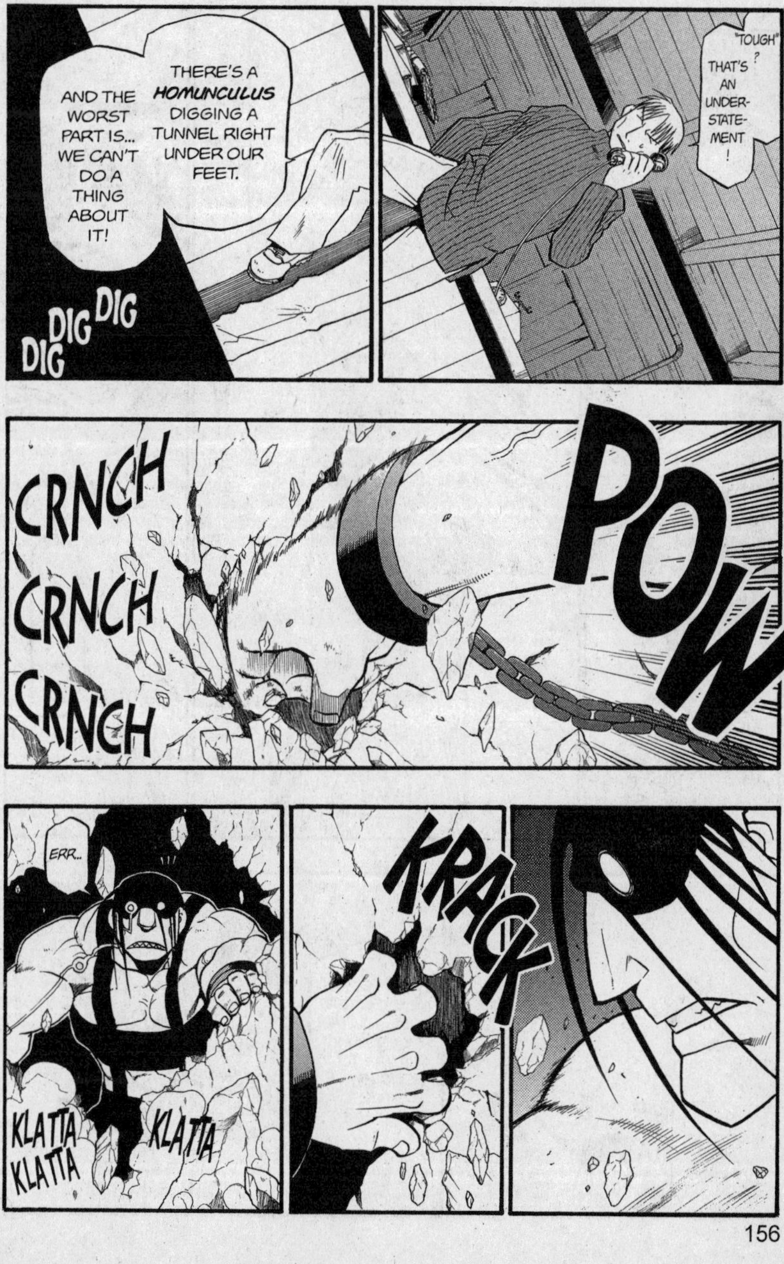
"TOUGH"? THAT'S AN UNDER-STATE-MENT!
THERE'S A **HOMUNCULUS** DIGGING A TUNNEL RIGHT UNDER OUR FEET.
AND THE WORST PART IS... WE CAN'T DO A THING ABOUT IT!
DIG DIG DIG
POW
CRNCH CRNCH CRNCH
KRACK
ERR..
KLATTA KLATTA KLATTA

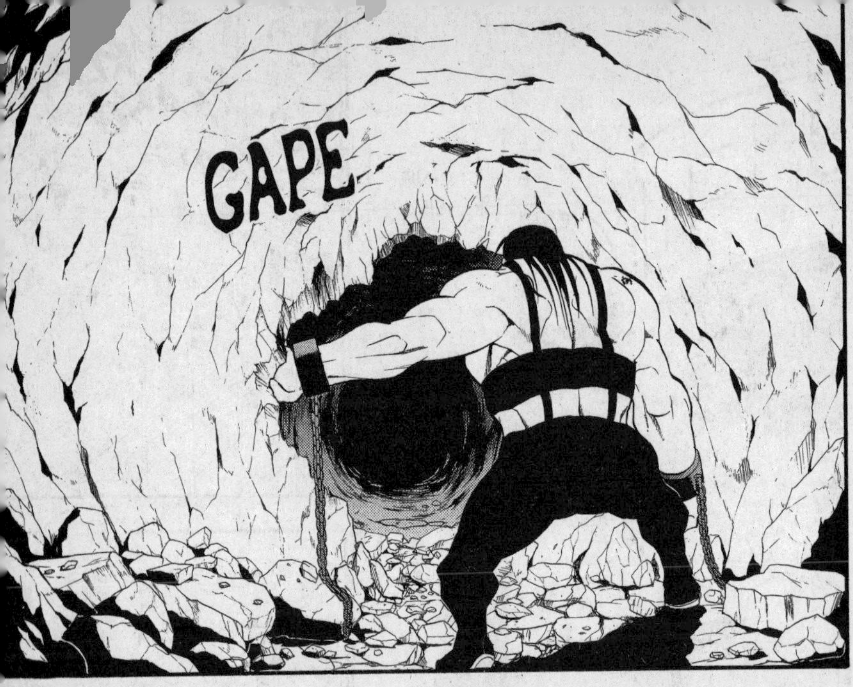
GAPE

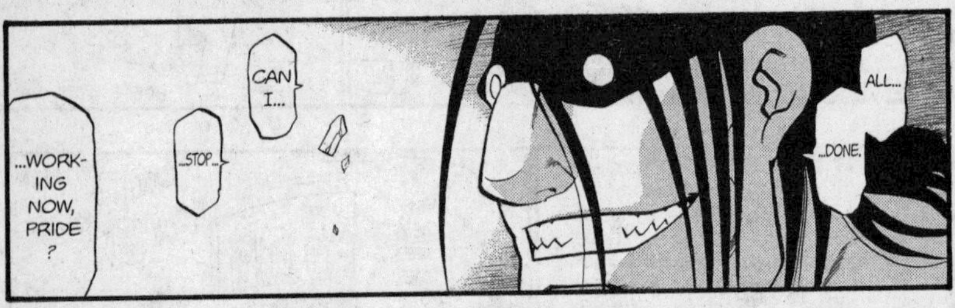
ALL...
...DONE.
CAN I...
...STOP...
...WORKING NOW, PRIDE?

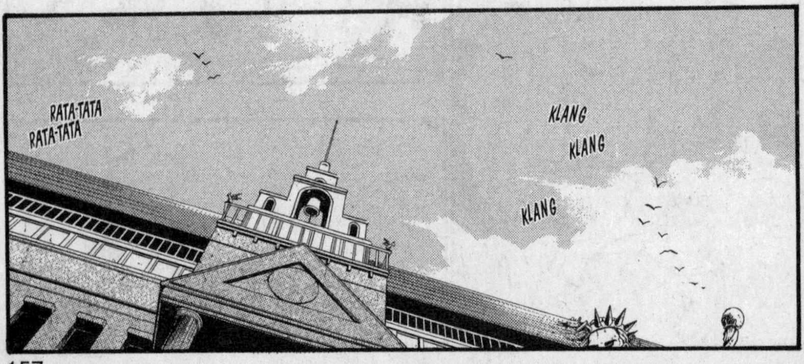
KLANG
KLANG
KLANG
RATA-TATA
RATA-TATA

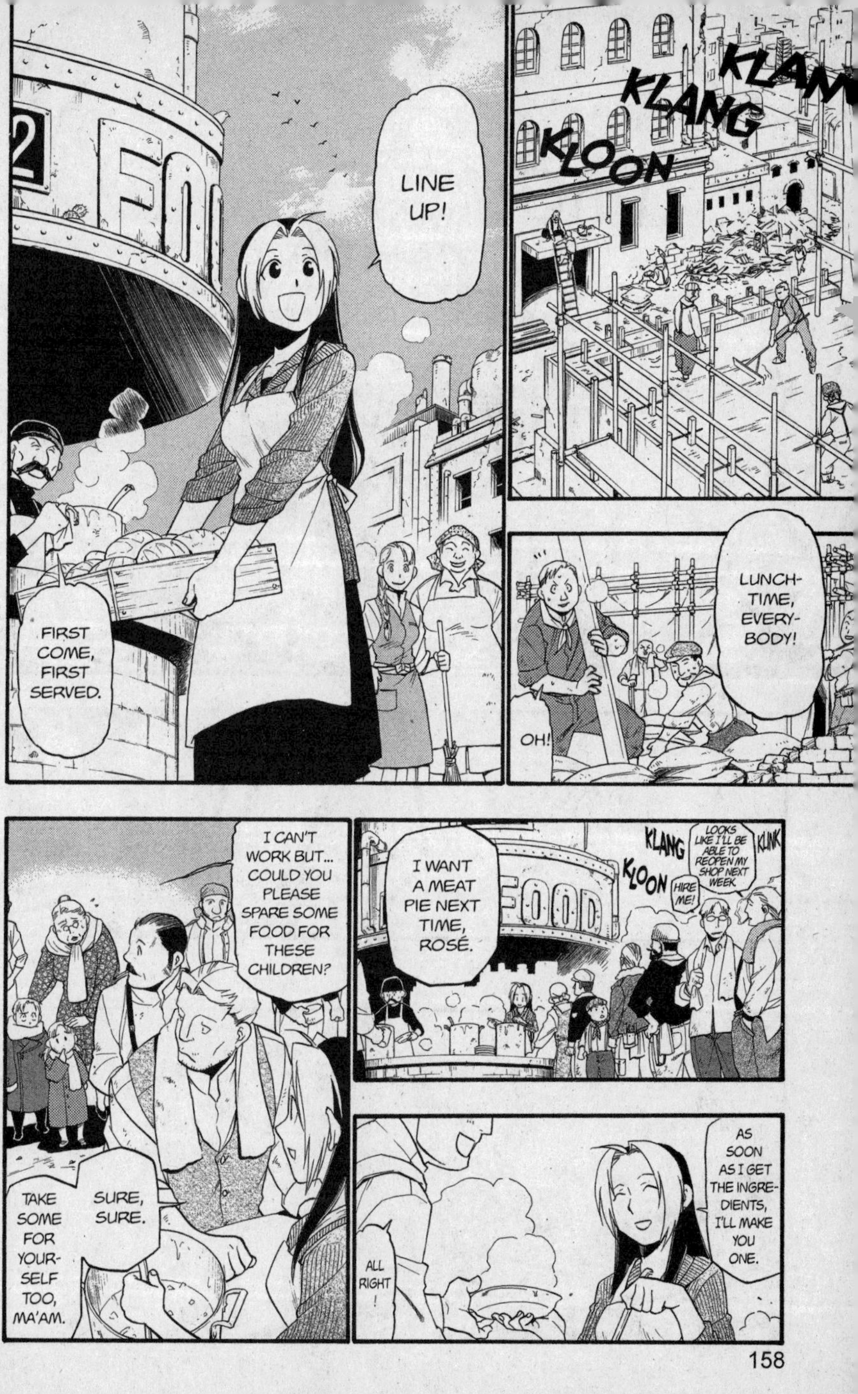
KLAM
KLANG
KLOON
LUNCH-TIME, EVERY-BODY!
OH!
LINE UP!
FIRST COME, FIRST SERVED.
KLUNK
LOOKS LIKE I'LL BE ABLE TO REOPEN MY SHOP NEXT WEEK.
KLANG
HIRE ME!
KLOON
I WANT A MEAT PIE NEXT TIME, ROSÉ.
AS SOON AS I GET THE INGRE-DIENTS, I'LL MAKE YOU ONE.
ALL RIGHT!
I CAN'T WORK BUT... COULD YOU PLEASE SPARE SOME FOOD FOR THESE CHILDREN?
SURE, SURE.
TAKE SOME FOR YOUR-SELF TOO, MA'AM.

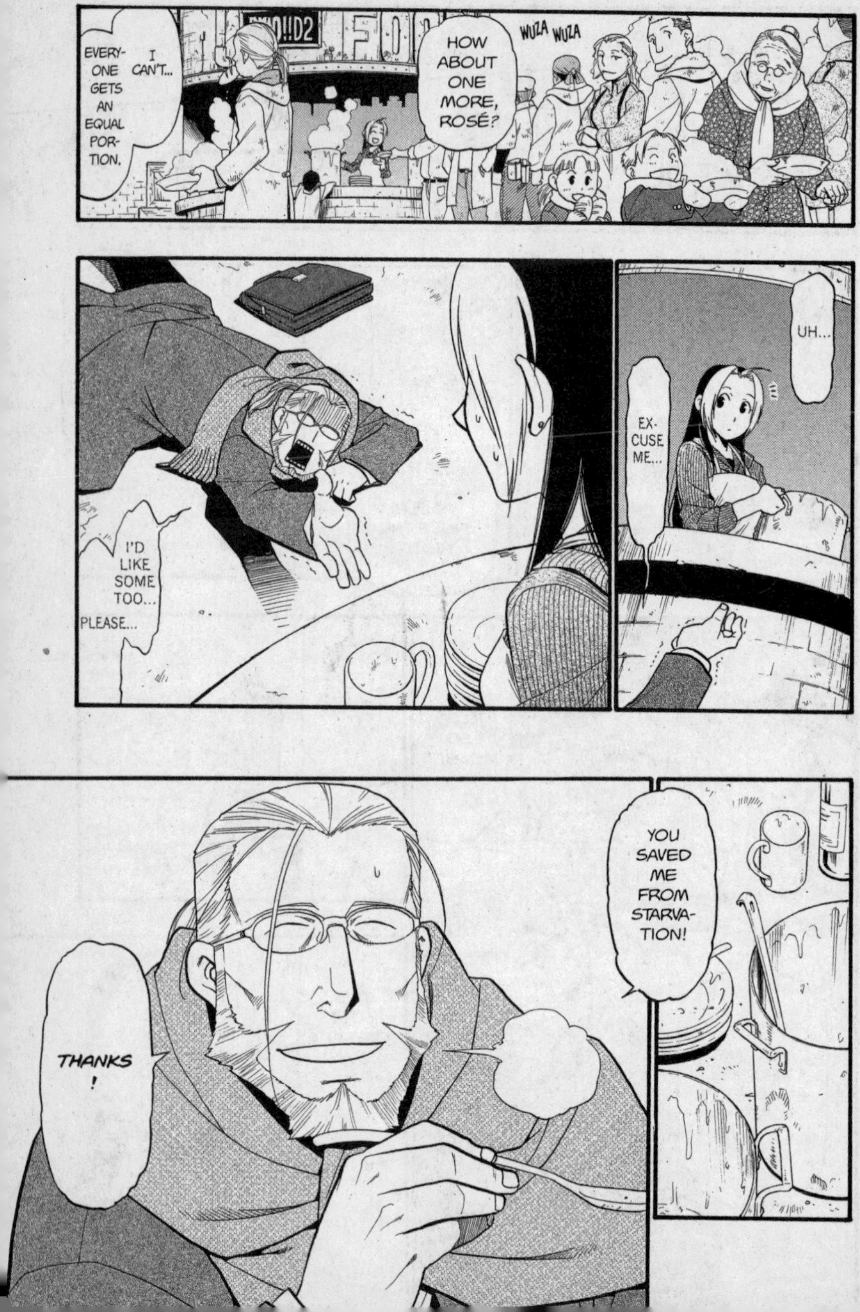
WUZA WUZA
HOW ABOUT ONE MORE, ROSÉ?
I CAN'T...
EVERYONE GETS AN EQUAL PORTION.
UH...
EXCUSE ME...
I'D LIKE SOME TOO... PLEASE...
YOU SAVED ME FROM STARVATION!
THANKS!

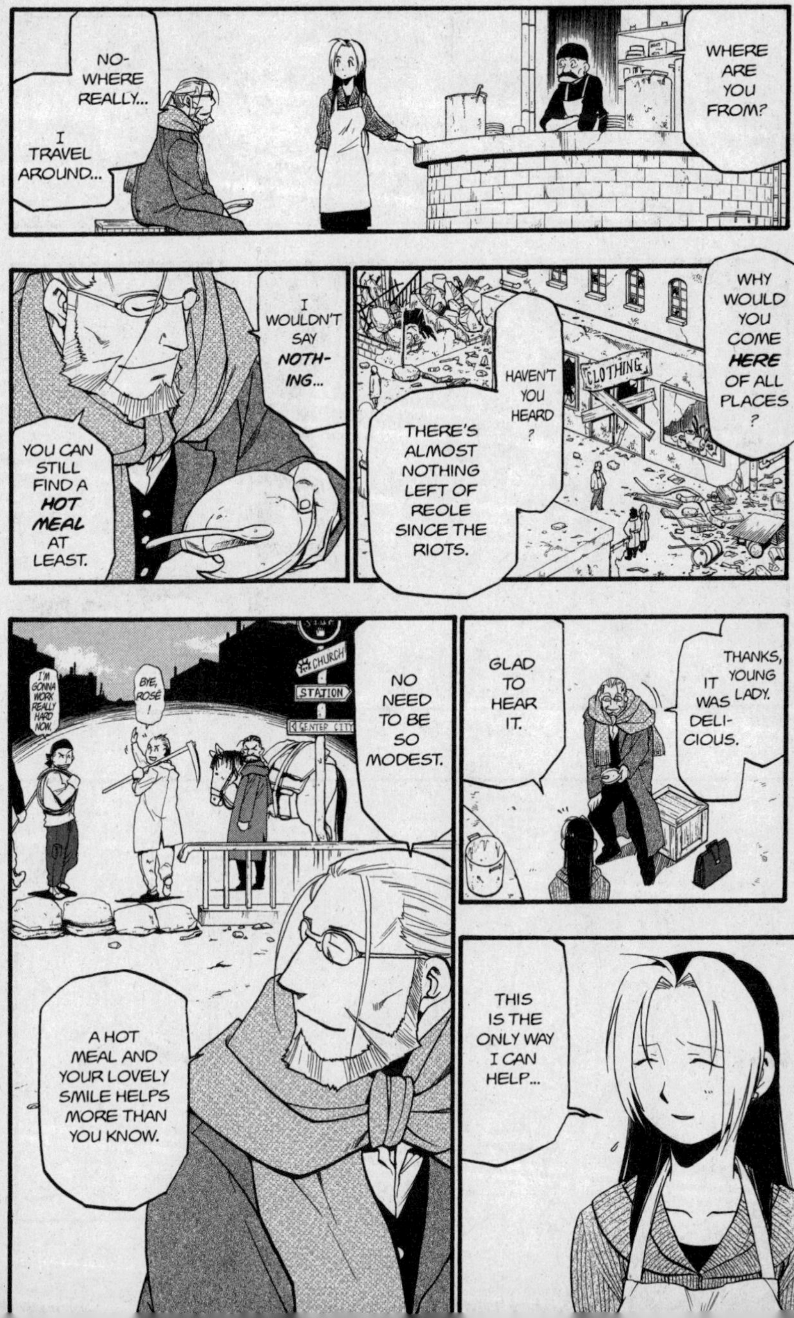
WHERE ARE YOU FROM?
NO-WHERE REALLY...
I TRAVEL AROUND...
WHY WOULD YOU COME HERE OF ALL PLACES?
CLOTHING
HAVEN'T YOU HEARD?
THERE'S ALMOST NOTHING LEFT OF REOLE SINCE THE RIOTS.
I WOULDN'T SAY NOTHING...
YOU CAN STILL FIND A HOT MEAL AT LEAST.
THANKS, YOUNG LADY.
IT WAS DELICIOUS.
GLAD TO HEAR IT.
THIS IS THE ONLY WAY I CAN HELP...
NO NEED TO BE SO MODEST.
CHURCH
STATION
CENTER CITY
BYE, ROSÉ!
I'M GONNA WORK REALLY HARD NOW.
A HOT MEAL AND YOUR LOVELY SMILE HELPS MORE THAN YOU KNOW.

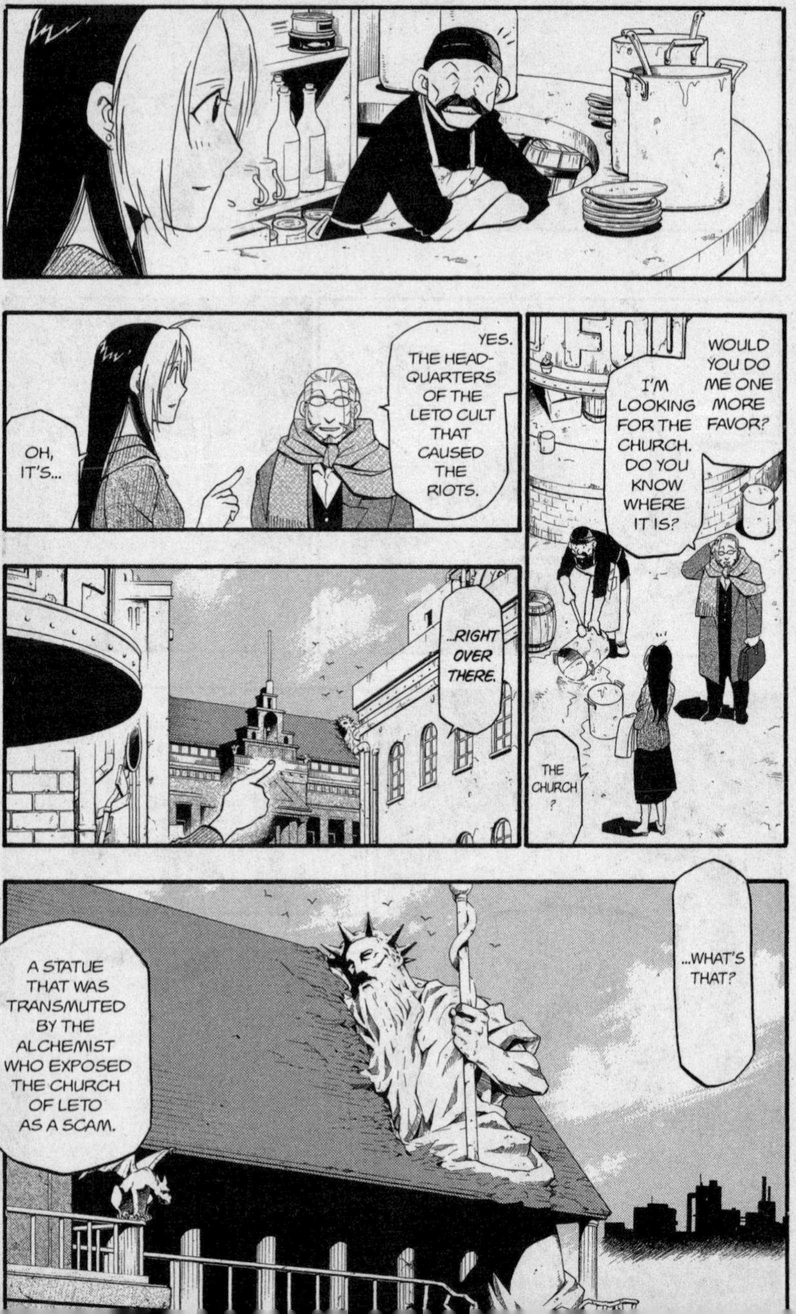
WOULD YOU DO ME ONE MORE FAVOR?
I'M LOOKING FOR THE CHURCH. DO YOU KNOW WHERE IT IS?
THE CHURCH?
YES. THE HEAD-QUARTERS OF THE LETO CULT THAT CAUSED THE RIOTS.
OH, IT'S...
...RIGHT OVER THERE.
...WHAT'S THAT?
A STATUE THAT WAS TRANSMUTED BY THE ALCHEMIST WHO EXPOSED THE CHURCH OF LETO AS A SCAM.

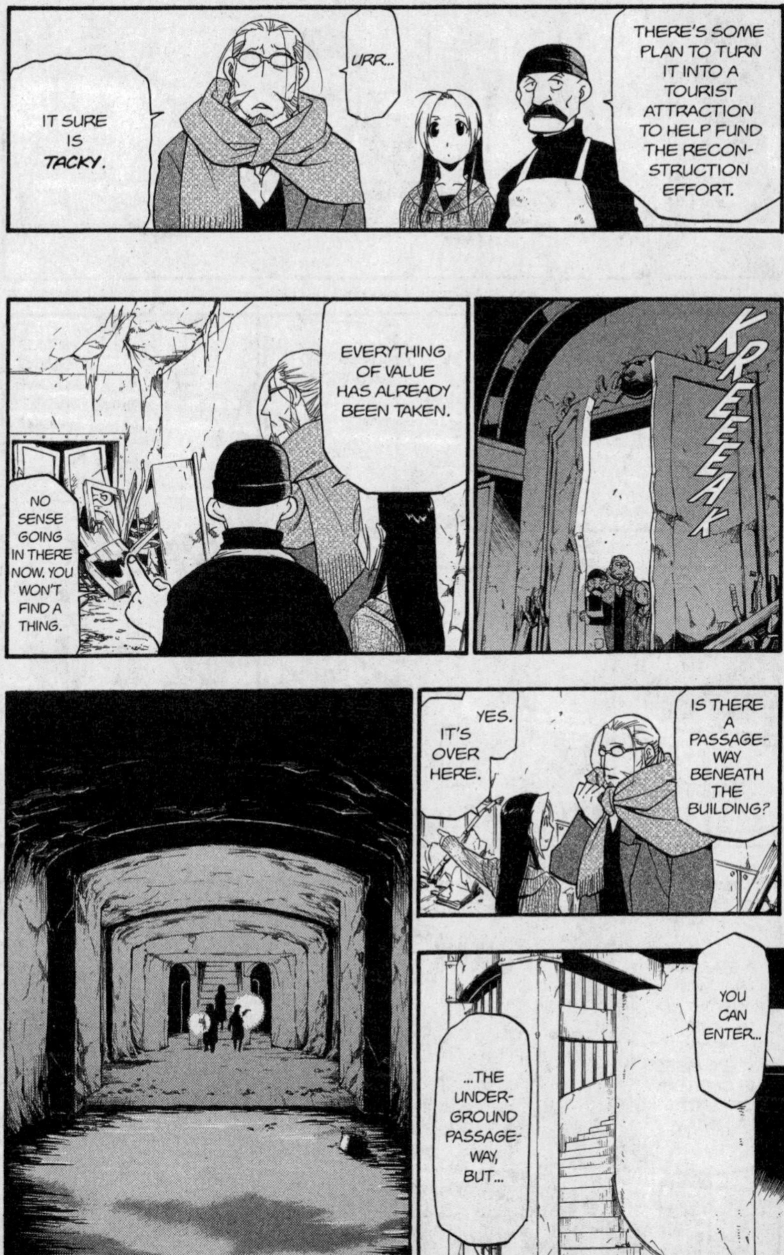
THERE'S SOME PLAN TO TURN IT INTO A TOURIST ATTRACTION TO HELP FUND THE RECON-STRUCTION EFFORT.
URR...
IT SURE IS *TACKY*.
KREEEAK
EVERYTHING OF VALUE HAS ALREADY BEEN TAKEN.
NO SENSE GOING IN THERE NOW. YOU WON'T FIND A THING.
IS THERE A PASSAGE-WAY BENEATH THE BUILDING?
YES. IT'S OVER HERE.
YOU CAN ENTER...
...THE UNDER-GROUND PASSAGE-WAY, BUT...

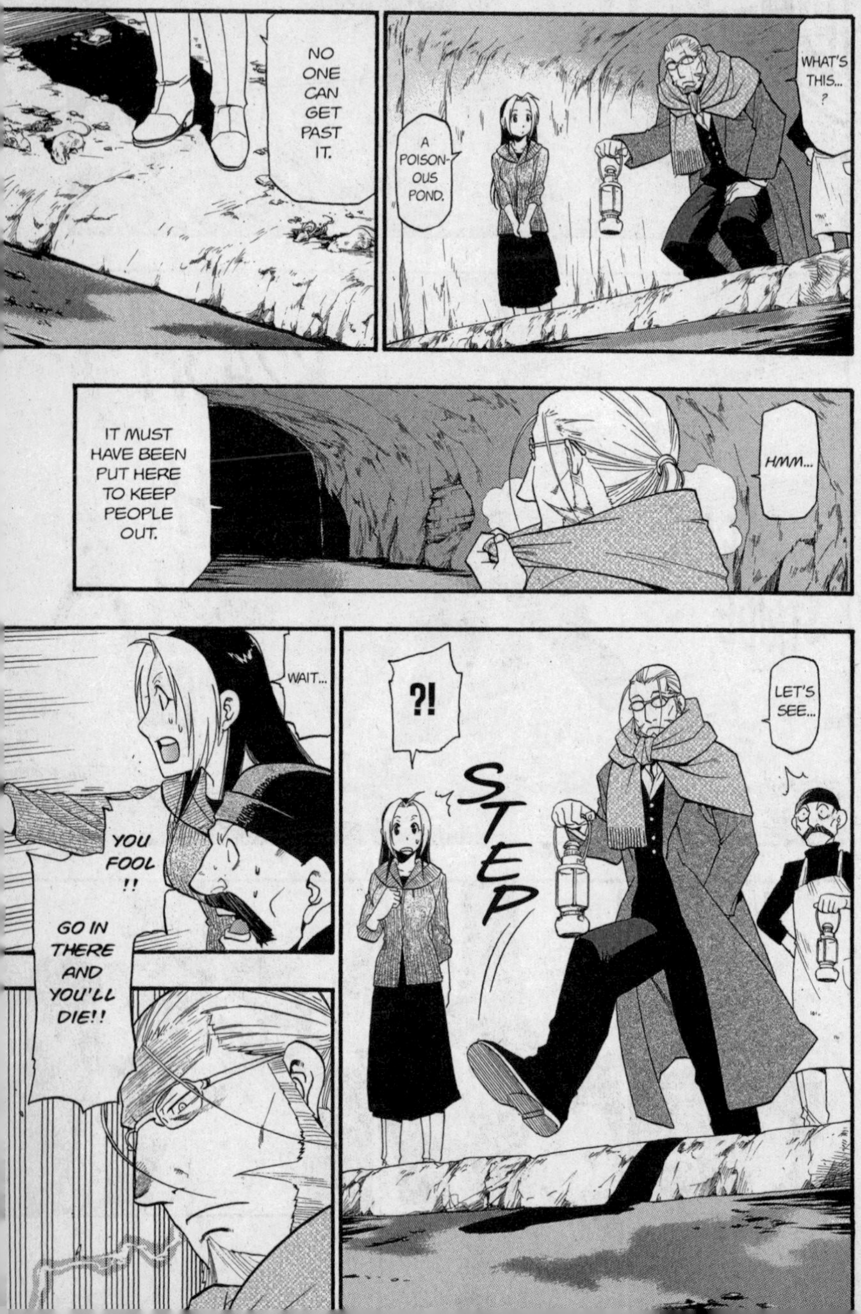
WHAT'S THIS... ?
A POISON-OUS POND.
NO ONE CAN GET PAST IT.
HMM...
IT MUST HAVE BEEN PUT HERE TO KEEP PEOPLE OUT.
LET'S SEE...
?!
STEP
WAIT...
YOU FOOL!!
GO IN THERE AND YOU'LL DIE!!

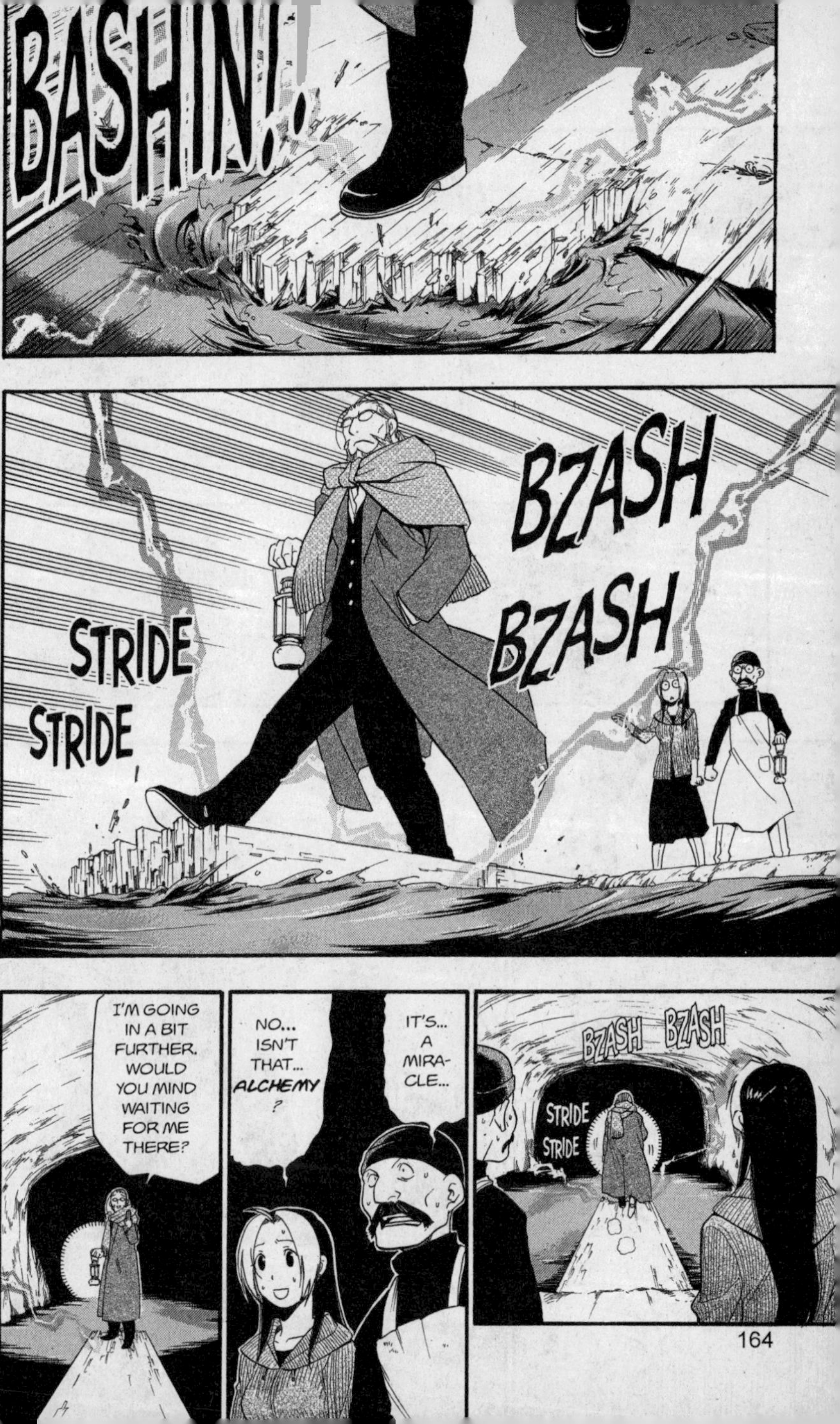
BASHIN!!
BZASH BZASH
STRIDE STRIDE
BZASH BZASH
STRIDE STRIDE
IT'S... A MIRA-CLE...
NO... ISN'T THAT... ALCHEMY?
I'M GOING IN A BIT FURTHER. WOULD YOU MIND WAITING FOR ME THERE?

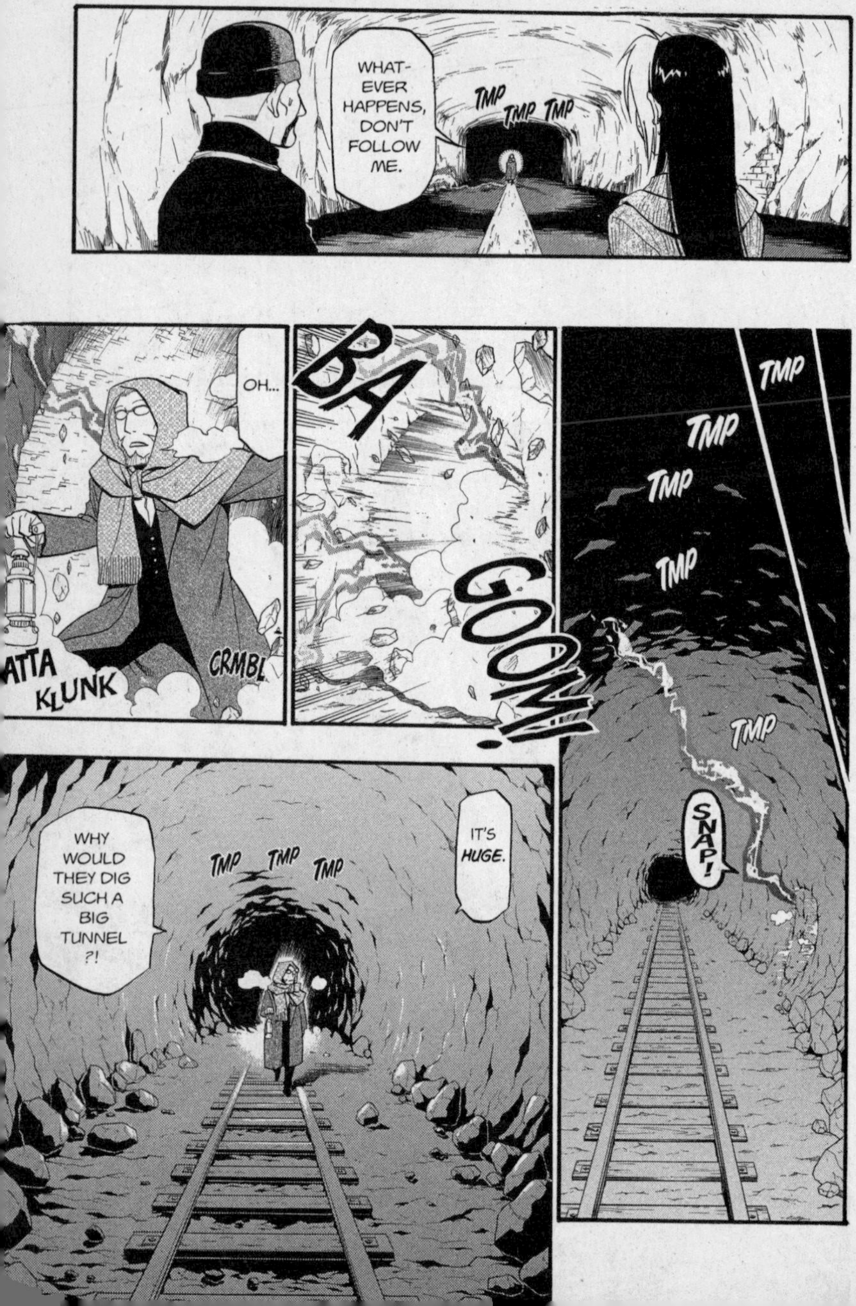
WHAT-EVER HAPPENS, DON'T FOLLOW ME.
TMP TMP TMP
TMP
TMP
TMP
TMP
TMP
SNAP!
BA
GOOM!
OH...
CRMBL
ATTA KLUNK
IT'S HUGE.
TMP TMP TMP
WHY WOULD THEY DIG SUCH A BIG TUNNEL?!

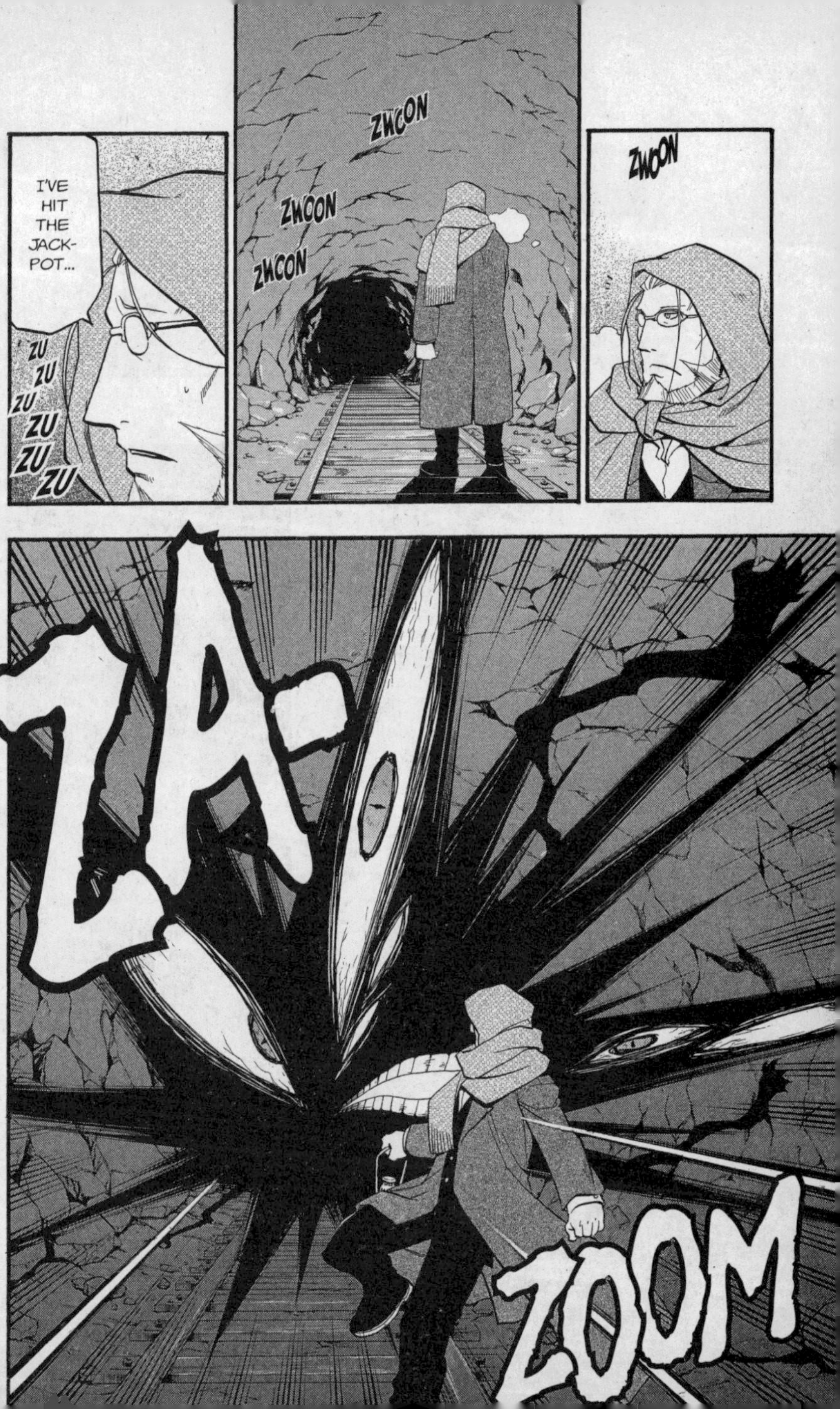
ZWOON
ZWOON
ZWOON
ZWOON
I'VE HIT THE JACK-POT...
ZU ZU ZU ZU ZU ZU
ZA
ZOOM

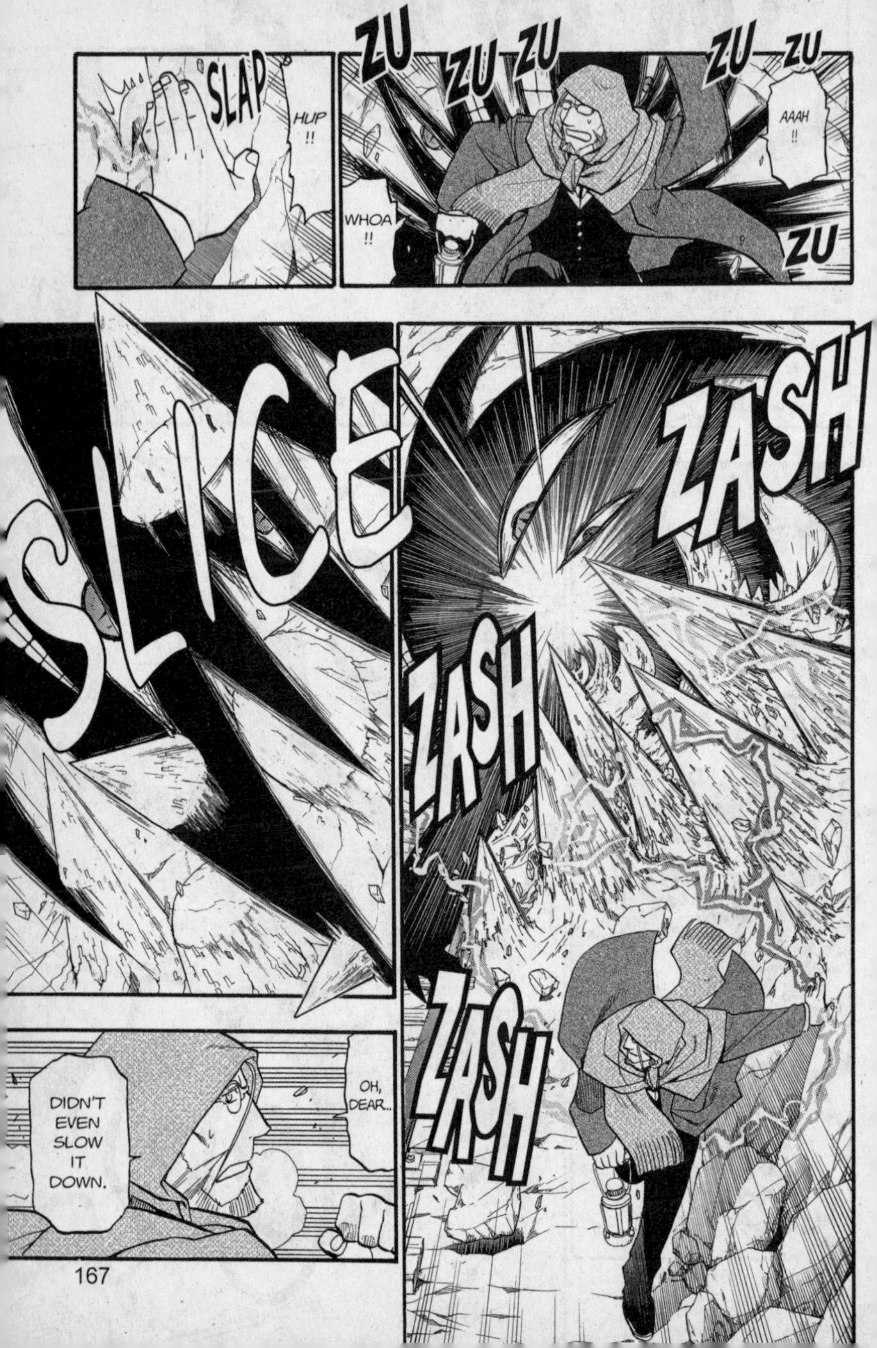
ZU
ZU ZU
ZU ZU
AAAH!!
WHOA!!
ZU
SLAP
HUP!!
ZASH
ZASH
ZASH
SLICE
OH, DEAR...
DIDN'T EVEN SLOW IT DOWN.

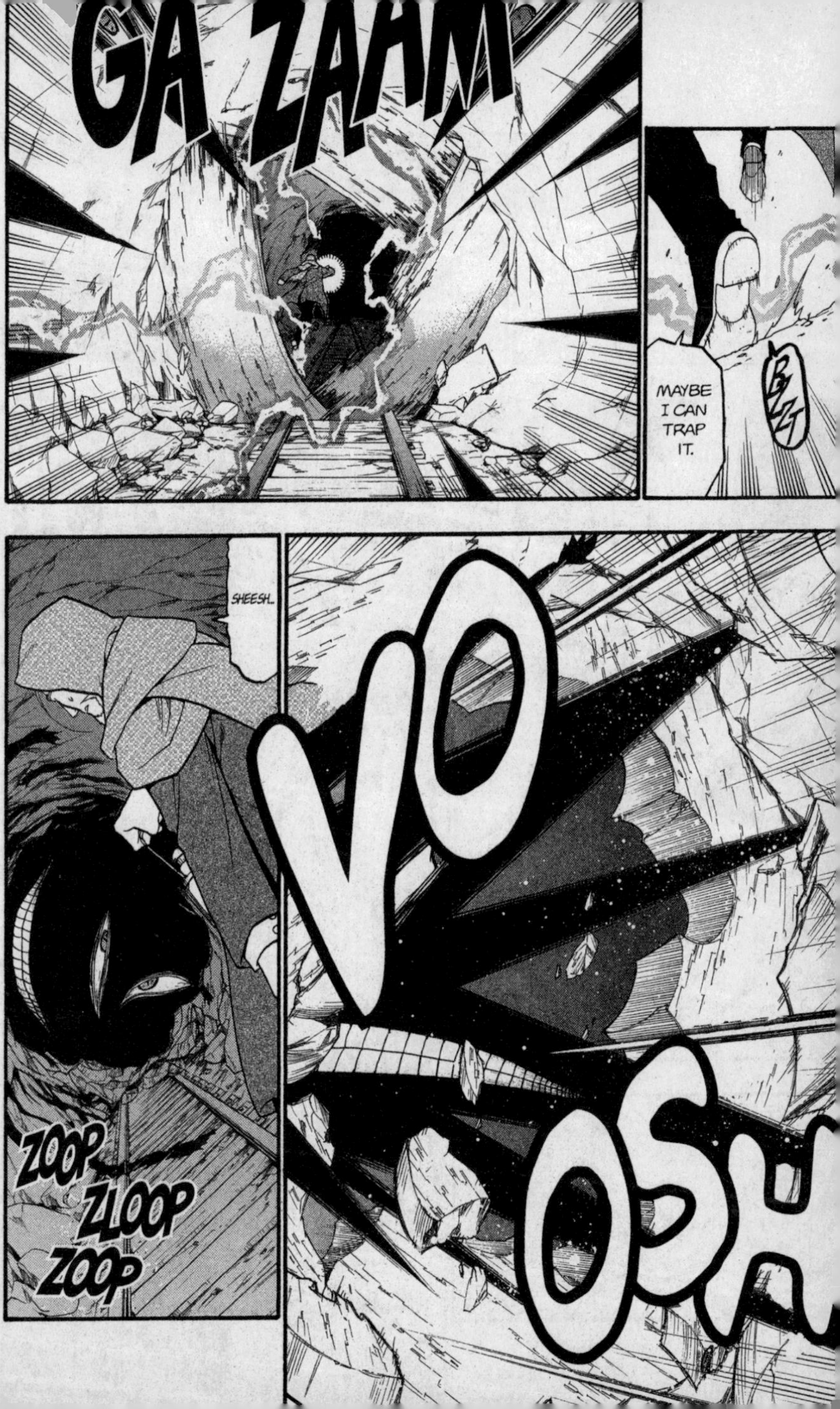

BZZT
MAYBE I CAN TRAP IT.
GA ZAAM
VOOOSH
SHEESH.
ZOOP
ZLOOP
ZOOP

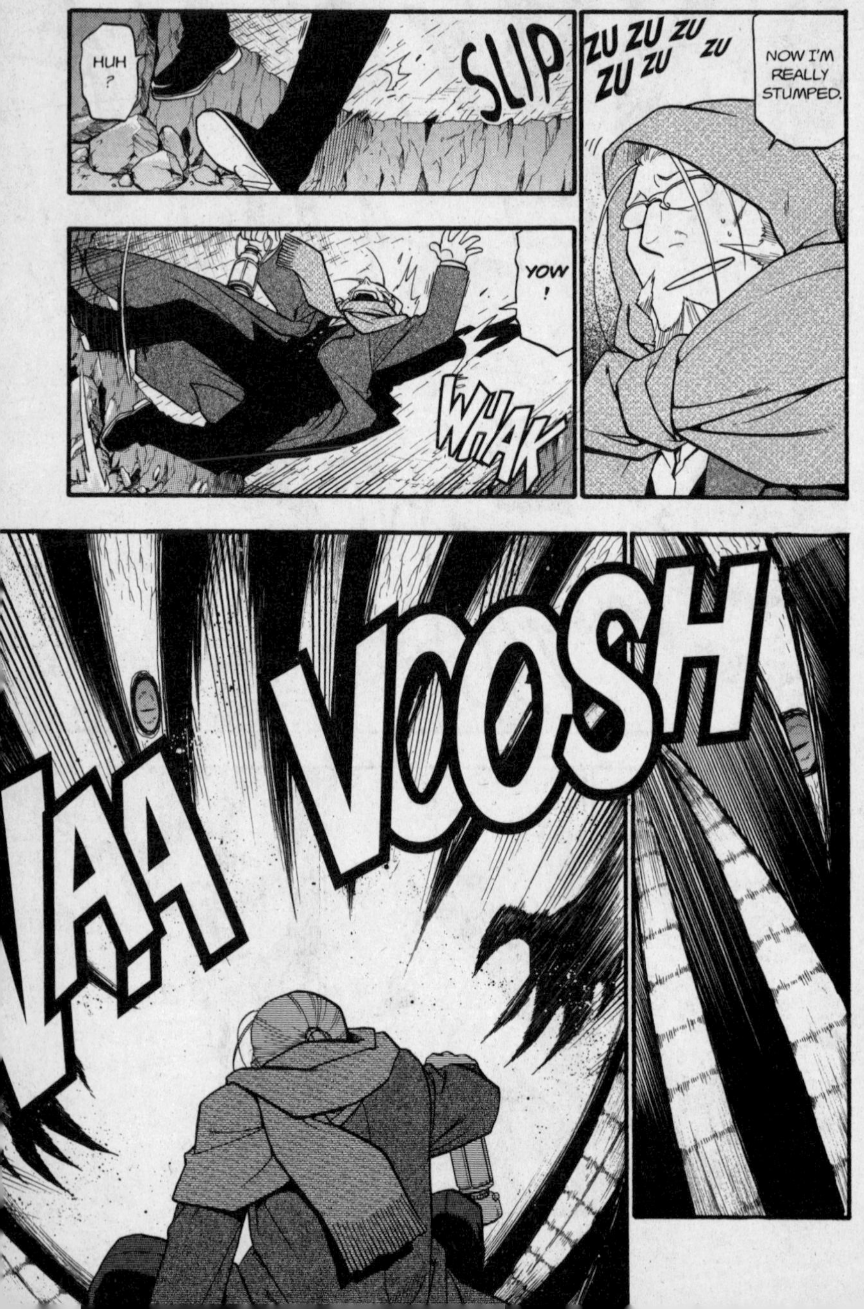
ZU ZU ZU ZU ZU ZU
NOW I'M REALLY STUMPED.
HUH ?
SLIP
YOW !
WHAK
VOOSH

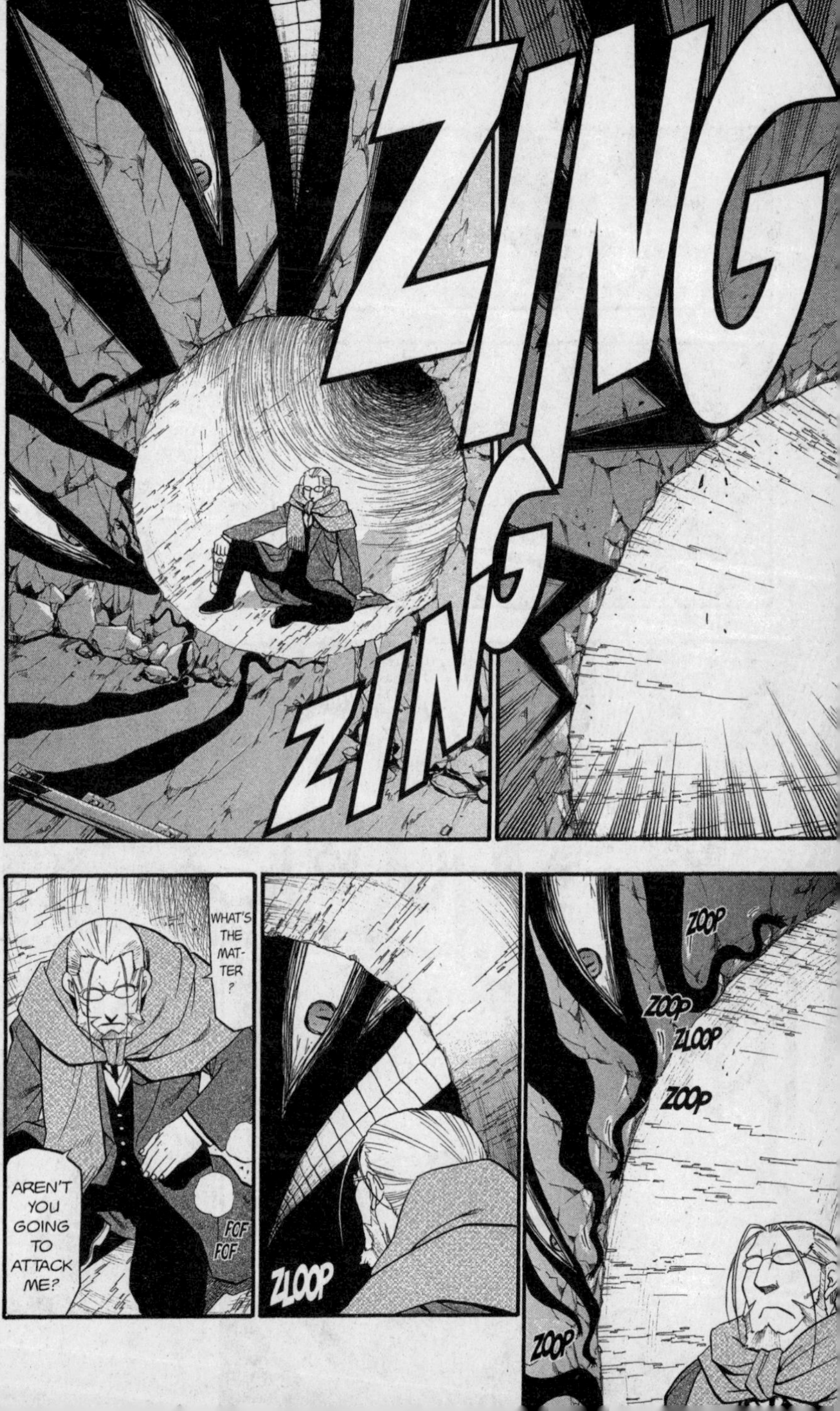
ZING
ZING
ZOOP
ZOOP
ZLOOP
ZOOP
ZOOP
ZLOOP
WHAT'S THE MAT-TER?
AREN'T YOU GOING TO ATTACK ME?
FOF FOF

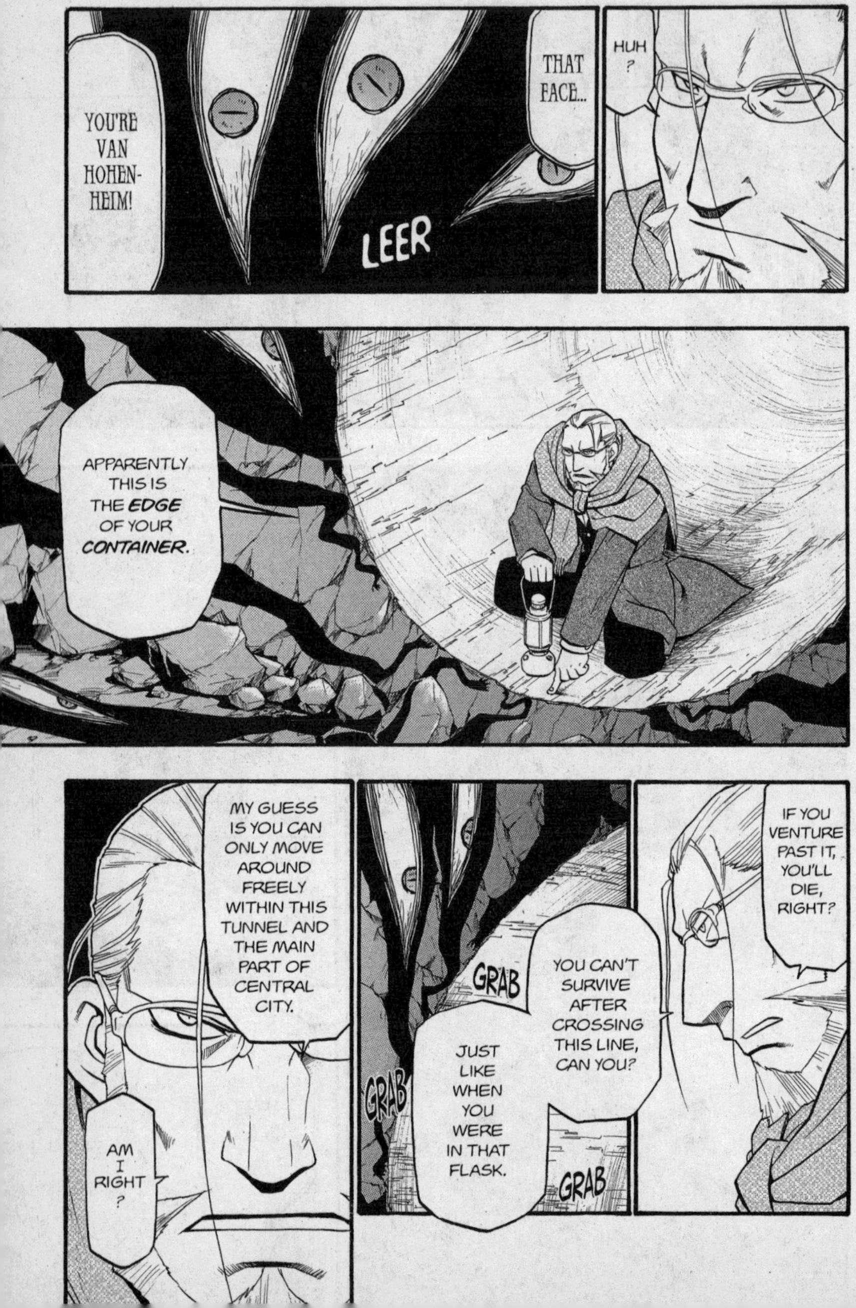
HUH?
THAT FACE...
YOU'RE VAN HOHENHEIM!
LEER
APPARENTLY THIS IS THE *EDGE* OF YOUR *CONTAINER*.
IF YOU VENTURE PAST IT, YOU'LL DIE, RIGHT?
YOU CAN'T SURVIVE AFTER CROSSING THIS LINE, CAN YOU?
GRAB
JUST LIKE WHEN YOU WERE IN THAT FLASK.
GRAB
GRAB
MY GUESS IS YOU CAN ONLY MOVE AROUND FREELY WITHIN THIS TUNNEL AND THE MAIN PART OF CENTRAL CITY.
AM I RIGHT?

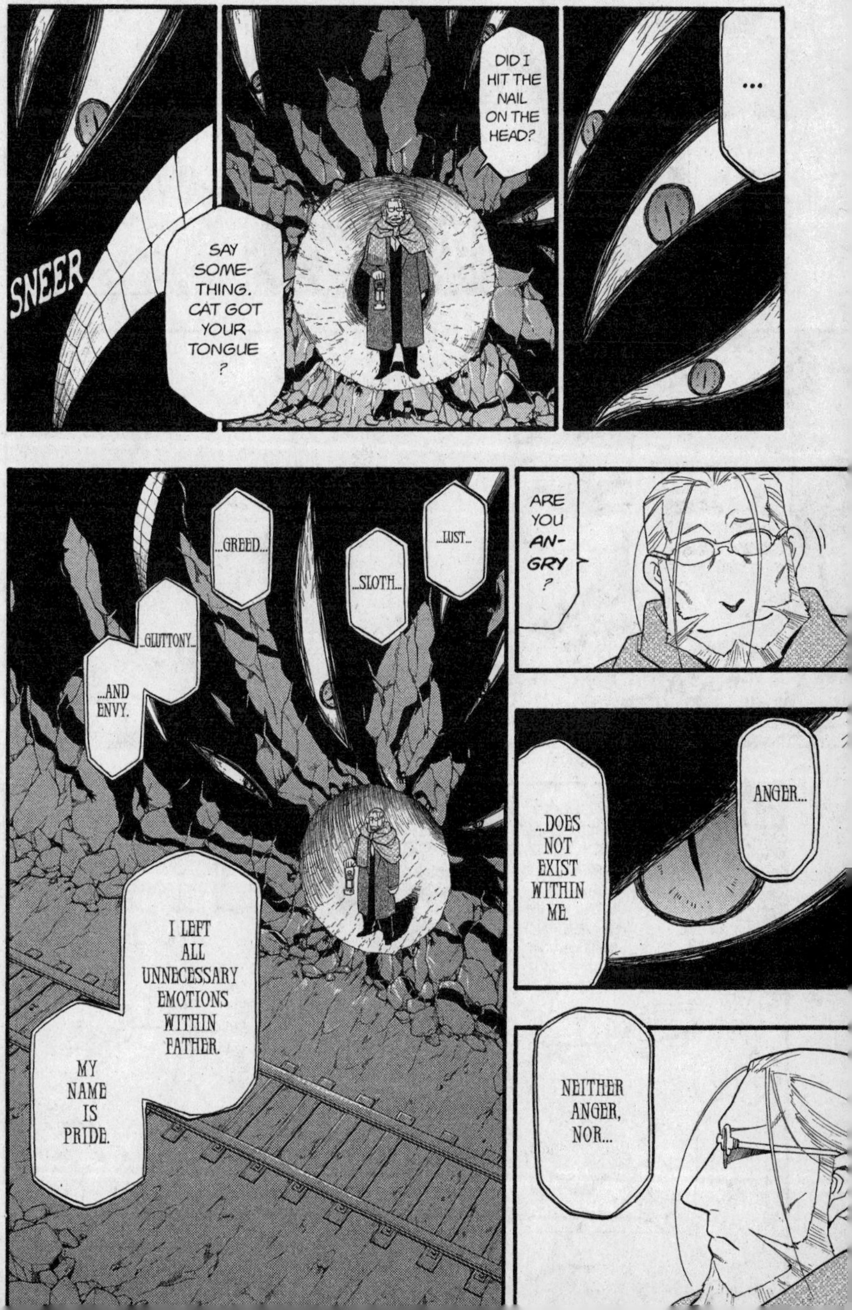
...
DID I HIT THE NAIL ON THE HEAD?
SAY SOME-THING. CAT GOT YOUR TONGUE?
SNEER
ARE YOU ANGRY?
ANGER...
...DOES NOT EXIST WITHIN ME.
NEITHER ANGER, NOR...
...LUST...
...SLOTH...
...GREED...
...GLUTTONY...
...AND ENVY.
I LEFT ALL UNNECESSARY EMOTIONS WITHIN FATHER.
MY NAME IS PRIDE.

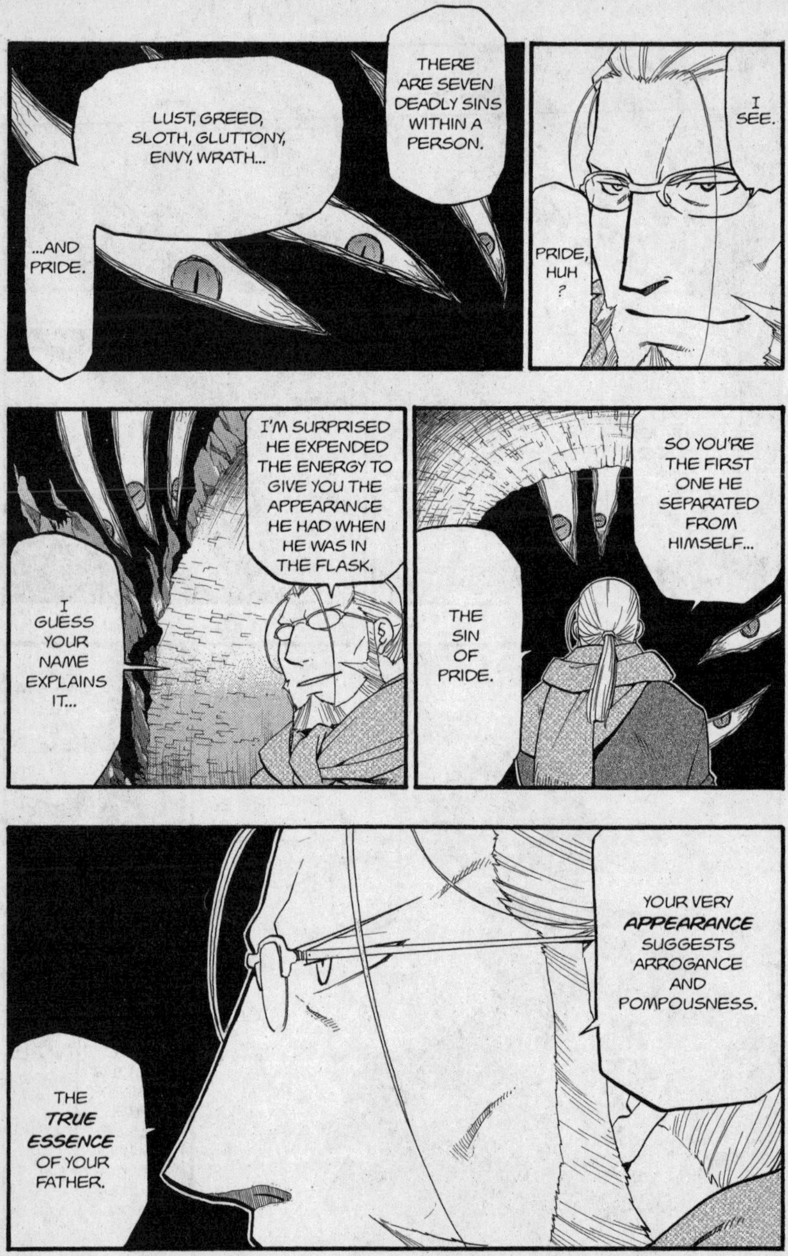
I SEE.
PRIDE, HUH?
THERE ARE SEVEN DEADLY SINS WITHIN A PERSON.
LUST, GREED, SLOTH, GLUTTONY, ENVY, WRATH...
...AND PRIDE.
SO YOU'RE THE FIRST ONE HE SEPARATED FROM HIMSELF...
THE SIN OF PRIDE.
I'M SURPRISED HE EXPENDED THE ENERGY TO GIVE YOU THE APPEARANCE HE HAD WHEN HE WAS IN THE FLASK.
I GUESS YOUR NAME EXPLAINS IT...
YOUR VERY ***APPEARANCE*** SUGGESTS ARROGANCE AND POMPOUSNESS.
THE ***TRUE ESSENCE*** OF YOUR FATHER.

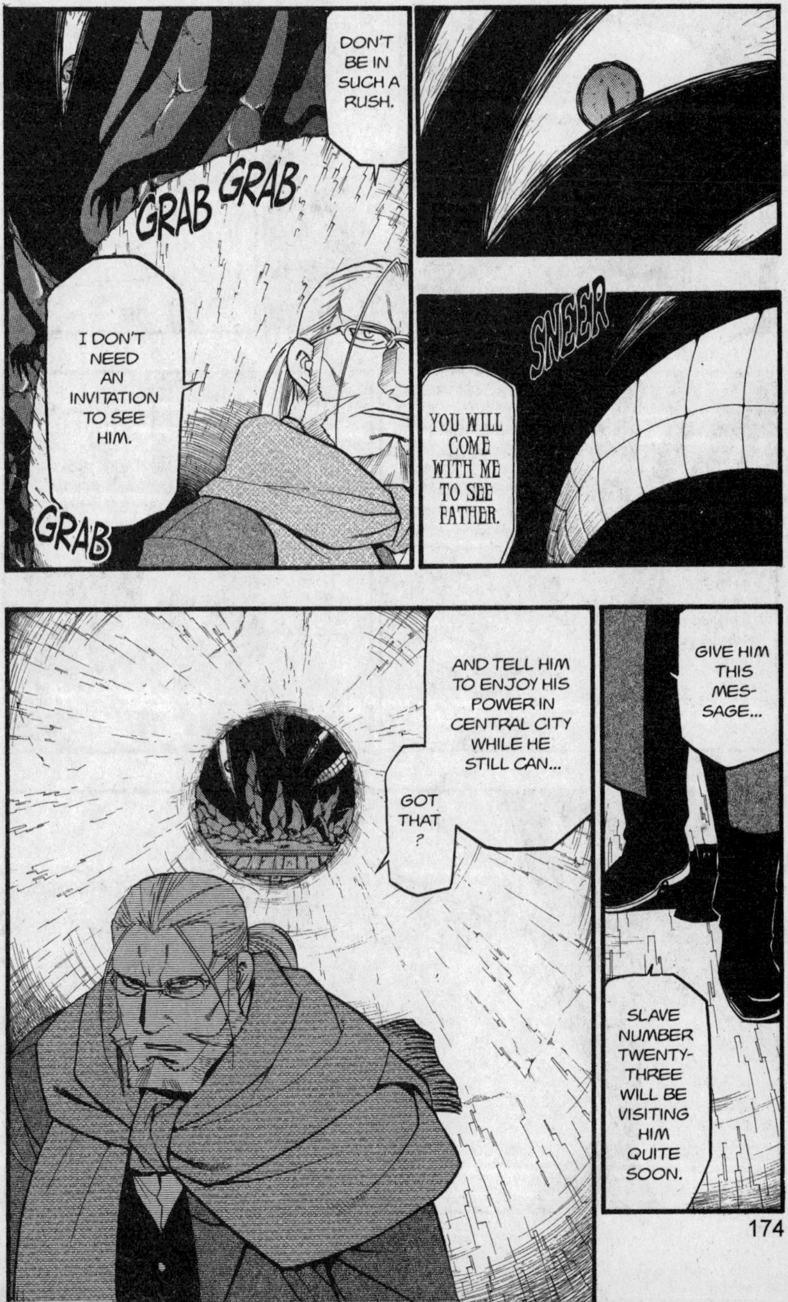
SNEER
YOU WILL COME WITH ME TO SEE FATHER.
DON'T BE IN SUCH A RUSH.
GRAB GRAB
I DON'T NEED AN INVITATION TO SEE HIM.
GRAB
GIVE HIM THIS MESSAGE...
SLAVE NUMBER TWENTY-THREE WILL BE VISITING HIM QUITE SOON.
AND TELL HIM TO ENJOY HIS POWER IN CENTRAL CITY WHILE HE STILL CAN...
GOT THAT?

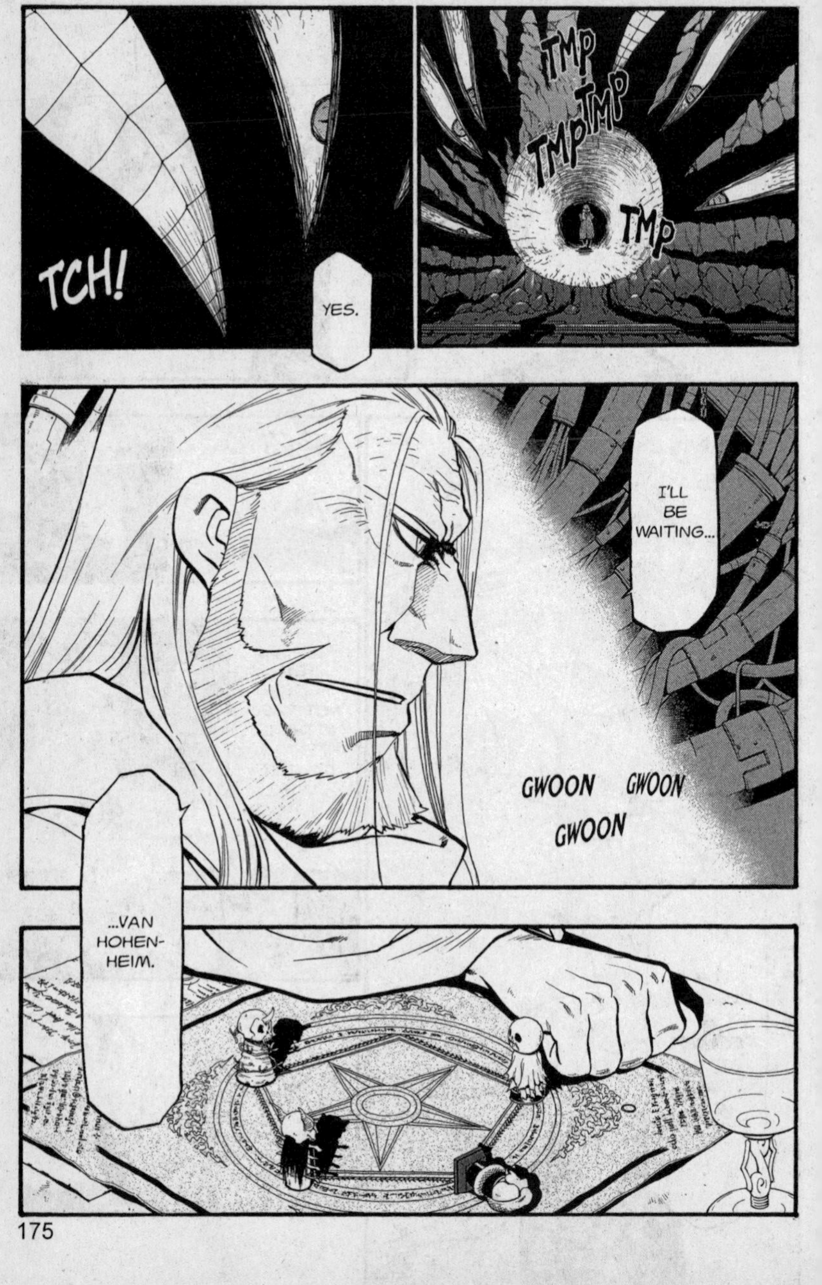
TMP TMP TMP TMP
YES.
TCH!
I'LL BE WAITING...
GWOON GWOON GWOON
...VAN HOHENHEIM.

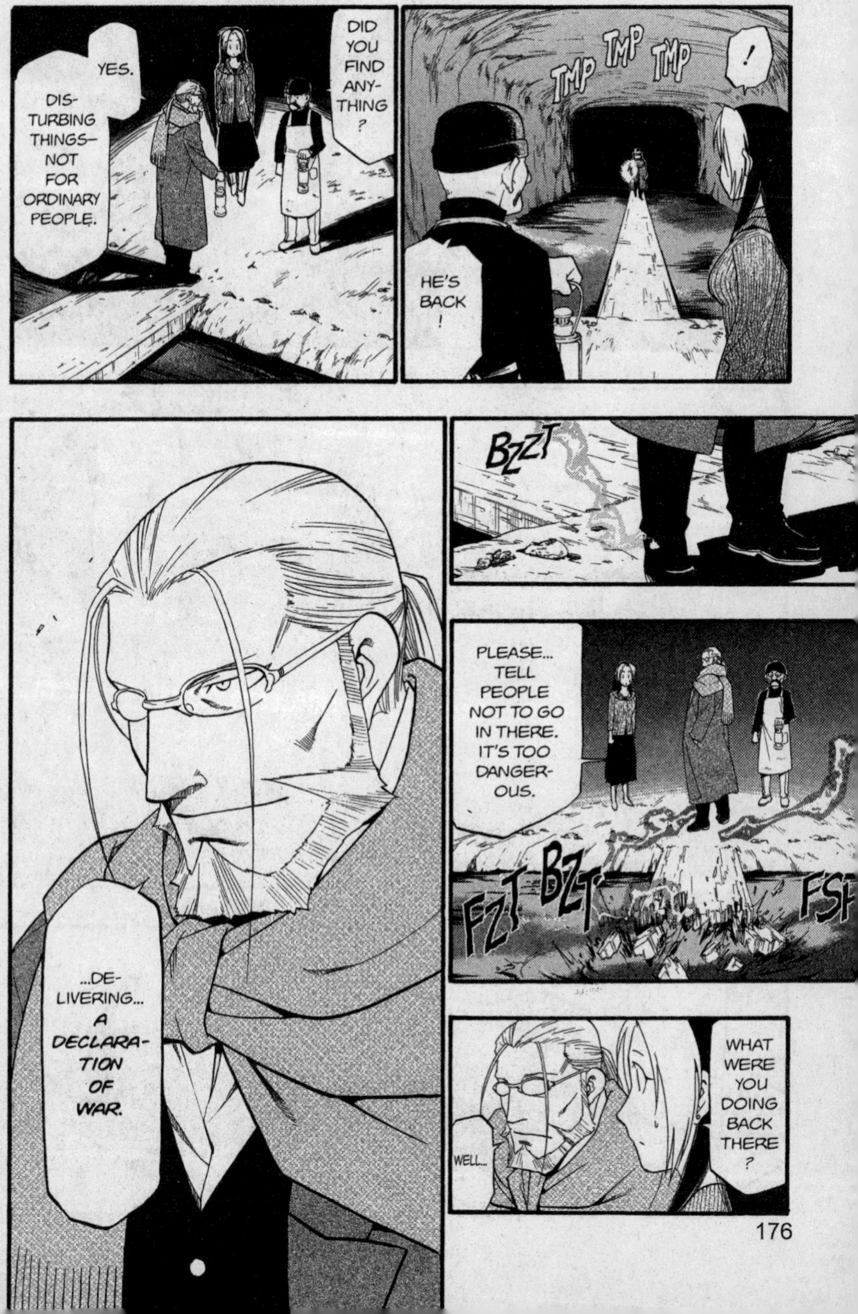
!
TMP TMP TMP
HE'S BACK!
DID YOU FIND ANYTHING?
YES.
DISTURBING THINGS—NOT FOR ORDINARY PEOPLE.
BZZT
PLEASE... TELL PEOPLE NOT TO GO IN THERE. IT'S TOO DANGEROUS.
FZT BZT
FSH
WHAT WERE YOU DOING BACK THERE?
WELL...
...DELIVERING... A DECLARATION OF WAR.

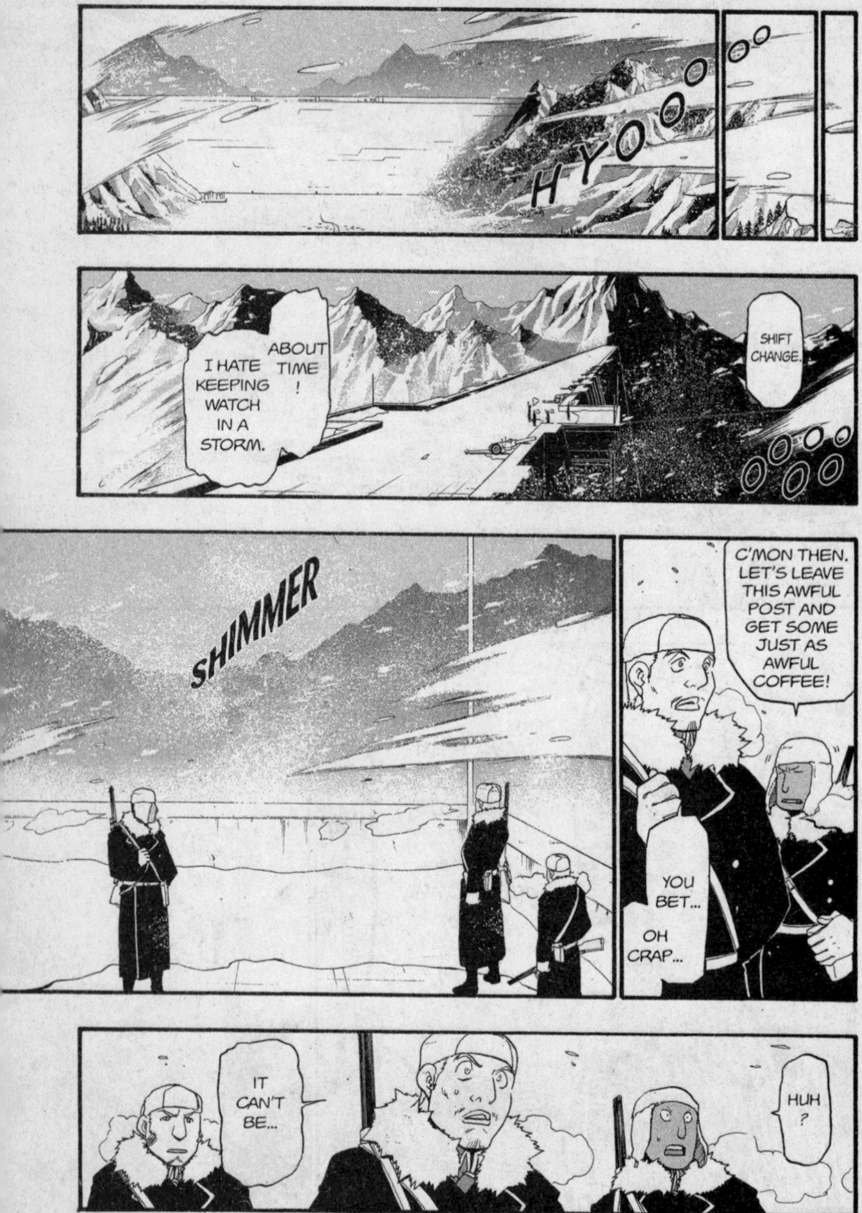
HYOOOOOO
SHIFT CHANGE.
ABOUT TIME!
I HATE KEEPING WATCH IN A STORM.
OOOOOO
C'MON THEN. LET'S LEAVE THIS AWFUL POST AND GET SOME JUST AS AWFUL COFFEE!
YOU BET...
OH CRAP...
SHIMMER
HUH?
IT CAN'T BE...

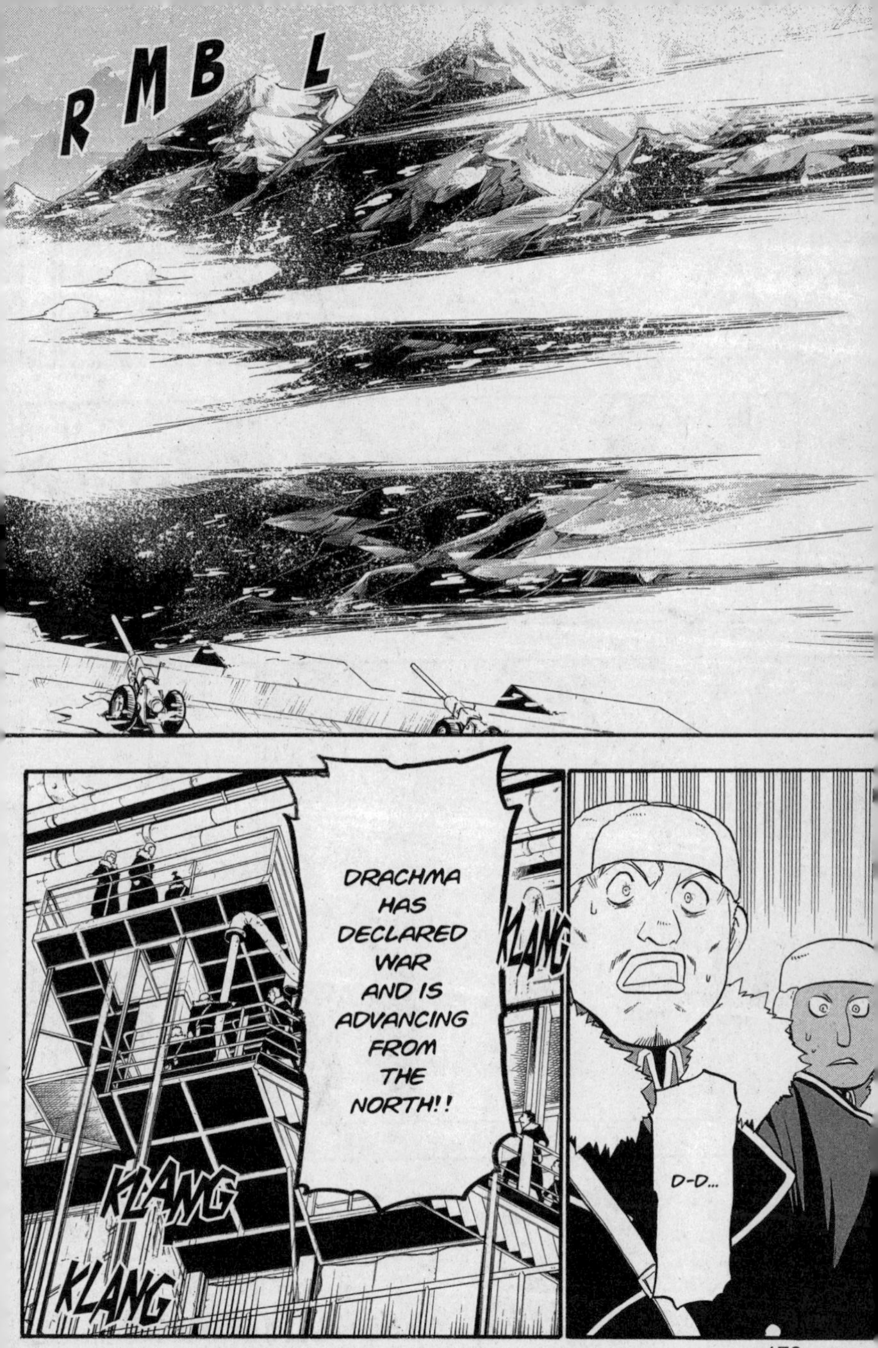
RMBL
D-D...
KLANG
DRACHMA HAS DECLARED WAR AND IS ADVANCING FROM THE NORTH!!
KLANG
KLANG

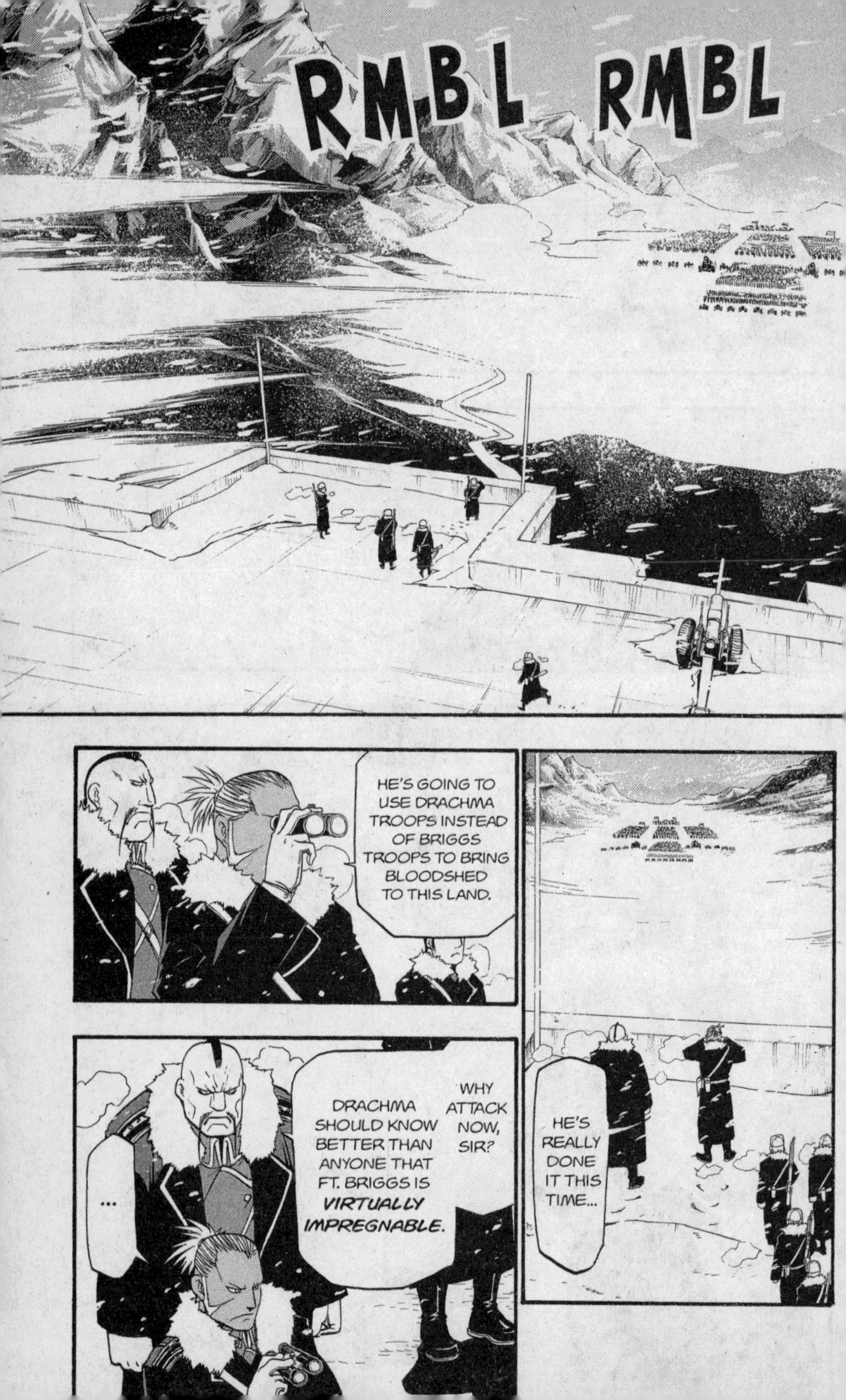
RMBL RMBL
HE'S REALLY DONE IT THIS TIME...
HE'S GOING TO USE DRACHMA TROOPS INSTEAD OF BRIGGS TROOPS TO BRING BLOODSHED TO THIS LAND.
WHY ATTACK NOW, SIR?
DRACHMA SHOULD KNOW BETTER THAN ANYONE THAT FT. BRIGGS IS ***VIRTUALLY IMPREGNABLE***.
...

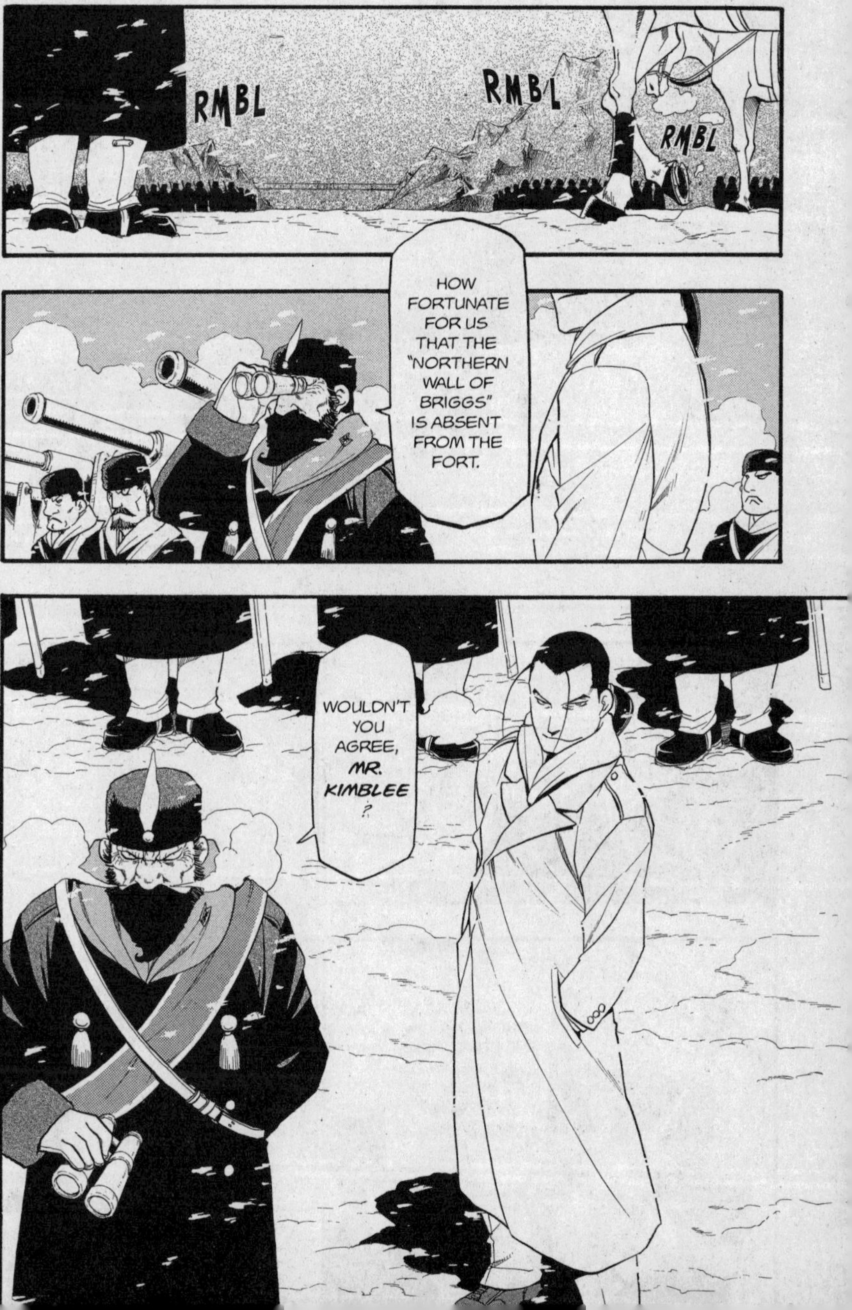
RMBL
RMBL
RMBL
HOW FORTUNATE FOR US THAT THE "NORTHERN WALL OF BRIGGS" IS ABSENT FROM THE FORT.
WOULDN'T YOU AGREE, MR. KIMBLEE?

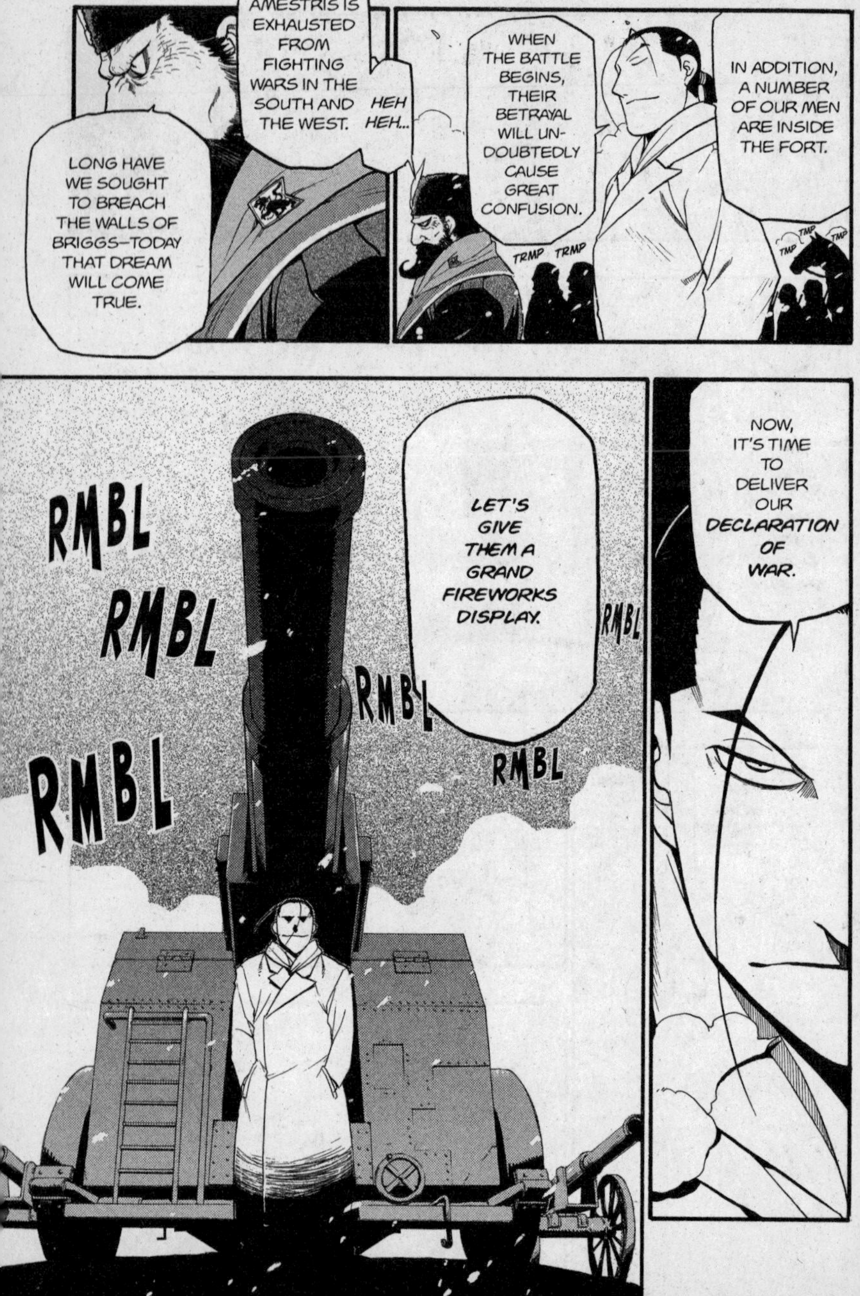
IN ADDITION, A NUMBER OF OUR MEN ARE INSIDE THE FORT.
TMP TMP TMP
WHEN THE BATTLE BEGINS, THEIR BETRAYAL WILL UNDOUBTEDLY CAUSE GREAT CONFUSION.
TRMP TRMP
AMESTRIS IS EXHAUSTED FROM FIGHTING WARS IN THE SOUTH AND THE WEST.
HEH HEH...
LONG HAVE WE SOUGHT TO BREACH THE WALLS OF BRIGGS—TODAY THAT DREAM WILL COME TRUE.
NOW, IT'S TIME TO DELIVER OUR *DECLARATION OF WAR.*
RMBL
LET'S GIVE THEM A GRAND FIREWORKS DISPLAY.
RMBL
RMBL
RMBL RMBL
RMBL

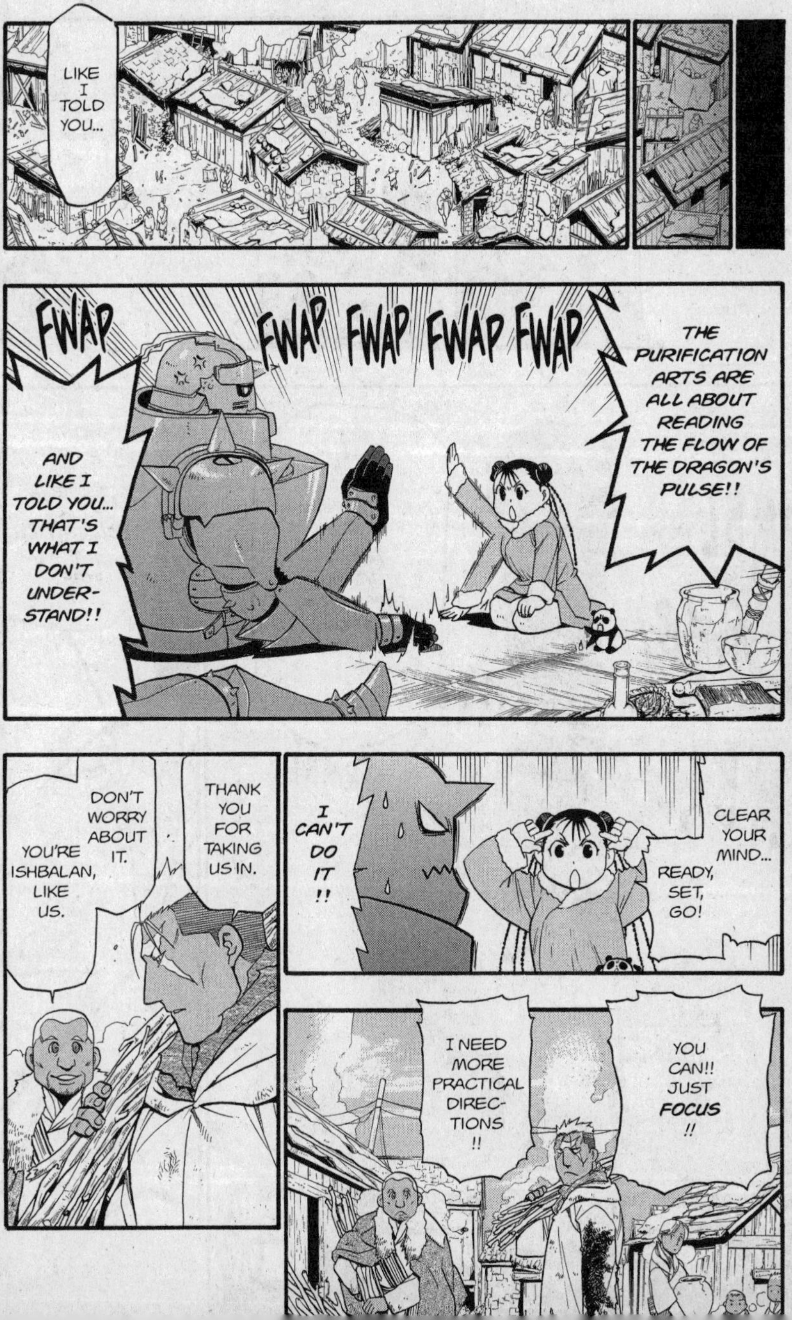

LIKE I TOLD YOU...
THE PURIFICATION ARTS ARE ALL ABOUT READING THE FLOW OF THE DRAGON'S PULSE!!
FWAP FWAP FWAP FWAP
FWAP
AND LIKE I TOLD YOU... THAT'S WHAT I DON'T UNDER-STAND!!
CLEAR YOUR MIND... READY, SET, GO!
I CAN'T DO IT!!
YOU CAN!! JUST FOCUS!!
I NEED MORE PRACTICAL DIREC-TIONS!!
THANK YOU FOR TAKING US IN.
DON'T WORRY ABOUT IT. YOU'RE ISHBALAN, LIKE US.

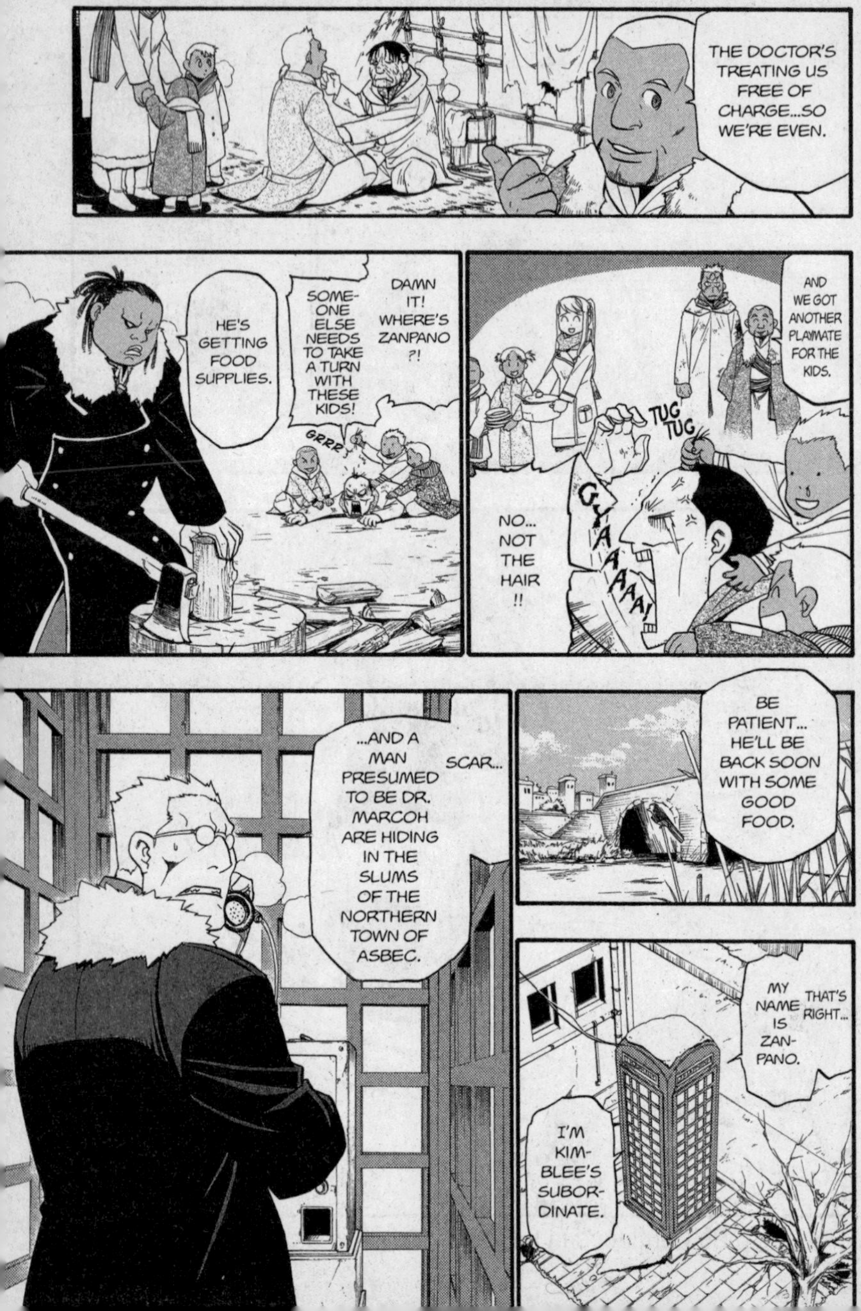
THE DOCTOR'S TREATING US FREE OF CHARGE...SO WE'RE EVEN.
AND WE GOT ANOTHER PLAYMATE FOR THE KIDS.
TUG TUG
GYAAAAAA!
NO... NOT THE HAIR!!
DAMN IT! WHERE'S ZANPANO?!
SOME-ONE ELSE NEEDS TO TAKE A TURN WITH THESE KIDS!
GRRR
HE'S GETTING FOOD SUPPLIES.
BE PATIENT... HE'LL BE BACK SOON WITH SOME GOOD FOOD.
THAT'S RIGHT...
MY NAME IS ZAN-PANO.
I'M KIM-BLEE'S SUBOR-DINATE.
SCAR...
...AND A MAN PRESUMED TO BE DR. MARCOH ARE HIDING IN THE SLUMS OF THE NORTHERN TOWN OF ASBEC.

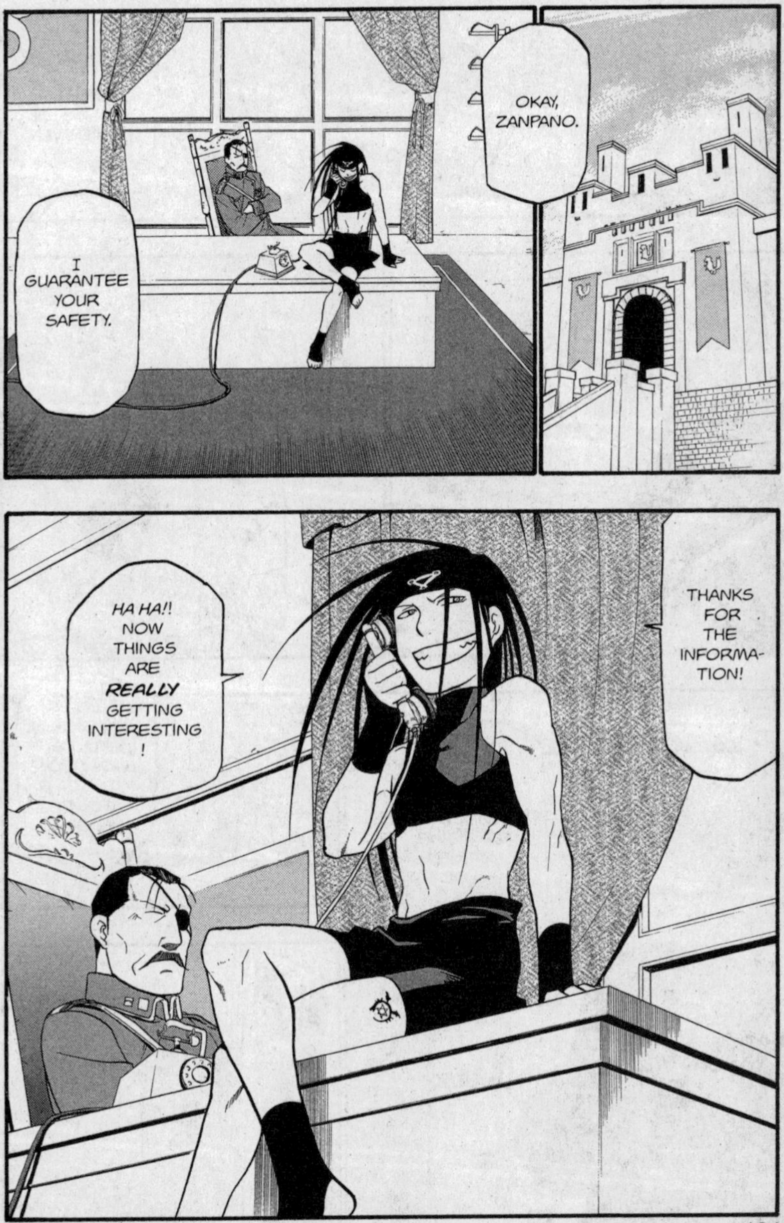
OKAY, ZANPANO.
I GUARANTEE YOUR SAFETY.
THANKS FOR THE INFORMATION!
HA HA!! NOW THINGS ARE REALLY GETTING INTERESTING!

To Be Continued in Fullmetal Alchemist Volume 20!

AN ENDANGERED SPECIES

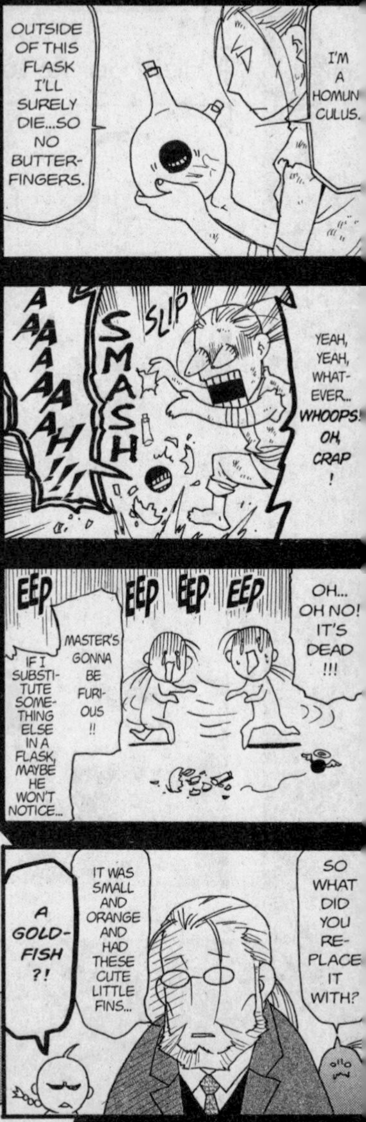
I'M A HOMUNCULUS.
OUTSIDE OF THIS FLASK I'LL SURELY DIE...SO NO BUTTER-FINGERS.
YEAH, YEAH, WHATEVER.. WHOOPS! OH, CRAP!
SLIP
SMASH
AAAAAAH!!!
OH... OH NO! IT'S DEAD!!!
EEP
EEP
EEP
EEP
MASTER'S GONNA BE FURIOUS!!
IF I SUBSTITUTE SOMETHING ELSE IN A FLASK, MAYBE HE WON'T NOTICE...
SO WHAT DID YOU REPLACE IT WITH?
IT WAS SMALL AND ORANGE AND HAD THESE CUTE LITTLE FINS...
A GOLDFISH?!

FULLMETAL ALCHEMIST 19

SPECIAL THANKS...

JUN TOHKO
NONO
MASASHI MIZUTANI
COUPON
NORIKO TSUBOTA
HARUHI NAKAMURA
MICHIKO SHISHIDO
KEI TAKANAMAZU
BIG BRO YOICHI KAMITONO
My Editor YUICHI SHIMOMURA

AND YOU!!

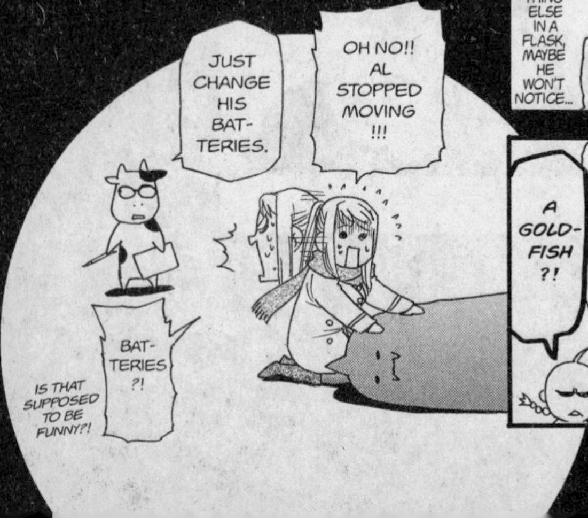
OH NO!! AL STOPPED MOVING!!!
JUST CHANGE HIS BATTERIES.
BATTERIES?!
IS THAT SUPPOSED TO BE FUNNY?!

A Field Guide to Briggs' Wildlife

Winter Coat

Summer Coat

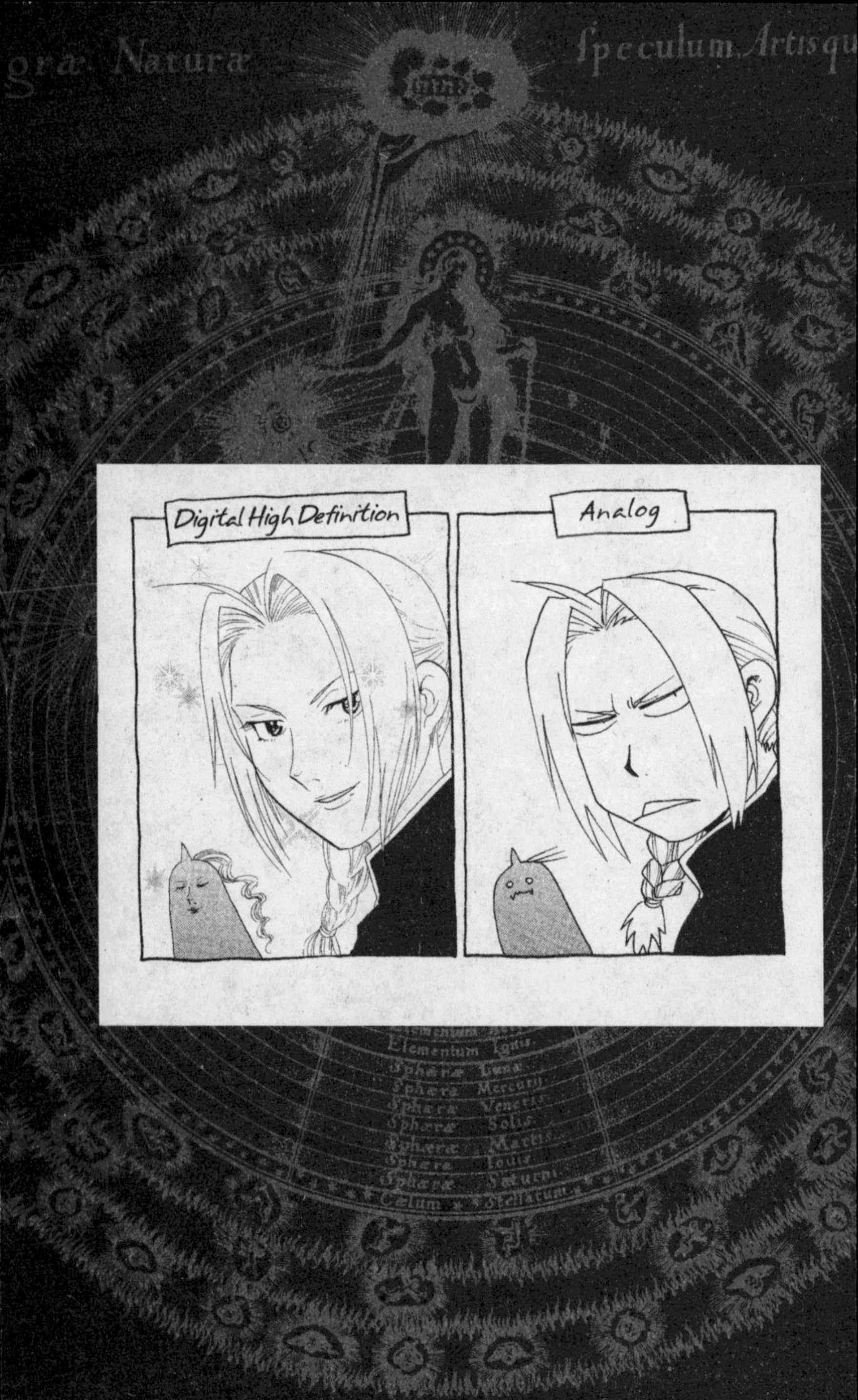
Digital High Definition
Analog

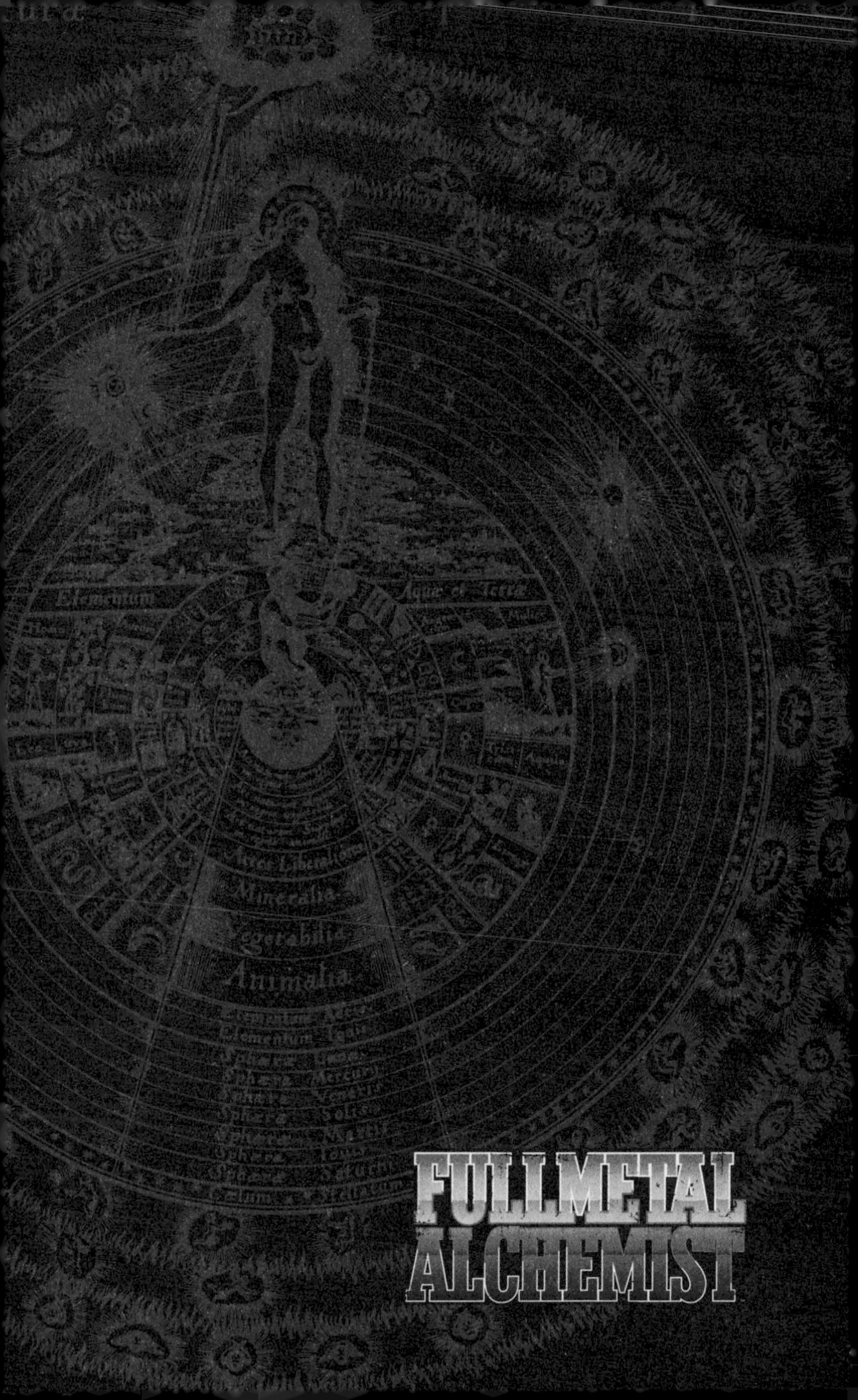
FULLMETAL
ALCHEMIST

FAREWELL COMRADES!

Recently, many of the items in my work space that have gone through good and bad times with me are breaking down, one after another. The pot that my assistants and I use to cook our lunch, the stereo, the ergonomic chair, etc.... You fools!! How dare you give up before the journey is done?! (sob)

—*Hiromu Arakawa, 2008*

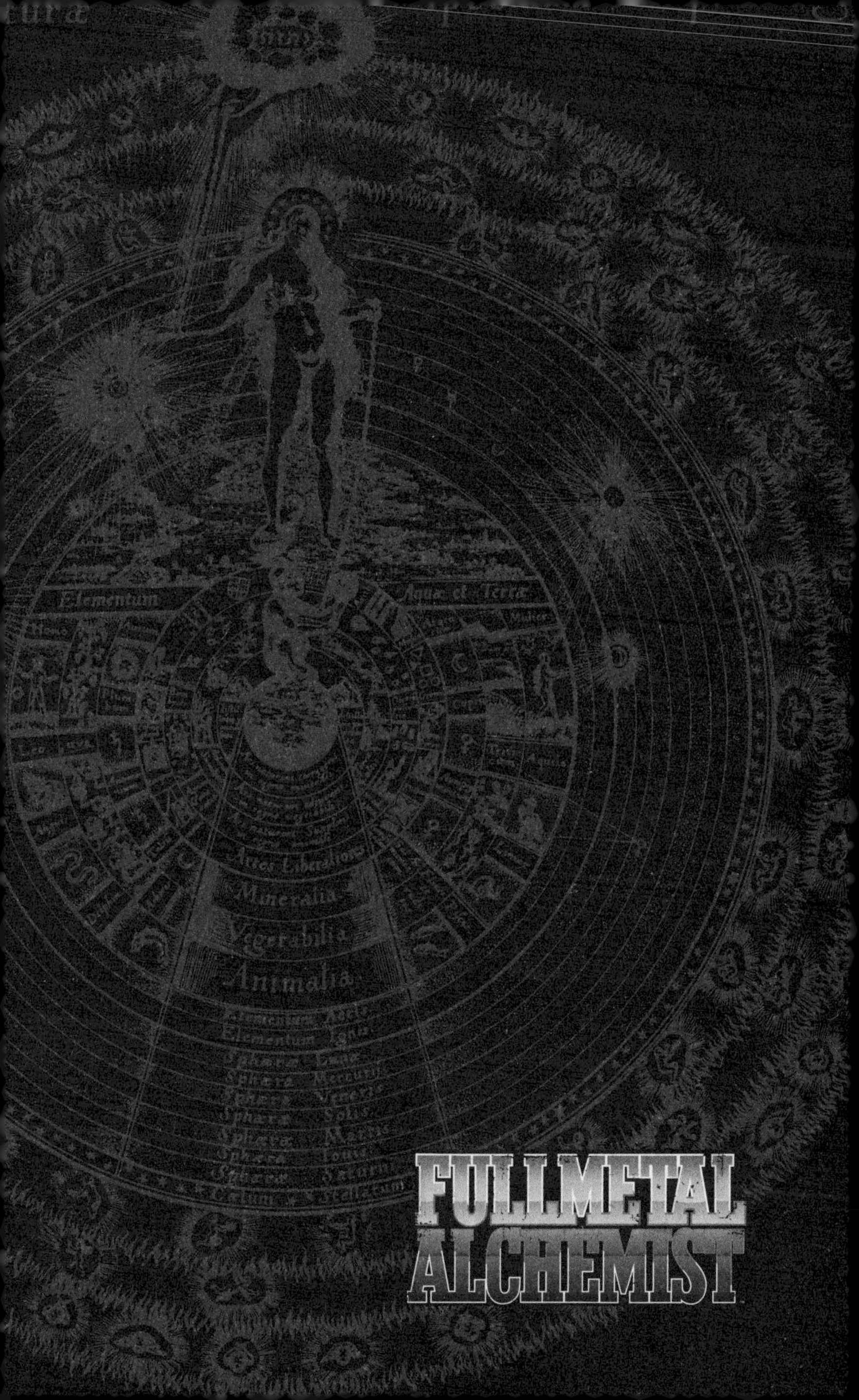
Elementum
Aquæ et Terræ
Mineralia
Vegetabilia
Animalia
FULLMETAL
ALCHEMIST

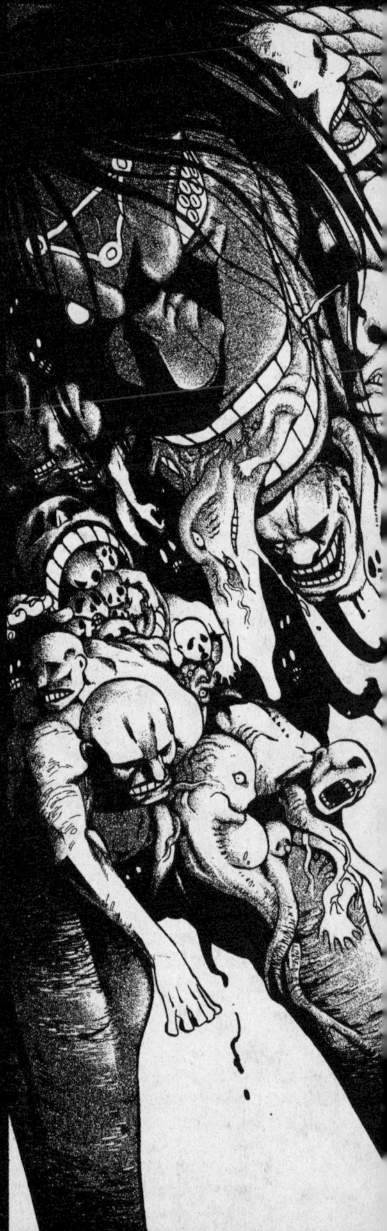

鋼の錬金術師
FULLMETAL ALCHEMIST

20

荒川弘
HIROMU ARAKAWA

■ アルフォンス・エルリック

Alphonse Elric

■ エドワード・エルリック

Edward Elric

■ アレックス・ルイ・アームストロング

Alex Louis Armstrong

■ ロイ・マスタング

Roy Mustang

OUTLINE
FULLMETAL ALCHEMIST

Using a forbidden alchemical ritual, the Elric brothers attempted to bring their dead mother back to life. But the ritual went wrong, consuming Edward Elric's leg and Alphonse Elric's entire body. At the cost of his arm, Edward was able to graft his brother's soul into a suit of armor. Equipped with mechanical "auto-mail" to replace his missing limbs, Edward becomes a state alchemist in the hopes of finding a way to restore their bodies. Their search embroils them in a deadly conspiracy that threatens to take the innocence, if not the lives, of everyone involved.

For decades, the nation of Amestris has slowly expanded its borders into the shape of an enormous transmutation circle with the Homunculi's "Father" at its center. Now the circle is complete and calculated bloody wars at key points sanctify the circle for a final transmutation. Long ago, when a similar ceremony was performed in the city of Cselkcess, thousands of souls were lost so that the original Homunculus could be free. Only one person survived the massacre–Van Hohenheim, Ed and Al's father. Now this Philosopher's Stone in the shape of a man might hold the key to stopping the Homunculi before an even greater massacre consumes the world…

鋼の錬金術師
FULLMETAL ALCHEMIST

CHARACTERS
FULLMETAL ALCHEMIST

■ ウィンリィ・ロックベル

Winry Rockbell

■ スカー

Scar

■ オリヴィエ・ミラ・アームストロング

Olivier Mira Armstrong

■ キング・ブラッドレイ

King Bradley

■ ヴァン・ホーエンハイム

Van Hohenheim

■ メイ・チャン

May Chang

CONTENTS

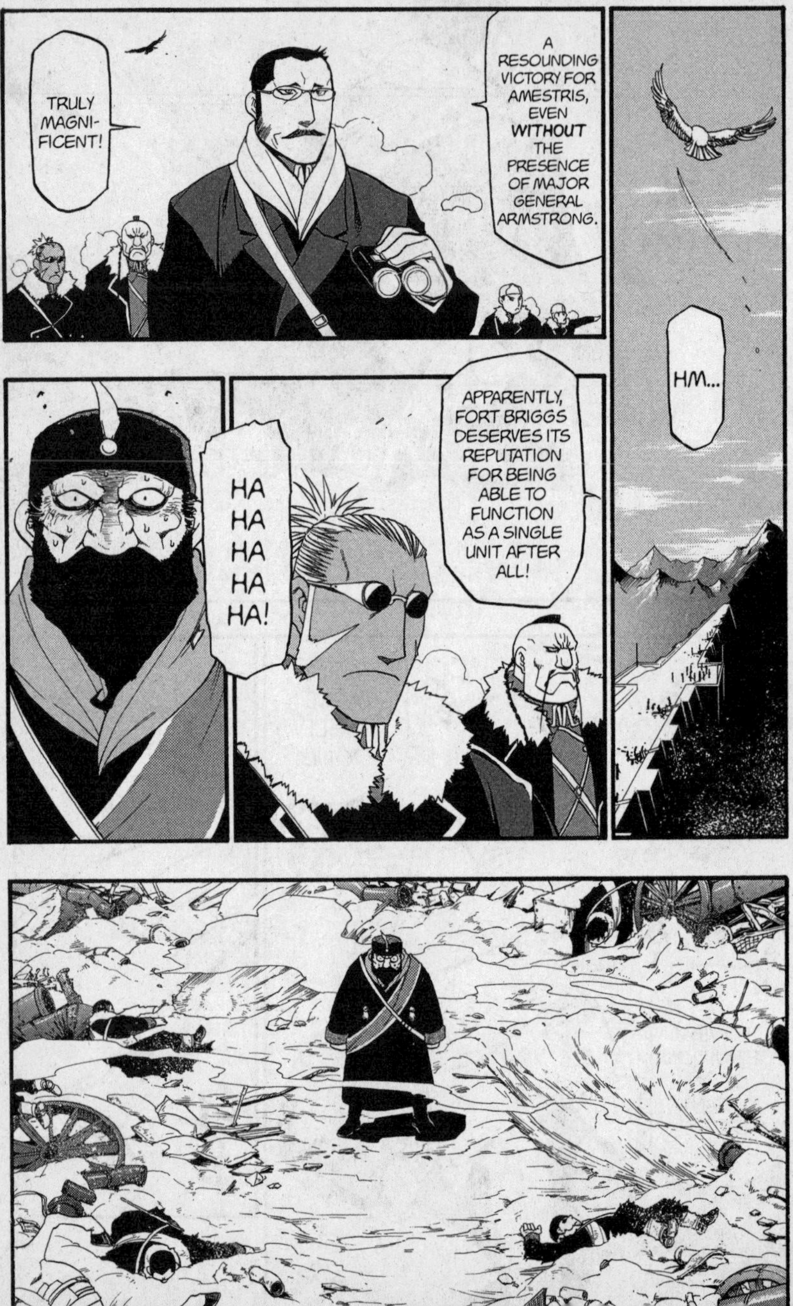
HM...
A RESOUNDING VICTORY FOR AMESTRIS, EVEN **WITHOUT** THE PRESENCE OF MAJOR GENERAL ARMSTRONG.
TRULY MAGNI-FICENT!
APPARENTLY, FORT BRIGGS DESERVES ITS REPUTATION FOR BEING ABLE TO FUNCTION AS A SINGLE UNIT AFTER ALL!
HA HA HA HA HA!

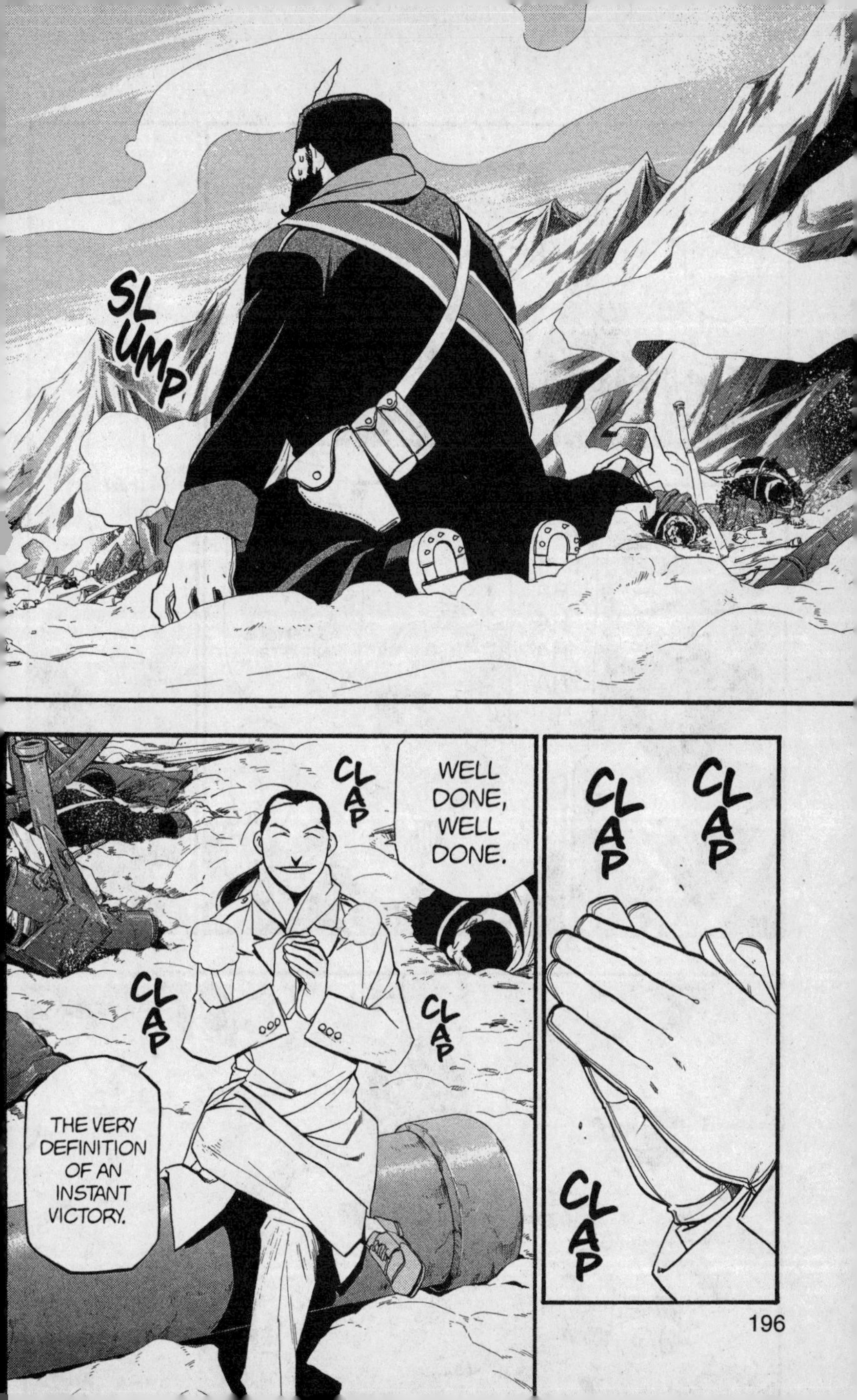
SLUMP
CLAP
CLAP
CLAP
WELL DONE, WELL DONE.
CLAP
CLAP
CLAP
THE VERY DEFINITION OF AN INSTANT VICTORY.

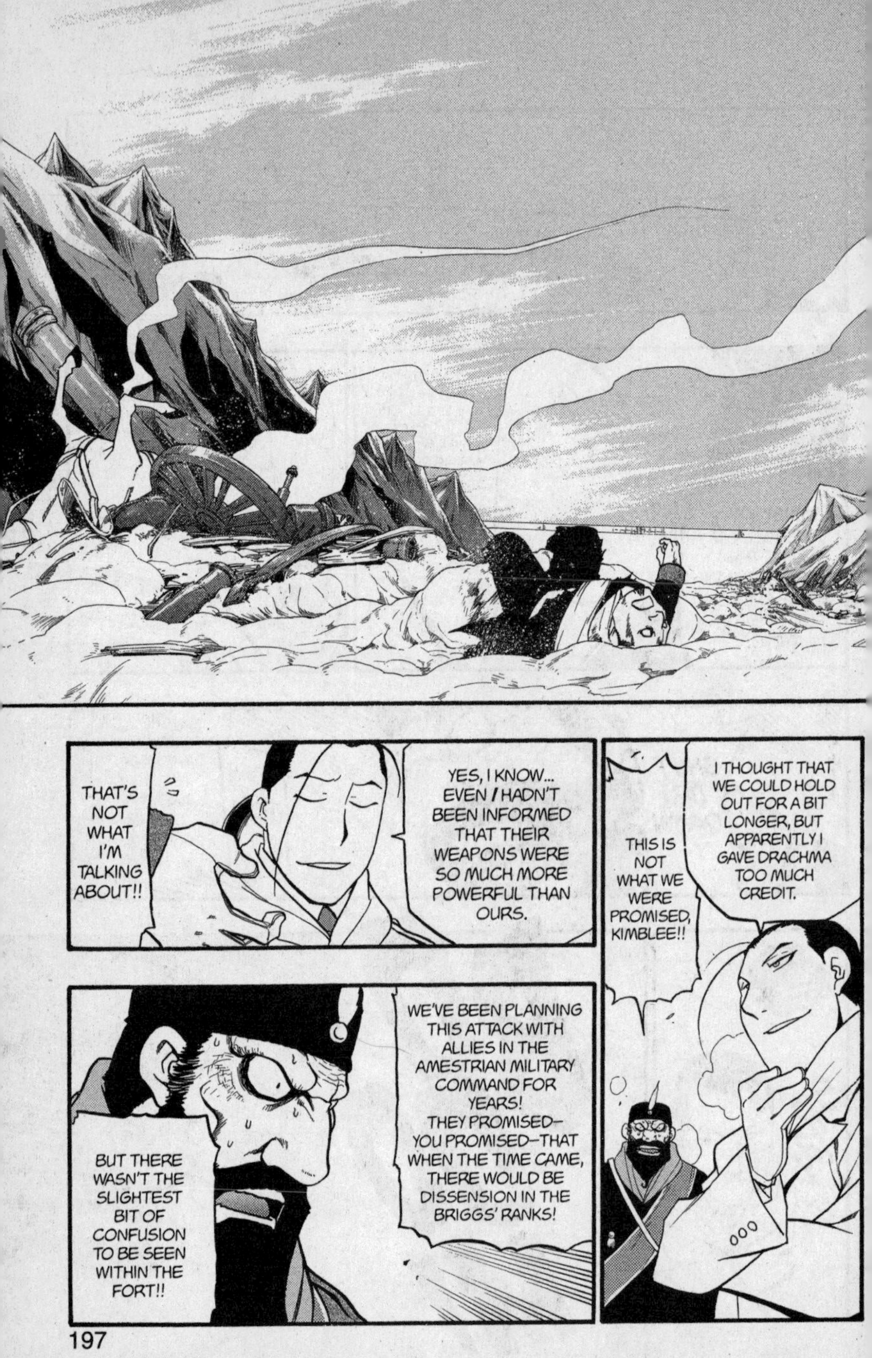
I THOUGHT THAT WE COULD HOLD OUT FOR A BIT LONGER, BUT APPARENTLY I GAVE DRACHMA TOO MUCH CREDIT.
THIS IS NOT WHAT WE WERE PROMISED, KIMBLEE!!
YES, I KNOW... EVEN I HADN'T BEEN INFORMED THAT THEIR WEAPONS WERE SO MUCH MORE POWERFUL THAN OURS.
THAT'S NOT WHAT I'M TALKING ABOUT!!
WE'VE BEEN PLANNING THIS ATTACK WITH ALLIES IN THE AMESTRIAN MILITARY COMMAND FOR YEARS!
THEY PROMISED—YOU PROMISED—THAT WHEN THE TIME CAME, THERE WOULD BE DISSENSION IN THE BRIGGS' RANKS!
BUT THERE WASN'T THE SLIGHTEST BIT OF CONFUSION TO BE SEEN WITHIN THE FORT!!

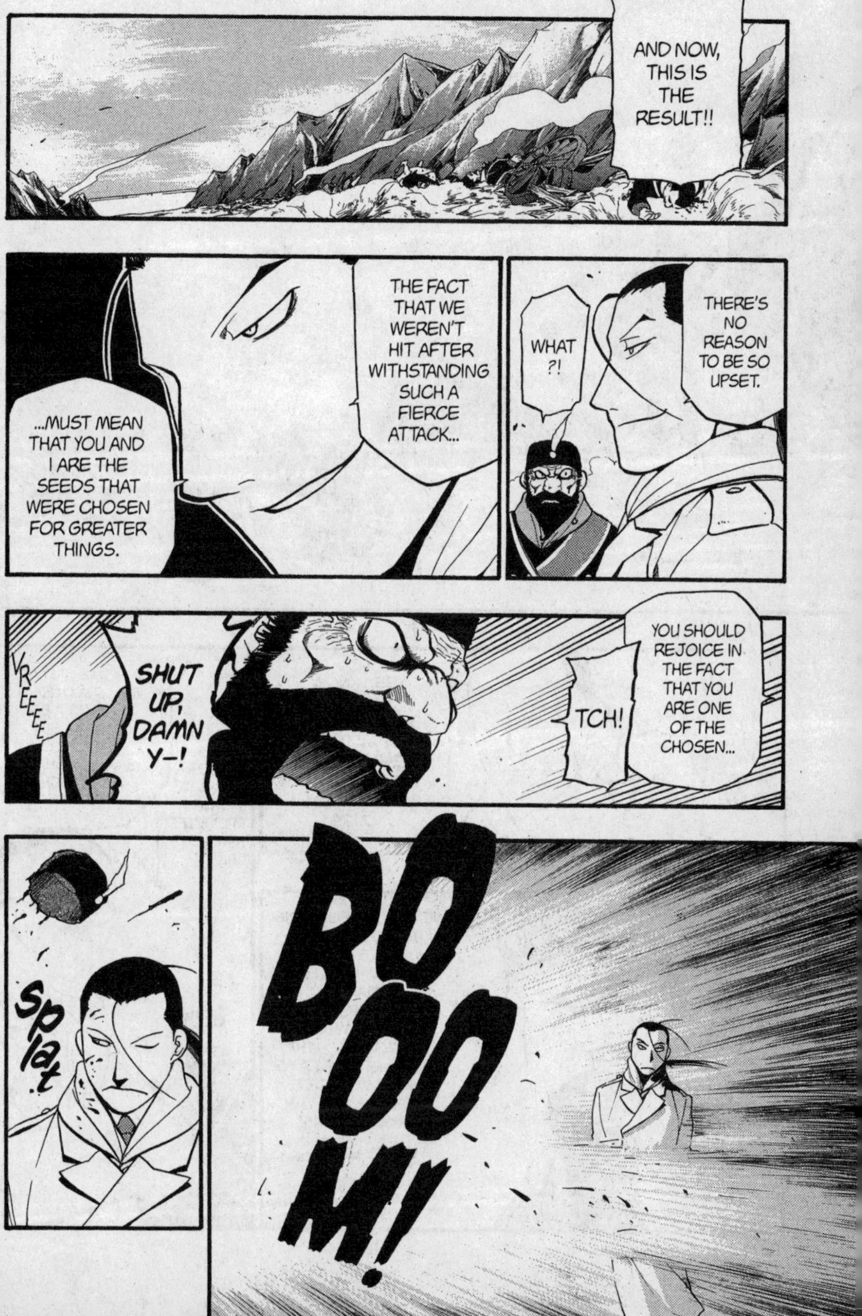
AND NOW, THIS IS THE RESULT!!
THERE'S NO REASON TO BE SO UPSET.
WHAT?!
THE FACT THAT WE WEREN'T HIT AFTER WITHSTANDING SUCH A FIERCE ATTACK...
...MUST MEAN THAT YOU AND I ARE THE SEEDS THAT WERE CHOSEN FOR GREATER THINGS.
YOU SHOULD REJOICE IN THE FACT THAT YOU ARE ONE OF THE CHOSEN...
TCH!
SHUT UP, DAMN Y-!
VREEEEE
BOOOOM!
splat

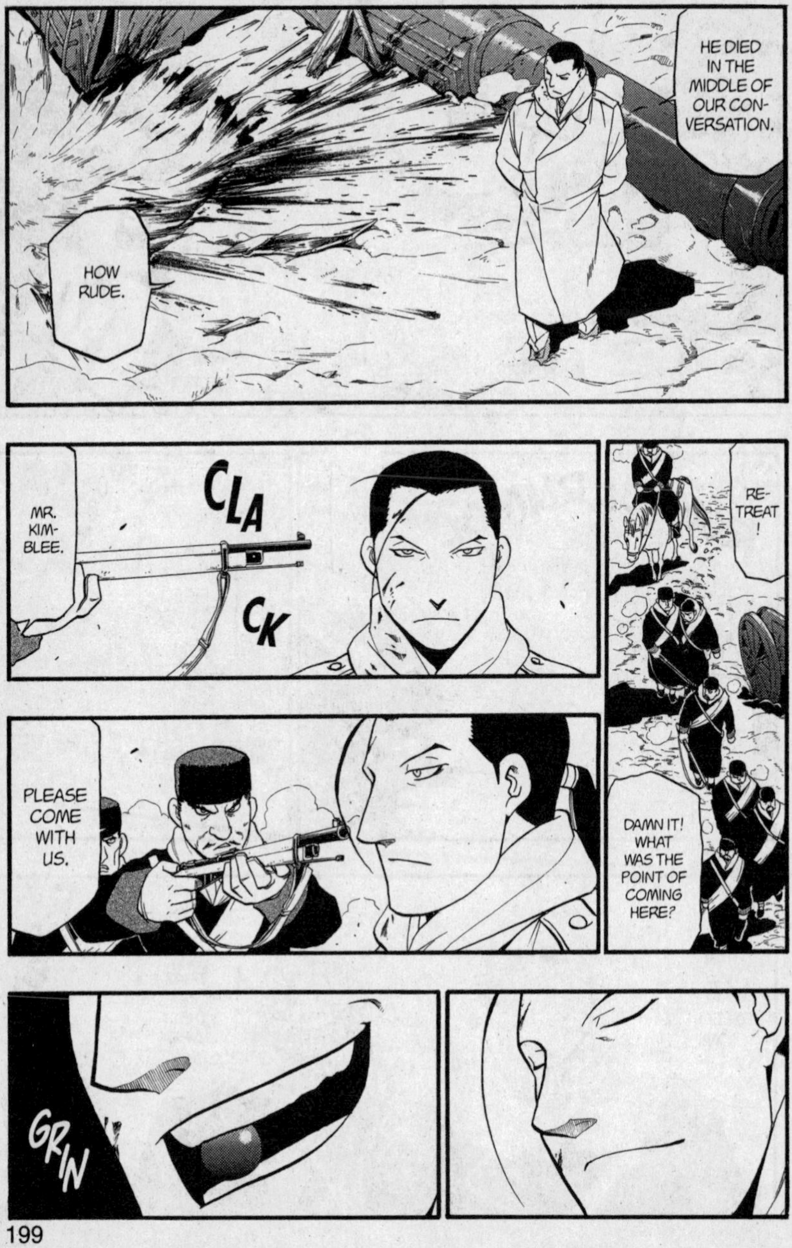
HE DIED IN THE MIDDLE OF OUR CON-VERSATION.
HOW RUDE.
RE-TREAT!
DAMN IT! WHAT WAS THE POINT OF COMING HERE?
MR. KIM-BLEE.
CLACK
PLEASE COME WITH US.
GRIN

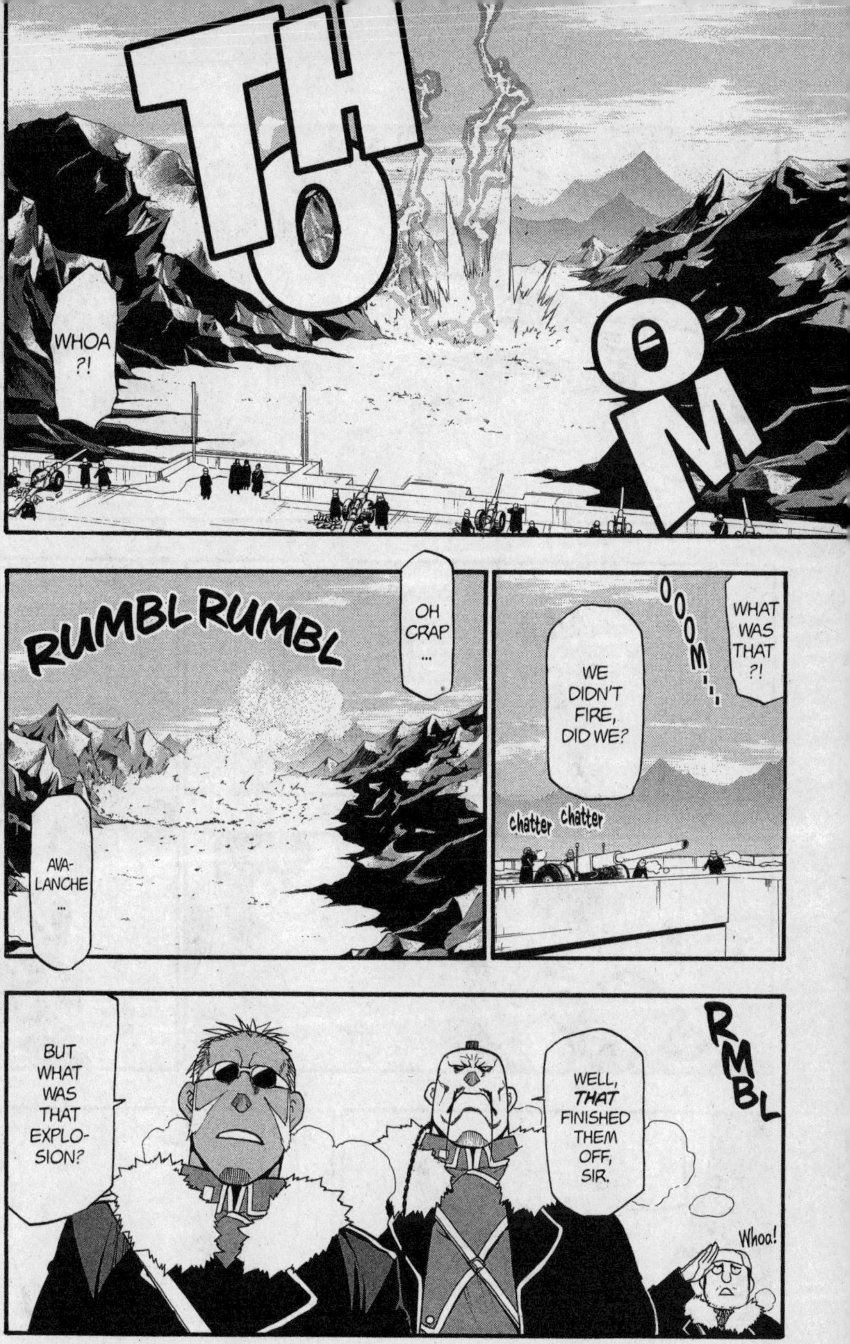
THOOM
WHOA?!
WHAT WAS THAT?!
OOOM...
WE DIDN'T FIRE, DID WE?
chatter chatter
OH CRAP...
RUMBL RUMBL
AVALANCHE...
RMBL
WELL, *THAT* FINISHED THEM OFF, SIR.
Whoa!
BUT WHAT WAS THAT EXPLOSION?

Chapter 79

Bug Bite

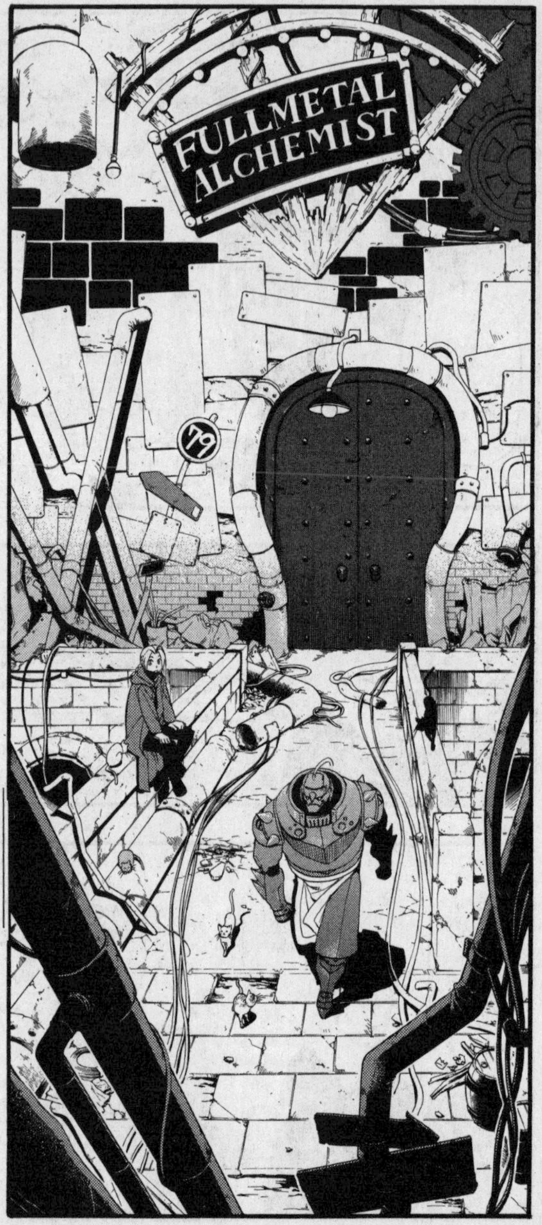
FULLMETAL ALCHEMIST
79

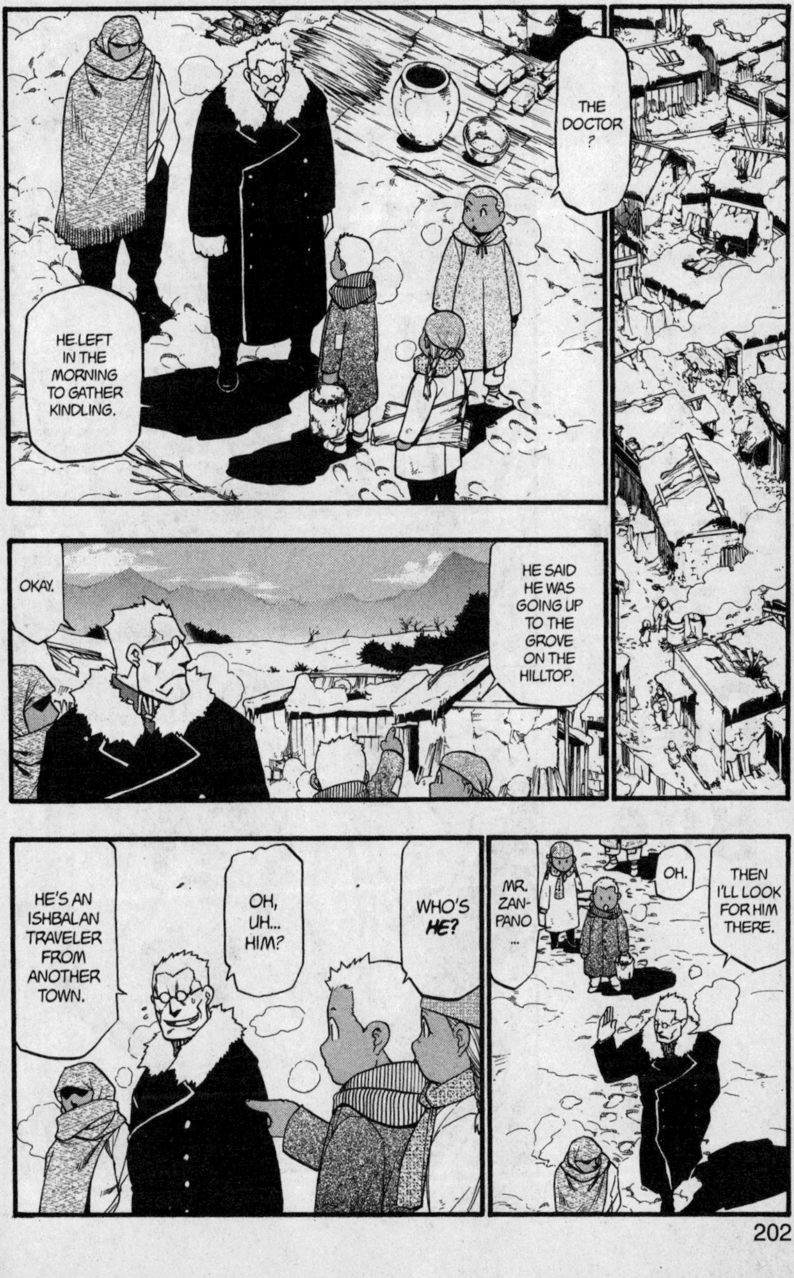
THE DOCTOR?
HE LEFT IN THE MORNING TO GATHER KINDLING.
HE SAID HE WAS GOING UP TO THE GROVE ON THE HILLTOP.
OKAY.
THEN I'LL LOOK FOR HIM THERE.
OH.
MR. ZAN-PANO...
WHO'S HE?
OH, UH... HIM?
HE'S AN ISHBALAN TRAVELER FROM ANOTHER TOWN.

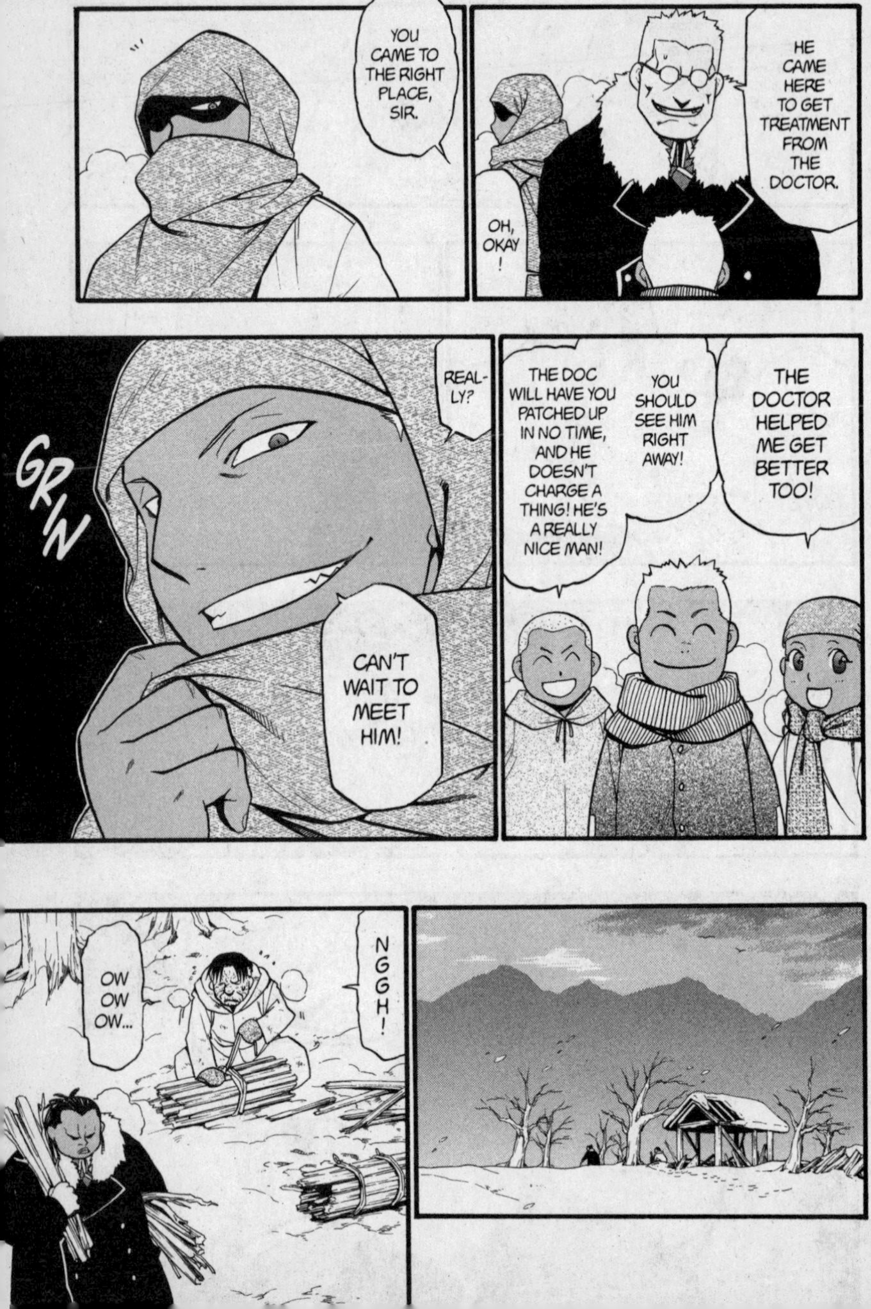
HE CAME HERE TO GET TREATMENT FROM THE DOCTOR.
OH, OKAY!
YOU CAME TO THE RIGHT PLACE, SIR.
THE DOCTOR HELPED ME GET BETTER TOO!
YOU SHOULD SEE HIM RIGHT AWAY!
THE DOC WILL HAVE YOU PATCHED UP IN NO TIME, AND HE DOESN'T CHARGE A THING! HE'S A REALLY NICE MAN!
REAL-LY?
GRIN
CAN'T WAIT TO MEET HIM!
NGGH!
OW OW OW...

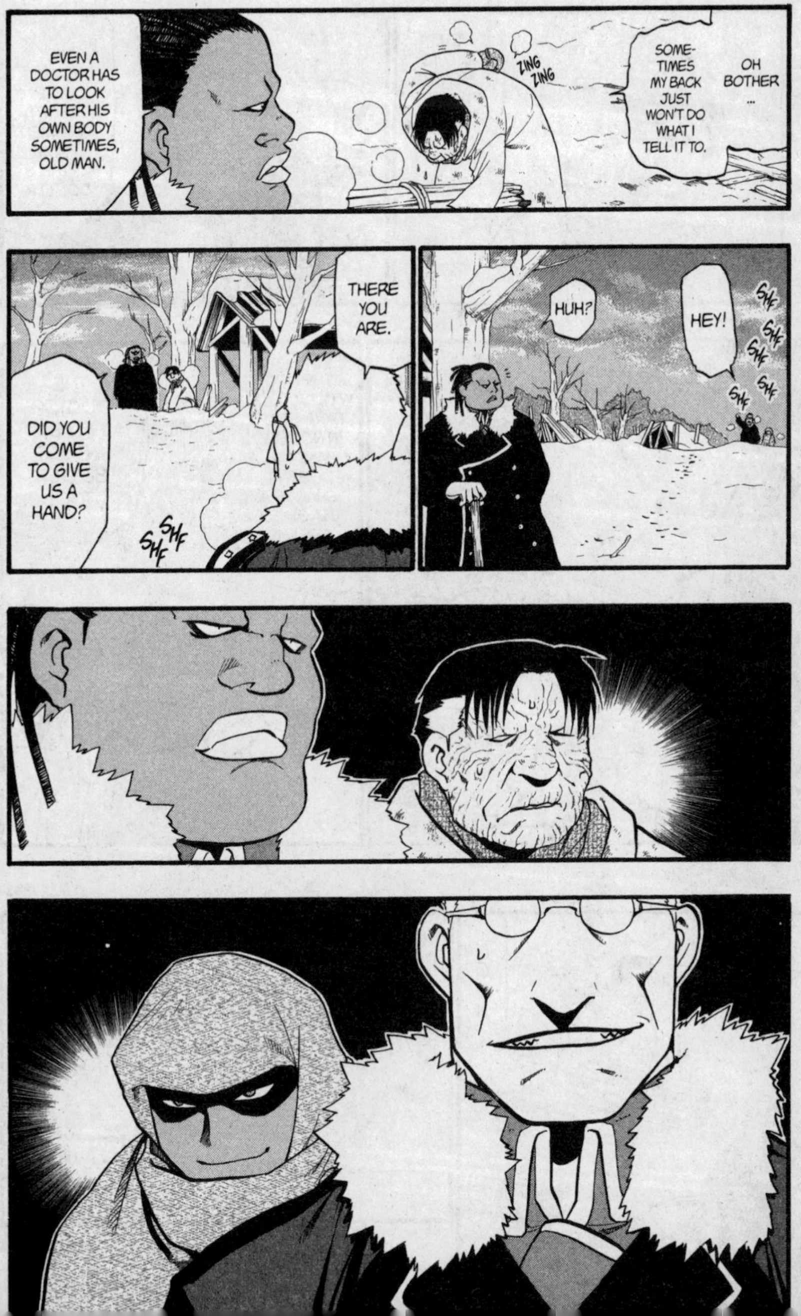
OH BOTHER ...
SOME-TIMES MY BACK JUST WON'T DO WHAT I TELL IT TO.
ZING ZING
EVEN A DOCTOR HAS TO LOOK AFTER HIS OWN BODY SOMETIMES, OLD MAN.
SHF SHF SHF SHF SHF
HEY!
HUH?
THERE YOU ARE.
DID YOU COME TO GIVE US A HAND?
SHF SHF

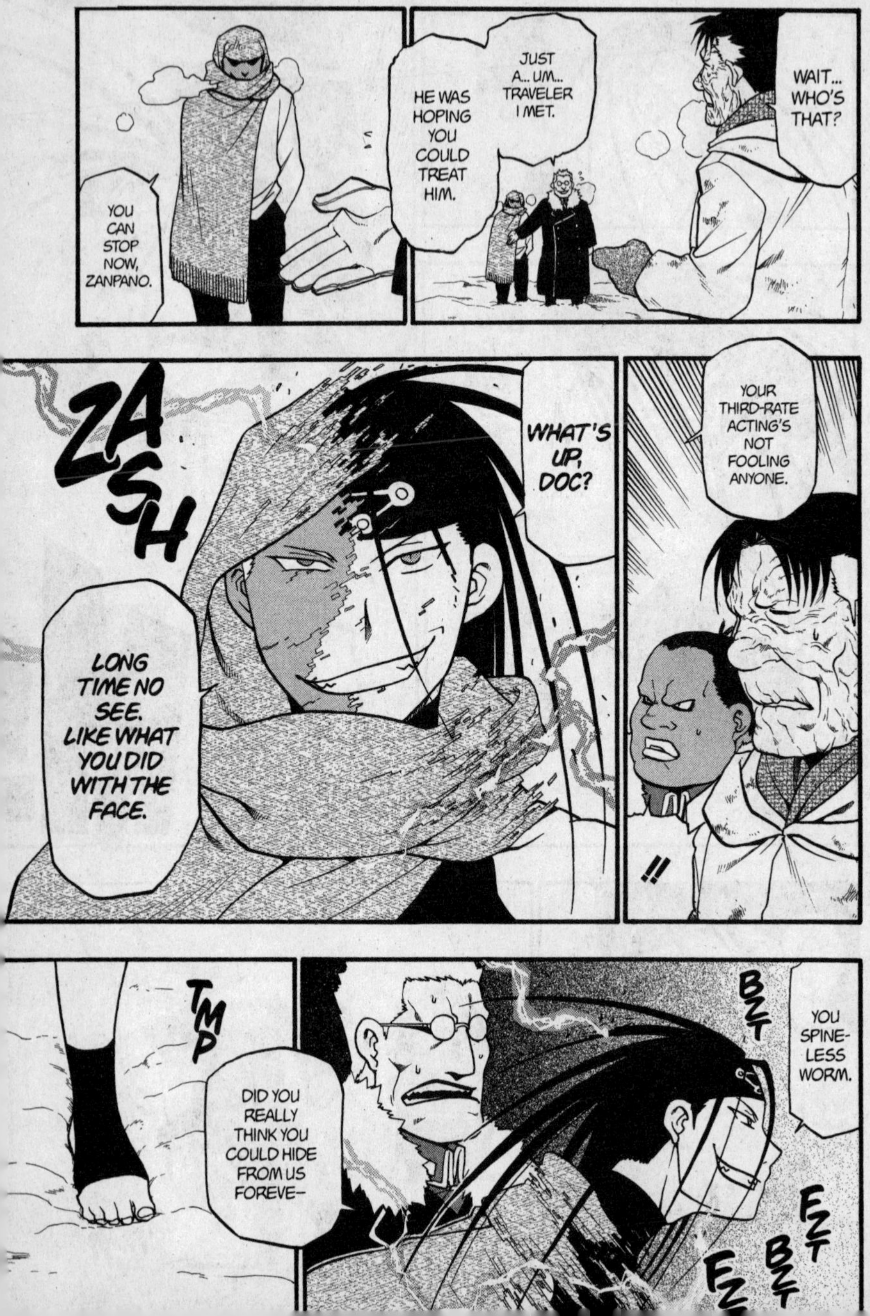
WAIT... WHO'S THAT?
JUST A... UM... TRAVELER I MET.
HE WAS HOPING YOU COULD TREAT HIM.
YOU CAN STOP NOW, ZANPANO.
YOUR THIRD-RATE ACTING'S NOT FOOLING ANYONE.
!!
WHAT'S UP, DOC?
ZASH
LONG TIME NO SEE. LIKE WHAT YOU DID WITH THE FACE.
BZZT
YOU SPINELESS WORM.
FZZT
BZZT
FZZ
DID YOU REALLY THINK YOU COULD HIDE FROM US FOREVE-
TMP

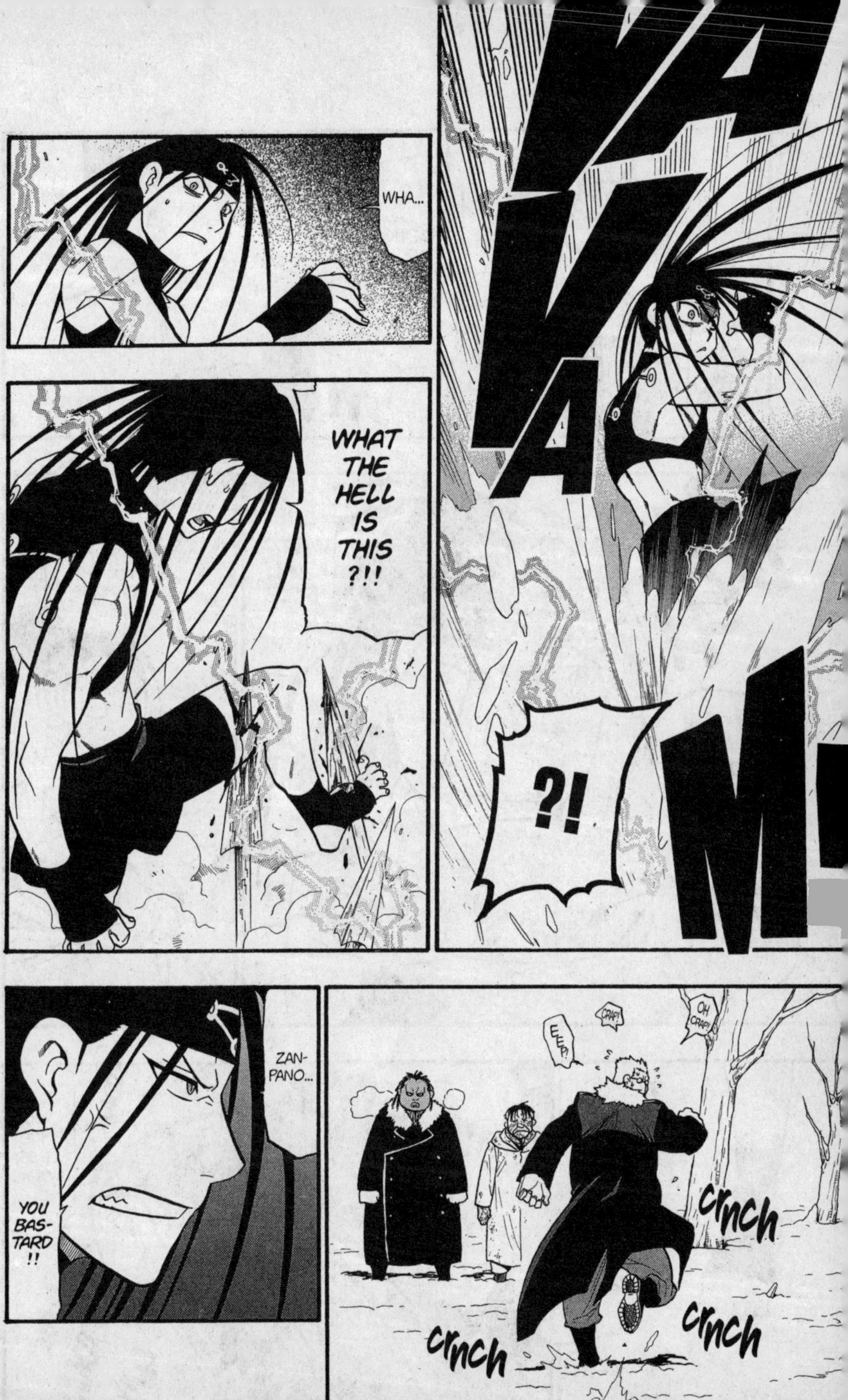
?!
WHA...
WHAT THE HELL IS THIS?!!
OH CRAP!
CRAP!
EEP!
crnch
crnch
crnch
ZAN-PANO...
YOU BAS-TARD!!

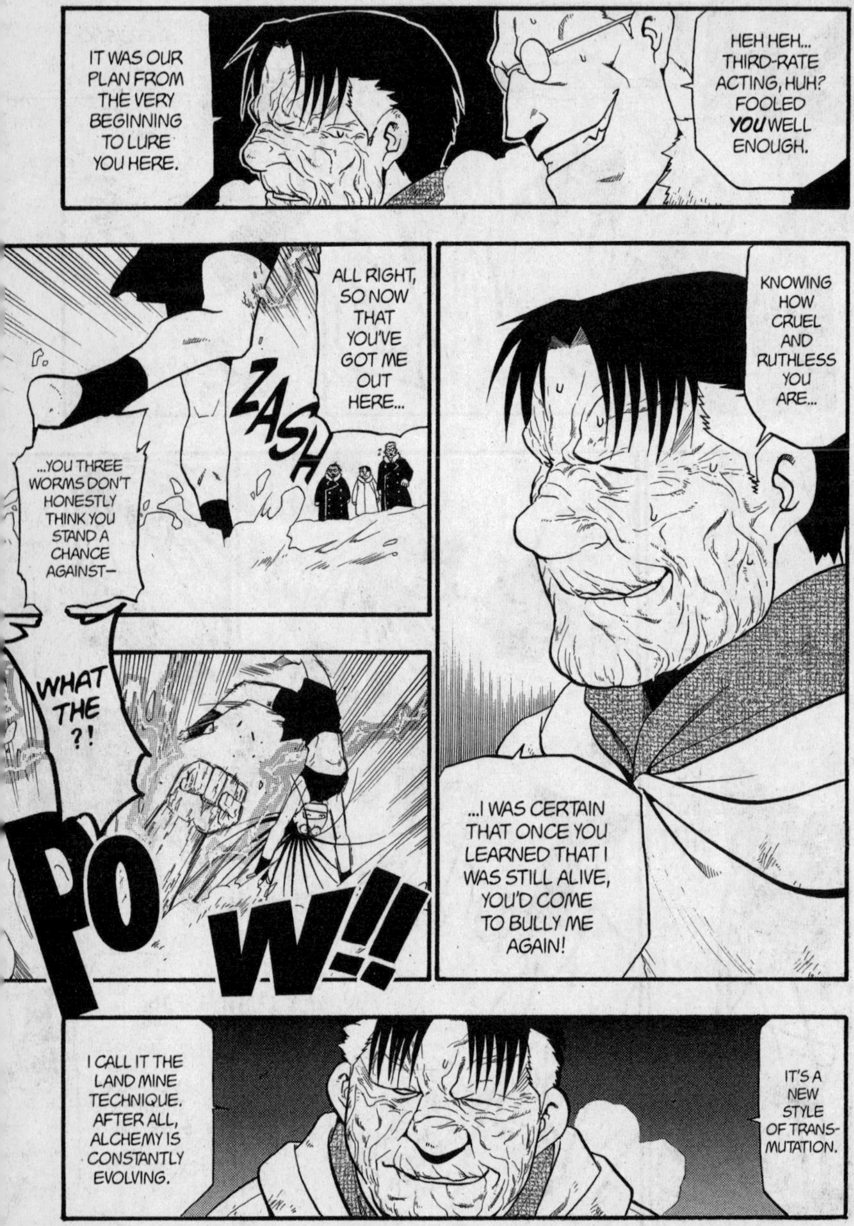
HEH HEH... THIRD-RATE ACTING, HUH? FOOLED YOU WELL ENOUGH.
IT WAS OUR PLAN FROM THE VERY BEGINNING TO LURE YOU HERE.
KNOWING HOW CRUEL AND RUTHLESS YOU ARE...
...I WAS CERTAIN THAT ONCE YOU LEARNED THAT I WAS STILL ALIVE, YOU'D COME TO BULLY ME AGAIN!
ALL RIGHT, SO NOW THAT YOU'VE GOT ME OUT HERE...
ZASH
...YOU THREE WORMS DON'T HONESTLY THINK YOU STAND A CHANCE AGAINST—
WHAT THE ?!
POW!!
IT'S A NEW STYLE OF TRANS-MUTATION.
I CALL IT THE LAND MINE TECHNIQUE. AFTER ALL, ALCHEMY IS CONSTANTLY EVOLVING.

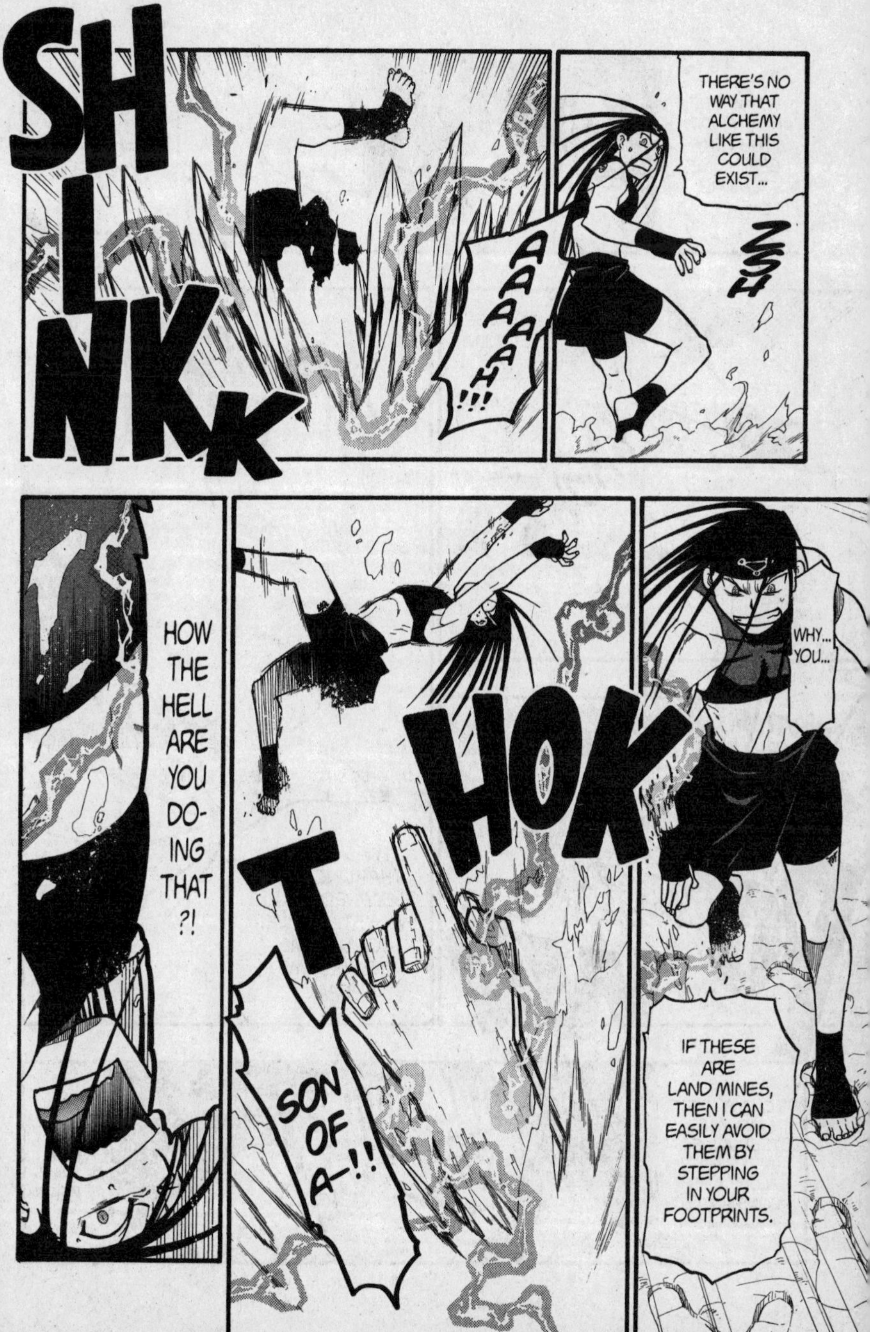
THERE'S NO WAY THAT ALCHEMY LIKE THIS COULD EXIST...
ZSH
AAAAAH!!!
SHLINKK
WHY... YOU...
IF THESE ARE LAND MINES, THEN I CAN EASILY AVOID THEM BY STEPPING IN YOUR FOOTPRINTS.
THOK
SON OF A—!!
HOW THE HELL ARE YOU DOING THAT?!

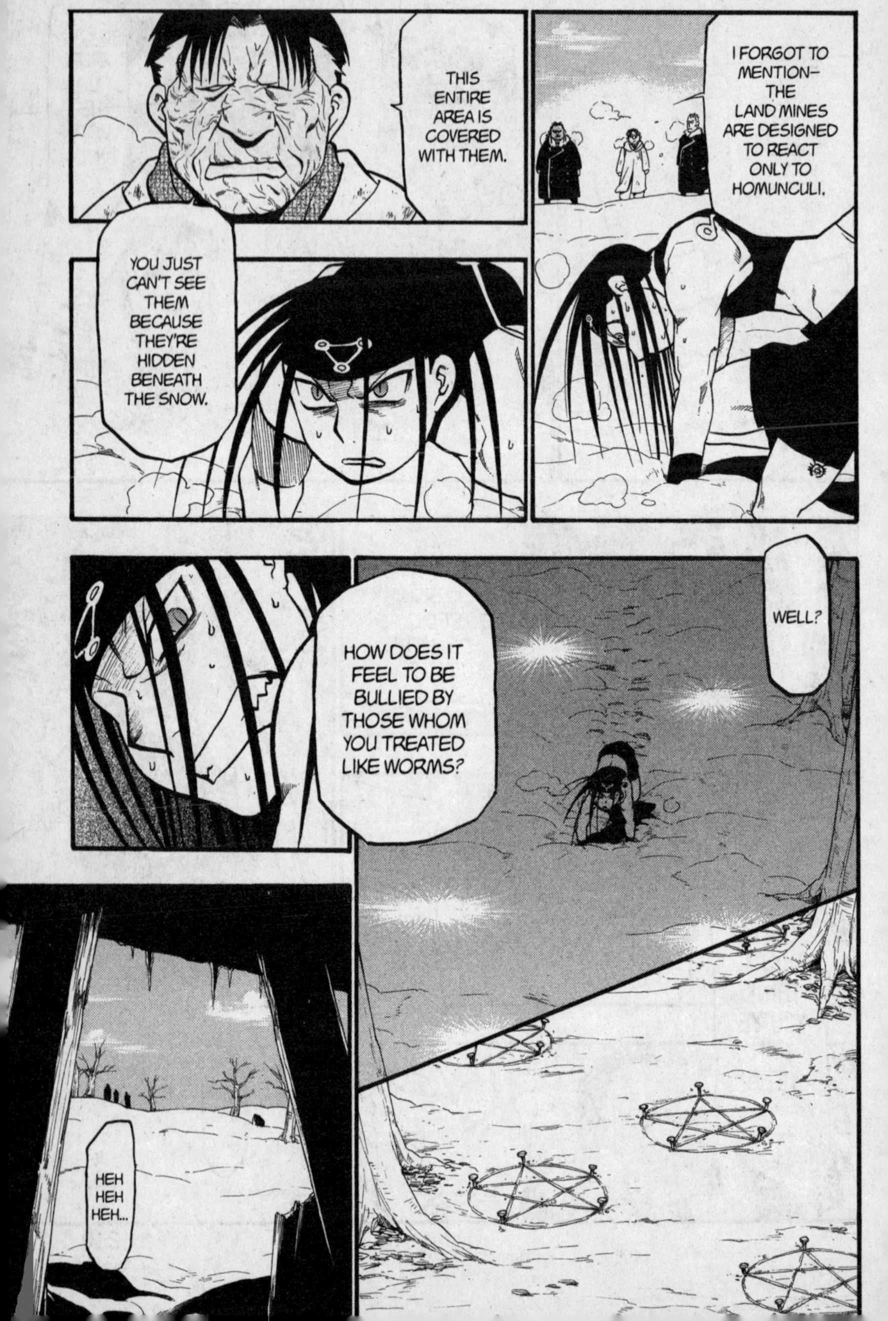
I FORGOT TO MENTION— THE LAND MINES ARE DESIGNED TO REACT ONLY TO HOMUNCULI.
THIS ENTIRE AREA IS COVERED WITH THEM.
YOU JUST CAN'T SEE THEM BECAUSE THEY'RE HIDDEN BENEATH THE SNOW.
WELL?
HOW DOES IT FEEL TO BE BULLIED BY THOSE WHOM YOU TREATED LIKE WORMS?
HEH HEH HEH...

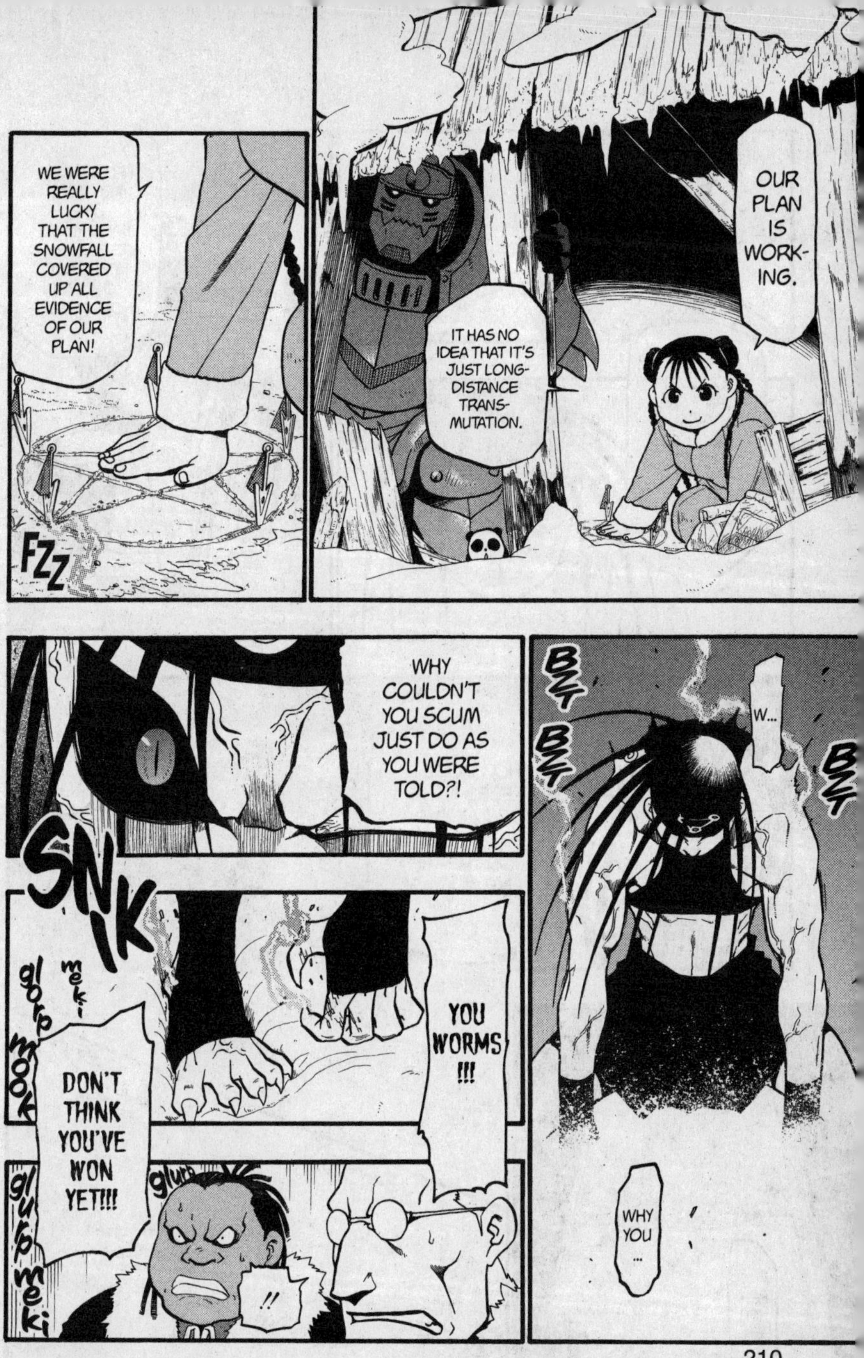
OUR PLAN IS WORKING.
IT HAS NO IDEA THAT IT'S JUST LONG-DISTANCE TRANSMUTATION.
WE WERE REALLY LUCKY THAT THE SNOWFALL COVERED UP ALL EVIDENCE OF OUR PLAN!
FZZ
BZT
BZT
BZT
W...
WHY YOU ...
WHY COULDN'T YOU SCUM JUST DO AS YOU WERE TOLD?!
SNIK
meki
glorp
mook
YOU WORMS !!!
DON'T THINK YOU'VE WON YET!!!
glurb
glurp
meki
!!

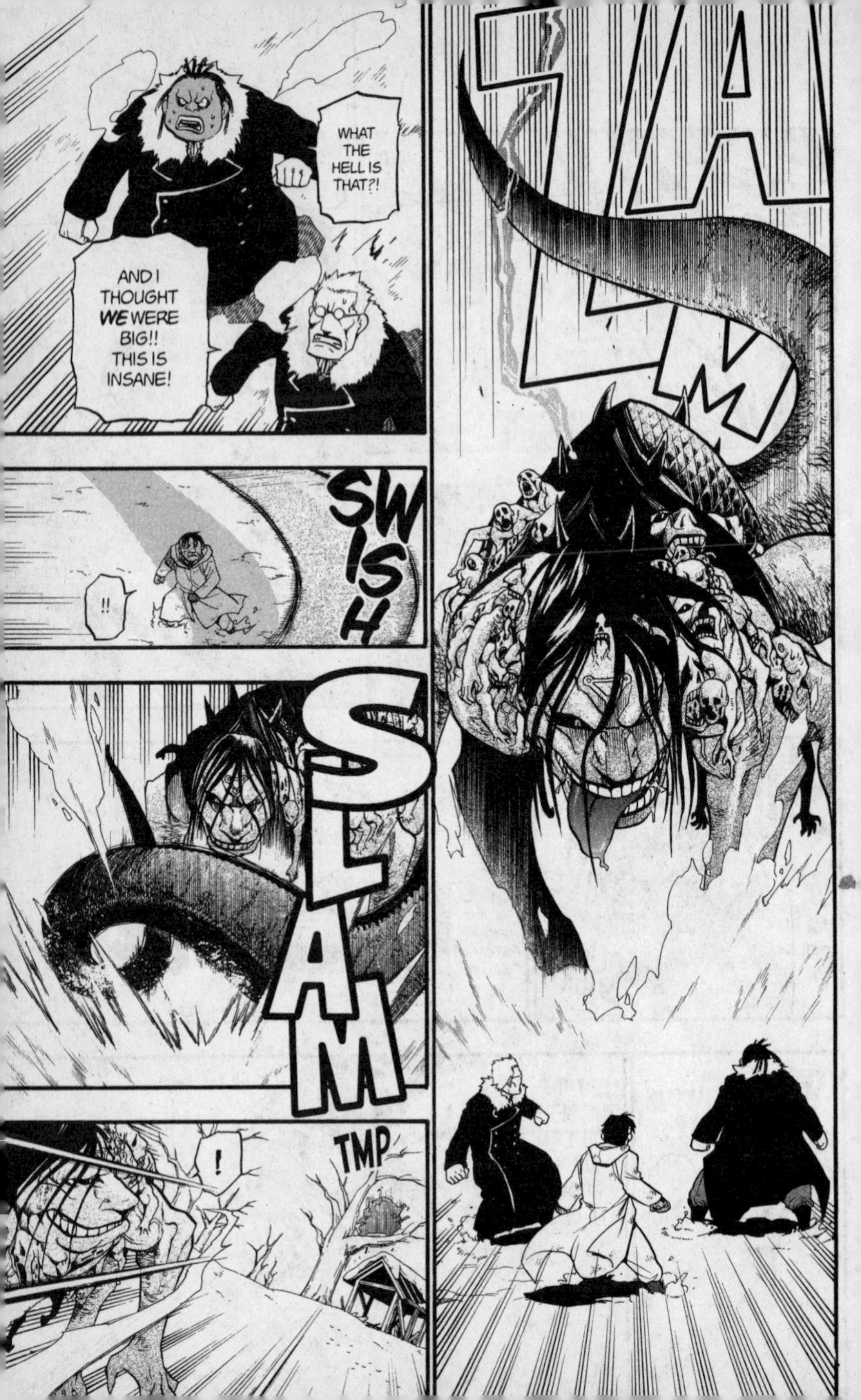
SLAM
WHAT THE HELL IS THAT?!
AND I THOUGHT WE WERE BIG!! THIS IS INSANE!
SWISH
!!
SLAM
TMP
!

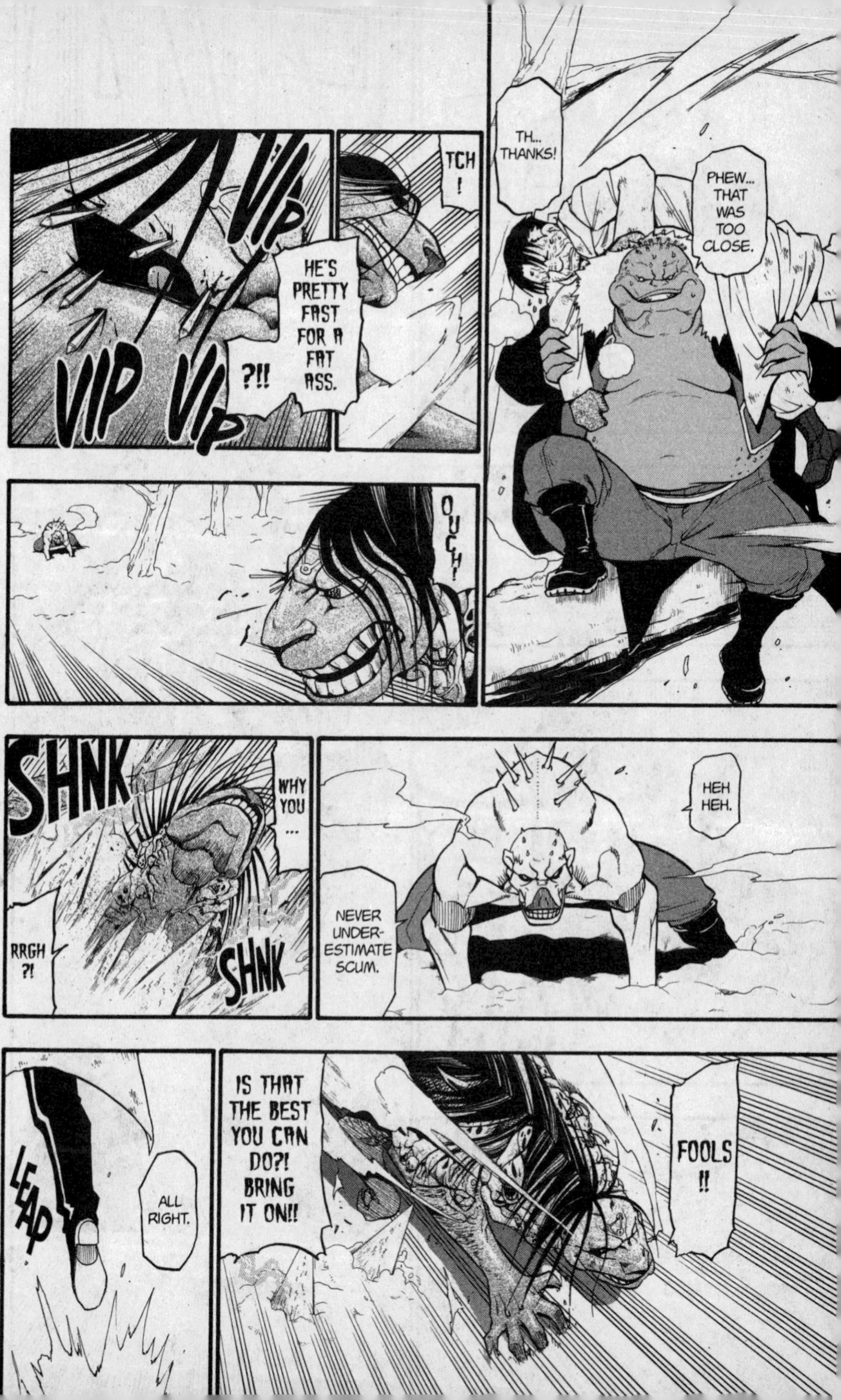
PHEW... THAT WAS TOO CLOSE.
TH... THANKS!
TCH!
HE'S PRETTY FAST FOR A FAT ASS.
?!!
VIP
VIP
VIP
OUCH!
HEH HEH.
NEVER UNDER-ESTIMATE SCUM.
WHY YOU...
SHNK
RRGH ?!
SHNK
FOOLS!!
IS THAT THE BEST YOU CAN DO?! BRING IT ON!!
ALL RIGHT.
LEAP

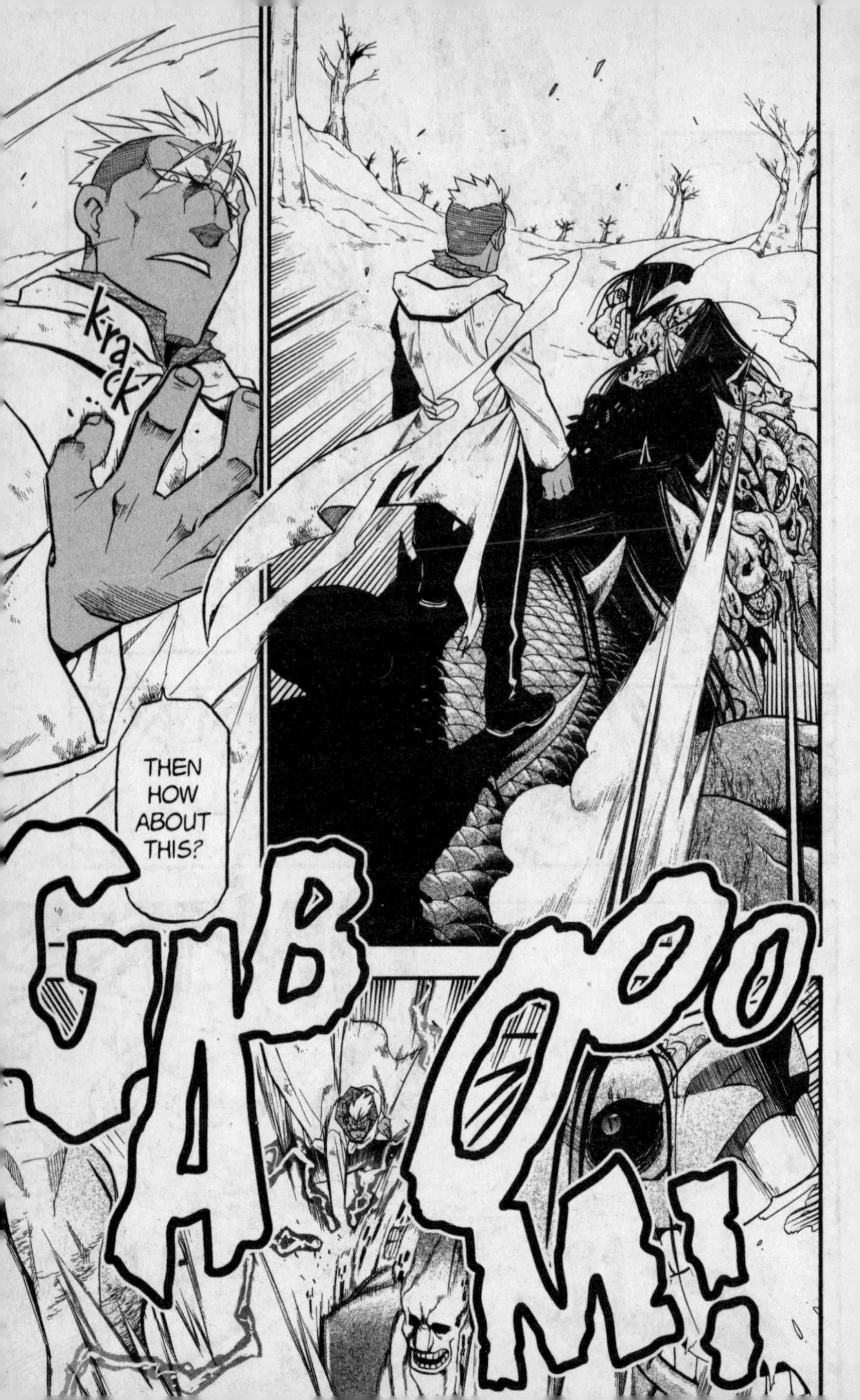
K-RACK
THEN HOW ABOUT THIS?
GABOOM!

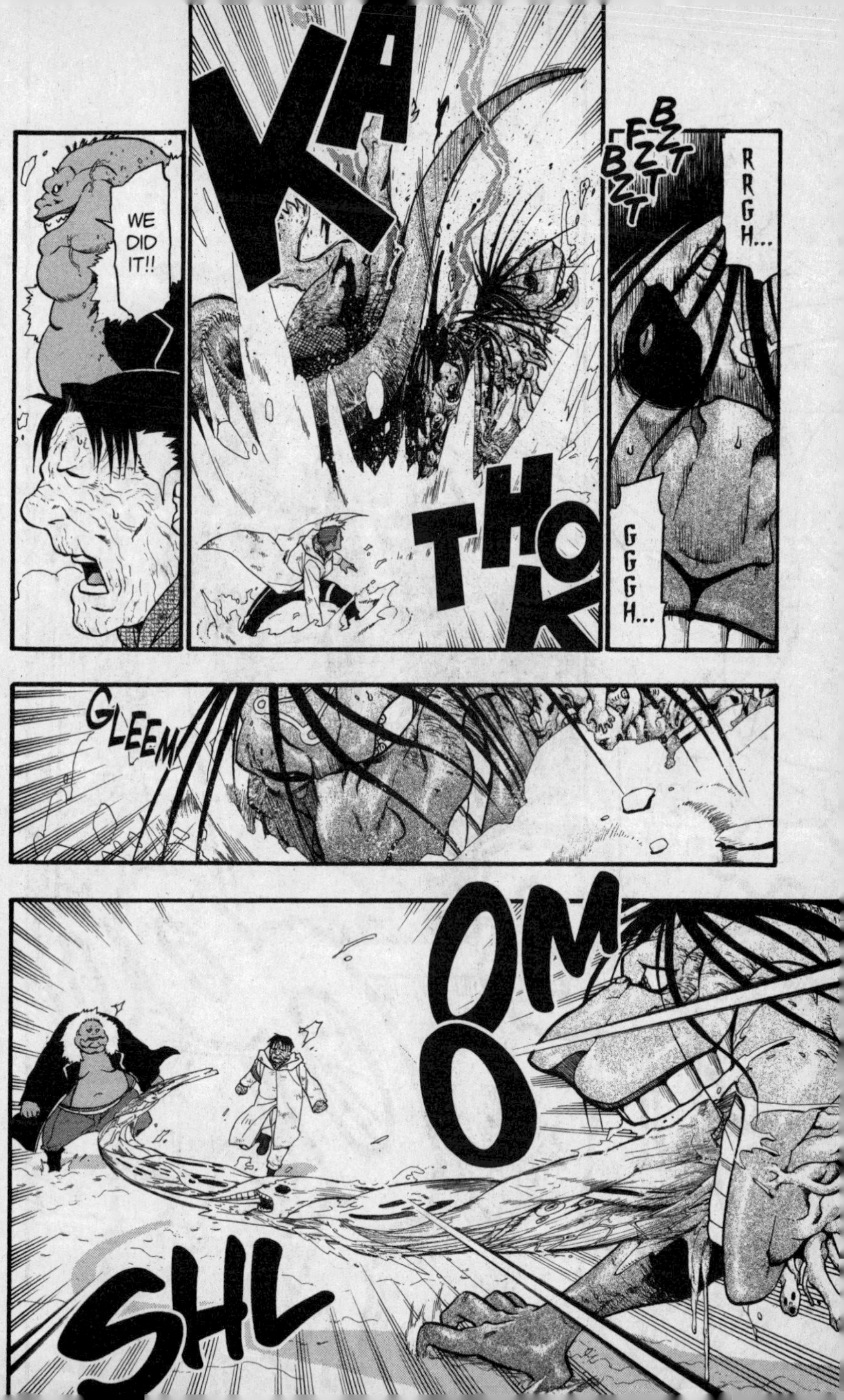
RRGH...
BZT
FZT
BZT
GGGH...
KA
THOK
WE DID IT!!
GLEEM
OM
O
SHL

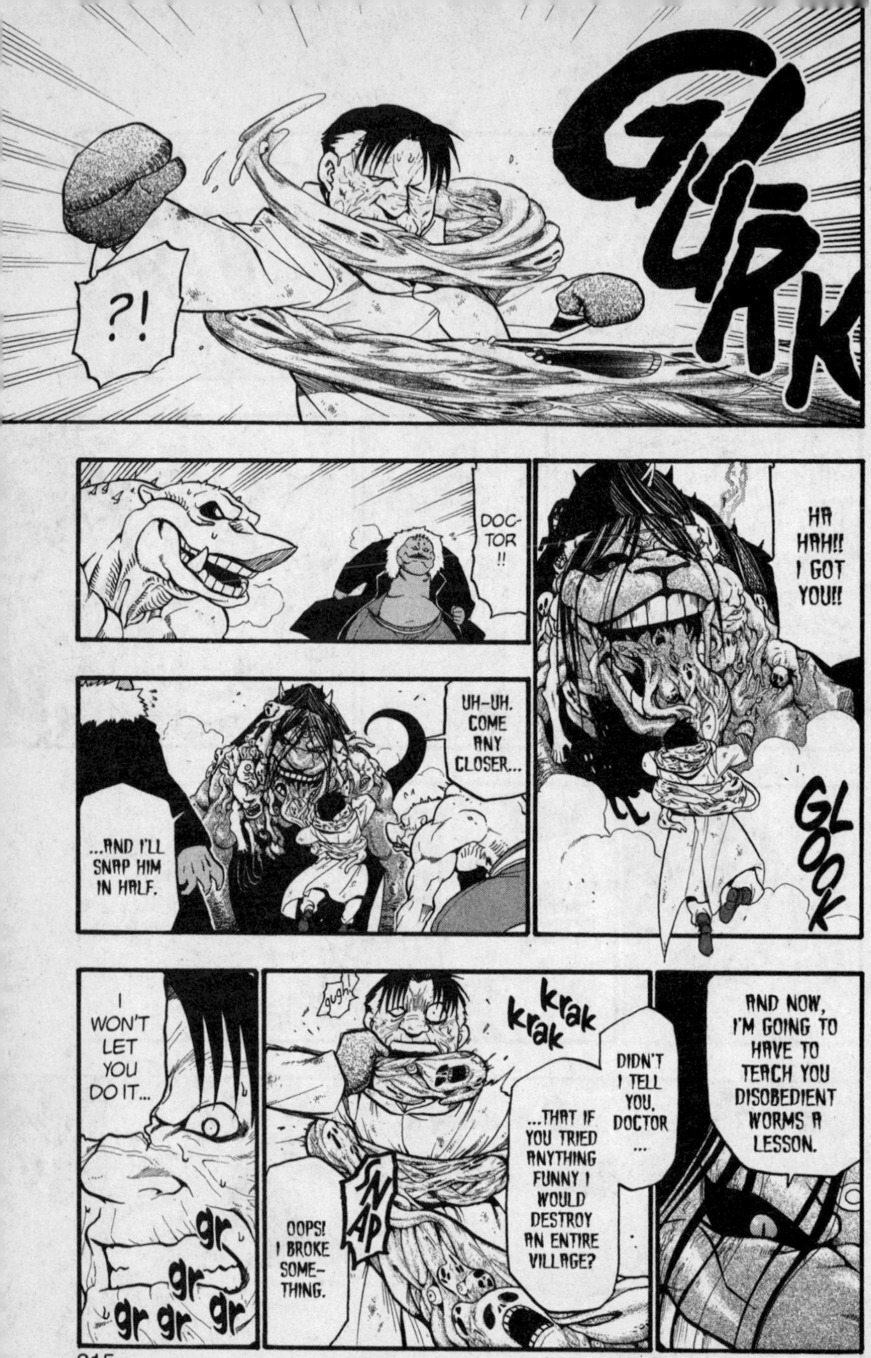
GLURK
?!
HA HAH!! I GOT YOU!!
GLOOOK
DOC-TOR!!
UH-UH. COME ANY CLOSER...
...AND I'LL SNAP HIM IN HALF.
AND NOW, I'M GOING TO HAVE TO TEACH YOU DISOBEDIENT WORMS A LESSON.
krak krak
gugh
DIDN'T I TELL YOU, DOCTOR...
...THAT IF YOU TRIED ANYTHING FUNNY I WOULD DESTROY AN ENTIRE VILLAGE?
SNAP
OOPS! I BROKE SOME-THING.
I WON'T LET YOU DO IT...
gr gr gr gr gr

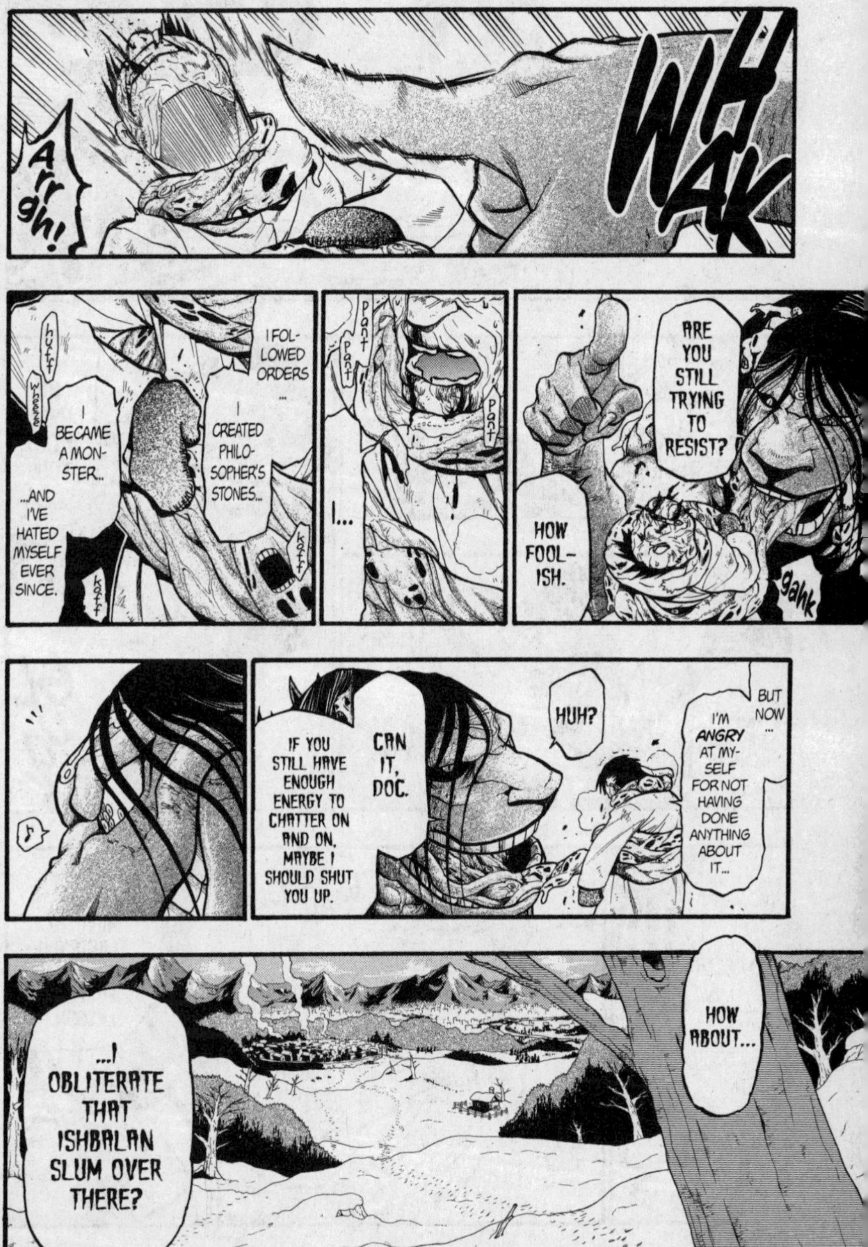
WHAK
Arrgh!
ARE YOU STILL TRYING TO RESIST?
HOW FOOLISH.
gahk
pant
pant
pant
I...
I FOLLOWED ORDERS...
I CREATED PHILOSOPHER'S STONES...
huff
wheeze
I BECAME A MONSTER..
...AND I'VE HATED MYSELF EVER SINCE.
koff
koff
BUT NOW...
I'M ANGRY AT MYSELF FOR NOT HAVING DONE ANYTHING ABOUT IT...
HUH?
CAN IT, DOC.
IF YOU STILL HAVE ENOUGH ENERGY TO CHATTER ON AND ON, MAYBE I SHOULD SHUT YOU UP.
♪
HOW ABOUT...
...I OBLITERATE THAT ISHBALAN SLUM OVER THERE?

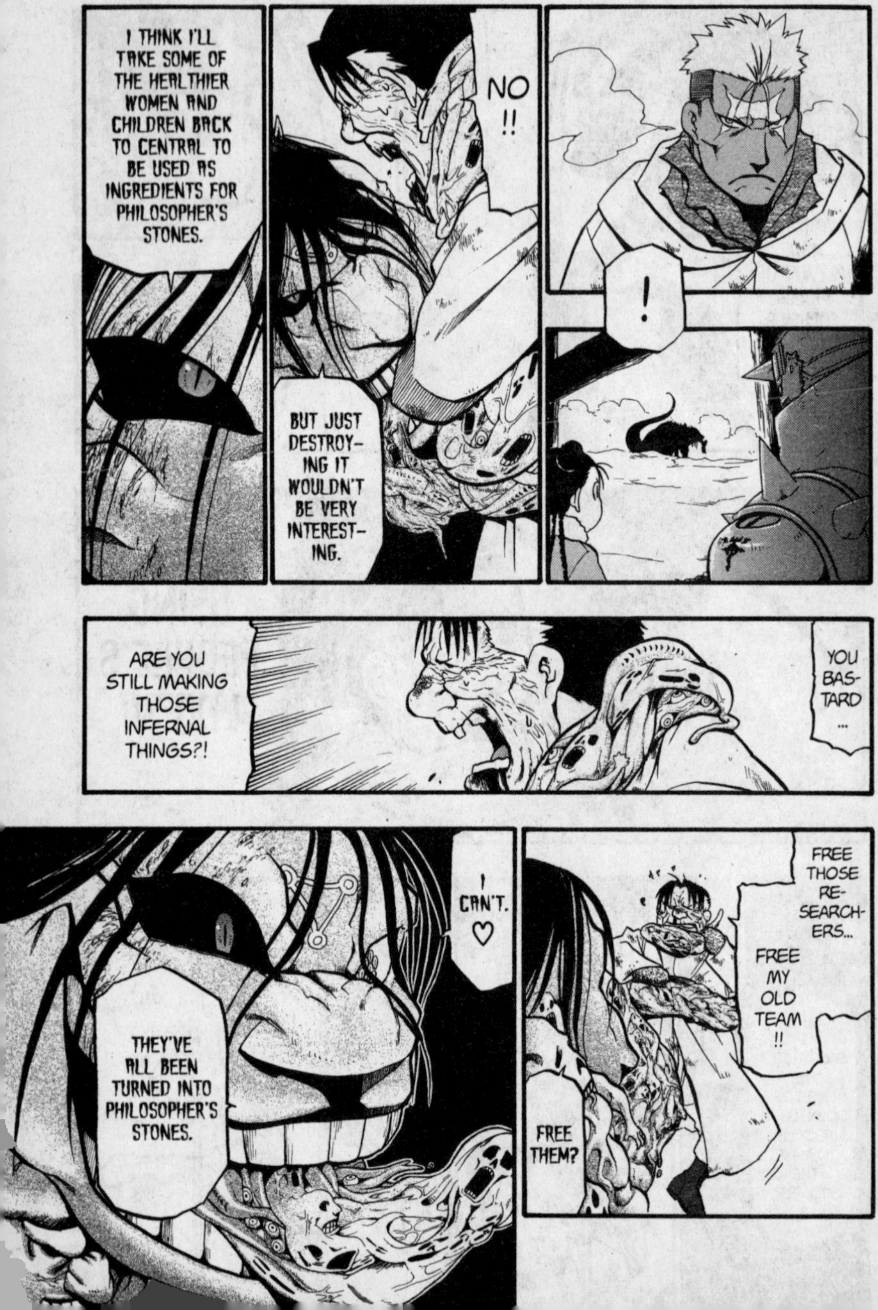

!
NO !!
BUT JUST DESTROYING IT WOULDN'T BE VERY INTERESTING.
I THINK I'LL TAKE SOME OF THE HEALTHIER WOMEN AND CHILDREN BACK TO CENTRAL TO BE USED AS INGREDIENTS FOR PHILOSOPHER'S STONES.
YOU BASTARD...
ARE YOU STILL MAKING THOSE INFERNAL THINGS?!
FREE THOSE RESEARCHERS...
FREE MY OLD TEAM !!
FREE THEM?
I CAN'T. ♡
THEY'VE ALL BEEN TURNED INTO PHILOSOPHER'S STONES.

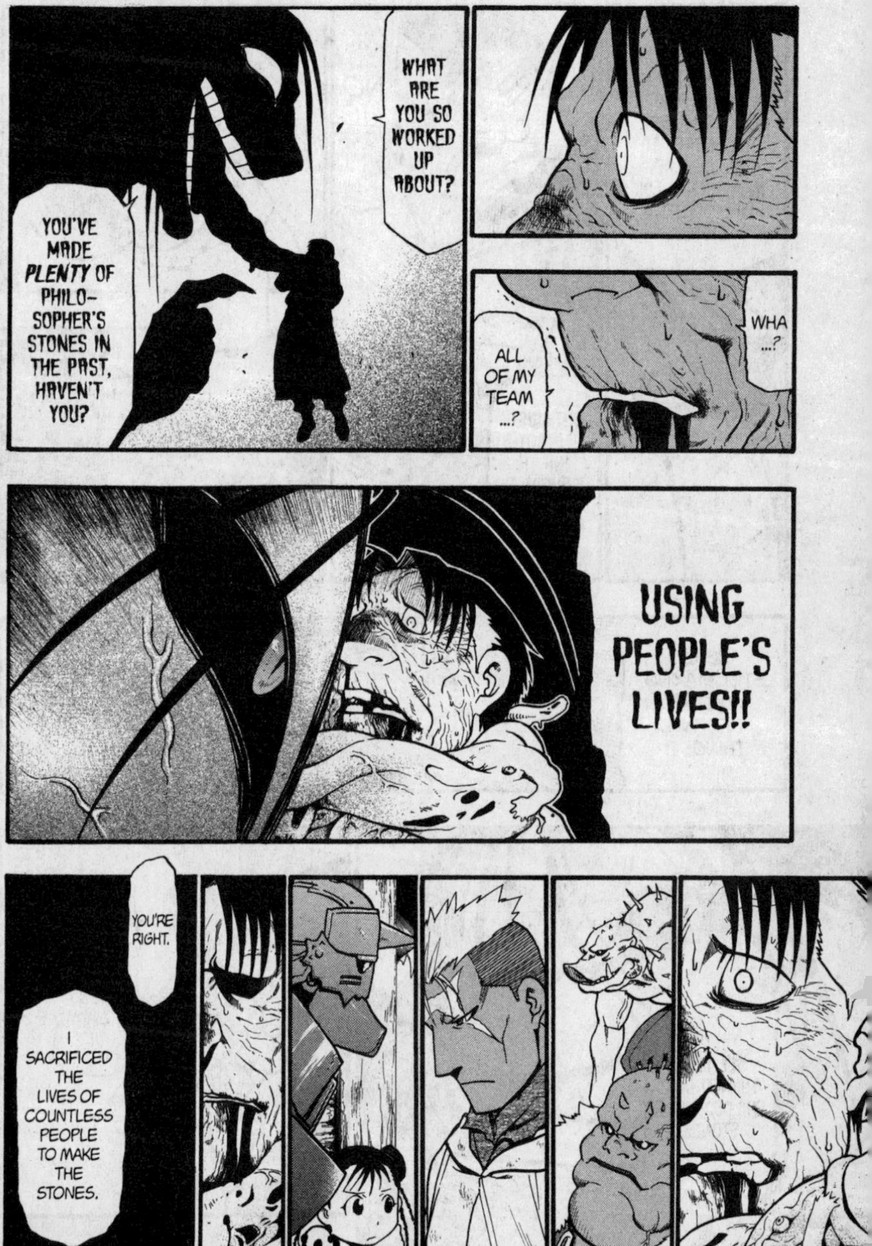
WHA ...?
ALL OF MY TEAM ...?
WHAT ARE YOU SO WORKED UP ABOUT?
YOU'VE MADE *PLENTY* OF PHILO-SOPHER'S STONES IN THE PAST, HAVEN'T YOU?
USING PEOPLE'S LIVES!!
YOU'RE RIGHT.
I SACRIFICED THE LIVES OF COUNTLESS PEOPLE TO MAKE THE STONES.

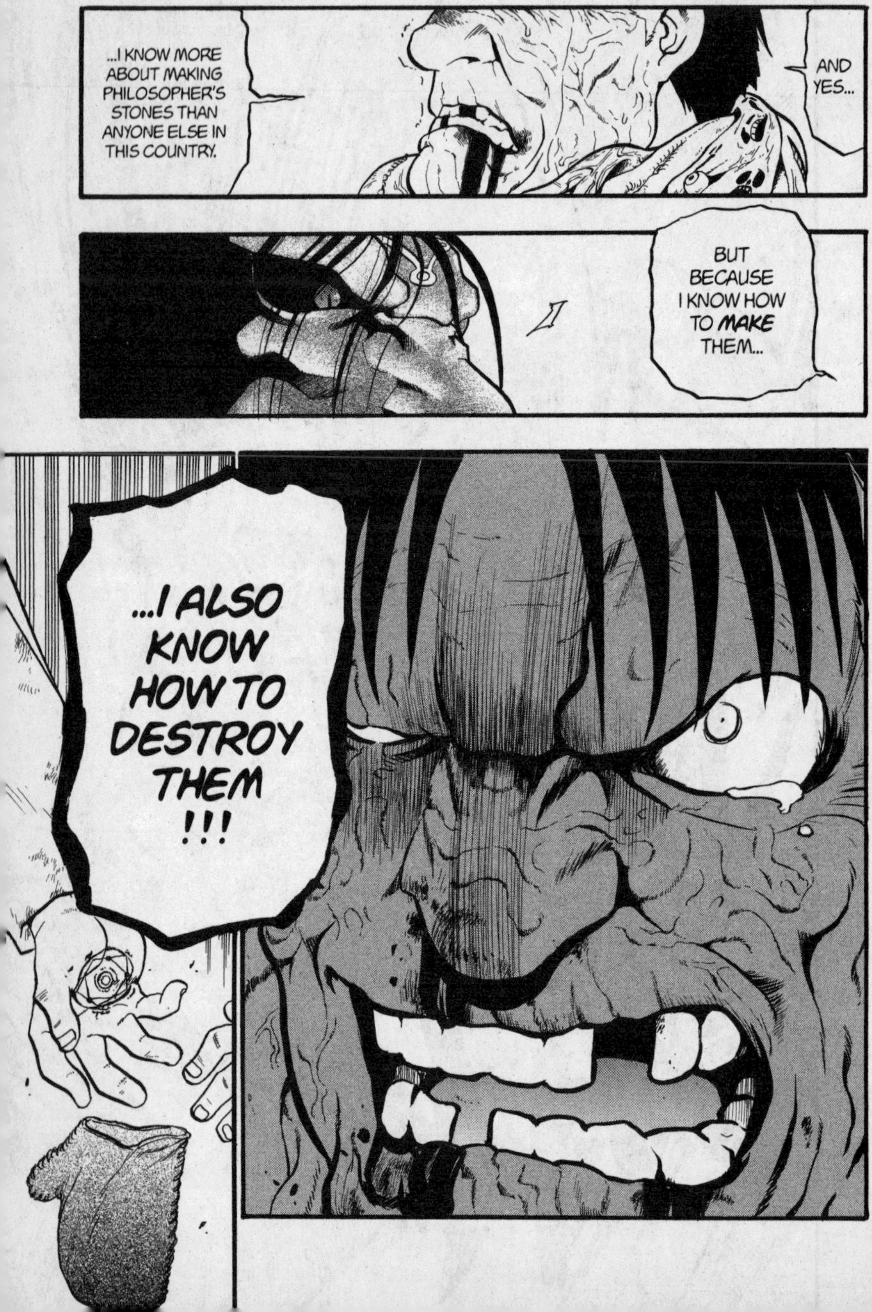
AND YES...
...I KNOW MORE ABOUT MAKING PHILOSOPHER'S STONES THAN ANYONE ELSE IN THIS COUNTRY.
BUT BECAUSE I KNOW HOW TO MAKE THEM...
...I ALSO KNOW HOW TO DESTROY THEM!!!

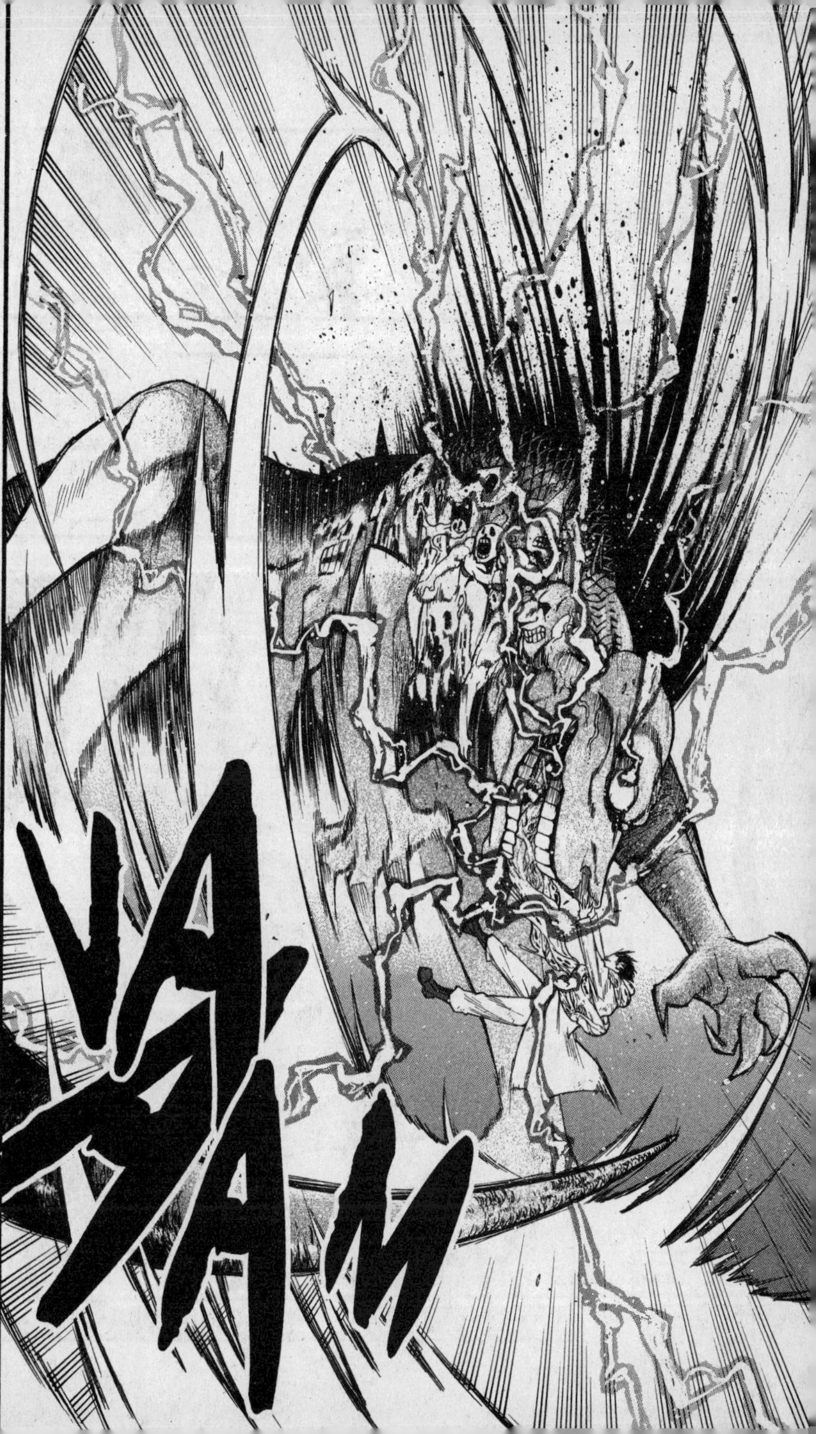
VA
BAM

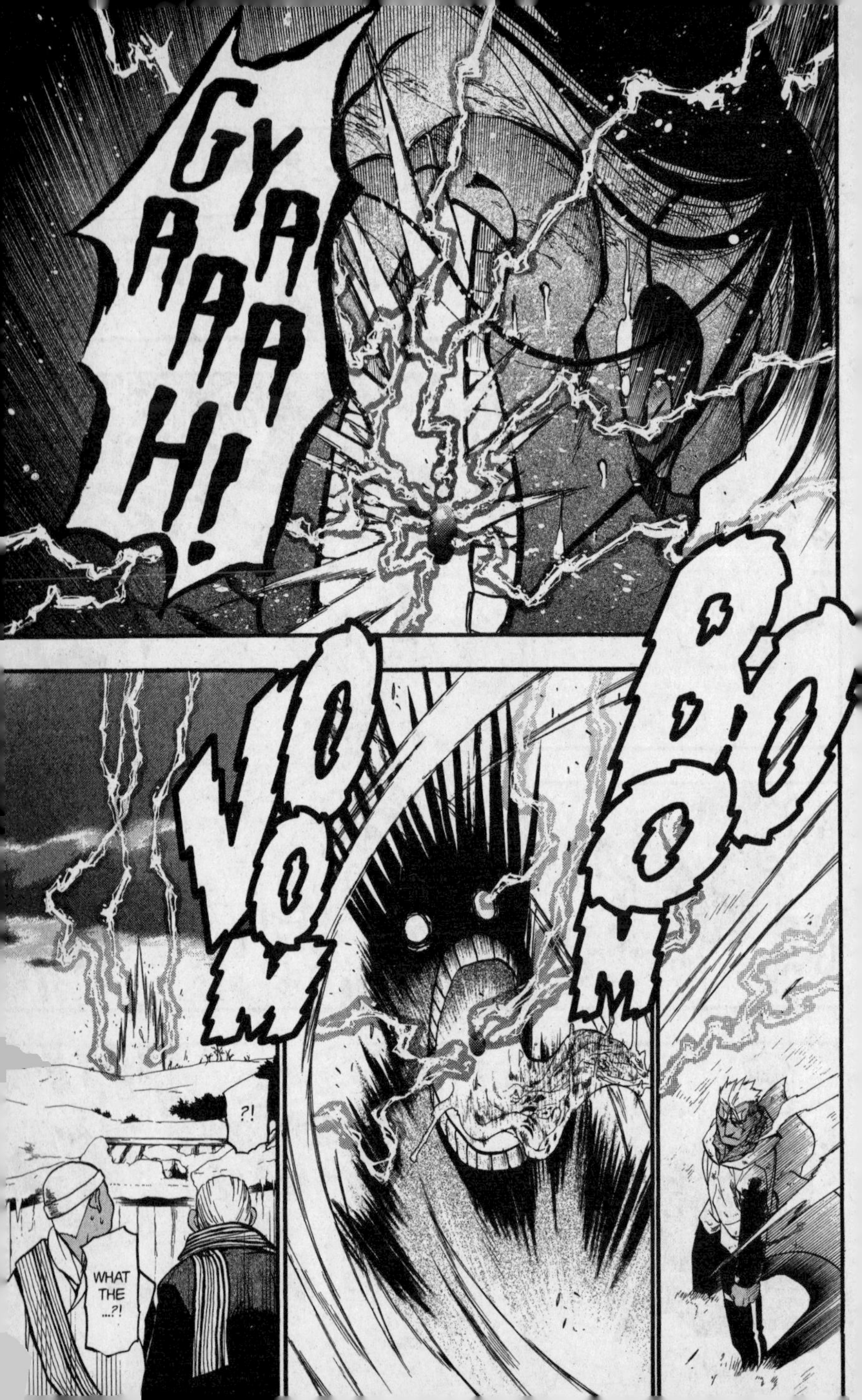
GYAAAAH!
VOOOOOM
VOOOOM
?!
WHAT THE ...?!

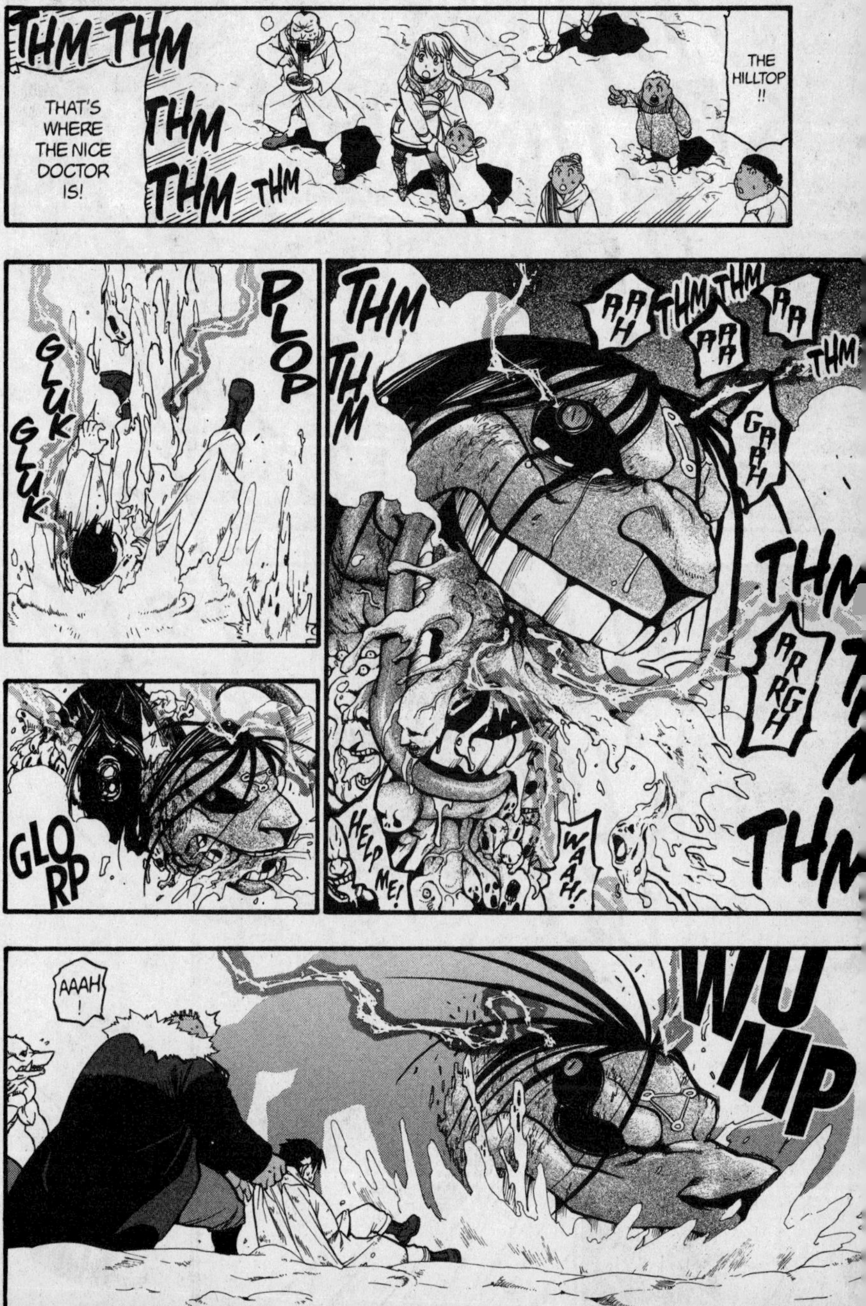
THE HILLTOP !!
THAT'S WHERE THE NICE DOCTOR IS!
THM THM THM THM THM
THM THM THM
AAH
THM THM
AA
AAA
THM
GAAH
THM
ARRGH
THM
WAAH!
HELP ME!
PLOP
GLUK GLUK
GLORP
WUMP
AAAH!

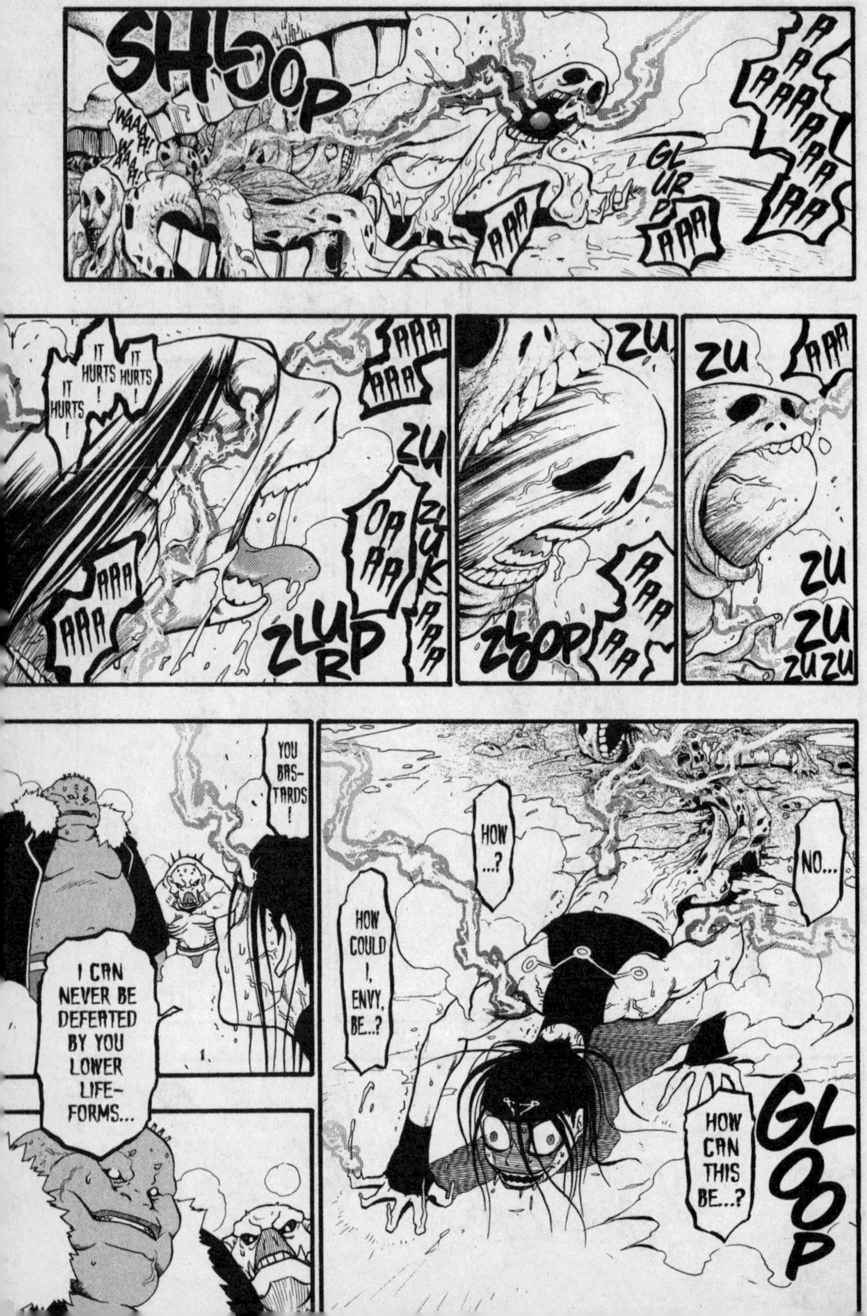
AAAAAAAAAAA
GLURP
AAA
AAA
SHLOOP
WAAAH! WAAAH!
ZU
AAA
ZU
ZU
ZUZU
ZU
AAAA
ZLOOP
AAA
AAA
ZU
OAAA
ZUZUK
AAA
IT HURTS!
IT HURTS!
IT HURTS!
AAA
AAA
ZLURP
NO...
HOW...?
HOW COULD I, ENVY, BE...?
HOW CAN THIS BE...?
GLOOP
YOU BASTARDS!
I CAN NEVER BE DEFEATED BY YOU LOWER LIFE-FORMS...

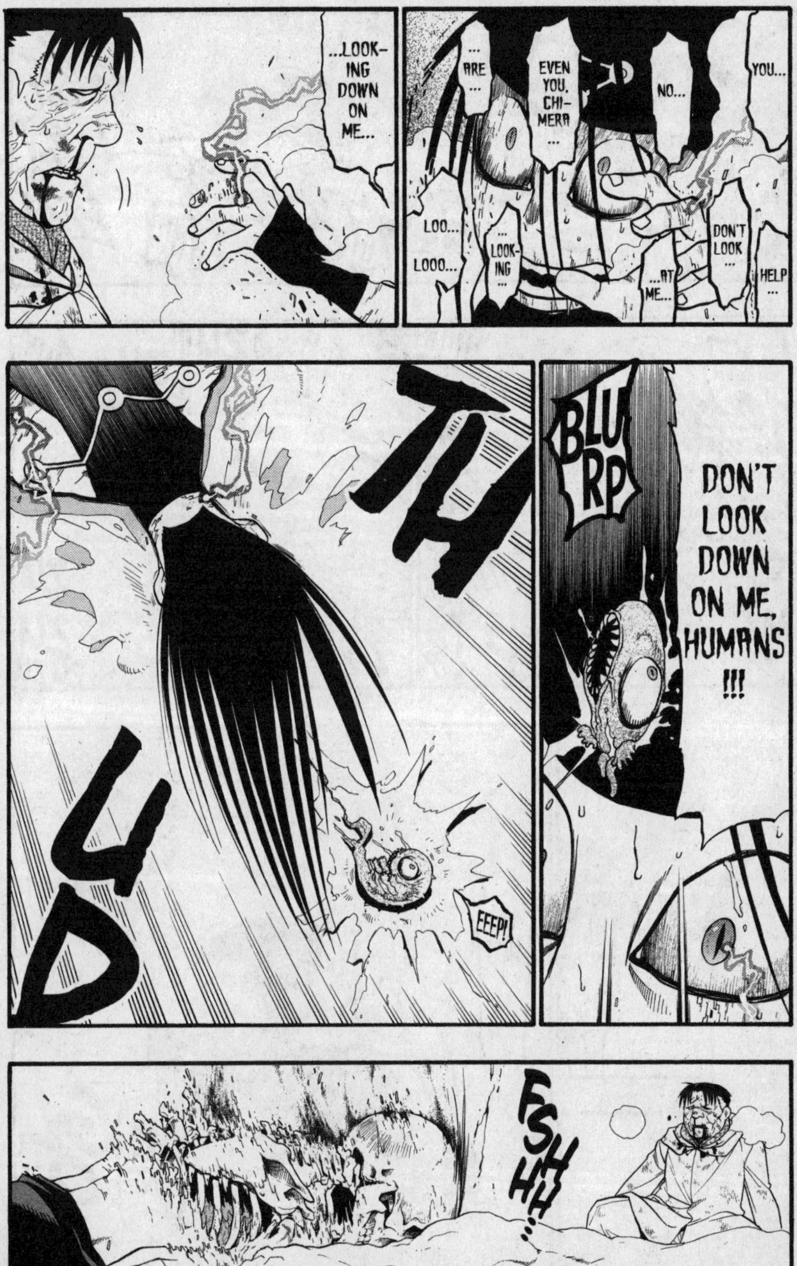
YOU...
NO...
EVEN YOU, CHIMERA...
...ARE...
HELP...
DON'T LOOK...
...AT ME...
...LOOKING...
LOO...
LOOO...
...LOOKING DOWN ON ME...
BLURP
DON'T LOOK DOWN ON ME, HUMANS!!!
THUD
EEEP!
FSHHH...

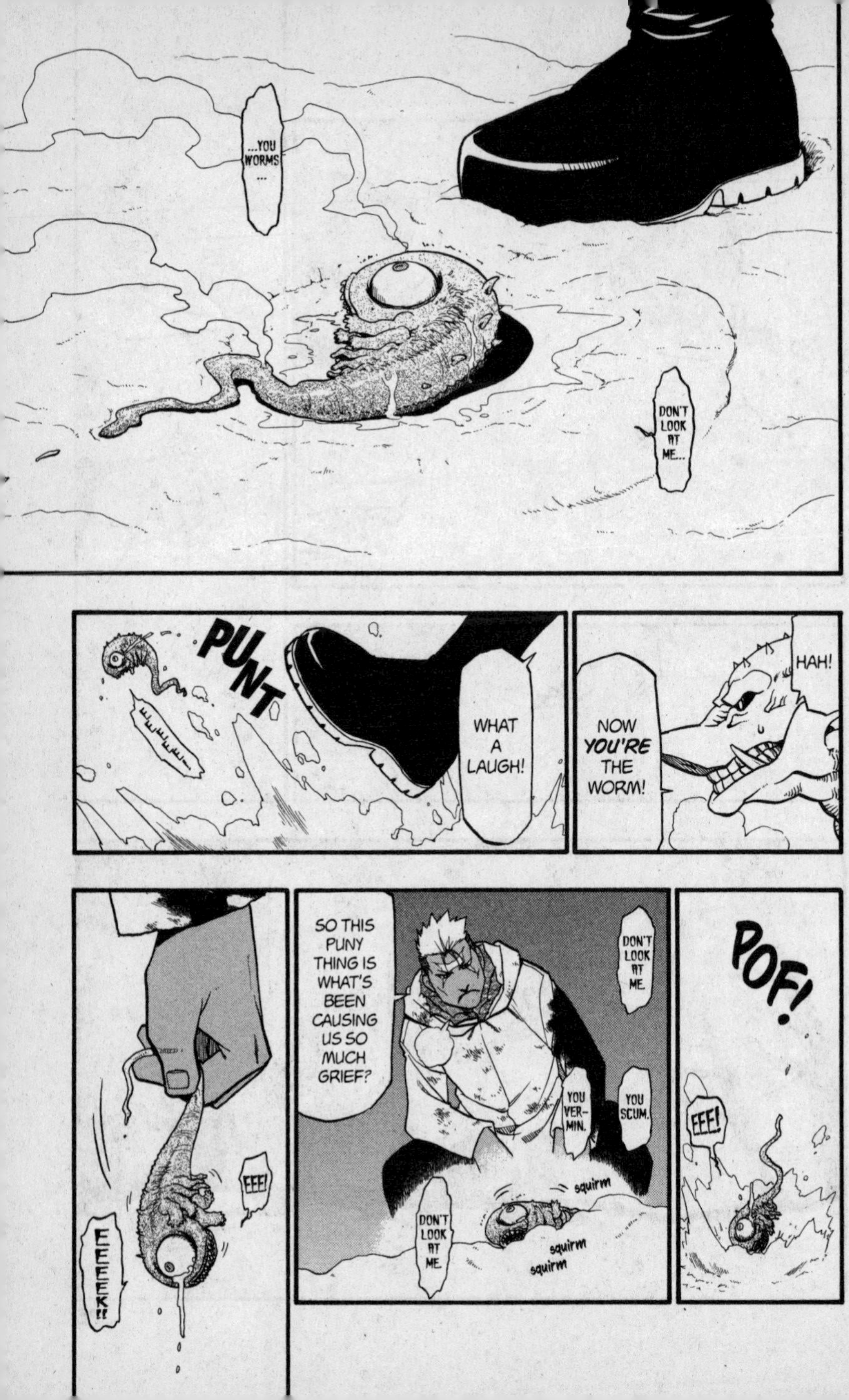
DON'T LOOK AT ME...
...YOU WORMS ...
HAH!
NOW YOU'RE THE WORM!
WHAT A LAUGH!
PUNT
POF!
EEE!
DON'T LOOK AT ME.
YOU SCUM.
YOU VERMIN.
SO THIS PUNY THING IS WHAT'S BEEN CAUSING US SO MUCH GRIEF?
DON'T LOOK AT ME.
squirm
squirm
squirm
EEE!
EEEEEK!!

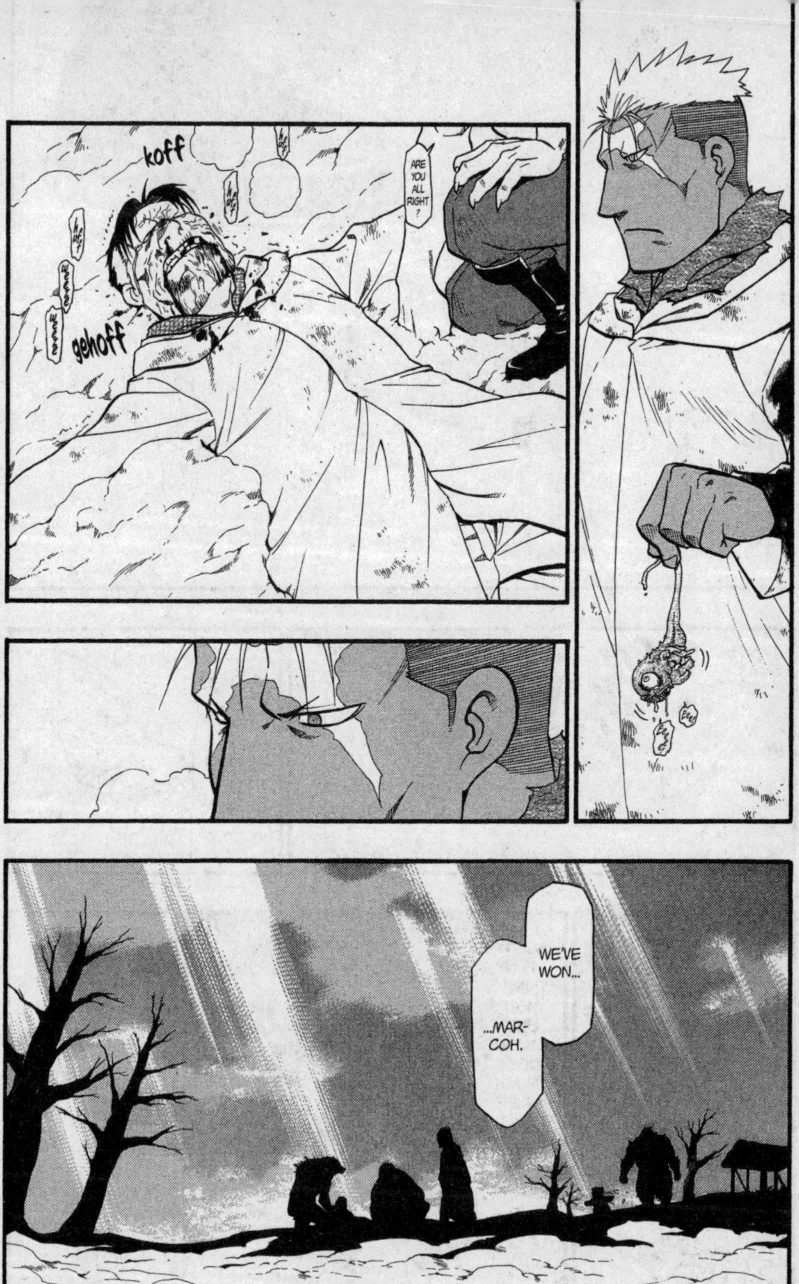
Eee!
Eeeee!
ARE YOU ALL RIGHT?
huff
huff
koff
huff
weeze
weeze
gehoff
WE'VE WON...
...MAR-COH.

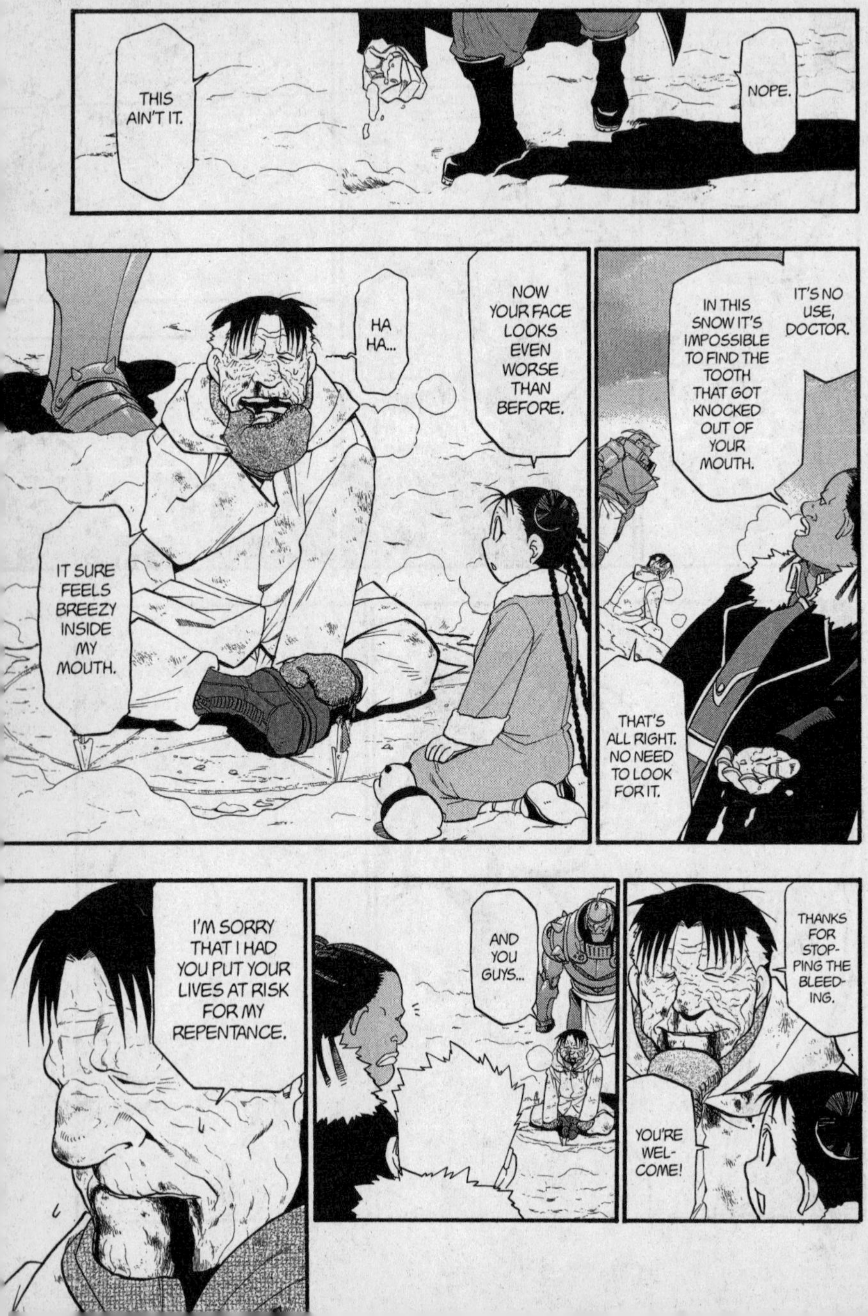
NOPE.
THIS AIN'T IT.
IT'S NO USE, DOCTOR.
IN THIS SNOW IT'S IMPOSSIBLE TO FIND THE TOOTH THAT GOT KNOCKED OUT OF YOUR MOUTH.
THAT'S ALL RIGHT. NO NEED TO LOOK FOR IT.
NOW YOUR FACE LOOKS EVEN WORSE THAN BEFORE.
HA HA...
IT SURE FEELS BREEZY INSIDE MY MOUTH.
THANKS FOR STOP-PING THE BLEED-ING.
YOU'RE WEL-COME!
AND YOU GUYS...
I'M SORRY THAT I HAD YOU PUT YOUR LIVES AT RISK FOR MY REPENTANCE.

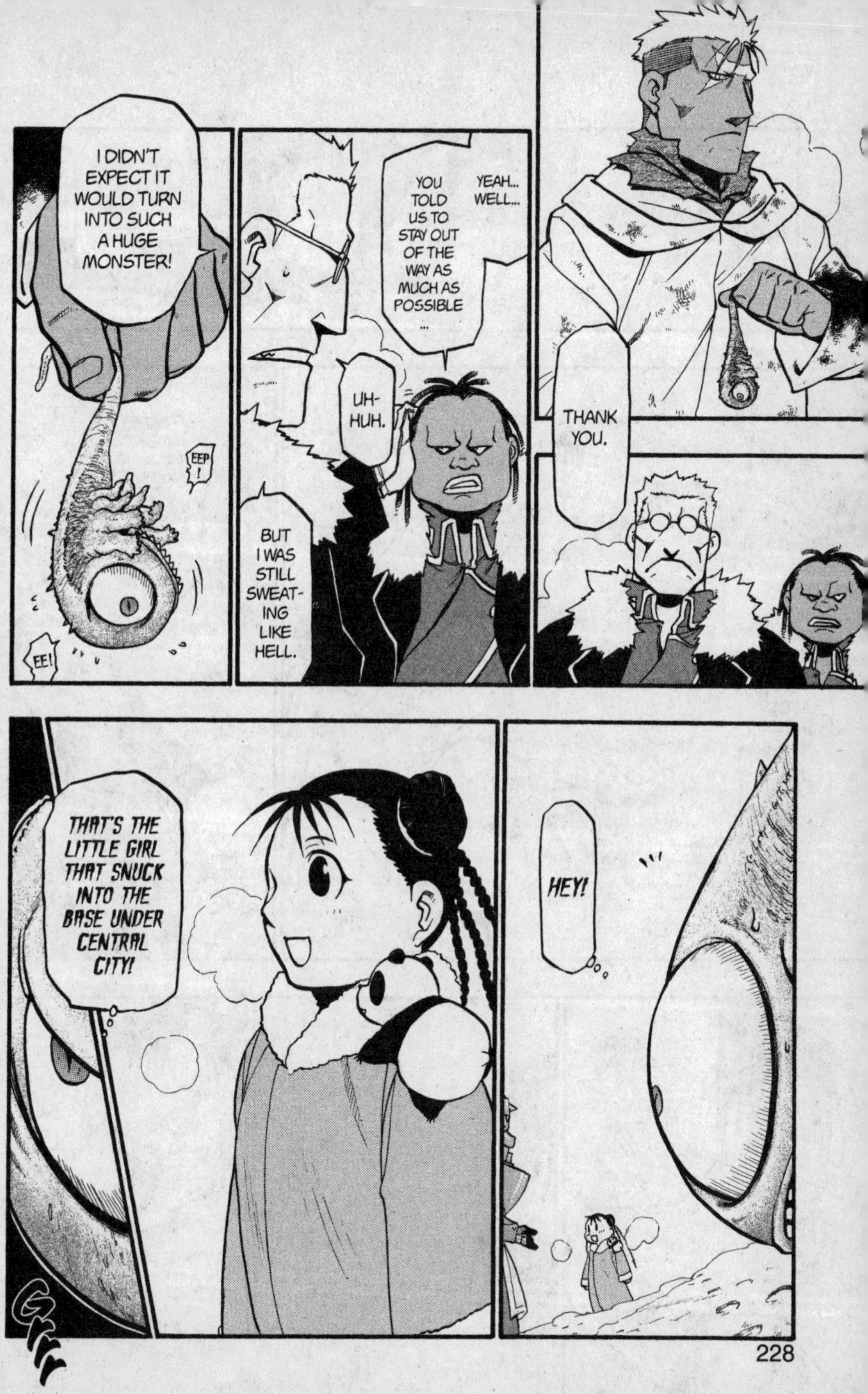
THANK YOU.
YEAH... WELL...
YOU TOLD US TO STAY OUT OF THE WAY AS MUCH AS POSSIBLE...
UH-HUH.
BUT I WAS STILL SWEATING LIKE HELL.
I DIDN'T EXPECT IT WOULD TURN INTO SUCH A HUGE MONSTER!
EEP!
EE!
HEY!
THAT'S THE LITTLE GIRL THAT SNUCK INTO THE BASE UNDER CENTRAL CITY!
Grrr

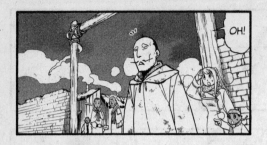

Chapter 80
The Prodigal Father Returns

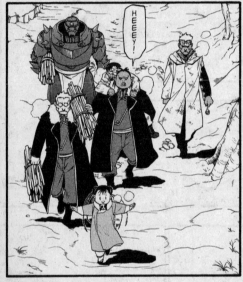

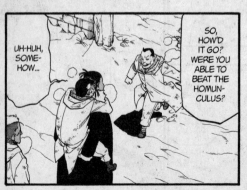

OH!
HEEEEY!
SO, HOW'D IT GO? WERE YOU ABLE TO BEAT THE HOMUN-CULUS?
UH-HUH, SOME-HOW...

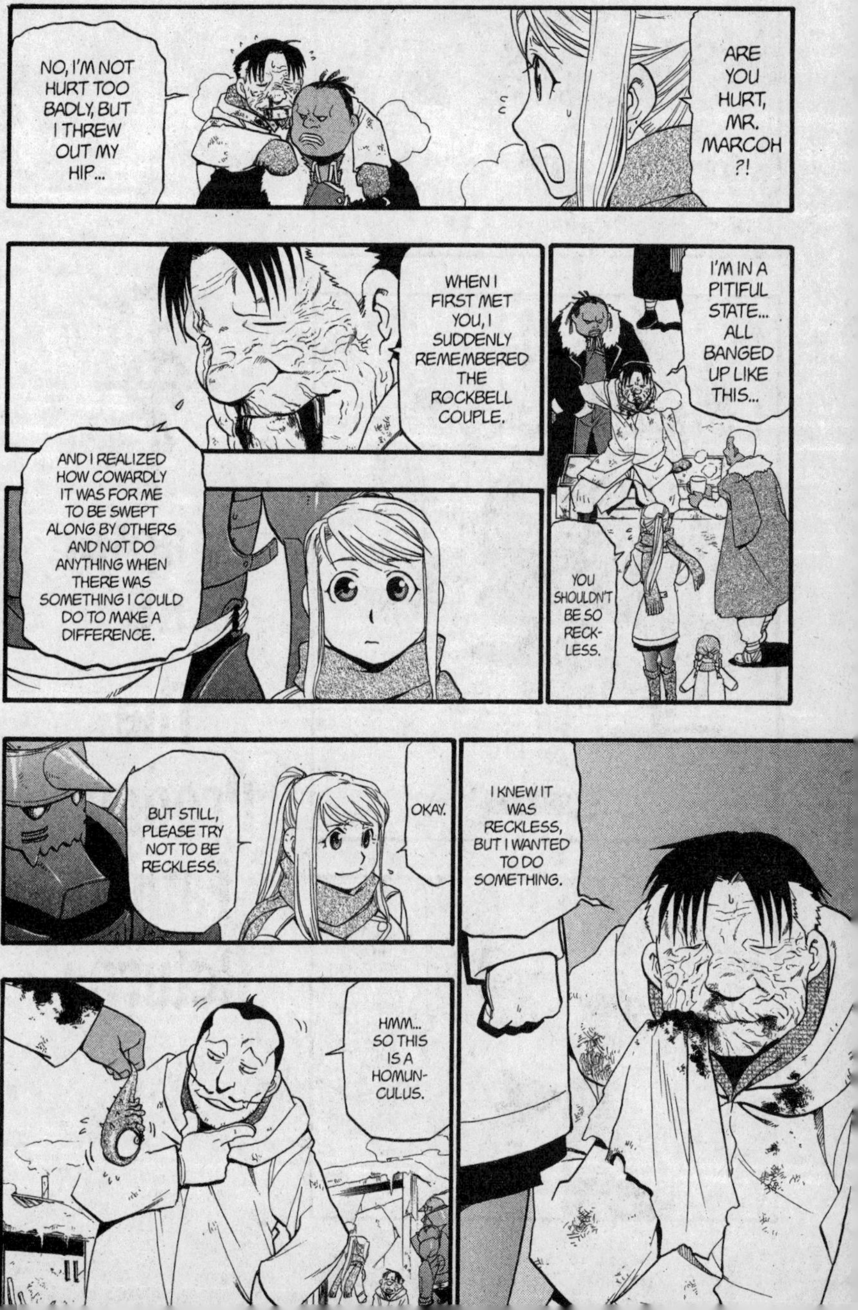
ARE YOU HURT, MR. MARCOH?!
NO, I'M NOT HURT TOO BADLY, BUT I THREW OUT MY HIP...
I'M IN A PITIFUL STATE... ALL BANGED UP LIKE THIS...
YOU SHOULDN'T BE SO RECKLESS.
WHEN I FIRST MET YOU, I SUDDENLY REMEMBERED THE ROCKBELL COUPLE.
AND I REALIZED HOW COWARDLY IT WAS FOR ME TO BE SWEPT ALONG BY OTHERS AND NOT DO ANYTHING WHEN THERE WAS SOMETHING I COULD DO TO MAKE A DIFFERENCE.
I KNEW IT WAS RECKLESS, BUT I WANTED TO DO SOMETHING.
OKAY.
BUT STILL, PLEASE TRY NOT TO BE RECKLESS.
HMM... SO THIS IS A HOMUNCULUS.

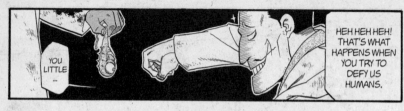

HEH HEH HEH! THAT'S WHAT HAPPENS WHEN YOU TRY TO DEFY US HUMANS.

YOU LITTLE ...

WHY, YOU ...

...WORM !!

EEP!

FLICK

SLIP

CHOOMP

OWWWWWW!!!

Aaiieee!!

?!

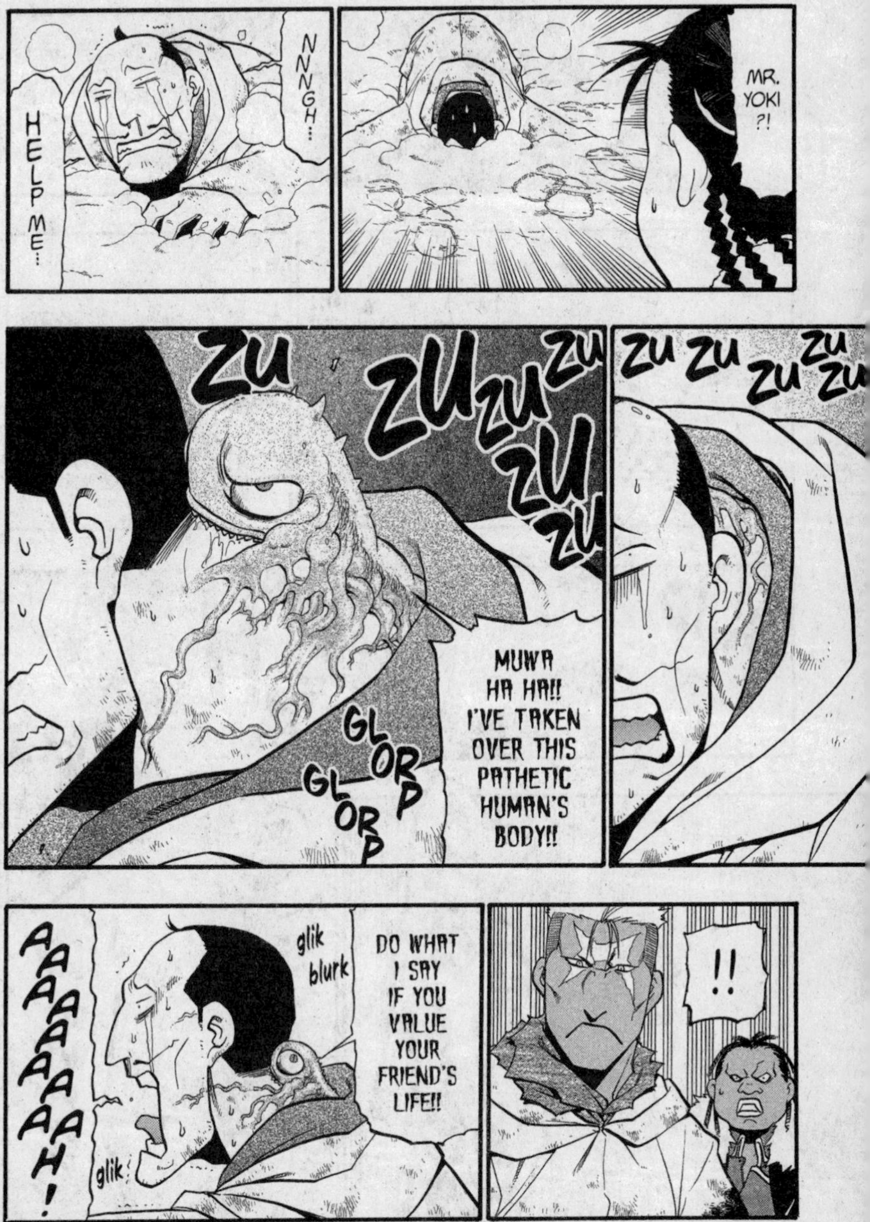
MR. YOKI ?!
NNNGH...
HELP ME...
ZU ZU ZU ZU ZU
ZU ZU ZU ZU ZU ZU
MUWA HA HA!! I'VE TAKEN OVER THIS PATHETIC HUMAN'S BODY!!
GLORP GLORP
!!
DO WHAT I SAY IF YOU VALUE YOUR FRIEND'S LIFE!!
glik blurk
AAAAAAAAH!
glik

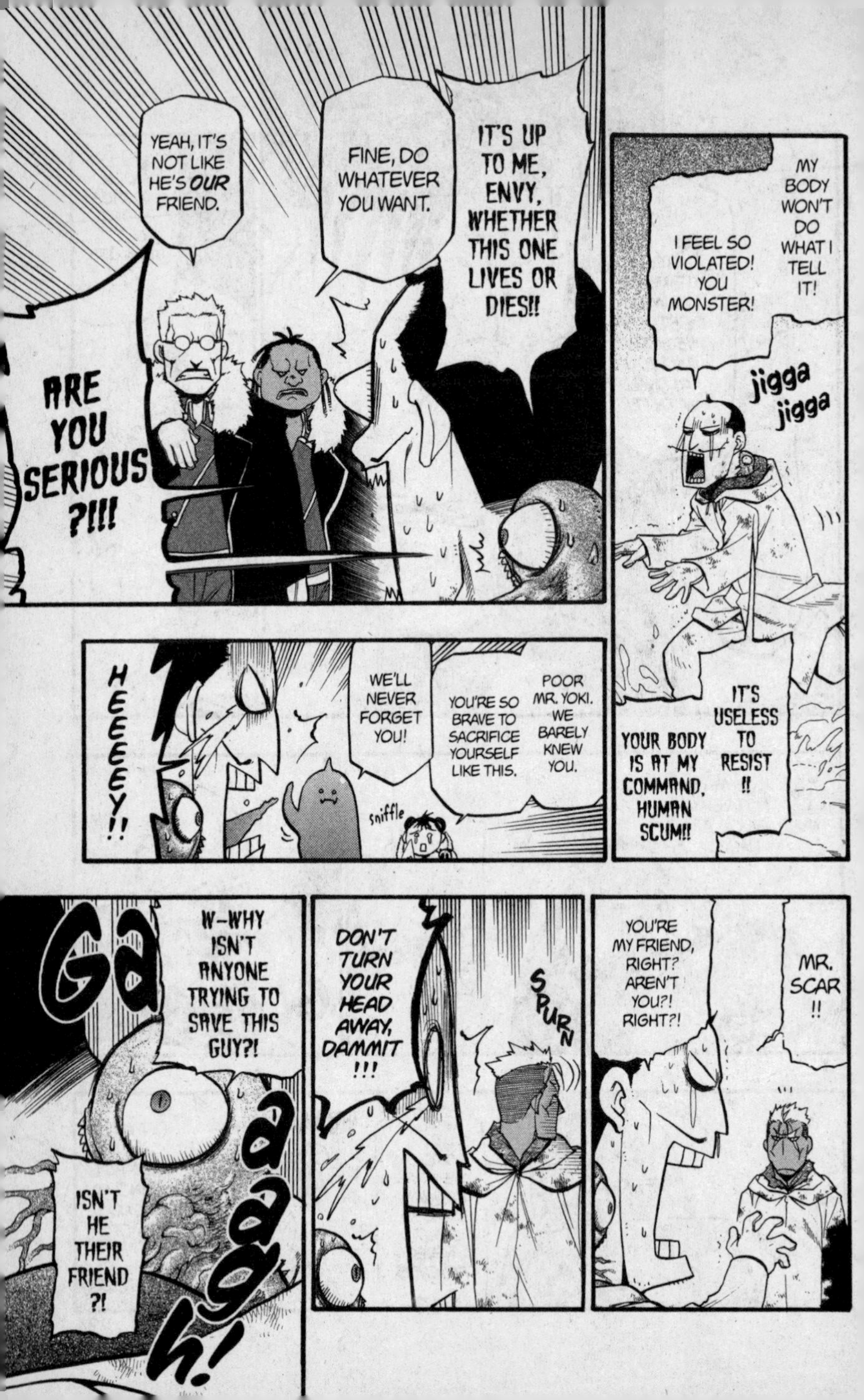
MY BODY WON'T DO WHAT I TELL IT!
I FEEL SO VIOLATED! YOU MONSTER!
jigga jigga
IT'S USELESS TO RESIST!!
YOUR BODY IS AT MY COMMAND, HUMAN SCUM!!
IT'S UP TO ME, ENVY, WHETHER THIS ONE LIVES OR DIES!!
FINE, DO WHATEVER YOU WANT.
YEAH, IT'S NOT LIKE HE'S OUR FRIEND.
ARE YOU SERIOUS?!!!
POOR MR. YOKI. WE BARELY KNEW YOU.
YOU'RE SO BRAVE TO SACRIFICE YOURSELF LIKE THIS.
WE'LL NEVER FORGET YOU!
sniffle
HEEEEEY!!
MR. SCAR!!
YOU'RE MY FRIEND, RIGHT? AREN'T YOU?! RIGHT?!
SPURN
DON'T TURN YOUR HEAD AWAY, DAMMIT!!!
W-WHY ISN'T ANYONE TRYING TO SAVE THIS GUY?!
Gaaagh!
ISN'T HE THEIR FRIEND?!

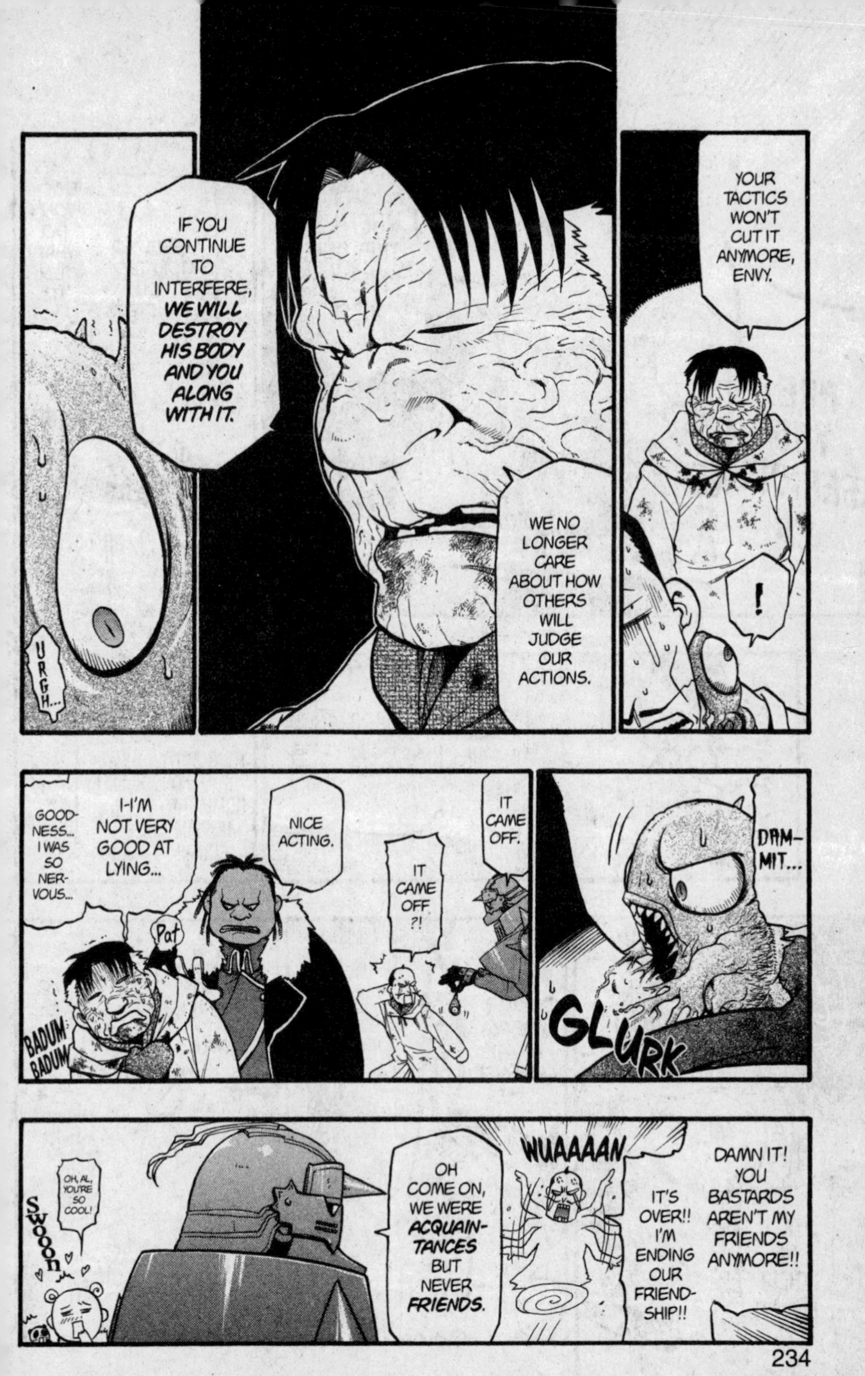
YOUR TACTICS WON'T CUT IT ANYMORE, ENVY.
!
WE NO LONGER CARE ABOUT HOW OTHERS WILL JUDGE OUR ACTIONS.
IF YOU CONTINUE TO INTERFERE, WE WILL DESTROY HIS BODY AND YOU ALONG WITH IT.
URGH...
DAM-MIT...
GLURK
IT CAME OFF.
IT CAME OFF ?!
NICE ACTING.
I-I'M NOT VERY GOOD AT LYING...
GOOD-NESS... I WAS SO NER-VOUS...
Pat
BADUM BADUM
DAMN IT! YOU BASTARDS AREN'T MY FRIENDS ANYMORE!!
IT'S OVER!! I'M ENDING OUR FRIEND-SHIP!!
WUAAAAN
OH COME ON, WE WERE ACQUAIN-TANCES BUT NEVER FRIENDS.
OH, AL, YOU'RE SO COOL!
Swooon

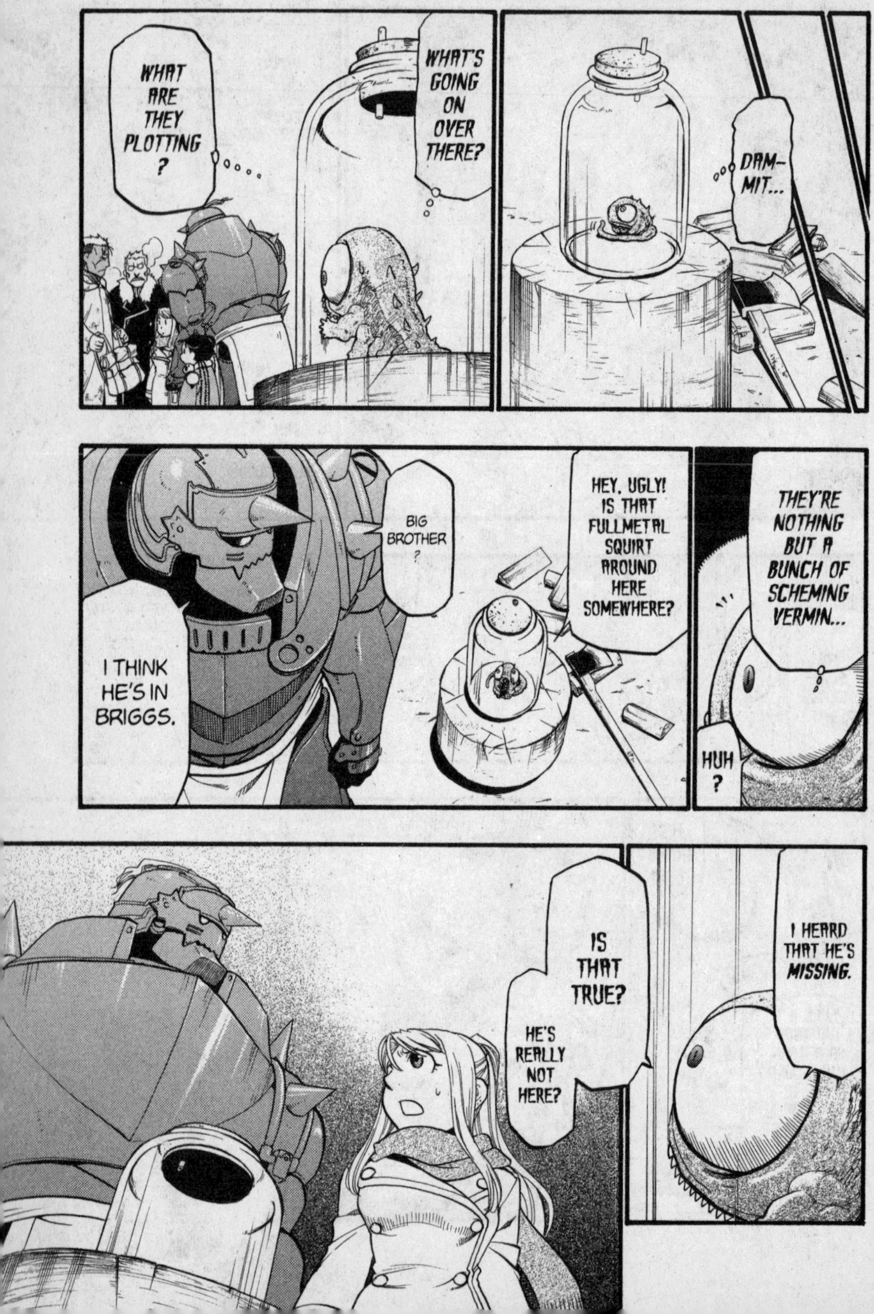
DAM-MIT...
WHAT'S GOING ON OVER THERE?
WHAT ARE THEY PLOTTING?
THEY'RE NOTHING BUT A BUNCH OF SCHEMING VERMIN...
HUH?
HEY, UGLY! IS THAT FULLMETAL SQUIRT AROUND HERE SOMEWHERE?
BIG BROTHER?
I THINK HE'S IN BRIGGS.
I HEARD THAT HE'S MISSING.
IS THAT TRUE?
HE'S REALLY NOT HERE?

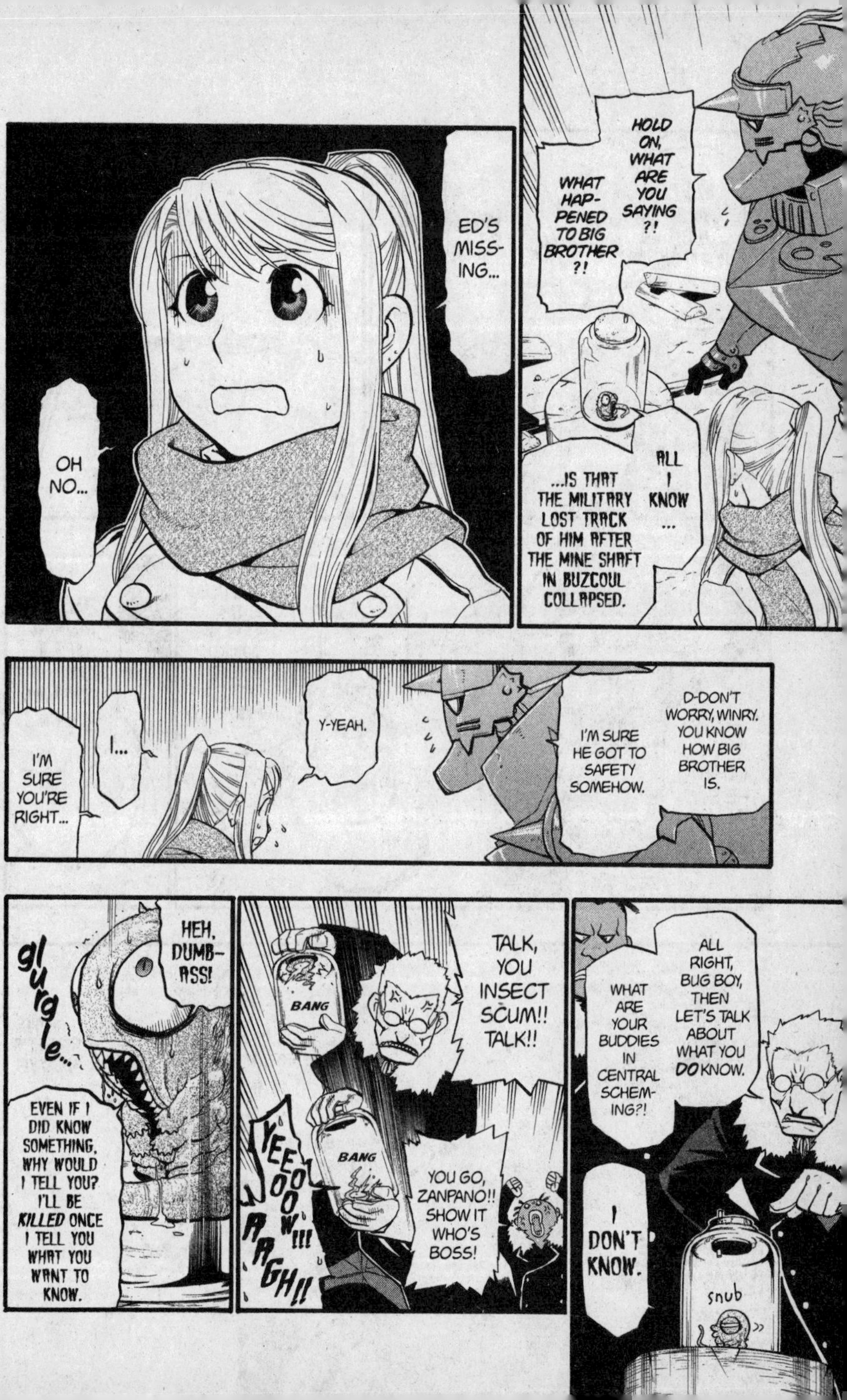
HOLD ON, WHAT ARE YOU SAYING?!
WHAT HAPPENED TO BIG BROTHER?!
ALL I KNOW...
...IS THAT THE MILITARY LOST TRACK OF HIM AFTER THE MINE SHAFT IN BUZCOUL COLLAPSED.
ED'S MISSING...
OH NO...
D-DON'T WORRY, WINRY. YOU KNOW HOW BIG BROTHER IS.
I'M SURE HE GOT TO SAFETY SOMEHOW.
Y-YEAH.
I...
I'M SURE YOU'RE RIGHT...
ALL RIGHT, BUG BOY, THEN LET'S TALK ABOUT WHAT YOU **DO** KNOW.
WHAT ARE YOUR BUDDIES IN CENTRAL SCHEMING?!
I DON'T KNOW.
snub
TALK, YOU INSECT SCUM!! TALK!!
BANG
BANG
YEEOOOOW!!! RAGH!!
YOU GO, ZANPANO!! SHOW IT WHO'S BOSS!
HEH, DUMBASS!
glurgle...
EVEN IF I DID KNOW SOMETHING, WHY WOULD I TELL YOU? I'LL BE ***KILLED*** ONCE I TELL YOU WHAT YOU WANT TO KNOW.

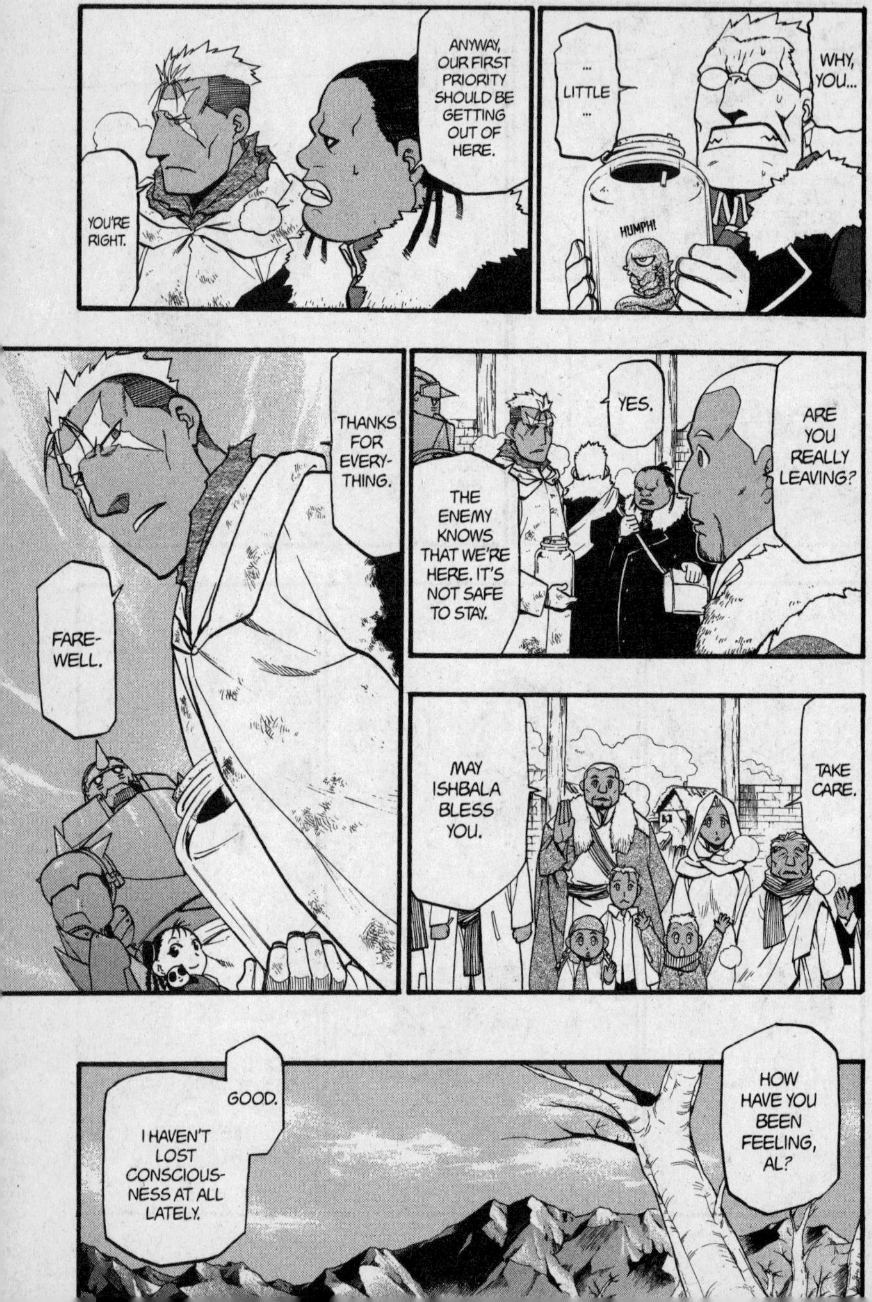
WHY, YOU...
... LITTLE ...
HUMPH!
ANYWAY, OUR FIRST PRIORITY SHOULD BE GETTING OUT OF HERE.
YOU'RE RIGHT.
ARE YOU REALLY LEAVING?
YES.
THE ENEMY KNOWS THAT WE'RE HERE. IT'S NOT SAFE TO STAY.
TAKE CARE.
MAY ISHBALA BLESS YOU.
THANKS FOR EVERYTHING.
FAREWELL.
HOW HAVE YOU BEEN FEELING, AL?
GOOD.
I HAVEN'T LOST CONSCIOUSNESS AT ALL LATELY.

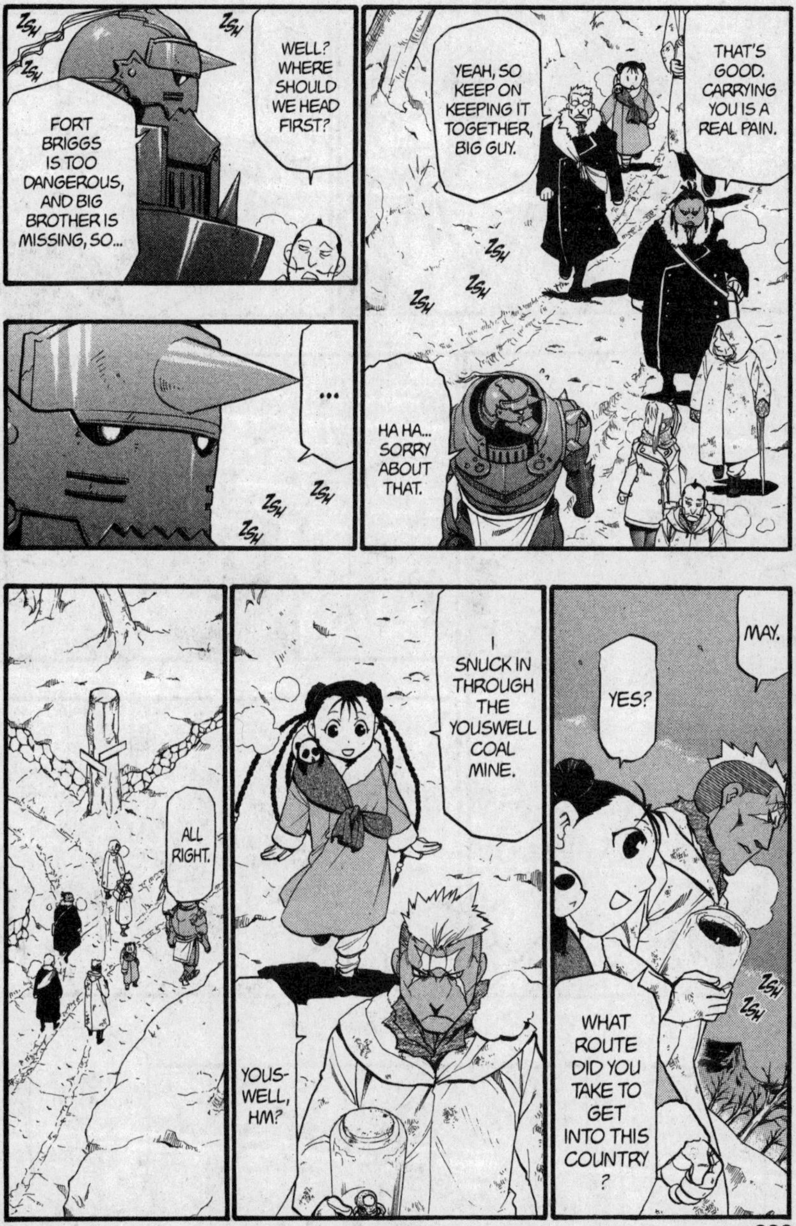
THAT'S GOOD. CARRYING YOU IS A REAL PAIN.
YEAH, SO KEEP ON KEEPING IT TOGETHER, BIG GUY.
ZSH
ZSH
ZSH
HA HA... SORRY ABOUT THAT.
ZSH
WELL? WHERE SHOULD WE HEAD FIRST?
ZSH
ZSH
FORT BRIGGS IS TOO DANGEROUS, AND BIG BROTHER IS MISSING, SO...
...
ZSH
ZSH
ZSH
MAY.
YES?
ZSH
ZSH
WHAT ROUTE DID YOU TAKE TO GET INTO THIS COUNTRY?
I SNUCK IN THROUGH THE YOUSWELL COAL MINE.
YOUS-WELL, HM?
ALL RIGHT.

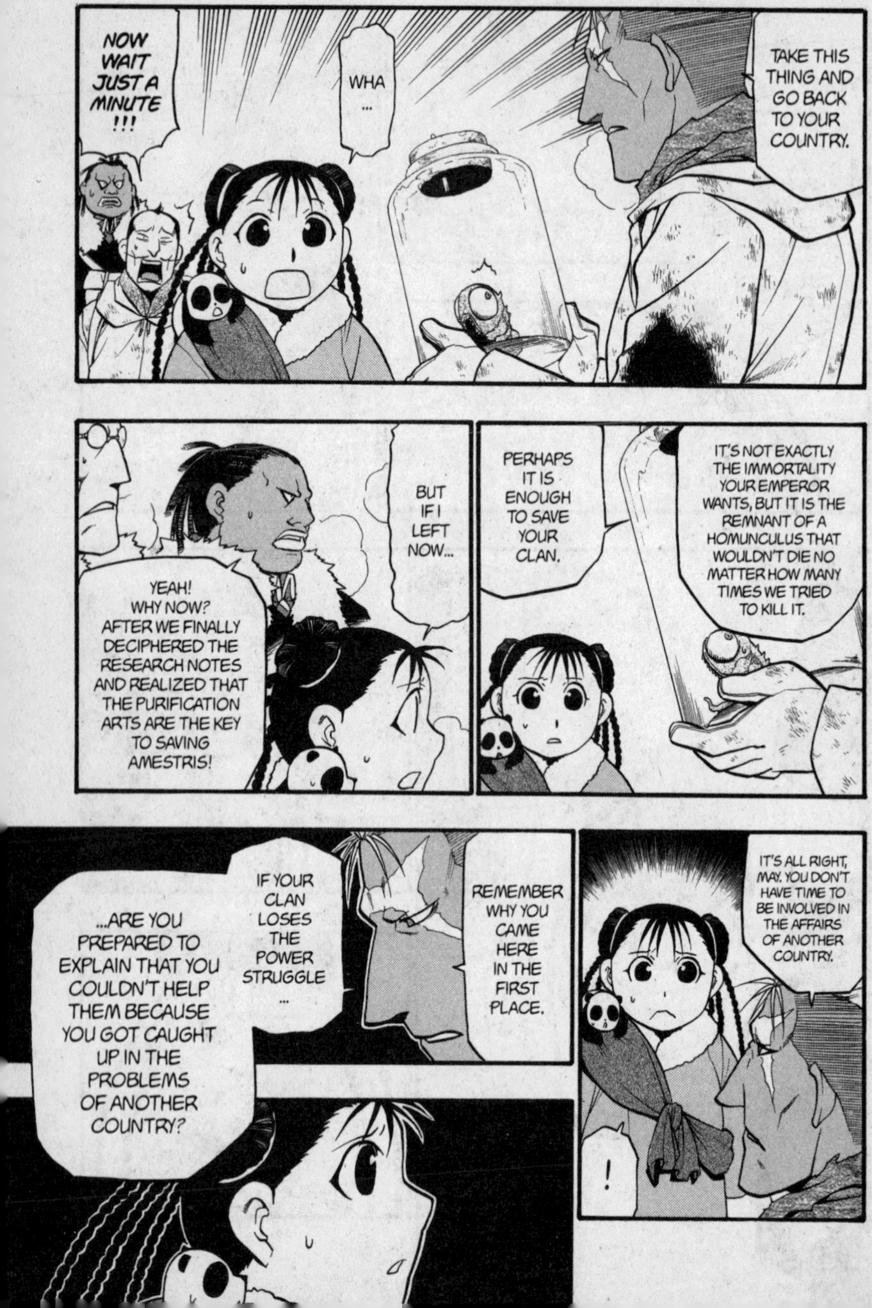
TAKE THIS THING AND GO BACK TO YOUR COUNTRY.
WHA ...
NOW WAIT JUST A MINUTE !!!
IT'S NOT EXACTLY THE IMMORTALITY YOUR EMPEROR WANTS, BUT IT IS THE REMNANT OF A HOMUNCULUS THAT WOULDN'T DIE NO MATTER HOW MANY TIMES WE TRIED TO KILL IT.
PERHAPS IT IS ENOUGH TO SAVE YOUR CLAN.
BUT IF I LEFT NOW...
YEAH! WHY NOW? AFTER WE FINALLY DECIPHERED THE RESEARCH NOTES AND REALIZED THAT THE PURIFICATION ARTS ARE THE KEY TO SAVING AMESTRIS!
IT'S ALL RIGHT, MAY. YOU DON'T HAVE TIME TO BE INVOLVED IN THE AFFAIRS OF ANOTHER COUNTRY.
!
REMEMBER WHY YOU CAME HERE IN THE FIRST PLACE.
IF YOUR CLAN LOSES THE POWER STRUGGLE ...
...ARE YOU PREPARED TO EXPLAIN THAT YOU COULDN'T HELP THEM BECAUSE YOU GOT CAUGHT UP IN THE PROBLEMS OF ANOTHER COUNTRY?

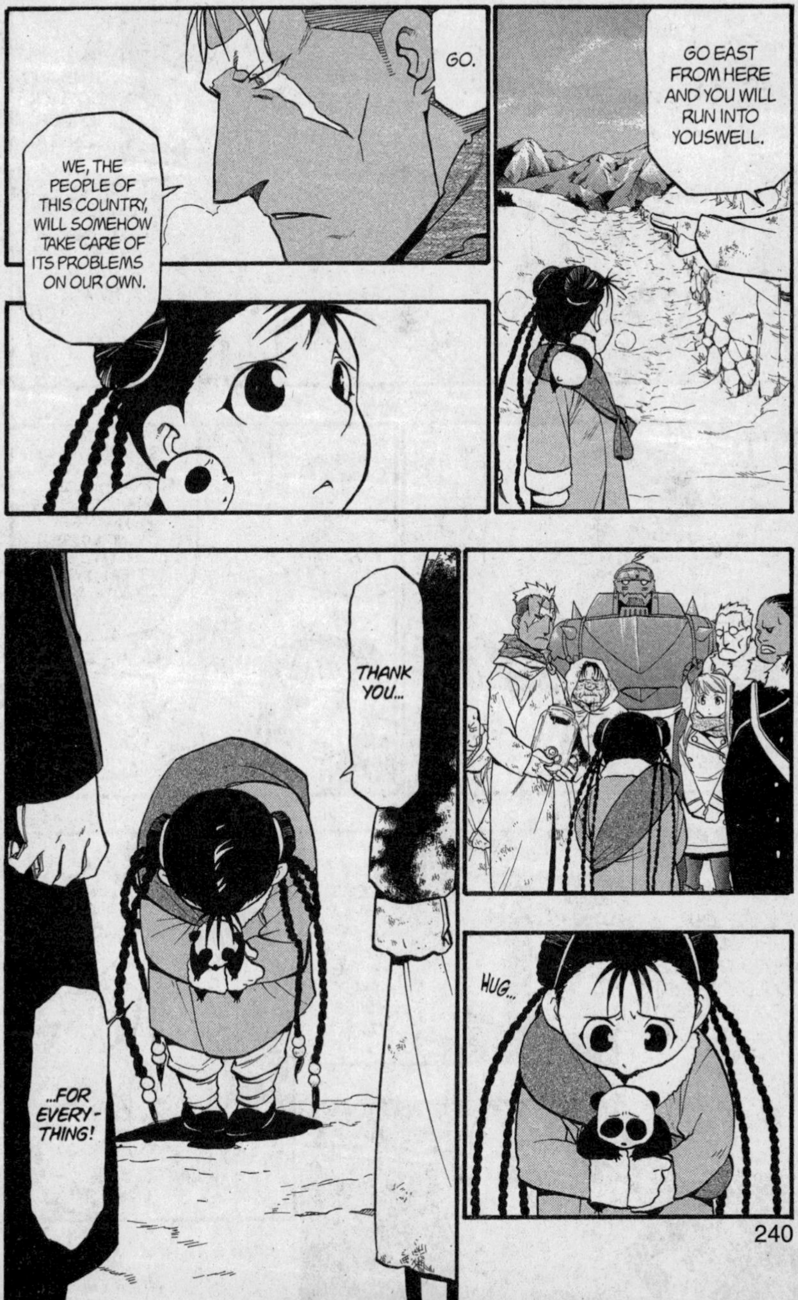
GO EAST FROM HERE AND YOU WILL RUN INTO YOUSWELL.
GO.
WE, THE PEOPLE OF THIS COUNTRY, WILL SOMEHOW TAKE CARE OF ITS PROBLEMS ON OUR OWN.
HUG...
THANK YOU...
...FOR EVERY-THING!

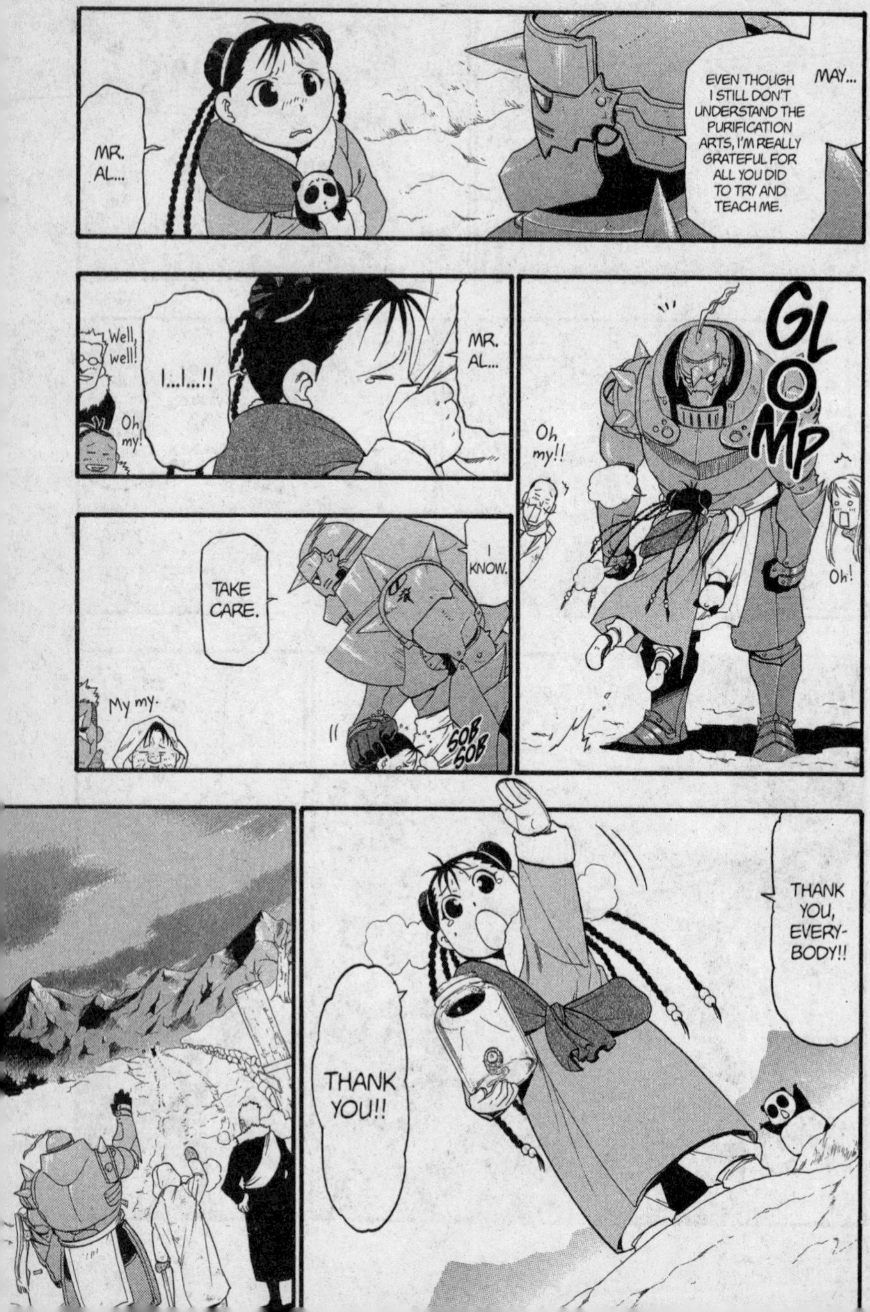
MAY...
EVEN THOUGH I STILL DON'T UNDERSTAND THE PURIFICATION ARTS, I'M REALLY GRATEFUL FOR ALL YOU DID TO TRY AND TEACH ME.
MR. AL...
GLOMP
Oh!
Oh my!!
MR. AL...
I...I...!!
Well, well!
Oh my!
I KNOW.
TAKE CARE.
SOB SOB
My my.
THANK YOU, EVERYBODY!!
THANK YOU!!

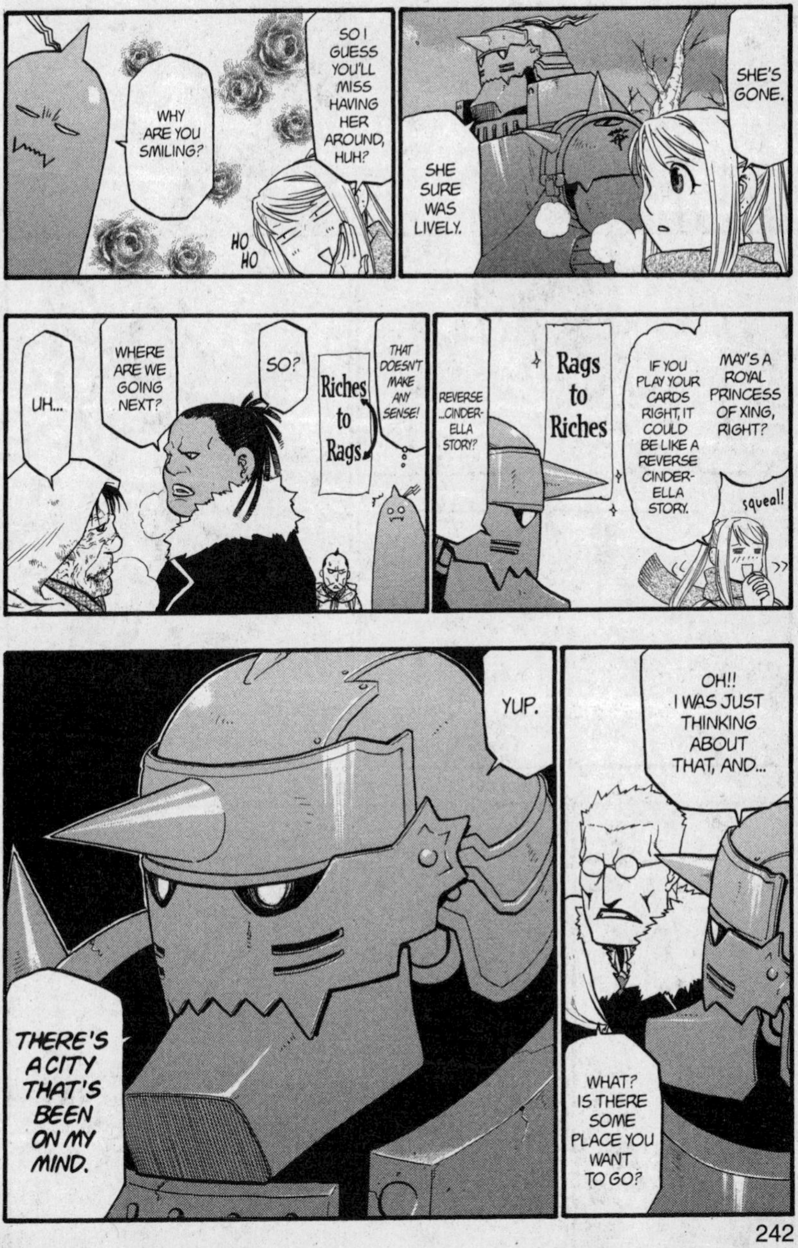
SHE'S GONE.
SHE SURE WAS LIVELY.
SO I GUESS YOU'LL MISS HAVING HER AROUND, HUH?
WHY ARE YOU SMILING?
HO HO
MAY'S A ROYAL PRINCESS OF XING, RIGHT?
IF YOU PLAY YOUR CARDS RIGHT, IT COULD BE LIKE A REVERSE CINDER-ELLA STORY.
Rags to Riches
squeal!
REVERSE ...CINDER-ELLA STORY?
THAT DOESN'T MAKE ANY SENSE!
Riches to Rags
SO?
WHERE ARE WE GOING NEXT?
UH...
OH!! I WAS JUST THINKING ABOUT THAT, AND...
WHAT? IS THERE SOME PLACE YOU WANT TO GO?
YUP.
THERE'S A CITY THAT'S BEEN ON MY MIND.

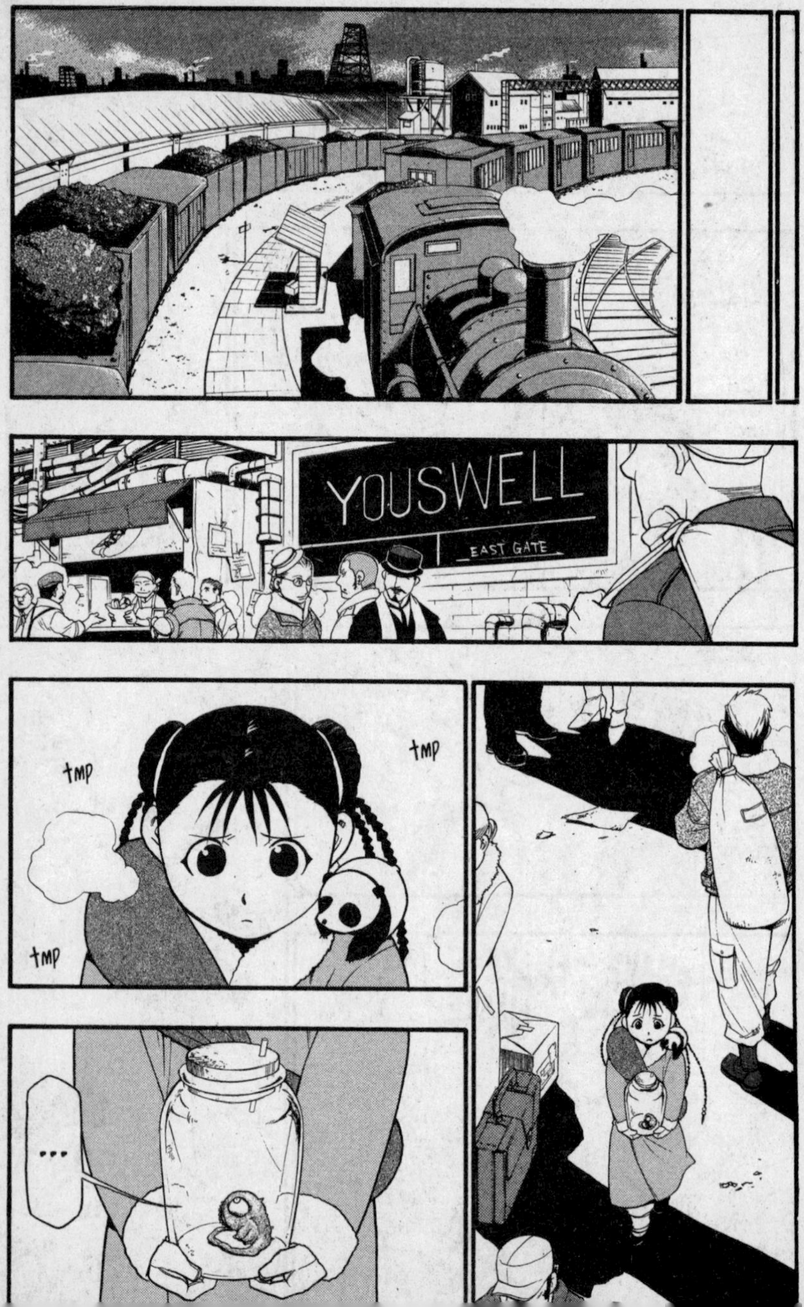
YOUSWELL
EAST GATE
tmp
tmp
tmp
...

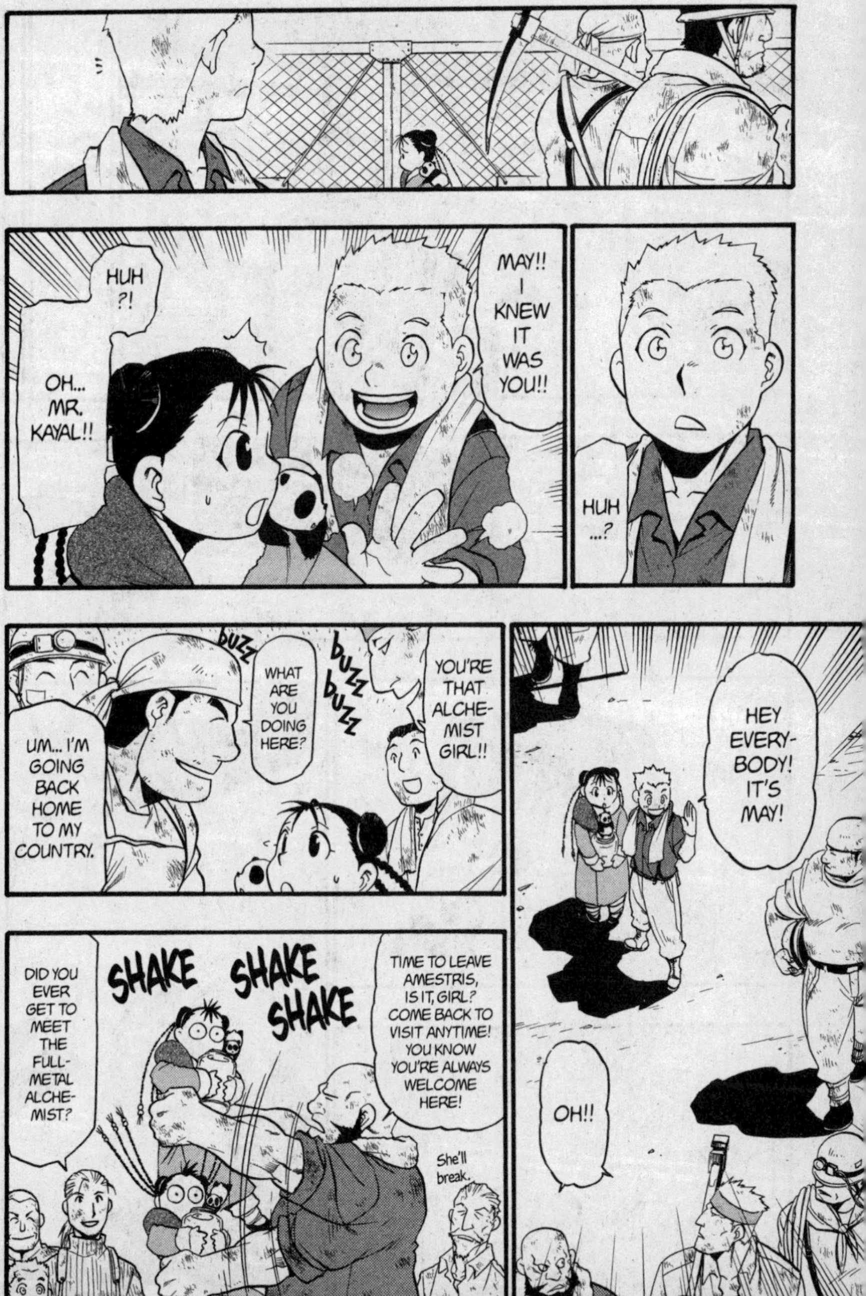
HUH ...?
MAY!! I KNEW IT WAS YOU!!
HUH ?!
OH... MR. KAYAL!!
HEY EVERY-BODY! IT'S MAY!
OH!!
YOU'RE THAT ALCHE-MIST GIRL!!
BUZZ BUZZ
WHAT ARE YOU DOING HERE?
BUZZ
UM... I'M GOING BACK HOME TO MY COUNTRY.
TIME TO LEAVE AMESTRIS, IS IT, GIRL? COME BACK TO VISIT ANYTIME! YOU KNOW YOU'RE ALWAYS WELCOME HERE!
SHAKE SHAKE SHAKE
She'll break.
DID YOU EVER GET TO MEET THE FULL-METAL ALCHE-MIST?

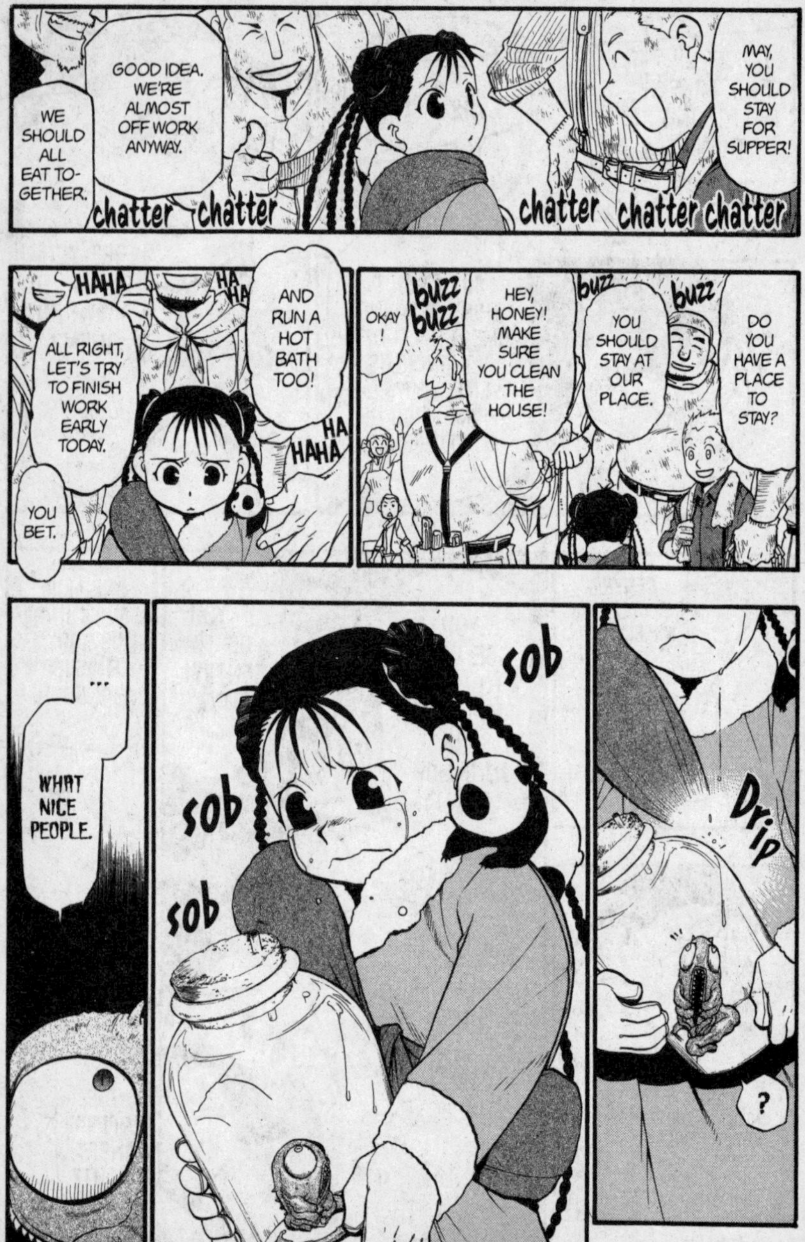
MAY, YOU SHOULD STAY FOR SUPPER!
chatter chatter
chatter
GOOD IDEA. WE'RE ALMOST OFF WORK ANYWAY.
chatter
WE SHOULD ALL EAT TO-GETHER.
chatter
DO YOU HAVE A PLACE TO STAY?
buzz
YOU SHOULD STAY AT OUR PLACE.
buzz
HEY, HONEY! MAKE SURE YOU CLEAN THE HOUSE!
buzz buzz
OKAY!
AND RUN A HOT BATH TOO!
HA HA
HAHA
ALL RIGHT, LET'S TRY TO FINISH WORK EARLY TODAY.
HA HAHA
YOU BET.
Drip
?
sob
sob
sob
...
WHAT NICE PEOPLE.

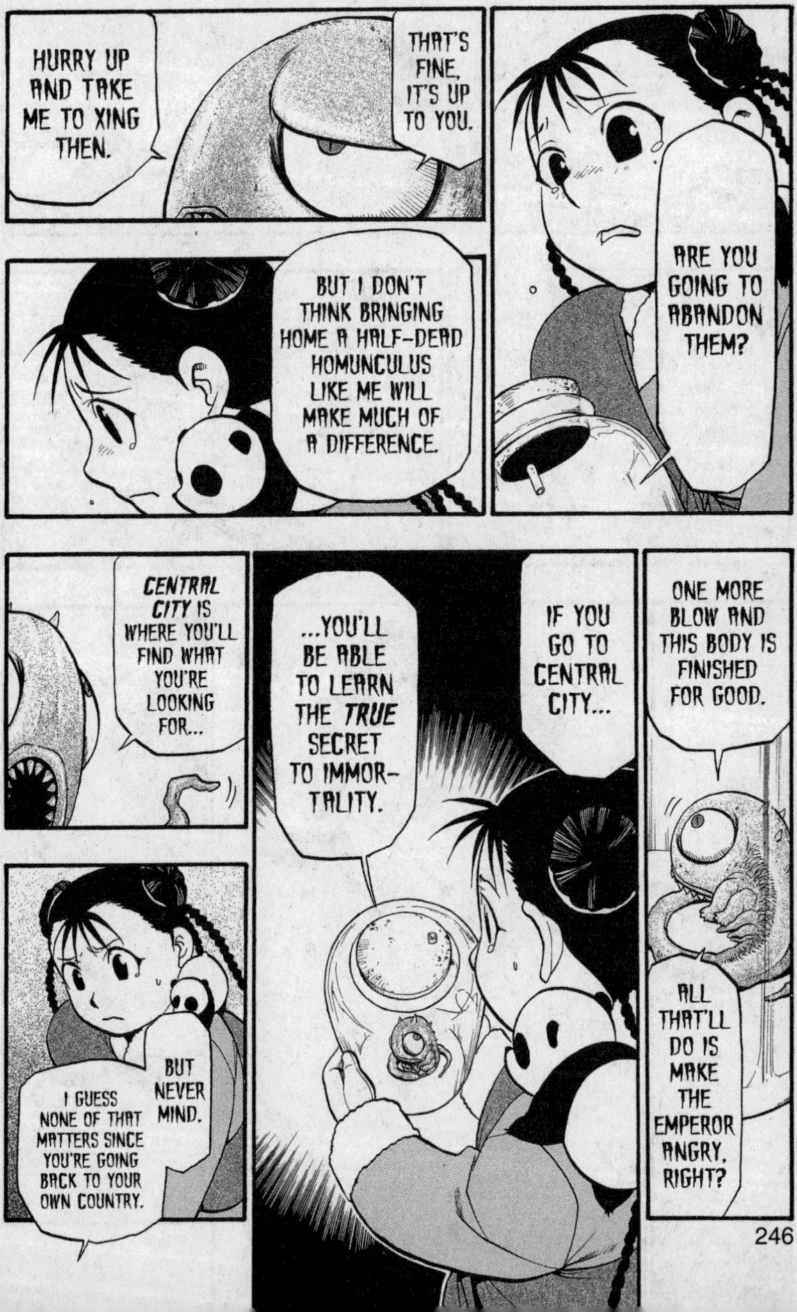
ARE YOU GOING TO ABANDON THEM?
THAT'S FINE, IT'S UP TO YOU.
HURRY UP AND TAKE ME TO XING THEN.
BUT I DON'T THINK BRINGING HOME A HALF-DEAD HOMUNCULUS LIKE ME WILL MAKE MUCH OF A DIFFERENCE.
ONE MORE BLOW AND THIS BODY IS FINISHED FOR GOOD.
ALL THAT'LL DO IS MAKE THE EMPEROR ANGRY, RIGHT?
IF YOU GO TO CENTRAL CITY...
...YOU'LL BE ABLE TO LEARN THE *TRUE* SECRET TO IMMORTALITY.
CENTRAL CITY IS WHERE YOU'LL FIND WHAT YOU'RE LOOKING FOR...
BUT NEVER MIND.
I GUESS NONE OF THAT MATTERS SINCE YOU'RE GOING BACK TO YOUR OWN COUNTRY.

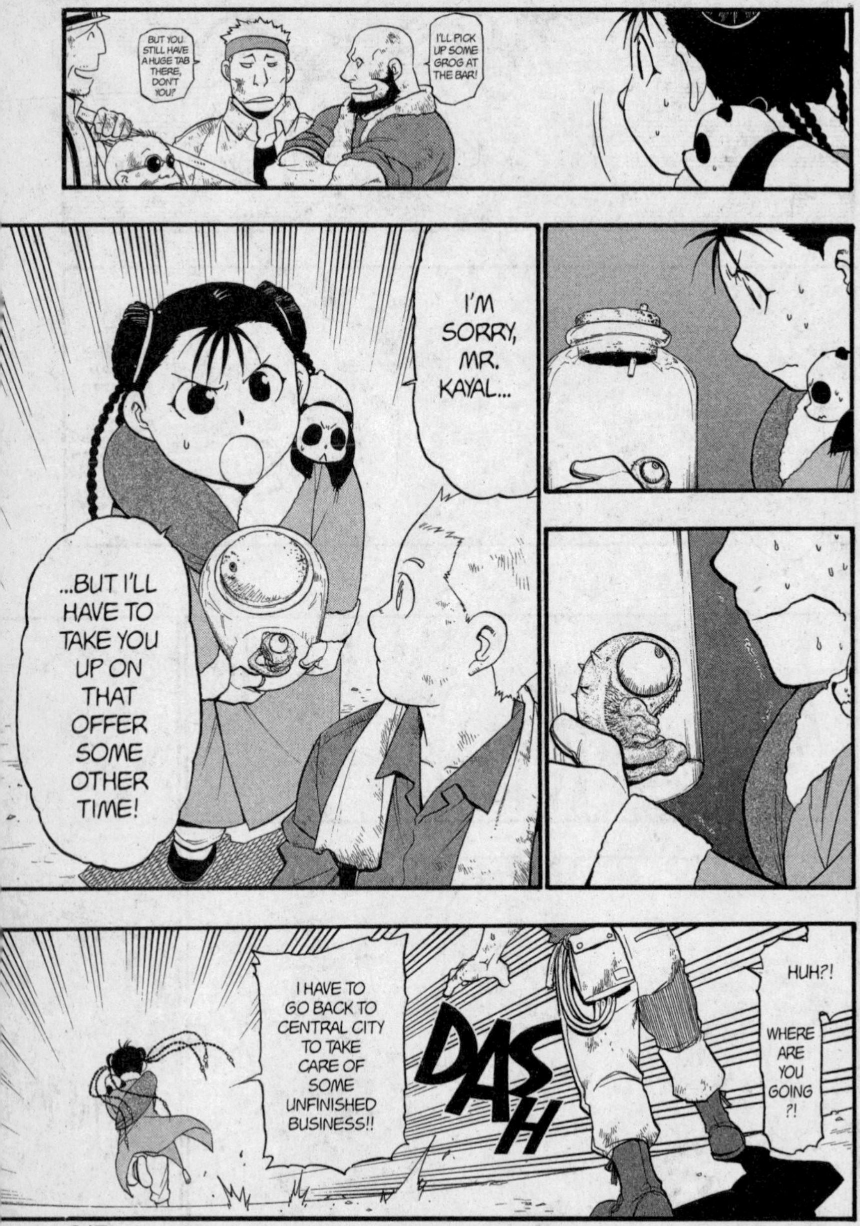
I'LL PICK UP SOME GROG AT THE BAR!
BUT YOU STILL HAVE A HUGE TAB THERE, DON'T YOU?
I'M SORRY, MR. KAYAL...
...BUT I'LL HAVE TO TAKE YOU UP ON THAT OFFER SOME OTHER TIME!
HUH?!
WHERE ARE YOU GOING?!
DASH
I HAVE TO GO BACK TO CENTRAL CITY TO TAKE CARE OF SOME UNFINISHED BUSINESS!!

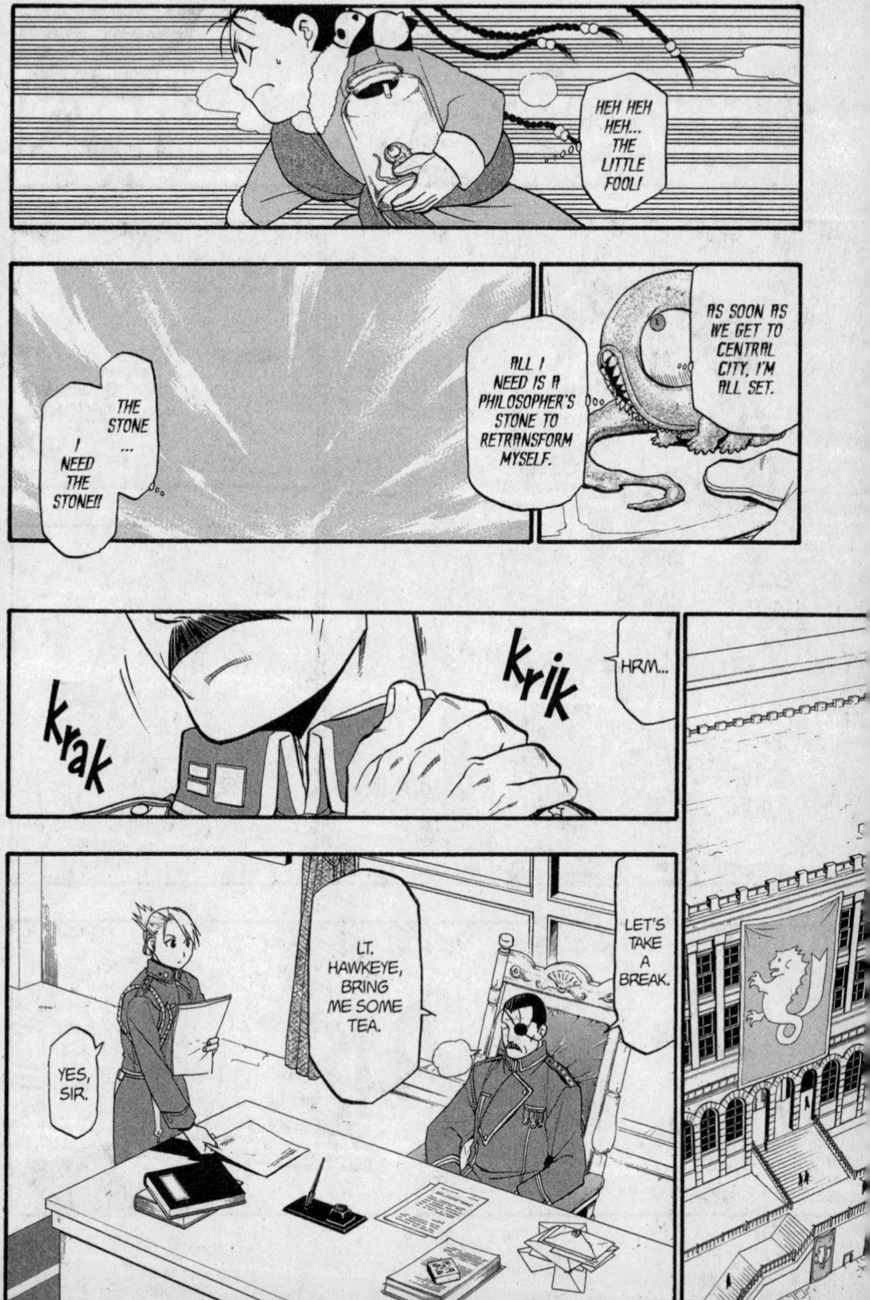
HEH HEH HEH... THE LITTLE FOOL!
AS SOON AS WE GET TO CENTRAL CITY, I'M ALL SET.
ALL I NEED IS A PHILOSOPHER'S STONE TO RETRANSFORM MYSELF.
THE STONE ...
I NEED THE STONE!!
HRM...
krik
krak
LET'S TAKE A BREAK.
LT. HAWKEYE, BRING ME SOME TEA.
YES, SIR.

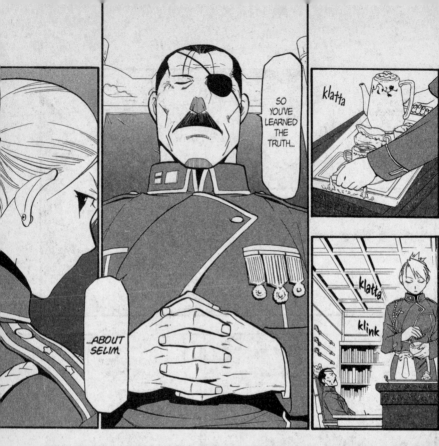

SO YOU'VE LEARNED THE TRUTH...

...ABOUT SELIM.

klatta

klatta

klink

YES, SIR.

AND YOU ALSO KNOW MY TRUE IDENTITY?

YES, SIR.

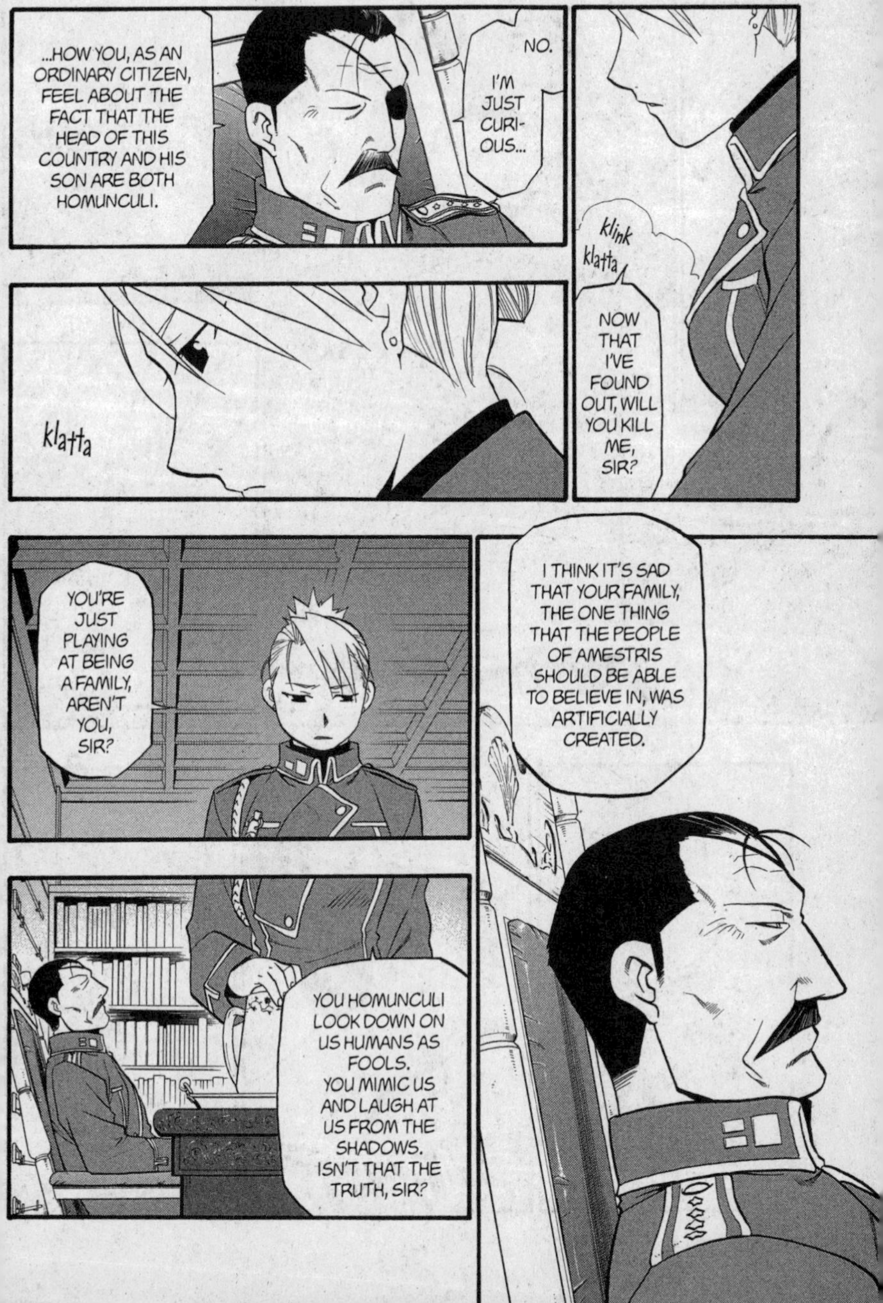
klink
klatta
NOW THAT I'VE FOUND OUT, WILL YOU KILL ME, SIR?
NO.
I'M JUST CURIOUS...
...HOW YOU, AS AN ORDINARY CITIZEN, FEEL ABOUT THE FACT THAT THE HEAD OF THIS COUNTRY AND HIS SON ARE BOTH HOMUNCULI.
klatta
I THINK IT'S SAD THAT YOUR FAMILY, THE ONE THING THAT THE PEOPLE OF AMESTRIS SHOULD BE ABLE TO BELIEVE IN, WAS ARTIFICIALLY CREATED.
YOU'RE JUST PLAYING AT BEING A FAMILY, AREN'T YOU, SIR?
YOU HOMUNCULI LOOK DOWN ON US HUMANS AS FOOLS. YOU MIMIC US AND LAUGH AT US FROM THE SHADOWS. ISN'T THAT THE TRUTH, SIR?

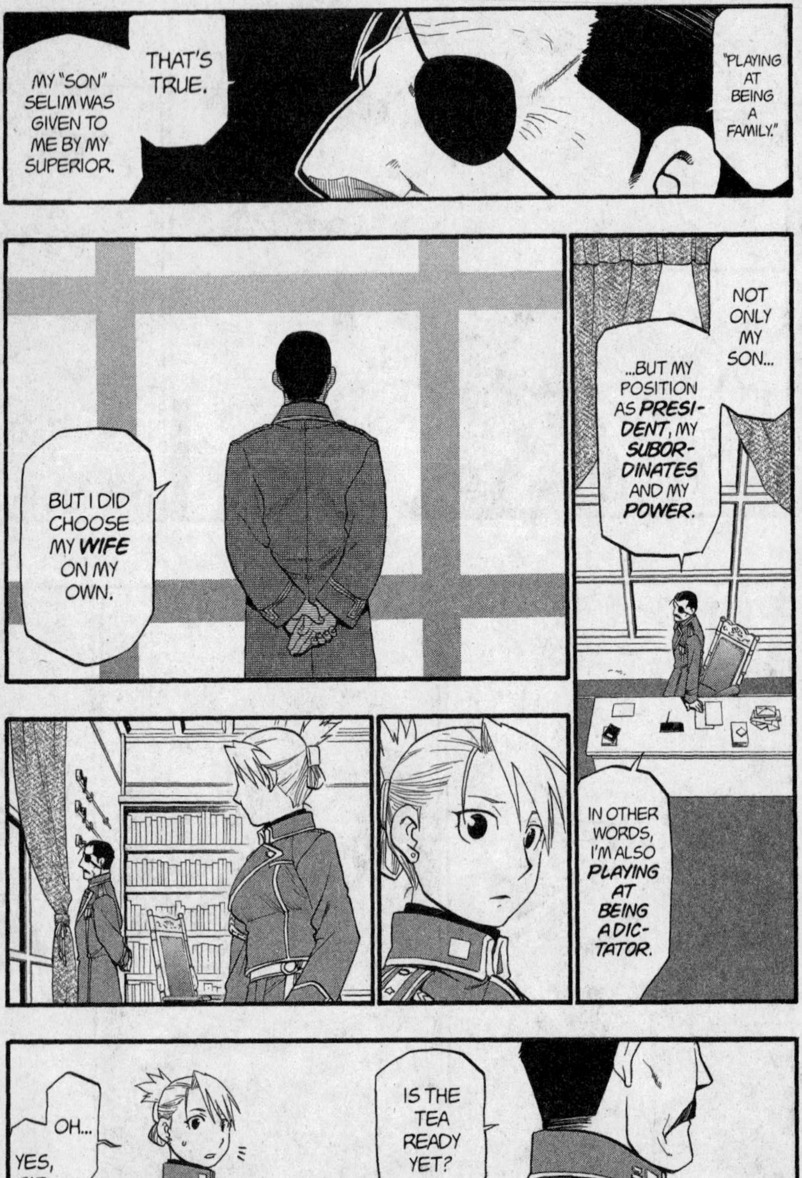
"PLAYING AT BEING A FAMILY."
THAT'S TRUE.
MY "SON" SELIM WAS GIVEN TO ME BY MY SUPERIOR.
NOT ONLY MY SON...
...BUT MY POSITION AS PRESIDENT, MY SUBORDINATES AND MY POWER.
IN OTHER WORDS, I'M ALSO PLAYING AT BEING A DICTATOR.
BUT I DID CHOOSE MY WIFE ON MY OWN.
IS THE TEA READY YET?
OH...
YES, SIR.

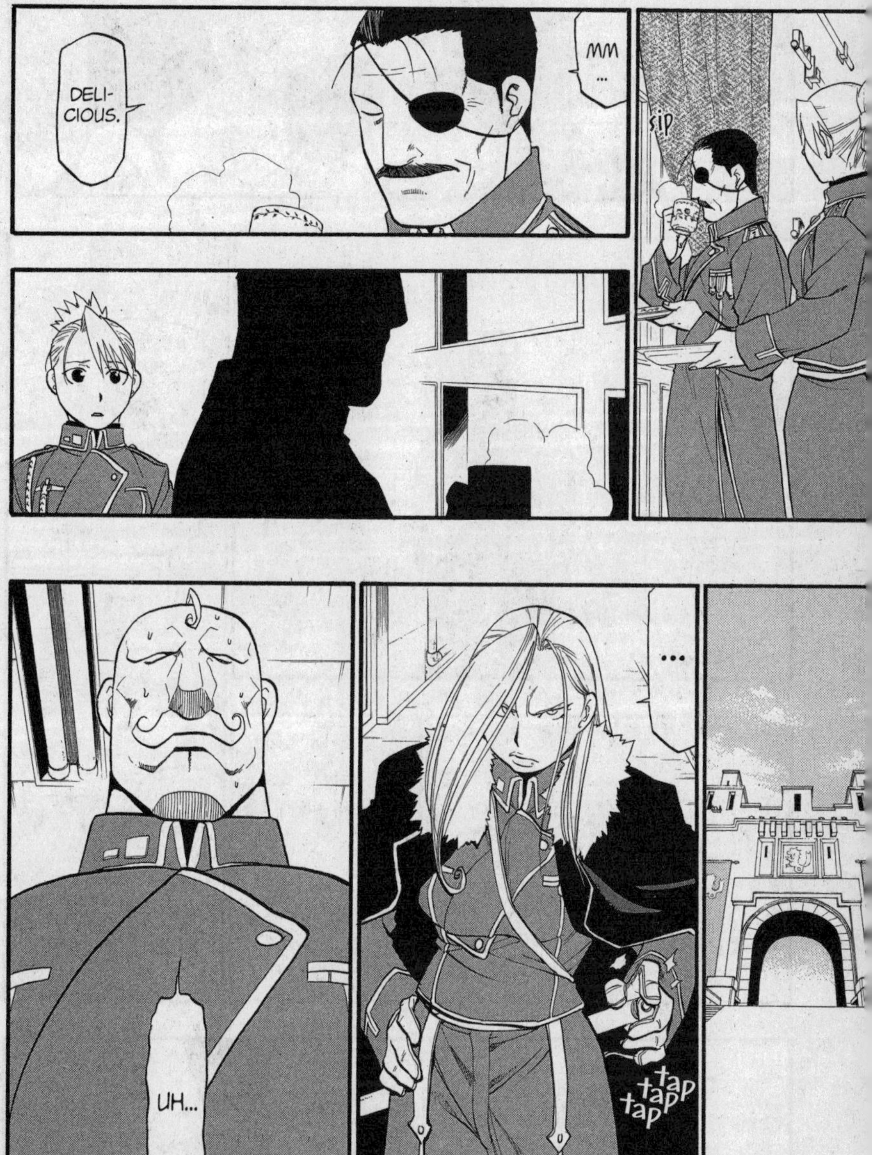
sip
MM ...
DELI-CIOUS.
...
tap tap tap
UH...

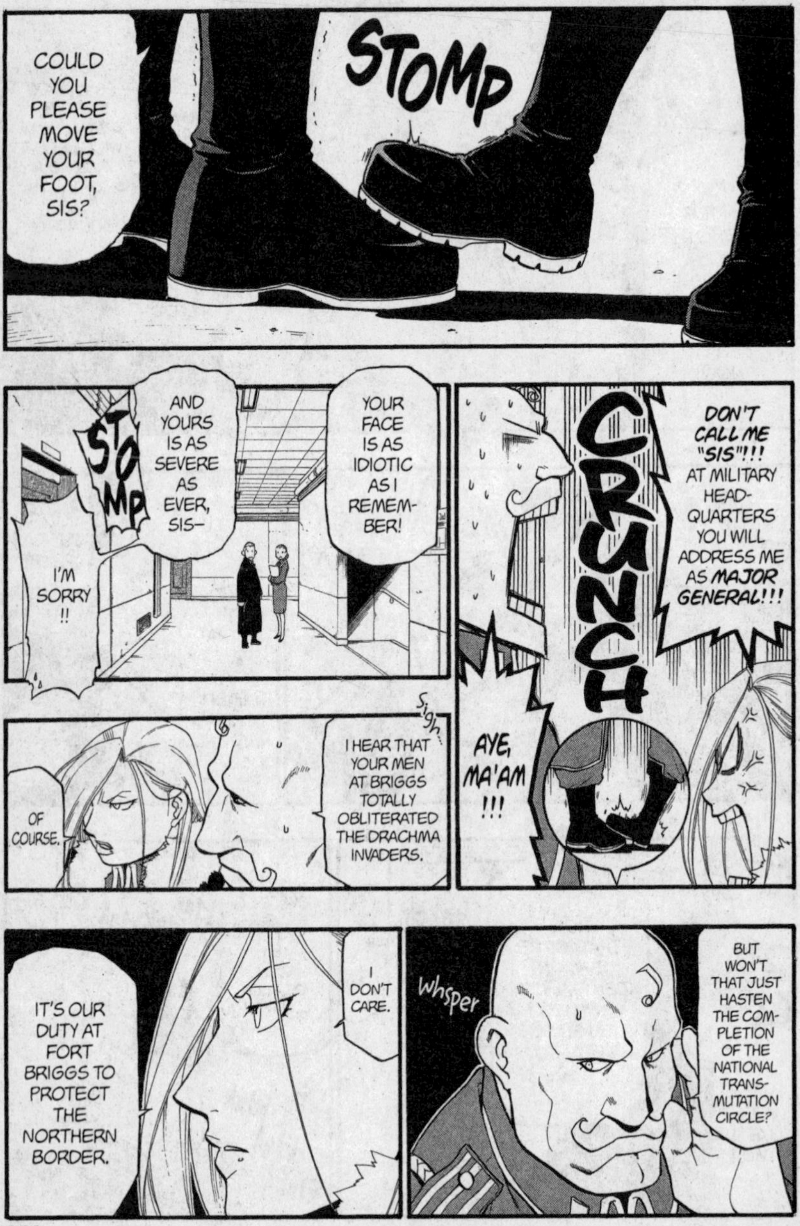
STOMP
COULD YOU PLEASE MOVE YOUR FOOT, SIS?
CRUNCH
DON'T CALL ME "SIS"!!! AT MILITARY HEADQUARTERS YOU WILL ADDRESS ME AS MAJOR GENERAL!!!
AYE, MA'AM!!!
YOUR FACE IS AS IDIOTIC AS I REMEMBER!
AND YOURS IS AS SEVERE AS EVER, SIS—
STOMP
I'M SORRY!!
Sigh...
I HEAR THAT YOUR MEN AT BRIGGS TOTALLY OBLITERATED THE DRACHMA INVADERS.
OF COURSE.
whsper
BUT WON'T THAT JUST HASTEN THE COMPLETION OF THE NATIONAL TRANSMUTATION CIRCLE?
I DON'T CARE.
IT'S OUR DUTY AT FORT BRIGGS TO PROTECT THE NORTHERN BORDER.

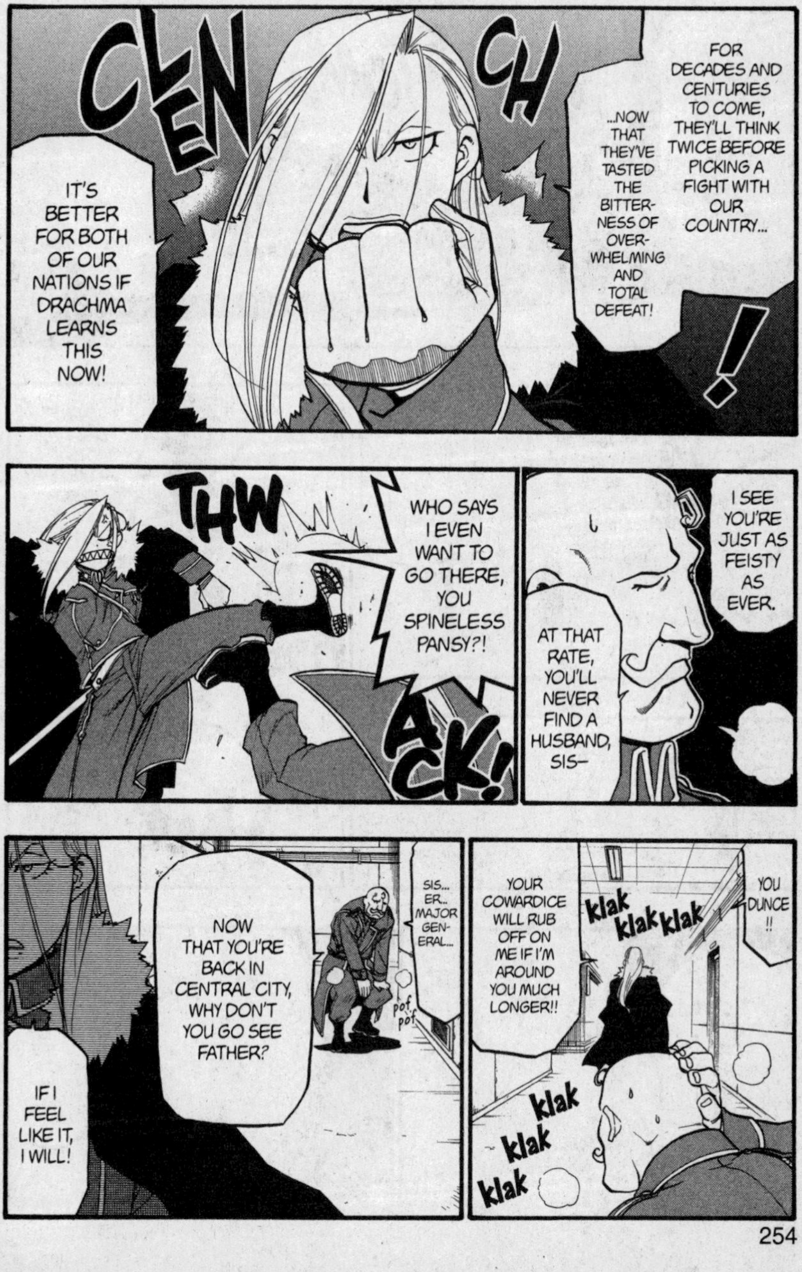
FOR DECADES AND CENTURIES TO COME, THEY'LL THINK TWICE BEFORE PICKING A FIGHT WITH OUR COUNTRY...
...NOW THAT THEY'VE TASTED THE BITTERNESS OF OVERWHELMING AND TOTAL DEFEAT!
CLENCH
IT'S BETTER FOR BOTH OF OUR NATIONS IF DRACHMA LEARNS THIS NOW!
!
I SEE YOU'RE JUST AS FEISTY AS EVER.
AT THAT RATE, YOU'LL NEVER FIND A HUSBAND, SIS—
WHO SAYS I EVEN WANT TO GO THERE, YOU SPINELESS PANSY?!
THWACK!
YOU DUNCE!!
klak klak klak
YOUR COWARDICE WILL RUB OFF ON ME IF I'M AROUND YOU MUCH LONGER!!
klak klak klak
SIS... ER... MAJOR GENERAL...
pof pof
NOW THAT YOU'RE BACK IN CENTRAL CITY, WHY DON'T YOU GO SEE FATHER?
IF I FEEL LIKE IT, I WILL!

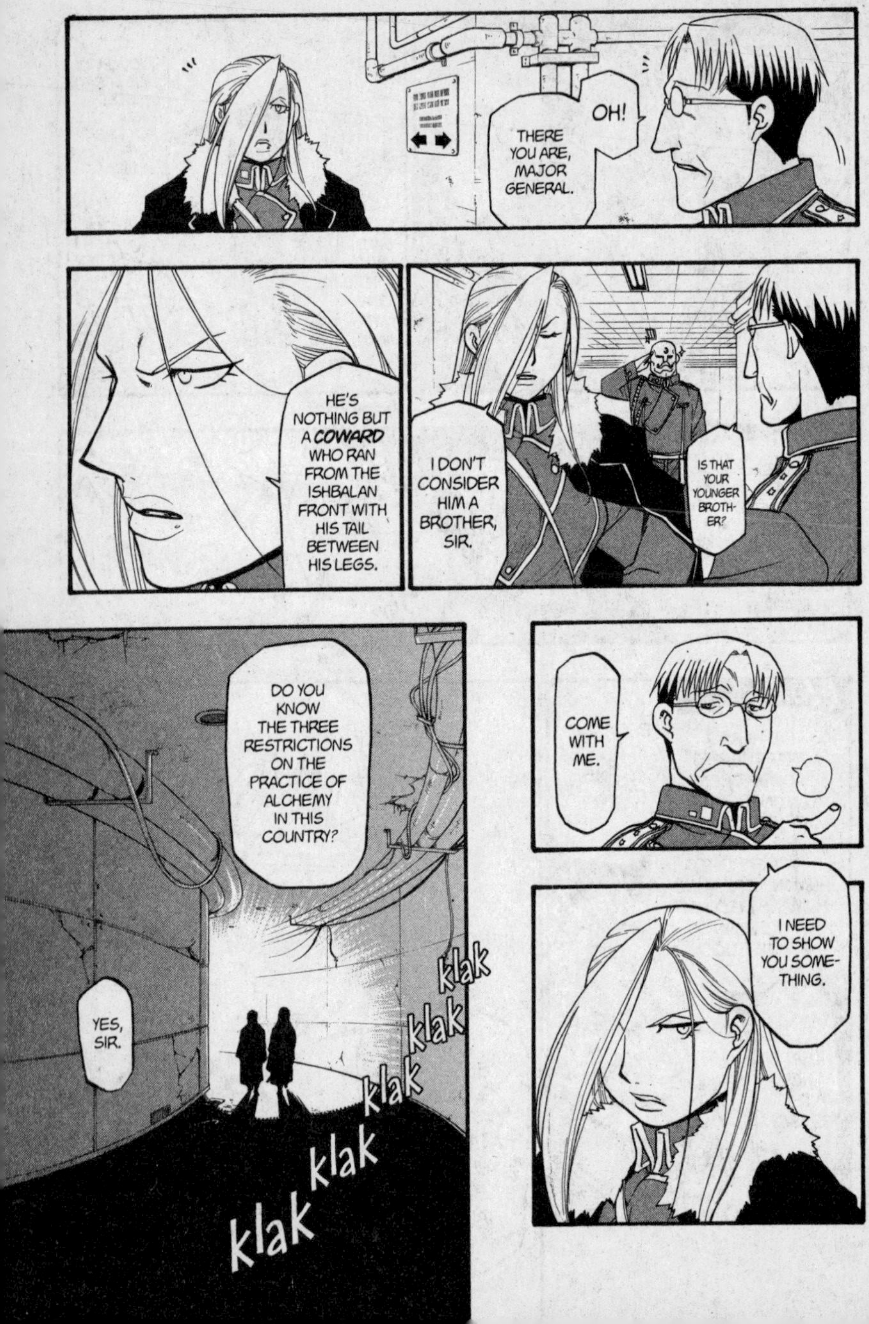
OH!
THERE YOU ARE, MAJOR GENERAL.
IS THAT YOUR YOUNGER BROTHER?
I DON'T CONSIDER HIM A BROTHER, SIR.
HE'S NOTHING BUT A **COWARD** WHO RAN FROM THE ISHBALAN FRONT WITH HIS TAIL BETWEEN HIS LEGS.
COME WITH ME.
I NEED TO SHOW YOU SOME-THING.
DO YOU KNOW THE THREE RESTRICTIONS ON THE PRACTICE OF ALCHEMY IN THIS COUNTRY?
YES, SIR.
klak
klak
klak
klak
klak

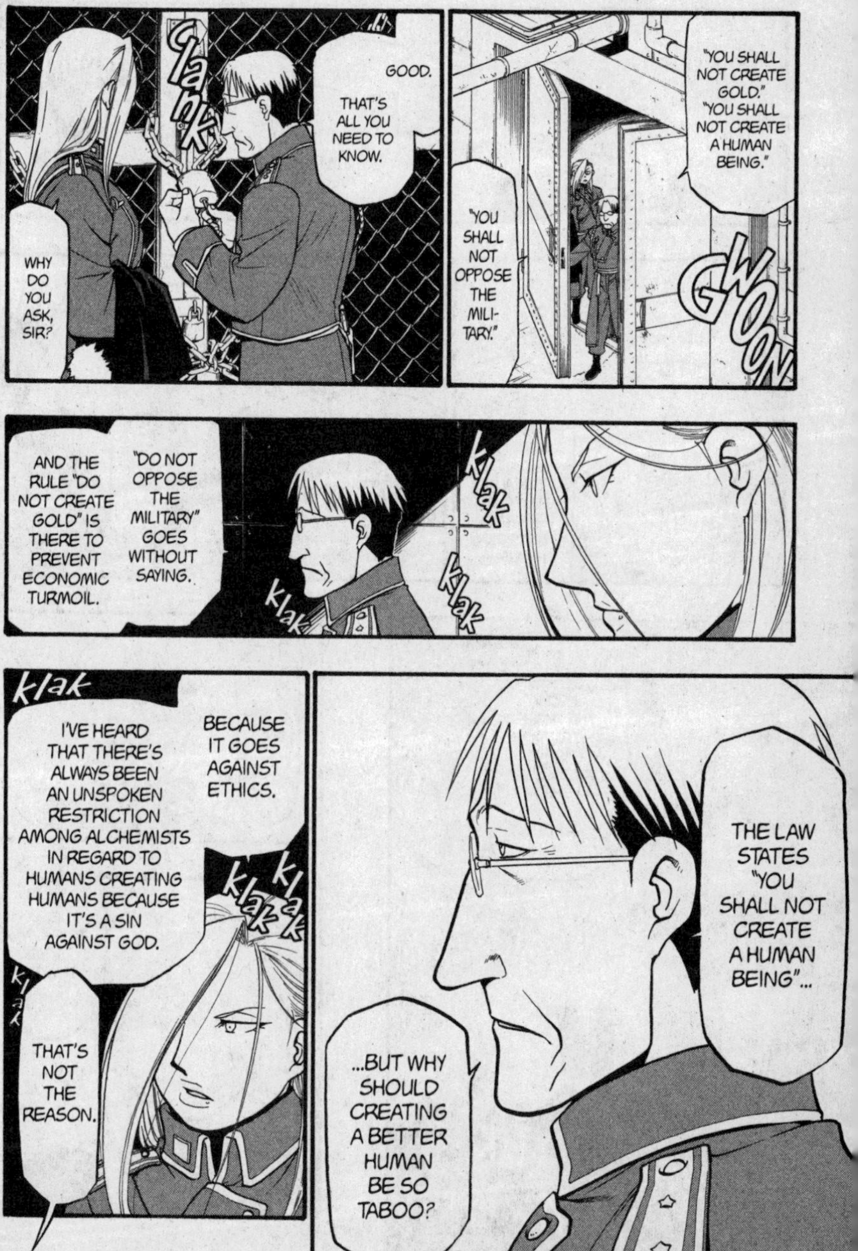
"YOU SHALL NOT CREATE GOLD." "YOU SHALL NOT CREATE A HUMAN BEING."
"YOU SHALL NOT OPPOSE THE MILITARY."
GWOON
CLANK
GOOD.
THAT'S ALL YOU NEED TO KNOW.
WHY DO YOU ASK, SIR?
KLAK
KLAK
KLAK
"DO NOT OPPOSE THE MILITARY" GOES WITHOUT SAYING.
AND THE RULE "DO NOT CREATE GOLD" IS THERE TO PREVENT ECONOMIC TURMOIL.
THE LAW STATES "YOU SHALL NOT CREATE A HUMAN BEING"...
...BUT WHY SHOULD CREATING A BETTER HUMAN BE SO TABOO?
KLAK
BECAUSE IT GOES AGAINST ETHICS.
I'VE HEARD THAT THERE'S ALWAYS BEEN AN UNSPOKEN RESTRICTION AMONG ALCHEMISTS IN REGARD TO HUMANS CREATING HUMANS BECAUSE IT'S A SIN AGAINST GOD.
KLAK
KLAK
KLAK
THAT'S NOT THE REASON.

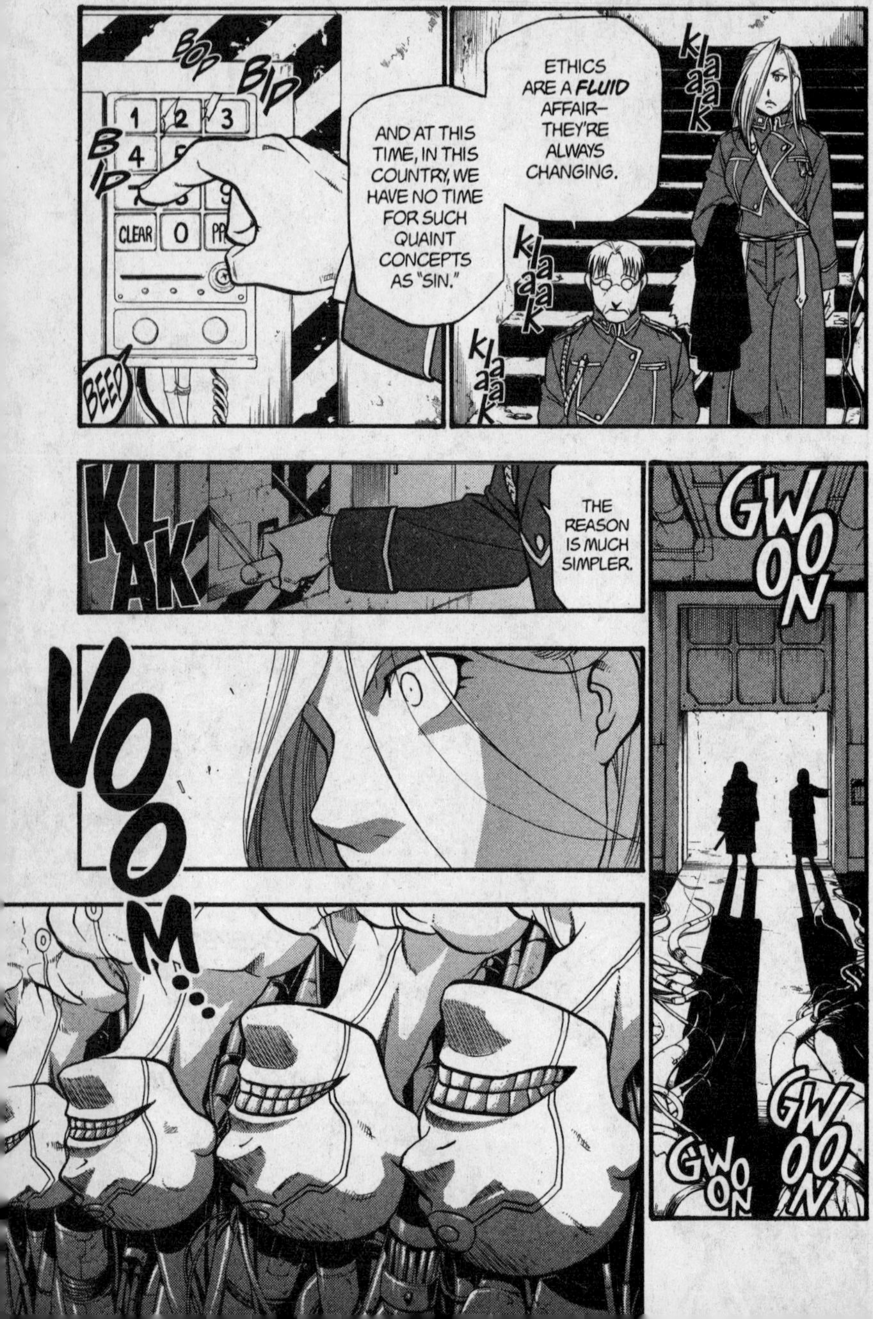

ETHICS ARE A FLUID AFFAIR— THEY'RE ALWAYS CHANGING.
KLAAAK
AND AT THIS TIME, IN THIS COUNTRY, WE HAVE NO TIME FOR SUCH QUAINT CONCEPTS AS "SIN."
KLAAAK
KLAAAK
BOOP
BIP
BIP
1
2
3
4
CLEAR
0
BEEP
GWOOON
GWOOON
GWOON
KLAK
THE REASON IS MUCH SIMPLER.
VOOOM...

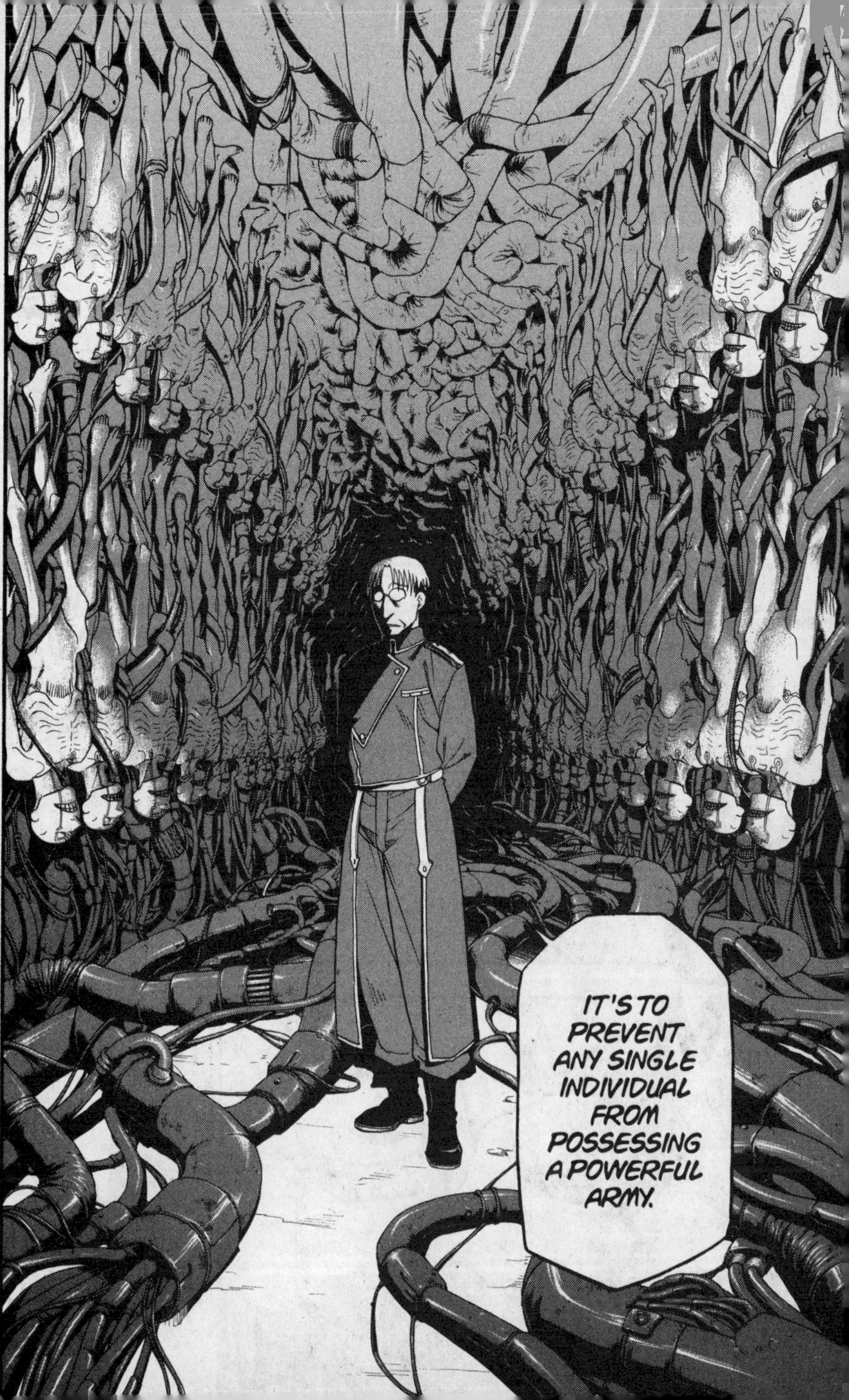
IT'S TO PREVENT ANY SINGLE INDIVIDUAL FROM POSSESSING A POWERFUL ARMY.

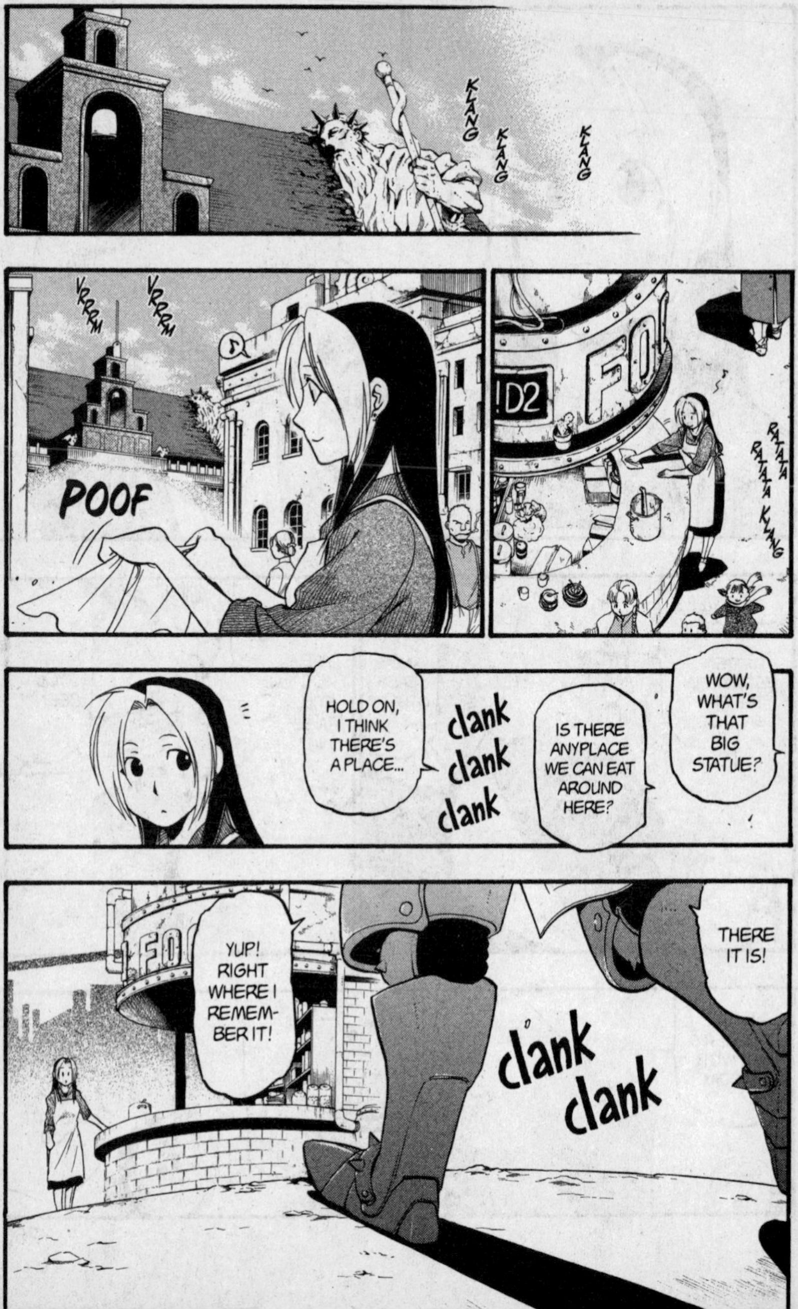
KLANG
KLANG
KLANG
RATATATA
RATATATA KLANG
VRRRM
VRRRM
POOF
WOW, WHAT'S THAT BIG STATUE?
IS THERE ANYPLACE WE CAN EAT AROUND HERE?
clank clank clank
HOLD ON, I THINK THERE'S A PLACE...
THERE IT IS!
clank clank
YUP! RIGHT WHERE I REMEMBER IT!

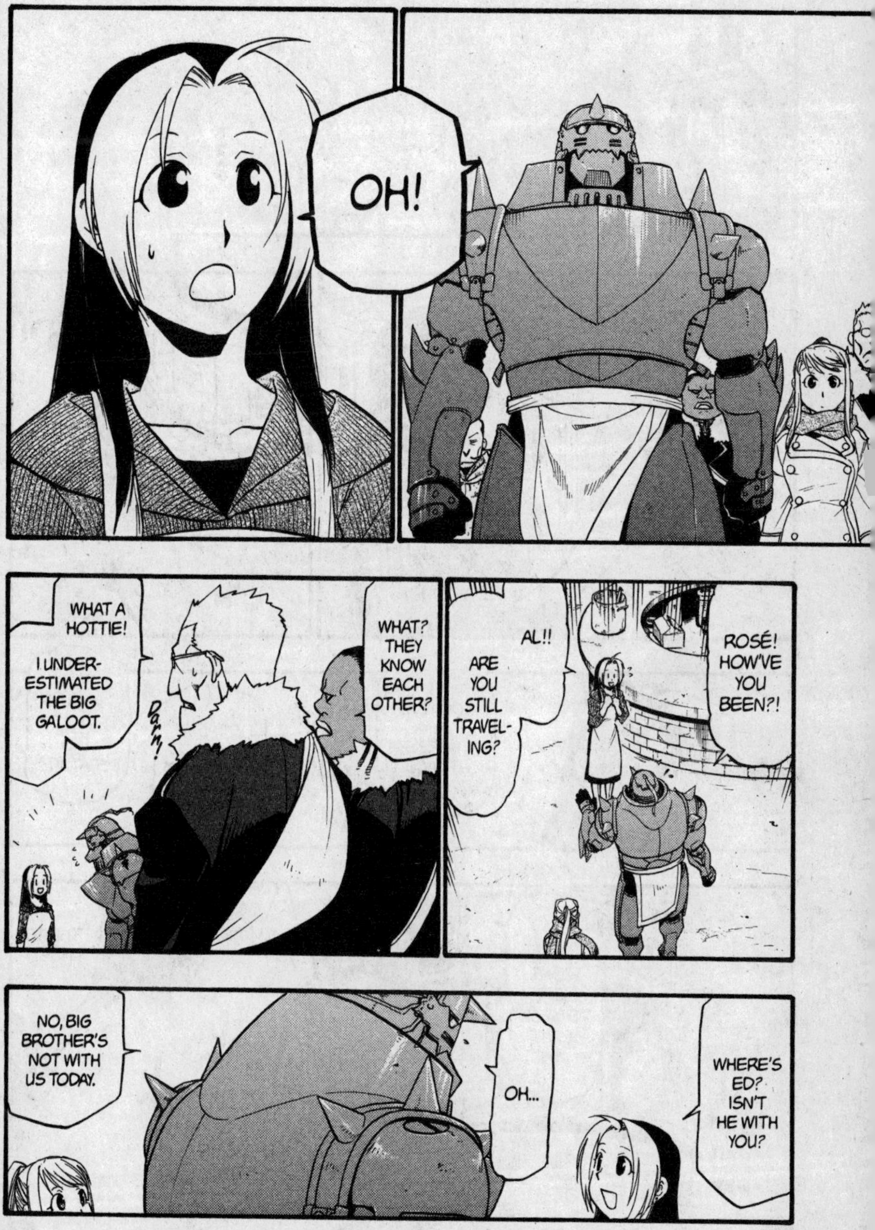
OH!
ROSÉ! HOW'VE YOU BEEN?!
AL!! ARE YOU STILL TRAVELING?
WHAT? THEY KNOW EACH OTHER?
WHAT A HOTTIE! I UNDERESTIMATED THE BIG GALOOT.
Darn!
WHERE'S ED? ISN'T HE WITH YOU?
OH...
NO, BIG BROTHER'S NOT WITH US TODAY.

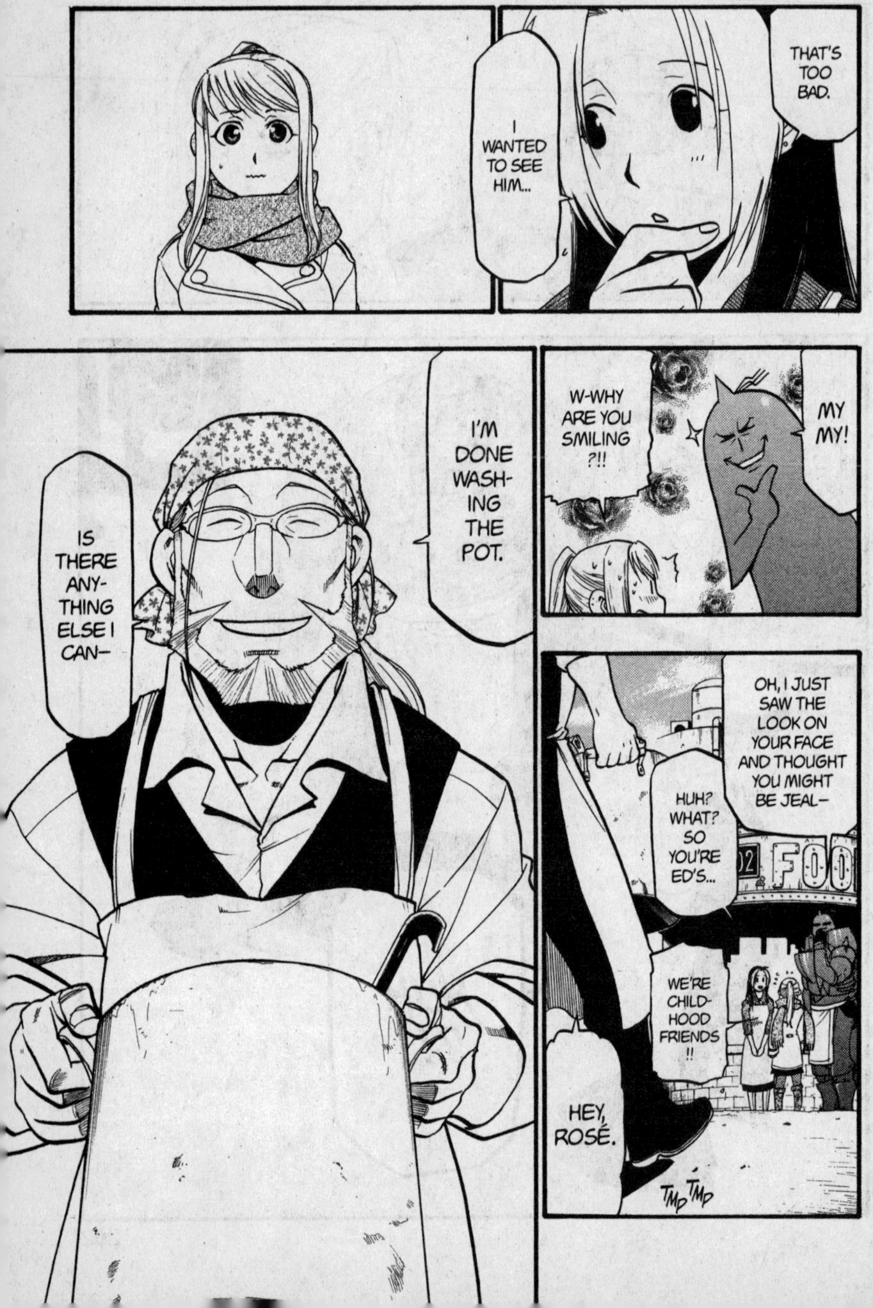
THAT'S TOO BAD.
I WANTED TO SEE HIM...
MY MY!
W-WHY ARE YOU SMILING ?!!
OH, I JUST SAW THE LOOK ON YOUR FACE AND THOUGHT YOU MIGHT BE JEAL—
HUH? WHAT? SO YOU'RE ED'S...
WE'RE CHILDHOOD FRIENDS !!
HEY, ROSÉ.
TMP TMP
I'M DONE WASHING THE POT.
IS THERE ANYTHING ELSE I CAN—

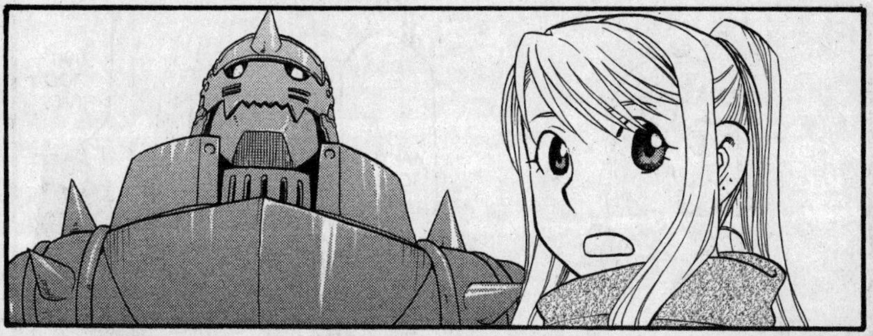

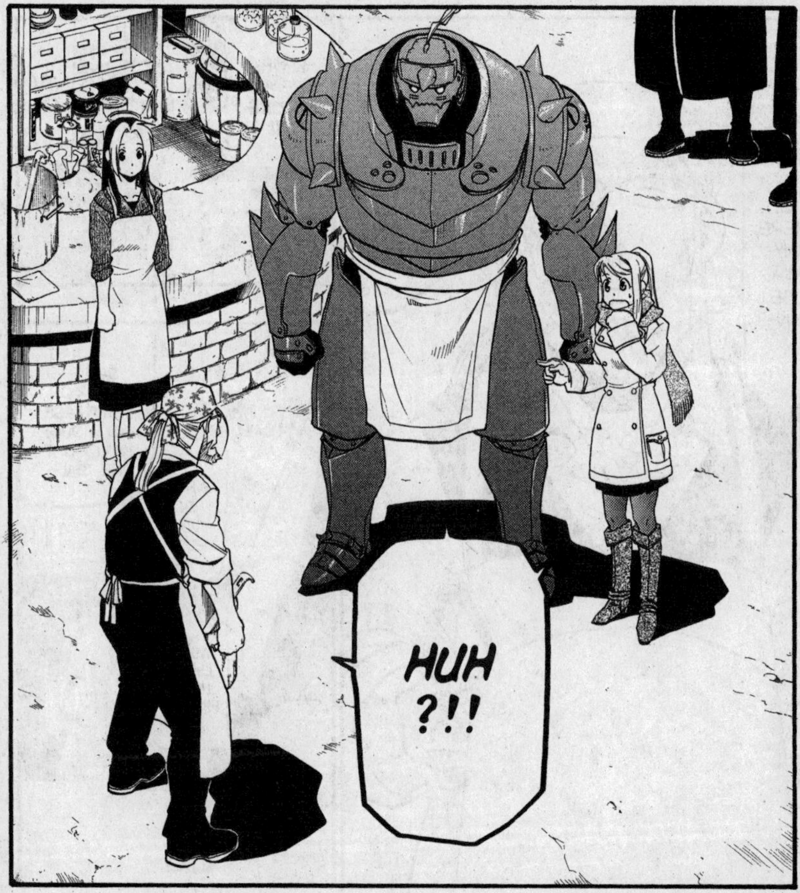
HUH ?!!

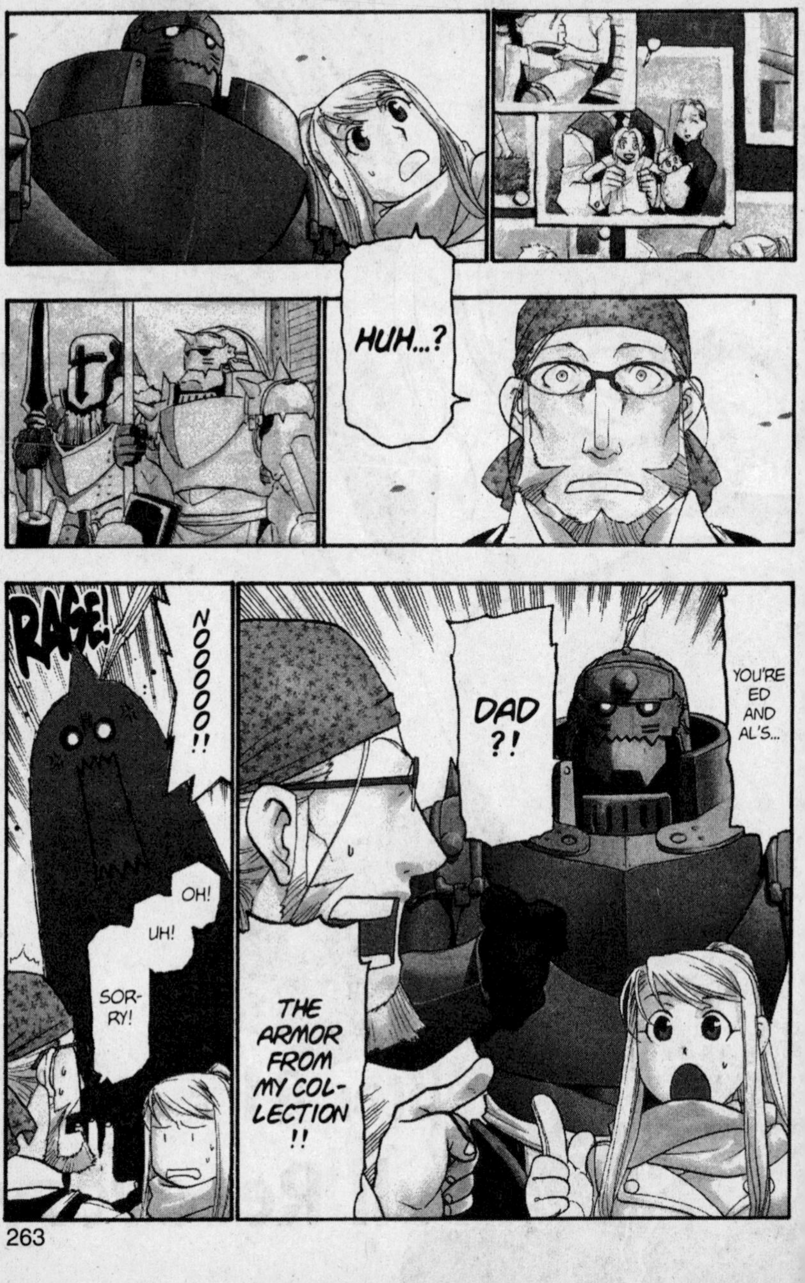
HUH...?
YOU'RE ED AND AL'S...
DAD ?!
THE ARMOR FROM MY COLLECTION !!
RAGE!
NOOOOOO!!
OH!
UH!
SOR-RY!

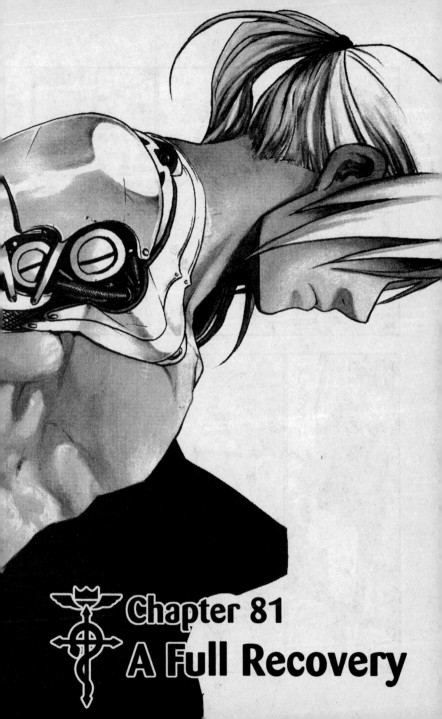

Chapter 81
A Full Recovery

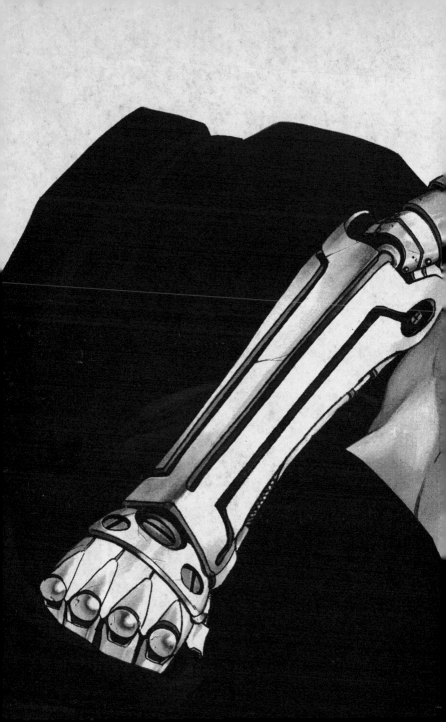

FULLMETAL
ALCHEMIST

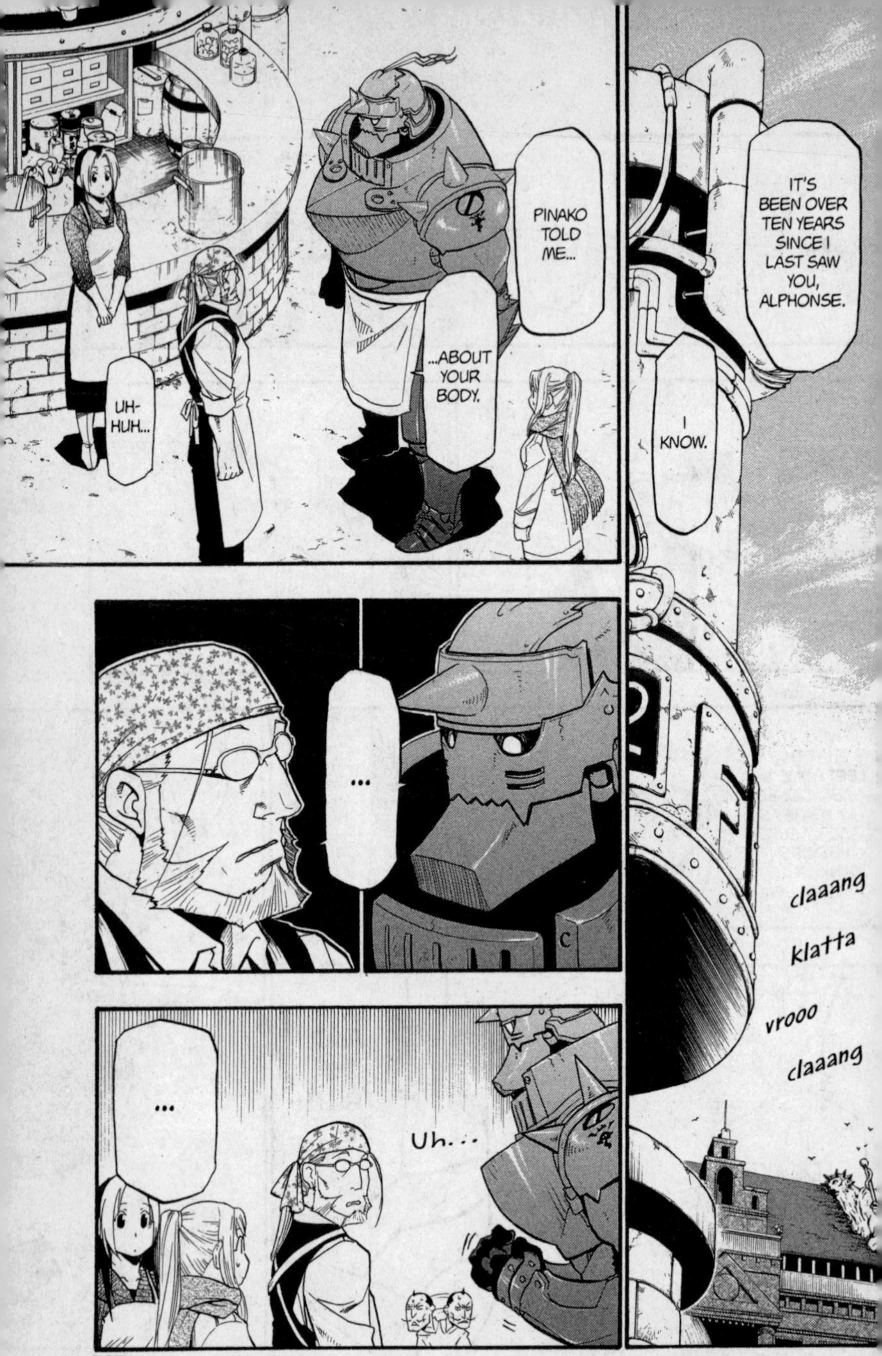
IT'S BEEN OVER TEN YEARS SINCE I LAST SAW YOU, ALPHONSE.
I KNOW.
claaang
klatta
vrooo
claaang
PINAKO TOLD ME...
...ABOUT YOUR BODY.
UH-HUH...
...
...
Uh...

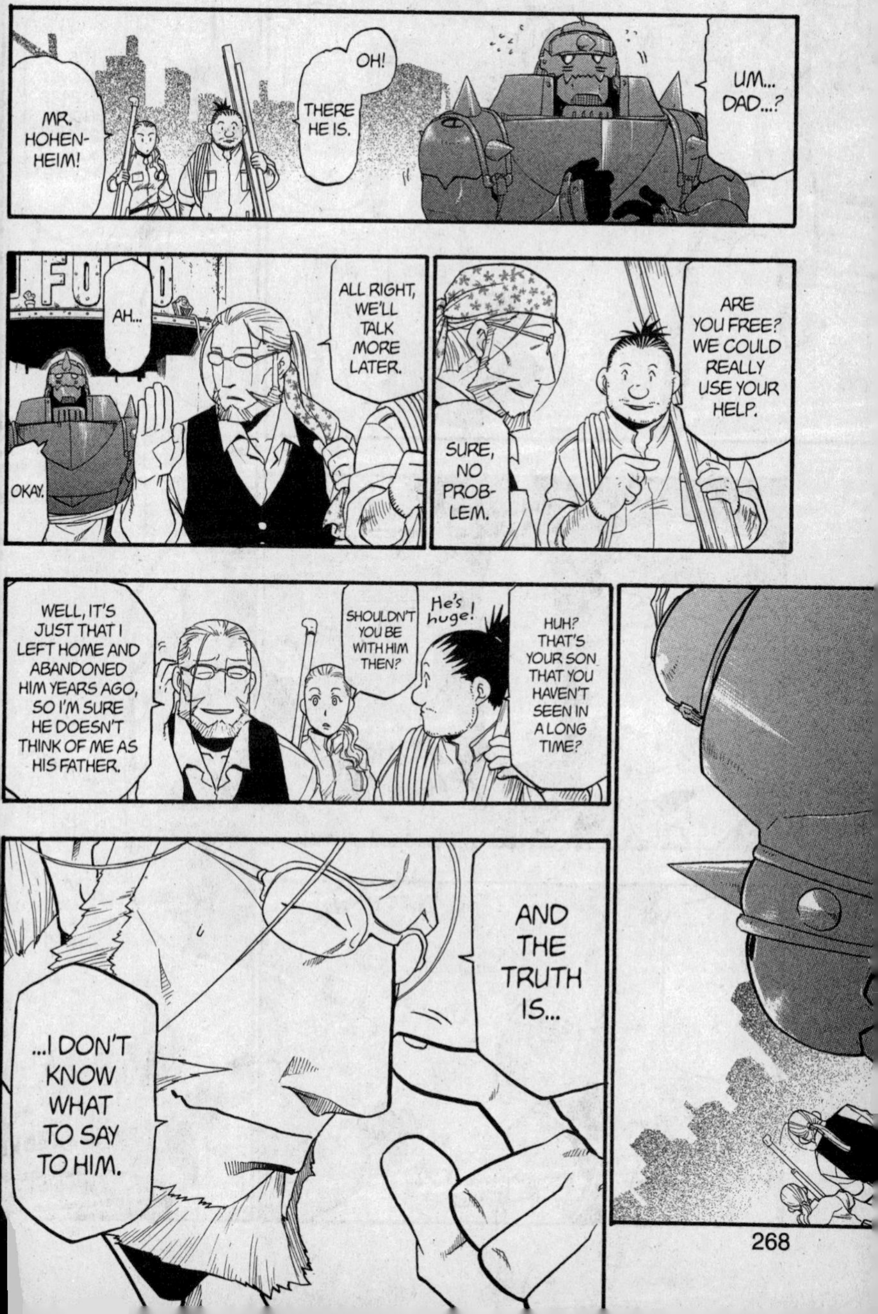
UM... DAD...?
OH!
THERE HE IS.
MR. HOHEN-HEIM!
ARE YOU FREE? WE COULD REALLY USE YOUR HELP.
SURE, NO PROB-LEM.
ALL RIGHT, WE'LL TALK MORE LATER.
AH...
OKAY.
HUH? THAT'S YOUR SON THAT YOU HAVEN'T SEEN IN A LONG TIME?
He's huge!
SHOULDN'T YOU BE WITH HIM THEN?
WELL, IT'S JUST THAT I LEFT HOME AND ABANDONED HIM YEARS AGO, SO I'M SURE HE DOESN'T THINK OF ME AS HIS FATHER.
AND THE TRUTH IS...
...I DON'T KNOW WHAT TO SAY TO HIM.

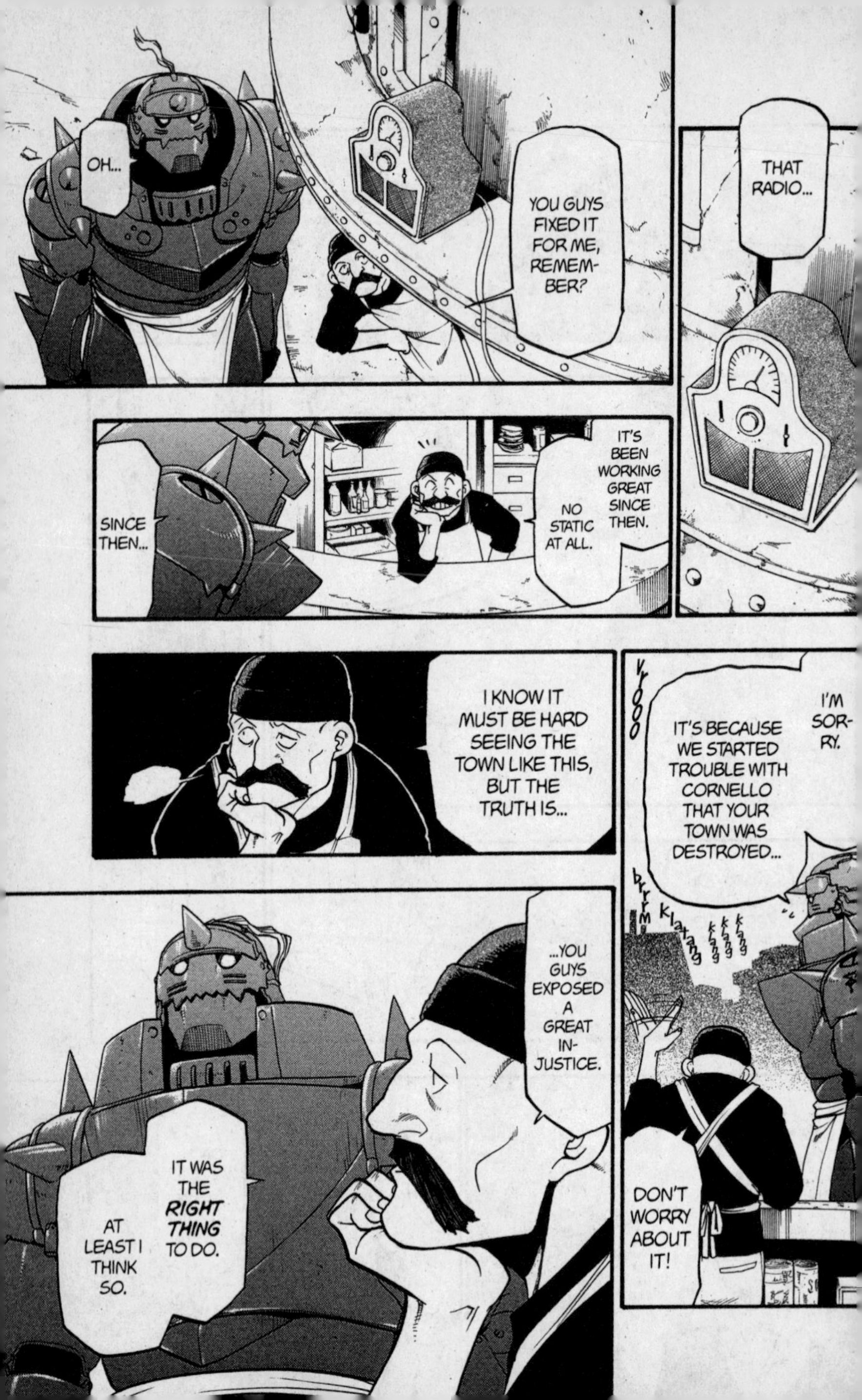
THAT RADIO...
YOU GUYS FIXED IT FOR ME, REMEMBER?
OH...
IT'S BEEN WORKING GREAT SINCE THEN.
NO STATIC AT ALL.
SINCE THEN...
I'M SORRY.
IT'S BECAUSE WE STARTED TROUBLE WITH CORNELLO THAT YOUR TOWN WAS DESTROYED...
vrooo
brrrm
klatang
klang klang klang
DON'T WORRY ABOUT IT!
I KNOW IT MUST BE HARD SEEING THE TOWN LIKE THIS, BUT THE TRUTH IS...
...YOU GUYS EXPOSED A GREAT INJUSTICE.
IT WAS THE *RIGHT THING* TO DO.
AT LEAST I THINK SO.

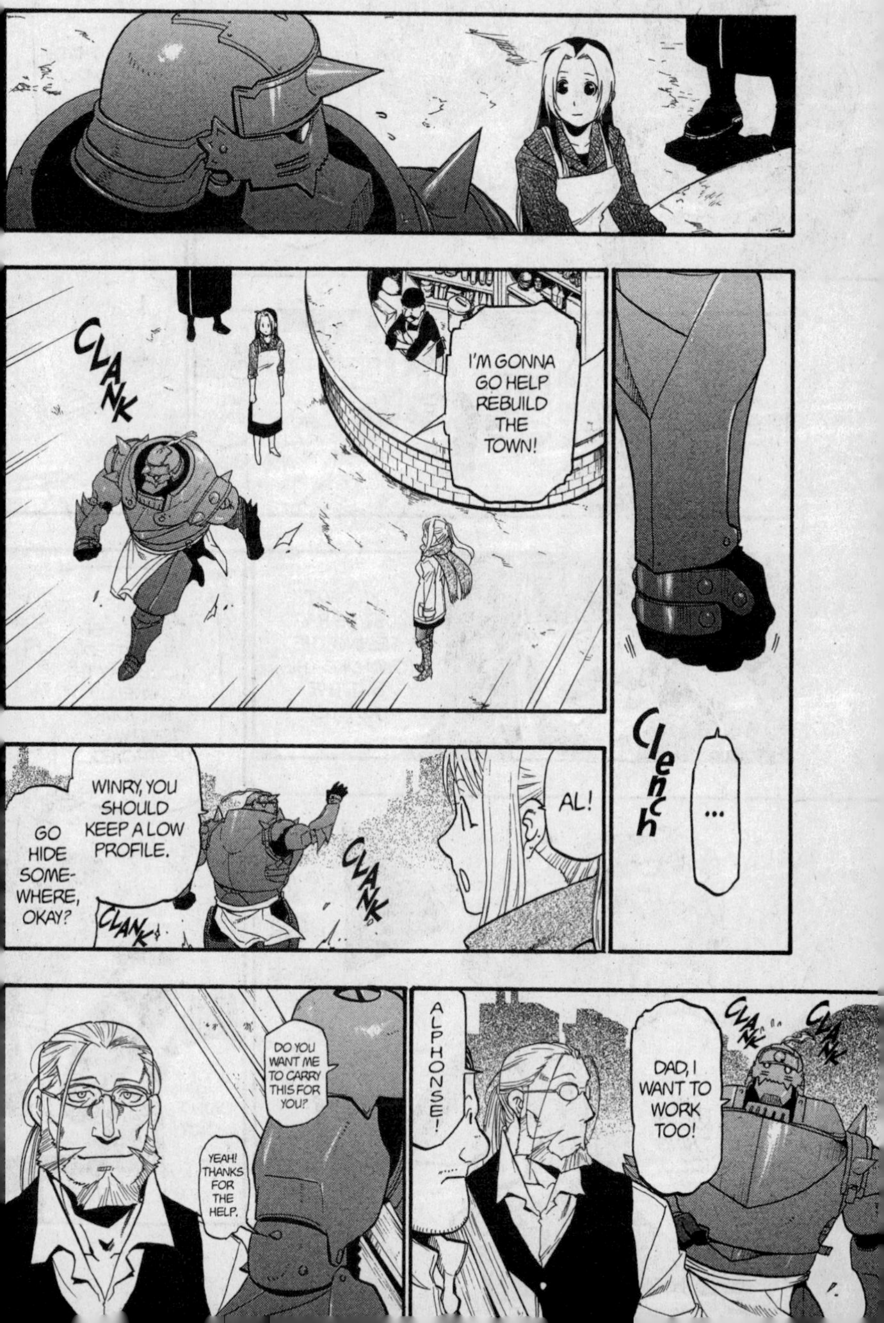
Clench
...
I'M GONNA GO HELP REBUILD THE TOWN!
CLANK
AL!
WINRY, YOU SHOULD KEEP A LOW PROFILE.
GO HIDE SOME-WHERE, OKAY?
CLANK
CLANK
CLANK
CLANK
DAD, I WANT TO WORK TOO!
ALPHONSE!
DO YOU WANT ME TO CARRY THIS FOR YOU?
YEAH! THANKS FOR THE HELP.

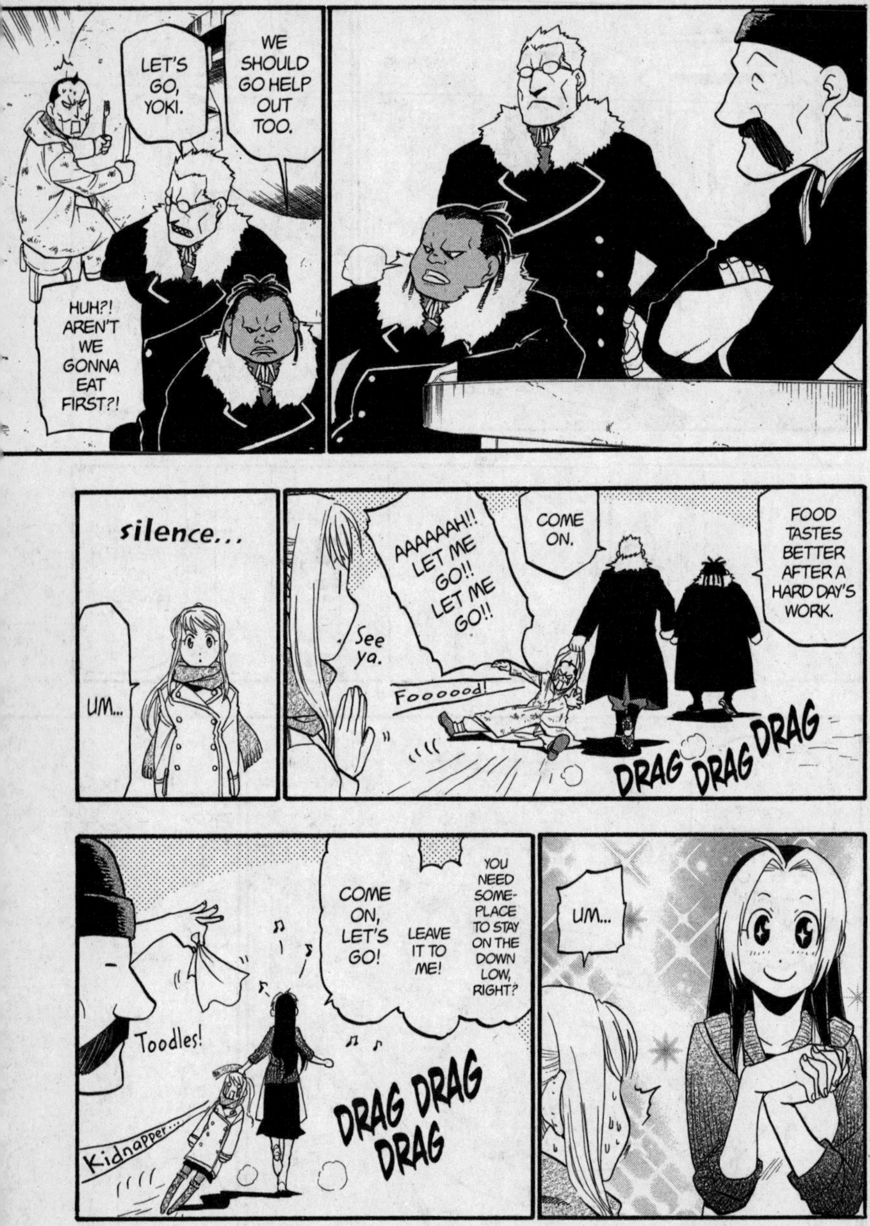
WE SHOULD GO HELP OUT TOO.
LET'S GO, YOKI.
HUH?! AREN'T WE GONNA EAT FIRST?!
FOOD TASTES BETTER AFTER A HARD DAY'S WORK.
COME ON.
AAAAAAH!! LET ME GO!! LET ME GO!!
See ya.
Foooood!
DRAG DRAG DRAG
silence...
UM...
UM...
YOU NEED SOME-PLACE TO STAY ON THE DOWN LOW, RIGHT?
LEAVE IT TO ME!
COME ON, LET'S GO!
Toodles!
DRAG DRAG DRAG
Kidnapper...

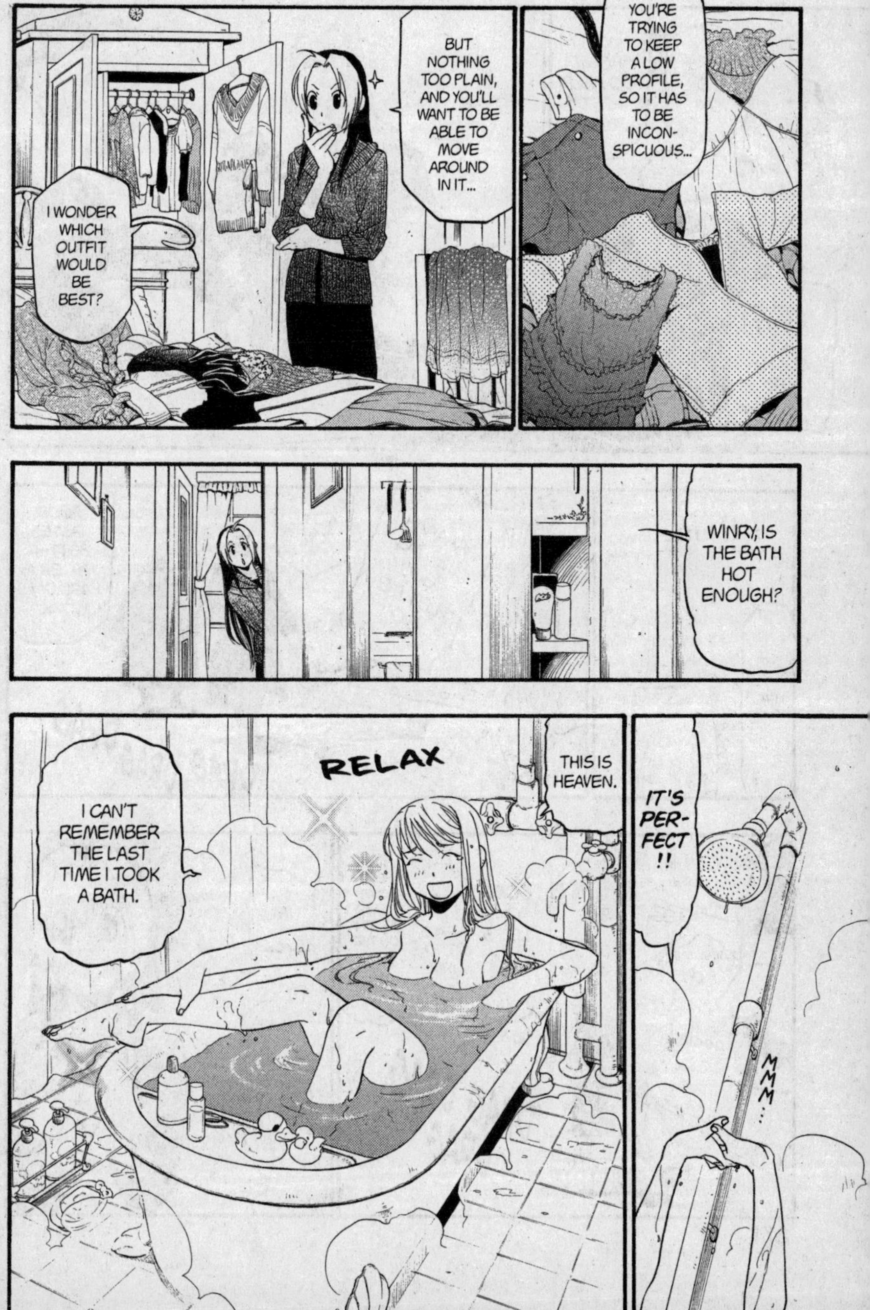
YOU'RE TRYING TO KEEP A LOW PROFILE, SO IT HAS TO BE INCON-SPICUOUS...
BUT NOTHING TOO PLAIN, AND YOU'LL WANT TO BE ABLE TO MOVE AROUND IN IT...
I WONDER WHICH OUTFIT WOULD BE BEST?
WINRY, IS THE BATH HOT ENOUGH?
IT'S PER-FECT!!
MMM...
THIS IS HEAVEN.
RELAX
I CAN'T REMEMBER THE LAST TIME I TOOK A BATH.

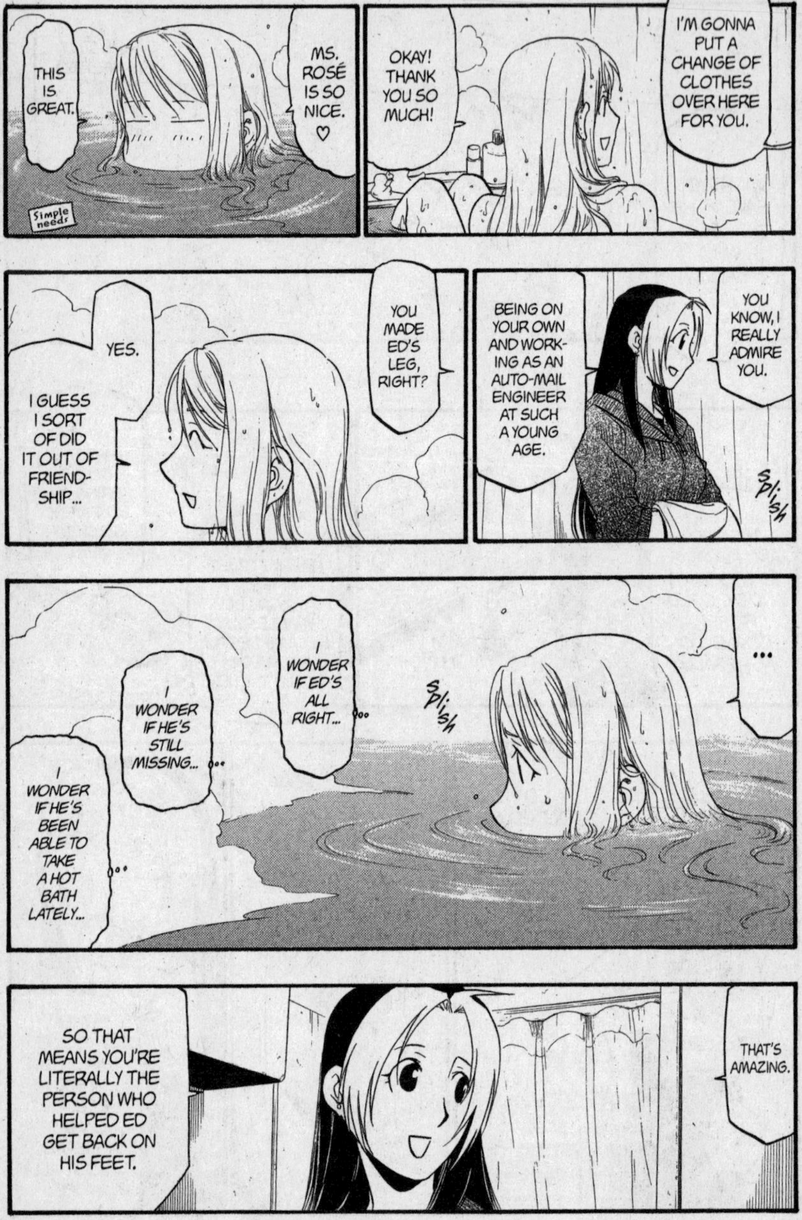
I'M GONNA PUT A CHANGE OF CLOTHES OVER HERE FOR YOU.
OKAY! THANK YOU SO MUCH!
MS. ROSÉ IS SO NICE. ♡
THIS IS GREAT.
Simple needs
YOU KNOW, I REALLY ADMIRE YOU.
BEING ON YOUR OWN AND WORKING AS AN AUTO-MAIL ENGINEER AT SUCH A YOUNG AGE.
splish
YOU MADE ED'S LEG, RIGHT?
YES.
I GUESS I SORT OF DID IT OUT OF FRIENDSHIP...
...
splish
I WONDER IF ED'S ALL RIGHT...
I WONDER IF HE'S STILL MISSING...
I WONDER IF HE'S BEEN ABLE TO TAKE A HOT BATH LATELY...
THAT'S AMAZING.
SO THAT MEANS YOU'RE LITERALLY THE PERSON WHO HELPED ED GET BACK ON HIS FEET.

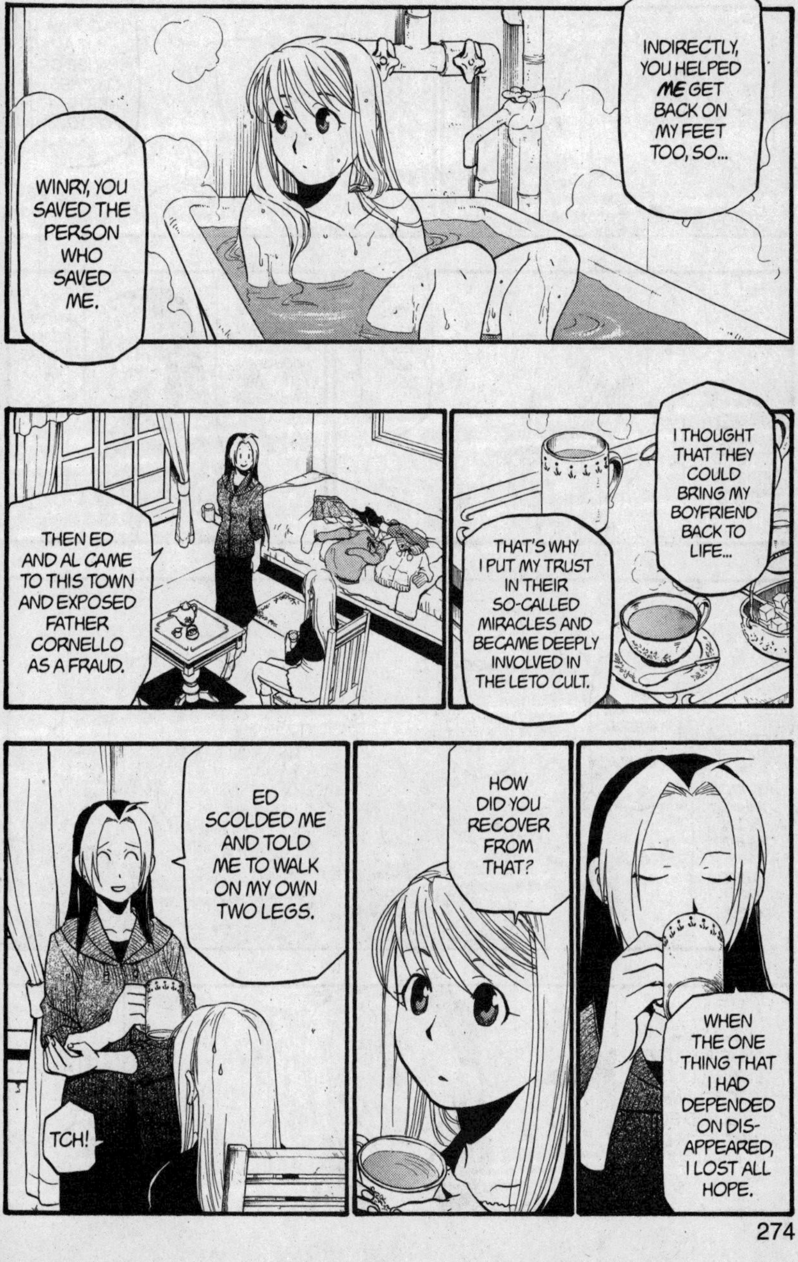
INDIRECTLY, YOU HELPED *ME* GET BACK ON MY FEET TOO, SO...
WINRY, YOU SAVED THE PERSON WHO SAVED ME.
I THOUGHT THAT THEY COULD BRING MY BOYFRIEND BACK TO LIFE...
THAT'S WHY I PUT MY TRUST IN THEIR SO-CALLED MIRACLES AND BECAME DEEPLY INVOLVED IN THE LETO CULT.
THEN ED AND AL CAME TO THIS TOWN AND EXPOSED FATHER CORNELLO AS A FRAUD.
WHEN THE ONE THING THAT I HAD DEPENDED ON DIS-APPEARED, I LOST ALL HOPE.
HOW DID YOU RECOVER FROM THAT?
ED SCOLDED ME AND TOLD ME TO WALK ON MY OWN TWO LEGS.
TCH!

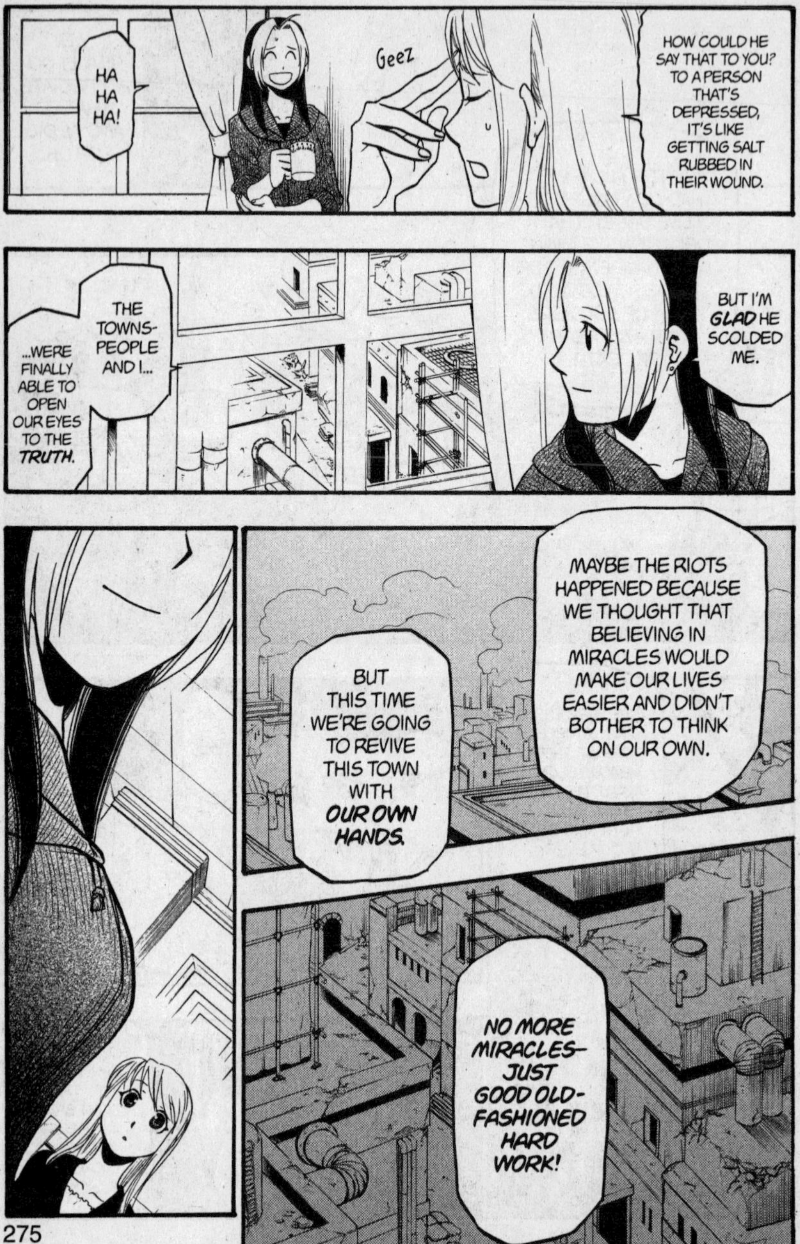
HOW COULD HE SAY THAT TO YOU? TO A PERSON THAT'S DEPRESSED, IT'S LIKE GETTING SALT RUBBED IN THEIR WOUND.
Geez
HA HA HA!
BUT I'M *GLAD* HE SCOLDED ME.
THE TOWNS-PEOPLE AND I...
...WERE FINALLY ABLE TO OPEN OUR EYES TO THE *TRUTH*.
MAYBE THE RIOTS HAPPENED BECAUSE WE THOUGHT THAT BELIEVING IN MIRACLES WOULD MAKE OUR LIVES EASIER AND DIDN'T BOTHER TO THINK ON OUR OWN.
BUT THIS TIME WE'RE GOING TO REVIVE THIS TOWN WITH *OUR OWN HANDS.*
NO MORE MIRACLES- JUST GOOD OLD-FASHIONED HARD WORK!

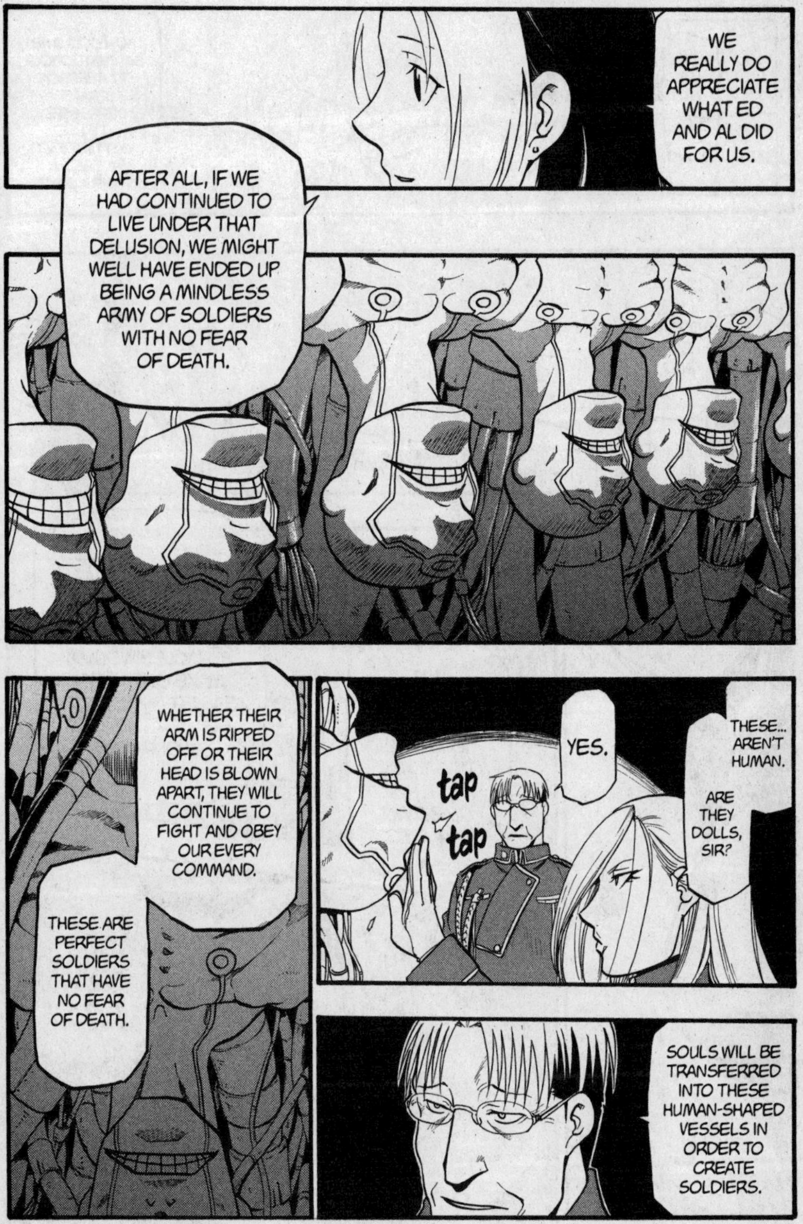
WE REALLY DO APPRECIATE WHAT ED AND AL DID FOR US.
AFTER ALL, IF WE HAD CONTINUED TO LIVE UNDER THAT DELUSION, WE MIGHT WELL HAVE ENDED UP BEING A MINDLESS ARMY OF SOLDIERS WITH NO FEAR OF DEATH.
THESE... AREN'T HUMAN.
ARE THEY DOLLS, SIR?
YES.
tap
tap
SOULS WILL BE TRANSFERRED INTO THESE HUMAN-SHAPED VESSELS IN ORDER TO CREATE SOLDIERS.
WHETHER THEIR ARM IS RIPPED OFF OR THEIR HEAD IS BLOWN APART, THEY WILL CONTINUE TO FIGHT AND OBEY OUR EVERY COMMAND.
THESE ARE PERFECT SOLDIERS THAT HAVE NO FEAR OF DEATH.

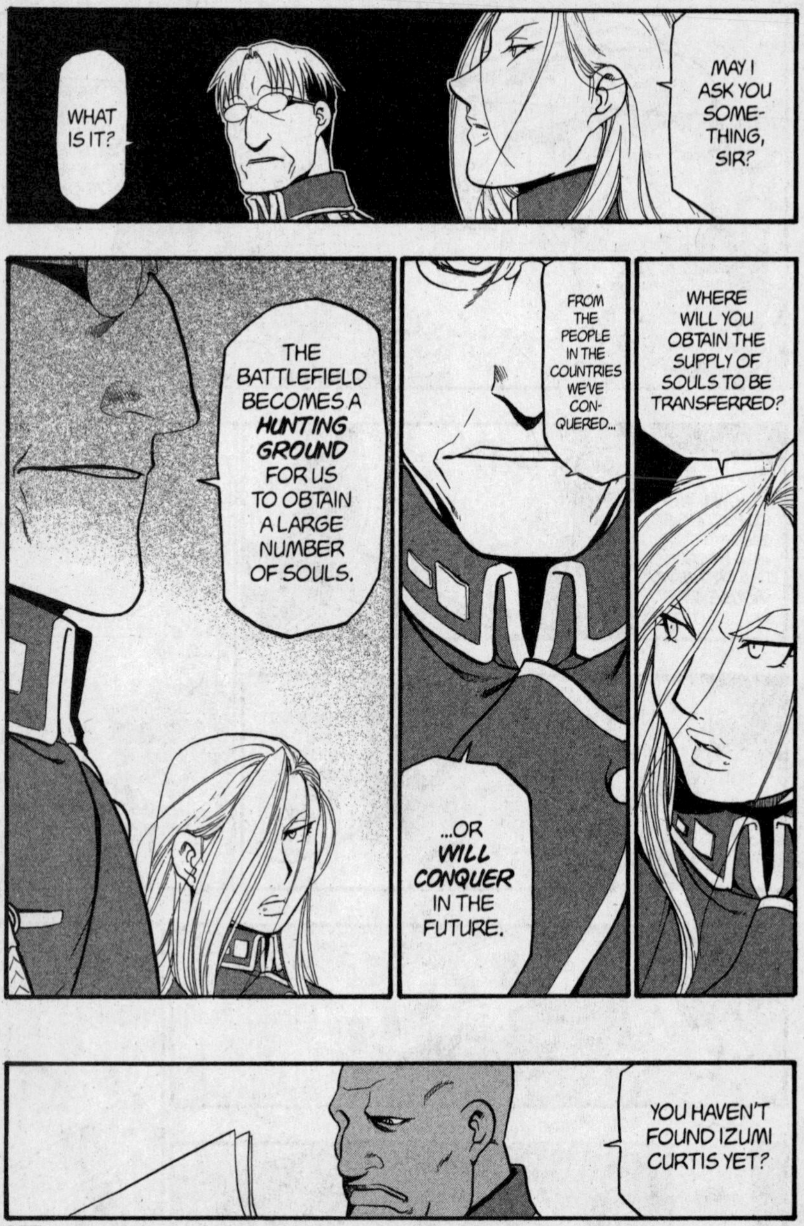
MAY I ASK YOU SOME-THING, SIR?
WHAT IS IT?
WHERE WILL YOU OBTAIN THE SUPPLY OF SOULS TO BE TRANSFERRED?
FROM THE PEOPLE IN THE COUNTRIES WE'VE CON-QUERED...
...OR **WILL CONQUER** IN THE FUTURE.
THE BATTLEFIELD BECOMES A **HUNTING GROUND** FOR US TO OBTAIN A LARGE NUMBER OF SOULS.
YOU HAVEN'T FOUND IZUMI CURTIS YET?

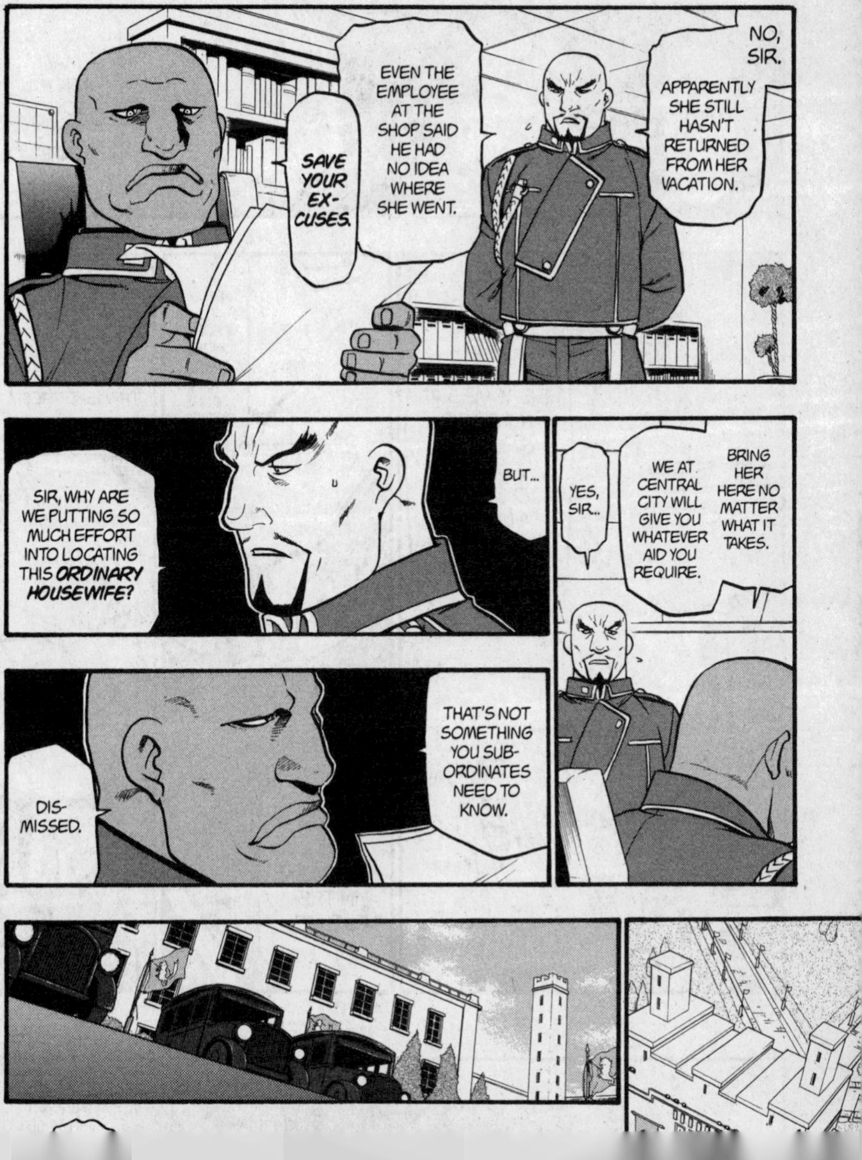
NO, SIR.
APPARENTLY SHE STILL HASN'T RETURNED FROM HER VACATION.
EVEN THE EMPLOYEE AT THE SHOP SAID HE HAD NO IDEA WHERE SHE WENT.
SAVE YOUR EX-CUSES.
BRING HER HERE NO MATTER WHAT IT TAKES.
WE AT CENTRAL CITY WILL GIVE YOU WHATEVER AID YOU REQUIRE.
YES, SIR...
BUT...
SIR, WHY ARE WE PUTTING SO MUCH EFFORT INTO LOCATING THIS ORDINARY HOUSEWIFE?
THAT'S NOT SOMETHING YOU SUB-ORDINATES NEED TO KNOW.
DIS-MISSED.

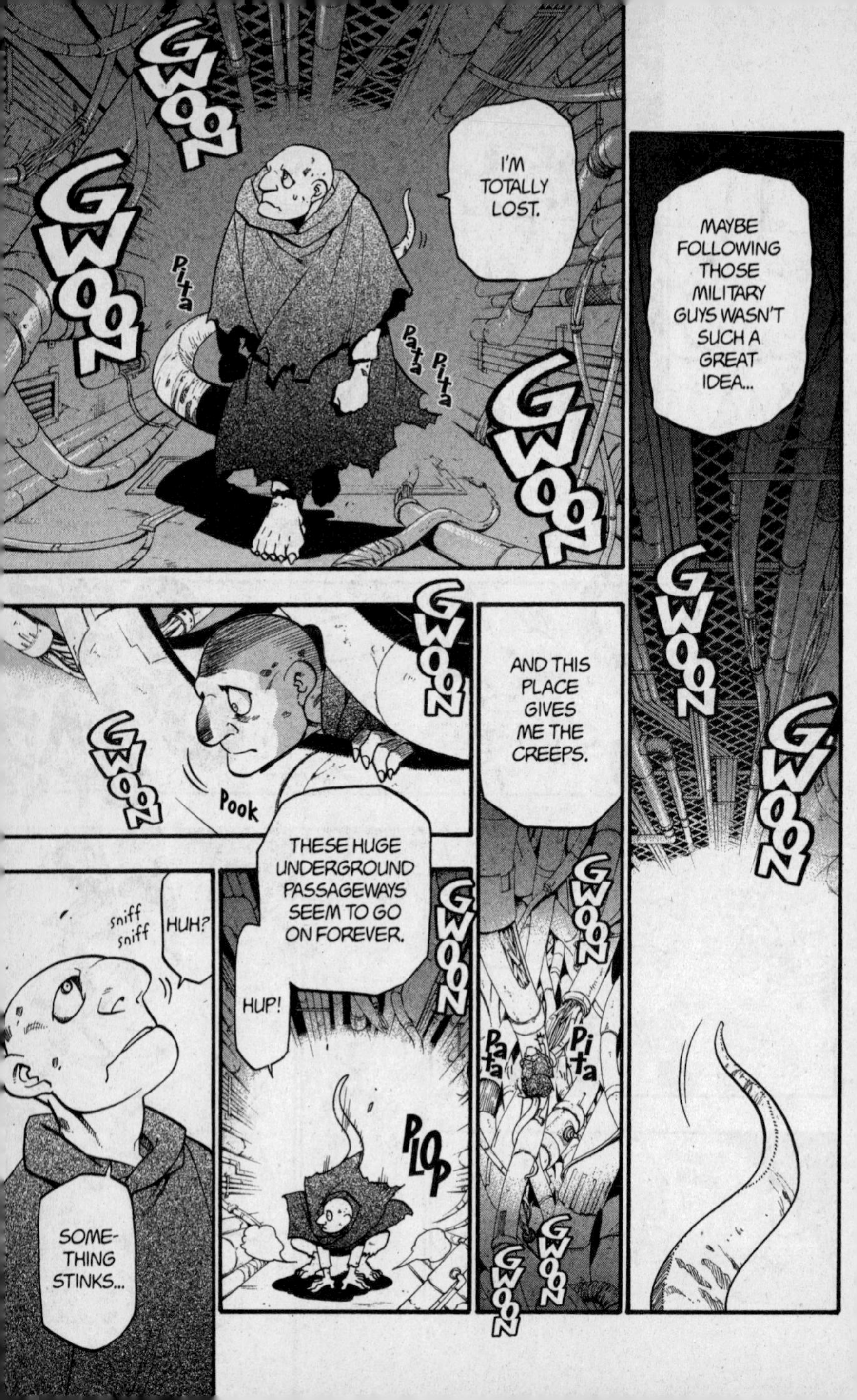
MAYBE FOLLOWING THOSE MILITARY GUYS WASN'T SUCH A GREAT IDEA...
GWOON
GWOON
GWOON
GWOON
I'M TOTALLY LOST.
Pita
Pata
Pita
GWOON
AND THIS PLACE GIVES ME THE CREEPS.
GWOON
Pita
Pata
GWOON
GWOON
GWOON
GWOON
Pook
THESE HUGE UNDERGROUND PASSAGEWAYS SEEM TO GO ON FOREVER.
GWOON
HUP!
PLOP
HUH?
sniff sniff
SOME-THING STINKS...

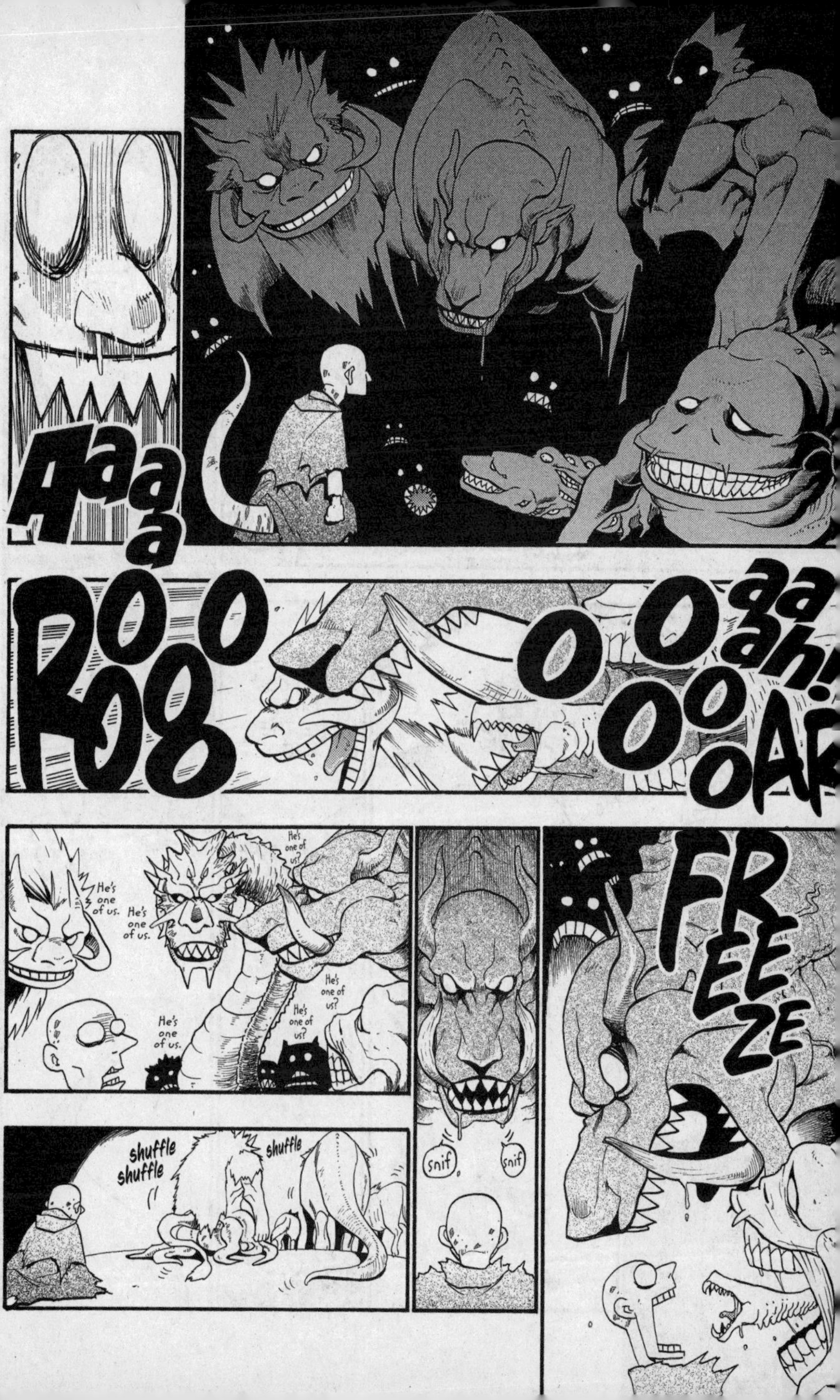
Aaaa
ROOOOOO
OOOaah!
OOOOAR
FREEZE
snif
snif
He's one of us?
He's one of us.
He's one of us.
He's one of us?
He's one of us?
He's one of us.
shuffle
shuffle shuffle

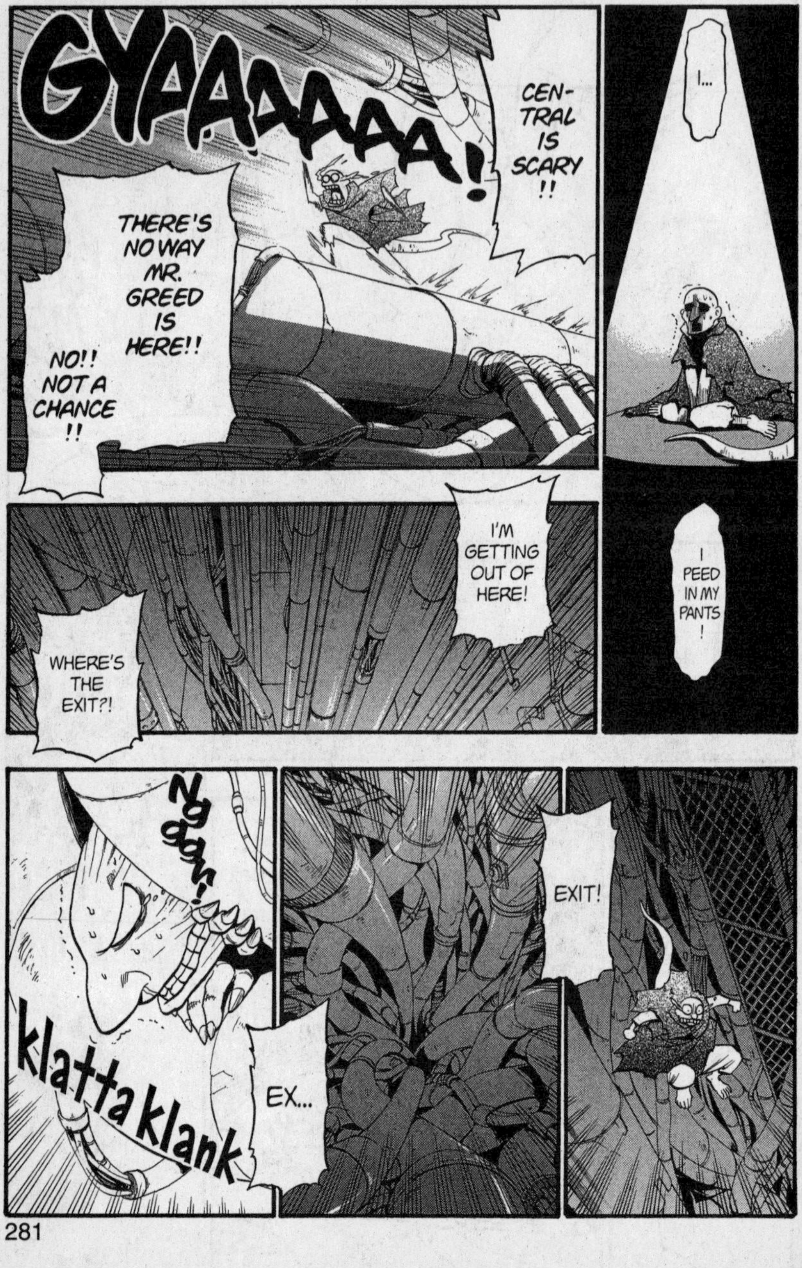
I...
I PEED IN MY PANTS!
GYAAAAAA!
CENTRAL IS SCARY!!
THERE'S NO WAY MR. GREED IS HERE!!
NO!! NOT A CHANCE!!
I'M GETTING OUT OF HERE!
WHERE'S THE EXIT?!
EXIT!
Nggah!
EX...
klatta klank

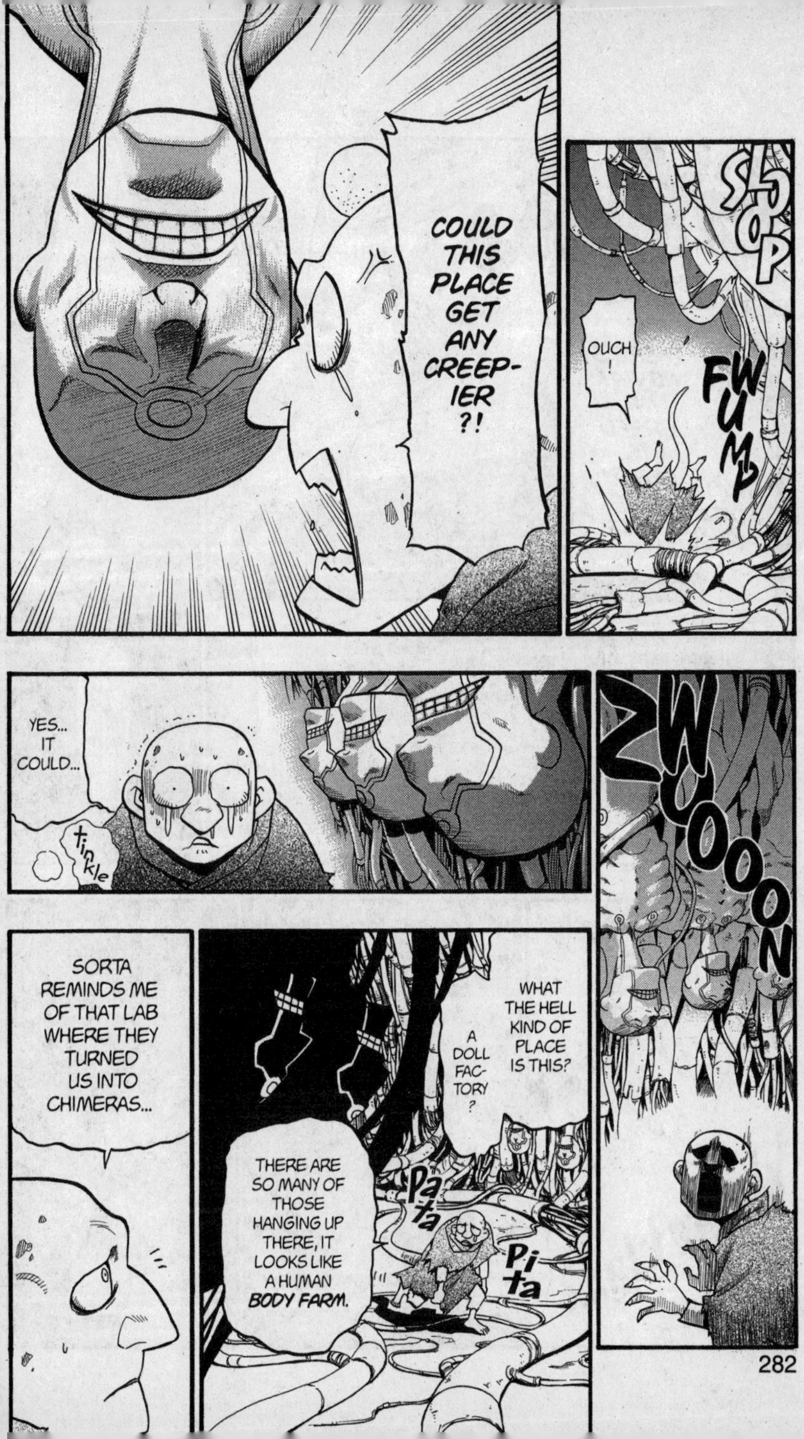
SLOOP
OUCH!
FWUMP
COULD THIS PLACE GET ANY CREEPIER?!
ZWOOOOON
YES... IT COULD...
tinkle
WHAT THE HELL KIND OF PLACE IS THIS?
A DOLL FACTORY?
THERE ARE SO MANY OF THOSE HANGING UP THERE, IT LOOKS LIKE A HUMAN *BODY FARM.*
Pata
Pita
SORTA REMINDS ME OF THAT LAB WHERE THEY TURNED US INTO CHIMERAS...

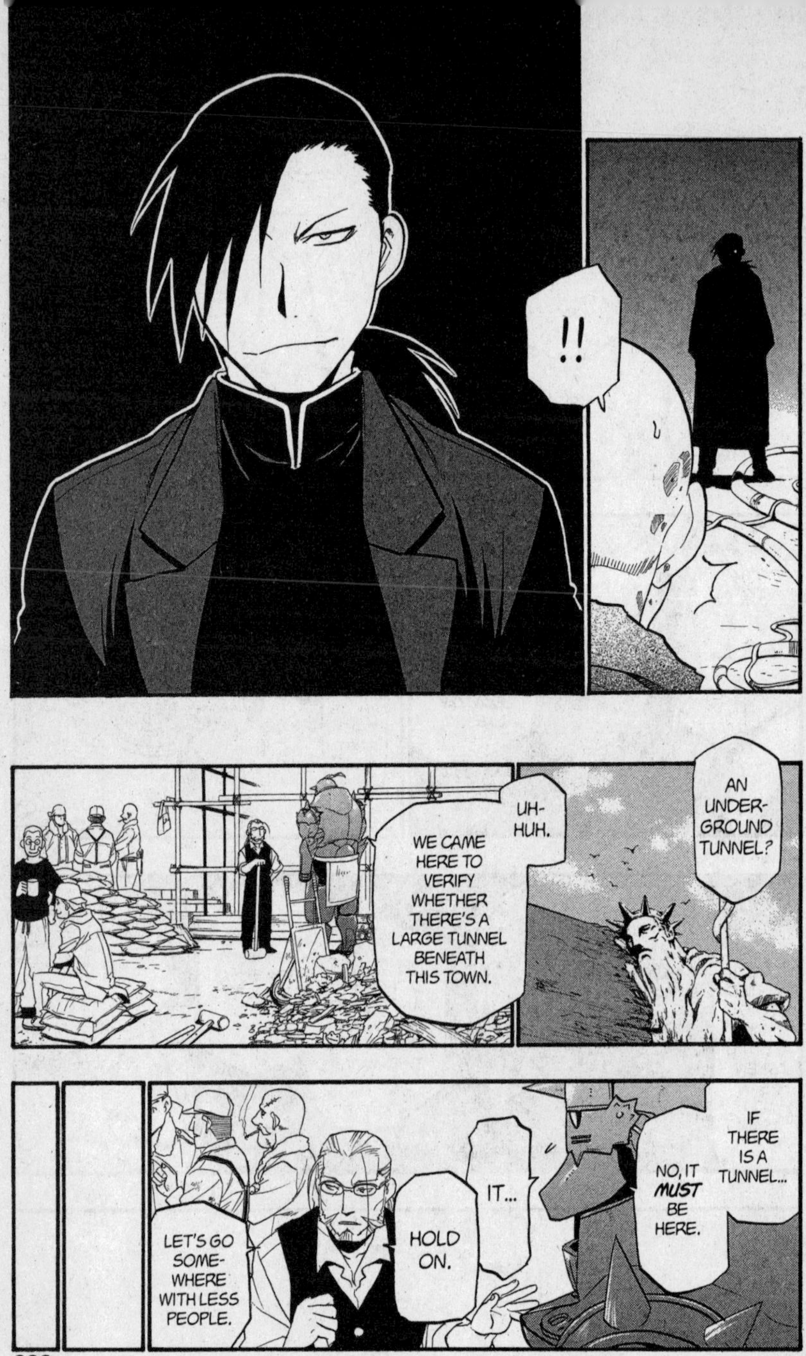
!!
AN UNDERGROUND TUNNEL?
UH-HUH.
WE CAME HERE TO VERIFY WHETHER THERE'S A LARGE TUNNEL BENEATH THIS TOWN.
IF THERE IS A TUNNEL...
NO, IT *MUST* BE HERE.
IT...
HOLD ON.
LET'S GO SOMEWHERE WITH LESS PEOPLE.

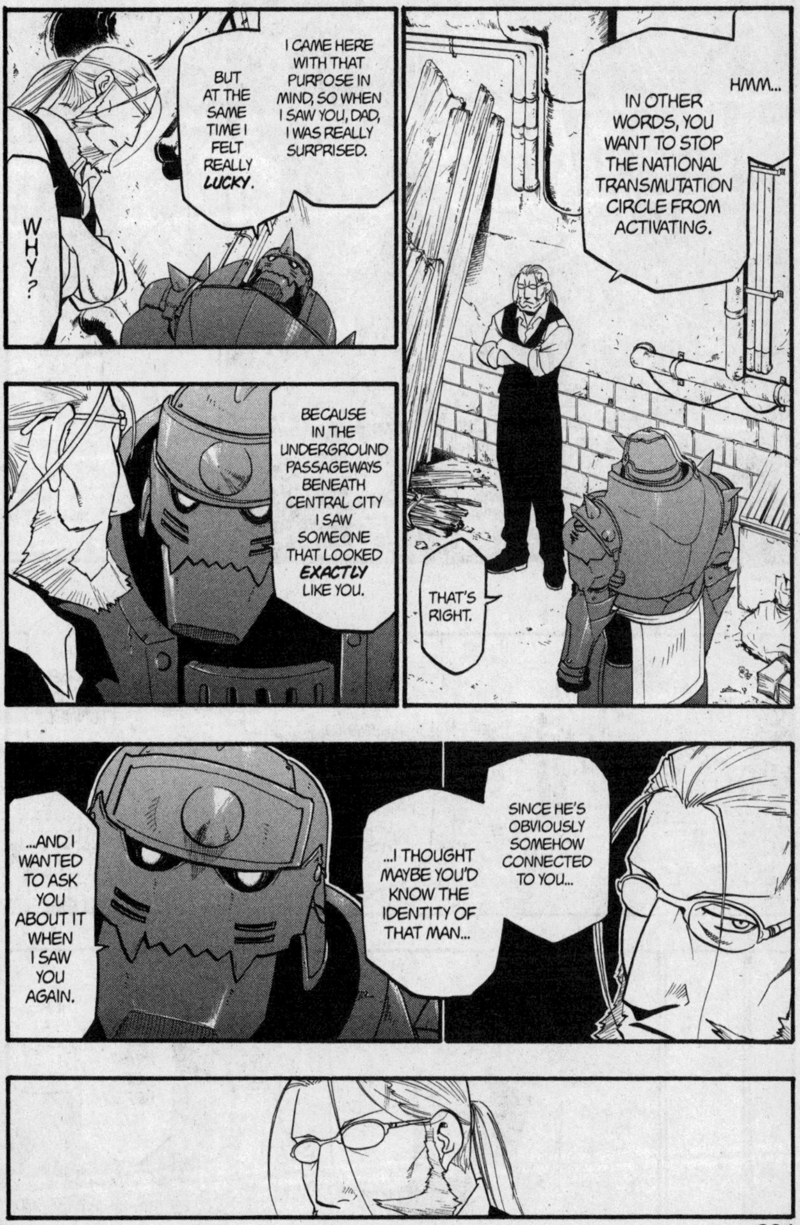
HMM...
IN OTHER WORDS, YOU WANT TO STOP THE NATIONAL TRANSMUTATION CIRCLE FROM ACTIVATING.
THAT'S RIGHT.
I CAME HERE WITH THAT PURPOSE IN MIND, SO WHEN I SAW YOU, DAD, I WAS REALLY SURPRISED.
BUT AT THE SAME TIME I FELT REALLY LUCKY.
WHY?
BECAUSE IN THE UNDERGROUND PASSAGEWAYS BENEATH CENTRAL CITY I SAW SOMEONE THAT LOOKED EXACTLY LIKE YOU.
SINCE HE'S OBVIOUSLY SOMEHOW CONNECTED TO YOU...
...I THOUGHT MAYBE YOU'D KNOW THE IDENTITY OF THAT MAN...
...AND I WANTED TO ASK YOU ABOUT IT WHEN I SAW YOU AGAIN.

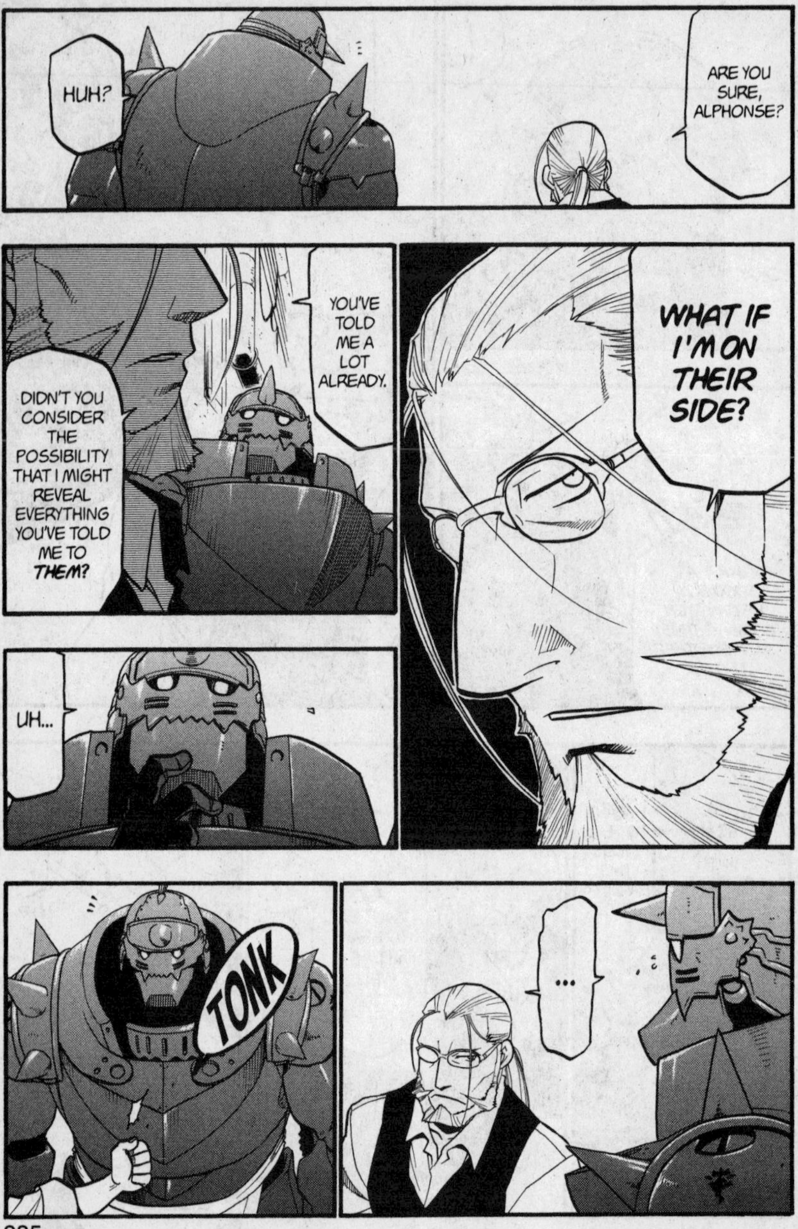
ARE YOU SURE, ALPHONSE?
HUH?
WHAT IF I'M ON THEIR SIDE?
YOU'VE TOLD ME A LOT ALREADY.
DIDN'T YOU CONSIDER THE POSSIBILITY THAT I MIGHT REVEAL EVERYTHING YOU'VE TOLD ME TO *THEM*?
UH...
...
TONK

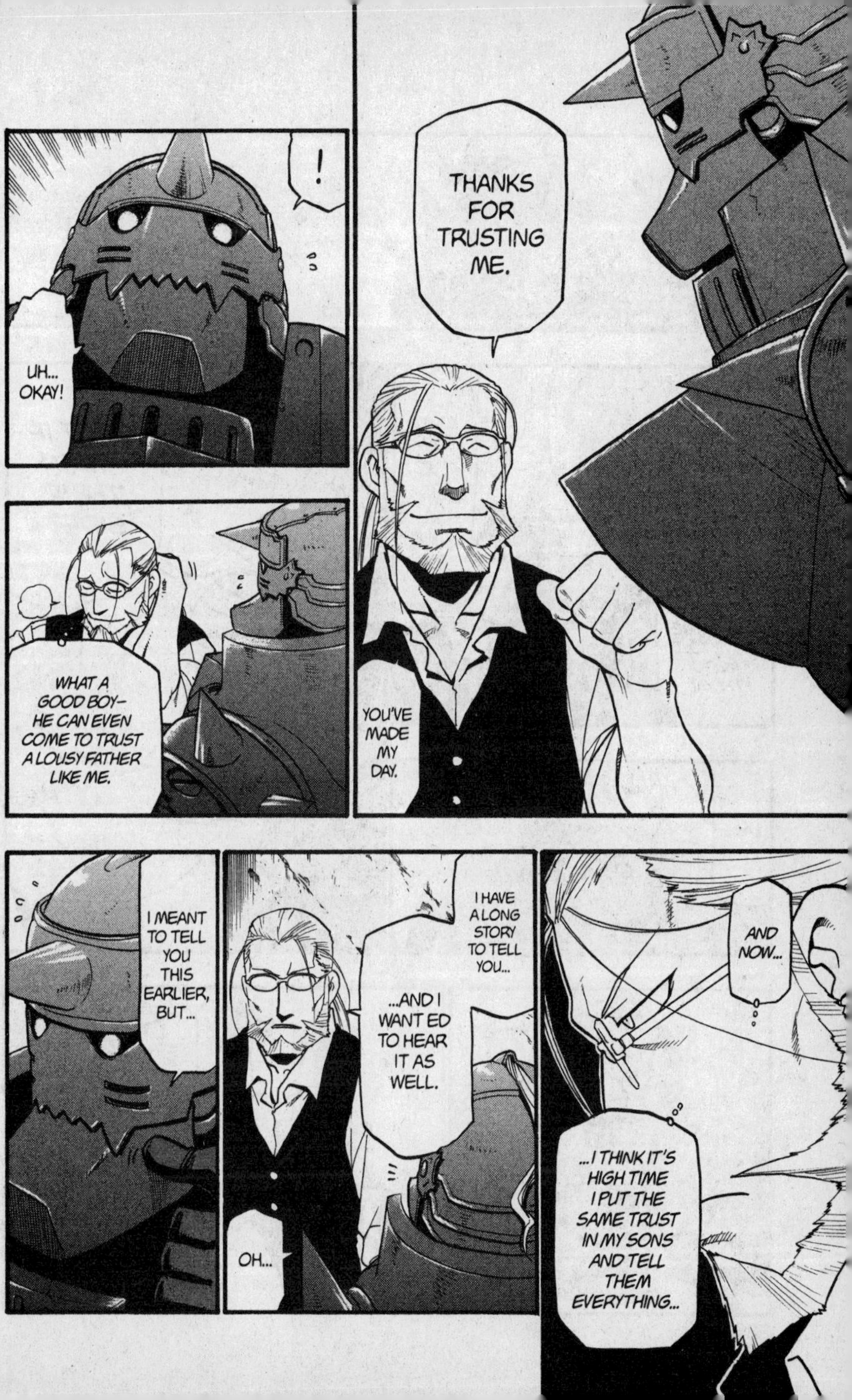
THANKS FOR TRUSTING ME.
YOU'VE MADE MY DAY.
!
UH... OKAY!
WHAT A GOOD BOY—HE CAN EVEN COME TO TRUST A LOUSY FATHER LIKE ME.
AND NOW...
...I THINK IT'S HIGH TIME I PUT THE SAME TRUST IN MY SONS AND TELL THEM EVERYTHING...
I HAVE A LONG STORY TO TELL YOU...
...AND I WANT ED TO HEAR IT AS WELL.
OH...
I MEANT TO TELL YOU THIS EARLIER, BUT...

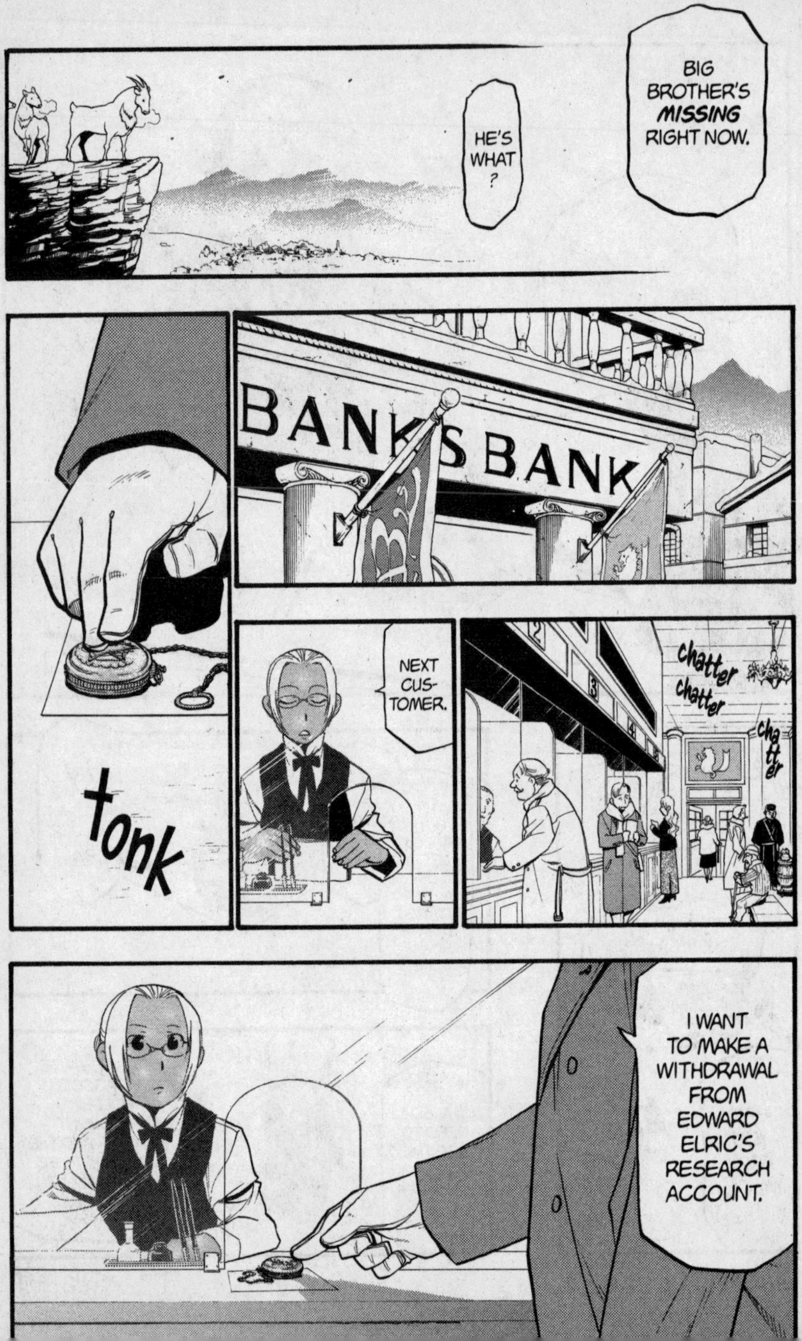
BIG BROTHER'S **MISSING** RIGHT NOW.
HE'S WHAT?
BANKS BANK
chatter chatter chatter
NEXT CUS-TOMER.
tonk
I WANT TO MAKE A WITHDRAWAL FROM EDWARD ELRIC'S RESEARCH ACCOUNT.

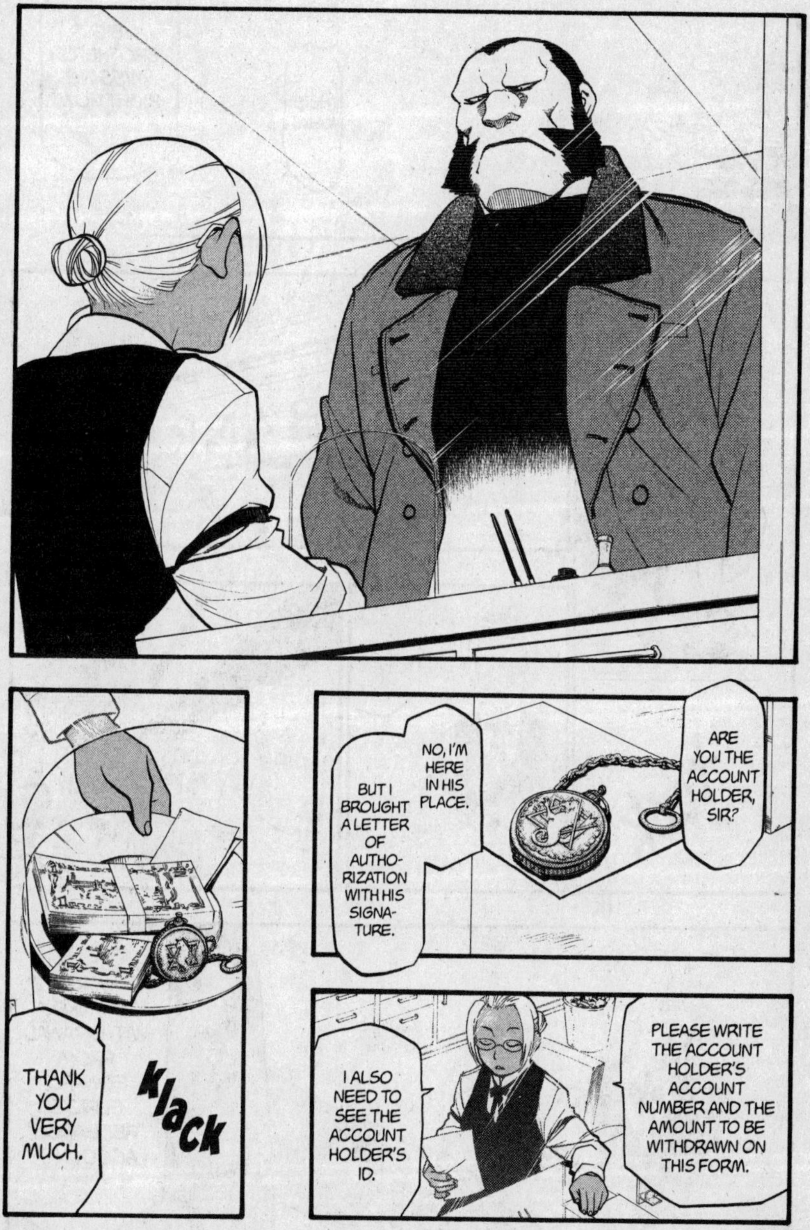
ARE YOU THE ACCOUNT HOLDER, SIR?
NO, I'M HERE IN HIS PLACE.
BUT I BROUGHT A LETTER OF AUTHORIZATION WITH HIS SIGNATURE.
PLEASE WRITE THE ACCOUNT HOLDER'S ACCOUNT NUMBER AND THE AMOUNT TO BE WITHDRAWN ON THIS FORM.
I ALSO NEED TO SEE THE ACCOUNT HOLDER'S ID.
THANK YOU VERY MUCH.
klack

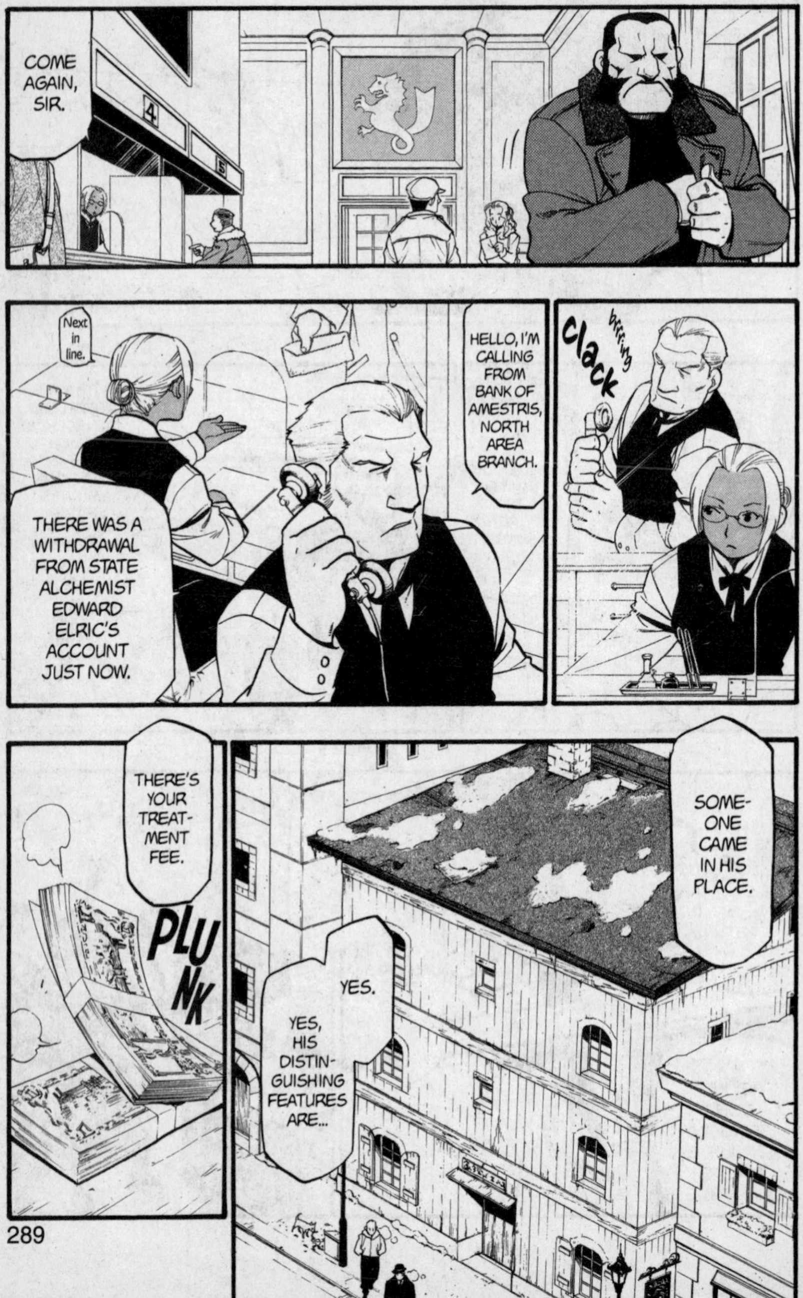
COME AGAIN, SIR.
brrring
clack
HELLO, I'M CALLING FROM BANK OF AMESTRIS, NORTH AREA BRANCH.
Next in line.
THERE WAS A WITHDRAWAL FROM STATE ALCHEMIST EDWARD ELRIC'S ACCOUNT JUST NOW.
SOME-ONE CAME IN HIS PLACE.
YES.
YES, HIS DISTIN-GUISHING FEATURES ARE...
THERE'S YOUR TREAT-MENT FEE.
PLUNK

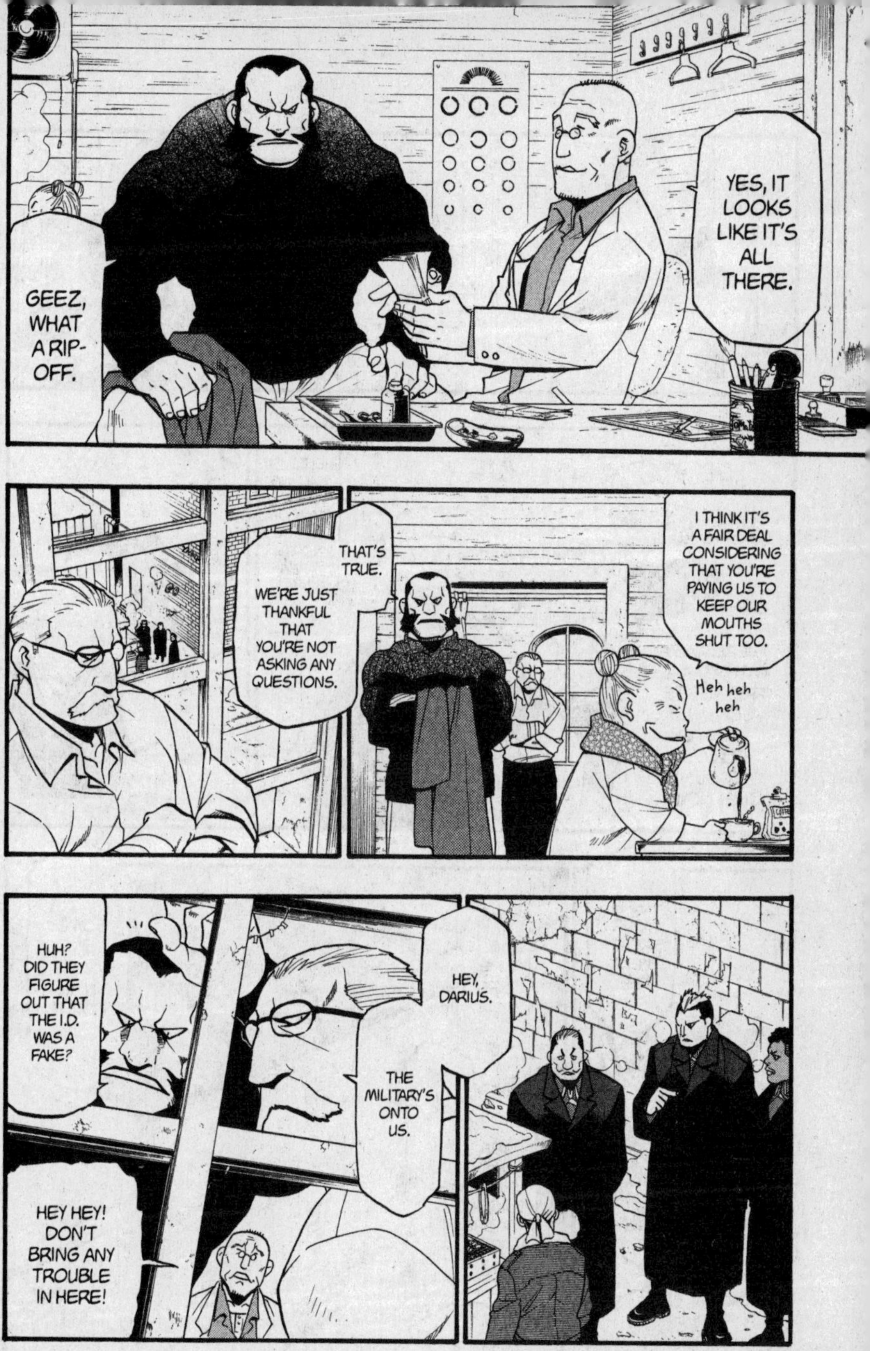
YES, IT LOOKS LIKE IT'S ALL THERE.
GEEZ, WHAT A RIP-OFF.
I THINK IT'S A FAIR DEAL CONSIDERING THAT YOU'RE PAYING US TO KEEP OUR MOUTHS SHUT TOO.
Heh heh heh
THAT'S TRUE.
WE'RE JUST THANKFUL THAT YOU'RE NOT ASKING ANY QUESTIONS.
HEY, DARIUS.
THE MILITARY'S ONTO US.
HUH? DID THEY FIGURE OUT THAT THE I.D. WAS A FAKE?
HEY HEY! DON'T BRING ANY TROUBLE IN HERE!

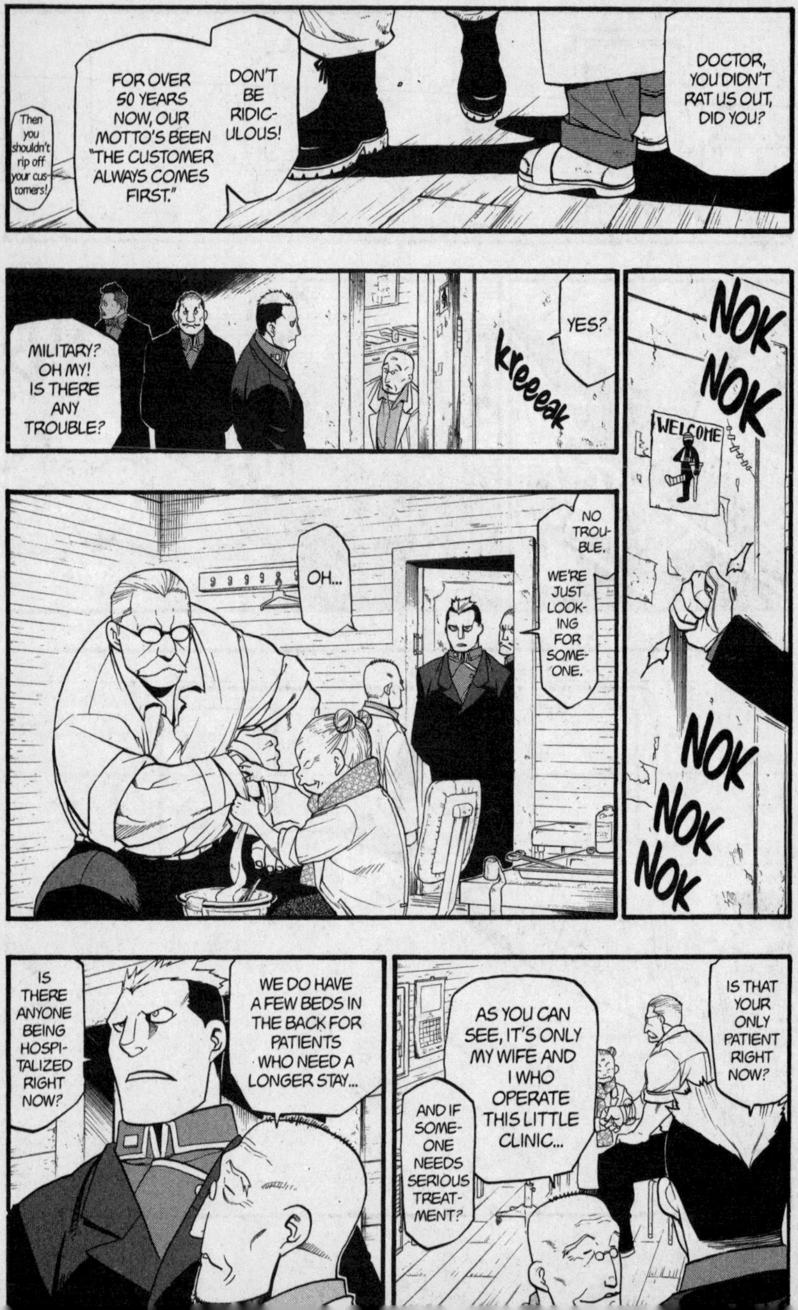
DOCTOR, YOU DIDN'T RAT US OUT, DID YOU?
DON'T BE RIDICULOUS!
FOR OVER 50 YEARS NOW, OUR MOTTO'S BEEN "THE CUSTOMER ALWAYS COMES FIRST."
Then you shouldn't rip off your customers!
NOK NOK
WELCOME
NOK NOK NOK
YES?
kreeeeak
MILITARY? OH MY! IS THERE ANY TROUBLE?
NO TROUBLE.
WE'RE JUST LOOKING FOR SOMEONE.
OH...
IS THAT YOUR ONLY PATIENT RIGHT NOW?
AS YOU CAN SEE, IT'S ONLY MY WIFE AND I WHO OPERATE THIS LITTLE CLINIC...
AND IF SOMEONE NEEDS SERIOUS TREATMENT?
WE DO HAVE A FEW BEDS IN THE BACK FOR PATIENTS WHO NEED A LONGER STAY...
IS THERE ANYONE BEING HOSPITALIZED RIGHT NOW?

WELL, THERE IS ONE PERSON...

...

ZISH

TMP TMP TMP TMP

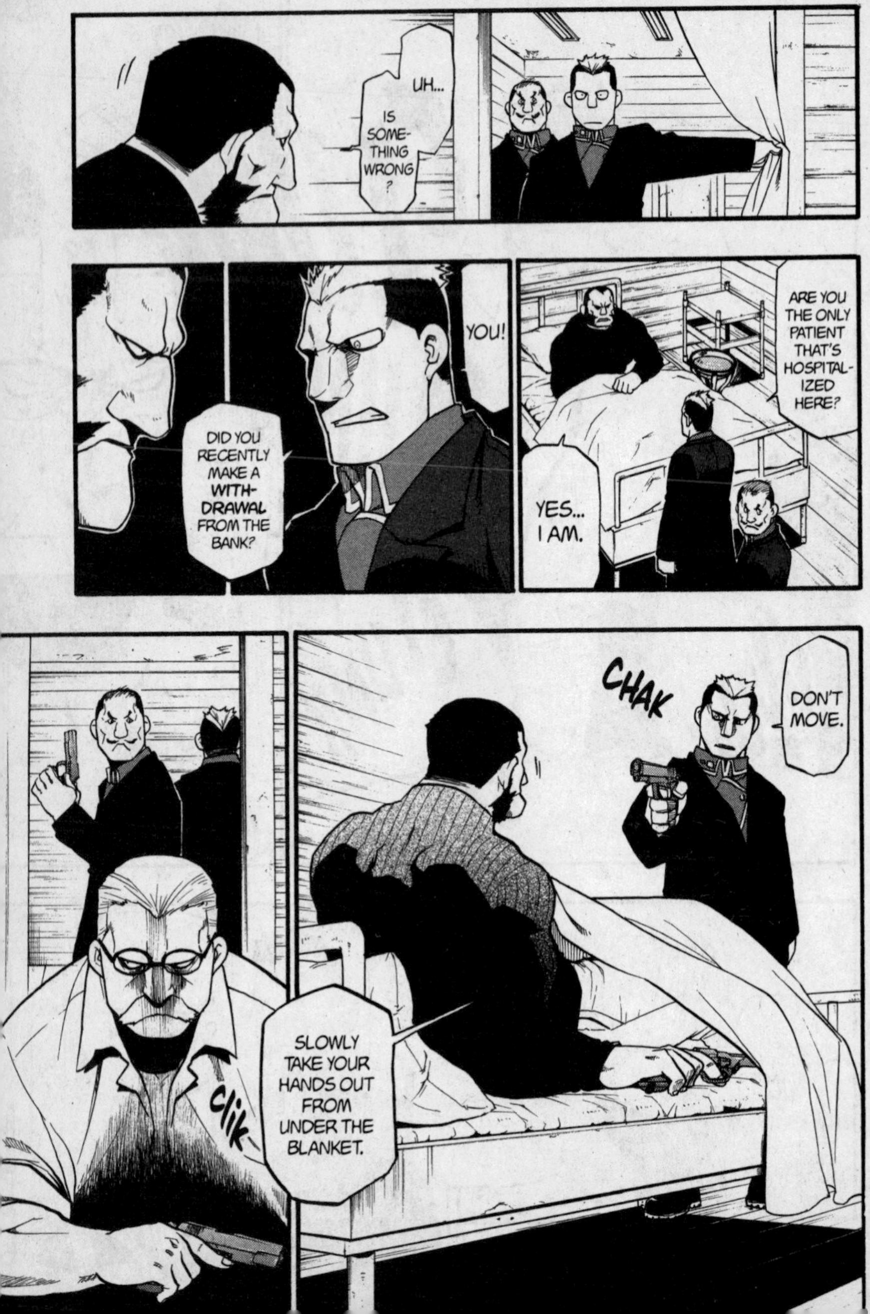
UH...
IS SOMETHING WRONG?
ARE YOU THE ONLY PATIENT THAT'S HOSPITALIZED HERE?
YES... I AM.
YOU!
DID YOU RECENTLY MAKE A WITHDRAWAL FROM THE BANK?
CHAK
DON'T MOVE.
SLOWLY TAKE YOUR HANDS OUT FROM UNDER THE BLANKET.
Clik

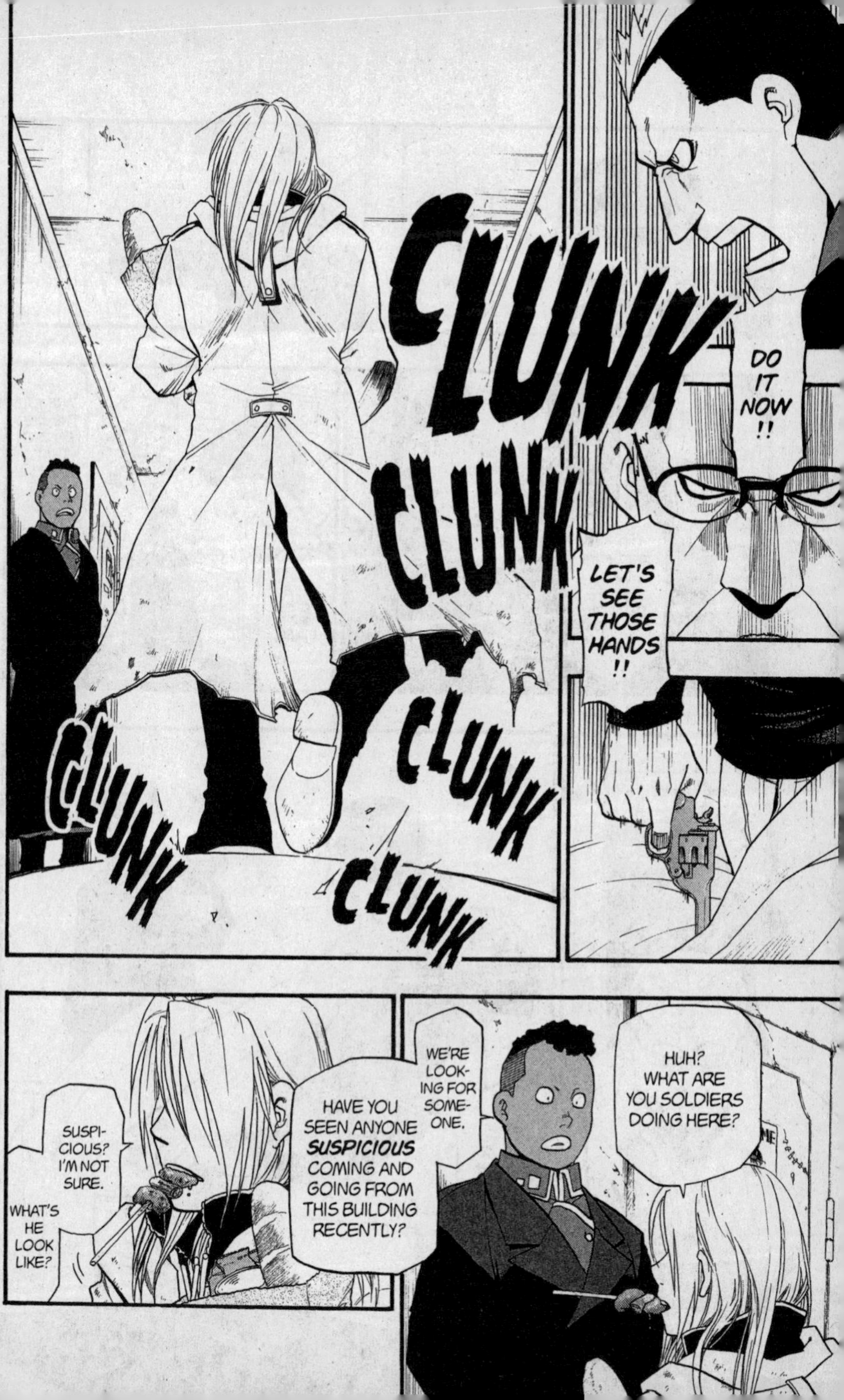
DO IT NOW!!
LET'S SEE THOSE HANDS!!
CLUNK
CLUNK
CLUNK
CLUNK
CLUNK
HUH? WHAT ARE YOU SOLDIERS DOING HERE?
WE'RE LOOKING FOR SOMEONE.
HAVE YOU SEEN ANYONE **SUSPICIOUS** COMING AND GOING FROM THIS BUILDING RECENTLY?
SUSPICIOUS? I'M NOT SURE.
WHAT'S HE LOOK LIKE?

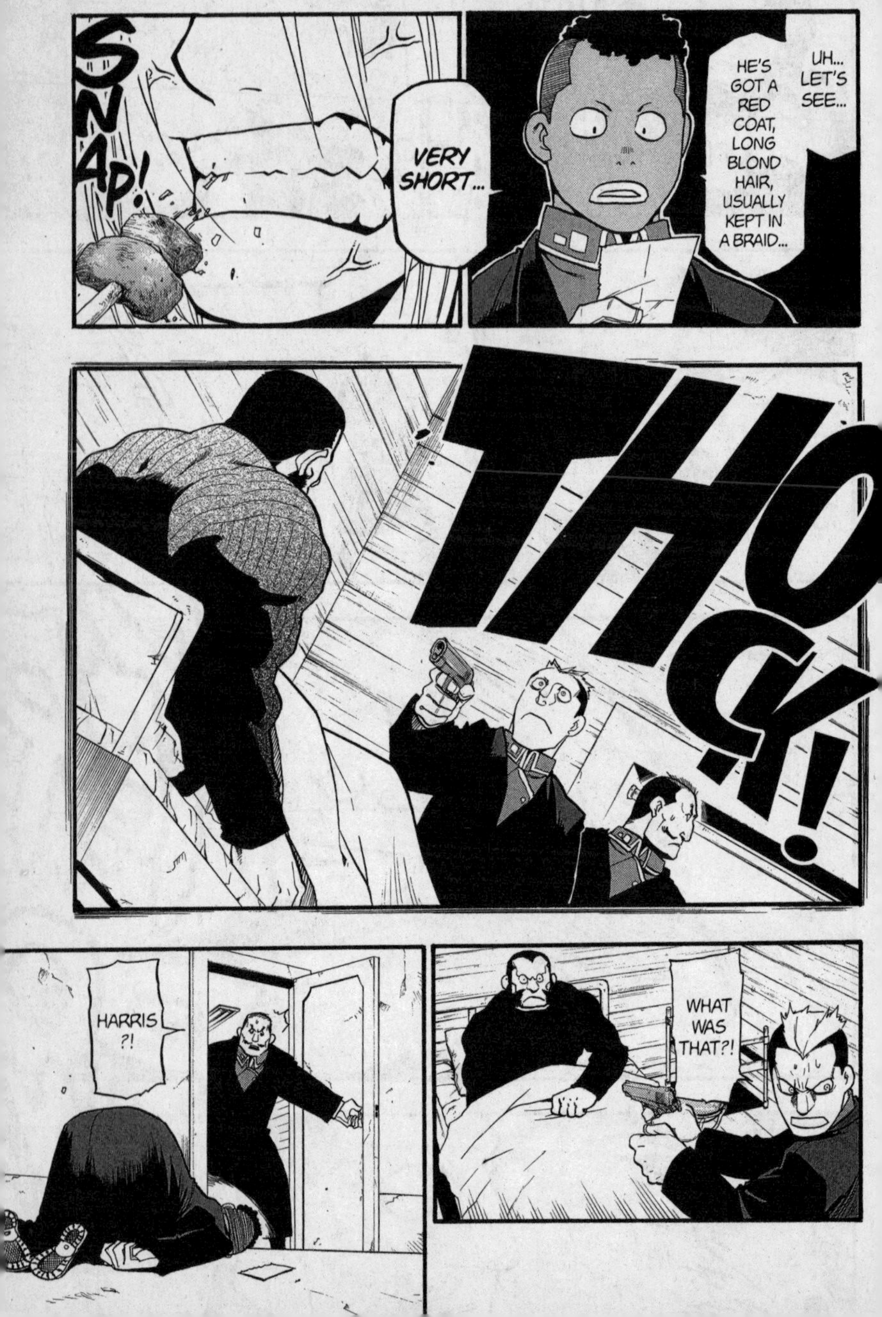
UH... LET'S SEE...
HE'S GOT A RED COAT, LONG BLOND HAIR, USUALLY KEPT IN A BRAID...
VERY SHORT...
SNAP!
THOCK!
WHAT WAS THAT?!
HARRIS ?!

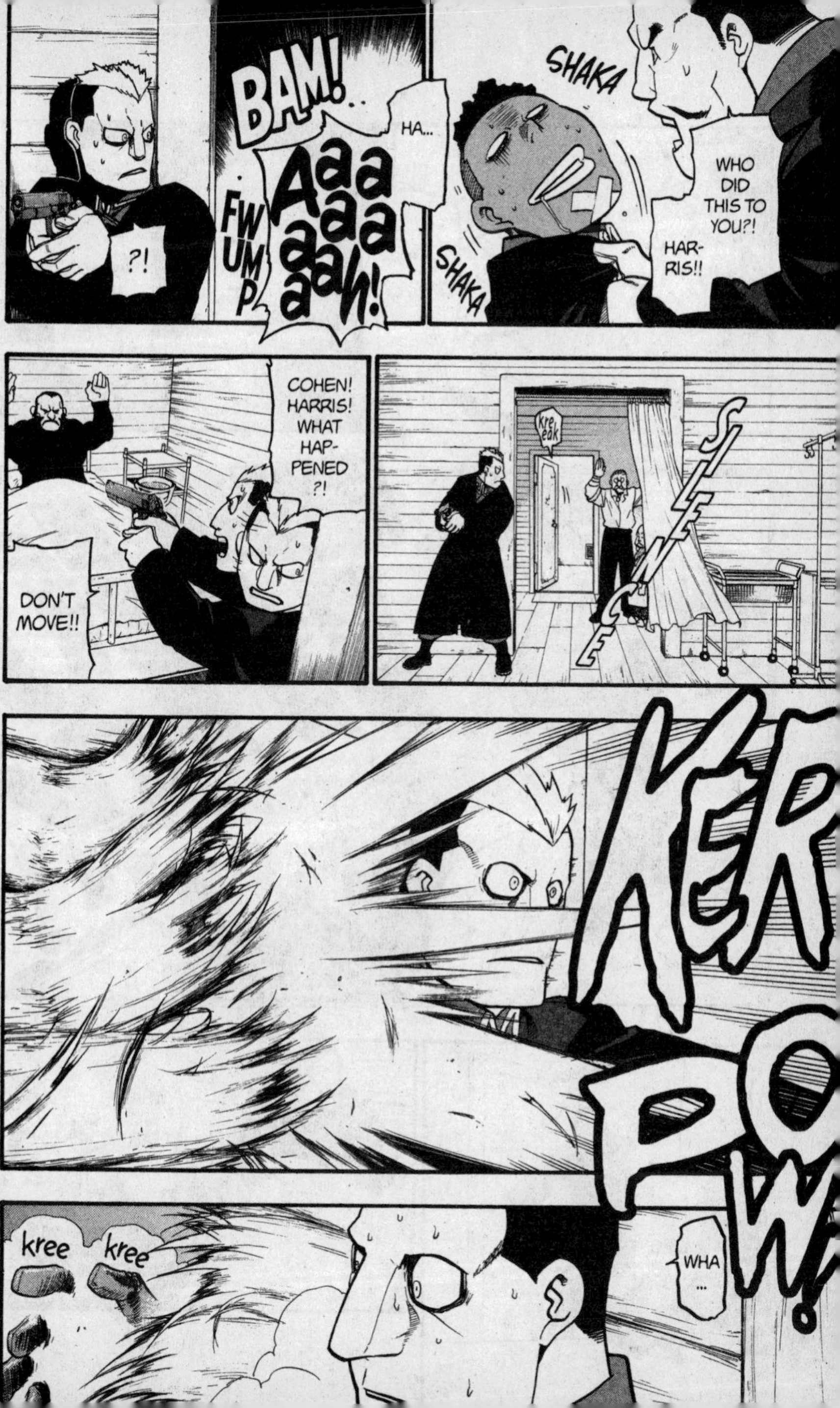
SHAKA
SHAKA
HAR-RIS!!
WHO DID THIS TO YOU?!
HA...
BAM!
Aaaaaaaaaah!
FWUMP
?!
SILENCE
kre eak
COHEN! HARRIS! WHAT HAP-PENED ?!
DON'T MOVE!!
KERPOW
WHA ...
kree
kree

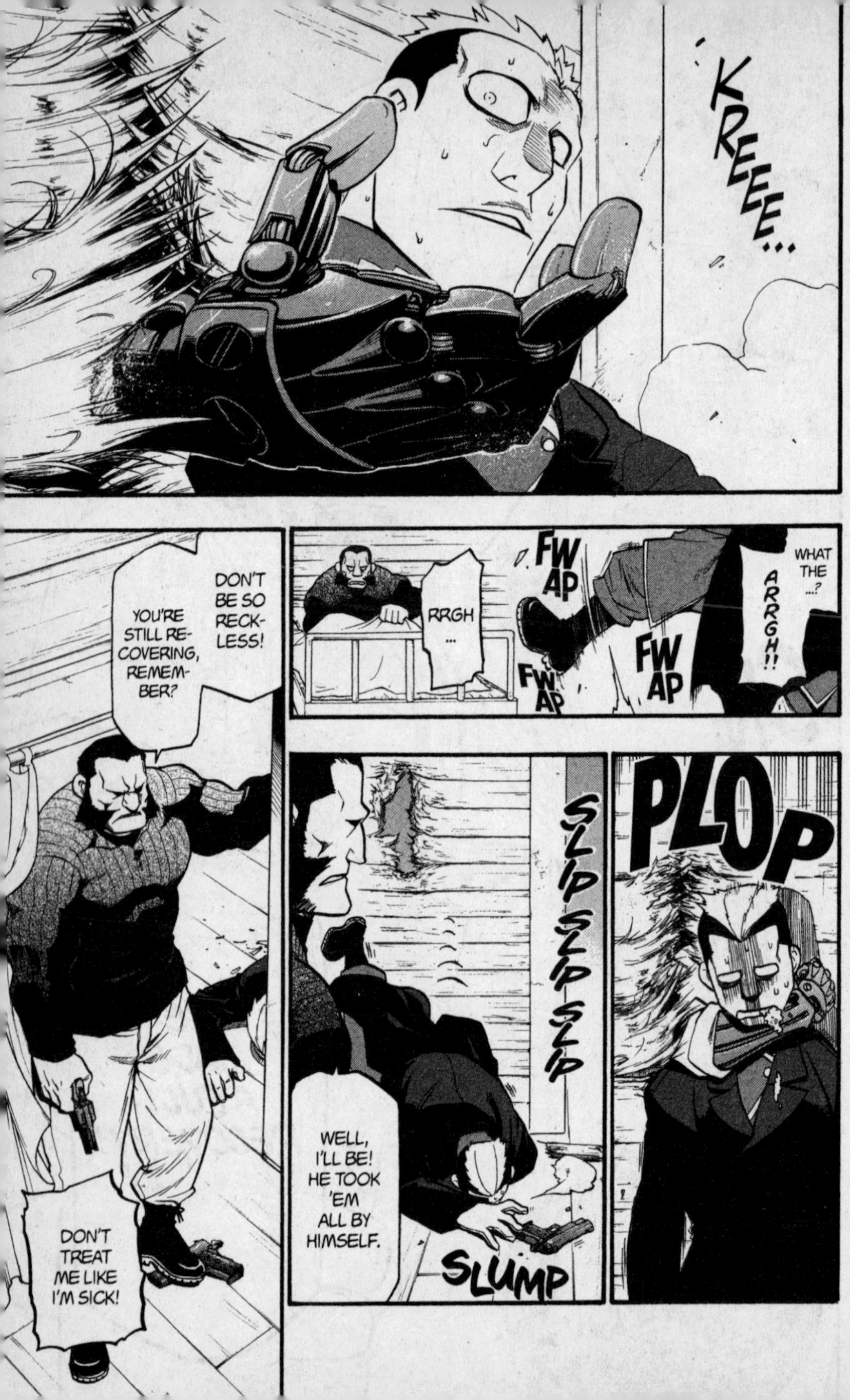
KREEEE...
WHAT THE ...?
ARRGH!!
FWAP
FWAP
FWAP
RRGH ...
PLOP
SLIP SLIP SLIP SLIP
WELL, I'LL BE! HE TOOK 'EM ALL BY HIMSELF.
SLUMP
DON'T BE SO RECKLESS! YOU'RE STILL RE-COVERING, REMEM-BER?
DON'T TREAT ME LIKE I'M SICK!

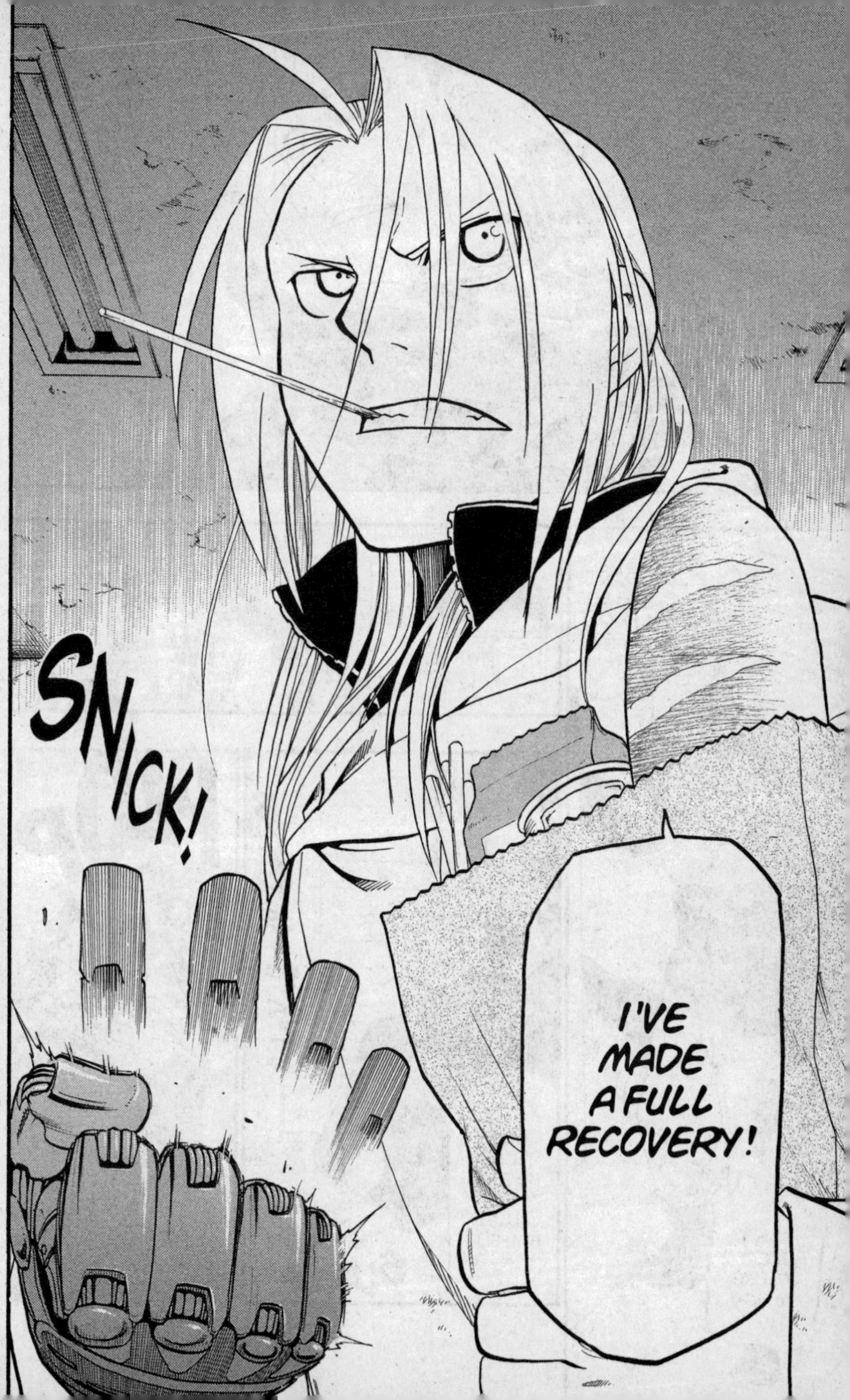
SNICK!
I'VE MADE A FULL RECOVERY!

Chapter 82
Family by Spirit

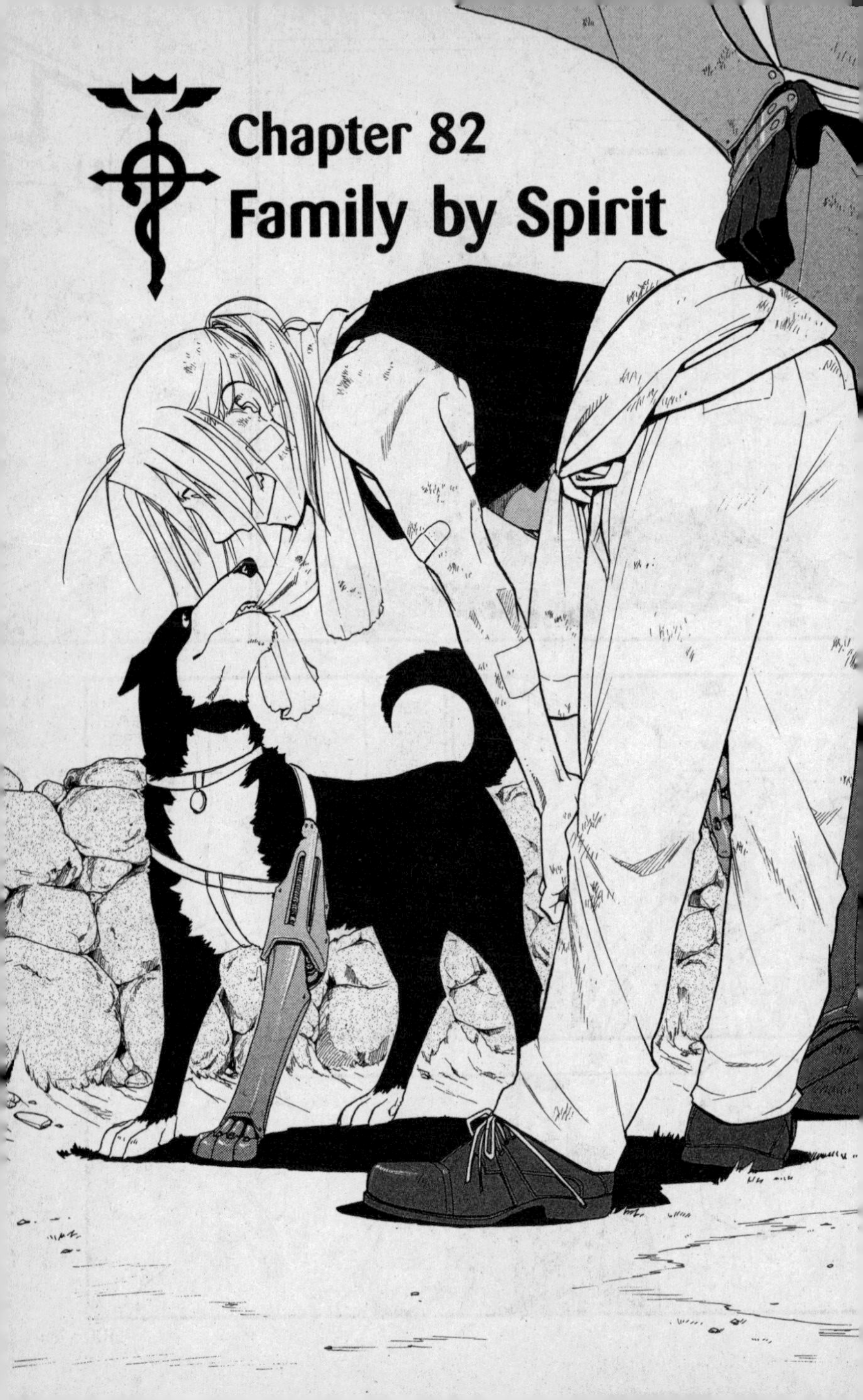

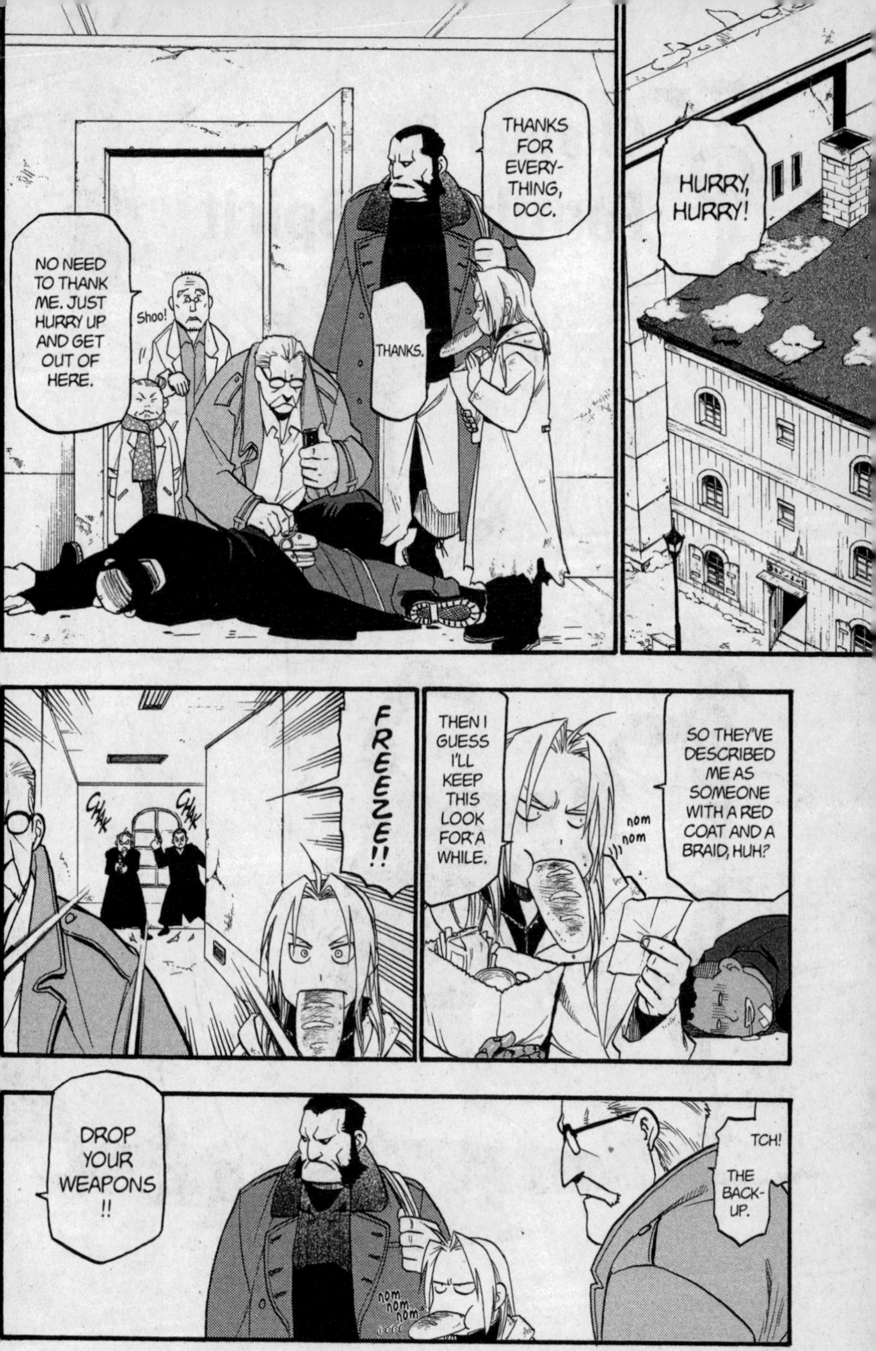
HURRY, HURRY!
THANKS FOR EVERY-THING, DOC.
THANKS.
NO NEED TO THANK ME. JUST HURRY UP AND GET OUT OF HERE.
Shoo!
SO THEY'VE DESCRIBED ME AS SOMEONE WITH A RED COAT AND A BRAID, HUH?
nom nom
THEN I GUESS I'LL KEEP THIS LOOK FOR A WHILE.
FREEZE!!
CHAK
CHAK
TCH!
THE BACK-UP.
DROP YOUR WEAPONS!!
nom nom nom

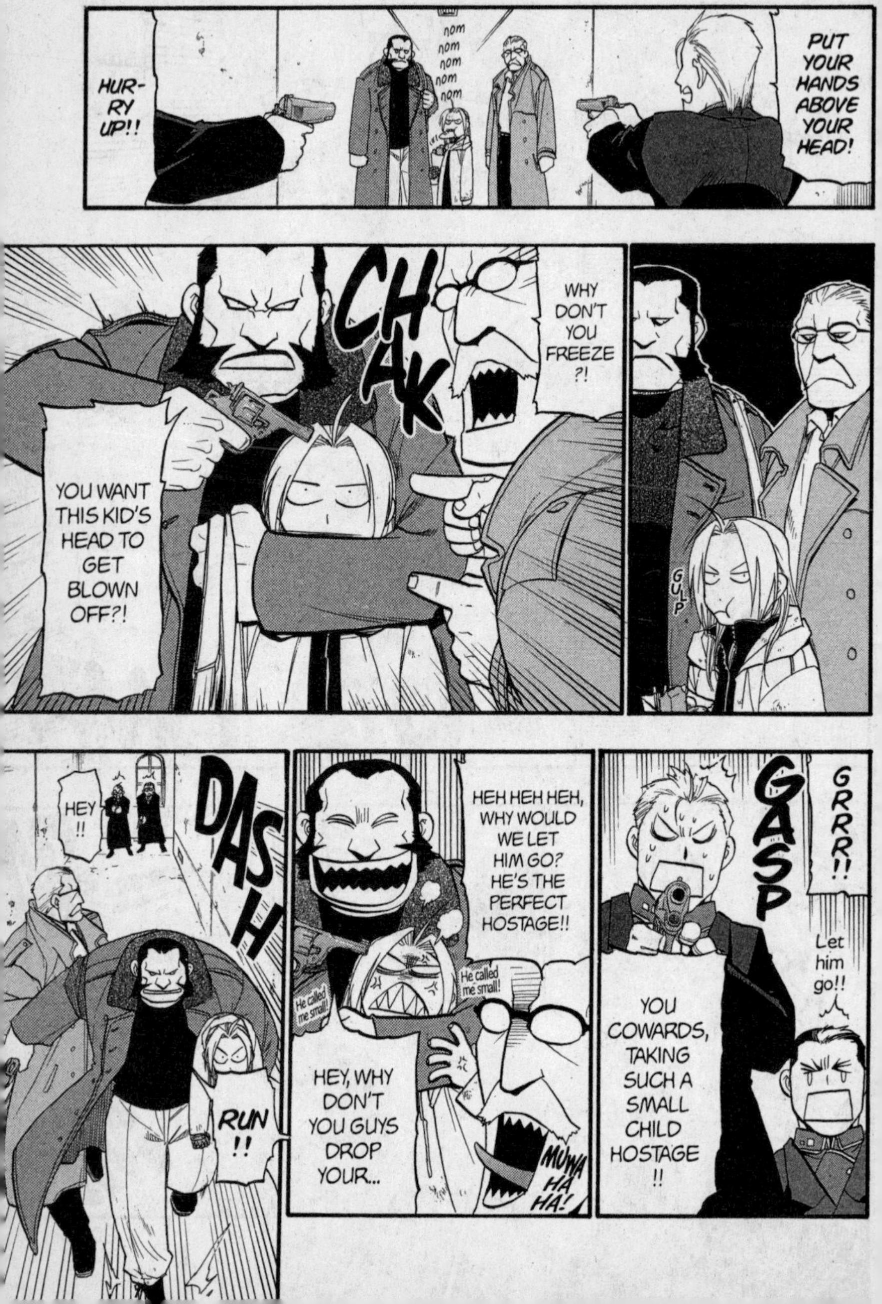
PUT YOUR HANDS ABOVE YOUR HEAD!
nom nom nom nom nom
HUR-RY UP!!
GULP
WHY DON'T YOU FREEZE?!
CHAK
YOU WANT THIS KID'S HEAD TO GET BLOWN OFF?!
GRRR!!
GASP
Let him go!!
YOU COWARDS, TAKING SUCH A SMALL CHILD HOSTAGE!!
HEH HEH HEH, WHY WOULD WE LET HIM GO? HE'S THE PERFECT HOSTAGE!!
He called me small!
He called me small!
HEY, WHY DON'T YOU GUYS DROP YOUR...
MUWA HA HA!
DASH
HEY!!
RUN!!

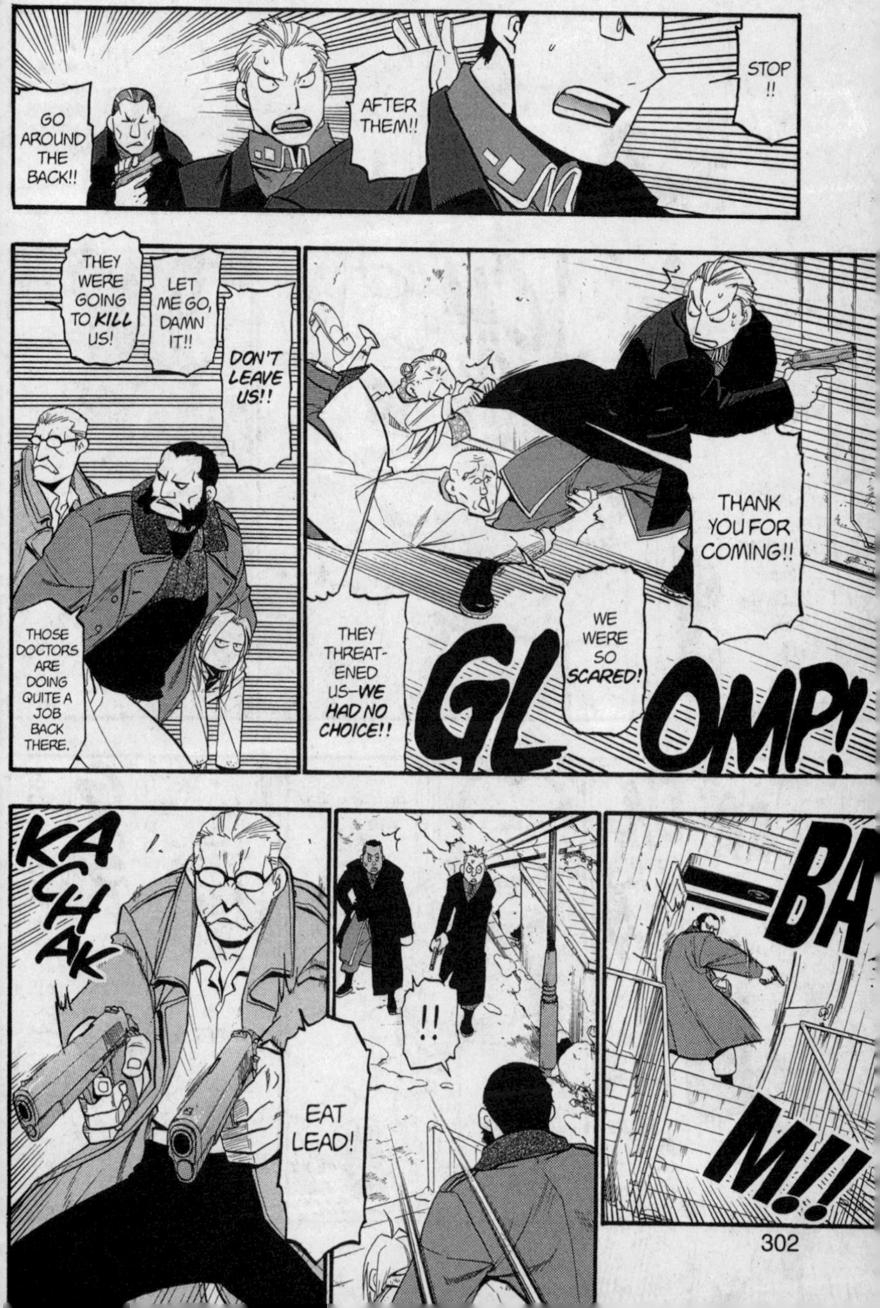
STOP!!
AFTER THEM!!
GO AROUND THE BACK!!
THANK YOU FOR COMING!!
WE WERE SO SCARED!
GLOMP!
THEY THREATENED US—WE HAD NO CHOICE!!
DON'T LEAVE US!!
LET ME GO, DAMN IT!!
THEY WERE GOING TO KILL US!
THOSE DOCTORS ARE DOING QUITE A JOB BACK THERE.
BAM!!
!!
KACHAK
EAT LEAD!

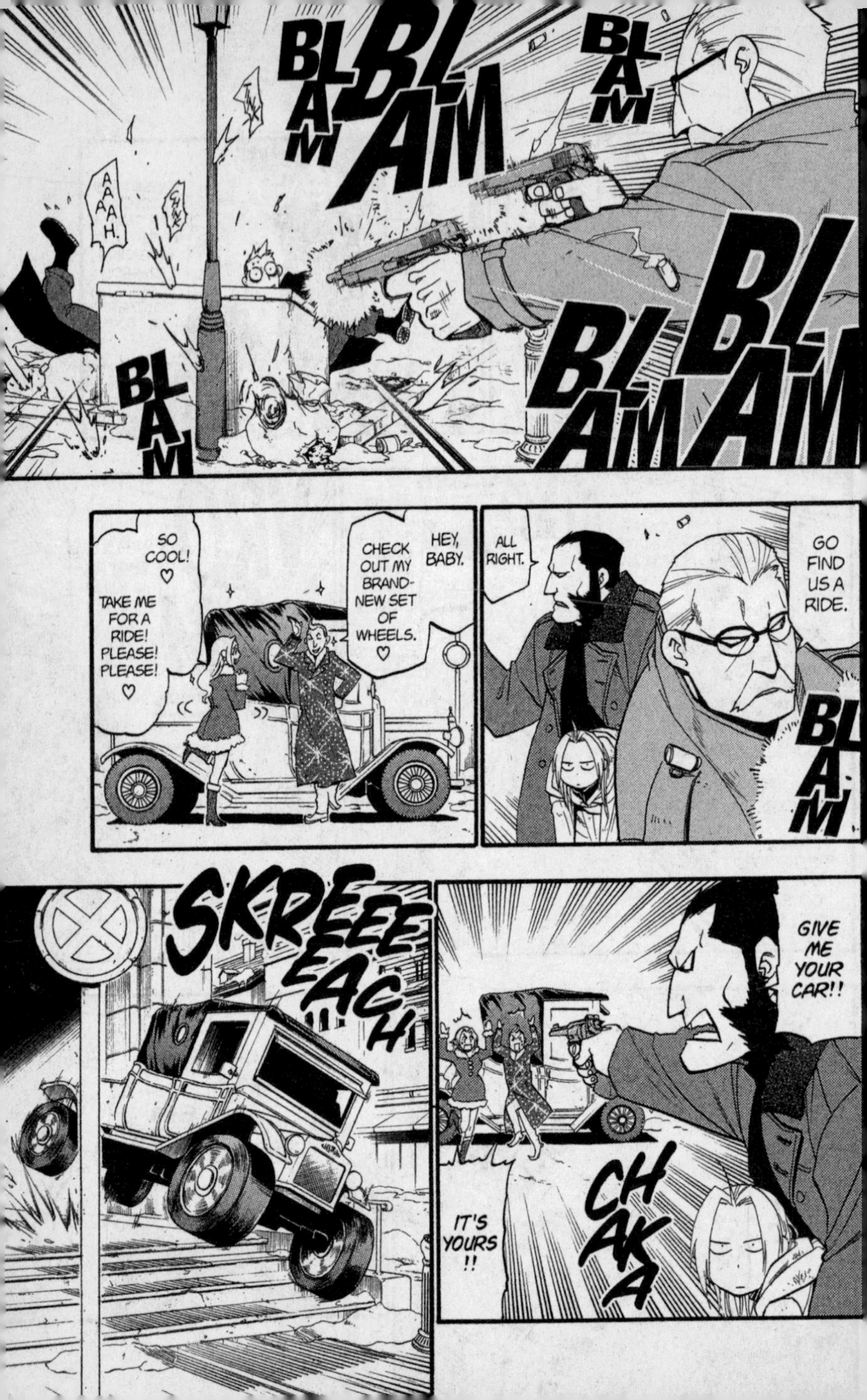
BLAM
BLAM
BLAM
AAAH.
BLAM
BLAM
BLAM
GO FIND US A RIDE.
ALL RIGHT.
BLAM
HEY, BABY.
CHECK OUT MY BRAND-NEW SET OF WHEELS. ♡
SO COOL! ♡
TAKE ME FOR A RIDE! PLEASE! PLEASE! ♡
GIVE ME YOUR CAR!!
CHAKA
IT'S YOURS!!
SKREEEEACH!!

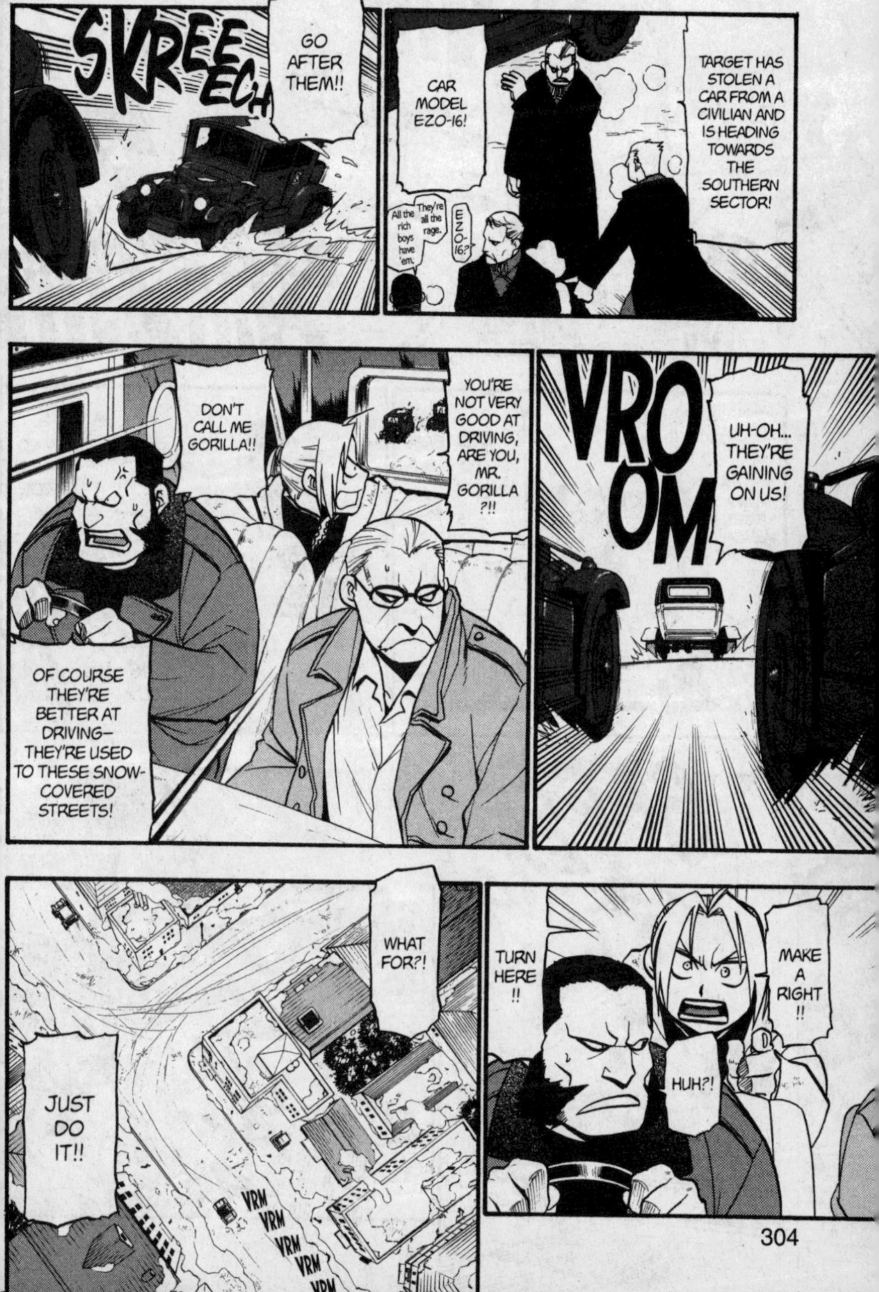

TARGET HAS STOLEN A CAR FROM A CIVILIAN AND IS HEADING TOWARDS THE SOUTHERN SECTOR!
CAR MODEL EZO-16!
EZO-16?
They're all the rage.
All the rich boys have 'em.
GO AFTER THEM!!
SKREEECH
VROOM
UH-OH... THEY'RE GAINING ON US!
YOU'RE NOT VERY GOOD AT DRIVING, ARE YOU, MR. GORILLA?!!
DON'T CALL ME GORILLA!!
OF COURSE THEY'RE BETTER AT DRIVING— THEY'RE USED TO THESE SNOW-COVERED STREETS!
MAKE A RIGHT!!
TURN HERE!!
HUH?!
WHAT FOR?!
JUST DO IT!!
VRM VRM VRM VRM VRM

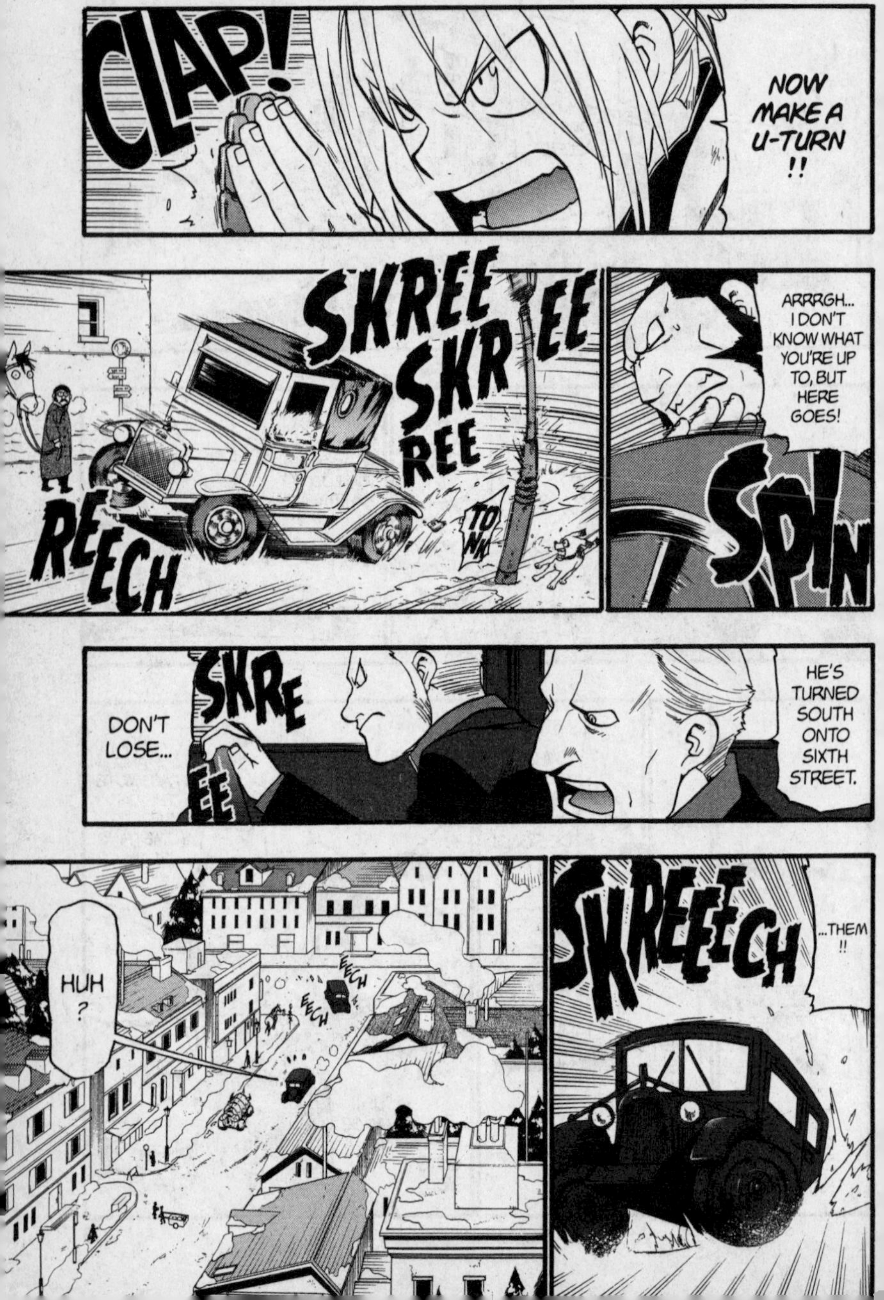
CLAP!
NOW MAKE A U-TURN !!
ARRRGH... I DON'T KNOW WHAT YOU'RE UP TO, BUT HERE GOES!
SPIN
SKREE
SKR
EE
REE
REECH
TONK
HE'S TURNED SOUTH ONTO SIXTH STREET.
SKREE
DON'T LOSE...
SKREEECH
...THEM !!
HUH ?
EECH
EECH

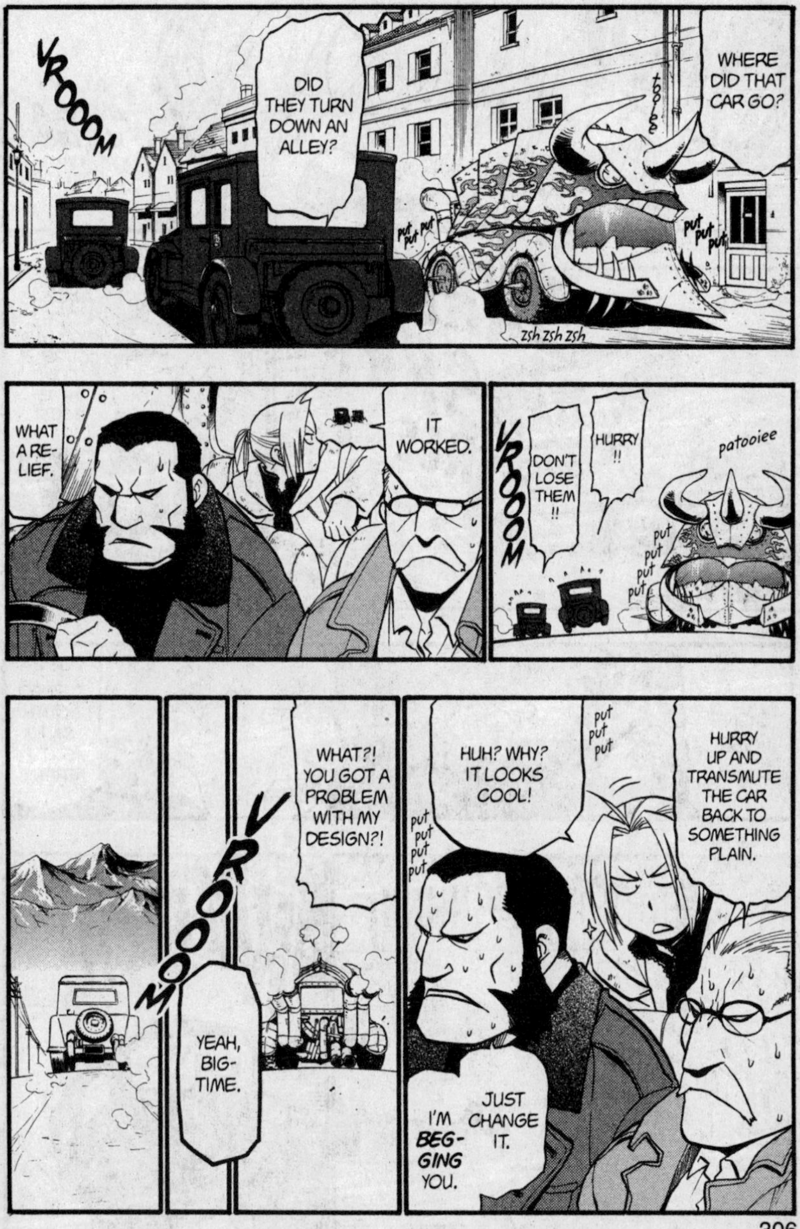
WHERE DID THAT CAR GO?
tooiee
put put put
DID THEY TURN DOWN AN ALLEY?
put put put
VROOOM
zsh zsh zsh
patooiee
HURRY!!
DON'T LOSE THEM!!
put put put put
VROOOM
IT WORKED.
WHAT A RE-LIEF.
HURRY UP AND TRANSMUTE THE CAR BACK TO SOMETHING PLAIN.
put put put
HUH? WHY? IT LOOKS COOL!
put put put put
JUST CHANGE IT.
I'M BEG-GING YOU.
WHAT?! YOU GOT A PROBLEM WITH MY DESIGN?!
VROOOOM
YEAH, BIG-TIME.

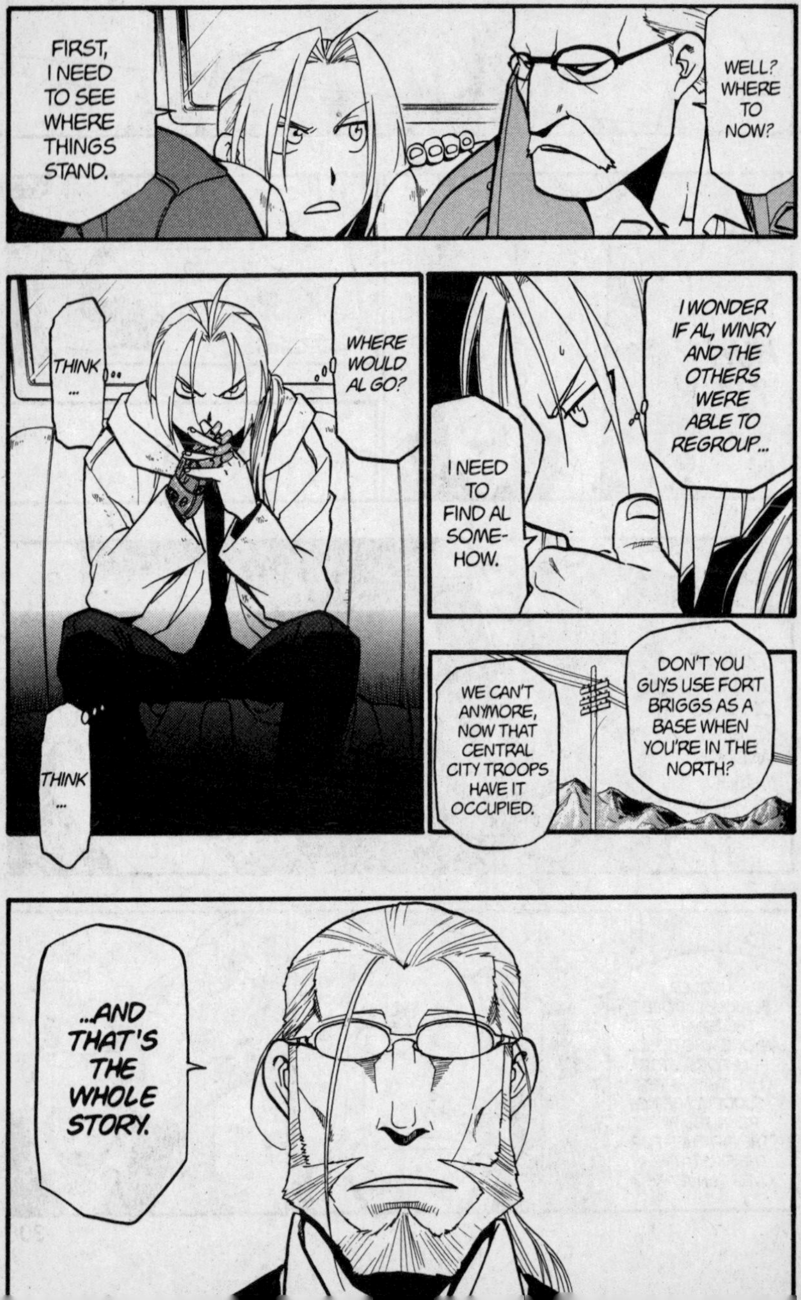
WELL? WHERE TO NOW?
FIRST, I NEED TO SEE WHERE THINGS STAND.
I WONDER IF AL, WINRY AND THE OTHERS WERE ABLE TO REGROUP...
I NEED TO FIND AL SOME-HOW.
DON'T YOU GUYS USE FORT BRIGGS AS A BASE WHEN YOU'RE IN THE NORTH?
WE CAN'T ANYMORE, NOW THAT CENTRAL CITY TROOPS HAVE IT OCCUPIED.
WHERE WOULD AL GO?
THINK ...
THINK ...
...AND THAT'S THE WHOLE STORY.

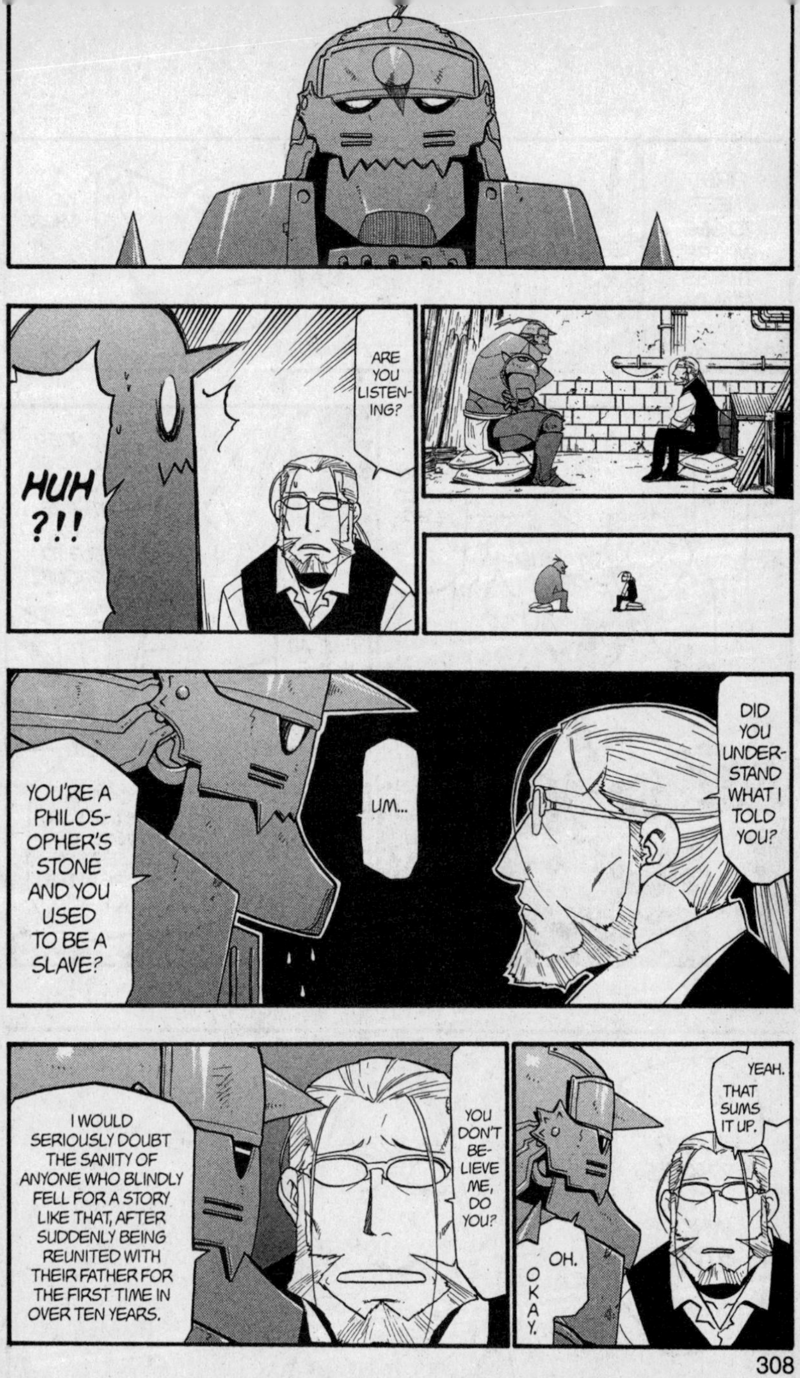
ARE YOU LISTENING?
HUH?!!
DID YOU UNDERSTAND WHAT I TOLD YOU?
UM...
YOU'RE A PHILOSOPHER'S STONE AND YOU USED TO BE A SLAVE?
YEAH. THAT SUMS IT UP.
OH.
OKAY.
YOU DON'T BELIEVE ME, DO YOU?
I WOULD SERIOUSLY DOUBT THE SANITY OF ANYONE WHO BLINDLY FELL FOR A STORY LIKE THAT, AFTER SUDDENLY BEING REUNITED WITH THEIR FATHER FOR THE FIRST TIME IN OVER TEN YEARS.

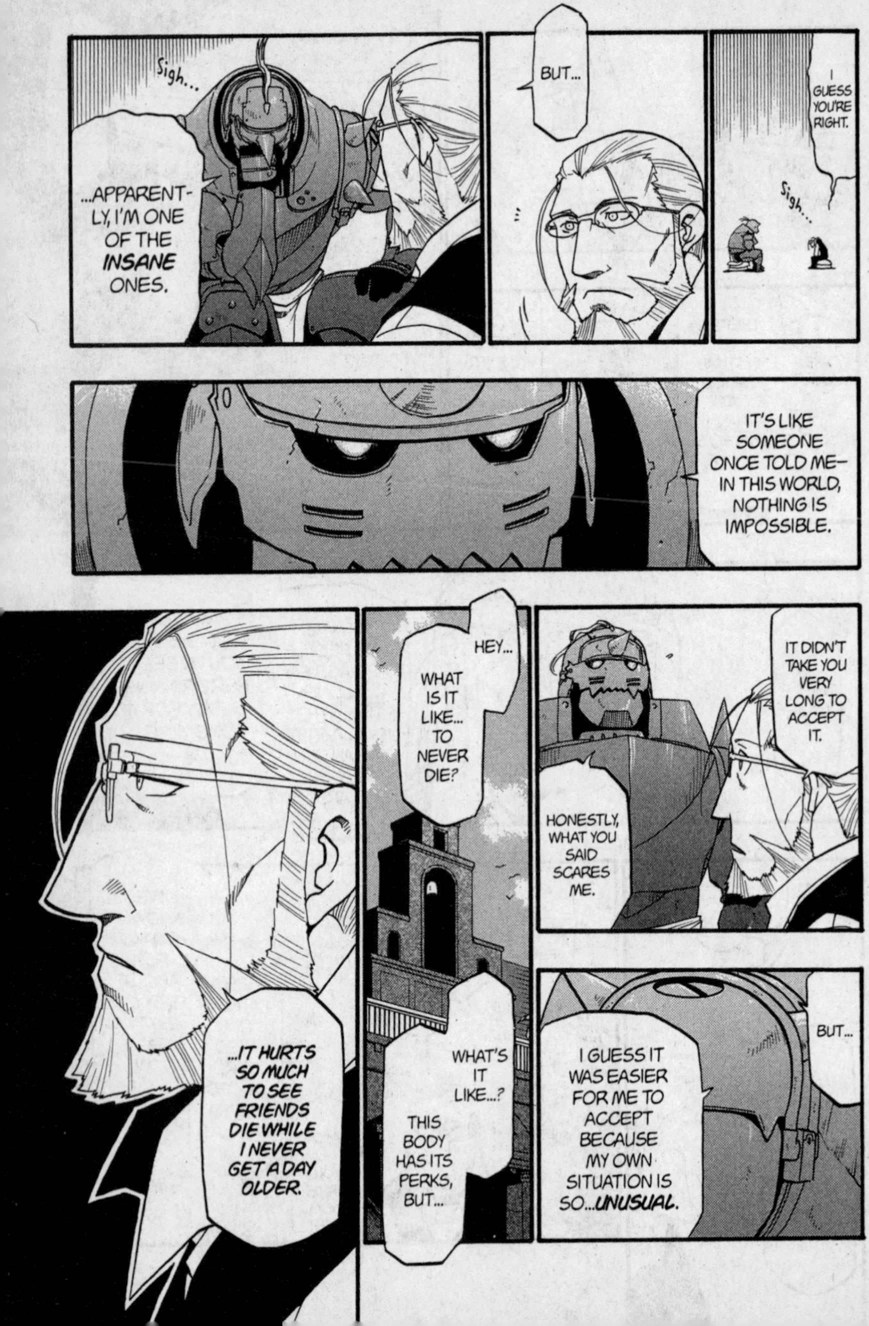
I GUESS YOU'RE RIGHT.
Sigh...
BUT...
Sigh...
...APPARENT-LY, I'M ONE OF THE INSANE ONES.
IT'S LIKE SOMEONE ONCE TOLD ME— IN THIS WORLD, NOTHING IS IMPOSSIBLE.
IT DIDN'T TAKE YOU VERY LONG TO ACCEPT IT.
HONESTLY, WHAT YOU SAID SCARES ME.
BUT...
I GUESS IT WAS EASIER FOR ME TO ACCEPT BECAUSE MY OWN SITUATION IS SO...UNUSUAL.
HEY...
WHAT IS IT LIKE... TO NEVER DIE?
WHAT'S IT LIKE...?
THIS BODY HAS ITS PERKS, BUT...
...IT HURTS SO MUCH TO SEE FRIENDS DIE WHILE I NEVER GET A DAY OLDER.

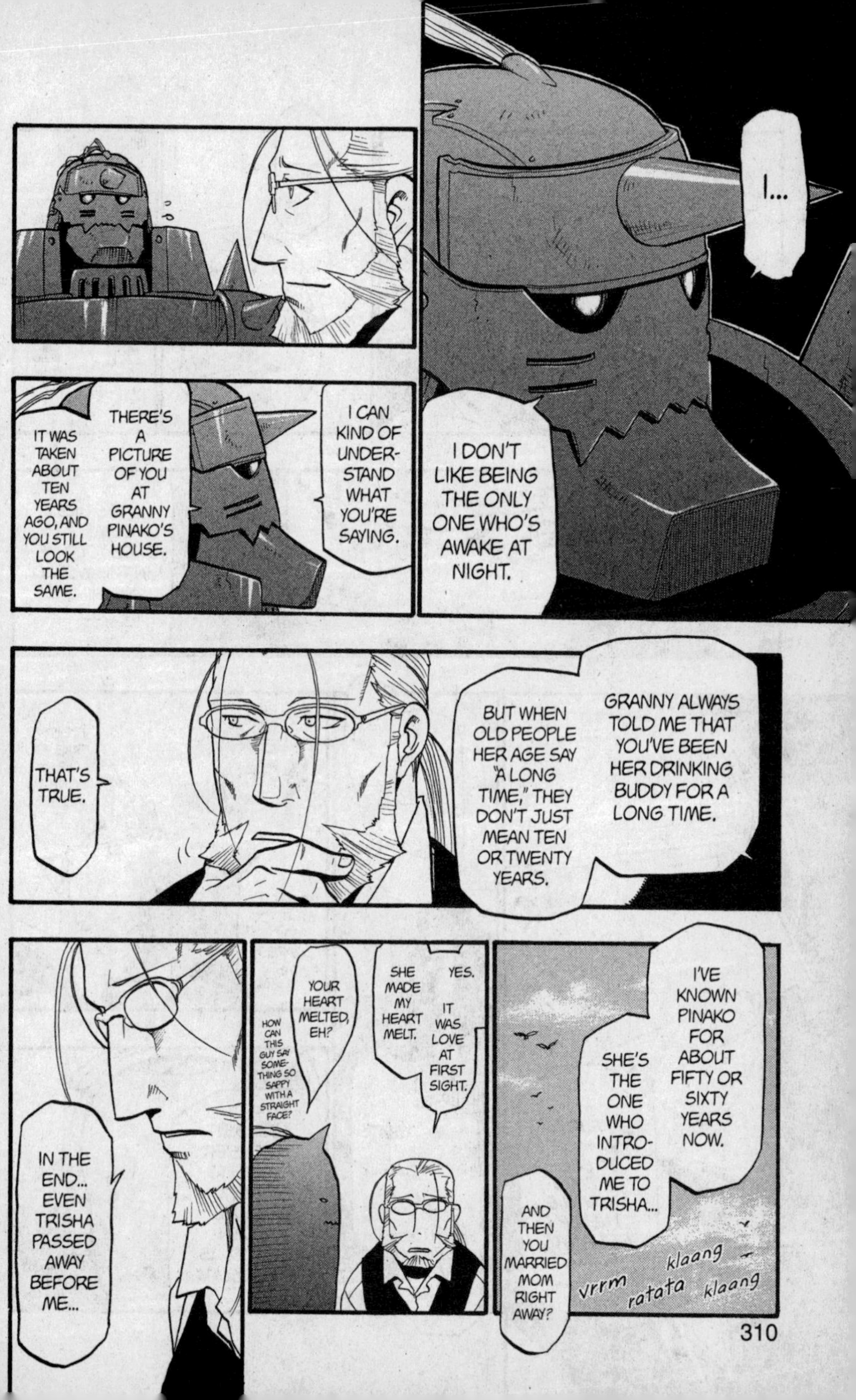
I...
I DON'T LIKE BEING THE ONLY ONE WHO'S AWAKE AT NIGHT.
I CAN KIND OF UNDERSTAND WHAT YOU'RE SAYING.
THERE'S A PICTURE OF YOU AT GRANNY PINAKO'S HOUSE.
IT WAS TAKEN ABOUT TEN YEARS AGO, AND YOU STILL LOOK THE SAME.
GRANNY ALWAYS TOLD ME THAT YOU'VE BEEN HER DRINKING BUDDY FOR A LONG TIME.
BUT WHEN OLD PEOPLE HER AGE SAY "A LONG TIME," THEY DON'T JUST MEAN TEN OR TWENTY YEARS.
THAT'S TRUE.
I'VE KNOWN PINAKO FOR ABOUT FIFTY OR SIXTY YEARS NOW.
SHE'S THE ONE WHO INTRODUCED ME TO TRISHA...
AND THEN YOU MARRIED MOM RIGHT AWAY?
vrrm
klaang
ratata
klaang
YES.
IT WAS LOVE AT FIRST SIGHT.
SHE MADE MY HEART MELT.
YOUR HEART MELTED, EH?
HOW CAN THIS GUY SAY SOMETHING SO SAPPY WITH A STRAIGHT FACE?
IN THE END... EVEN TRISHA PASSED AWAY BEFORE ME...

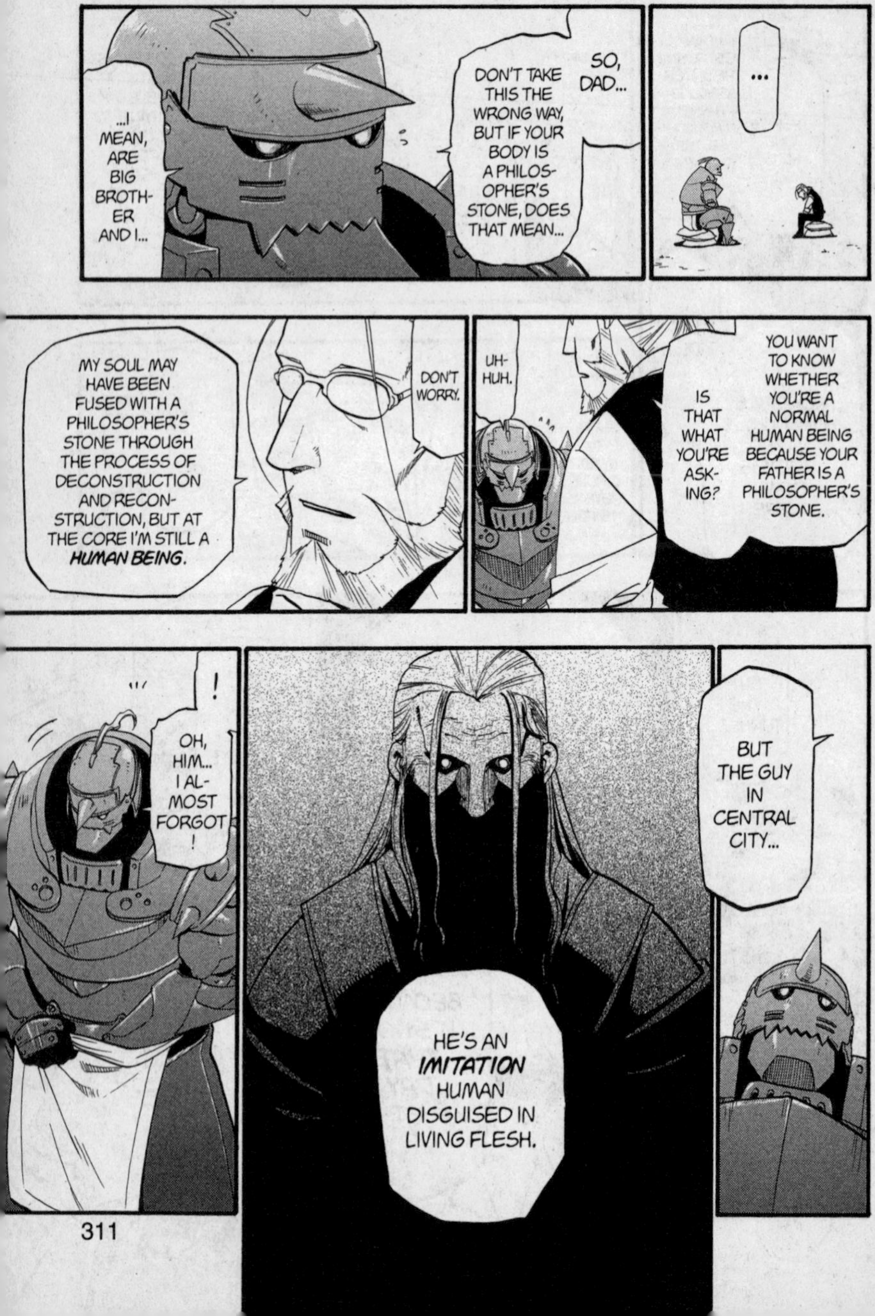
...
SO, DAD...
DON'T TAKE THIS THE WRONG WAY, BUT IF YOUR BODY IS A PHILOSOPHER'S STONE, DOES THAT MEAN...
...I MEAN, ARE BIG BROTHER AND I...
YOU WANT TO KNOW WHETHER YOU'RE A NORMAL HUMAN BEING BECAUSE YOUR FATHER IS A PHILOSOPHER'S STONE.
IS THAT WHAT YOU'RE ASKING?
UH-HUH.
DON'T WORRY.
MY SOUL MAY HAVE BEEN FUSED WITH A PHILOSOPHER'S STONE THROUGH THE PROCESS OF DECONSTRUCTION AND RECONSTRUCTION, BUT AT THE CORE I'M STILL A ***HUMAN BEING***.
BUT THE GUY IN CENTRAL CITY...
HE'S AN ***IMITATION*** HUMAN DISGUISED IN LIVING FLESH.
!
OH, HIM... I ALMOST FORGOT!

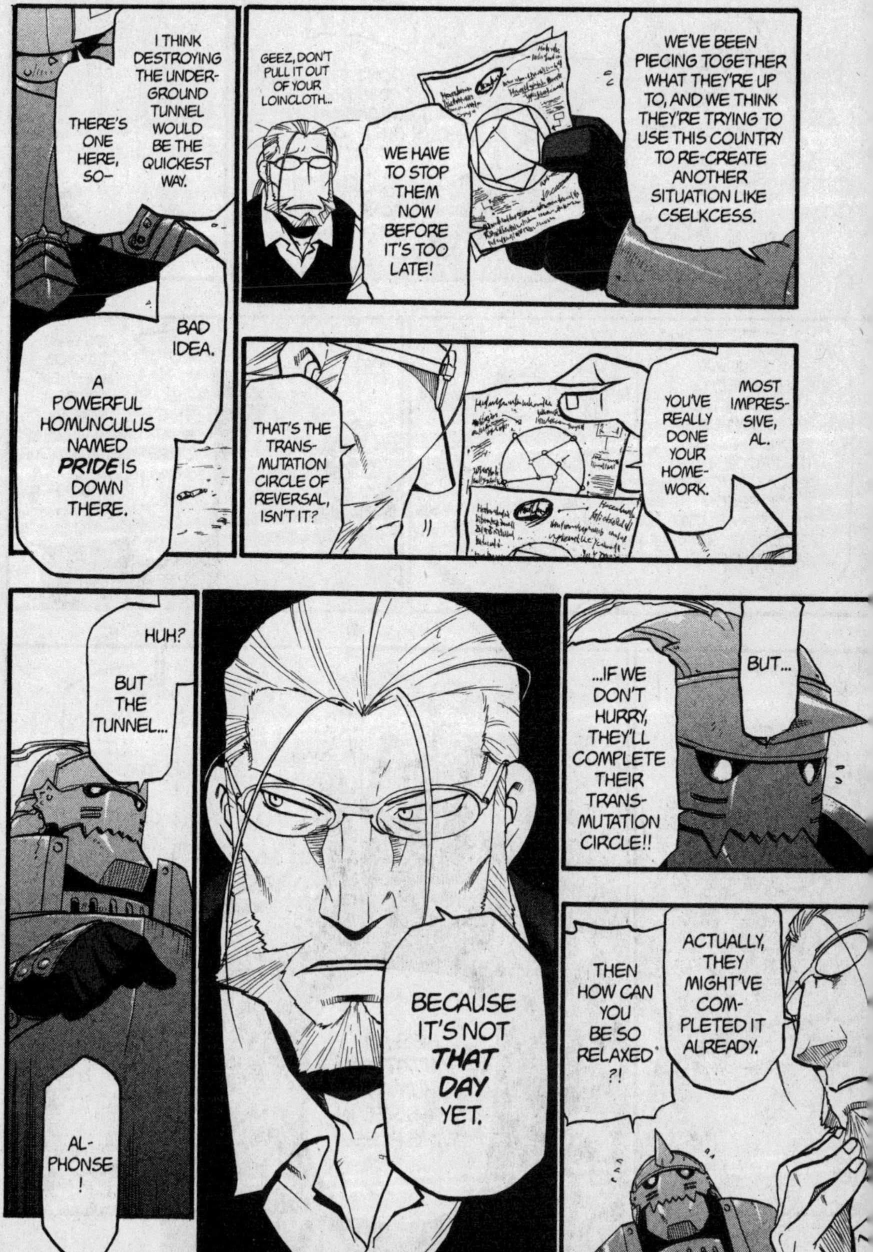
WE'VE BEEN PIECING TOGETHER WHAT THEY'RE UP TO, AND WE THINK THEY'RE TRYING TO USE THIS COUNTRY TO RE-CREATE ANOTHER SITUATION LIKE CSELKCESS.
WE HAVE TO STOP THEM NOW BEFORE IT'S TOO LATE!
GEEZ, DON'T PULL IT OUT OF YOUR LOINCLOTH...
MOST IMPRESSIVE, AL.
YOU'VE REALLY DONE YOUR HOMEWORK.
THAT'S THE TRANSMUTATION CIRCLE OF REVERSAL, ISN'T IT?
I THINK DESTROYING THE UNDERGROUND TUNNEL WOULD BE THE QUICKEST WAY.
THERE'S ONE HERE, SO—
BAD IDEA.
A POWERFUL HOMUNCULUS NAMED PRIDE IS DOWN THERE.
BUT...
...IF WE DON'T HURRY, THEY'LL COMPLETE THEIR TRANSMUTATION CIRCLE!!
ACTUALLY, THEY MIGHT'VE COMPLETED IT ALREADY.
THEN HOW CAN YOU BE SO RELAXED?!
BECAUSE IT'S NOT THAT DAY YET.
HUH?
BUT THE TUNNEL...
ALPHONSE!

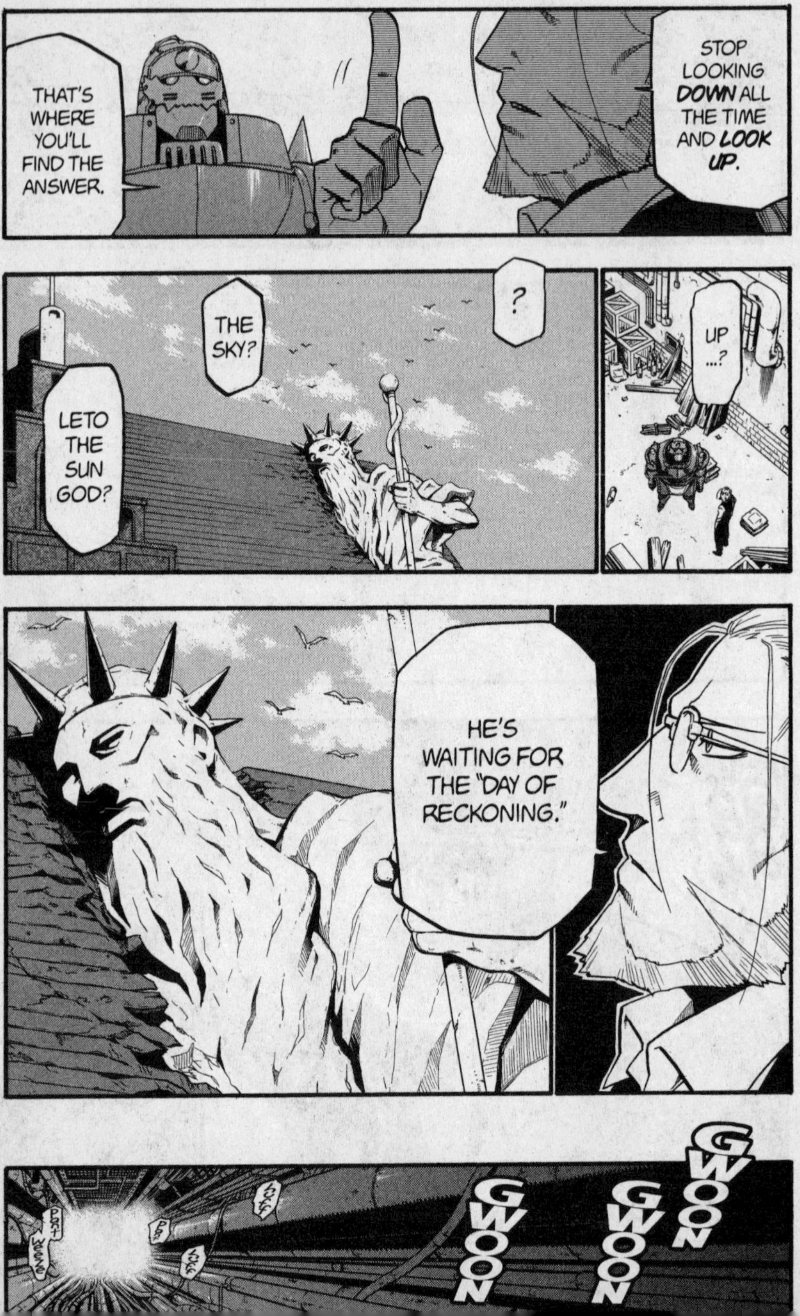
STOP LOOKING **DOWN** ALL THE TIME AND **LOOK UP**.
THAT'S WHERE YOU'LL FIND THE ANSWER.
UP ...?
?
THE SKY?
LETO THE SUN GOD?
HE'S WAITING FOR THE "DAY OF RECKONING."
GWOON
GWOON
GWOON
huff
pant
huff
pant
weeze

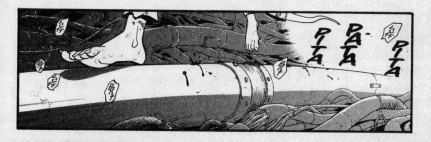

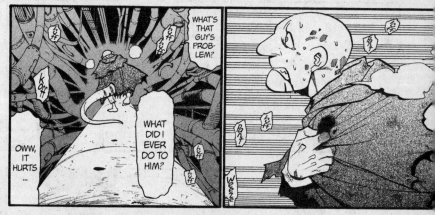

PITA
PATA
PITA
Weeze
WHAT'S THAT GUY'S PROB-LEM?
WHAT DID I EVER DO TO HIM?
K'off
OWW, IT HURTS ...
Ei!
ZASH!
Aaaaaah!!

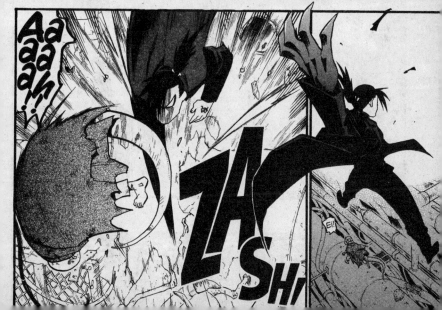

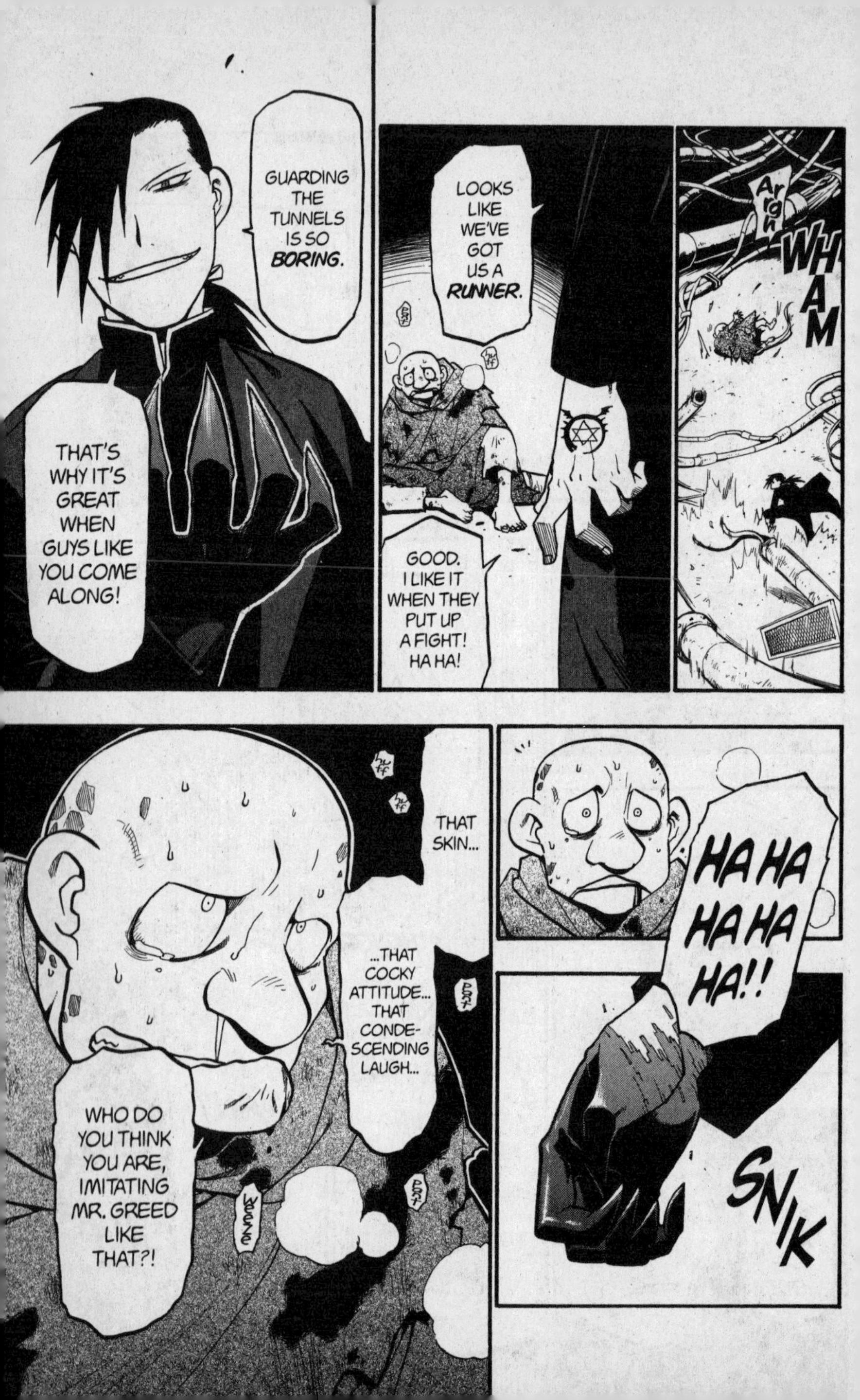
Argh
WHAM
LOOKS LIKE WE'VE GOT US A RUNNER.
GOOD. I LIKE IT WHEN THEY PUT UP A FIGHT! HA HA!
GUARDING THE TUNNELS IS SO BORING.
THAT'S WHY IT'S GREAT WHEN GUYS LIKE YOU COME ALONG!
HA HA HA HA HA!!
SNIK
THAT SKIN...
...THAT COCKY ATTITUDE... THAT CONDE-SCENDING LAUGH...
WHO DO YOU THINK YOU ARE, IMITATING MR. GREED LIKE THAT?!

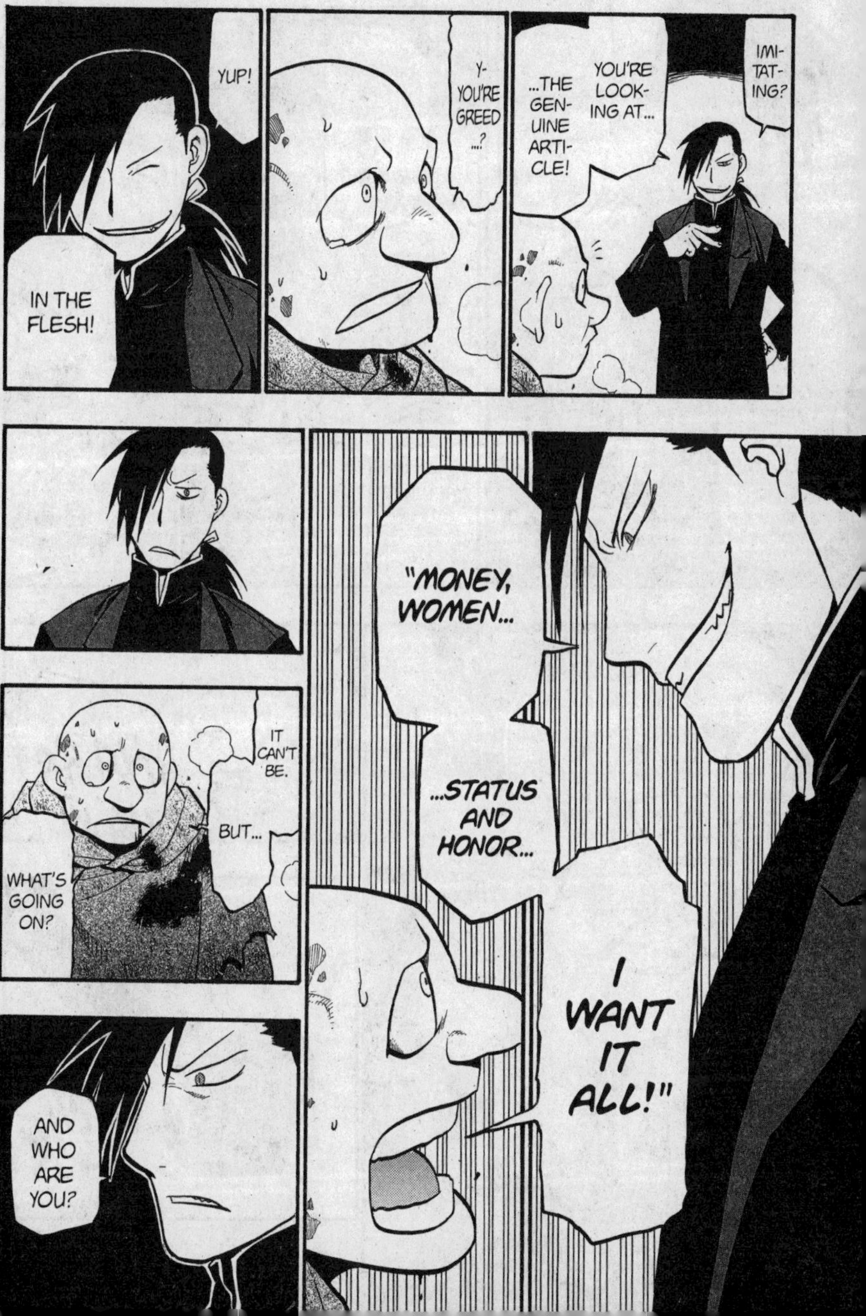

IMITATING?
YOU'RE LOOKING AT...
...THE GENUINE ARTICLE!
Y-YOU'RE GREED...?
YUP!
IN THE FLESH!
"MONEY, WOMEN...
...STATUS AND HONOR...
I WANT IT ALL!"
IT CAN'T BE.
BUT...
WHAT'S GOING ON?
AND WHO ARE YOU?

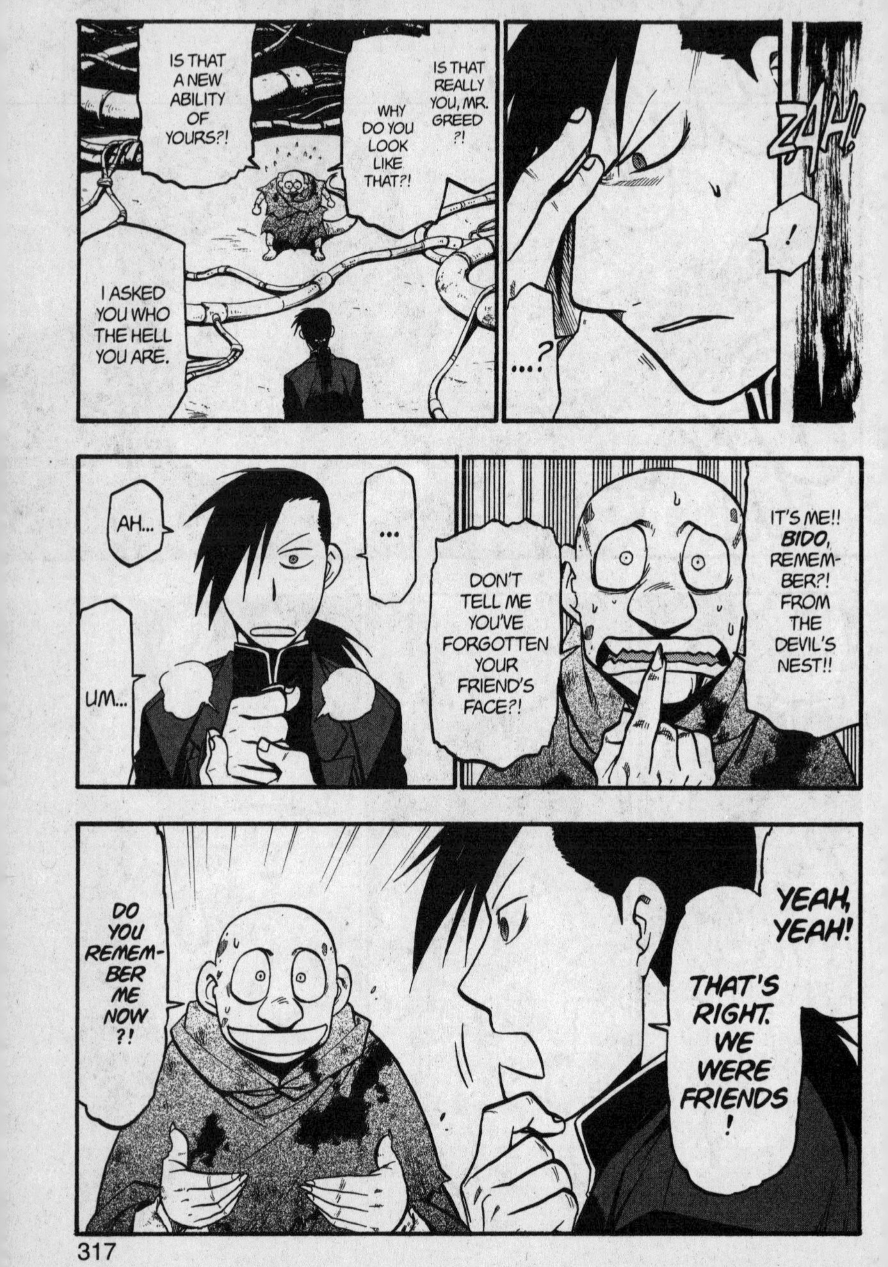
ZAH!
!
...?
IS THAT REALLY YOU, MR. GREED?!
WHY DO YOU LOOK LIKE THAT?!
IS THAT A NEW ABILITY OF YOURS?!
I ASKED YOU WHO THE HELL YOU ARE.
IT'S ME!! BIDO, REMEMBER?! FROM THE DEVIL'S NEST!!
DON'T TELL ME YOU'VE FORGOTTEN YOUR FRIEND'S FACE?!
...
AH...
UM...
YEAH, YEAH!
THAT'S RIGHT. WE WERE FRIENDS!
DO YOU REMEMBER ME NOW?!

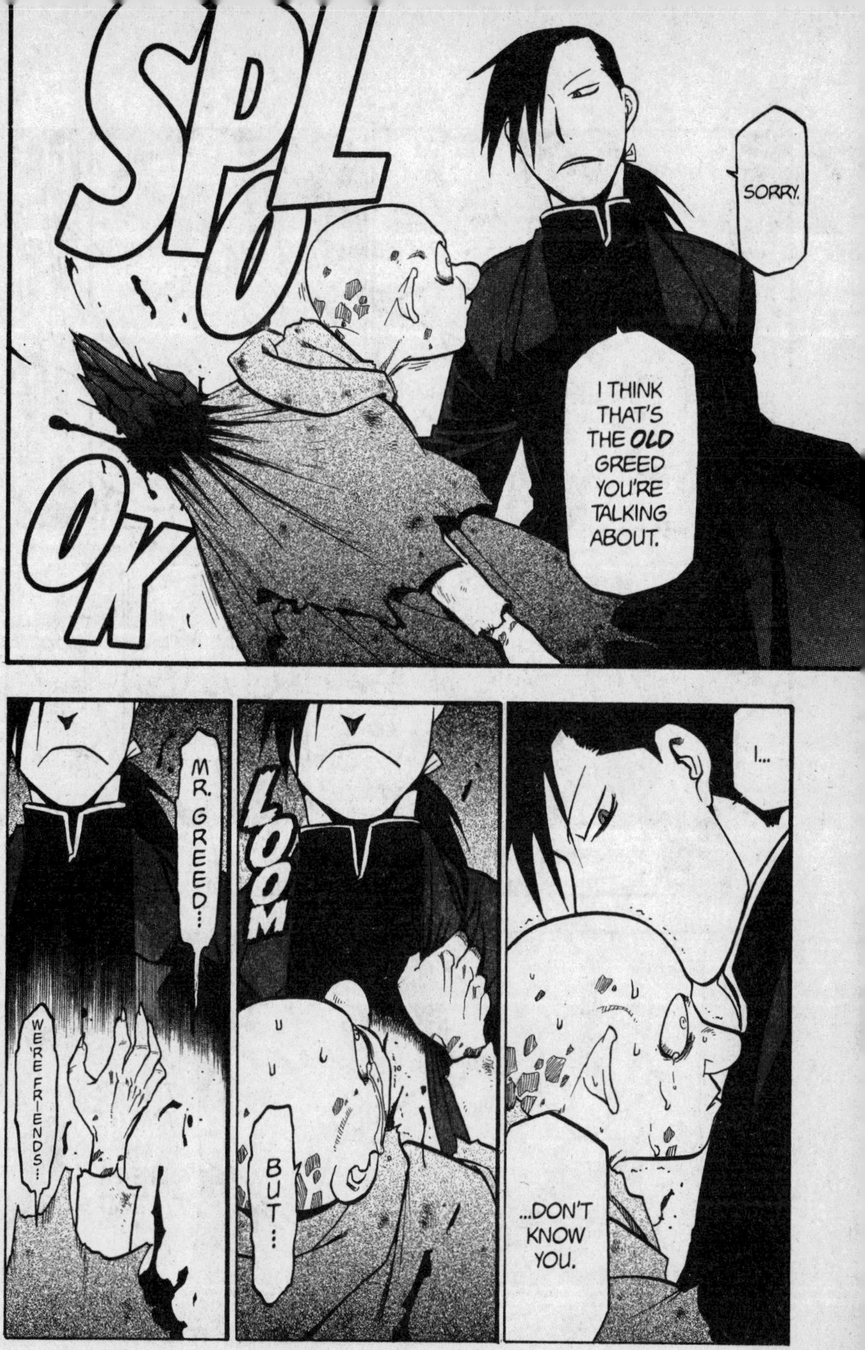
SPLOOK
SORRY.
I THINK THAT'S THE OLD GREED YOU'RE TALKING ABOUT.
I...
...DON'T KNOW YOU.
LOOM
BUT...
MR. GREED...
WE'RE FRIENDS...

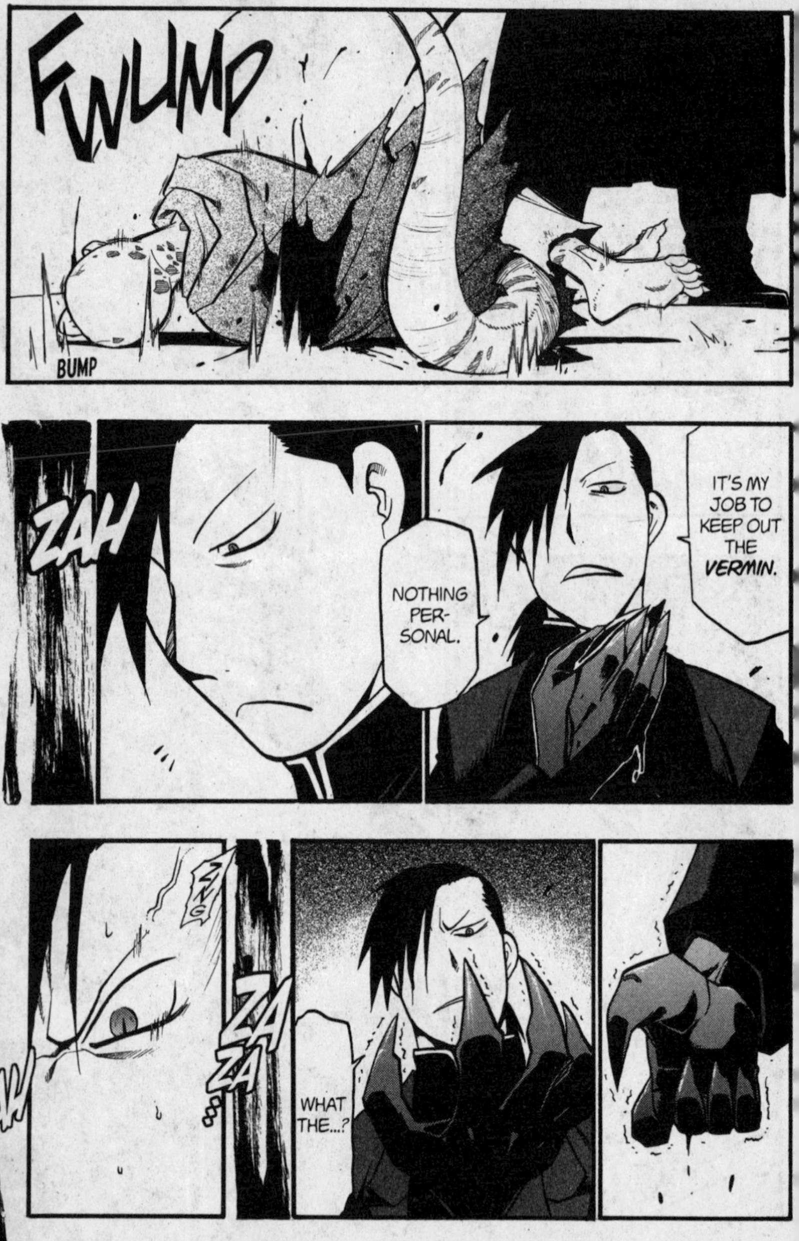
FWUMP
BUMP
IT'S MY JOB TO KEEP OUT THE VERMIN.
NOTHING PERSONAL.
ZAH
WHAT THE...?
ZA ZA
ZING
ZAH

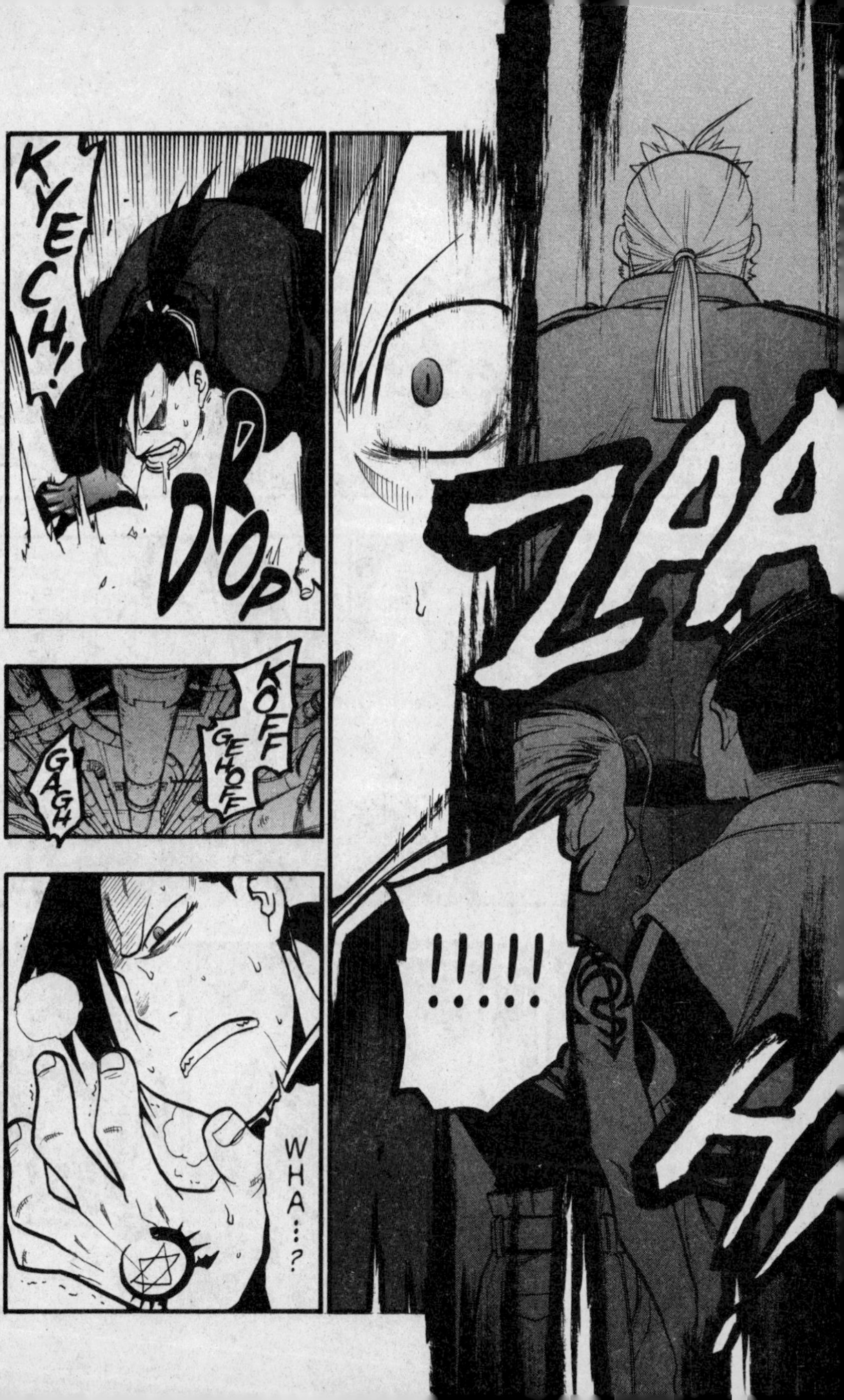
ZAP
!!!!!
KYECH!
DROP
KOFF
GEHOFF
GAGH
WHA...?

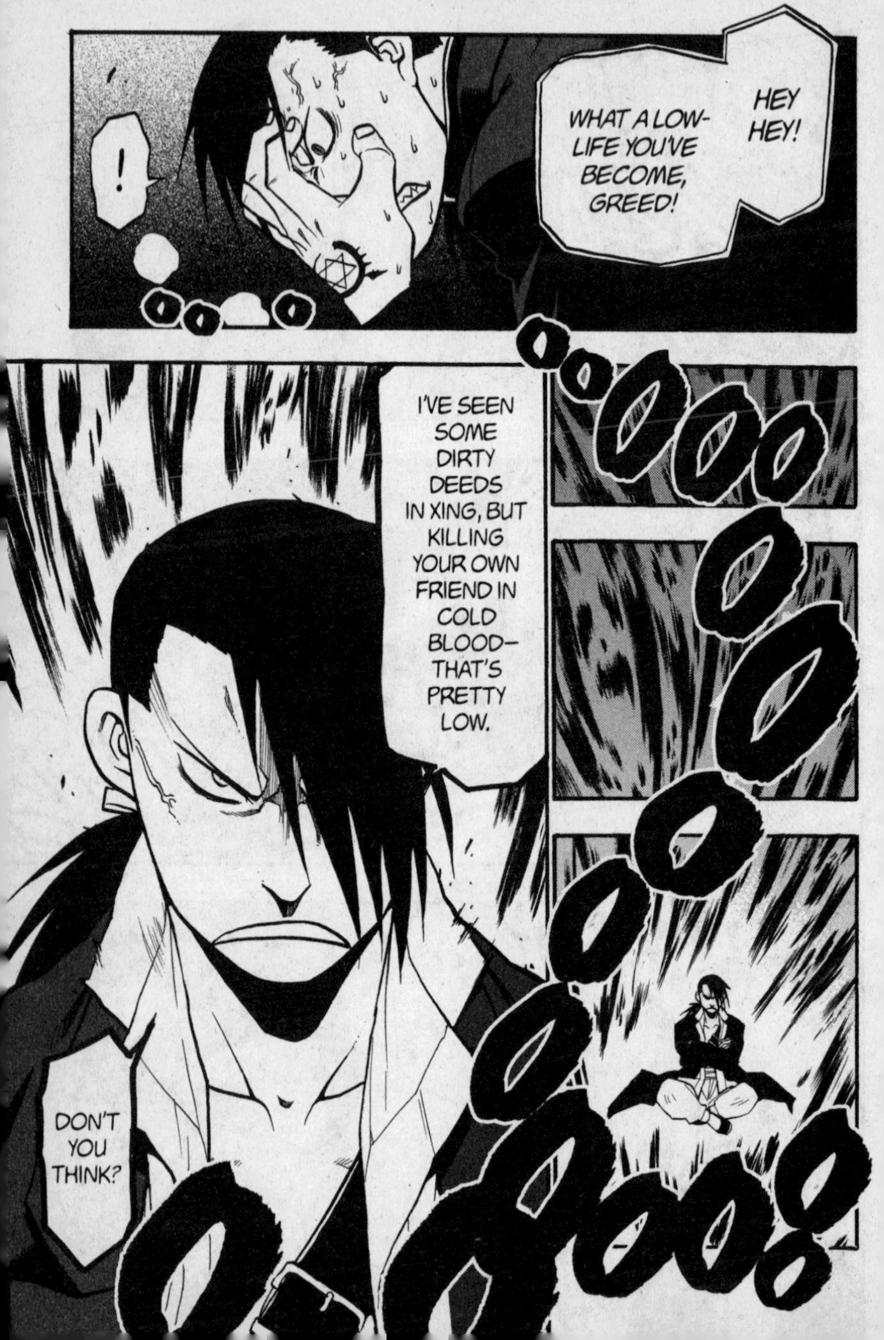
HEY HEY!
WHAT A LOW-LIFE YOU'VE BECOME, GREED!
!
I'VE SEEN SOME DIRTY DEEDS IN XING, BUT KILLING YOUR OWN FRIEND IN COLD BLOOD—THAT'S PRETTY LOW.
DON'T YOU THINK?

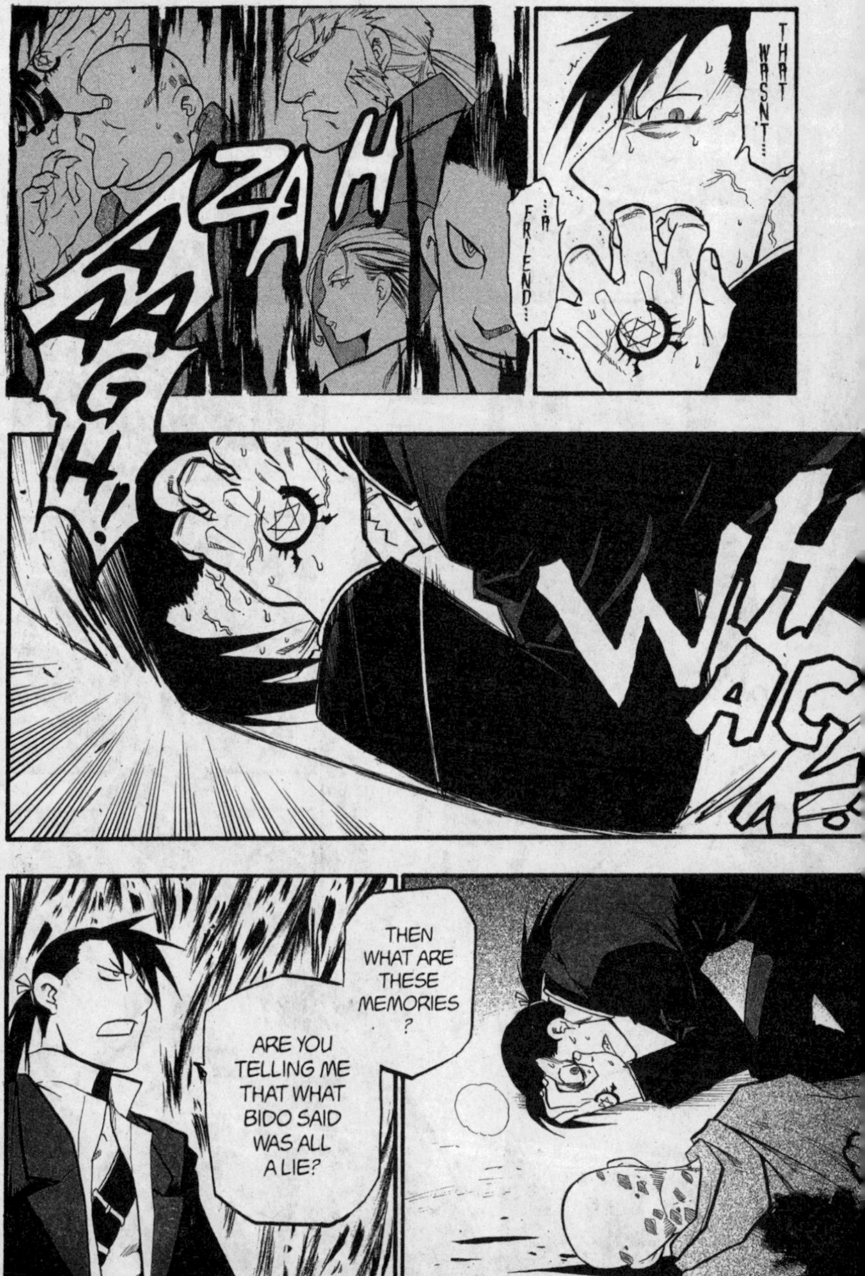
THAT WASN'T...
...A FRIEND...
ZAH
AAAGH!
WHACK
THEN WHAT ARE THESE MEMORIES?
ARE YOU TELLING ME THAT WHAT BIDO SAID WAS ALL A LIE?

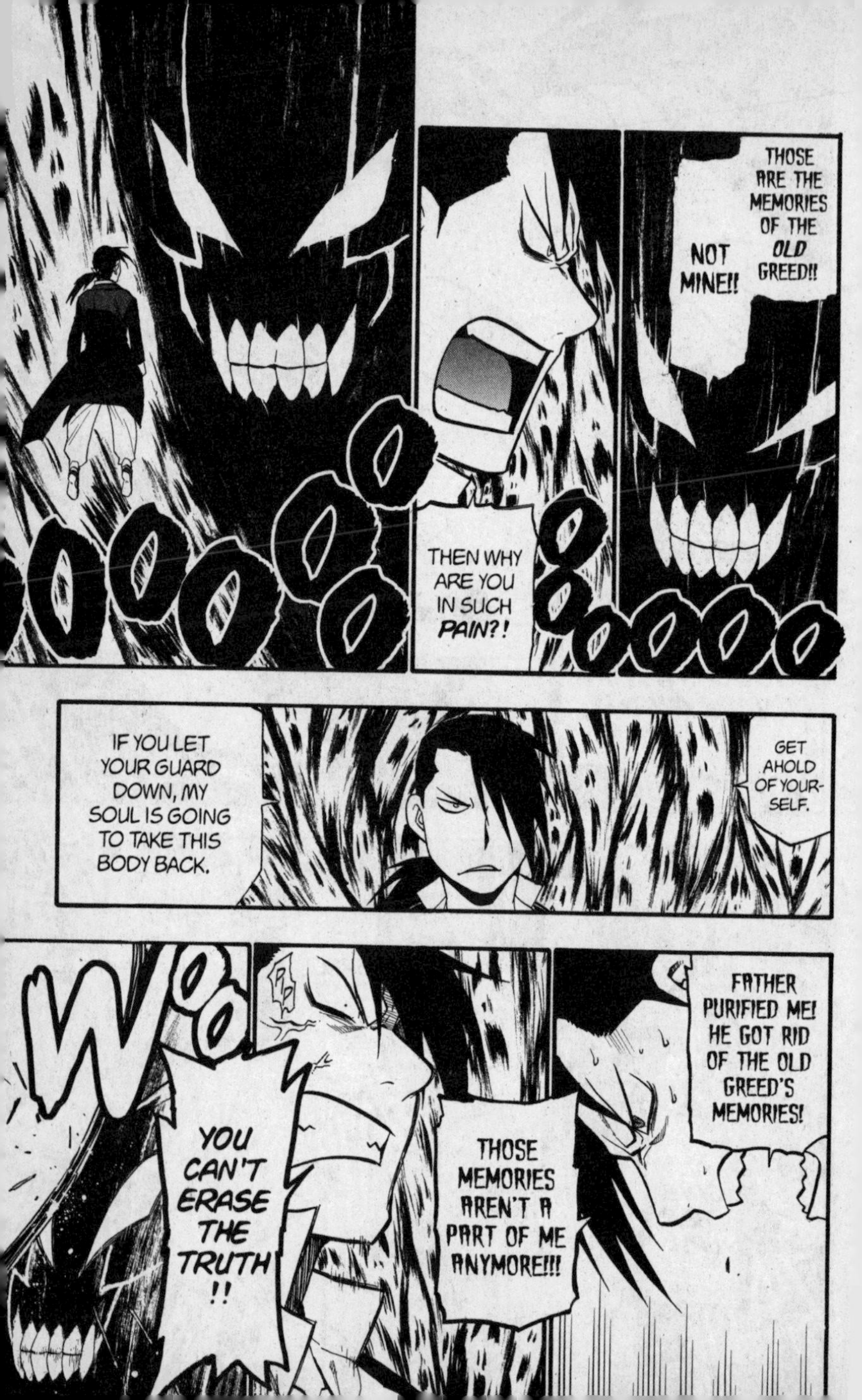
THOSE ARE THE MEMORIES OF THE *OLD* GREED!!
NOT MINE!!
THEN WHY ARE YOU IN SUCH *PAIN?!*
GET AHOLD OF YOURSELF.
IF YOU LET YOUR GUARD DOWN, MY SOUL IS GOING TO TAKE THIS BODY BACK.
FATHER PURIFIED ME! HE GOT RID OF THE OLD GREED'S MEMORIES!
THOSE MEMORIES AREN'T A PART OF ME ANYMORE!!!
YOU CAN'T ERASE THE TRUTH!!
WOO

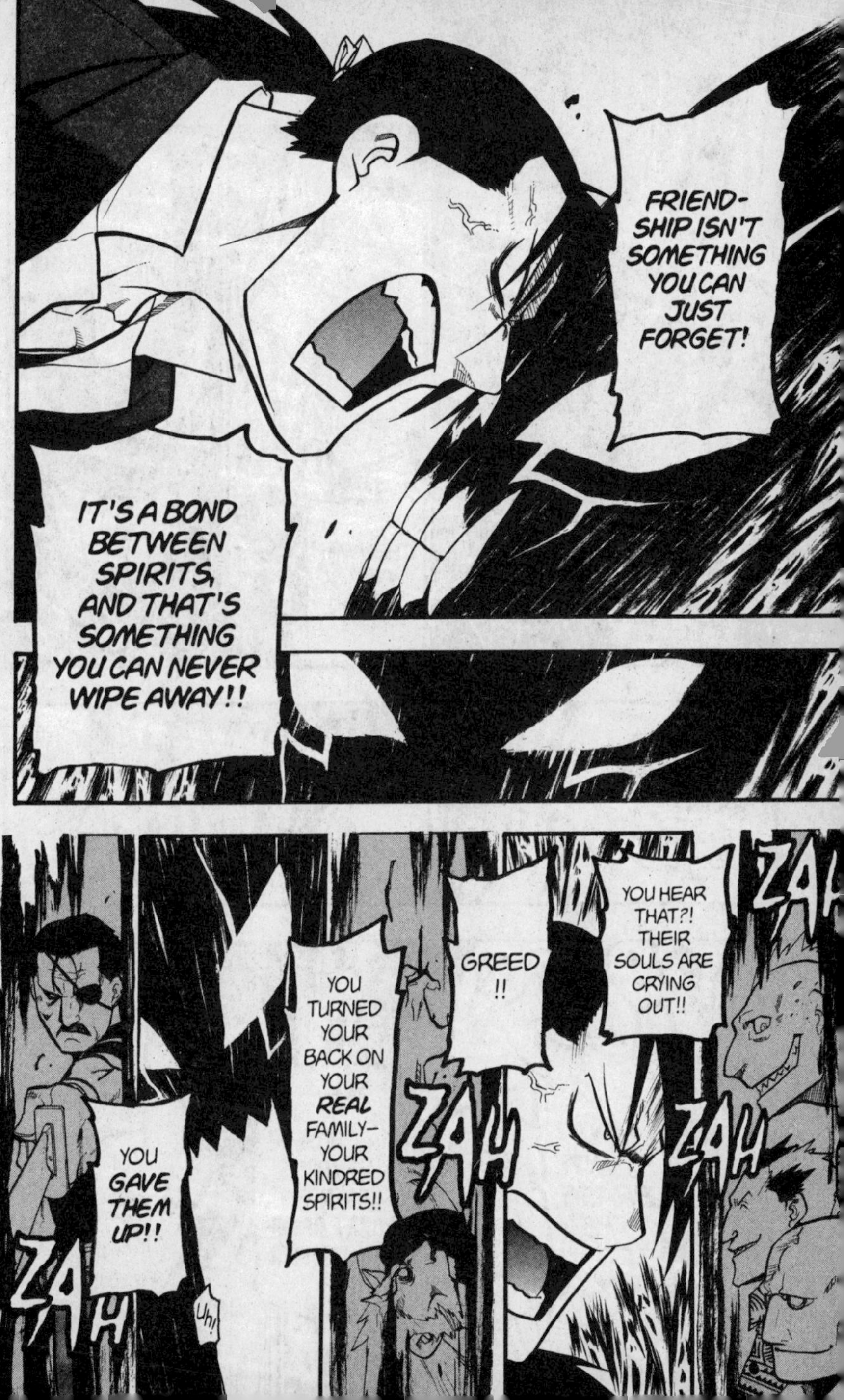
FRIEND-SHIP ISN'T SOMETHING YOU CAN JUST FORGET!
IT'S A BOND BETWEEN SPIRITS, AND THAT'S SOMETHING YOU CAN NEVER WIPE AWAY!!
ZAH
YOU HEAR THAT?! THEIR SOULS ARE CRYING OUT!!
GREED !!
ZAH
YOU TURNED YOUR BACK ON YOUR REAL FAMILY—YOUR KINDRED SPIRITS!!
ZAH
YOU GAVE THEM UP!!
Uh!
ZAH

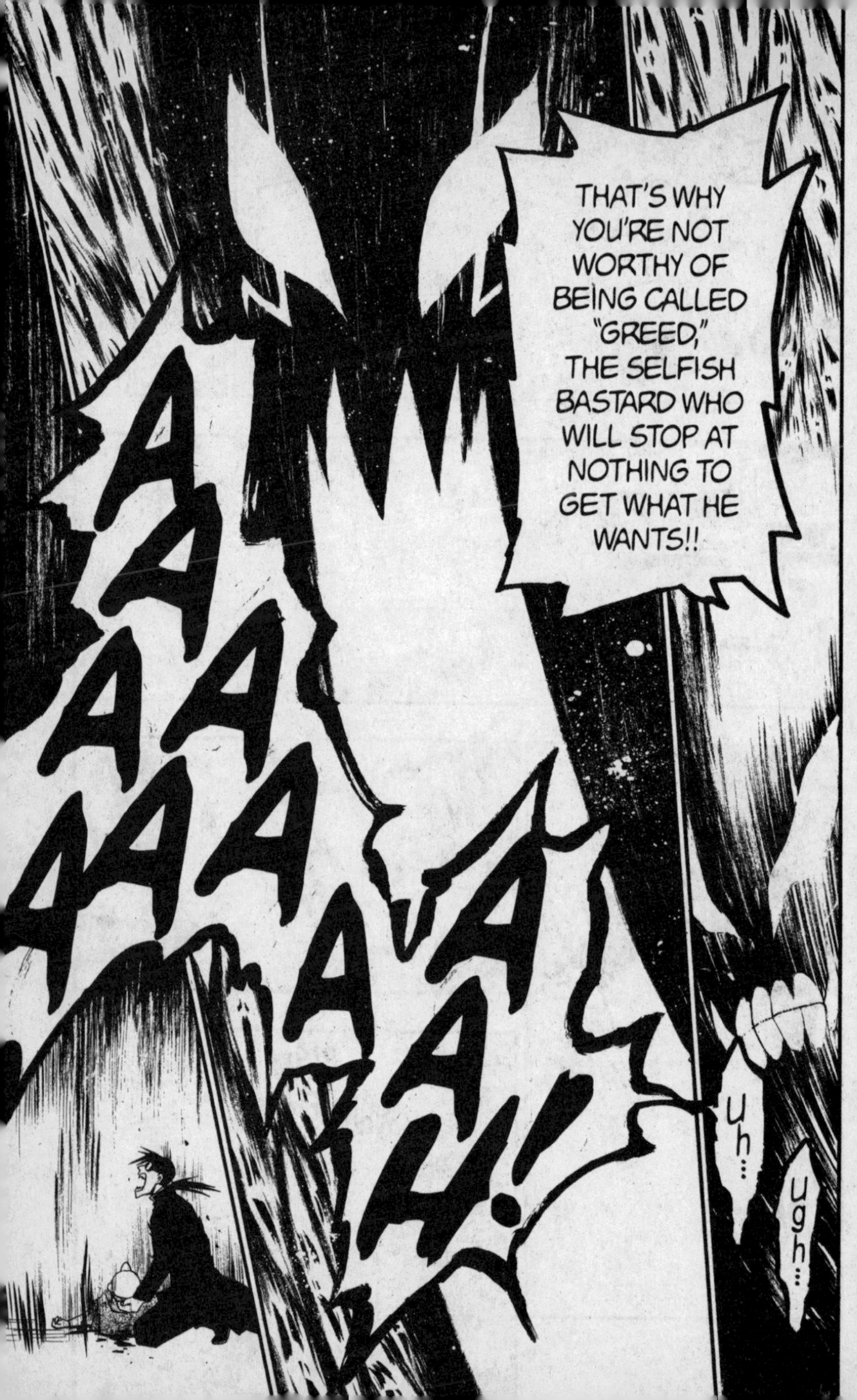
THAT'S WHY YOU'RE NOT WORTHY OF BEING CALLED "GREED," THE SELFISH BASTARD WHO WILL STOP AT NOTHING TO GET WHAT HE WANTS!!
AAAAAAAAAAAAAH!!
Uh...
Ugh...

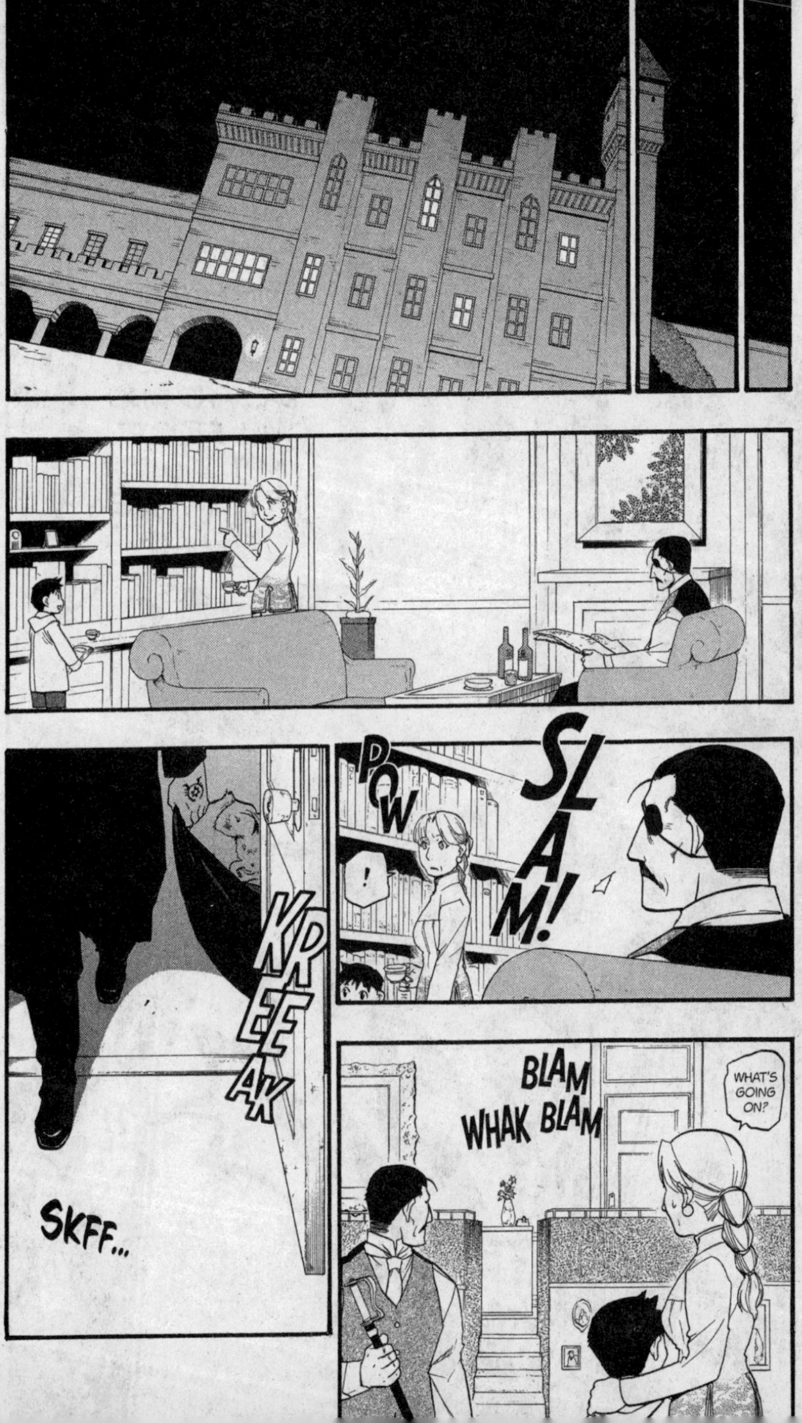
SLAM!
POW
!
WHAT'S GOING ON?
BLAM
WHAK BLAM
KREEAK
SKFF...

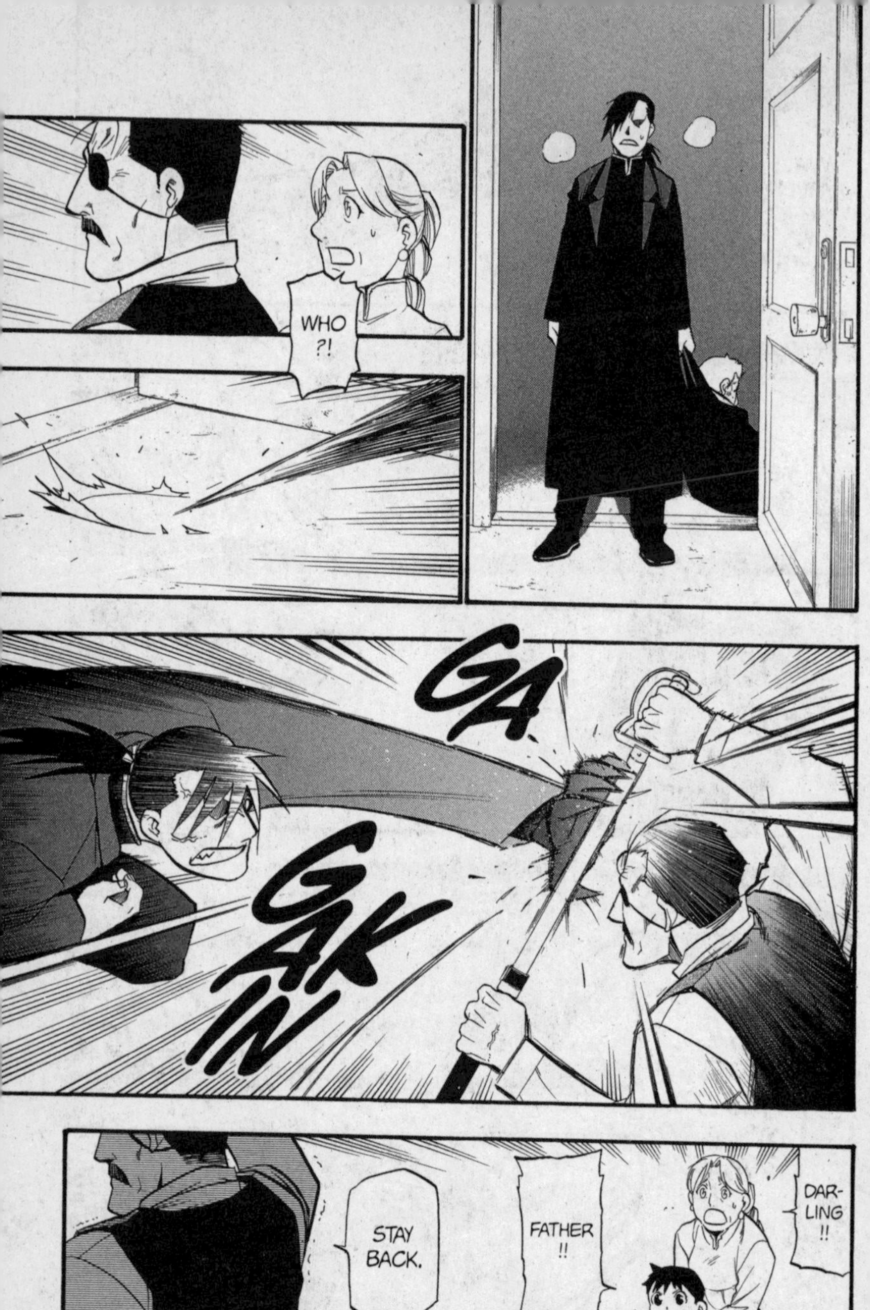
WHO ?!
GA
GAKIN
DAR-LING !!
FATHER !!
STAY BACK.

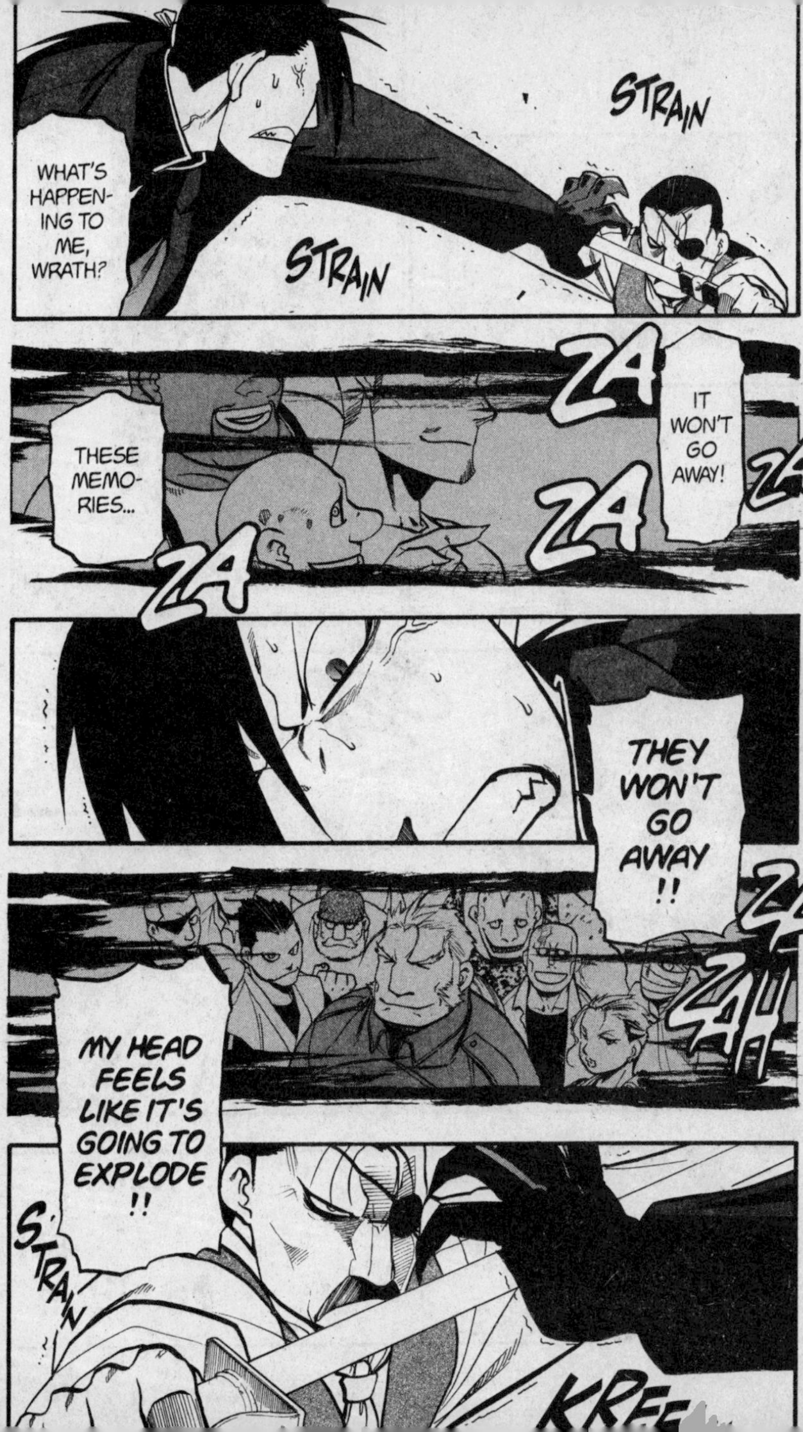
STRAIN
WHAT'S HAPPENING TO ME, WRATH?
STRAIN
ZA
IT WON'T GO AWAY!
ZA
ZA
THESE MEMORIES...
ZA
THEY WON'T GO AWAY!!
ZA
ZAH
MY HEAD FEELS LIKE IT'S GOING TO EXPLODE!!
KREE
STRAIN

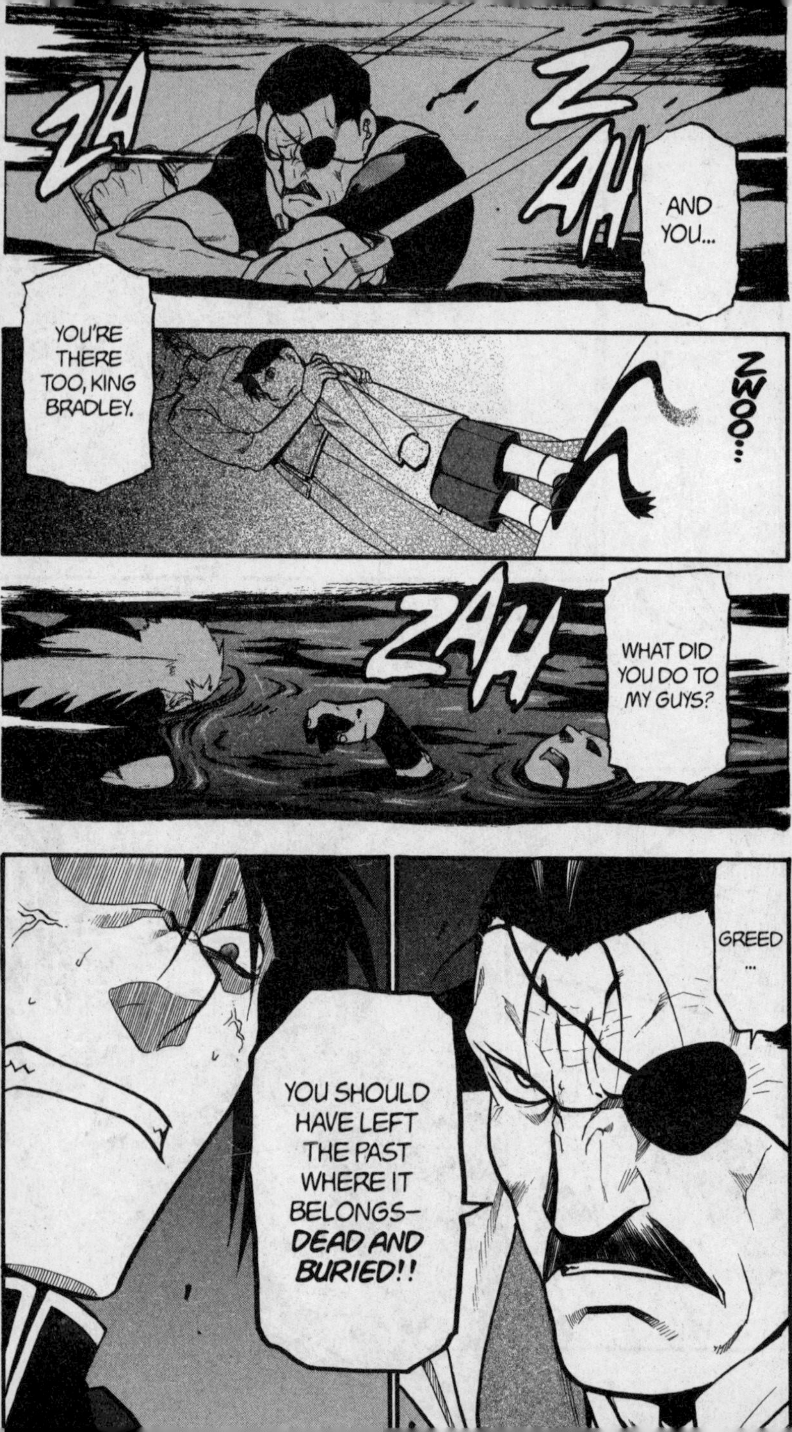
AND YOU...
ZAH
ZA
YOU'RE THERE TOO, KING BRADLEY.
ZWOO...
WHAT DID YOU DO TO MY GUYS?
ZAH
GREED...
YOU SHOULD HAVE LEFT THE PAST WHERE IT BELONGS— DEAD AND BURIED!!

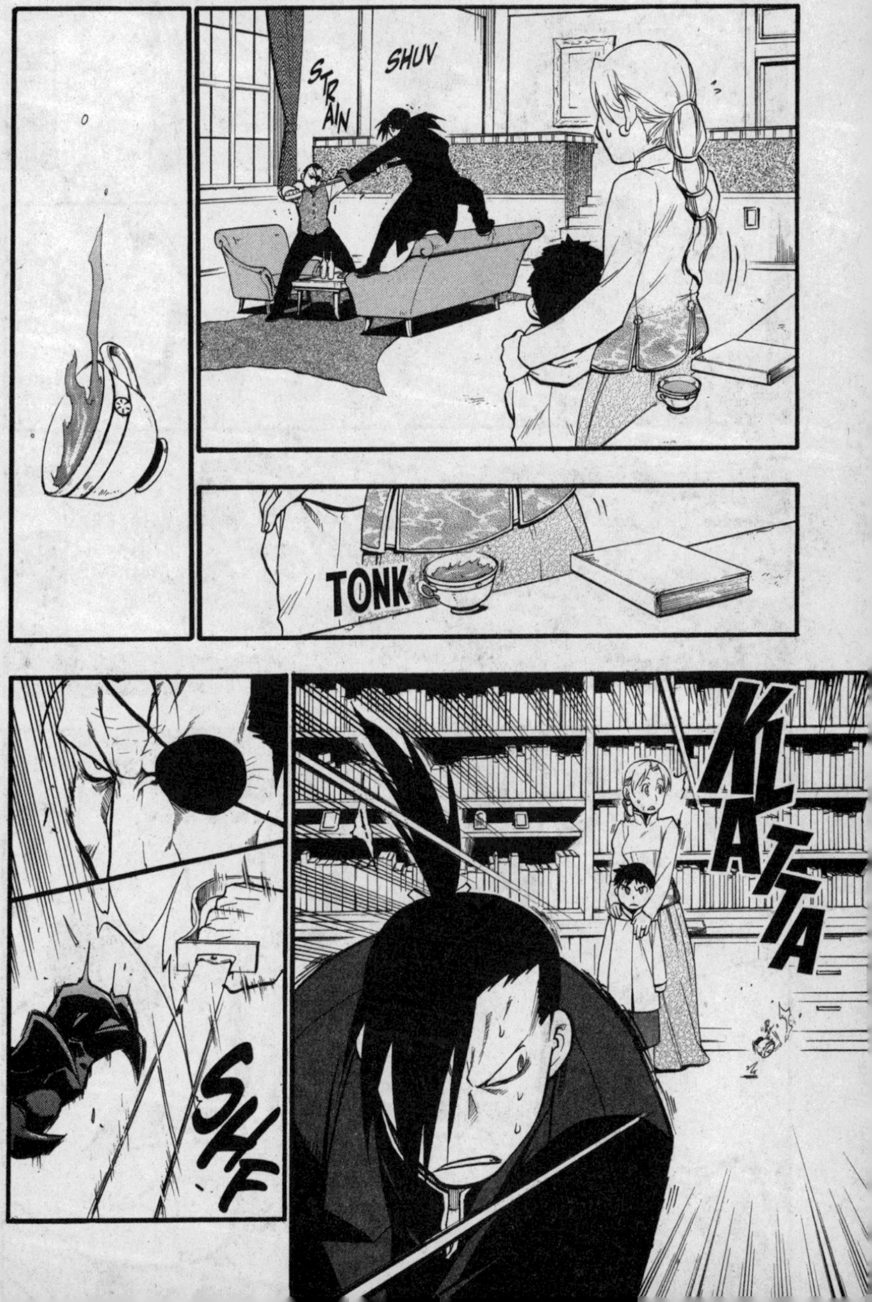
SHUV
STRAIN
TONK
KLATTA
SHF

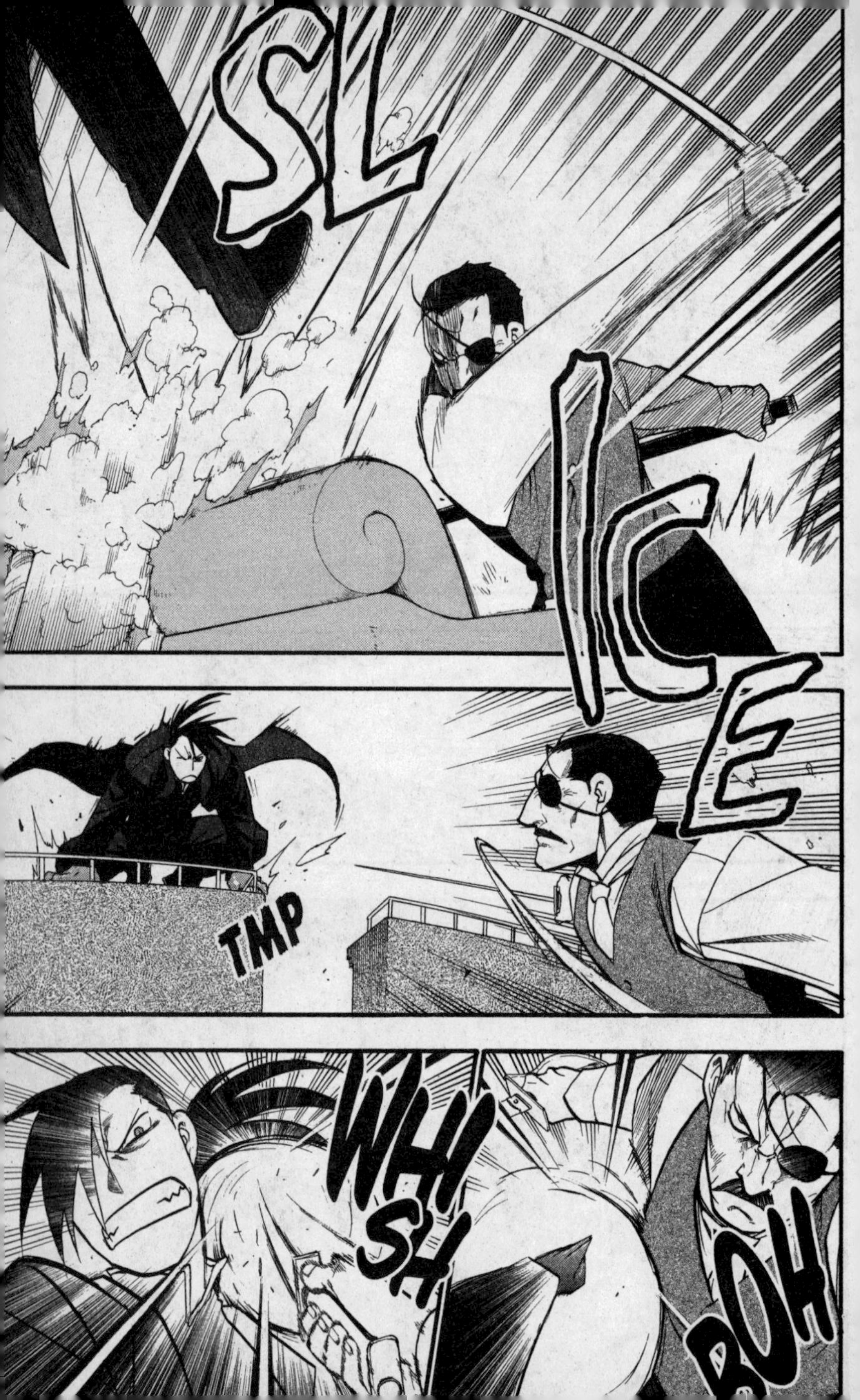
SLICE
TMP
BOH
WHISH

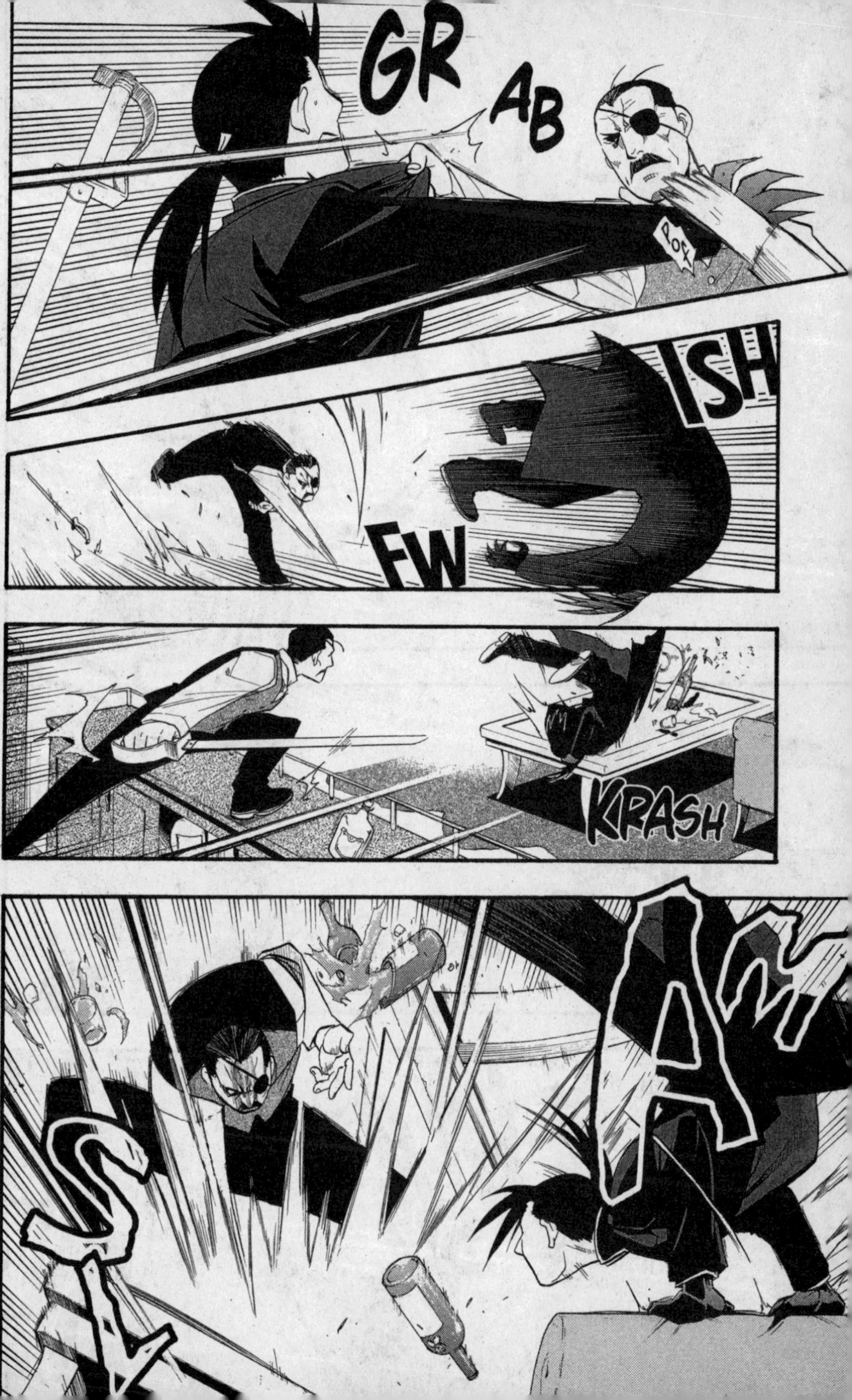
GRAB
POF
FWISH
KRASH

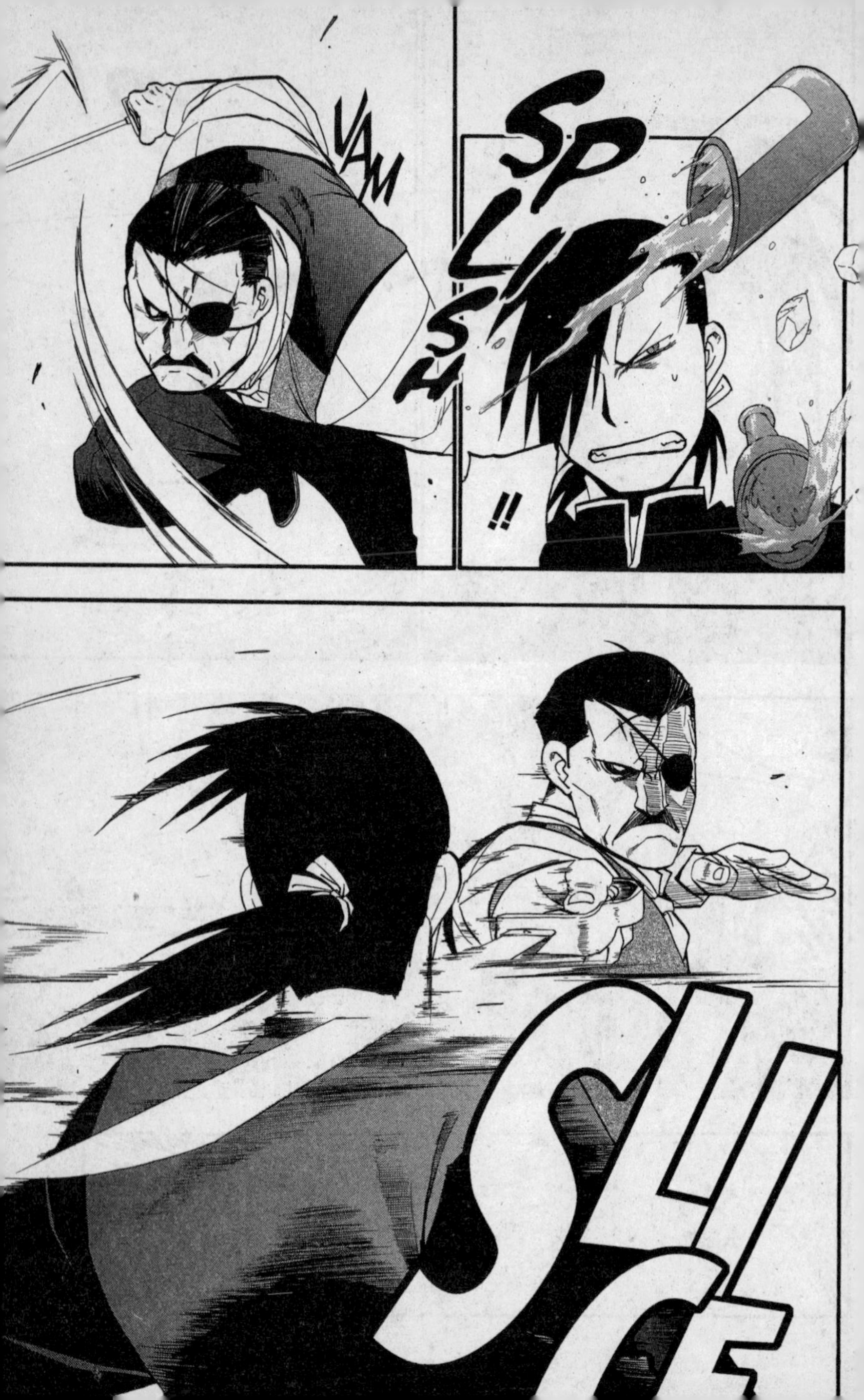
SPLISH
!!
VAM
SLICE

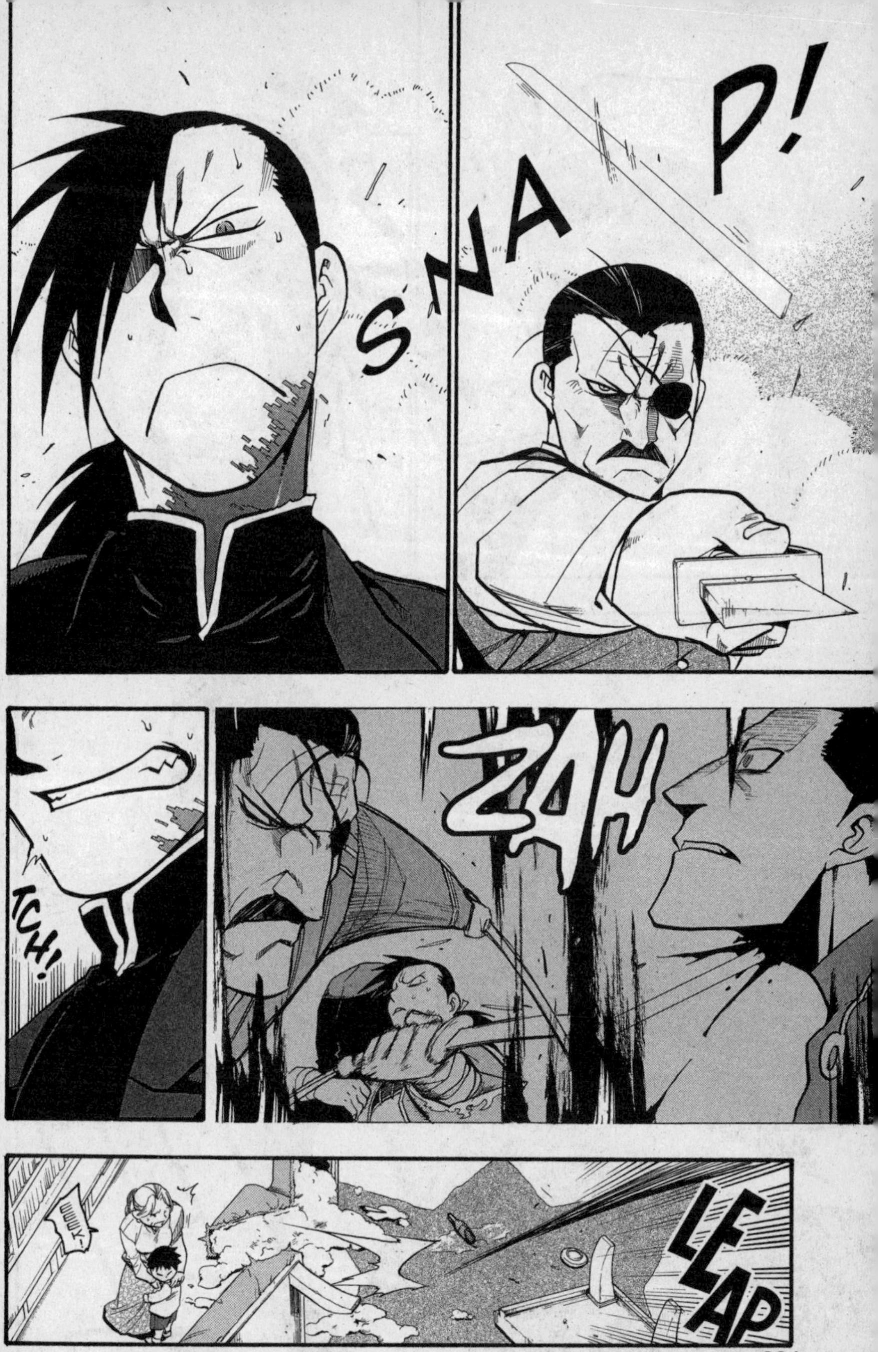
SNAP!
ZAH
TCH!
LEAP
EEEEK!

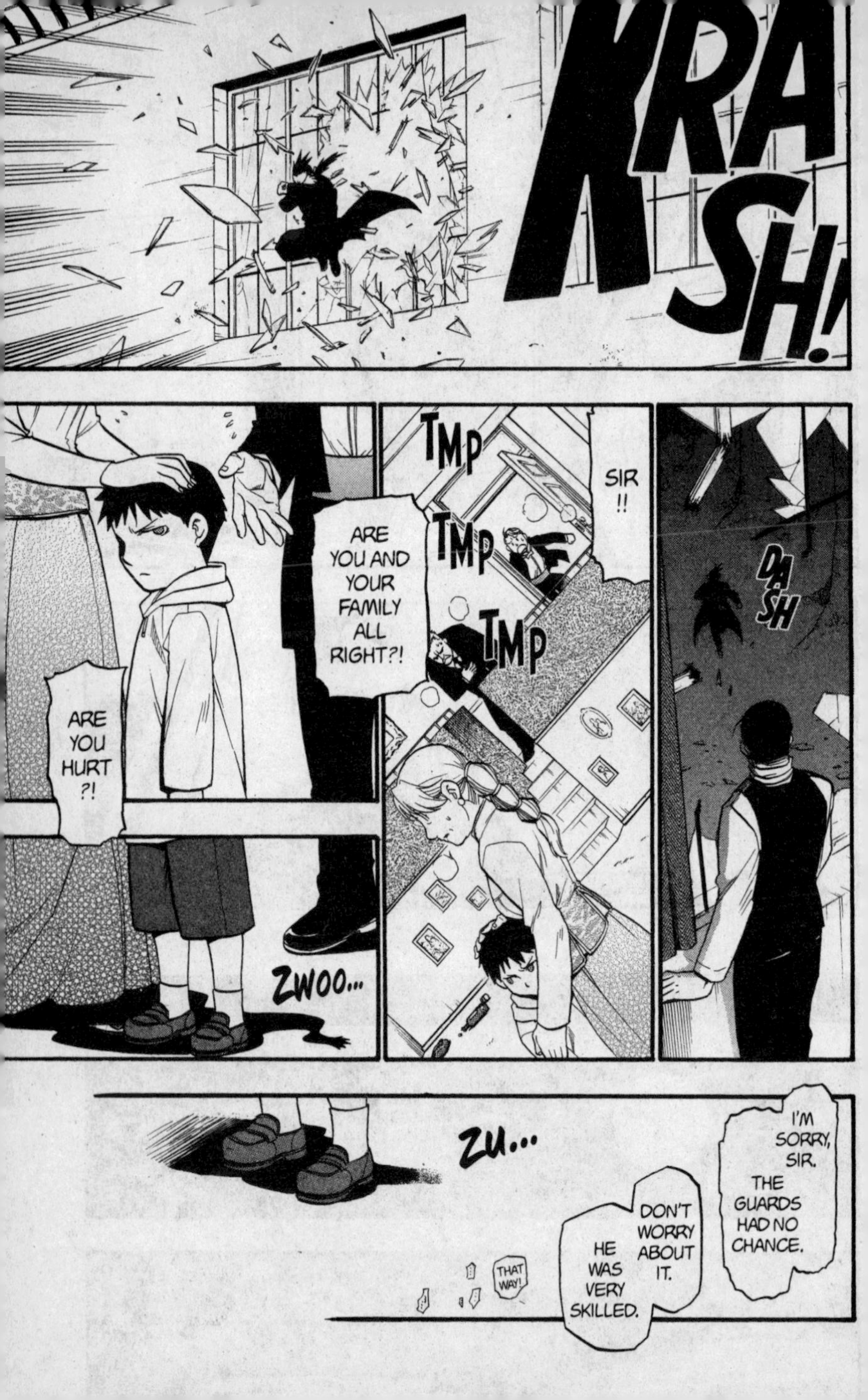
KRASH!
DASH
SIR!!
TMP
TMP
ARE YOU AND YOUR FAMILY ALL RIGHT?!
TMP
ARE YOU HURT?!
ZWOO...
I'M SORRY, SIR. THE GUARDS HAD NO CHANCE.
DON'T WORRY ABOUT IT.
HE WAS VERY SKILLED.
THAT WAY!
ZU...

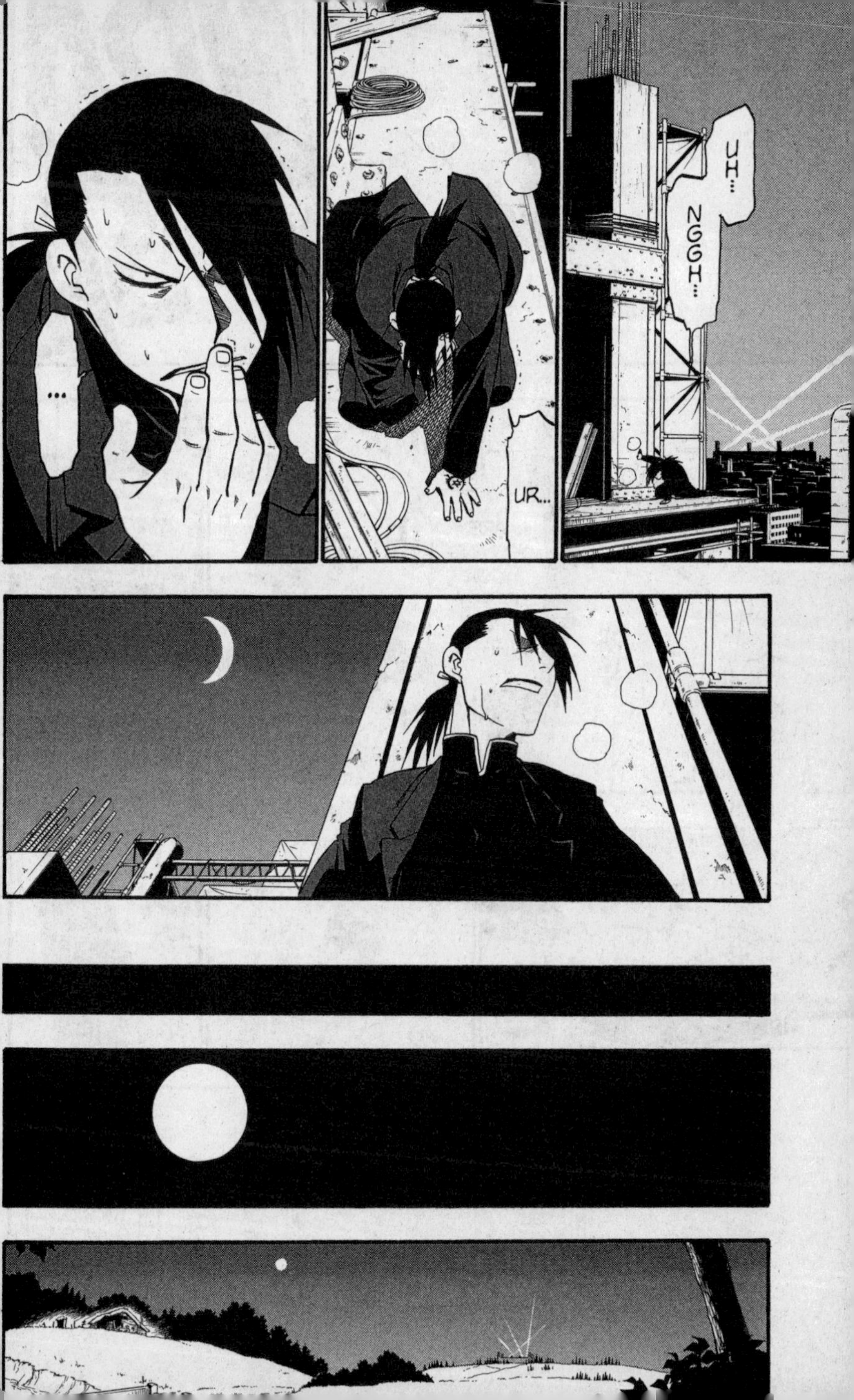
UH... NGGH...
UR...
...

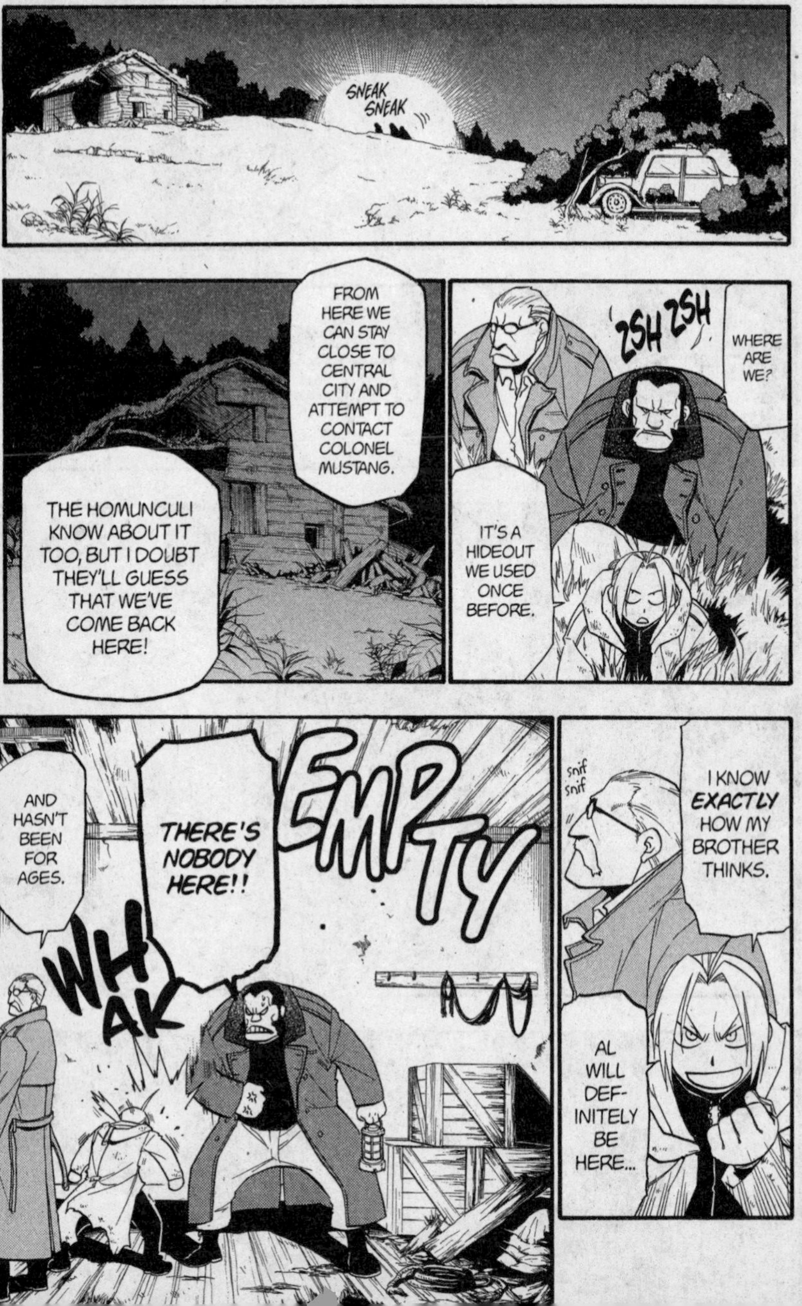
SNEAK SNEAK
WHERE ARE WE?
ZSH ZSH
IT'S A HIDEOUT WE USED ONCE BEFORE.
FROM HERE WE CAN STAY CLOSE TO CENTRAL CITY AND ATTEMPT TO CONTACT COLONEL MUSTANG.
THE HOMUNCULI KNOW ABOUT IT TOO, BUT I DOUBT THEY'LL GUESS THAT WE'VE COME BACK HERE!
snif snif
I KNOW EXACTLY HOW MY BROTHER THINKS.
AL WILL DEF-INITELY BE HERE...
EMPTY
THERE'S NOBODY HERE!!
AND HASN'T BEEN FOR AGES.
WHAK

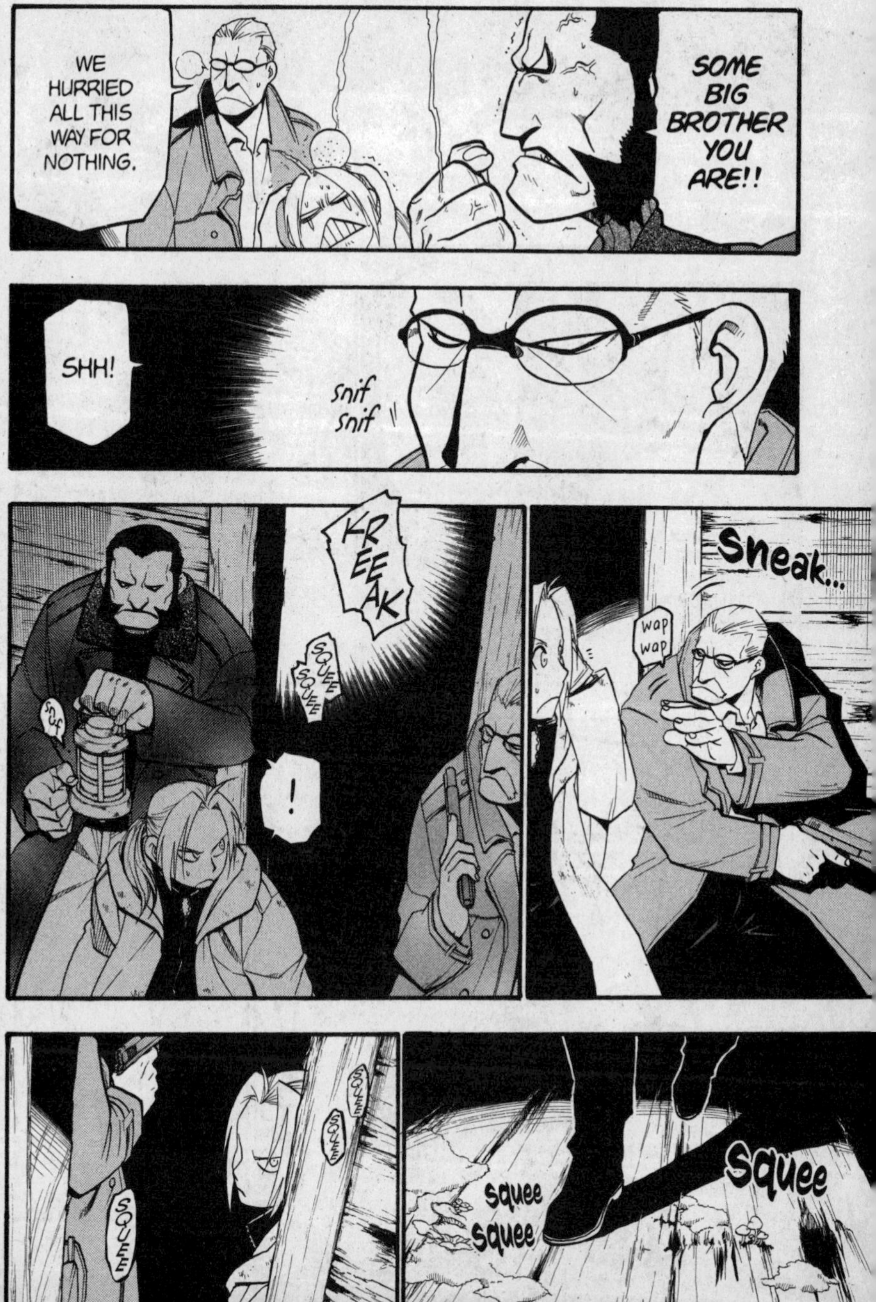
SOME BIG BROTHER YOU ARE!!
WE HURRIED ALL THIS WAY FOR NOTHING.
snif snif
SHH!
Sneak...
wap wap
KREEEAK
SQUEE SQUEE
!
snuf
Squee
squee squee
SQUEE SQUEE
SQUEE

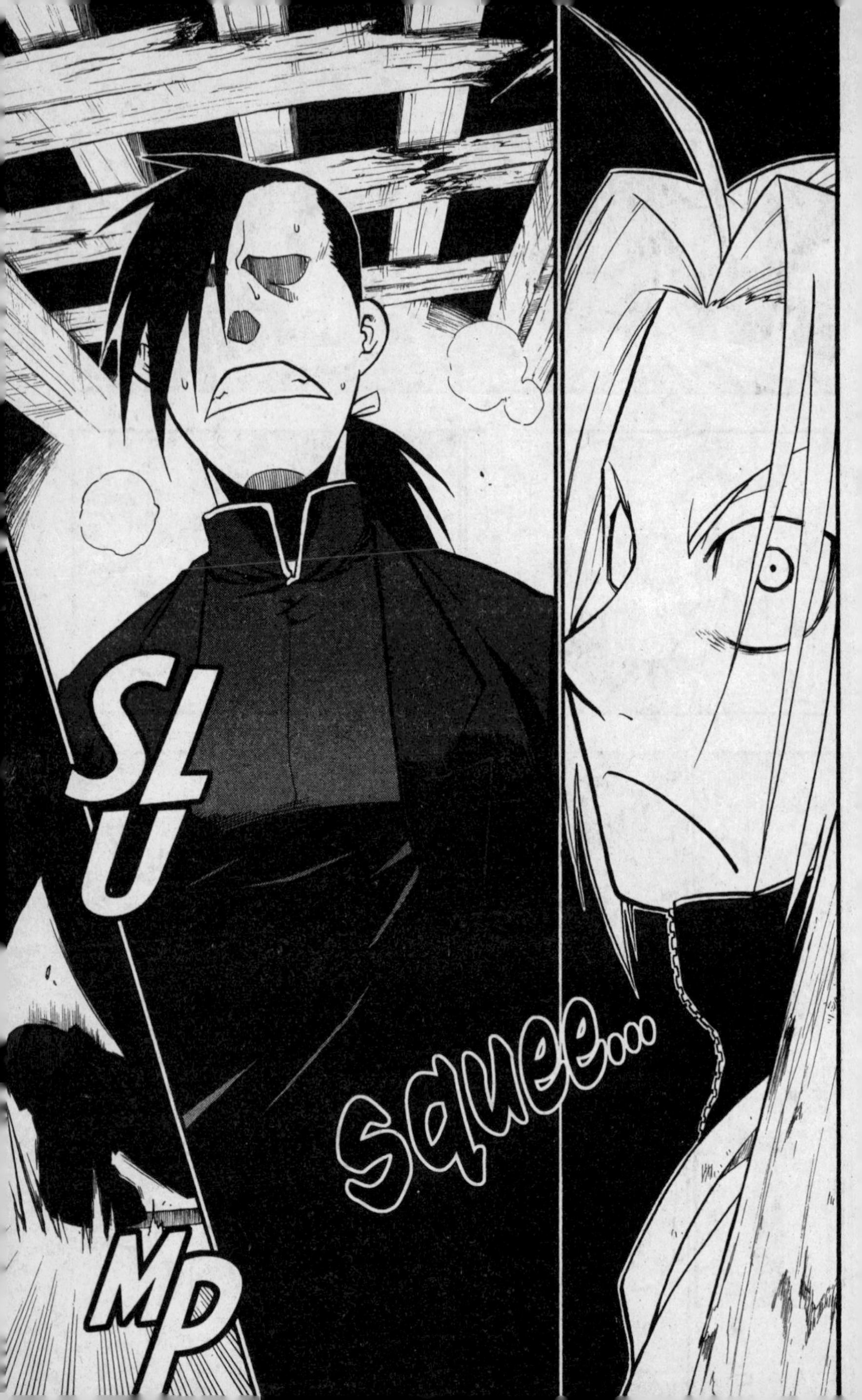
squee...
SLUMP

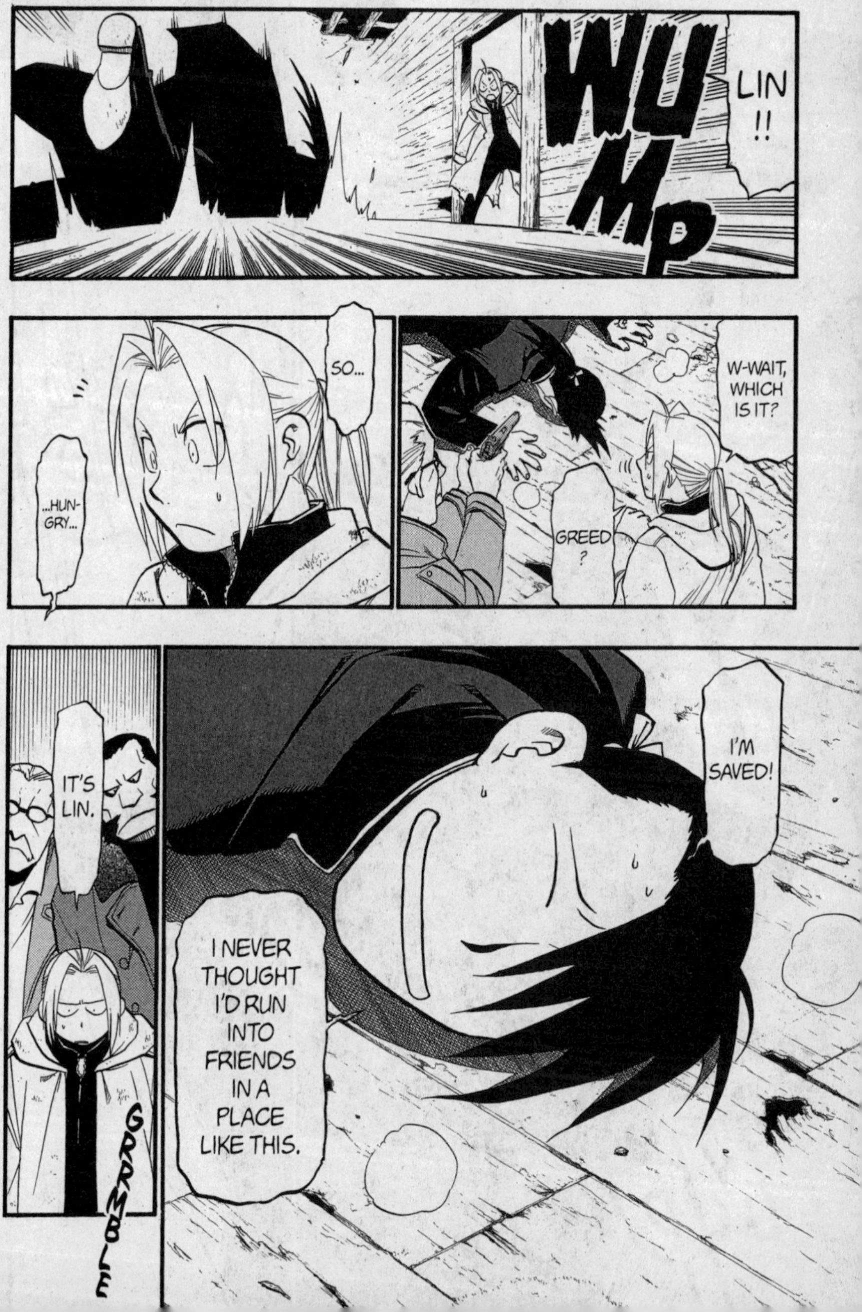
LIN !!
WUMP
W-WAIT, WHICH IS IT?
GREED?
SO...
...HUN-GRY...
I'M SAVED!
I NEVER THOUGHT I'D RUN INTO FRIENDS IN A PLACE LIKE THIS.
IT'S LIN.
GRRMBLE

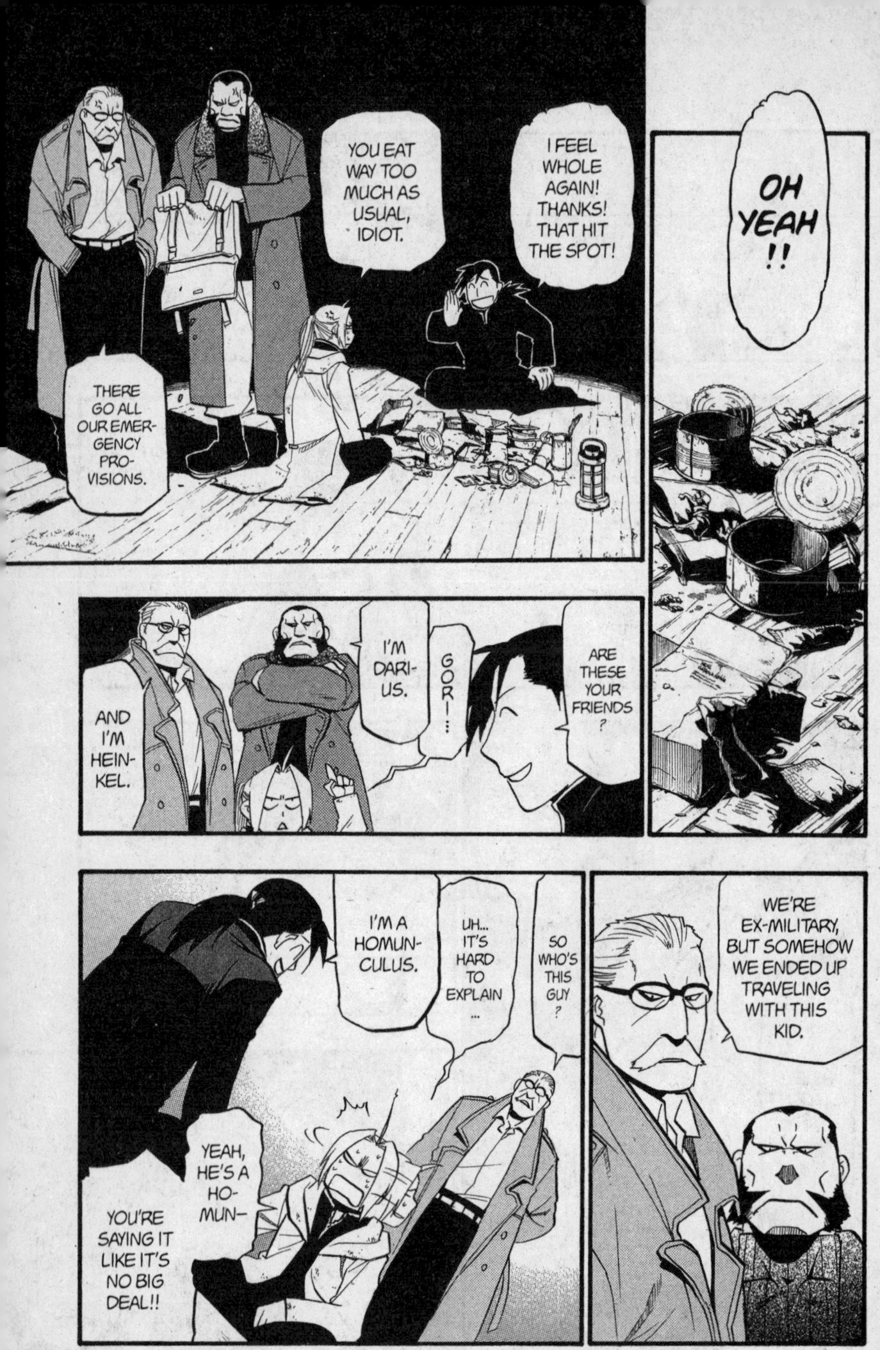
OH YEAH!!
I FEEL WHOLE AGAIN! THANKS! THAT HIT THE SPOT!
YOU EAT WAY TOO MUCH AS USUAL, IDIOT.
THERE GO ALL OUR EMERGENCY PROVISIONS.
ARE THESE YOUR FRIENDS?
GORI...
I'M DARIUS.
AND I'M HEINKEL.
WE'RE EX-MILITARY, BUT SOMEHOW WE ENDED UP TRAVELING WITH THIS KID.
SO WHO'S THIS GUY?
UH... IT'S HARD TO EXPLAIN...
I'M A HOMUNCULUS.
YEAH, HE'S A HOMUN-
YOU'RE SAYING IT LIKE IT'S NO BIG DEAL!!

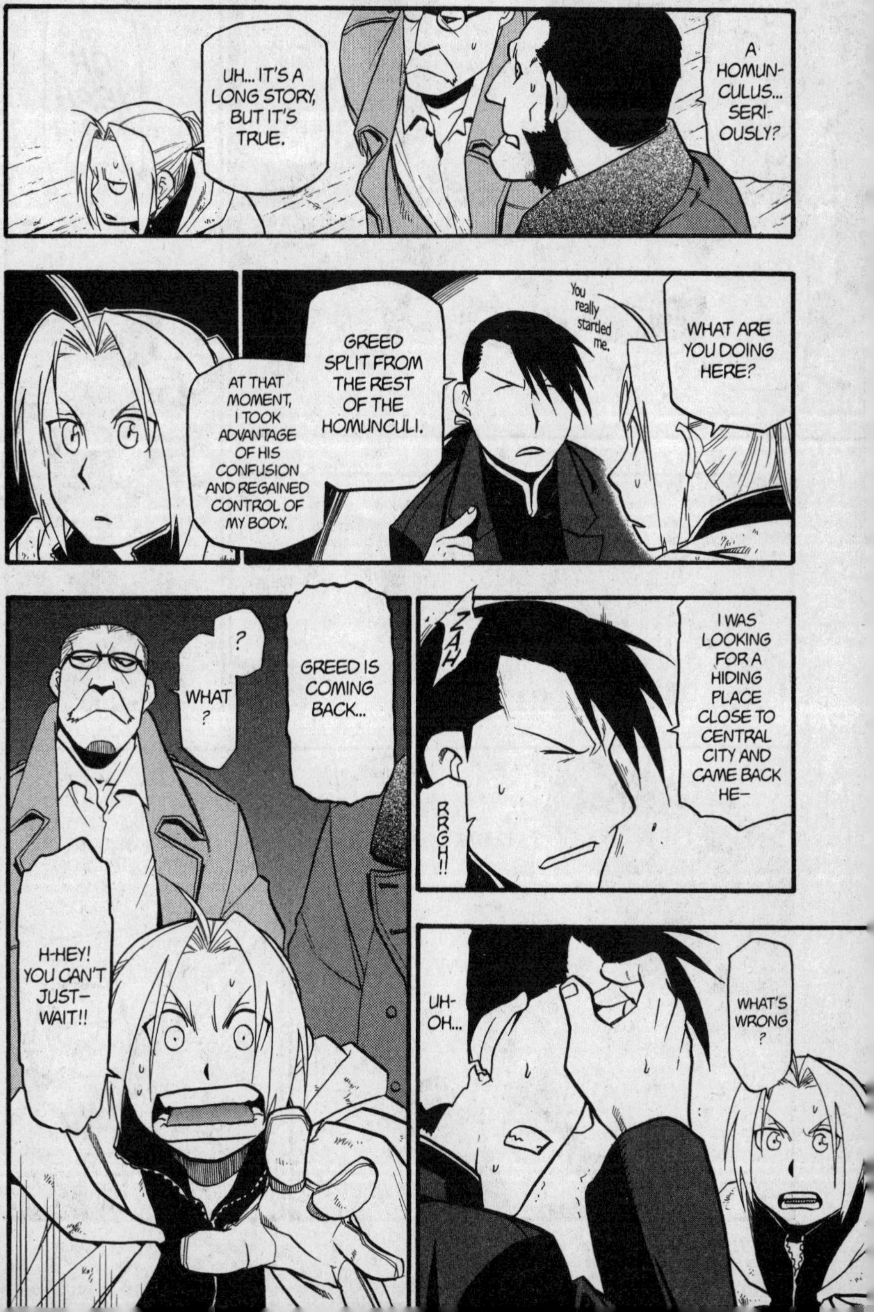
A HOMUNCULUS... SERIOUSLY?
UH... IT'S A LONG STORY, BUT IT'S TRUE.
WHAT ARE YOU DOING HERE?
You really startled me.
GREED SPLIT FROM THE REST OF THE HOMUNCULI.
AT THAT MOMENT, I TOOK ADVANTAGE OF HIS CONFUSION AND REGAINED CONTROL OF MY BODY.
I WAS LOOKING FOR A HIDING PLACE CLOSE TO CENTRAL CITY AND CAME BACK HE—
ZAH
RRGH!!
WHAT'S WRONG?
UH-OH...
GREED IS COMING BACK...
WHAT?
?
H-HEY! YOU CAN'T JUST— WAIT!!

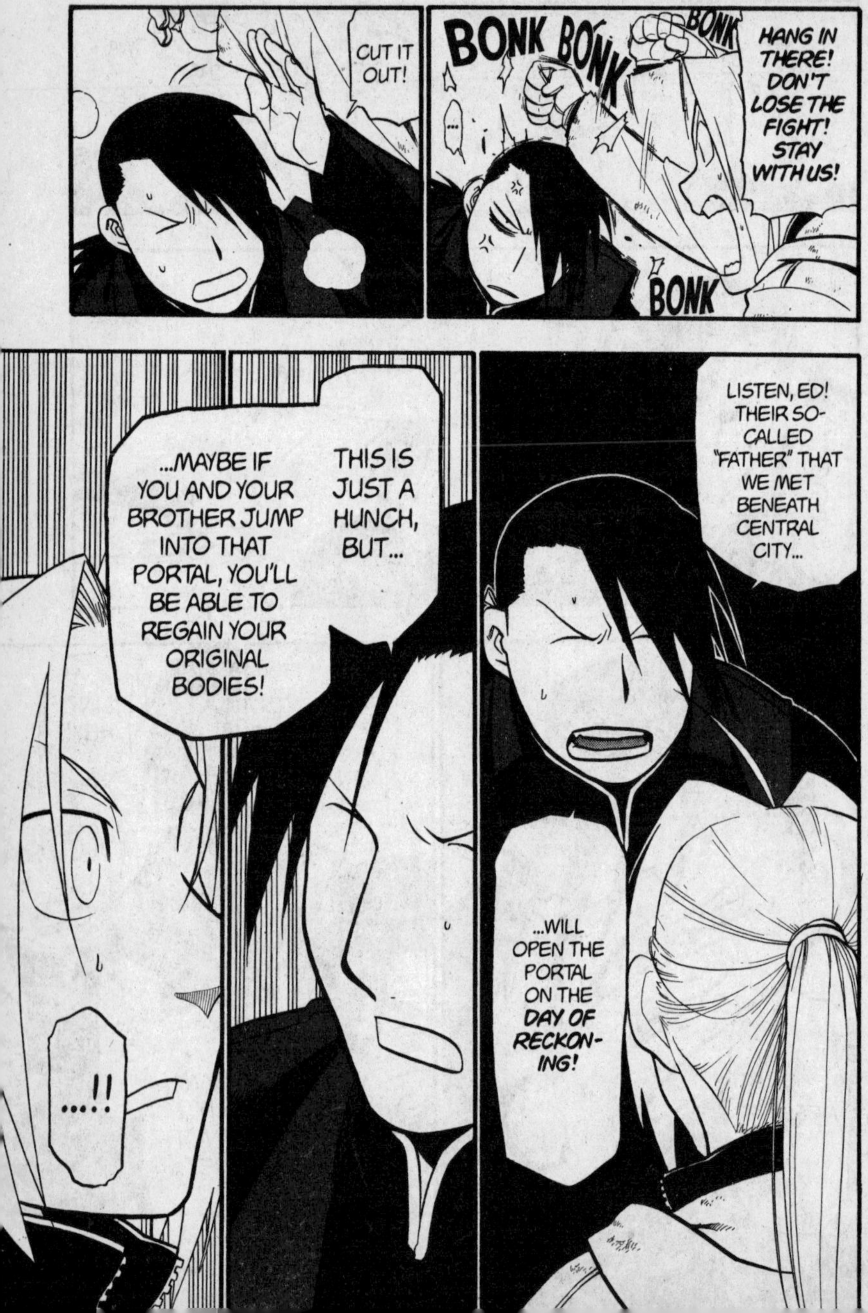
HANG IN THERE! DON'T LOSE THE FIGHT! STAY WITH US!
BONK
BONK
BONK
...
CUT IT OUT!
LISTEN, ED! THEIR SO-CALLED "FATHER" THAT WE MET BENEATH CENTRAL CITY...
...WILL OPEN THE PORTAL ON THE DAY OF RECKONING!
THIS IS JUST A HUNCH, BUT...
...MAYBE IF YOU AND YOUR BROTHER JUMP INTO THAT PORTAL, YOU'LL BE ABLE TO REGAIN YOUR ORIGINAL BODIES!
....!!

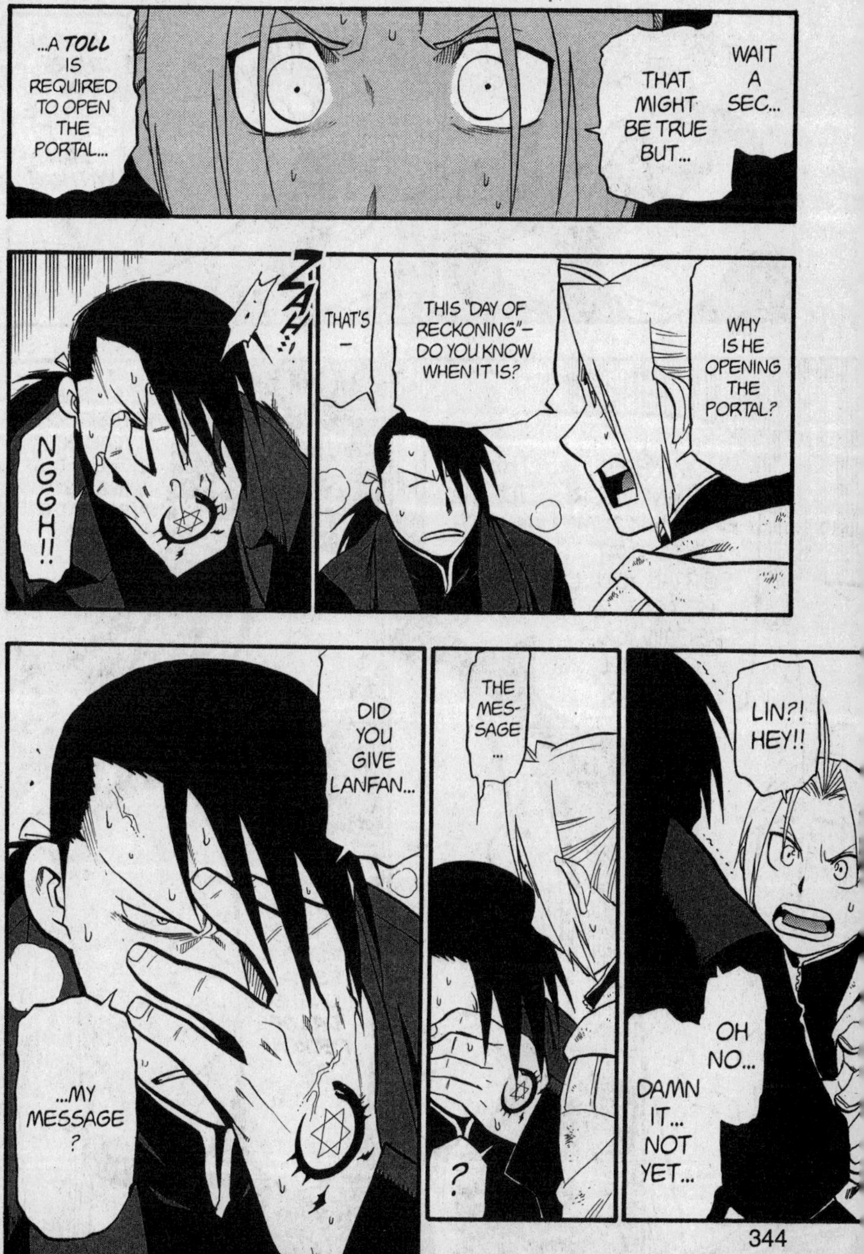
WAIT A SEC...
THAT MIGHT BE TRUE BUT...
...A TOLL IS REQUIRED TO OPEN THE PORTAL...
WHY IS HE OPENING THE PORTAL?
THIS "DAY OF RECKONING"— DO YOU KNOW WHEN IT IS?
THAT'S —
ZAP
NGGH!!
LIN?! HEY!!
OH NO...
DAMN IT... NOT YET...
THE MES-SAGE ...
?
DID YOU GIVE LANFAN...
...MY MESSAGE?

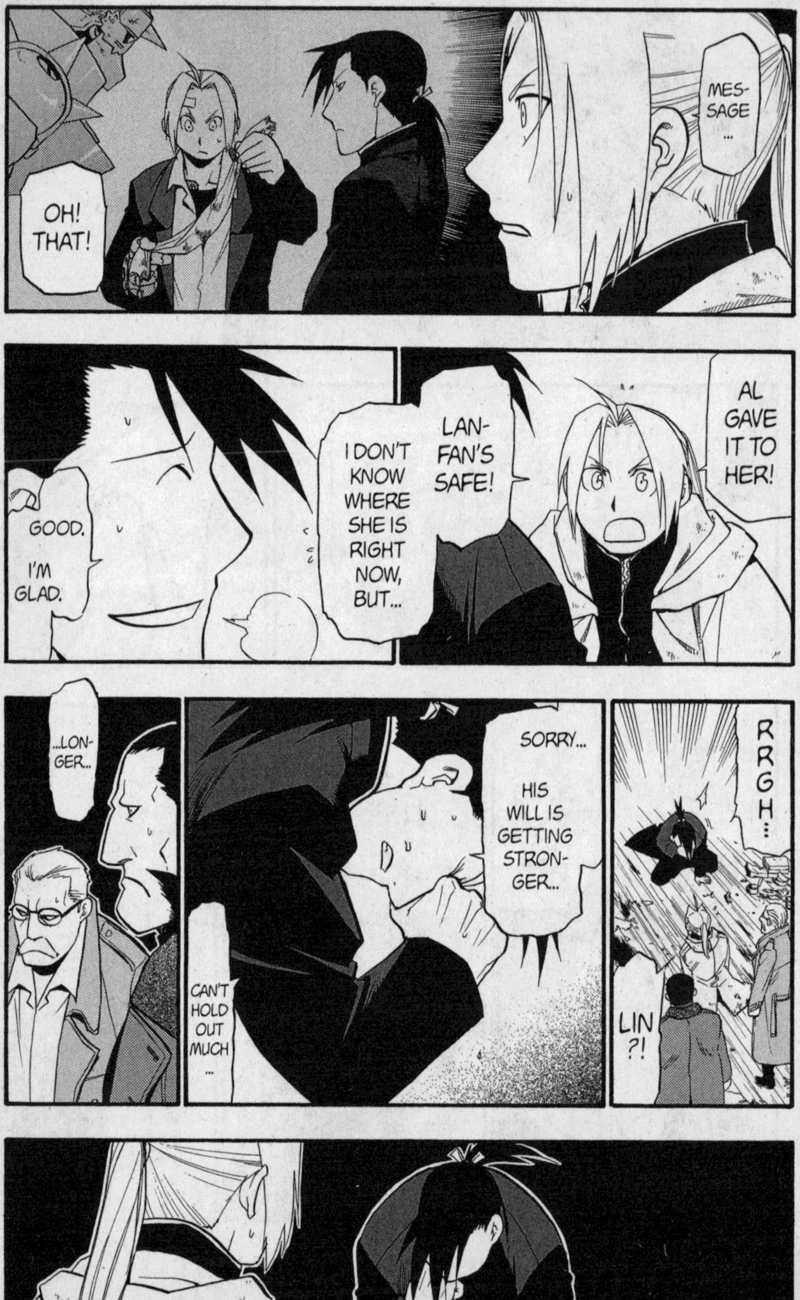
MES-SAGE...
OH! THAT!
AL GAVE IT TO HER!
LAN-FAN'S SAFE!
I DON'T KNOW WHERE SHE IS RIGHT NOW, BUT...
GOOD. I'M GLAD.
RRGH...
LIN?!
SORRY... HIS WILL IS GETTING STRON-GER...
CAN'T HOLD OUT MUCH...
...LON-GER...

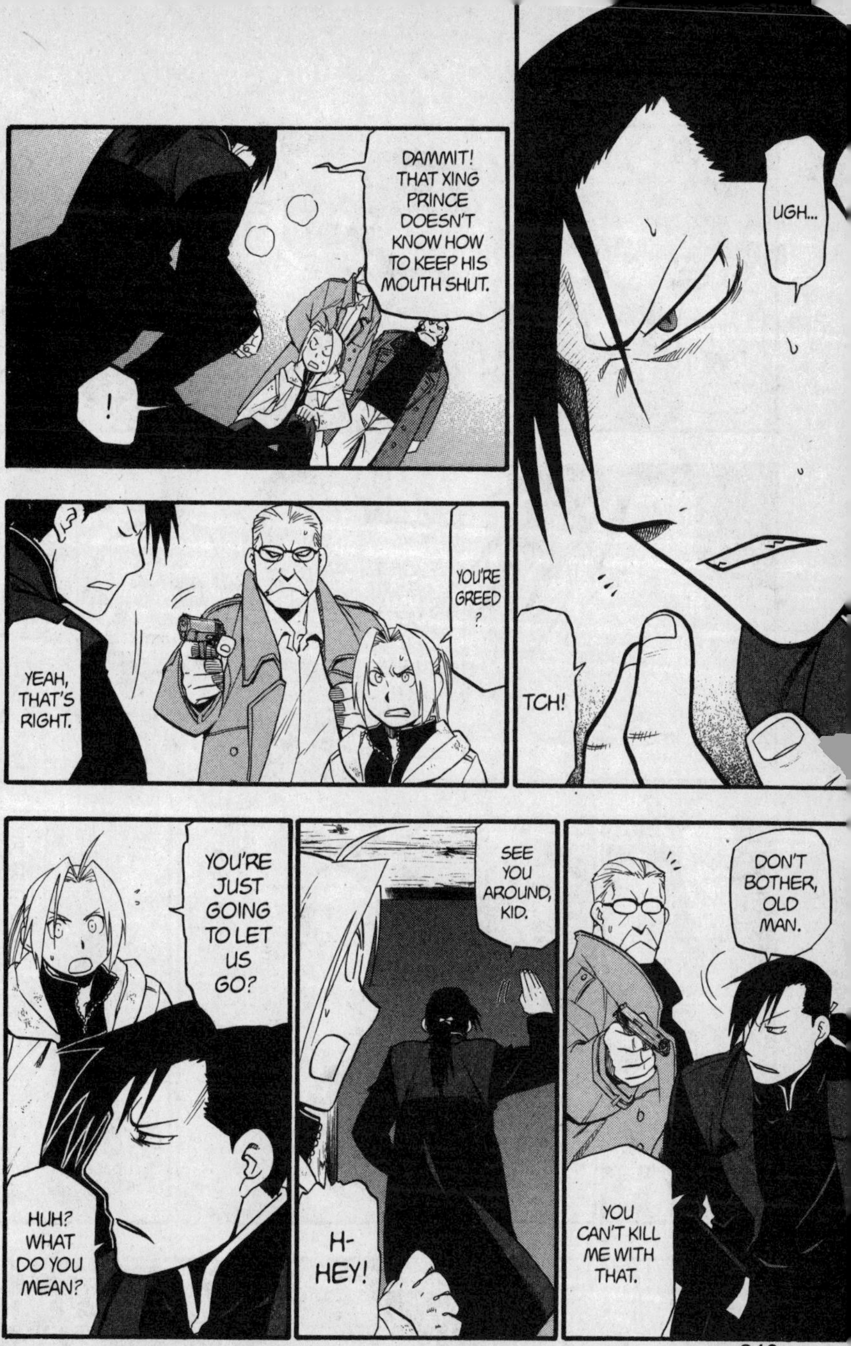
UGH...
TCH!
DAMMIT! THAT XING PRINCE DOESN'T KNOW HOW TO KEEP HIS MOUTH SHUT.
!
YOU'RE GREED?
YEAH, THAT'S RIGHT.
DON'T BOTHER, OLD MAN.
YOU CAN'T KILL ME WITH THAT.
SEE YOU AROUND, KID.
H- HEY!
YOU'RE JUST GOING TO LET US GO?
HUH? WHAT DO YOU MEAN?

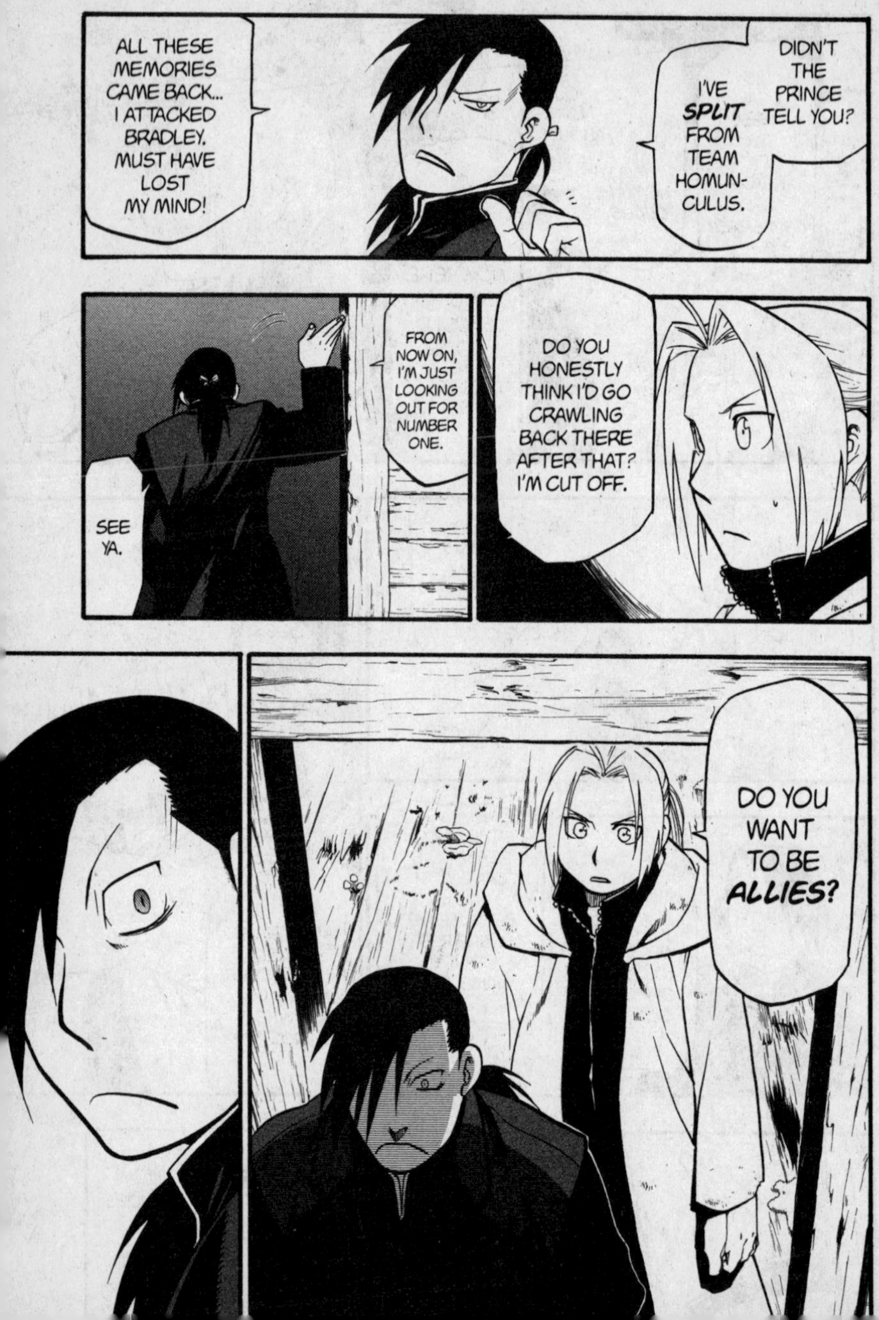
DIDN'T THE PRINCE TELL YOU?
I'VE **SPLIT** FROM TEAM HOMUN-CULUS.
ALL THESE MEMORIES CAME BACK... I ATTACKED BRADLEY. MUST HAVE LOST MY MIND!
DO YOU HONESTLY THINK I'D GO CRAWLING BACK THERE AFTER THAT? I'M CUT OFF.
FROM NOW ON, I'M JUST LOOKING OUT FOR NUMBER ONE.
SEE YA.
DO YOU WANT TO BE **ALLIES?**

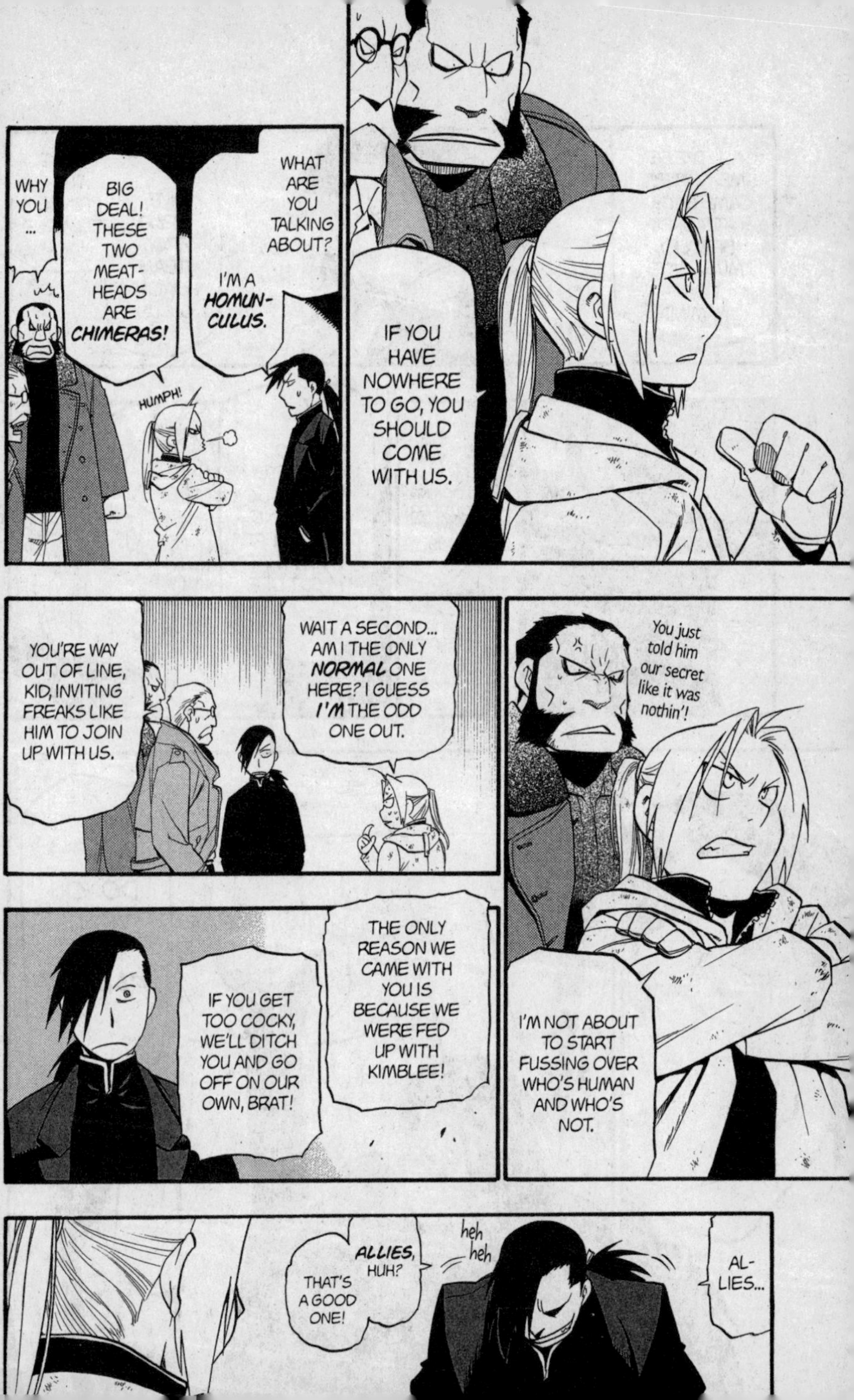
IF YOU HAVE NOWHERE TO GO, YOU SHOULD COME WITH US.
WHAT ARE YOU TALKING ABOUT?
I'M A **HOMUNCULUS.**
BIG DEAL! THESE TWO MEATHEADS ARE **CHIMERAS!**
WHY YOU ...
HUMPH!
You just told him our secret like it was nothin'!
I'M NOT ABOUT TO START FUSSING OVER WHO'S HUMAN AND WHO'S NOT.
WAIT A SECOND... AM I THE ONLY **NORMAL** ONE HERE? I GUESS ***I'M*** THE ODD ONE OUT.
YOU'RE WAY OUT OF LINE, KID, INVITING FREAKS LIKE HIM TO JOIN UP WITH US.
THE ONLY REASON WE CAME WITH YOU IS BECAUSE WE WERE FED UP WITH KIMBLEE!
IF YOU GET TOO COCKY, WE'LL DITCH YOU AND GO OFF ON OUR OWN, BRAT!
AL-LIES...
heh heh
ALLIES, HUH?
THAT'S A GOOD ONE!

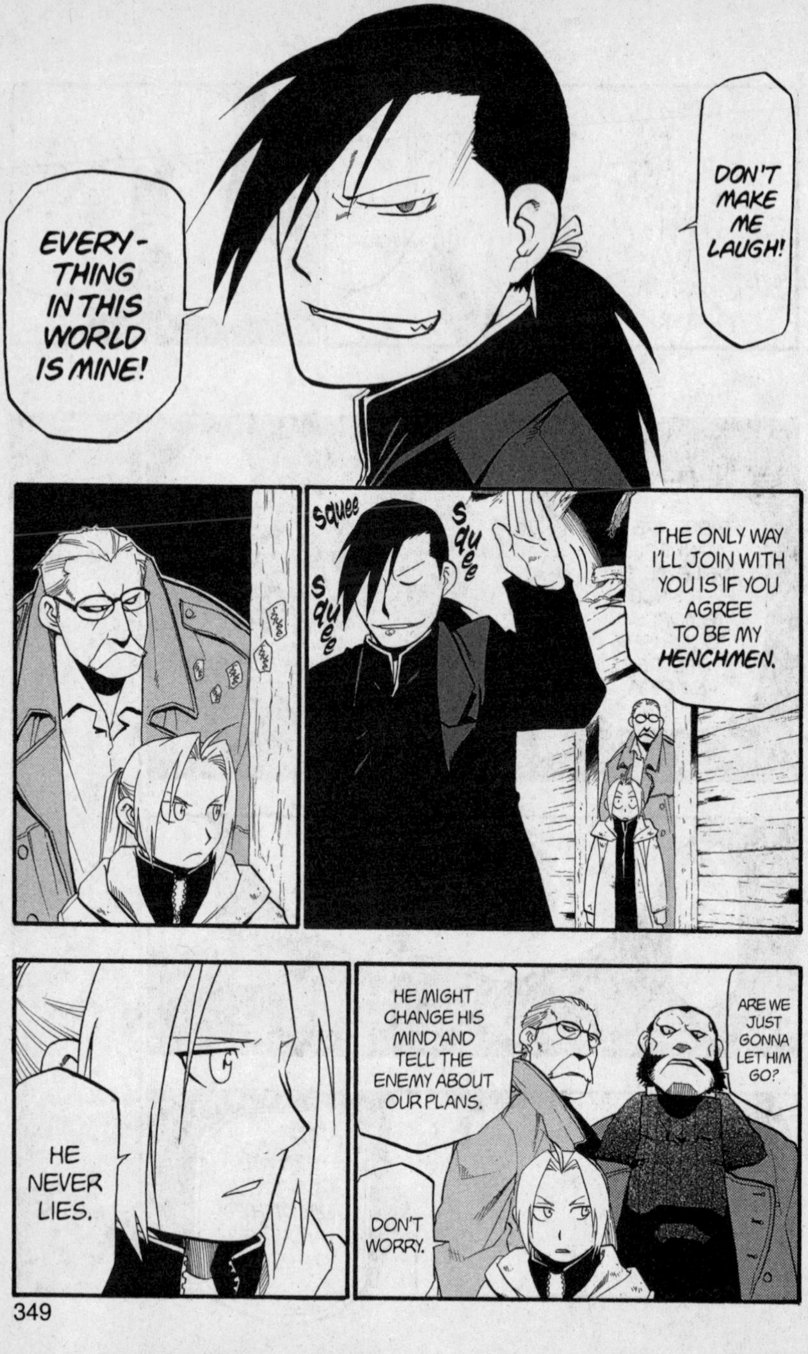
DON'T MAKE ME LAUGH!
EVERY-THING IN THIS WORLD IS MINE!
THE ONLY WAY I'LL JOIN WITH YOU IS IF YOU AGREE TO BE MY **HENCHMEN.**
squee
squee
squee
ARE WE JUST GONNA LET HIM GO?
HE MIGHT CHANGE HIS MIND AND TELL THE ENEMY ABOUT OUR PLANS.
DON'T WORRY.
HE NEVER LIES.

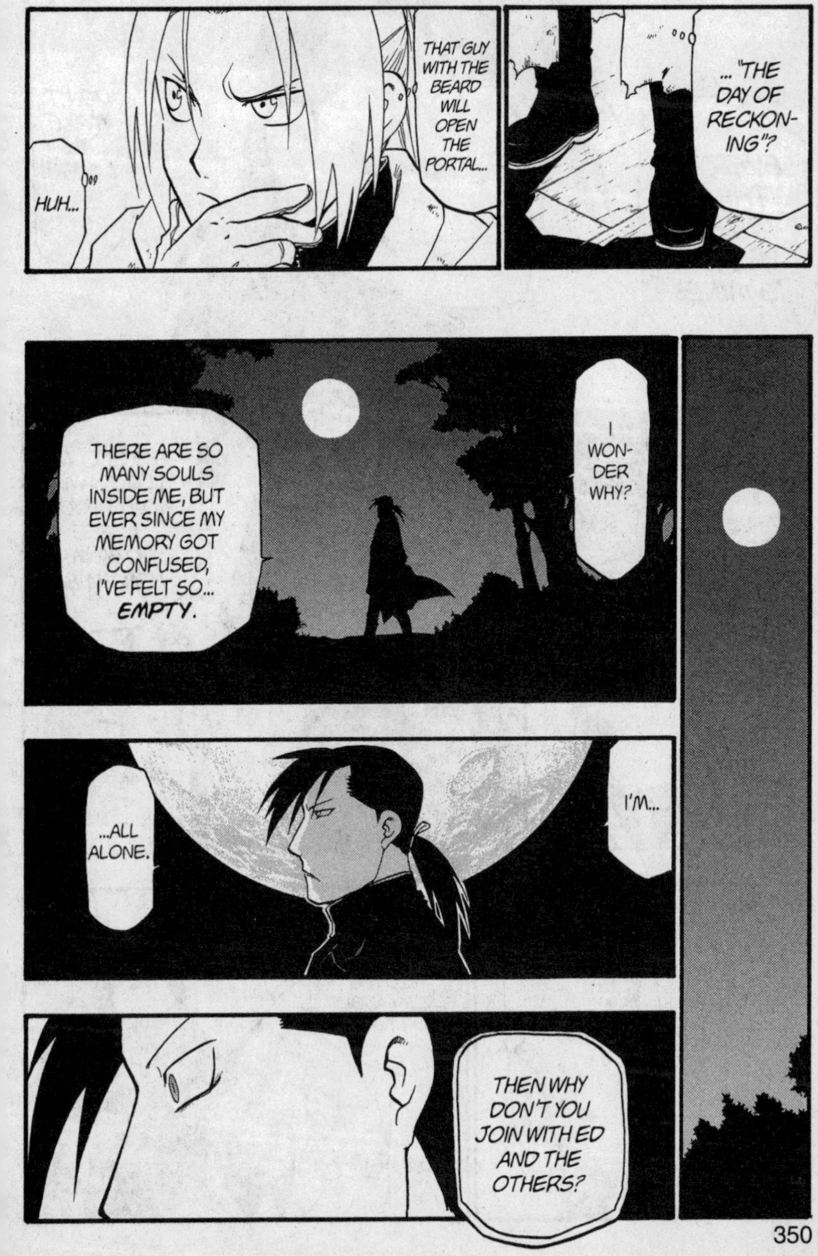
..."THE DAY OF RECKON-ING"?
THAT GUY WITH THE BEARD WILL OPEN THE PORTAL...
HUH...
I WON-DER WHY?
THERE ARE SO MANY SOULS INSIDE ME, BUT EVER SINCE MY MEMORY GOT CONFUSED, I'VE FELT SO... **EMPTY**.
I'M...
...ALL ALONE.
THEN WHY DON'T YOU JOIN WITH ED AND THE OTHERS?

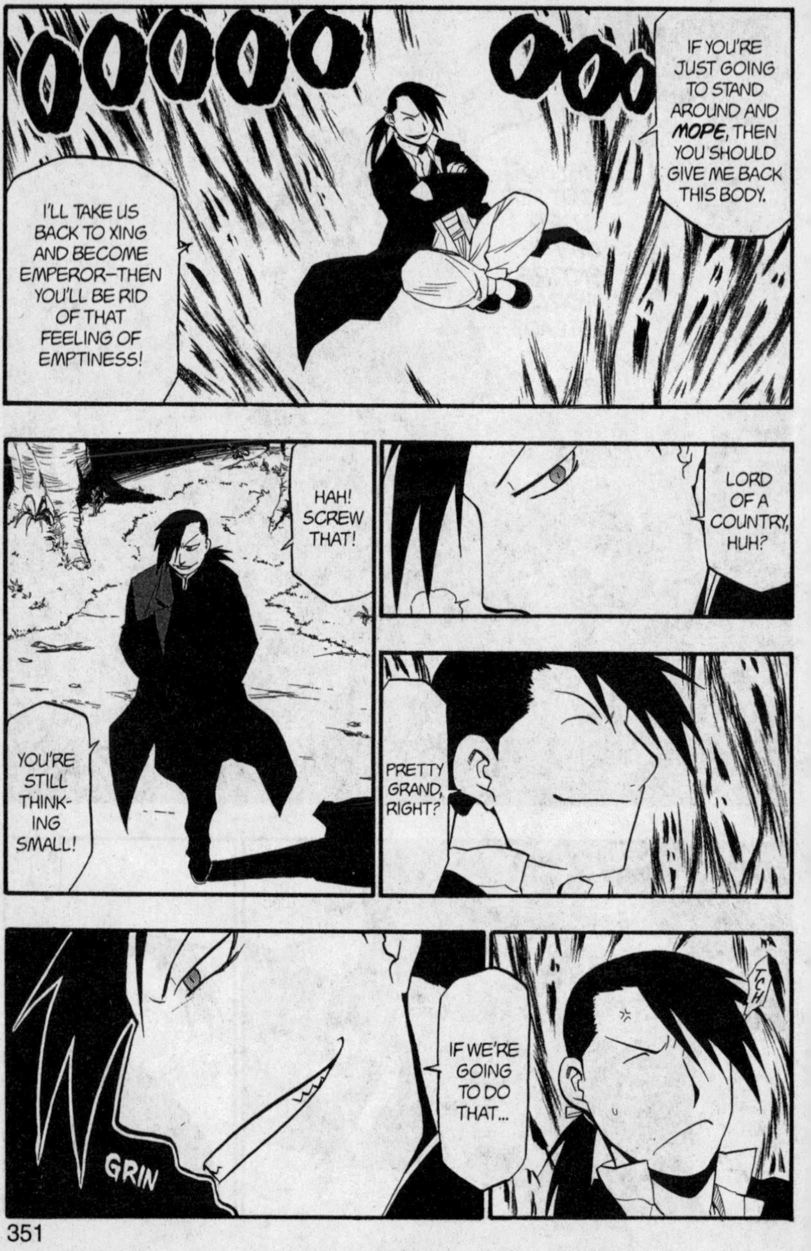

IF YOU'RE JUST GOING TO STAND AROUND AND MOPE, THEN YOU SHOULD GIVE ME BACK THIS BODY.
I'LL TAKE US BACK TO XING AND BECOME EMPEROR—THEN YOU'LL BE RID OF THAT FEELING OF EMPTINESS!
LORD OF A COUNTRY, HUH?
PRETTY GRAND, RIGHT?
HAH! SCREW THAT!
YOU'RE STILL THINKING SMALL!
TCH
IF WE'RE GOING TO DO THAT...
GRIN

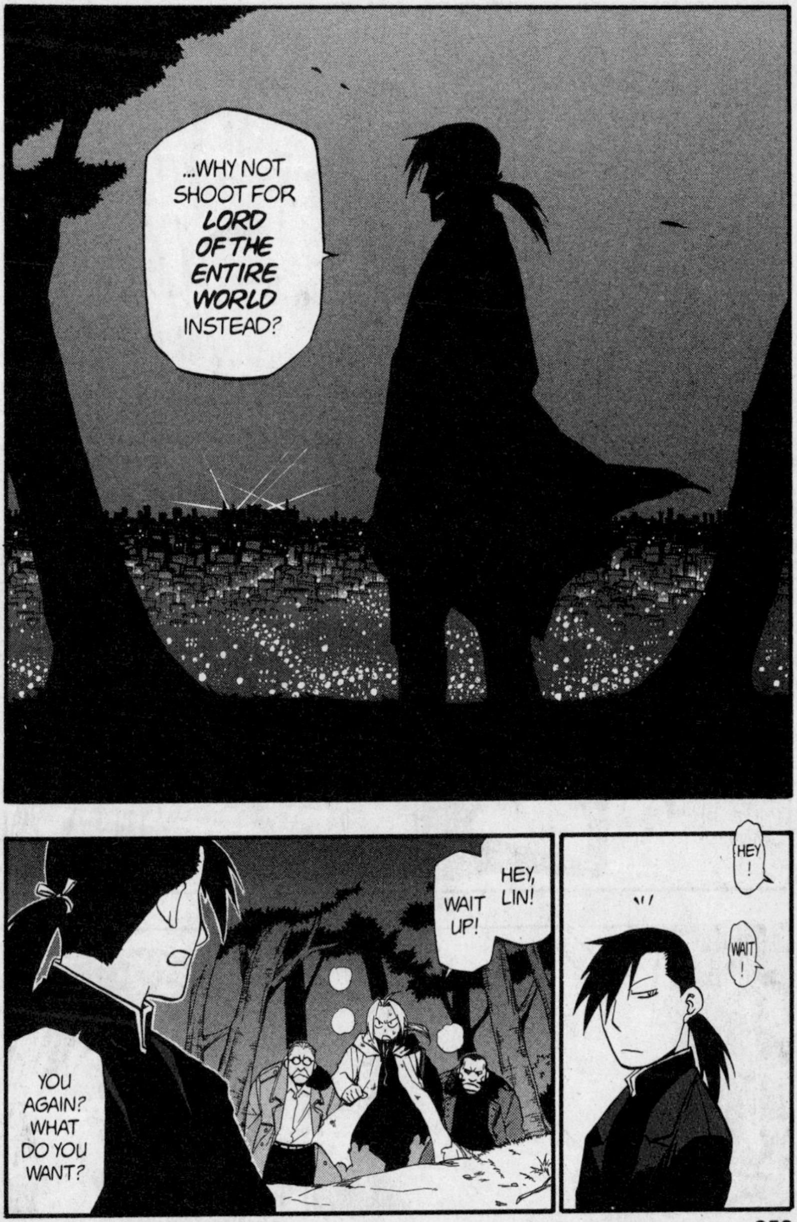
...WHY NOT SHOOT FOR LORD OF THE ENTIRE WORLD INSTEAD?
HEY!
WAIT!
HEY, LIN!
WAIT UP!
YOU AGAIN? WHAT DO YOU WANT?

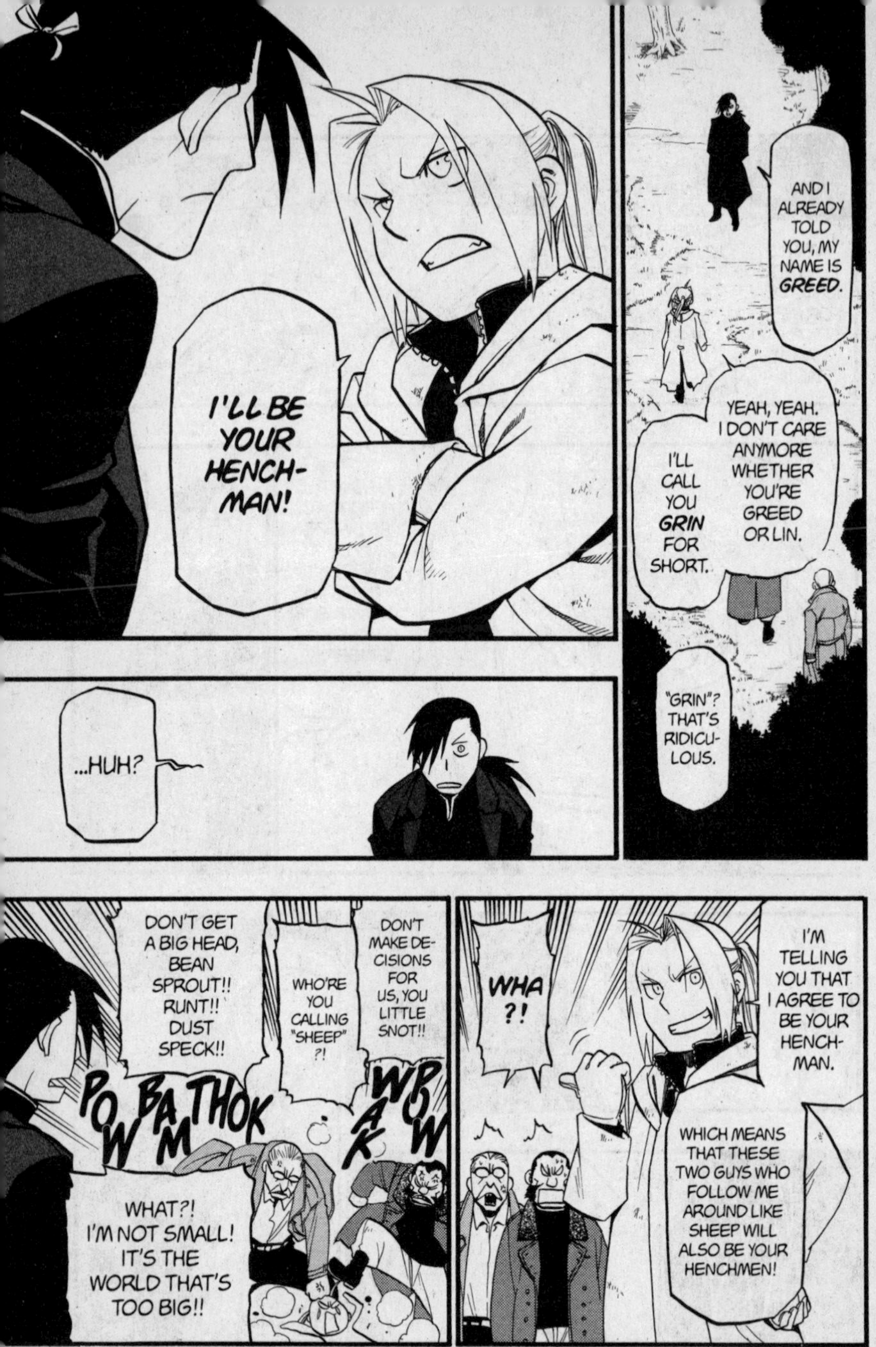
AND I ALREADY TOLD YOU, MY NAME IS GREED.
YEAH, YEAH. I DON'T CARE ANYMORE WHETHER YOU'RE GREED OR LIN.
I'LL CALL YOU GRIN FOR SHORT.
"GRIN"? THAT'S RIDICULOUS.
I'LL BE YOUR HENCHMAN!
...HUH?
I'M TELLING YOU THAT I AGREE TO BE YOUR HENCHMAN.
WHICH MEANS THAT THESE TWO GUYS WHO FOLLOW ME AROUND LIKE SHEEP WILL ALSO BE YOUR HENCHMEN!
WHA?!
DON'T MAKE DECISIONS FOR US, YOU LITTLE SNOT!!
WHO'RE YOU CALLING "SHEEP"?!
DON'T GET A BIG HEAD, BEAN SPROUT!! RUNT!! DUST SPECK!!
WPOW
WAK
THOK
BAM
POW
WHAT?! I'M NOT SMALL! IT'S THE WORLD THAT'S TOO BIG!!

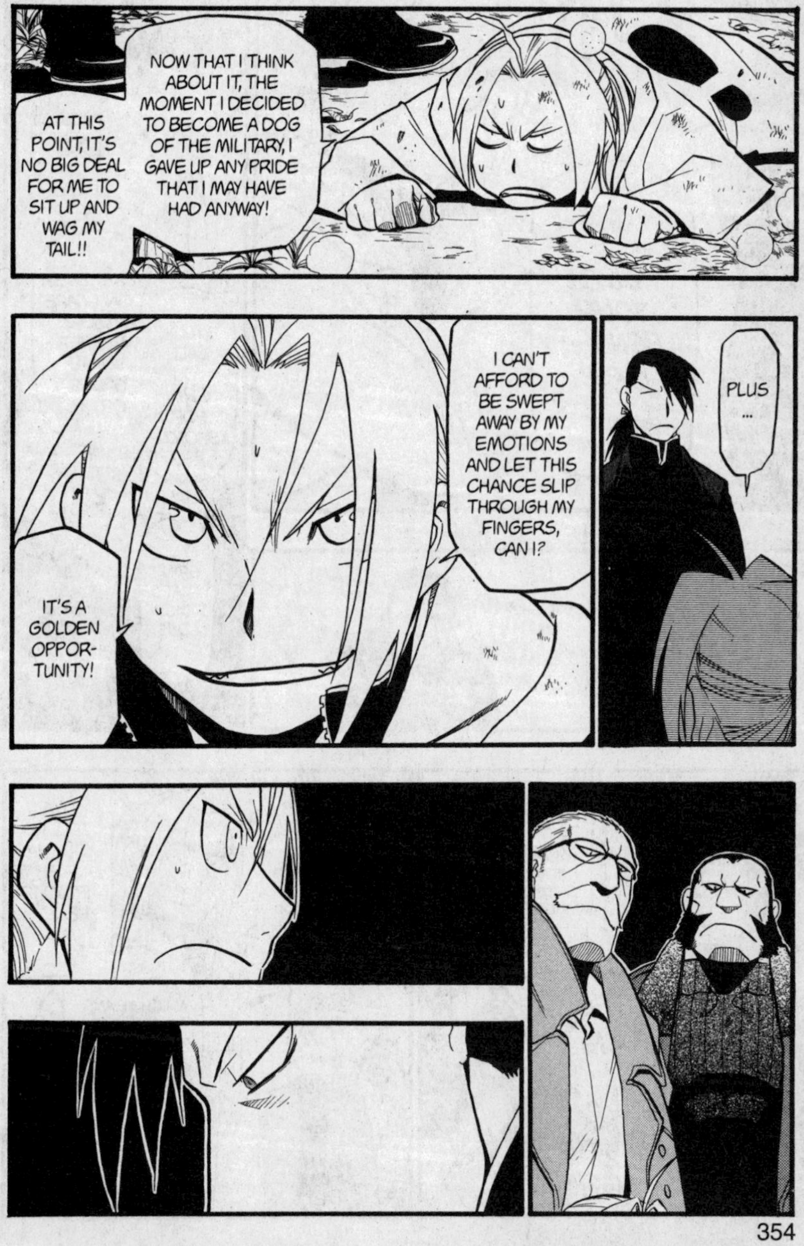
NOW THAT I THINK ABOUT IT, THE MOMENT I DECIDED TO BECOME A DOG OF THE MILITARY, I GAVE UP ANY PRIDE THAT I MAY HAVE HAD ANYWAY!
AT THIS POINT, IT'S NO BIG DEAL FOR ME TO SIT UP AND WAG MY TAIL!!
PLUS ...
I CAN'T AFFORD TO BE SWEPT AWAY BY MY EMOTIONS AND LET THIS CHANCE SLIP THROUGH MY FINGERS, CAN I?
IT'S A GOLDEN OPPOR-TUNITY!

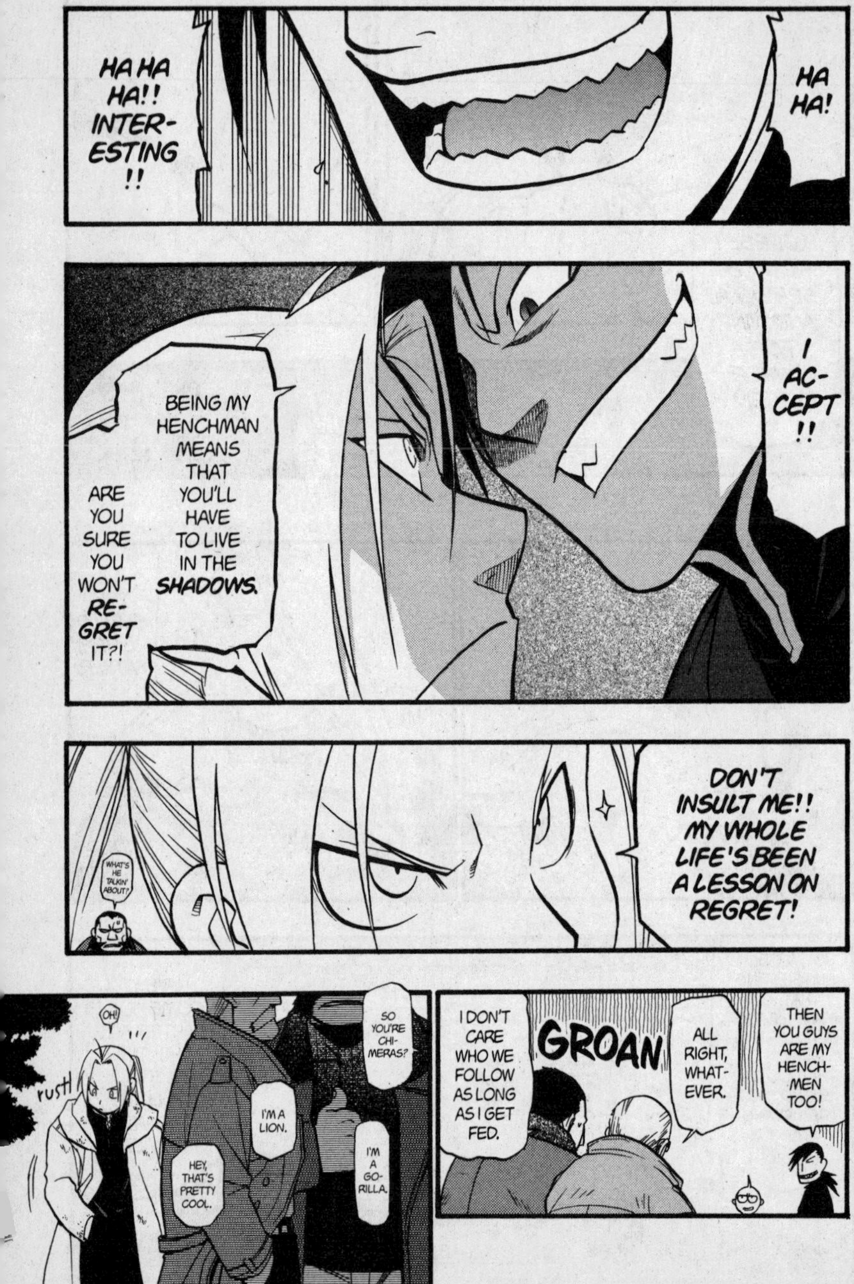
HA HA!
HA HA HA!! INTER-ESTING!!
I AC-CEPT!!
BEING MY HENCHMAN MEANS THAT YOU'LL HAVE TO LIVE IN THE SHADOWS.
ARE YOU SURE YOU WON'T RE-GRET IT?!
DON'T INSULT ME!! MY WHOLE LIFE'S BEEN A LESSON ON REGRET!
WHAT'S HE TALKIN' ABOUT?
THEN YOU GUYS ARE MY HENCH-MEN TOO!
ALL RIGHT, WHAT-EVER.
GROAN
I DON'T CARE WHO WE FOLLOW AS LONG AS I GET FED.
SO YOU'RE CHI-MERAS?
OH!
rustl
I'M A LION.
I'M A GO-RILLA.
HEY, THAT'S PRETTY COOL.

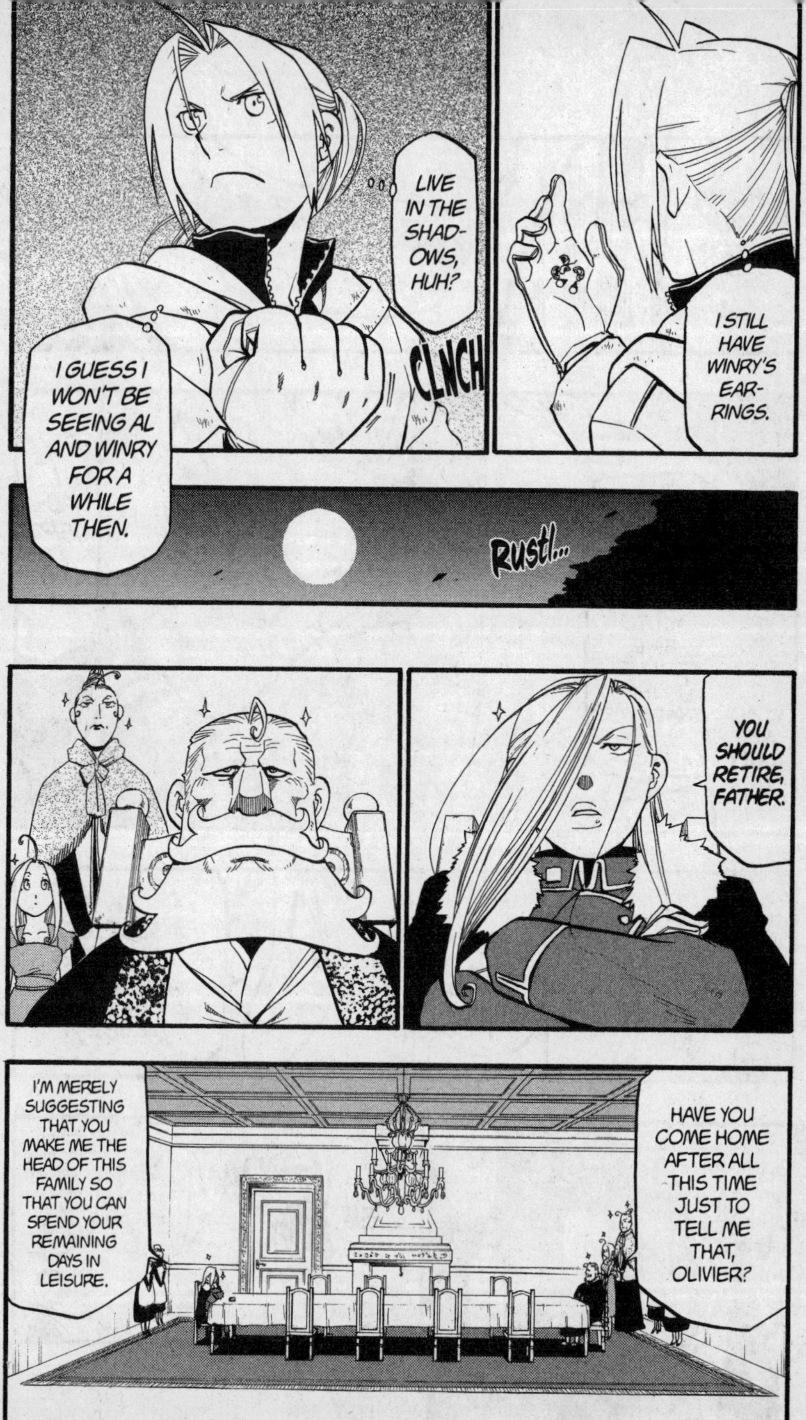
I STILL HAVE WINRY'S EAR-RINGS.
LIVE IN THE SHAD-OWS, HUH?
CLNCH
I GUESS I WON'T BE SEEING AL AND WINRY FOR A WHILE THEN.
Rustl...
YOU SHOULD RETIRE, FATHER.
HAVE YOU COME HOME AFTER ALL THIS TIME JUST TO TELL ME THAT, OLIVIER?
I'M MERELY SUGGESTING THAT YOU MAKE ME THE HEAD OF THIS FAMILY SO THAT YOU CAN SPEND YOUR REMAINING DAYS IN LEISURE.

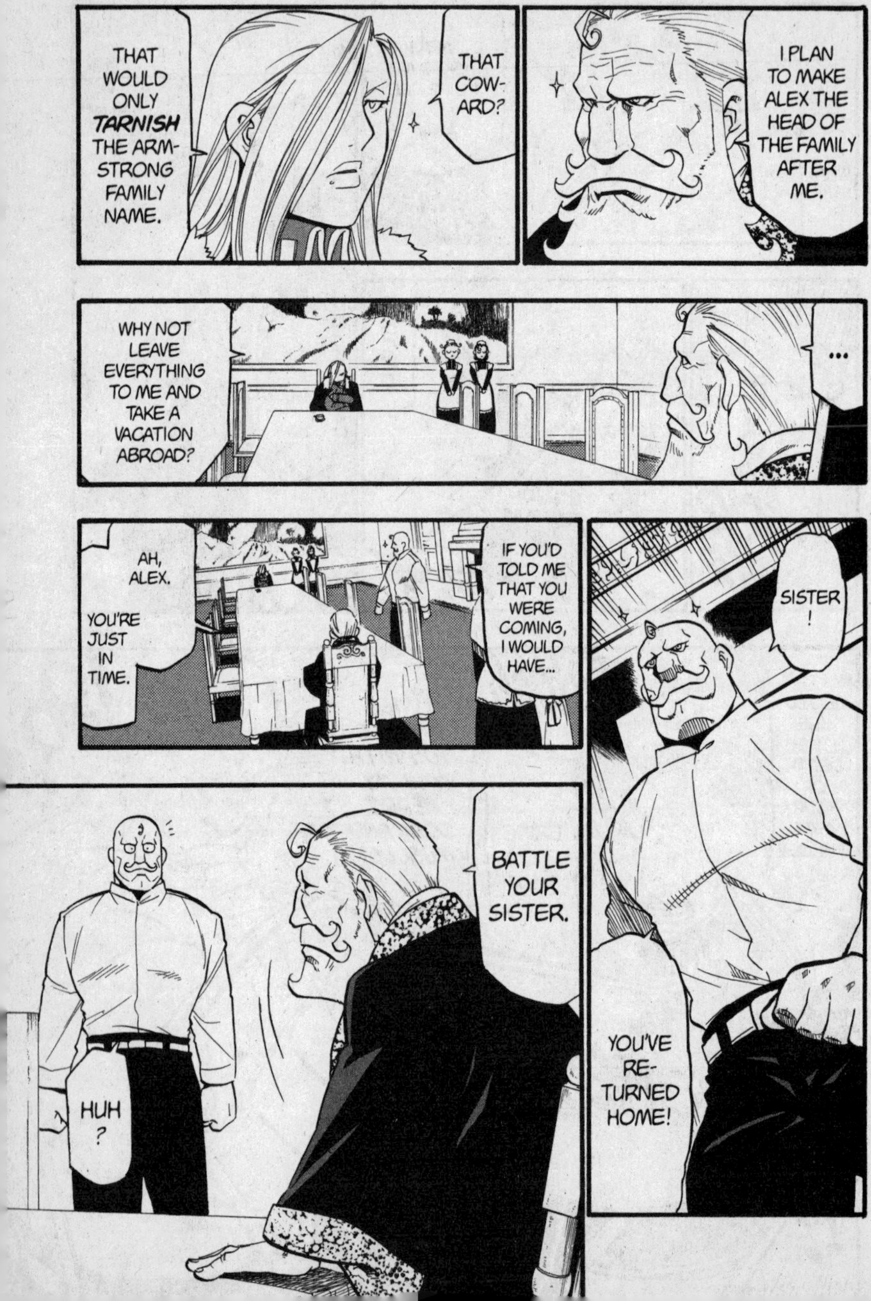
I PLAN TO MAKE ALEX THE HEAD OF THE FAMILY AFTER ME.
THAT COWARD?
THAT WOULD ONLY **TARNISH** THE ARMSTRONG FAMILY NAME.
...
WHY NOT LEAVE EVERYTHING TO ME AND TAKE A VACATION ABROAD?
SISTER!
YOU'VE RETURNED HOME!
IF YOU'D TOLD ME THAT YOU WERE COMING, I WOULD HAVE...
AH, ALEX.
YOU'RE JUST IN TIME.
BATTLE YOUR SISTER.
HUH?

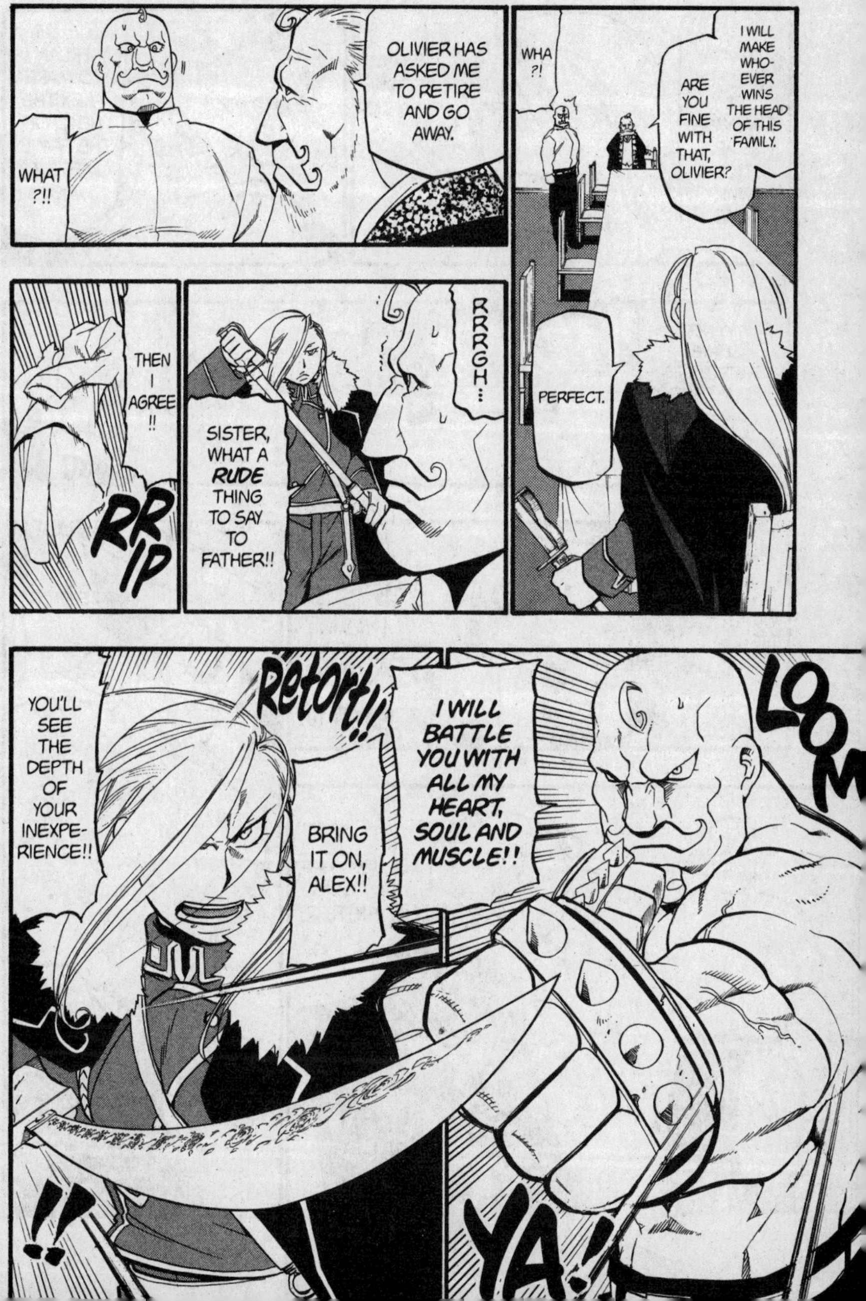
I WILL MAKE WHO-EVER WINS THE HEAD OF THIS FAMILY.
ARE YOU FINE WITH THAT, OLIVIER?
WHA ?!
PERFECT.
OLIVIER HAS ASKED ME TO RETIRE AND GO AWAY.
WHAT ?!!
RRRGH...
SISTER, WHAT A RUDE THING TO SAY TO FATHER!!
THEN I AGREE !!
RRIP
LOOM
I WILL BATTLE YOU WITH ALL MY HEART, SOUL AND MUSCLE!!
YA!
Retort!!
BRING IT ON, ALEX!!
YOU'LL SEE THE DEPTH OF YOUR INEXPE-RIENCE!!
!!

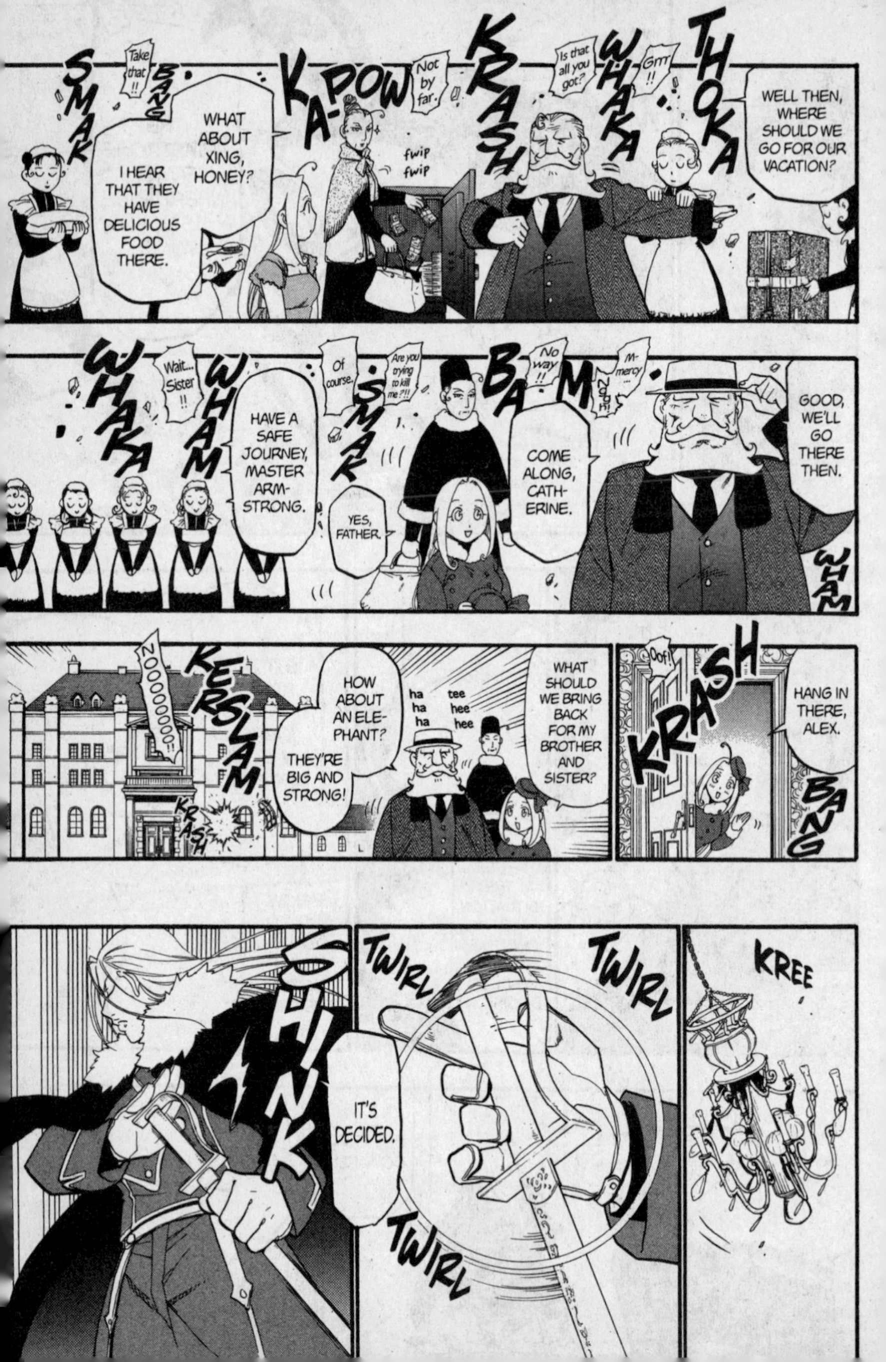
WELL THEN, WHERE SHOULD WE GO FOR OUR VACATION?
THOKA
Grrr!!
WHAKA
Is that all you got?
KRASH
Not by far.
KA-POW
fwip fwip
WHAT ABOUT XING, HONEY?
I HEAR THAT THEY HAVE DELICIOUS FOOD THERE.
BANG
Take that!!
SMAK
GOOD, WE'LL GO THERE THEN.
WHAM
M-mercy...
Nngh!!
No way!!
BAM
COME ALONG, CATHERINE.
YES, FATHER.
Are you trying to kill me?!!
Of course.
SMAK
HAVE A SAFE JOURNEY, MASTER ARMSTRONG.
WHAM
Wait... Sister!!
WHAKA
HANG IN THERE, ALEX.
BANG
KRASH
Oof!
WHAT SHOULD WE BRING BACK FOR MY BROTHER AND SISTER?
tee hee hee
ha ha ha
HOW ABOUT AN ELEPHANT?
THEY'RE BIG AND STRONG!
KERSLAM
NOOOOOOOO!!
KRASH
KREE
TWIRL
TWIRL
TWIRL
SHINK
IT'S DECIDED.

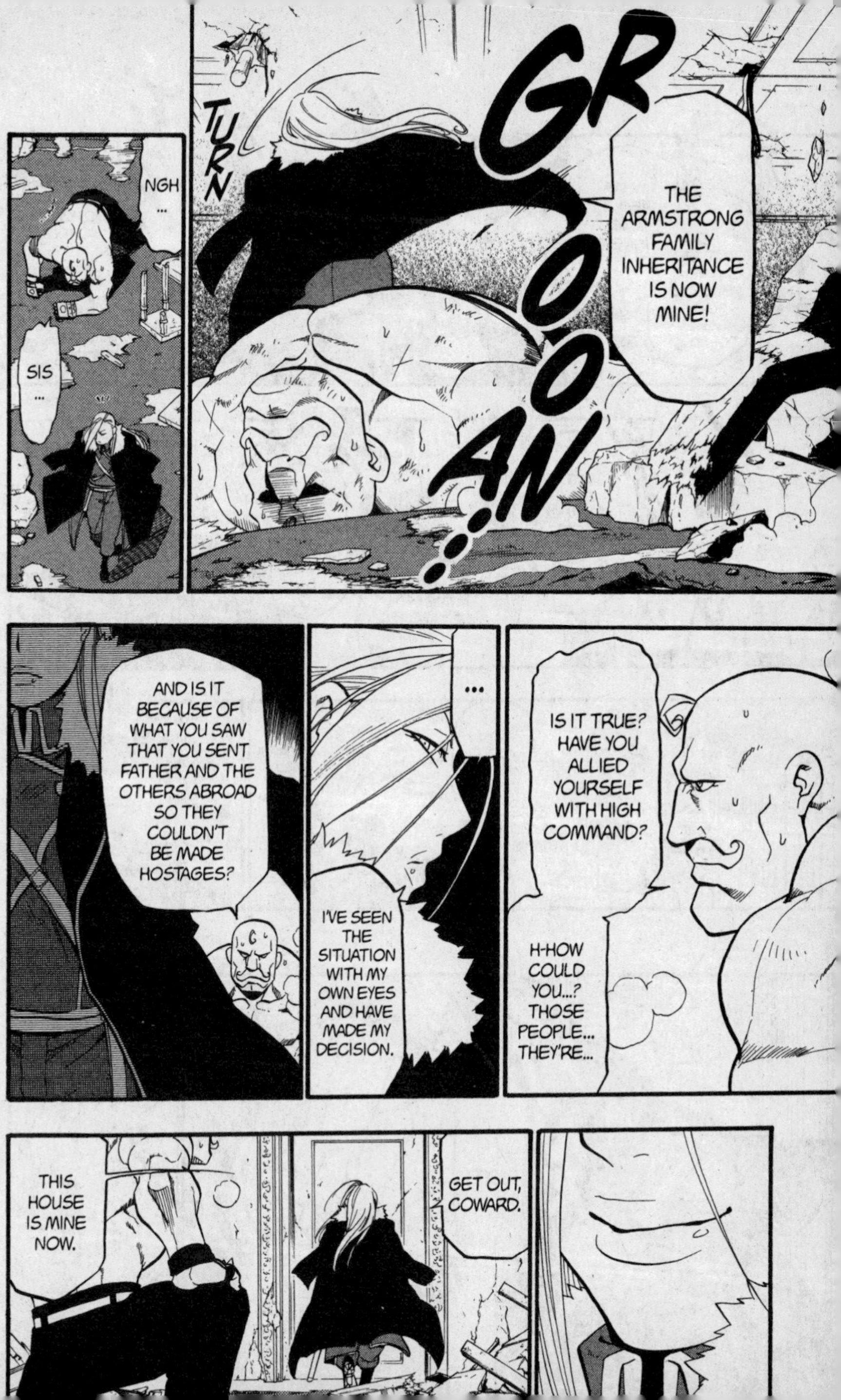
GROOOAN...
THE ARMSTRONG FAMILY INHERITANCE IS NOW MINE!
TURN
NGH...
SIS...
IS IT TRUE? HAVE YOU ALLIED YOURSELF WITH HIGH COMMAND?
H-HOW COULD YOU...? THOSE PEOPLE... THEY'RE...
...
I'VE SEEN THE SITUATION WITH MY OWN EYES AND HAVE MADE MY DECISION.
AND IS IT BECAUSE OF WHAT YOU SAW THAT YOU SENT FATHER AND THE OTHERS ABROAD SO THEY COULDN'T BE MADE HOSTAGES?
GET OUT, COWARD.
THIS HOUSE IS MINE NOW.

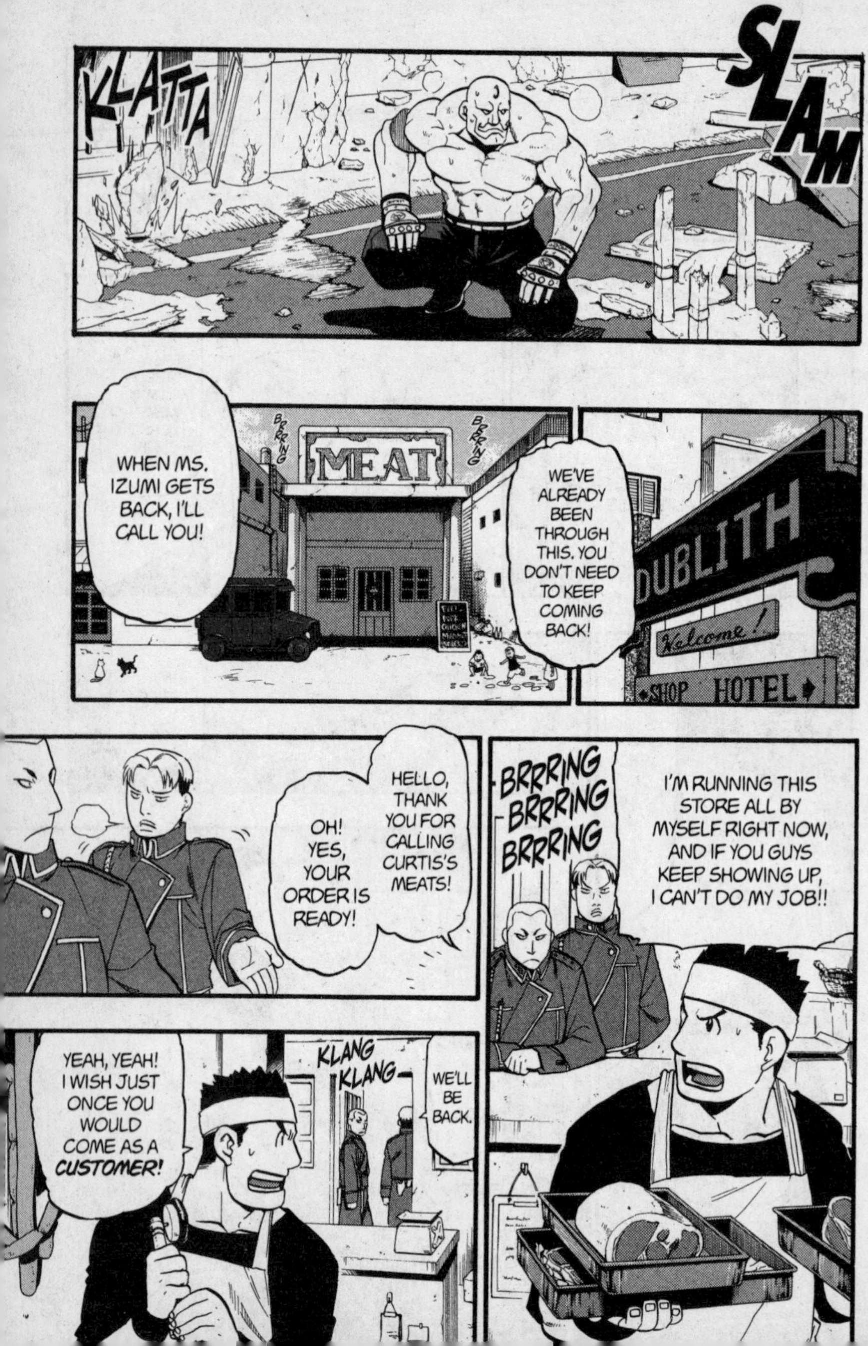
SLAM
KLATTA
DUBLITH
Welcome!
SHOP HOTEL
WE'VE ALREADY BEEN THROUGH THIS. YOU DON'T NEED TO KEEP COMING BACK!
BRRRING
BRRRING
MEAT
WHEN MS. IZUMI GETS BACK, I'LL CALL YOU!
I'M RUNNING THIS STORE ALL BY MYSELF RIGHT NOW, AND IF YOU GUYS KEEP SHOWING UP, I CAN'T DO MY JOB!!
BRRRING BRRRING BRRRING
HELLO, THANK YOU FOR CALLING CURTIS'S MEATS!
OH! YES, YOUR ORDER IS READY!
WE'LL BE BACK.
KLANG KLANG
YEAH, YEAH! I WISH JUST ONCE YOU WOULD COME AS A CUSTOMER!

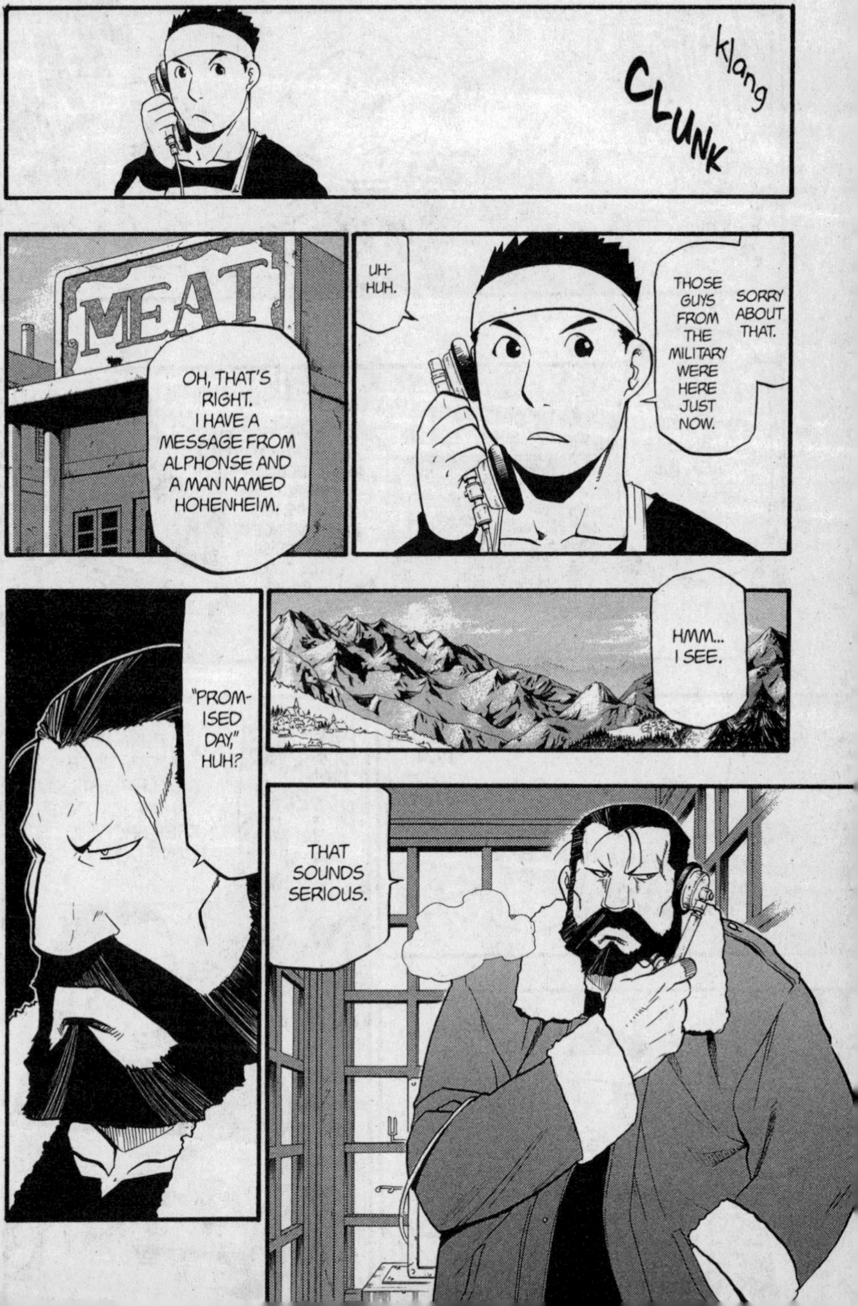
klang
CLUNK
SORRY ABOUT THAT.
THOSE GUYS FROM THE MILITARY WERE HERE JUST NOW.
UH-HUH.
OH, THAT'S RIGHT. I HAVE A MESSAGE FROM ALPHONSE AND A MAN NAMED HOHENHEIM.
HMM... I SEE.
THAT SOUNDS SERIOUS.
"PROMISED DAY," HUH?

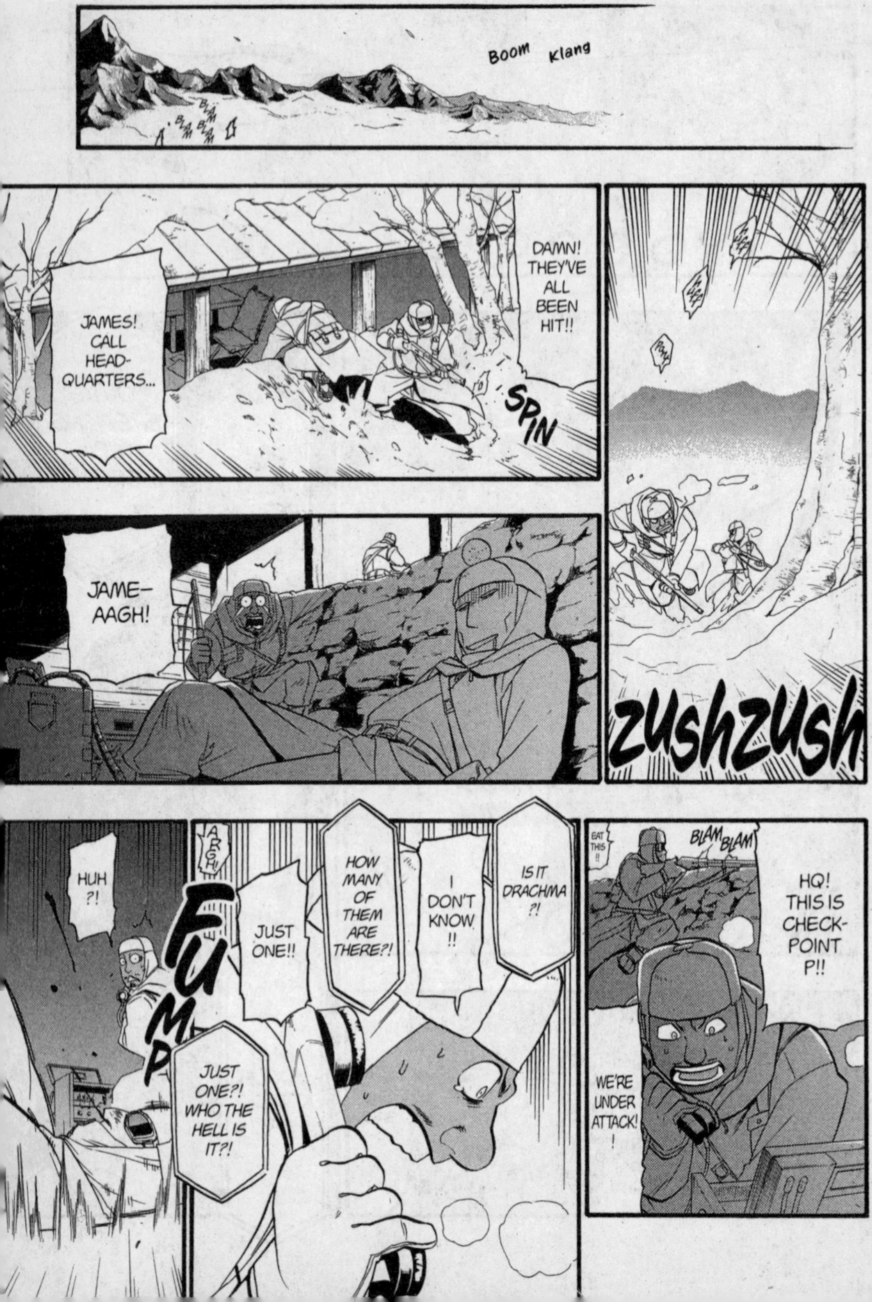
Boom
Klang
BLAM BLAM BLAM BLAM
ZUSHZUSH
DAMN! THEY'VE ALL BEEN HIT!!
JAMES! CALL HEAD-QUARTERS...
SPIN
JAME— AAGH!
EAT THIS!!
BLAM BLAM
HQ! THIS IS CHECK-POINT P!!
WE'RE UNDER ATTACK!!
IS IT DRACHMA?!
I DON'T KNOW!!
HOW MANY OF THEM ARE THERE?!
JUST ONE!!
JUST ONE?! WHO THE HELL IS IT?!
AARGH!!
FUMP
HUH?!

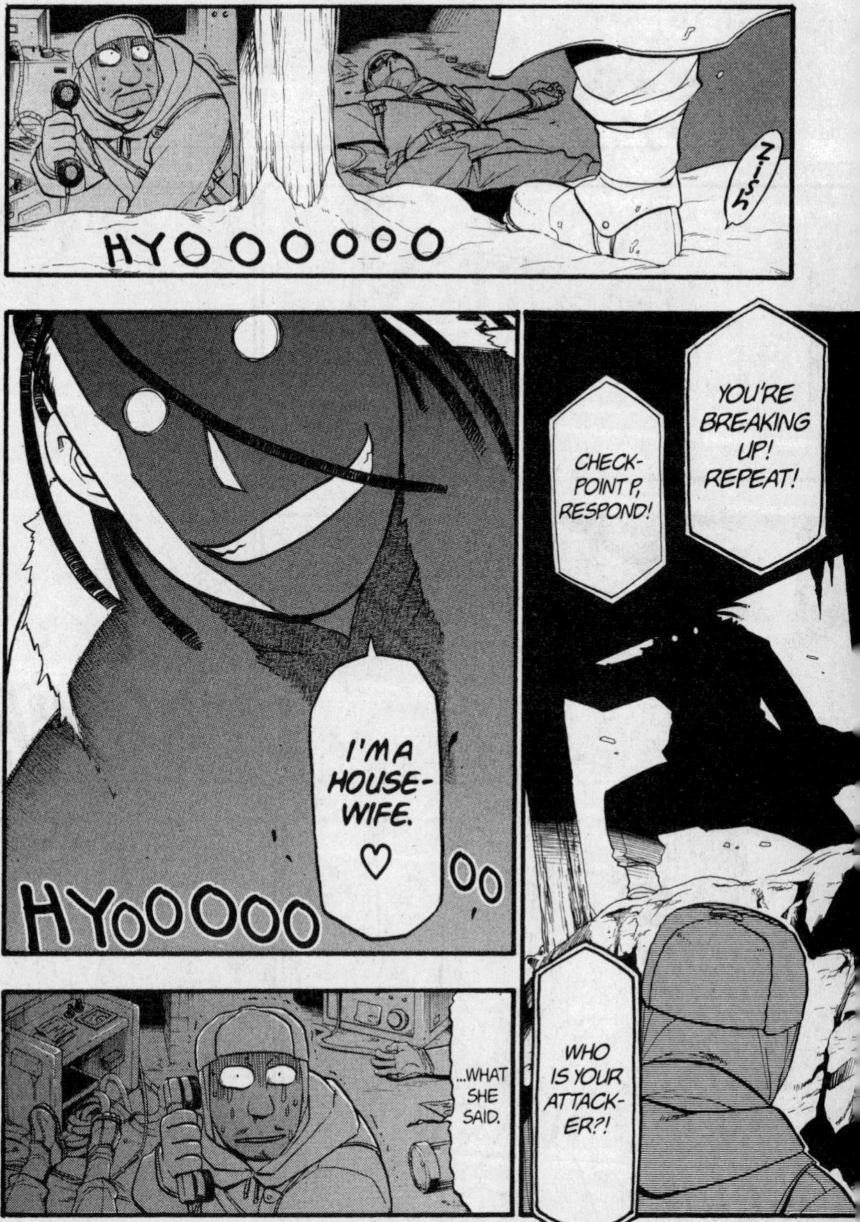
Zish
HYOOOOOO
YOU'RE BREAKING UP! REPEAT!
CHECK-POINT P, RESPOND!
WHO IS YOUR ATTACKER?!
I'M A HOUSE-WIFE. ♡
HYOOOOOOO
...WHAT SHE SAID.

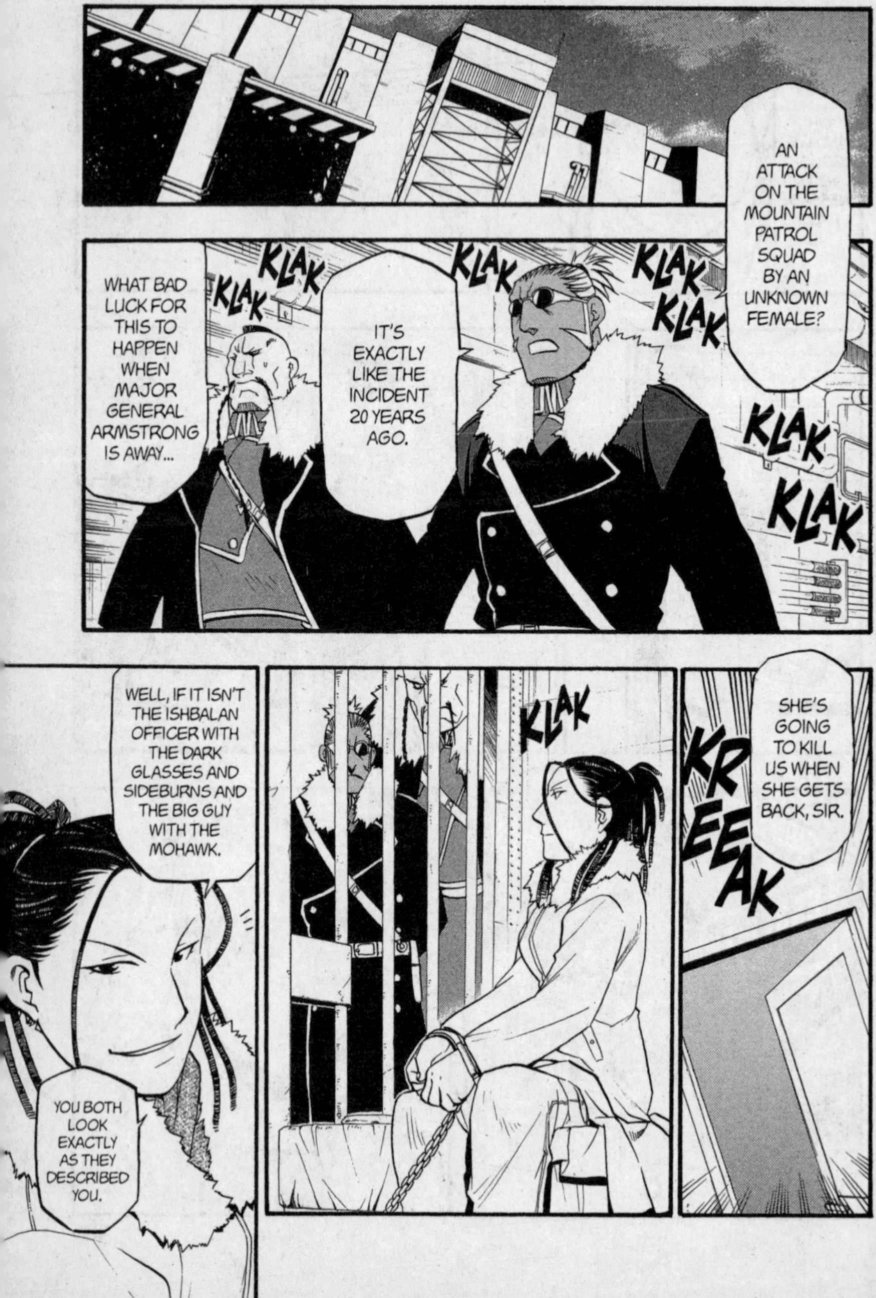
AN ATTACK ON THE MOUNTAIN PATROL SQUAD BY AN UNKNOWN FEMALE?
KLAK KLAK
KLAK
KLAK
KLAK
IT'S EXACTLY LIKE THE INCIDENT 20 YEARS AGO.
KLAK
KLAK
WHAT BAD LUCK FOR THIS TO HAPPEN WHEN MAJOR GENERAL ARMSTRONG IS AWAY...
SHE'S GOING TO KILL US WHEN SHE GETS BACK, SIR.
KREEEAK
KLAK
WELL, IF IT ISN'T THE ISHBALAN OFFICER WITH THE DARK GLASSES AND SIDEBURNS AND THE BIG GUY WITH THE MOHAWK.
YOU BOTH LOOK EXACTLY AS THEY DESCRIBED YOU.

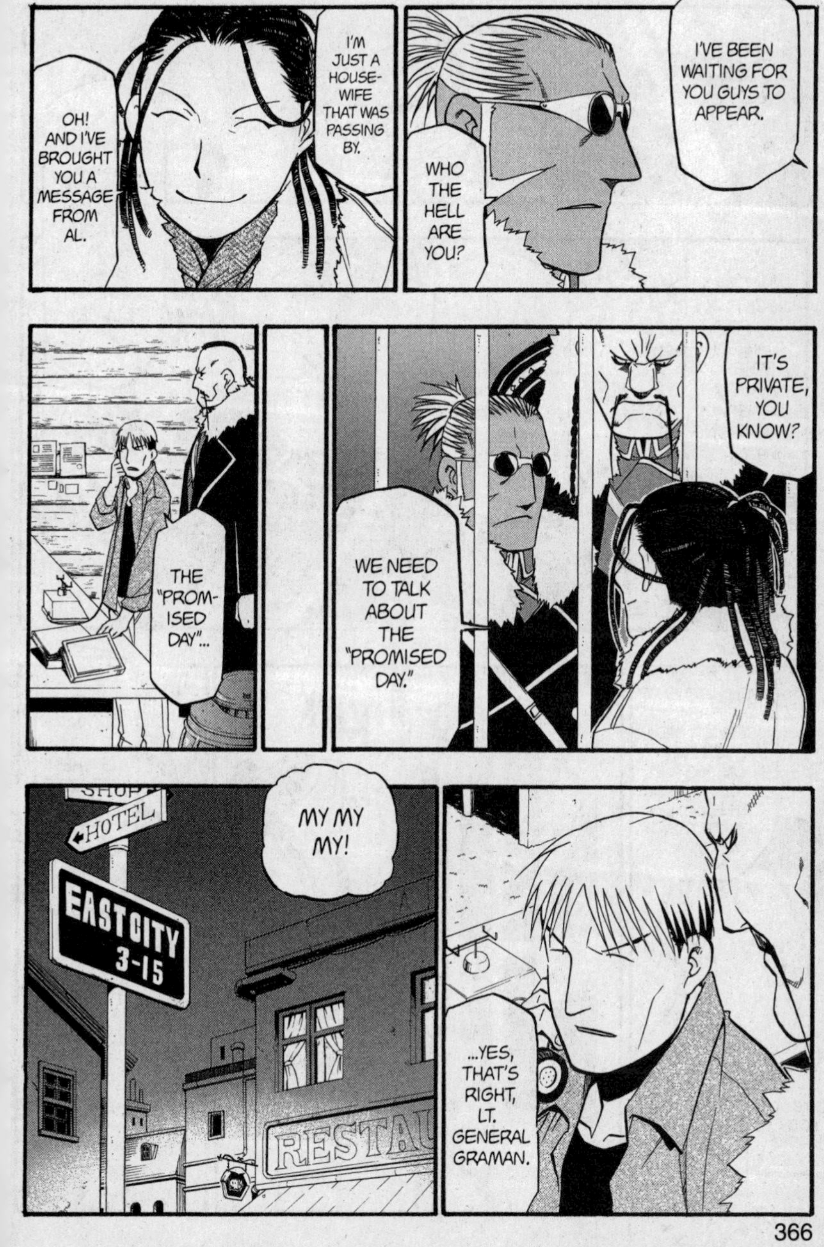
I'VE BEEN WAITING FOR YOU GUYS TO APPEAR.
WHO THE HELL ARE YOU?
I'M JUST A HOUSE-WIFE THAT WAS PASSING BY.
OH! AND I'VE BROUGHT YOU A MESSAGE FROM AL.
IT'S PRIVATE, YOU KNOW?
WE NEED TO TALK ABOUT THE "PROMISED DAY."
THE "PROM-ISED DAY"...
...YES, THAT'S RIGHT, LT. GENERAL GRAMAN.
MY MY MY!
HOTEL
EAST CITY 3-15
RESTAU

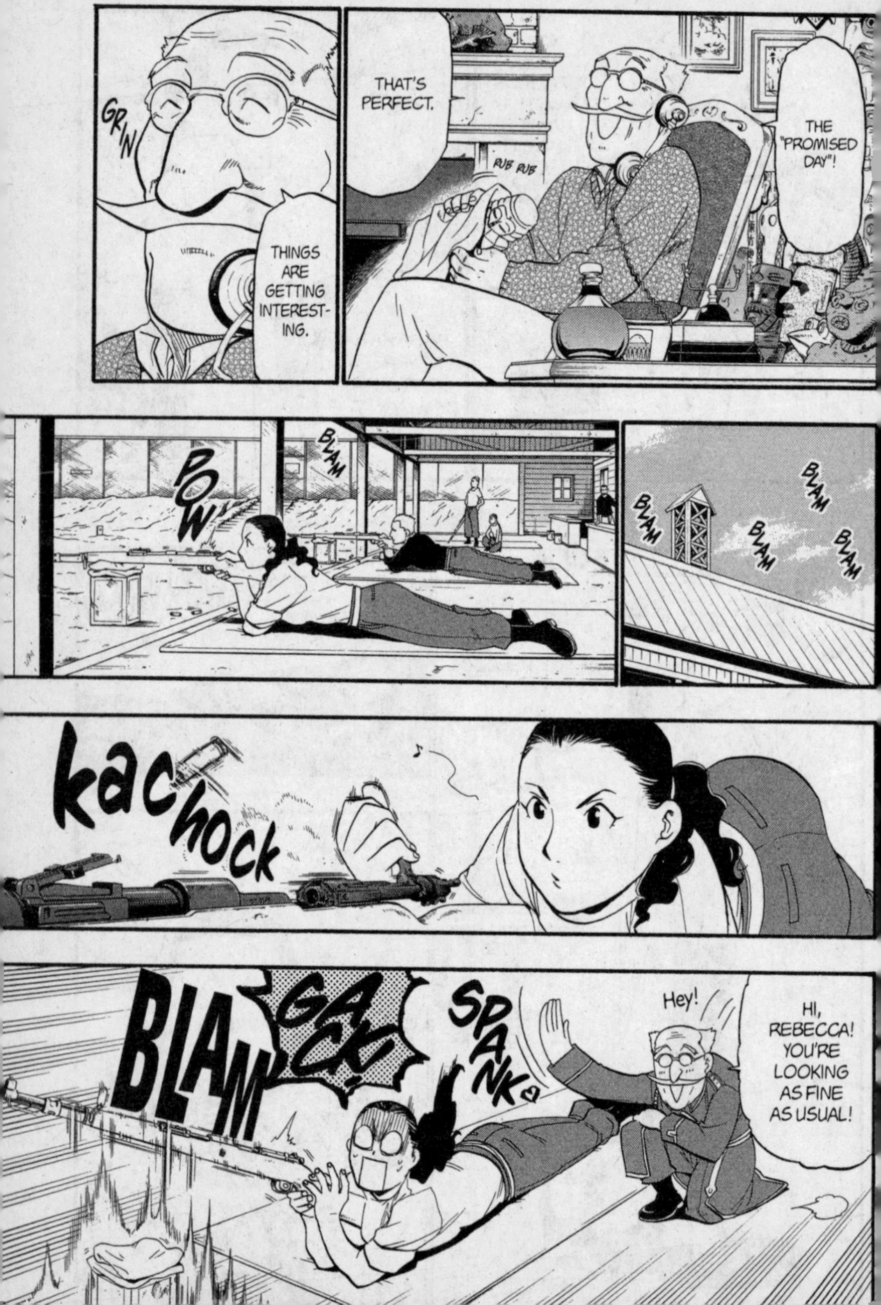
THE "PROMISED DAY"!
THAT'S PERFECT.
RUB RUB
GRIN
THINGS ARE GETTING INTEREST-ING.
BLAM
BLAM
BLAM
BLAM
BLAM
POW
kachock
HI, REBECCA! YOU'RE LOOKING AS FINE AS USUAL!
Hey!
SPANK♡
GACK!
BLAM

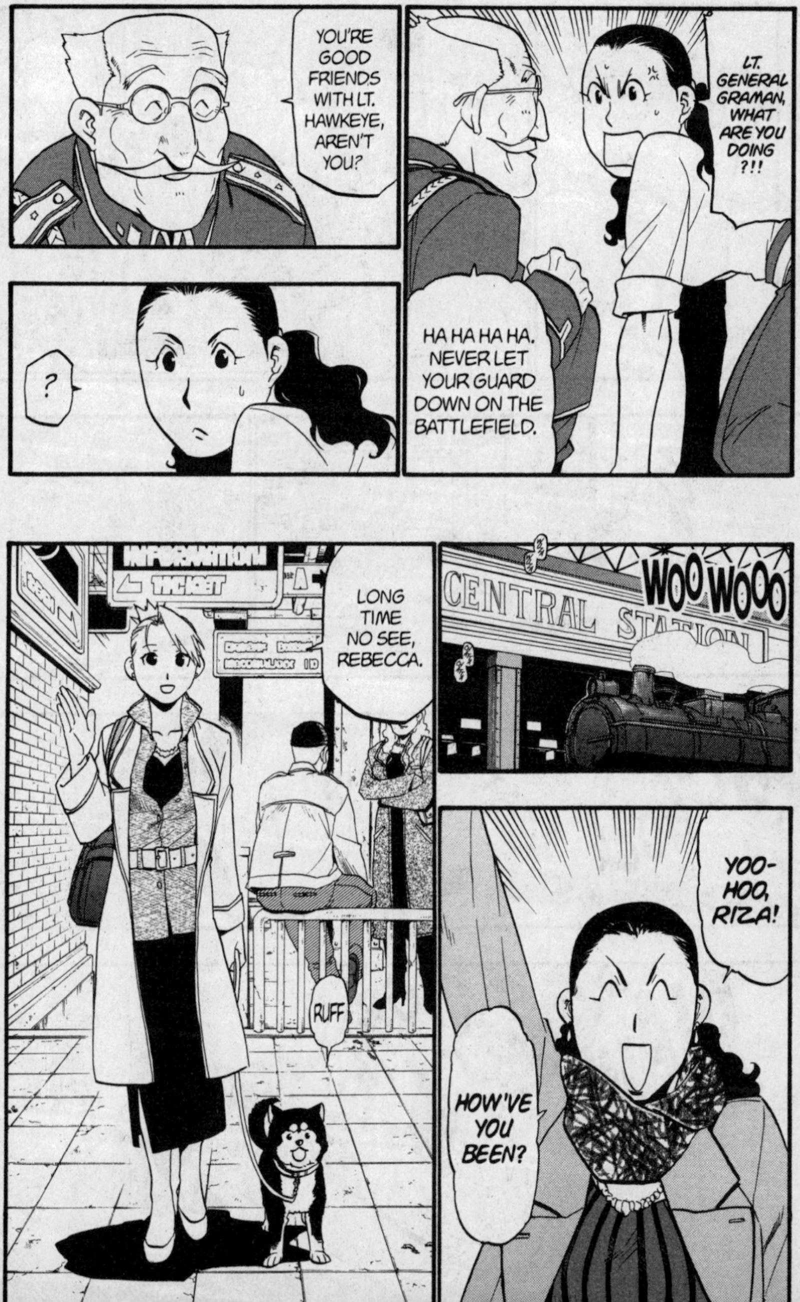
LT. GENERAL GRAMAN, WHAT ARE YOU DOING?!!
HA HA HA HA. NEVER LET YOUR GUARD DOWN ON THE BATTLEFIELD.
YOU'RE GOOD FRIENDS WITH LT. HAWKEYE, AREN'T YOU?
?
WOO WOOO
CENTRAL STATION
YOO-HOO, RIZA!
HOW'VE YOU BEEN?
LONG TIME NO SEE, REBECCA.
RUFF

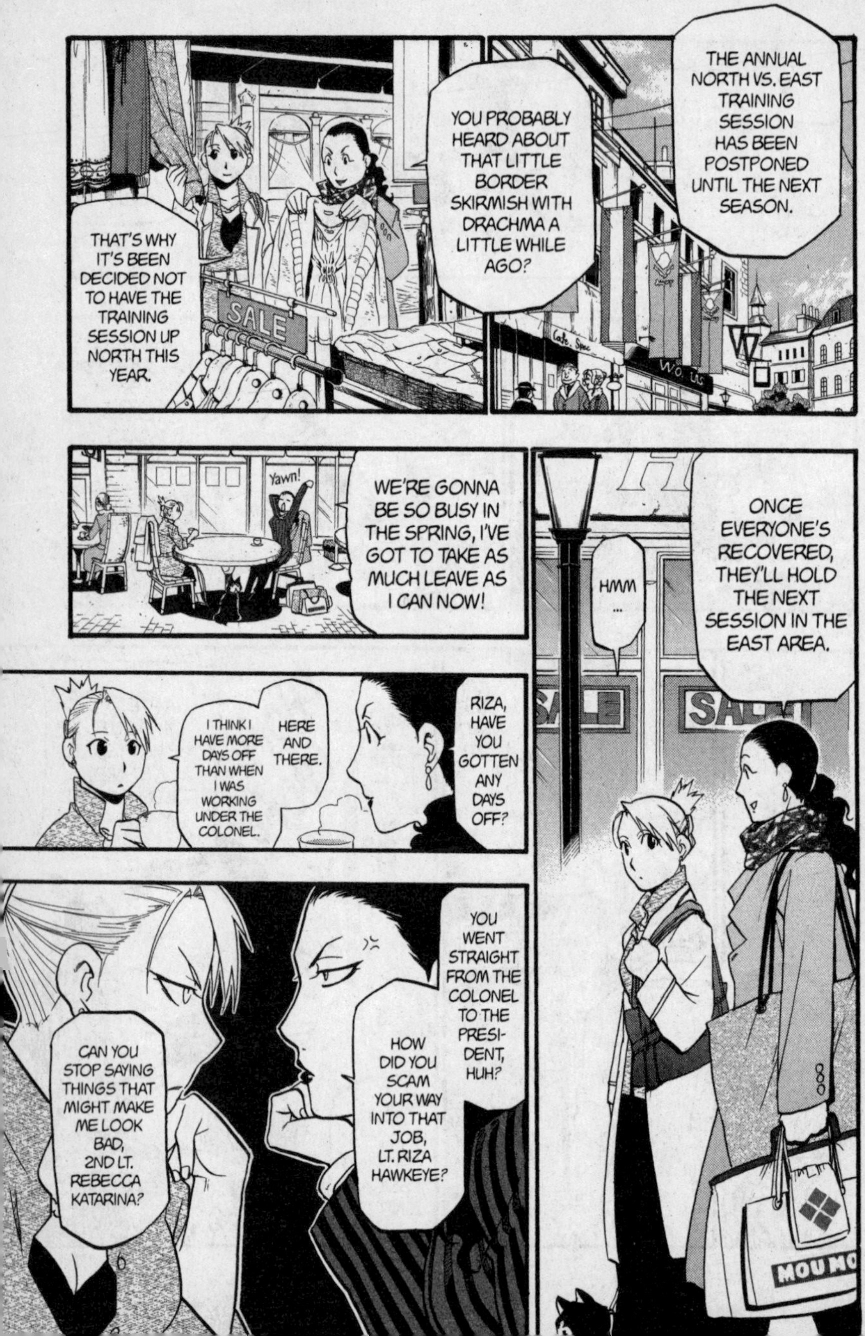
THE ANNUAL NORTH VS. EAST TRAINING SESSION HAS BEEN POSTPONED UNTIL THE NEXT SEASON.
YOU PROBABLY HEARD ABOUT THAT LITTLE BORDER SKIRMISH WITH DRACHMA A LITTLE WHILE AGO?
SALE
THAT'S WHY IT'S BEEN DECIDED NOT TO HAVE THE TRAINING SESSION UP NORTH THIS YEAR.
ONCE EVERYONE'S RECOVERED, THEY'LL HOLD THE NEXT SESSION IN THE EAST AREA.
HMM...
WE'RE GONNA BE SO BUSY IN THE SPRING, I'VE GOT TO TAKE AS MUCH LEAVE AS I CAN NOW!
Yawn!
RIZA, HAVE YOU GOTTEN ANY DAYS OFF?
HERE AND THERE.
I THINK I HAVE MORE DAYS OFF THAN WHEN I WAS WORKING UNDER THE COLONEL.
YOU WENT STRAIGHT FROM THE COLONEL TO THE PRESI-DENT, HUH?
HOW DID YOU SCAM YOUR WAY INTO THAT JOB, LT. RIZA HAWKEYE?
CAN YOU STOP SAYING THINGS THAT MIGHT MAKE ME LOOK BAD, 2ND LT. REBECCA KATARINA?

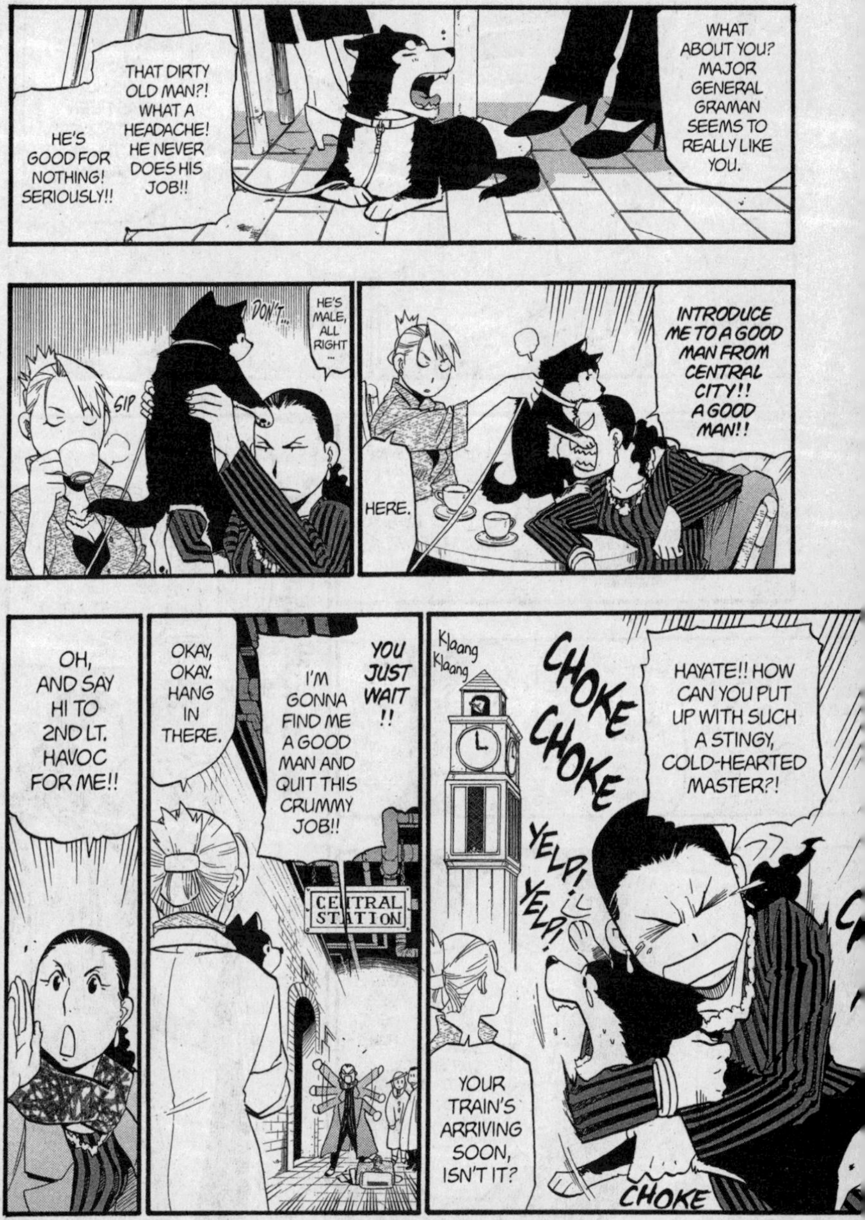
WHAT ABOUT YOU? MAJOR GENERAL GRAMAN SEEMS TO REALLY LIKE YOU.
THAT DIRTY OLD MAN?! WHAT A HEADACHE! HE NEVER DOES HIS JOB!!
HE'S GOOD FOR NOTHING! SERIOUSLY!!
INTRODUCE ME TO A GOOD MAN FROM CENTRAL CITY!! A GOOD MAN!!
HERE.
HE'S MALE, ALL RIGHT ...
DON'T...
SIP
Klaang Klaang
CHOKE CHOKE
HAYATE!! HOW CAN YOU PUT UP WITH SUCH A STINGY, COLD-HEARTED MASTER?!
YELP! YELP!
YOUR TRAIN'S ARRIVING SOON, ISN'T IT?
CHOKE
YOU JUST WAIT!!
I'M GONNA FIND ME A GOOD MAN AND QUIT THIS CRUMMY JOB!!
OKAY, OKAY. HANG IN THERE.
CENTRAL STATION
OH, AND SAY HI TO 2ND LT. HAVOC FOR ME!!

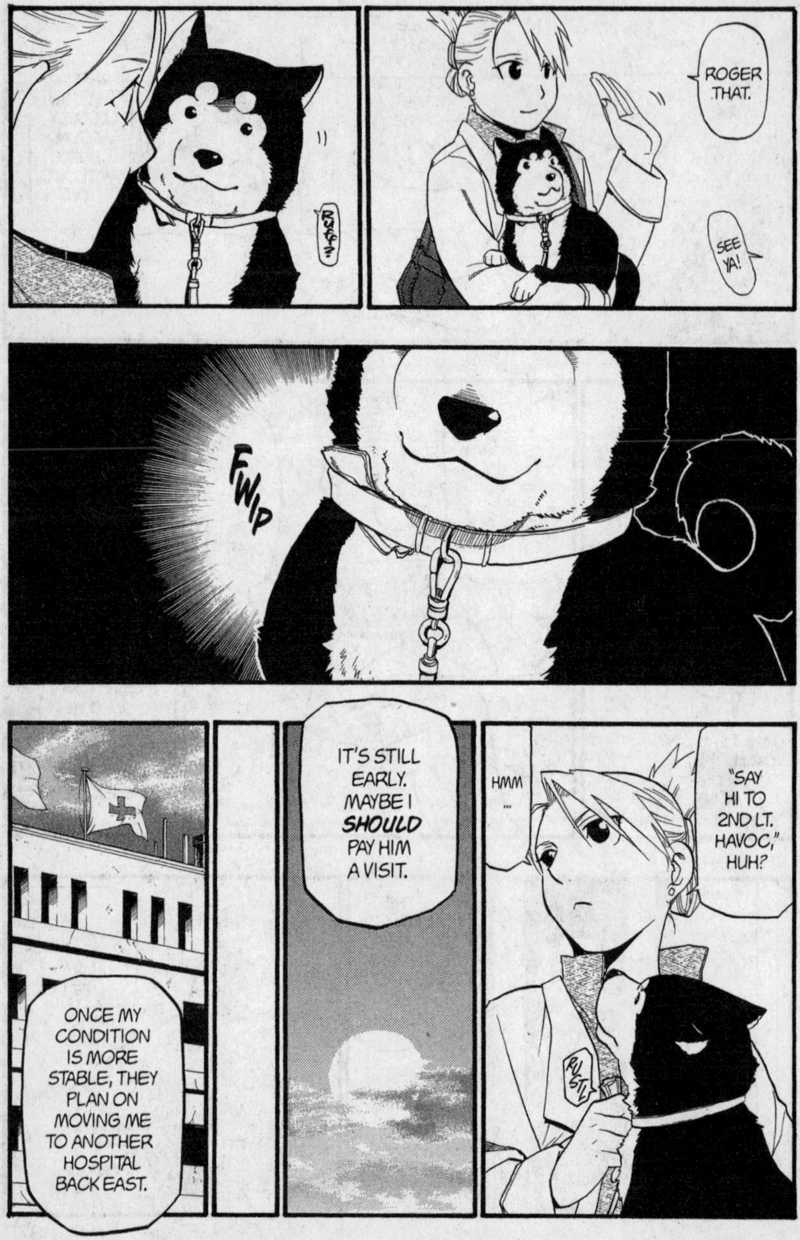
ROGER THAT.
SEE YA!
RUFF?
FWIP
"SAY HI TO 2ND LT. HAVOC," HUH?
HMM ...
RUSTL
IT'S STILL EARLY. MAYBE I **SHOULD** PAY HIM A VISIT.
ONCE MY CONDITION IS MORE STABLE, THEY PLAN ON MOVING ME TO ANOTHER HOSPITAL BACK EAST.

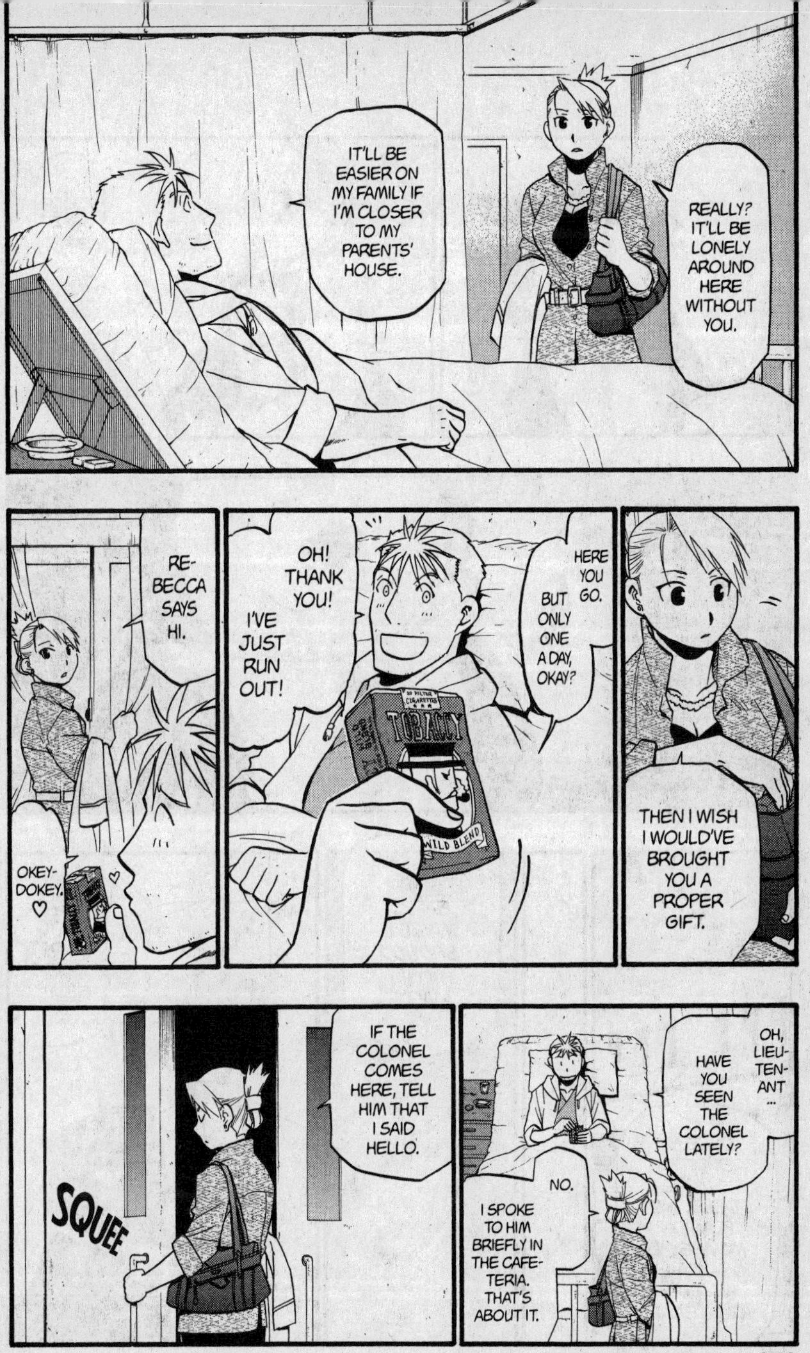
IT'LL BE EASIER ON MY FAMILY IF I'M CLOSER TO MY PARENTS' HOUSE.
REALLY? IT'LL BE LONELY AROUND HERE WITHOUT YOU.
THEN I WISH I WOULD'VE BROUGHT YOU A PROPER GIFT.
HERE YOU GO.
BUT ONLY ONE A DAY, OKAY?
OH! THANK YOU!
I'VE JUST RUN OUT!
20 FILTER CIGARETTES
TOBACCY
WILD BLEND
RE-BECCA SAYS HI.
OKEY-DOKEY. ♡
OH, LIEU-TEN-ANT ...
HAVE YOU SEEN THE COLONEL LATELY?
NO.
I SPOKE TO HIM BRIEFLY IN THE CAFE-TERIA. THAT'S ABOUT IT.
IF THE COLONEL COMES HERE, TELL HIM THAT I SAID HELLO.
SQUEE

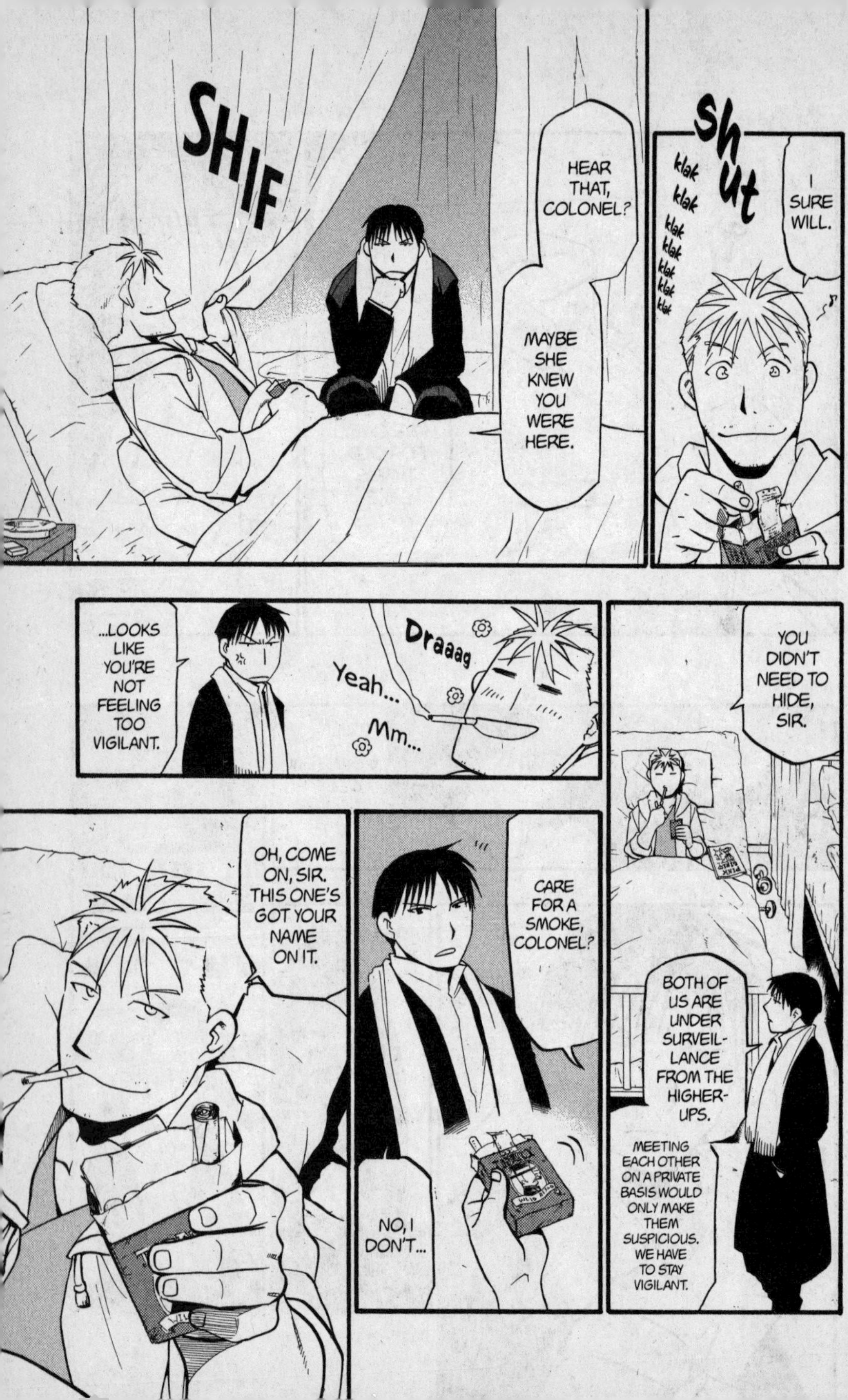
I SURE WILL.
Shut
klak klak klak klak klak klak klak
SHIF
HEAR THAT, COLONEL?
MAYBE SHE KNEW YOU WERE HERE.
YOU DIDN'T NEED TO HIDE, SIR.
BOTH OF US ARE UNDER SURVEIL-LANCE FROM THE HIGHER-UPS.
MEETING EACH OTHER ON A PRIVATE BASIS WOULD ONLY MAKE THEM SUSPICIOUS. WE HAVE TO STAY VIGILANT.
Draaag
Yeah...
Mm...
...LOOKS LIKE YOU'RE NOT FEELING TOO VIGILANT.
CARE FOR A SMOKE, COLONEL?
NO, I DON'T...
OH, COME ON, SIR. THIS ONE'S GOT YOUR NAME ON IT.

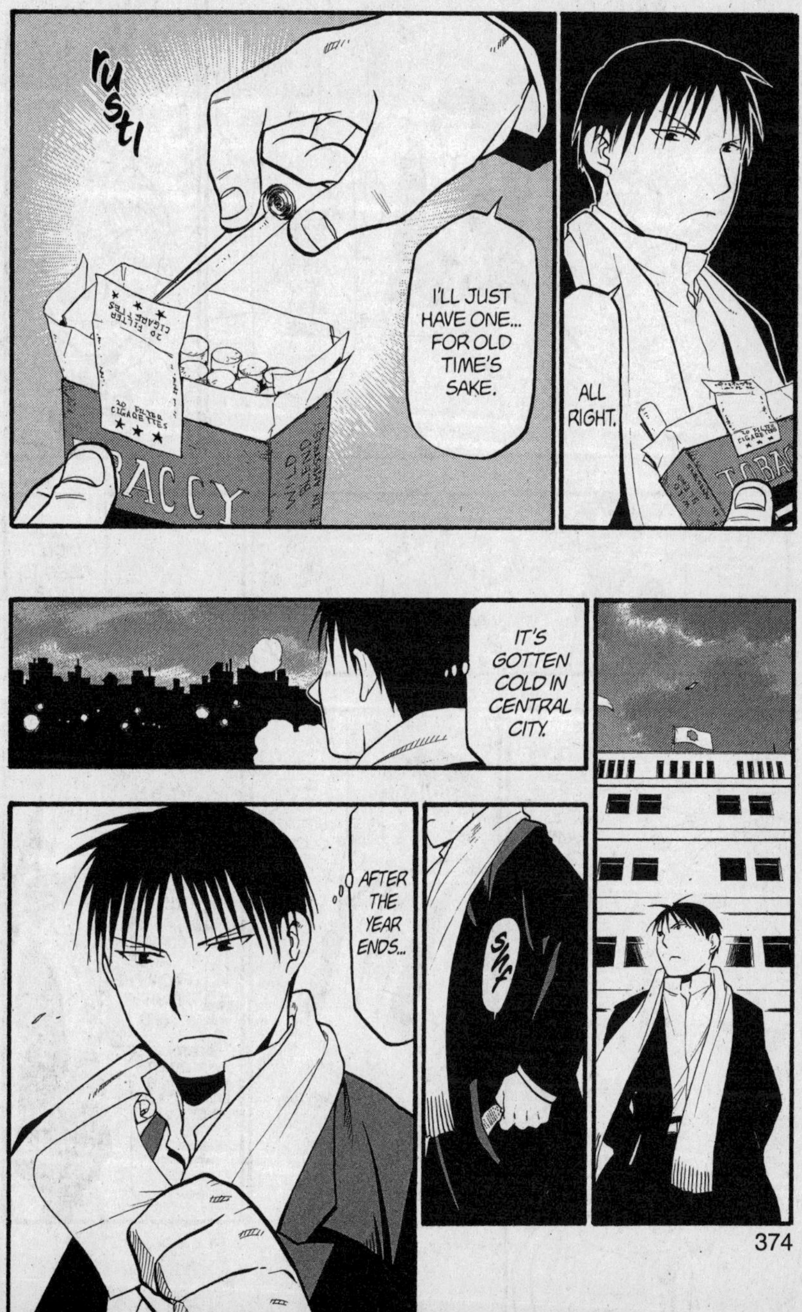
ALL RIGHT.
rustl
20 FILTER CIGARETTES
I'LL JUST HAVE ONE... FOR OLD TIME'S SAKE.
IT'S GOTTEN COLD IN CENTRAL CITY.
sniff
AFTER THE YEAR ENDS...

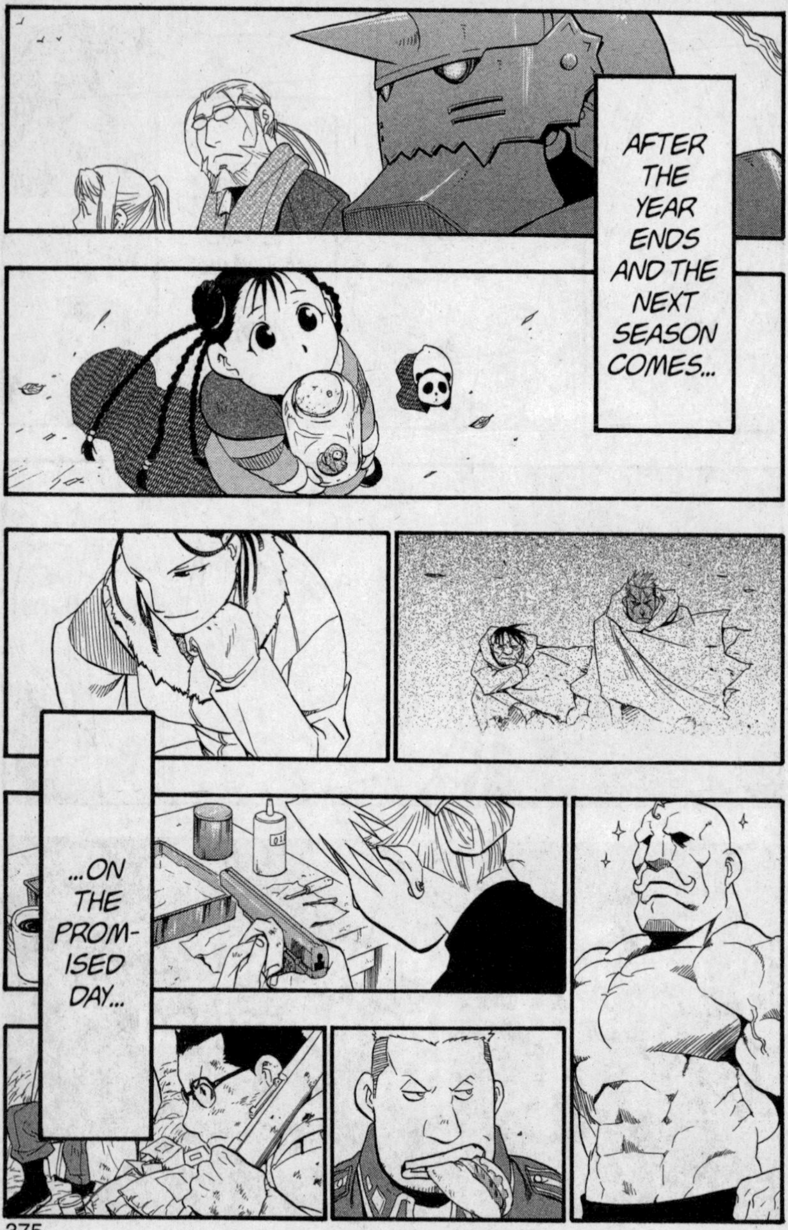
AFTER THE YEAR ENDS AND THE NEXT SEASON COMES...
...ON THE PROM-ISED DAY...

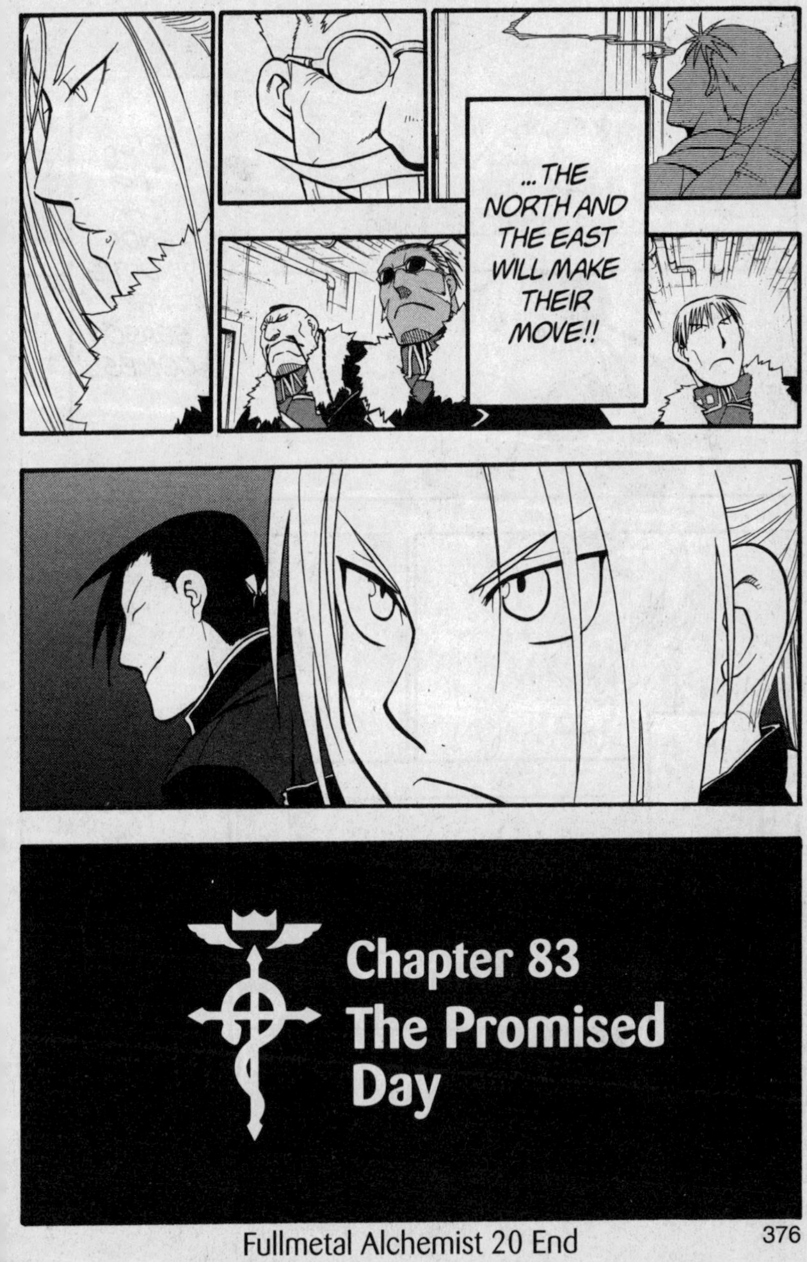
...THE NORTH AND THE EAST WILL MAKE THEIR MOVE!!

Chapter 83
The Promised Day

Fullmetal Alchemist 20 End

What if?

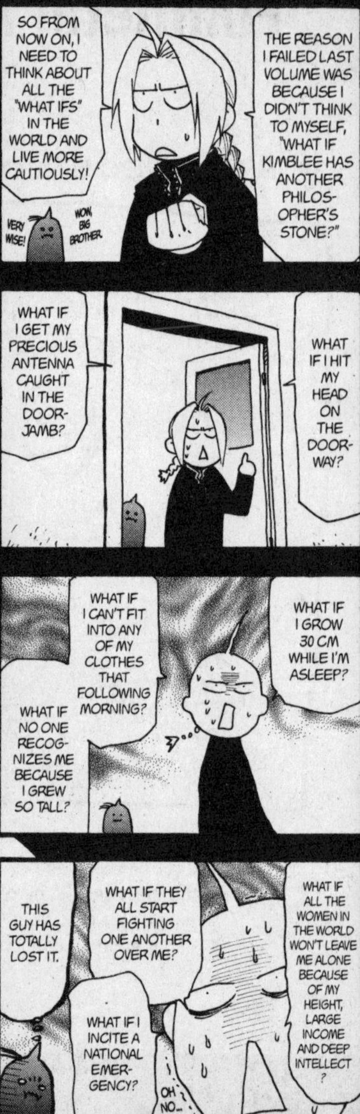
THE REASON I FAILED LAST VOLUME WAS BECAUSE I DIDN'T THINK TO MYSELF, "WHAT IF KIMBLEE HAS ANOTHER PHILOS-OPHER'S STONE?"
SO FROM NOW ON, I NEED TO THINK ABOUT ALL THE "WHAT IFS" IN THE WORLD AND LIVE MORE CAUTIOUSLY!
WOW, BIG BROTHER
VERY WISE!
WHAT IF I HIT MY HEAD ON THE DOOR-WAY?
WHAT IF I GET MY PRECIOUS ANTENNA CAUGHT IN THE DOOR-JAMB?
WHAT IF I GROW 30 CM WHILE I'M ASLEEP?
WHAT IF I CAN'T FIT INTO ANY OF MY CLOTHES THAT FOLLOWING MORNING?
WHAT IF NO ONE RECOGNIZES ME BECAUSE I GREW SO TALL?
WHAT IF ALL THE WOMEN IN THE WORLD WON'T LEAVE ME ALONE BECAUSE OF MY HEIGHT, LARGE INCOME AND DEEP INTELLECT?
WHAT IF THEY ALL START FIGHTING ONE ANOTHER OVER ME?
WHAT IF I INCITE A NATIONAL EMER-GENCY?
THIS GUY HAS TOTALLY LOST IT.
OH NO...

Fullmetal Alchemist 20

Special Thanks

Jun Tohko

Nono

Masashi Mizutani

Coupon

Noriko Tsubota

Haruhi Nakamura

Kazufumi Kaneko

Mitsuri Sakano

Kei Takanamazu

Big bro Yoichi Kamitono

Aiyaball Sensei

Michiko Shishido Sensei

My Editor,
Yuichi Shimomura

AND YOU!!

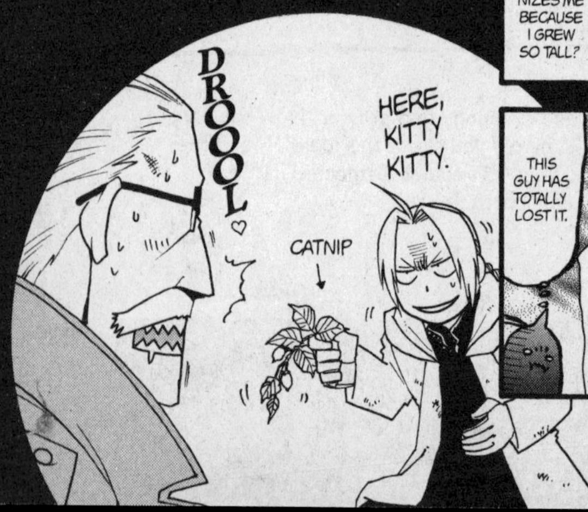
HERE, KITTY KITTY.
CATNIP
DROOOL ♡

Fullmetal Alchemist 20

A rejected state alchemist character

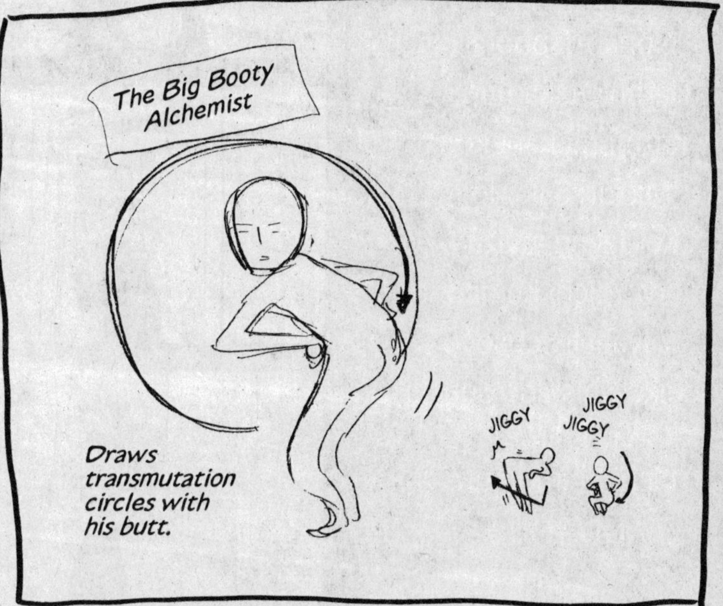

The Big Booty Alchemist
Draws transmutation circles with his butt.
JIGGY
JIGGY JIGGY

I found this while cleaning out a drawer. Now the part of me that asks, "Why did you reject this idea?!!" and the part of me that says, "Of course I rejected it!!" are engaged in an epic battle.

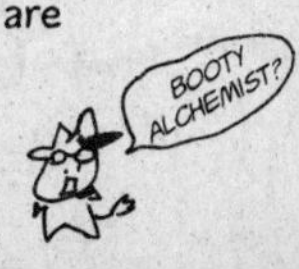

BOOTY ALCHEMIST?

—ARAKAWA

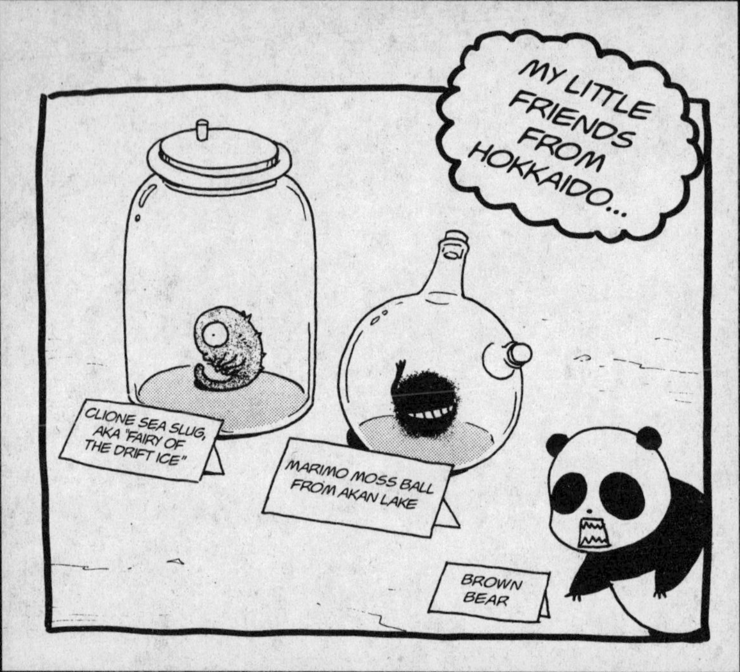
MY LITTLE FRIENDS FROM HOKKAIDO...
CLIONE SEA SLUG, AKA "FAIRY OF THE DRIFT ICE"
MARIMO MOSS BALL FROM AKAN LAKE
BROWN BEAR

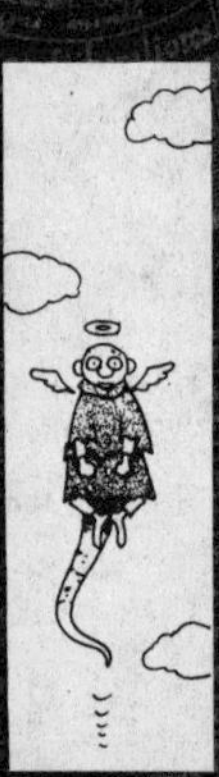

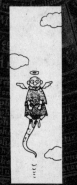

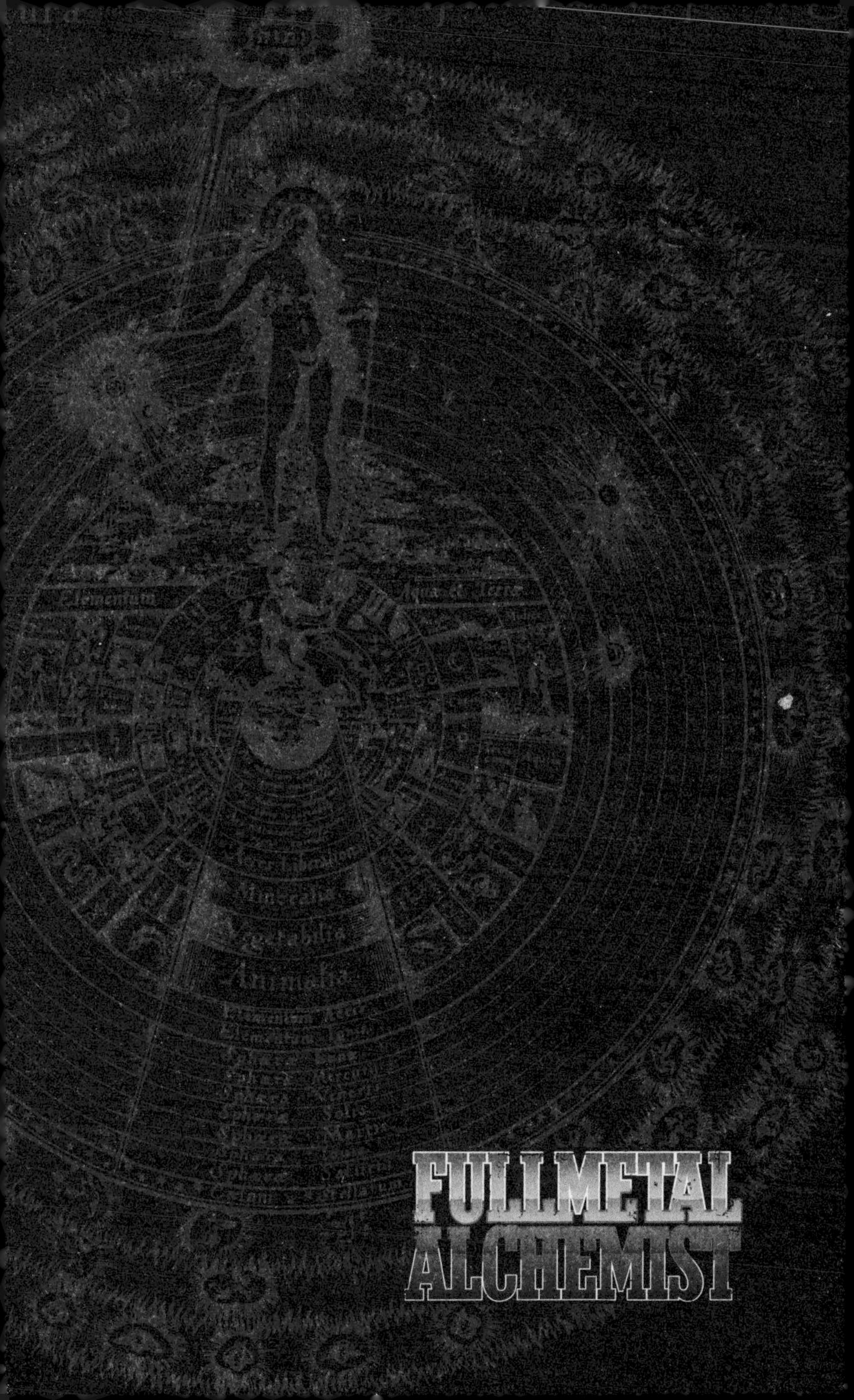
FULLMETAL
ALCHEMIST

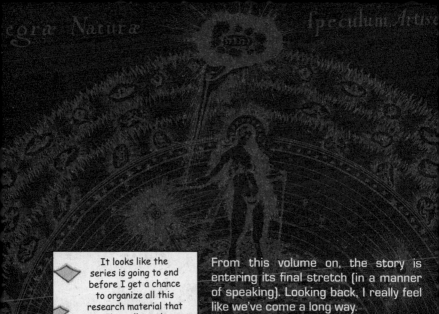

It looks like the series is going to end before I get a chance to organize all this research material that I've collected.

From this volume on, the story is entering its final stretch (in a manner of speaking). Looking back, I really feel like we've come a long way.

—Hiromu Arakawa, 2009

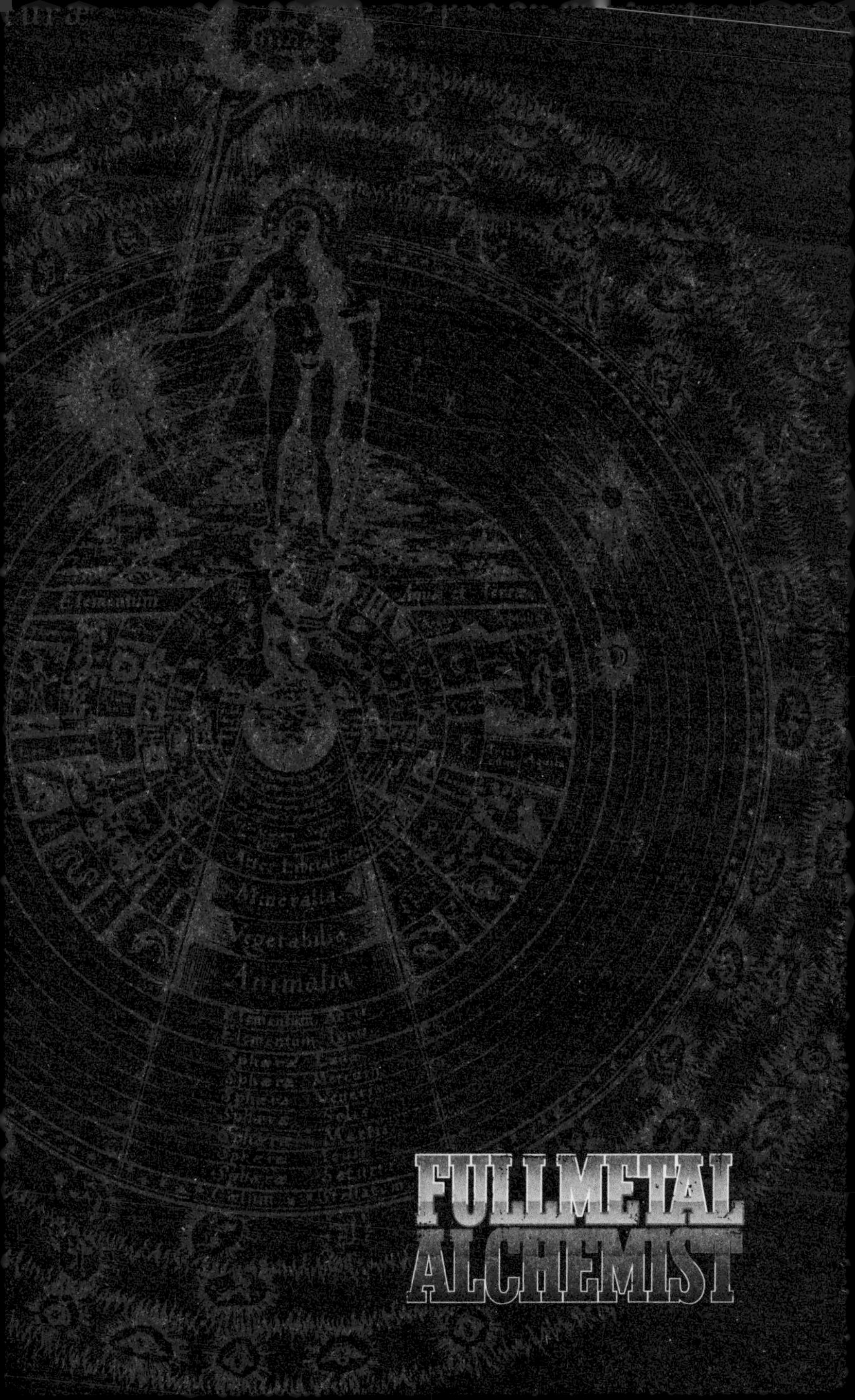
FULLMETAL
ALCHEMIST

鋼の錬金術師

FULLMETAL ALCHEMIST

HIROMU ARAKAWA

荒川弘

21

■ アルフォンス・エルリック
Alphonse Elric

■ エドワード・エルリック
Edward Elric

■ アレックス・ルイ・アームストロング
Alex Louis Armstrong

■ ロイ・マスタング
Roy Mustang

OUTLINE
FULLMETAL ALCHEMIST

Using a forbidden alchemical ritual, the Elric brothers attempted to bring their dead mother back to life. But the ritual went wrong, consuming Edward Elric's leg and Alphonse Elric's entire body. At the cost of his arm, Edward was able to graft his brother's soul into a suit of armor. Equipped with mechanical "auto-mail" to replace his missing limbs, Edward becomes a state alchemist in hopes of finding a way to restore their bodies. Their search embroils them in a deadly conspiracy that threatens to take the innocence, if not the lives, of everyone involved.

As the "Day of Reckoning" approaches, an intricate chess game has emerged in Amestris. On one side stand the Elrics, Mustang's crew, Olivier Armstrong and a ragtag bunch of chimeras; on the other, Military Command, Kimblee, the Homunculi and their mysterious "Father." At stake—the lives and souls of every last person in the country! But there is one "piece" who refuses to take sides—Prince Lin of Xing, now fused with the Homunculus Greed. With time running out, Ed swears fealty to Greed in the hopes of tipping the balance. Will the gambit pay off…?

鋼の錬金術師
FULLMETAL ALCHEMIST

CHARACTERS
FULLMETAL ALCHEMIST

■ ウィンリィ・ロックベル

Winry Rockbell

■ スカー

Scar

■ オリヴィエ・ミラ・アームストロング

Olivier Mira Armstrong

■ キング・ブラッドレイ

King Bradley

■ ヴァン・ホーエンハイム

Van Hohenheim

■ リン・ヤオ（グリード）

Lin Yao (Greed)

CONTENTS

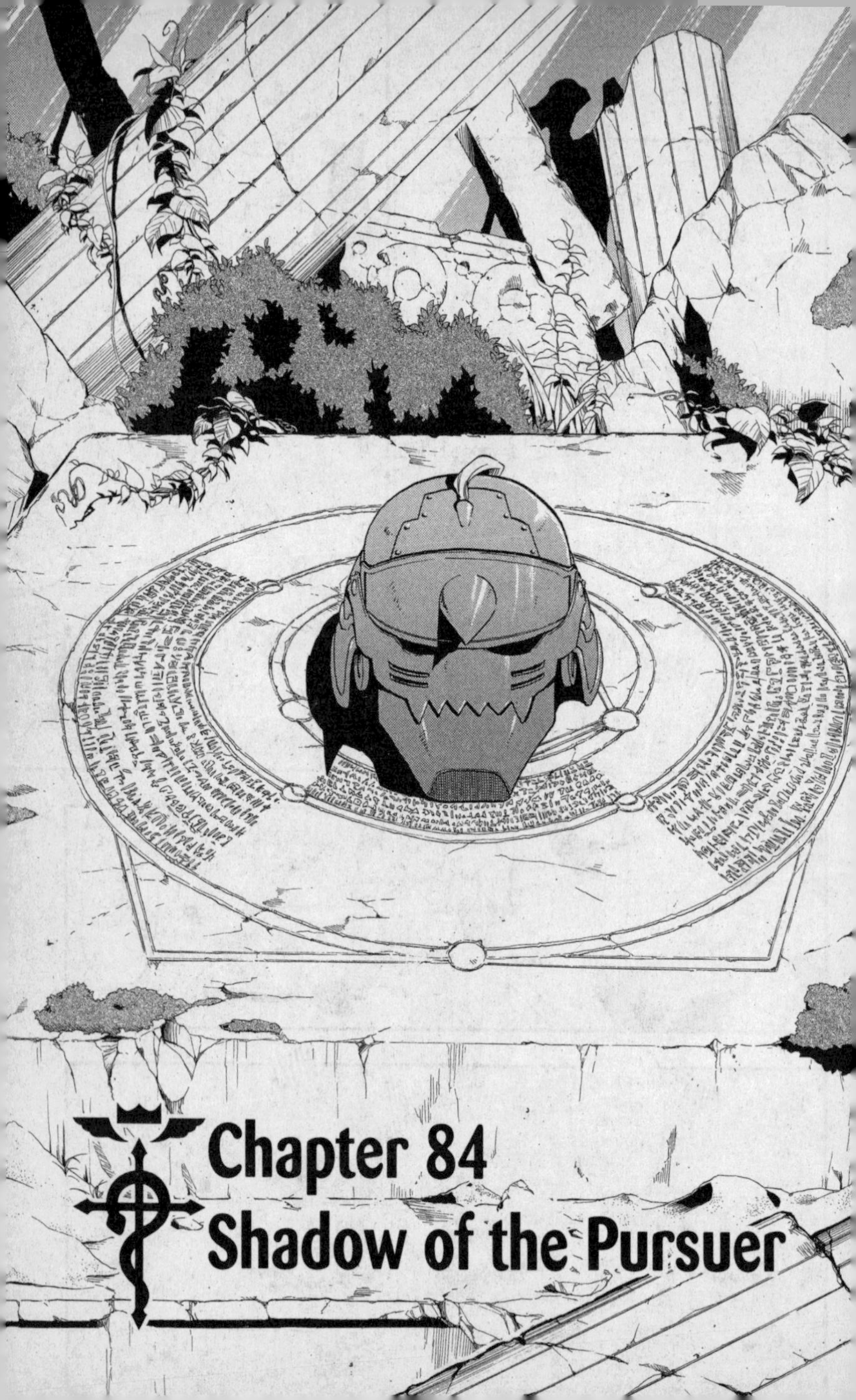
Chapter 84
Shadow of the Pursuer

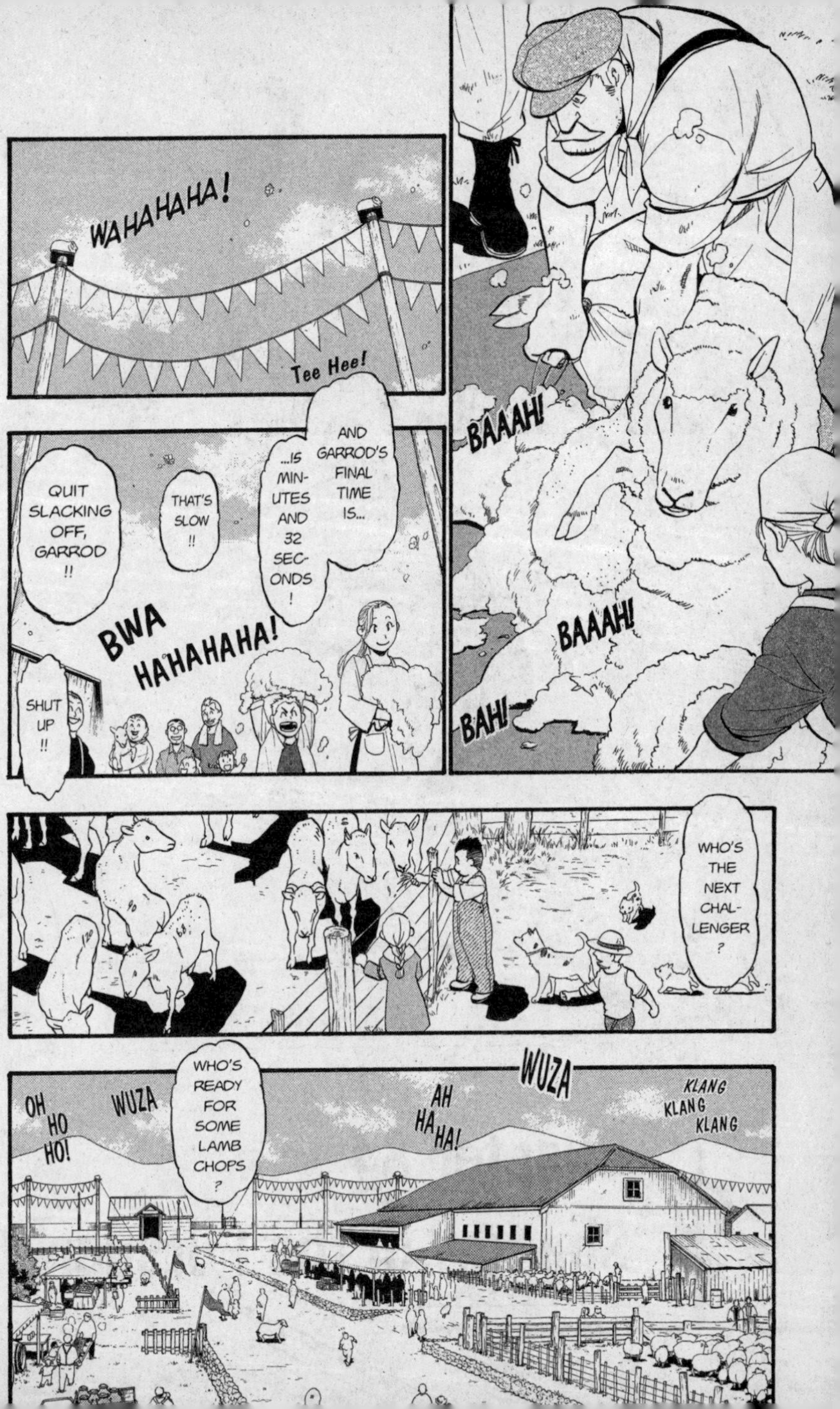
BAAAH!
BAAAH!
BAH!
WAHAHAHA!
Tee Hee!
AND GARROD'S FINAL TIME IS...
...IS MIN- UTES AND 32 SEC- ONDS!
THAT'S SLOW!!
QUIT SLACKING OFF, GARROD!!
BWA HAHAHAHA!
SHUT UP!!
WHO'S THE NEXT CHAL- LENGER?
KLANG KLANG KLANG
WUZA
AH HA HA!
WHO'S READY FOR SOME LAMB CHOPS?
WUZA
OH HO HO!

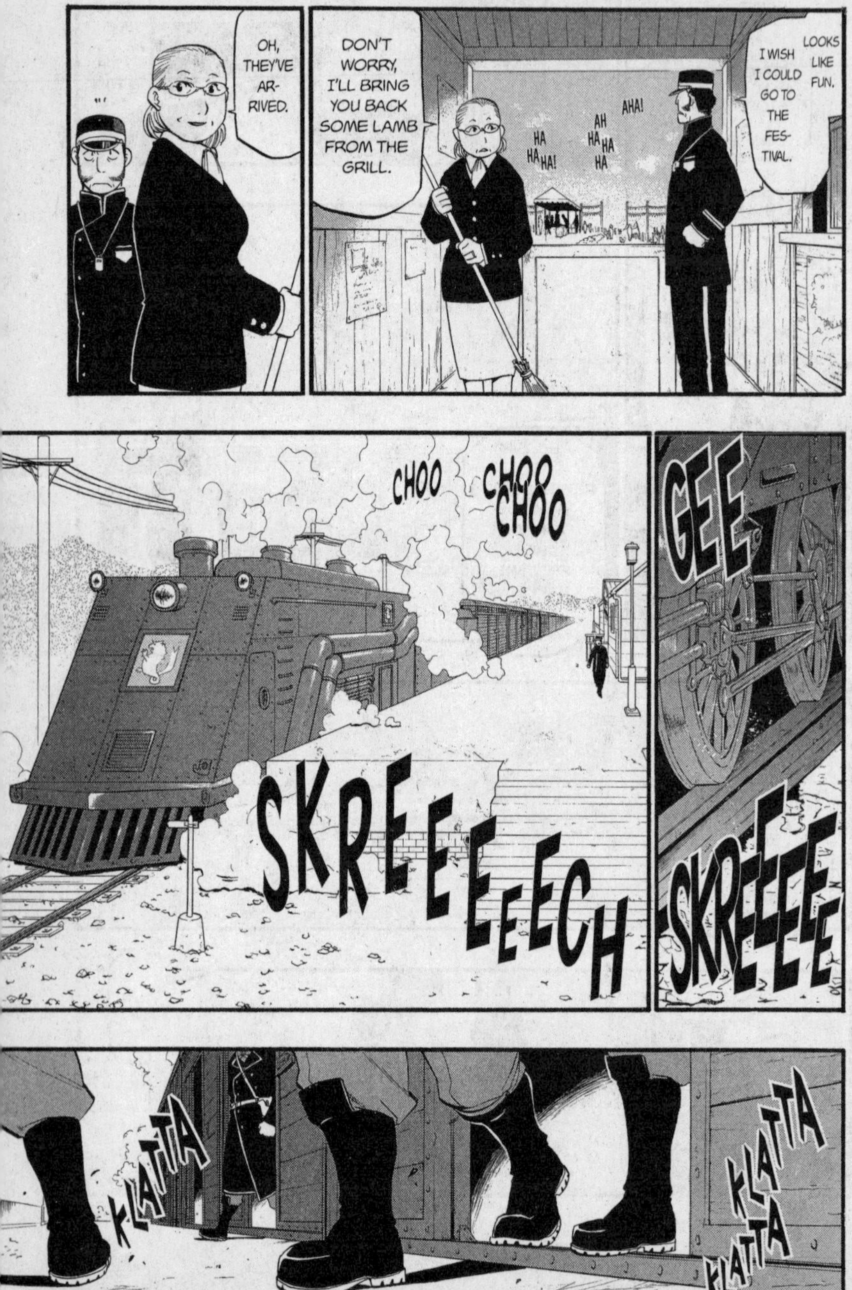
LOOKS LIKE FUN.
I WISH I COULD GO TO THE FES-TIVAL.
AHA!
AH HA HA HA HA
HA HA HA!
DON'T WORRY, I'LL BRING YOU BACK SOME LAMB FROM THE GRILL.
OH, THEY'VE AR-RIVED.
GEE
SKREEEEE
CHOO CHOO CHOO
SKREEEEEECH
KLATTA KLATTA
KLATTA

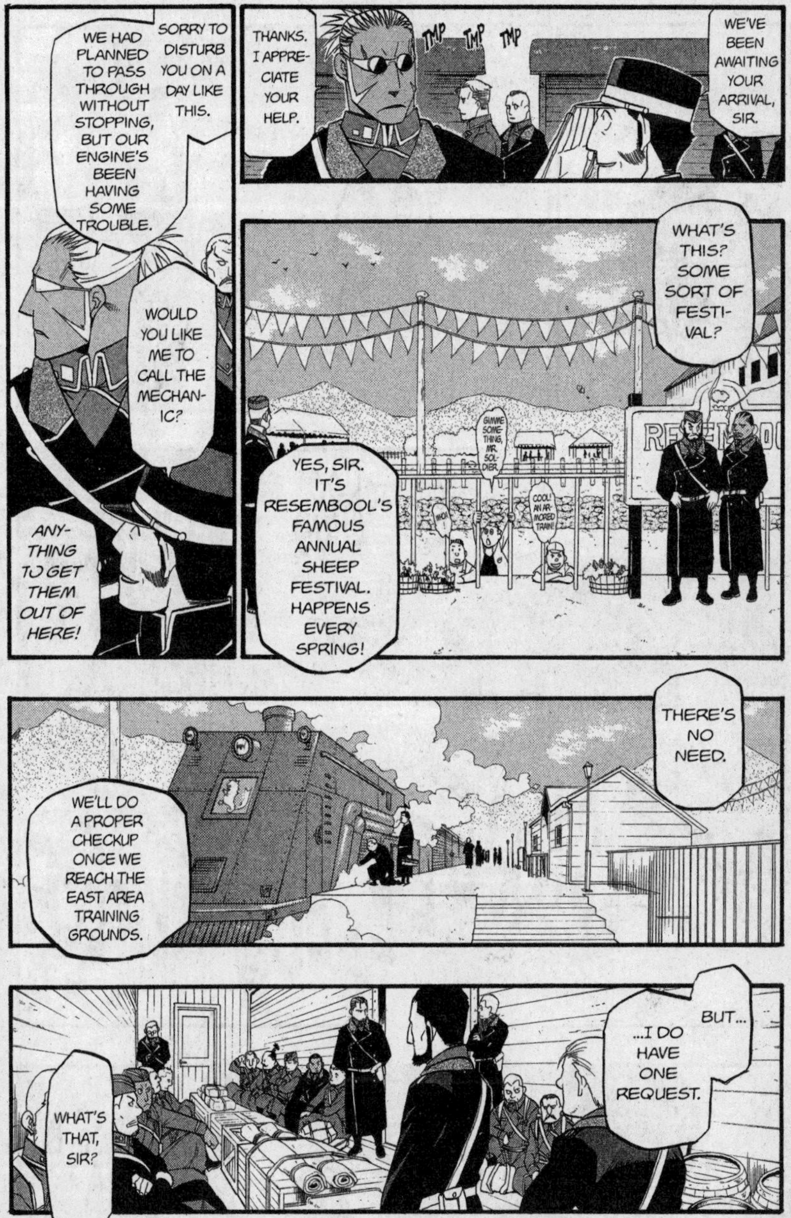
WE'VE BEEN AWAITING YOUR ARRIVAL, SIR.
TMP TMP TMP
THANKS. I APPRECIATE YOUR HELP.
WHAT'S THIS? SOME SORT OF FESTIVAL?
GIMME SOMETHING, MR. SOLDIER
COOL! AN ARMORED TRAIN!
WHOA!
YES, SIR. IT'S RESEMBOOL'S FAMOUS ANNUAL SHEEP FESTIVAL. HAPPENS EVERY SPRING!
SORRY TO DISTURB YOU ON A DAY LIKE THIS.
WE HAD PLANNED TO PASS THROUGH WITHOUT STOPPING, BUT OUR ENGINE'S BEEN HAVING SOME TROUBLE.
WOULD YOU LIKE ME TO CALL THE MECHANIC?
ANYTHING TO GET THEM OUT OF HERE!
THERE'S NO NEED.
WE'LL DO A PROPER CHECKUP ONCE WE REACH THE EAST AREA TRAINING GROUNDS.
BUT...
...I DO HAVE ONE REQUEST.
WHAT'S THAT, SIR?

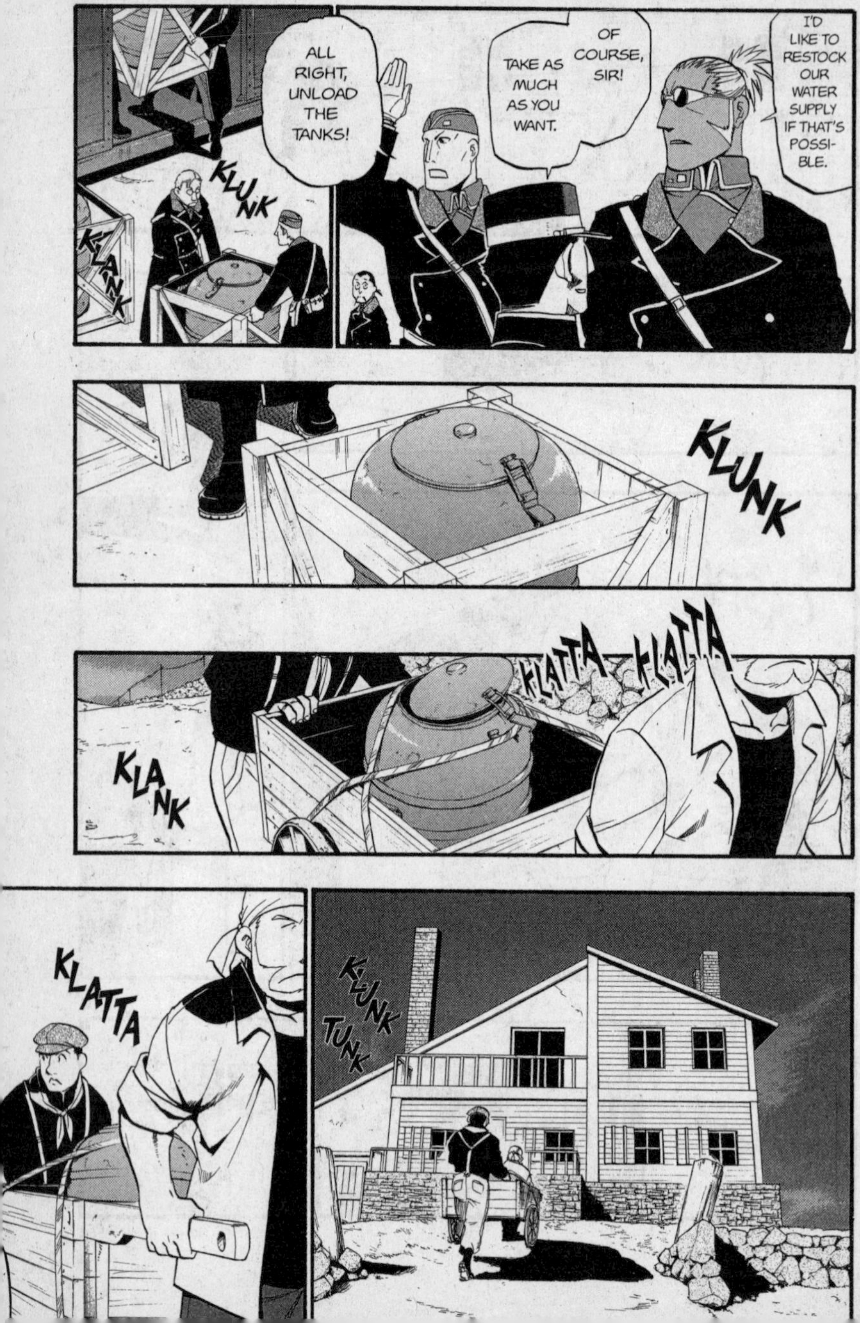

I'D LIKE TO RESTOCK OUR WATER SUPPLY IF THAT'S POSSIBLE.
OF COURSE, SIR!
TAKE AS MUCH AS YOU WANT.
ALL RIGHT, UNLOAD THE TANKS!
KLUNK
KLANK
KLUNK
KLATTA KLATTA
KLANK
KLUNK TUNK
KLATTA

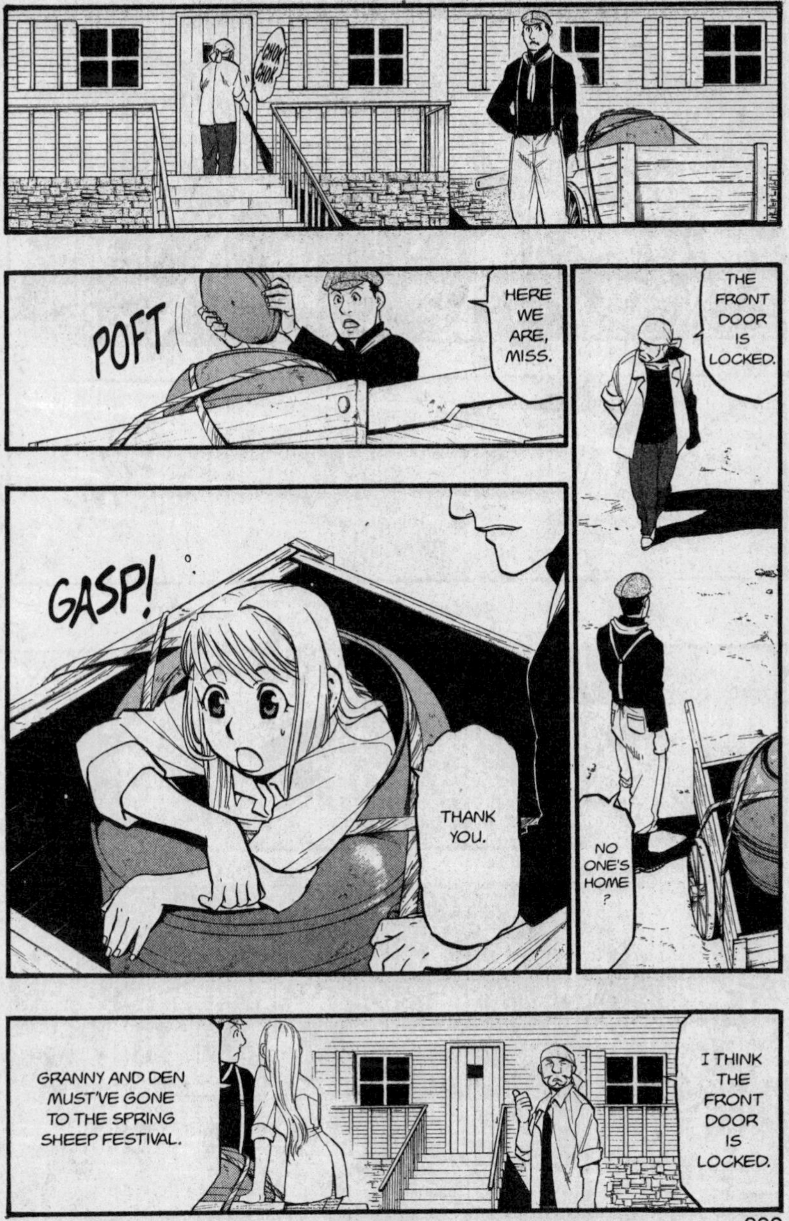
CHOK CHOK
THE FRONT DOOR IS LOCKED.
NO ONE'S HOME?
POFT
HERE WE ARE, MISS.
GASP!
THANK YOU.
I THINK THE FRONT DOOR IS LOCKED.
GRANNY AND DEN MUST'VE GONE TO THE SPRING SHEEP FESTIVAL.

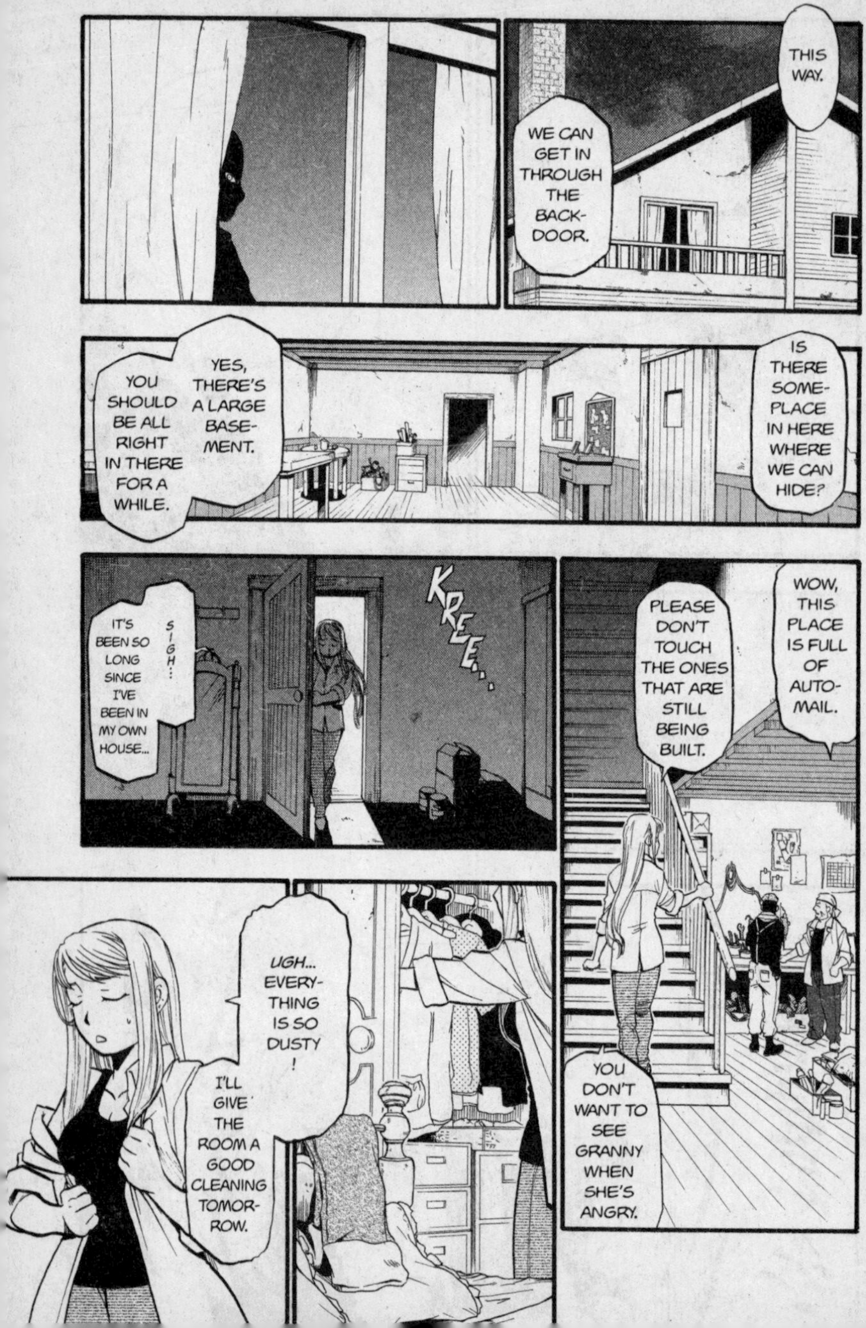
THIS WAY.
WE CAN GET IN THROUGH THE BACKDOOR.
IS THERE SOMEPLACE IN HERE WHERE WE CAN HIDE?
YES, THERE'S A LARGE BASEMENT.
YOU SHOULD BE ALL RIGHT IN THERE FOR A WHILE.
WOW, THIS PLACE IS FULL OF AUTOMAIL.
PLEASE DON'T TOUCH THE ONES THAT ARE STILL BEING BUILT.
YOU DON'T WANT TO SEE GRANNY WHEN SHE'S ANGRY.
KREEE...
SIGH...
IT'S BEEN SO LONG SINCE I'VE BEEN IN MY OWN HOUSE...
UGH... EVERYTHING IS SO DUSTY!
I'LL GIVE THE ROOM A GOOD CLEANING TOMORROW.

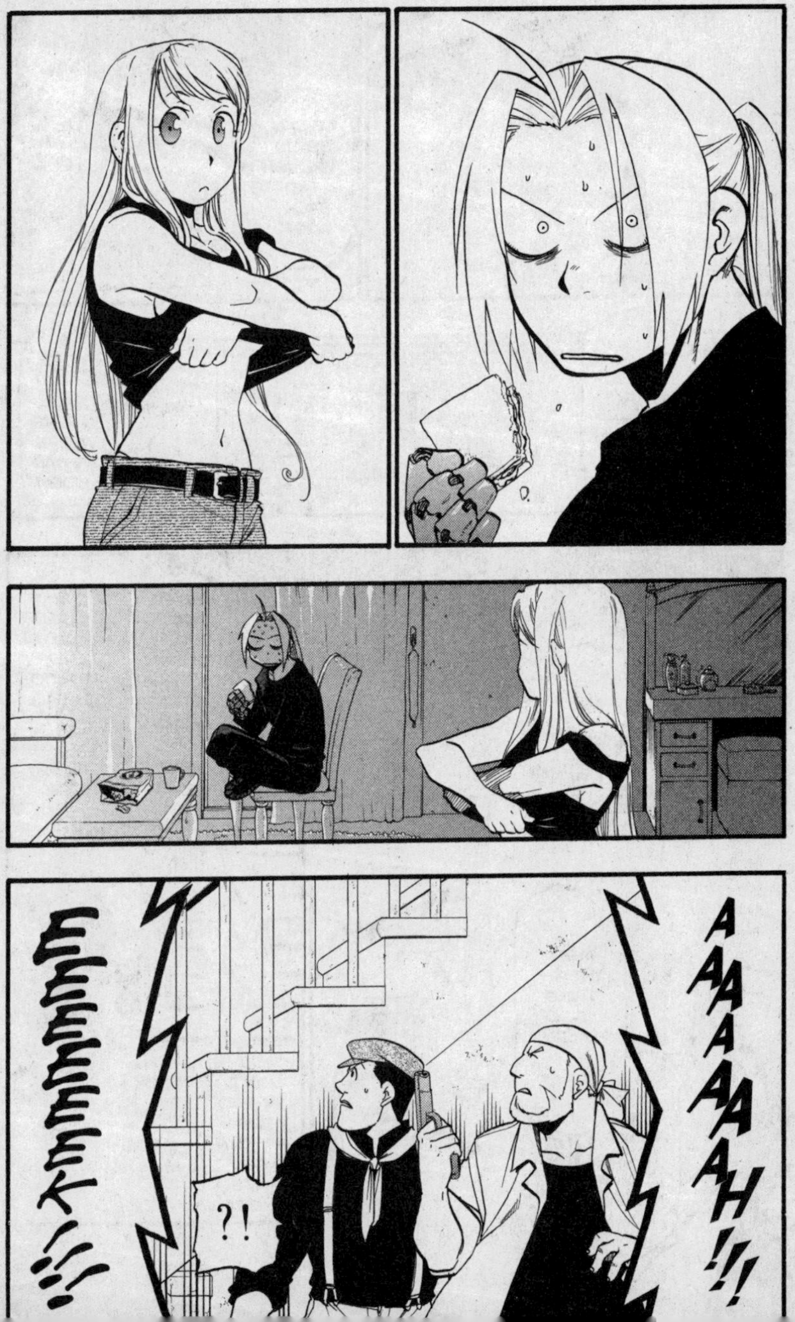
AAAAAAAAH!!!
?!
EEEEEEEEK!!!!

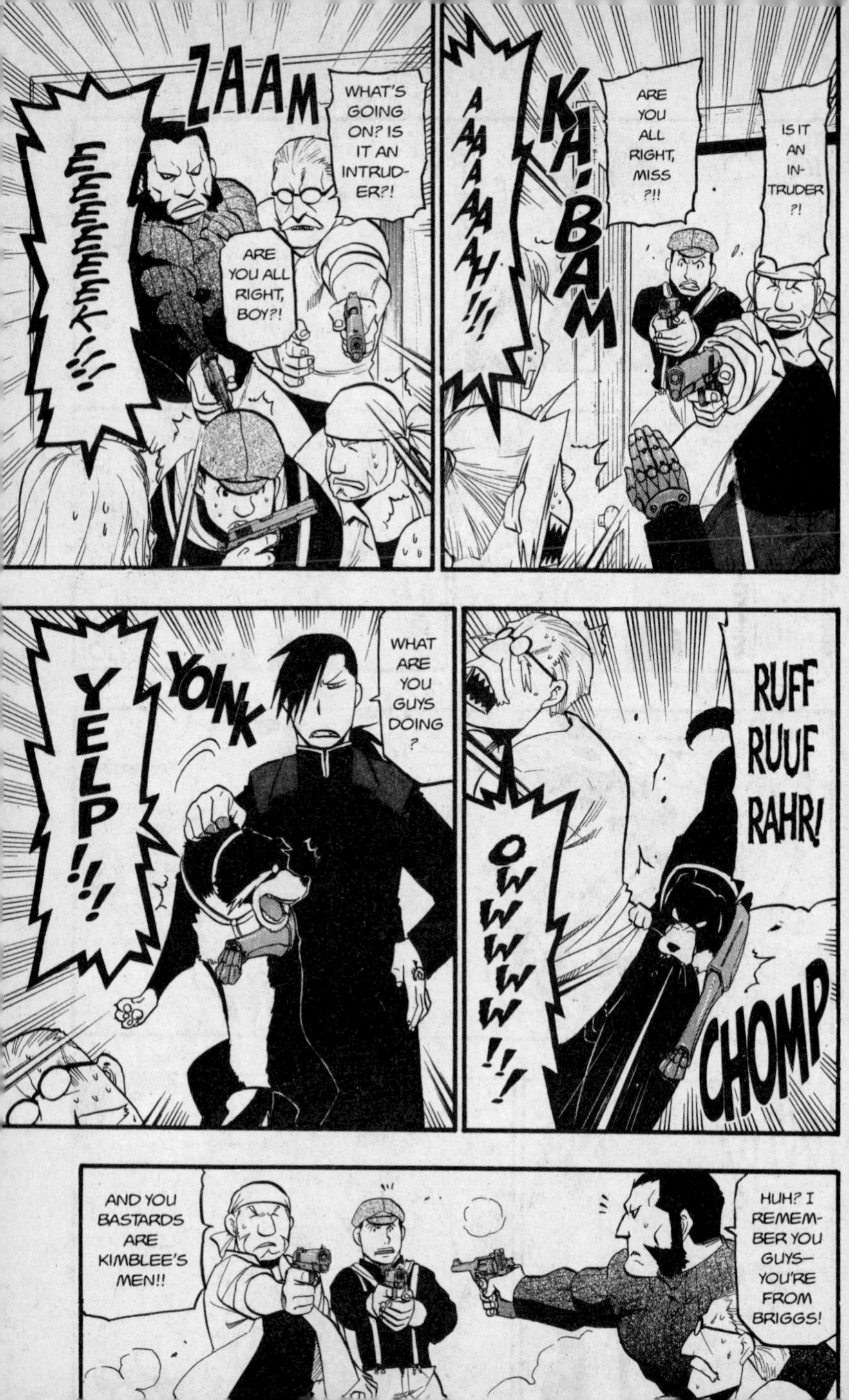
IS IT AN IN-TRUDER?!
ARE YOU ALL RIGHT, MISS?!!
KA-BAM
AAAAAAAH!!!
WHAT'S GOING ON? IS IT AN INTRUD-ER?!
ZAAM
EEEEEEEK!!!
ARE YOU ALL RIGHT, BOY?!
RUFF RUUF RAHR!
OWWWWW!!!
CHOMP
WHAT ARE YOU GUYS DOING?
YOINK
YELP!!!
HUH? I REMEM-BER YOU GUYS— YOU'RE FROM BRIGGS!
AND YOU BASTARDS ARE KIMBLEE'S MEN!!

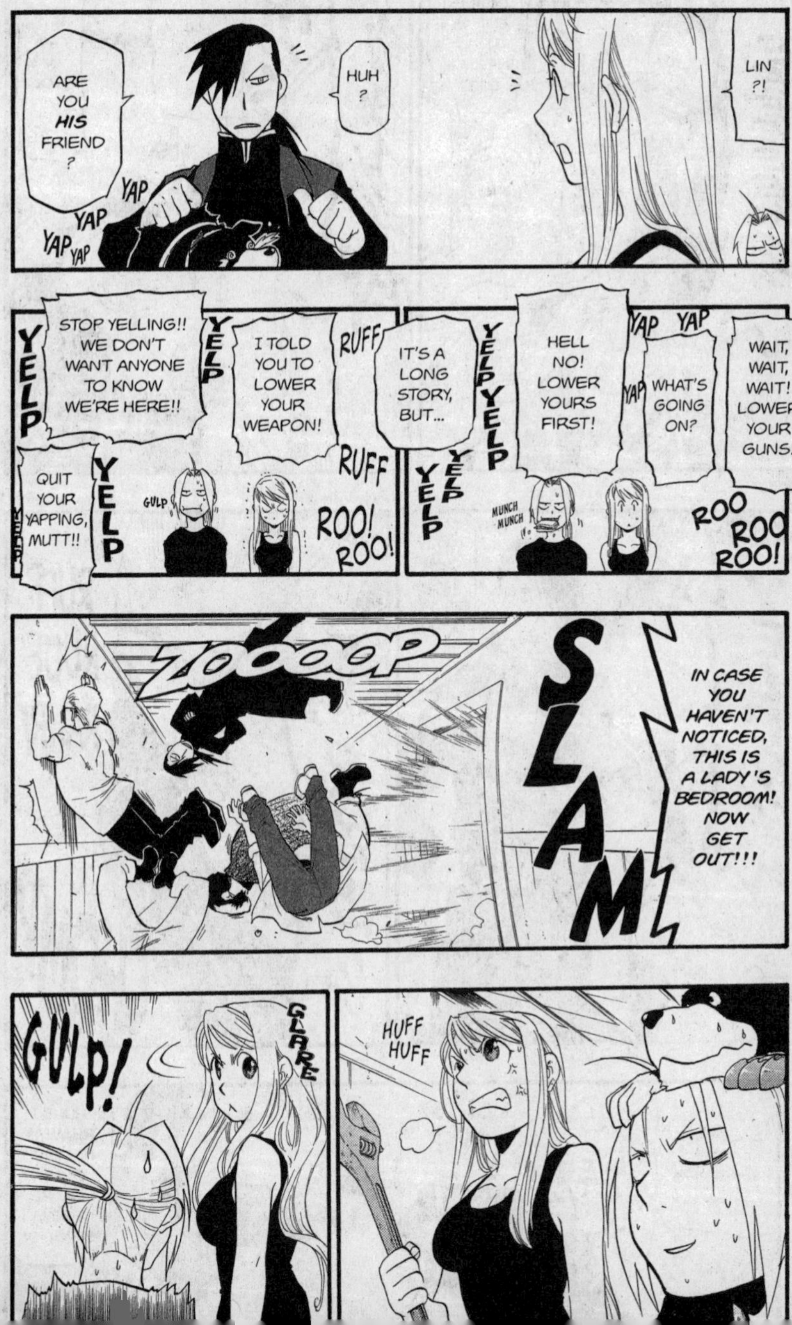
LIN ?!
HUH ?
ARE YOU HIS FRIEND ?
YAP
YAP
YAP YAP
WAIT, WAIT, WAIT! LOWER YOUR GUNS.
YAP YAP
WHAT'S GOING ON?
YAP
HELL NO! LOWER YOURS FIRST!
YELP
YELP
IT'S A LONG STORY, BUT...
YELP
YELP
MUNCH MUNCH
ROO ROO ROO!
RUFF
I TOLD YOU TO LOWER YOUR WEAPON!
YELP
STOP YELLING!! WE DON'T WANT ANYONE TO KNOW WE'RE HERE!!
YELP
RUFF
YELP
QUIT YOUR YAPPING, MUTT!!
GULP
ROO! ROO!
SLAM
IN CASE YOU HAVEN'T NOTICED, THIS IS A LADY'S BEDROOM! NOW GET OUT!!!
ZOOOOP
HUFF HUFF
GLARE
GULP!

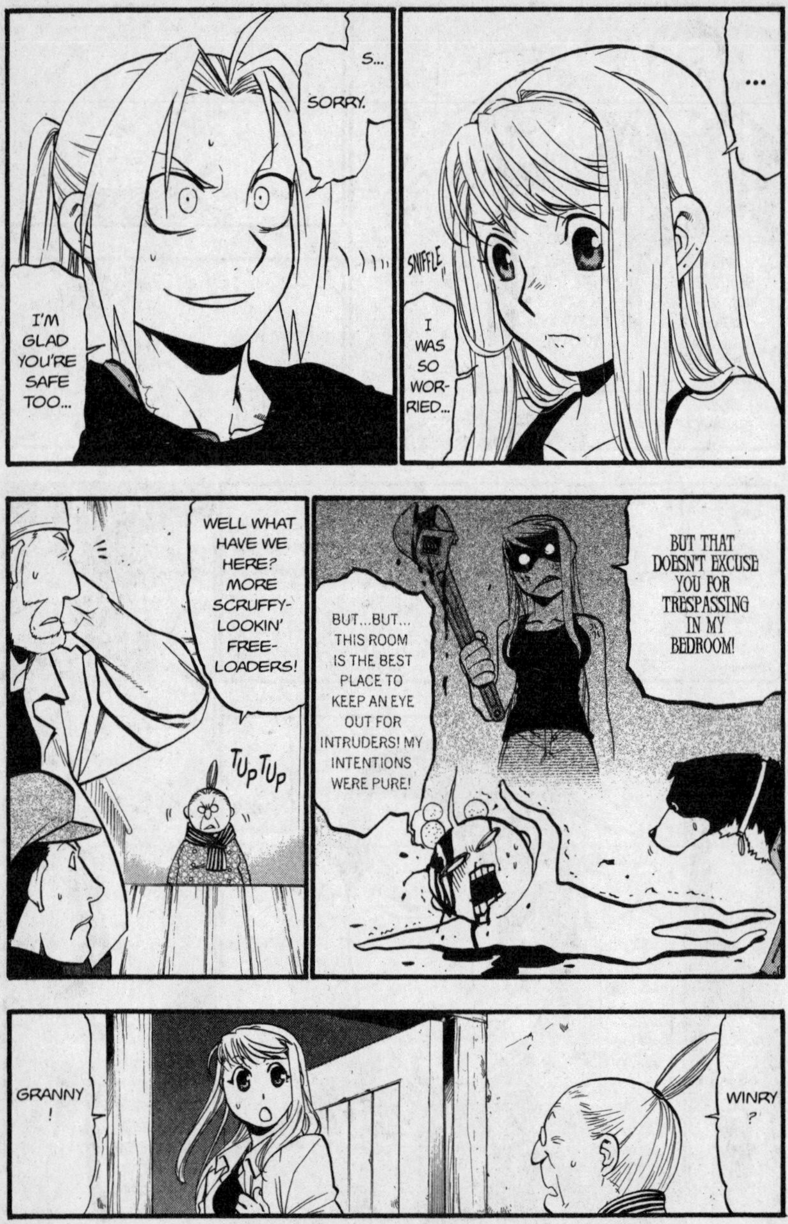
...
SNIFFLE
I WAS SO WORRIED...
S...
SORRY.
I'M GLAD YOU'RE SAFE TOO...
BUT THAT DOESN'T EXCUSE YOU FOR TRESPASSING IN MY BEDROOM!
BUT...BUT... THIS ROOM IS THE BEST PLACE TO KEEP AN EYE OUT FOR INTRUDERS! MY INTENTIONS WERE PURE!
WELL WHAT HAVE WE HERE? MORE SCRUFFY-LOOKIN' FREE-LOADERS!
TUP TUP
WINRY?
GRANNY!

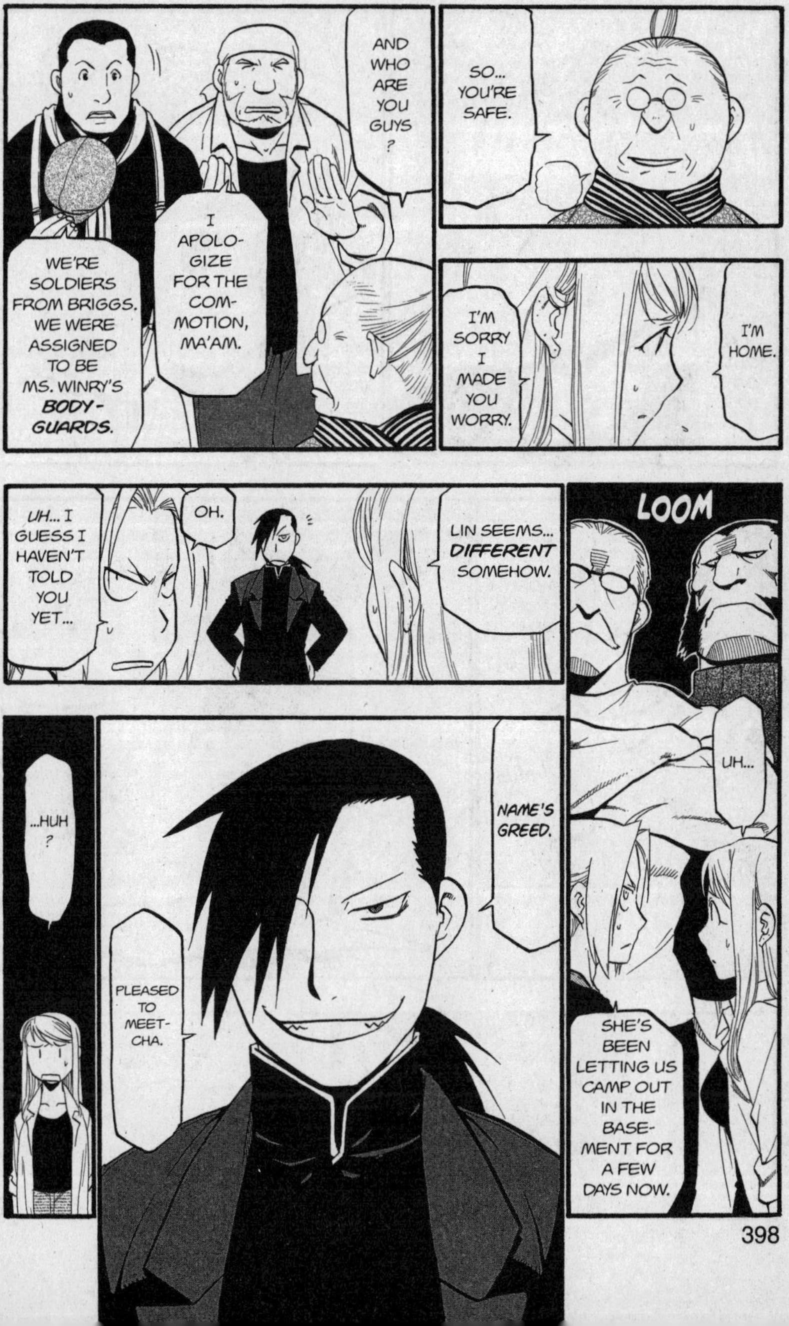
SO... YOU'RE SAFE.
I'M HOME.
I'M SORRY I MADE YOU WORRY.
AND WHO ARE YOU GUYS?
I APOLOGIZE FOR THE COMMOTION, MA'AM.
WE'RE SOLDIERS FROM BRIGGS. WE WERE ASSIGNED TO BE MS. WINRY'S ***BODYGUARDS.***
LOOM
UH...
SHE'S BEEN LETTING US CAMP OUT IN THE BASEMENT FOR A FEW DAYS NOW.
LIN SEEMS... ***DIFFERENT*** SOMEHOW.
OH.
UH... I GUESS I HAVEN'T TOLD YOU YET...
NAME'S GREED.
PLEASED TO MEET-CHA.
...HUH?

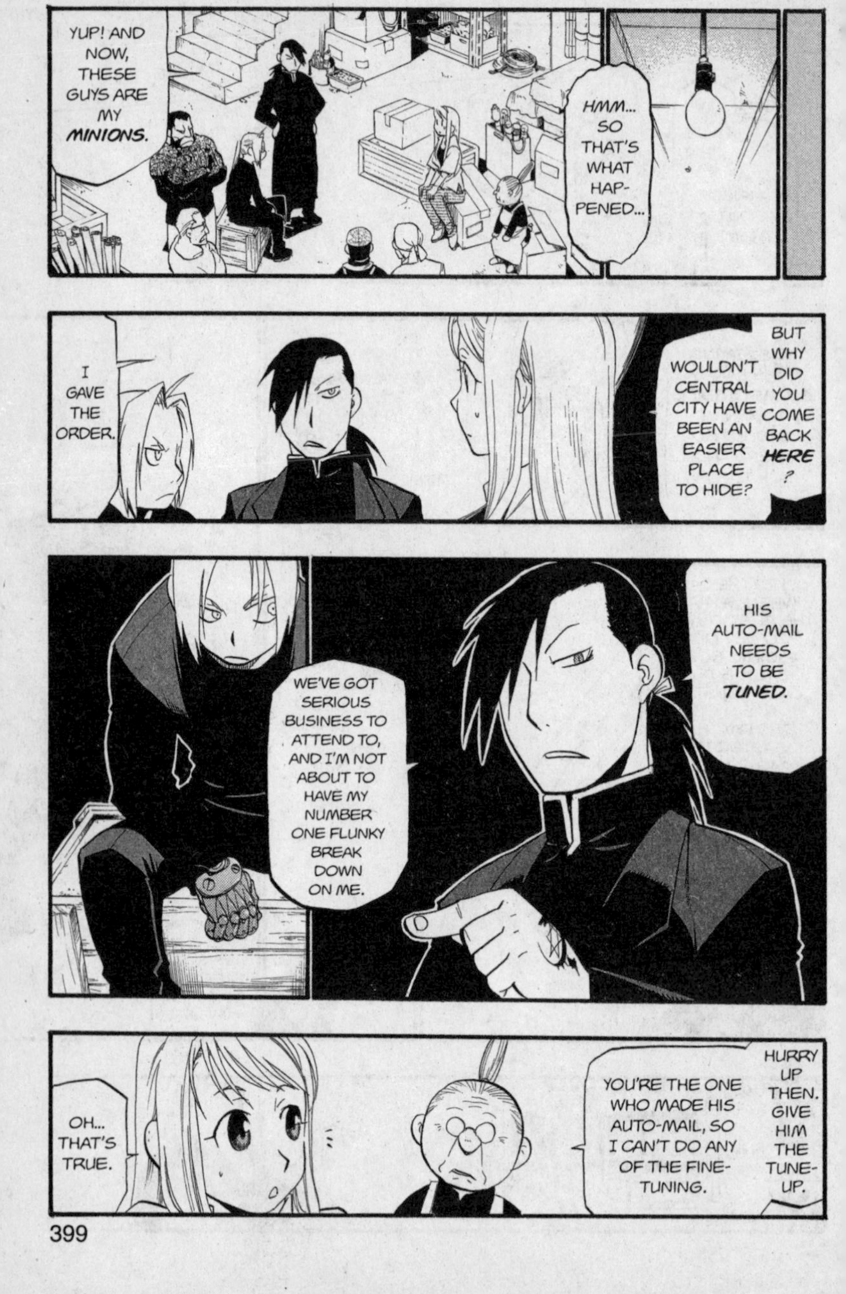
HMM... SO THAT'S WHAT HAP-PENED...
YUP! AND NOW, THESE GUYS ARE MY MINIONS.
BUT WHY DID YOU COME BACK HERE?
WOULDN'T CENTRAL CITY HAVE BEEN AN EASIER PLACE TO HIDE?
I GAVE THE ORDER.
HIS AUTO-MAIL NEEDS TO BE TUNED.
WE'VE GOT SERIOUS BUSINESS TO ATTEND TO, AND I'M NOT ABOUT TO HAVE MY NUMBER ONE FLUNKY BREAK DOWN ON ME.
HURRY UP THEN. GIVE HIM THE TUNE-UP.
YOU'RE THE ONE WHO MADE HIS AUTO-MAIL, SO I CAN'T DO ANY OF THE FINE-TUNING.
OH... THAT'S TRUE.

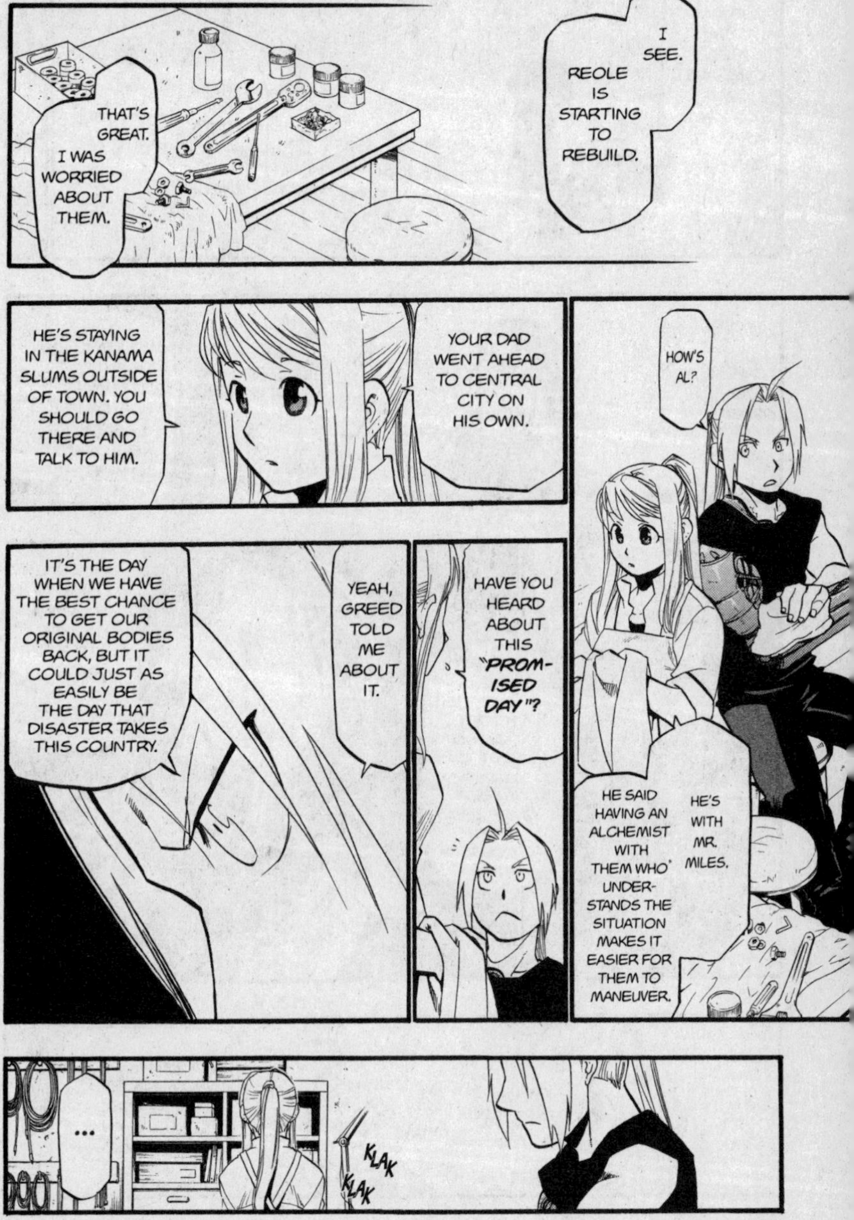
I SEE. REOLE IS STARTING TO REBUILD.
THAT'S GREAT. I WAS WORRIED ABOUT THEM.
HOW'S AL?
HE'S WITH MR. MILES.
HE SAID HAVING AN ALCHEMIST WITH THEM WHO UNDERSTANDS THE SITUATION MAKES IT EASIER FOR THEM TO MANEUVER.
YOUR DAD WENT AHEAD TO CENTRAL CITY ON HIS OWN.
HE'S STAYING IN THE KANAMA SLUMS OUTSIDE OF TOWN. YOU SHOULD GO THERE AND TALK TO HIM.
HAVE YOU HEARD ABOUT THIS "PROMISED DAY"?
YEAH, GREED TOLD ME ABOUT IT.
IT'S THE DAY WHEN WE HAVE THE BEST CHANCE TO GET OUR ORIGINAL BODIES BACK, BUT IT COULD JUST AS EASILY BE THE DAY THAT DISASTER TAKES THIS COUNTRY.
KLAK
KLAK
...

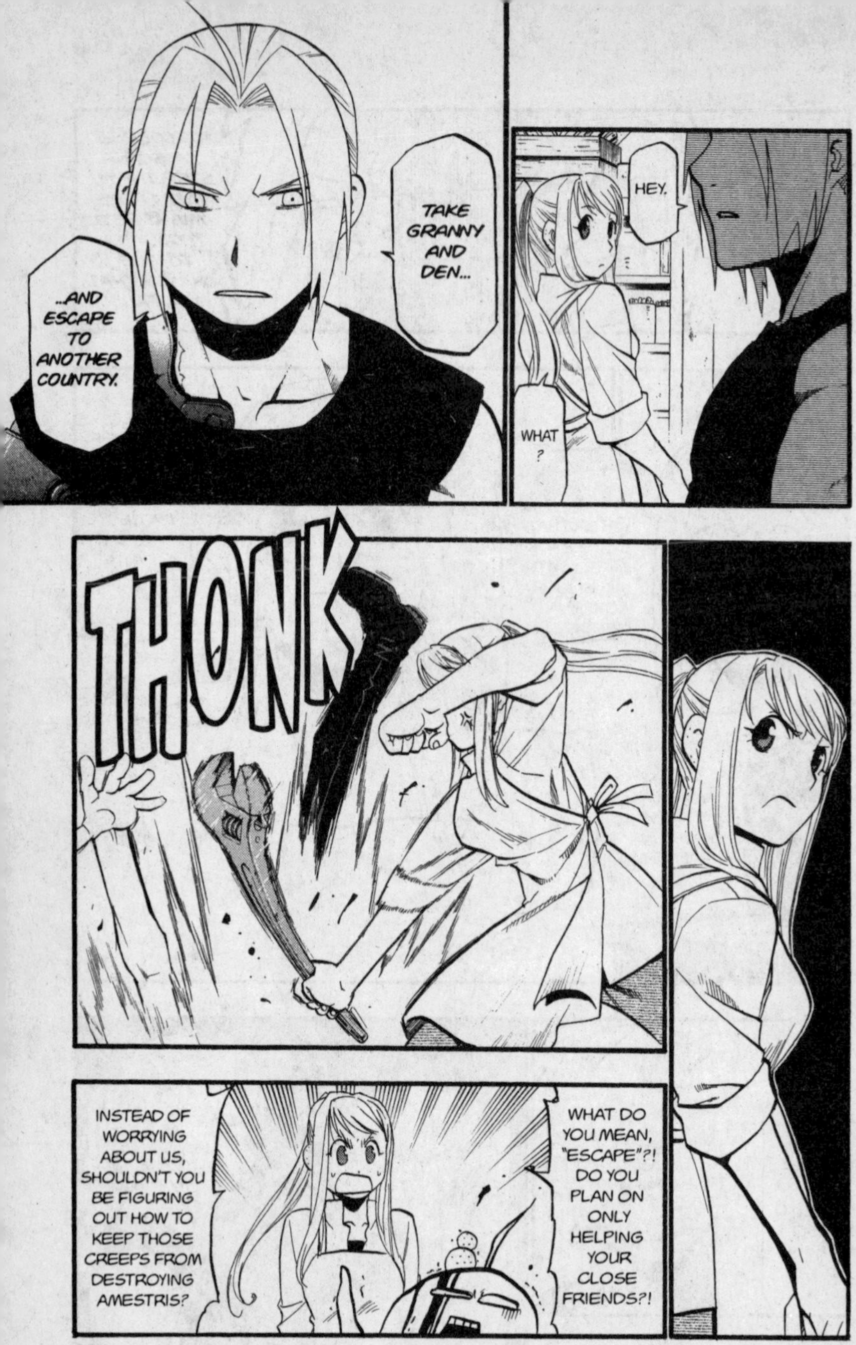
HEY.
WHAT?
TAKE GRANNY AND DEN...
...AND ESCAPE TO ANOTHER COUNTRY.
THONK
WHAT DO YOU MEAN, "ESCAPE"?! DO YOU PLAN ON ONLY HELPING YOUR CLOSE FRIENDS?!
INSTEAD OF WORRYING ABOUT US, SHOULDN'T YOU BE FIGURING OUT HOW TO KEEP THOSE CREEPS FROM DESTROYING AMESTRIS?

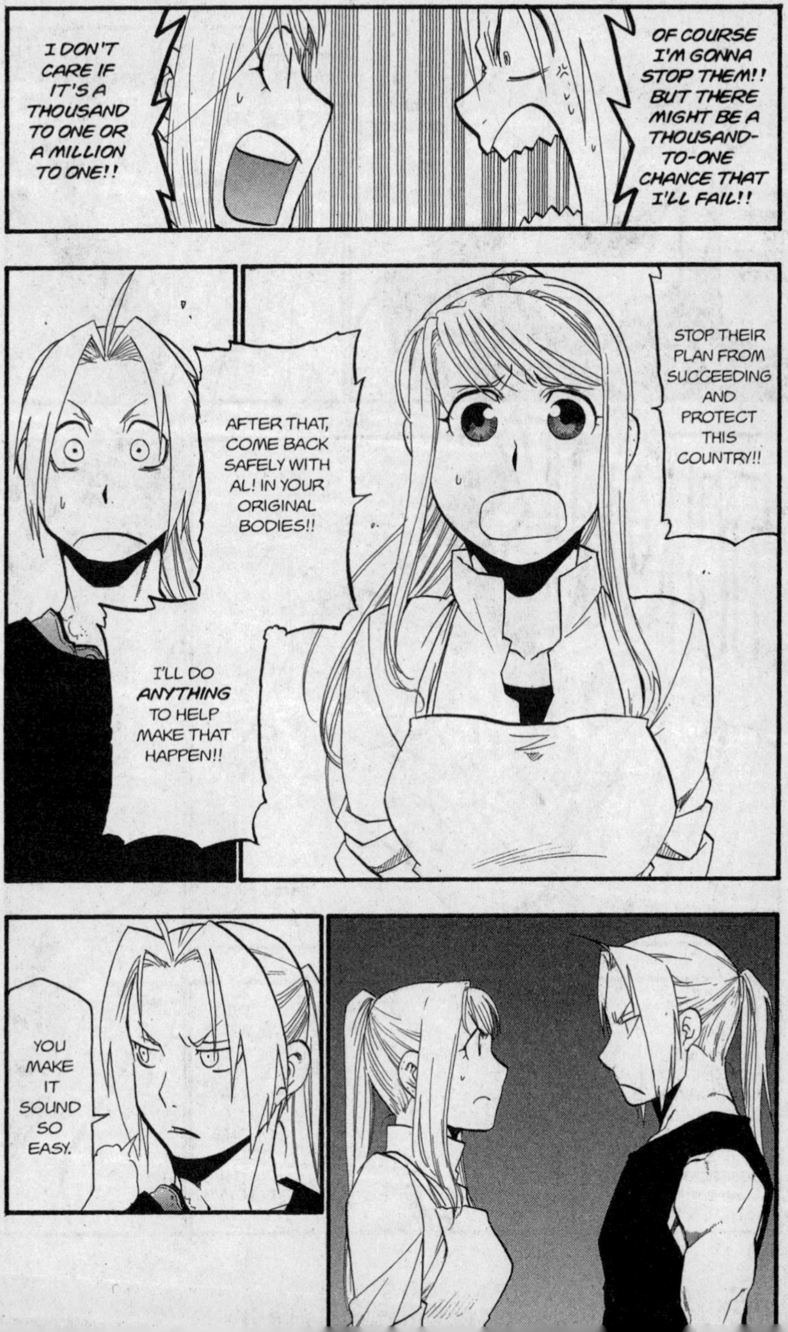
OF COURSE I'M GONNA STOP THEM!! BUT THERE MIGHT BE A THOUSAND-TO-ONE CHANCE THAT I'LL FAIL!!
I DON'T CARE IF IT'S A THOUSAND TO ONE OR A MILLION TO ONE!!
STOP THEIR PLAN FROM SUCCEEDING AND PROTECT THIS COUNTRY!!
AFTER THAT, COME BACK SAFELY WITH AL! IN YOUR ORIGINAL BODIES!!
I'LL DO ANYTHING TO HELP MAKE THAT HAPPEN!!
YOU MAKE IT SOUND SO EASY.

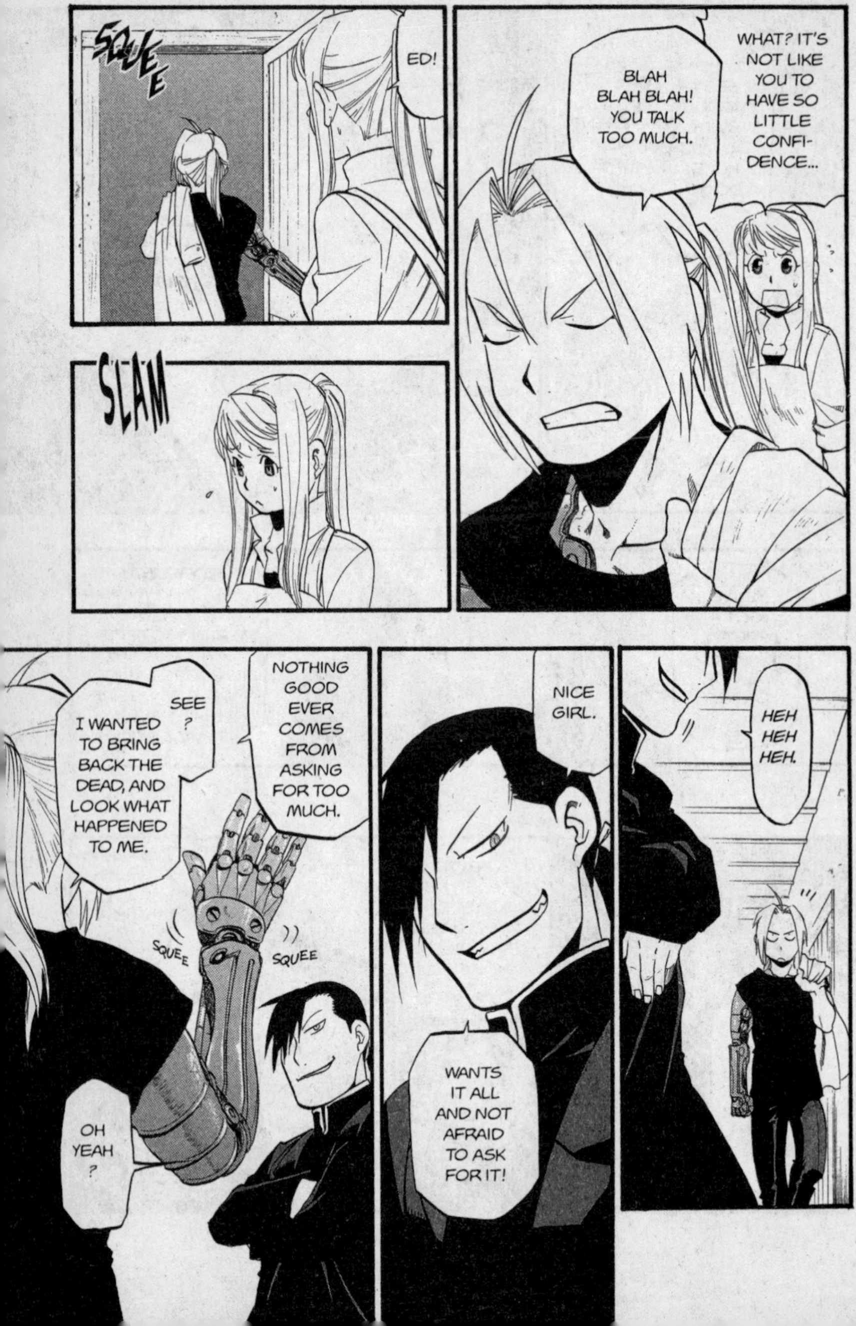
WHAT? IT'S NOT LIKE YOU TO HAVE SO LITTLE CONFIDENCE...
BLAH BLAH BLAH! YOU TALK TOO MUCH.
ED!
SQUEEE
SLAM
HEH HEH HEH.
NICE GIRL.
WANTS IT ALL AND NOT AFRAID TO ASK FOR IT!
NOTHING GOOD EVER COMES FROM ASKING FOR TOO MUCH.
SEE?
I WANTED TO BRING BACK THE DEAD, AND LOOK WHAT HAPPENED TO ME.
SQUEE
SQUEEE
OH YEAH?

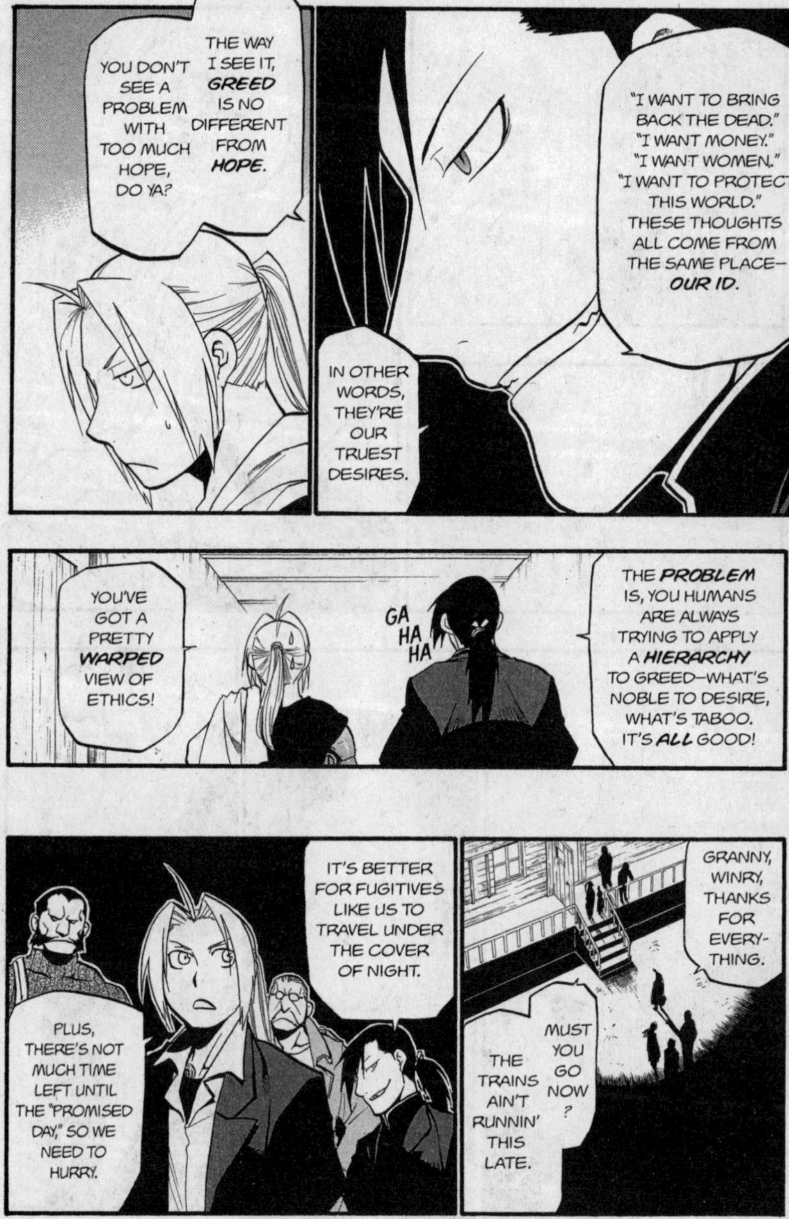
"I WANT TO BRING BACK THE DEAD." "I WANT MONEY." "I WANT WOMEN." "I WANT TO PROTECT THIS WORLD." THESE THOUGHTS ALL COME FROM THE SAME PLACE— OUR ID.
IN OTHER WORDS, THEY'RE OUR TRUEST DESIRES.
THE WAY I SEE IT, GREED IS NO DIFFERENT FROM HOPE.
YOU DON'T SEE A PROBLEM WITH TOO MUCH HOPE, DO YA?
THE PROBLEM IS, YOU HUMANS ARE ALWAYS TRYING TO APPLY A HIERARCHY TO GREED—WHAT'S NOBLE TO DESIRE, WHAT'S TABOO. IT'S ALL GOOD!
GA HA HA
YOU'VE GOT A PRETTY WARPED VIEW OF ETHICS!
GRANNY, WINRY, THANKS FOR EVERYTHING.
MUST YOU GO NOW?
THE TRAINS AIN'T RUNNIN' THIS LATE.
IT'S BETTER FOR FUGITIVES LIKE US TO TRAVEL UNDER THE COVER OF NIGHT.
PLUS, THERE'S NOT MUCH TIME LEFT UNTIL THE "PROMISED DAY," SO WE NEED TO HURRY.

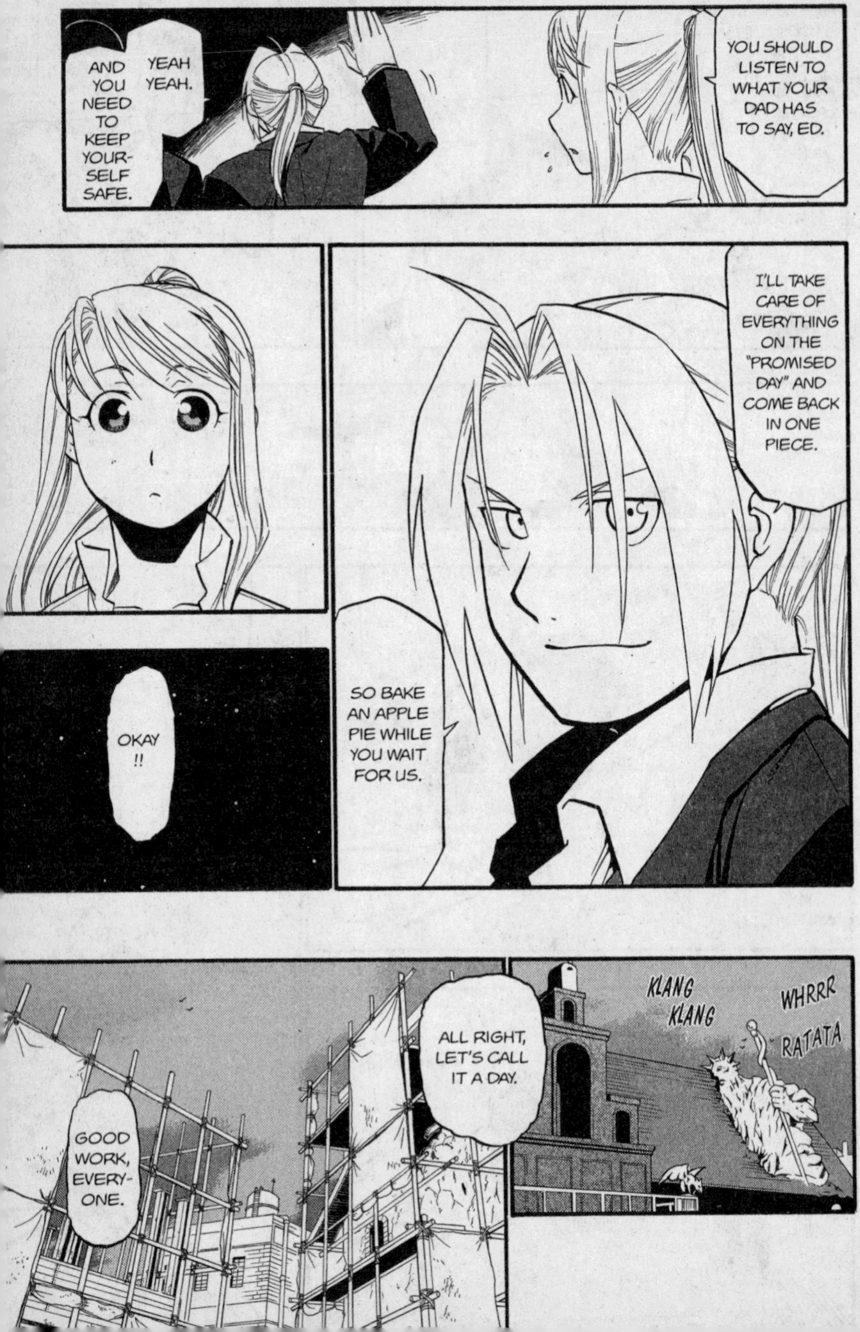
YOU SHOULD LISTEN TO WHAT YOUR DAD HAS TO SAY, ED.
YEAH YEAH.
AND YOU NEED TO KEEP YOURSELF SAFE.
I'LL TAKE CARE OF EVERYTHING ON THE "PROMISED DAY" AND COME BACK IN ONE PIECE.
SO BAKE AN APPLE PIE WHILE YOU WAIT FOR US.
OKAY !!
WHRRR
RATATA
KLANG KLANG
ALL RIGHT, LET'S CALL IT A DAY.
GOOD WORK, EVERYONE.

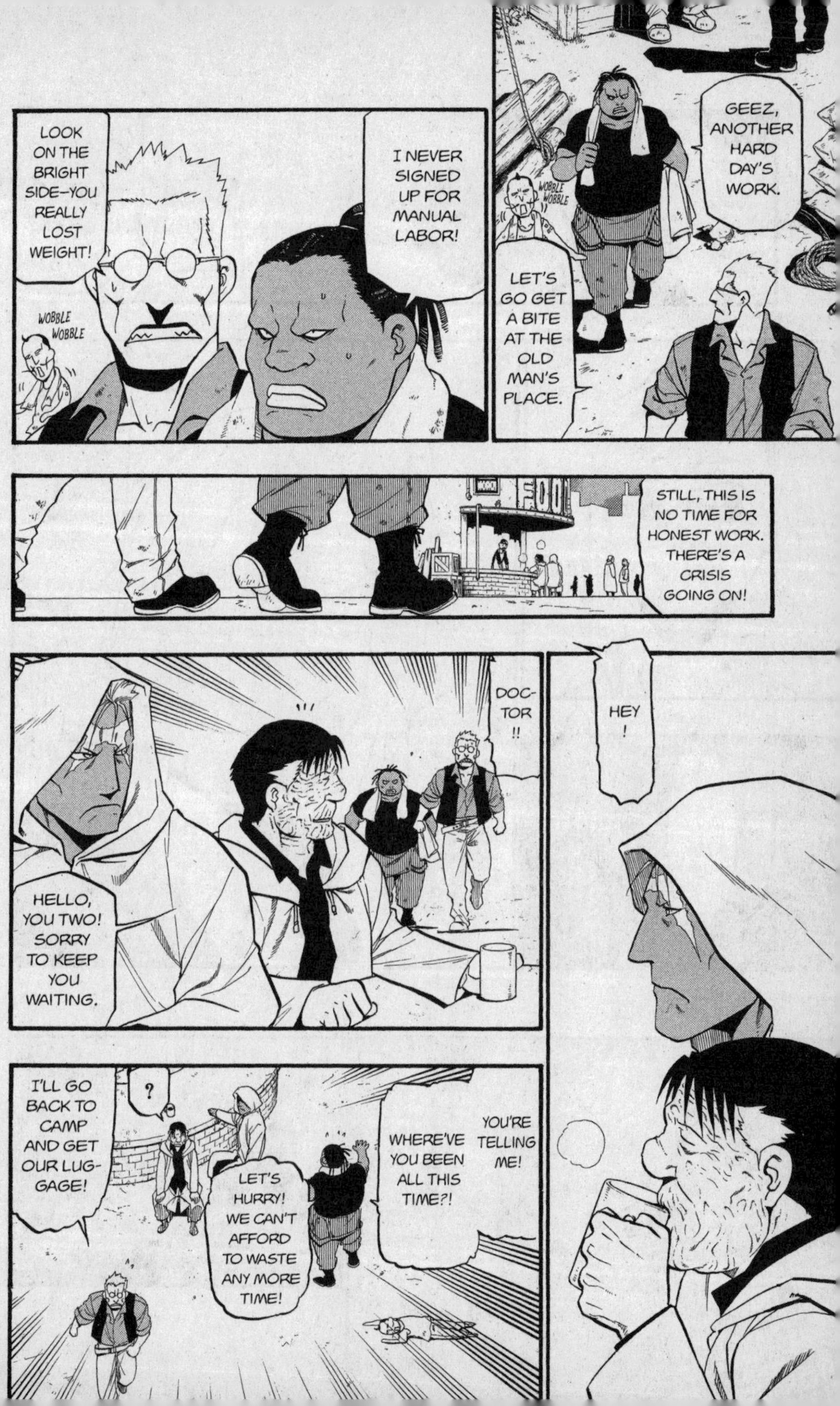
GEEZ, ANOTHER HARD DAY'S WORK.
WOBBLE WOBBLE
LET'S GO GET A BITE AT THE OLD MAN'S PLACE.
I NEVER SIGNED UP FOR MANUAL LABOR!
LOOK ON THE BRIGHT SIDE—YOU REALLY LOST WEIGHT!
WOBBLE WOBBLE
STILL, THIS IS NO TIME FOR HONEST WORK. THERE'S A CRISIS GOING ON!
HEY!
DOCTOR!!
HELLO, YOU TWO! SORRY TO KEEP YOU WAITING.
YOU'RE TELLING ME!
WHERE'VE YOU BEEN ALL THIS TIME?!
?
LET'S HURRY! WE CAN'T AFFORD TO WASTE ANY MORE TIME!
I'LL GO BACK TO CAMP AND GET OUR LUGGAGE!

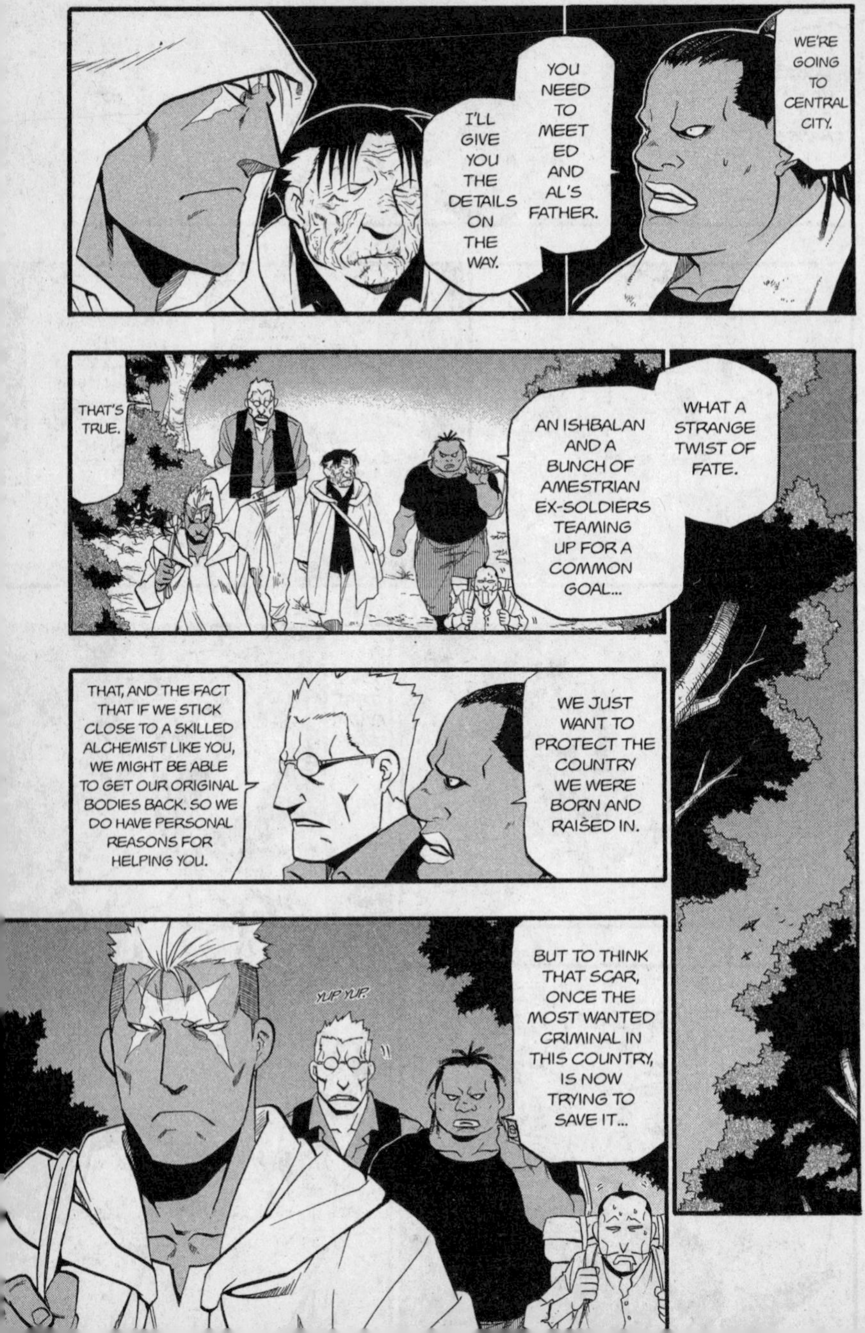
WE'RE GOING TO CENTRAL CITY.
YOU NEED TO MEET ED AND AL'S FATHER.
I'LL GIVE YOU THE DETAILS ON THE WAY.
WHAT A STRANGE TWIST OF FATE.
AN ISHBALAN AND A BUNCH OF AMESTRIAN EX-SOLDIERS TEAMING UP FOR A COMMON GOAL...
THAT'S TRUE.
WE JUST WANT TO PROTECT THE COUNTRY WE WERE BORN AND RAISED IN.
THAT, AND THE FACT THAT IF WE STICK CLOSE TO A SKILLED ALCHEMIST LIKE YOU, WE MIGHT BE ABLE TO GET OUR ORIGINAL BODIES BACK. SO WE DO HAVE PERSONAL REASONS FOR HELPING YOU.
BUT TO THINK THAT SCAR, ONCE THE MOST WANTED CRIMINAL IN THIS COUNTRY, IS NOW TRYING TO SAVE IT...
YUP YUP.

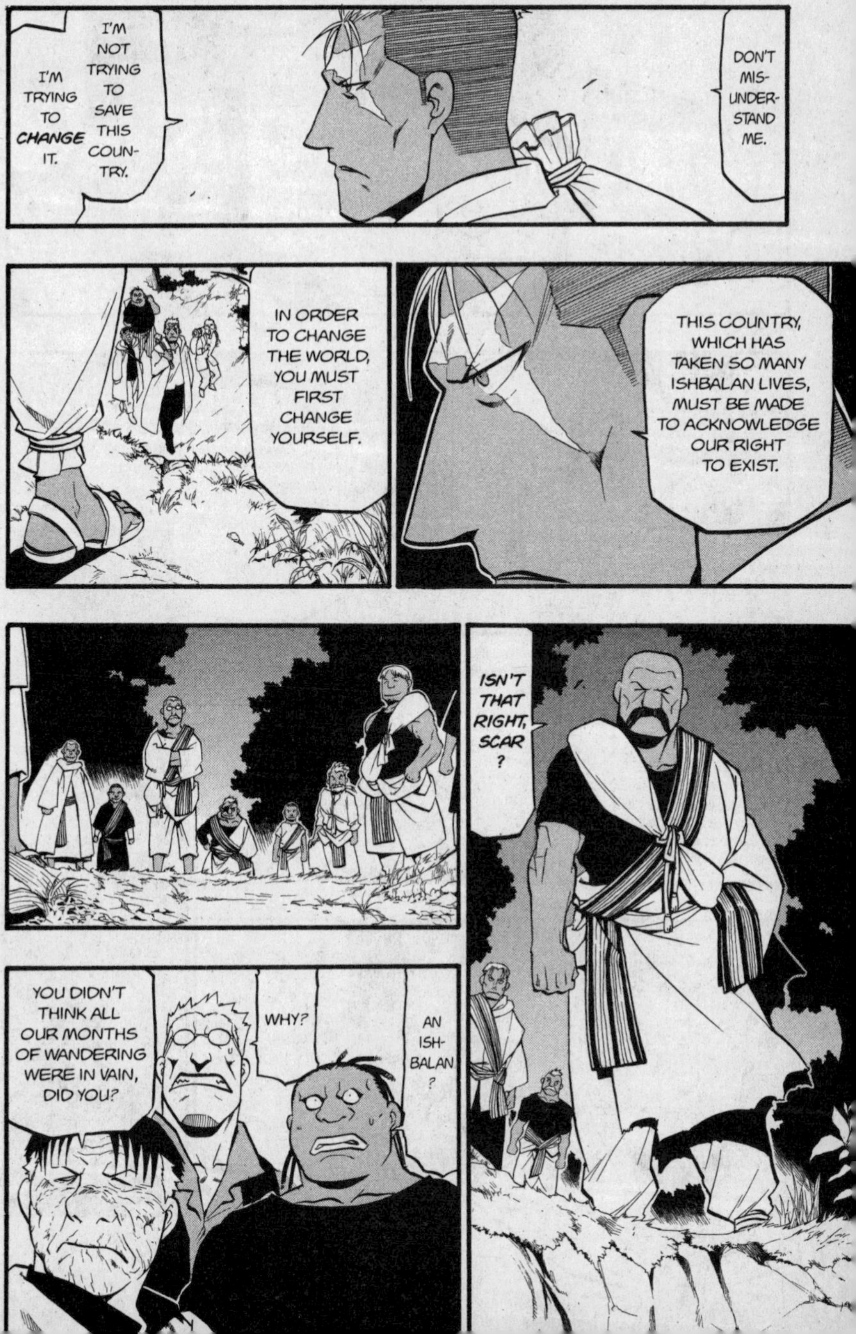
DON'T MIS-UNDER-STAND ME.
I'M NOT TRYING TO SAVE THIS COUN-TRY.
I'M TRYING TO CHANGE IT.
THIS COUNTRY, WHICH HAS TAKEN SO MANY ISHBALAN LIVES, MUST BE MADE TO ACKNOWLEDGE OUR RIGHT TO EXIST.
IN ORDER TO CHANGE THE WORLD, YOU MUST FIRST CHANGE YOURSELF.
ISN'T THAT RIGHT, SCAR?
AN ISH-BALAN?
WHY?
YOU DIDN'T THINK ALL OUR MONTHS OF WANDERING WERE IN VAIN, DID YOU?

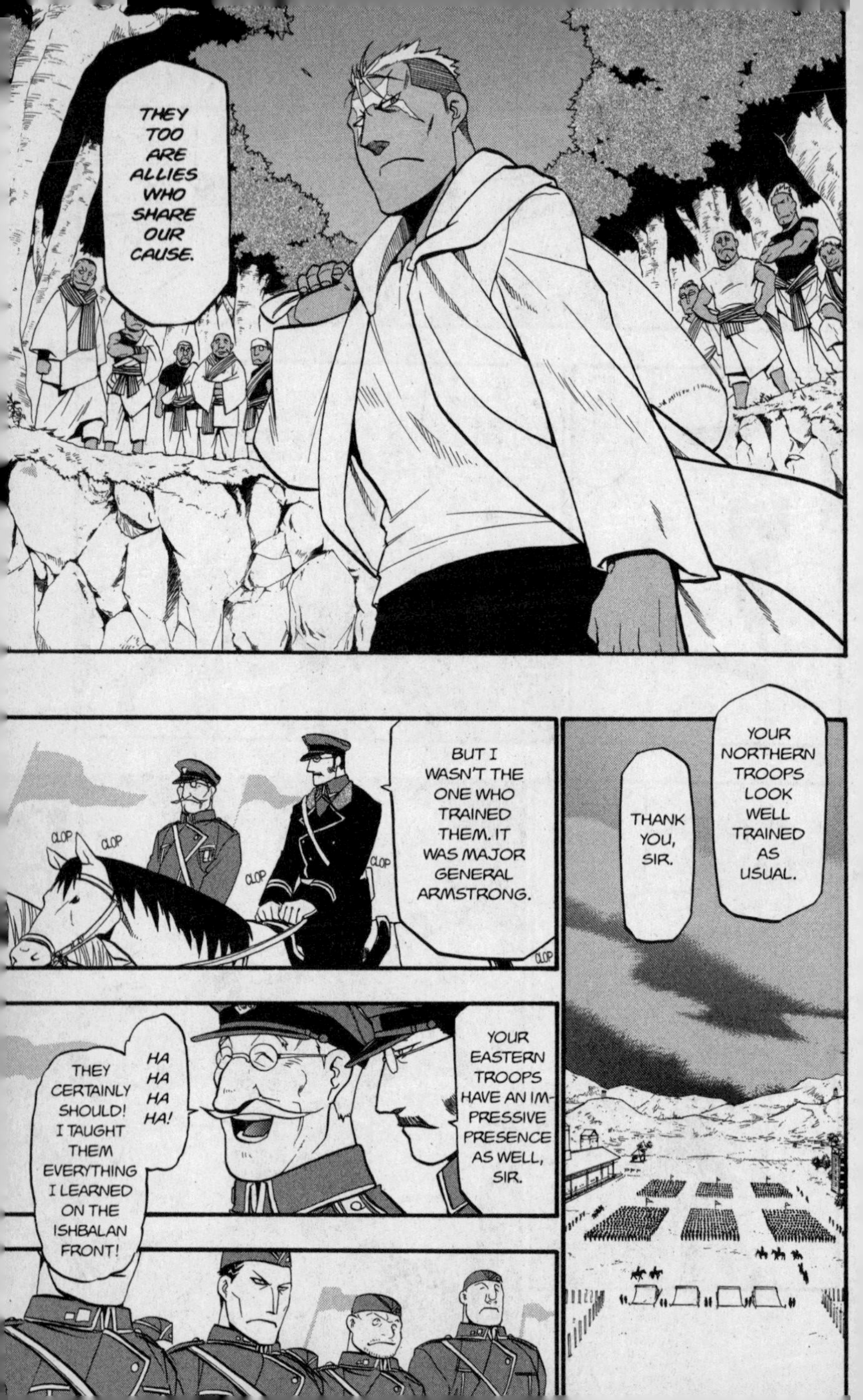
THEY TOO ARE ALLIES WHO SHARE OUR CAUSE.
YOUR NORTHERN TROOPS LOOK WELL TRAINED AS USUAL.
THANK YOU, SIR.
BUT I WASN'T THE ONE WHO TRAINED THEM. IT WAS MAJOR GENERAL ARMSTRONG.
CLOP
CLOP
CLOP
CLOP
CLOP
YOUR EASTERN TROOPS HAVE AN IMPRESSIVE PRESENCE AS WELL, SIR.
HA HA HA HA!
THEY CERTAINLY SHOULD! I TAUGHT THEM EVERYTHING I LEARNED ON THE ISHBALAN FRONT!

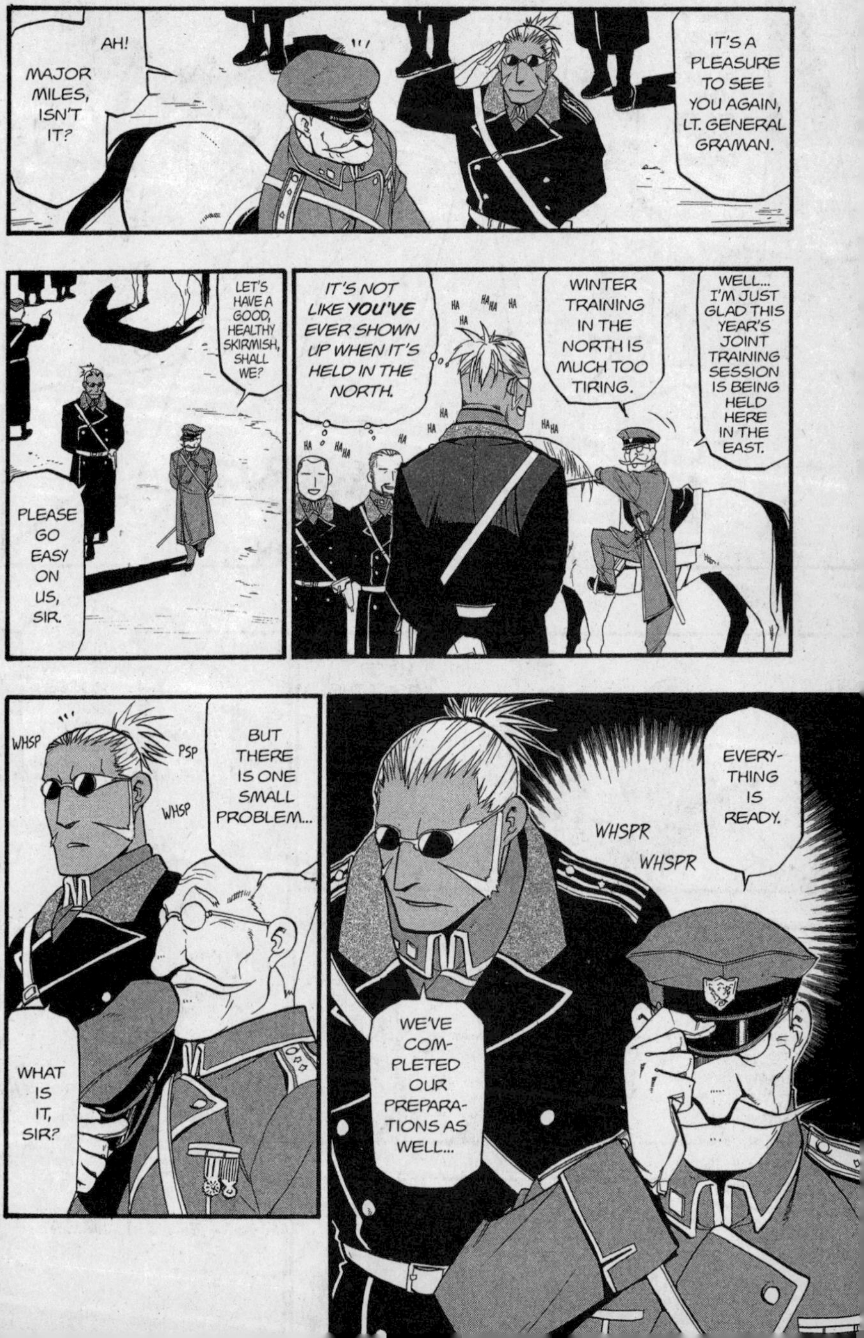
IT'S A PLEASURE TO SEE YOU AGAIN, LT. GENERAL GRAMAN.
AH!
MAJOR MILES, ISN'T IT?
WELL... I'M JUST GLAD THIS YEAR'S JOINT TRAINING SESSION IS BEING HELD HERE IN THE EAST.
WINTER TRAINING IN THE NORTH IS MUCH TOO TIRING.
HA HAHA HA HA
IT'S NOT LIKE **YOU'VE** EVER SHOWN UP WHEN IT'S HELD IN THE NORTH.
HA HA HAHA HA HA HA HAHA
LET'S HAVE A GOOD, HEALTHY SKIRMISH, SHALL WE?
PLEASE GO EASY ON US, SIR.
EVERY-THING IS READY.
WHSPR
WHSPR
WE'VE COM-PLETED OUR PREPARA-TIONS AS WELL...
BUT THERE IS ONE SMALL PROBLEM...
WHSP
PSP
WHSP
WHAT IS IT, SIR?

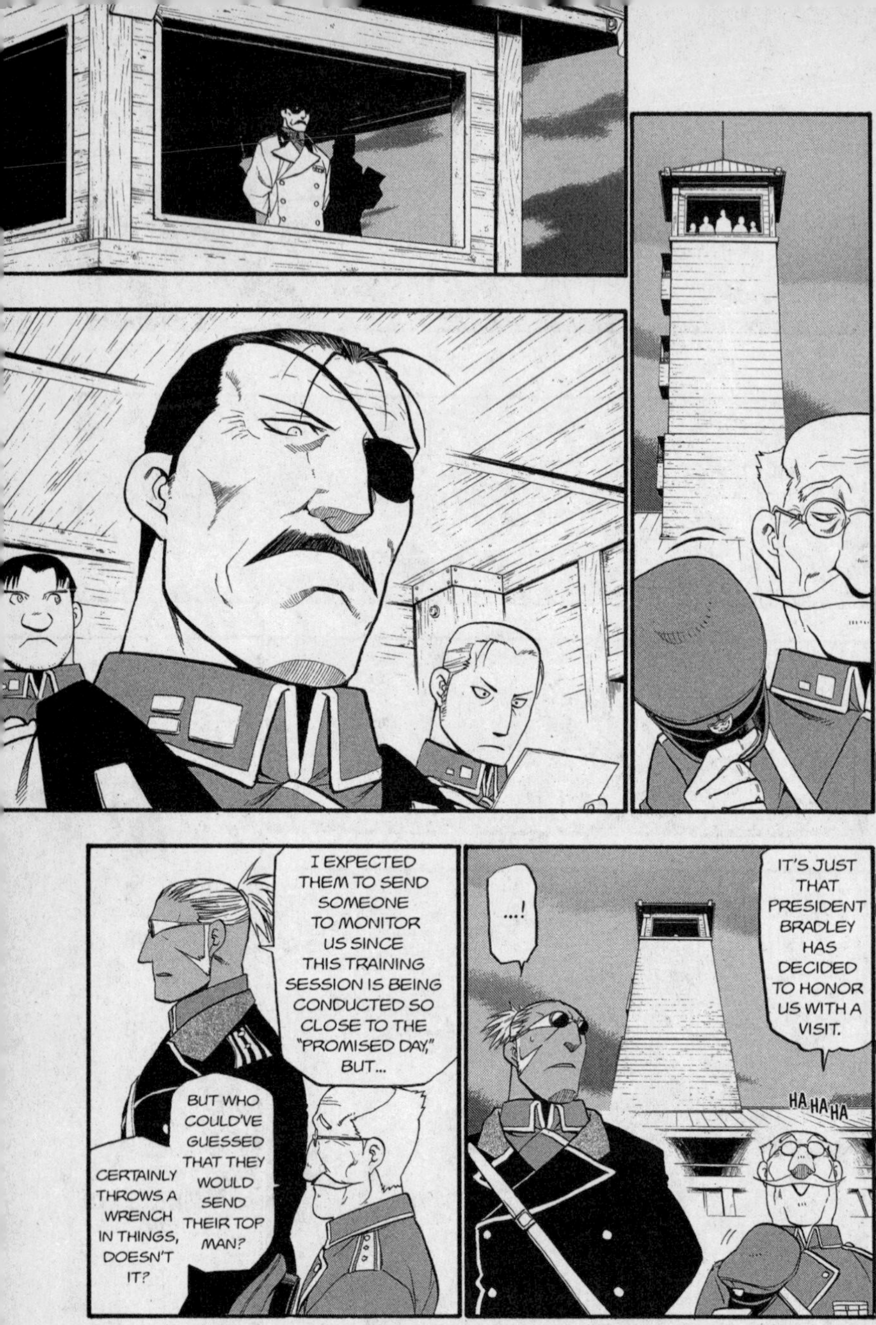
IT'S JUST THAT PRESIDENT BRADLEY HAS DECIDED TO HONOR US WITH A VISIT.
HA HA HA
....!
I EXPECTED THEM TO SEND SOMEONE TO MONITOR US SINCE THIS TRAINING SESSION IS BEING CONDUCTED SO CLOSE TO THE "PROMISED DAY," BUT...
BUT WHO COULD'VE GUESSED THAT THEY WOULD SEND THEIR TOP MAN?
CERTAINLY THROWS A WRENCH IN THINGS, DOESN'T IT?

I GUESS WE'LL JUST HAVE TO FIGURE SOMETHING OUT.

WELL.

RRGH...

TWITCH

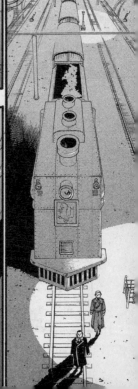

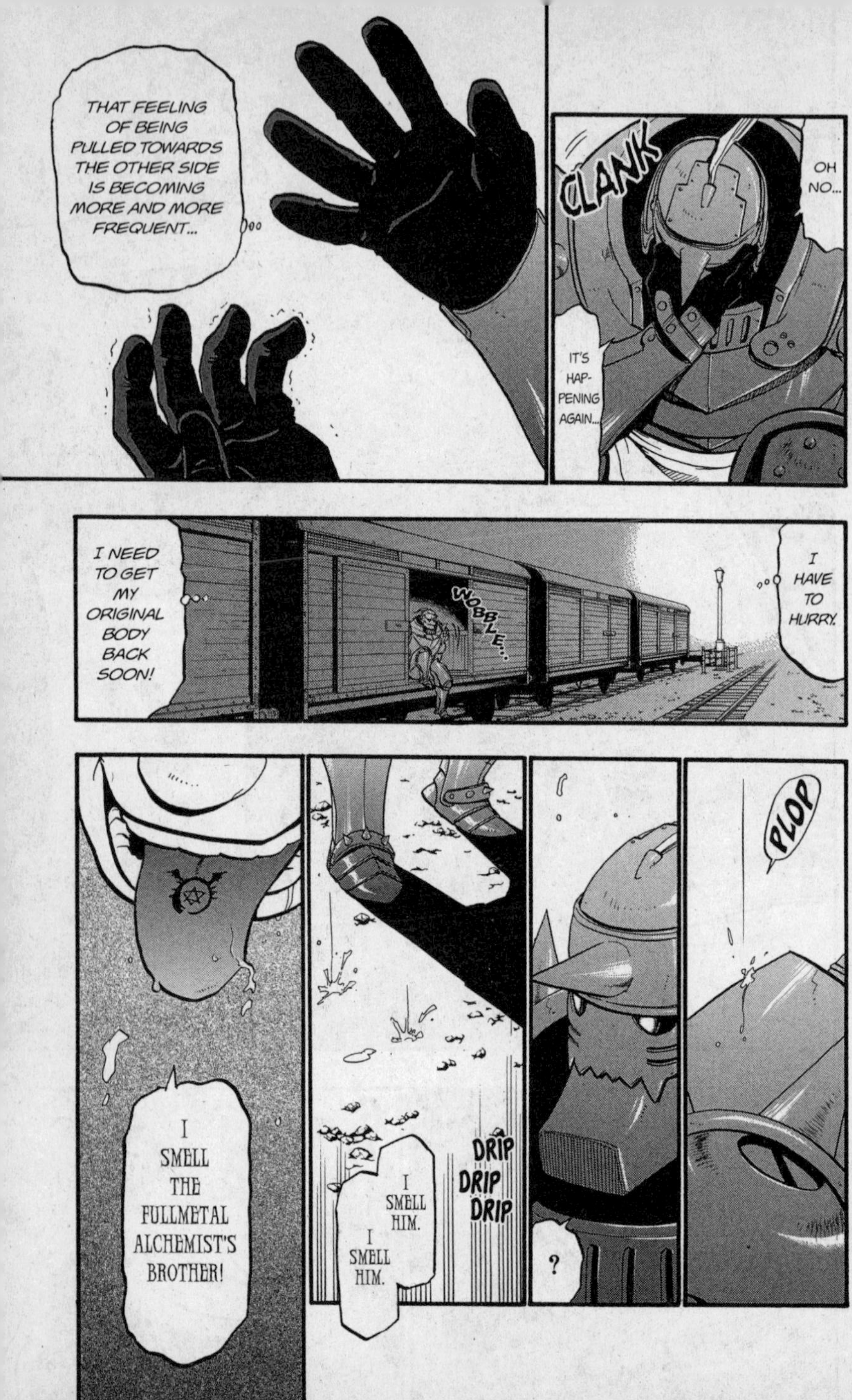
CLANK
OH NO...
IT'S HAPPENING AGAIN...
THAT FEELING OF BEING PULLED TOWARDS THE OTHER SIDE IS BECOMING MORE AND MORE FREQUENT...
I HAVE TO HURRY.
WOBBLE...
I NEED TO GET MY ORIGINAL BODY BACK SOON!
PLOP
?
DRIP DRIP DRIP
I SMELL HIM.
I SMELL HIM.
......
I SMELL THE FULLMETAL ALCHEMIST'S BROTHER!

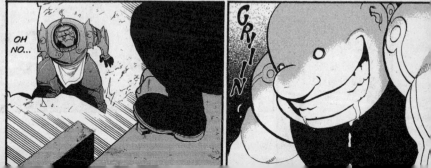

OH NO...

GRIIIN

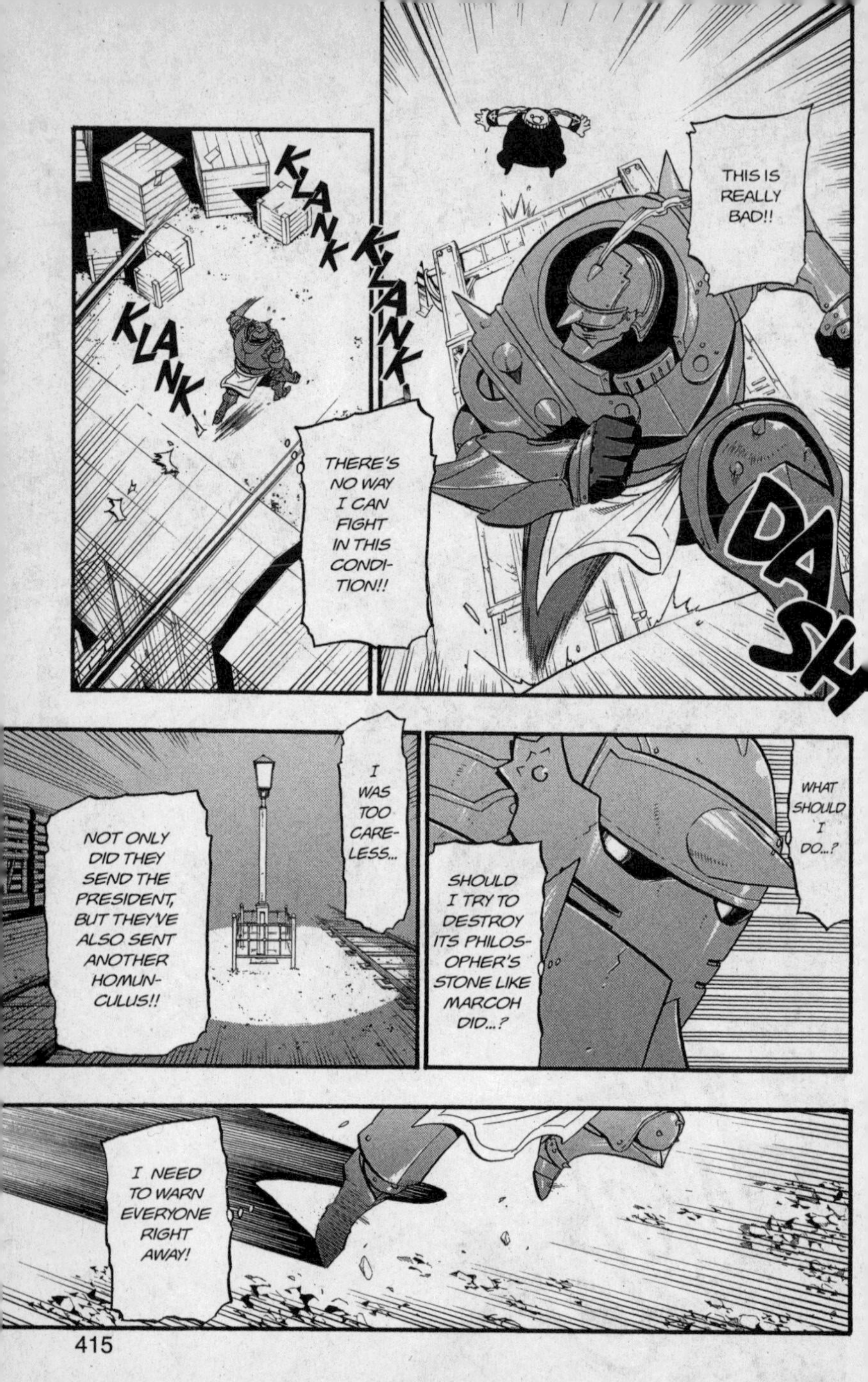
THIS IS REALLY BAD!!
DASH
KLANK
KLANK
KLANK
THERE'S NO WAY I CAN FIGHT IN THIS CONDITION!!
WHAT SHOULD I DO...?
SHOULD I TRY TO DESTROY ITS PHILOSOPHER'S STONE LIKE MARCOH DID...?
I WAS TOO CARELESS...
NOT ONLY DID THEY SEND THE PRESIDENT, BUT THEY'VE ALSO SENT ANOTHER HOMUNCULUS!!
I NEED TO WARN EVERYONE RIGHT AWAY!

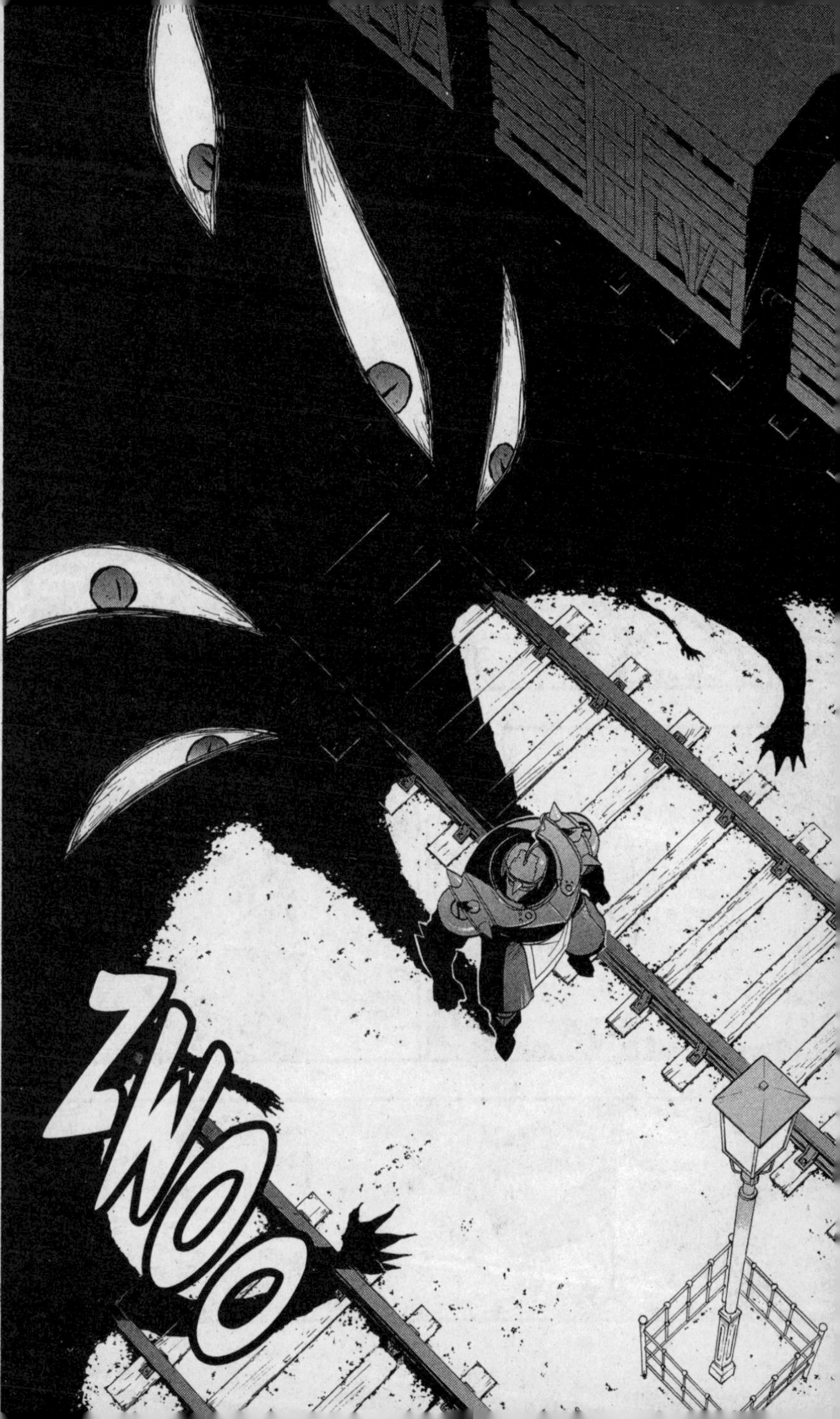
ZWOO

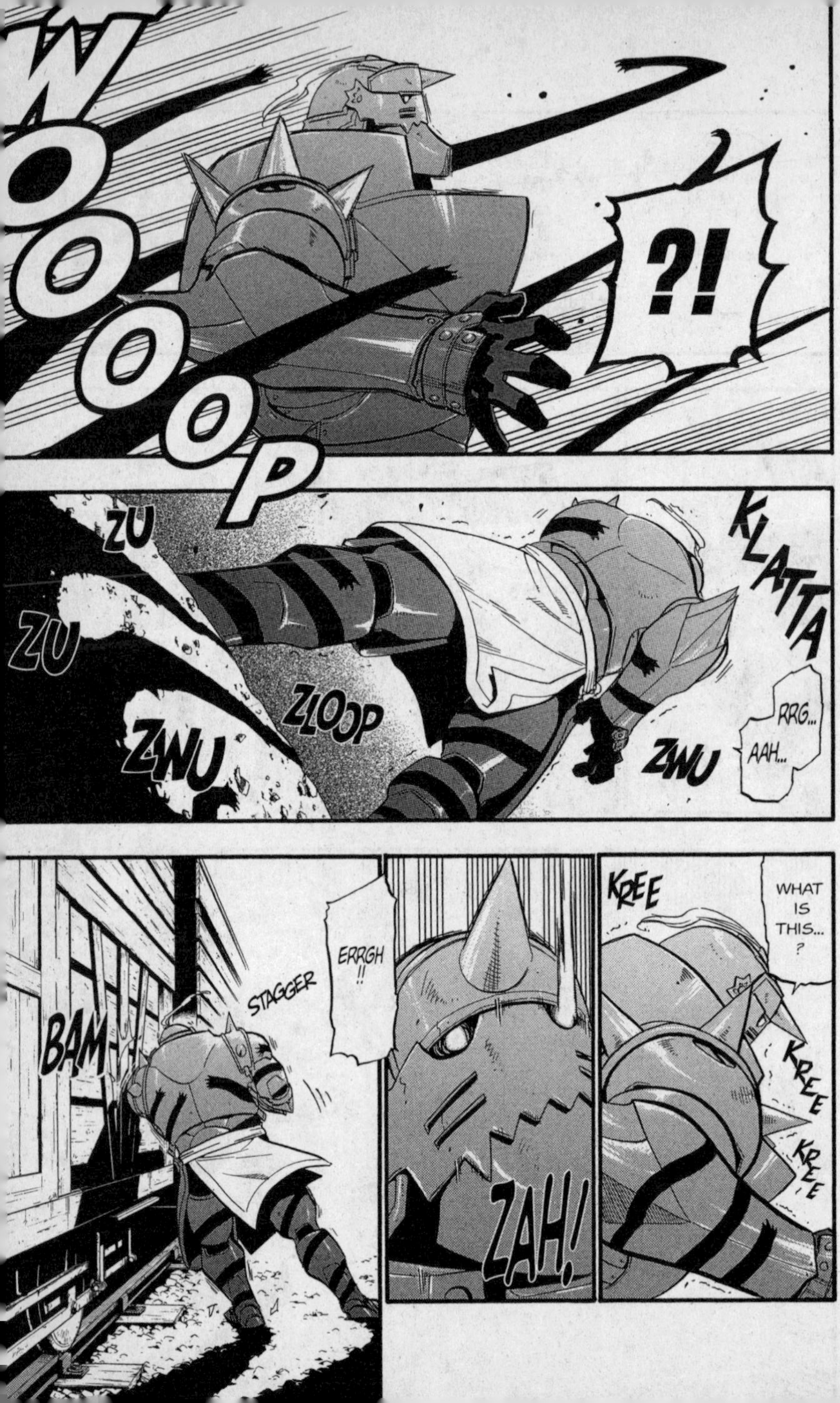
?!
WOOOOP
KLATTA
RRG... AAH...
ZWU
ZLOOP
ZU
ZU
ZWU
KREE
WHAT IS THIS...?
KREE
KREE
ZAH!
ERRGH!!
STAGGER
BAM

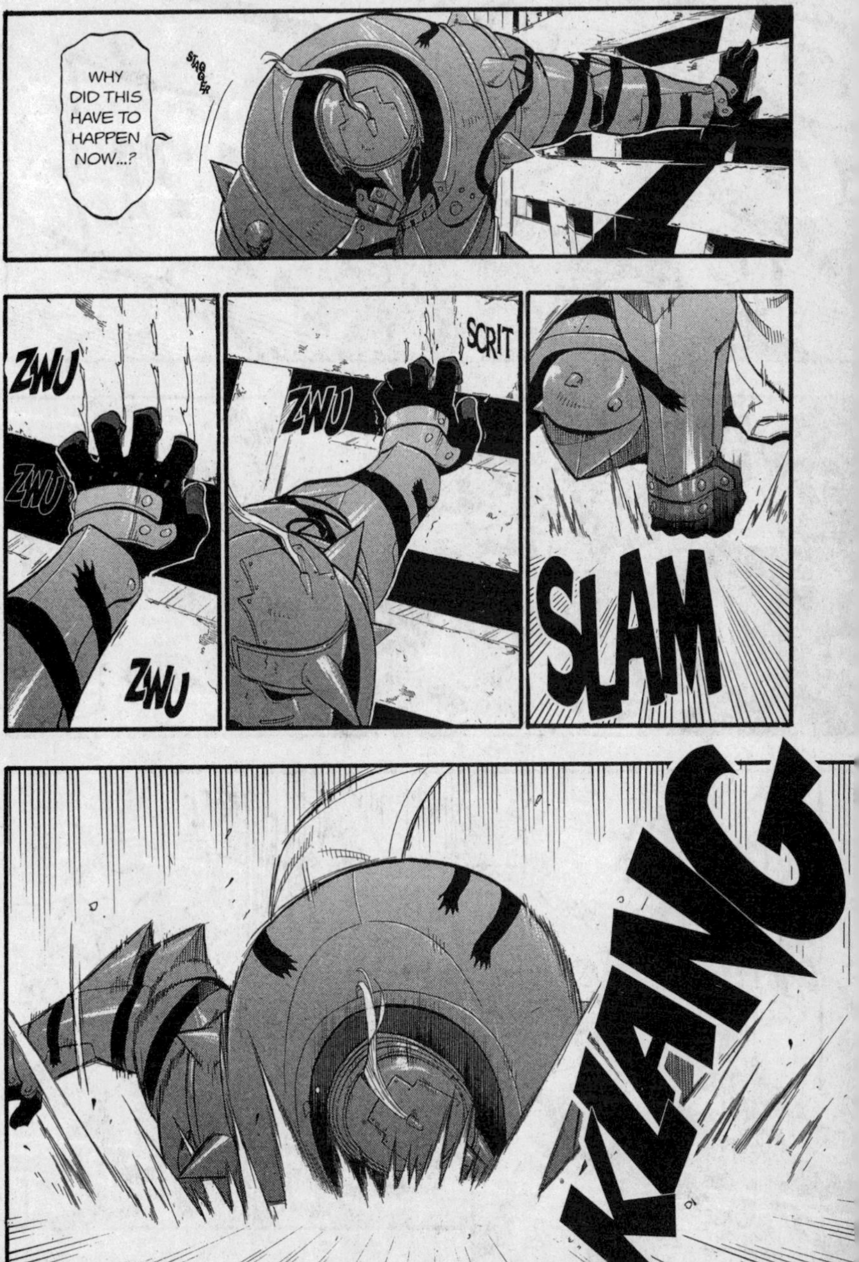

STAGGER
WHY DID THIS HAVE TO HAPPEN NOW...?
SLAM
SCRIT
ZWU
ZWU
ZWU
ZWU
KLANG

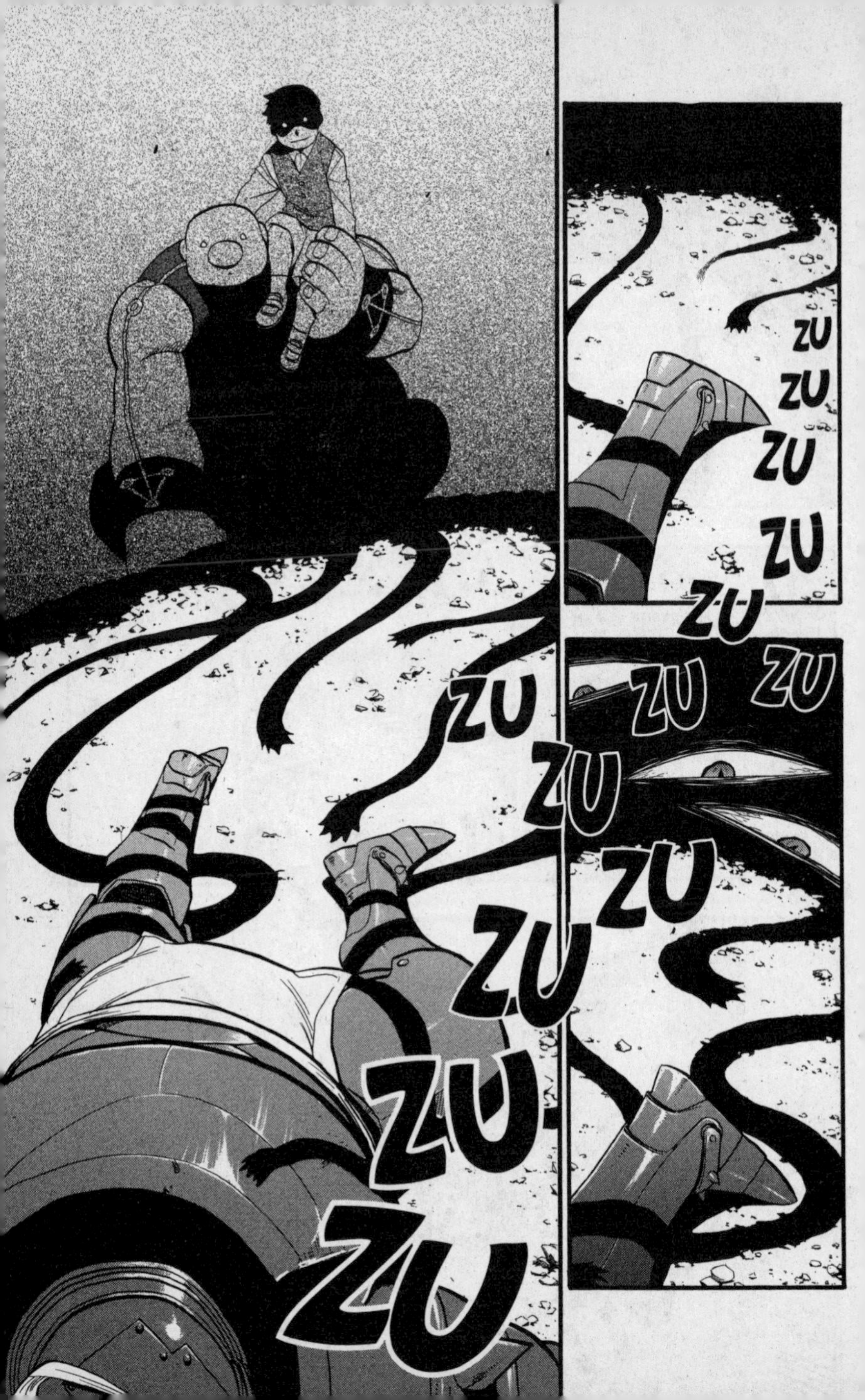
ZU
ZU
ZU
ZU
ZU
ZU
ZU
ZU
ZU
ZU
ZU
ZU
ZU

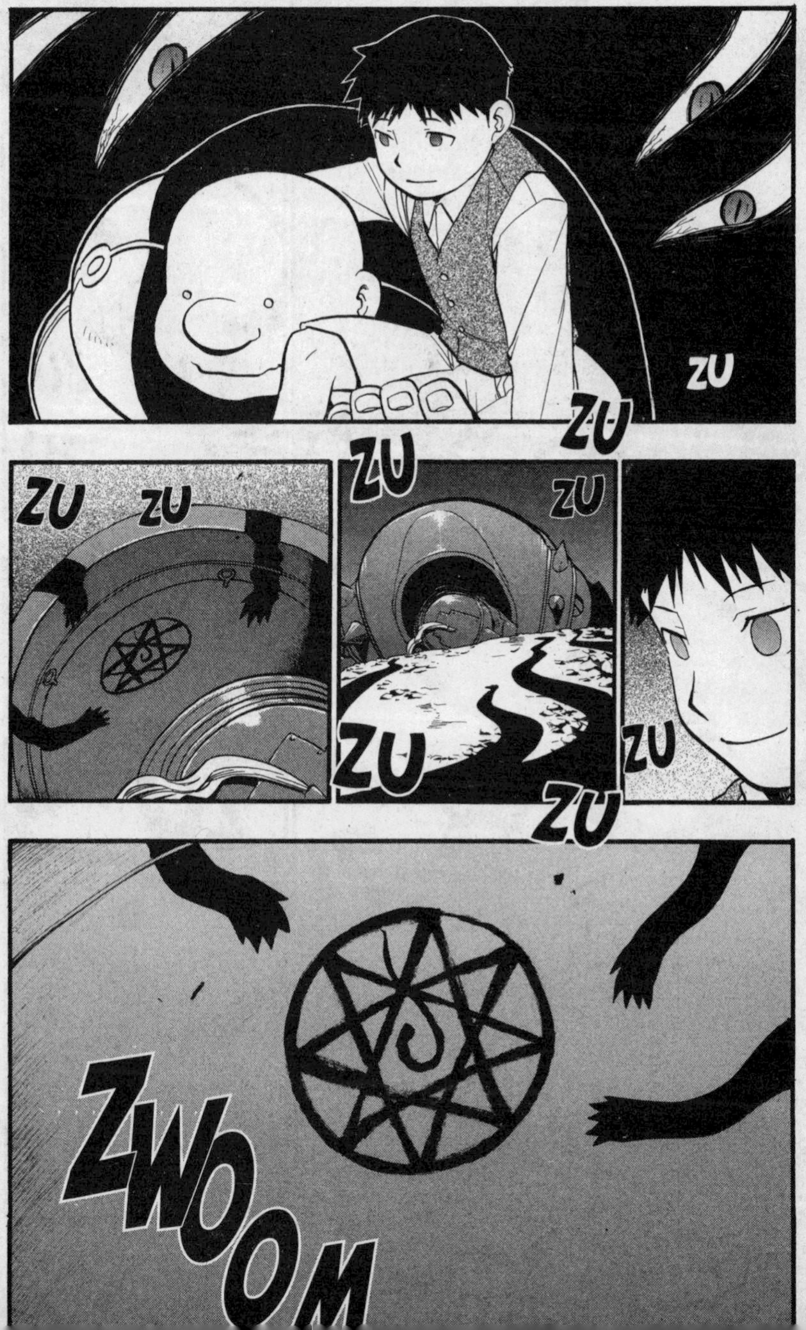
ZU
ZU
ZU
ZU
ZU
ZU
ZU
ZU
ZU
ZWOOM

FULLMETAL
ALCHEMIST

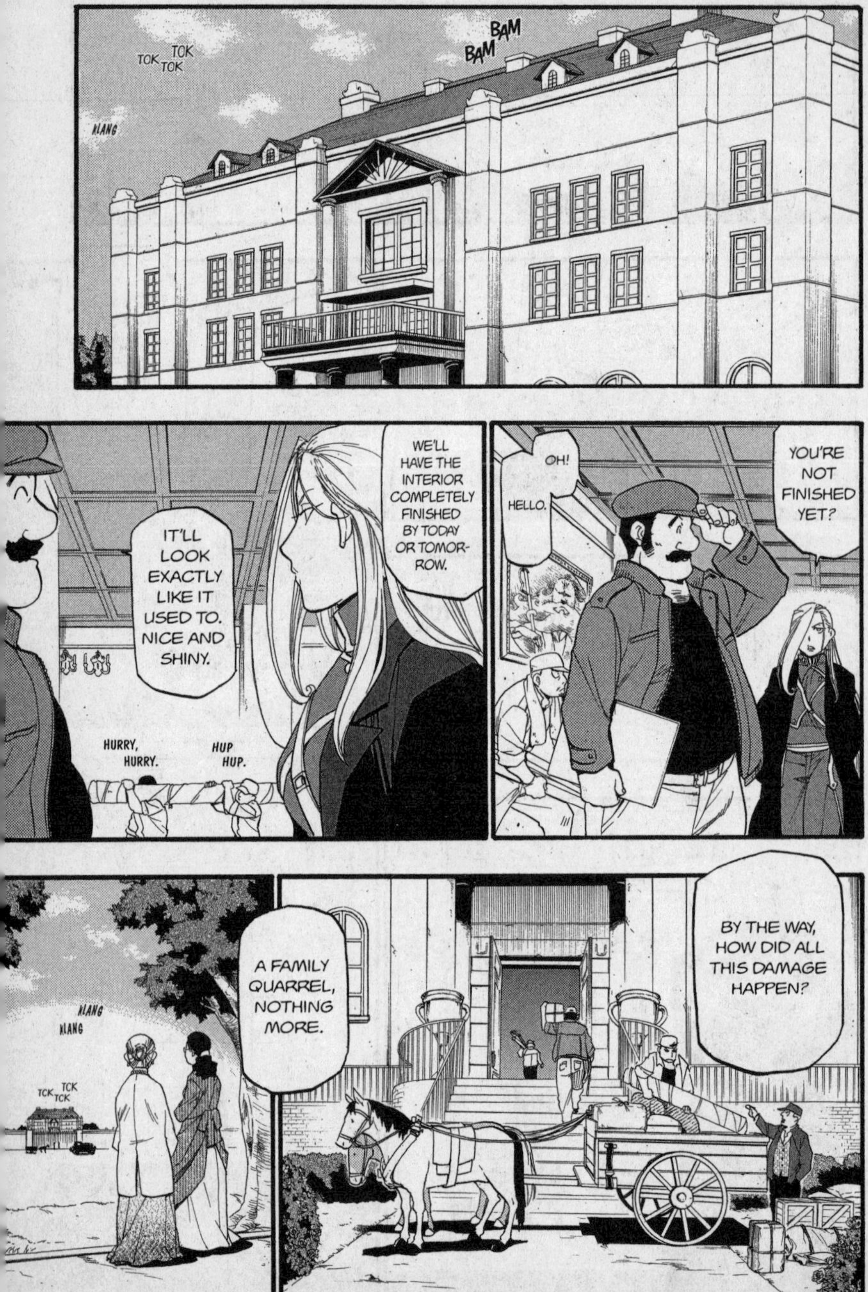
TOK TOK TOK
BAM BAM
KLANG
YOU'RE NOT FINISHED YET?
OH!
HELLO.
WE'LL HAVE THE INTERIOR COMPLETELY FINISHED BY TODAY OR TOMORROW.
IT'LL LOOK EXACTLY LIKE IT USED TO. NICE AND SHINY.
HUP HUP.
HURRY, HURRY.
BY THE WAY, HOW DID ALL THIS DAMAGE HAPPEN?
A FAMILY QUARREL, NOTHING MORE.
KLANG KLANG
TCK TCK TCK

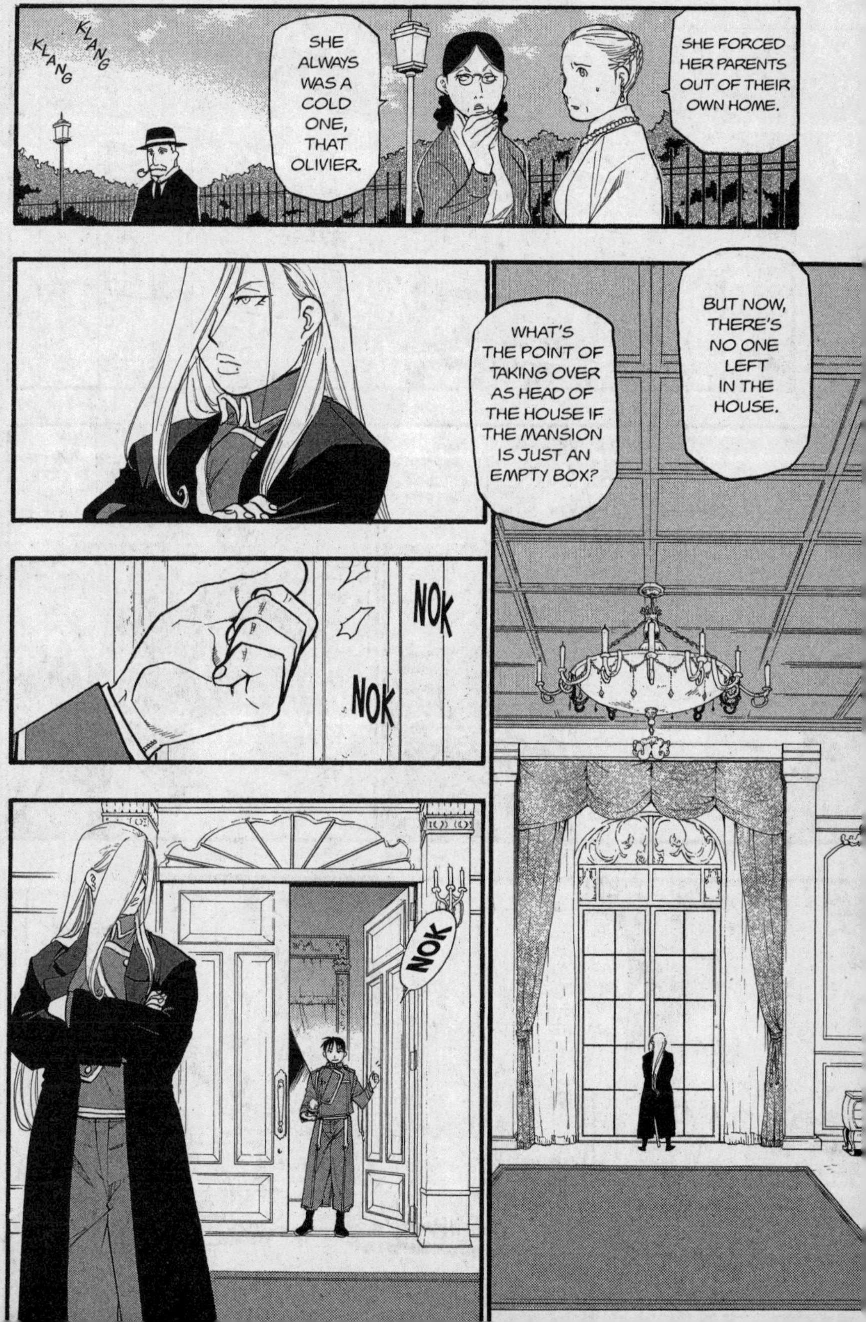
SHE FORCED HER PARENTS OUT OF THEIR OWN HOME.
SHE ALWAYS WAS A COLD ONE, THAT OLIVIER.
KLANG
KLANG
BUT NOW, THERE'S NO ONE LEFT IN THE HOUSE.
WHAT'S THE POINT OF TAKING OVER AS HEAD OF THE HOUSE IF THE MANSION IS JUST AN EMPTY BOX?
NOK
NOK
NOK

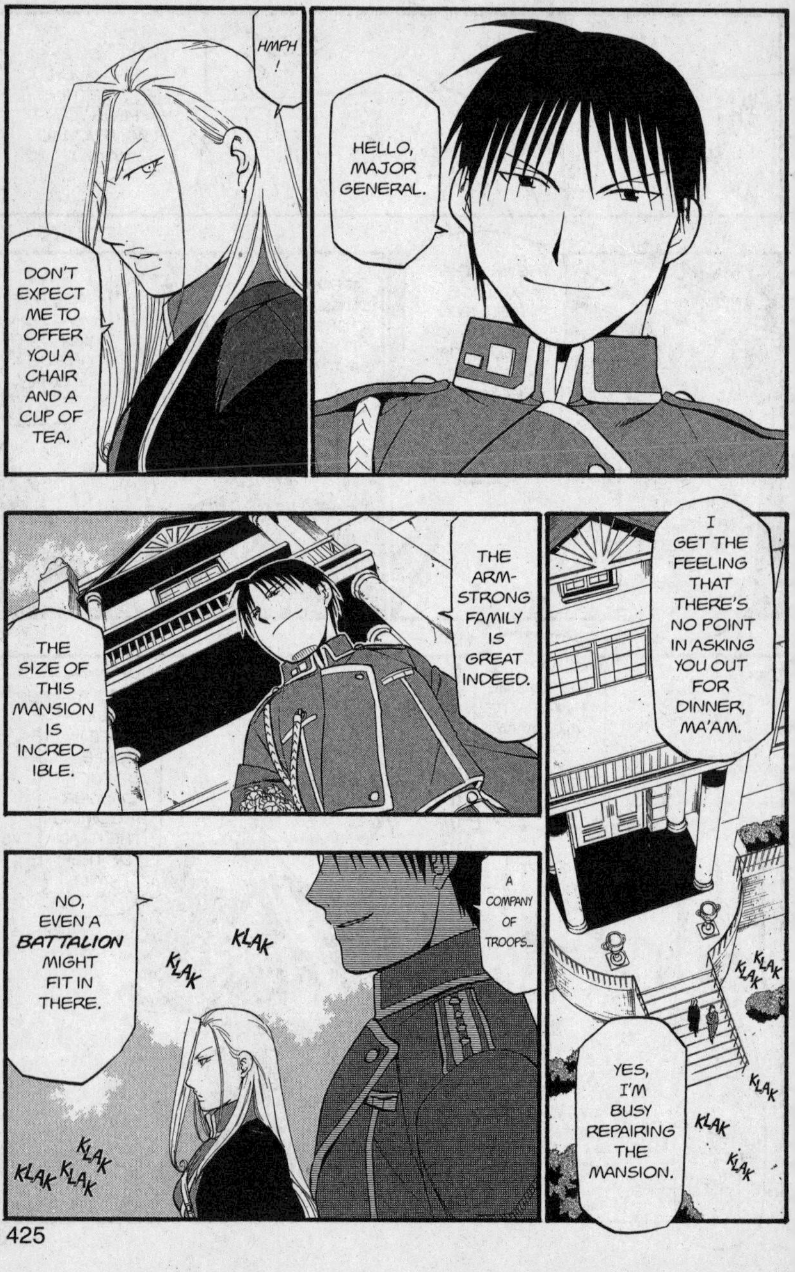
HELLO, MAJOR GENERAL.
HMPH!
DON'T EXPECT ME TO OFFER YOU A CHAIR AND A CUP OF TEA.
I GET THE FEELING THAT THERE'S NO POINT IN ASKING YOU OUT FOR DINNER, MA'AM.
KLAK KLAK
YES, I'M BUSY REPAIRING THE MANSION.
KLAK
KLAK
KLAK
THE ARMSTRONG FAMILY IS GREAT INDEED.
THE SIZE OF THIS MANSION IS INCREDIBLE.
A COMPANY OF TROOPS...
NO, EVEN A ***BATTALION*** MIGHT FIT IN THERE.
KLAK
KLAK
KLAK KLAK KLAK

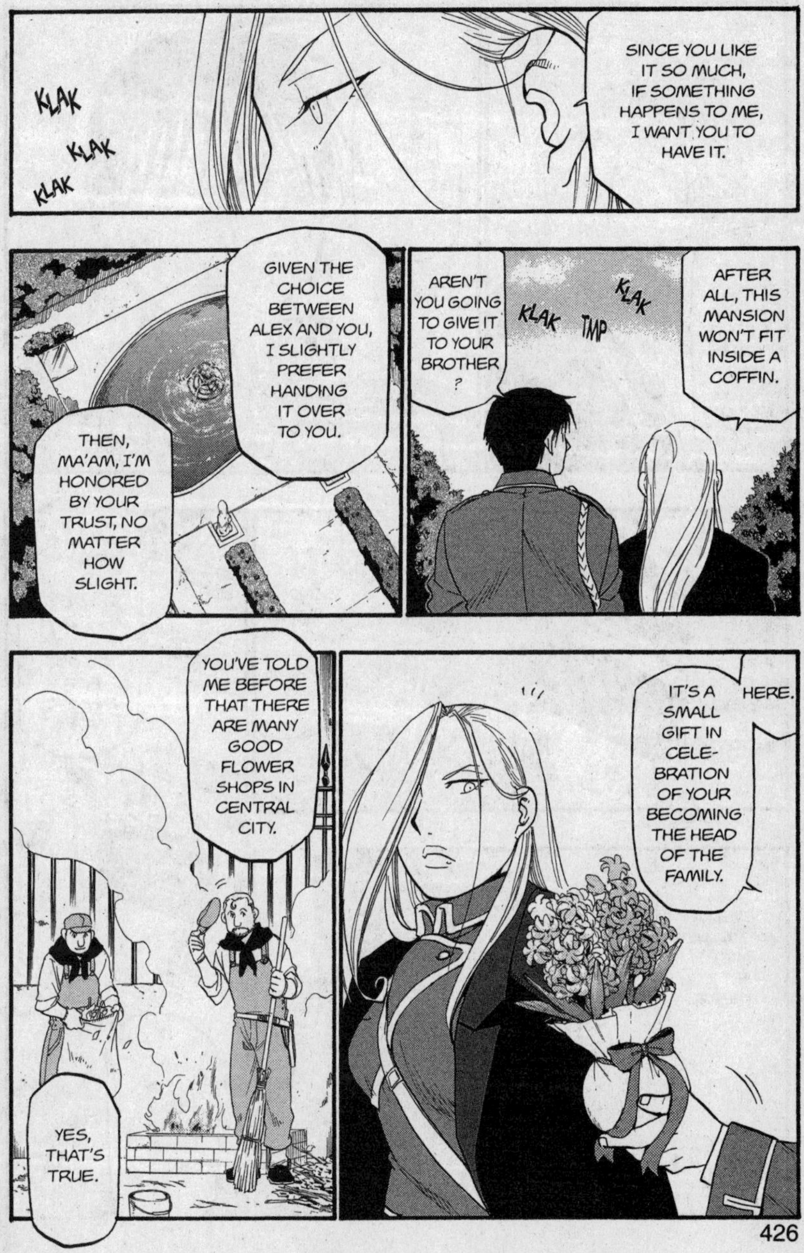
SINCE YOU LIKE IT SO MUCH, IF SOMETHING HAPPENS TO ME, I WANT YOU TO HAVE IT.
KLAK
KLAK
KLAK
AFTER ALL, THIS MANSION WON'T FIT INSIDE A COFFIN.
KLAK
TMP
KLAK
AREN'T YOU GOING TO GIVE IT TO YOUR BROTHER?
GIVEN THE CHOICE BETWEEN ALEX AND YOU, I SLIGHTLY PREFER HANDING IT OVER TO YOU.
THEN, MA'AM, I'M HONORED BY YOUR TRUST, NO MATTER HOW SLIGHT.
HERE.
IT'S A SMALL GIFT IN CELE-BRATION OF YOUR BECOMING THE HEAD OF THE FAMILY.
YOU'VE TOLD ME BEFORE THAT THERE ARE MANY GOOD FLOWER SHOPS IN CENTRAL CITY.
YES, THAT'S TRUE.

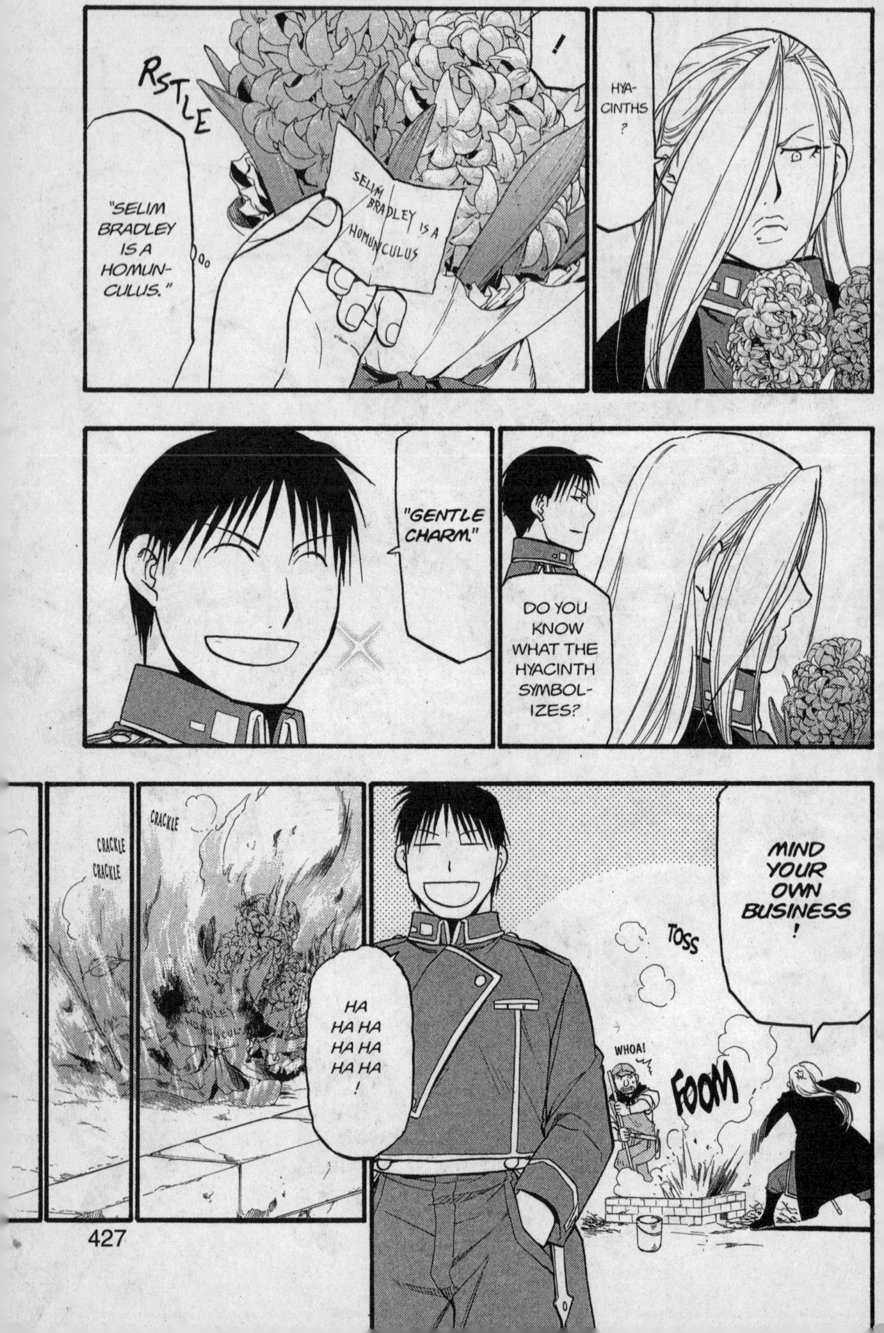
HYA-CINTHS?
!
RSTLE
SELIM BRADLEY IS A HOMUNCULUS
"SELIM BRADLEY IS A HOMUN-CULUS."
DO YOU KNOW WHAT THE HYACINTH SYMBOL-IZES?
"GENTLE CHARM."
MIND YOUR OWN BUSINESS!
TOSS
WHOA!
FOOM
HA HA HA HA HA HA HA HA!
CRACKLE
CRACKLE CRACKLE

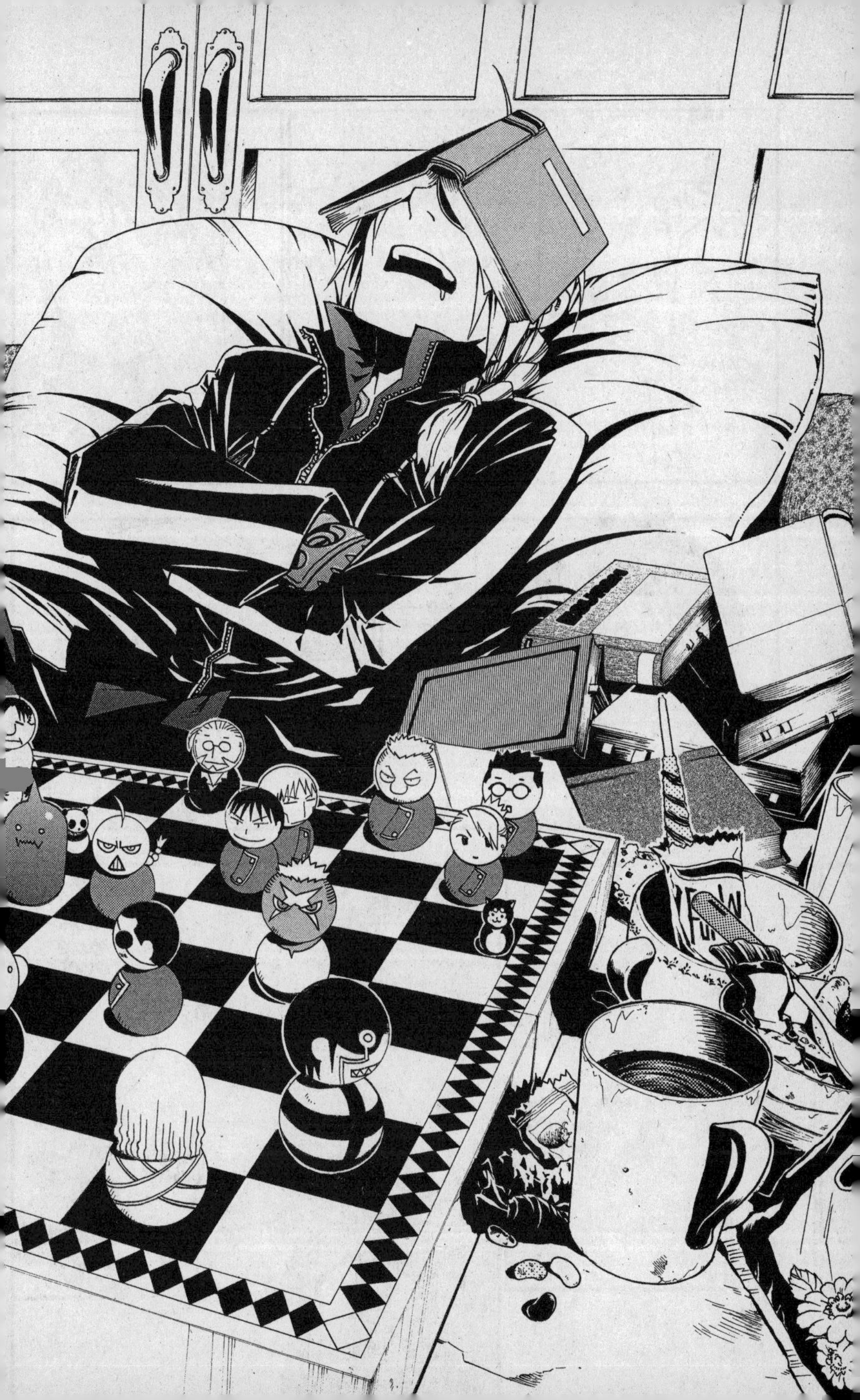

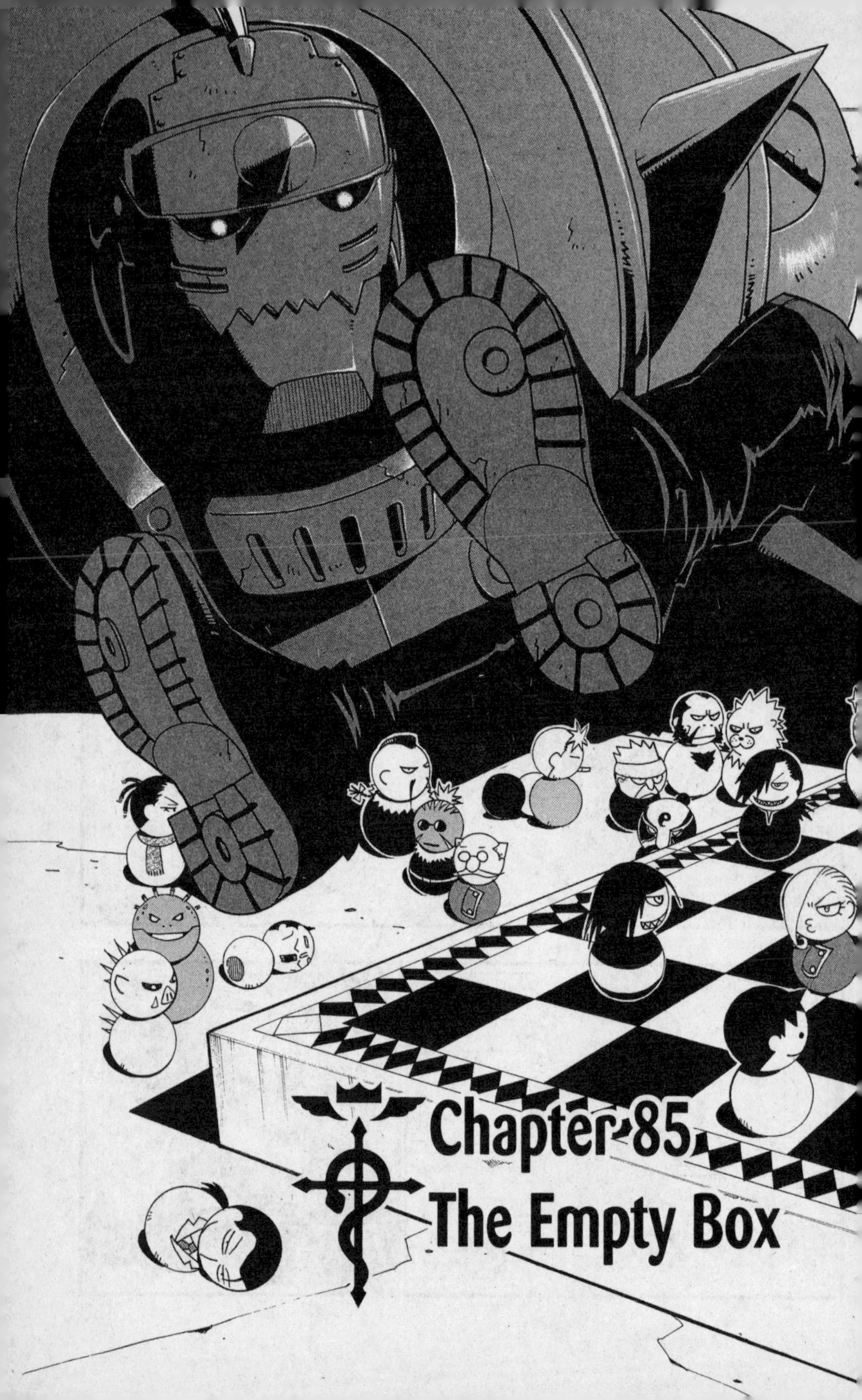
Chapter 85
The Empty Box

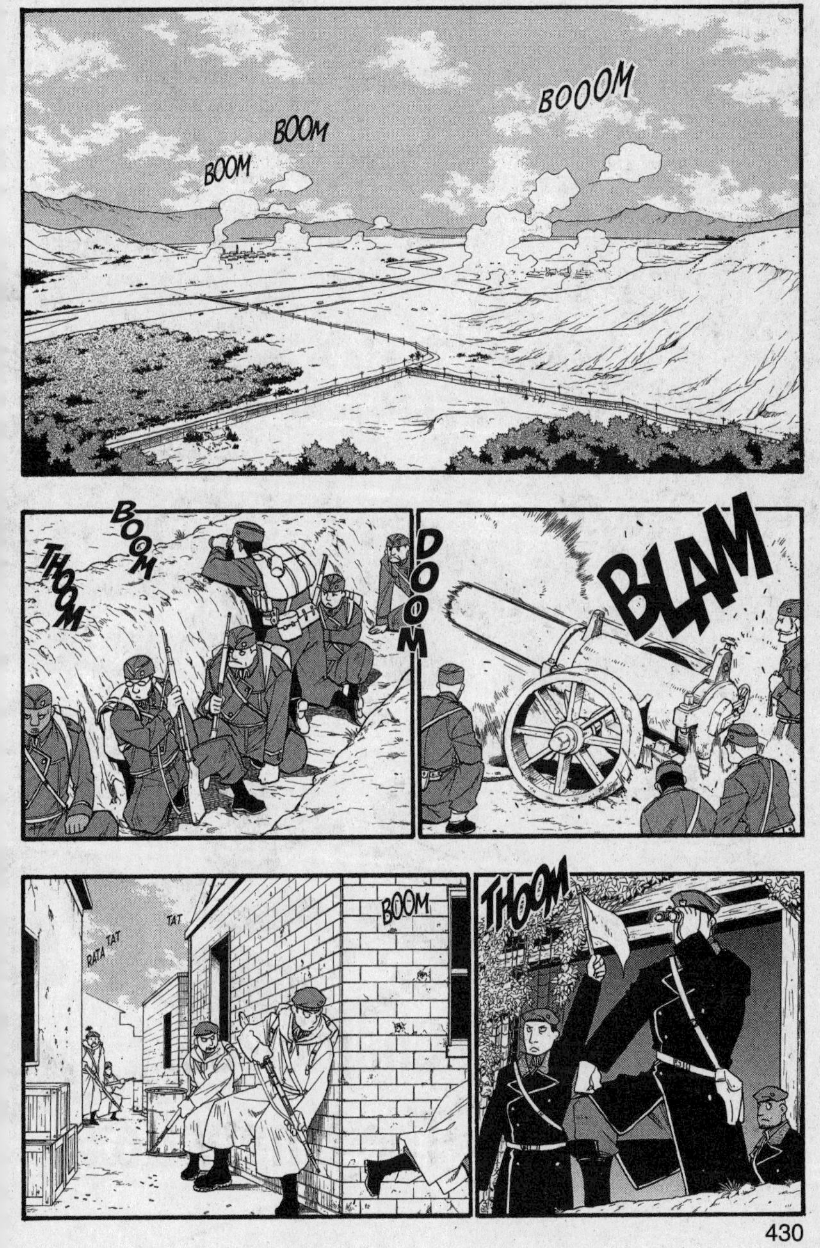
BOOOM
BOOM
BOOM
BLAM
DOOM
BOOM
THOOM
THOOM
BOOM
TAT
RATA TAT

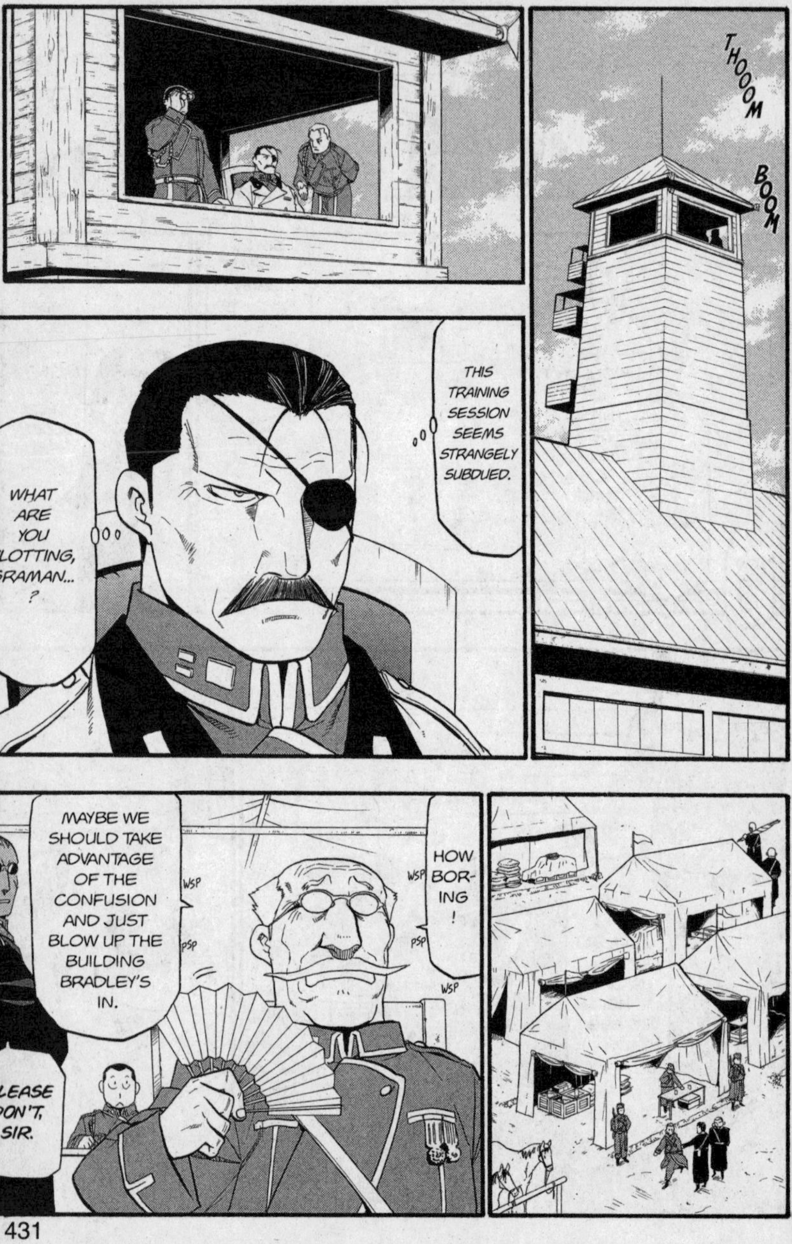
THOOOM
BOOM
THIS TRAINING SESSION SEEMS STRANGELY SUBDUED.
WHAT ARE YOU PLOTTING, GRAMAN...?
WSP
HOW BORING!
PSP
WSP
WSP
MAYBE WE SHOULD TAKE ADVANTAGE OF THE CONFUSION AND JUST BLOW UP THE BUILDING BRADLEY'S IN.
PSP
PLEASE DON'T, SIR.

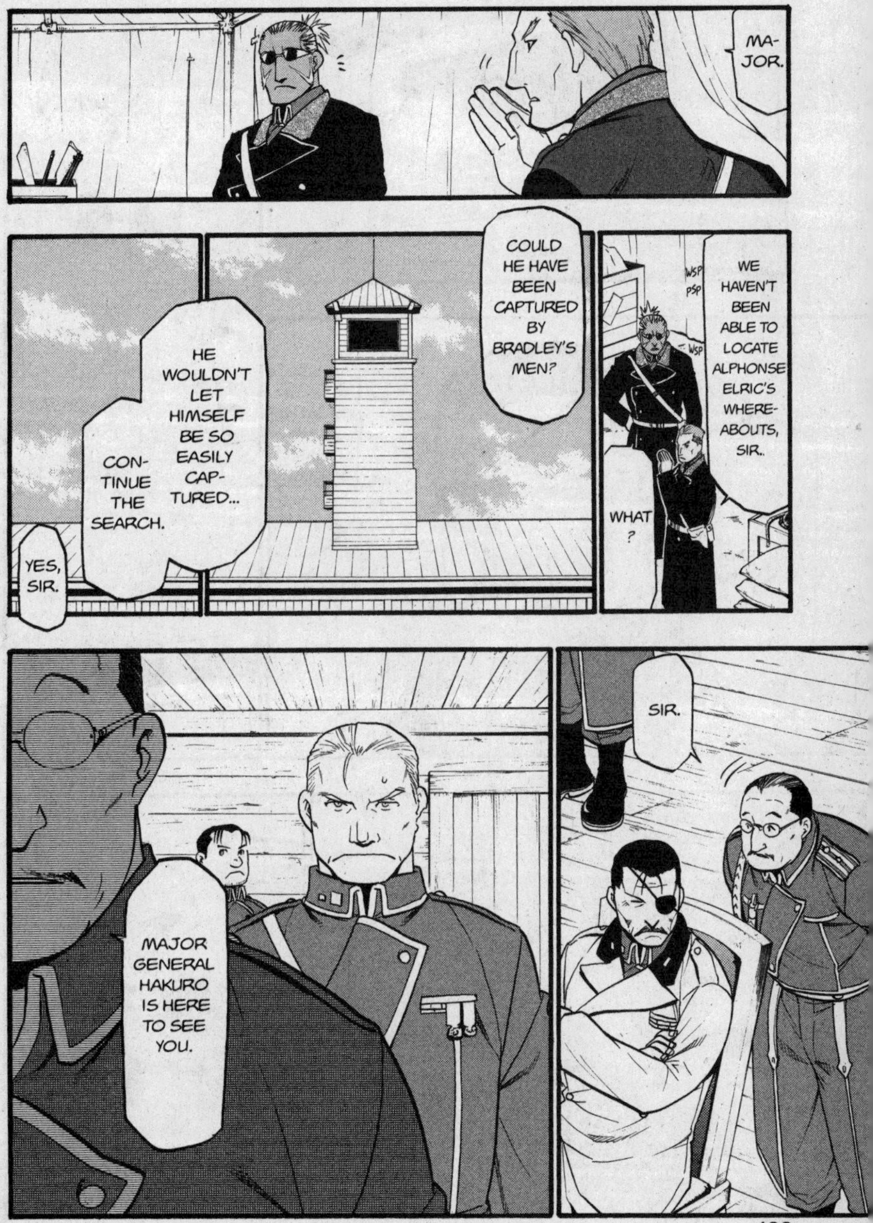
MAJOR.
WSP
PSP
WSP
WE HAVEN'T BEEN ABLE TO LOCATE ALPHONSE ELRIC'S WHEREABOUTS, SIR..
WHAT?
COULD HE HAVE BEEN CAPTURED BY BRADLEY'S MEN?
HE WOULDN'T LET HIMSELF BE SO EASILY CAPTURED...
CONTINUE THE SEARCH.
YES, SIR.
SIR.
MAJOR GENERAL HAKURO IS HERE TO SEE YOU.

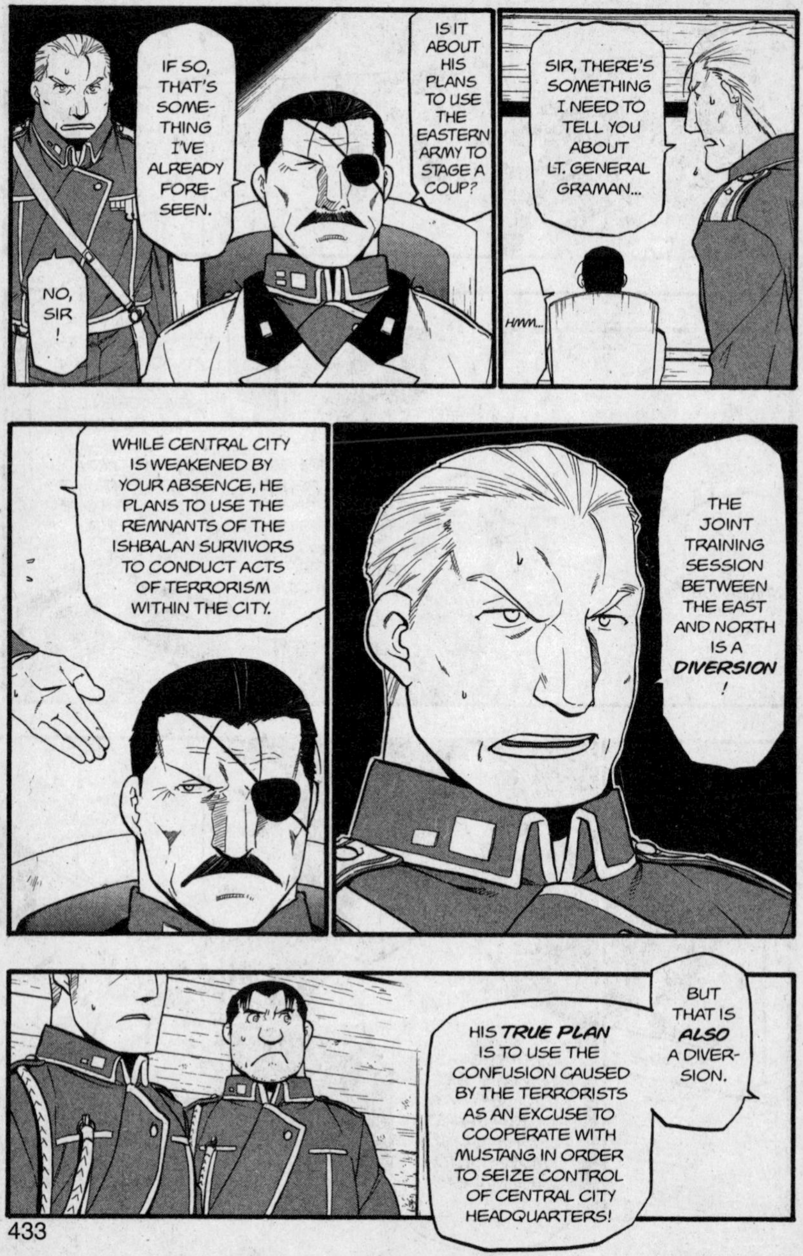
SIR, THERE'S SOMETHING I NEED TO TELL YOU ABOUT LT. GENERAL GRAMAN...
HMM...
IS IT ABOUT HIS PLANS TO USE THE EASTERN ARMY TO STAGE A COUP?
IF SO, THAT'S SOME-THING I'VE ALREADY FORE-SEEN.
NO, SIR!
THE JOINT TRAINING SESSION BETWEEN THE EAST AND NORTH IS A *DIVERSION*!
WHILE CENTRAL CITY IS WEAKENED BY YOUR ABSENCE, HE PLANS TO USE THE REMNANTS OF THE ISHBALAN SURVIVORS TO CONDUCT ACTS OF TERRORISM WITHIN THE CITY.
BUT THAT IS *ALSO* A DIVER-SION.
HIS *TRUE PLAN* IS TO USE THE CONFUSION CAUSED BY THE TERRORISTS AS AN EXCUSE TO COOPERATE WITH MUSTANG IN ORDER TO SEIZE CONTROL OF CENTRAL CITY HEADQUARTERS!

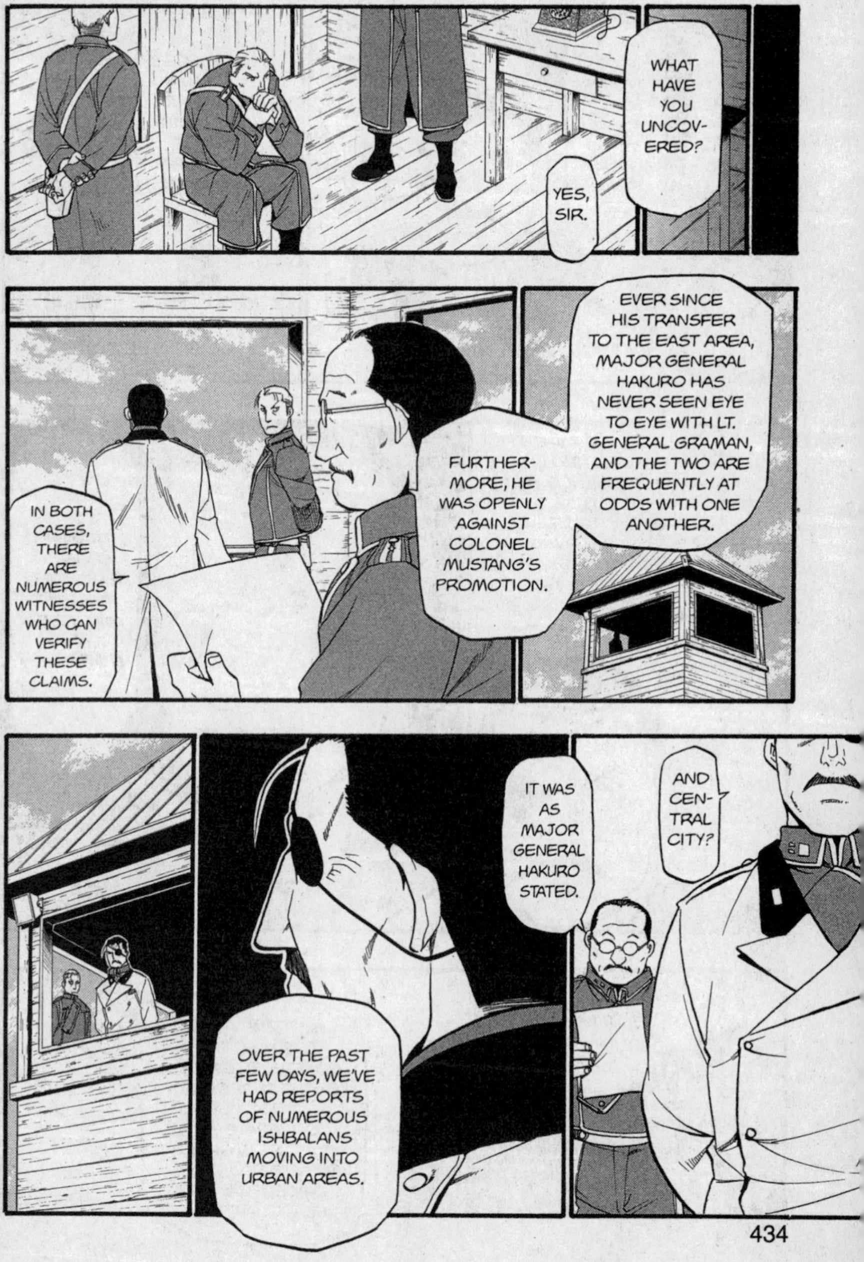
WHAT HAVE YOU UNCOVERED?
YES, SIR.
EVER SINCE HIS TRANSFER TO THE EAST AREA, MAJOR GENERAL HAKURO HAS NEVER SEEN EYE TO EYE WITH LT. GENERAL GRAMAN, AND THE TWO ARE FREQUENTLY AT ODDS WITH ONE ANOTHER.
FURTHERMORE, HE WAS OPENLY AGAINST COLONEL MUSTANG'S PROMOTION.
IN BOTH CASES, THERE ARE NUMEROUS WITNESSES WHO CAN VERIFY THESE CLAIMS.
AND CENTRAL CITY?
IT WAS AS MAJOR GENERAL HAKURO STATED.
OVER THE PAST FEW DAYS, WE'VE HAD REPORTS OF NUMEROUS ISHBALANS MOVING INTO URBAN AREAS.

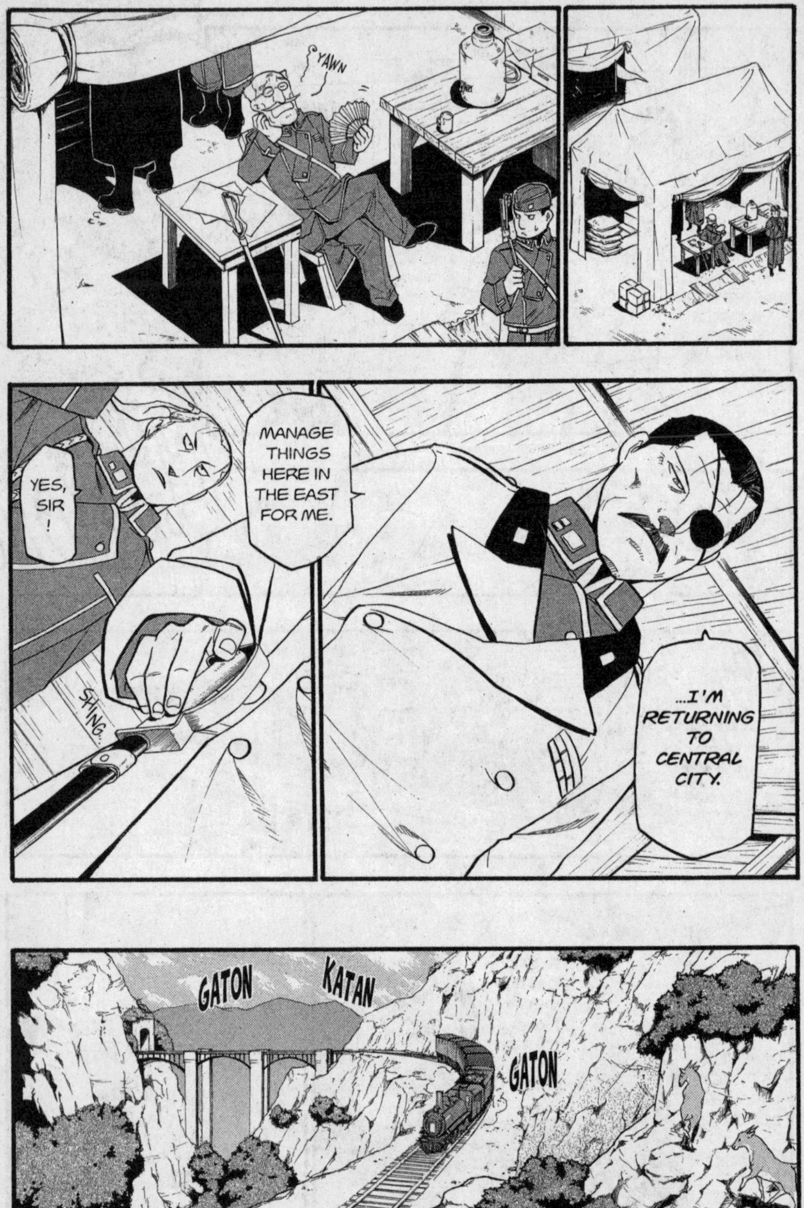
YAWN
...I'M RETURNING TO CENTRAL CITY.
MANAGE THINGS HERE IN THE EAST FOR ME.
YES, SIR!
SHING...
GATON
KATAN
GATON

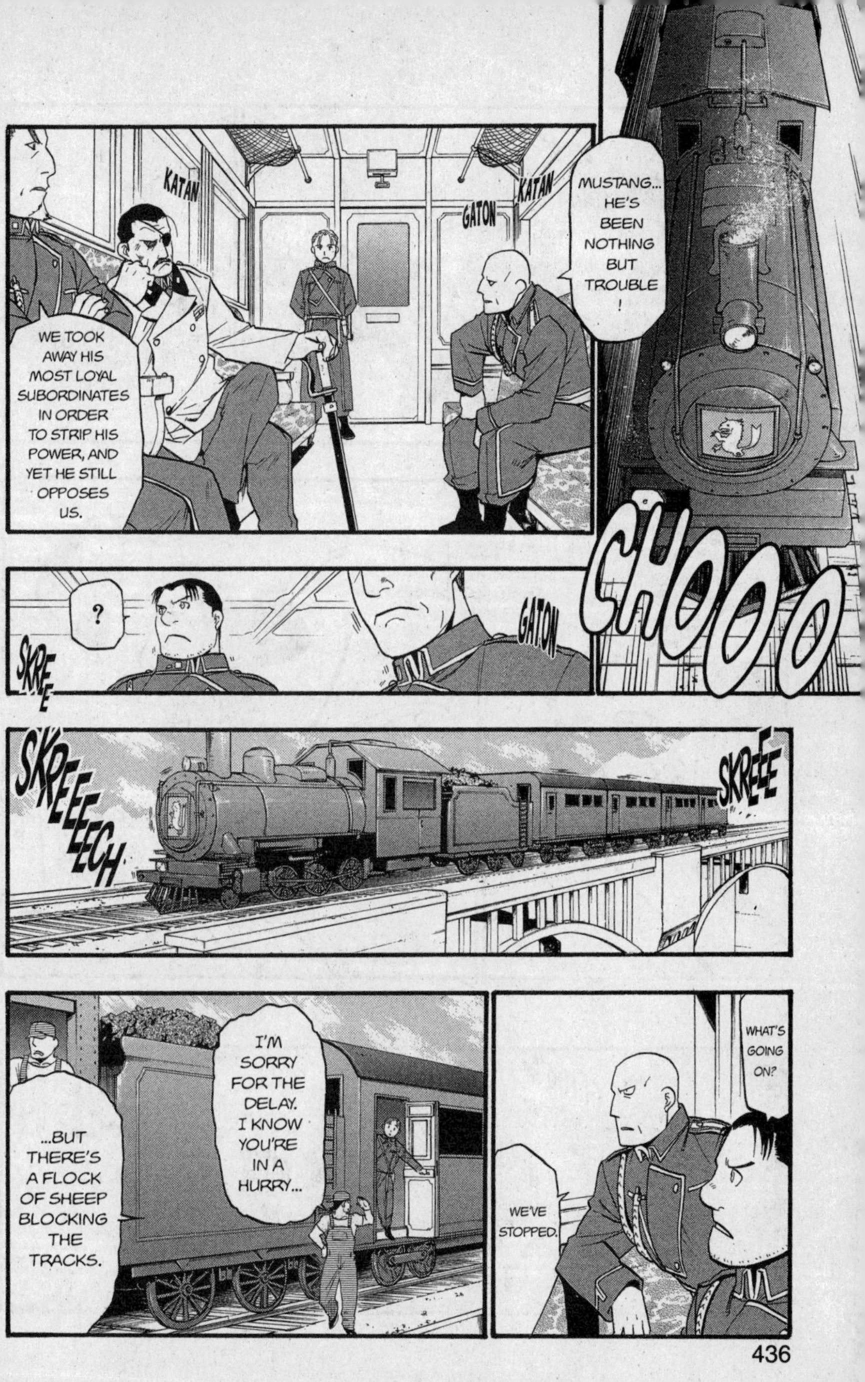
CHOOOO
MUSTANG... HE'S BEEN NOTHING BUT TROUBLE!
KATAN
GATON
KATAN
WE TOOK AWAY HIS MOST LOYAL SUBORDINATES IN ORDER TO STRIP HIS POWER, AND YET HE STILL OPPOSES US.
GATON
?
SKREE
SKREEE
SKREEEEECH
WHAT'S GOING ON?
WE'VE STOPPED.
I'M SORRY FOR THE DELAY. I KNOW YOU'RE IN A HURRY...
...BUT THERE'S A FLOCK OF SHEEP BLOCKING THE TRACKS.

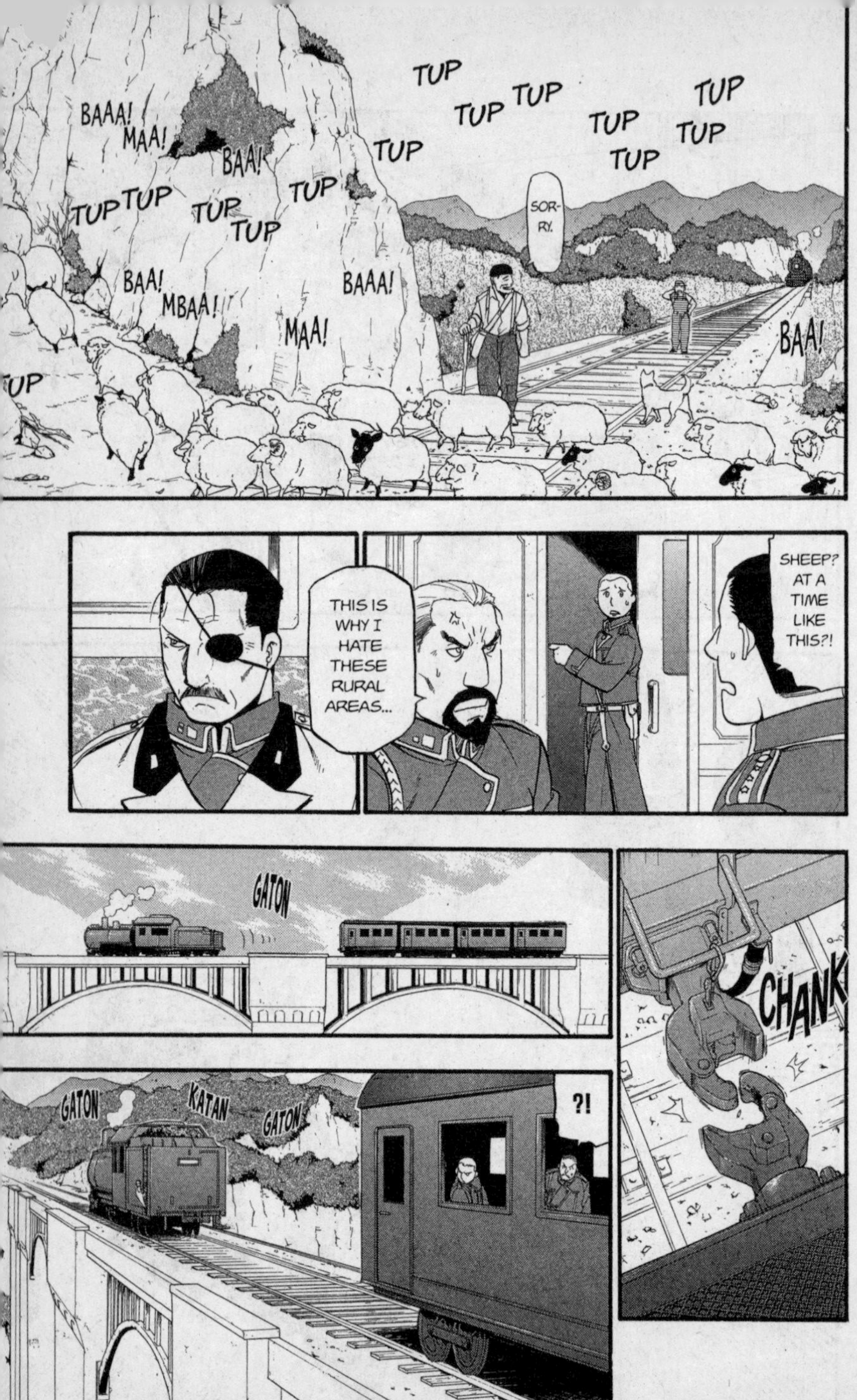
TUP
TUP
TUP
TUP TUP
TUP
TUP
TUP
BAA!
SOR-RY.
TUP
BAAA!
MAA!
BAA!
TUP
TUP TUP
TUP
TUP
BAAA!
BAA!
MBAA!
MAA!
UP
SHEEP? AT A TIME LIKE THIS?!
THIS IS WHY I HATE THESE RURAL AREAS...
CHANK
GATON
?!
GATON
KATAN
GATON

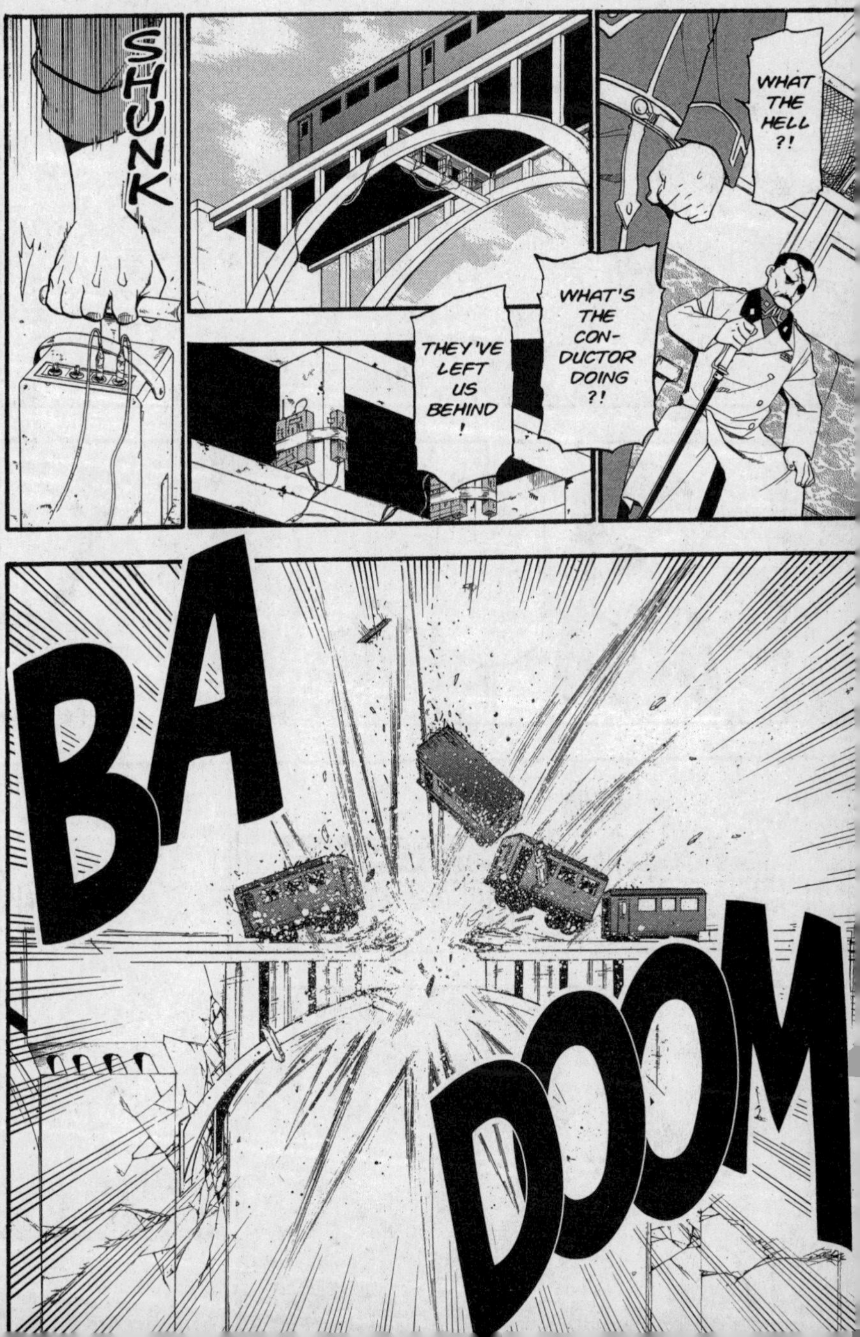
WHAT THE HELL ?!
WHAT'S THE CON-DUCTOR DOING ?!
THEY'VE LEFT US BEHIND !
SHUNK
BA
DOOM

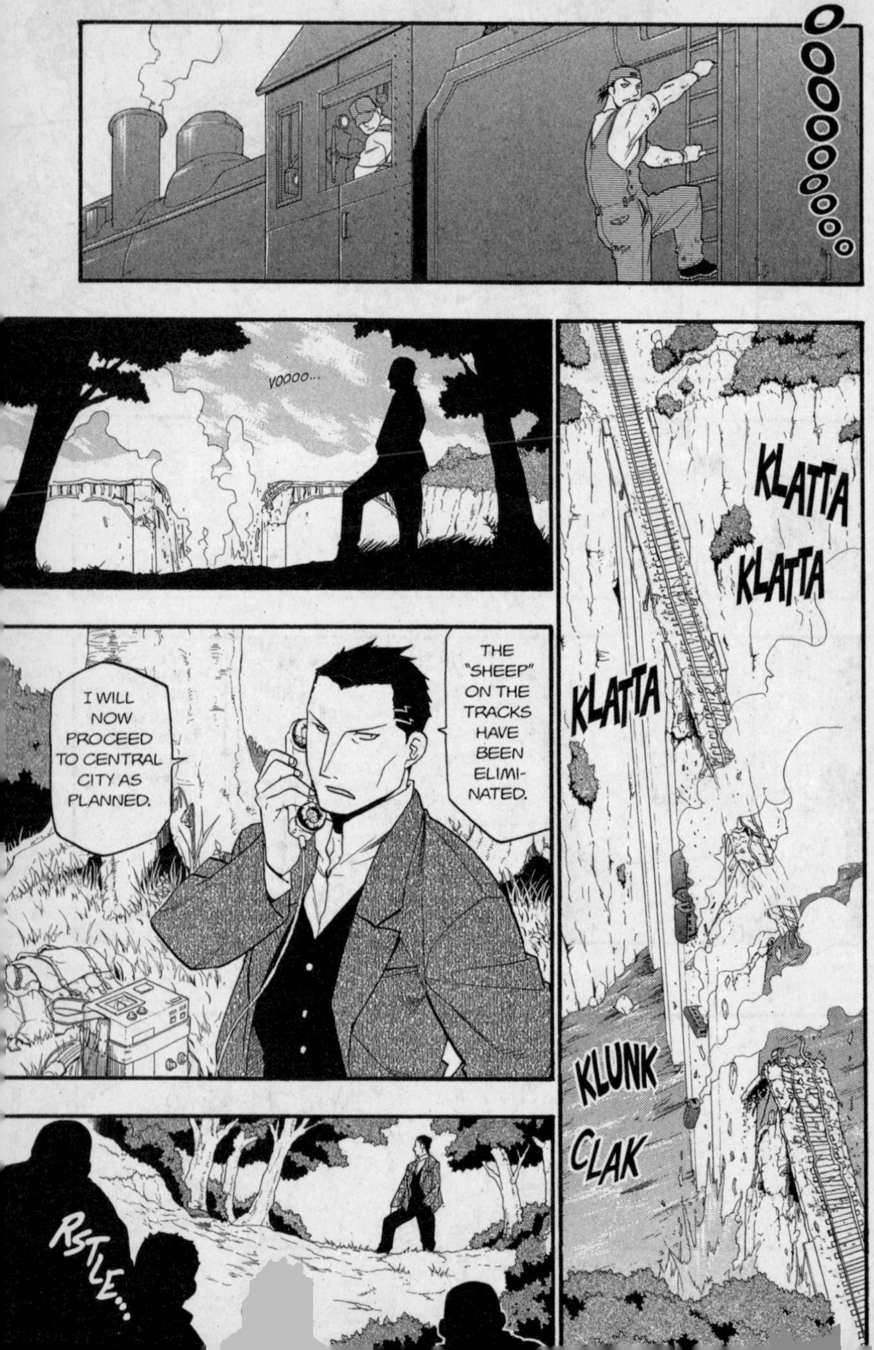
OOOOOOOOOO
KLATTA
KLATTA
KLATTA
KLUNK
CLAK
VOOOO...
THE "SHEEP" ON THE TRACKS HAVE BEEN ELIMINATED.
I WILL NOW PROCEED TO CENTRAL CITY AS PLANNED.
RSTLE...

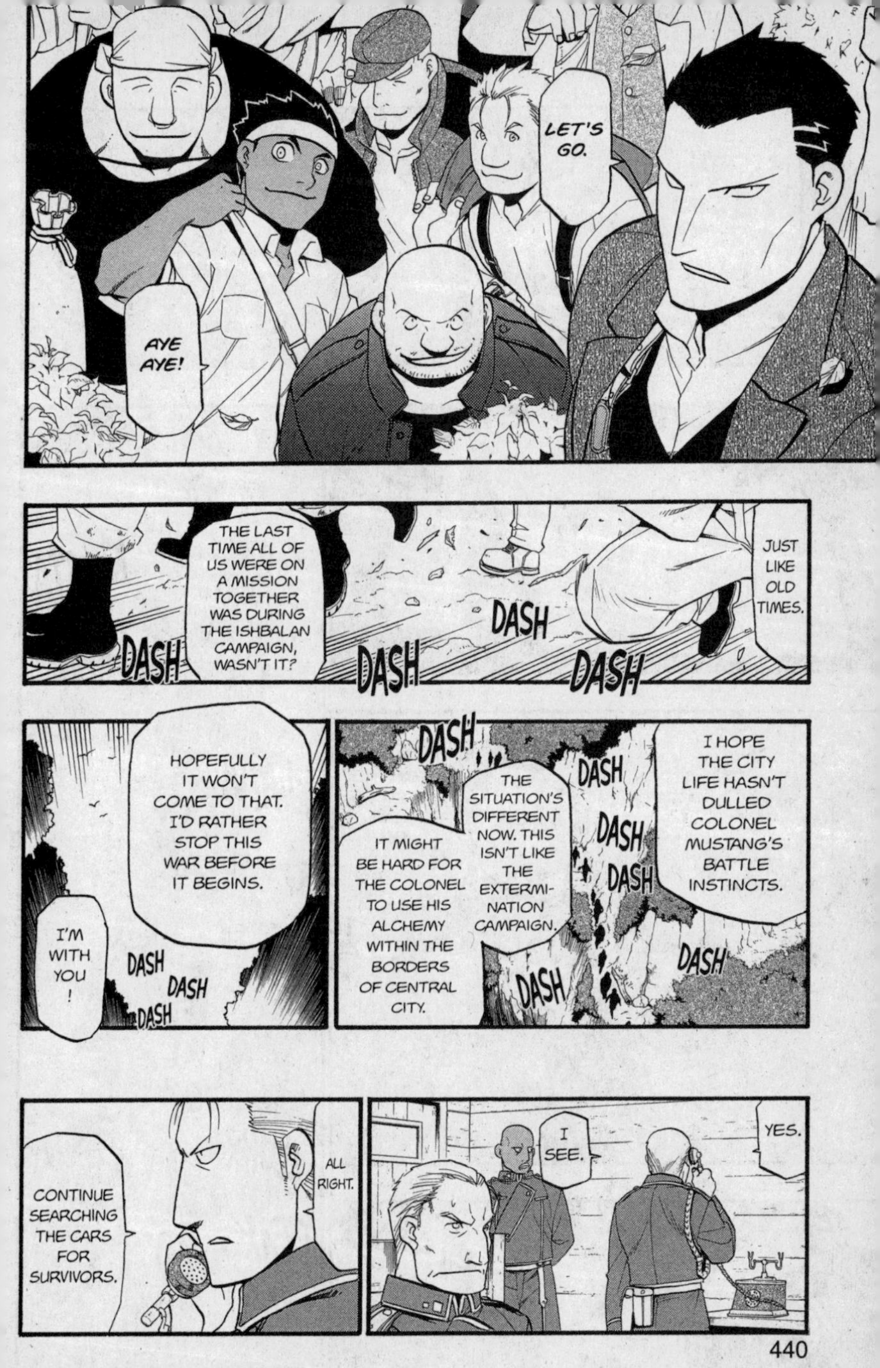
LET'S GO.
AYE AYE!
JUST LIKE OLD TIMES.
DASH
DASH
DASH
DASH
THE LAST TIME ALL OF US WERE ON A MISSION TOGETHER WAS DURING THE ISHBALAN CAMPAIGN, WASN'T IT?
I HOPE THE CITY LIFE HASN'T DULLED COLONEL MUSTANG'S BATTLE INSTINCTS.
DASH
DASH
DASH
DASH
DASH
DASH
THE SITUATION'S DIFFERENT NOW. THIS ISN'T LIKE THE EXTERMINATION CAMPAIGN.
IT MIGHT BE HARD FOR THE COLONEL TO USE HIS ALCHEMY WITHIN THE BORDERS OF CENTRAL CITY.
HOPEFULLY IT WON'T COME TO THAT. I'D RATHER STOP THIS WAR BEFORE IT BEGINS.
I'M WITH YOU!
DASH
DASH
DASH
YES.
I SEE.
ALL RIGHT.
CONTINUE SEARCHING THE CARS FOR SURVIVORS.

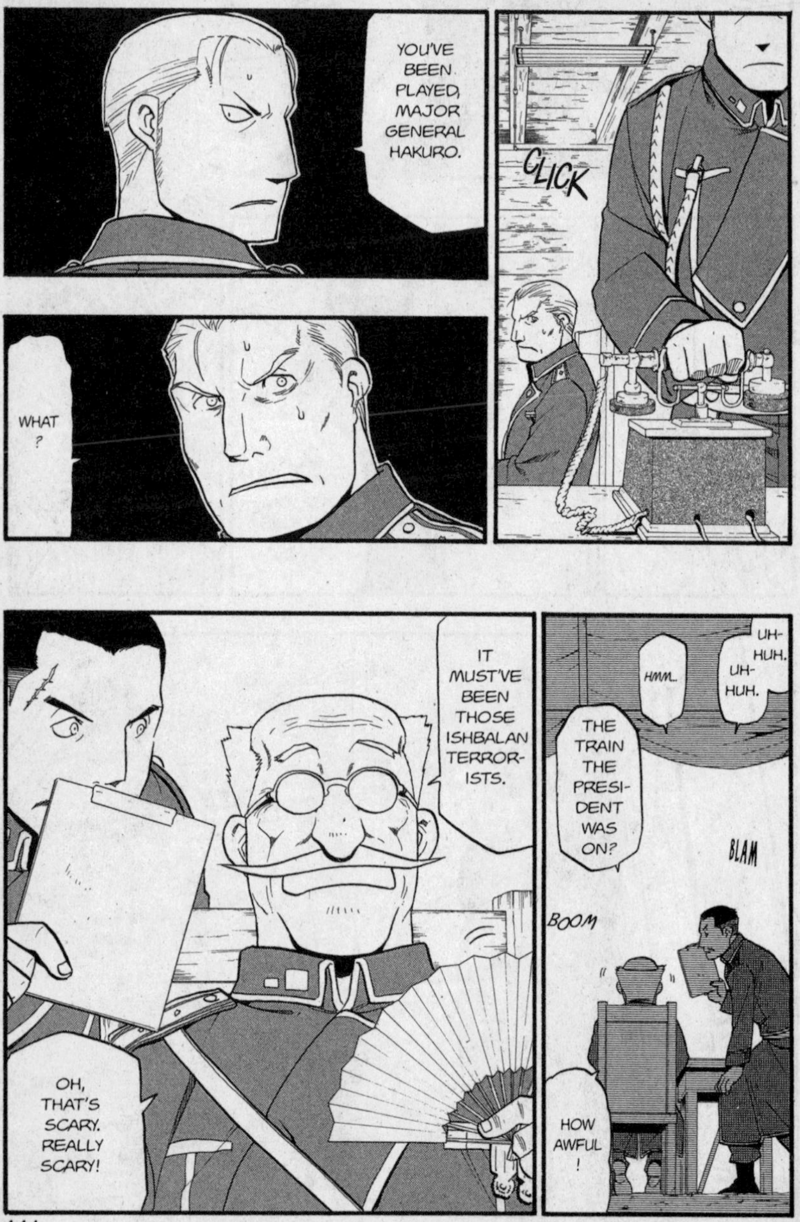
CLICK
YOU'VE BEEN PLAYED, MAJOR GENERAL HAKURO.
WHAT?
UH-HUH. UH-HUH.
HMM..
THE TRAIN THE PRESIDENT WAS ON?
BLAM
BOOM
HOW AWFUL!
IT MUST'VE BEEN THOSE ISHBALAN TERRORISTS.
OH, THAT'S SCARY. REALLY SCARY!

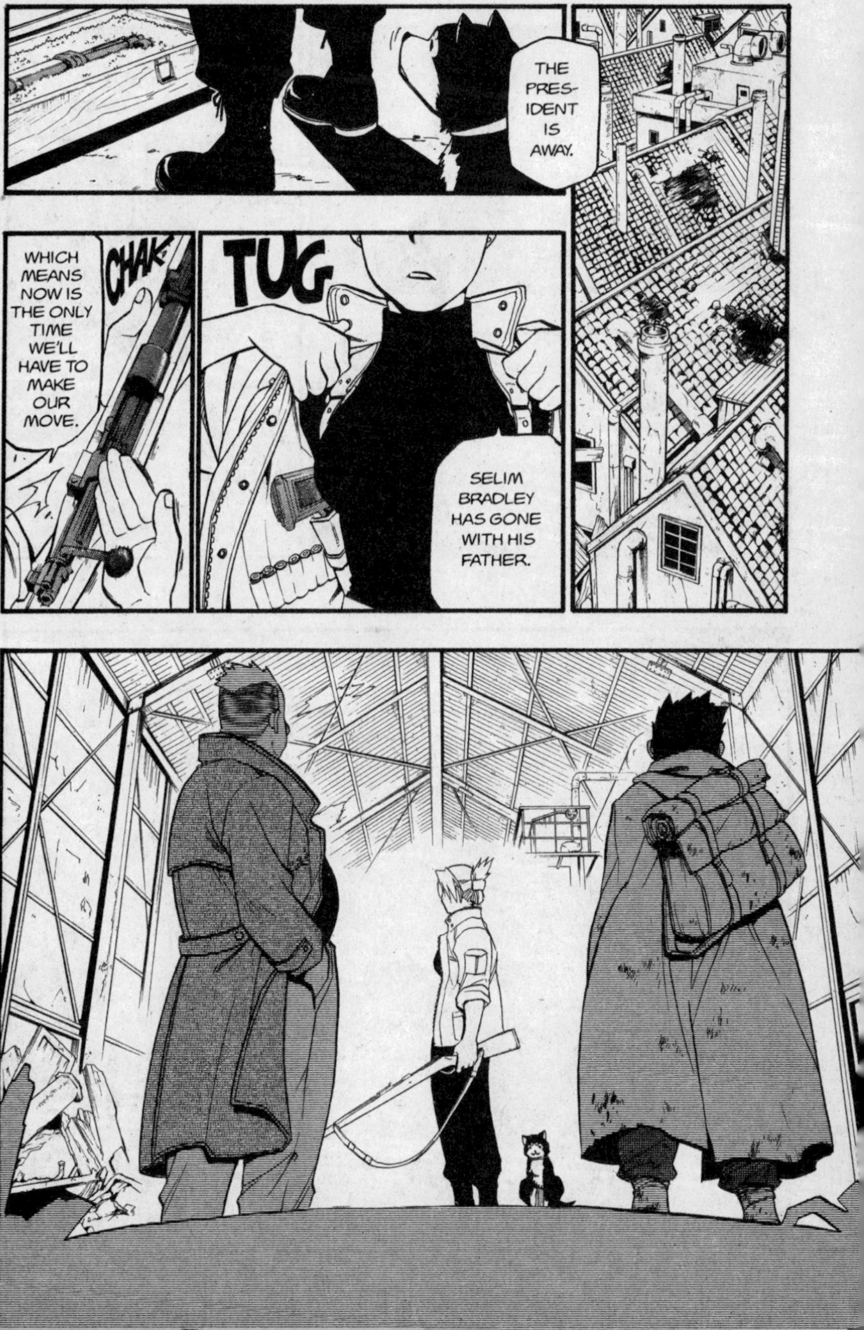
THE PRES-IDENT IS AWAY.
TUG
SELIM BRADLEY HAS GONE WITH HIS FATHER.
CHAK
WHICH MEANS NOW IS THE ONLY TIME WE'LL HAVE TO MAKE OUR MOVE.

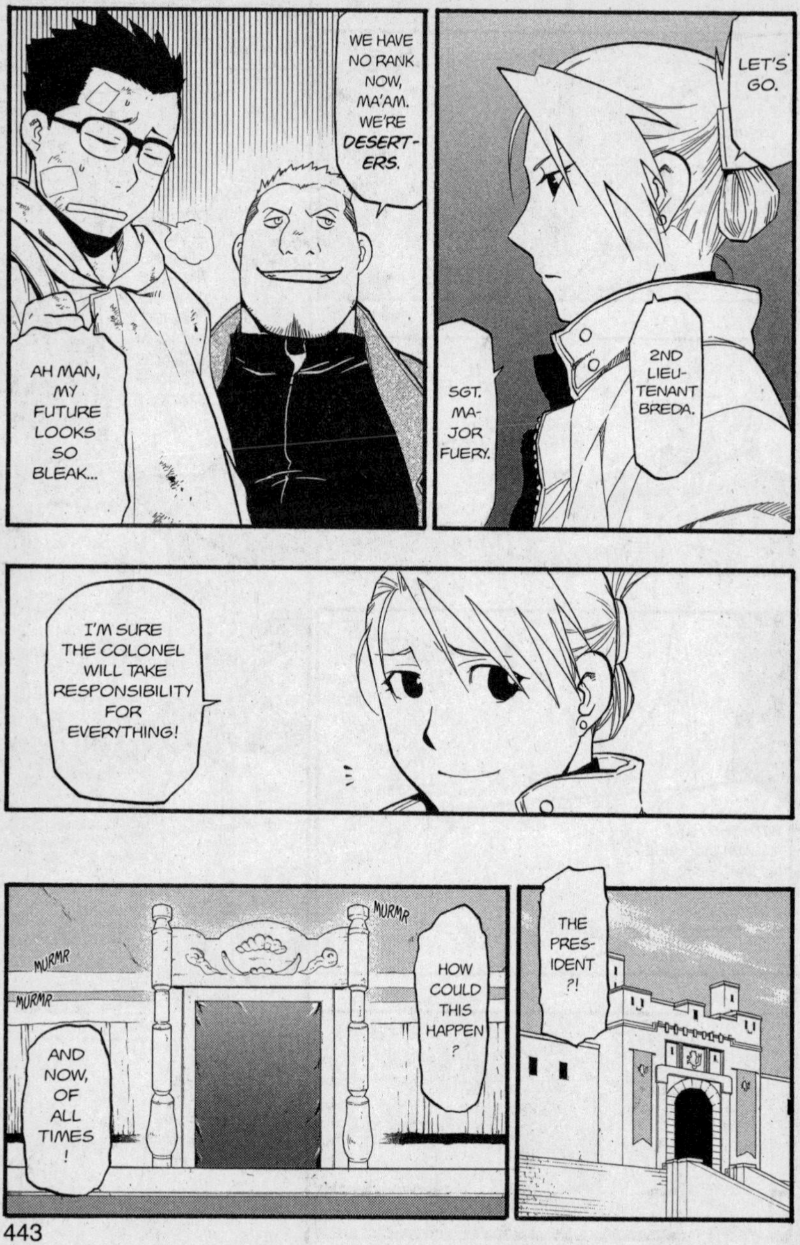
LET'S GO.
2ND LIEUTENANT BREDA.
SGT. MAJOR FUERY.
WE HAVE NO RANK NOW, MA'AM. WE'RE *DESERTERS.*
AH MAN, MY FUTURE LOOKS SO BLEAK...
I'M SURE THE COLONEL WILL TAKE RESPONSIBILITY FOR EVERYTHING!
THE PRESIDENT?!
MURMR
HOW COULD THIS HAPPEN?
MURMR
MURMR
AND NOW, OF ALL TIMES!

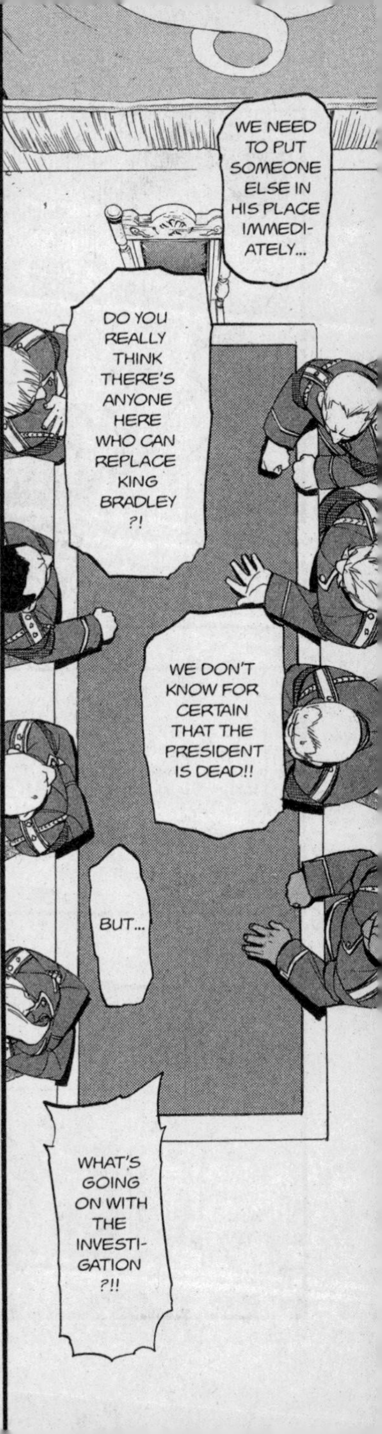
WE NEED TO PUT SOMEONE ELSE IN HIS PLACE IMMEDIATELY...
DO YOU REALLY THINK THERE'S ANYONE HERE WHO CAN REPLACE KING BRADLEY?!
WE DON'T KNOW FOR CERTAIN THAT THE PRESIDENT IS DEAD!!
BUT...
WHAT'S GOING ON WITH THE INVESTIGATION?!!

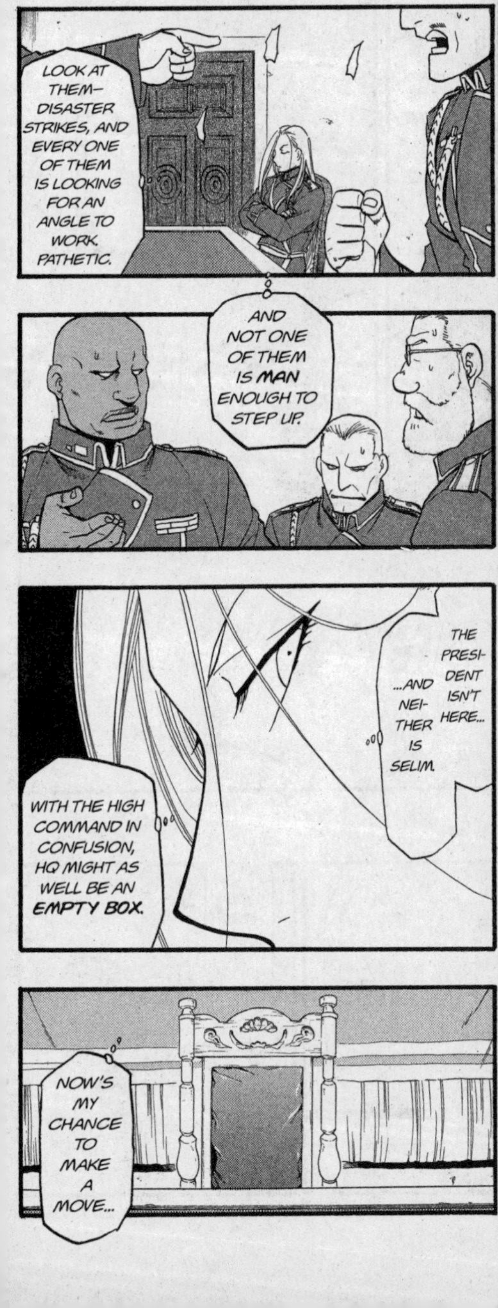
LOOK AT THEM— DISASTER STRIKES, AND EVERY ONE OF THEM IS LOOKING FOR AN ANGLE TO WORK. PATHETIC.
AND NOT ONE OF THEM IS MAN ENOUGH TO STEP UP.
THE PRESIDENT ISN'T HERE...
...AND NEITHER IS SELIM.
WITH THE HIGH COMMAND IN CONFUSION, HQ MIGHT AS WELL BE AN EMPTY BOX.
NOW'S MY CHANCE TO MAKE A MOVE...

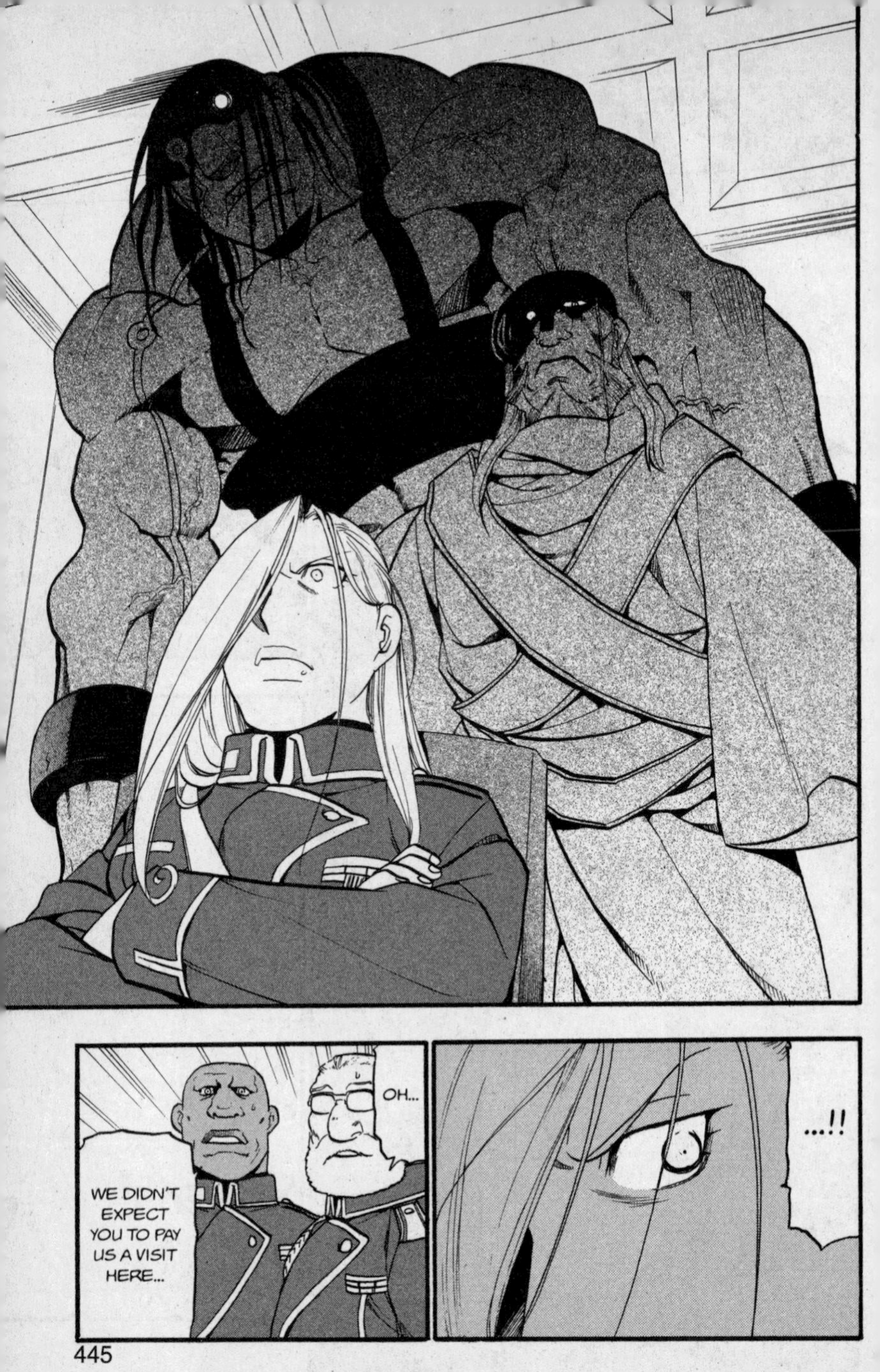
...!!
OH...
WE DIDN'T EXPECT YOU TO PAY US A VISIT HERE...

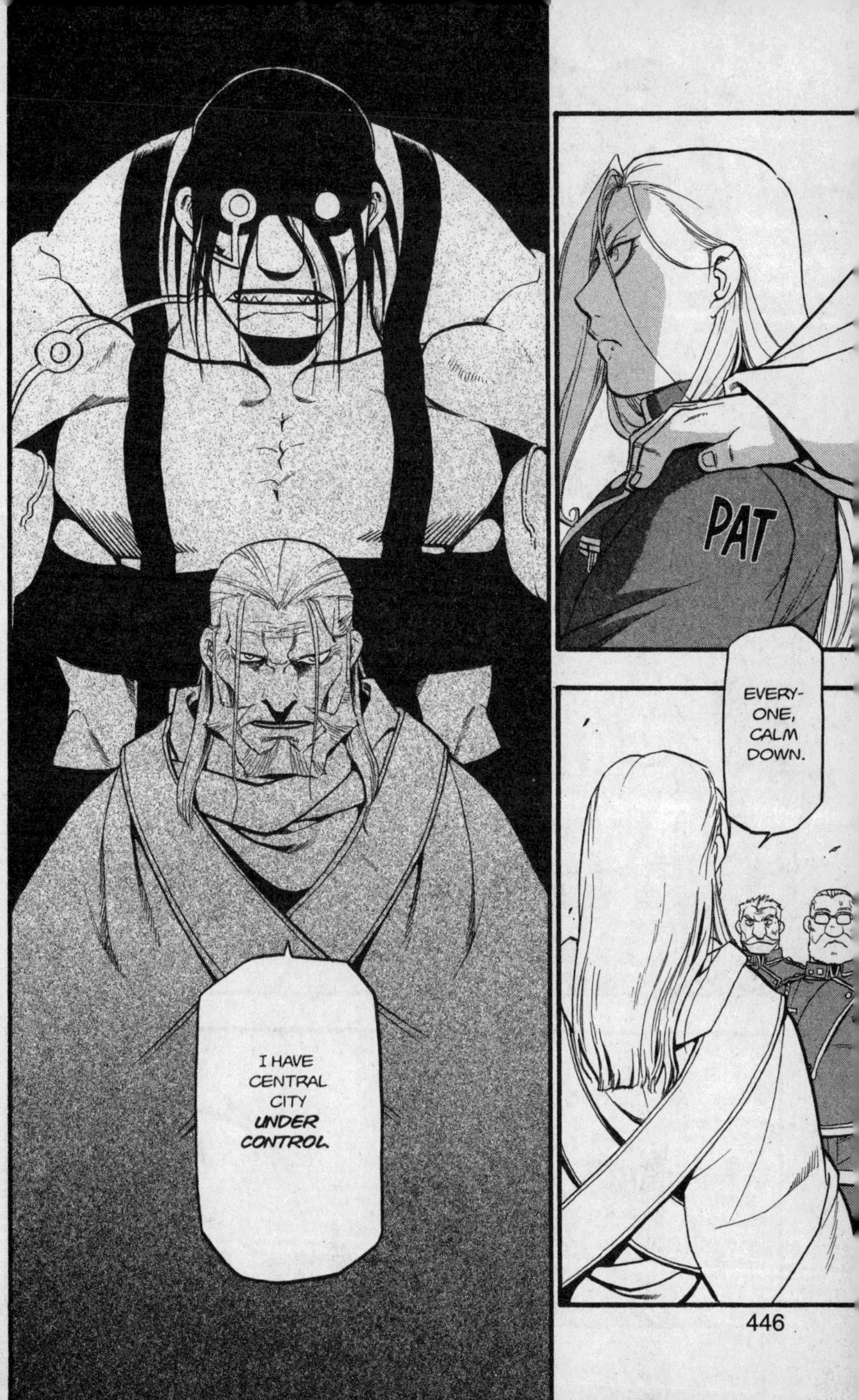
PAT
EVERYONE, CALM DOWN.
I HAVE CENTRAL CITY UNDER CONTROL.

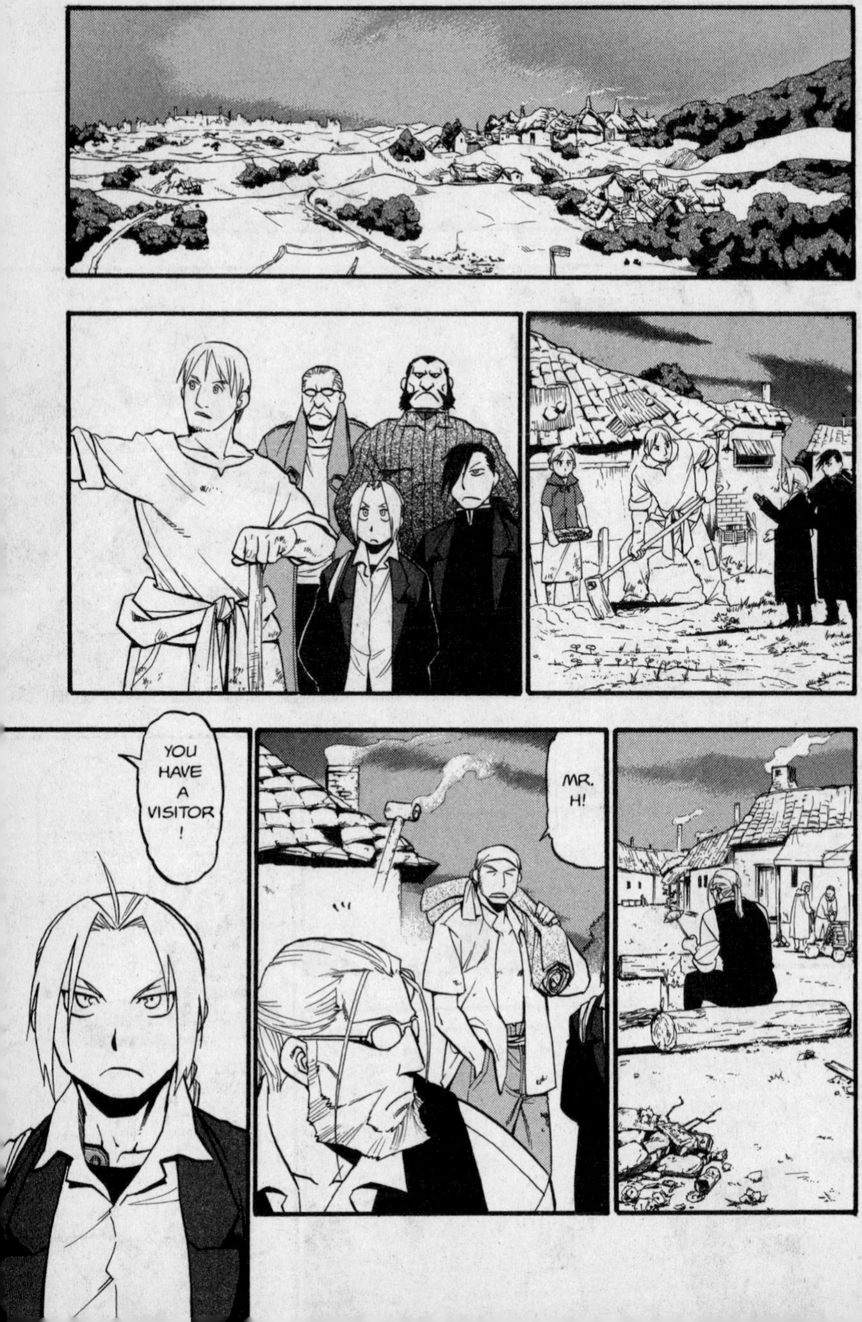
MR. H!
YOU HAVE A VISITOR!

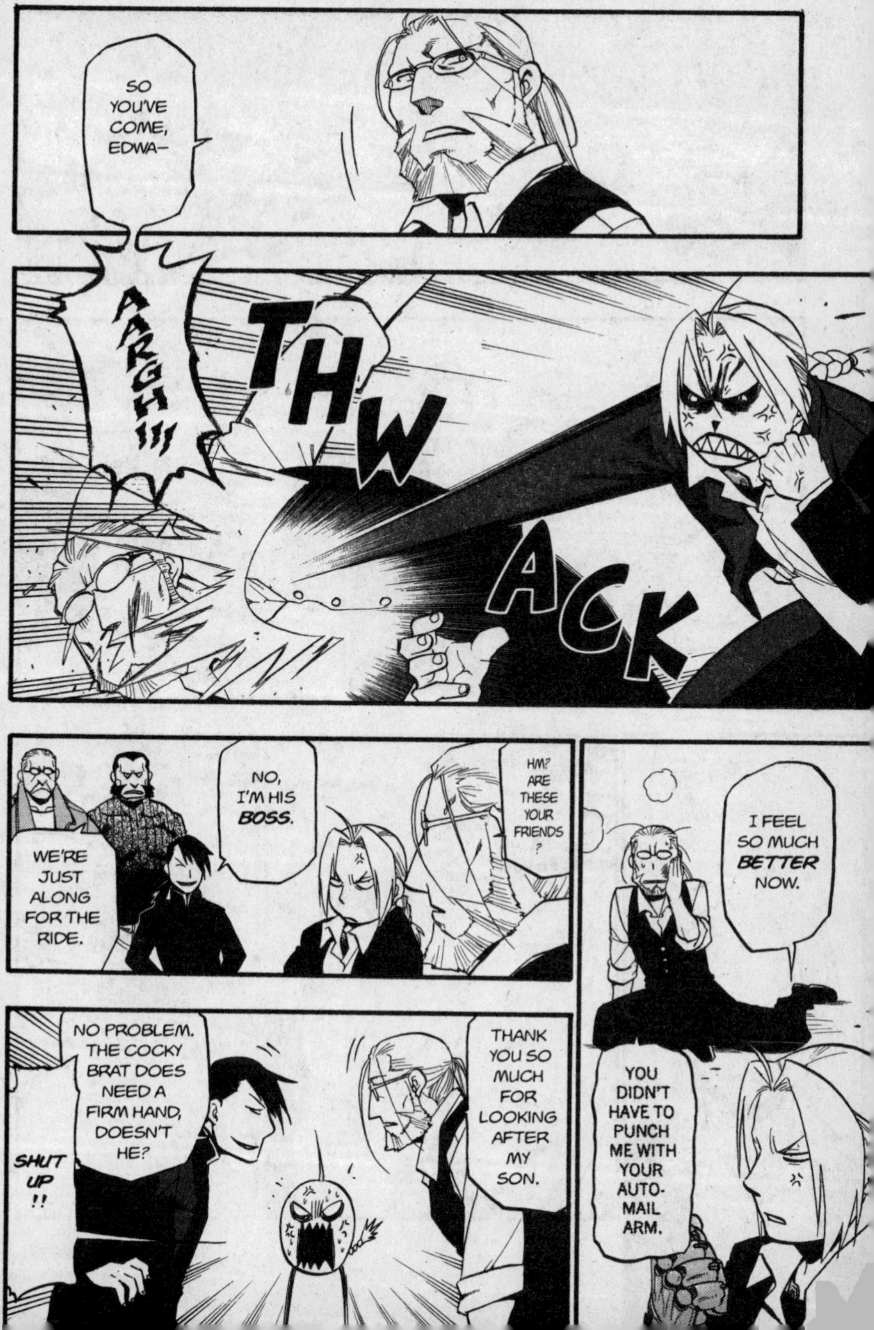
SO YOU'VE COME, EDWA—
THWACK
AARGH!!!
I FEEL SO MUCH BETTER NOW.
YOU DIDN'T HAVE TO PUNCH ME WITH YOUR AUTO-MAIL ARM.
HM? ARE THESE YOUR FRIENDS?
NO, I'M HIS BOSS.
WE'RE JUST ALONG FOR THE RIDE.
THANK YOU SO MUCH FOR LOOKING AFTER MY SON.
NO PROBLEM. THE COCKY BRAT DOES NEED A FIRM HAND, DOESN'T HE?
SHUT UP!!

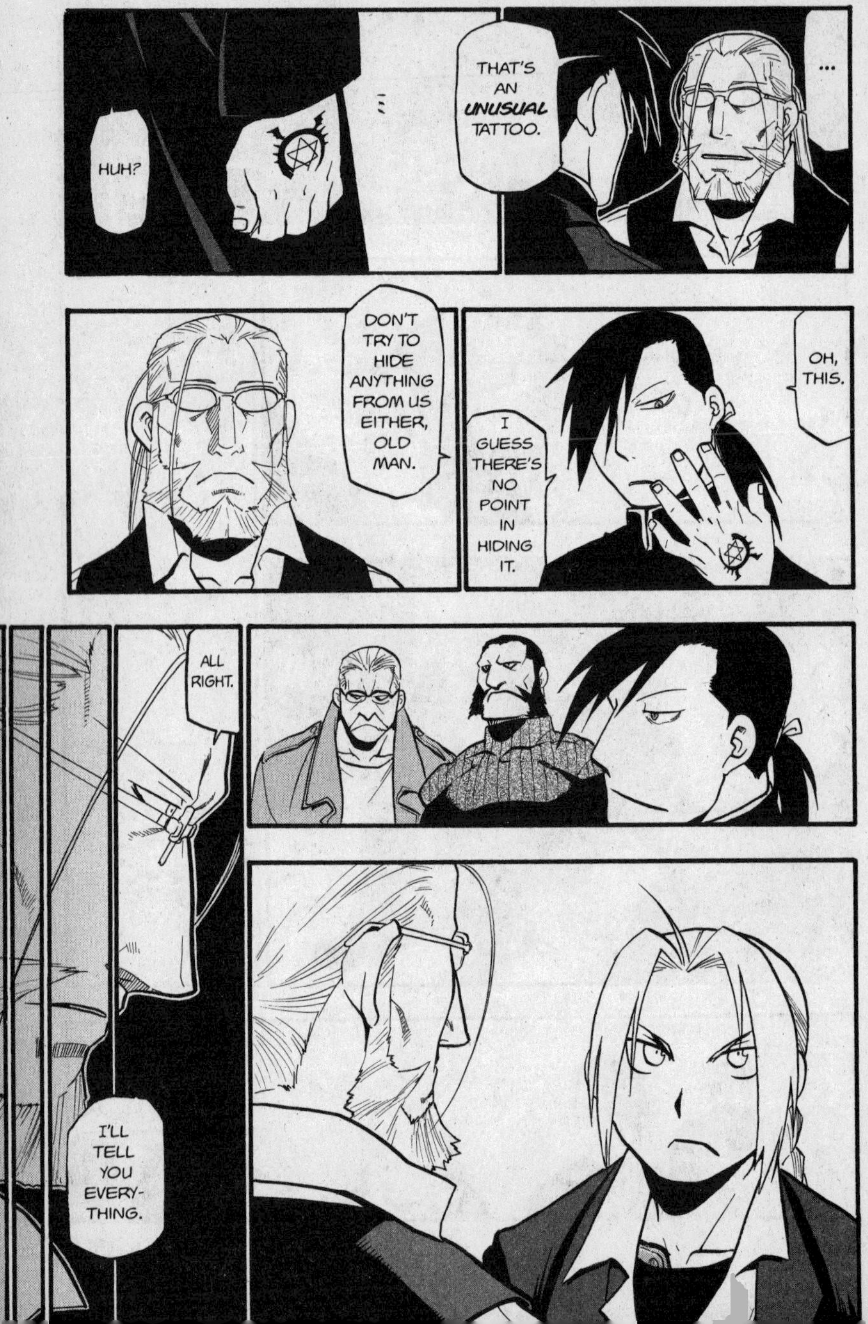
...
THAT'S AN *UNUSUAL* TATTOO.
HUH?
OH, THIS.
I GUESS THERE'S NO POINT IN HIDING IT.
DON'T TRY TO HIDE ANYTHING FROM US EITHER, OLD MAN.
ALL RIGHT.
I'LL TELL YOU EVERY-THING.

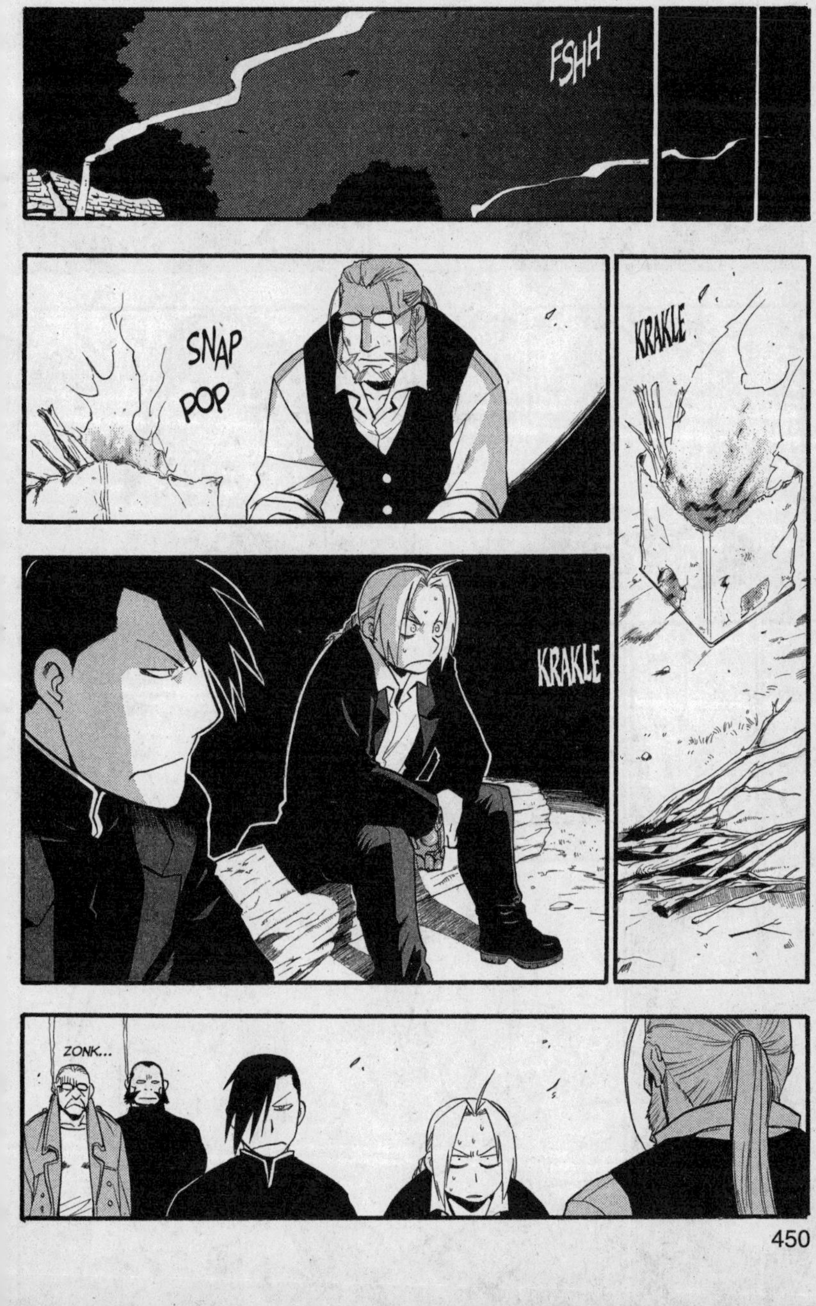
FSHH
KRAKLE
SNAP
POP
KRAKLE
ZONK...

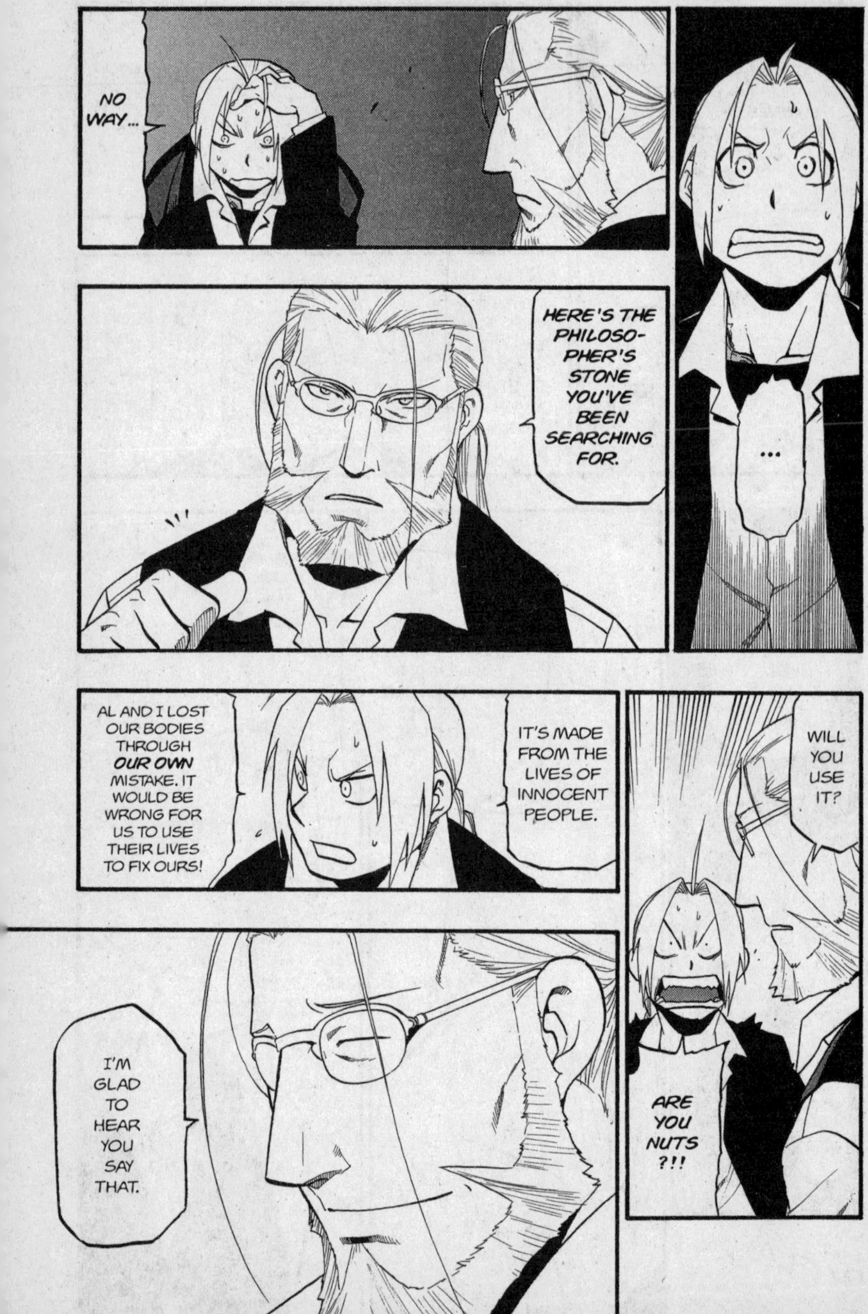
...
NO WAY...
HERE'S THE PHILOSOPHER'S STONE YOU'VE BEEN SEARCHING FOR.
WILL YOU USE IT?
ARE YOU NUTS?!!
IT'S MADE FROM THE LIVES OF INNOCENT PEOPLE.
AL AND I LOST OUR BODIES THROUGH OUR OWN MISTAKE. IT WOULD BE WRONG FOR US TO USE THEIR LIVES TO FIX OURS!
I'M GLAD TO HEAR YOU SAY THAT.

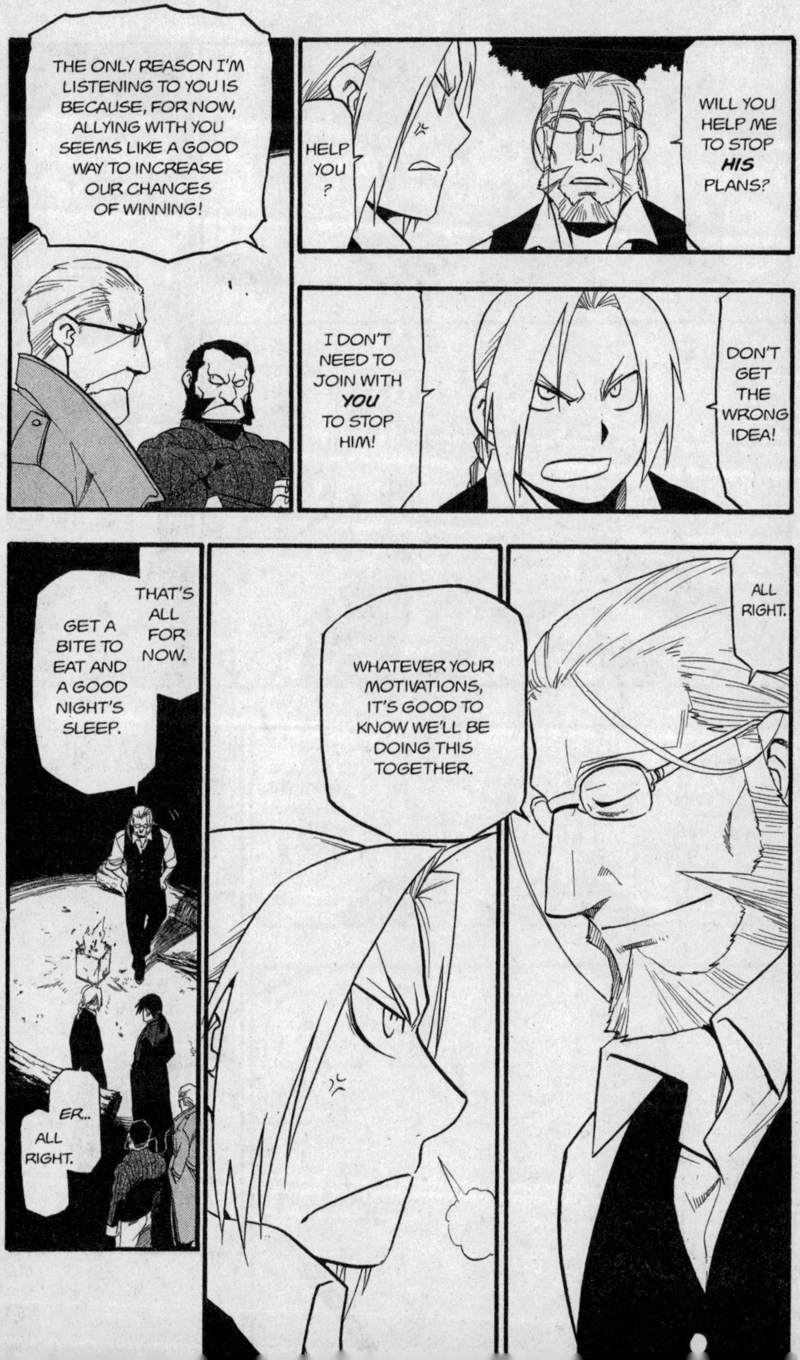
WILL YOU HELP ME TO STOP **HIS** PLANS?
HELP YOU ?
DON'T GET THE WRONG IDEA!
I DON'T NEED TO JOIN WITH **YOU** TO STOP HIM!
THE ONLY REASON I'M LISTENING TO YOU IS BECAUSE, FOR NOW, ALLYING WITH YOU SEEMS LIKE A GOOD WAY TO INCREASE OUR CHANCES OF WINNING!
ALL RIGHT.
WHATEVER YOUR MOTIVATIONS, IT'S GOOD TO KNOW WE'LL BE DOING THIS TOGETHER.
THAT'S ALL FOR NOW.
GET A BITE TO EAT AND A GOOD NIGHT'S SLEEP.
ER... ALL RIGHT.

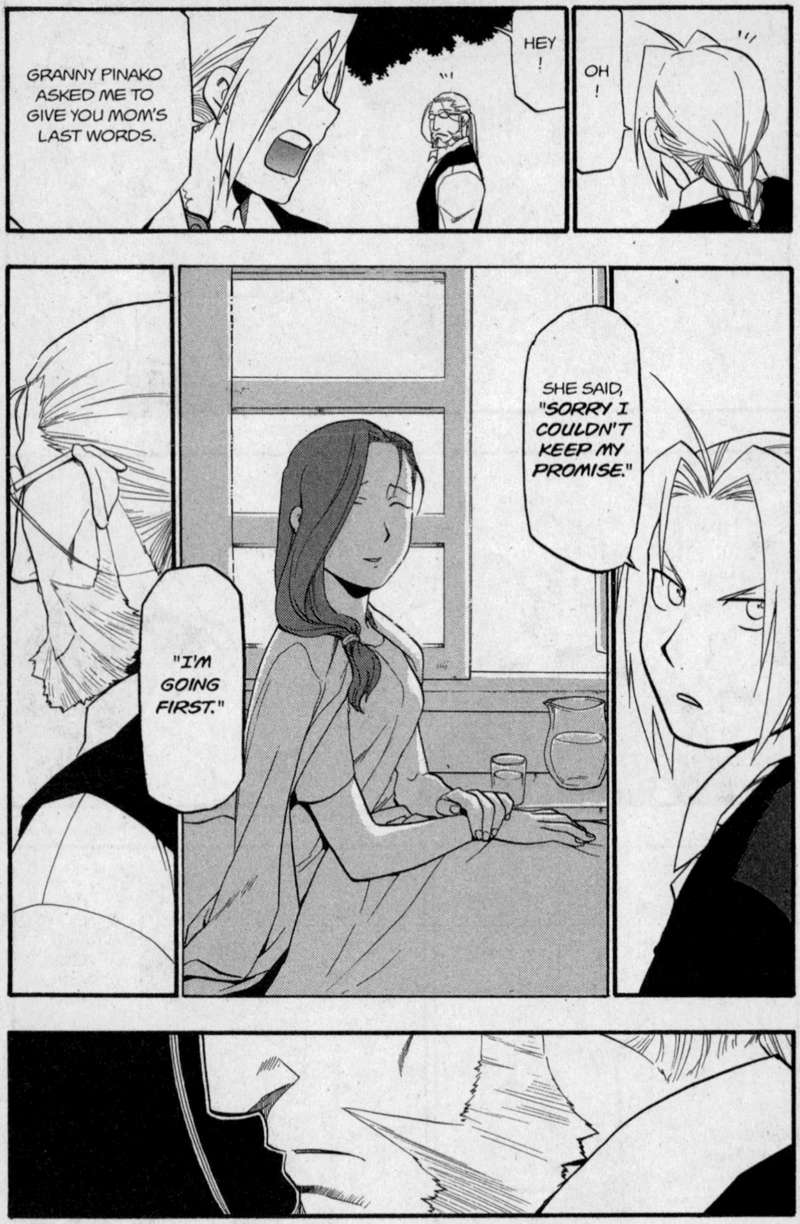
OH !
HEY !
GRANNY PINAKO ASKED ME TO GIVE YOU MOM'S LAST WORDS.
SHE SAID, "SORRY I COULDN'T KEEP MY PROMISE."
"I'M GOING FIRST."

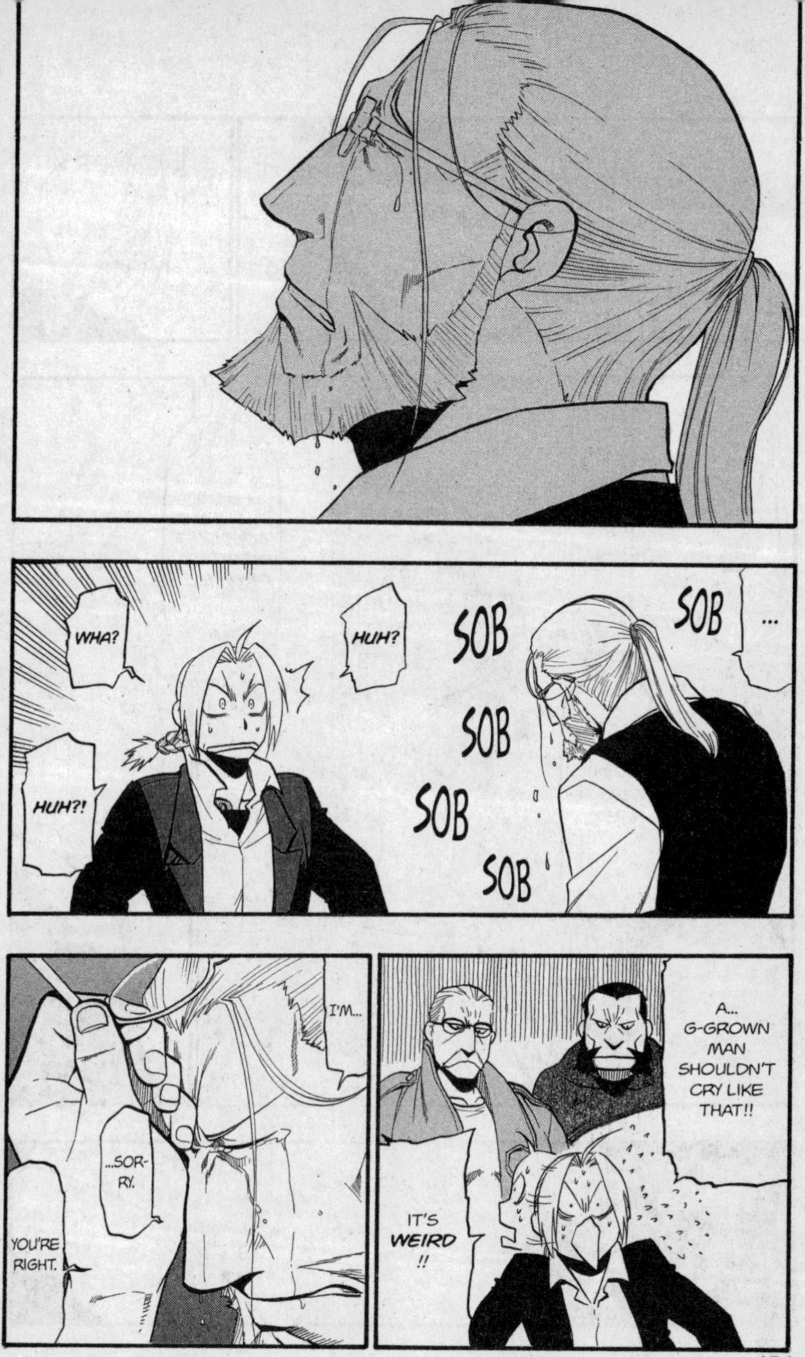
...
SOB
SOB
SOB
SOB
SOB
HUH?
WHA?
HUH?!
A... G-GROWN MAN SHOULDN'T CRY LIKE THAT!!
IT'S WEIRD !!
I'M...
...SOR-RY.
YOU'RE RIGHT.

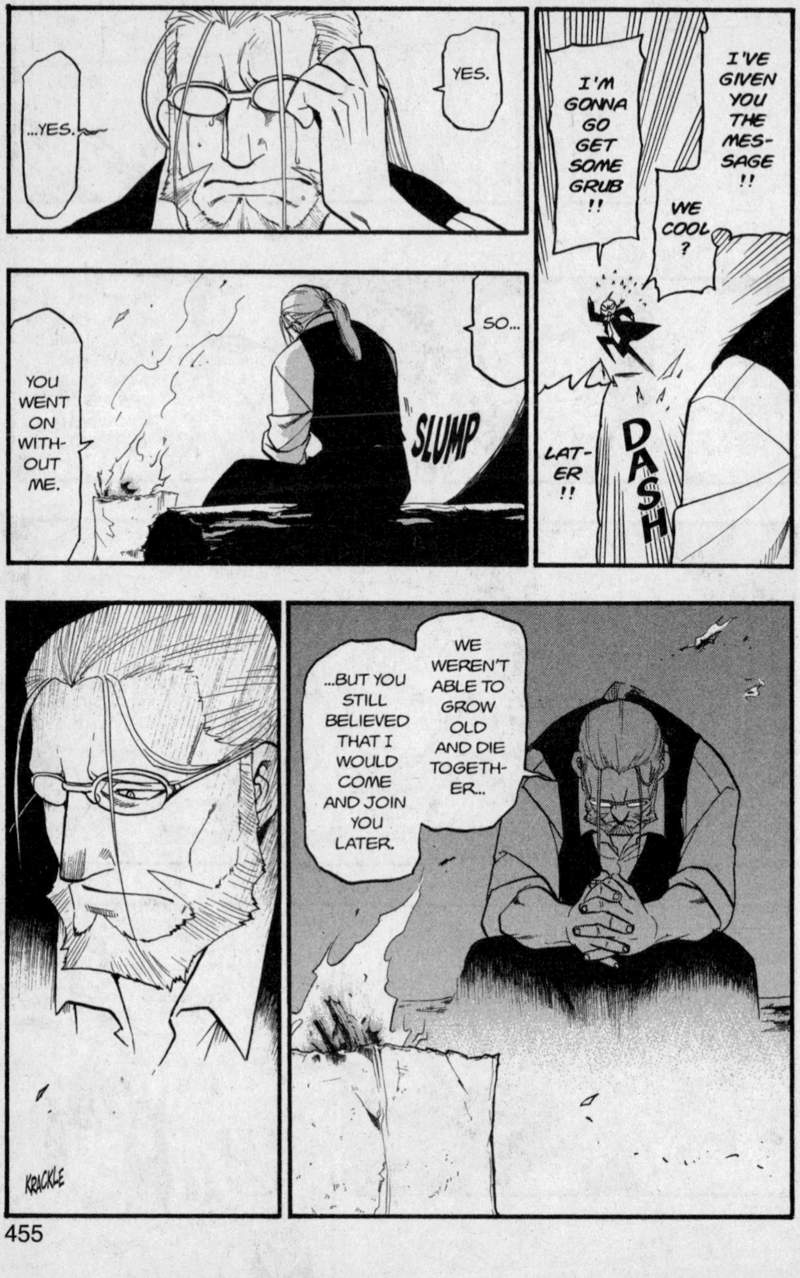
I'VE GIVEN YOU THE MESSAGE!!
I'M GONNA GO GET SOME GRUB!!
WE COOL?
DASH
LATER!!
YES.
...YES.
SO...
SLUMP
YOU WENT ON WITHOUT ME.
WE WEREN'T ABLE TO GROW OLD AND DIE TOGETHER...
...BUT YOU STILL BELIEVED THAT I WOULD COME AND JOIN YOU LATER.
KRACKLE

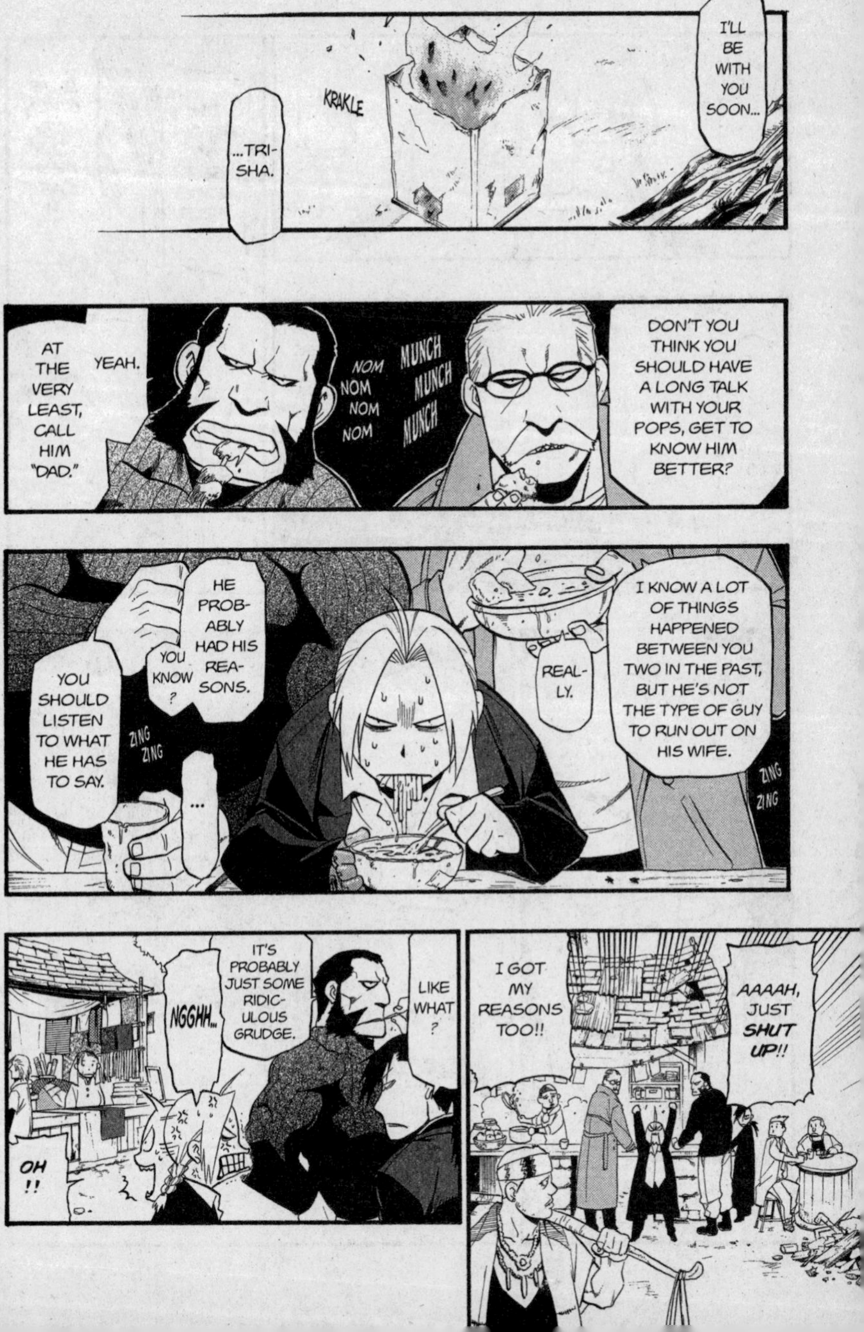

I'LL BE WITH YOU SOON...
KRAKLE
...TRI-SHA.
DON'T YOU THINK YOU SHOULD HAVE A LONG TALK WITH YOUR POPS, GET TO KNOW HIM BETTER?
MUNCH MUNCH MUNCH
NOM NOM NOM NOM
YEAH.
AT THE VERY LEAST, CALL HIM "DAD."
I KNOW A LOT OF THINGS HAPPENED BETWEEN YOU TWO IN THE PAST, BUT HE'S NOT THE TYPE OF GUY TO RUN OUT ON HIS WIFE.
ZING ZING
REAL-LY.
HE PROB-ABLY HAD HIS REA-SONS.
YOU KNOW?
YOU SHOULD LISTEN TO WHAT HE HAS TO SAY.
ZING ZING
...
AAAAH, JUST **SHUT UP!!**
I GOT MY REASONS TOO!!
LIKE WHAT?
IT'S PROBABLY JUST SOME RIDIC-ULOUS GRUDGE.
NGGHH...
OH!!

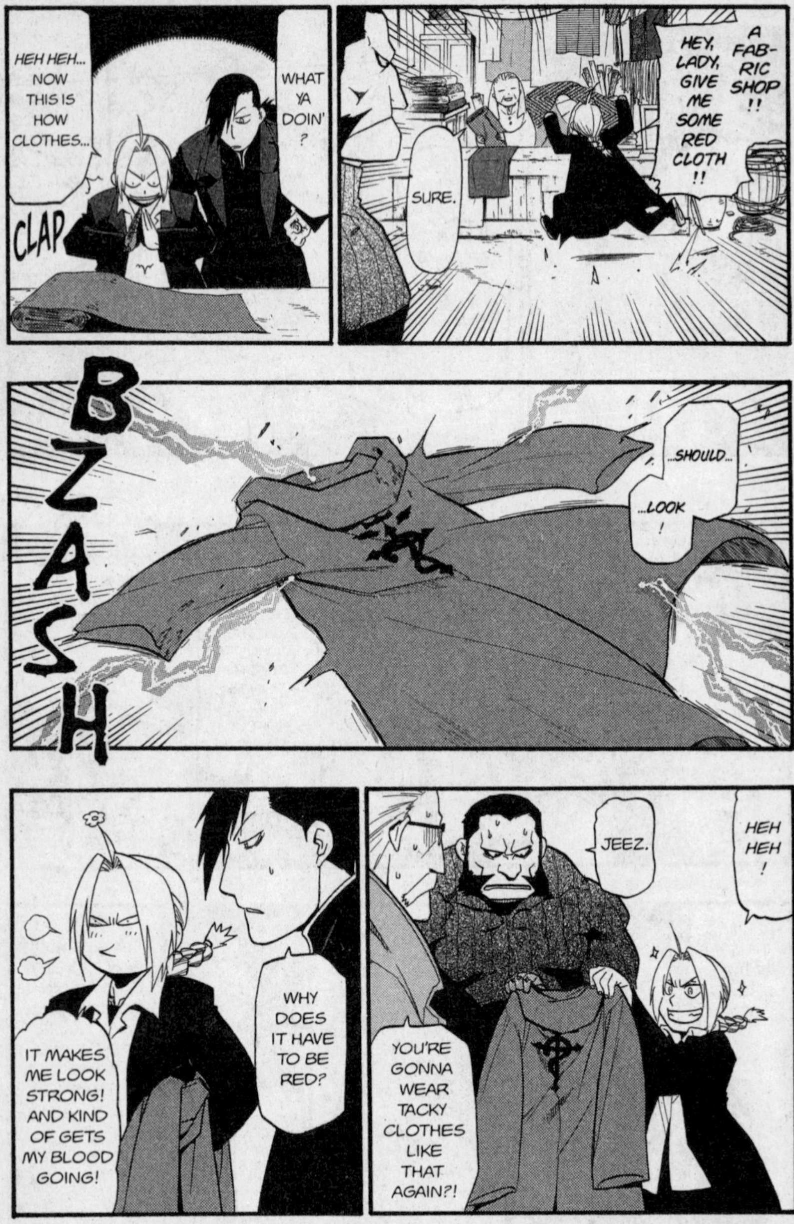
A FAB-RIC SHOP!!
HEY, LADY, GIVE ME SOME RED CLOTH!!
SURE.
WHAT YA DOIN'?
HEH HEH... NOW THIS IS HOW CLOTHES...
CLAP
...SHOULD...
...LOOK!
BZASH
HEH HEH!
JEEZ.
YOU'RE GONNA WEAR TACKY CLOTHES LIKE THAT AGAIN?!
WHY DOES IT HAVE TO BE RED?
IT MAKES ME LOOK STRONG! AND KIND OF GETS MY BLOOD GOING!

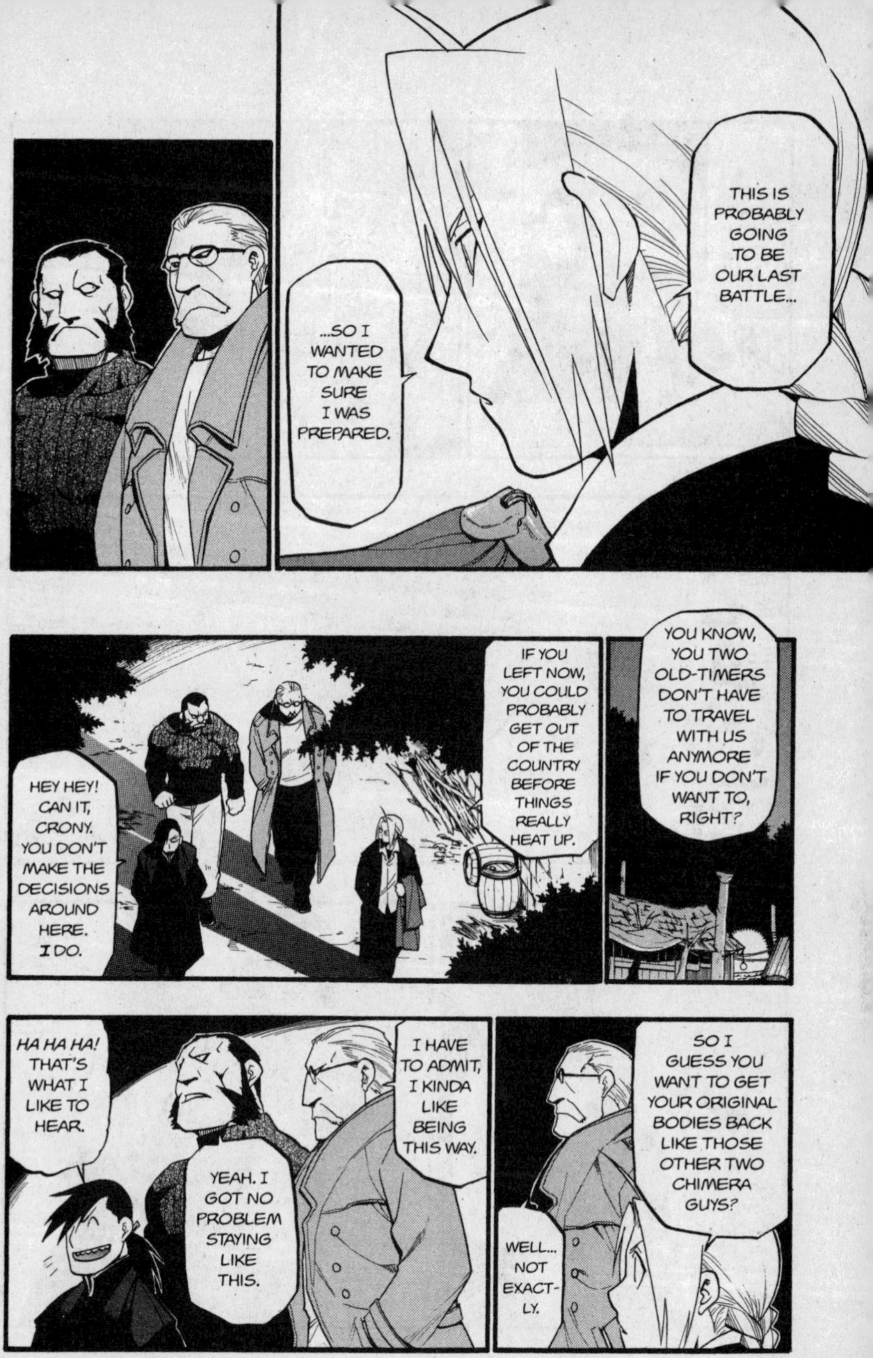
THIS IS PROBABLY GOING TO BE OUR LAST BATTLE...
...SO I WANTED TO MAKE SURE I WAS PREPARED.
YOU KNOW, YOU TWO OLD-TIMERS DON'T HAVE TO TRAVEL WITH US ANYMORE IF YOU DON'T WANT TO, RIGHT?
IF YOU LEFT NOW, YOU COULD PROBABLY GET OUT OF THE COUNTRY BEFORE THINGS REALLY HEAT UP.
HEY HEY! CAN IT, CRONY. YOU DON'T MAKE THE DECISIONS AROUND HERE. I DO.
SO I GUESS YOU WANT TO GET YOUR ORIGINAL BODIES BACK LIKE THOSE OTHER TWO CHIMERA GUYS?
WELL... NOT EXACT-LY.
I HAVE TO ADMIT, I KINDA LIKE BEING THIS WAY.
YEAH. I GOT NO PROBLEM STAYING LIKE THIS.
HA HA HA! THAT'S WHAT I LIKE TO HEAR.

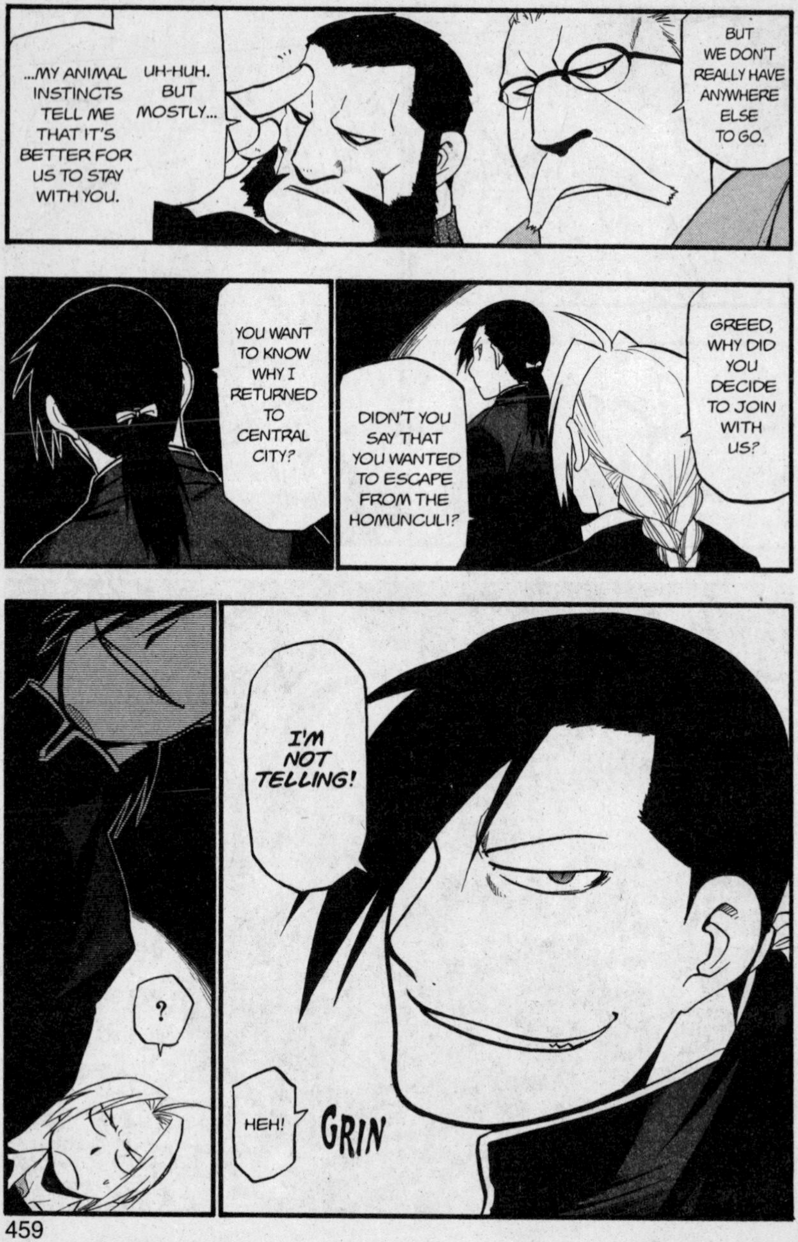
BUT WE DON'T REALLY HAVE ANYWHERE ELSE TO GO.
UH-HUH. BUT MOSTLY...
...MY ANIMAL INSTINCTS TELL ME THAT IT'S BETTER FOR US TO STAY WITH YOU.
GREED, WHY DID YOU DECIDE TO JOIN WITH US?
DIDN'T YOU SAY THAT YOU WANTED TO ESCAPE FROM THE HOMUNCULI?
YOU WANT TO KNOW WHY I RETURNED TO CENTRAL CITY?
I'M NOT TELLING!
HEH!
GRIN
?

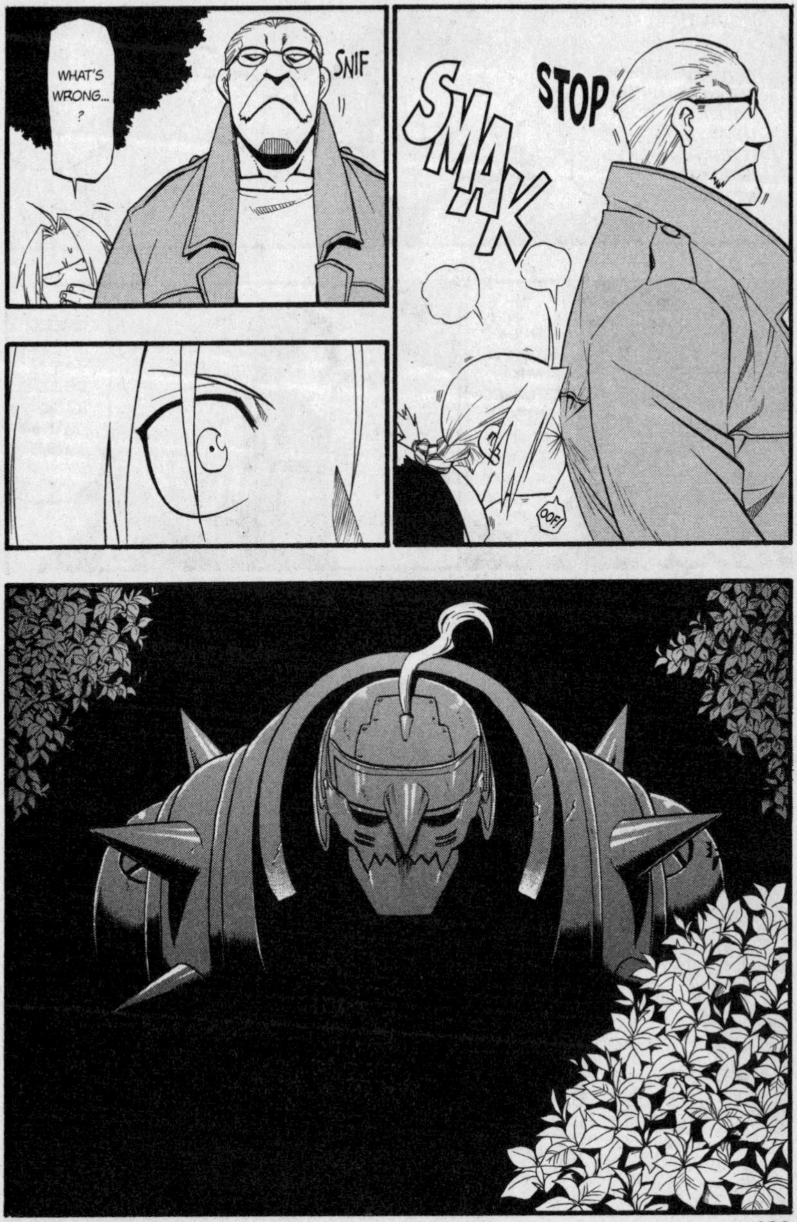
STOP
SMAK
OOF!
WHAT'S WRONG... ?
SNIF

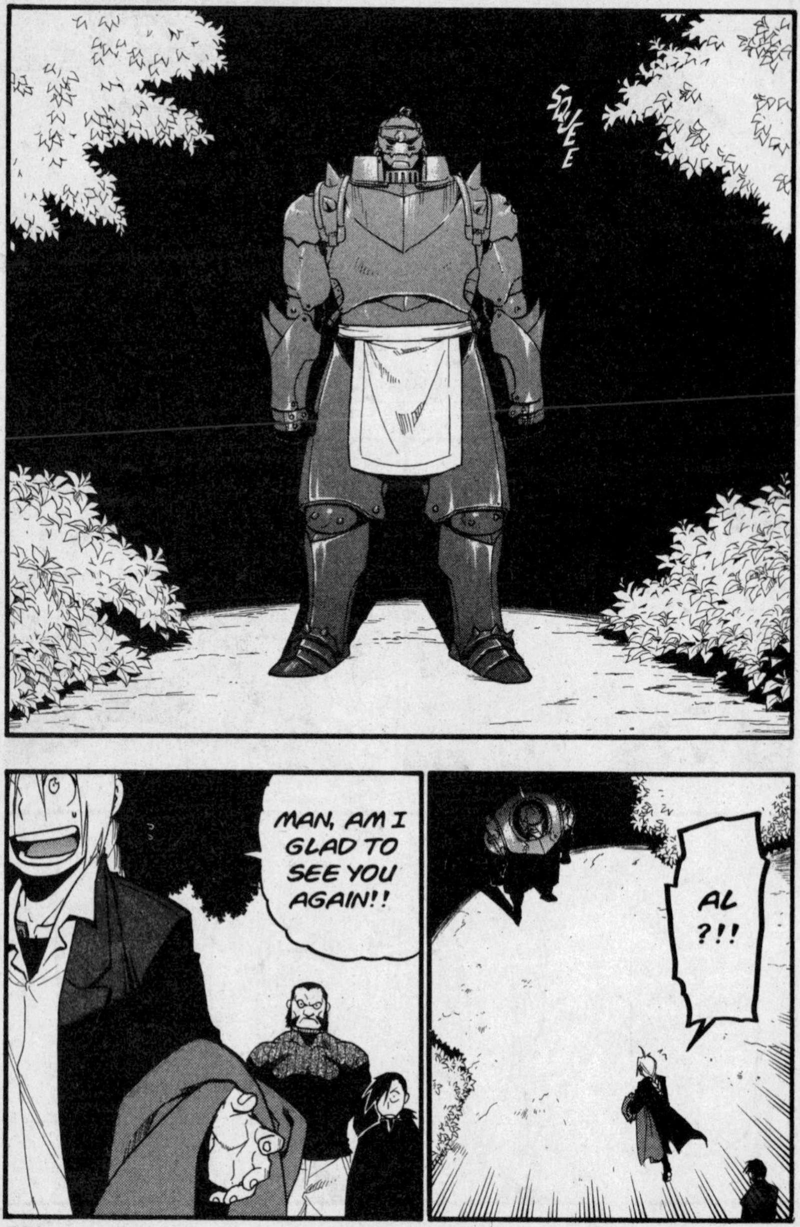
SQUEEE
AL ?!!
MAN, AM I GLAD TO SEE YOU AGAIN!!

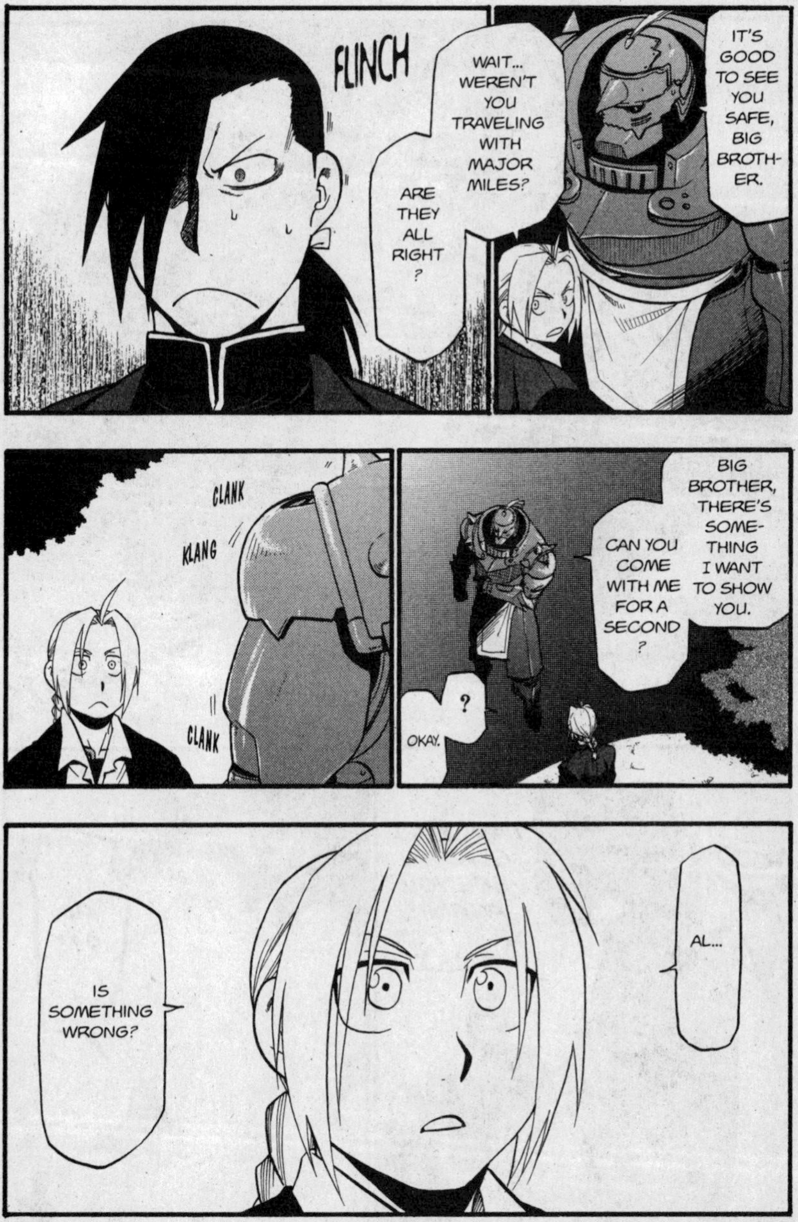
IT'S GOOD TO SEE YOU SAFE, BIG BROTHER.
WAIT... WEREN'T YOU TRAVELING WITH MAJOR MILES?
FLINCH
ARE THEY ALL RIGHT?
BIG BROTHER, THERE'S SOMETHING I WANT TO SHOW YOU.
CAN YOU COME WITH ME FOR A SECOND?
?
OKAY.
CLANK
KLANG
CLANK
AL...
IS SOMETHING WRONG?

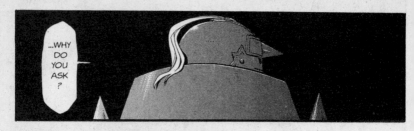

...WHY DO YOU ASK?

ED!!

...JUST A FEEL-ING...

IT'S...

GET AWAY FROM HIM!

HE'S A...

IT'S A...

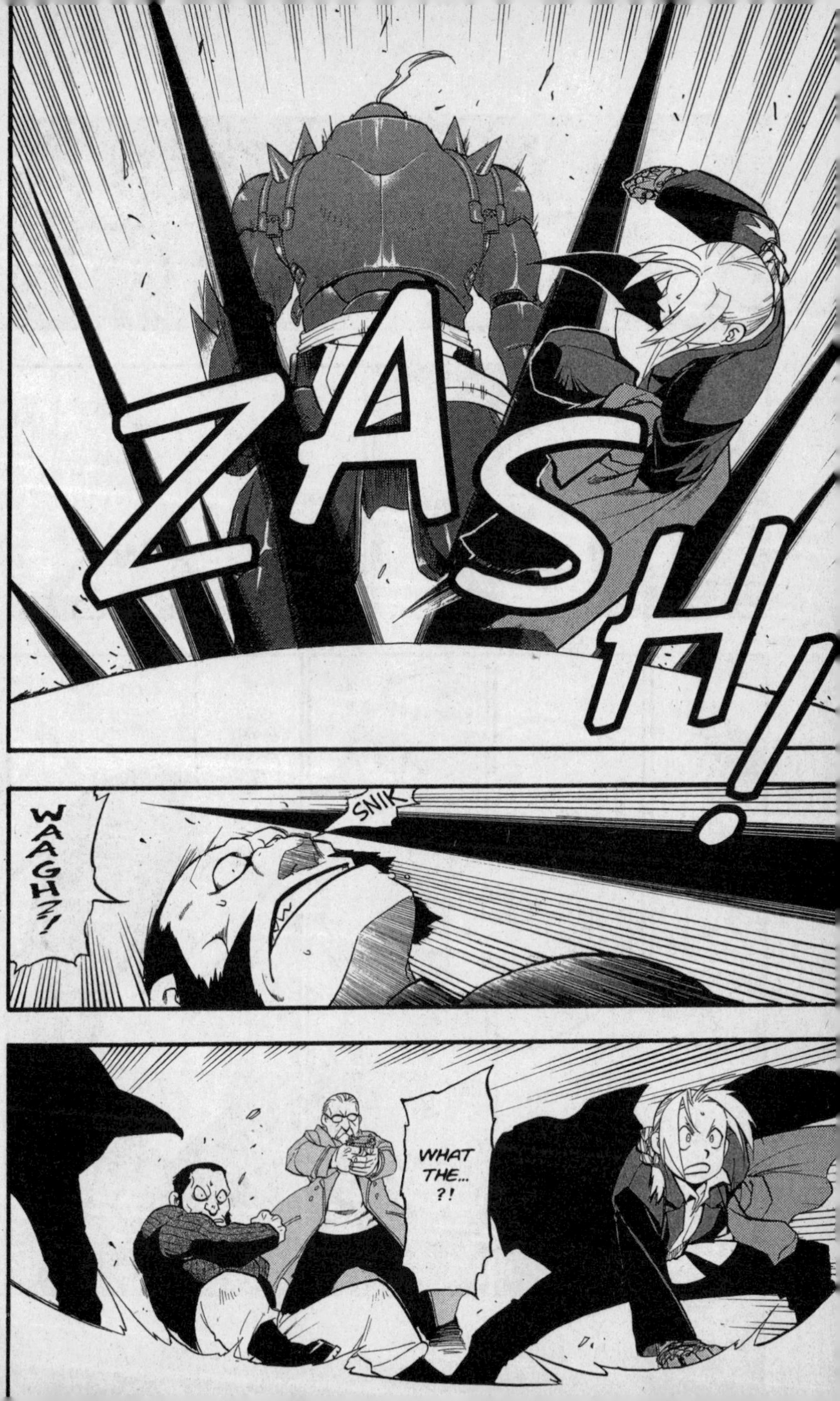
ZASH!
SNIK
WAAGH?!
WHAT THE...?!

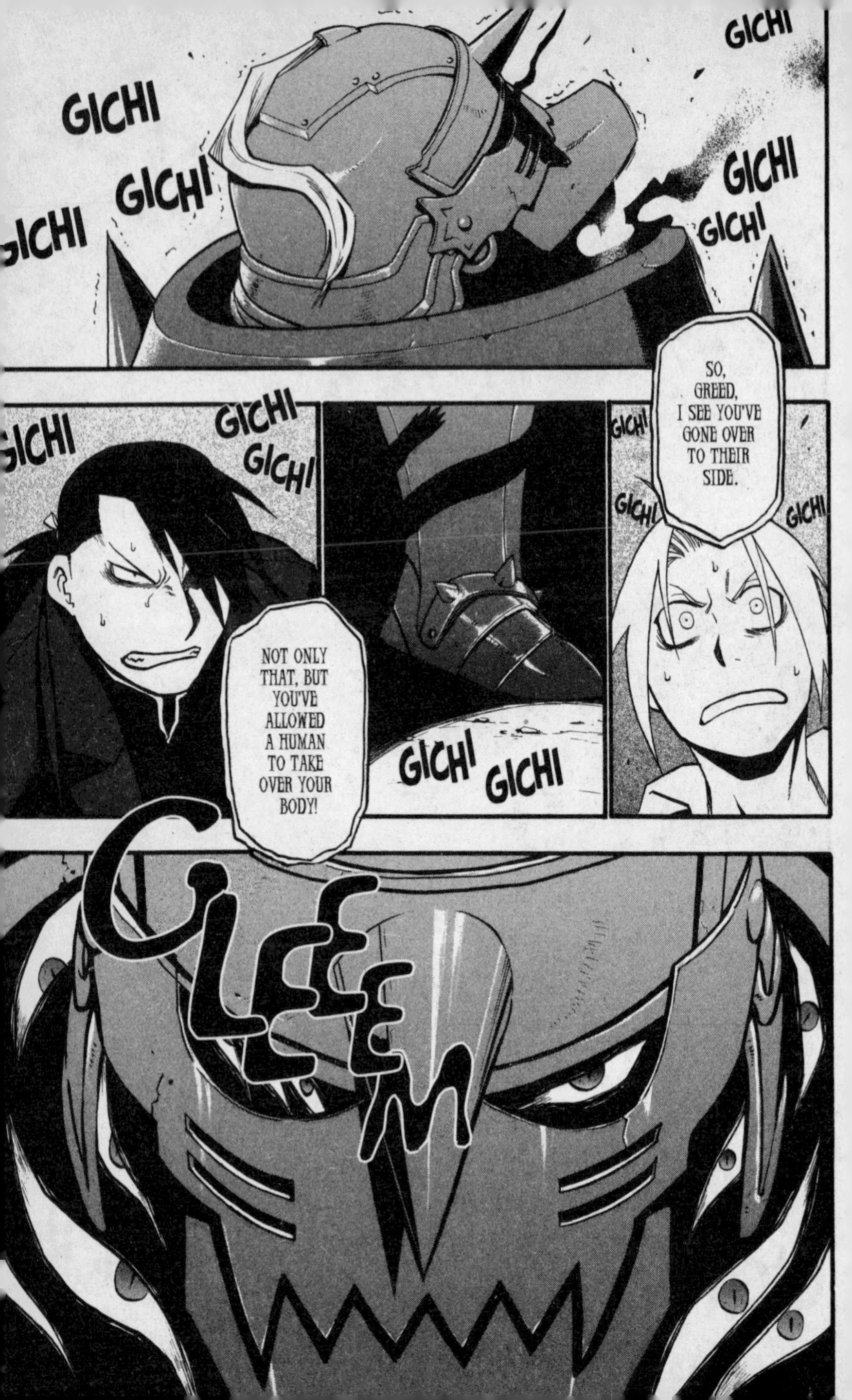
GICHI
GICHI
GICHI
GICHI
GICHI
GICHI
SO, GREED, I SEE YOU'VE GONE OVER TO THEIR SIDE.
GICHI
GICHI
GICHI
GICHI
GICHI
GICHI
GICHI
NOT ONLY THAT, BUT YOU'VE ALLOWED A HUMAN TO TAKE OVER YOUR BODY!
GLEEEM

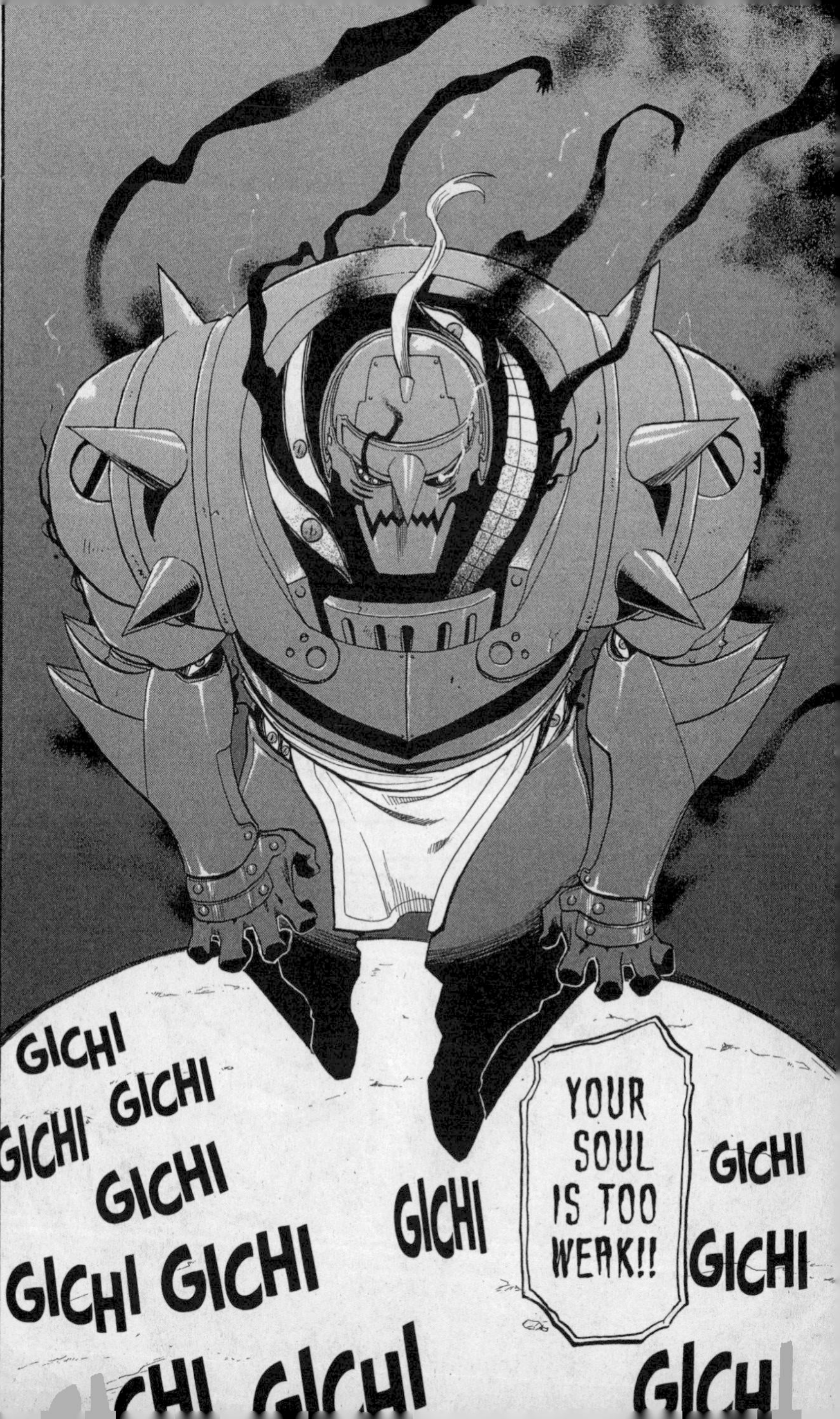
GICHI
GICHI
GICH
YOUR SOUL IS TOO WEAK!!
GICHI
GICHI
GICHI
GICHI
GICHI
GICHI
GICHI
GICHI

FULLMETAL
ALCHEMIST

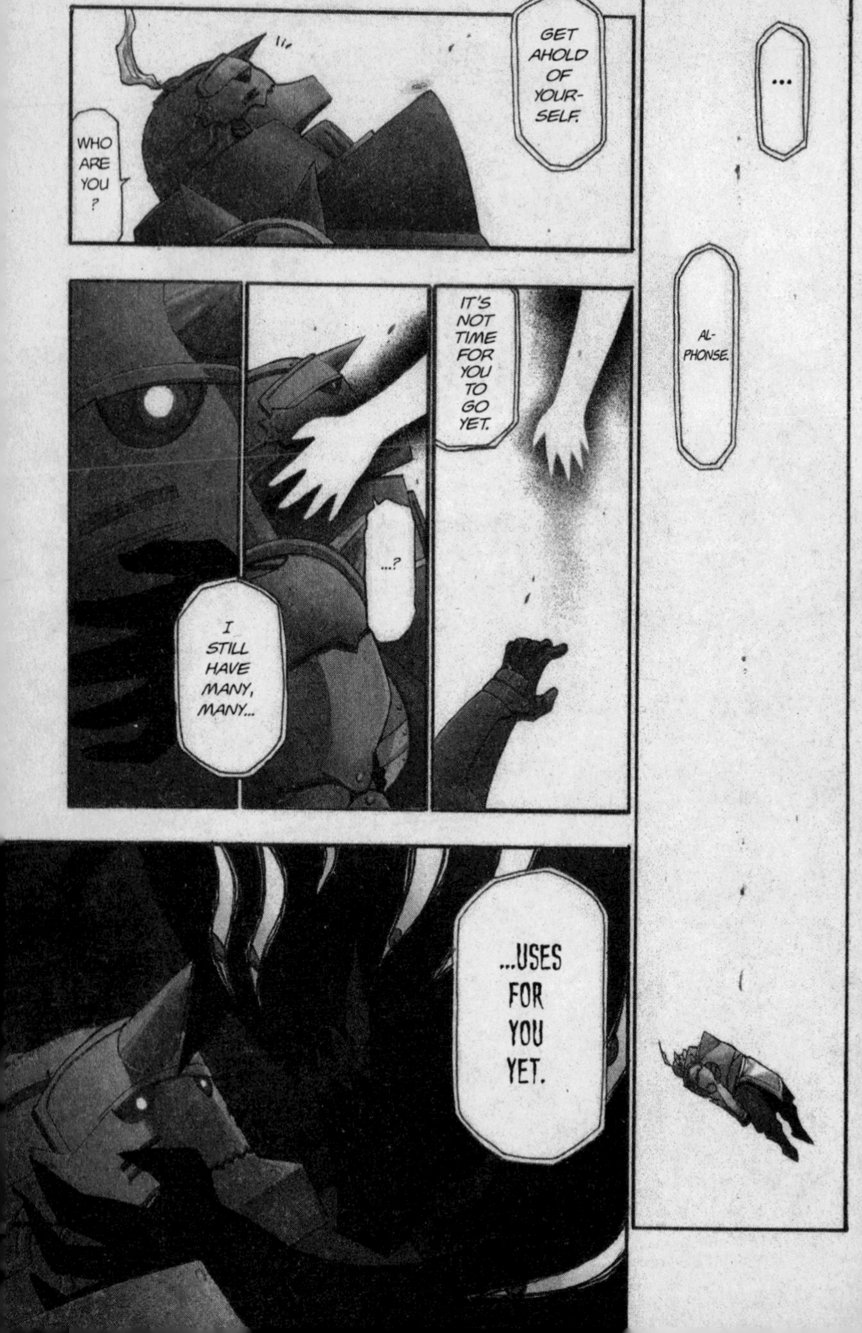
...
AL-PHONSE.
GET AHOLD OF YOUR-SELF.
WHO ARE YOU?
IT'S NOT TIME FOR YOU TO GO YET.
...?
I STILL HAVE MANY, MANY...
...USES FOR YOU YET.

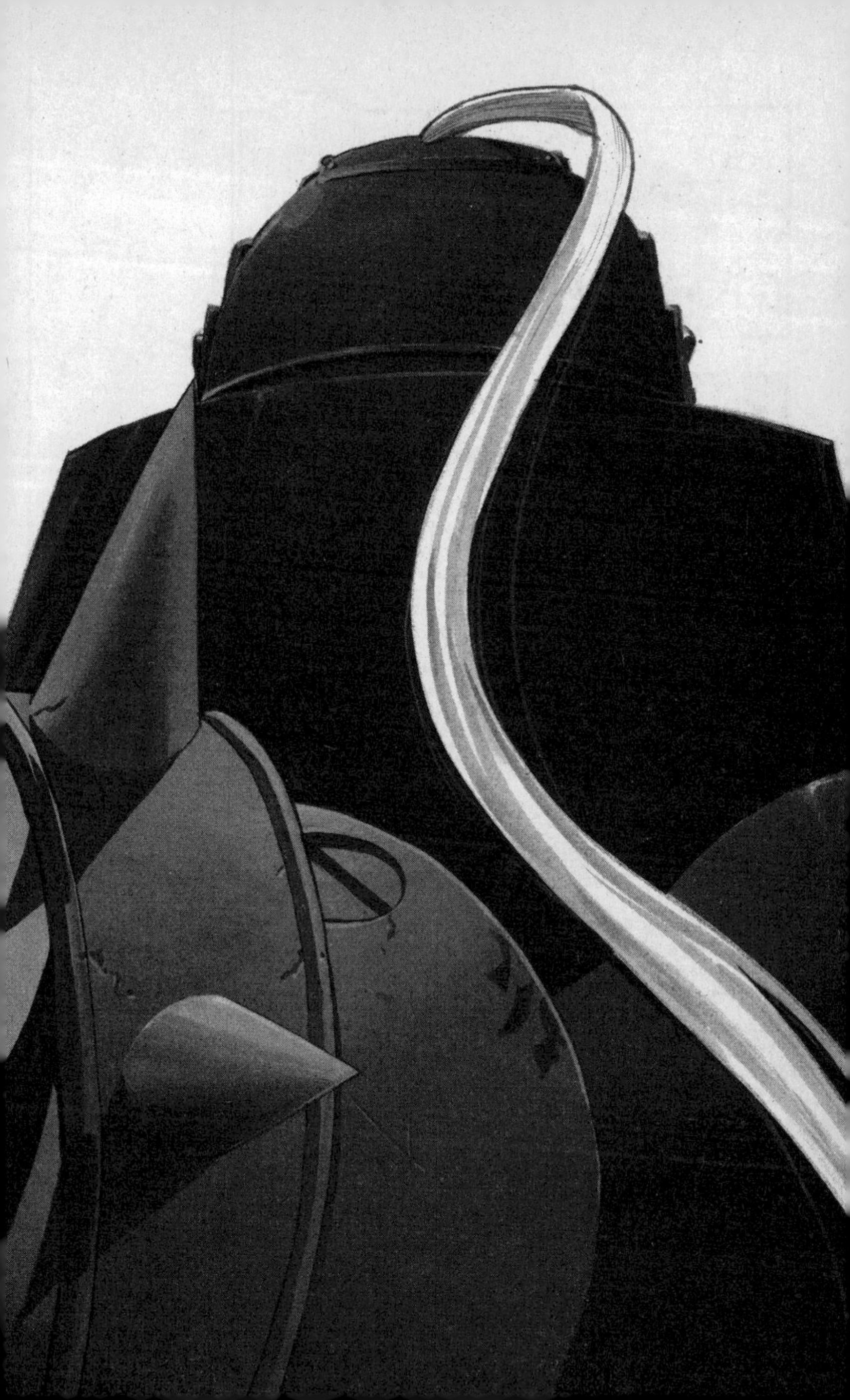

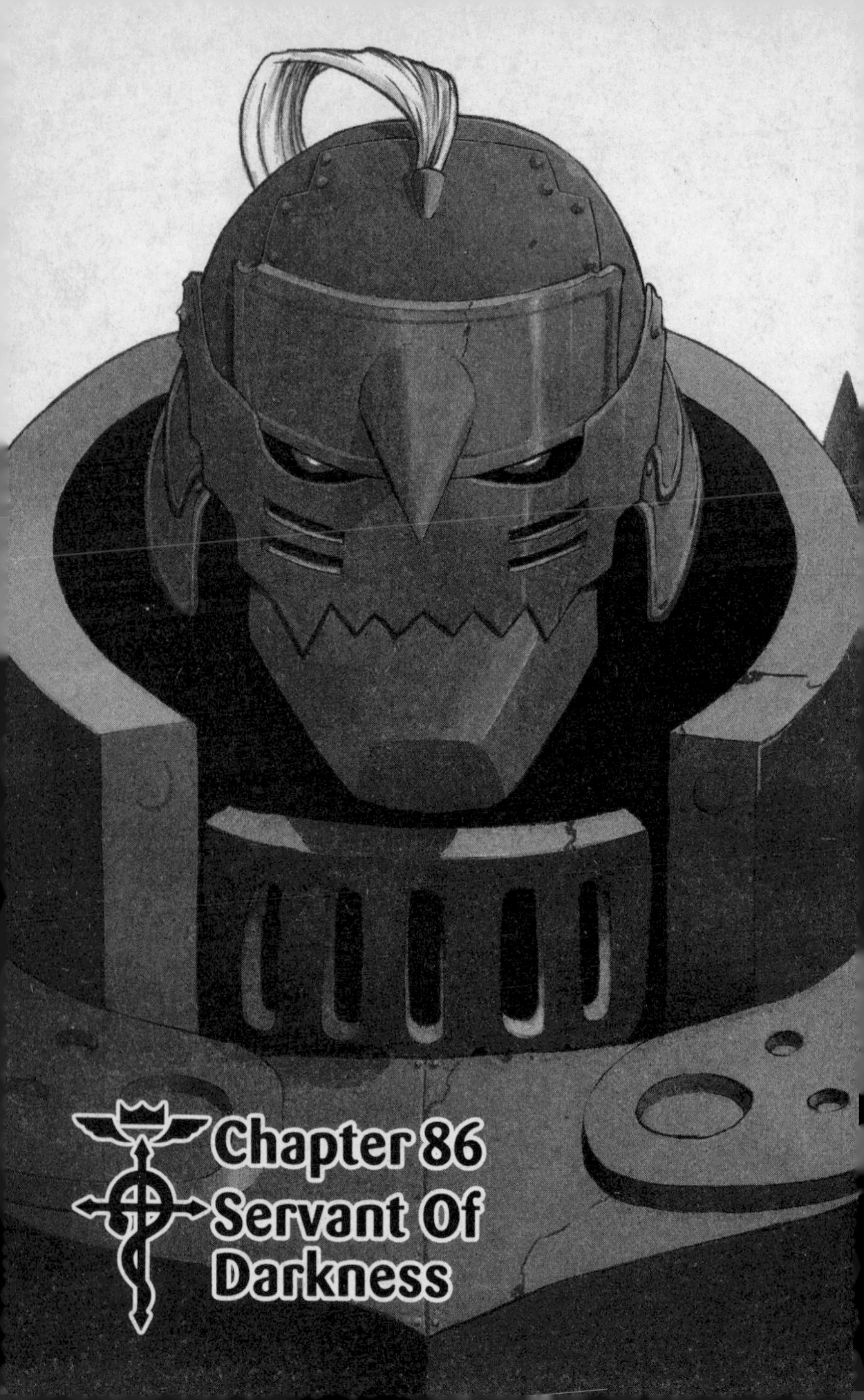
Chapter 86
Servant Of
Darkness

FULLMETAL
ALCHEMIST

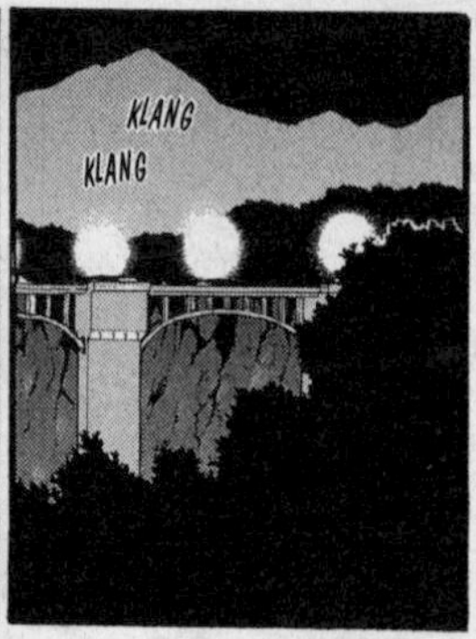
KLANG
KLANG
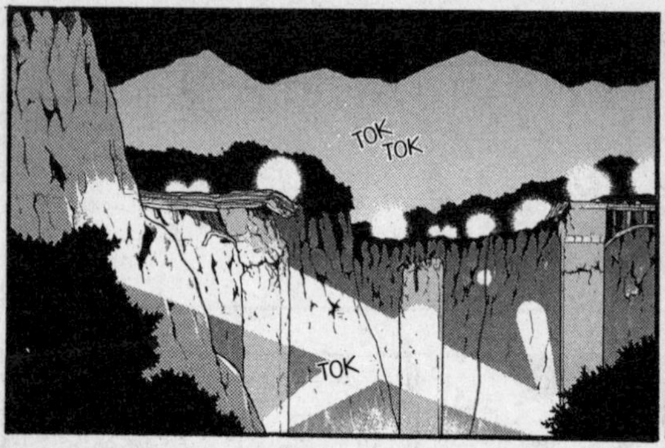
TOK TOK
TOK
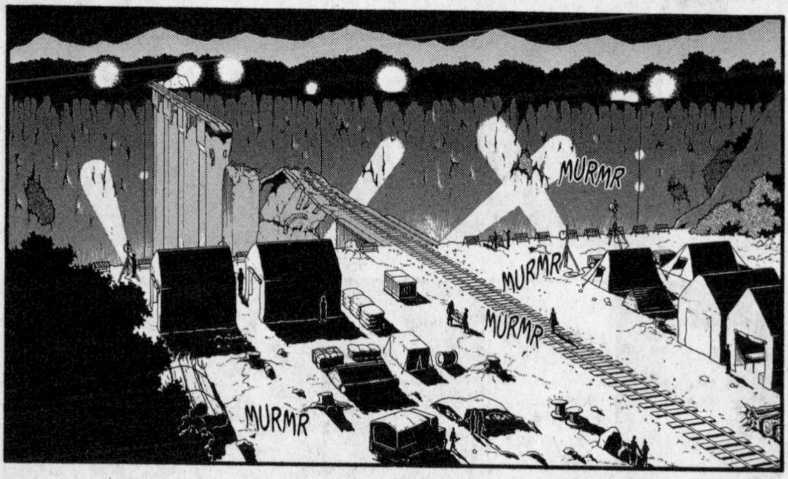
MURMR
MURMR
MURMR
MURMR
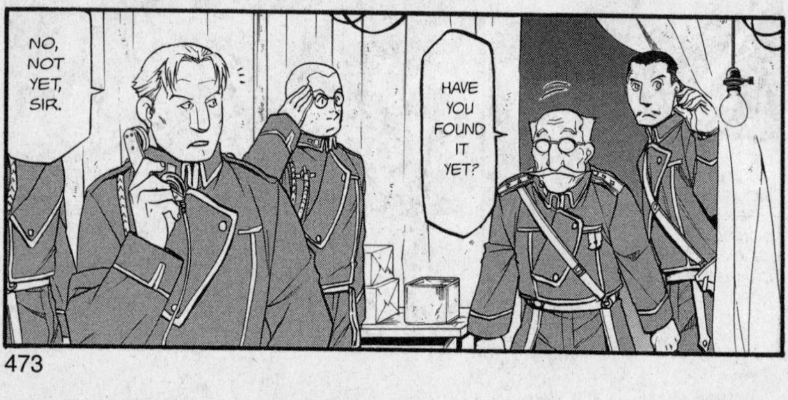
HAVE YOU FOUND IT YET?
NO, NOT YET, SIR.

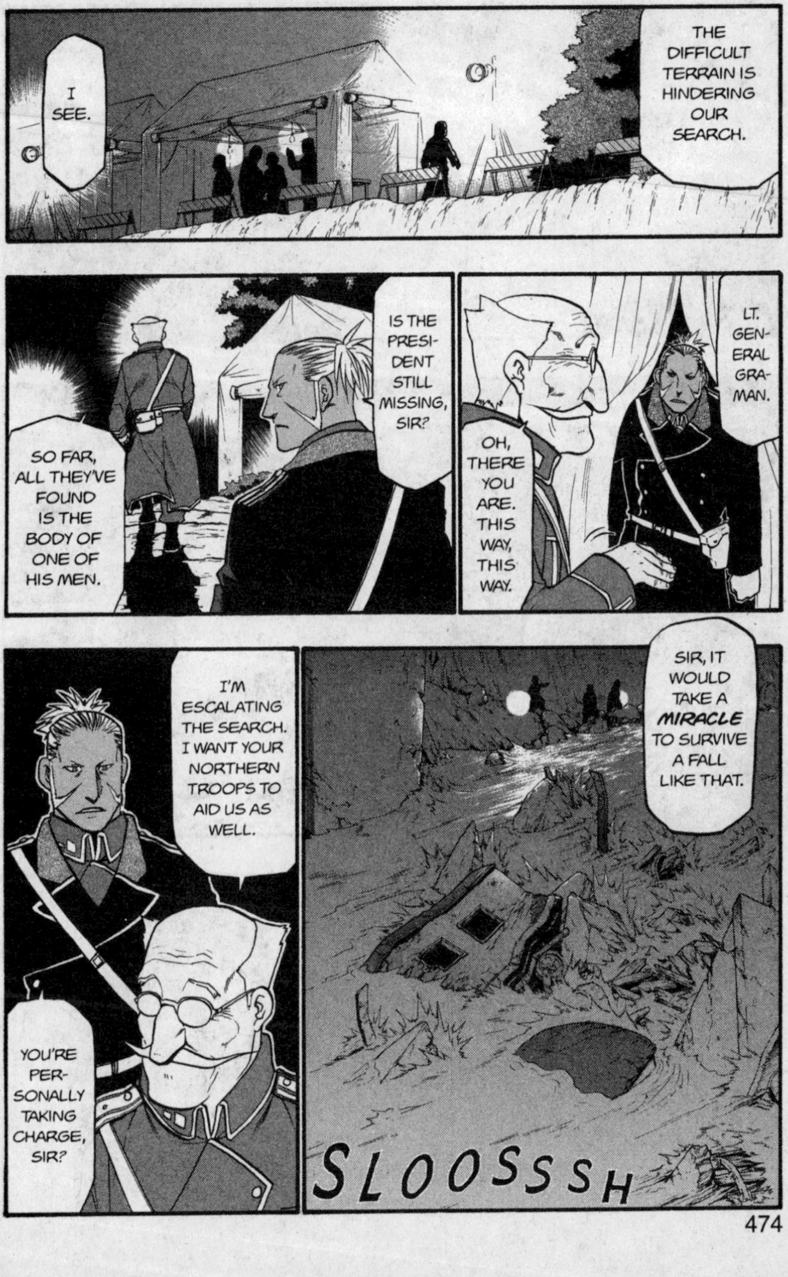
THE DIFFICULT TERRAIN IS HINDERING OUR SEARCH.
I SEE.
LT. GENERAL GRAMAN.
OH, THERE YOU ARE. THIS WAY, THIS WAY.
IS THE PRESIDENT STILL MISSING, SIR?
SO FAR, ALL THEY'VE FOUND IS THE BODY OF ONE OF HIS MEN.
SIR, IT WOULD TAKE A *MIRACLE* TO SURVIVE A FALL LIKE THAT.
SLOOSSSH
I'M ESCALATING THE SEARCH. I WANT YOUR NORTHERN TROOPS TO AID US AS WELL.
YOU'RE PERSONALLY TAKING CHARGE, SIR?

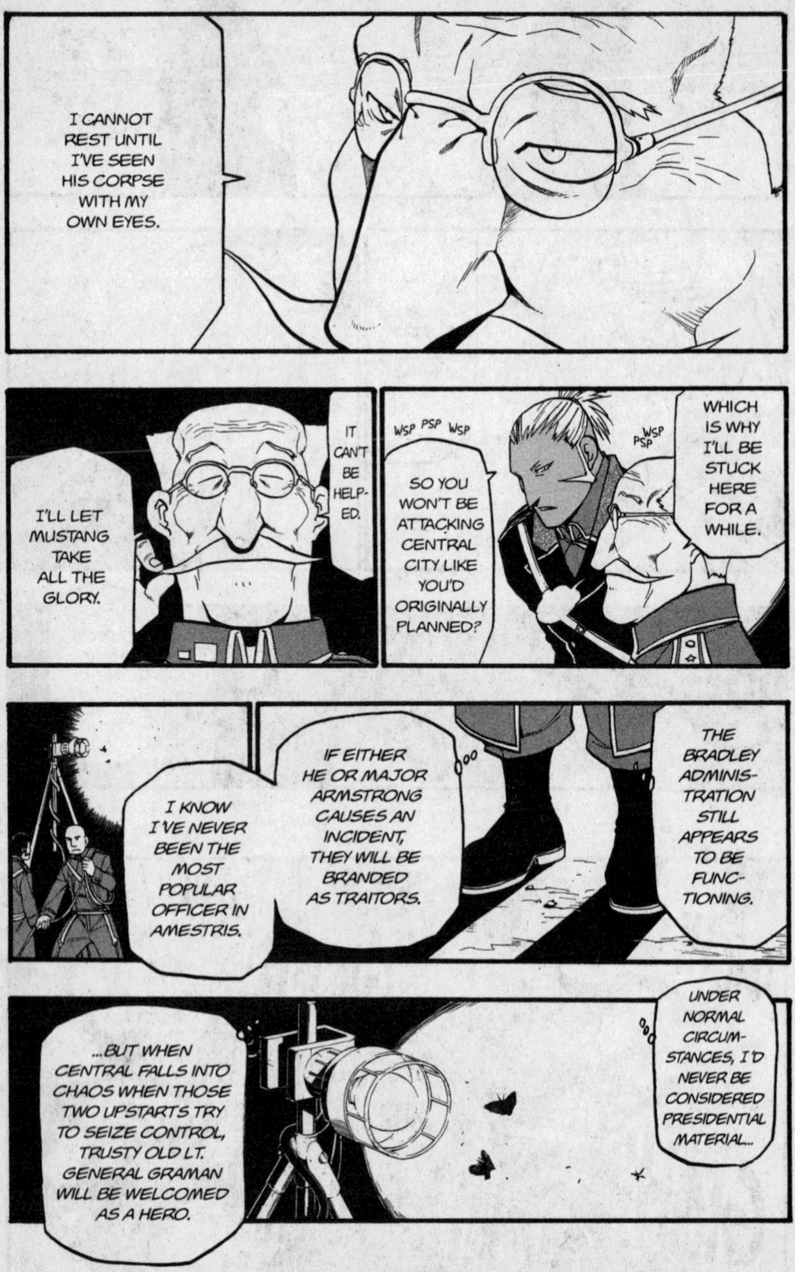
I CANNOT REST UNTIL I'VE SEEN HIS CORPSE WITH MY OWN EYES.
WHICH IS WHY I'LL BE STUCK HERE FOR A WHILE.
PSP WSP
WSP PSP WSP
SO YOU WON'T BE ATTACKING CENTRAL CITY LIKE YOU'D ORIGINALLY PLANNED?
IT CAN'T BE HELP-ED.
I'LL LET MUSTANG TAKE ALL THE GLORY.
THE BRADLEY ADMINIS-TRATION STILL APPEARS TO BE FUNC-TIONING.
IF EITHER HE OR MAJOR ARMSTRONG CAUSES AN INCIDENT, THEY WILL BE BRANDED AS TRAITORS.
I KNOW I'VE NEVER BEEN THE MOST POPULAR OFFICER IN AMESTRIS.
UNDER NORMAL CIRCUM-STANCES, I'D NEVER BE CONSIDERED PRESIDENTIAL MATERIAL...
...BUT WHEN CENTRAL FALLS INTO CHAOS WHEN THOSE TWO UPSTARTS TRY TO SEIZE CONTROL, TRUSTY OLD LT. GENERAL GRAMAN WILL BE WELCOMED AS A HERO.

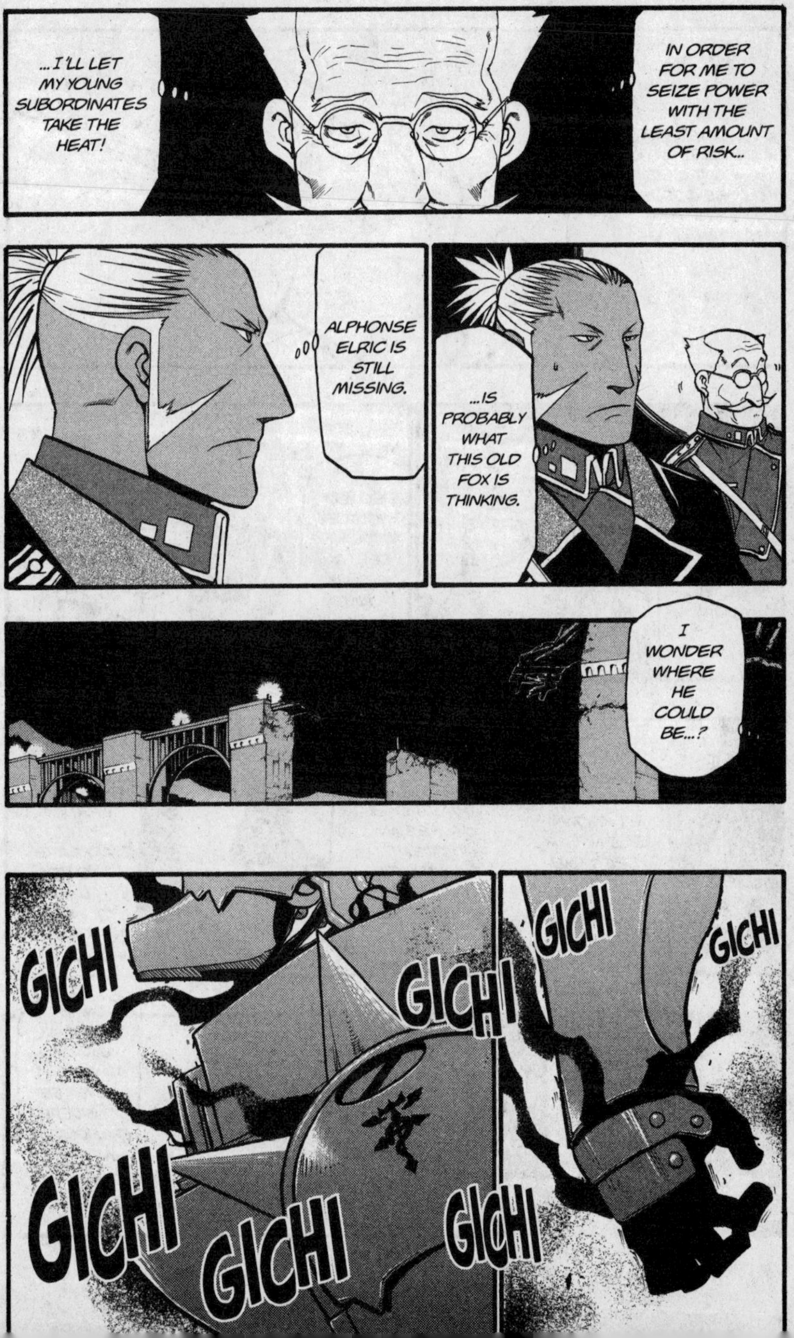
IN ORDER FOR ME TO SEIZE POWER WITH THE LEAST AMOUNT OF RISK..
...I'LL LET MY YOUNG SUBORDINATES TAKE THE HEAT!
...IS PROBABLY WHAT THIS OLD FOX IS THINKING.
ALPHONSE ELRIC IS STILL MISSING.
I WONDER WHERE HE COULD BE...?
GICHI
GICHI
GICHI
GICHI
GICHI
GICHI
GICHI

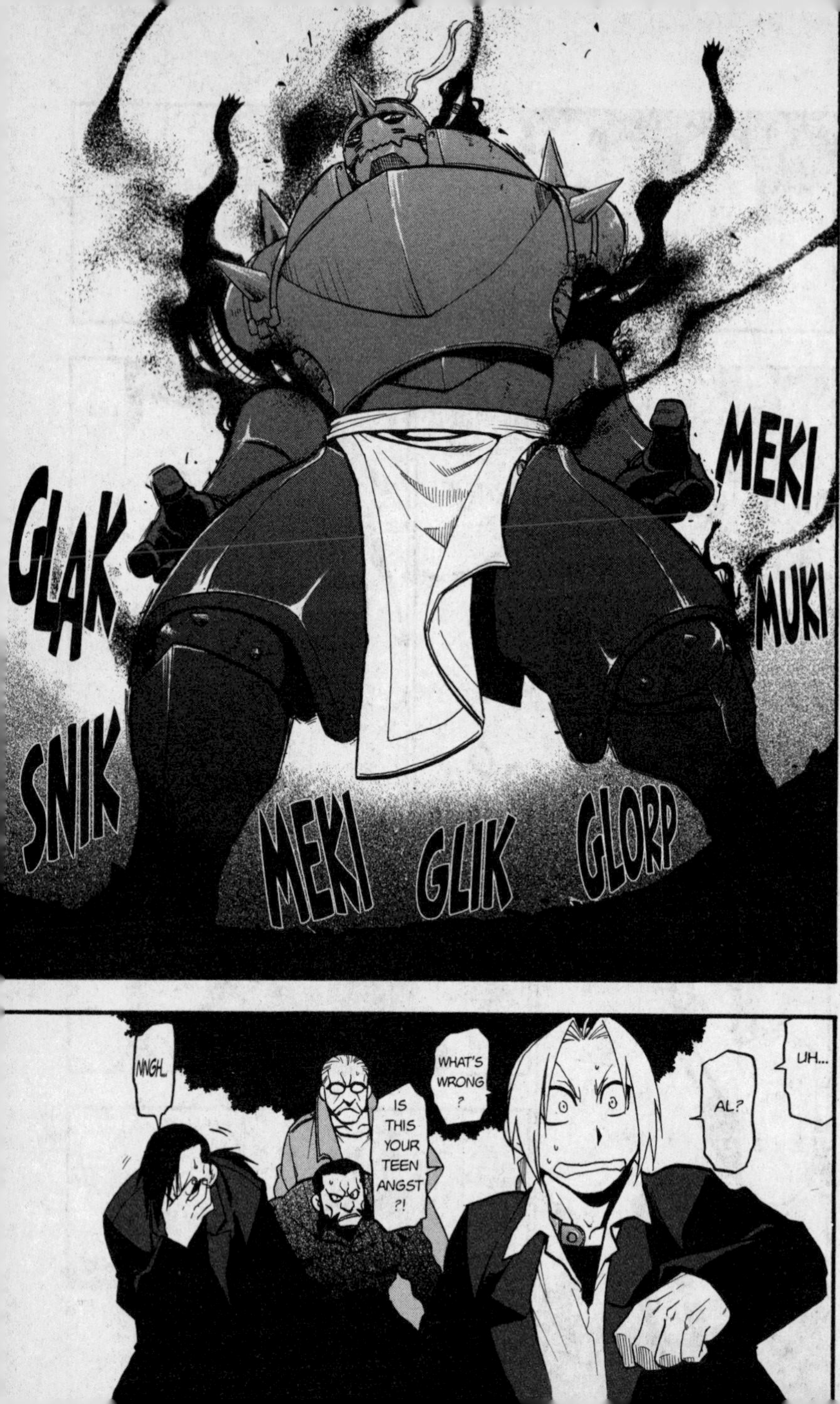
MEKI
MUKI
GLAK
SNIK
GLORP
GLIK
MEKI
UH...
AL?
WHAT'S WRONG?
IS THIS YOUR TEEN ANGST?!
NNGH...

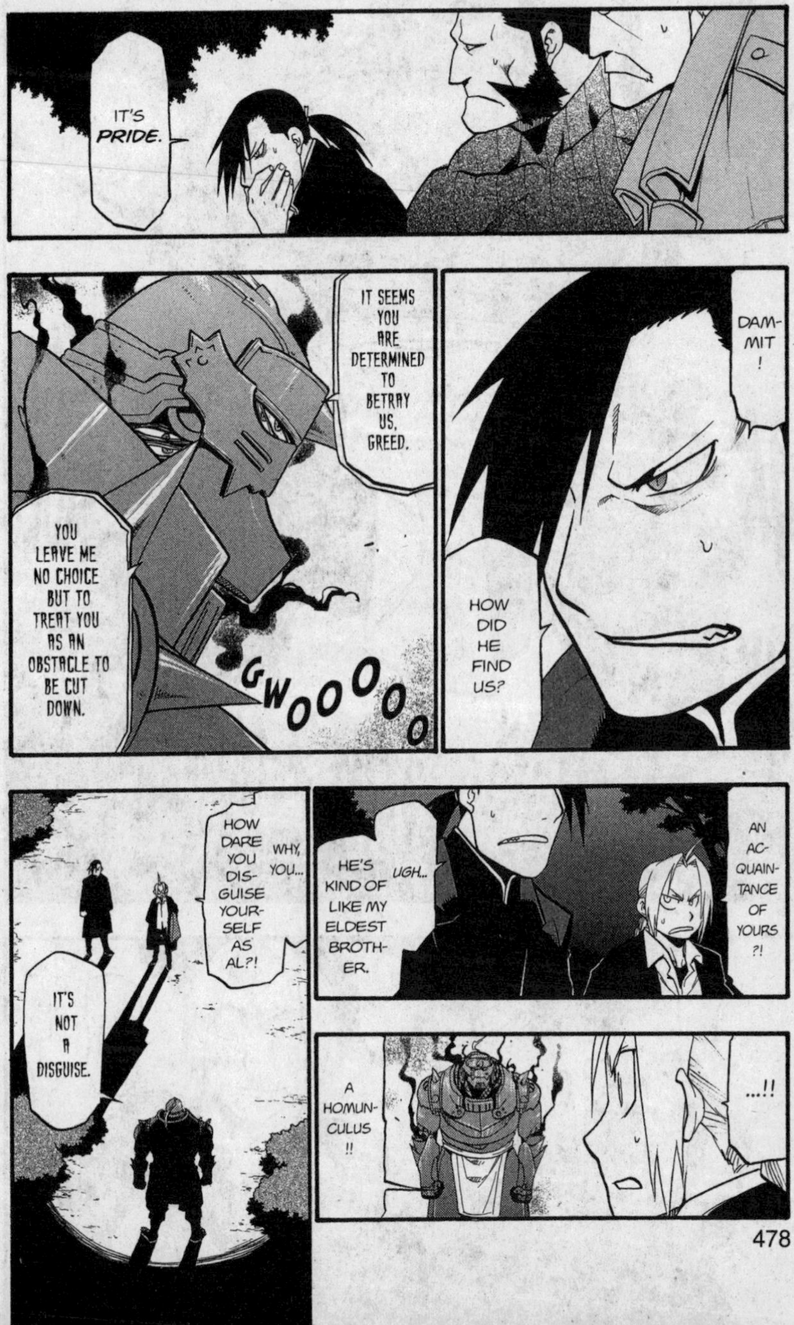
IT'S PRIDE.
DAM-MIT!
HOW DID HE FIND US?
IT SEEMS YOU ARE DETERMINED TO BETRAY US, GREED.
YOU LEAVE ME NO CHOICE BUT TO TREAT YOU AS AN OBSTACLE TO BE CUT DOWN.
GWOOOOOO
AN AC-QUAIN-TANCE OF YOURS?!
UGH...
HE'S KIND OF LIKE MY ELDEST BROTH-ER.
...!!
A HOMUN-CULUS!!
WHY, YOU...
HOW DARE YOU DIS-GUISE YOUR-SELF AS AL?!
IT'S NOT A DISGUISE.

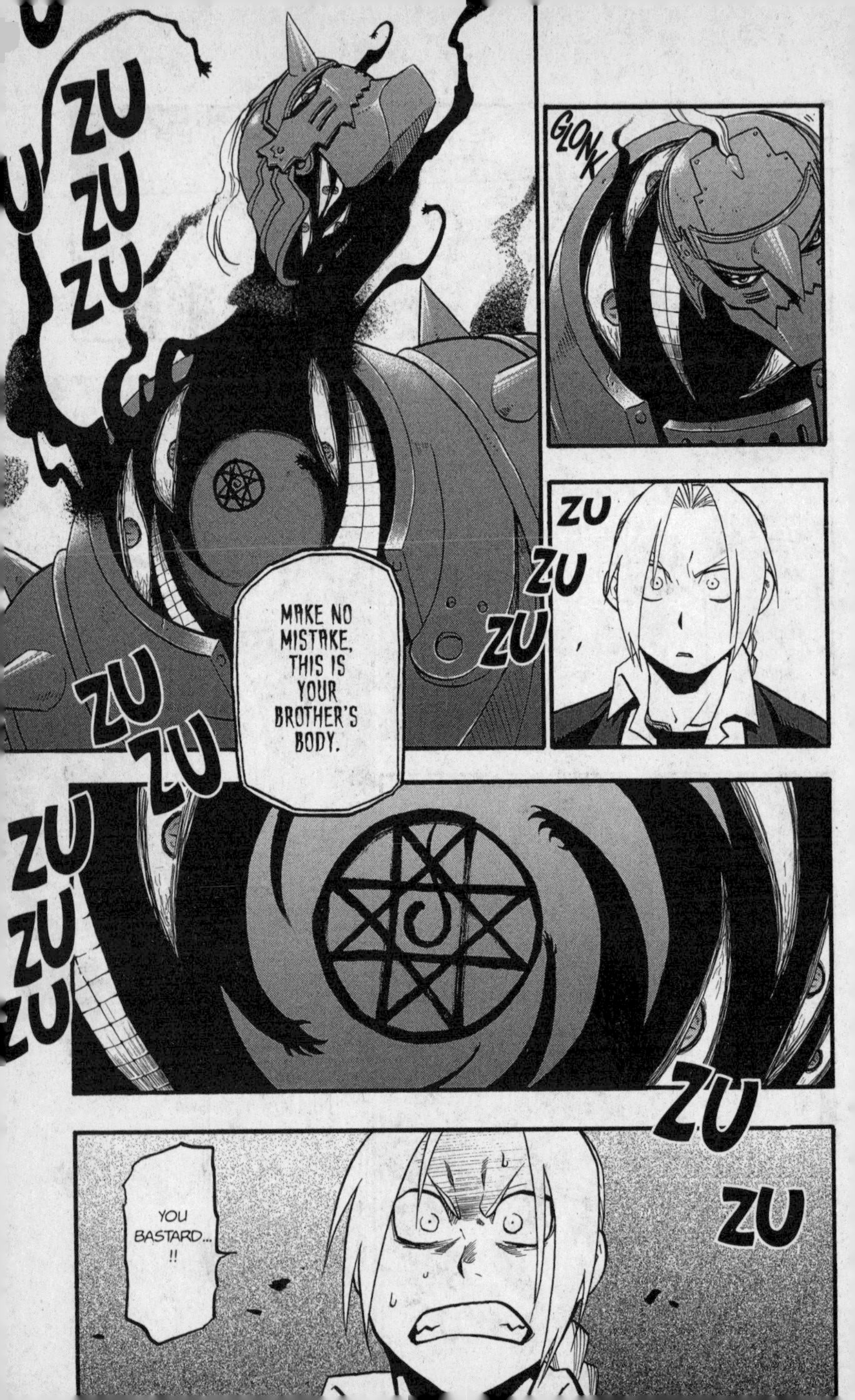
GLONK
ZU
ZU
ZU
U
ZU
ZU
ZU
MAKE NO MISTAKE, THIS IS YOUR BROTHER'S BODY.
ZU
ZU
ZU
ZU
ZU
ZU
ZU
ZU
YOU BASTARD... !!

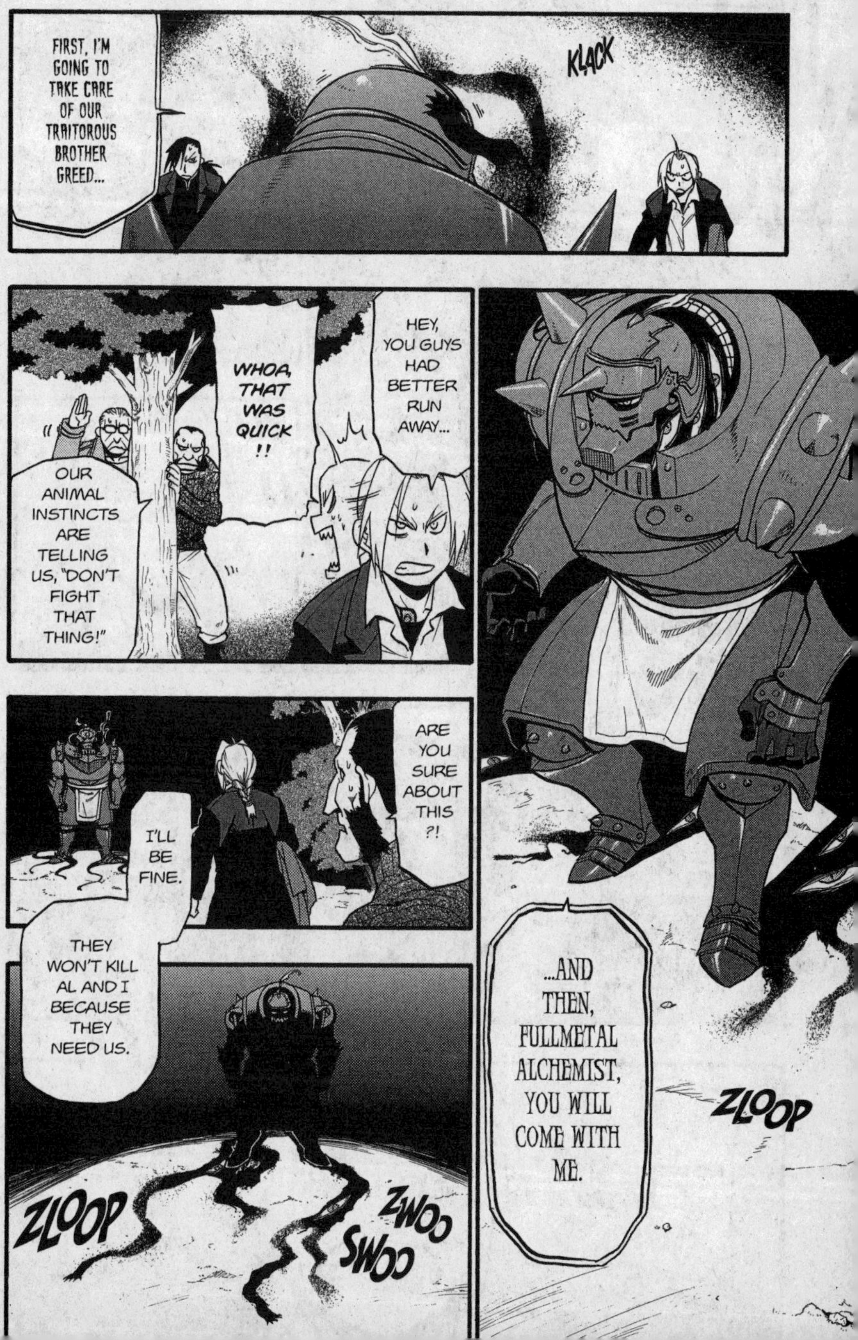
KLACK
FIRST, I'M GOING TO TAKE CARE OF OUR TRAITOROUS BROTHER GREED...
...AND THEN, FULLMETAL ALCHEMIST, YOU WILL COME WITH ME.
ZLOOP
HEY, YOU GUYS HAD BETTER RUN AWAY...
WHOA, THAT WAS QUICK!!
OUR ANIMAL INSTINCTS ARE TELLING US, "DON'T FIGHT THAT THING!"
ARE YOU SURE ABOUT THIS?!
I'LL BE FINE.
THEY WON'T KILL AL AND I BECAUSE THEY NEED US.
ZWOO
SWOO
ZLOOP

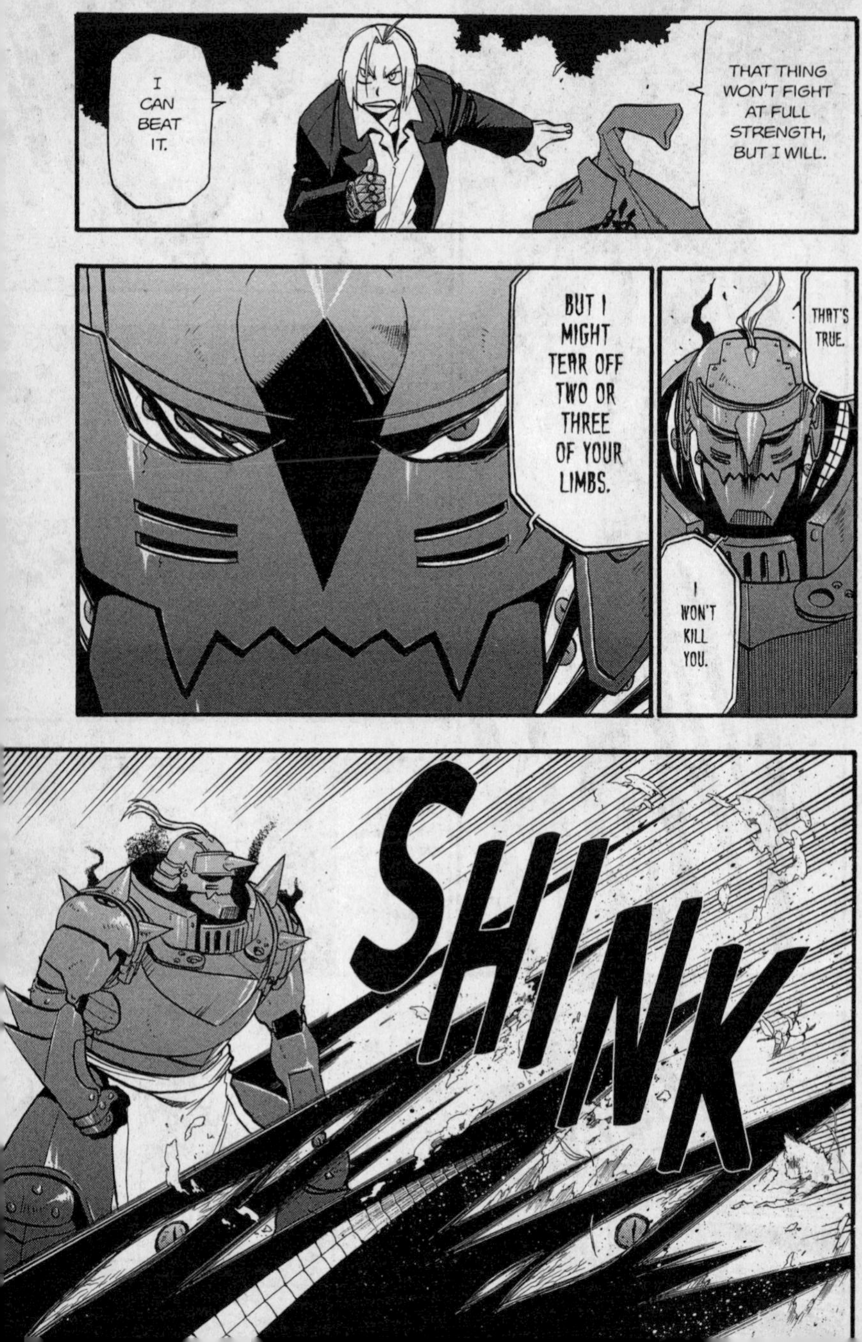
THAT THING WON'T FIGHT AT FULL STRENGTH, BUT I WILL.
I CAN BEAT IT.
THAT'S TRUE.
I WON'T KILL YOU.
BUT I MIGHT TEAR OFF TWO OR THREE OF YOUR LIMBS.
SHINK

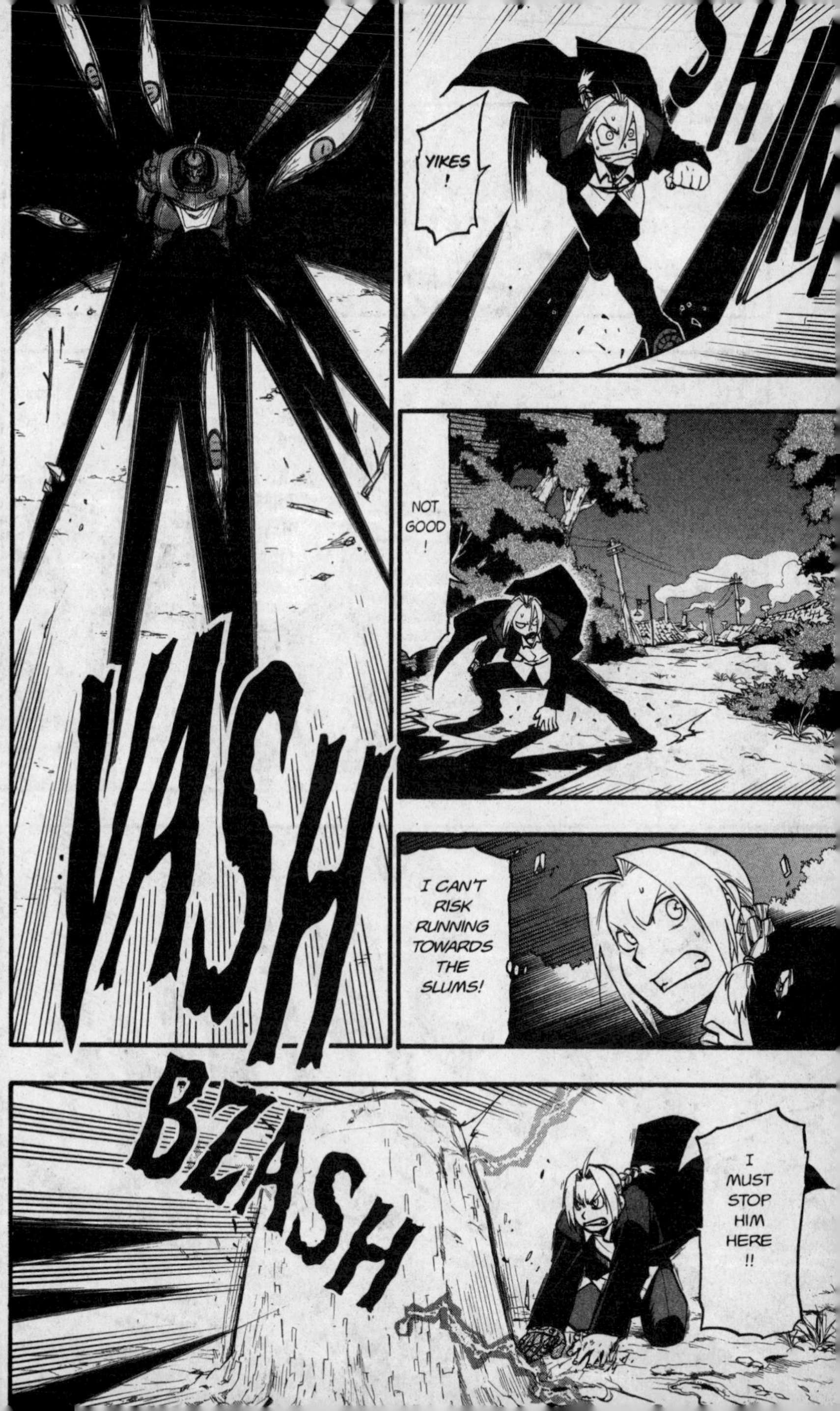
YIKES!
NOT GOOD!
I CAN'T RISK RUNNING TOWARDS THE SLUMS!
VASH
I MUST STOP HIM HERE!!
BZASH

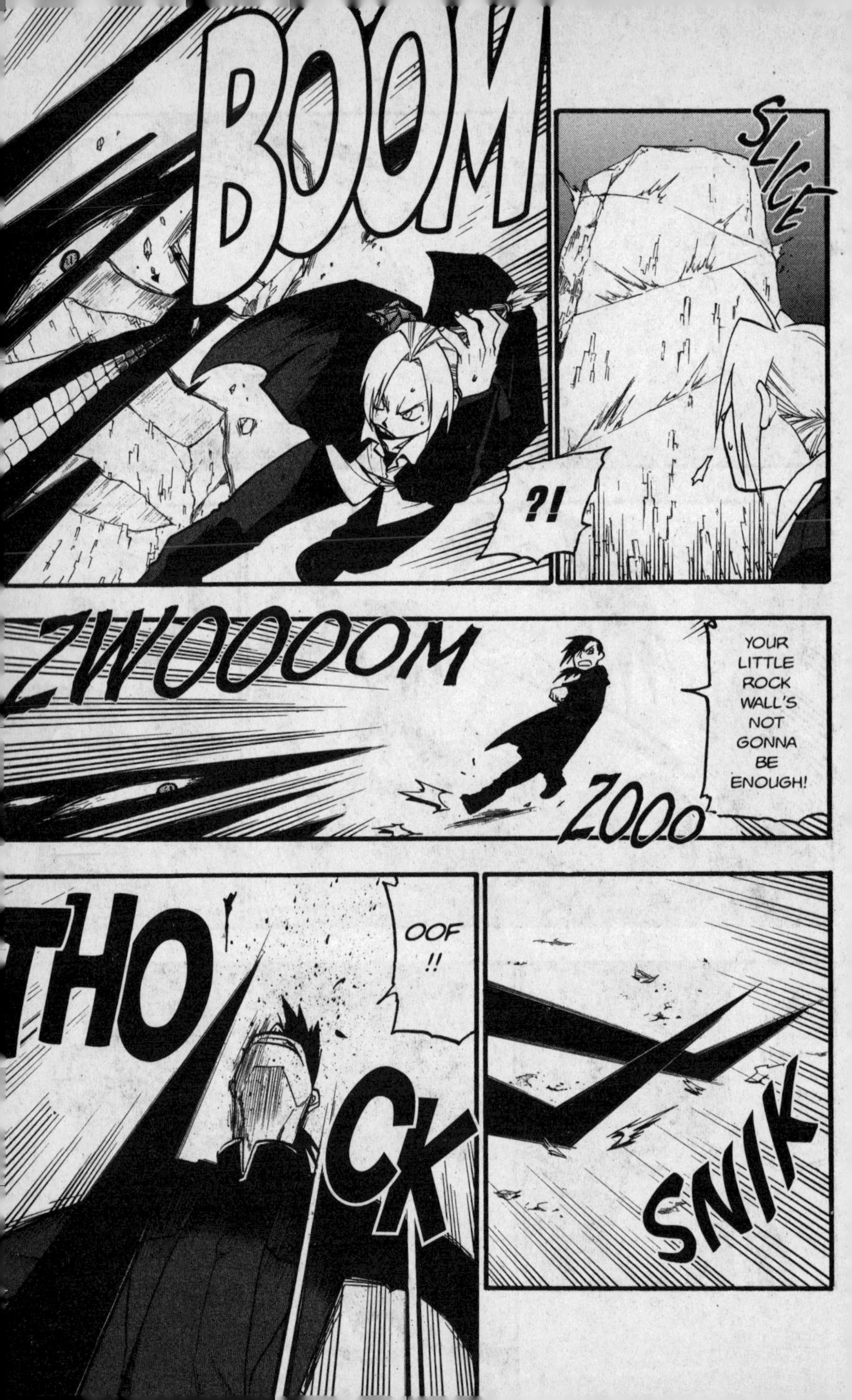
SLICE
BOOM
?!
YOUR LITTLE ROCK WALL'S NOT GONNA BE ENOUGH!
ZOOO
ZWOOOOOM
SNIK
OOF !!
THOCK

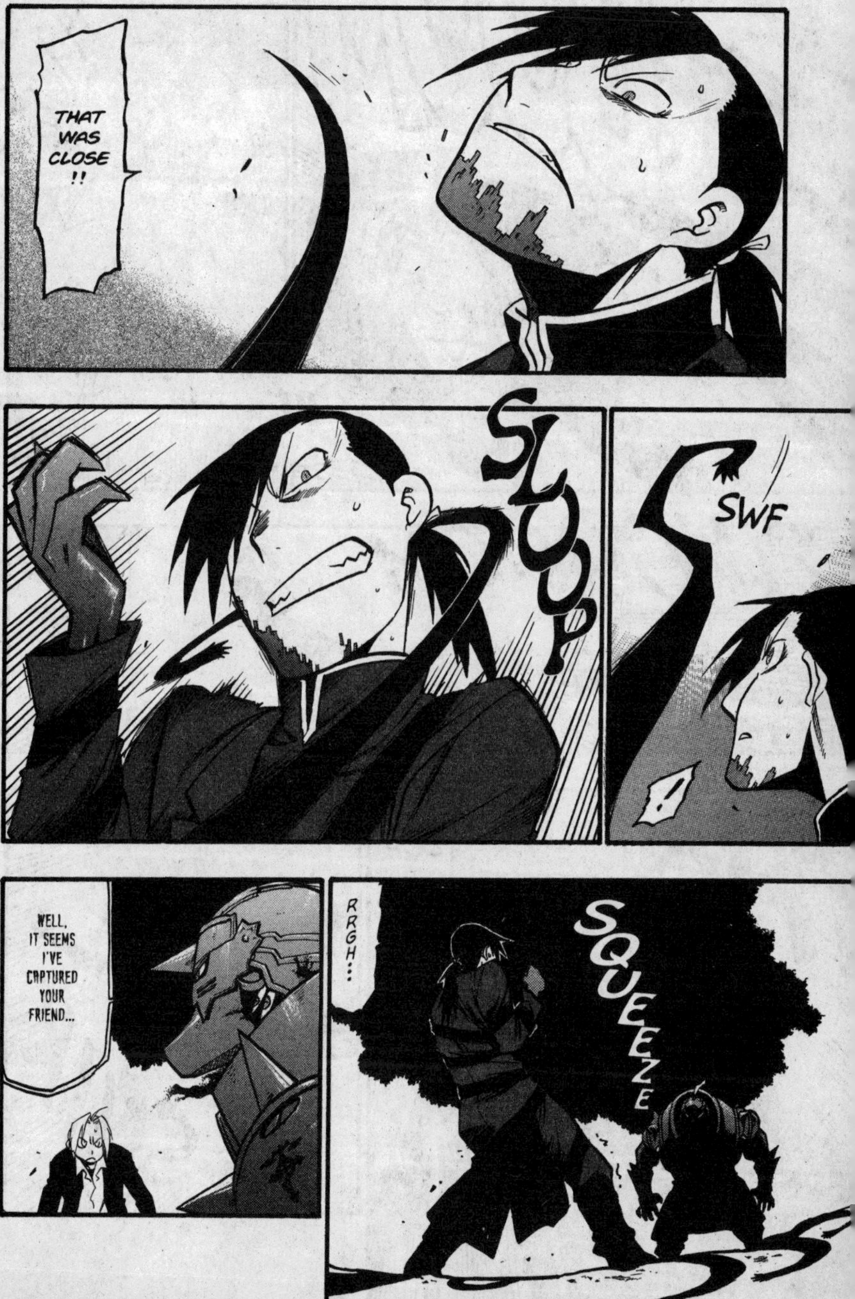
THAT WAS CLOSE !!
SWF
SLUUP!
RRGH...
SQUEEZE
WELL, IT SEEMS I'VE CAPTURED YOUR FRIEND...

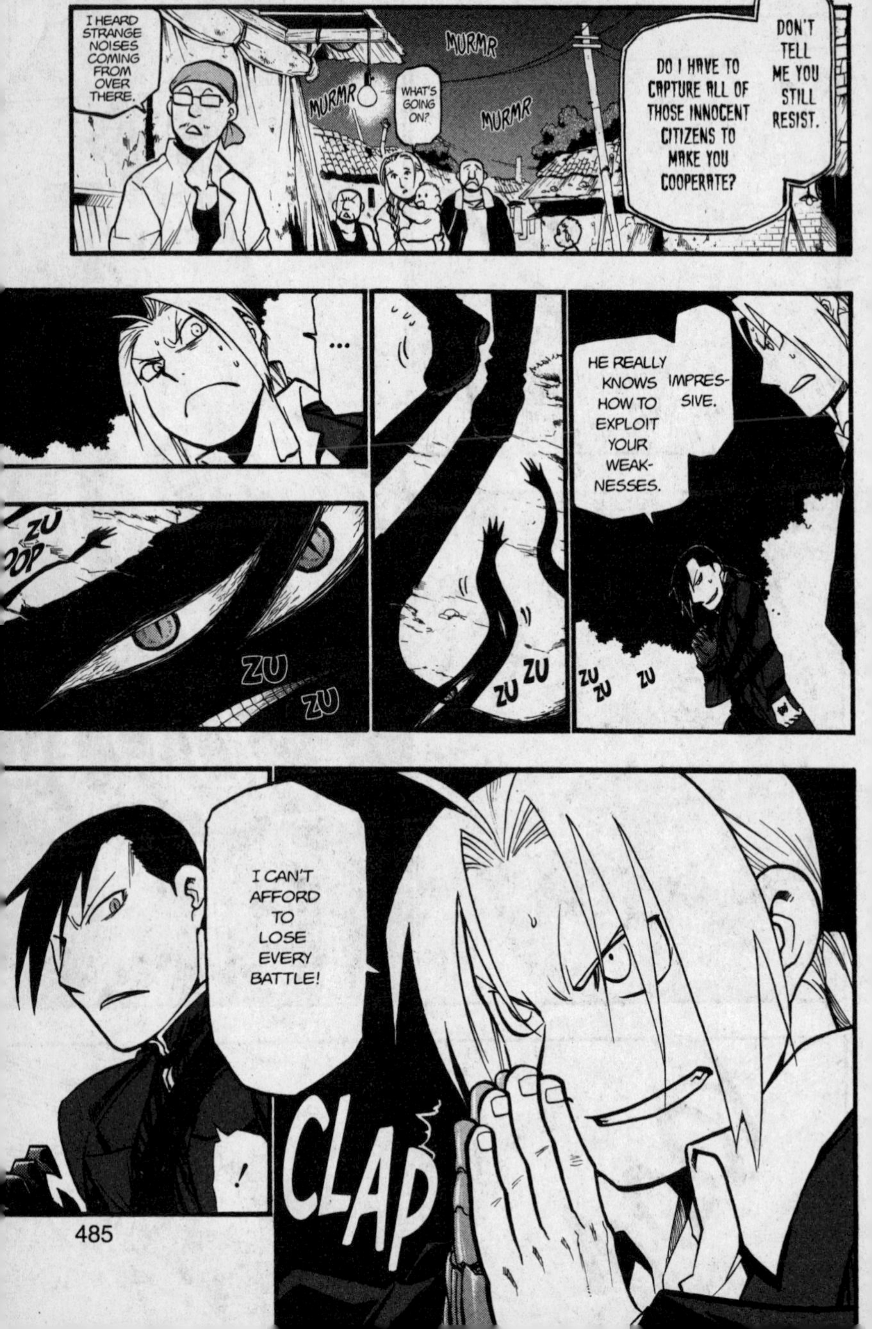
DON'T TELL ME YOU STILL RESIST.
DO I HAVE TO CAPTURE ALL OF THOSE INNOCENT CITIZENS TO MAKE YOU COOPERATE?
MURMR
MURMR
WHAT'S GOING ON?
MURMR
I HEARD STRANGE NOISES COMING FROM OVER THERE.
IMPRESSIVE.
HE REALLY KNOWS HOW TO EXPLOIT YOUR WEAKNESSES.
ZU ZU ZU
ZU ZU
...
ZU ZU
ZU POP
I CAN'T AFFORD TO LOSE EVERY BATTLE!
CLAP
!

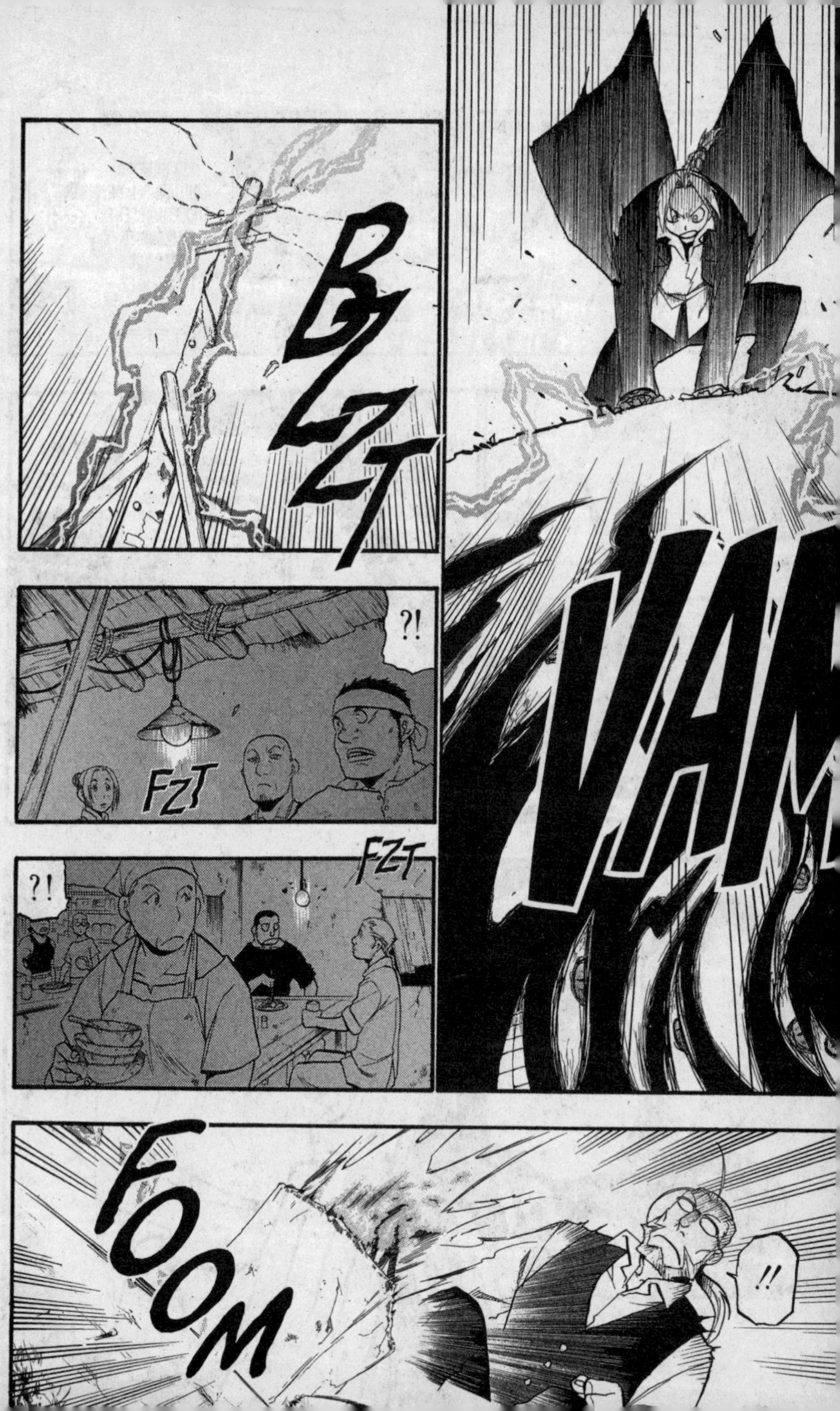
VAM
BZZT
?!
FZT
FZT
?!
!!
FOOM

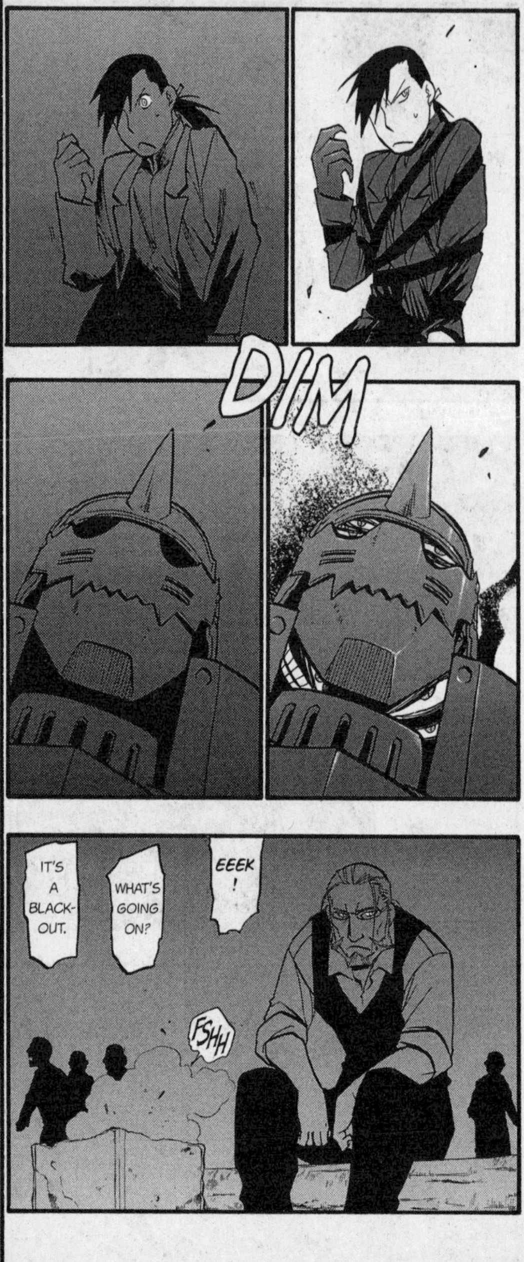
DIM
EEEK!
WHAT'S GOING ON?
IT'S A BLACK-OUT.
FSHH
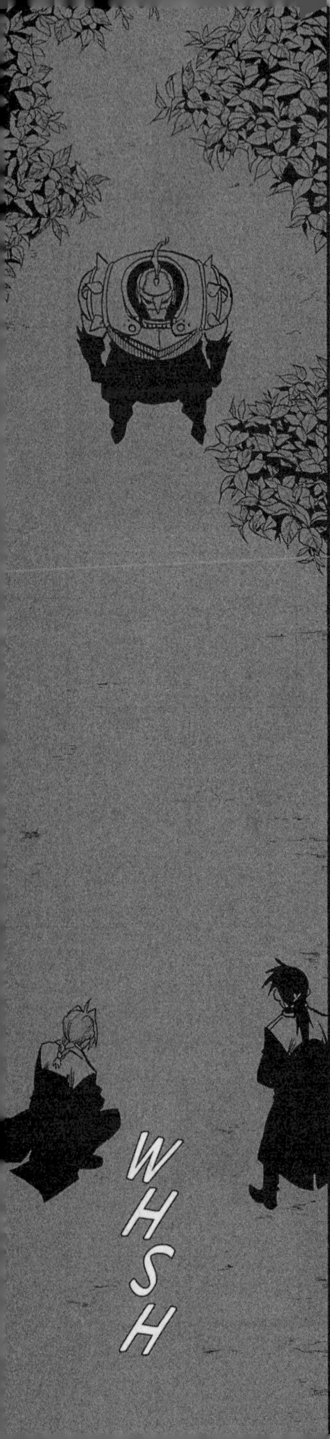
WHSH

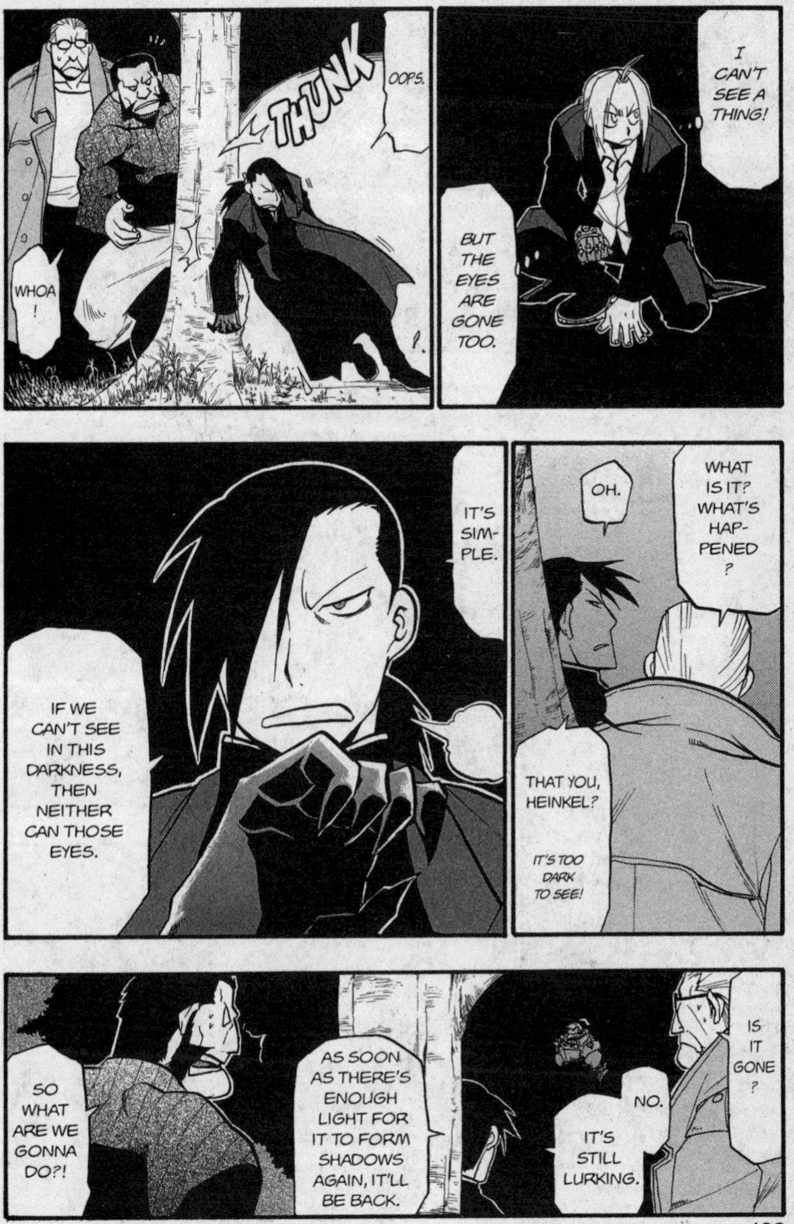
I CAN'T SEE A THING!
BUT THE EYES ARE GONE TOO.
THUNK
OOPS.
WHOA!
WHAT IS IT? WHAT'S HAPPENED?
OH.
THAT YOU, HEINKEL?
IT'S TOO DARK TO SEE!
IT'S SIMPLE.
IF WE CAN'T SEE IN THIS DARKNESS, THEN NEITHER CAN THOSE EYES.
IS IT GONE?
NO.
IT'S STILL LURKING.
AS SOON AS THERE'S ENOUGH LIGHT FOR IT TO FORM SHADOWS AGAIN, IT'LL BE BACK.
SO WHAT ARE WE GONNA DO?!

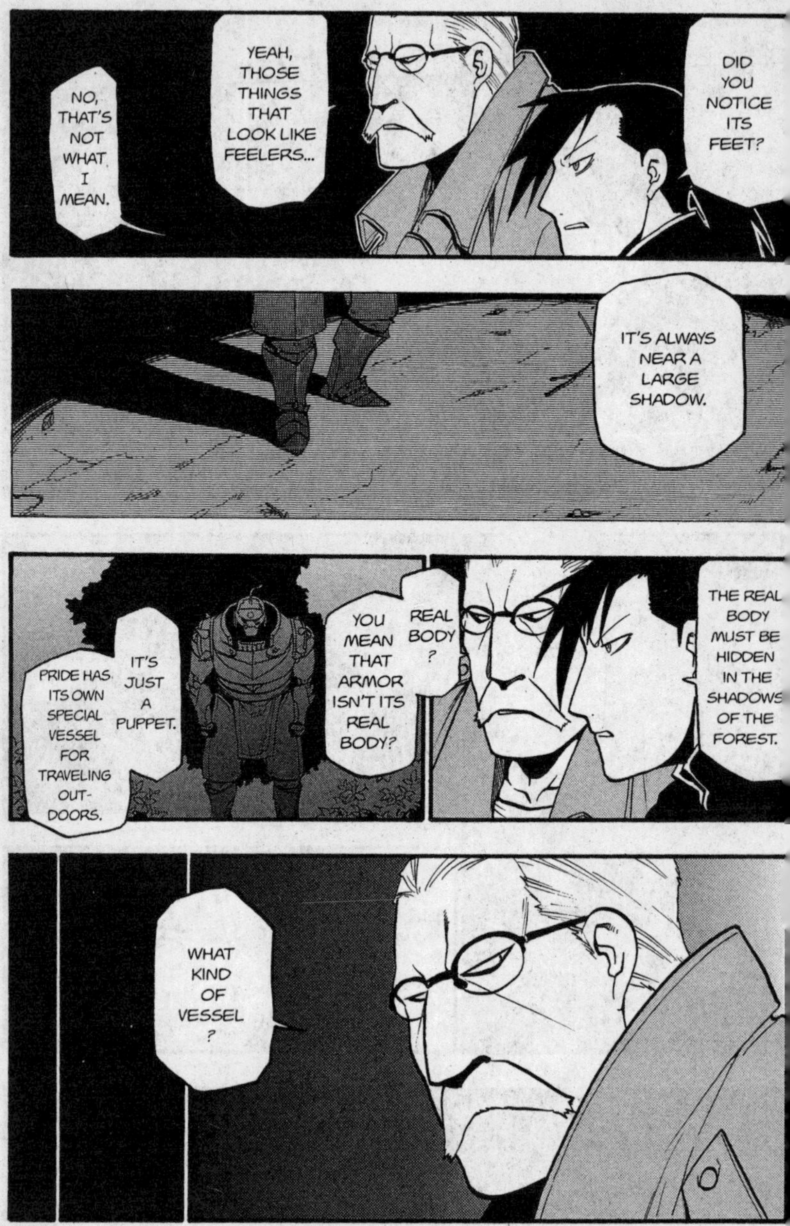
DID YOU NOTICE ITS FEET?
YEAH, THOSE THINGS THAT LOOK LIKE FEELERS...
NO, THAT'S NOT WHAT I MEAN.
IT'S ALWAYS NEAR A LARGE SHADOW.
THE REAL BODY MUST BE HIDDEN IN THE SHADOWS OF THE FOREST.
REAL BODY?
YOU MEAN THAT ARMOR ISN'T ITS REAL BODY?
IT'S JUST A PUPPET.
PRIDE HAS ITS OWN SPECIAL VESSEL FOR TRAVELING OUT-DOORS.
WHAT KIND OF VESSEL?

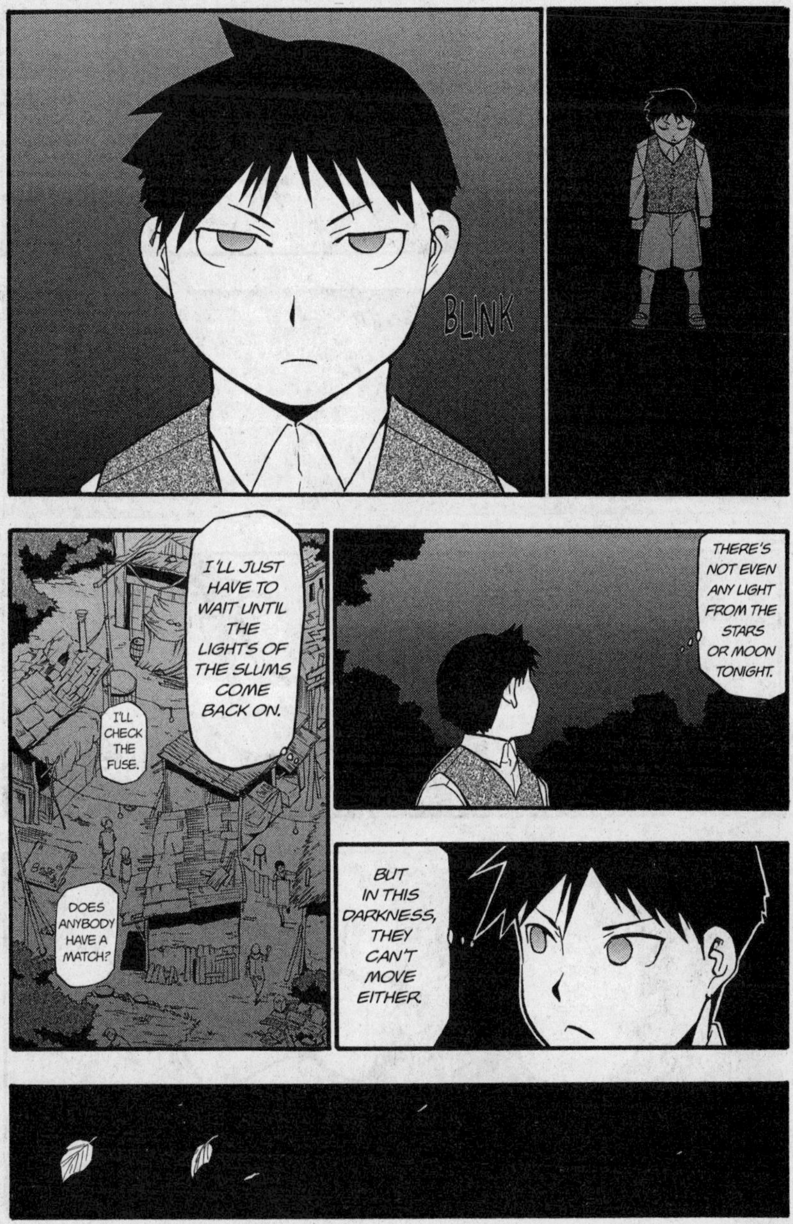
BLINK
THERE'S NOT EVEN ANY LIGHT FROM THE STARS OR MOON TONIGHT.
BUT IN THIS DARKNESS, THEY CAN'T MOVE EITHER.
I'LL JUST HAVE TO WAIT UNTIL THE LIGHTS OF THE SLUMS COME BACK ON.
I'LL CHECK THE FUSE.
DOES ANYBODY HAVE A MATCH?

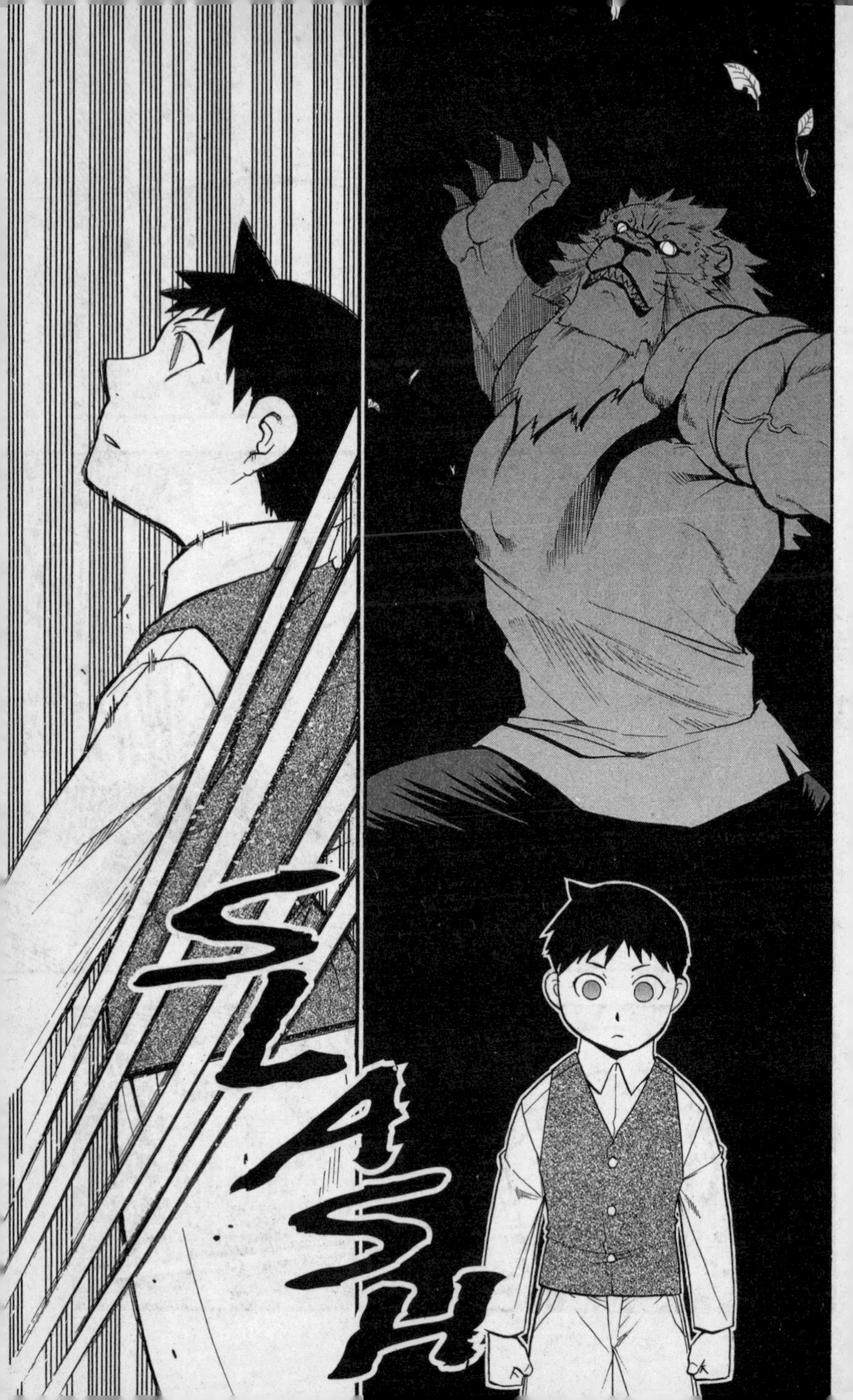
SLASH

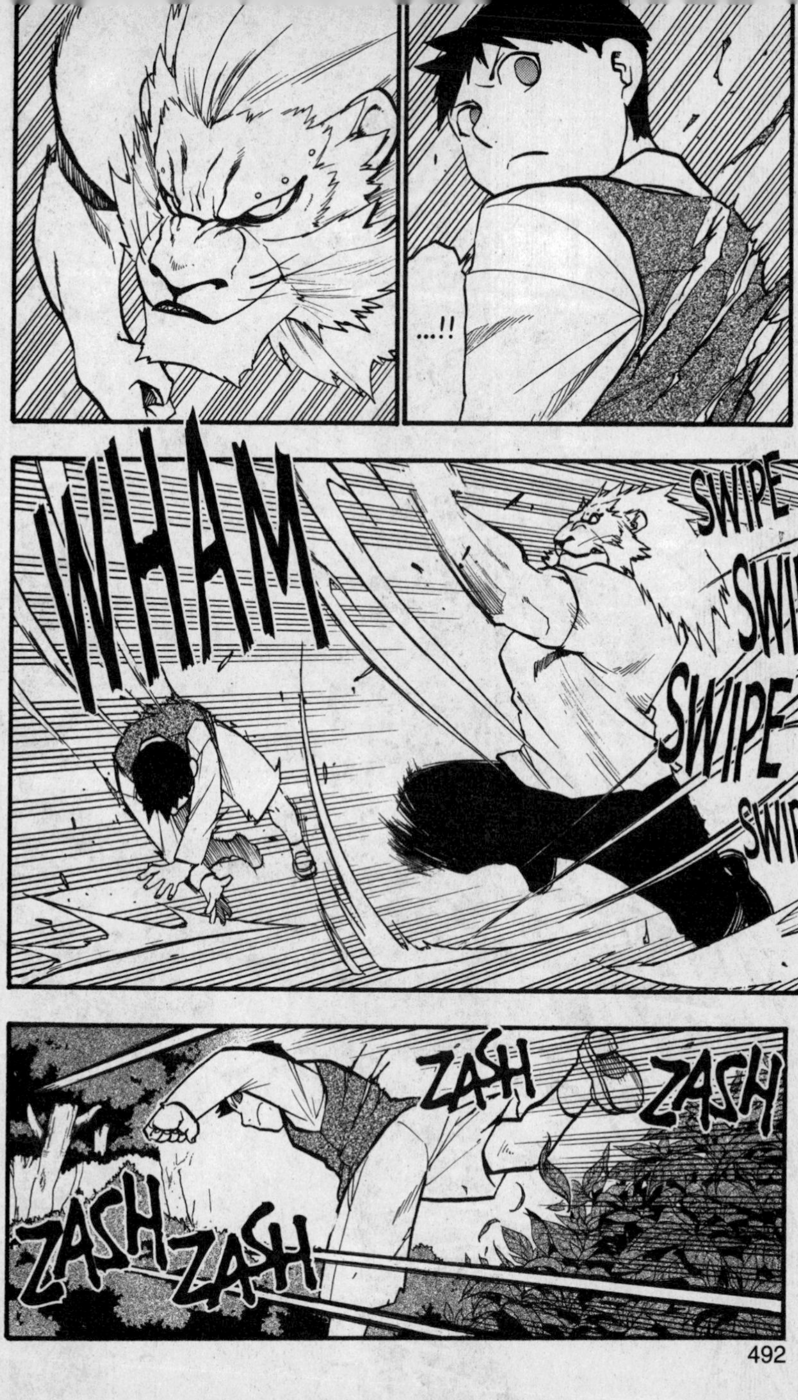
...!!
SWIPE
SWIPE
SWIPE
SWIPE
WHAM
ZASH
ZASH
ZASH
ZASH

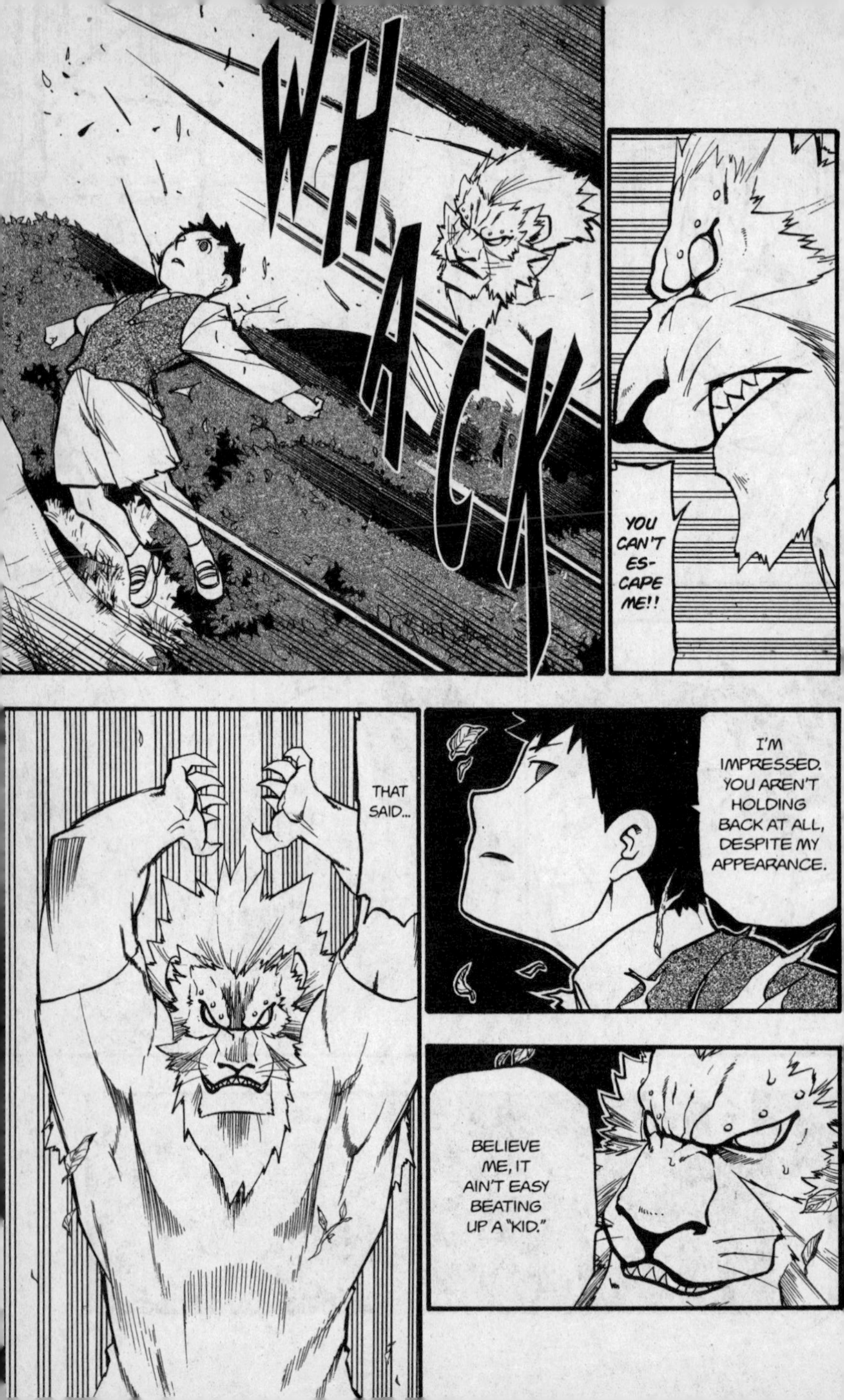
YOU CAN'T ES-CAPE ME!!
WHACK
I'M IMPRESSED. YOU AREN'T HOLDING BACK AT ALL, DESPITE MY APPEARANCE.
BELIEVE ME, IT AIN'T EASY BEATING UP A "KID."
.....
THAT SAID...

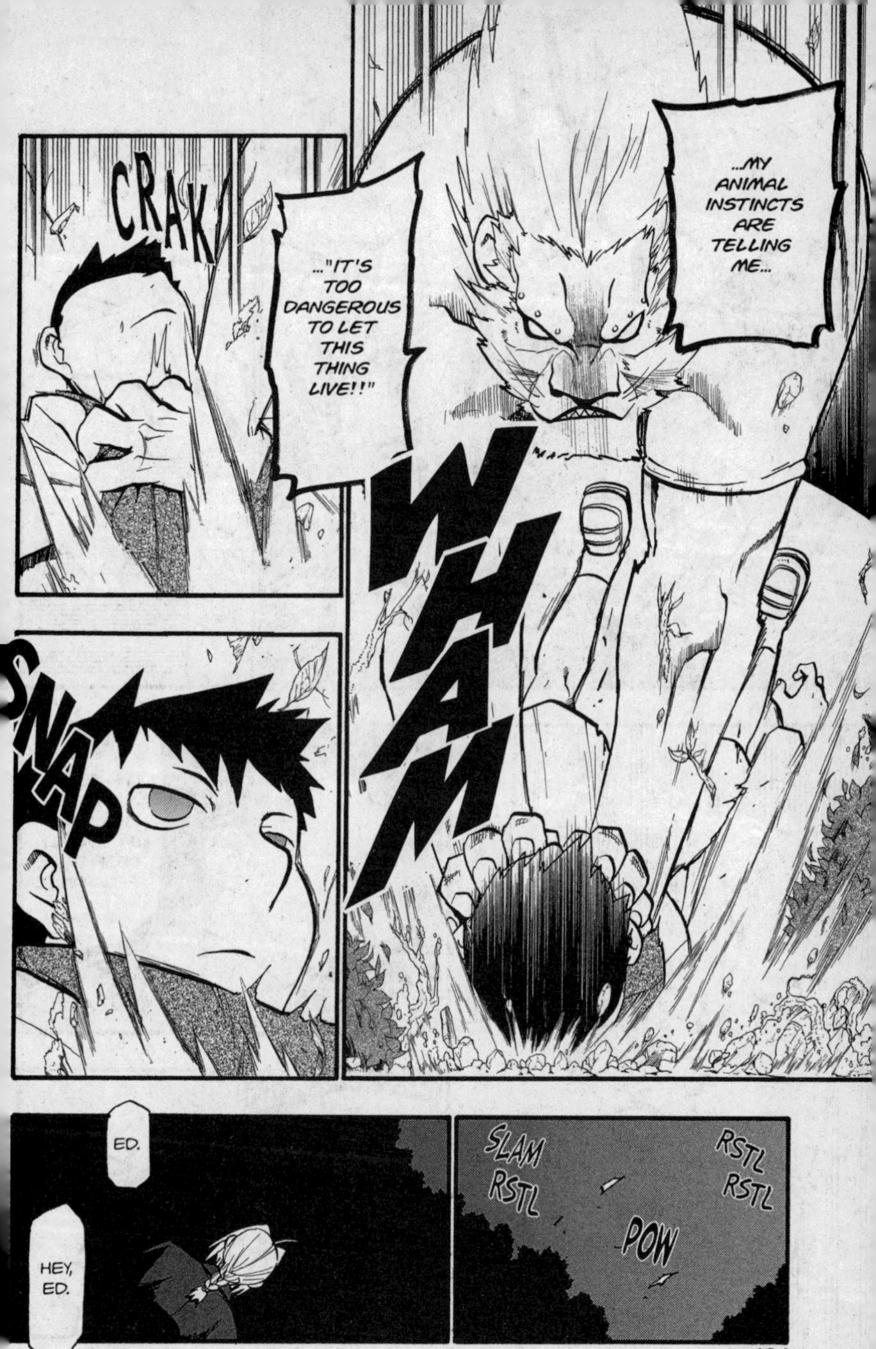
...MY ANIMAL INSTINCTS ARE TELLING ME...
..."IT'S TOO DANGEROUS TO LET THIS THING LIVE!!"
WHAM
CRAK
SNAP
RSTL RSTL
SLAM RSTL
POW
ED.
HEY, ED.

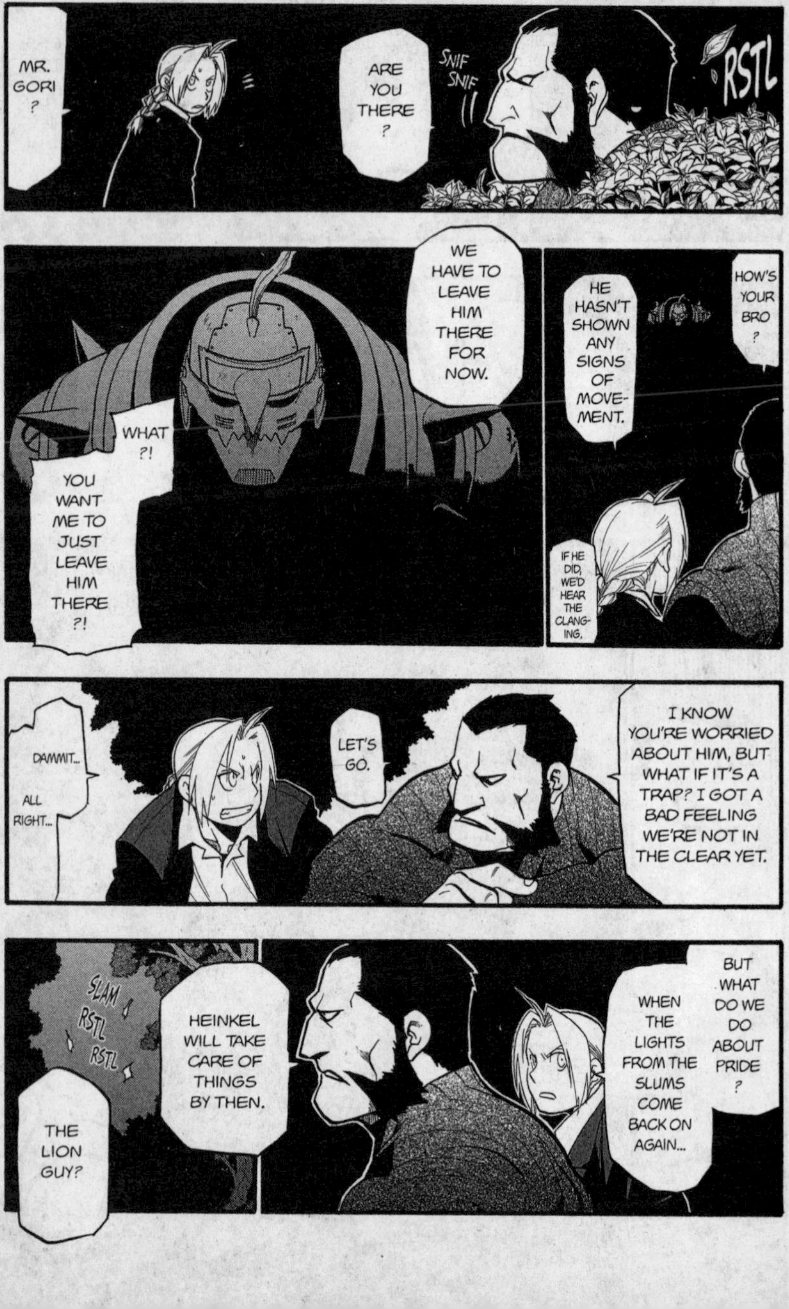
RSTL
SNIF SNIF
ARE YOU THERE?
MR. GORI?
HOW'S YOUR BRO?
HE HASN'T SHOWN ANY SIGNS OF MOVEMENT.
IF HE DID, WE'D HEAR THE CLANGING.
WE HAVE TO LEAVE HIM THERE FOR NOW.
WHAT?!
YOU WANT ME TO JUST LEAVE HIM THERE?!
I KNOW YOU'RE WORRIED ABOUT HIM, BUT WHAT IF IT'S A TRAP? I GOT A BAD FEELING WE'RE NOT IN THE CLEAR YET.
LET'S GO.
DAMMIT... ALL RIGHT...
BUT WHAT DO WE DO ABOUT PRIDE?
WHEN THE LIGHTS FROM THE SLUMS COME BACK ON AGAIN...
HEINKEL WILL TAKE CARE OF THINGS BY THEN.
SLAM
RSTL RSTL
THE LION GUY?

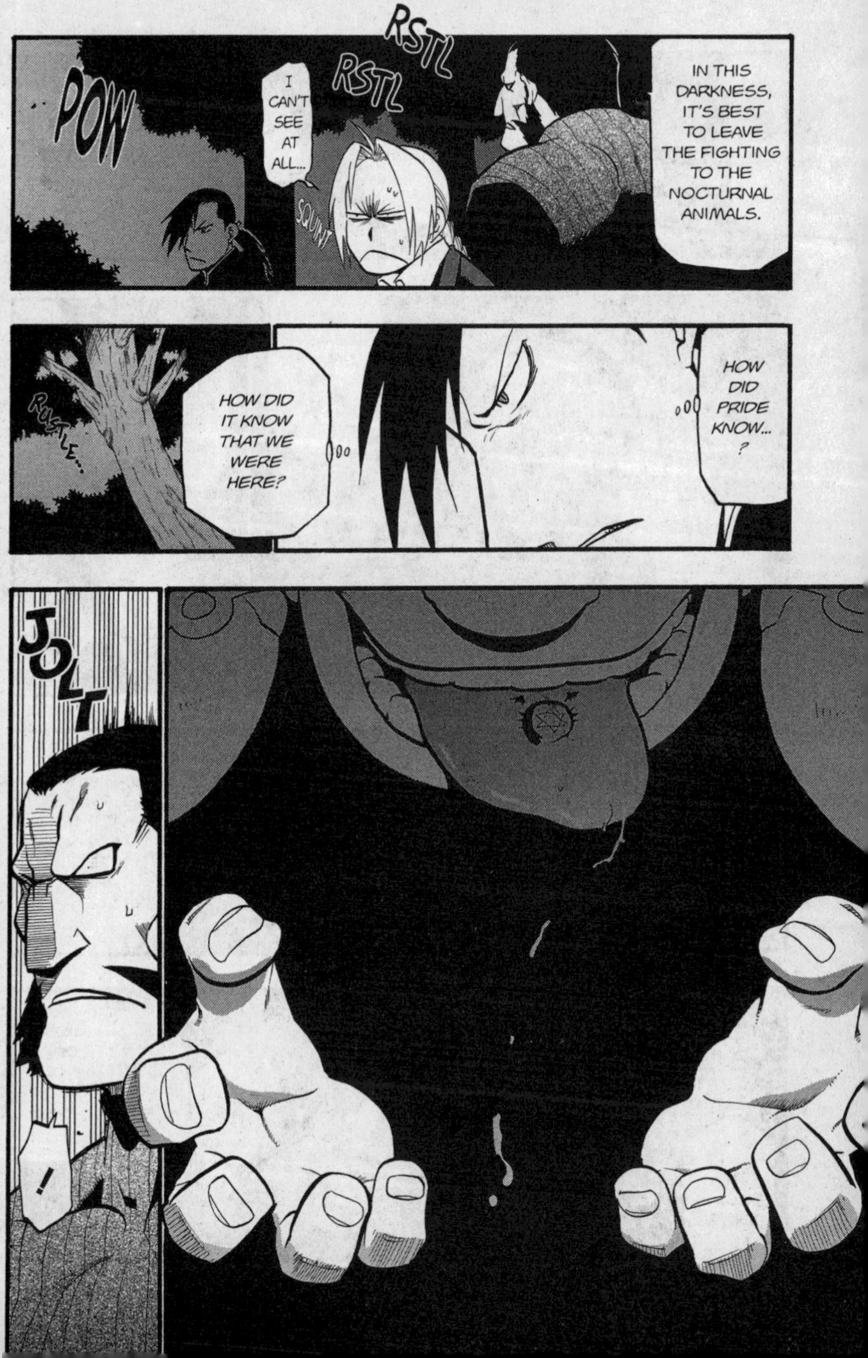
IN THIS DARKNESS, IT'S BEST TO LEAVE THE FIGHTING TO THE NOCTURNAL ANIMALS.
RSTL
RSTL
I CAN'T SEE AT ALL...
SQUINT
POW
HOW DID PRIDE KNOW...?
HOW DID IT KNOW THAT WE WERE HERE?
RUSTLE...
JOLT
!

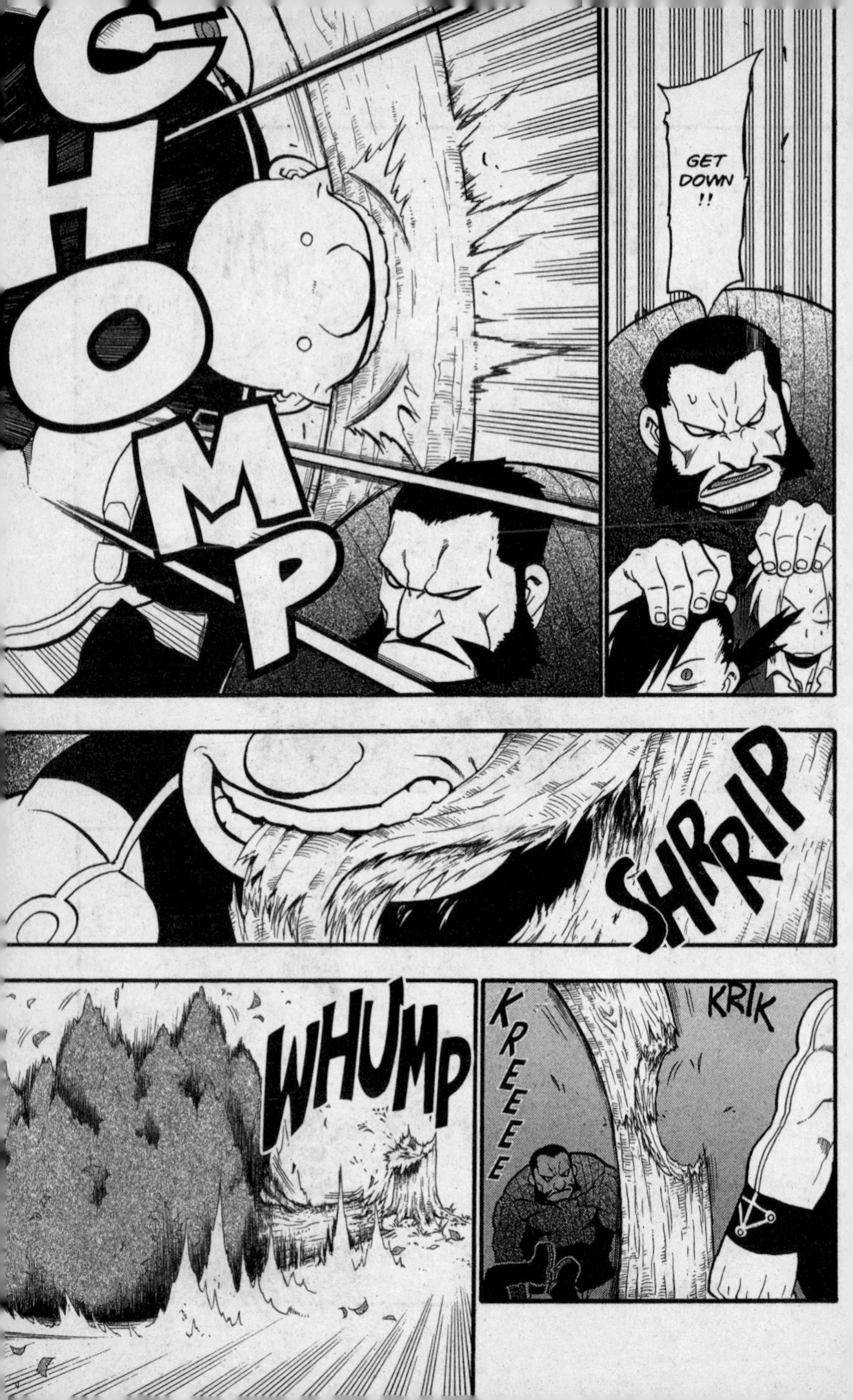
GET DOWN !!
CHOMP
SHRIP
KRIK
KREEEEE
WHUMP

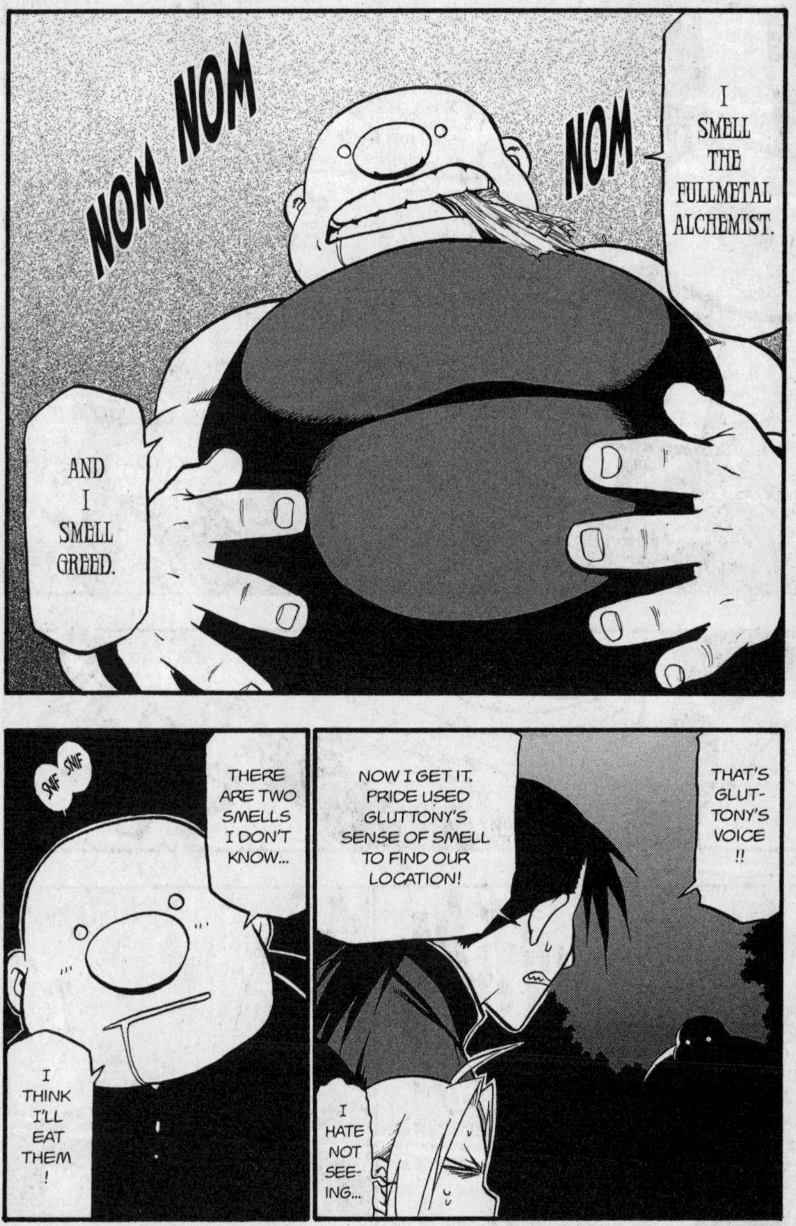
I SMELL THE FULLMETAL ALCHEMIST.
NOM
NOM NOM
AND I SMELL GREED.
THAT'S GLUTTONY'S VOICE!!
NOW I GET IT. PRIDE USED GLUTTONY'S SENSE OF SMELL TO FIND OUR LOCATION!
I HATE NOT SEEING...
SNIF SNIF
THERE ARE TWO SMELLS I DON'T KNOW...
I THINK I'LL EAT THEM!

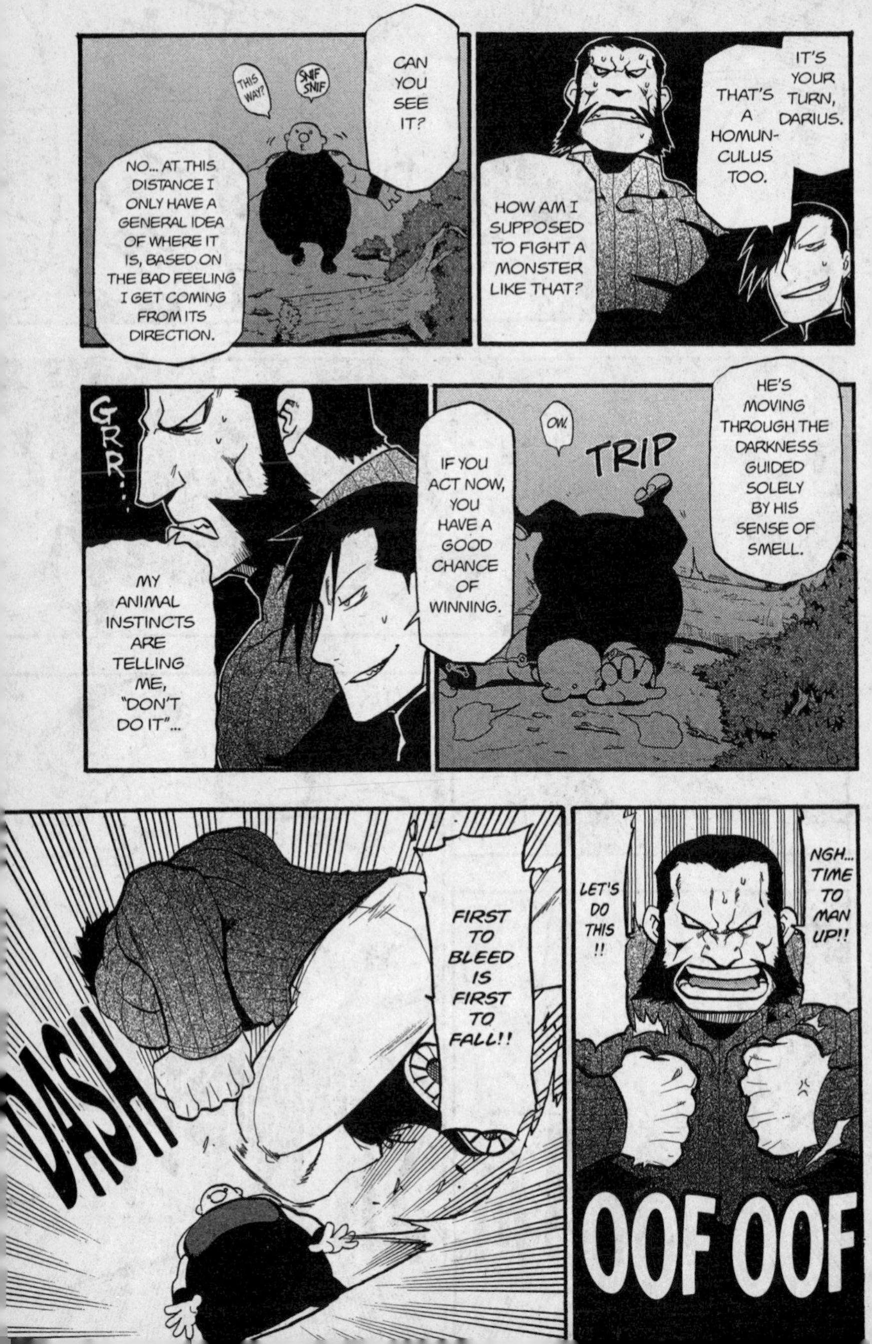
IT'S YOUR TURN, DARIUS.
THAT'S A HOMUNCULUS TOO.
HOW AM I SUPPOSED TO FIGHT A MONSTER LIKE THAT?
CAN YOU SEE IT?
SNIF SNIF
THIS WAY?
NO... AT THIS DISTANCE I ONLY HAVE A GENERAL IDEA OF WHERE IT IS, BASED ON THE BAD FEELING I GET COMING FROM ITS DIRECTION.
HE'S MOVING THROUGH THE DARKNESS GUIDED SOLELY BY HIS SENSE OF SMELL.
TRIP
OW.
IF YOU ACT NOW, YOU HAVE A GOOD CHANCE OF WINNING.
GRR...
MY ANIMAL INSTINCTS ARE TELLING ME, "DON'T DO IT"...
NGH... TIME TO MAN UP!!
LET'S DO THIS!!
OOF OOF
FIRST TO BLEED IS FIRST TO FALL!!
DASH

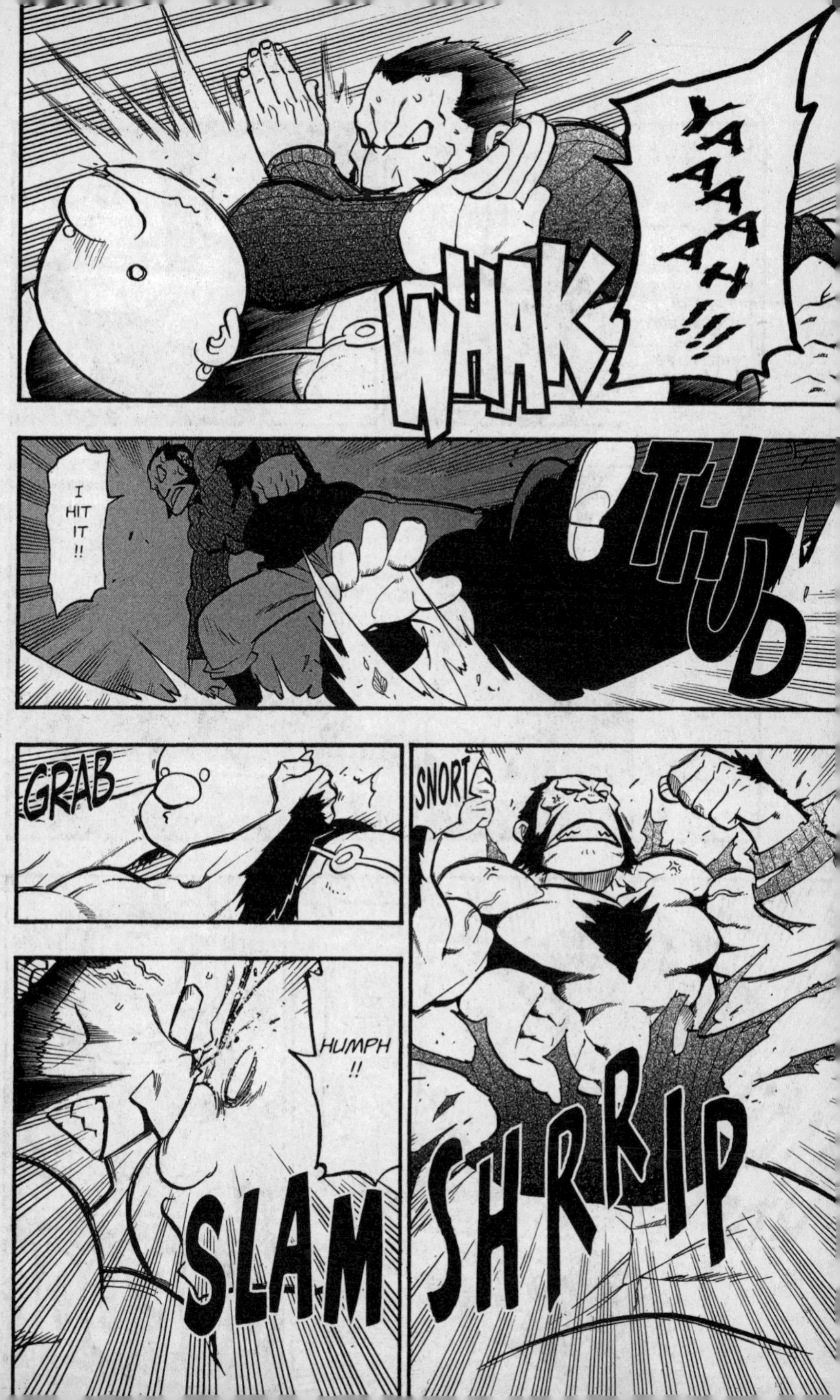
YAAAAAH!!!
WHAK
THUD
I HIT IT!!
SNORT
SHRRIP
GRAB
HUMPH!!
SLAM

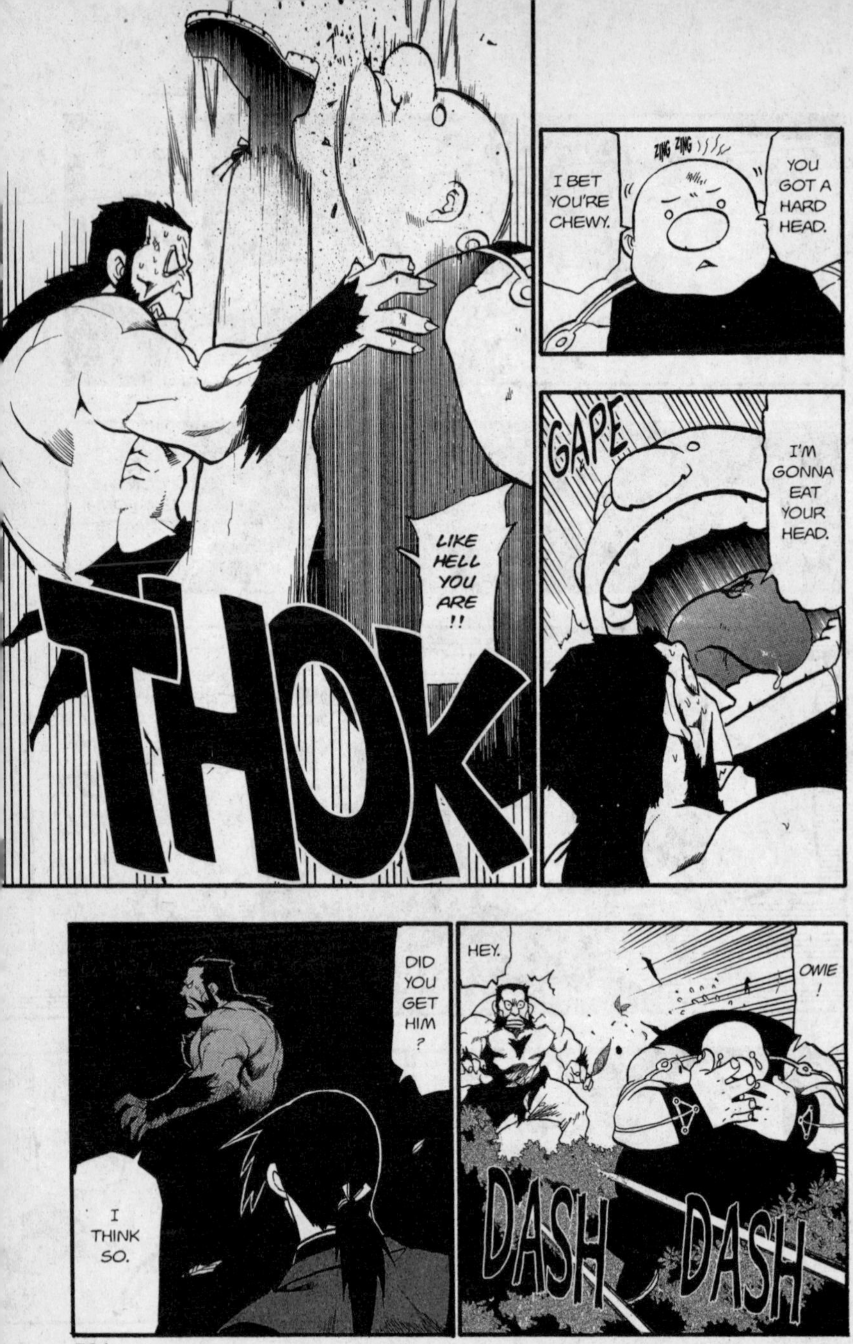
ZING ZING
YOU GOT A HARD HEAD.
I BET YOU'RE CHEWY.
I'M GONNA EAT YOUR HEAD.
GAPE
LIKE HELL YOU ARE!!
THOK
OWIE!
HEY.
DASH DASH
DID YOU GET HIM?
I THINK SO.

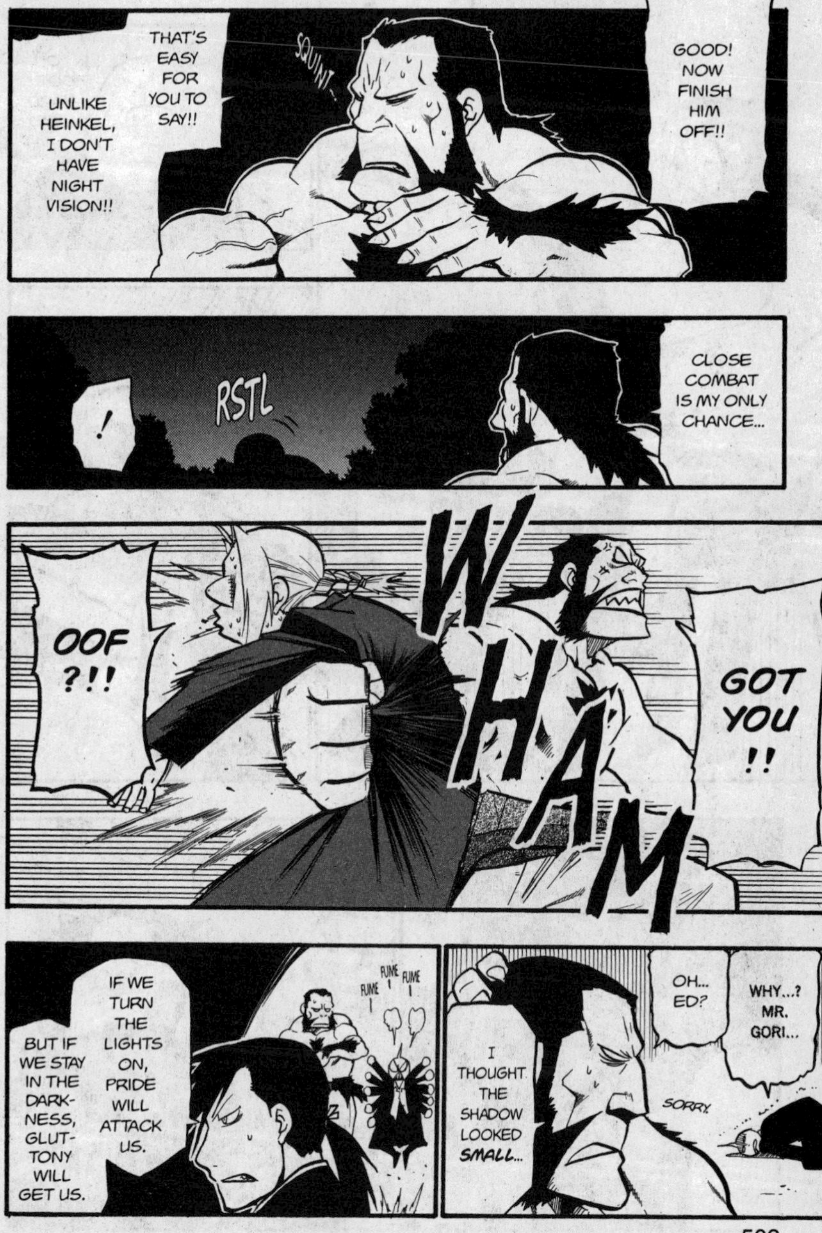
GOOD! NOW FINISH HIM OFF!!
SQUINT
THAT'S EASY FOR YOU TO SAY!!
UNLIKE HEINKEL, I DON'T HAVE NIGHT VISION!!
CLOSE COMBAT IS MY ONLY CHANCE...
RSTL
!
GOT YOU!!
WHAM
OOF?!!
WHY...? MR. GORI...
OH... ED?
SORRY.
I THOUGHT THE SHADOW LOOKED SMALL...
FUME
FUME
FUME
IF WE TURN THE LIGHTS ON, PRIDE WILL ATTACK US.
BUT IF WE STAY IN THE DARKNESS, GLUTTONY WILL GET US.

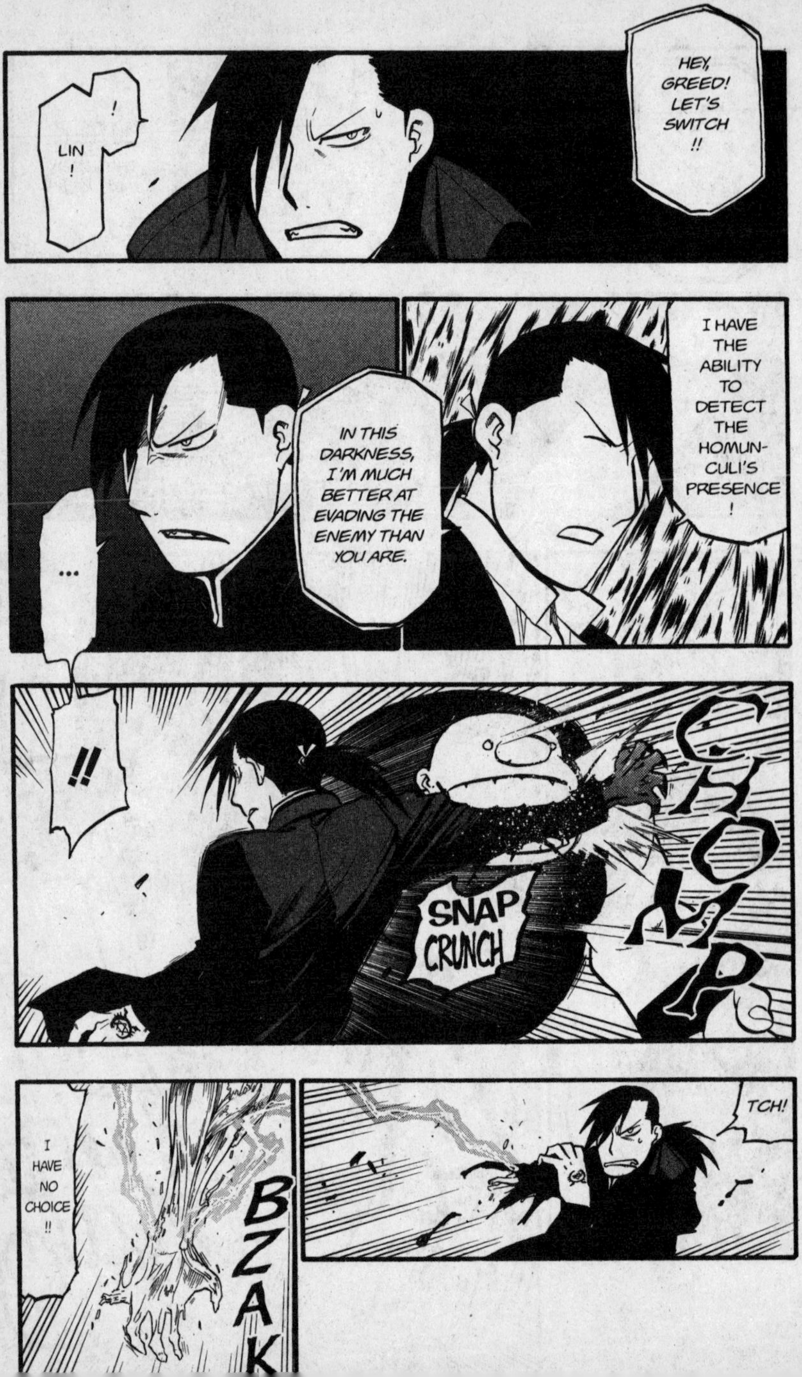
HEY, GREED! LET'S SWITCH !!
! LIN !
I HAVE THE ABILITY TO DETECT THE HOMUN-CULI'S PRESENCE !
IN THIS DARKNESS, I'M MUCH BETTER AT EVADING THE ENEMY THAN YOU ARE.
...
CHOMP
SNAP CRUNCH
!!
TCH!
I HAVE NO CHOICE !!
BZAK

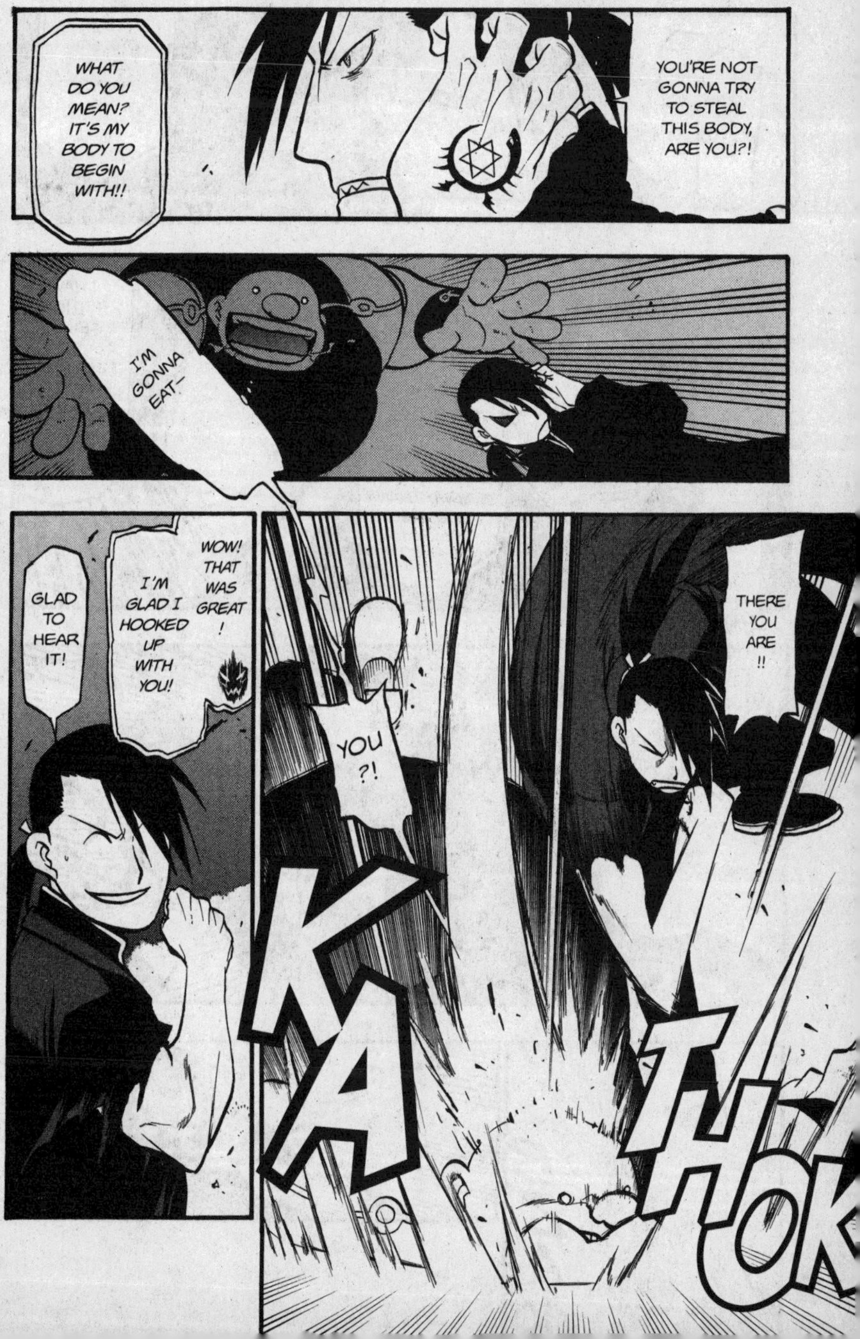
YOU'RE NOT GONNA TRY TO STEAL THIS BODY, ARE YOU?!
WHAT DO YOU MEAN? IT'S MY BODY TO BEGIN WITH!!
I'M GONNA EAT—
THERE YOU ARE!!
YOU?!
KA-THOK
WOW! THAT WAS GREAT!
I'M GLAD I HOOKED UP WITH YOU!
GLAD TO HEAR IT!

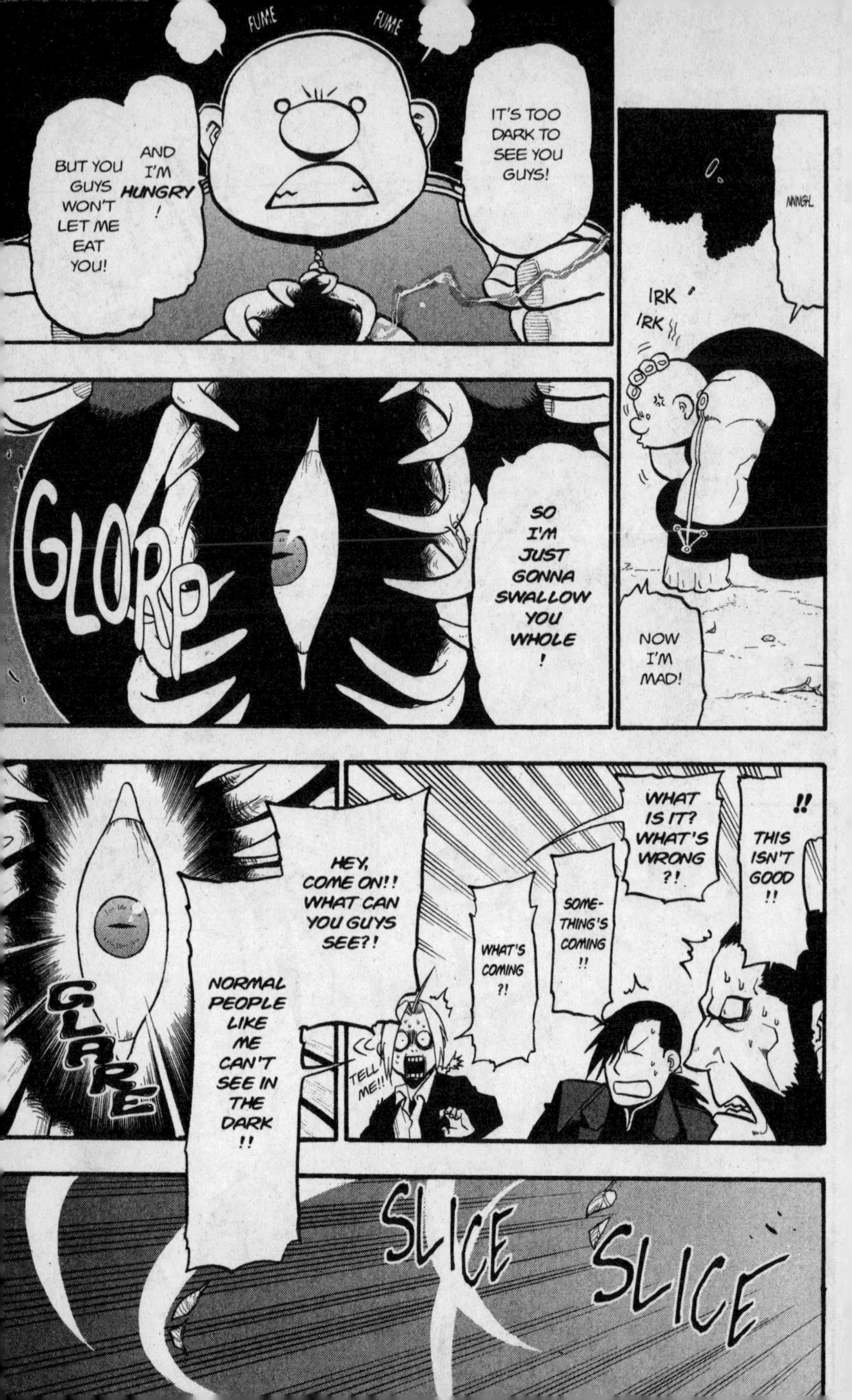
NNNGH.
IRK IRK
NOW I'M MAD!
FUME FUME
IT'S TOO DARK TO SEE YOU GUYS!
AND I'M HUNGRY!
BUT YOU GUYS WON'T LET ME EAT YOU!
SO I'M JUST GONNA SWALLOW YOU WHOLE!
GLORP
!! THIS ISN'T GOOD!!
WHAT IS IT? WHAT'S WRONG?!
SOME-THING'S COMING!!
WHAT'S COMING?!
HEY, COME ON!! WHAT CAN YOU GUYS SEE?!
TELL ME!!
NORMAL PEOPLE LIKE ME CAN'T SEE IN THE DARK!!
GLARE
SLICE
SLICE

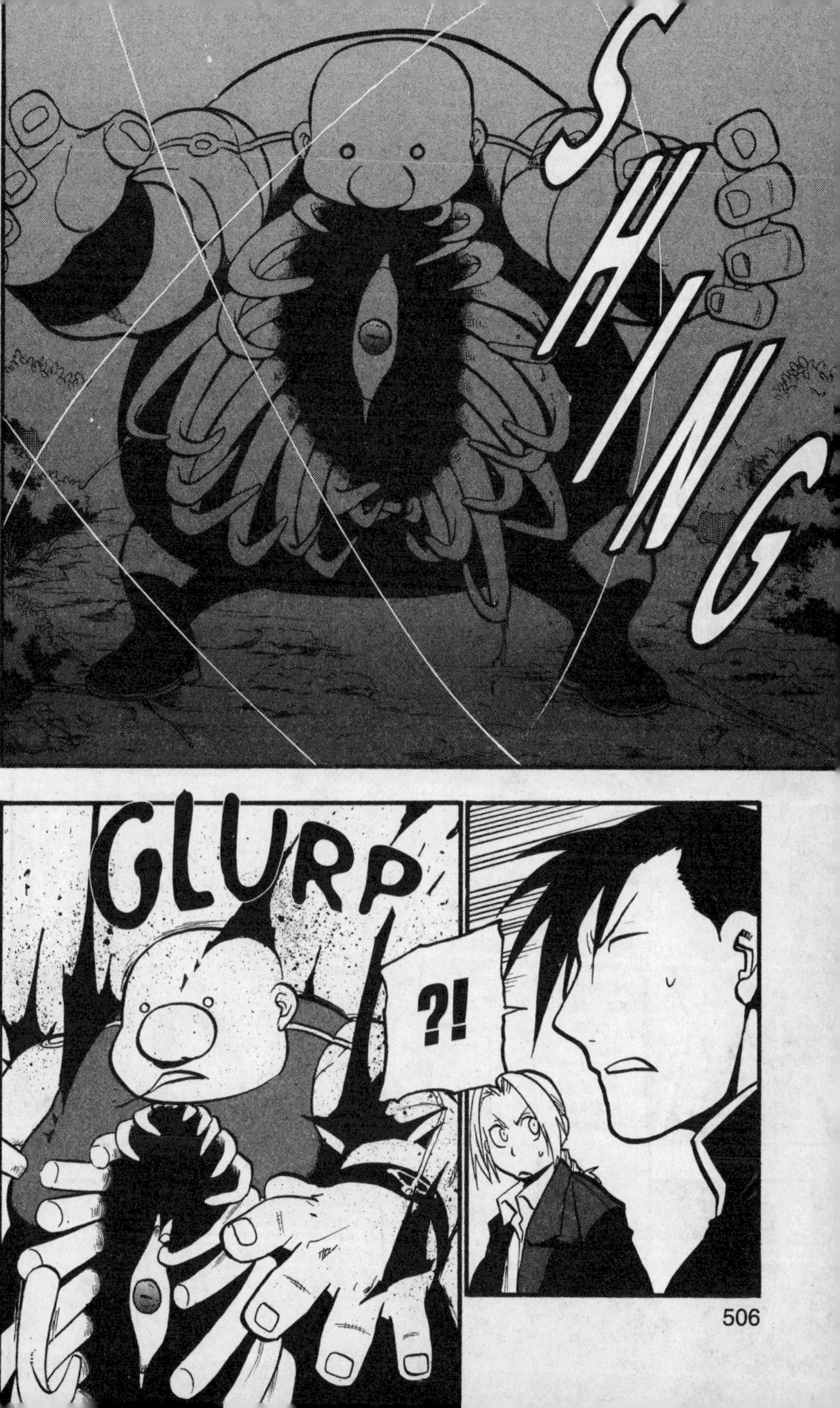
SHING
?!
GLURP

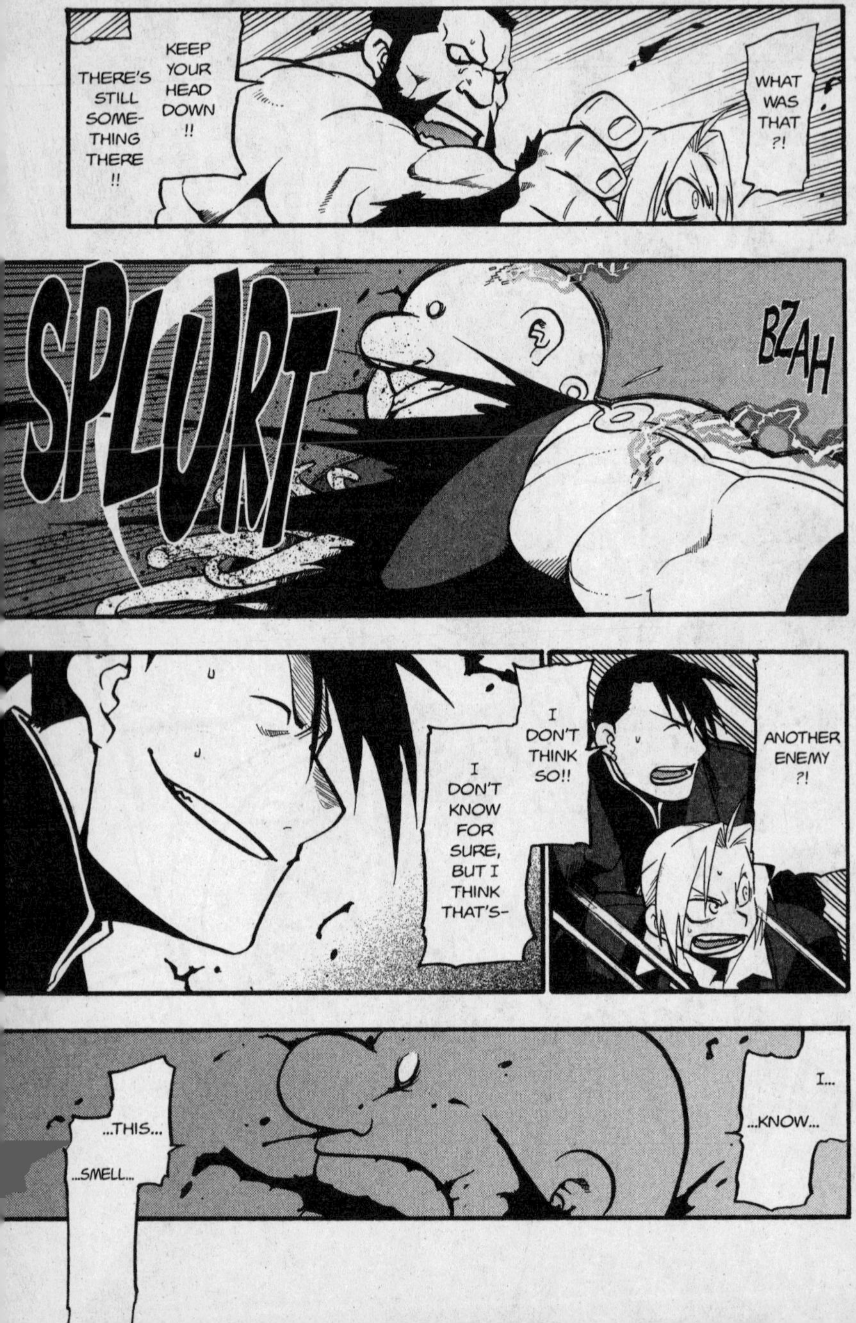
WHAT WAS THAT ?!
KEEP YOUR HEAD DOWN !!
THERE'S STILL SOME-THING THERE !!
BZAH
SPLURT
ANOTHER ENEMY ?!
I DON'T THINK SO!!
I DON'T KNOW FOR SURE, BUT I THINK THAT'S-
I... ...KNOW...
...THIS... ...SMELL...

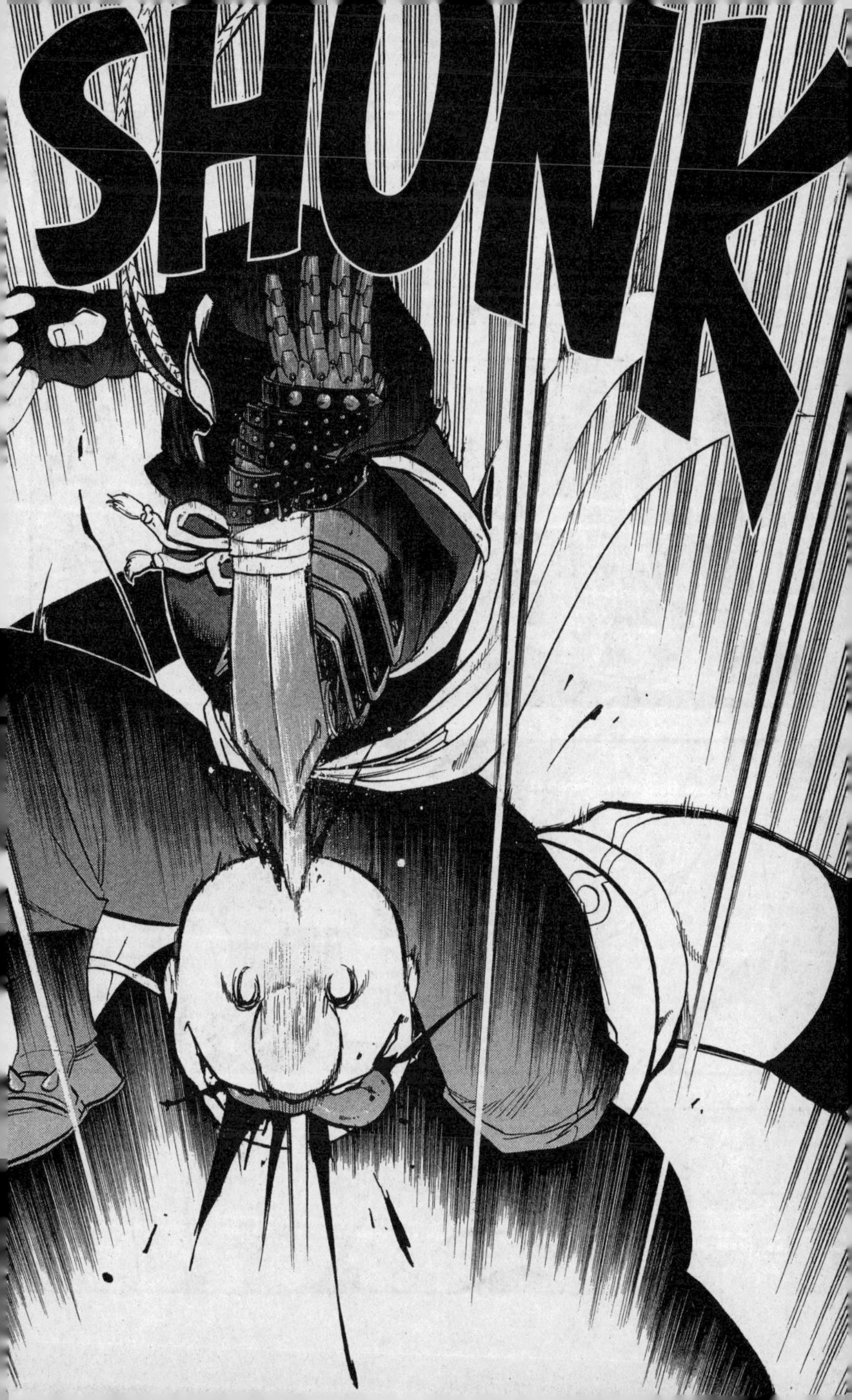
SHUNK

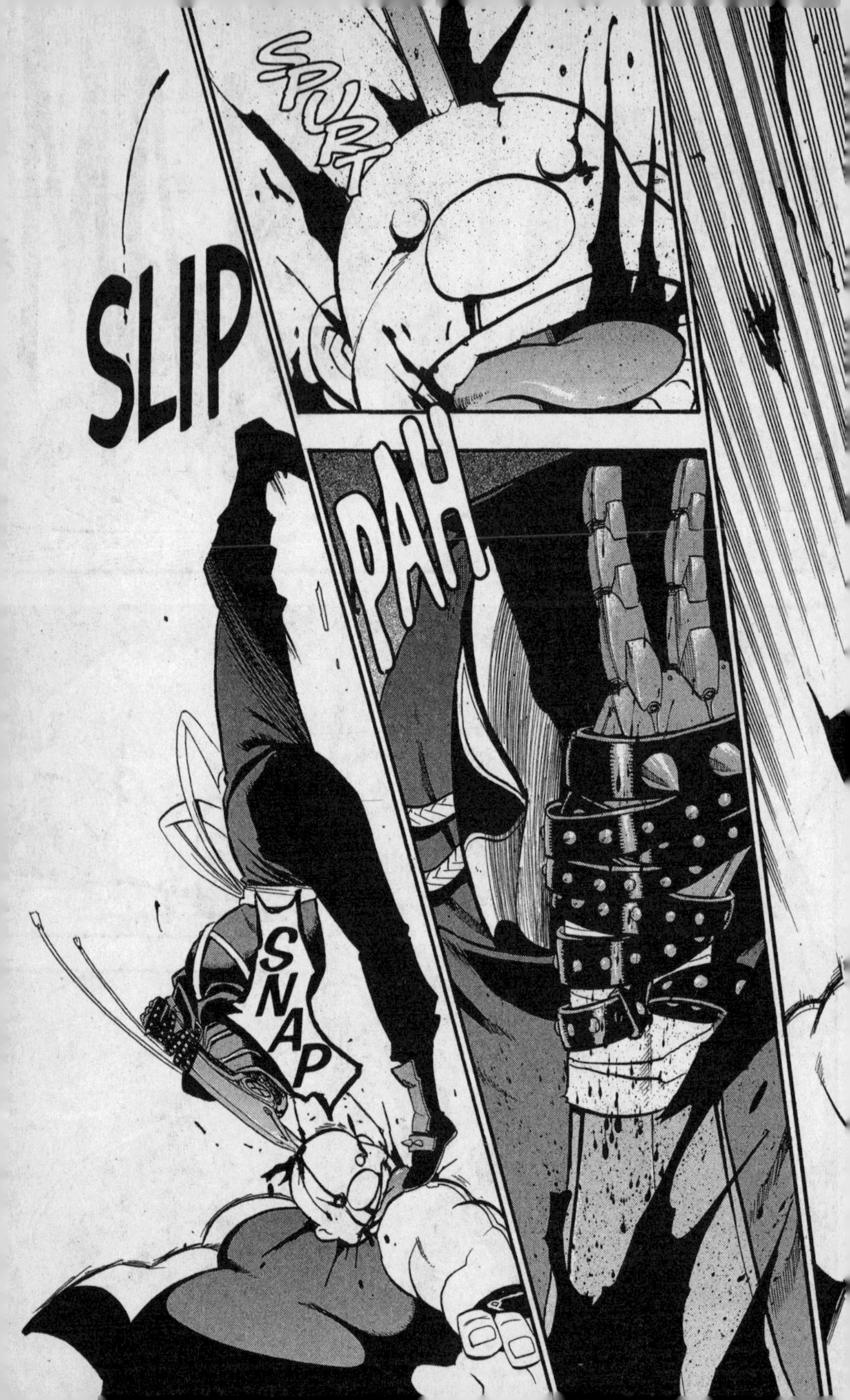
SPURT
PAH
SLIP
SNAP

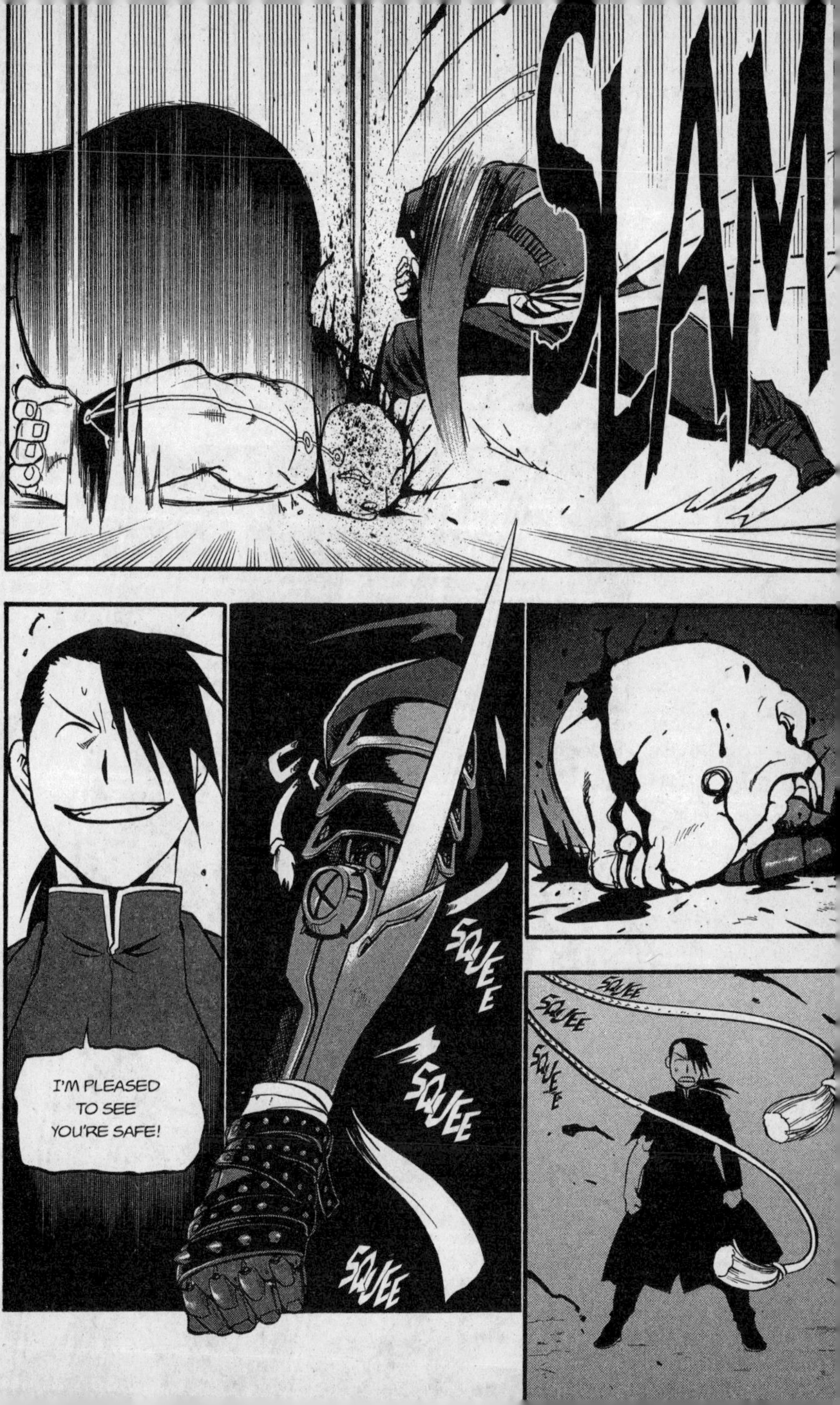
SLAM
SQUEE
SQUEE
SQUEE
SQUEEE
SQUEE
SQUEE
I'M PLEASED TO SEE YOU'RE SAFE!

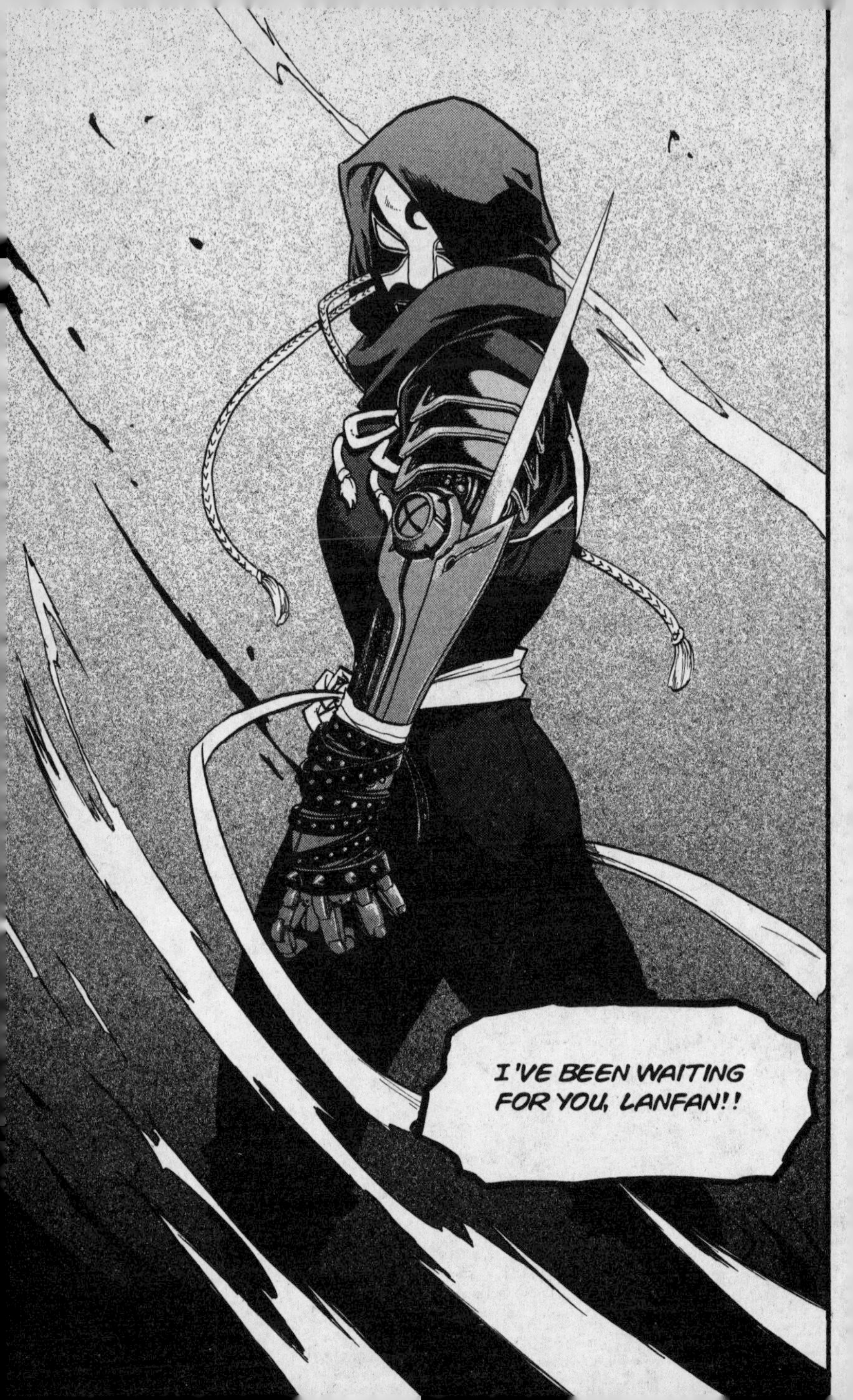
I'VE BEEN WAITING FOR YOU, LANFAN!!

FULLMETAL
ALCHEMIST

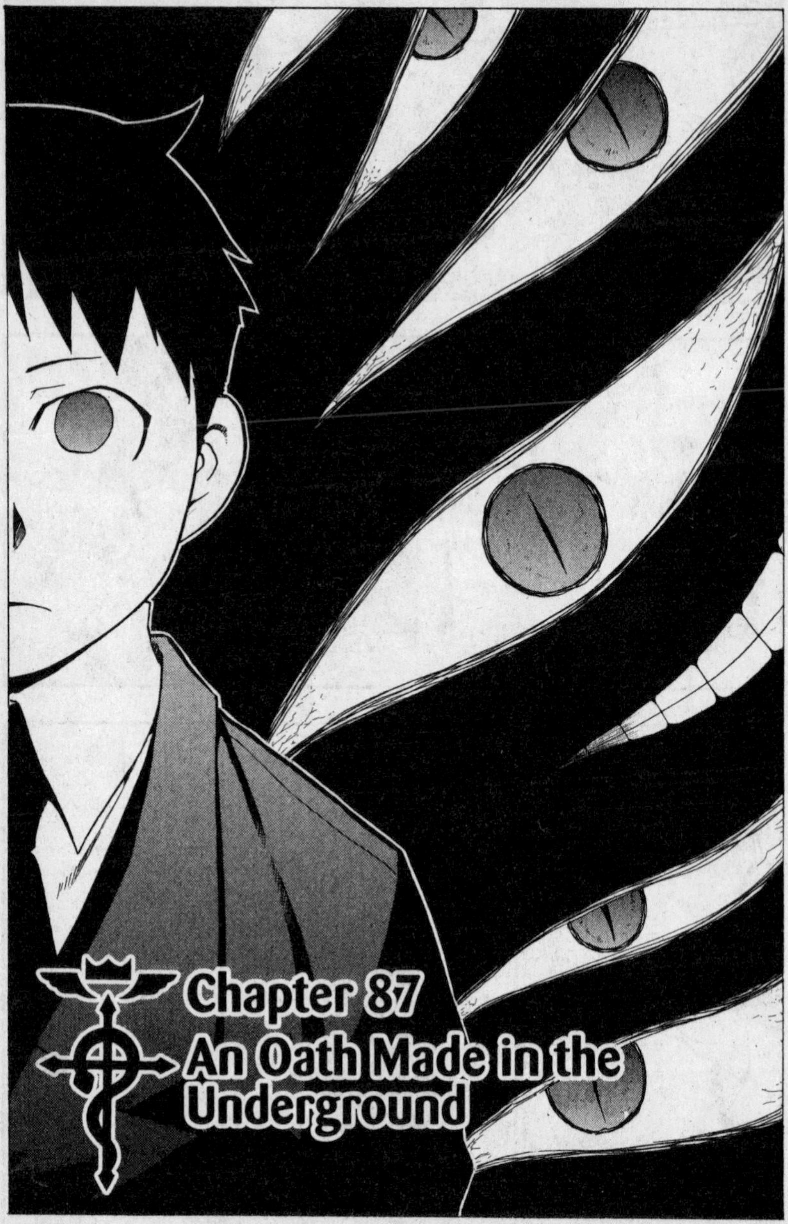
Chapter 87
An Oath Made in the Underground

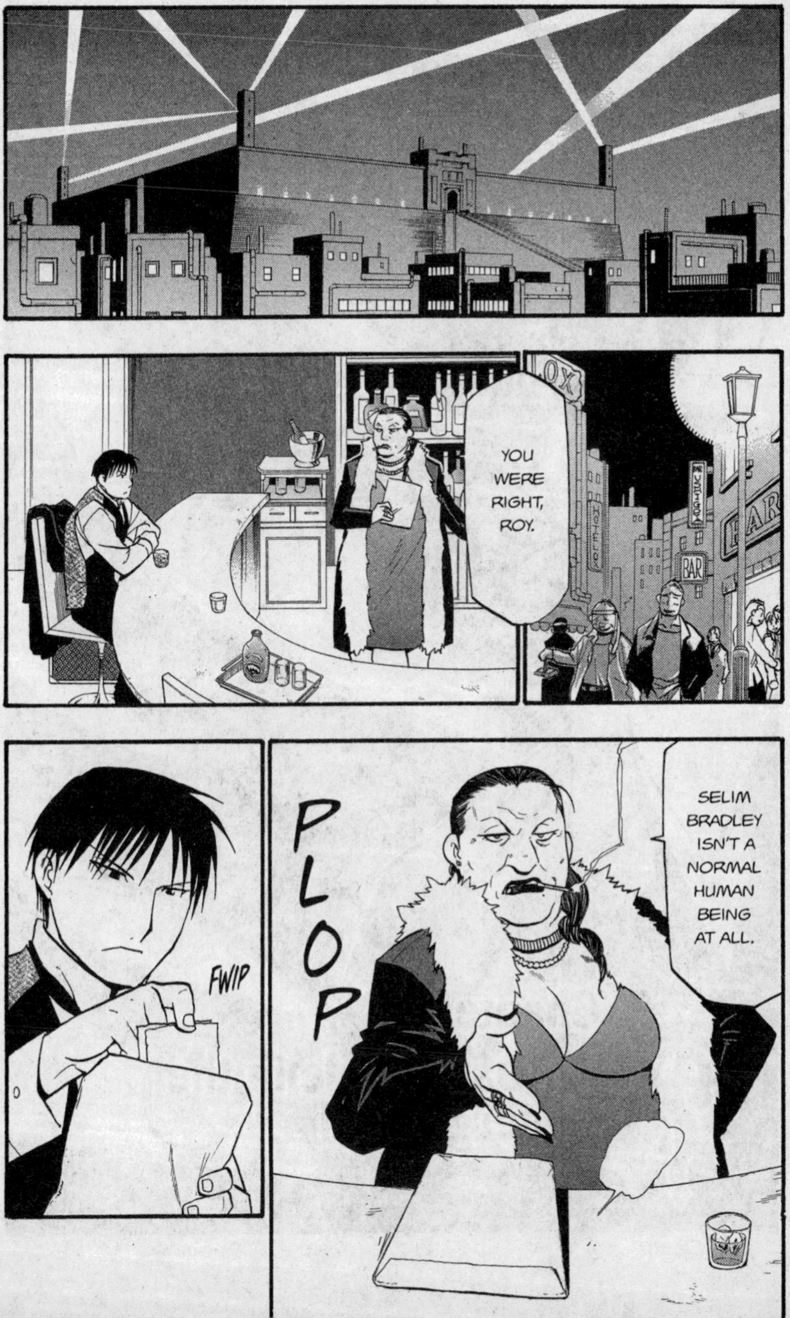
BAR
YOU WERE RIGHT, ROY.
PLOP
SELIM BRADLEY ISN'T A NORMAL HUMAN BEING AT ALL.
FWIP

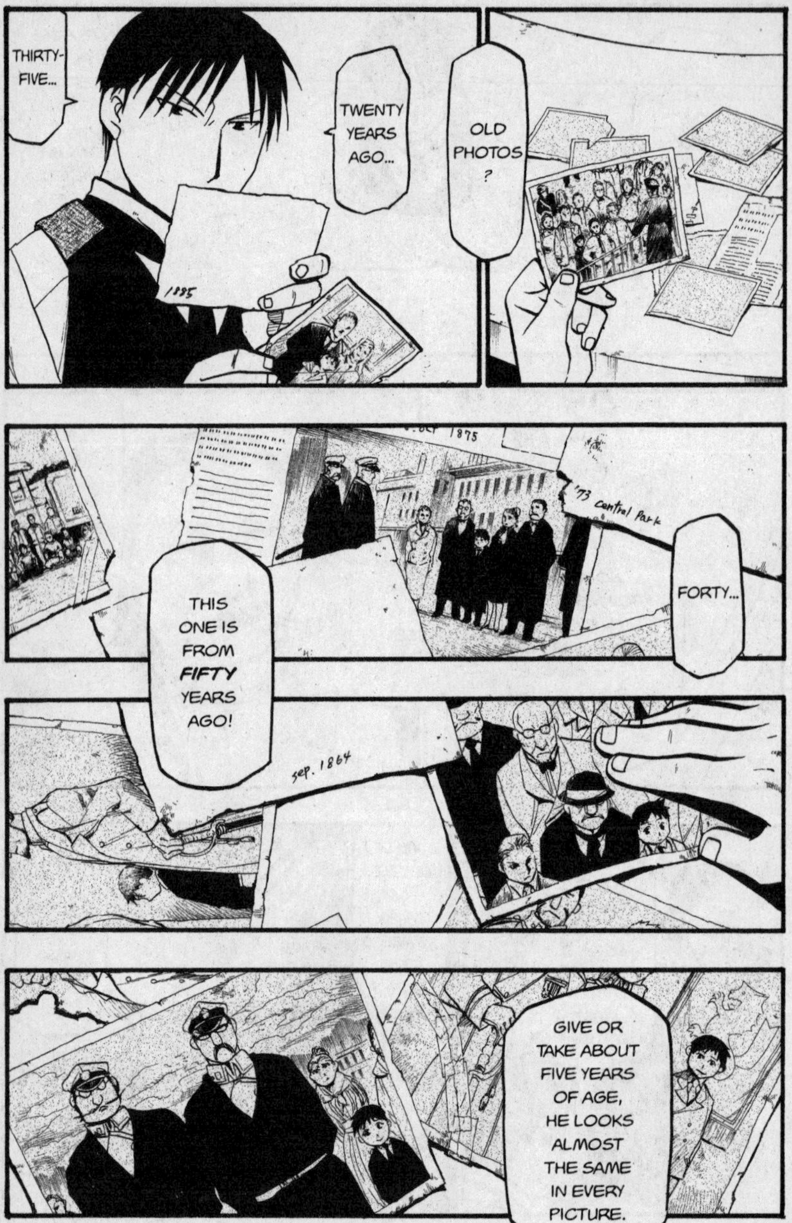
OLD PHOTOS?
TWENTY YEARS AGO...
THIRTY-FIVE...
1885
'73 Central Park
FORTY...
THIS ONE IS FROM *FIFTY* YEARS AGO!
sep. 1864
GIVE OR TAKE ABOUT FIVE YEARS OF AGE, HE LOOKS ALMOST THE SAME IN EVERY PICTURE.

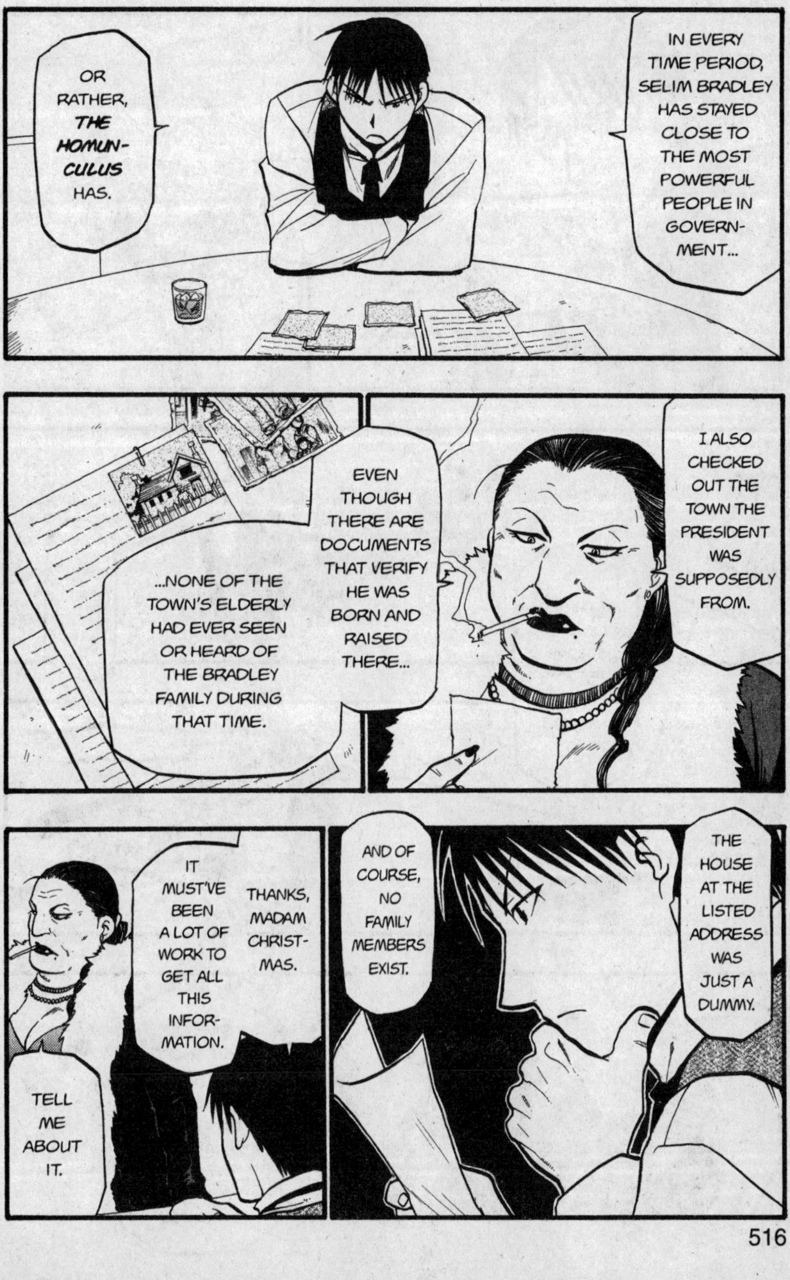
IN EVERY TIME PERIOD, SELIM BRADLEY HAS STAYED CLOSE TO THE MOST POWERFUL PEOPLE IN GOVERNMENT...
OR RATHER, ***THE HOMUNCULUS*** HAS.
I ALSO CHECKED OUT THE TOWN THE PRESIDENT WAS SUPPOSEDLY FROM.
EVEN THOUGH THERE ARE DOCUMENTS THAT VERIFY HE WAS BORN AND RAISED THERE...
...NONE OF THE TOWN'S ELDERLY HAD EVER SEEN OR HEARD OF THE BRADLEY FAMILY DURING THAT TIME.
THE HOUSE AT THE LISTED ADDRESS WAS JUST A DUMMY.
AND OF COURSE, NO FAMILY MEMBERS EXIST.
THANKS, MADAM CHRISTMAS.
IT MUST'VE BEEN A LOT OF WORK TO GET ALL THIS INFORMATION.
TELL ME ABOUT IT.

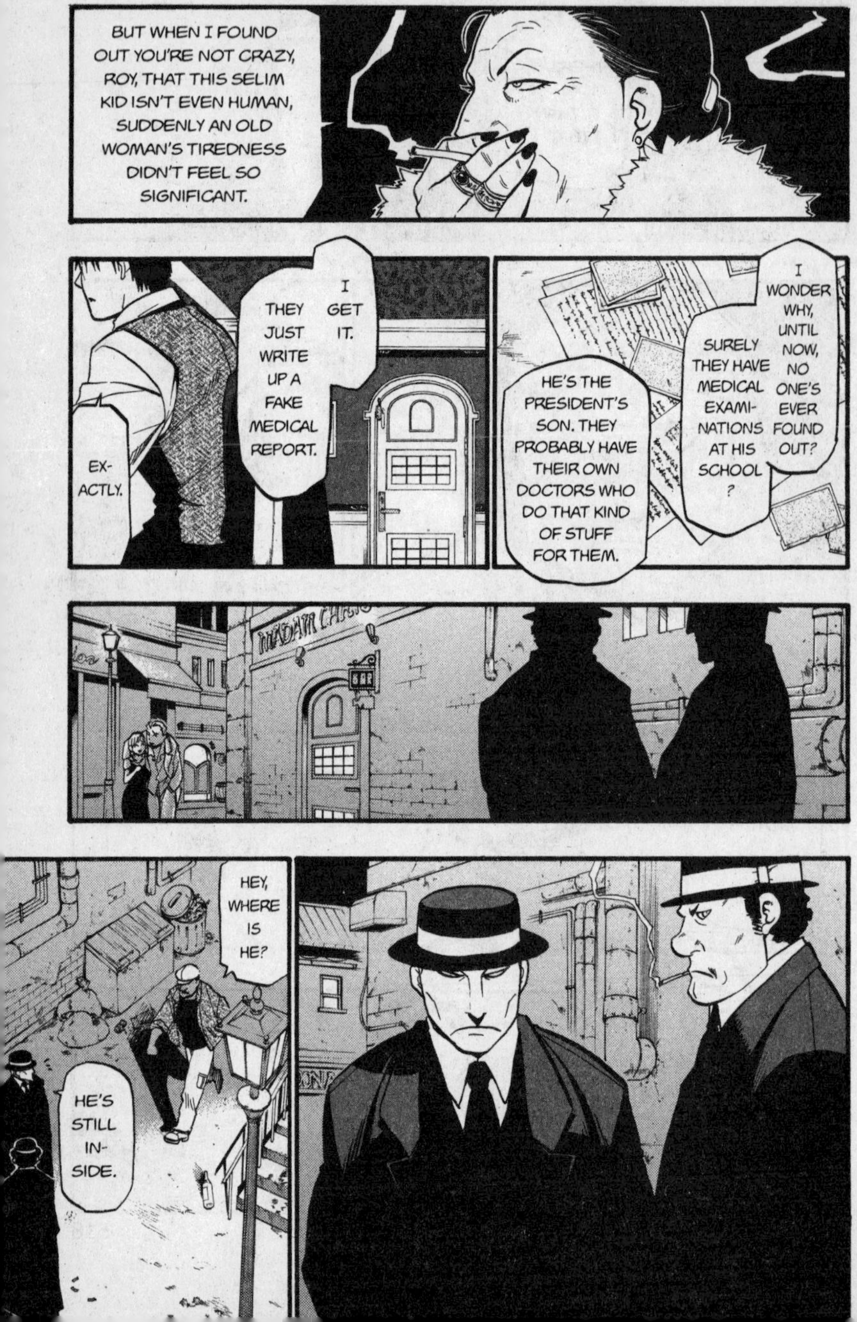
BUT WHEN I FOUND OUT YOU'RE NOT CRAZY, ROY, THAT THIS SELIM KID ISN'T EVEN HUMAN, SUDDENLY AN OLD WOMAN'S TIREDNESS DIDN'T FEEL SO SIGNIFICANT.
I WONDER WHY, UNTIL NOW, NO ONE'S EVER FOUND OUT?
SURELY THEY HAVE MEDICAL EXAMINATIONS AT HIS SCHOOL?
HE'S THE PRESIDENT'S SON. THEY PROBABLY HAVE THEIR OWN DOCTORS WHO DO THAT KIND OF STUFF FOR THEM.
I GET IT.
THEY JUST WRITE UP A FAKE MEDICAL REPORT.
EX-ACTLY.
HEY, WHERE IS HE?
HE'S STILL IN-SIDE.

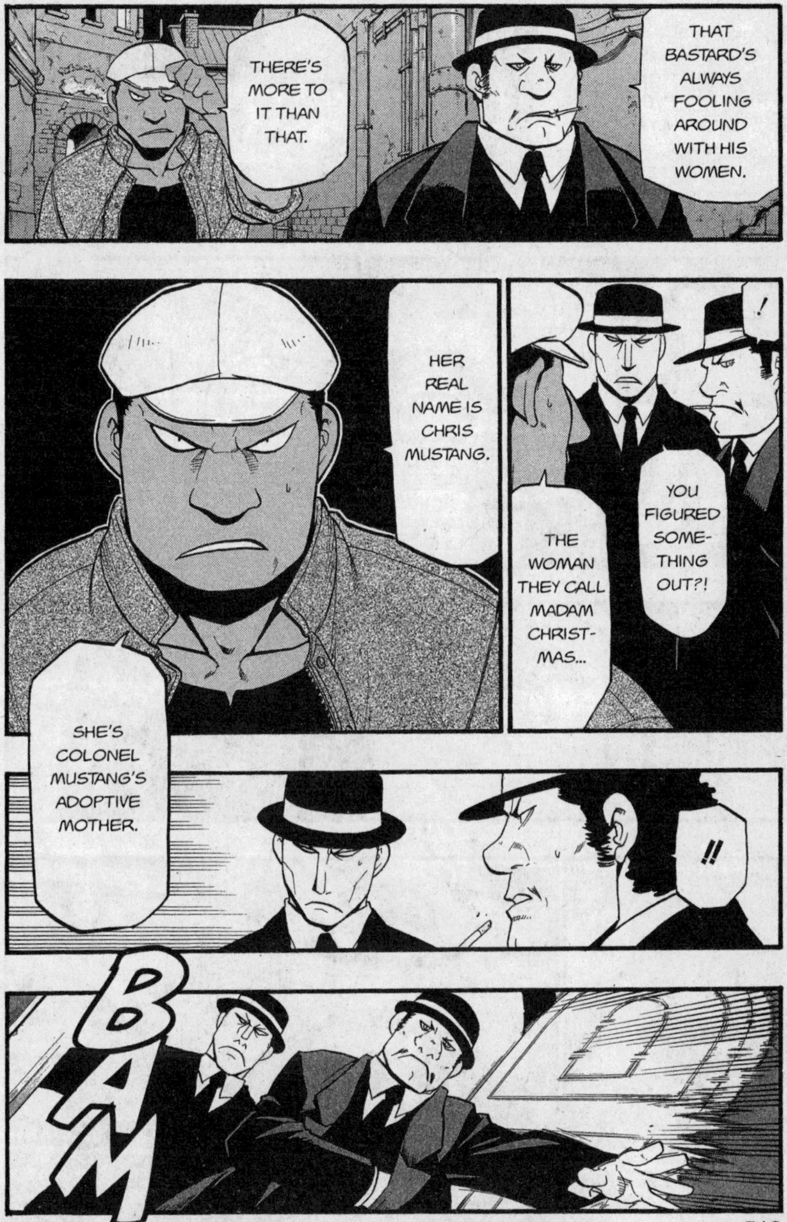
THAT BASTARD'S ALWAYS FOOLING AROUND WITH HIS WOMEN.
THERE'S MORE TO IT THAN THAT.
!
YOU FIGURED SOMETHING OUT?!
THE WOMAN THEY CALL MADAM CHRISTMAS...
HER REAL NAME IS CHRIS MUSTANG.
SHE'S COLONEL MUSTANG'S ADOPTIVE MOTHER.
!!
BAM

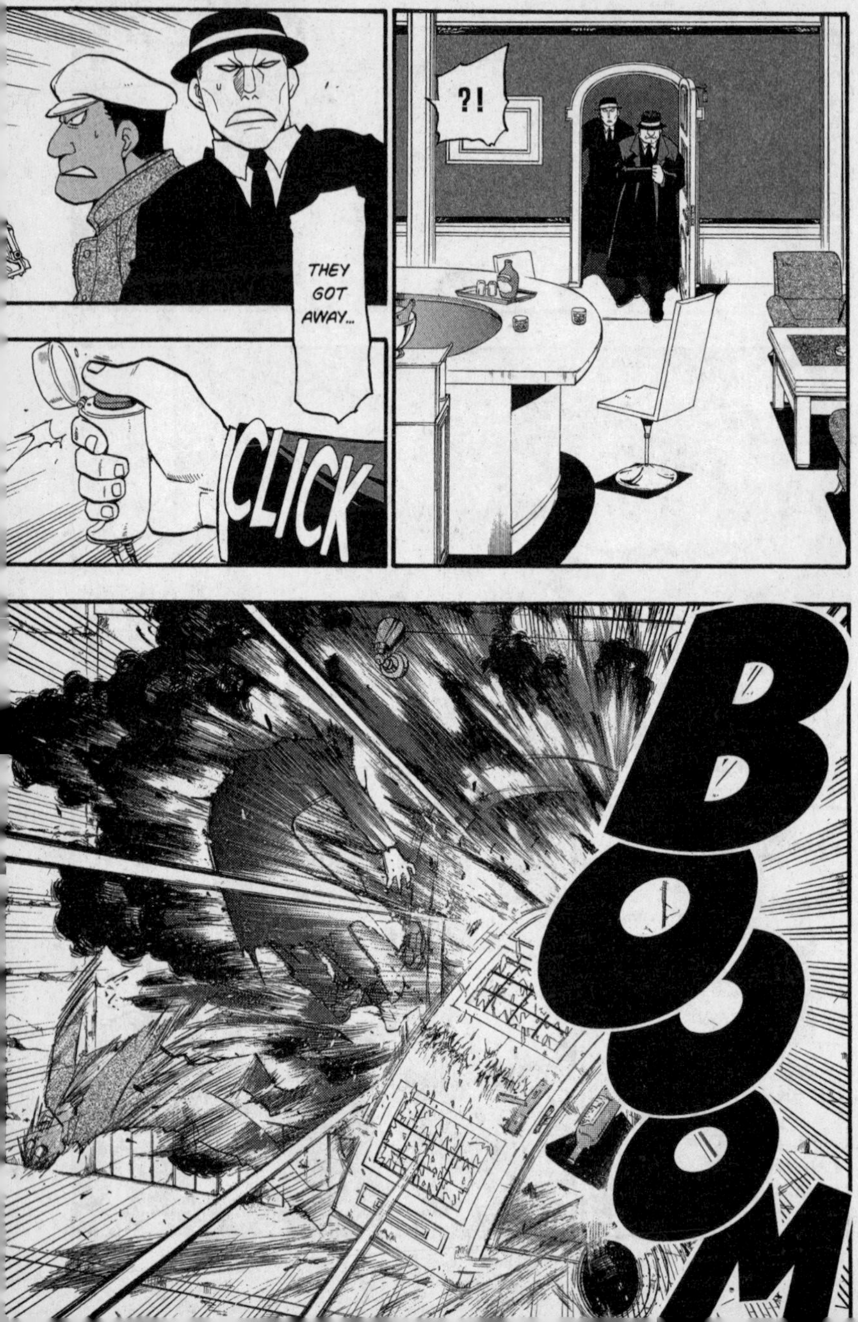
?!
THEY GOT AWAY...
CLICK
BOOOOM

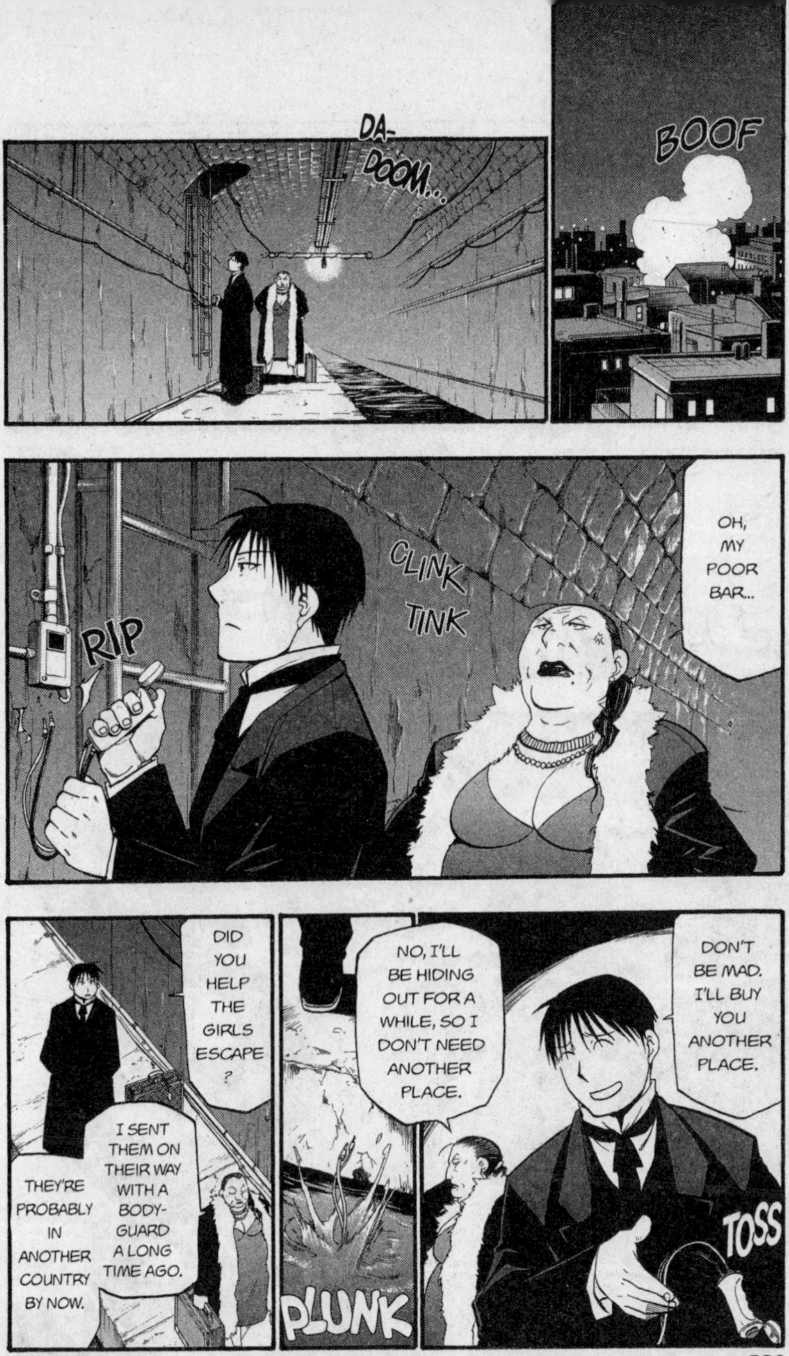
BOOF
DA-DOOM...
OH, MY POOR BAR...
CLINK
TINK
RIP
DON'T BE MAD. I'LL BUY YOU ANOTHER PLACE.
TOSS
NO, I'LL BE HIDING OUT FOR A WHILE, SO I DON'T NEED ANOTHER PLACE.
PLUNK
DID YOU HELP THE GIRLS ESCAPE?
I SENT THEM ON THEIR WAY WITH A BODY-GUARD A LONG TIME AGO.
THEY'RE PROBABLY IN ANOTHER COUNTRY BY NOW.

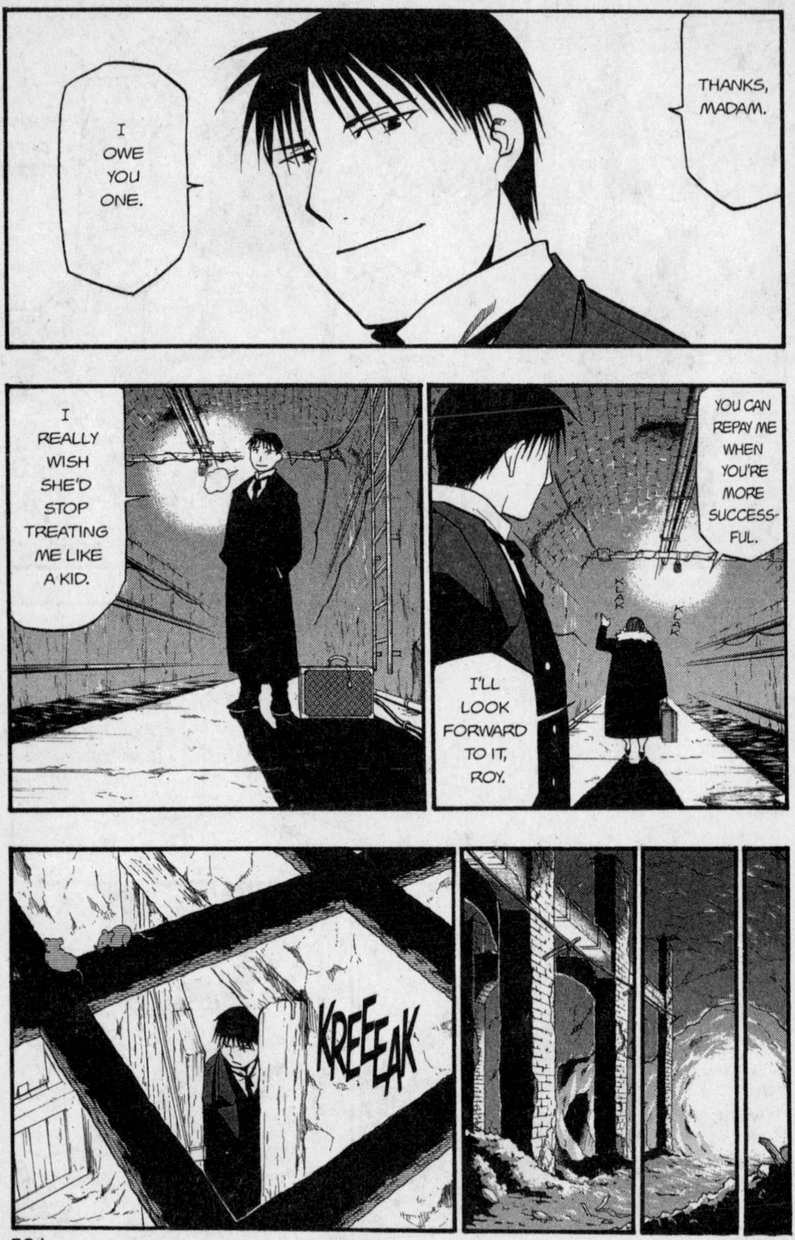
THANKS, MADAM.
I OWE YOU ONE.
YOU CAN REPAY ME WHEN YOU'RE MORE SUCCESSFUL.
KLAK
KLAK
I'LL LOOK FORWARD TO IT, ROY.
I REALLY WISH SHE'D STOP TREATING ME LIKE A KID.
KREEEEAK

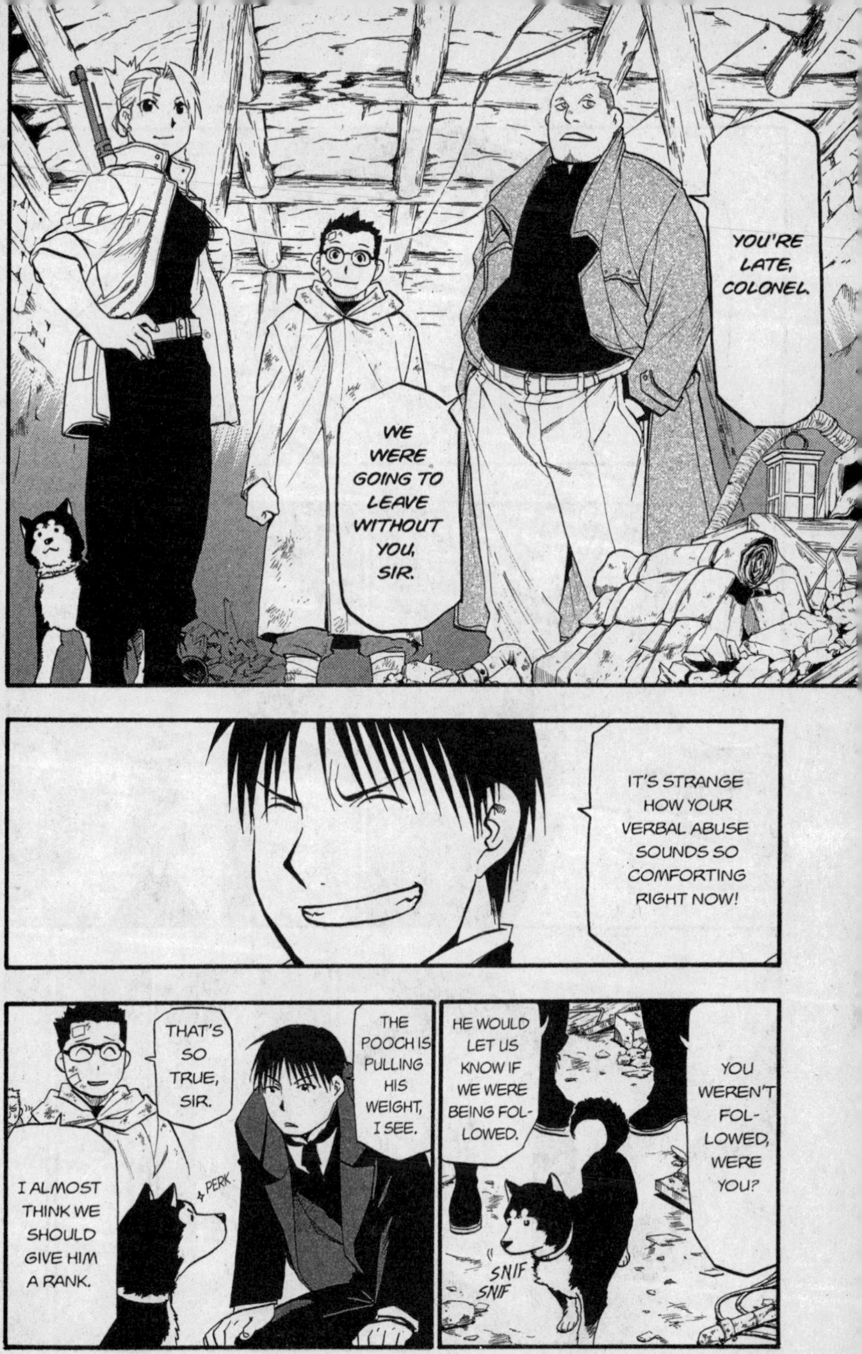
YOU'RE LATE, COLONEL.
WE WERE GOING TO LEAVE WITHOUT YOU, SIR.
IT'S STRANGE HOW YOUR VERBAL ABUSE SOUNDS SO COMFORTING RIGHT NOW!
YOU WEREN'T FOL-LOWED, WERE YOU?
HE WOULD LET US KNOW IF WE WERE BEING FOL-LOWED.
SNIF SNIF
THE POOCH IS PULLING HIS WEIGHT, I SEE.
PERK
THAT'S SO TRUE, SIR.
I ALMOST THINK WE SHOULD GIVE HIM A RANK.

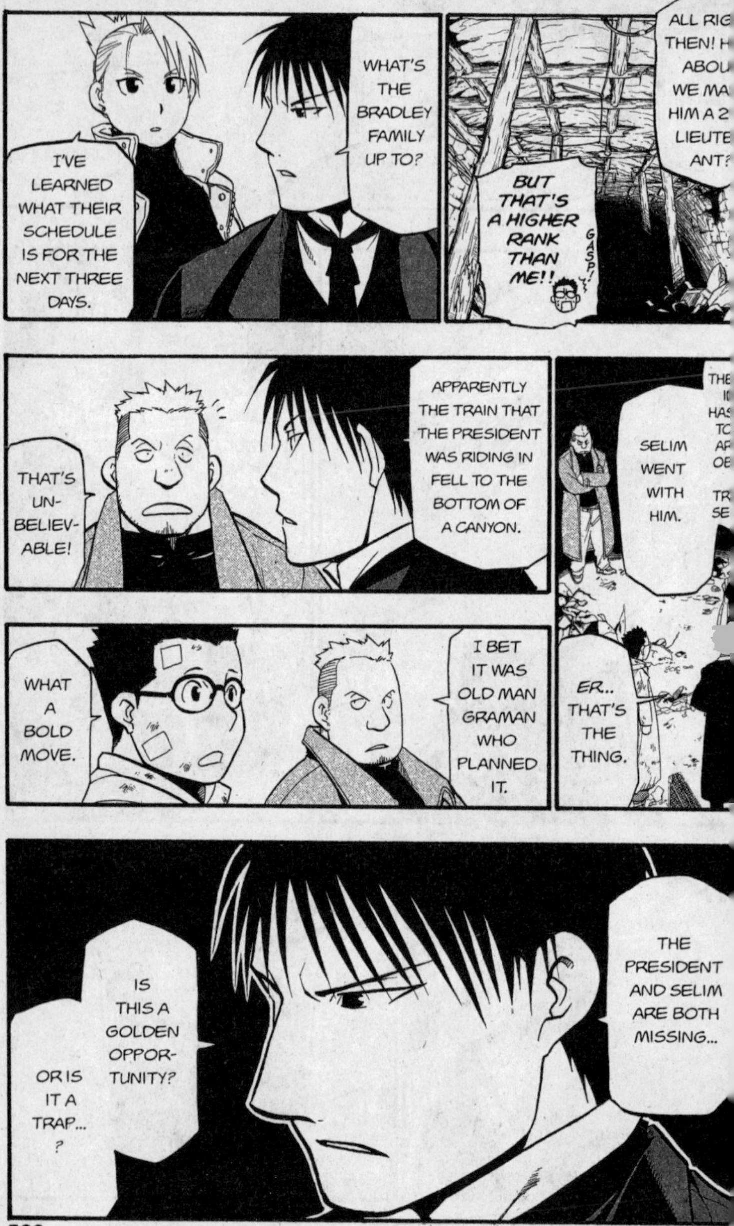
BUT THAT'S A HIGHER RANK THAN ME!!
GASP!
WHAT'S THE BRADLEY FAMILY UP TO?
I'VE LEARNED WHAT THEIR SCHEDULE IS FOR THE NEXT THREE DAYS.
SELIM WENT WITH HIM.
ER.. THAT'S THE THING.
APPARENTLY THE TRAIN THAT THE PRESIDENT WAS RIDING IN FELL TO THE BOTTOM OF A CANYON.
THAT'S UN-BELIEV-ABLE!
I BET IT WAS OLD MAN GRAMAN WHO PLANNED IT.
WHAT A BOLD MOVE.
THE PRESIDENT AND SELIM ARE BOTH MISSING...
IS THIS A GOLDEN OPPOR-TUNITY?
OR IS IT A TRAP... ?

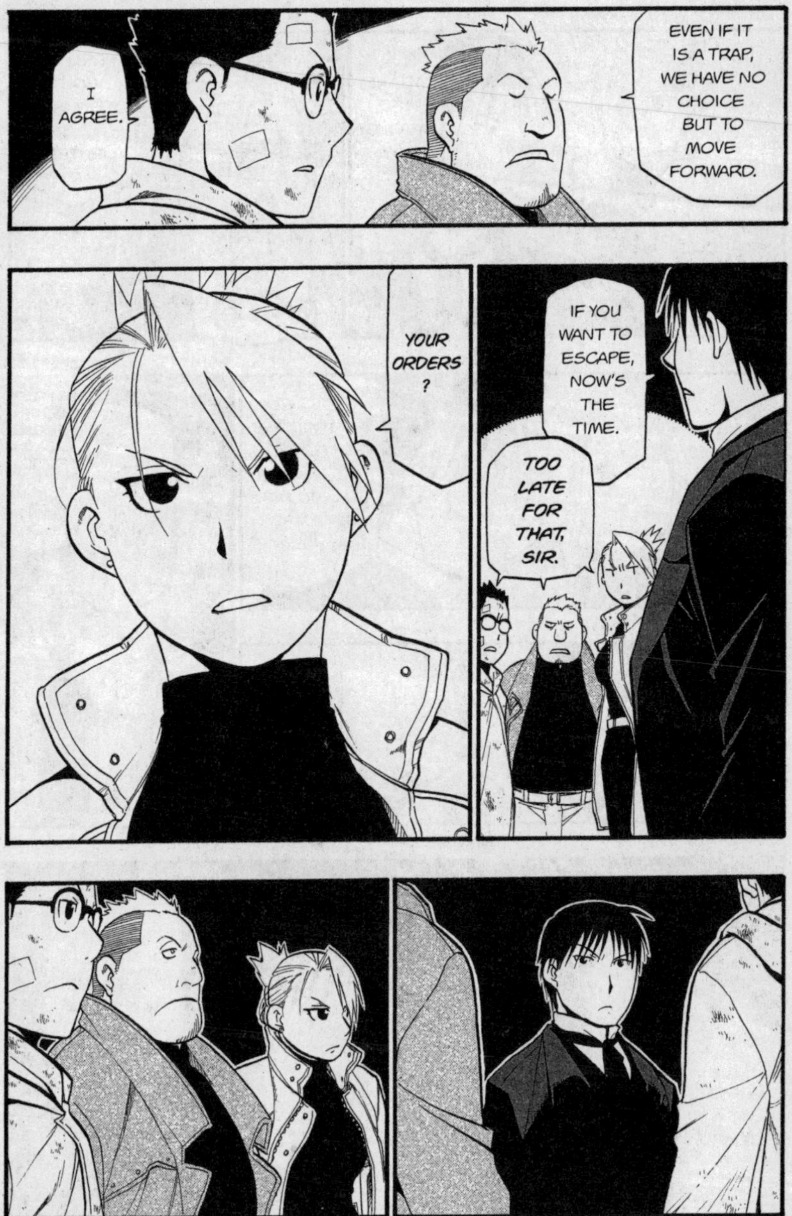
EVEN IF IT IS A TRAP, WE HAVE NO CHOICE BUT TO MOVE FORWARD.
I AGREE.
IF YOU WANT TO ESCAPE, NOW'S THE TIME.
TOO LATE FOR THAT, SIR.
YOUR ORDERS ?

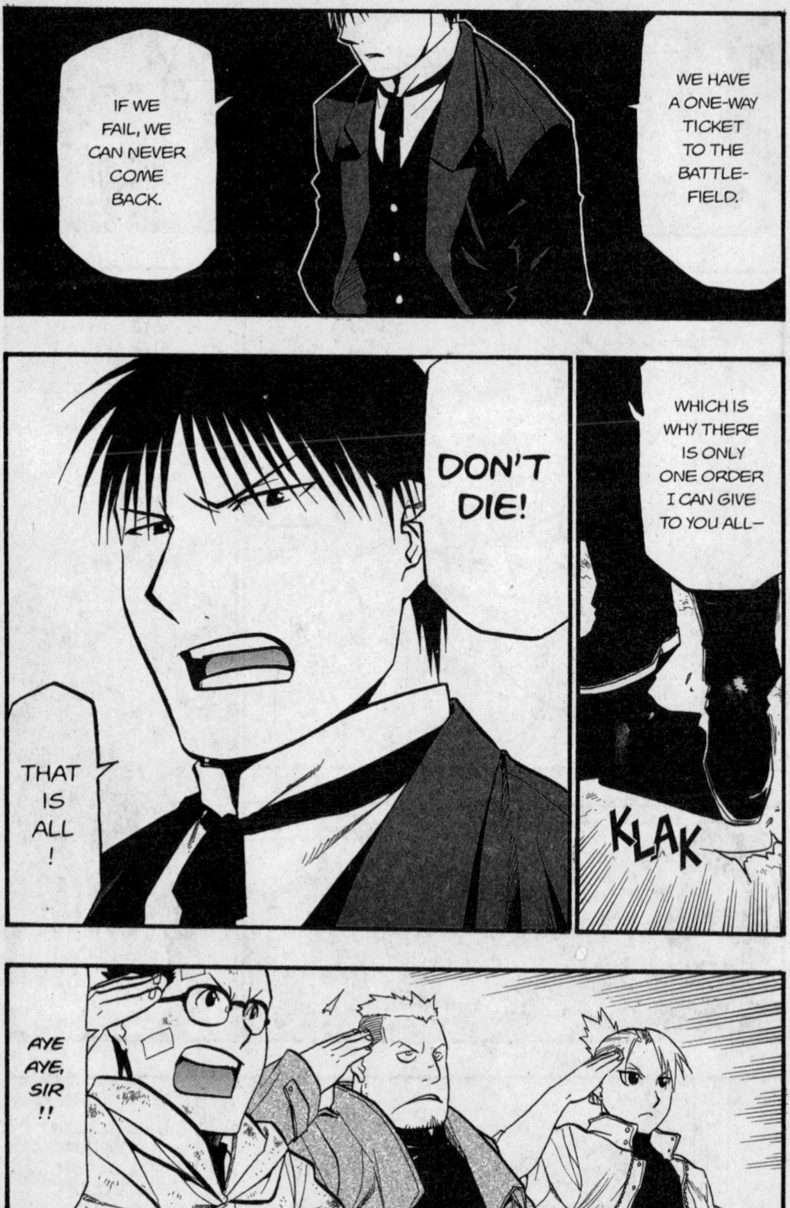
WE HAVE A ONE-WAY TICKET TO THE BATTLE-FIELD.
IF WE FAIL, WE CAN NEVER COME BACK.
WHICH IS WHY THERE IS ONLY ONE ORDER I CAN GIVE TO YOU ALL—
KLAK
DON'T DIE!
THAT IS ALL!
AYE AYE, SIR!!

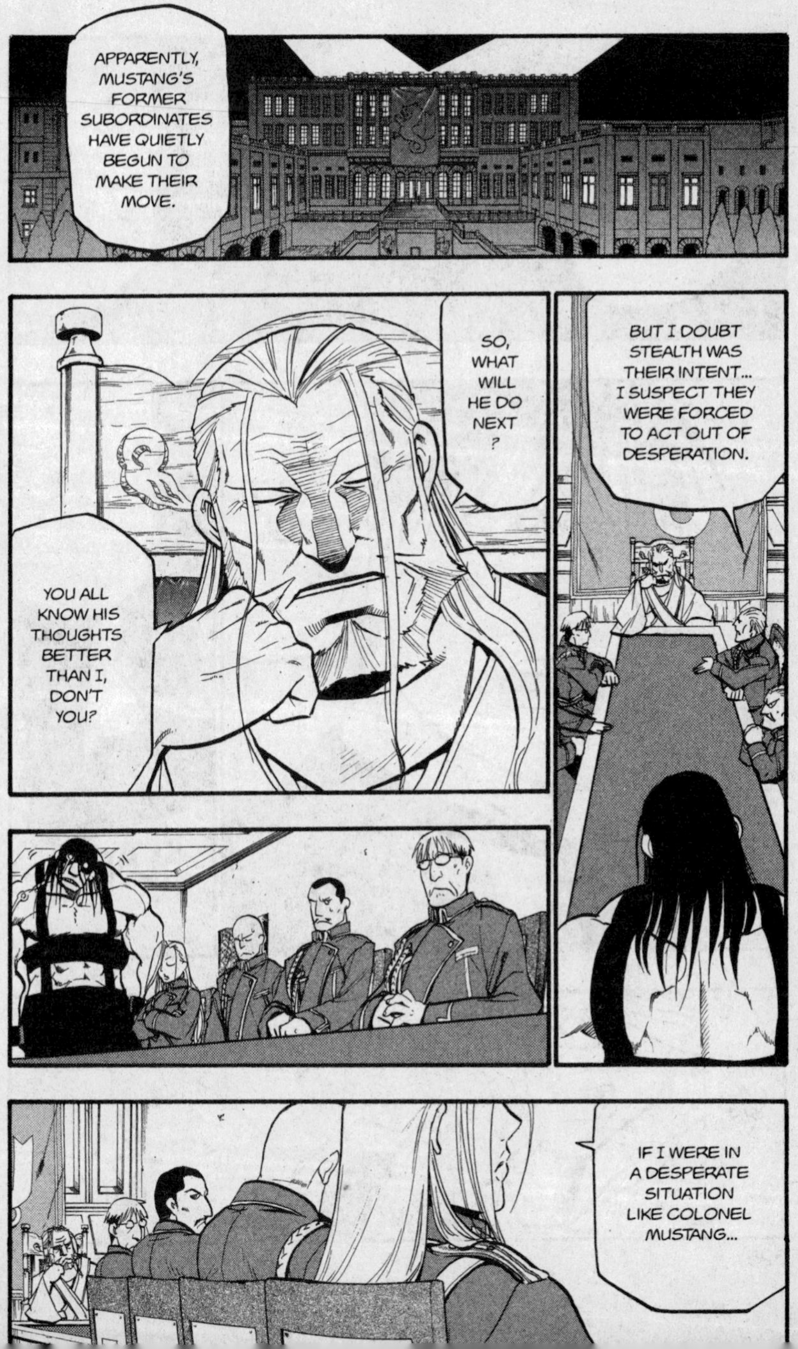
APPARENTLY, MUSTANG'S FORMER SUBORDINATES HAVE QUIETLY BEGUN TO MAKE THEIR MOVE.
BUT I DOUBT STEALTH WAS THEIR INTENT... I SUSPECT THEY WERE FORCED TO ACT OUT OF DESPERATION.
SO, WHAT WILL HE DO NEXT?
YOU ALL KNOW HIS THOUGHTS BETTER THAN I, DON'T YOU?
IF I WERE IN A DESPERATE SITUATION LIKE COLONEL MUSTANG...

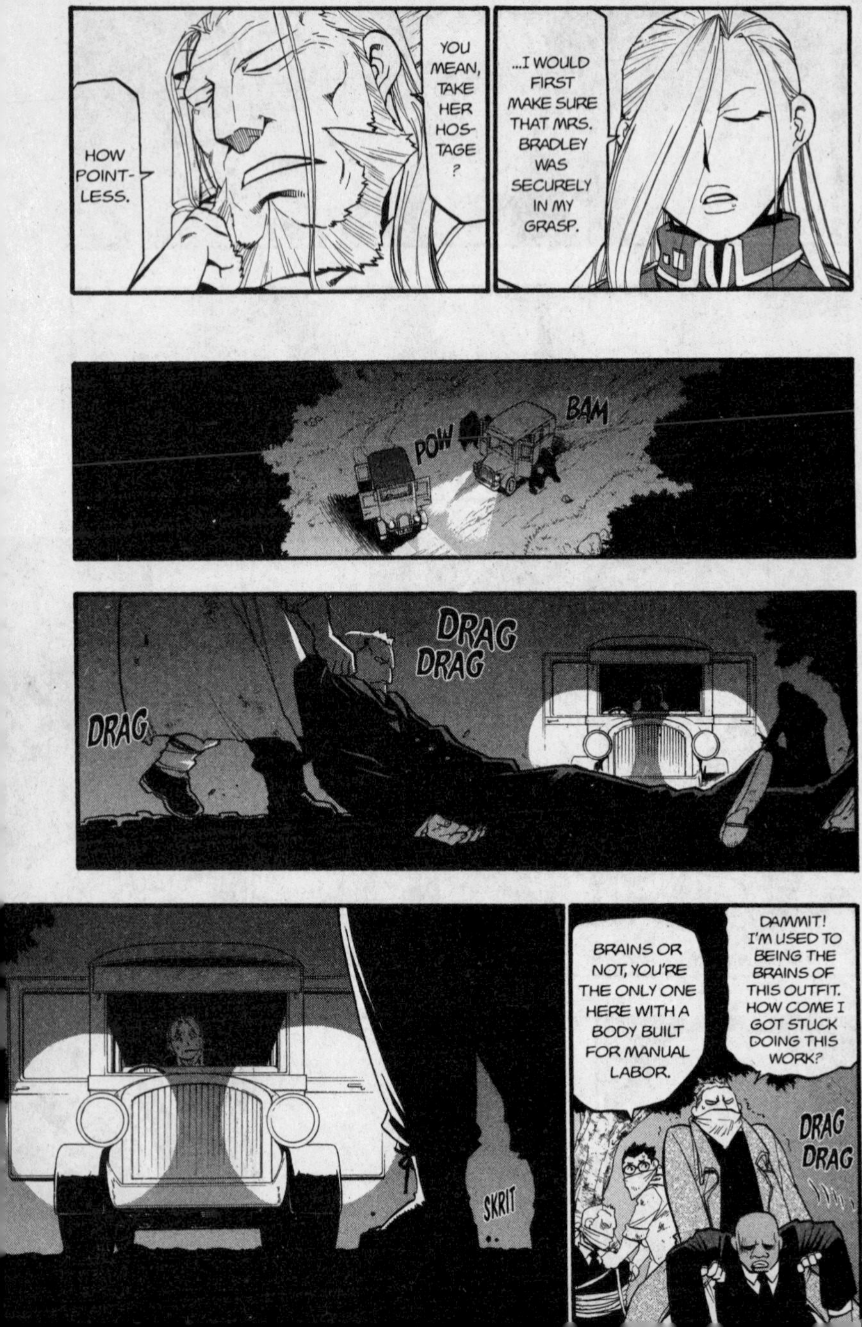
...I WOULD FIRST MAKE SURE THAT MRS. BRADLEY WAS SECURELY IN MY GRASP.
YOU MEAN, TAKE HER HOSTAGE?
HOW POINTLESS.
BAM
POW
DRAG DRAG
DRAG
DAMMIT! I'M USED TO BEING THE BRAINS OF THIS OUTFIT. HOW COME I GOT STUCK DOING THIS WORK?
BRAINS OR NOT, YOU'RE THE ONLY ONE HERE WITH A BODY BUILT FOR MANUAL LABOR.
DRAG DRAG
SKRIT

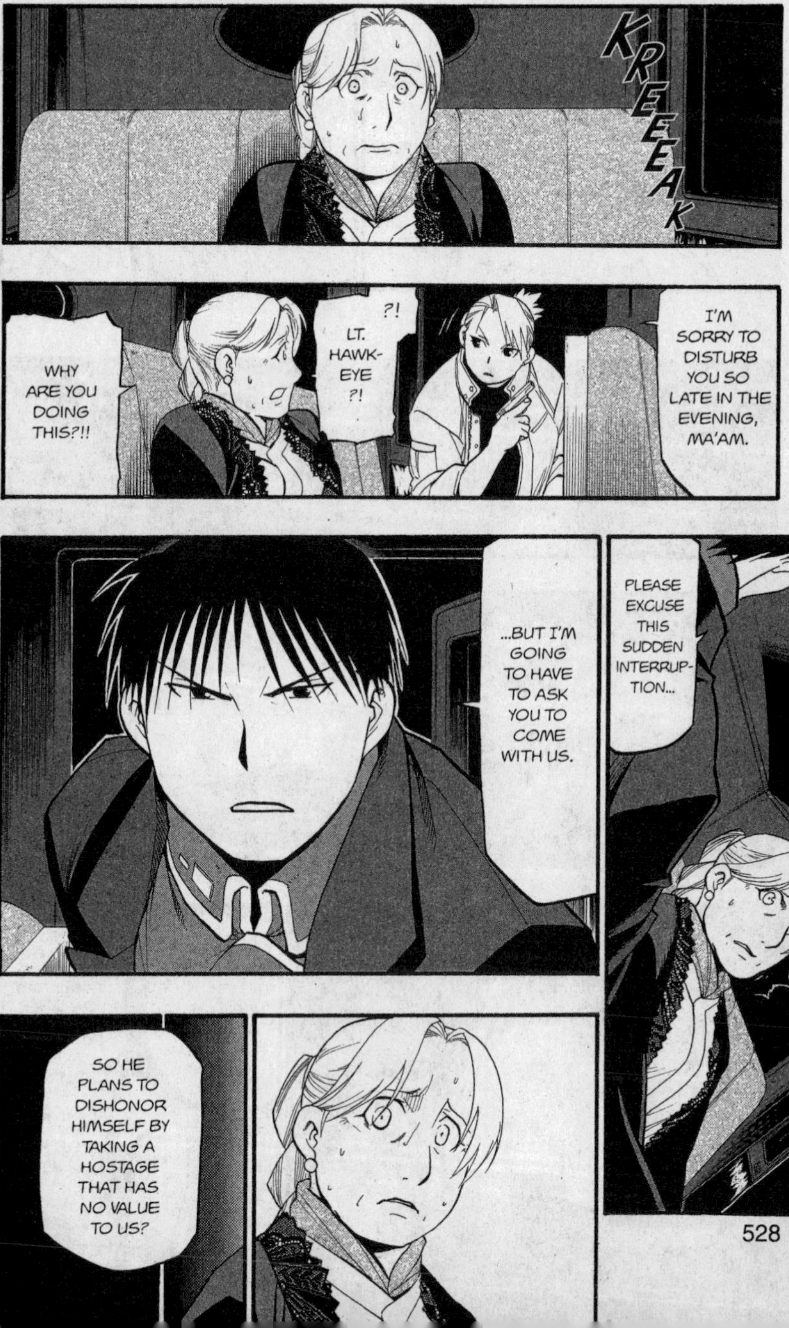
KREEEAK
I'M SORRY TO DISTURB YOU SO LATE IN THE EVENING, MA'AM.
?! LT. HAWK-EYE ?!
WHY ARE YOU DOING THIS?!!
PLEASE EXCUSE THIS SUDDEN INTERRUP-TION...
...BUT I'M GOING TO HAVE TO ASK YOU TO COME WITH US.
SO HE PLANS TO DISHONOR HIMSELF BY TAKING A HOSTAGE THAT HAS NO VALUE TO US?

HUMANS ARE TRULY BEYOND SALVATION.

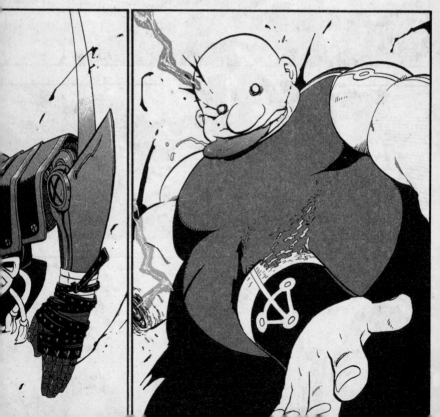

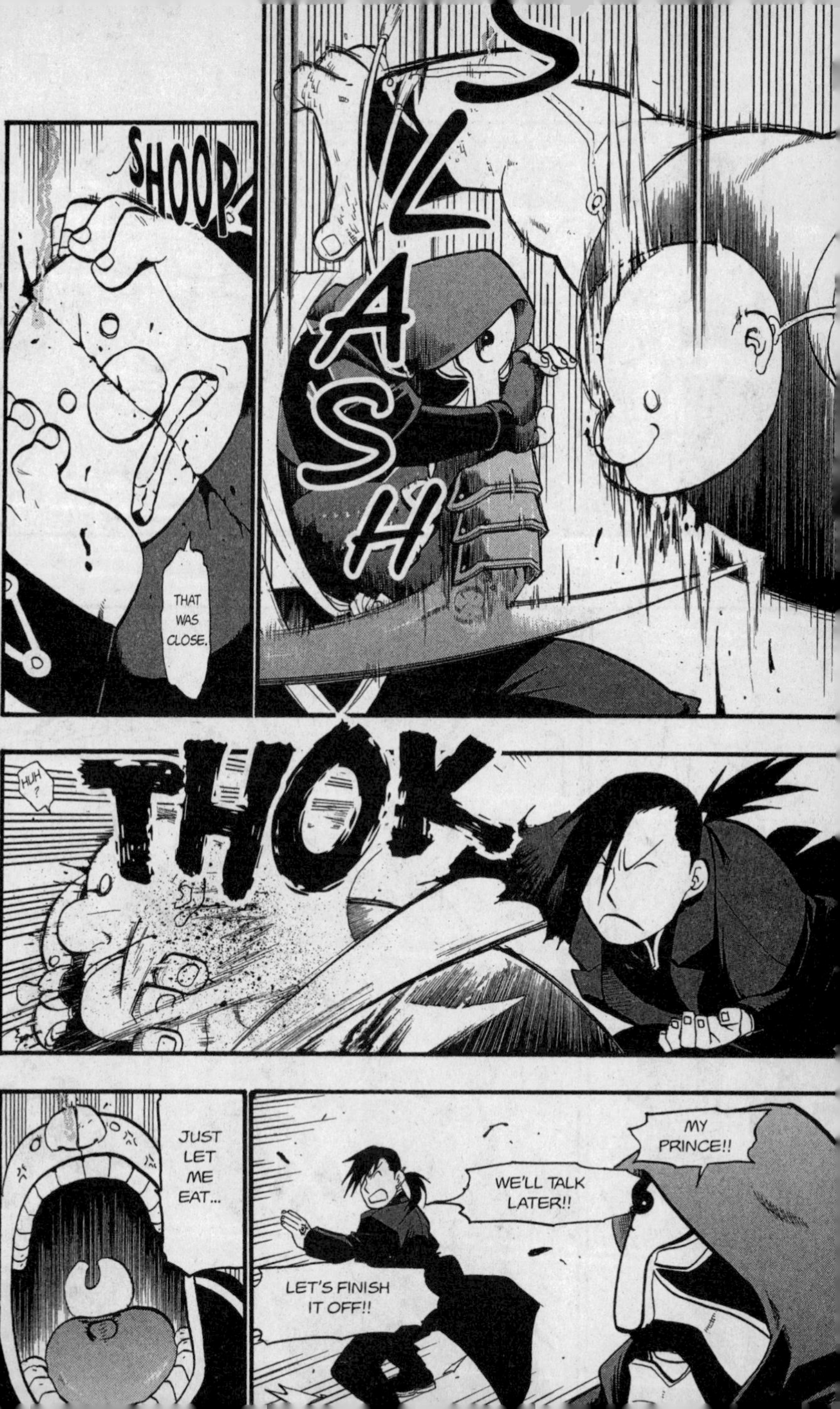
SLASH
SHOOP
THAT WAS CLOSE.
THOK
HUH?
MY PRINCE!!
WE'LL TALK LATER!!
LET'S FINISH IT OFF!!
JUST LET ME EAT...

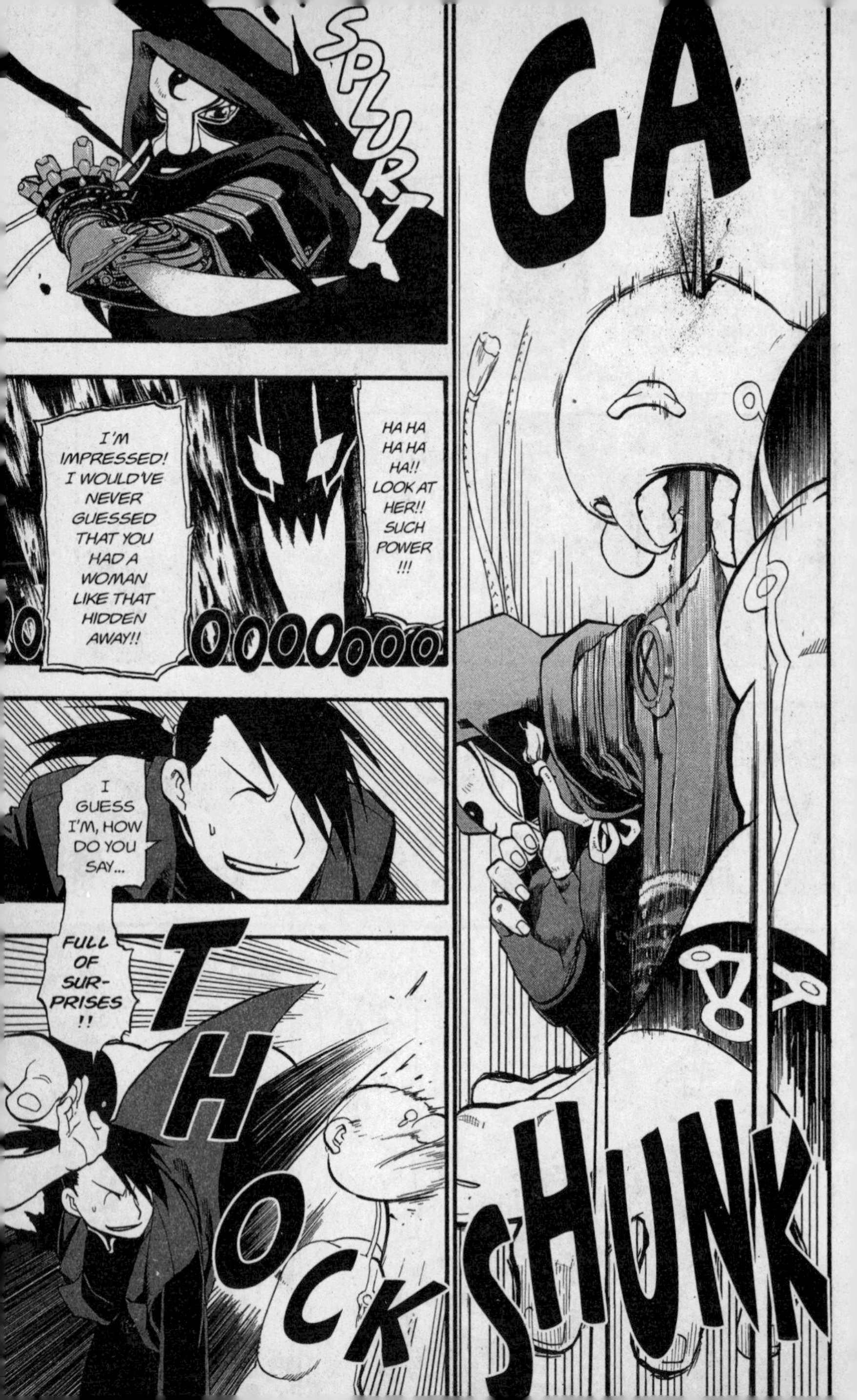
GA
SHUNK
SPLURT
HA HA HA HA HA!! LOOK AT HER!! SUCH POWER!!!
I'M IMPRESSED! I WOULD'VE NEVER GUESSED THAT YOU HAD A WOMAN LIKE THAT HIDDEN AWAY!!
OOOOOOOO
I GUESS I'M, HOW DO YOU SAY...
FULL OF SUR-PRISES!!
THOCK

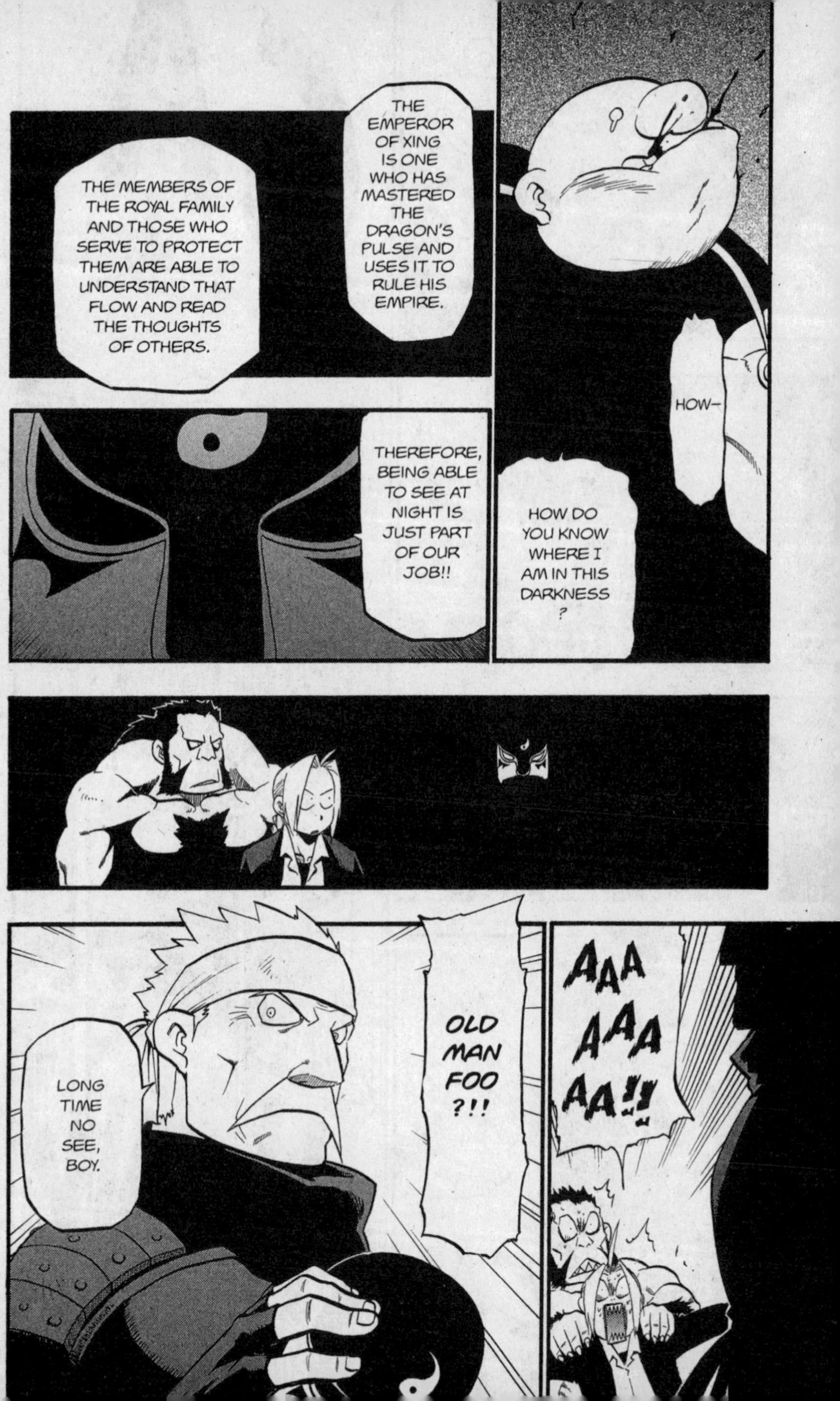
HOW—
HOW DO YOU KNOW WHERE I AM IN THIS DARKNESS ?
THE EMPEROR OF XING IS ONE WHO HAS MASTERED THE DRAGON'S PULSE AND USES IT TO RULE HIS EMPIRE.
THE MEMBERS OF THE ROYAL FAMILY AND THOSE WHO SERVE TO PROTECT THEM ARE ABLE TO UNDERSTAND THAT FLOW AND READ THE THOUGHTS OF OTHERS.
THEREFORE, BEING ABLE TO SEE AT NIGHT IS JUST PART OF OUR JOB!!
AAAAAAAA!!
OLD MAN FOO ?!!
LONG TIME NO SEE, BOY.

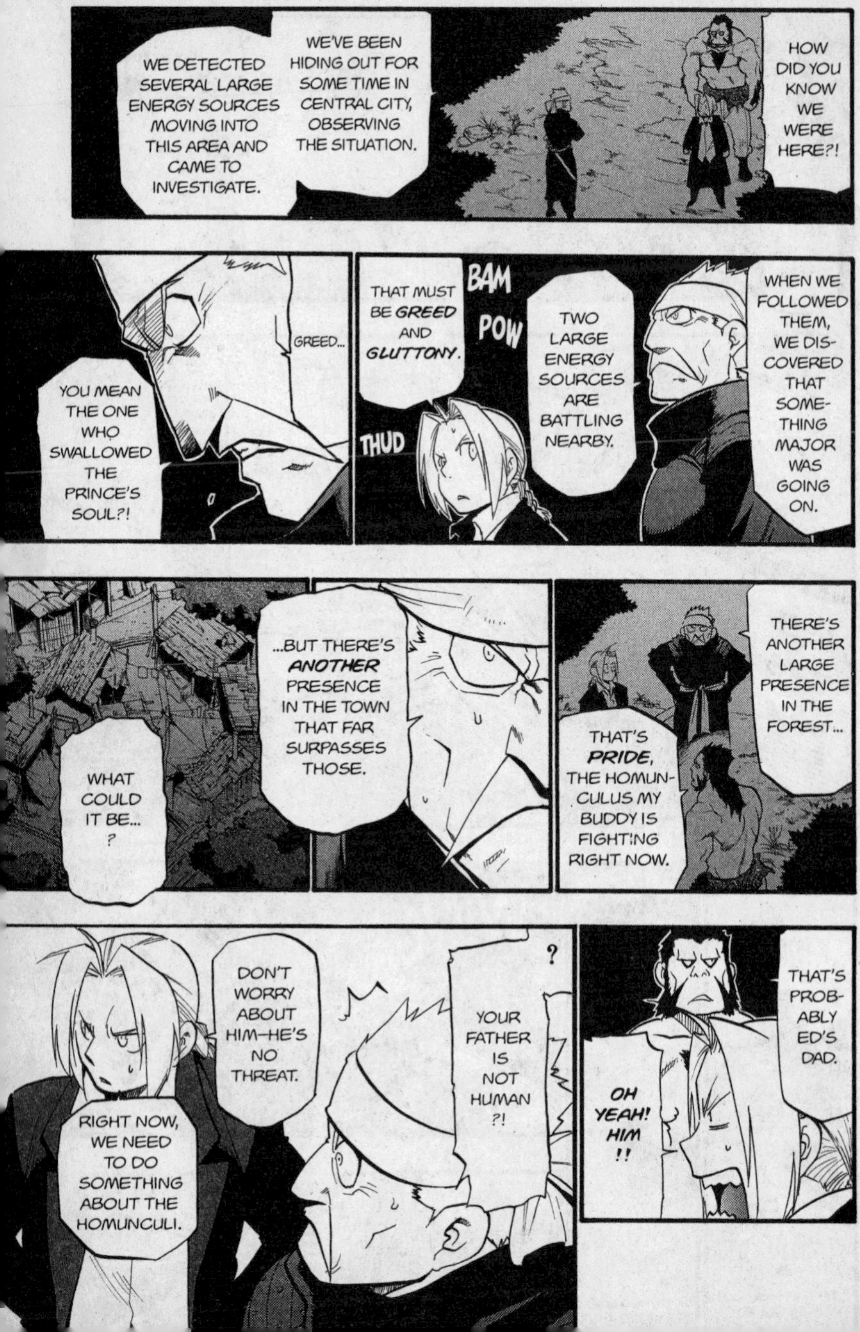
HOW DID YOU KNOW WE WERE HERE?!
WE'VE BEEN HIDING OUT FOR SOME TIME IN CENTRAL CITY, OBSERVING THE SITUATION.
WE DETECTED SEVERAL LARGE ENERGY SOURCES MOVING INTO THIS AREA AND CAME TO INVESTIGATE.
WHEN WE FOLLOWED THEM, WE DISCOVERED THAT SOMETHING MAJOR WAS GOING ON.
TWO LARGE ENERGY SOURCES ARE BATTLING NEARBY.
BAM
POW
THAT MUST BE **GREED** AND **GLUTTONY**.
THUD
GREED...
YOU MEAN THE ONE WHO SWALLOWED THE PRINCE'S SOUL?!
THERE'S ANOTHER LARGE PRESENCE IN THE FOREST...
THAT'S **PRIDE**, THE HOMUNCULUS MY BUDDY IS FIGHTING RIGHT NOW.
...BUT THERE'S **ANOTHER** PRESENCE IN THE TOWN THAT FAR SURPASSES THOSE.
WHAT COULD IT BE...?
THAT'S PROBABLY ED'S DAD.
OH YEAH! HIM!!
?
YOUR FATHER IS NOT HUMAN?!
DON'T WORRY ABOUT HIM—HE'S NO THREAT.
RIGHT NOW, WE NEED TO DO SOMETHING ABOUT THE HOMUNCULI.

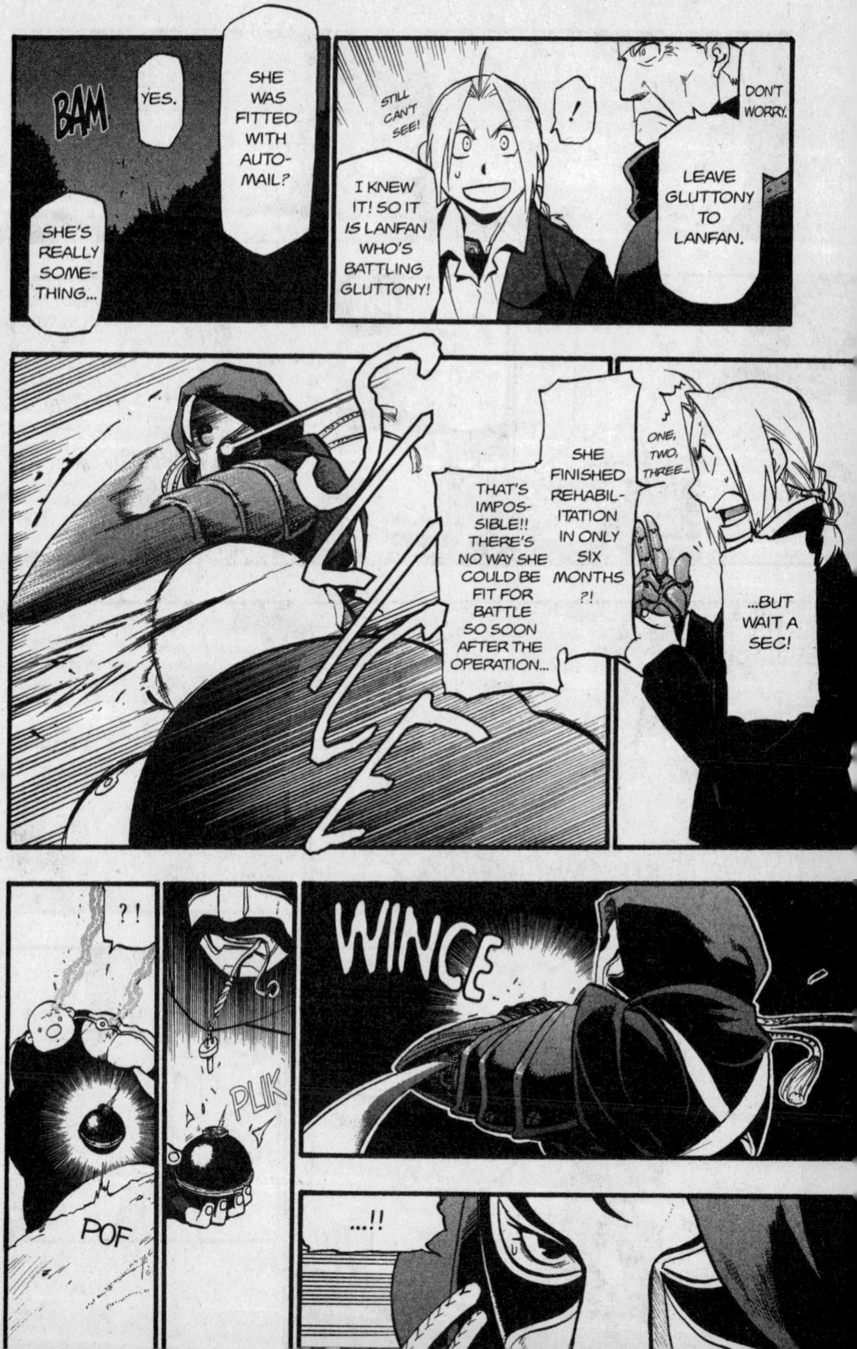
DON'T WORRY.
LEAVE GLUTTONY TO LANFAN.
!
STILL CAN'T SEE!
I KNEW IT! SO IT IS LANFAN WHO'S BATTLING GLUTTONY!
SHE WAS FITTED WITH AUTO-MAIL?
YES.
BAM
SHE'S REALLY SOME-THING...
ONE, TWO, THREE...
...BUT WAIT A SEC!
SHE FINISHED REHABIL-ITATION IN ONLY SIX MONTHS ?!
THAT'S IMPOS-SIBLE!! THERE'S NO WAY SHE COULD BE FIT FOR BATTLE SO SOON AFTER THE OPERATION...
WINCE
...!!
PLIK
?!
POF

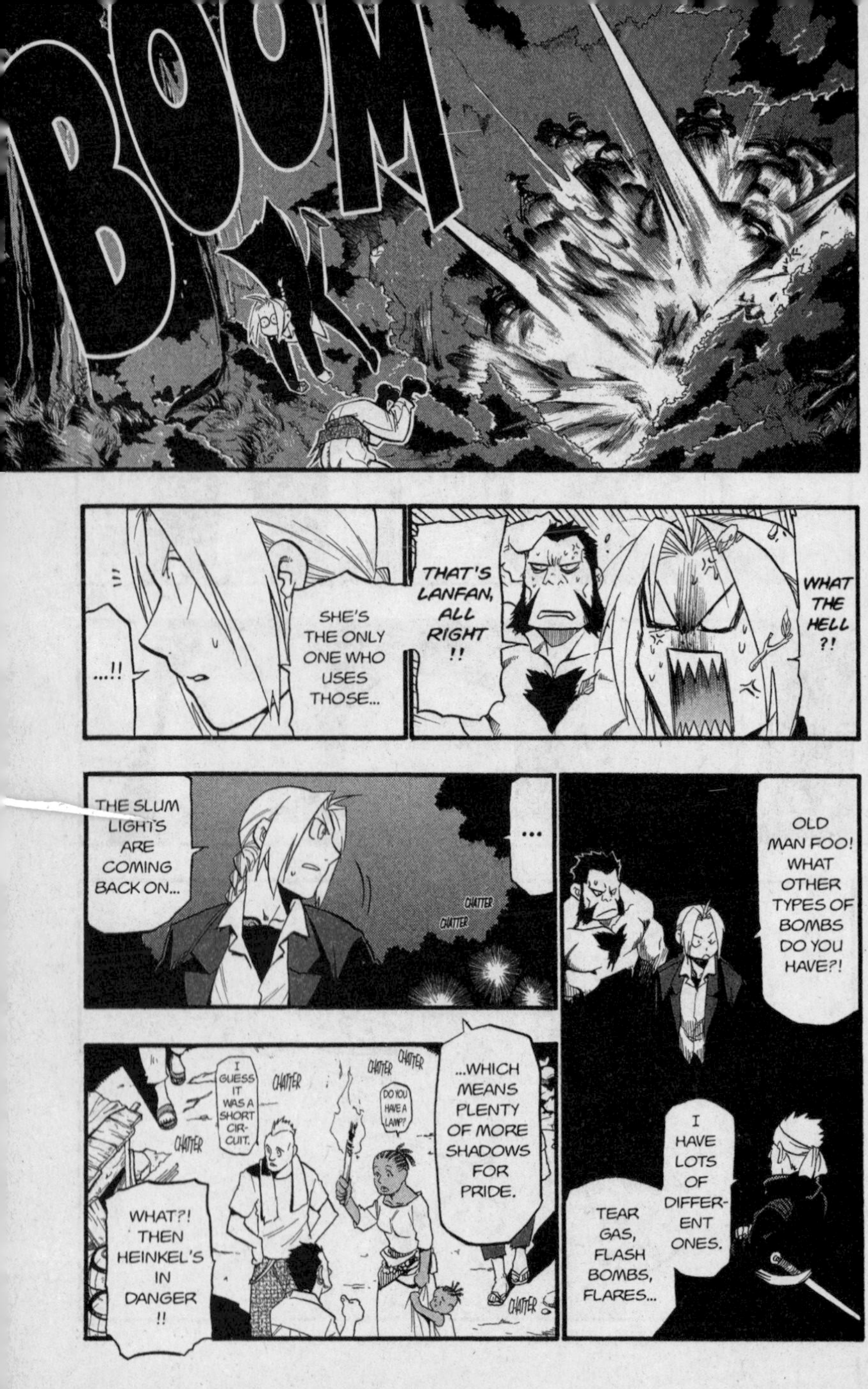
BOOM
WHAT THE HELL?!
THAT'S LANFAN, ALL RIGHT!!
SHE'S THE ONLY ONE WHO USES THOSE...
...!!
OLD MAN FOO! WHAT OTHER TYPES OF BOMBS DO YOU HAVE?!
I HAVE LOTS OF DIFFER-ENT ONES.
TEAR GAS, FLASH BOMBS, FLARES...
...
THE SLUM LIGHTS ARE COMING BACK ON...
CHATTER
CHATTER
...WHICH MEANS PLENTY OF MORE SHADOWS FOR PRIDE.
CHATTER
CHATTER
DO YOU HAVE A LAMP?
CHATTER
I GUESS IT WAS A SHORT CIR-CUIT.
CHATTER
WHAT?! THEN HEINKEL'S IN DANGER!!
CHATTER

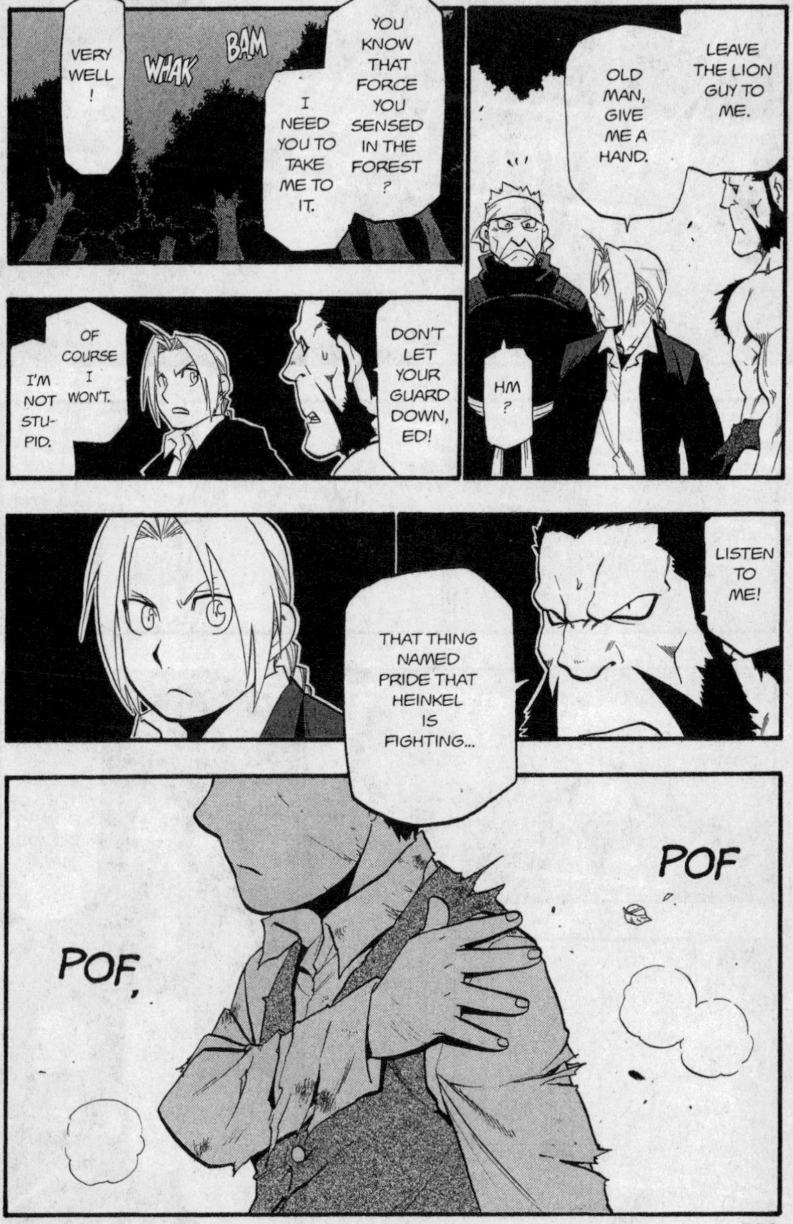
LEAVE THE LION GUY TO ME.
OLD MAN, GIVE ME A HAND.
HM ?
YOU KNOW THAT FORCE YOU SENSED IN THE FOREST ?
BAM
I NEED YOU TO TAKE ME TO IT.
WHAK
VERY WELL !
DON'T LET YOUR GUARD DOWN, ED!
OF COURSE I WON'T.
I'M NOT STUPID.
LISTEN TO ME!
THAT THING NAMED PRIDE THAT HEINKEL IS FIGHTING...
POF
POF,

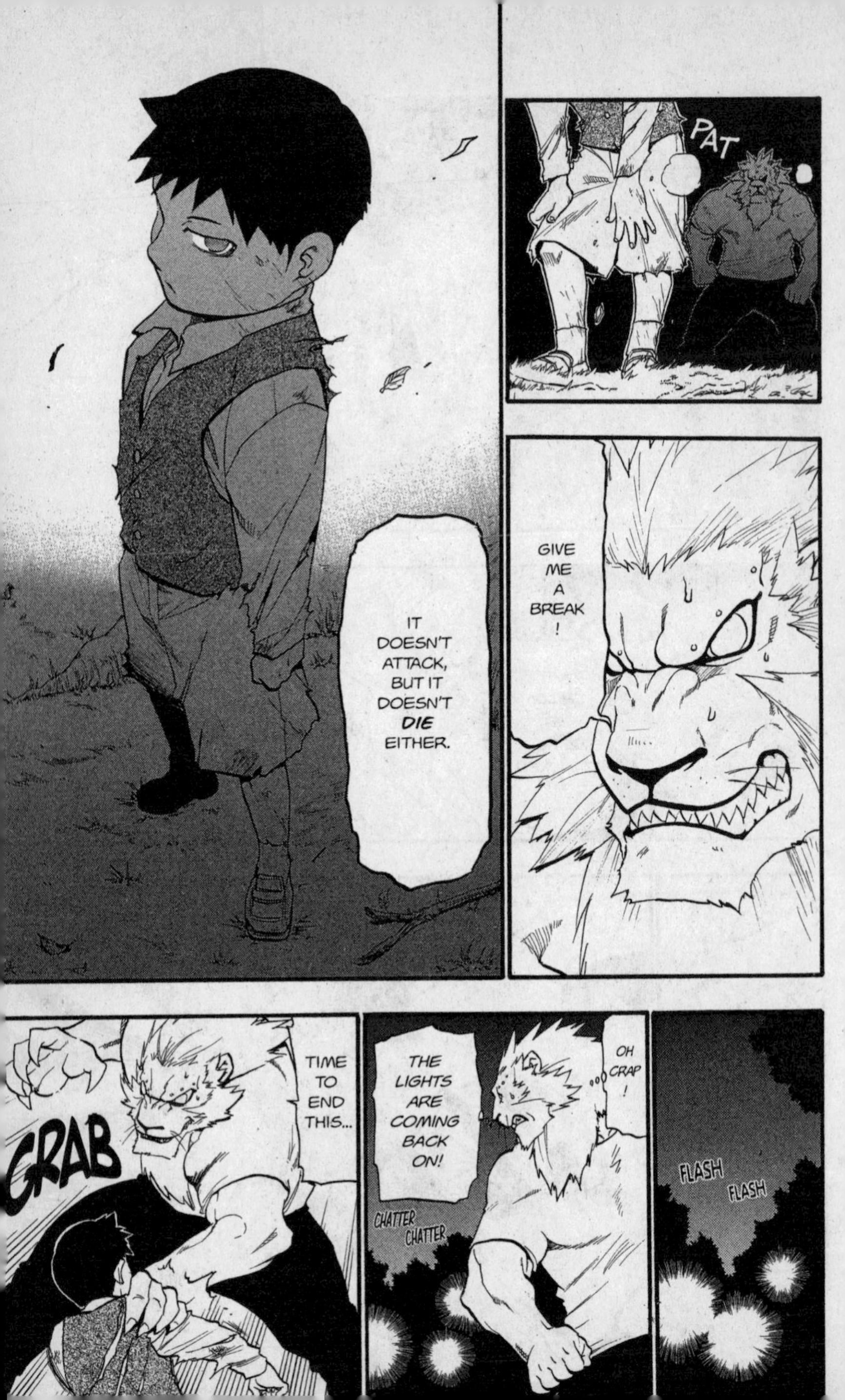
PAT
GIVE ME A BREAK!
IT DOESN'T ATTACK, BUT IT DOESN'T **DIE** EITHER.
FLASH
FLASH
OH CRAP!
THE LIGHTS ARE COMING BACK ON!
CHATTER CHATTER
TIME TO END THIS...
GRAB

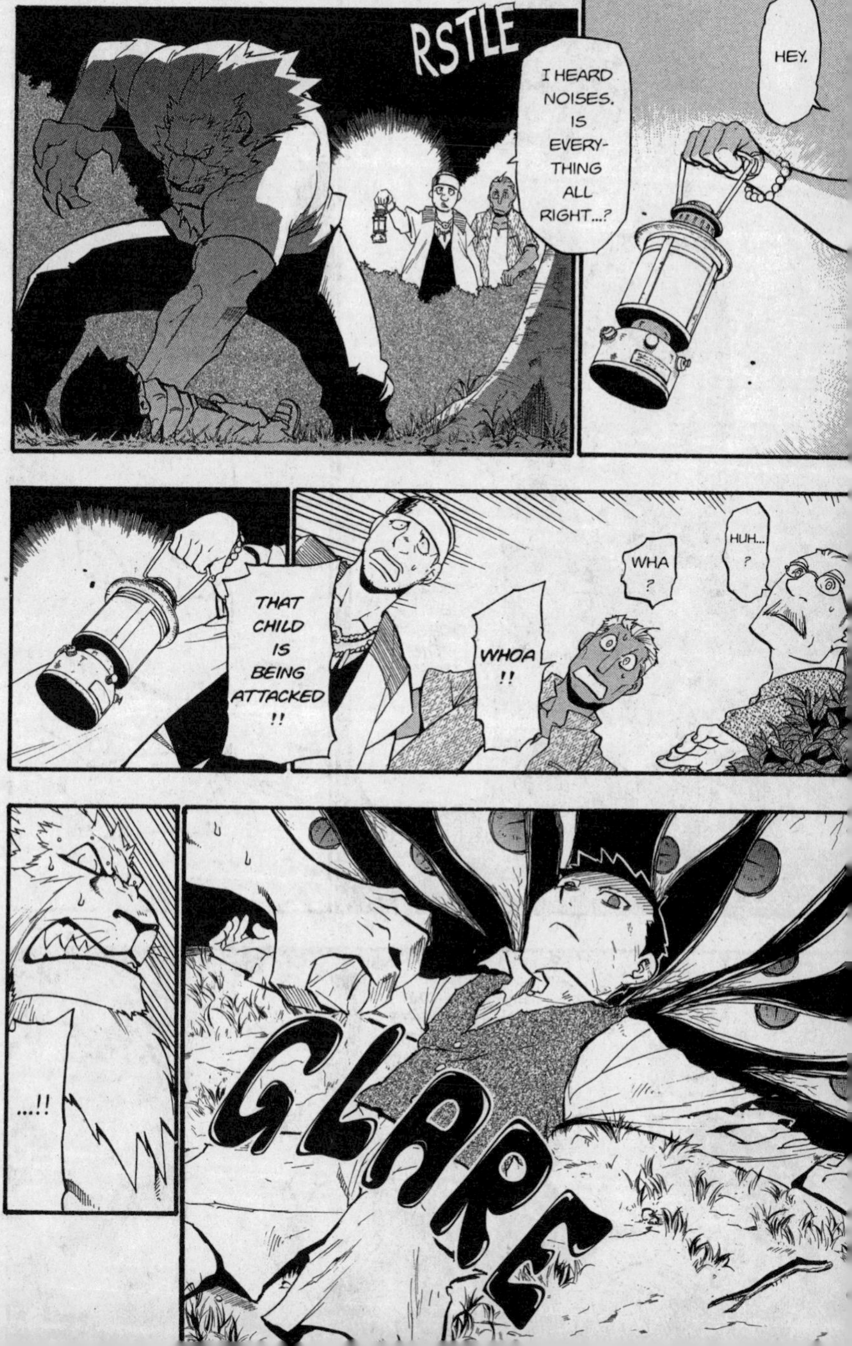
HEY.
RSTLE
I HEARD NOISES. IS EVERY-THING ALL RIGHT...?
HUH... ?
WHA ?
WHOA !!
THAT CHILD IS BEING ATTACKED !!
GLARE
...!!

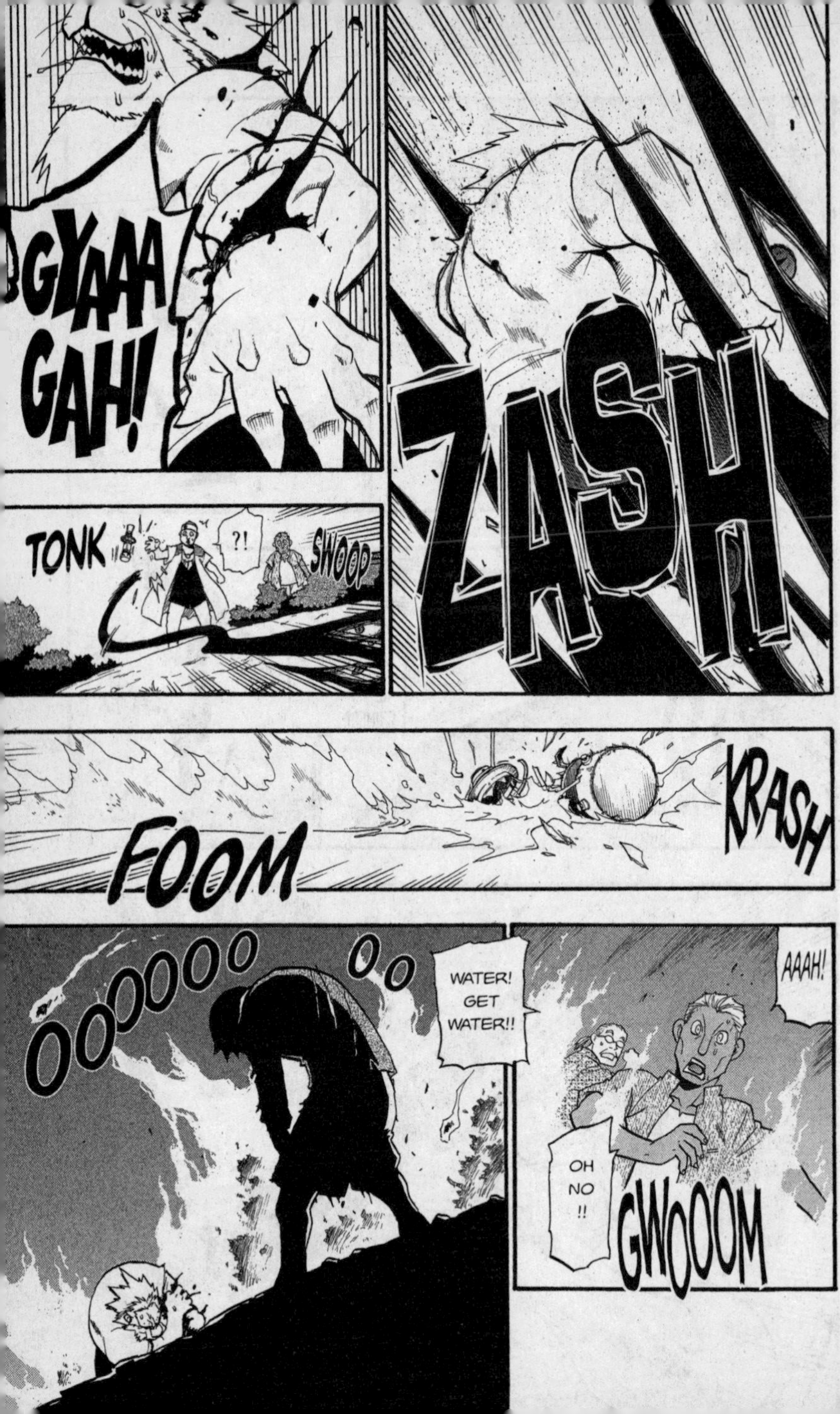
ZASH
GYAAA GAH!
SWOOP
?!
TONK
KRASH
FOOM
AAAH!
OH NO !!
GWOOOM
WATER! GET WATER!!
OOOOOOO
OO

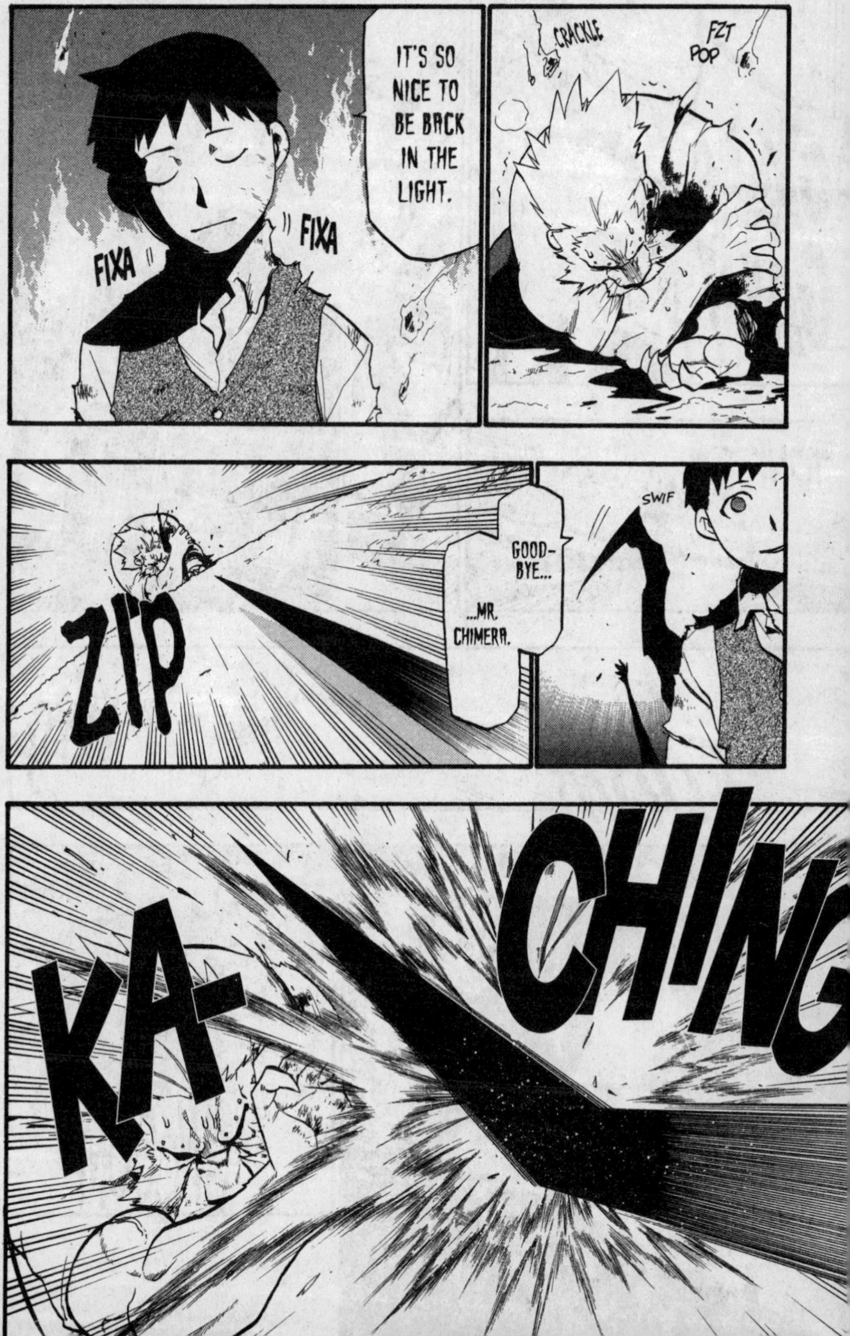
CRACKLE
FZT
POP
IT'S SO NICE TO BE BACK IN THE LIGHT.
FIXA
FIXA
SWIF
GOOD-BYE...
...MR. CHIMERA.
ZIP
KA-
CHING

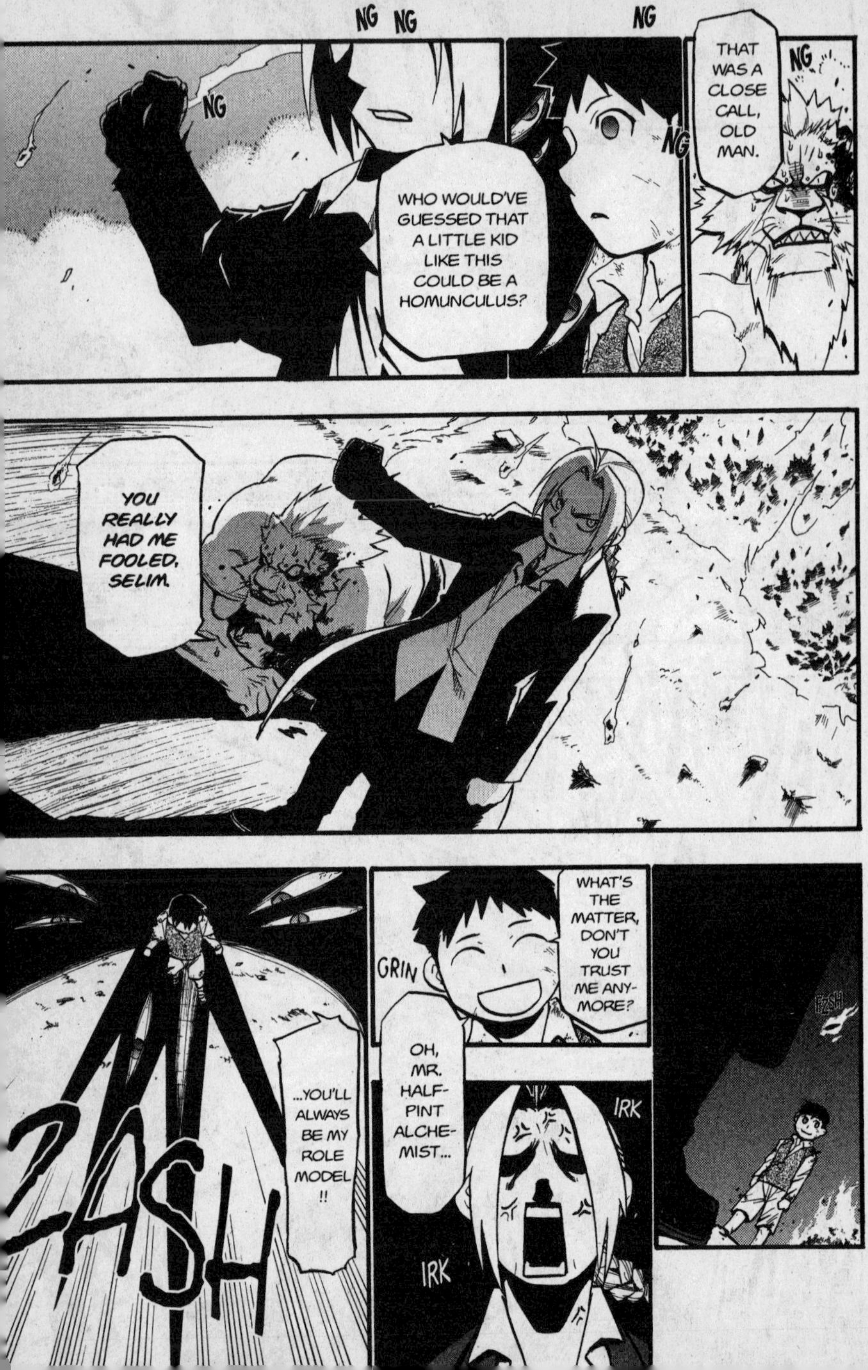
NG
THAT WAS A CLOSE CALL, OLD MAN.
NG
NG
WHO WOULD'VE GUESSED THAT A LITTLE KID LIKE THIS COULD BE A HOMUNCULUS?
NG NG
NG
YOU REALLY HAD ME FOOLED, SELIM.
FZSH
WHAT'S THE MATTER, DON'T YOU TRUST ME ANY-MORE?
GRIN
OH, MR. HALF-PINT ALCHE-MIST...
IRK
IRK
...YOU'LL ALWAYS BE MY ROLE MODEL!!
ZASH

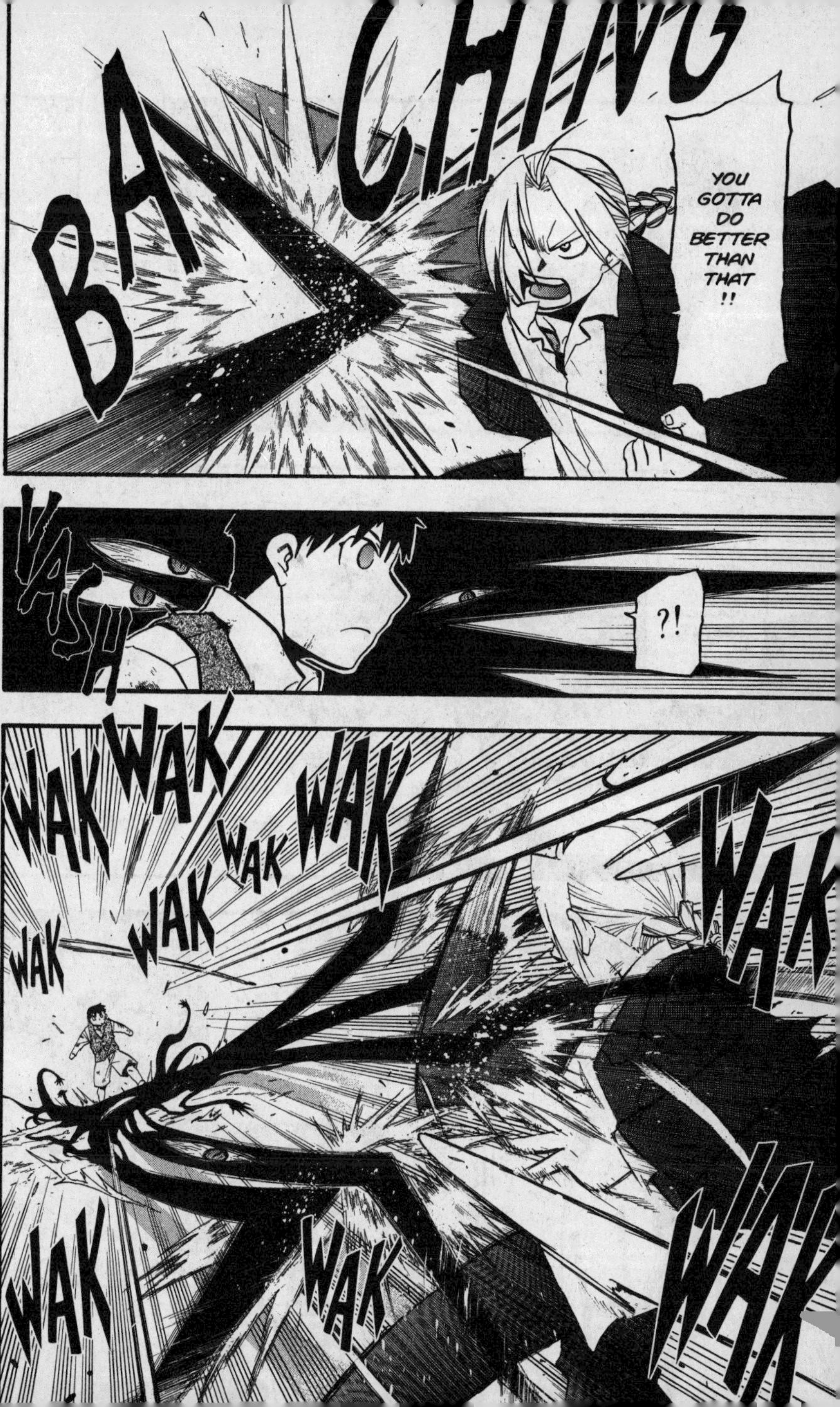
BA CHING
YOU GOTTA DO BETTER THAN THAT!!
VASH
?!
WAK
WAK WAK WAK WAK WAK WAK
WAK
WAK
WAK WAK

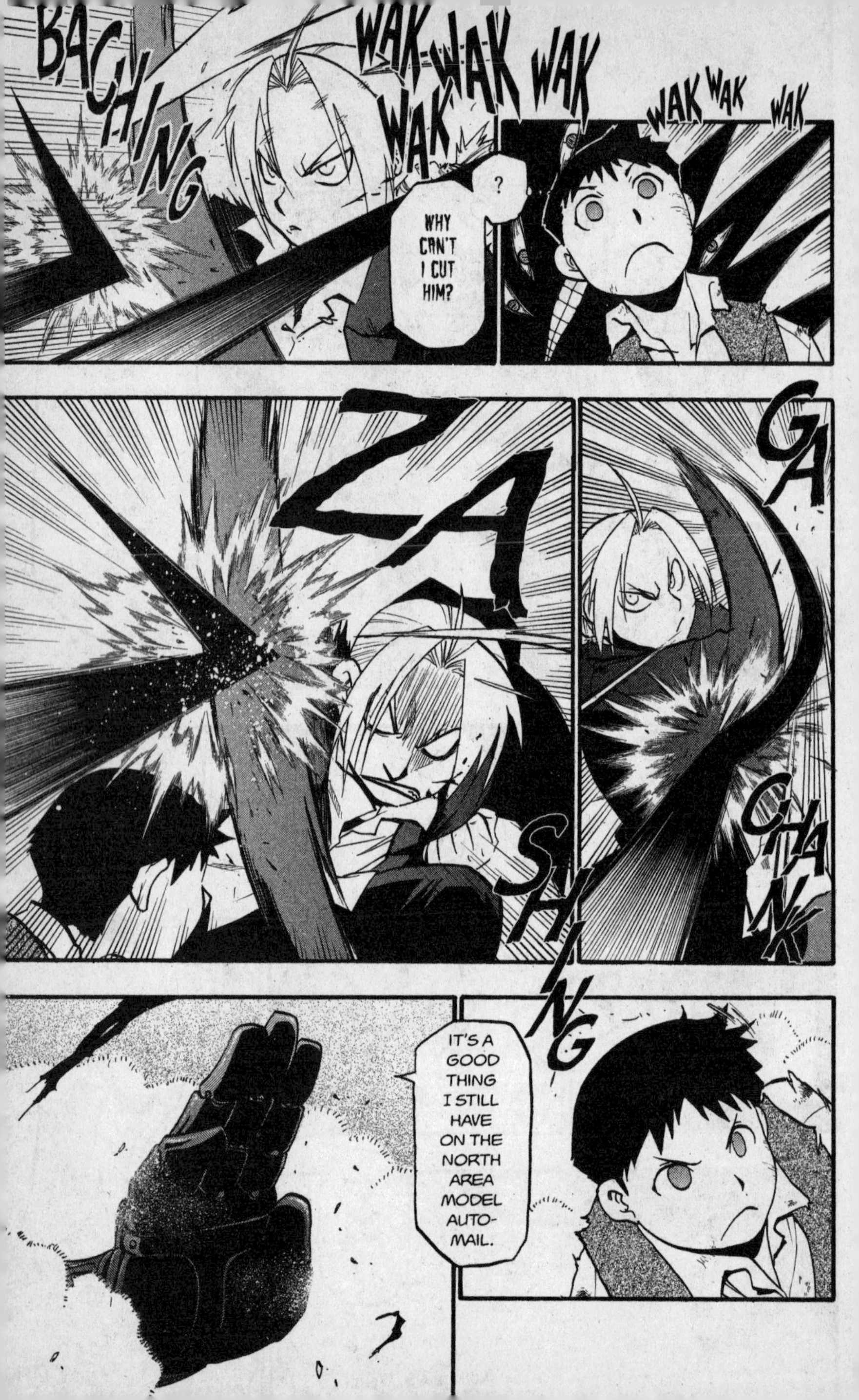
WAK WAK WAK
?
WAK-WAK WAK WAK WAK
BACHING
WHY CAN'T I CUT HIM?
GA CHANK
ZA SHING
IT'S A GOOD THING I STILL HAVE ON THE NORTH AREA MODEL AUTO-MAIL.

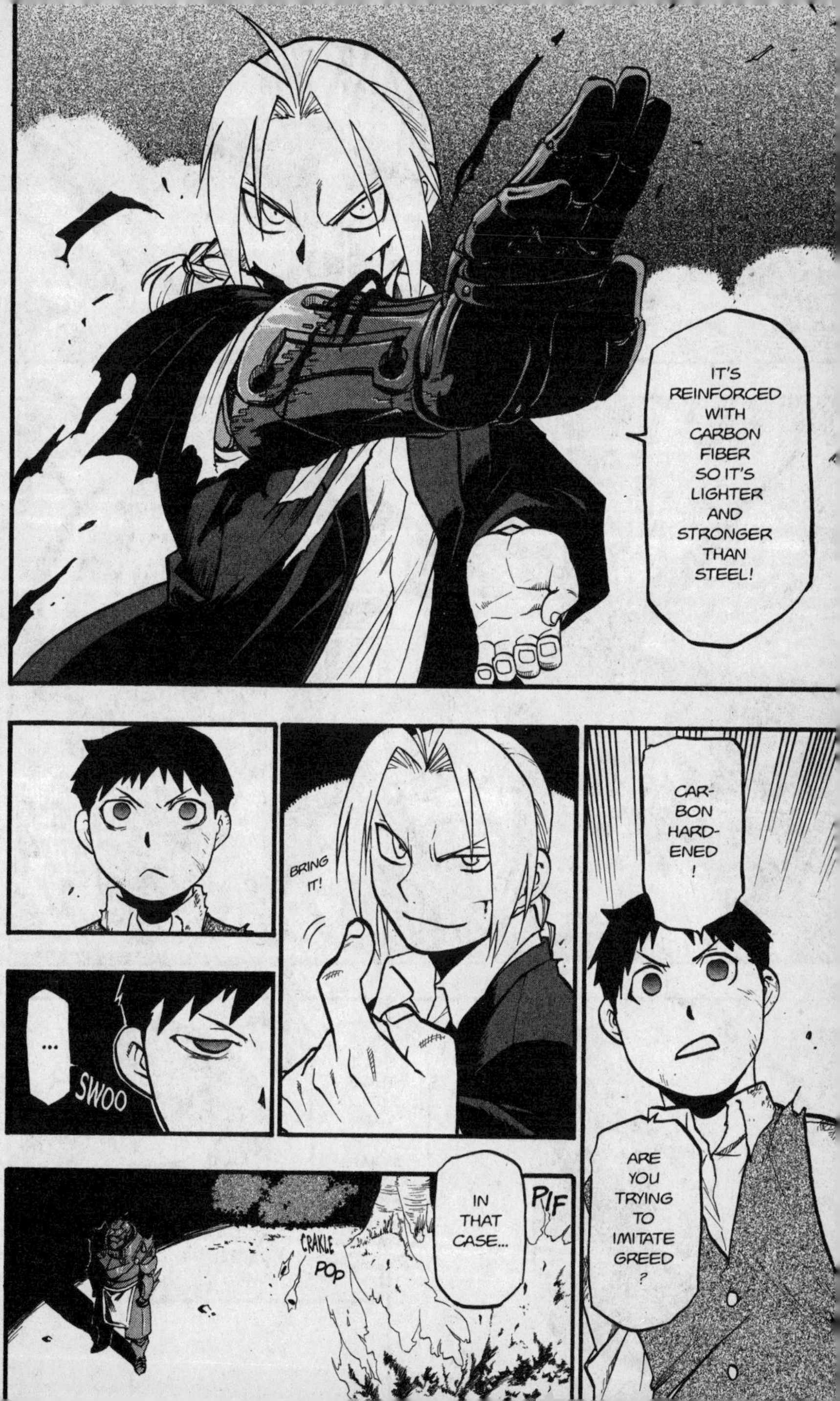
IT'S REINFORCED WITH CARBON FIBER SO IT'S LIGHTER AND STRONGER THAN STEEL!
CAR-BON HARD-ENED!
ARE YOU TRYING TO IMITATE GREED?
BRING IT!
...
SWOO
PIF
IN THAT CASE...
CRAKLE
POP

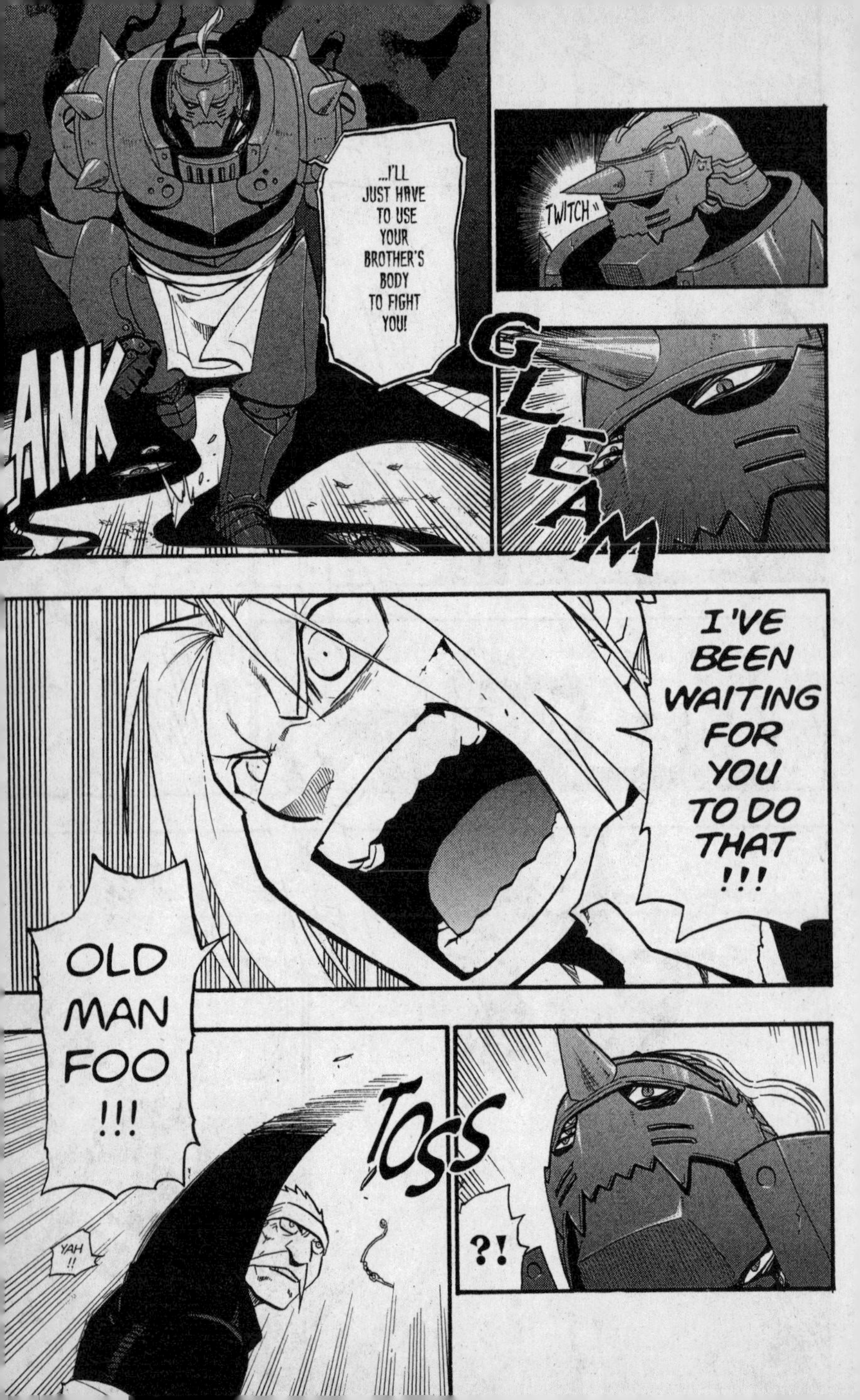
TWITCH
GLEAM
...I'LL JUST HAVE TO USE YOUR BROTHER'S BODY TO FIGHT YOU!
ANK
I'VE BEEN WAITING FOR YOU TO DO THAT!!!
OLD MAN FOO!!!
?!
TOSS
YAH!!

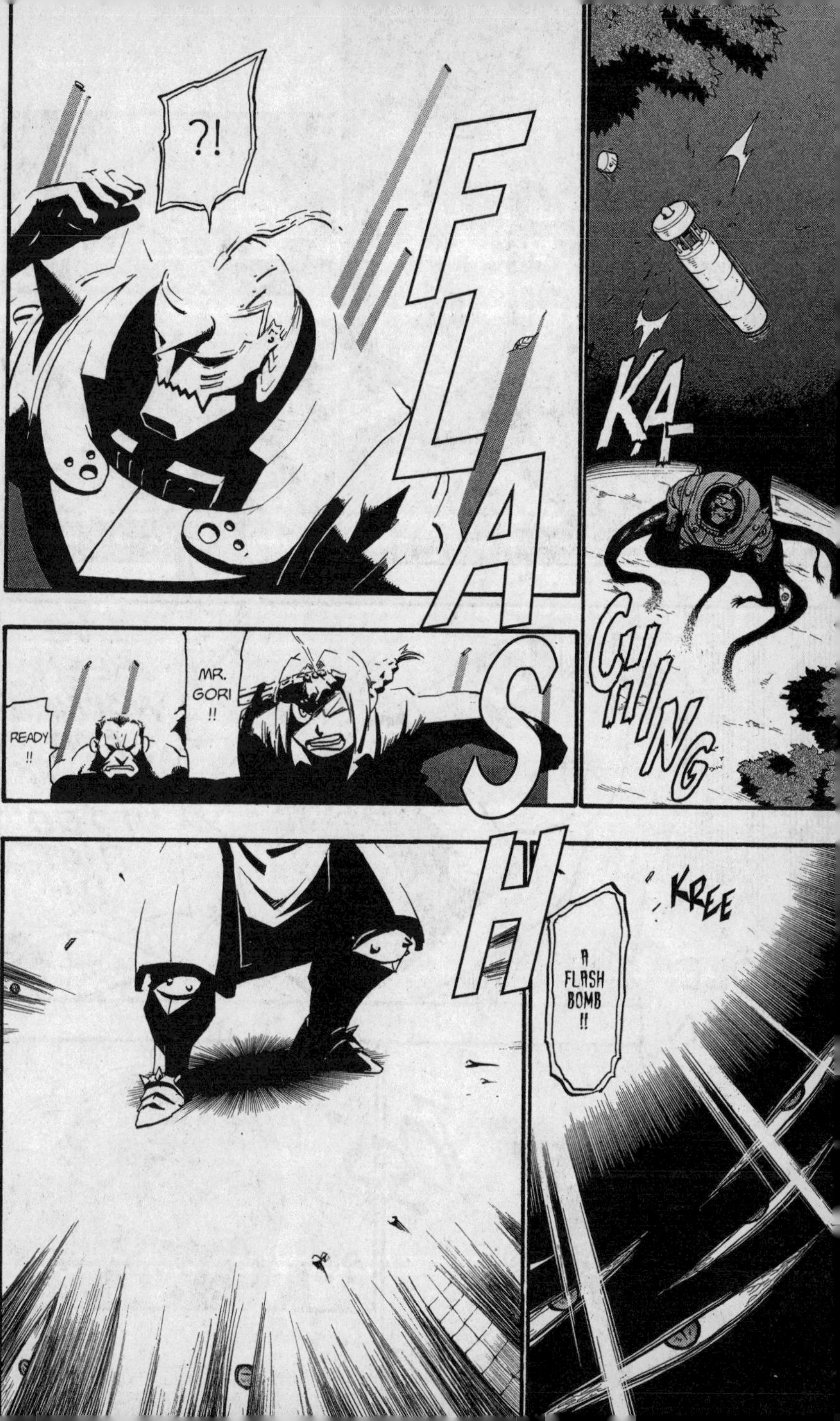
KA-CHING
?!
FLASH
MR. GORI !!
READY !!
KREE
A FLASH BOMB !!

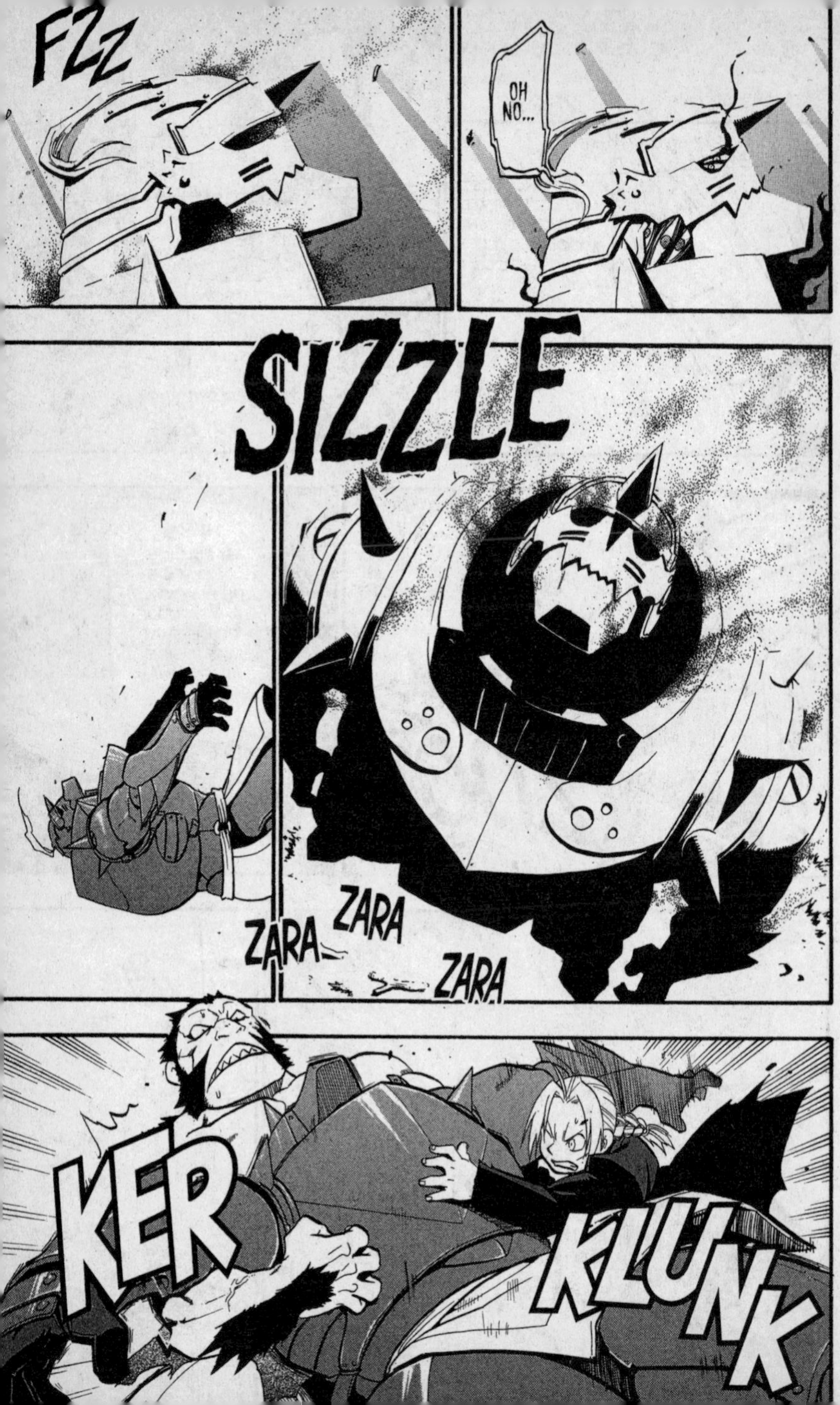
OH NO...
FZZ
SIZZLE
ZARA
ZARA
ZARA
KER
KLUNK

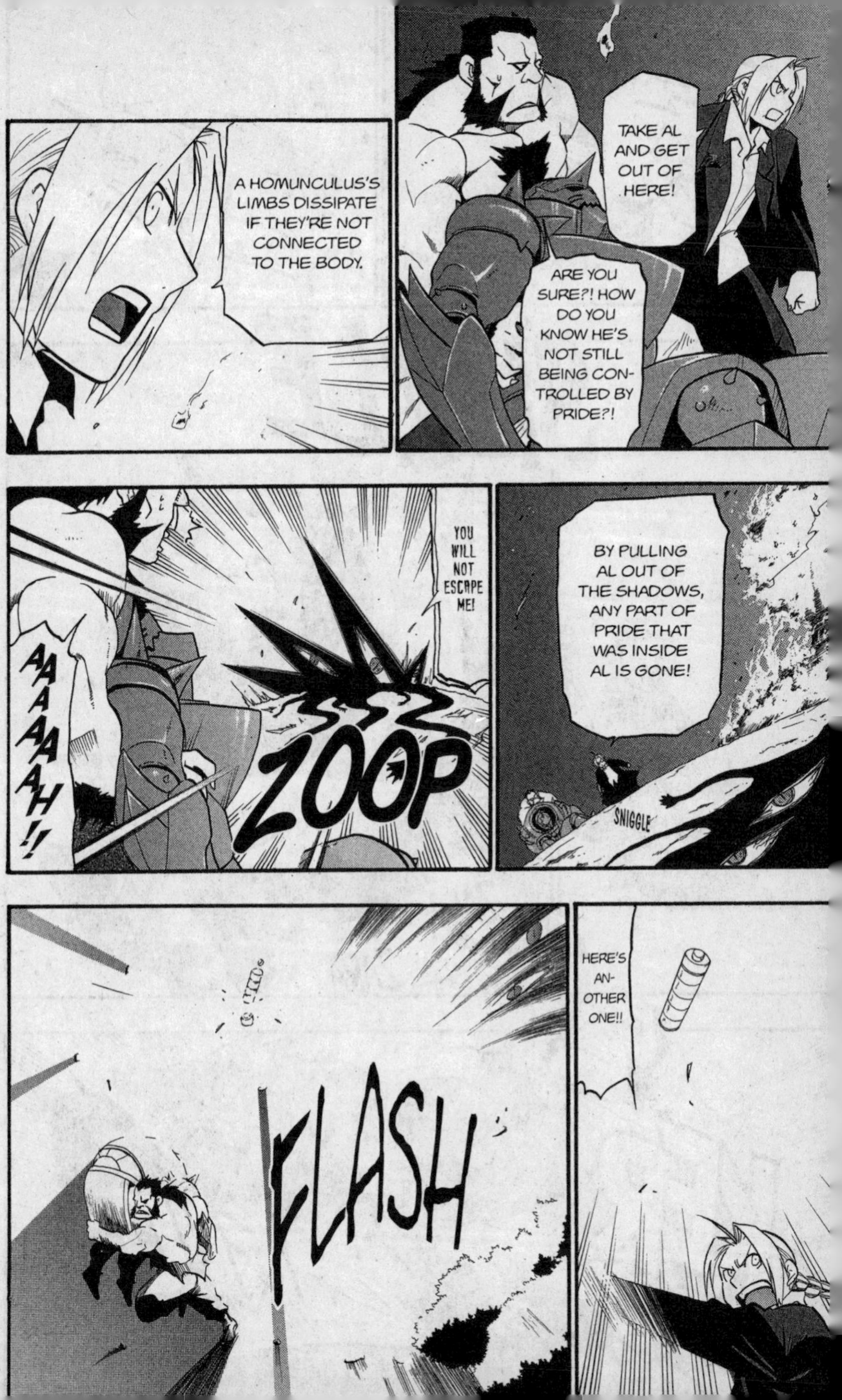
TAKE AL AND GET OUT OF HERE!
ARE YOU SURE?! HOW DO YOU KNOW HE'S NOT STILL BEING CON-TROLLED BY PRIDE?!
A HOMUNCULUS'S LIMBS DISSIPATE IF THEY'RE NOT CONNECTED TO THE BODY.
BY PULLING AL OUT OF THE SHADOWS, ANY PART OF PRIDE THAT WAS INSIDE AL IS GONE!
SNIGGLE
YOU WILL NOT ESCAPE ME!
ZOOP
AAAAAAH!!
HERE'S AN-OTHER ONE!!
FLASH

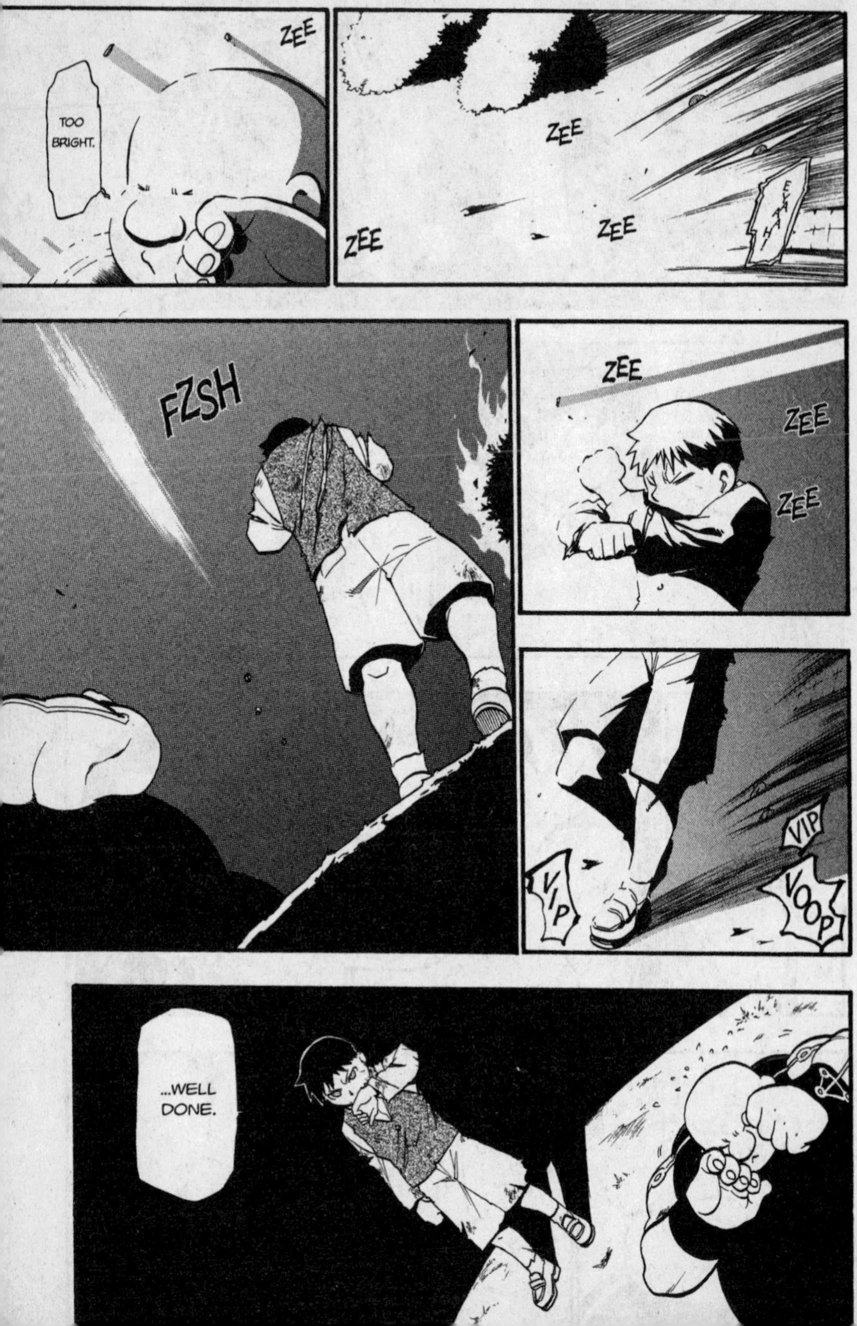
ZEE
EYAAH!
ZEE
ZEE
ZEE
ZEE
TOO BRIGHT.
ZEE
ZEE
ZEE
VIP
VOOP
VIP
FZSH
...WELL DONE.

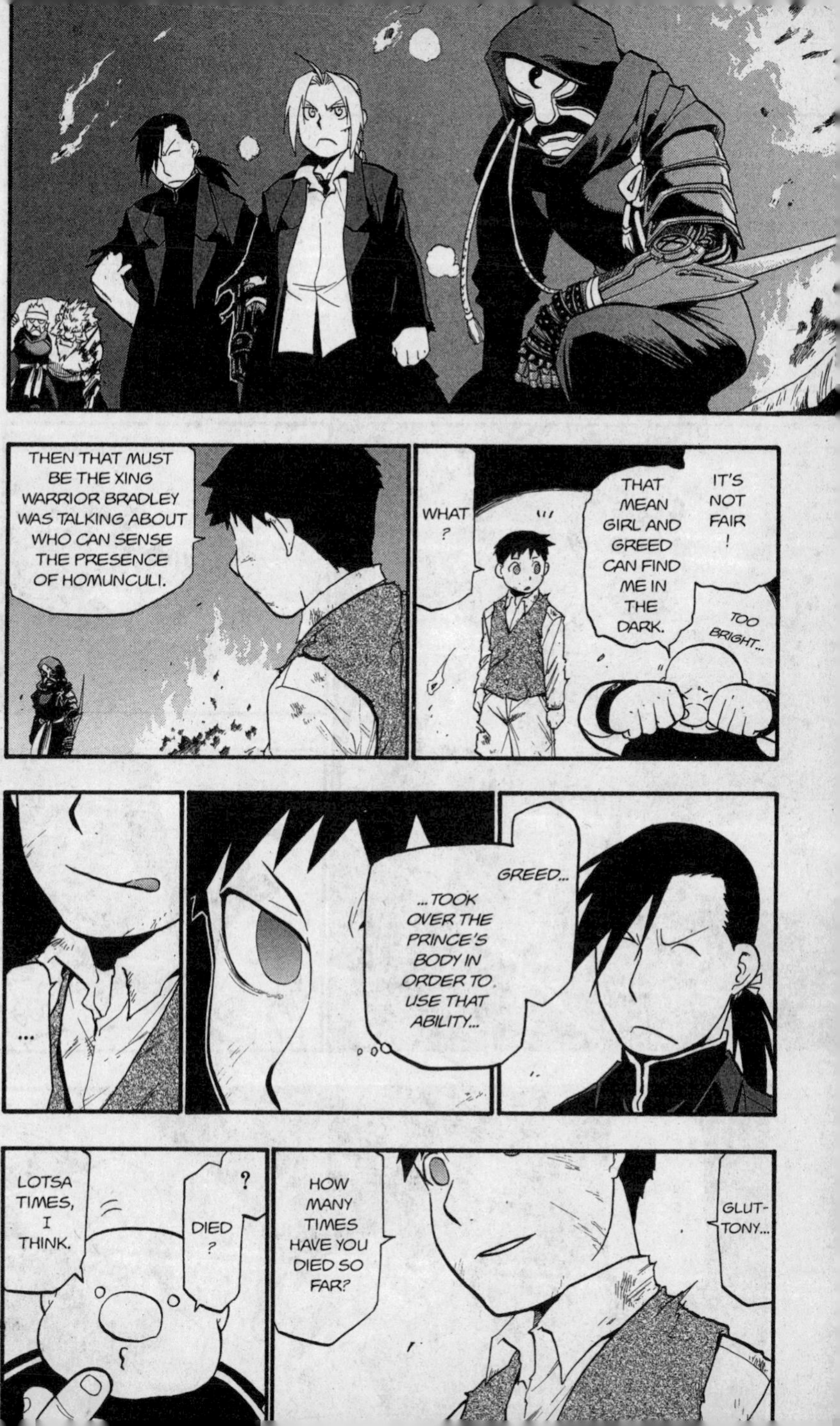
IT'S NOT FAIR!
THAT MEAN GIRL AND GREED CAN FIND ME IN THE DARK.
WHAT?
TOO BRIGHT...
THEN THAT MUST BE THE XING WARRIOR BRADLEY WAS TALKING ABOUT WHO CAN SENSE THE PRESENCE OF HOMUNCULI.
GREED...
...TOOK OVER THE PRINCE'S BODY IN ORDER TO USE THAT ABILITY...
...
GLUT-TONY...
HOW MANY TIMES HAVE YOU DIED SO FAR?
DIED?
LOTSA TIMES, I THINK.

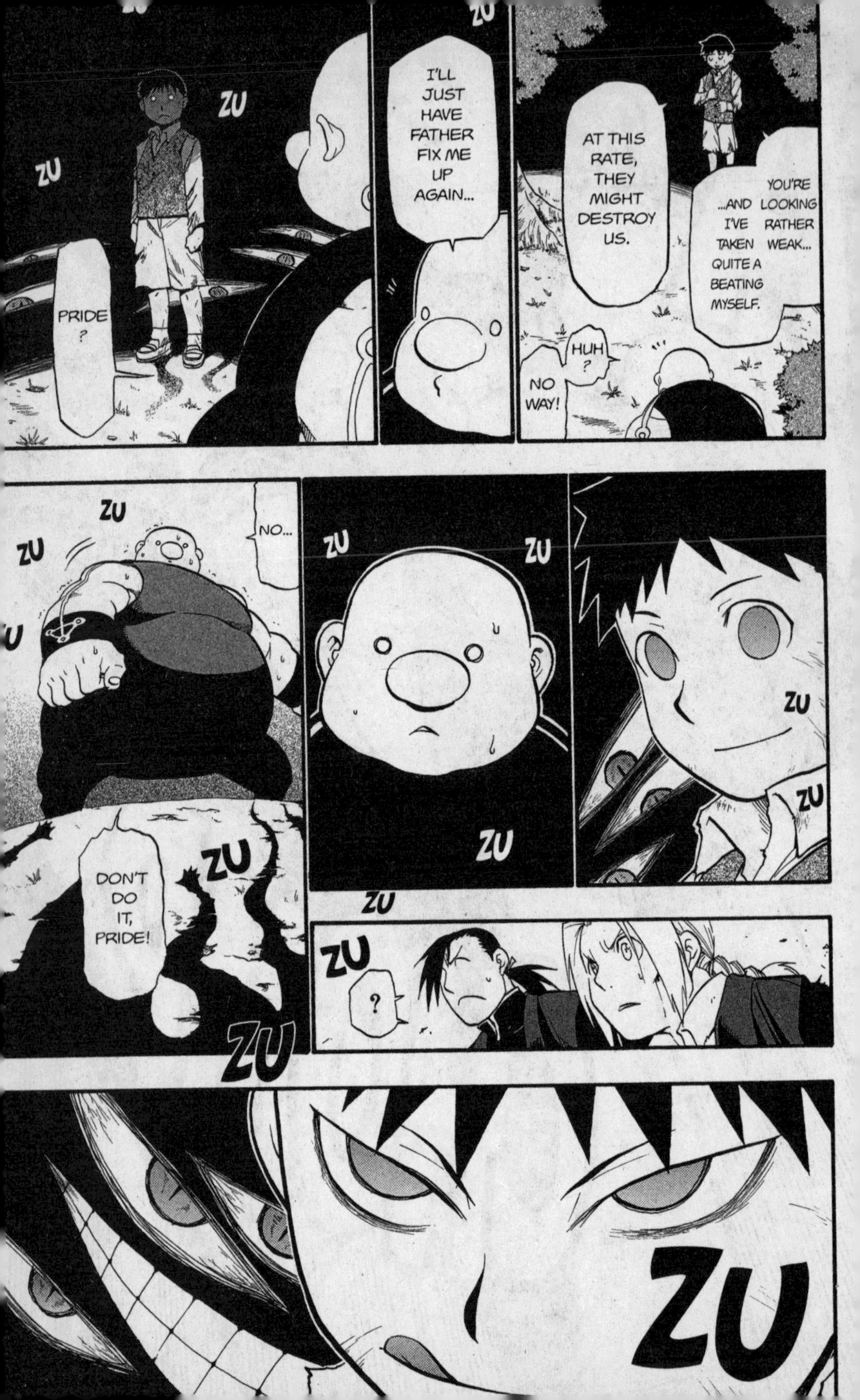
YOU'RE LOOKING RATHER WEAK...
...AND I'VE TAKEN QUITE A BEATING MYSELF.
AT THIS RATE, THEY MIGHT DESTROY US.
HUH?
NO WAY!
ZU
I'LL JUST HAVE FATHER FIX ME UP AGAIN...
ZU
ZU
PRIDE?
ZU
ZU
ZU
ZU
ZU
NO...
ZU
ZU
DON'T DO IT, PRIDE!
ZU
ZU
ZU
ZU
?
ZU

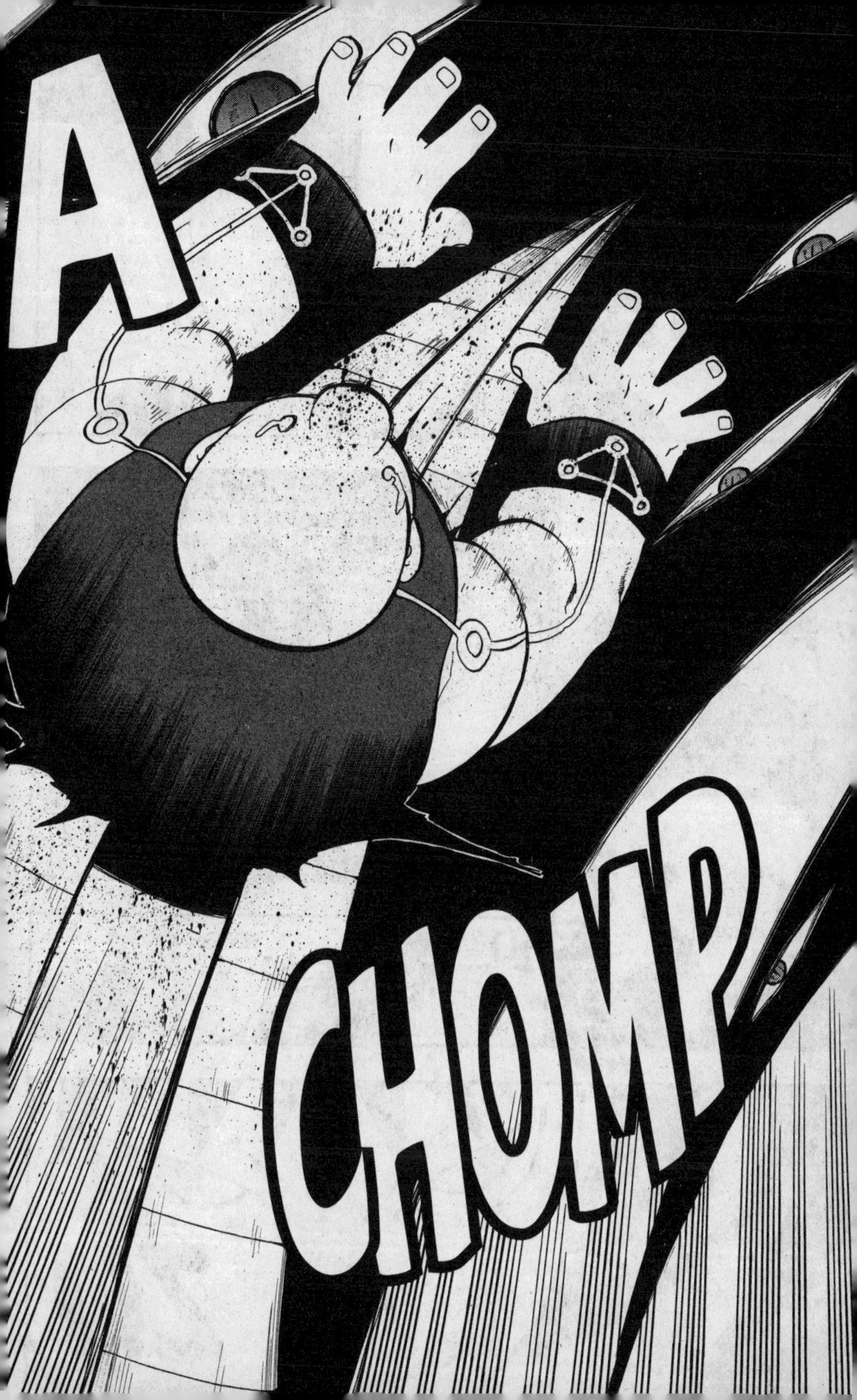
A
CHOMP

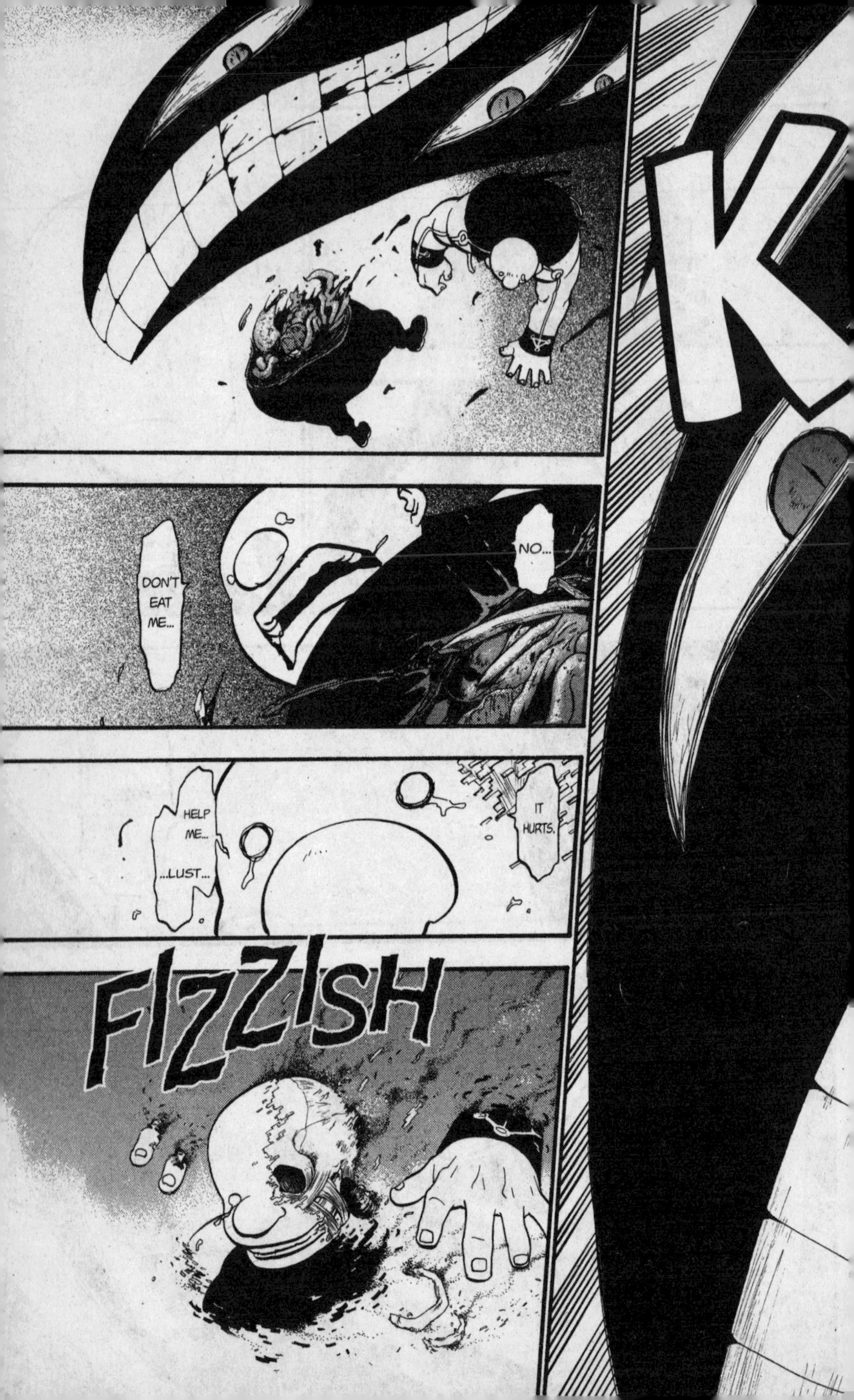
K
NO...
DON'T EAT ME...
IT HURTS.
HELP ME... ...LUST...
FIZZISH

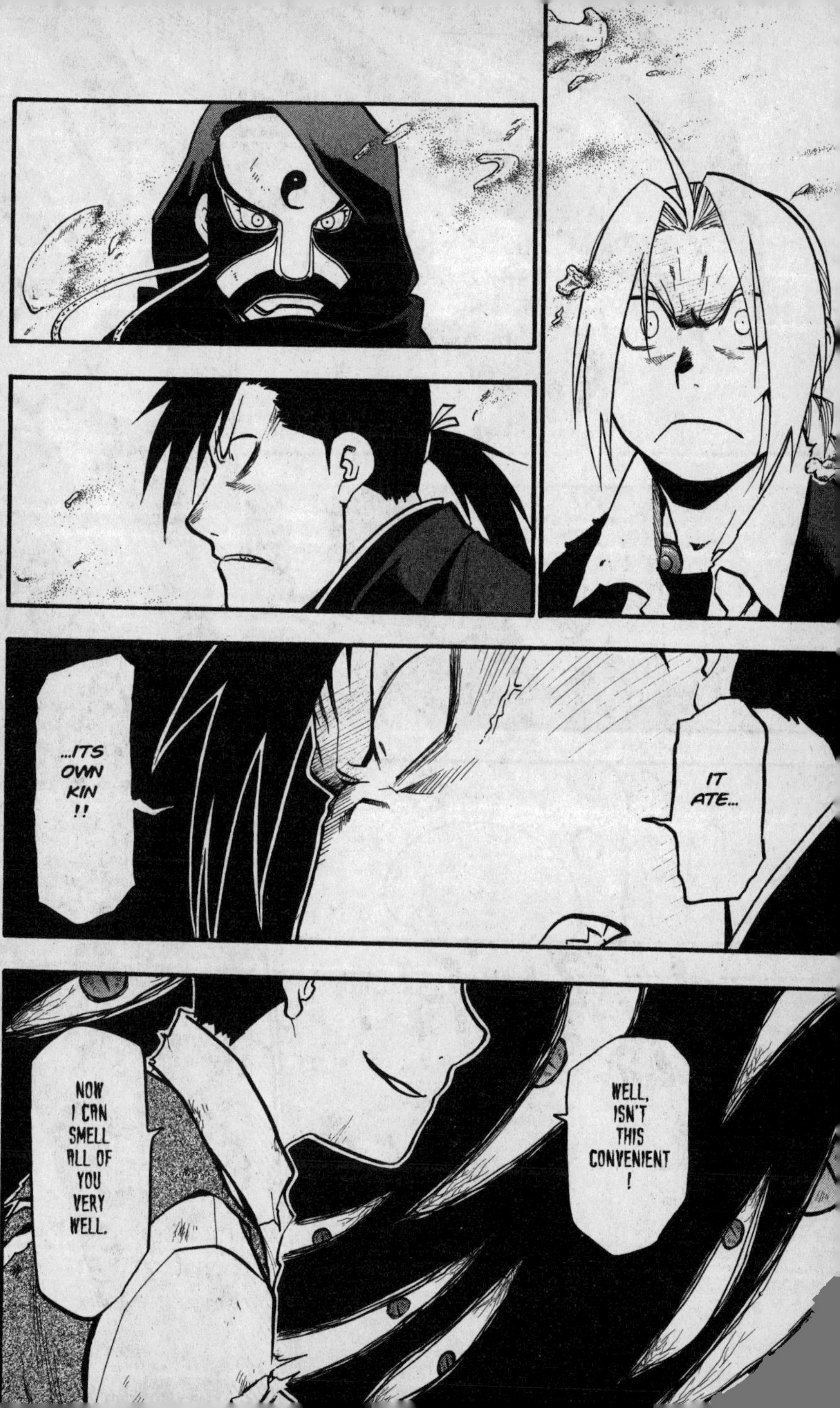
IT ATE...
...ITS OWN KIN!!
WELL, ISN'T THIS CONVENIENT!
NOW I CAN SMELL ALL OF YOU VERY WELL.

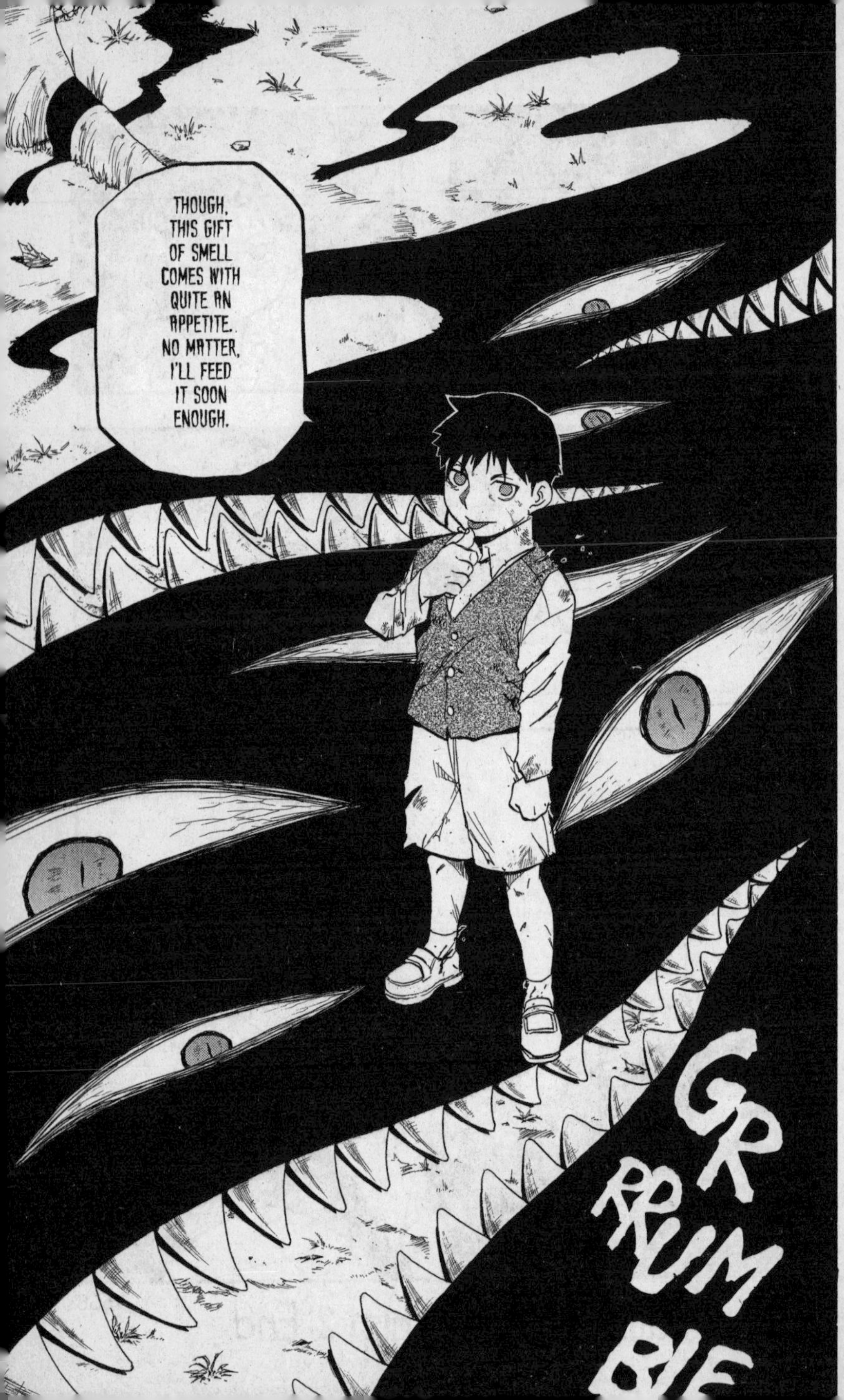
THOUGH, THIS GIFT OF SMELL COMES WITH QUITE AN APPETITE. NO MATTER, I'LL FEED IT SOON ENOUGH.
GRRRUMBLE

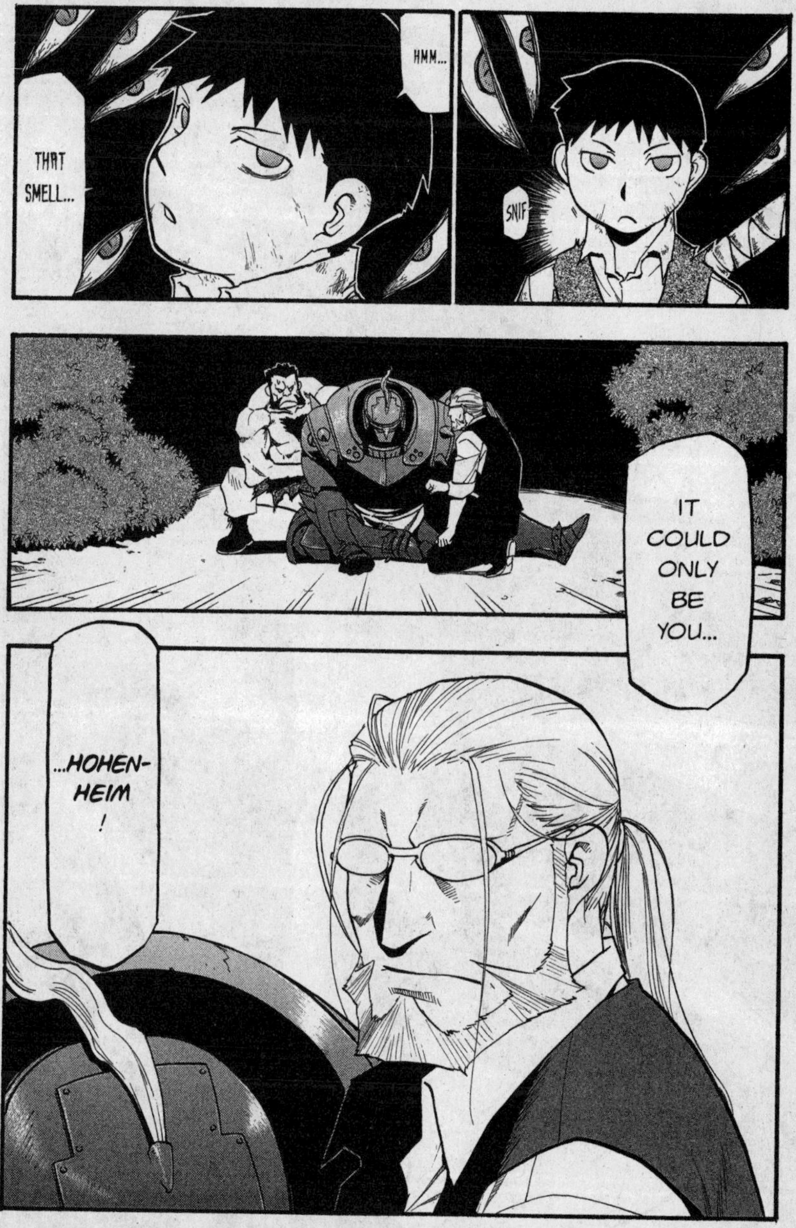
SNIF
HMM...
THAT SMELL...
IT COULD ONLY BE YOU...
...HOHEN-HEIM!

Fullmetal Alchemist 21 End

FULLMETAL
ALCHEMIST

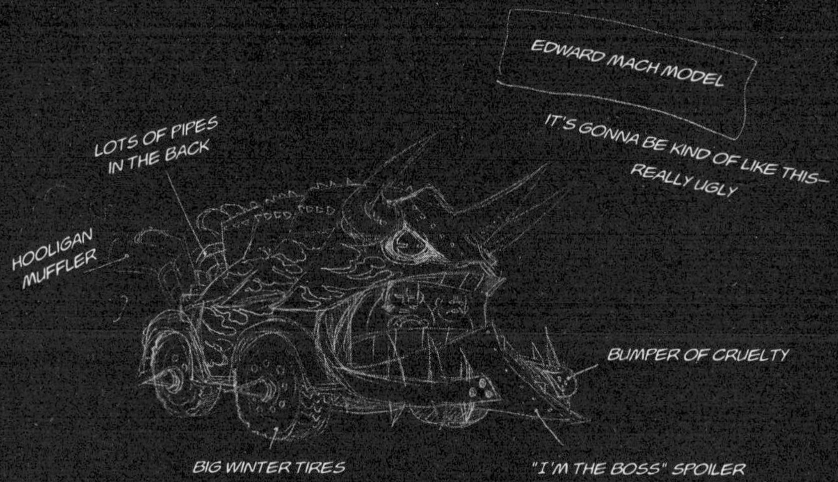
EDWARD MACH MODEL
IT'S GONNA BE KIND OF LIKE THIS—
REALLY UGLY
LOTS OF PIPES
IN THE BACK
HOOLIGAN
MUFFLER
BUMPER OF CRUELTY
BIG WINTER TIRES
"I'M THE BOSS" SPOILER

EXTRAS

THAT SMELL...
SNIF SNIF
IT COULD ONLY BE YOU, HO...
POOT
AAAAAAAH!!
IT STINKS !!
AAAAAAAH!!
SQUIRM SQUIRM
?

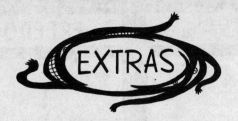

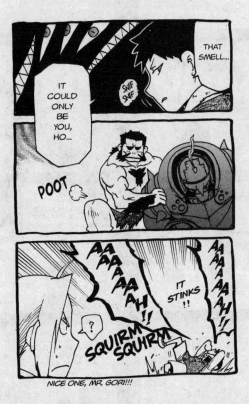

NICE ONE, MR. GORI!!!

FREEDOM

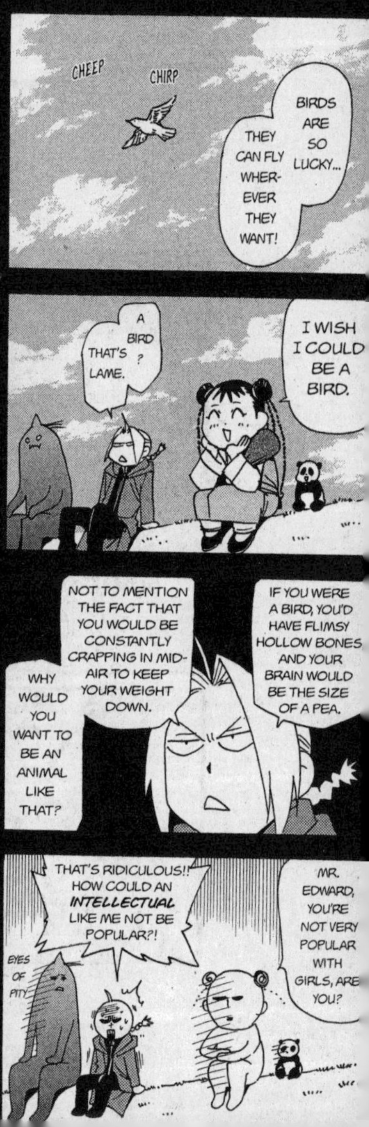
BIRDS ARE SO LUCKY...
THEY CAN FLY WHEREVER THEY WANT!
CHIRP
CHEEP
I WISH I COULD BE A BIRD.
A BIRD? THAT'S LAME.
IF YOU WERE A BIRD, YOU'D HAVE FLIMSY HOLLOW BONES AND YOUR BRAIN WOULD BE THE SIZE OF A PEA.
NOT TO MENTION THE FACT THAT YOU WOULD BE CONSTANTLY CRAPPING IN MID-AIR TO KEEP YOUR WEIGHT DOWN.
WHY WOULD YOU WANT TO BE AN ANIMAL LIKE THAT?
MR. EDWARD, YOU'RE NOT VERY POPULAR WITH GIRLS, ARE YOU?
THAT'S RIDICULOUS!! HOW COULD AN INTELLECTUAL LIKE ME NOT BE POPULAR?!
EYES OF PITY

THE GREAT "GET POPULAR" PLAN

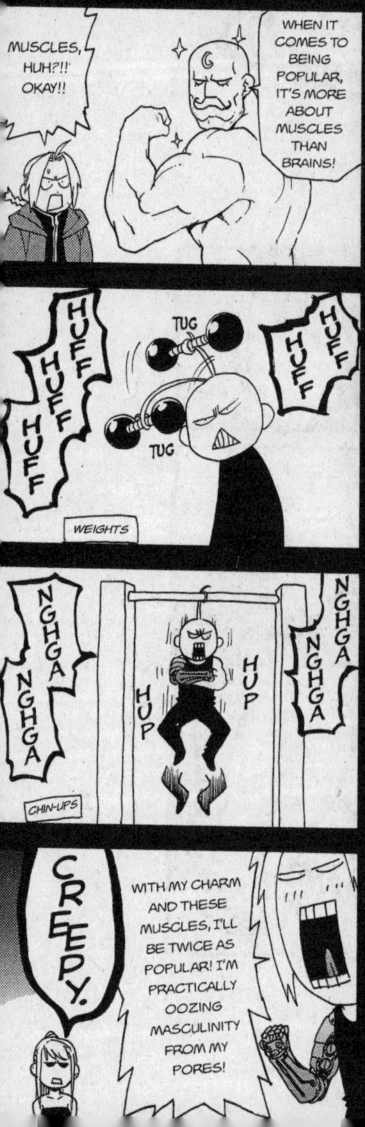
WHEN IT COMES TO BEING POPULAR, IT'S MORE ABOUT MUSCLES THAN BRAINS!
MUSCLES, HUH?!! OKAY!!
HUFF HUFF
TUG
TUG
HUFF HUFF HUFF
WEIGHTS
NGHGA NGHGA
HUP
HUP
NGHGA NGHGA
CHIN-UPS
WITH MY CHARM AND THESE MUSCLES, I'LL BE TWICE AS POPULAR! I'M PRACTICALLY OOZING MASCULINITY FROM MY PORES!
CREEPY.

HAWKEYE'S HOMECOMING

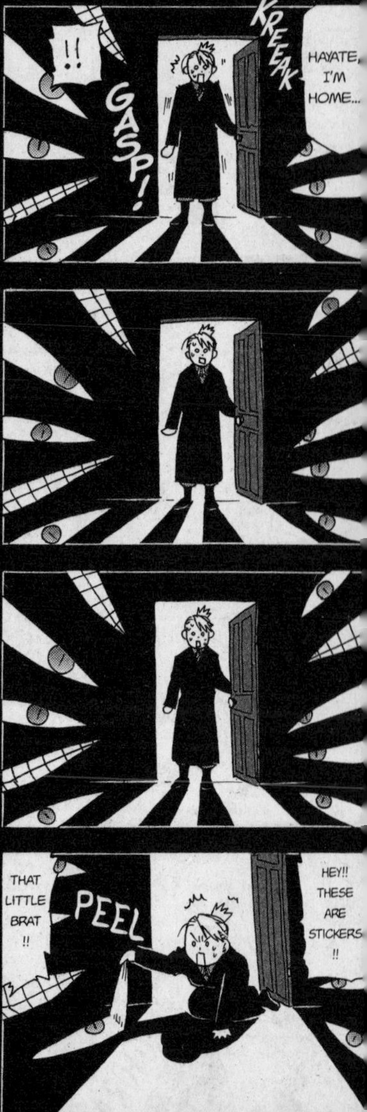
KREEAK
HAYATE, I'M HOME...
!!
GASP!
HEY!! THESE ARE STICKERS!!
THAT LITTLE BRAT!!
PEEL

MUGGER

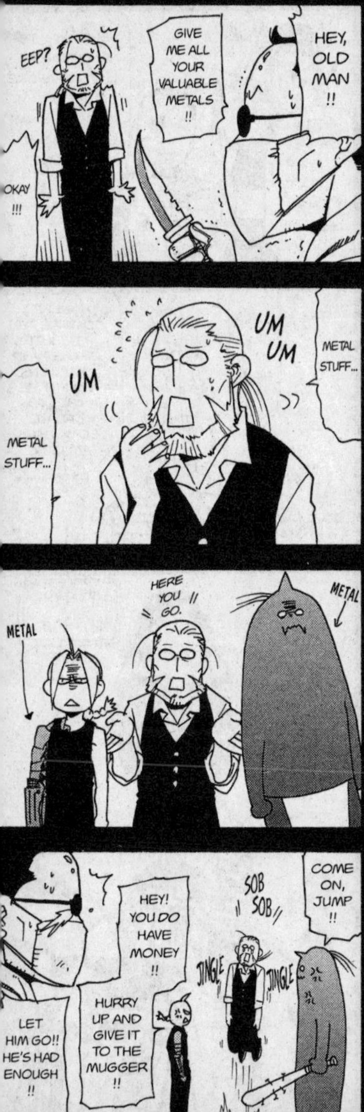
HEY, OLD MAN!!
GIVE ME ALL YOUR VALUABLE METALS!!
EEP?
OKAY!!!
METAL STUFF...
UM UM
UM
METAL STUFF...
METAL
HERE YOU GO.
METAL
COME ON, JUMP!!
SOB SOB
HEY! YOU DO HAVE MONEY!!
JINGLE
JINGLE
HURRY UP AND GIVE IT TO THE MUGGER!!
LET HIM GO!! HE'S HAD ENOUGH!!

EXTREME HOMUNCULUS

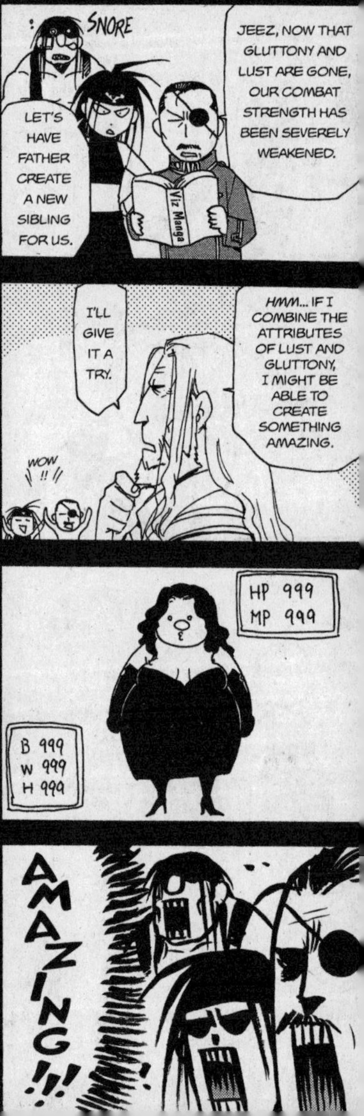
JEEZ, NOW THAT GLUTTONY AND LUST ARE GONE, OUR COMBAT STRENGTH HAS BEEN SEVERELY WEAKENED.
SNORE
LET'S HAVE FATHER CREATE A NEW SIBLING FOR US.
Viz Manga
HMM... IF I COMBINE THE ATTRIBUTES OF LUST AND GLUTTONY, I MIGHT BE ABLE TO CREATE SOMETHING AMAZING.
I'LL GIVE IT A TRY.
WOW !!
HP 999
MP 999
B 999
W 999
H 999
AMAZING!!!

HERO FOR A DAY

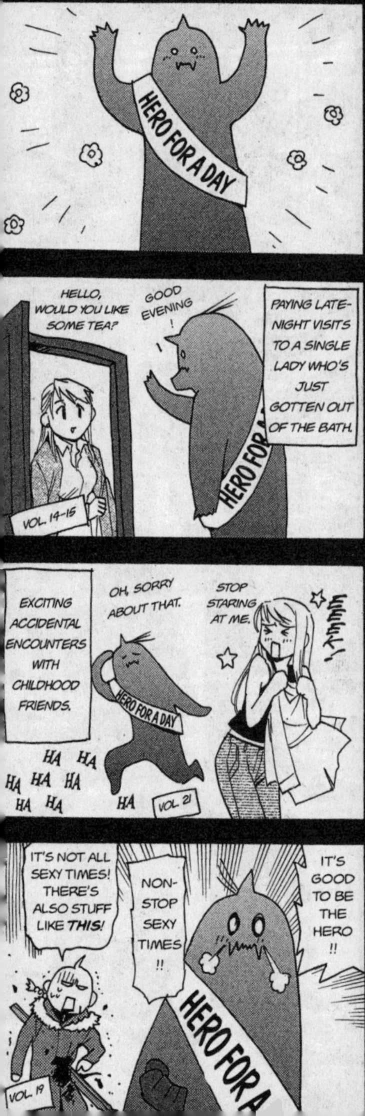
HERO FOR A DAY
PAYING LATE-NIGHT VISITS TO A SINGLE LADY WHO'S JUST GOTTEN OUT OF THE BATH.
GOOD EVENING !
HELLO, WOULD YOU LIKE SOME TEA?
HERO FOR A
VOL. 14-15
STOP STARING AT ME.
OH, SORRY ABOUT THAT.
EXCITING ACCIDENTAL ENCOUNTERS WITH CHILDHOOD FRIENDS.
HERO FOR A DAY
HA HA HA HA HA HA HA HA
VOL. 21
IT'S GOOD TO BE THE HERO !!
NON-STOP SEXY TIMES !!
IT'S NOT ALL SEXY TIMES! THERE'S ALSO STUFF LIKE *THIS*!
HERO FOR A
VOL. 19

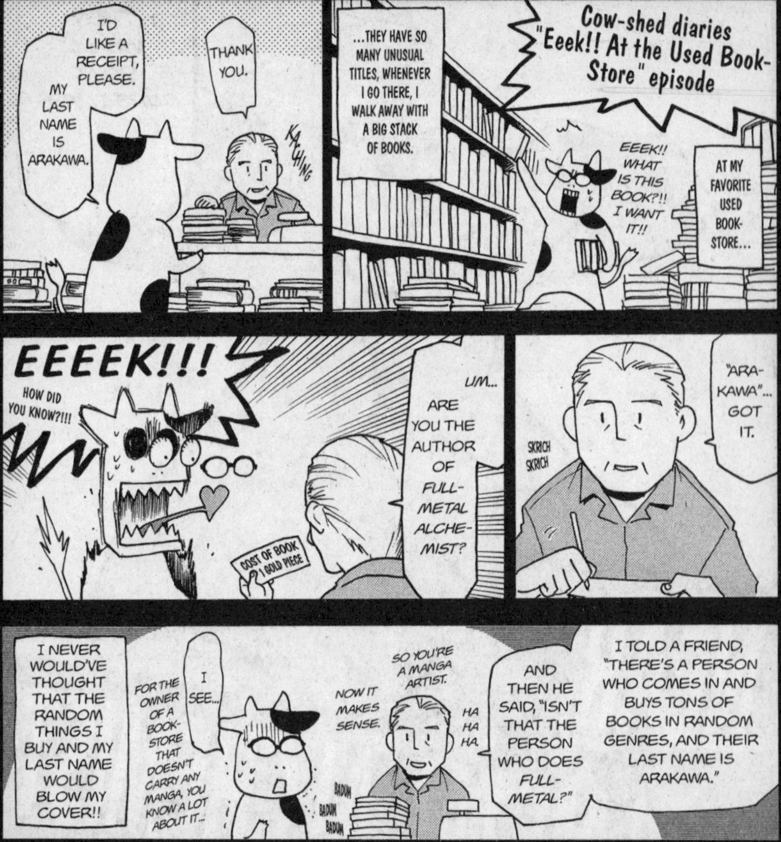
Cow-shed diaries "Eeek!! At the Used Book-Store" episode
AT MY FAVORITE USED BOOK-STORE...
EEEK!! WHAT IS THIS BOOK?!! I WANT IT!!
...THEY HAVE SO MANY UNUSUAL TITLES, WHENEVER I GO THERE, I WALK AWAY WITH A BIG STACK OF BOOKS.
THANK YOU.
KACHING
I'D LIKE A RECEIPT, PLEASE.
MY LAST NAME IS ARAKAWA.
"ARA-KAWA"... GOT IT.
SKRICH SKRICH
UM... ARE YOU THE AUTHOR OF FULL-METAL ALCHE-MIST?
EEEEK!!!
HOW DID YOU KNOW?!!!
COST OF BOOK 1 GOLD PIECE
I TOLD A FRIEND, "THERE'S A PERSON WHO COMES IN AND BUYS TONS OF BOOKS IN RANDOM GENRES, AND THEIR LAST NAME IS ARAKAWA."
AND THEN HE SAID, "ISN'T THAT THE PERSON WHO DOES FULL-METAL?"
HA HA HA.
SO YOU'RE A MANGA ARTIST.
NOW IT MAKES SENSE.
BADUM BADUM BADUM
I SEE...
FOR THE OWNER OF A BOOK-STORE THAT DOESN'T CARRY ANY MANGA, YOU KNOW A LOT ABOUT IT...
I NEVER WOULD'VE THOUGHT THAT THE RANDOM THINGS I BUY AND MY LAST NAME WOULD BLOW MY COVER!!

FULLMETAL ALCHEMIST 21

SPECIAL THANKS to:

Jun Tohko
Noriko Tsubota
Mitsuri Sakano
Masashi Mizutani
Haruhi Nakamura
Manatsu Sakura
Coupon
Kazufumi Kaneko
Kei Takanamazu
Editor—Yuichi Shimomura

AND YOU!!

Fullmetal Alchemist
Preview

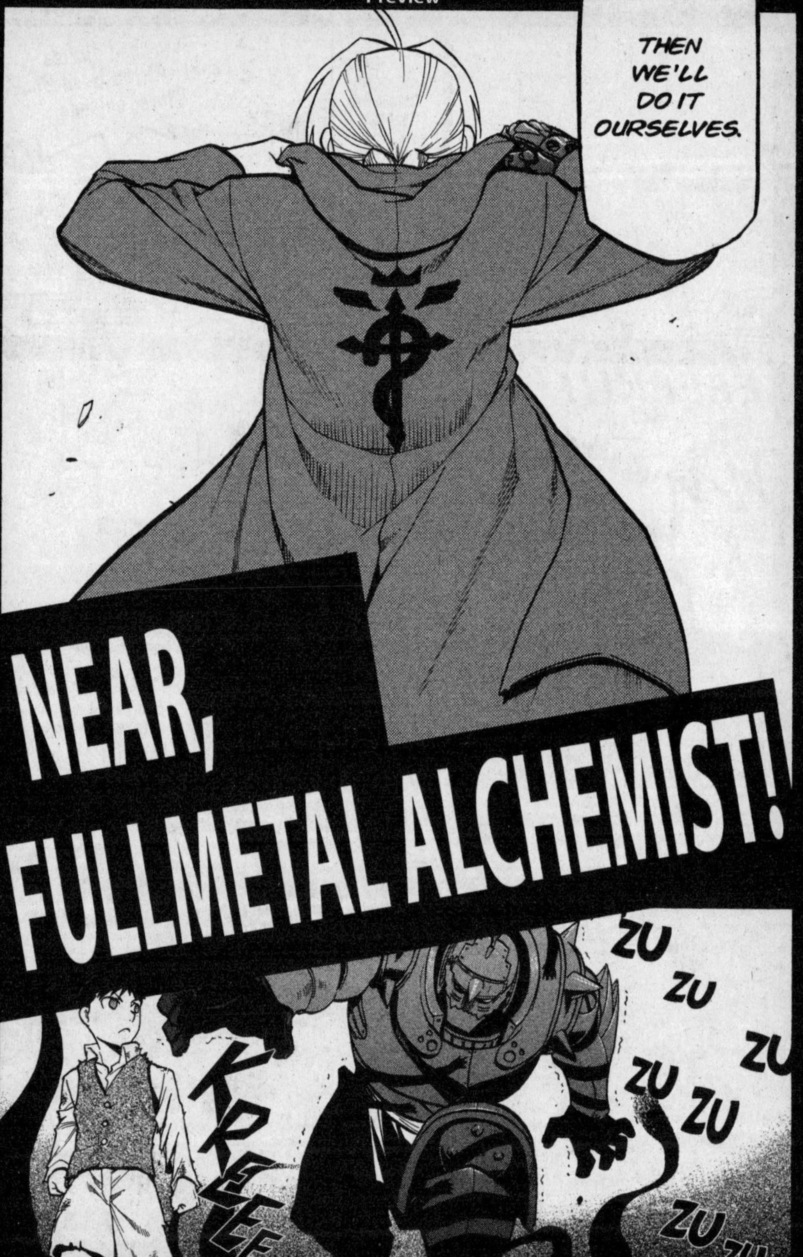
THEN WE'LL DO IT OURSELVES.
NEAR, FULLMETAL ALCHEMIST!
ZU ZU ZU ZU ZU ZU ZU ZU
KREEEE

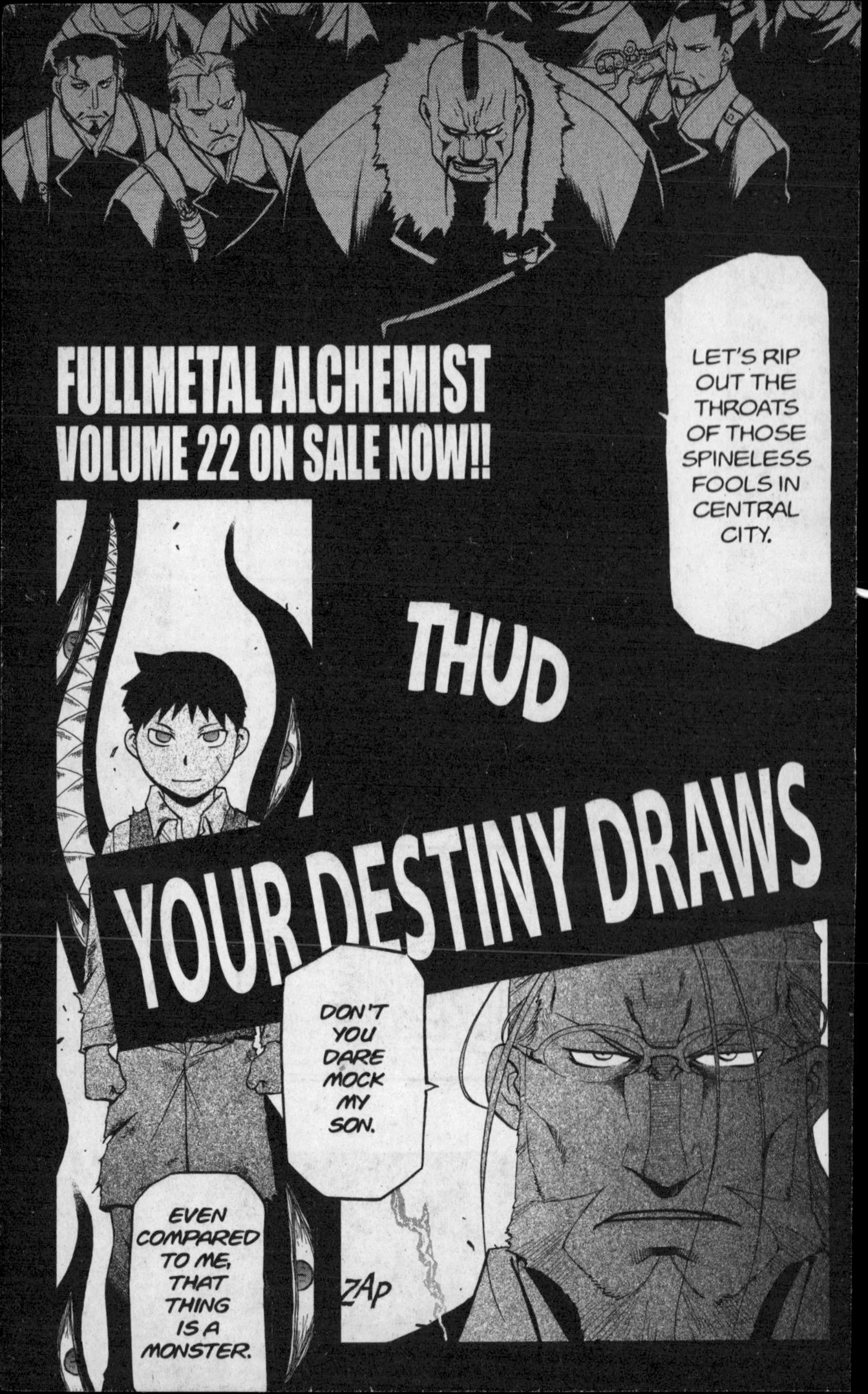
FULLMETAL ALCHEMIST
VOLUME 22 ON SALE NOW!!
LET'S RIP OUT THE THROATS OF THOSE SPINELESS FOOLS IN CENTRAL CITY.
THUD
YOUR DESTINY DRAWS
DON'T YOU DARE MOCK MY SON.
ZAP
EVEN COMPARED TO ME, THAT THING IS A MONSTER.

Fullmetal Alchemist 21

A DAY IN THE LIFE OF FATHER

OH BOY, OH BOY! TOMORROW IS THE "DAY OF RECKONING!" ☆
JITTER JITTER
I'M SO EXCITED! I CAN'T SLEEP!!
NEXT DAY...
CHEEP
CHEEP
CHEEP
...I OVER-SLEPT!!!
CHEEP CHEEP

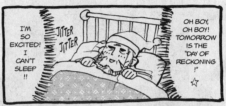

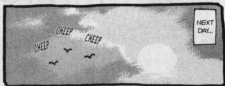

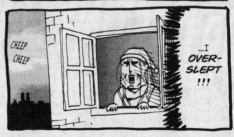

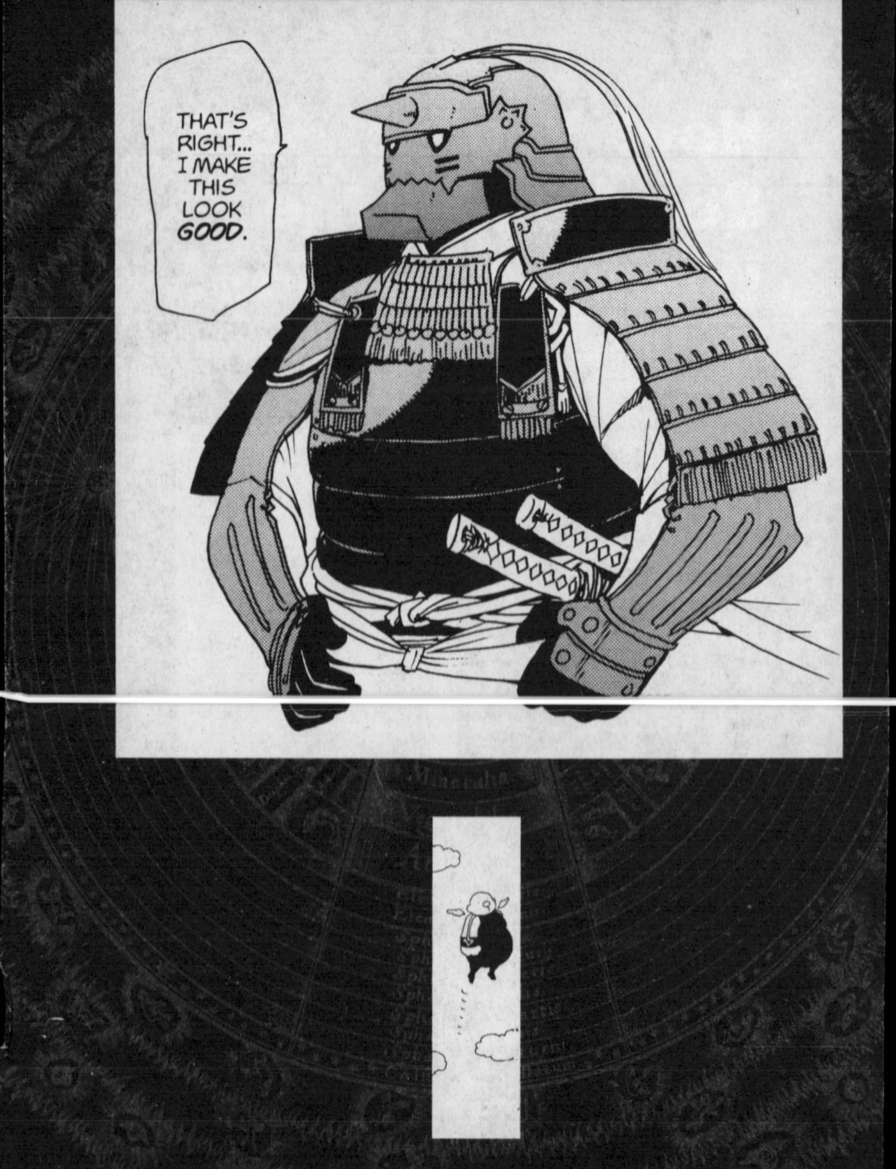
THAT'S RIGHT... I MAKE THIS LOOK GOOD.

SO-AWD-272

Hey! You're
Reading in the
Wrong Direction!

This is the *end* of this graphic novel!

To properly enjoy this
VIZ graphic novel,
please turn it around
and begin reading
from *right to left*.

Unlike English,
Japanese is read right
to left, so Japanese
comics are read in
reverse order from the
way English comics
are typically read.

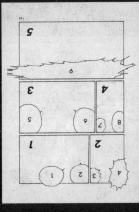

Follow the action this way

This book has been printed in the original Japanese
format in order to preserve the orientation of the
original artwork. Have fun with it!